SMART ENGINEERING SYSTEM DESIGN:

NEURAL NETWORKS, FUZZY LOGIC,

EVOLUTIONARY PROGRAMMING,

COMPLEX SYSTEMS AND ARTIFICIAL LIFE

VOLUME 14

ASME PRESS SERIES ON INTELLIGENT ENGINEERING SYSTEMS THROUGH ARTIFICIAL NEURAL NETWORKS

EDITOR

C.H. Dagli, University of Missouri-Rolla, Rolla, Missouri, USA

Intelligent Engineering Systems Through Artificial Neural Networks, Volume 1, edited by Cihan H. Dagli, Soundar R.T. Kumara, and Yung C. Shin, 1991

Intelligent Engineering Systems Through Artificial Neural Networks, Volume 2, edited by Cihan H. Dagli, Laura I. Burke, and Yung C. Shin, 1992

Intelligent Engineering Systems Through Artificial Neural Networks, Volume 3, edited by Cihan H. Dagli, Laura I. Burke, Benito Fernandez, and Joydeep Ghosh, 1993

Intelligent Engineering Systems Through Artificial Neural Networks, Volume 4, edited by Cihan H. Dagli, Benito Fernandez, Joydeep Ghosh, and R.T. Soundar Kumara, 1994

Intelligent Engineering Systems Through Artificial Neural Networks, Volume 5, edited by Cihan H. Dagli, Metin Akay, C.L. Phillip Chen, Benito Fernandez, and Joydeep Ghosh, 1

Intelligent Engineering Systems Through Artificial Neural Networks, Volume 6, edited by Cihan H. Dagli, Metin Akay, C.L. Phillip Chen, Benito Fernandez, and Joydeep Ghosh, 1

Intelligent Engineering Systems Through Artificial Neural Networks: Smart Engineering Systems: Neural Networks, Fuzzy Logic, Data Mining and Evolutionary Programming, Vo 7, edited by Cihan H. Dagli, Metin Akay, Okan Ersoy, Benito Fernandez, and Alice Smith 1997

Intelligent Engineering Systems Through Artificial Neural Networks: Smart Engineering Systems: Neural Networks, Fuzzy Logic, Evolutionary Programming, Data Mining and Ro Sets, Volume 8, edited by Cihan H. Dagli, Metin Akay, Anna L. Buczak, Okan Ersoy, and Benito Fernandez, 1998

Intelligent Engineering Systems Through Artificial Neural Networks: Smart Engineering System Design: Neural Networks, Fuzzy Logic, Evolutionary Programming, Data Mining Complex Systems, Volume 9, edited by Cihan H. Dagli, Anna L. Buczak, Joydeep Ghosh, Mark Embrechts and Okan Ersoy, 1999

Intelligent Engineering Systems Through Artificial Neural Networks: Smart Engineering System Design: Neural Networks, Fuzzy Logic, Evolutionary Programming, Data Mining Complex Systems, Volume 10, edited by Cihan H. Dagli, Anna L. Buczak, Joydeep Ghos Mark Embrechts, Okan Ersoy and Stephen Kercel, 2000

Intelligent Engineering Systems Through Artificial Neural Networks: Smart Engineering System Design: Neural Networks, Fuzzy Logic, Evolutionary Programming, Data Mining Complex Systems, Volume 11, edited by Cihan H. Dagli, Anna L. Buczak, Joydeep Ghos Mark Embrechts, Okan Ersoy and Stephen Kercel, 2001

Intelligent Engineering Systems Through Artificial Neural Networks: Smart Engineering System Design: Neural Networks, Fuzzy Logic, Evolutionary Programming, Complex Syst and Artificial Life, Volume 12, edited by Cihan H. Dagli, Anna L. Buczak, Joydeep Ghosh Mark Embrechts, Okan Ersoy and Stephen Kercel, 2002 ntelligent Engineering Systems Through Artificial Neural Networks: Smart Engineering ystem Design: Neural Networks, Fuzzy Logic, Evolutionary Programming, Complex Systems nd Artificial Life, Volume 14, edited by Cihan H. Dagli, Anna L. Buczak, David L. Enke, lark Embrechts and Okan Ersoy, 2004

SMART ENGINEERING SYSTEM DESIGN:

Neural Networks, Fuzzy Logic, Evolutionary Programming, Complex Systems and Artificial Life

VOLUME 14

Proceedings of the Artificial Neural Networks in Engineering Conference (ANNIE 2004) held November 7-10, 2004, in St. Louis, Missouri, U.S.A.

EDITORS
Cihan H. Dagli
Department of Engineering Management and Systems Engineering
University of Missouri-Rolla

Anna L. Buczak
Lockheed Martin
Camden, New Jersey

David L. Enke
Department of Engineering Management and System Engineering
University of Missouri - Rolla

Mark Embrechts
Rensselaer Polytechnic Institute, RPI
Troy, New York

Okan Ersoy
Purdue University
West Lafayette, Indiana

ASME PRESS NEW YORK 2004

Library of Congress 92-30949
ISBN 0-7918-0228-0

Contents

PREFACE

As a follow up to the previous twelfth volumes of Intelligent Engineering Systems Through Artificial Neural Networks, edited by Dagli, C.H. et. al., this volume contains the edited versions of the technical presentations of ANNIE 2004. The thirteenth international gathering of researchers interested in Smart Engineering System Design using neural networks, fuzzy logic, evolutionary programming, data mining and artificial life, was held on November 7-10, 2004 in St. Louis, Missouri, USA. The conference covered the theory of neural networks, fuzzy logic, evolutionary programming, data mining, and artificial life; and their applications in the engineering domain. The papers included in this volume provide a forum for researchers in the field to exchange ideas on smart engineering systems design.

An extended version of each paper selected for inclusion was reviewed by two referees, then revised, edited, and condensed to the format herein. The papers in this edited book are grouped into eleven categories:

- Architectures
- Artificial Life
- Evolutionary Programming
- Fuzzy Systems
- Adaptive Control
- Data Mining
- Pattern Recognition
- Civil Engineering
- Financial Engineering
- Smart Engineering Systems
- Bio-Medical Engineering

There were six plenary sessions scheduled for ANNIE 2004. Lee Giles gave a presentation for the Monday morning plenary talk entitled "CiteSeer, The Next Generation" followed by the Monday luncheon plenary talk by Hojjat Adeli who's talk was entitled " A Multi-Paradigm Approach to Complexity: Chaos-Dynamic Neural Network-Wavelet Models with Applications in Intelligent Transportation Systems". Juergen Schmidhuber gave the Tuesday morning plenary talk that was entitled "How to Learn Algorithm: Optimal Universal Learners, Goedel Machines & Recurrent Nets, followed by the Wednesday luncheon plenary talk by Dr. Stefan Kremer which was entitled "Machine Learning Techniques in Bioinformatics: Bio-Hacking for Fun and Profit". Vladimir Cherkassky gave the Wednesday morning plenary talk entitled " Alternative Formulations for Predictive Learning, followed by the Wednesday luncheon plenary talk that was given by Dr. Wunsch entitled, No "Not Invented Here": An Engineering Approach to Computational Intelligence.

Our Banquet Plenary Speaker for this year's ANNIE was Dr. John Mclean, he gave he's talk entitled "AI & IA: The Use of Artificial Intelligence in High Assurance Systems. John McLean is the Superintendent of the Navel Research Laboratory's Information Technology Division (ITD).He became Acting Superintendent in 2002, and he was confirmed as Superintendent and appointed to the Government's Senior Executive Service in 2003. Prior to becoming Superintendent, Dr. McLean was a member of the Government's Senior Science and Technology Service and NRL's Senior Scientist for Information Assurance.

Dr. McLean came to NRL in 1980 as a Research Computer Scientist. Serving as Principal Investigator for several projects, he published widely in the areas of formal methods and formal modeling for computer security. In 1988 he helped create ITD's Center for High Assurance Computer Systems, establishing and heading the Center's Formal Methods Section. In 1984 he became Director of the Center, which during his tenure transitioned technological advances into several successful products, including IPSec, IPv6, devices that support a variety of MSL architectures, and the worlds's first Type 1 programmable cryptologic device. While at NRL, he has also held positions as an Adjunct Professor of Computer Science for the University of Maryland, the National Cryptologic School, and Troisieme Cycle Romand d'Informatique.

Dr. McLean is an Associate Editor of Distributed Computing, Journal of Computer Security, and ACM Transactions on Information and System Security. He is a member of the Steering Committee of the IEEE Computer Security Foundations Workshop and a US Navy Representative to the Technical Cooperation Program (TTCP) C31 Group, where he previously served as the Chair and US National Leader of the Group's Technical Panel on High Assurance Systems and Defensive Information Welfare.

During his career at NRL, Dr. McLean has served as a Senior Research Fellow of the University of Cambridge's Centre for Communications Systems Research and as a member of the Scientific Advisory Committee of Cambridge's Issac Newton Instituite Program in Computer Security, Cryptology and Coding Theory. He has been Conference Chair for the IEEE Symposium on Research in Security and Privacy and Program Chair for that conference, the IEEE Computer Security Foundations Workshop, and COMPASS, where he was also a member of the conference's Board of Director's. He is the recipient of an Outstanding Paper Award for the IEEE Computer Society and three Alan Berman Research Publication Awards form NRL.

Dr. McLean graduated from Oberlin College in 1974 with a B.A. in Mathematics. He received an M.S. in Computer Science in 1980 and an M.A. and Ph.D. in Philosophy in 1976 and 1980, respectively, all from the University of North Carolina at Chapel Hill where his research interests were computer science, mathematical logic, and the philosophy of science.

The editors would like to once again thank the plenary speakers, and the authors for their contributions. We would also like to recognize the organizing committee members of ANNIE 2004 for their excellent support in promoting the conference internationally. Further, we wish to express our gratitude to all the referees for their excellent and timely review efforts, which made this edited book possible within a short period of time.

Although space will not permit for the recognition of all contributors special thanks goes to the session chairs, whom contributed to the quality of the discussions in the presentations. We would also like to mention our appreciation to Andrea Bramel. Her ownership of the ANNIE 04 Conference, the excellent ability to communicate with authors all over the world, her superb organizing capabilities, the ability to pay attention to details, along with putting this volume together, made her an integral part of the ANNIE Conference.

Lastly, but most importantly, we would like to thank all of our families for their patience and sustenance during the many long hours that it took to create yet another ANNIE, ANNIE 2004, and subsequently, this book.

Cihan H. Dagli
University of Missouri-Rolla

Anna Buczak
Lockheed Martin

David L. Enke
University of Missouri - Rolla

Mark Embrechts
Rensselaer Polytechnic Institute, RPI

Okan Ersoy
Purdue University

PART I: ARCHITECTURES

SYNCHRONIZATION OF SPIKING NEURONS MODELING INHIBITION/EXCITATION FIRING

IREN VALOVA
Computer and Information Sciences
University of Massachusetts Dartmouth
285 Old Westport Rd, North Dartmouth, MA 02747

NATACHA GUEORGUIEVA
Computer Science
CSI/City University of New York
2800 Victory Blvd.
Staten Island, NY 10314

FRANK TROESCHER
Computer and Information Sciences
University of Massachusetts Dartmouth
285 Old Westport Rd, North Dartmouth, MA 02747

ABSTRACT
Spiking neural systems are based on biologically inspired neural models of computation since they take into account the precise timing of spike events and therefore are suitable to analyze dynamical aspects of neuronal signal transmission. These systems gained increasing interest because they are more sophisticated than simple neuron models found in artificial neural systems; they are closer to biophysical models of neurons, synapses, and related elements and their synchronized firing of neuronal assemblies could serve the brain as a code for feature binding and pattern segmentation.
Our simulations showed that the inter-neuron transmission delay controls the size of spatial variations of the input and also smoothes the network response. Our integrate-and-fire extended model proves to be a useful basis from which we can study more sophisticated features as complex pattern formation and, global stability and chaos of OB dynamics.

ANATOMICAL DESCRIPTION OF OLFACTORY BULB

Smell is based on physical stimulation of odor receptor cells by volatile, chemical substances. The olfactory system evolved an extremely large repertoire of seven-transmembrane-domain receptors that are encoded by about 1000 different odor receptor genes [1]. These odor receptor cells located in the epithelium are connected to the olfactory sensory neurons (OSNs), which are located in the olfactory epithelium. The axons of the OSNs reach down into an area of the forebrain that is called the olfactory bulb (OB). Molecular-genetic studies have shown that all the OSN expressing the same or similar, type of odor receptors converge to a single region of the OB, the glomerulus [1, 2]. The glomerulus is a complex area of axonal and dendritic branches for the synaptic connection between the receptor cells and the mitral cells. There are about 10,000 glomeruli, each having axonal input from approximately 2,000 receptor cells [3]. There are also two other main cell types in the OB, periglomerular cells and granule cells. They are used for lateral information processing between mitral cells. Periglomerular cells contact multiple primary mitral cell dendrites within the glomeruli. Besides the input from receptor cells the olfactory has an input from higher regions of the brain. There are pathways from the olfactory cortex and the anterior commissure to the OB. Those pathways mostly end at granule cells. It is therefore believed that the granule cells have a modulatory effect on the OB [4].

OLFACTORY BULB DYNAMICS BASED ON THE INTEGRATE-AND-FIRE NEURON

The spiking neuron models can show the same dynamics like biological neurons but the parameter space is very broad. It can help to determine, how this functions of the olfactory bulb are achieved in detail. Certain parameters of the spiking neuron model can be used to model these dynamics [5, 6, 7, 8]. Two forms of connectivity in the study of OB dynamics have been used: all-to-all coupling and receptive field style coupling.

All-to-all coupling [5] is described briefly in this section. The model is a large homogeneous population of neurons, as presented in Fig. 1.

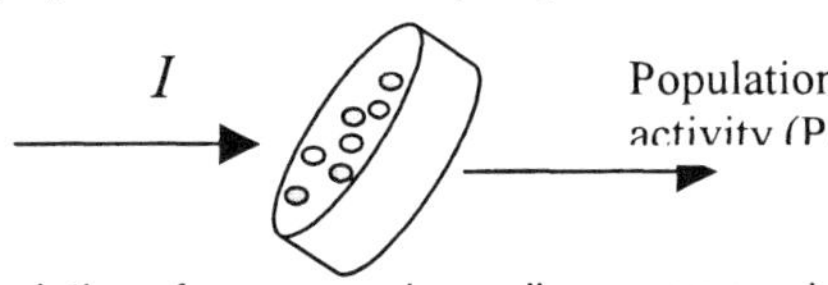

Figure 1. Population of neurons, where all neurons receive the same input I , which results in time dependent population activity.

The homogeneous property of the system means that all neurons are identical and receive the same external input I .

If we represent the strength between the neurons as S_{tn}, the following assumptions are derived: S_{tn} is uniform between all the neurons, and $S_{tn} = f$ (excitatory and inhibitory coupling between all homogeneous neurons). This function *f*, represents the all-to-all coupling between the neurons. Model neurons are described by formal spiking neurons as introduced in previous sections. In the case of leaky integrate-and-fire neurons the transformed (1) becomes:

$$\tau_m \frac{d}{dt} u_i = -u_i + RI(t) \tag{2}$$

Where homogeneous network implies that all neurons have the same input resistance *R,* same membrane time constant, as well as identical threshold and reset values. The input current *I* takes care of both the external drive and synaptic coupling

$$I_n = \sum_{j=1}^{N} \sum_{f} S_{tn_{nj}} \lambda\left(t - t_j^{(f)}\right) + I(t) \tag{3}$$

Here we have assumed that each input spike generates a postsynaptic current with some generic time course $\lambda\left(t - t_j^{(f)}\right)$. The sum on the right-hand side of (3) runs over all firing times of all neurons. Because of the homogeneous all-to-all coupling, the total input current is identical for all neurons.

Therefore the total input current is:

$$I(t) = Con * \int_0^{\propto} \alpha(s) PA(t-s) ds + I(t)$$

where Con is a parameter. For $Con = 0$ all neurons are independent; a value $Con > 0$ ($Con < 0$) implies excitatory (inhibitory) all-to-all coupling.

In the case of receptive field coupling [9], each neuron gets to fire at most once per input signal. For input I and number of neurons n, and let $\vec{x}_i = \{x_{i1}, x_{i2}, \ldots\ldots, x_{ik}\}$ be receptive field of neuron I, and $t_i^{\vec{I}}$ be the time when neuron i spikes when input $\vec{I}$ is present, then the potential of neuron i : u_i at time t is given by $u_i = \vec{x}_i * \vec{I}t$.

If a neuron fires when its potential reaches some threshold, then $u_i\left(t_i^{\vec{I}}\right) = \vec{x}_i\vec{x}_i$ and the time can be represented as $t_i^{\vec{I}} = \vec{x}_i\vec{x}_i / \vec{x}_i\vec{I}$

This threshold property is very significant for our studies because, if the input signal is identical to the neurons receptive field, then the neuron will fire at t=1, independent of the magnitude of the receptive field.

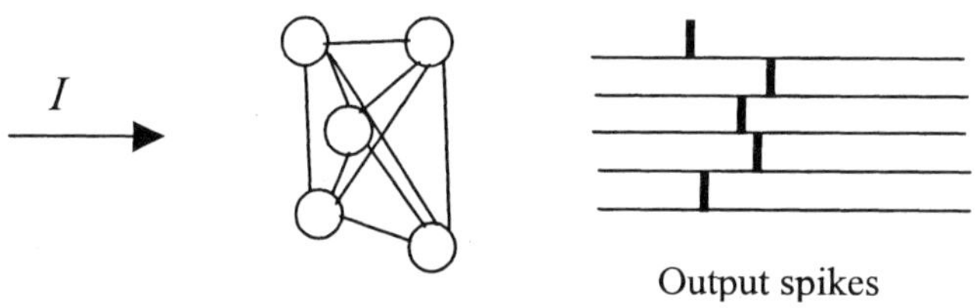

Figure 2. Neurons Responses

The input odor will be recognized by the olfactory system as $\vec{R} = \sum_{i=1}^{N} \frac{\vec{x}_i}{t_i^{\vec{I}}}$

where R is the recognized odor.

If at time t, k neurons have fired, then the partial recognition of the odor R_k can be found as $\vec{R}_k = \sum_{i=1}^{k} \frac{\vec{x}_i}{t_i^{\vec{I}}}$.

At this point the neurons that did not fired yet, decide when they should fire to best recognize the odor input signal. The optimal time of firing is the time at which the error of odor recognition is minimized, where the error is given by:

$$E_k = \left(\vec{R}_k - \vec{I}\right)^2$$

The first neuron that fires, decides to fire at the moment when best recognition of the input signal will be achieved, therefore:

$\forall k \frac{\partial}{\partial t_k^{\vec{I}}} E_k = 0$ and with some rearrangements:

$$t_k^{\vec{I}} = \vec{x}_k\vec{x}_k \Big/ \vec{I}\cdot\vec{x}_k - \sum_{i=1}^{k-1}\frac{\vec{x}_i\vec{x}_k}{t_i^{\vec{I}}}$$

In this model, the neurons still should act almost like an IF neuron, except that it is inhibited whenever its neighbors fire in a time dependent retroactive fashion. Neuron k should have an integration rate, which starts at $\vec{I} * \vec{x}_k$. When neighbor i fires, it subtracts from this rate $\vec{x}_k\vec{x}_k / t_i^{\vec{I}}$. When its rate times the current time equals the threshold, it fires.

For this model one of the disadvantages is the stabilization process of the receptive field and the second one is how well the neuron signaled correlates with the input by waiting certain amount of time before firing.

SIMULATION

Figure 3 shows the general architecture of the spiking neuron network for modeling the dynamics of the mitral and granule cells. The network consists of three main layers, the input layer, the mitral layer and the granule layer. Each layer has three cells that are connected with each other via synapses, e.g. is $i1$ from the input layer connected with $m1$ through $s1$. The plus and minus symbols indicate whether the connection is excitatory or inhibitory. In this network, the cells of the input layer produce spike trains and can be compared to the input of receptors to a glomerulus in the olfactory bulb. There is no influence between neighboring mitral layer cells through the input of the cells of the input layer. Connections between the input layer and the mitral layer are excitatory. In opposite to input-mitral connections, mitral-granule bidirectional connections are influencing neighboring mitral cells. Each mitral cell is connected with every granule cell and vice versa. The synaptic connections are weighted, whereby connections to neighboring cells are weaker. Connections between $m1$ and $g1$ have the weight 0.5 and -0.5 respectively and connections between $m1$ and $g2$ and between $m1$ and $g3$ are weaker and have a weight of 0.2 and -0.2. Membrane time constant is set to 25-100ms [4].

The circular connection of mitral and granule cells in the model and weighting the synapses of the granule-mitral connection negative enable the simulation of reciprocal inhibitory effects in the olfactory bulb. By changing the weight, one can impact the strength of this inhibitory effect. Sidewise connections of mitral cells through granule cells in the model allow modeling the lateral inhibition of mitral cells. The weight of the connection between $m1$ and $g1$ is 0.5 for the mitral-granule connection and -0.5 for the granule-mitral connection, whereas the connection between $m1$ and $g2$ and also between $m1$ and $g3$ have weights of 0.2 and -0.2. We model the saturation of the mitral layer by introducing a saturation layer. It is basically another reciprocal connection that inhibits the mitral layer that has the effect of saturation. Therefore we included in the model neurons $sa1$, $sa2$ and $sa3$ that have bidirectional connections with $m1$, $m2$ and $m3$.

For simulations in Fig. 3 the input of $m1$, $m2$ and $m3$ are two spike trains of the same length. In the graph of the membrane potential of $m1$ one can observe a decreasing potential after a spike train because of the inhibitory effect of the newly introduced layer. The result is the suppression of parts of the second spike train, which corresponds to a long-term depression.

The simulations show the saturation of mitral cells, where $m1$, $m2$ have the same input and $m3$ a different one (Fig.4, 5). As one can see there is saturation for $m1$ and $m2$, but not for $m3$. Both spike trains of the input of $m3$ result in the same output. The reason that there is no saturation for $m3$ is that the input spike train is too short so that the saturation level is not reached. The fact that the output of $m3$ is so short is because of the lateral inhibition of $m1$ and $m2$.

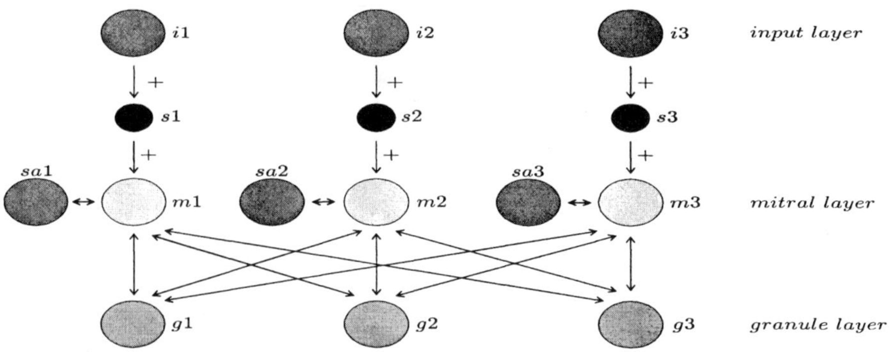

Figure 3. The neural network topology of our olfactory bulb simulator

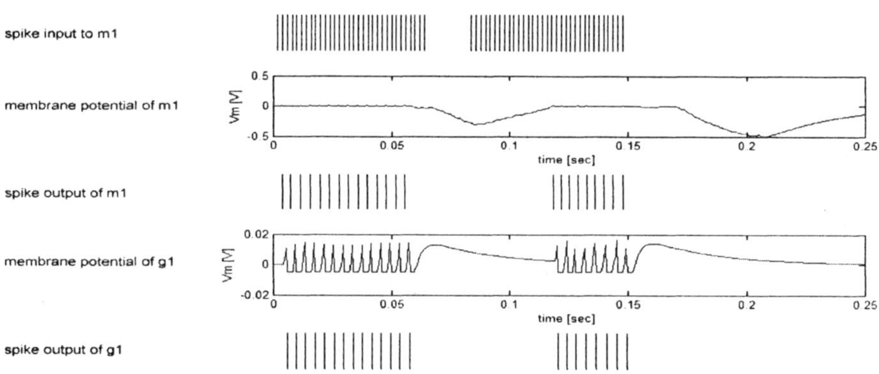

Figure 4. Saturation of mitral cells

CONCLUSIONS

This research shows that spiking neuron networks are very powerful and capable of modeling dynamics within the olfactory bulb. The proposed approach enables us to build spiking neuron networks and to produce reasonable outputs for various scenarios. Those scenarios reflect the three main dynamics - reciprocal inhibition, lateral inhibition and saturation of mitral cells - occurring in the olfactory bulb.

The circular connection of mitral and granule cells in the model and weighting the synapses of the granule-mitral connection negative enable the simulation of reciprocal inhibitory effects in the olfactory bulb. By changing the weight one can impact the strength of this inhibitory effect.

As with reciprocal connections changing weights and delays of the synapses result in an earlier or later inhibition with various strengths. Changing the weight and/or the delay of the synapses of the connection results in a different timing and strength of saturation.

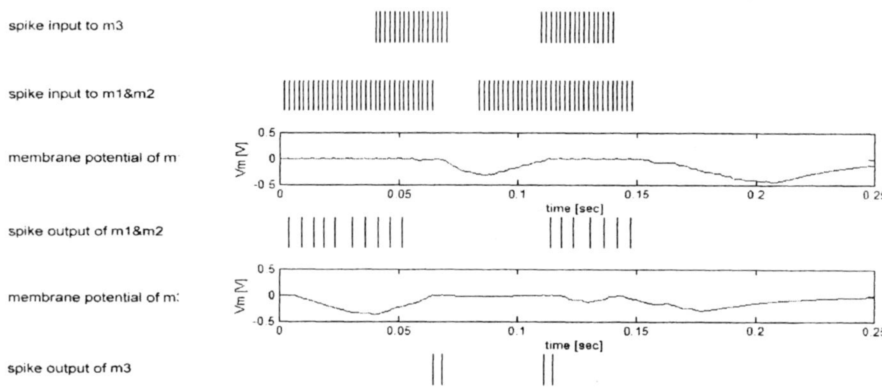

Figure 5. Saturation of mitral cells having different input

ACKNOWLEDGEMENTS

This work was partially supported by Dean of College of Engineering Grant with University of Masssachusetts Dartmouth (UMD). The authors acknowledge the work of the following UMD graduate students: Plamen Tchimev, Martin Prokop, Supreet Chana, towards the preliminary experimental results.

REFERENCES

[1] S. Firestein, *How the olfactory system makes sense of scents*, Nature, 413 (2001), pp. 211-218.

[2] K. Mori, *Relation of chemical structure to specificity of response in olfactory glomeruli*, Current Opinion in Neurobiology, 5 (1995), pp. 467-474.

[3] S. M. Nagel and L. K. Grant, *Tutorial: The Olfactory System*, Athabasca University, 2002.

[4] K. Mori, *Membrane and synaptic properties of identified neurons in the olfactory bulb*, *Prog. Neurobiol.* 29: 275-320, 1987.

[5] W. Gerstner and W. M. Kistler, *Spiking Neuron Models, Single Neurons, Populations, Plasticity*, Cambridge University Press, 2002.

[6] Sterratt, D.C., Spikes, synchrony, sequences and Schistocerca's sense of smell, PhD Thesis, University of Edinburgh, 2001.

[7] W. Maas and B. Ruf, *The Computational Power of Spiking Neurons Depends on the Shape of the Postsynaptic Potentials*, 2002.

[8] Shaw, J., Temporal Sparse Coding with Spiking Neurons without Synfire Chains, Technical Report with University of Rochester, March 2004.

DATA CLUSTERING WITH SPIKING NEURONS

NATACHA GUEORGUIEVA
Computer Science
CSI/City University of New York
2800 Victory Blvd.
Staten Island, NY 10314

IREN VALOVA
Computer and Information Sciences
University of Massachusetts
Dartmouth
285 Old Westport Rd,
North Dartmouth, MA 02747

GEORGI GEORGIEV
Computer Science
University of Wisconsin Oshkosh
800 Algoma Blvd.,
Oshkosh, WI 54901

ABSTRACT

A spiking neuron is a simplified model of the biological neuron as the input, output and internal representation of information, which is the relative timing of individual spikes, is more closely related to that of a biological network.
In this paper we present a biologically plausible unsupervised learning rule for clustering data with spiking neurons based on the idea presented in [2] that a radial basis function (RBF) neuron encodes a particular input spike pattern in the delays available across its synapses. We develop an algorithm for learning the delays by using locally available information as the time difference between the pre- and post- synaptic spike. The computer simulations were performed for RBF neural networks with 20 inputs and the delay interval of 15 ms.

INTRODUCTION

Many application and scientific research areas require analysis of large data sets which becomes a difficult task when the data space is high dimensional, i.e. when the number of features that characterize each point is very large. Often the solution of these problems relies exclusively on the distances between the data points. This is the basis of many clustering methods that use these distances as a dissimilarity measure.

A spiking neurons network (SNN) with their input, output and internal representation of information based on the relative timing of individual spikes is closely related to the biological network. Spiking neurons, receiving temporally encoded inputs, can compute RBFs by storing the relevant information in their delays which can be learned using the time difference between the pre- and post-synaptic spike [1].

Hopfield approach [2] for discovering clusters in an input space based on RBFs with spiking neurons was motivated by many neurobiological findings [3]. The basic idea of the Hopfield model is that an RBF neuron encodes a particular input spike pattern in the delays available across its synapses. If an input pattern is close to the center of the RBF neuron which encoded spike pattern of an RBF neuron, the delays balance out the differences of the firing times of the input neurons such that the RBF neuron fires.

The learning mechanism introduced for a single RBF neuron in [4, 5] is based on the assumption that there are several paths with different delays between each input and each RBF neuron. The choice of the appropriate delays, which encode the center of an RBF neuron, depends on a neuronal learning rule which increases the efficacy of synapses with corresponding suitable delays and decreases the efficacy of other synapses.

Natschläger and Ruf [6] extended the Hopfield idea by proposing a learning algorithm that performs unsupervised clustering in spiking neural networks using spike times as input. Their model encodes the input patterns in the delays across its synapses. It is reliable in finding the centers of high-dimensional clusters but shows some limitations in both cluster capacity as well as in precision.

Here we extend this approach by taking into consideration not only the firing of a neuron but also its firing time and delays. We show how on the basis of these ideas networks of such RBF neurons can be constructed and trained to divide the input space into several clusters, where the selection of the proper delays depends on the difference between pre- and postsynaptic firing time. Using the evidence that temporal coding of biological systems relays on the timing of single spikes [4] we develop a learning algorithm for spiking neurons realizing multiple layers RBF based on temporal spike-time coding.

SPIKING NEURONS: A MATHEMATICAL MODEL

The state of neuron j is described by the internal state variable $u_j(t)$, which models the neuron's membrane potential at time t. A spike is generated whenever $u_j(t)$ crosses the threshold θ. Let us denote by $\boldsymbol{F}_j = \{t_j^1, t_j^2, t_j^3, ...\}$ is the set of firing times (the moment of threshold crossing) of neuron j. The total postsynaptic potential $h_j(t)$, represented by (1), is a linear superposition of the postsynaptic potentials (PSPs) represented by the kernel $\varepsilon(t-(t_j^k+d_{ij}))$, where t_j^k is the presynaptic firing time and d_{ij} models the delay from the occurrence of a spike in neuron j and the beginning of it's effect on neuron i.

$$h_j(t) = \sum_{j \in \boldsymbol{\Gamma}_i} \sum_{t_j^K \in F_j} w_{ij} \varepsilon(t-(t_j^k+d_{ij})) \tag{1}$$

where w_{ij} models the synaptic efficacy between neurons i and j; $(t_j^k+d_{ij})$ is the time when the k'th spike from neuron j started affecting neuron i and $\boldsymbol{\Gamma}_i$ is the set of neurons sending outputs to neuron j.

Therefore, the membrane potential $u_j(t)$ can be presented with the following formula:

$$u_j(t \mid t_j^{last\_fire}) = \mu_j(t - t_j^{last\_fire}) + h_j(t) \tag{2}$$

where t^{last_time} is the last firing time of neuron j and $\mu_j(t - t_j^{last\_fire})$ is the negative contribution to the neuron membrane potential $u_j(t)$ after the spike. Thus, t^{last_time} can be obtained from the following equation:

$$t^{last\_fire} = max\{t_j^{(n)} \mid t_j^{(n)} > t\} \tag{3}$$

NEURAL NETWORK TOPOLOGY OF RBF WITH SPIKING NEURONS

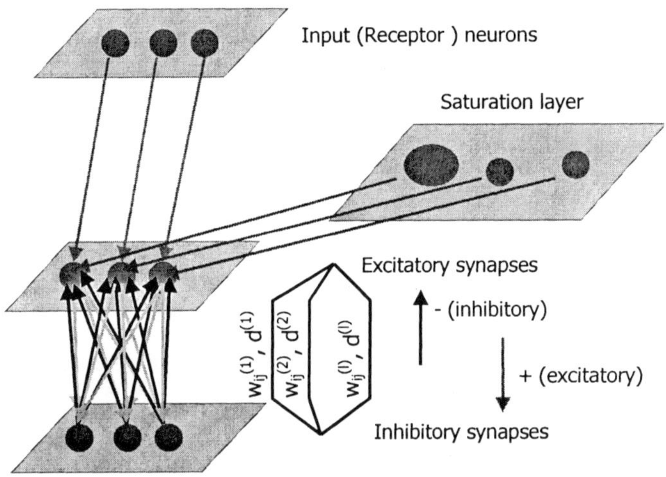

Figure 1. Neural Network Topology of RBF with Spiking Neurons

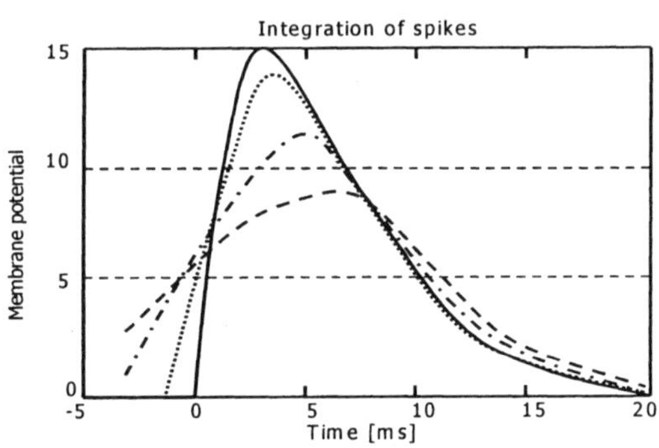

Figure 2. Membrane potential as a result of four 15-dimentional objects

We demonstrate how the system of leaky integrate-and-fire neurons can be used to perform a clustering task, relying on the fact that the neuron fires if its excitatory input is strong enough to push the postsynaptic potential above its threshold [7, 8].

The n-dimensional input patterns $X^{(j)} = (x_1^{(j)}, x_2^{(j)}, ..., x_n^{(j)})$ are encoded with input (sensory) spiking neurons $u_1, u_2, ..., u_n$ which are connected to a single RBF layer of output spiking neurons $v_1, v_2, \ldots, v_n$ shown in Fig.1. For the purposes of clusterization, the temporal coding of data assumes that each sensory neuron emits exactly one spike when the pattern is presented to the NN, e.g., the spike from u_j is delayed by x_j ms. Thus, the 3-dimentional input (3, 7, 1) will be coded by u_3 firing after 1 ms, u_1 firing after 3 ms and u_2 firing after 7 ms.

If we consider the case of multiple synapses and constant delays, $h_j(t)$ will be presented as:

$$h_j(t) = \sum_{j \in \Gamma_i} \sum_{t_j^K \in F_j} \sum_{d=1}^{D} w_{ij}^{(d)} \varepsilon(t - (t_j^k + d)) \qquad (4)$$

Fig. 2 shows membrane potential as a result of four 15-dimentional input patterns. The thick solid line is the response to a pattern directly at the center of the RBF, the thin dashed line is the response to an input slightly off the center and the other two patterns are farther away. If the threshold is set to 10, the neuron will react fastest to the pattern which is at the center. When presented with the furthermost pattern from the center (thick dashed line) it will not reach the threshold, and therefore not fire at all.

When comparing the reaction of v_j to an input pattern which is at it's center and an input pattern which is slightly off it's center, we can see that the first pattern causes a higher peak in v_j's membrane potential and the membrane potential crosses the threshold. When a pattern is far from the center, the peak will be lower then the threshold and no spike will be generated. The neuron realizes a radial basis function which is symmetric around the center defined above and whose input is an m-dimensional pattern and output is the time till it emits a spike.

LEARNING ALGORITHM FOR CLUSTERING WITH RBF USING SPIKING NEURONS

The learning rule is a variant of the Hebb law. It is applied to the synaptic weights of the neuron that fired when the input was presented to the network. The weights are changed in a way that moves the RBF neuron's center closer to the input pattern following the rule: synapses which contributed to the neuron's firing are strengthened and synapses which did not contribute are weakened. We distinguish two types of synapses:

- Those of the synapses who started affecting the postsynaptic neuron slightly before the neuron actually crossed the threshold contribute to the neuron's firing.
- The ones who affected the membrane potential much earlier or much later did not contribute to the neuron's firing.

During the learning process the weight $w_{ij}^{(q)}$ of the synapse between input neuron u_i and RBF spiking neuron v_j with delay $d^{(q)}$ is updated, where the change in the synaptic weight is presented by the following learning rule:

$$\Delta w_{ij}^{(q)} = \eta L((t_i + d^{(q)}) - (t_j + d^{(r)})) \tag{5}$$

where η determines the learning rate; t_i is the time since neuron i fired; t_j is the time since neuron j fired; $d^{(q)}$ is the synaptic delay and $d^{(r)}$ shows the time used by the postsynaptic spike to propagate backwards to the synapses.

SIMULATIONS WITH ARTIFICIAL DATA SETS

In order to study how our RBF SNN behaves on a high-dimensional space we perform six sets of simulations based on artificial data for clusterization where the number of RBF was different or equal to the number of clusters. These simulations were organized with the following common parameters: the length of coding interval was 10 ms and the delay interval was 15 ms such that the available delays were 1 ms, 2 ms, ..., 16 ms; every 50 ms a new learning cycle started by presenting a new vector X to the neural network; there was no overlap between the clusters.

In the first set of experiments - Fig. 3, the number of RBF was equal to the number of clusters. After 30 learning cycles from each cluster each RBF spiking neuron had converged to one cluster. We also observed that as the absolute refractory period increased, the postsynaptic response for each spike decreased on average and increased current input was required on the pre-synaptic neuron to trigger a synaptic discharge (a spike). After learning the cluster, the RBF neuron started to fire significantly earlier when a sample from this cluster is presented.

SIMULATIONS WITH IRIS DATA

We implemented our RBF neural network based on spiking neurons to the Iris data set consisting of 150 data points belonging to 3 groups of the same size. There are three varieties of Iris: Setosa, Versicolor and Virginica. The original problem is to classify a new Iris flower into one of these three types on the basis of four attributes (petal and sepal length and width). The input groups for our experiments are 3 species of iris and each of the data points is described by 4 features: petal-length, petal-width, sepal-length, and sepal-width. By using the proposed RBF neural network based on spiking neurons we were able to classify correctly 89% of the data points what is comparable with other powerful algorithms.

CONCLUSIONS

The data clusterization based on the presented NN algorithm with RBF and leaky integrate-and-fire type showed that: a) The RBF neurons converged very reliably to the centers of the clusters even in the presence of noise; b) If during the learning process clusters were added or removed the RBF neurons were able to reconfigure dynamically what is of particular importance for biological systems.

ACKNOWLEDGEMENTS

This work was partially supported by CREW/NSF grant, City University of New York/CSI President Award Grant, University of Wisconsin Oshkosh Faculty Development Grant.

REFERENCES

[1] Maas W., Networks Of Spiking Neurons: The Third Generation Of Neural Network Models. *Neural Networks*, 10(9):1659-1671, 1998.

[2] Hopfield J. J., Pattern Recognition Computation Using Action Potential Timing For Stimulus Representation. *Nature*, 376: 33-36, 1995.

[3] O'Keefe and Reece, M. L., Phase Relationship Between Hippocampal Place Units And The EEG Theta Rhythm. *Hippocampus*, 3(3): 3317-30, 1993.

[4] Bohte, S. M., Han A. P. and Kok N. K., Unsupervised Clustering With Spiking Neurons By Sparse Temporal Coding And Multi-Layer RBF Networks. *Proceedings of the IEEE-INNS-ENNS International Joint Conference on Neural Networks,* 2000.

[5] Maas W., Lower Bounds For The Computational Power Of Networks Of Spiking Neurons. *Neural Computation* 8: 1-40, 1996.

[6] Natschläger T. and B. Ruf B., Spatial And Temporal Pattern Analysis Via Spiking Neurons. *Network: Computation in Neural Systems*, 9(3): 319-332, 1998.

[7] Guedalia I.D., London M., and Werman M., An On-Line Agglomerative Clustering Method For Nonstationary Data. *Neural Comp.*, vol. 11, no. 2, pp. 521–540, 1999.

[8] Mattia M. and Del Giudice P., Efficient event-driven simulation of large networks of spiking neurons and dynamical synapses. *Neural Computation*, vol. 12, no. 10, pp. 2305–2329, 2000.

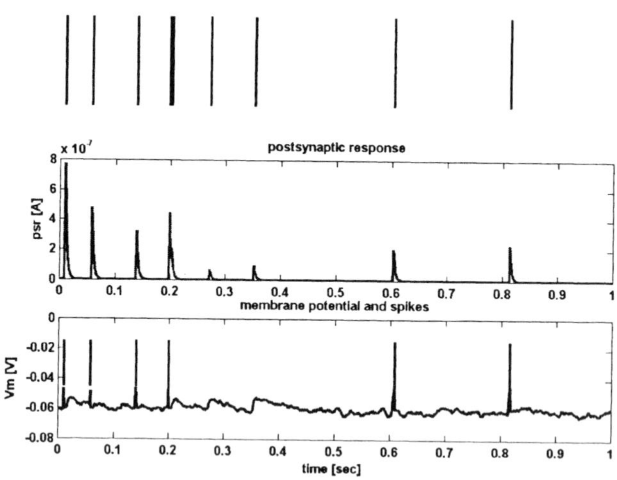

Figure 3. The number of clusters and RBFs is equal

WHAT CAN SVMS TEACH EACH OTHER?

OLCAY KURŞUN
School of Computer Science
University of Central Florida
Orlando, FL 32816, USA
Email: kursun@cs.ucf.edu

OLEG V. FAVOROV
Dept. of Biomedical Engineering
University of North Carolina
Chapel Hill, NC 27599, USA
Email: favorov@bme.unc.edu

ABSTRACT

Causal factors operating in a studied system can be discovered through a search for highly correlated functions of any kind over disjoint subsets of the observed variables, since such correlated functions must have a reason for their statistical interdependence, a causal source in the domain of the data. Based on this mutual-information maximization principle (*Imax*), a pair of SVMs, set up to use each other's output as their own training signal, can teach each other higher-order features of the data that reveal hidden causal factors controlling the observed phenomena. When applied to a database of human face images, this method extracts such facial features that enable performance on a face recognition task superior to that of other comparable methods.

INTRODUCTION

Developing an understanding of a new studied subject commonly involves creation of new, subject-specific concepts that reveal deeper relations, interdependencies among the subject's observed phenomena. One central function of concepts is to express hidden causal factors, which – once recognized – serve to reduce complexity of the observed relations. Hidden factors can vary greatly in the extent of their impact on the studied systems, from factors that impact behaviors of just one or a few observed variables to factors that impact behaviors of most or even all of the observed variables. Hidden factors that are reflected in the behaviors of sufficiently large numbers of the observed variables can, in principle, be extracted from them through some computation. And they should be extracted: their reflectance in behaviors of multiple observed variables implies that these factors play prominent and central roles in the organization and functioning of the studied system. In this paper we describe how SVMs can be used in extraction of hidden factors, and illustrate their use by extracting individual-distinguishing facial features from photographs of a large set of human faces.

SINBAD METHOD FOR EXTRACTING HIDDEN FACTORS

Recently we have developed SINBAD – a novel computational method of nonlinear factor analysis designed specifically for finding deeply hidden factors (Ryder and Favorov, 2001; Favorov et al., 2003; Kursun and Favorov, 2003, 2004; Favorov and Ryder, 2004). SINBAD belongs to the class of unsupervised learning algorithms that are based on the *Imax* principle of maximization of mutual information among disjoint sources of information (Becker and Hinton, 1992). The basic idea is to set up two or more computational modules that look at separate but related parts of the sensory input, and to make these 'search' modules teach each other to produce outputs that match their own as closely as possible. In this way the modules will learn to perform different operations (i.e., functions) on their different inputs so as to yield correlated outputs. Such correlated outputs must have a reason for their statistical interdependence, a causal source in the domain of the data. Therefore, the correlated functions over different subsets of variables express a previously unrecognized feature (a hidden factor) that is responsible for the correlation (Becker and Hinton, 1992; Phillips and Singer, 1997; Ryder and Favorov, 2001; Favorov and Ryder, 2004).

In the original SINBAD design (Favorov and Ryder, 2004), each learning module – called a "dendrite"– was implemented in a form of an error backpropagation network. In this paper we replace backprop nets with SVMs. Backprop nets, and neural networks in general, are vulnerable to over-fitting when applied to datasets with large numbers of variables and small numbers of samples, which is typical of real-life problems. SVMs are better suited for such conditions (Burges, 1998; Scholkopf and Smola, 2002).

For its use as a SINBAD dendrite, we used a simple implementation of SVM regressor, SVM^{light} (Joachims, 1999). This SVM regressor works in batch mode. Other versions of SVMs for regression can be used as well. In a basic design, a SINBAD cell has two SVMs for its two dendrites, each receiving different, non-overlapping sets of input channels. Output of one SVM is used as the training signal for the other SVM, and vice versa, which means that the SVMs are set up to teach each other to produce maximally correlated outputs in response to their different inputs. As a result, the SVMs are driven to tune to the causal source (a hidden factor) responsible for the correlation.

To train SVMs, at the start each SVM is assigned randomly chosen values to be its output in response to the training set of input vectors. During training, outputs of each SVM are autoscaled first; i.e., normalized to zero-mean and unit standard deviation. Then SVM^{ligh} regressor is run in a batch mode over all the training data samples, using the autoscaled outputs of the other SVM as the training signal. After regression of both SVMs, their outputs are re-computed (updated) and autoscaled, and the training cycle (of regression and autoscaling) is repeated until outputs of the two SVMs converge as much as possible.

SINBAD cells are powerful discoverers of hidden factors. For a quick illustration we created a toy problem with four observed variables (Fig. 1). These variables are pixels taken from corresponding locations in four images shown in Fig. 1. Each pixel in image IM2 is a nonlinear function of identically located pixels in images IM1 and IM5 (scaled between 0 and 1): $IM2xy = IM1xy + IM5xy - 2 \cdot IM1xy \cdot IM5xy$. The same holds for image IM3 – each pixel in IM3 is the analogous function of identically located pixels in images IM4 and, again, IM5. Thus, image IM5 is a hidden factor determining the contents of images IM2 and IM3. To discover this hidden factor, SINBAD cell is trained on the values of identically located pixels in images 1, 2, 3, 4. Pixels from images IM1 and IM2 are given to SVM_1, pixels from images IM3 and IM4 are given to SVM_2. SINBAD cell gradually learns – without any guidance – to output the value of the identically located pixel in the hidden image IM5 (compare IM5 with the image below the cell). Thus, although image IM5 was so well hidden in images IM2 and IM3 as to be invisible there, SINBAD cell nevertheless was able to easily detect its presence and extract its content.

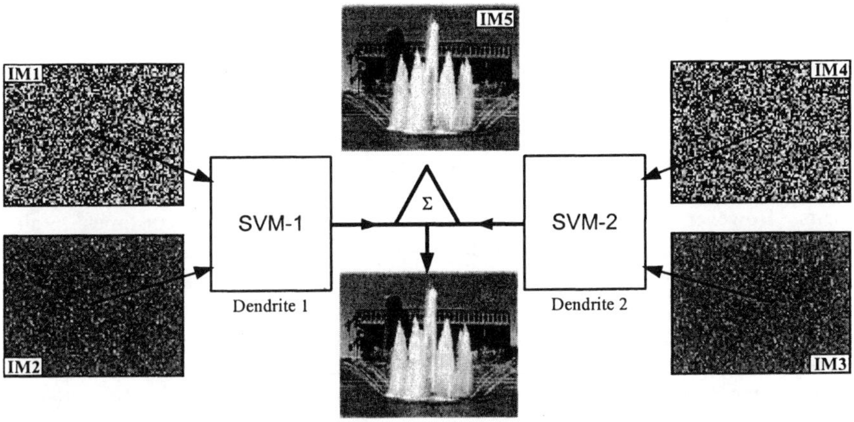

Figure 1. The SINBAD cell with two SVM dendrites. Each SVM receives input via two channels from identically positioned pixels in two images. The cell's output is a sum of outputs of the two SVMs. Output of one SVM is used as a teaching signal for the other SVM. The hidden image is a photo taken from the University of Central Florida - main campus in Orlando.

EXTRACTING FACIAL FEATURES WITH SINBAD

The field of Machine Learning has many examples of promising new algorithms performing well on simple, artificially constructed ("toy") problems, but showing only limited success when applied in practice to more challenging real-life problems. To evaluate the potential of SINBAD to perform on realistically challenging problems, we applied it to the problem of human face recognition. We used AT&T face database (AT&T Laboratories, Cambridge) for our face recognition experiments. This database, formerly known as ORL face database, is composed of 400 gray scale images obtained from 40 different individuals, ten different images per a person. The images were taken at different times, varying the lighting, the viewing angle (frontal or more or less semi-frontal view), facial expressions (open or closed eyes, smiling or not smiling), and facial details (e.g., glasses or no glasses). All images were taken against a dark homogeneous background with the subjects in an upright position, with tolerance for some side movement. The size of each original image is 92x112 pixels, with 256 gray levels per pixel. To reduce the computational load for our exercise, we down-sampled each image to 23x28 pixels by bilinear interpolation.

One of the central goals of face-processing research is to identify informative higher-order facial features that can effectively characterize and distinguish human faces independent of variations of viewing conditions, such as, for example, viewing angle, illumination, or facial expression. Such features constitute hidden factors – they are variables that are present in face images, but hidden in the spatial patterns of pixels across the image and require computational extraction. In extracting such hidden variables using SINBAD approach, we sought to take advantage of the presence in the database of ten different images of the same face. That is, these images differ from one another at the pixel level (due to variations of viewing conditions), but not at the level of higher-order facial features (which are determined by the identity of the photographed individual). Consequently, we can train SINBAD dendrites by concurrently exposing two or more dendrites of the same SINBAD cell to different images of the same individual, thus forcing the dendrites to discover some higher-order variable that does not change across different images of the same individual, i.e., an *individual-specific facial feature.*

Although we can use the basic two-dendrite SINBAD cell described above in this task, it would be computationally more efficient to adapt the SINBAD design to specifics of this project. The first step in efficiency is to give a SINBAD cell 10 dendrites, so that all 10 images of the same individual can be presented at the same time, rather than in 90 pairs. However, since each dendrite ought to be exposed, at different times, to all 10 images, it means that 10 different dendrites will end up being exposed to exactly the same set of images and required to produce exactly the same outputs to them. That means that the 10 dendrites will be functionally identical and can be replaced with a single dendrite. Operating in a batch mode, the SVM that implements this dendrite should be exposed in a sequence to all the images in the dataset, all the outputs should be auto-scaled (as before), and then the SVM should be trained on the teaching signal T. For image j of individual i, the teaching signal $T_{i,j}$ is:

$$T_{i,j} = \left(\sum_{\substack{k=1 \\ k \neq j}}^{n} OUTPUT_{i,k} \right) / (n-1), \tag{1}$$

where n is the number of images per one individual in the training set and $OUTPUT_{i,k}$ is the output of the SVM to image k of individual i.

For our exercise, we chose to develop 15 facial features. Therefore we trained 15 SINBAD cells (each with one SVM dendrite). To ensure that different SINBAD cells learn different facial features, we used cascaded anti-Hebbian inhibition among the cells (Favorov and Ryder, 2004); i.e., the first cell inhibited all the rest, the second cell inhibited all but the first cell, and so on, each successive cell inhibiting all the following cells. In this scheme, the first cell is free to learn any facial feature and prevents all the other cells from learning the same feature, the second cell is free to learn any other feature and prevents the rest from learning it as well, and so on. For each cell, its training signal for image j of individual i, $T_{i,j}$, was adjusted by subtracting inhibition $I_{i,j}$ from it. $I_{i,j}$ was computed as:

$$I_{i,j} = \iota \cdot \sum_{s} \rho_s \cdot OUTPUT_{s,i,j}, \tag{2}$$

where ι is a scaling constant ($\iota = 0.25$ in our exercise), s is one of the cells inhibiting the target cell, ρ_s is correlation coefficient of outputs of the target cell and cell s, and $OUTPUT_{s,i,j}$ is the output of cell s in response to image j of individual i.

The 15 SINBAD cells were trained on 9 out of 10 images of each individual, saving one image for later testing. The study was repeated 10 times (10 runs) to determine the reproducibility of outcomes. For the SVMs of SINBAD cells we used radial basis function (RBF) kernels with σ=0.01 (standard deviation) and C=10 (trade-off between training error and margin). All 15 SINBAD cells were successful in learning facial features, as judged by the fact that each cell learned to produce nearly the same outputs to different images of the same individual, and different outputs to images of different individuals (coefficient of correlation between a cell's output to a test image and the other images of the same individual – the ones used in training – was in 0.85-0.95 range).

How meaningful are the facial features learned by the SINBAD cells? To answer this question will require evaluation of the usefulness of these features in various face-processing tasks. In this paper we report on their performance in one such task, which has received much attention; namely, the individual-recognition task. For this task, we describe each image in the dataset by a vector of 15 SINBAD-learned features. This 15-dimensional feature vector is used as an input to 40 new binary SVMs (Joachims 1999) with RBF-kernels with σ=0.5 and C=5. Each SVM was trained to respond with +1 output to images of one particular individual and with –1 output to images of all 39 other individuals. Thus, for each individual in the dataset we set up a separate SVM dedicated to his/her recognition. These individual-recognizing SVMs were trained only on those images that were used in training SINBAD cells to learn facial features. To test the recognition performance of these SVMs, the set-aside "test" images (one per each individual) were shown to the 40 SVMs, and the SVM that produced the highest output was taken as the "winner," thus deciding the identity of the individual in the presented image. Although this leave-one-out winner-take-all testing method is not the most efficient one, it is simple and sensitive enough to give us an approximate estimate of the usefulness of SINBAD features for this individual-recognition task.

The error rate of 2.50% we obtained in this task using SINBAD facial features compare favorably to other published approaches: the nearest neighbor classifier (11.00%) (Lee et al., 2003), Eigenfaces/PCA (4.75%) (Yankun and Chongqing, 2002), multi-class SVMs on PCA+LDA subspace (6.75%) (Lee et al., 2003), and binary-tree SVMs (3.00%) (Guodong et al., 2000). To appreciate the level of difficulty of identifying an individual from an image at which our SINBAD method produced errors, Fig. 2 shows 10 images of two particular individuals who were responsible for the majority of misidentification errors. These two individuals, indeed, strongly resemble each other. In conclusion, the results of this study demonstrate the definite usefulness of SINBAD-learned facial features in, at least, the individual-recognition task.

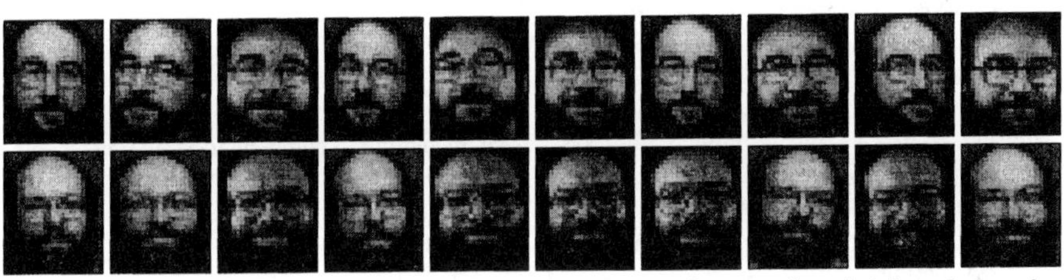

Figure 2. Images of the two individuals who were most frequently mistaken for each other in the individual-recognition task that utilized SINBAD-learned facial features.

Better classification accuracies on the AT&T face database, about 1-2% error, have been reported by Xi et al. (2002) and Heisele et al. (2003) However, their methods involved supervised hand-labeling for extraction of local features, such as eyes, nose, mouth, etc. SINBAD method can readily be extended to enable it also to extract local – as opposed to, at present, global – features, and do it in unsupervised manner (Kursun and Favorov, 2004). Thus, we believe that with additional work unsupervised SINBAD extraction of local facial features is feasible and it should further improve our performance on face-recognition tasks.

CONCLUSIONS

Identification of the descriptive/explanatory features/factors in the data is one of the central tasks of data processing. It is also one of the most difficult tasks. SINBAD offers a promising method for accomplishing this task. It is based on search for correlated functions over different sets of inputs, therefore tuning to a hidden source responsible for this correlation. Use of SVMs as a part of the SINBAD architecture, to perform the search for correlated functions, significantly expands the capabilities of the SINBAD approach, especially in its application to real-life subjects characterized by large numbers of raw variables, limited numbers of observations, and rich in multivariate and nonlinear relations.

ACKNOWLEDGEMENTS

The authors wish to acknowledge helpful discussions with Niels da Vitoria Lobo and Jamal Alzeban. This work was supported, in part, by US Army Research Office grant P43077-LS.

REFERENCES

Becker S, Hinton GE, 1992, "A self-organizing neural network that discovers surfaces in random-dot stereograms," *Nature,* Vol. 355, pp. 161-163.

Burges CJC, 1998, "A tutorial on support vector machines for pattern recognition," *Data Mining Knowledge Discovery,* Vol. 2, pp. 121-167.

Favorov OV, Ryder D, 2004, "SINBAD: A neocortical mechanism for discovering environmental variables and regularities hidden in sensory input," *Biological Cybernetics,* Vol. 90, pp. 191-202.

Favorov OV, Ryder D, Hester JT, Kelly DG, Tommerdahl M, 2003, "The cortical pyramidal cell as a set of interacting error backpropagating networks: a mechanism for discovering nature's order," *Computational Models for Neuroscience,* Hecht-Nielsen R and McKenna T (ed.), Springer Verlag, London, pp.25-64.

Guodong G, Li SZ, Chan K, 2000, "Face recognition by support vector machines," *Proceedings of Fourth IEEE International Conference on Automatic Face and Gesture Recognition (FGR'00),* Grenoble, France.

Heisele B, Ho P, Wu J, Poggio T, 2003, "Face recognition: component-based versus global approaches," *Computer Vision and Image Understanding,* Vol. 91(2), pp. 6-21.

Joachims T, 1999, "Making large-scale SVM learning practical," *Advances in Kernel Methods - Support Vector Learning,* B. Schölkopf and C. Burges and A. Smola (ed.), MIT-Press, Cambridge.

Kursun O, Favorov OV, 2003, "Single-frame super-resolution by inference from learned features," *Istanbul University Journal of Electrical & Electronics Engineering,* Vol. 3(1), pp. 673-681.

Kursun O, Favorov O, 2004, "SINBAD automation of scientific discovery: from factor analysis to theory synthesis," *Natural Computing,* Vol. 3, pp. 207-233.

Lee CH, Park SW, Chang W, Park JW, 2003, "Improving the Performance of Multi-Class SVMs in Face Recognition with Nearest Neighbor Rule," *Proceedings of the 15th IEEE International Conference on Tools with Artificial Intelligence (ICTAI'03),* Sacramento, CA.

Phillips WA, Singer W, 1997, "In search of common foundations for cortical computation," *Behavioral and Brain Sciences,* Vol. 20, pp. 657-722.

Ryder D, Favorov OV, 2001, "The new associationism: a neural explanation for the predictive powers of cerebral cortex," *Brain and Mind,* Vol. 2, pp. 161-194.

Scholkopf B and Smola AJ, 2002, *"Learning with Kernels,"* Cambridge, MA: MIT Press.

Xi D, Podolak IT, Lee SW, 2002, "Facial component extraction and face recognition with support vector machines," *Proceedings of the Fifth IEEE International Conference on Automatic Face and Gesture Recognition (FGR'02),* Washinton D.C., Washington.

Yankun Z, Chongqing L, 2002, "Face Recognition Using Kernel Principal Component Analysis And Genetic Algorithms," *IEEE International Workshop on Neural Networks for Signal Processing,* Martigny, Switzerland.

SPARSE VS DENSE DATA REPRESENTATIONS IN KERNEL METHODS

N. ANCONA, R. MAGLIETTA, E. STELLA

Istituto di Studi sui Sistemi Intelligenti per l'Automazione - C.N.R
Via G. Amendola, 122/D-I - 70126 – Bari – Italy
{ancona, maglietta, stella}@ba.issia.cnr.it

ABSTRACT

This paper focuses on the problem of how data representation influences the generalization error of kernel based learning machines like Support Vector Machines (SVM) for classification. Frame theory provides a well founded mathematical framework for representing data in many different ways. We analyze the effects of sparse and dense data representations on the generalization error of such learning machines measured by using leave-one-out error given a finite number of training data. We show that, in the case of sparse data representation, the generalization capacity of an SVM trained by using polynomial or Gaussian kernel functions is equal to the one of a linear SVM. We show that sparse data representations reduce the generalization error as long as the representation is not too sparse, as in the case of very large dictionaries. Very sparse representations increase drastically the generalization error of kernel based methods. Dense data representations, on the contrary, reduce the generalization error also in the case of very large dictionaries.

INTRODUCTION

The problem of data representation is one of the most critical issues concerning the realization of intelligence machines which are able to solve real life problems [1]. In this paper we analyze how different data representation models influence the generalization capacity of kernel based learning machines, in particular of Support Vector Machines (SVM) for classification [2]. Data representation is the problem of finding an appropriate set of coefficients or features for numerically describing the data. In general such representations involve linear or not linear transformations of the original data. In this paper we focus on transformations of the former type. Hence, the features $(c_j)_{j\in J}$ are generated projecting the data (signal) f on a suitable system of vectors or functions $(\varphi_j)_{j\in J}$, i.e. $c_j = \langle f, \varphi_j \rangle$, with given properties, where the symbol $\langle \cdot, \cdot \rangle$ denotes the scalar product defined in the space where these objects live. It is important that the features $(c_j)_{j\in J}$ relative to the signal f characterize the signal itself, in the sense that if $\langle f_1, \varphi_j \rangle = \langle f_2, \varphi_j \rangle$ for all $j\in J$, then $f_1 \equiv f_2$. This is equivalent to say that any signal f can be expressed by using the system of functions. This means that the system $(\varphi_j)_{j\in J}$ is *complete*. When the system $(\varphi_j)_{j\in J}$ is the smallest set of functions spanning the whole space, we say that it constitutes a *basis*. In this case, the basis functions $(\varphi_j)_{j\in J}$ are linearly independent and the representation of any signal with respect to the given basis is *unique* [3]. In this paper we require that the system of functions $(\varphi_j)_{j\in J}$ to be complete only, and not to be a basis. We require that the system span the whole space, and that the elements of the system are linearly dependent. In fact such systems, in general, are constituted by much more elements than the ones present in a basis, and for this reason they are called *overcomplete* or *redundant* systems of functions. The main difference with respect to a basis is that now there is not a unique representation for each element of the space. On the contrary, there is a plurality of possible representations. Overcomplete dictionaries of functions or vectors are called *frames* [4]. We refer the reader to [6] for a review of the frame theory in generic Hilbert spaces. At this aim, we consider a family of vectors $(\varphi_j)_{j\in J}$ of $\Re^n$. In some contexts [7], the family is called *dictionary* and the elements of the family are called *atoms*. By definition, the family of vectors $(\varphi_j)_{j\in J}$ constitutes a frame if there exist two constants $A>0$ and $B<\infty$ such that, for all $u\in\Re^n$ we have: $A||u||^2\leq \Sigma_{j\in J} (\langle u, \varphi_j \rangle)^2 \leq B||u||^2$. We call A and B *frame bounds*.

We have considered two different representation techniques of data in terms of elements of overcomplete dictionaries. *Method of frames* (MOF) proposed by I. Daubechies in [4] provides a dense representation of data obtained projecting the data onto all the atoms of the dictionary. *Matching pursuit* (MP) introduced by S. Mallat in [5] provides, on the contrary, a sparse representation of data with a very few number of coefficients different from zero. We analyze the representations of data obtained with these two methods by using overcomplete dictionaries of Haar and Gabor functions, with a different number of center frequencies and spacing.

METHOD OF FRAME AND MATCHING PURSUIT

Let F be a l x n matrix having the frame vectors as its rows. The matrix F is the *frame operator*. Let $c\in\Re^l$ be the vector obtained when we apply the frame operator F to the vector $u\in\Re^n$, that is: $c=Fu$. Once we have computed the coefficients c, projecting the signal on the frame elements, there is a unique way to recover the signal u: $u=F^+c$, where $F^+ = (F^T F)^{-1}F^T$ is the *pseudoinverse* of F. F, also called *analysis operator*, associates a vector of coefficients c (features) to a signal u, projecting the signal through the atoms of the dictionary. This operation involves a l x n matrix. F^+, also called *synthesis operator*, builds up a signal u as a superposition of the atoms of the dual dictionary weighted with coefficients c. This operation involves a n x l matrix. Note that the columns of F^+ are the elements of the dual frame. In [6] we show (see also [7]) that, among all representations of a signal in terms of the frame elements, MOF selects the one whose coefficients have minimum l^2 norm. Note that the method of frame is not sparsity preserving: in fact each atom having a non zero scalar product with the signal contributes to the solution, and so the corresponding component of c is different from zero.

Matching pursuit [5] is a non linear algorithm that decomposes a signal into a linear expansion of waveforms that, in general, belong to a overcomplete dictionary of functions. It is an iterative procedure which, at each step, selects the atom of the dictionary which best reduces the residual between the current approximation of the signal and the signal itself. We analyse the method in the case of a signal $u\in\Re^n$. Let $(\varphi_j)_{j\in J}$ be a frame of vectors of $\Re^n$, with $||\varphi_j||=1$ for all $j=1, 2,..l$. At stage $k=0$, let $u^{(0)} = 0$ be the current approximation of the signal u

with residual $R^{(0)}$ given by $R^{(0)}=u-u^{(0)}$. The algorithm selects the dictionary atom that best correlates with the residual. In general, at stage k the algorithm builds the approximation $u^{(k)}$ of u given by $u^{(k)}=u^{(k-1)}+\langle R^{(k-1)}, \varphi_{jk}\rangle$ with $j_k=\arg\max_{(j\in J)} |\langle R^{(k-1)}, \varphi_j\rangle|$ with residual $R^{(k)}=u-u^{(k)}$. From the residual at the stage k-th we have: $u=u^{(k)}+R^{(k)}$. Recursively, at the stage k we have:

$$u=\sum_{i=1}^{k}\langle R^{(i-1)},\varphi_{j_i}\rangle\varphi_{j_i}+R^{(k)}$$

Hence matching pursuit represents the signal u as linear combination of the dictionary atoms with coefficients computed minimizing at each step the residual. Some considerations are in order. In general the algorithm ends after a fixed number of iterations or when the residual is less than a given threshold. Matching pursuit is an example of a more general class of methods known as *greedy algorithms*: they do the best thing at every step. The algorithm provides a sparse representation of the signal.

KERNELS AND FRAME OPERATORS

In this section we analyze what happens when we apply SVM on the features obtained by projecting the original examples on a frame. We are given a training set $S=\{x_1, x_2, ..., x_N\}$ of size N where $x_i\in\Re^n$, for $i=1,2, ..., N$. Let F be a frame operator of size l x n. Let us consider the feature vectors obtained applying the analysis operator F to the examples x_i: $c_i = F x_i$. Hence we have a training set $S_c=\{c_1, c_2, ..., c_N\}$ in the feature space. SVM [2] classifies a new data, evaluating the decision function *f(c)*:

$$f(c)=\sum_{i=1}^{N}\lambda_i^* y_i K(c_i,c)+b$$

where $y_i=\{-1, 1\}$ for $i=1,2, ..., N$, λ^*_i are the solution of the classical quadratic programming (QP) problem of SVM, b is *bias term* and K is the kernel function of SVM. In the case of linear kernel function we have:

$$K(c_i,c_j)=\langle c_i,c_j\rangle=c_i^T c_j=(Fx_i)^T Fx_j=x_i^T F^T Fx_j$$

Such a function computes scalar products in the feature space without having to explicitly map the input vectors in this space. This property is particularly useful when the number l of atoms in the dictionary is extremely high. Such a property holds true also in the case of polynomial and Gaussian kernel functions. So we can conclude that, in the case of features generated by method of frame, the application of the frame operator F on the input patterns can be synthesized in the kernel function K.

EXPERIMENTAL RESULTS

For analyzing the influence of the sparsity on the generalization error, we use a popular benchmark data set: the "sonar data set" from the UCI Repository (http//www.ics.uci.edu/~mlearn/MLRepository.html). It consists of 208 examples, 111 positive and 97 negative, each one having $n=60$ components in the range [0,1], representing the sonar return produced by a metal cylinder or by a cylindrically shaped rock in the same environment. For measuring the behaviour of different learning machines, with the aforementioned representation schemes by using different overcomplete dictionaries, we use the loo-error. Table I shows the loo-error for SVM with $K_1(x,y) = x \cdot y$ and $K_2(x,y)=(1+ x \cdot y)^2$ on the original data, where $x \cdot y = \langle x,y \rangle$. For each experiment, we report the minimum loo-error obtained varying the parameter C in an interval. A typical behaviour of the loo-error function with respect to C is shown in figure 1. Note that after having reached the minimum value, the loo-error increases as C increases, showing that for high values of C overfitting occurs. In the successive table, l indicates the number of atoms in the dictionary, B/A is the frame bound ratio, S is the mean sparsification ratio of the training examples as represented by MP with the dictionary. For representing an example x, MP ends if $\|R^{(k)}\|/\|x\| \leq 10^{-4}$. We have verified that error thresholds smaller than this do not modify the loo-error. Moreover, we report the minimum loo-error of SVM with kernels K_1 and K_2 trained on examples represented with MOF and MP techniques. For having a number of components of the training vectors equals to a power of two, we have symmetrically extended each vector from 60 to 64 components.

We consider three types of dictionaries: Haar, Gabor evenly spaced frequencies, and Gabor b octave dictionaries. The Haar dictionary is made of all the translated versions of the Haar functions at each scale. MP does not produce very sparse data representations in this case. Moreover, with this dictionary, it produces features which increase the loo-error of SVM with both kernels. This worsening is much more evident in the case of SVM with polynomial kernel function. The reason of this fact, common to all the experiments, will be explained at the end of the section. MOF, on the contrary, produces features which leave unchanged the loo-error of SVM with K_1, but they reduce the error of SVM with K_2.

The Gabor dictionary is made of all the translated versions of Gabor functions having evenly spaced center frequencies (for a review see [8]). Their main property is that the Fourier transform is a shifted Gaussian function, centered at the frequency ω_0. Thus, applying the frame operator F to a signal is equivalent to convolve the signal with a pass band filter bank with equal passing bandwidths. Experiments show that the loo-error is proportional to the inverse of S. The lower the sparsification ratio, the higher the loo-error. Also here, this phenomenon is much more evident in the case of SVM with K_2. MOF generates features which reduce the error of SVM with K_1, but leave unchanged the loo-error of SVM with K_2.

The Gabor b octave dictionary is made of all the translated versions of Gabor functions having passing bandwidths of b octaves (for a review see [8]). The main difference with the previous dictionary is that here the passing bandwidth of the filter is proportional to the center frequency. In this case, MOF produces features which reduce the loo-error of SVM with both K_1 and K_2 kernels. Also MP performs well also if limited to the case of SVM with linear kernel.

For brevity we illustrate here only the best performances obtained with Gabor b octave dictionaries, see table II. f_0 indicates the number of center frequencies (i.e. functions) used in the dictionary. The empty fields in table II are due to the impossibility for MP of representing the data with the specified error threshold, with the dictionary generated with f_0=5 and b=0.5.

Hence very sparse data representations increase drastically the generalization error of SVM as the experimental results show. Let c_i, $c_j \in \Re^l$ be the feature vectors produced by MP on training examples x_i and x_j by using a given dictionary; let $\phi(c) \in \Re^h$ be the mapping function in the feature space such that: $K(c_i, c_j) = \phi(c_i) \cdot \phi(c_j) = (1 + c_i \cdot c_j)$. As figure 2 shows, a sparsity S_c of 20% in the input space corresponds to a sparsity $S_{\phi(c)}$ of less than 5% in the feature space for a dictionary of l=320 atoms and the ratio $S_{\phi(c)}/S_c$ becomes smaller and smaller as S_c tends to zero. Thus, if c is sparse then $\phi(c)$ is much more sparse. Moreover, any polinomial kernel function of d degree can be written:

$$K(c_i, c_j) = \left(1 + c_i \cdot c_j\right)^d = \sum_{k=0}^{d} \binom{d}{k} \left(c_i \cdot c_j\right)^k$$

Since c_i and c_j are sparse then $c_i \cdot c_j \approx 0$ because only few components are different from zero at the same time. Therefore the kernel function becomes: $K(c_i, c_j) \approx 1 + d(c_i \cdot c_j)$. Hence if the representation of the data is sparse then using polynomial kernel functions of any degree is equivalent to using linear kernel functions, and so the optimal separating hyperplane found by SVM in the feature space induced by polynomial kernels has a generalization capacity very similar to the one of the hyperplane found by SVM in the input space. The experiments confirm this result. In fact, as all the tables show, with features generated by MP, the loo-errors of the optimal separating hyperplanes found by SVM with K_1 and K_2 coincide.

CONCLUSIONS

We have shown that different types of data representations heavily influence the generalization capacity of kernel based learning machines as SVM. In the case of very sparse data representations obtainned with MP, the generalization capacity of an SVM trained by using polynomial or Gaussian kernel functions reduce to the one of a linear SVM. In fact, in this case, polynomial kernel functions of any degree and Gaussian kernel functions collapse to linear kernels. With data representations sparse moderately the generalization capacity increases. Dense data representations, on the contrary, reduce the generalization error also in the case ofvery large dictionaries.

FIGURE 1

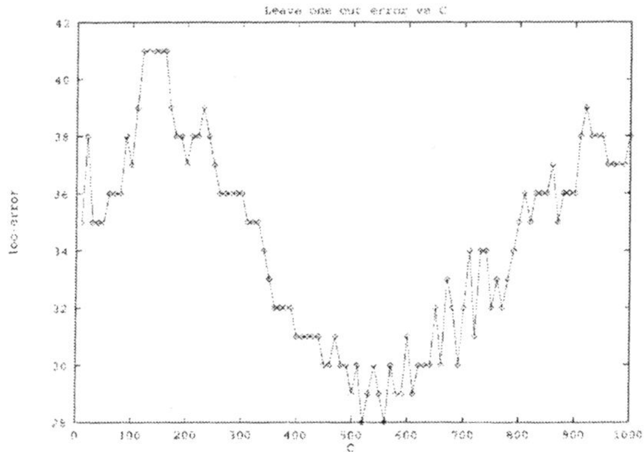

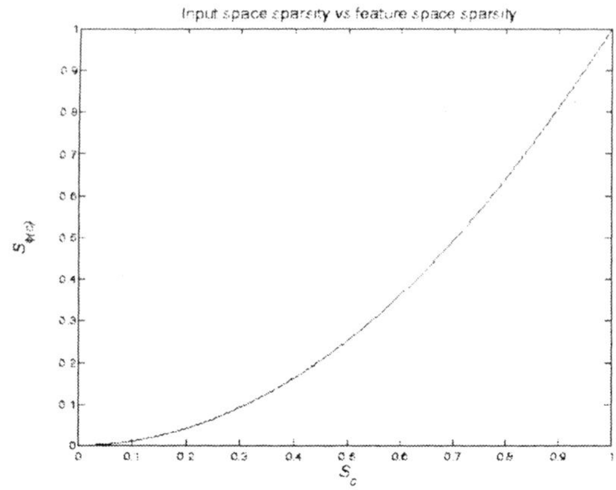

FIGURE 2

REFERENCES

[1] Avrim Blum and Pat Langley, Selection of relevant features and examples in machine learning, Artificial Intelligence, 97:245-271, 1997.

[2] V.Vapnik, Statistical Learning Theory, John Wiley & Sons, INC., 1998.

[3] A.N. Kolmogorov and S.V. Fomin, Introductory real analysis, Dover Publications, INC., 1970.

[4] I.Daubechies, Ten lectures on wavelets, CBMS-NSF Regional Conferences Series in Applied Mathematics, SIAM, Philadelphia, PA, 1992.

[5] S.Mallat and Z.Zhang, Matching pursuit in a time-frequency dictionary, IEEE Transactions on Signal Processing, 41:3397-3415, 1993.

[6] N.Ancona and E.Stella, Image representations with overcomplete dictionaries for object detection, Technical Report R.I.-IESI/CNR-Nr.02/2003, Istituto di Studi sui Sistemi Intelligenti per l'Automazione – Consiglio Nazionale delle Ricerche, Bari, Italy, 2003. (available at the URL: http://www.ba.cnr.it/~iesina18/).

[7] S.Chen, D.Donoho, and M.Saunders, Atomic decomposition by basis pursuit, Technical Report Technical report 479, Dept of Statistics, Stanford University, 1995.

[8] C.Mandriota and N.Ancona, Gabor function analysis, Technical Report R.I.-IESI/CNR-Nr.02/2002, Istituto di Studi sui Sistemi Intelligenti per l'Automazione – Consiglio Nazionale delle Ricerche, Bari, Italy, 2002. (available at the URL:http://www.ba.cnr.it/~iesina18/).

K1	*K2*
46	28

TABLE I

					K1		*K2*	
f_0	σ	*l*	*B/A*	*S(%)*	MOF	MP	MOF	MP
5	1	320	$5x10^4$		54		53	
10	1	640	63.3	13.1	47	68	**23**	66
20	1	1280	66.1	6.1	47	60	28	60
40	1	2560	130.6	3.1	47	58	30	58
5	2	320	271.3	27.9	**39**	46	24	46
10	2	640	44.1	10.8	44	65	30	63
20	2	1280	89.6	5.4	44	60	31	63
40	2	2560	142.1	2.7	50	71	32	73
5	4	320	15.4	19.1	47	49	25	48
10	4	640	32.7	9.6	47	**40**	29	**40**
20	4	1280	52.4	4.8	51	50	28	49
40	4	2560	142.1	2.4	55	50	31	49

TABLE II

August 2, 2004 14:37

TARGET IDENTIFICATION THROUGH TIME USING HIDDEN MARKOV MODELS

TIMOTHY W. ALBRECHT*
Dept. of Operational Sciences
Air Force Institute of Technology
Wright-Patterson AFB, OH 45433
timothy.albrecht@afit.edu

KENNETH W. BAUER
Dept. of Operational Sciences
Air Force Institute of Technology
Wright-Patterson AFB, OH 45433

ABSTRACT

Hidden Markov models (HMMs) are statistical models used to study time series data. This paper introduces hidden Markov models and applies HMMs in an automatic target recognition (ATR) scenario using synthetic aperture radar (SAR) target data taken at multiple aspect angles. The relationship between model complexity and model performance is examined and the fusion of multiple classifiers across features is studied.

HIDDEN MARKOV MODELS

Hidden Markov models (HMMs) fit into a broad class of statistical signal models which also includes Gaussian processes, Poisson processes and Markov processes. These models seek to characterize a signal as a parametric random process whose parameters can be estimated in a well-defined manner [1].

HMMs are statistical representations of time series data. An HMM is used to represent probability distributions given a sequence, or many sequences, of observations. The fundamental property of HMMs is the assumption that the sequence of observations is a noisy function of a Markov chain which is not directly observed, or hidden.

In developing the theory of HMMs we begin with a stochastic process $\{X_n, n \geq 0\}$, where X_n denotes the state of the system at time n and where, for all $n \geq 0$, X_n is a random variable taking values in set S. We further assume $\{X_n, n \geq 0\}$ is a discrete-time Markov chain (DTMC) with finite state space S, thus

1. for all $n \geq 0, X_n \in S$ with probability 1,
2. $P\{X_{n+1} = j | X_n = i, X_{n-1} = i_{n-1}, \ldots, X_0 = i_0\} = P\{X_{n+1} = j | X_n = i\}$ for all $n \geq 0$ and $i, j \in S$. This is the first order Markov property.

Next we introduce the idea of time-homogeneity. A DTMC is time-homogeneous when the conditional probabilities $P\{X_{n+1} = j | X_n = i\}$ are independent of time, $n \geq 0$, for all $i, j \in S$.

In an HMM the finite-state space, time-homogeneous DTMC $\{X_n, n \geq 0\}$ is hidden and can only be observed through an additional stochastic process, $\{Y_n, n \geq 0\}$, which is a

*Address all correspondence to this author.

sequence of conditionally independent random variables with the conditional distribution of Y_n depending on the hidden DTMC $\{X_n, n \geq 0\}$ only through the state at time n, X_n. In a discrete HMM the state space of Y_n is finite.

Thus, the discrete-time stochastic process $\{(X_n, Y_n), n \geq 0\}$ forms a hidden Markov model where $\{X_n, n \geq 0\}$ is a hidden time-homogeneous DTMC with finite state space and $\{Y_n, n \geq 0\}$ is an observation sequence dependent on the state of the hidden DTMC at time n.

To parameterize a discrete HMM a stochastic transition matrix, $A = [a_{ij}]$, where $a_{ij} = P\{X_{n+1} = j | X_n = i\}$, is used to represent the hidden Markov chain. In addition to the hidden state transition matrix, A, an observation distribution matrix, B, is defined by $[b_{ji}] = P\{Y_n = i | X_n = j\}$ where each observation Y_n of the sequence $\{Y_n, n \geq 0\}$ is one of Q possible values. Finally, the parameterization of a discrete HMM must include an initial state distribution, $\pi_i = P\{X_0 = i\}$, which provides the starting point for the hidden Markov chain. The complete set of parameters for a given model is written, $\lambda = (A, B, \pi)$.

Rabiner [1] discusses three basic problems associated with HMMs:

1. Given a model, λ, find the probability of producing a specified observation sequence of length T, $Y \in \{Y_n\}_1^T$. Or written mathematically, $P\{Y|\lambda\}$. Note we have adjusted the time index to begin at $n = 1$ so that a sequence from time $n = 1$ to $n = T$ is of length T and not $T + 1$.
2. Given a model, λ, and an observations sequence, $Y \in \{Y_n\}_1^T$, find the best state sequence, $X \in \{X_n\}_1^T$, that explains Y.
3. Given an observation sequence, or set of observation sequences, $\{Y\}$, parameterize an HMM, $\lambda^* = (A, B, \pi)$, such that it is the most likely model to have produced the given data. This amounts to training an HMM given observation data.

The standard practice when employing HMMs in a classification experiment is to train an HMM for each class using a set of class-specific training sequences. Once trained, a test sequence of unknown class is evaluated by each HMM. The result of each evaluation is the likelihood that the test sequence was produced by the class-specific HMM.

HMMS AS SAR TARGET CLASSIFIER

The classification of three types of ground vehicle targets from the publicly-available MSTAR (Moving and Stationary Target Acquisition and Recognition) database [2] is investigated using HMMs. This work extends to two classifiers an earlier work by Albrecht and Gustafson [3]. Here, two HMM-based classifiers employ separate training sets; the first comprised of six power spectrum features extracted from High Range Resolution (HRR) radar profiles of the targets, and the second comprised of 7 peak magnitudes of HRR range bins. Classification performance is examined in both the case of separate classifiers and the case of fused classifiers. Classification accuracy versus numbers of hidden states (3-30), sequence lengths (10, 30 and 100), and discretization levels of the features (3, 10 and 30 levels) is explored using training and testing data.

The HMM classifier acts on time series data; features drawn from targets at a sequence of aspect angles. The analogy is to an airborne sensor moving relative to a ground target while collecting information. Increasing sequence length adds to the aspect angle window across which the target is observed and relates to a greater observation period.

Figure 1. Processed SAR returns of T-72, BMP-2, and BTR-70 vehicles.

SAR data of three targets are used: the T-72 main battle tank, the BMP-2 armored personnel carrier, and the BTR-70 armored personnel carrier. The training data were collected from an airborne platform whose sensor operated at a 17 degree depression angle relative to the horizontal flight path. The test data were collected at a 15 degree depression angle, thus presenting a different target SAR signature. Figure 1 shows SAR data which has been converted to target images.

The HMM-based classifiers employ features extracted from High Range Resolution (HRR) profiles of the SAR target data. The U.S. Air Force has sponsored research into target recognition based on HRR profiles [4–6], and Liao et al have applied HMMs to HRR profiles with some success [7, 8]. HRR waveforms are generated by tracking radars and, depending on the pulse-width employed by the transmitter, can determine relative range between independent target scattering centers. HRR samples can then be related to physical characteristics of the target. Each SAR target chip is converted to a 1-D HRR profile.

The data universe includes approximately 230 images of each target in the training set and approximately 150 images of each target in the testing set. However, not all aspect angles are covered by the sets of target data: there are "holes" in the aspect angle coverage for each target type. Of relevance here is the need to train and test the HMMs using information from aspect angle sequences as similar as possible across target types. The feature sets are interpolated across the available aspect angles. Interpolating the data provides representative target data at 1 degree intervals from 0-359 degrees for both training and testing sets. Figure 2 shows example feature data across aspect angle.

The first feature set is comprised of the first six frequency bins of the FFT-transformed HRR profile of each target at each aspect angle. The second feature set is comprised of the peak magnitude return at each of seven range bins of the HRR profile of each target at each aspect angle. Thus, two feature sets are drawn from the HRR profiles of the targets, the first in the frequency domain and the second in the spatial domain.

The training input to each HMM-based classifier derives from two feature sets, power-bin and range-bin, extracted as described above from target HRR profiles. Using the T-72 target as an example, the HRR profile and power spectra for each of the available 234 aspect angles are calculated. The feature data are interpolated to fill in aspect angle holes. From the power spectra, six training sequences corresponding to each of the six features (frequency bin signals) are derived. These sequences are the magnitudes of the power spectra at the respective frequency bins at each of the 360 degree aspect angles. The process repeats for the 7 range-bin features. Thus, two feature sets of training records capture target information across all sample aspect angles.

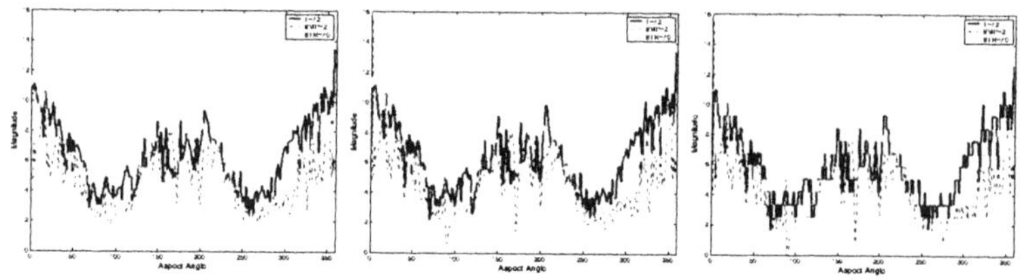

Figure 2. The left plot shows the magnitude of the first bin of feature set 1 training data across aspect angle for each of the three target types (approx. 230 data points per target). The middle plot interpolates the data at each degree of aspect angle (360 data points per target). The right plot discretizes the interpolated data magnitude into 20 bins. The feature data is discretized in order to implement discrete HMM classification.

Five testing methodologies were used in the experiment. Once trained, the HMM classifiers were given test sequences to evaluate producing a log-likelihood. The five testing methodologies handled the HMM outputs in different ways:

1. Methodology 1 took feature set 1 (power-bin) as input to the HMMs and compared HMM output log-likelihoods using a committee of experts system to determine the target classification.
2. Methodology 2 also took feature set 1 as input but used a mean log-likelihood across the 6 features to determine the most likely target.
3. Methodology 3 took feature set 2 (range-bin) as inputs and used a committee of experts system to determine target classification.
4. Methodology 4 also took feature set 2 as input but used a mean log-likelihood across the 7 features to determine the most likely target.
5. Methodology 5 fused feature sets 1 and 2 using the mean log-likelihood across all 13 features to determine the most likely target.

Each experiment consists of 100 test sequences and results in a probability of correct selection influenced by a set of parameters which determine model complexity (number of hidden states), the size of the observation space (discretization level), and the sequence length (number of aspect angles comprising the test sequence). Parameter settings for the results reported here are: number of hidden states (3-30), discretization level (3 10 30), and sequence length (10 30 100).

Sequence length impacts the experiment in two ways. For a sequence length of 10, a test sequence has 10 elements. Thus a sequence length of 10 captures information at 10 different aspect angles in an ascending series incremented by 1 degree. Suppose the sequence is randomly chosen to begin at 35 degrees. Then the 10 element sequence has data from target images at 35, 36, 37, ..., and 44 degrees. In the case of feature set 1 the full input test set consists of 6 vectors of length 10 with each vector containing information from its respective frequency bin of the power spectra for the transformed HRR profile.

The second way sequence length impacts the classification experiment is the manner in which the training sets are formed. Each of the three target sets requires the training of

HMMs corresponding to the number of features in the feature set (6 for power-bin, 7 for range-bin). By moving a window of width equal to the chosen sequence length across the 0-359 degree training sequence, additional training sequences are created: each successive movement of the window creates another training sequence. Each training sequence is closely related to its predecessor, differing only in the first and last elements and the shift in the intermediate elements.

CONCLUSIONS

Figure 3 shows representative results. The top two plots compare results from a single testing methodology (no. 5 Fusion) at two discretization levels; 10 on the left, and 30 on the right. The bottom two plots compare results from two testing methodologies (no. 3 range-bin committee of experts on the left, and no. 4 range-bin mean log-likelihood on the right) at the same discretization level.

The results do not support the conclusion that increasing model complexity (i.e. greater number of hidden states) improves classification performance. Indeed, the best performance occurs with 10 or fewer hidden states indicating either the complexity of the phenomena being modeled can be captured with an HMM of moderate complexity (10 or fewer states), or there is insufficient training data to adequately train an HMM of greater complexity (10 or more states).

The results show performance at the finer discretization setting (30) typically fell below the performance at 10. A finer setting means a larger discrete observation space for the HMM, and, thus, a greater number of parameters to train.

No single testing methodology dominates the rest. Methodology no. 5, fusion, mitigates poor performance in its component feature sets but does not outperform the component methodologies at all experiment settings.

The results support the use of HMMs to capture temporal information contained within sequences of target images, and point to several areas, such as HMM hidden state structure, training mechanisms, and feature selection, where performance improvement can be sought.

ACKNOWLEDGMENT

The views expressed in this thesis are those of the authors and do not reflect the official policy or position of the United States Air Force, Department of Defense, or the United States Government.

REFERENCES

[1] Rabiner, L., 1989. "A tutorial on hidden markov models and selected applications in speech recognition". *Proceedings of the IEEE*, 77, pp. 257–285.

[2] SENSOR DATA MANAGEMENT SYSTEM, 1995. *MSTAR Database*. Air Force Research Laboratory, Wright-Patterson AFB, OH. `http://www.mbvlab.wpafb.af.mil/public/sdms/additional.htm`.

[3] Albrecht, T., and Gustafson, S., 2004. "Hidden markov models for classifying sar target images". In Proceedings of SPIE. in publication.

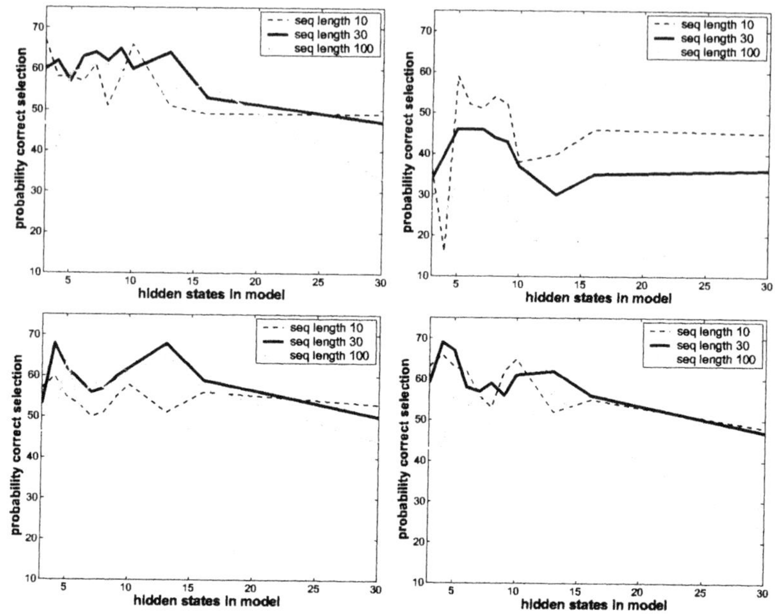

Figure 3. Plots of percentage of correct selection versus number of hidden states. The plots in the top row show results for testing methodology 5 (fusion) at discretization level 10 (on right) and 30 (on left). The plots on the bottom row show results at discretization level 10 for testing methodology 3 (range-bin feature, committee of experts) on the left, and testing methodology 4 (range-bin feature, mean log-likelihood), on the right.

[4] DeWitt, M., 1992. High range resolution radar target identification using the prony model and hidden markov models. Master's thesis, Air Force Institute of Technology, Wright-Patterson AFB, OH.

[5] MacDonald, A., 1999. Classification of high range resolution radar returns using hidden markov and gaussian mixture models. Master's thesis, Air Force Institute of Technology, Wright-Patterson AFB, OH.

[6] Zumwalt, M., 2000. Robust high range resolution radar for target classification. Master's thesis, Air Force Institute of Technology, Wright-Patterson AFB, OH.

[7] Liao, X., Runkle, P., Jiao, Y., and Carin, L., 2001. "Identification of ground targets from sequential hrr radar signatures". In Proceedings of IEEE International Conference on Acoustics, Speech, and Signal Processing, pp. 2897–2900.

[8] Liao, X., Runkle, P., and Carin, L., 2002. "Identification of ground targets from sequential high-range-resolution radar signatures". IEEE Transactions on Aerospace and Electronic Systems, **38** (4), pp. 1230–1242.

ANALYSIS OF THE ERROR SURFACE OF SIMPLE RECURRENT NEURAL NETWORKS

JASON M. HORN
Oklahoma State University
School of Electrical and
Computer Engineering
202 Engineering South
Stillwater, OK, 74078-5032, USA

MARTIN T. HAGAN
Oklahoma State University
School of Electrical and
Computer Engineering
202 Engineering South
Stillwater, OK, 74078-5032, USA

ABSTRACT
In this paper we demonstrate that the error surfaces for recurrent neural networks commonly contain "spurious" valleys – valleys that are unrelated to the functional that the recurrent network is being trained to approximate. These valleys make training more difficult, especially for gradient-based optimization algorithms. These steep, narrow valleys in the error surface can cause network training to stop prematurely. In some cases, the form of the valley is a cusp, so that the slope increases as the minimum is approached. This paper presents detailed analyses of the error surfaces for several simple recurrent networks. We show that the spurious valleys are caused by a number of different mechanisms. Some of the valleys are caused by characteristics of the input sequence, and are not related to the network architecture. Other valleys are specific to the network architecture. The paper will demonstrate procedures that can be used to predict regions in the error surface where these valleys are most likely to occur and where the locations of the valleys are most likely to interfere with proper network training.

INTRODUCTION

Recurrent neural networks have been successfully used in the identification and control of dynamic systems. Unfortunately, these networks have proven difficult to train due to the characteristics of the error surfaces. Steep, narrow valleys cause training algorithms to get "stuck" and stop without finding optimal or even acceptable values for the weights of the network (De Jesus, Horn & Hagan, 2001).

Methods such as switching input/output data used for training, regularization, and randomly setting initial conditions have been used to work around this problem with some success. In order to make further improvements to the training procedure, however, a more complete understanding of the cause of the problem is needed.

In this paper we will identify several types of valleys that occur in the error surface of two simple recurrent networks. We will explain the cause of each type of valley and present algorithms that predict the locations of the valleys for a given network and input sequence. This information can be used to help evaluate the results of training and determine whether the weights reached are likely to be incorrectly chosen due to one of these valleys in the error surface.

FIRST ORDER LINEAR RECURRENT NETWORK

To begin investigating this problem, we decided to look for the simplest possible recurrent network with an error surface that contained these spurious valleys. This turned out to be the simplest possible recurrent network, illustrated in Fig 1.

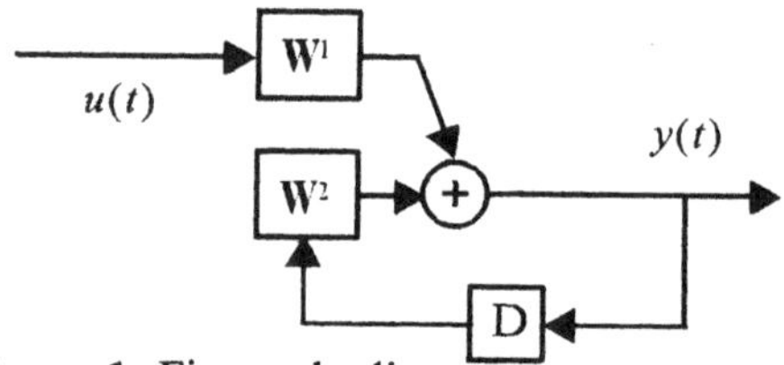

Figure 1: First order linear recurrent network

In order to generate training data for this network, a network of this type was created and its weights were set to $\mathbf{W}^1 = 0.5$ and $\mathbf{W}^2 = 0.5$. Random input sequences were generated and used as input to this network with zero initial condition, resulting in input/output data that could be used to train another network with the same architecture. By using this method, the optimal weights were known to be the weights used to generate the data.

Although this network architecture is simple, the error surfaces generated by these networks have spurious valleys similar to those encountered in more complicated networks. Figure 2 illustrates these valleys and the structure of the error surface.

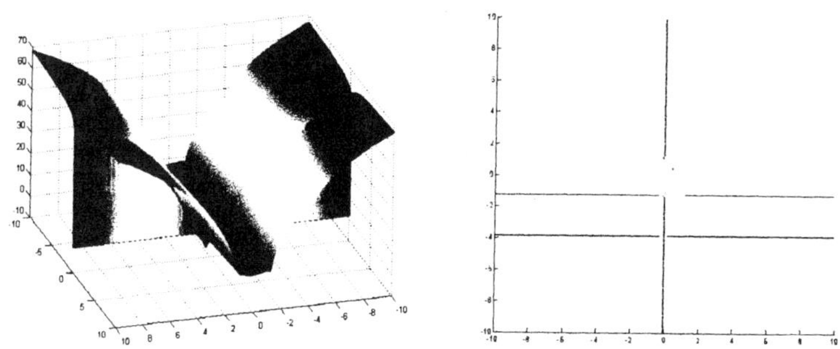

Figure 2: Error surface (log scale) and valleys for first order linear network

Two types of valleys were seen in error surfaces generated using this method. One valley occurs for all values of $\mathbf{W}^2$ along the line $\mathbf{W}^1 = 0$. This valley is easily explained because when $\mathbf{W}^1 = 0$, the output of the network is always 0. This causes the error to be constant no matter what the value of $\mathbf{W}^2$ is. The other type of valley is not so simple, and the mathematics behind the output of the network must be analyzed to provide an explanation. Other valleys, such as the ones seen in Fig 2, were also appearing for all values of $\mathbf{W}^1$ when $\mathbf{W}^2$ was equal to some non-zero value that was different for different input sequences. The output equation for the network is given in Eq. (1).

$$\begin{aligned} y(k) &= \mathbf{W}^1 u(k) + \mathbf{W}^2 y(k-1) \\ &= \mathbf{W}^1 \Big\{ u(k) + \mathbf{W}^2 u(k-1) + (\mathbf{W}^2)^2 u(k-2) + \\ &\quad \ldots + (\mathbf{W}^2)^{k-1} u(1) \Big\} \end{aligned} \tag{1}$$

The output at each time k is a polynomial of order $k-1$ in the parameter $\mathbf{W}^2$. The coefficients of this polynomial are related to the input sequence and $\mathbf{W}^1$. When $\mathbf{W}^2$ is close to a root of this polynomial, the output at that time point will be very near zero. Because the coefficients of the polynomials that correspond to each time k are related, the roots of the polynomials are close together. This means that the output of the network will be small, even though $\mathbf{W}^2$ may be large. The result of this phenomenon is a steep, narrow valley in the error surface that is dependent only on the value of $\mathbf{W}^2$.

Comprehensive prediction of valleys for this first order linear recurrent network is relatively simple, since only two types of valleys were encountered. First, we predict a valley where $\mathbf{W}^1$ is equal to zero. Second, we predict valleys where $\mathbf{W}^2$ is equal to the value of a real root of the polynomial which has the input sequence as its coefficients. The second valley will only be significant if the root has a magnitude larger than one. If the magnitude of the root is not greater than one, then the output will not be significantly higher for values on either side of the root than for values at the root.

FIRST ORDER NONLINEAR RECURRENT NETWORK

In addition to the first order linear recurrent network, we analyzed the error surface of this network, illustrated in Fig 3. It is similar to that of the linear recurrent network but includes a sigmoid nonlinearity.

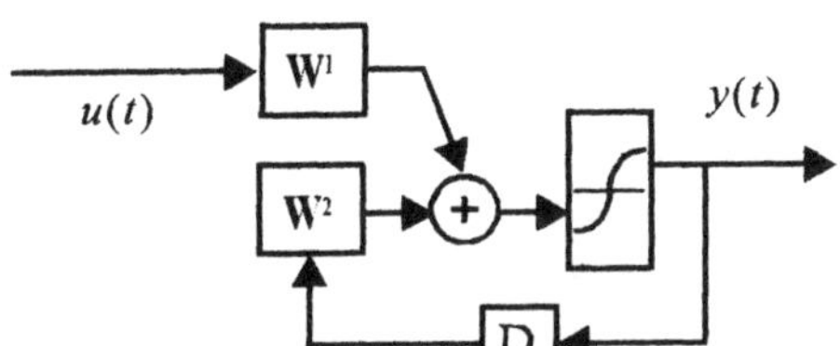

Figure 3: First order nonlinear recurrent network

The same method that was used to generate training data for the linear recurrent network was used for this network as well. The error surface and valleys seen in Fig 4 were generated using the same input sequence that generated the error surface and valleys seen in Fig 2, when used as input to the linear recurrent network. As you can see, the addition of the nonlinearity to the network significantly complicates the error surface.

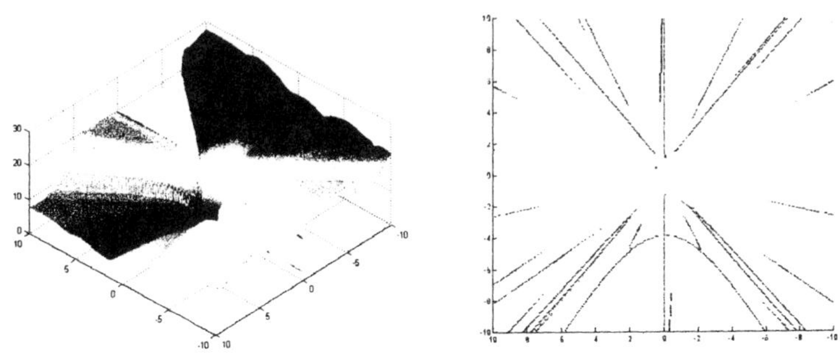

Figure 4: Error surface and valleys for first order nonlinear network

Four types of valleys were identified in the error surfaces of the nonlinear recurrent network that were generated using this method. Like the linear network, a valley appears along the line $\mathbf{W}^1 = 0$. The cause of this valley is the same in the nonlinear case as it is in the linear case: the output of the network is zero for all values of $\mathbf{W}^2$. The error is therefore limited to the sum of the squares of the output data used to train the network. The other three types of valleys differ from those encountered in the linear network.

Equation (2) gives the output equation for the nonlinear recurrent network.

$$y(k) = tansig(\mathbf{W}^1 u(k) + \mathbf{W}^2 y(k-1)) \tag{2}$$

For small values of $\mathbf{W}^1$, the argument of the *tansig* function is small, and this equation reduces to that of the linear recurrent network. It is therefore not surprising that the valleys that were seen in the linear case related to the roots of the polynomial in Eq. (1) appear in the nonlinear case for small values of $\mathbf{W}^1$ as well. As the value of $\mathbf{W}^1$ increases, however, the nonlinearity causes the behavior of the valley to differ from the linear case.

As soon as $\mathbf{W}^1$ reaches a certain threshold, which can be determined by the magnitude of the terms in the input sequence and the magnitude of $\mathbf{W}^2$ at which the valley occurs, a term in the output begins to saturate as the network leaves the linear operating region of the *tansig* function. This point saturates and begins approaching the value of one or negative one. The output for all following points in time, which is still small enough to be operating in the approximately linear region of the *tansig* function, can be approximated by Eq. (3)

$$y(t+k) \approx \mathbf{W}^1 \Big\{ u(k) + \mathbf{W}^2 u(k-1) + (\mathbf{W}^2)^2 u(k-2) + \ldots + (\mathbf{W}^2)^{k-1} u(t+1) \Big\} + (\mathbf{W}^2)^k y(t) \tag{3}$$

We again have a polynomial in the parameter $\mathbf{W}^2$, but in this case there is an additional term which does not include $\mathbf{W}^1$. This means that the root of the polynomial is dependent on $\mathbf{W}^1$, so as $\mathbf{W}^1$ increases, the root will increase as well. The valley found in the nonlinear network follows the curve of this increasing root. As $\mathbf{W}^1$ increases further, more points in the input sequence will saturate and cause additional valleys. This brings us to the third type of valleys encountered, which occur as $\mathbf{W}^1$ and $\mathbf{W}^2$ increase enough to cause saturation in most of the outputs of the network. Figure 5 illustrates both of these types of valleys.

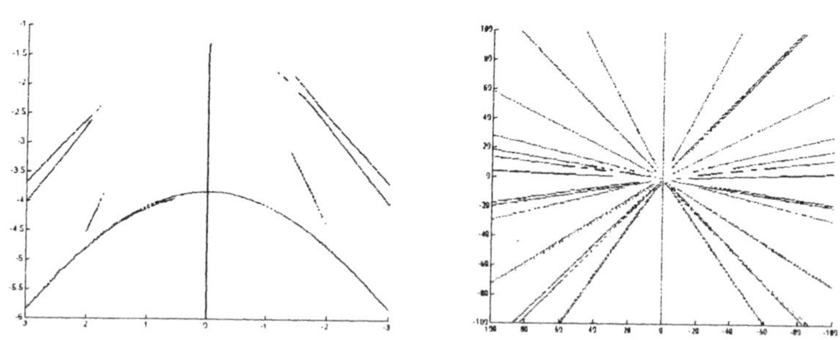

Figure 5: Valleys in the error surface of the third and fourth type

When the output of the network at time *k-1* is saturated near one or negative one, then the output of the network at time *k* becomes a function of $\mathbf{W}^1$ and $\mathbf{W}^2$. For some combinations of weights the output will be near one, and for others it will be near negative one.

There is a period of transition, however, while it is switching between positive and negative saturation at which it will cross the desired output of the network. Because the output at all other points is saturated and unchanging, changing this one output (at one time point) to equal the output of the training data will cause a valley in the error surface. The possible locations of this valley can be found by substituting one or negative one for *y(k-1)* and the desired output (or zero if this is not available) for *y(k)* in the output equation of the network and solving for $\mathbf{W}^1$ in terms of $\mathbf{W}^2$. This gives us Eq. (4):

$$\mathbf{W}^1 = \frac{y_{desired}(t) \pm \mathbf{W}^2}{u(k)} \tag{4}$$

To make matters worse, a shift of the output at time *k-1* between positive and negative one also has the potential to cause the output at time *k* to shift between positive and negative one. This can cause another valley, and also can cause the output at time *k+1* to shift between positive and negative one. This cycle has the potential to continue until the final input is reached, so a single shift at time *k* in an input sequence of length *n* has the potential to cause *n-k+1* valleys near the line given by Eq. (4).

Fortunately, not all of these potential valleys actually appear on the error surface. To determine which valleys will occur, a simple algorithm can be written which keeps track of the sign of the output at each time and determines which outputs will shift between positive and negative one as $\mathbf{W}^1/\mathbf{W}^2$ varies from -Inf to 0 and from 0 to Inf. Only the outputs that actually shift will cause valleys to occur. Using this method, we were able to predict accurately the locations of all valleys of this type that actually would occur for a given input/output sequence of training data.

The fourth and final type of valley that we identified and analyzed in the error surface of the nonlinear recurrent network is also related to the effects of saturation. When $\mathbf{W}^1$ is small and $\mathbf{W}^2$ is large, then the output of the network for early points in time will be near zero. As time progresses, however, the power to which $\mathbf{W}^2$ is raised increases, and the output will eventually saturate to positive or negative one, depending on the input sequence and the signs of $\mathbf{W}^1$ and $\mathbf{W}^2$. Like the case where an output was switching between positive and negative saturation, the transition between zero and the saturated value may cause the output to equal the desired output for some combination of $\mathbf{W}^1$ and $\mathbf{W}^2$. All other points in the input sequence remain near zero or saturated near this combination, so a valley is formed. These valleys are illustrated in Fig 6.

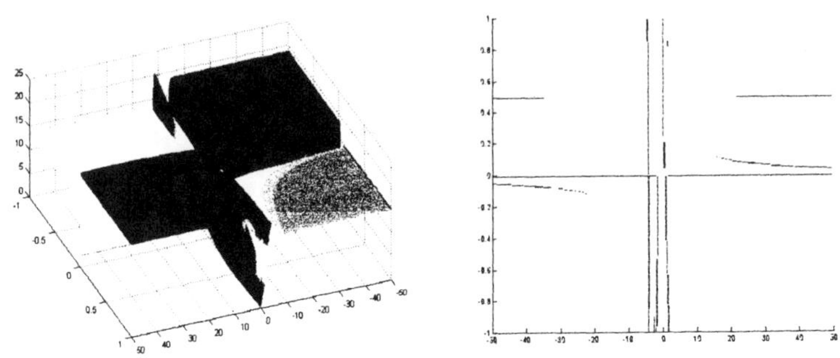

Figure 6: Error surface and valleys for small $\mathbf{W}^1$ for first order nonlinear network

In order to predict the location of these valleys, a simplification of the output equation at time *k* is necessary. Because the output is near zero at all time less than *k* , it can be assumed to operate in the linear region of the sigmoid function. The output equation at time

k then reduces to that of the linear network, given in Eq. (1). For large values of $\mathbf{W}^2$ and small values of $\mathbf{W}^1$, the output will be approximately equal to the desired output when Eq. (5) is satisfied.

$$\mathbf{W}^1 = \frac{y(k)}{(\mathbf{W}^2)^{k-1} u(1)} \tag{5}$$

This equation was reached by solving for $\mathbf{W}^1$ and eliminating all other terms, which are insignificant compared to $(\mathbf{W}^2)^{k-1}$ because $\mathbf{W}^2$ is large. This equation can be used to predict accurately and reliably all valleys of this type that will occur in the error surface for given input/output training data.

Comprehensive prediction of all valleys that will occur in an error surface for the first order nonlinear network can now be achieved by combining the prediction methods for each of the four types of valleys that occur. The constraints mentioned for each type of valley must be followed, so valleys should not be predicted for real roots of the input sequence that have a magnitude less than one. Valleys predicted by Eq. (4) and Eq. (5) will only occur for large values of $\mathbf{W}^2$.

CONCLUSIONS

Certain types of valleys in the error surfaces of recurrent neural networks cause problems when attempting to train the network. These valleys can cause the training to stop without reaching the optimal weights. This paper presents a complete analysis of the error surfaces of one linear and one nonlinear first order recurrent network. The reasons that the valleys occur are explained and tools necessary to predict the locations of the valleys are developed. This paper demonstrates that even very simple recurrent networks can have many spurious valleys.

In order to make practical use of the information presented in this paper, it must first be extended to apply to larger networks. Preliminary research has indicated that methods similar to those used to analyze these error surfaces can be used on more complicated networks to achieve good prediction of valley locations. This information can then be used to assist the training algorithm by attempting to avoid such valleys or, if a valley is encountered, recognizing the valley and starting training again from another location.

NOMENCLATURE

D - Delay in a neural network.
$\mathbf{W}^i$ - Connection weight in a neural network.
$u(t)$ - Input sequence to a neural network
$y(t)$ - Output sequence from a neural network.

REFERENCES

De Jesus, O., Horn, J. M., and Hagan, M. T., 2001, "Analysis of Recurrent Network Training and Suggestions for Improvements," *Proceedings of the INNS/IEEE International Joint Conference on Neural Networks*, IEEE, Washington D.C., Vol. 4, pp. 2632-2637

Hagan, M. T., Demuth, H. B., 1999, "Neural Networks for Control," *Proceedings of the 1999 American Control Conference*, IEEE, San Diego,CA, pp. 1642-1656

INTRODUCTION TO FUNCTIONAL SET THEORY AND ITS PRINCIPLES

DJAMEL BOUCHAFFRA

Department of Computer Science & Engineering
131 Dodge Hall, Oakland University
Rochester, MI, 48309, USA
Telephone: (248) 370-2242
dbouchaffra@ieee.org

ABSTRACT:
We propose a novel mathematical domain that we named "functional set theory" (f-set theory). It extends traditional set theory by considering all possible mappings between objects in a traditional set. Because of our need to search structural information, f-set theory focuses more on relationships between objects and less on the objects themselves. We developed the notions of "role" assigned to mappings between objects and membership values assigned to objects. We introduce some functional-set theoretic operations as well as the notion of functional reasoning. We show some significant impacts of f-set theory in the area of artificial intelligence, and soft computing.

1. INTRODUCTION

From Aristotle to Cantor, the focus of human research was mainly behind the idea of counting, membership and infinity. The notion of infinity was one of the most important foci and challenges for the Greek scientists at that time. It was with Cantor's work however, that set theory came to be put on a proper mathematical basis. Cantor stated: "a set is a collection into a whole of definite and separate objects of our intuition or thought" [Dauwben, 1979; Johnson, 1972]. However, to remove paradoxes in the set axiomatization conducted by Russell and Whitehead, Russell added: "... such that given an object x and a set S, it is possible to state unequivocally that x either *belongs* to the set S, or x does *not belong* to S" [Garciadiego, 1992]. *However, since many years the use of set theory had focused more on objects than on relations between objects.* In other words, the notion of structure[1] formed by the objects (or elements) of a set has always been lacking. In fact, no inter-relationships between objects are emphasized in many applications of set theory. Cantor's definition requires the objects to be separate *but did not exclude inter-relationships between the objects.* In addition, the Russel and Whitehead axiomatization of set theory did remove paradoxes but limited significantly the interaction of an object with the set that contains it. Fuzzy set theory developed more recently by Zadeh extended the notion of membership of an element within a set [Zadeh, 1962] but suffers similarly from the inability to capture structural information. Fuzzy set

---

[1] A structure refers to a certain arrangement of objects in a definite pattern of organization.

theory does not account for structural information between the elements that form the fuzzy set. The "subjective" membership functions introduced in fuzzy set theory do not unfold the hidden structure formed by the objects themselves. Ideally researchers would like to have a solution to a pattern recognition (PR) problem that consists of the following stages: (i) find a feature vector x, (ii) train a system using a set of training patterns whose classification is *a priori* known, and (iii) classify unknown incoming patterns. Unfortunately, for most practical problems, this approach is not feasible. The reason is that a pattern contains some *relational information* from which it is difficult and sometimes impossible to derive appropriate feature vector. *Therefore, the analytical approaches which process the patterns only on a quantitative basis but ignore the inter-relationships (or structure) between the components of the patterns quite often fail.* Several approaches have been attempted to circumvent this serious obstacle. The first alternative that accounts for structural information is syntactical pattern recognition [Fu, 1982]. This concept establishes a connection between formal languages and pattern recognition, but it is quite difficult to represent continuous and complex patterns using a finite set of rules. A second alternative is the Bayesian belief networks [Buntine, 1996; Pearl, 1988] that use conditional probabilities and priors to express causal and sometimes non causal relationships. However, the structural information we are considering is more general and cannot always be represented through a Bayesian network.

The thrust in this paper is to develop a new mathematical domain that the author named *"Functional Set Theory" (FST)* which answers this challenge. We show that object of the traditional set theory can be enriched by adding its connections (or mappings) with other objects within the same set. Each mapping is assigned to a *role* "played" in a functional set (f-set). This role introduces the notion of *fuzzy membership* assigned to each object of the f-set. The roles impact the membership values of the objects. Because of the existence of the mathematical properties of the mappings between objects and their roles, FST will unravel the interaction between the traditional use of set theory and fuzzy set theory. An example of impact is in artificial intelligence and pattern recognition [Duda, Hart and Stork, 2001] where the hidden Markov models will be transformed into structural hidden Markov models (SHMM's). These models introduced by the author and his Ph.D student has been recently established within the computational intelligence and pattern recognition community [Bouchaffra and Tan, 2004, 2003[1], 2003[2]]. The *structural* hidden Markov models help us better understand the shape of a sequence of patterns in a traditional HMM. We believe this new vision strengthened by "everyday" more powerful computers will leapfrog the current state-of-the-art models.

2. INTRODUCTION TO FUNCTIONAL SET THEORY AND ITS PRINCIPLES

Our goal is to develop a new mathematical theory that incorporates structural information within the f-set axiomatic. Our goal is to develop a definition of a structure and devise ways to learn it. Our development of functional set theory is driven by the followings: (i) the need to create structural relationships between the objects that constitute the f-set. Instead of just being able to relate each element of a set to the set itself, we will be able to characterize and understand the type of structural relationships that exist between the elements themselves. (ii) the need of capturing imprecision, or fuzziness within a set through a non crisp membership operator. (iii) the need of viewing structures at different levels of resolution. Therefore, objects in a set are not necessarily atomic but are either atomic or are recursively f-sets. We now define an f-set (a functional set):

Definition 1: *Let E be a ground set of objects a_i of cardinality n, an f-set Ω is a finite collection of functions $f_{i;j}$: $S_i \rightarrow S_j$, where S_i and $S_j \in P(E)$ (power set of E) and whose element membership values in the f-set Ω depend on the functions $f_{i;j}$.*

A possible representation of an f-set is: $\Omega = \{f_{1;2}\langle S_1;S_2\rangle, f_{3;4}\langle S_3;S_4\rangle, \ldots, f_{u;v}\langle S_u;S_v\rangle\}$ where: $f_{i;j} \in F(S_i; S_j)$ (set of all mappings from the fuzzy set S_i to the fuzzy set S_j).

2.1 Some Examples of F-Sets

The first example of an f-set is the following: Let $E = \{1, 2, 4\}$ then $P(E) = \{\emptyset, \{1\}, \{2\}, \{4\}, \{1, 2\}, \{1, 4\}, \{2, 4\}, E\}$, a possible f-set Ω is formed by mappings from one member of $P(E)$ to another member of $P(E)$. A possible mapping is $f_1 : \{1, 2\} \rightarrow \{1, 4\}$ such that $\forall n \in \{1, 2\}, f_1(n) = n^2 \in \{1, 4\}$. Another mapping is $f_2 : \{1, 2\} \rightarrow \{2, 4\}$ such that: $\forall n \in \{1, 2\}, f_2(n) = 2n \in \{2, 4\}$. In case there are no possible mappings between members of $P(E)$, identity functions that map each member to itself are used. The second example describes an f-set where the objects are non mathematical and the mappings are graphical representations rather than mathematical functions: Let E = {fax/scanner1, fax/scanner2,computer1,computer2,cell-phone1,cell-phone2,rugby-ball} be the ground set. Some members of $P(E)$ are: S_1 = {fax/scanner1,fax/scanner}, S_2 = {computer1,computer2}, S_3 ={cell-phone1,cell-phone2}, and S_4 = {rugby-ball}, then possible elements of this f-set are: $f_{1;2} = Plug\langle S_1; S_2\rangle$: "plug a fax/scanner to a computer", $f_{2;1} = Transmit\langle S_2; S_1\rangle$: "transmit information from a computer to a fax/scanner", $f_{3;2} = Connect\langle S_3; S_2\rangle$: "connect a cellular phone to a computer using a wireless communication protocol" and $f_{2;3} = Redirect\langle S_2; S_3\rangle$: "redirect information from a computer server to a cell-phone". The isolated object "rugby-ball" is mapped to itself. We can write: $f_4 = Id\langle S_4\rangle$. Figure 1 provides an illustration of this f-set.

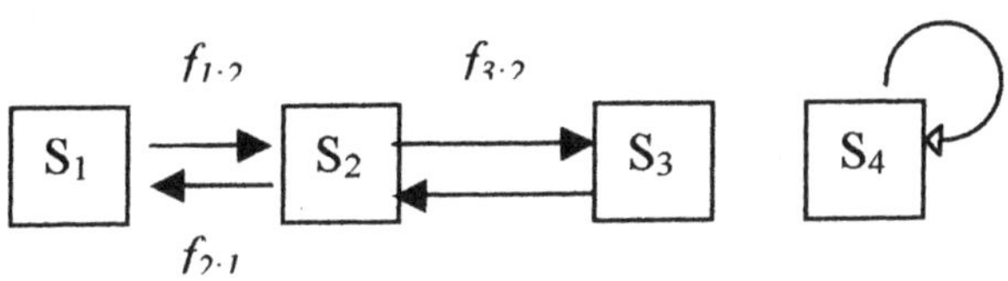

Figure 1: A graphical representation of an f-set.

The third example is in handwriting recognition. Let's consider E as a ground set that contains images of digits from 0-9 (handwritten by different persons) with their feature representations using various feature extraction techniques. This ground set contains different ways of writing a digit. For example, some zeros are round, while others may be elliptical, flat, or some other shape. A possible collection of mappings between members of $P(E)$ are the different feature extraction techniques that are applied on these images. These mappings are for example: a polynomial representation of the external contour, which attempts to approximate each stroke of the external contour of the digit by a polynomial expression, or a vector representation such as Fourier descriptors or a chain code representation. All these functions map a digit image to a digit representation in a feature space. Similarly, other mappings from the feature space to itself are obtained by mapping a digit feature representation to one of the ten template feature representations. These mappings are classification techniques such as "Neural Network", "Genetic Algorithms", and others. The f-set Ω is a *pattern recognition system* composed of feature extraction functions, and pattern classification functions.

2.2 Roles of Mappings and Object Memberships

The notion of mapping between two members of *P(E)* is crucial in FST. The "role" the mappings play provides the most relevant information about the inner structure contained in an f-set. However, a role is different from a membership. Memberships apply to objects with respect to an f-set whereas roles apply to mappings. *If the role value assigned to a mapping between two members of P(E) is high then the membership values of these objects in the f-set are also high and vice versa. In other words, unlike fuzzy set theory, functional set theory focuses on the roles played by the functions and not only on the objects themselves.* These membership values *are derived from these role values.* Because the role value assigned to the identity mapping on a member of *P(E)* is very low, therefore the objects contained in this fuzzy set have very low membership values to belong to the whole f-set. Conversely, the objects of fuzzy sets that are sources or targets of several mappings with *highest roles* have high membership values to belong to the f-set. These latter fuzzy sets contribute prominently to the global structure of the f-set. We can express physical structures such as the "statue of liberty", logical such as "a particular combination of words makes a sentence" or temporal structures such as "a sequence of objects ordered by time. For example, any group of organs of a human body considered as a fuzzy set has a membership value different from 0. The vital biological functions[2] between the heart and the brain considered both as fuzzy sets will provide these two organs with high membership values to belong to the whole human body f-set. Conversely, the finger and the arm will be assigned low membership values because the biological functions between these two organs are not vital. If the mappings are dynamic functions with respect to time, then using functional set theory, we will be able to predict the parts of cybernetic systems (including species) that will change or even disappear over time because of a change in their environment.

Definition 2: *The membership of an object a_i in the f-set Ω is determined by the roles of the mappings that relate two fuzzy sets that contain a_i (as a source or as a target). We write $\mu(a_i \in \Omega) = \alpha$ to state that the membership value of the object a_i in Ω is equal to α.*

2.3 Functional-Set Theoretic Operations

For now, we will introduce only the complement and the intersection for now. Given an f-set Ω and an f-subset $A \subseteq \Omega$, the complement of A in Ω is the f-subset B of all mappings that belong to Ω but not to A. The intersection of two f-sets A and B is the f-set C containing those mappings in both A and B. If: $A = \{f_1\langle S_1; S_2\rangle, f_2\langle S_3; S_4\rangle\}$ and $B = \{f_1\langle S_1; S_2\rangle\}$, then the intersection $C = A \wedge B = \{f_1\langle S_1; S_2\rangle\}$ with the following membership values: $\mu_{A \wedge B}(a_i) = \min\{\mu_A(a_i); \mu_B(a_i)\}\ \forall\ a_i \in S_i$.

2.4 The Notion of Functional Class

Our goal in this section is to extract well-organized patterns that are parts of a whole entity. This is done through the definition of "a functional class" (f-class).

Definition 3: *An f-class is an f-subset of an f-set Ω that involves only members of P(E) that are related through at least one mapping. That is, all non-related members (or fuzzy sets) are dropped. Figure 1 depicts one f-class that involves $\{S_1, S_2, S_3\}$ and another f-class that involves $\{S_4\}$.*

---

[2] We mean very complex biochemical interactions between the two organs.

Definition 4: *An f-structure of order β ($\beta \in \Re$) is an f-class that is represented by the mappings between members of P(E) with role values $\geq \beta$. The lists of mappings that have* the highest roles *are called* the invariants *(or descriptors) of the f-structure.*

"A human face" can be viewed as an f-structure since it is made of "a nose", "a mouth", "two eyes", etc., all viewed as f-substructures. The structural invariants are *particular qualities or properties* that mappings between fuzzy subsets of objects from the same f-class share. *They represent a particular class of functions with high roles.* The structural invariants capture the core of the structure. For example, these invariants might characterize features pertaining to the ancestors of species and are found in a higher level in a taxonomy tree of species. They are key answers to the questions: "what makes a hawk close to an eagle?" and "what makes a tiger close to a lion?"

3. LEARNING WITHIN FUNCTIONAL SET THEORY

The learning process within the FST paradigm consists roughly of (i) determining whether components or groups of objects are forming different whole entities (or f-classes) or whether they form a single entity, and (ii) discovering the parts of the entity that are most "important" in the sense they have higher fuzzy membership values in the f-class. These important parts constitute *the structure*, they are determined by the *invariants* of the f-class. The learning algorithm starts with random mappings that relate members of $P(E)$ where E is a ground set. As the system evolves, it gets more relevant information, by adding, modifying or removing some mappings between members of $P(E)$. The mappings are improved with respect to a criterion. At this stage some f-classes have emerged from the initial configuration (the initial cloud). Once the f-classes are identified, the algorithm will focus on finding the structure of each f-class. Through these mapping updates, the roles are being increased. In a supervised mode, the expert will provide better mappings within an iteration of the learning algorithm in order to enhance their roles. The process will continue iteratively and stop after a predefined learning threshold is reached. At this stage, the algorithm has identified the "optimal mappings" called "invariants" as well as the "optimal fuzzy membership values" of the objects in the f-class. *Therefore, the structure has emerged and the f-set algorithm has learned.* Reasoning under FST is called *functional reasoning* (FR) by the author. It is conducted in order to extract the different f-classes contained in a functional set. The power set $P(E)$, enables view the cloud of data from different views in order to detect eventual "best connections" between these views. The idea is similar to the puzzle game principle. By arranging the puzzle pieces in a certain way, a larger well-organized pattern will be unraveled.

4. IMPACTS OF F-SET THEORY

There are many areas on which f-set theory has an impact. Some of them are:

Logic: Functional set theory brings a new vision of logic that enables human to better communicate with machines. The logical formalism of FST is more appropriate to human reasoning than the binary logical formalism. In a long-term, we will be able to design a new type of chips based on FST that will open a door to a new generation of more intelligent machines that better understand humans.

Fuzzy Set Theory: The incorporation of FST will extend fuzzy set theory that also does not account for structural information. *There are no relations or mappings between objects in the fuzzy set theory.* FST introduces the notion of "role" of a mapping that impacts the degree of membership of objects that are being mapped in the f-set.

Hidden Markov Models: Traditional HMM's *have a clear conceptual framework and the ability to learn statistically, but they are unable to account for structural information of the sequence.* Because the symbols of an input sequence are assumed to be conditionally independent, therefore HMM's make no use of structure, either topological or conceptual. Structural hidden Markov models (SHMM's) developed by the author and his student extend HMM's by searching this underlying structure. *A structural HMM is then composed of several f-structures that are connected through mappings to form a bigger f-structure.* For example, if $E = \{o_1, o_2, \ldots, o_k, c_1, c_2, \ldots, c_p\}$ is the ground set, an f-structure might be composed of mappings between some members S_i of $P(E)$ (group of evidences o_i) and some conclusions c_k. SHMM's merge statistics with syntax in a natural and seamless way. We have applied the concept of SHMM to help design engineers map external car designs to customer's preferences. SHMM has outperformed the classical HMM with 10% of difference in prediction accuracy [Bouchaffra, and Jun, 2004].

5. CONCLUSION

We have introduced in this paper a new mathematical domain that we called f-set theory. Our goal is to emphasize the relationships between objects rather than the objects themselves. We believe that this "functional approach" is a must for a better understanding of the notion of structure. We have introduced the notion of role assigned to mappings between fuzzy sets as well as the notion of fuzzy membership value assigned to an object in an f-set. We introduced the notion of f-class from which we derived the notion of a structure. Our intuition is driven by the fact that mappings provide more information about structures than the objects alone. This research is promising since it impacts so many areas such as mathematics, computer science, and biology.

REFERENCES

D. Bouchaffra and J. Tan "Introduction to the Concept of Structural Hidden Markov Model: Application to Mining Customers' Preferences for Automotive Designs", in Proceedings of the 17th International Conference on Pattern Recognition (ICPR), Cambridge, UK, 23-26-07-2004.

D. Bouchaffra and J. Tan, "Structural HMM modeling and its Applications in Automotive Industry", in: Proceedings of the 5th International Conference on Enterprise Information Systems, Angers, France 23-26, 2003[1].

D. Bouchaffra and J. Tan, "Mapping Designs to User Perceptions using a Structural HMM: Application to Kansei-Engineering", in: Proceedings of the International Conference on Computational Intelligence for Modeling, Control and Automation - CIMCA'2003, Vienna, Austria, 12-14 February 2003[2].

W. Buntine, "A Guide to the Literature on Learning Probabilistic Networks from Data", in: IEEE Transactions on Knowledge and Data Engineering, 8(2): 195-210, 1996.

J. W. Dauwben, "Georg Cantor's Creation of Transfinite Set Theory: Personality and Psychology in the History of Mathematics", Papers in Mathematics, New York, 1979.

R. Duda, P. Hart, and D. Stork, "Pattern Classification", Wiley, New York, 2001.

K.S. Fu, "Syntactic Pattern Recognition and Applications", Prentice-Hall, Englewood Cliffs, N.J., 1982.

A. Garciadiego, "Bertrand Russell and the Origins of the Set Theory Paradoxes", Basel 1992.

P.E. Johnson, "A History of Set Theory" (Boston, Mass., 1972).

J. Pearl, "Probabilistic Reasoning in Intelligent Systems: Networks of Plausible Inference", Morgan Kaufmann, San Mateo, CA, 1988.

L. Zadeh, "Fuzzy Sets", in: Information and Control, 8(3), 338-53, 1962.

AN ADAPTIVE HYBRID GENETIC ANNEALING TECHNIQUE APPLIED TO BAYESIAN NETWORKS

ASHRAF M. ABDELBAR and MANAR I. HOSNY
Dept. of Computer Science, American University in Cairo

ABSTRACT

Bayesian belief networks (BBN's) are a popular graphical representation for reasoning under (probabilistic) uncertainty. An important, and $\mathcal{NP}$-complete, problem on BBN's is the *maximum a posteriori* (MAP) assignment problem, in which the goal is find the network assignment with highest conditional probability given a set of observances, or evidence. In this paper, we present an adaptive hybrid technique combining genetic algorithms and simulated annealing, and apply it to a 100-node Bayesian network. Simulated annealing is used as a type of mutation within the framework of the genetic algorithm, and the parameters of the annealing schedule are themselves adapted by the genetic algorithm.

INTRODUCTION

Bayesian networks [6], also known as Bayesian belief networks, influence diagrams, and causal networks, are a connectionist structure which meets common definitions of a neural network and is popular in the AI community for reasoning under uncertainty. They have been applied to a wide variety of domains.

Bayesian belief networks (BBN's) [6] are a popular graphical representation for reasoning under (probabilistic) uncertainty. They have been applied to domains ranging from natural language understanding to medical diagnosis to computer vision. An important problem on BBN's is the *maximum a posteriori* (MAP) assignment problem, also known as the Most Probable Explanation (MPE) problem, which is concerned with finding the highest probability assignment, or explanation, $\mathcal{A}$ for a BBN B that is consistent with a set of observations, or evidence, $\mathcal{E}$.

For the special-case of singly-connected BBN's, exact polynomial-time (linear-time, in fact) algorithms [6] exist for finding the MPE. However, for multiply-connected BBN's, the problem is $\mathcal{NP}$-hard [10] and even approximating it with a bounded degree of accuracy has recently been shown to be $\mathcal{NP}$-hard [2, 3].

BAYESIAN BELIEF NETWORKS

A BBN is a triple (V, E, P), where V is a set of random variables representing problem-domain events or hypotheses, E is a set of edges (representing causal relationships among domain variables) such that (V, E) is a directed acyclic graph, and $P = \{P_v | v \in V\}$ is a set of conditional probability distributions, where P_v specifies the conditional probability of every possible instantiation of v given every possible instantiation of v's parents, denoted $\pi(v)$. The dag (V, E) is assumed to be an independency map, i.e. that each node is conditionally independent, given its parents, of all its non-descendants.

Each conditional distribution P_v for a node v with k parents must specify 2^{k+1} probabilities. For example, if node v is identified with a binary-valued random variable and has two binary-valued parents, say u and w, then P_v must specify for each of the four possible instantiations of $\pi(v)$, (i.e. $\{u \leftarrow \mathbf{T}, w \leftarrow \mathbf{T}\}$, $\{u \leftarrow \mathbf{F}, w \leftarrow \mathbf{T}\}$,$\{u \leftarrow \mathbf{T}, w \leftarrow \mathbf{F}\}$, and $\{u \leftarrow \mathbf{F}, w \leftarrow \mathbf{F}\}$,) the two probabilities $P(v = \mathbf{T}|\pi(v))$ and $P(v = \mathbf{F}|\pi(v))$.

In this paper, as a notational device, we will assume that each P_v is represented as a series of *lines*, each line ℓ corresponding to a specific instantiation of the node v and of its parents $\pi(v)$. We will let $\ell(v)$ denote the value that the line ℓ assigns to v and if $\pi(v) = \{z_1, \ldots, z_k\}$, then $\ell(z_i)$ will denote the value that ℓ assigns to z_i. $P(\ell)$ will denote the probability that is associated with the line ℓ. In this paper, we will restrict our attention to binary-valued variables.

An instantiation, or full assignment, $\mathcal{A}$ of a binary-valued belief network defined over a set of variables V is a mapping which assigns a truth value to each member of V. A partial assignment $\mathcal{E}$ of a subset of the nodes of a belief network assigns truth values to the members of the subset.

Based on the assumption that a belief network's underlying graph is an independency map of the network variables, Pearl [6] has shown that the joint probability of any given full instantiation, $\mathcal{A} : V \mapsto v_1, \ldots, v_n$, of the network variables can be computed according to

$$P(v_1, v_2, \ldots, v_n) = \prod_{i=1}^{n} P(v_i \mid \pi(v_i)) \ . \qquad (1)$$

The MAP problem is an optimization problem where we are given a belief network B and partial assignment $\mathcal{E}$ of B which represents "real-world" observations, or evidence, for which we seek an explanation. The problem is undefined if $P(\mathcal{E}) = 0$, i.e. if the evidence is impossible. The objective is to find the full assignment which is most probable given the evidence at hand. In other words, it is required to find the instantiation $\mathcal{A}$ with *maximum a posteriori* probability $P(\mathcal{A}|\mathcal{E})$. This is equivalent to maximizing $P(\mathcal{A}, \mathcal{E})$ or maximizing $P(\mathcal{A})$ under the constraint that $\mathcal{E} \subseteq \mathcal{A}$. If the evidence set is empty, then the objective is to find the network assignment $\mathcal{A}$ with highest unconditional probability $P(\mathcal{A})$. The problem remains $\mathcal{NP}$-hard even for the case where the evidence set is null, i.e. finding the instantiation $\mathcal{A}$ with highest unconditional joint probability. For simplicity, in this paper, we focus on the case where the evidence $\mathcal{E}$ is null; however, it is not difficult to generalize these techniques to non-empty evidence sets.

PREVIOUS WORK

The first application of genetic algorithms to BBN's appears to be [8, 9]. In [1], a parallel combination of a genetic algorithm and simulated annealing was applied to a 14-node BBN that was an extension of one of the networks used in [8]. Using PVM to implement parallelism, one central processor ran a genetic algorithm on a single population. A number of satellite processors, ranging from one to eight, would, asynchronously, as soon as one was idle, request a random individual from the population of the central processor. The random individual

Table 1: The best, and the average, fitness in the population at the end of the evolutionary process for the three techniques.

Technique	Pop. Best	Pop. Average	Generations
Adaptive hybrid	8.71×10^{-15}	1.18×10^{-15}	666
Non-adaptive hybrid	3.27×10^{-15}	6.40×10^{-16}	2227
GA Alone	7.10×10^{-16}	1.76×10^{-16}	1136

would then be used as the start state of a simulated annealing process by the satelite processor. The result of the annealing process would then be returned to the central population, where it would compete for a place in the population based on its fitness.

Here, our interest is not the parallelization potential of combining genetic algorithms and simulated annealing but rather in the potential for the combination being able to reach deeper optima than either technique separately. In the standard genetic metaphor, random crossover and random mutation are meant to simulate a large number of generations of evolution. The simulated annealing operator can be thought of as an "intelligent," or a directed, mutation operator compared to the random (undirected) mutation operator. The advantage of random mutation is that it is typically very cheap computationally, which allows a large number of generations of slow evolution to be achieved. On the other hand, the simulated annealing operator can be viewed as simulating "evolutionary spurts," which occur infrequently relative to random mutation, of some elements of the population.

TECHNIQUE

In previous work [1], we used simulated annealing as a genetic operator. Here, we make the simulated annealing process adaptive: the parameters of the simulated annealing process will evolve and change according to the needs of the evolutionary process. Our technique belongs to a family of methods that combine aspects of evolutionary computation (EC) and simulated annealing (SA).

For implementation, we use the popular MIT class-library `GALib`, which provides a number of genome types and crossover and mutation operators, and implement simulated annealing as a special case of mutation. A call to the mutation operator is, with a probability P_{SA}, diverted to the simulated annealing procedure; with the inverse probability the standard mutation operator is called. The chromosome passed to the annealing procedure is used as the start state of the annealing search and the final state is returned as the result of the mutation. The simulated annealing process uses the genetic algorithm's mutation operator to find neighboring states and uses its fitness function to evaluate the quality of each state. The annealing schedule is based on reducing the temperature T by a fixed factor f_{SA} at the end of each iteration.

Each chromosome in the genetic algorithm population contains n boolean bits, where n is the number of BBN nodes, representing a candidate assignment to the BBN, in addition to two real-valued fields: f_{SA} (the annealing temperature cooling factor), and P_{SA} (the probability that a given call to mutation will call the simulated annealing directed mutation instead of the standard mutation).

The two SA-related chromosome fields of course do not play a direct role in the computation of a chromosome's fitness, but they play an indirect role in the evolutionary process. Intuitively, good annealing parameters will produce good solutions that will be more likely to survive longer in the population and therefore to produce more offspring. Consequently, good annealing parameters, although they are not directly involved in the computation of fitness, will live longer and bad parameters will die out faster.

The fitness function is based on Equation (1). Given an assignment $\mathcal{A}$, the line in the probability table, for each node in the network, consistent with $\mathcal{A}$ is found and the corresponding probabilities are multiplied to obtain the overall joint probability of the truth assignment $\mathcal{A}$.

The crossover operator is based on the cluster-based operator used in [8, 9], which was also used in [1]. In this technique, a random BBN node is selected as the center of a cluster, and then all nodes that fall within a certain number of links of the center of the cluster are exchanged between the two chromosomes being mated.

As parameters to the hybrid technique, the user selects the probabilities of mutation P_{mut}, and crossover P_{cross} for the n boolean bits, and probability of mutation P'_{mut} and crossover P'_{cross} for the two real-valued fields representing the annealing parameters. We recommend $P'_{mut} = P_{mut}/10$ and $P'_{cross} = P_{cross}/10$.

EXPERIMENTAL RESULTS AND ANALYSIS

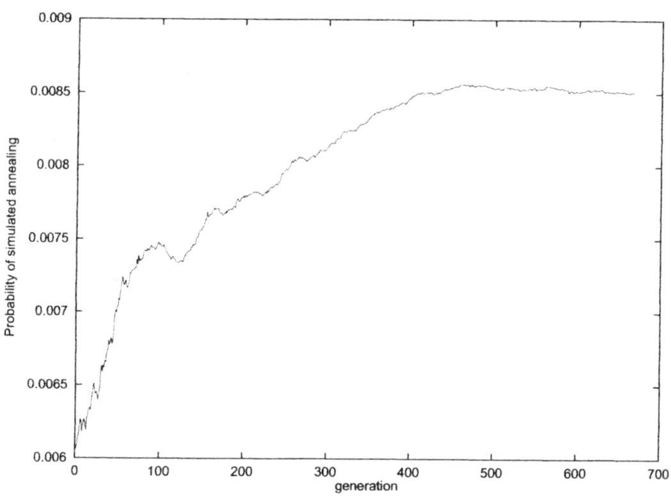

Figure 1: Population average value for P_{SA} versus generation number

We used a steady-state GA with a population replacement factor of 10%. We compared three techniques: a stand-alone GA without annealing, a non-adaptive hybrid GA-SA which uses fixed annealing parameters (this basically corresponds to the technique presented in [1]), and the adaptive hybrid technique described in the previous section. We used a large, randomly-generated 100-node BBN, with a maximum number of parents per node of 15.

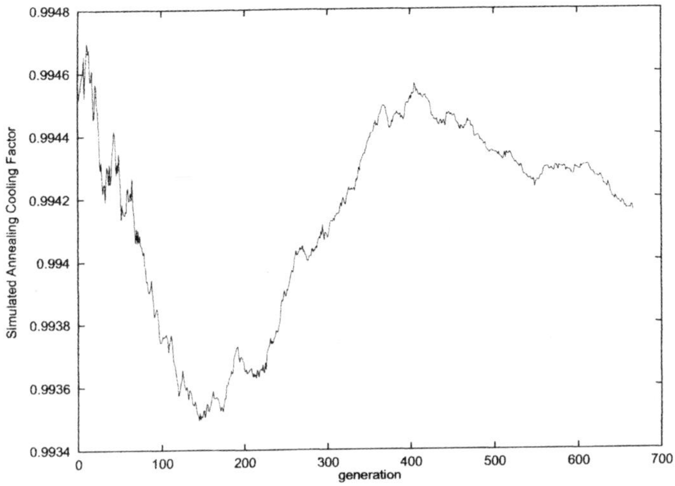

Figure 2: Population average value for cooling factor f_{SA} versus generation number

Table 2: Run-time behavior of the adaptive hybrid technique.

Statistic	Value
Number of generations	666
Total CPU time	104 min
Total calls to obj. func.	4.75×10^6 calls
Calls to obj. func. from within GA	9.33×10^5 calls
Calls to obj. func. from within SA	3.82×10^6 calls
Calls to SA module	1.07×10^3 calls
Total CPU time of all obj. func. evaluations	55.66 min
Total CPU time of all calls to annealing	65.77 min
Total GA processing time (excluding SA time)	38.23 min

Table 1 shows the best, and the average fitness in the population at the end of the evolutionary process for the three techniques. Figures 1 and 2 show plots of the average population value for P_{SA} and for f_{SA}, respectively, versus generation number for the adaptive hybrid. Over the entire run, 92.92% of the calls to annealing returned an improved solution; 6.24% returned a solution of lower fitness; and, 0.84% returned a solution of the same fitness as the solution with which it was called. Table 2 shows a breakdown of how much time was spent inside each module of the adaptive hybrid technique.

Examining Figure 1, we observe that the average population P_{SA} tended to increase for the first half of the evolutionary computation, and then remained more or less steady for the second half of the computation. Examining Figure 2, we observe that the average population f_{SA} tended to decrease rapidly for the first 150 generations, and then tended to increase rapidly for the next 250 generations. Finally, it tended to decrease more slowly for the final third of the computation.

DISCUSSION AND CONCLUSION

We have presented a hybrid adaptive technique that combines genetic algorithms and simulated annealing. Experimental results on a large 100-node Bayesian belief network suggest that the presented technique is effective compared to a stand-alone GA and to a non-adaptive hybrid.

Table 2 presents a profile of the run-time behavior of the adaptive hybrid. Although we did not record a similar profile for the stand-alone GA, important information can be deduced from Table 2. We can see that the total processing time is 104 minutes, of which 65.77 minutes were spent inside calls to annealing, and 38.23 minutes were consumed by the GA's own processing. This indicates that the GA alone would take 0.057 minutes per generation. We can see, from Table 1, that the stand-alone GA ran for 1136 generations, which would take 65.21 minutes.

This means the adaptive hybrid took less than twice the processing time of the standalone GA but returned a solution whose probability (8.71×10^{-15}) is more than an order of magnitude higher than the probability (7.10×10^{-16}) of the solution returned by the stand-alone GA.

References

[1] A.M. Abdelbar, and S.M. Hedetniemi, "A Parallel Hybrid Genetic Algorithm Simulated Annealing Approach to Finding Probable Explanations on Bayesian Belief Networks," *Proceedings IEEE International Conference on Neural Networks,* Vol. I, 1997, pp. 450-455.

[2] A.M. Abdelbar, and S.M. Hedetniemi, "Approximating MAPs for Belief Networks is NP-hard and Other Theorems," *Artificial Intelligence,* Vol. 102, 1998, 21-38.

[3] A.M. Abdelbar, S.T. Hedetniemi, and S. M. Hedetniemi, "The Complexity of Approximating MAPs for Belief Networks with Bounded Probabilities," *Artificial Intelligence*, Vol. 124, 2000, 283-288.

[4] J. Pearl, *Probabilistic Reasoning in Intelligence Systems: Networks of Plausible Inference,* Morgan-Kaufmann, San Mateo, 1988.

[5] C. Rojas-Guzman and M.A. Kramer, "GALGO: A Genetic ALGOrithm Decision Support Tool for Complex Uncertain Systems Modeled with Bayesian Belief Networks," *Proceedings Ninth Conference on Uncertainty in AI*, 1993.

[6] C. Rojas-Guzman and M.A. Kramer, "Remote Diagnosis and Monitoring of Complex Industrial Systems Using a Genetic Algorithms Approach," *Proceedings IEEE International Symposium on Industrial Electronics,* pp. 363-367, 1994.

[7] S.E. Shimony, "Finding MAPs for Belief Networks Is NP-hard," *Artificial Intelligence,* 68, 399, 1994.

ARTIFICIAL NEURAL NETWORK DEVELOPMENT USING P2P NETWORKS*

AARON HARWOOD, ANTHONY SENYARD†, MINH TRI TRUONG
Department of Computer Science and Software Engineering
University of Melbourne
Victoria, AUSTRALIA

ABSTRACT

There are many choices when creating an effective artificial neural network for a given problem. The artificial neurons and connections to be used, the network topology, the learning algorithm, the problem representation, all with unique parameters. These choices are continuously enhanced by neural network researchers. The approach taken in this paper is to search through this space of choices and associated parameters using human guidance and experience until an effective combination is found. A peer-to-peer software tool has been implemented to perform this search, called the ANN Grid Toolset. Our toolset allows researchers to share their computing resources, share their learning algorithms and to collectively view the progress of neural network creation. Peer-to-Peer technologies ensures that our toolset is scalable, allowing a large number of resources to be harnessed. We believe that our approach successfully addresses the problem of making appropriate choices for creating an effective artificial neural network.

INTRODUCTION

The aim of this paper is to argue that a distributed computing tool specifically designed for neural network learning, when combined with an appropriate development process, is of significant use to neural network developers. We first establish the major problem with neural network development as we see it. A single method for creating a neural network that satisfies precision and accuracy goals for a given problem has presented a far greater challenge to neural network developers than solving individual problems. That is, despite the wide range of solved problems, no predictable, repeatable and problem-domain independent process for developing specific neural networks has been created and adopted. This motivated us to define a software engineering styled development process for creating neural networks. Following this, we outline the details of our distributed computing tool (based on peer-to-peer networks) and how it can be used in this process. Finally, we describe further work to enhance the tool and development process.

*Funded in part by the Australian Research Council, grant number DP0451936.

†Author for correspondence.

Development Process

The current development process used by most developers can essentially be characterized as the following. First, select some specific neural network parameters. These parameters could include, the type of artificial neurons to use , the number of layers , the number of neurons in the layers , the connection structure , the learning algorithm (and associated parameters) as well as the problem representation and others. Secondly, using neural network tools, create a neural network based on these parameters. Third, if successful, finish, otherwise, if that particular combination of parameters did not achieve the precision and accuracy goals, try another. By varying one or more parameters another combination [1] of parameters can be used for creation. The process continues until a successful combination is found or development is abandoned.

There are three main problems with this approach. Firstly, the process above is not fully defined. New developers who wish to create neural networks must discover the development process and experience any problems without the knowledge of experienced developers. Secondly, at the outset of development the appropriate neural network parameters are unknown and a search is required. To select the appropriate neural network parameters for a particular problem requires a search through an exponentially increasing set of combinations of parameters. The future of such searches faces the problem of an increasing range of choices for parameters as more elaborate models of neural networks are proposed by researchers. Finally, the search is unbounded and unpredictable. Establishing when to give up the search is undefined (except once the desired precision and accuracy goals are met) and determining the resources requirements is unknown.

Numerous approaches for creating a neural network have been proposed based on technical solutions, such as evolutionary computing or genetic algorithms [8] Such approaches are exciting as potential solutions to the problem of creating neural networks. However, these approaches do not address the issue of predicting or bounding the resources required and do not exploit the experience and knowledge of developers and problem domain experts. In the work of Senyard et. al. [4] a thorough review of current practice is performed and a novel neural network development process is proposed.

In the Senyard process a human guided enumeration and subsequent investigation of the neural network parameters associated with creation is suggested. The developer begins by listing all potential combinations of parameters they think will be most effective in creating a neural network to meet the precision and accuracy goals. These decisions are documented by the developer for future reference and communication purposes. The creation of this list is guided by the experience of the developer and a problem domain expert (for the creation and selection of data representations).

This approach directly addresses the problems with current practice previously identified. Firstly, it is generic and exploits the expertise of the developer and problem domain expert rather than being based solely on technique. This knowledge can be communicated through publication of the details of the parameters listed in the Problem Specification phase and the effectiveness of combinations used in the Parameter Exploration step. This provides guidance to developers who wish to develop neural networks and repeat the success of others.

Secondly, rather than an unguided search, a systematic search is conducted through an enumeration of the desired parameter combinations. This allows the neural network development process to move toward a true engineering discipline. This can be accomplished through timing the individual learning tasks and then

---

[1] Combination is used to refer to both new combinations of parameters and permutations formed through varying one parameter in an existing combination.

predicting the resources required for future trials based upon these timings. In this way, the development process can consume a bounded amount of resources through following the plan established in the Problem Specification phase and Parameter Exploration step.

In our development process, a number of neural network learning tasks [2] can be carried out in parallel to speed up the Parameter Exploration step. The tool we have created allows for an arbitrary program executable (depending only on platform) to be used in the learning tasks. This is why our distributed computing tool has potential for neural network developers.

We have previously contributed comprehensive studies of the ANN development process. Separately we have also contributed significant developments of distributed architecture, namely peer-to-peer, for complex applications. In this work we combine our separate contributions to develop an ANN Grid Toolset (that uses the peer-to-peer paradigm). In particular our ANN Grid Toolset is: (i) A new software tool for developing neural networks, not just a simulation system; (ii) A tool which is integrated into a development process but allows for the use of arbitrary software by individual developers; and (iii) A tool which has been engineered using software engineering methods and process.

ANN GRID TOOLSET REQUIREMENTS

The neural network development process leads to a rich set of functional requirements for distributed processing. Developers primarily require the ability to: **[P1]** Distribute or farm out multiple instances of an algorithm, called task farming, with different parameters over a set of resources; and **[P2]** Monitor the learning progress of each task, as the task executes, to decide whether the task should be terminated early or be allowed to continue execution.

Secondary requirements include: **[S1]** An ability to make use of existing programming languages and executables as is, **[S2]** The possibility to connect, disconnect/reconnect from the system without interrupting learning tasks, **[S3]** Use of a consistent naming convention and index for the learning tasks **[S4]** Access for multiple researchers to share resources and learning algorithms and to monitor the progress of each others development. Further to the functional requirements of the development process, we may list some non-functional requirements of a modern distributed system [3], in general: dynamicity , fault tolerance , scalability , efficiency and security.

ANN GRID TOOLSET DESIGN

Compare to orthodox grid methodology which is based on hierarchies, the recent emergence of alternative distributed systems, namely peer-to-peer (P2P) systems, shows a different approach to large scale integration, with astonishing success [1]. In this case, the hierarchical structure is abandoned and replaced by a self-organized structure or network that supports efficient data sharing among simple autonomous entities called peers. For example, the SETI@home reports an average of roughly 40TFlops of computing power which compares to the world's largest supercomputers. Our other work is concerned with the use of P2P for applications such as interactive virtual world's and we have already substantial developments of P2P technology [7]. On this basis, we selected P2P as our underlying architecture.

[2] A neural network learning task means the execution of a particular set of neural network parameters to create a neural network.

Most applications that are built upon a P2P network make use of the data sharing or key-based routing capabilities, as a kind of distributed shared-memory or communication system. P2P networks are well known for their ability to share data, that supports the secondary requirements.

Task farming and monitoring

A *task farming* tool and a *task monitoring* tool are the primary tools used by a developer. The farming tool allows the developer to select the learning tasks from a local repository and to select parameter files that describe the parameters for each task. Selected tasks and associated parameters can then be "farmed" out to resources for execution, with the results being captured and stored locally. The monitoring tool allows the developer to inspect the output of currently executing tasks and to signal early termination of tasks that do not show promising results. These tools satisfy the primary requirements.

The secondary requirements provide interesting extensions to the tools. The farming tool allows learning tasks and parameter files to be uploaded into a shared space and allows developers to choose learning tasks and parameter files from this shared space rather than from their local repositories. This simultaneously requires a systemic naming convention for learning tasks and their associated parameter files. For example, a version of a Hopfield network constructed by Senyard may be named `Hopfield-Senyard-type1`. Also, the results of a learning task when run with a given parameter file needs to follow the same conventions. Over time, a database of tasks, parameters and results arises which is both shared and (perhaps partially) stored locally by each developer.

The overall architecture is depicted in Fig. 1 and will be explained further in the following sections. The ANN Grid Toolset may connect to any of the peers, but typically the developer will connect to the peer that is local.

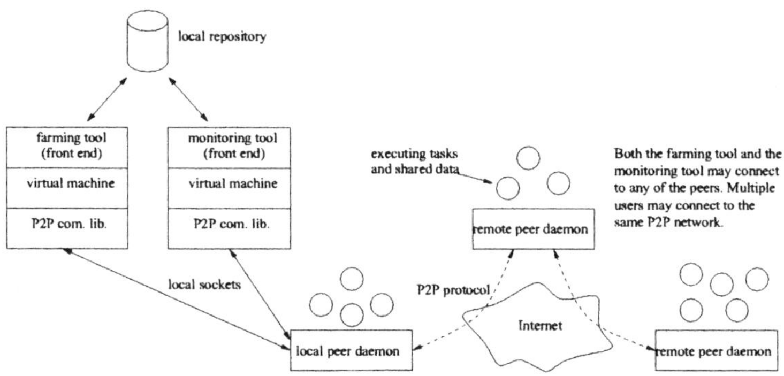

Figure 1: Overall architecture of the neural network grid

Virtual machine

We choose to keep the tools separated from the P2P network so that changes to the tools or to the P2P network can transparently take place. To do this, we use a middle layer of abstraction, in this case called the *virtual machine* (VM). The VM concept is not new, for example the Parallel Virtual Machine (PVM) system of [6] allows tasks to be spawned and managed over a heterogeneous set of resources. However the implementation of a VM over a P2P network is a challenging task, largely due to the dynamicity (unreliability) and required scale of the network, that is not addressed by previous efforts and they are infeasible to adapt. These details are the topic of our other research.

We should emphasize here that the VM concept is not intended to mimic cluster computing or grid computing concepts, where resources are managed by users and distribution is strictly controlled. A striking feature of the P2P paradigm is that the total number of peers in a P2P network is not required to be known (indeed it would be extremely difficult to track).

Peer-to-peer infrastructure

The VM layer communicates via a P2P I/O library to a peer daemon process. The tool is a "peer-client" that does not join a P2P network but rather requests services from a peer which is connected to a P2P network. It is equally possible to build tools that are themselves peers and would first join a P2P network before obtaining service. The separation of tools from the network allows the network to remain in continual service when the tools are not being used, thereby ensuring that the P2P network resources are available for other purposes.

We have developed a P2P architecture that in principle allows multiple P2P protocols and networks to be used. For now, we have implemented a variation of the Chord protocol [5], originally conceived by Ian Stoica and currently used as the basis for the Cooperative File System [2]. The purpose of the protocol is to provide an abstract layer of routing, called key-based routing. Tasks and data are associated with keys and the P2P protocol is used to distribute them over the P2P network. When a peer joins, a small fraction (roughly inversely proportional to the total number of peers) of the total keys are migrated to that peer. Any keys that a leaving peer owns are migrated to other peers before leaving.

ANN GRID TOOLSET APPLICATION

The first step is to identify a problem to be solved and then conduct a variety of activities involving problem description, data collection, data analysis, preprocessing data, determining problem representations, devising testing and training strategies, creating testing and training datasets and numerous other activities. The ANN Grid Toolset is then started and each combination of parameters is farmed out to the peers on the P2P network. The results of the learning tasks are monitored and specific learning tasks can be terminated if performance is lower than expected. Once the Parameter Exploration step is completed more extensive learning on the promising parameter combinations can occur. The resources required to achieve the desired accuracy and precision goals can be estimated using the resource utilization revealed during the Parameter Exploration step.

Using the ANN Grid Toolset involves both maintaining a network of peer daemons and a local repository of learning tasks and parameter files. Peer daemons are started on Internet hosts, much like HTTP daemons, and remain active continuously until explicitly shutdown. Peers may be started only for the period of development by the developer and shutdown after each session if the developer does not want to maintain a presence in the network. Given a network of peers, each tool requires the network address of an existing peer before it can make use of the virtual machine services.

CONCLUSIONS AND FUTURE WORK

Our neural network development process is a significant improvement over ad-hoc practices. Ad-hoc practices do not posses the level of maturity required of an engineering process. Our process is further improved by provided tools which support the process. This tool utilizes an appropriate distributed computing technology, namely P2P networks, with a virtual machine concept to create what we call an ANN Grid Toolset.

Our ANN Grid Toolset provides a neural network developer with the fundamental functions of farming and monitoring neural network learning tasks. P2P properties support the sharing of learning tasks and parameter files among a continually changing and growing community of developers.

We have currently built and tested the components of the ANN Grid Toolset, including the key interfaces, task farming and monitoring functionality. The virtual machine ensures that the distributed architecture and tools can be independently maintained and developed - a basic principle of layered software design.

Further work continues on various aspects of our ANN Grid Toolset. At the highest layer we can improve the development process by refining the conventions that facilitate cooperative research and system development. In the middle layer we can enrich the virtual machine interface, thereby increasing the capacity of the developer to perform development. At the lowest layer we can investigate P2P protocols that better support the requirements of higher layers. In time, the widespread use of a systematic development process will improve best practice. Combined with this improved practice is an ANN Grid Toolset which leads to significant time savings in the development process.

References

[1] D. Clark. Face-to-face with peer-to-peer networking. *IEEE Computer*, 34:18–21, January 2001.

[2] F. Dabek, M. F. Kaashoek, D. Karger, R. Morris, and I. Stoica. Wide-area cooperative storage with CFS. In *Proceedings of the ACM SOSP'01*, pages 202–215, Banff, AL, October 2001. ACM Press.

[3] D. Nessett. Massively distributed systems: Design issues and challenges. In *Proceedings of the Embedded Systems Workshop*. USENIX Association, March 1999.

[4] S. L. Senyard, A. and K. E. Software engineering methods for neural networks. *Proceedings of the Tenth Asia Pacific Software Engineering Conference*, December 2003.

[5] I. Stoica, R. Morris, D. Liben-Nowell, D. R. Karger, F. D. M. F. Kaasheoek, and H. Balakrishnan. Chord: a scalable peer-to-peer lookup protocol for internet applications. *IEEE/ACM Transactions on Network*, 11(1):17–32, Feb. 2003.

[6] V. S. Sunderam. PVM: A framework for parallel distributed computing. *Concurrency: Practice and Experience*, 2(4):315–339, 1990.

[7] M. Truong and A. Harwood. Distributed shell over peer-to-peer networks. In *Proceeding of the International Conference on Parallel and Distributed Processing Techniques and Applications*, pages 269–275, Las Vegas, NV, 2003.

[8] Yao, Williams, and Riessen. Pepnet: Parallel evolutionary programming for constructing artificial neural networks. *Evolutionary Programming VI*, 1213, 1997.

AN EFFICIENT AND FAULT TOLERANT ALGORITHM FOR MULTILAYER NEURAL NETWORK

RAFIC A. AYOUBI
University of Balamand
Faculty of Engineering
Tripoli, Lebanon
rafic.ayoubi@balamand.edu.lb

HAISSAM A. ZIADE
Lebanese University
Faculty of Engineering I
Tripoli, Lebanon
hziade@ul.edu.lb

MAGDY A. BAYOUMI
University of Louisiana
CACS
Lafayette, Louisiana
mab@cacs.louisiana.edu

ABSTRACT
In this paper, we present the simulation results obtained for a modified back-error propagation algorithm for multi-layer perceptron model (MLP) implemented on MasPar massively parallel machine. The obtained results show that our modified algorithm is more tolerant to weight faults than the standard backprop algorithm. Moreover, the improvement of the proposed algorithm is more than 50% over the classical one.

1. INTRODUCTION

Researchers have followed two ways in studying the reliability and robustness of neural networks. Many researchers have studied the fault tolerance of ANN models and tried to find ways to improve their reliability [1, 2, 3, 4, 5, 6]. This approach is justified by the fact that biological neural networks are known to be remarkably tolerant of failures, as well as of noise in input sensory data. Other researchers applied conventional fault tolerant techniques such as redundancy and retraining of the networks in the presence of faulty components [2, 7].

Deodhare, Vidyasagar, and Keerthikaza in [8] formulated the fault tolerance problem for a feedforward network as a constrained minimax optimization problem. Two different methods were used to solve it. In the first method,the constrained minimax optimization problem is converted to a sequence of unconstrained least-squares optimization problems.In the second method a different approach is used to convert the problem to a single unconstrained minimization problem .

Hammadi and Ito in [9] proposed a new learning algorithm to enhance fault tolerance ability of the feedforward neural networks. The algorithm focuses on the weights that may cause errors at the output when they are open faults. The relevance of the synaptic weights to the output error are estimated in each training cycle of the standard backpropagation using Taylor expansion of the output around fault free weights. Then the weight giving the maximum relevance is decreased.

Emmerson and Damper [7] trained two layered networks to solve a pattern recognition task. They showed that increasing the number of neurons in the hidden layer did not increase the fault tolerance of the network. They suggested what they called an "augmented MLP" that improves the fault tolerance of the model by increasing the number of neurons in the hidden layer following a specific procedure. However, their method is very expensive in terms of hardware, because the number of hidden units with their connections is excessive.

Clay and Sequin [10] suggested a variation of the standard back-error propagation by faulting units during training. The argument for training with faults is to imbue a neural network with resistance to those particular faults. However, unit faults are too abstract and unlikely to be representative of the effect of physical faults in an implemented MLP.

Murray and Edwards [4] demonstrated that injection of random noise onto multilayer perceptron weights during learning enhances fault tolerance without additional supervision.

This paper is organized as follows. In Section 2, a brief description of multilayer perceptron network is presented. We briefly describe the visualization of fault in MLP in Section 3. In Section 4, we present our proposed fault tolerant algorithm for MLP network. Section 5 gives a brief description of the MasPar machine used for simulation. In Section 6, we discuss our simulation results. Finally, Section 7 concludes the paper.

2 THE PROPOSED FAULT TOLERANT ALGORITHM FOR MLP NETWORK

The traditional view that MLPs are intrinsically fault tolerant, since they are distributed parallel processing elements with each node contributing to the final output response, is not valid. In this section, we will show that standard back-error propagation algorithm used to train MLPs is not fault tolerant.

Most fault tolerance techniques used in the literature for MLP networks employ some randomized procedure, such as random noise injection or random weights/units faulting. The rationale is to distribute the weights so that there is no "unimportant weight". All weights are more or less evenly distributed. However, it is not always true that training with random noise or random weights faulting will improve the fault tolerance of the system. It might lead, in some cases, to a less fault tolerant system.

The fault tolerant algorithm is described below:

1. While the system is not close to convergence do
2. Apply input, $a[0] = I^{p}$
3. Propagate the signal forward to compute the output $a[L]$ using:

$$a_{i}^{p}[l] = f\left(\sum_{j} w_{ij}[l]\ a_{j}^{p}[l-1]\right),\ \text{for } l = 1,2,\ldots,L$$

4. Compute the deltas for the output layer,
   $\delta_i[L] = f'\left(h_i[l]\right)\left(t_i^p - a_i^p[L]\right)$
5. Compute the deltas for the preceding layers by propagating the error backwards,
   $\delta_i[l-1] = f'(h_i[l-1])\sum_j w_{ji}[l]\delta_j[l]$, for $l = L, L-1,...,2$
6. Adjust all weights according to:
   $\Delta w_{ij}[l] = \eta\delta_i[l]a_j[l-1]$
   $w_{ij}^{new}[l] = w_{ij}^{old}[l] + \Delta w_{ij}[l]$
7. find maximum weight in each weight vector,
   divide each maximum by a large specified scalar;
8. Repeat from Step 2 for the next input until all patterns are presented.
9. enddo;
10. Apply input, $a[0] = I^p$
11. Propagate the signal forward to compute the output $a[L]$ using:
    $a_i^p[l] = f\left(\sum_j w_{ij}[l]\, a_j^p[l-1]\right)$, for $l = 1, 2, ..., L$
12. Compute the deltas for the output layer,
    $\delta_i[L] = f'\left(h_i[l]\right)\left(t_i^p - a_i^p[L]\right)$
13. Compute the deltas for the preceding layers by propagating the error backwards,
    $\delta_i[l-1] = f'(h_i[l-1])\sum_j w_{ji}[l]\delta_j[l]$, for $l = L, L-1,...,2$
14. Adjust all weights according to:
    $\Delta w_{ij}[l] = \eta\delta_i[l]a_j[l-1]$
    $w_{ij}^{new}[l] = w_{ij}^{old}[l] + \Delta w_{ij}[l]$
15. Repeat from Step 10 for the next input until all patterns are presented.
16. Repeat from Step 10 for the first input pattern until convergence (i.e. when the difference between the desired output and the computed output is less than epsilon for all patterns, where epsilon $\ll 1$).

Fig. 3: Enhanced fault tolerant BackProp learning algorithm.

In brief, after every few iterations we interrupt the standard back-error propagation training and find the maximum weight components in each weight vector, and divide them by a large scalar to bring their values down to become closer to other weight components. This procedure will be repeated again until the system is close to convergence. At this time, training, using standard back-error propagation algorithm, is continued without interruption until the system fully converges. At the end of the training session, the components of each weight vector become very close in absolute value. Therefore, the weights are more evenly distributed than those of standard back-error propagation algorithm and there are no weights that are more important than others. Rather, each weight is contributing a little to the final output response.

The tendency of neural networks to show an indication of approaching failure due to graceful degradation will still be exhibited, since as more weight faults affect a unit, its absolute activation will decrease into the region of the squashing function's co-domain, where the function transitions between asymptotic values. Simulations have been carried out for different network sizes for different problems to support our theory.

3. SIMULATION RESULTS OF OUR FAULT TOLERANT MODEL

We have carried out several types of simulations in order to assess the effectiveness of our fault tolerant MLP models.

Simulations were carried out for both standard back-error propagation and our proposed algorithms running on different problems. These experiments were done on 8-3 and 16-4 encoder-decoder as well as on a 20-7 Arabic character recognition problem. The number of hidden units varied from 4 to 8 and 8 to 16 for the 8–3 and 16-4 encoder-decoder, respectively, and from 5 to 24 for the Arabic character recognition.

In order to make our simulations more realistic, we decided to fault weights randomly with equal probability until all input patterns are misclassified. We recorded the maximum number of weight faults when no misclassification occurred. Then, we recorded the maximum number of weight faults with 1 misclassification, 2 misclassifications, etc. until all input patterns were misclassified. This procedure was repeated 50 times; each time the weight faulting starts randomly at a different weight using different seed. At the end of the 50 runs, we averaged the results for no misclassification, 1 misclassification, …, all misclassifications.

Initially, we faulted weights only in the hidden layer. Then we carried out the same procedure, but for the output layer only. That was done 50 times, as explained above, and averaged for 8, 9, 10, 11, 12, and 16 hidden units for both standard and improved algorithms. One persistent result was that faulting in the hidden layer gave better classification both in the standard and improved algorithm for all different number of hidden units used. Figure 4 shows the comparison of hidden to output for improved algorithm for 16–8–4 encoder-decoder problem. Since faulting randomly with equal probability is more realistic than faulting in the hidden layer only or the output layer only, we will only show the graphs for the first scenario from here on. Figures 5 and 6 show how the fault tolerance of networks trained with both standard and improved algorithms changes as more hidden units are added to the MLP network. It can be seen that the fault tolerance increases as more hidden units are added for both the standard and improved algorithm. As expected, the fault tolerance of the improved MLP networks is higher than the original. A bar graph is shown in Figure 7 for the 16–4 encoder-decoder problem. This graph shows, for different hidden layer sizes, the number of weights removed before the network falls below 50% correct classification. Again, as can be seen, as the number of hidden units increases the fault tolerance increases.

Moreover, we have run similar simulations for the 8–3 encoder-decoder problem and Arabic character recognition, and obtained consistent results with that of 16–4 encoder-decoder problem. However, only two bar graphs are shown in Figures 8 and 9 for 8–3 problem and Arabic character recognition, respectively. These graphs represent the number of weight faults before the network falls below 50% correct classification. They also show that our improved algorithm is more fault tolerant than the standard back-error propagation algorithm.

CONCLUSIONS

In this work, we have shown the implementation of a modified backprop algorithm for MLP on MasPar machine. The experimental results obtained for different MLPs are shown and demonstrate the efficiency and fault tolerance of our model. In comparison with standard backprop algorithm, the simulation results show an improvement of more than 50%.

REFERENCES

[1] D. S. Phatak and I. Koren, "Complete and partial fault tolerance of feedforward neural nets," IEEE Transactions on Neural Networks, vol.6, no. 2, pp. 446-456, 1995.

[2] C. H. Sequin and R. D. Clay, "Fault tolerance in artificial neural networks," in Proceedings of International Joint Conference on Neural Networks, vol. 1, (San Diego, CA), pp. 703–708, 1990.

[3] K. Matsuoka, "Noise injection into inputs in back-propagation learning," IEEE Transactions on Systems, Man, and Cybernetics, vol. 22, no. 3, pp. 436–440, 1992.

[4] A. F. Murray and P. J. Edwards, "Synaptic weight noise during multilayer perceptron training: Fault tolerance and training improvements," IEEE Transactions on Neural Networks, vol. 4, no. 4, pp. 722–725, 1993.

[5] G. R. Bolt, "Assessing the reliability of artificial neural networks," in Proceedings of International Joint Conference on Neural Networks, vol. 1, (Singapore), pp. 578–583, 1991.

[6] Bernier, J. Ortega, A. Prieto, "A Modified Backpropagation Algorithm to Tolerate Weight Errors", Lecture Notes in Computer Science, vol. 1240, pp. 763-771, Springer-Verlag, June 1997.

[7] M. D. Emmerson and R. I. Damper, "Determining and improving the fault tolerance of multilayer perceptrons in a pattern-recognition application," IEEE Transactions on Neural Networks, vol. 4, no. 5, pp. 788–793, 1993.

[8] D. Deodhare, M. Vidyasagar, and S. S. Keerthi, "Synthesis of fault-tolerant feedforward neural networks using minimax optimization," IEEE Transactions on Neural Networks, vol. 9, no. 5, pp. 891-900, 1998.

[9] N. C. Hammadi and H. Ito, "A learning algorithm for fault tolerant feedforward neural networks," IEEE Transactions on Information and Systems, vol. E80-D, no.1, pp. 21-27, 1997.

[10] R. D. Clay and C. H. Sequin, "Fault tolerance training improves generalization and robustness," in Proceedings of International Joint Conference on Neural Networks, vol. 1, (Baltimore, MD), pp. 769–774, 1992.

[11] MasPar Computer Corporation, Sunnyvale, CA, MasPar MP-1 Hardware Manuals, 1992.

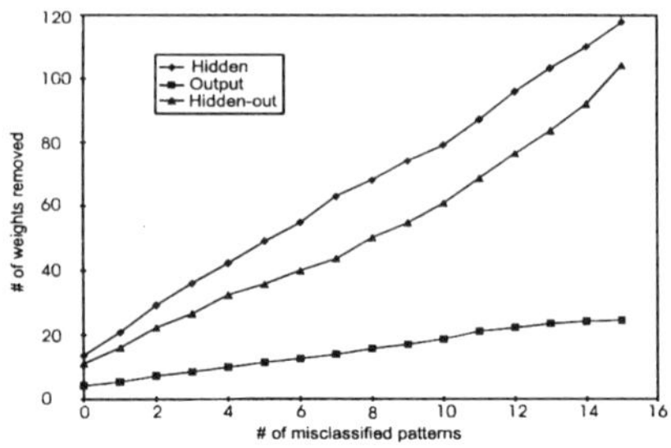

Fig 4: Comparison of the effect of faults in hidden, output, and hidden-output using improved backprop algorithm for a 16x8x4 netwrok.

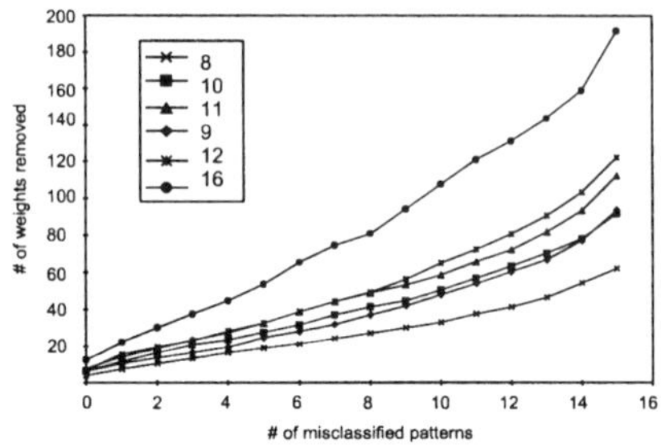

Fig 5: Comparison of the effect of faults for various numbers of hidden units for standard backprop algorithm.

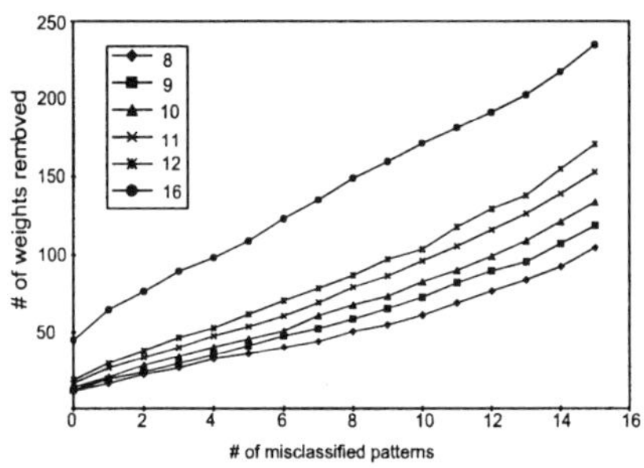

Fig 6: Comparison of the effect of faults for various numbers of hidden units for improved backprop algorithm.

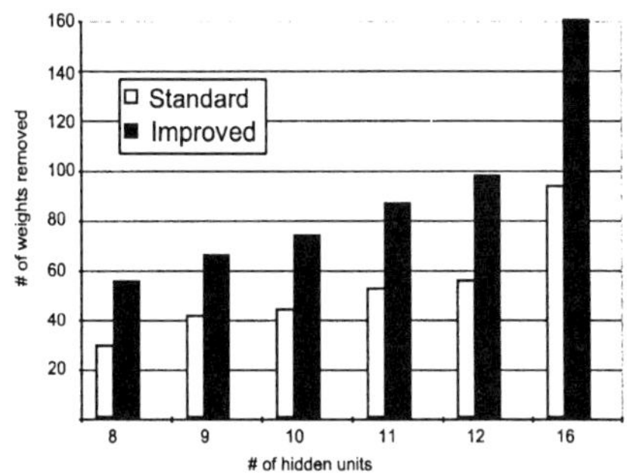

Fig 7: Comparison of the effect of faults for standard and improved algorithms when correct classification is 50% for a 16x4 network.

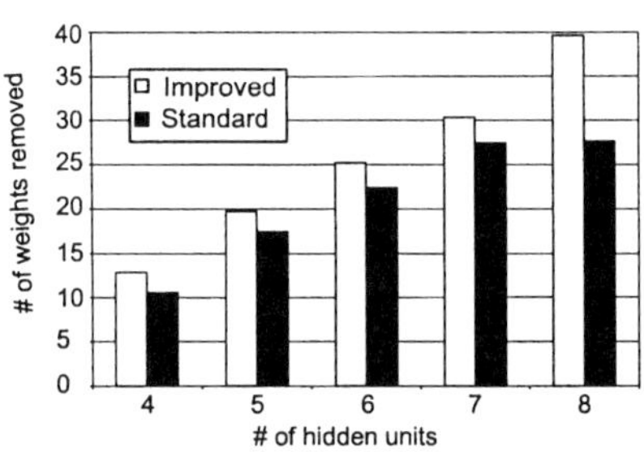

Fig 8: Comparison of the effect of faults for standard and improved algorithms when correct classification is 50% for 8x3 network.

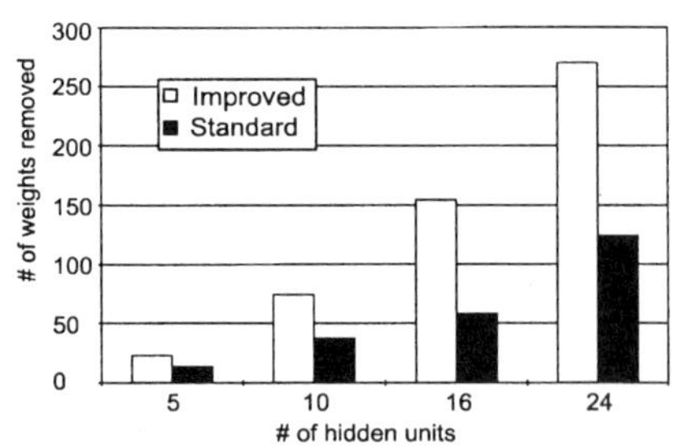

Fig 9: Comparison of the effect of faults for standard and improved algorithms when correct classification is 50% for 20x7 network for Arabic character recognition.

FAST, STABLE AND ONLINE TRAINING OF FUZZY ARTMAP USING A NOVEL, CONSERVATIVE, SLOW-LEARNING STRATEGY

K. CARR
Department of ECE, University of Central Florida, Orlando, FL 32826

K. CANNAVA
Department of ECE, University of Central Florida, Orlando, FL 32826

R. PESCATORE
Department of ECE, University of Central Florida, Orlando, FL 32826

M. GEORGIOPOULOS
Department of ECE, University of Central Florida, Orlando, FL 32826

G. C. ANAGNOSTOPOULOS
Department of ECE, Florida Institute of Technology, Melbourne, FL 32901

ABSTRACT

In this paper we present a novel variant of an on-line learning ART neural network algorithm. More specifically, we equip the semi-supervised Fuzzy ARTMAP classifier with a new learning strategy encompassing a new, *slow-learning* rule and a new type of *match tracking*, according to which category updates or creations are reduced to a minimum to control the proliferation of categories, while maintaining the on-line and stable learning characteristics of the original ART architectures. We have conducted a number of experiments on artificial and real databases to demonstrate the advantages of our proposed ART neural network algorithm.

1. INTRODUCTION

NEURAL networks have been used extensively and successfully to address a wide variety of problems. The ones that are of interest to us in this work are the class of neural network architectures referred to as ART neural networks. ART neural networks are based on the adaptive resonance theory developed by Grossberg (1976). Two of the ART neural network architectures that are important in this work is the Fuzzy ARTMAP neural network (Carpenter, et al., 1992) and the class of semi-supervised ART neural network architectures discussed in Anagnostopoulos, et al. (2002b). Fuzzy ARTMAP is considered the benchmark for supervised ART neural network architecture. Semi-supervised versions of ART were introduced (Anagnostopoulos, et al., 2003) to remedy the category proliferation problem in ART and to eliminate the zero post-training error that Fuzzy ARTMAP exhibits. The category proliferation problem is the problem encountered in the original ART architectures where many ART categories were unnecessarily created in the cases where the network was exposed to noisy and/or overlapping data. Remedies to the category proliferation problem in ART have been suggested by a variety of researchers (Williamson, 1996; Verzi, et al., 1998; Gomez-Sanchez, et al., 2002; and Anagnostopoulos et al., 2002b, and 2003).

The category proliferation problem was the main motivation behind the modification of ssFAM. We refer to the resulting architecture as *stable slow-learning FAM (sssFAM)*. A ssFAM category is essentially a representation of a cluster of the input data. In general, we wish to keep the numbers of the categories to a minimum. Our contribution is an attempt to decrease the amount of categories created and the size of these categories. We expand upon the modifications that were made with the semi-supervised FAM, and implement a slow-learning approach to category updates as well as the opportunity for minimum updates or no updates at all, if these are deemed unnecessary.

The organization of this document is as follows. In section 2 we describe the special features of sssFAM and contrast them to the ones of ssFAM. In section 3 we elaborate on the experimental results conducted that allows us to compare sssFAM versions and ssFAM. Finally, in section 4 we summarize our work and we emphasize some concluding remarks.

2. STABLE SLOW-LEARNING FAM (SSSFAM)

As stated earlier sssFAM differs with respect to ssFAM in the way match tracking is performed and when category updates occur. Below we present the pseudo-code of sssFAM and then we will elaborate on the features that make it different than the FAM and ssFAM counterparts. Note that CCF stands for category choice function (also knows as F_2 layer activation function) and CMF for category match function. The reader is referred to (Carpenter, et al., 1992) and (Anagnostopoulos & Georgiopoulos, 2002) and (Anagnostopoulos, et al., 2002b) for more details on the FAM and ssFAM architectures.

Choose a training pattern
Calculate the CCF values of every node in the category representation layer;
Find the node with the maximum CCF value;
Calculate the CMF value of the node with maximum CCF value;
Perform the Vigilance Test (VT) and the Commitment Test (CT);
Find the winning node (node with maximum CCF value that passes the VT and the CT)
Perform the Prediction Test (PT) for the winning node

If the winning node passes the PT

> *Perform <u>new threshold vigilance test</u>;*
> *if it passes update via fast learning; otherwise do nothing*

If the winning node fails PT

> *Perform <u>new match tracking</u> (i.e., temporarily raise the vigilance value and perform the <u>new vigilance test</u> for the category with the same label as the input pattern and of maximum CMF value)*
> *If the category, thus chosen, passes the vigilance test and the new threshold vigilance test update via fast learning; otherwise update via <u>slow learning</u>*

Let us first focus on the new match tracking rule. According to the old match tracking rule utilized in FAM and ssFAM, if a category of the wrong label is accessed (the category fails the PT), the vigilance is increased and another category that maximizes the CCF value and passes the new VT is examined. In turn, this category might be of the wrong label and the match tracking process is invoked once again. sssFAM avoids these repeated invocations of the match tracking rule by immediately examining, after the first match tracking pass, the node with the maximum CMF value, which would pass the PT with respect to the specific input pattern. This guarantees that only one match tracking pass will be necessary.

Our second focus is the new vigilance threshold test. The threshold vigilance is calculated using a parameter r in [0, 1], which in turn affects the maximum size a category is allowed to have. In particular, a comparison is made between the category's CMF value and a threshold value, as indicated below.

$$\rho(J \mid \mathbf{x}) \geq \bar{\rho}_{thres} = 1 - r(1 - \bar{\rho}) \qquad (1)$$

If Eq. (1) is satisfied, category J will be updated using fast learning; otherwise no update of the category occurs. In essence, if the updated. In essence, if the updated category's size does not exceed a certain size limit, controlled via the r parameter, then perform fast learning. Otherwise, do not perform an update.

In the case, where match tracking has already been invoked, this new threshold vigilance check is performed in the exact same fashion. However, instead of deciding whether or not to update the category, we are deciding of whether or not to update it using slow learning with a minimum learning rate calculation or to update it using fast learning. Once more, we update using fast learning if the new vigilance threshold test is passed and we update it using slow learning (with a minimum learning rate) if the new vigilance threshold test is violated. The minimum learning rate is calculated as

$$\gamma_{\min} = \left(1 - \frac{T_{J'}}{T_J}\right) \frac{\lfloor M_a - s(w_{J'}^a) + \beta_a \rfloor}{dis(w_{J'}^a, I)} \qquad (2)$$

where T_J is the CCF value of the category J that previously failed the PT, while $T_{J'}$ is the CCF value of the category J' with maximum CMF value that will pass the PT. The $\gamma_{\min}$ value is the minimum learning that needs to be applied to category J' so that, when the same input pattern is immediately presented again, category J' will have the highest CCF value of all other categories (including category J).

Before experimentation began, two different versions of stable ssFAM were considered. Stable ssFAM version 1 (sssFAM v.1) is the algorithm described above. On the other hand, version 2 differs from version 1 as follows: it allows updates via fast learning if a category passes the threshold vigilance test and if the category to be updated is a point category. In that sense, version 2 is slightly more conservative than version 1.

3. EXPERIMENTAL RESULTS

In order to show the advantages of sssFAM (versions 1 and 2) we conducted a collection of experiments using artificially generated data sets, as well as real databases. We separated the data of a database into three distinct sets: a training set, a cross-validation set and a test set. The training set was used to train the neural network architectures, the cross-validation set was used to find the "optimum" network parameter values, and the test set was used to produce the performance results of the networks with the "optimum" network parameter values. The "optimum" network parameter values were defined to be the ones that attained the 100 best generalization performances of the trained network on the cross-validation set. Justifiably, the resulting networks were referred to as the "best" networks. To find the "best" networks we experimented with various values of the network parameters, such as baseline vigilance, choice parameter, error tolerance and orders of pattern presentation (for ssFAM), and all of these parameters plus the additional parameter for sssFAM version 1 and 2 (r). For the 100 "best" generalization-performing networks, we also identified the number of categories created.

Artificial Databases

The advantage of using artificial databases is that we can generate as many training, cross-validation, and test data, as we desire. Working with enough cross validation data-points allowed us to safely state that, the best (with respect to generalization) network parameter values found are indeed optimal. The other advantage of the artificial databases is that we can experiment with different input domain dimensionalities, the number of output classes and the amount of inter-class overlap. In this paper we kept the dimensionality of the input patterns in the simulated data fixed, and equal to 2, and we experimented with the number of output classes (2, 4, or 6) and the amount of overlap amongst data belonging to different classes (overlap values of 5%, 15%, 30% and 40% were used). The artificial databases consisted of Gaussianly-distributed data. Input patterns were drawn from either 2 or 4 or 6 classes. Qualitatively the overlap can be classified as low (5%), medium (15%) or high (30% or 40%). The amount of overlap of the simulated data was defined to be the error rate of the optimum Bayes classifier pertinent to the data. For instance, if the Bayes classifier for a simulated data set exhibited a misclassification rate of x%, then the amount of overlap corresponding to this data-set was defined to be x%. For each one of the above 12 sets of artificial data (3 different number of classes × 4 different degrees of class overlap) we generated a training set, a validation set and a test set of 500, 5,000 and 5,000 data-points, respectively.

Our results show a definite improvement of sssFAM (versions 1 and 2) over ssFAM for 2,4,6-class for the Gaussian databases. Both new FAM versions (sssFAM (v.1) and sssFAM (v.2)) show a definite improvement over ssFAM, exhibiting lower percentage of incorrect classification and creating less categories. In particular, we witnessed that the number of categories created by the sssFAM versions (best 100 networks) are mostly located in the interval [0, 40] with very few outliers. On the other hand, the number of categories created by ssFAM are mostly located within the interval of [40, 920]. More specifically, the average number of categories for the best 100 networks created by sssFAM (v.1), sssFAM (v.2) and ssFAM are 24, 30 and 42, respectively. In a similar fashion, the PIC (percent incorrect classification) exhibited by the best 100 networks for the sssFAM versions lie in the range [31.5, 32.5]. On the contrary the PIC attained by ssFAM (best 100 networks) are within the interval [32, 34]. Actually the average PIC for the best 100 networks of sssFAM (v.1), sssFAM (v.2), and ssFAM are 32%, 32.1%, and 33.1%, respectively. Similar conclusions are valid for the 2-class and 6-class Gaussian problems and other amounts of overlap.

Real Databases

To verify the results obtained with the artificial databases, we conducted similar experiments using a real database (Abalone). This database was chosen from the UCI Machine Learning repository to test the credibility of the proposed algorithms. The training data set consists of 500 data points selected from the database in a way that reflects the distribution of classes in the database. The selection of the training patterns within each class is, however, arbitrary. The number of patterns remaining in the database, after extracting the training data set, is equally divided to form the test data set and the cross validation data set.

The Abalone database pertains to predicting the age of abalone shells from physical measurements. This is pursued to avoid an alternate, more cumbersome method, to do the same. The database has 8 attributes representing the sex, length, diameter, height, weight etc., and consists of 4177 data points. In our experiments, we used 1000 training patterns, 2133 cross validations patterns and 1044 test patterns. The number of rings in the shell of the abalone indicates the age. The database was treated as a classification problem by grouping the number of rings into three categories (1-8, 9-10, and 11-greater) and using the three groups as output classes. Experiments with the Abalone database have been conducted using the aforementioned grouping strategy. In our experiments, the first attribute representing the sex of the abalone was discarded since it was non-numerical. We conjecture that the Abalone dataset has high overlap among its output classes since the best generalization results reported in the literature are around 60%.

The results obtained with the Abalone database were similar with the results observed with the Gaussian databases. The best 100 networks for sssFAM showed improvement in both the percent correct classification as well as the number of categories created. In particular, the average PIC of the best 100 networks created by sssFAM (v.1), sssFAM (v.2) and ssFAM were found to be 45.35%, 45.5%, and 45.9%, respectively. Furthermore, the average number of categories of the best 100 networks created by sssFAM (v.1), sssFAM (v.2) and ssFAM were 3.6, 3.35, and 4.6, respectively. Although the improvement in generalization performance attained by the sssFAM versions, compared to ssFAM, is minimal, one could not but notice that the sssFAM versions reduced the average number of categories created, despite the excellent ssFAM performance. To be more specific, the minimum number of categories that a network could create without sacrificing generalization performance on the Abalone data (3-class problem) is 3. The average number of categories created by the best ssFAM network is 4.6 (very close to 3), but still sssFAM (v.1) manages to reduce this average number by almost a category resulting in a 25% reduction.

4. SUMMARY

We introduced a new ART algorithm named stable slow-learning Fuzzy ARTMAP (sssFAM), which extends the semi-supervised Fuzzy ARTMAP (ssFAM) architecture and which is introduced under the premise of expanding the ART categories by the least amount required, thus avoiding making assumptions about the data where data do not exist. In a way we expected that this sssFAM property would avoid the category proliferation problem observed in ART architectures. We have performed experiments to compare two sssFAM variations against the original ssFAM classifier. The experiments were performed on simulated data as well as on real data. The major conclusion from this comparison is that sssFAM creates networks with fewer categories than ssFAM, and it may slightly improve the observed generalization performance.

Acknowledgment: Michael Georgiopoulos acknowledges the support from the CRCD NSF grant 0203446 and Georgios C. Anagnostopoulos acknowledges the partial support from the CCLI-EMD NSF grant 0341601.

REFERENCES

[1] Anagnostopoulos, G.C., and Georgiopoulos, M., "Category Regions as New Geometrical Concepts in Fuzzy ART and Fuzzy ARTMAP," *Neural Networks*, 15(10), pp. 1205-1221, 2002.

[2] Anagnostopoulos, G. C., Georgiopoulos, M., Verzi, S., and Heileman, G. L., "Reducing generalization error and category proliferation in ellipsoid ARTMAP via tunable misclassification error tolerance: Boosted Ellipsoid ARTMAP, " *Proceedings of the 2002 International Joint Conference on Neural Networks (IJCNN 2002)*, May 12-17, Honolulu, Hawaii, 2002b.

[3] Anagnostopoulos, G. C., Bharadwaj, M., Georgiopoulos, M., Verzi, S. J., Heileman, G. L., "Exemplar-based pattern recognition via semi-supervised learning," *International Joint Conference on Neural Networks (IJCNN 2003)*, Portland, Oregon, July 20-24, Volume 4, pp. 2782-2787, 2003.

[4] Carpenter, G. A., Grossberg, S., Markuzon, N., Reynolds, J. H., "Fuzzy ARTMAP: A neural network architecture for incremental supervised learning of analog multi-dimensional maps," *IEEE Transactions on Neural Networks*, Vol. 3, No. 5, pp. 698-713, 1992.

[5] Gomez-Sanchez, E.; Dimitriadis, Y.A.; Cano-Izquierdo, J.M.; Lopez-Coronado, J., "μARTMAP: use of mutual information for category reduction in Fuzzy ARTMAP", *IEEE Transactions on Neural Networks*, Volume: 13, Issue:1, pp. 58-69, Jan. 2002.

[6] Grossberg, S., "Adaptive pattern recognition and universal recoding II: Feedback, expectation, olfaction, and illusions," *Biological Cybernetics*, 23, pp. 187-202, 1976.

[7] Verzi, S.J., Heileman, G.L., Georgiopoulos, M., Healy, M.J., "Boosted ART and Boosted ARTMAP," *Neural Networks Proceedings*, Vol. 1, 4-9 May 1998 pp. 396-401.

[8] Williamson, J. R., "Gaussian ARTMAP: A Neural Network for Fast Incremental Learning of Noisy Multi-Dimensional Maps," *Neural Networks*, Vol. 9, No. 5, pp. 881-897, 1996.

PIPELINING OF FUZZY ARTMAP (FAM) WITHOUT MATCH TRACKING

JOSE CASTRO(*), JIMMY SECRETAN(**), MICHAEL GEORGIOPOULOS(**), RONALD F. DEMARA (*), GEORGIOS ANAGNOSTOPOULOS(***), AVELINO GONZALEZ (**)
(*) Comp Eng., Instituto Tecnológico de Costa Rica, Cartago, Costa Rica
(**) Dept. of ECE, University of Central Florida, Orlando, FL 32816
(***) Dept. of ECE, Florida Institute of Technology, Melbourne, FL 32901

ABSTRACT
Fuzzy ARTMAP (FAM) is a neural network architecture that can establish the correct mapping between real-valued input patterns and correct labels in a variety of classification problems. Nevertheless, as the size of the dataset grows to thousands and hundreds of thousands, FAM's convergence time slows down considerably. In this paper we focus on a FAM variant called no-match tracking FAM (NMT-FAM). We propose a coarse grain parallelization of the NMT-FAM, based on a pipeline, and show that the parallelization strategy achieves linear speed-up in the order of p (number of processors). Experiments on the Covertype database support our results. We have also shown, but not included in this paper, that the parallelized NMT-FAM is equivalent to the sequential NMT-FAM, it also possesses a number of good properties. Our work in this paper is an effort in the direction of demonstrating that FAM can, through appropriate parallelization strategies, be used to mine data from large databases.

1. INTRODUCTION

Neural network algorithms have prohibitively slow training times, especially when they learn from large databases. Even Fuzzy ARTMAP (Carpenter, 1992), one of the fastest neural network algorithms in terms of training time, tends to exhibit slow convergence time as the size of the network increases. One way to address this problem is extensive use of parallelization. One of the works related to the parallelization of ART that is worth mentioning is the work by Manolakos (1998), where he has implemented a non-supervised ART neural network (ART1) on a ring of processors. Fuzzy ARTMAP has many desirable characteristics, such as on-line learning capabilities, fast training time, the ability to solve any mapping (classification) problem, an ease to provide explanations for the answers that it produces, etc. But Fuzzy ARTMAP's potential is compromised by the fact that its convergence speed to a solution, decreases considerably for problems with large datasets. This paper addresses this issue, the issue of Fuzzy ARTMAP parallelization so that it becomes more efficient, when confronted with the training of large datasets.

2. FAM AND NO MATCH-TRACKING FAM ALGORITHMS

The Fuzzy ARTMAP architecture consists of three layers or fields of nodes (see Figure 1). It is assumed here that the reader is familiar with the Fuzzy ARTMAP layers, their functionality, and the associated Fuzzy ARTMAP weights. It is also assumed here that the reader is familiar with the two network parameters in FAM, the choice parameter β_a, and the baseline vigilance parameter $\overline{\rho}_a$. The terminology that we have adopted is to designate inputs by **I**, outputs by **O**, template weights by $\mathbf{w}_j^a$ and inter-ART weights by $\mathbf{W}_j^{ab}$. Fuzzy ARTMAP can operate in two distinct phases: the *training phase* and the *performance phase*. In the training phase, Fuzzy ARTMAP is presented with a sequence of input/output pairs and it goes through a set of designated operations (to be described below) to learn the correct mapping from inputs to desired outputs. In this paper, only the on-line training phase of Fuzzy ARTMAP is considered, where an input output pair from the training set is only presented once. In the performance phase the trained Fuzzy ARTMAP is presented with an input pattern and it is required to produce a response (predicted output pattern). In this phase Fuzzy ARTMAP is usually presented with a list of input patterns whose correct output (response) is known; this way the trained Fuzzy ARTMAP's performance can be assessed. Prior to initiating the training phase of Fuzzy ARTMAP the top–down weights (the w_{ji}^a's) are chosen equal to 1. There are three major operations that take place during the presentation of a training input/output pair (e.g., $(\mathbf{I}^r, \mathbf{O}^r)$) to Fuzzy ARTMAP. One of the specific operands involved in all of these operations is the *fuzzy min operand*, designated by the symbol ^. Actually, the fuzzy min operation of two vectors **x**, and **y**, designated as **x^y**, is a vector whose components are equal to the minimum of components of **x** and **y**. Another specific operand involved in these equations is designated by the symbol $|\bullet|$. In particular, $|\mathbf{x}|$ is the size of a vector **x** and is defined to be the sum of its components.

Operation 1: Calculation of bottom up inputs to every node *j* in F_2^a, as follows:

$$T_j^a = \frac{\left|\mathbf{I}^r \wedge \mathbf{w}_j^a\right|}{\left|\mathbf{w}_j^a\right| + \beta_a} \tag{1}$$

after calculation of the bottom up inputs the node $j_{\max}$ with the maximum bottom up input is chosen.

Operation 2: The node $j_{\max}$ with the maximum bottom up input is examined to determine whether it passes the vigilance criterion. A node passes the vigilance criterion if the following condition is met:

$$\frac{\left|\mathbf{I}^r \wedge \mathbf{w}_j^a\right|}{\left|\mathbf{I}^r\right|} \geq \rho_a \tag{2}$$

if the vigilance criterion is satisfied we proceed with operation 3 otherwise node $j_{\max}$ is disqualified and we find the next node in sequence in F_2^a that maximizes the bottom up input. Eventually we will end up with a node $j_{\max}$ that maximizes the bottom up input and passes the vigilance criterion.

Operation 3: This operation is implemented only after we have found a node $j_{\max}$ that maximizes the bottom-up input of the remaining nodes in competition and that passes the vigilance criterion. Operation 3 determines whether this node $j_{\max}$ passes the prediction test. The prediction test checks if the inter--ART weight vector emanating from node $j_{\max}$

$$\text{ie. } \mathbf{W}_{j_{\max}}^{ab} = \left(W_{j_{\max}1}^{ab}, W_{j_{\max}2}^{ab}, \cdots, W_{j_{\max},N_b}^{ab}\right) \tag{3}$$

matches exactly the desired output vector $\mathbf{O}^r$ (if it does this is referred to as *passing the prediction test*). If the node does *not* pass the prediction test, the vigilance parameter ρ_a is increased to the level of

$$\rho_a \leftarrow \frac{\left|\mathbf{I}^r \wedge \mathbf{w}^a_{j\max}\right|}{\left|\mathbf{I}^r\right|} + \varepsilon \tag{4}$$

where ε is a very small number. Then, node j_{max} is disqualified, and the next in sequence node that maximizes the bottom-up input and passes the vigilance is chosen. The above operation of FAM is called match-tracking operation. If, on the other hand, node j_{max} passes the predictability test, the weights in Fuzzy ARTMAP are modified as follows:

$$\mathbf{w}^a_{j_{max}} \leftarrow \mathbf{w}^a_{j_{max}} \wedge \mathbf{I}^r, \mathbf{W}^{ab}_{j_{max}} \leftarrow \mathbf{O}^r \tag{5}$$

A modification of Fuzzy ARTMAP that is amenable to parallelization is the "no match-tracking" Fuzzy ARTMAP. This modification was proposed by Anagnostopoulos (2003) and it was shown that it can actually improve the performance of Fuzzy ARTMAP on some databases. The no-match tracking Fuzzy ARTMAP algorithm is the same as Fuzzy ARTMAP but it bypasses the match-tracking operation (described above). That is if a node that maximizes the bottom-up input and satisfies the vigilance is selected and this node does not pass the prediction test a new node (uncommitted node) in the category representation layer of Fuzzy ARTMAP is activated.

3. PARALLEL, NO-MATCH TRACKING FAM IMPLEMENTATION

Anagnostopoulos's FAM variant is particular amenable to production-line style pipeline parallel implementation since patterns can be evenly distributed among the nodes in the pipeline. The elimination of match-tracking makes the learning of the pattern a one-pass over the pipeline procedure, and different patterns can be processed on the different pipeline steps to achieve optimum parallelization. For the implementation of the no-match tracking FAM we first introduce a number of definitions. The algorithm itself (parallel, no-match tracking FAM implementation) is shown after the definitions are introduced. In the description of the parallel no-match tracking FAM the initialization procedure *(INIT(p))* and *WINNER* are not described due to lack of space. More details about these procedures as well as the algorithm presented here can be found in (Castro, 2004).

n : number of processors in the pipeline

k : index of current process, $k \in \{0,1,\ldots,n-1\}$

p : packet size, number of patterns sent downstream, 2p = number of templates sent upstream

$\mathbf{I}^i$: input pattern i of the current packet in the pipeline. $i \in \{1,2,\ldots,p\}$.

w^i : current best candidate template for input pattern $\mathbf{I}^i$.

T^i : current maximum activation for input pattern $\mathbf{I}^i$.

$myTemplates$: :set of templates that belong to the current processor.

$nodes$: variable local to the current processor that holds the total number of templates the process is aware of (its own plus the templates of other processors)

$myShare$: amount of templates that the current process should have.

w^i_{k-1} : template i coming from previous process in the pipeline.

w^i_{k+1} : template i coming from next process in the ring.

w^i : template i going to next process in the ring.

$w^i_{to(k-1)}$: template i going to previous process in the pipeline.

$\mathbf{I}.class$: class label associated with a given input pattern.

$w.class$: class label associated with a given input template.

$index(w)$: sequential index assigned to the template.

$newNodes$: number of created nodes on a given iteration to communicate upstream in the pipeline.

$newNodes_{k+1}$: number of created nodes on a given iteration communicated from processor k+1 in the pipeline.

Process $(k, n, \overline{\rho}_a, \beta_a, p)$

INIT (p)
while *continue*
do
    while $|myTemplates| > myShare$
    do
      EXTRACT-TEMPLATE $\left(myTemplates, \{w^i_{to(k-1)}\}\right)$
    SEND-NEXT $\left(k, n, \{(w^i, \mathbf{I}^i, T^i) : i = 1, \ldots, p\}\right)$
    RECV-NEXT $\left(k, n, \{w^i_{k+1} : i = 1, \ldots, 2p\}, newNodes_{k+1}\right)$
    SEND-NEXT $\left(k, \{w^i_{to(k-1)} : i = 1, \ldots, 2p\}, newNodes\right)$
    RECV-NEXT $\left(k, \{(w^i_{(k-1)}, \mathbf{I}^i_{k-1}, T^i_{k-1}) : i = 1, \ldots, p\}\right)$
    $newNodes \leftarrow newNodes_{k+1}$
    $S \leftarrow \{w^i_{k+1}\}$
    for each i **in** $\{1, 2, \ldots, p\}$
    do $WINNER\left(\mathbf{I}^i, w^i, T^i, \overline{\rho}_a, \beta_a, S\right)$
      $myTemplates \leftarrow myTemplates \cup S$
      if $\mathbf{I}^i_{k-1} =$ EOF
        then *continue* $\leftarrow$ FALSE
        else $S \leftarrow \{w^i_{to(k-1)}\}$
            for each i **in** $\{1, 2, \ldots, p\}$
            do $WINNER\left(\mathbf{I}^i_{k-1}, w^i_{k-1}, T^i_{k-1}, \rho_a, \beta_a, S\right)$
                $\left(\mathbf{I}^i, w^i, T^i\right) \leftarrow \left(\mathbf{I}^i_{k-1}, w^i_{k-1}, T^i_{k-1}\right)$
            for each i **in** $\{1, 2, \ldots, p\}$
            do $WINNER\left(\mathbf{I}^i, w^i, T^i, \overline{\rho}_a, \beta_a, myTemplates\right)$
                if $k = n - 1$

then if $class(\mathbf{I}^i) = class(w^i)$
then
$myTemplates \leftarrow myTemplates \cup \{\mathbf{I}^i \wedge w^i\}$
else $newTemplate \leftarrow \mathbf{I}^i$
$index(newTemplate) \leftarrow newNodes + nodes$
$myTemplates \leftarrow myTemplates \cup \{\mathbf{I}^i, w^i\}$
$newNodes \leftarrow newNodes + 1$
if $newNodes > 0$
then
$nodes \leftarrow nodes + newNodes$
$myShare \leftarrow \left\lceil \frac{nodes}{n} \right\rceil$
SEND-NEXT $(k, n, \{(\text{none}, \text{none}, 0)\})$
RECV-NEXT $(k, n, \{w_{k+1}^i : i = 1, \ldots, 2p\}, newNodes_{k+1})$
$myTemplates \leftarrow myTemplates \cup \{w_{k+1}^i : i = 1, \ldots, 2p\}$

4. EXPERIMENTS

The database used for testing the performance of the parallel, no-match tracking FAM was the Forest Covertype database, provided by Blackard, and donated to the UCI Repository. The experiments were run on OPCODE, a 96 node Beowulf cluster, connected by a fast Ethernet network. The database consists of a total of 581,012 patterns, each one associated with 1 of 7 different forest tree cover-types. The number of attributes of each pattern is 54, but this number is misleading since attributes 11 through 14 are actually a binary tabulation of the attribute *Wilderness-Area,* and attributes 15 to 54 (40 of them) are a binary tabulation of the attribute *Soil-Type*. The original database values are not normalized to fit in the unit hypercube (FAM requires normalization of input values, so that they lie in the interval [0, 1]). Hence, we normalized the input values. Patterns 1 through 512,000 were used for the training of the NMT-FAM. Patterns 561,001 to 581, 000 (20,000 of them) were used for testing. Training set sizes of $1000\ 2^i,\ i \in \{5, 6, \ldots, 9\}$ were used for the training of the no-match tracking FAM. The number of processors in the pipeline varied from *p=1* to *p*=32, in powers of 2. The metrics used to measure the performance of the pipelined approach were: (a) Classification performance of the pipelined no-match tracking FAM, and (b) Speed-up of the pipelined no-match tracking FAM versus sequential no-match tracking FAM. Results of the speed-up for this database can be seen in Figure 2. We observe from this figure that the speed-up is linear. For large training set sizes (i.e., 128,000 patterns) the speed-up is slightly above linear which suggests that the memory issues are a concern when few processes are in the pipeline. The classification performance of the Forest Covertype ranges from 70% to 79% as the training set size changes from 32,000 patterns to 512,000 patterns. It is worth mentioning that the classification performance of the no-match tracking FAM is comparable to the performance of the original FAM algorithm and better than the performance of other algorithms reported in the literature (best performance found was around 75%).

5. CONCLUSIONS

We have implemented a pipelined Fuzzy ARTMAP variant (called no-match tracking FAM). This FAM variant allowed us to focus on the parallelization of the competition process in Fuzzy ARTMAP. We have showed that this parallel implementation of the FAM variant is theoretically sound (results were omitted due to lack of space) and exhibits good workload balancing properties. We also showed experimentally (by working with the Covertype database) that this algorithm exhibited linear speed-up when the number of processors in the pipeline is increased. Furthermore, the generalization performance of this parallel no-matchtracking FAM was better than the performance of any other algorithm (from results reported in the literature) and similar to the performance of the original FAM. Finally, it is worth mentioning that, to the best of our knowledge, this is the first implementation of a Fuzzy ARTMAP-like algorithm on a Beowulf cluster.

ACKNOWLEDGEMENTS: Jose Castro and Michael Georgiopoulos would like to acknowledge the partial support of the NSF CRCD grant, no: 0203446. Georgios Anagnostopoulos and Michael Georgiopoulos would also like to acknowledge the partial support of the NSF CCLI grant, no: 0341601.

REFERENCES

Anagnostopoulos, G. C., and Georgiopoulos, M., "Putting the utility of match-tracking in Fuzzy ARTMAP to the test," In Proceedings of the Seventh International Conference on Knowledge-based Intelligent Information Engineering, Vol. 2, pp. 1-6, KES, 2003.

Carpenter, G. A., Grossberg, S. Markuzon, N., Reynolds, J. H., Rosen, D. B., "Fuzzy ARTMAP: A neural network architecture for incremental learning of analog multi-dimensional maps," IEEE Transactions on Neural Networks, Vol. 3, No. 5. pp. 698-713, 1992.

Castro, J., "Modifications of the Fuzzy-ARTMAP Algorithms for Distributed Learning in Large Data Sets," PhD. Dissertation, University of Central Florida, Summer 2004.

Manolakos, E. S., "Parallel Implementation of ART1 neural networks on Processor Ring Architectures", in Parallel Architectures for Artificial Neural Networks, editors N. Sundararajan and P. Saratchandran, IEEE Computer Society Press, 1998.

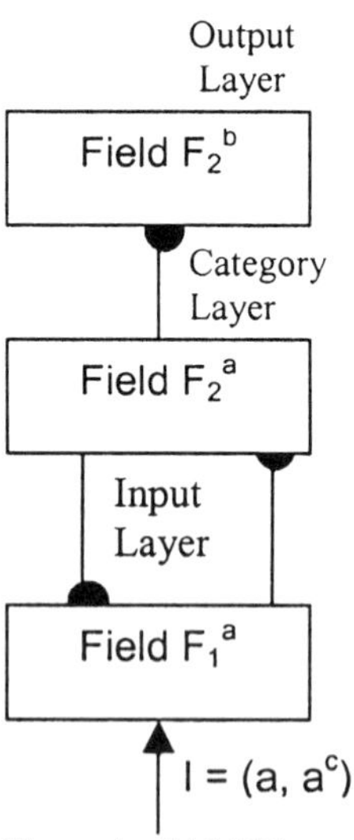

Figure 1. FAM Diagram.

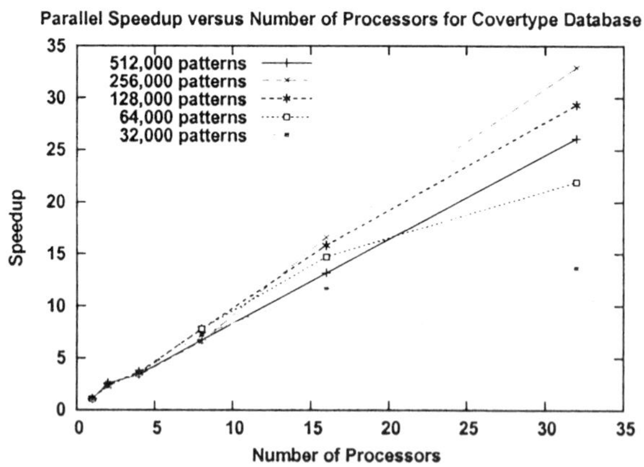

Figure 2. Performance of Pipelined NMT-FAM.

Mathematically Inspired Environment Classification and Identification: Simplicial Complex Hierarchy

Robert Woodley, Christina Welch, Matt Insall and Levent Acar
Department of Electrical and Computer Engineering,
Department of Mathematics and Statistics and
Intelligent Systems Center
University of Missouri-Rolla

ABSTRACT:
We provide a mathematical foundation for a biologically inspired hierarchical identification and classification system. We describe lines detected by the visual cortex in terms of natural basis elements, upon which simplicial complexes are erected to describe simple objects. Simple objects are basis elements in the next level of the hierarchy, and objects are described simply in terms of them. This is continued through several levels of the hierarchy, and each level identifies somewhat more complex objects than the previous level. Projections of the identified objects onto a manifold provides a natural and useful representation of the system's environment.

1 Introduction

Geometric objects are commonly modeled using simplicial complexes (Blelloch, Burch, Crary, Harper, Miller, and Walkington, 2001): The face of an object is decomposed into triangular regions. Points identified on the object are the zero simplicies. Interconnecting lines between points are one simplicies. The triangles are two simplicies and the collection of the simplicies is the simplicial complex (Stanley, 1996; Greenberg and Harper, 1981; Spanier, 1966).

Simplicial complexes are used in more abstract spaces also. They are the points of an algebraic structure that allows manipulation and storage of an organized system of information about the space. One uses a given set of basis elements which may be denoted as the 0-simplices, or vertices, of the simplicial complex space (Stanley, 1996; Greenberg and Harper, 1981; Spanier, 1966).

Simplicial complexes can be embedded into a hierarchical structure. Each level of the hierarchy uses as a basis, the complex formed in the previous level. In the first level, four basis elements describe the first objects-lines.

Performing the identification task independent of a fixed coordinate system is a main goal for our system; thus, a non-coordinate system will be used at all levels. In the hierarchy, the lower levels describe lines and objects retinocentrically. At the first layer, a reference point is selected based on the image and is not a fixed point on the retina. Using the reference point, objects are identified according to the retina position. The next layers identify objects in the scene. Subsequent layers place the objects in regions of a manifold. The highest level is the full manifold identifying three-dimensional characteristics of the objects and the relations between objects.

We embed the simplicial complexes in a hierarchy, use novel biologically motivated basis elements, and identify objects using a non-coordinate system. Unlike (Edelsbrunner and Shah, 1997), in which a set of fixed basis elements is used at each level, our system has dynamically described basis elements causing the system to react differently according to its environment, as found in nature. Our basis is based on biologically available data supplied by the visual cortex: angles of lines, lengths of lines, measure from a focal point, and a rotation around the focal point (Zeki, 1993). We use the manifold to automatically make adjustments from the body centered world to the real world, without performing a change of axis. This use of a coordinate free environment accellerates object identification.

2 Basis Elements

Recall that in our hierarchy four basis elements describe lines: From our existing Artificial Cortex, the retinal length is determined by summing the number of cortex neurons that are activated (Grossberg, Mingolla, and Viswanathan, 2001), and orientation (angle) of a line can be obtained, since orientationally selective cells exist within the cortex that identify lines at a particular angle (Hubel, 1988).

Basically, a measure that quantifies the distance from an object to a reference helps locate the object. Further, given the nature of brain structures, the metric will likely be symmetric, leading to unique descriptions via rotational angles of objects around the reference.

Lemma 1 *Line segments are uniquely describable by four coordinates: the distance from and rotation about a given reference point, together with length and orientation.*

The line segment lies on a line segment that is at the same angle, but twice as long with its center located at the distance and rotation point described above. We can then uniquely describe the line. QED.

3 Vanishing Point

We use the natural (Livingstone, 2002) vanishing point of a scene for the reference point. The eye can be viewed as a simple pin-hole camera (Horn, 1986). Light from an object passing through the lens converges on the retina, which is thought of as a two dimensional plane: parallel lines that recede from the viewer appear on the retinal plane as two converging lines.

Thereom 1 *A vanishing point may be used as a reference point by which objects may be identified.*

To illustrate Theorem 1 a set of simulated retinal images were created. The object being viewed is a wire-frame cube whose edges are all visible. Figure 1 shows the 2-dimensional retinal image of the cube when viewed directly with zero pan and tilt angles. Figure 2 shows the cube after the camera has been panned by 10 degrees. The object has moved on the retina, but the vanishing point remains directly in the center of the object as it did in Figure 1. This shows that the vanishing point is rotationally invariant.

Figure 3 shows the cube at a zero degree pan and tilt angle, however, the camera has been translated to the right. The vanishing point is now also further left then when the cube was viewed from the center. Figure 4 shows the same camera position, with a pan angle of 10 degrees. The vanishing point remains at the same location on the object, even though the object changes retinal position.

Vanishing points were also selected as the reference points based an physiological data.

Thereom 2 *The visual cortex model can identify the vanishing point.*

Proof

There are five rules by which a vanishing point can be identified.

1. Extend lines to an intersection: Two non-parallel lines will excite certain neurons. Another set of lines that point to the same intersection will excite the same neurons, acting as summation of the weights.
2. Set a tolerance around the intersection: There will be more than one excited neuron, arranged in a cluster. Another pair of lines will excite an additional cluster. If the two sets of lines excite enough of the same cluster, they point to the same intersection.
3. Weight non-linearly by line length: The output of the cortex model creates small segments; each sends a portion of the signal to the line neuron. The more segments, the stronger the output of the line neuron, which has a saturation to create the non-linear behavior.
4. Inhibit the weight if a real intersection exists: It is shown in (Woodley, 2004) how the cortex model can determine if two lines intersect, so it can produce an inhibiting signal to reduce the strength of the signals coming from the lines.
5. Sum the weights.

Since all these can be done by our cortex model, it can identify vanishing points. QED.

In addition to Theorem 2, there is evidence that perspective and thereby vanishing points are detected at very early levels of the human cortex (Schwartz, 1999). Vanishing points are identified in early vision as is evidenced by optical illusions that are created by perspective. The classic example (Kellogg, 1995) is that of two identically sized objects seen as not equal because of the perspective, which is imposed by the perspective lines that create the vanishing point.

4 Distance of an Object to the Vanishing Point

Certain criteria are required for an appropriate metric. The metric must be biologically feasible. Also, we must calculate distances not only between points, but also objects. Finally, the metric must be coordinate free. The Hausdorff metric satisfies these conditions.

For (X, d) a metric space, $A \subset X$ and $\varepsilon > 0$, $U(A, \varepsilon)$ is the ε-neighborhood of A, $\mathcal{H}$ is the collection of all non-empty closed, bounded subsets of X. If $A, B \in \mathcal{H}$, then the Hausdorff distance between A and B is defined as follows:

$$\mathbf{d}(A, B) = inf\{\varepsilon | A \subset U(B, \varepsilon) \text{ } and \text{ } B \subset U(A, \varepsilon)\} \quad (1)$$

Thereom 3 *The Hausdorff metric can be implemented by biologically inspired models of the cortex,*

Proof

An object excites neuron clusters (Grossberg, Mingolla, and Viswanathan, 2001). A separate object will excite a different group of neurons. Horizontal connections in the cortex models send out information on the excitation of the neuron (Grossberg and Raizada, 2003). Neuron clusters originate from specific areas, so the strength of the horizontal signal combined with distance traveled indicate the relative closeness of the objects. Subsequent cortex model levels use this information to obtain distances between objects. QED.

Theorem 3 also shows that the metric is adaptable to many levels of the cortex, thus, the same structures can be used to identify the distances of more complicated objects. This is the second reason the Hausdorff metric was selected. In (Chen, Tian, Shen, and Ouhyoung, 2003), the distance from an object's centroid to another object's centroid is treated as the distance. This adds another layer of processing that is not needed in the Hausdorff metric. Additionally, the centroid idea is hard to abstract to non-geometric entities. The Hausdorff metric is actually based upon sets, and therefore abstracts very easily, and it is a coordinate free metric, which is our third criterion.

The Hausdorff distance from a point to a point is trivial: it is the straight distance between points. Figure 5 shows the metric from a point to a line, which is just the distance from the point to the farthest point on the line. This is the case in which we are interested for the vanishing point problem. The problem of a particular point being identified on a line is eliminated with the Hausdorff metric. All other points on the line will be less than ϵ from the vanishing point.

5 Rotation Around the Vanishing Point

Multiple lines may have the same Hausdorff distance as shown in Figure 6. However, the Hausdorff distance from the vanishing point has a property needed to uniquely describe a line. From Lemma 1 it is known that it takes four basis elements to describe a line. The Hausdorff metric from a point turns out to be the distance to the farthest point on the line, and this gives us what we need to identify the line.

We identify a line by the rotation around the vanishing point of the point on the line that sets the Hausdorff distance. We can identify where the point is and which direction the line proceeds from the other basis elements. In case both ends of the line are at the Hausdorff distance from the vanishing point, two distinct representations will describe the same line. Duplicate descriptions are eliminated in the hierarchy. Distinct lines will have the distinct basis representations.

We can further classify the process by thinking of the basis in terms of vectors. A line in Euclidean space is determined by the end point coordinates, or just by two vectors that give length and orientation. Here, our first vector is composed of the length and orientation of the line. Our second vector is composed of the Hausdorff distance to the farthest point and the angle with respect to vertical the point rotates around the vanishing point.

As a consequence of Theorems 2 and 3, we have

Thereom 4 *Identification of the rotation of the farthest point of a line from the vanishing point is possible in the cortex model.*

6 Hierarchical Structure

We can now describe the hierarchy. Consciousness develops over many levels (Zeki, 1993). Each section in the brain leads to a piece of the sensation of consciousness. Damage to a section may not lead to unconsciousness, but may adversely affect perception.

Our hierarchical structure is different: objects may be described at different levels according to complexity. A simple object may be described at low levels, but a more complex object is described at higher levels. We can, therefore, see an object and describe it as a whole from a top level, or describe its components from lower levels.

Our main tool will be the use of simplicial complexes, which allow us to construct simple objects from simple line descriptions. Simple objects are the simplexes for the next level. This continues until no more complexes can be constructed.

7 Manifold Theory of Environment Description

From (Gray, 1993), a regular surface in n-dimensions may be covered by 2-dimensional manifolds. The vanishing point, a fixed point on the manifold, will inject the hierarchical representation. When a scene is processed into the hierarchy, the vanishing point is the reference point of all the objects. However, because the vanishing point is related to the systems location, it is also a reference for the manifold. When the system moves, the vanishing point changes position, and everything in the hierarchy is referenced from the new vanishing point. Determining the relationship between the systems movement and the position of the vanishing point describes associations between the two scenes, thereby, forming a new section on the manifold.

Thereom 5 *The vanishing point, the system coordinates, the system orientation, and motion of the system will describe the environment of the system on the manifold.*

References

Blelloch, G., Burch, H., Crary, K., Harper, R., Miller, G., and Walkington, N. (2001). Persistent triangulations. *Journal of Functional Programming 11*(5), 441–466.

Chen, D.-Y., Tian, X.-P., Shen, Y.-T., and Ouhyoung, M. (2003). On visual similarity based 3d model retrieval. In *Proceeings of the 2003 Eurographics*, 223–233.

Edelsbrunner, H. and Shah, N. R. (1997). Triangulating topological spaces. *International Journal of Computational Geometry and Applications 7*(4), 365–378.

Gray, A. (1993). *Modern differential geometry of curves and surfaces.* Boca Raton, CRC Press.

Greenberg, M. J. and Harper, J. R. (1981). *Algebraic topology a first course.* Reading, The Benjamin/Cummings Publishing Company, Inc.

Grossberg, S., Mingolla, E., and Viswanathan, L. (2001). Neural dynamics of motion integration and segmentation within and across apertures. *Vision Research 41*, 2521–2553.

Grossberg, S. and Raizada, R. D. S. (2003). Towards a theory of the laminar architecture of cerebral cortex: Computational clues from the visual system. *Cerebral Cortex 13*, 100–113.

Horn, B. (1986). *Robot vision.* Cambridge, MIT Press.

Hubel, D. (1988). *Eye, brain, and vision.* New York, Scientific American Library.

Kellogg, R. T. (1995). *Cognitive psychology.* Thousand Oaks, Sage Publication, Inc.

Livingstone, M. (2002). *Vision and art the biology of seeing.* New York, Harry N. Abrams, Inc.

Schwartz, S. H. (1999). *Visual perception, second edition.* Stamford, Appleton & Lange.

Spanier, E. H. (1966). *Algebraic topology.* New York, McGraw-Hill, Inc.

Stanley, R. P. (1996). *Combinatorics and commutative algebra, 2nd edition.* Birkhäuser Boston.

Woodley, R. S. (2004). *Biologically inspired identification and classification of a system's environment through artificial vision.* Ph. D. thesis, University of Missouri-Rolla.

Zeki, S. (1993). *A vision of the brain.* Oxford, Blackwell Scientific Publications.

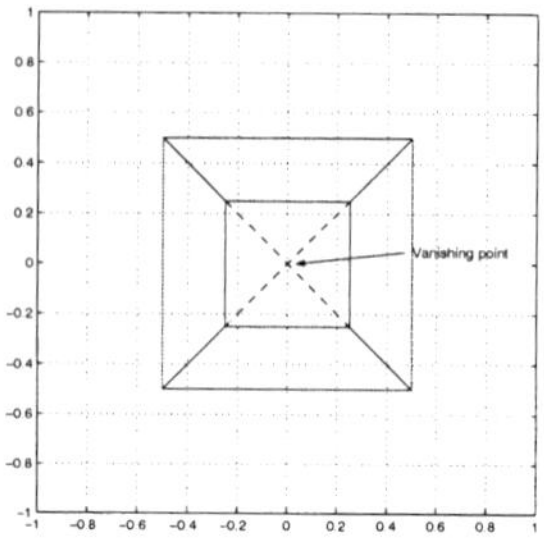

Figure 1: The 2-dimensional retinal image of the cube when viewed directly with zero pan and tilt angles.

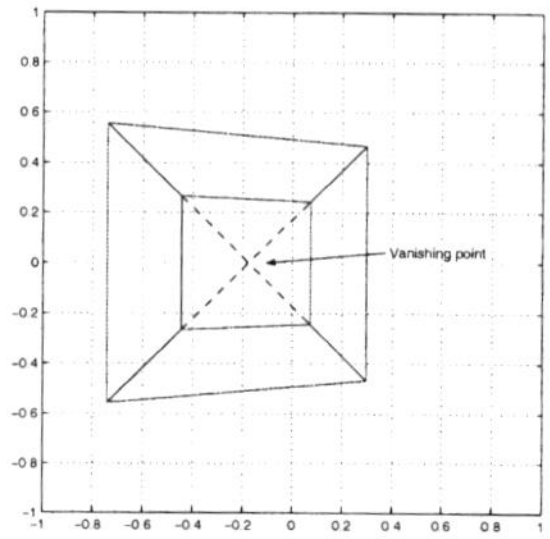

Figure 2: The 2-dimensional retinal image of the cube when viewed with a pan angle of 10 degrees and a tilt angle of zero.

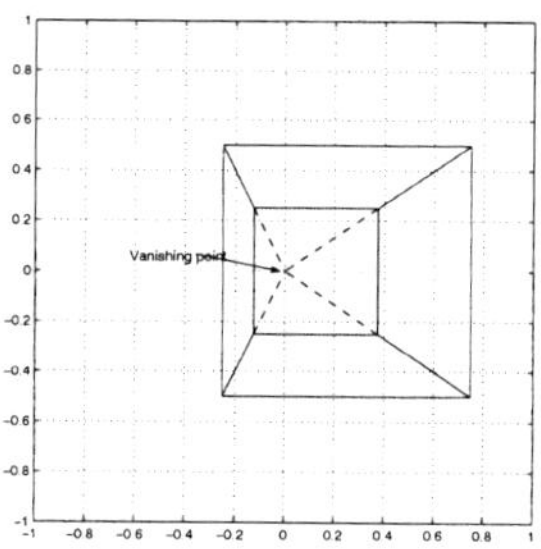

Figure 3: The 2-dimensional retinal image of the cube when viewed shifted to the right with a zero pan and zero tilt angles.

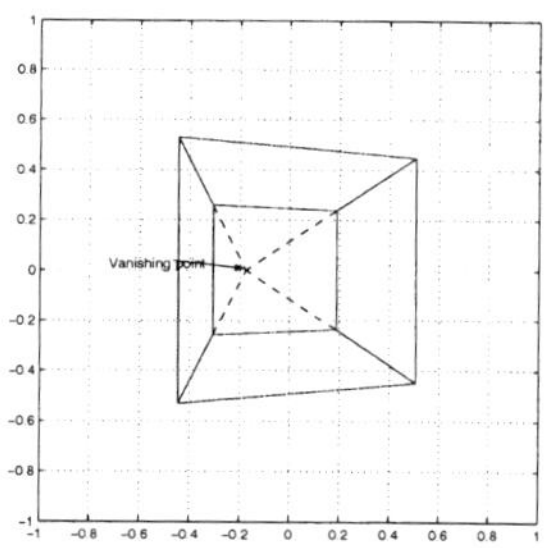

Figure 4: The 2-dimensional retinal image of the cube when viewed shifted to the right with a 10 degree pan and zero tilt angles.

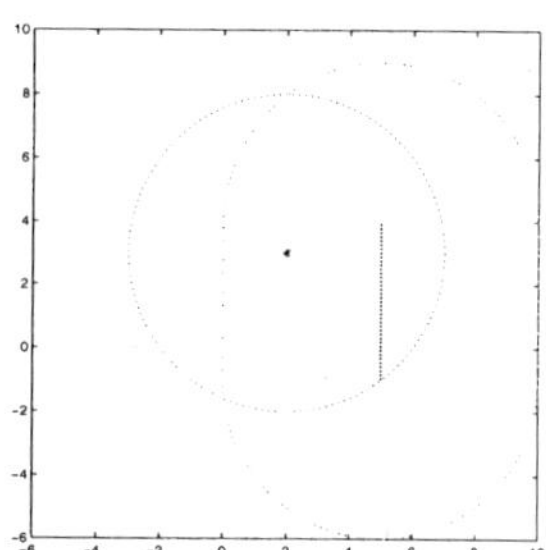

Figure 5: Hausdorff metric example from a point to a line. The dotted lines indicate the ϵ-neighborhood.

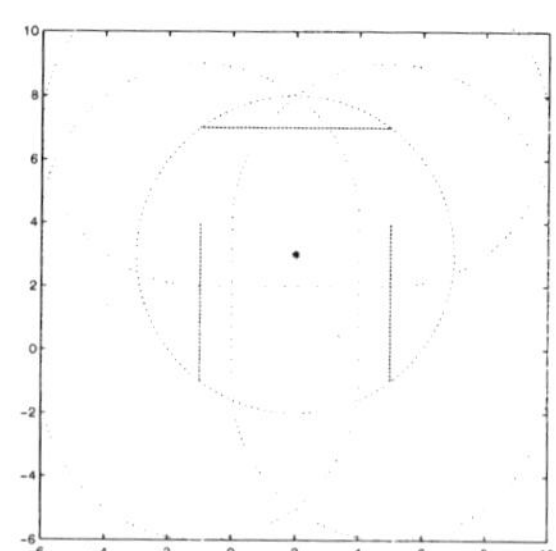

Figure 6: Hausdorff metric example from a point to several lines. All three lines have the same Hausdorff distance.

OPTIMIZATION OF THE ERROR ENTROPY MINIMIZATION ALGORITHM FOR NEURAL NETWORK CLASSIFICATION

JORGE M. SANTOS
Instituto de Engenharia Biomédica, Porto, Portugal.
Instituto Superior de Engenharia do Porto, Dep. Matemática, Porto, Portugal; jms@isep.ipp.pt

JOAQUIM MARQUES DE SÁ
Instituto de Engenharia Biomédica, Porto, Portugal.
Faculdade de Engenharia da Universidade do Porto, DEEC, Porto, Portugal

LUÍS A. ALEXANDRE
Instituto de Engenharia Biomédica, Porto, Portugal.
IT - Networks and Multimedia Group, Covilhã, Portugal

FERNANDO SERENO
Escola Superior de Educação, Instituto Politécnico do Porto, Porto, Portugal

ABSTRACT

One way of using entropy criteria in learning systems is to minimize the entropy of the error between the output of the learning system and the desired targets. In our last work, we introduced the Error Entropy Minimization (EEM) algorithm for neural network classification. There are some sensible aspects in the optimization of the EEM algorithm: the size of the Parzen Window (smoothing parameter) and the value of the learning rate parameter are the two most important. In this paper, we show how to optimize the EEM algorithm by using a variable learning rate during the training phase.

INTRODUCTION

The Error Entropy Minimization (EEM) algorithm minimizes the Reniy's Quadratic Entropy of the error between the output of the neural network and the desired targets. Reniy's Quadratic Entropy is used because, when using a non-parametric estimate of the probability density function (pdf) by the Parzen Window method, a simplified expression for the entropy is obtained.

The size of the Kernel window, *h*, used in Parzen Window method is one of the two most sensible aspects in the implementation of the EEM algorithm. The other important aspect is the backpropagation learning rate. We implemented a variable learning rate, similar to the one used in the MSE algorithm, and the results were better than the ones obtained with the previous algorithm.

RENYI'S QUADRATIC ENTROPY AND BACK-PROPAGATION ALGORITHM

Renyi extended the concept of entropy introduced by Shanon and defined the Renyi's α entropy, applied to continuos random variables, as (Renyi 1976):

$$H_{R\alpha} = -\log \int_C [f(x)]^\alpha dx \qquad (1)$$

Renyi's Quadratic Entropy, $\alpha = 2$, in conjunction with the Parzen Window pdf estimation with gaussian kernel allows, the determination of entropy in a non-parametric, practical and computationally efficient way. The Parzen window method estimates the pdf $f(x)$ as

$$f(x) = \frac{1}{Nh^m} \sum_{i=1}^{N} K\left(\frac{x - x_i}{h}\right) \tag{2}$$

where N is the number of data points, K is a kernel function, m is the dimensionality of vectors x ($x \in \Re^m$) and h the bandwidth or smoothing parameter. We usualy use the simplest Gaussian kernel with zero mean and Σ equal to $\boldsymbol{I}$ (the identity matrix)

$$G(x, \boldsymbol{I}) = \frac{1}{(2\pi)^{\frac{m}{2}}} \exp\left(-\frac{1}{2} x^T x\right) \tag{3}$$

Let $a = a_i \in \Re^m$, be a set of samples from x. Reniy's Quadratic Entropy can be estimated, applying the integration of Gaussian kernels (Xu and Principe, 1999), by

$$\hat{H}_{R2} = -\log\left[\frac{1}{N^2 h^{2m-1}} \sum_{i=1}^{N} \sum_{j=1}^{N} G\left(\frac{a_i - a_j}{h}, 2\boldsymbol{I}\right)\right] = -\log V(a) \tag{4}$$

Principe (1998) calls $V(a)$ the *information potential* in analogy with the potential field in physics. For the same reason he also calls the derivative of $V(a)$ the *information force F*. Therefore

$$F_i = -\frac{1}{2N^2 h^{2m+1}} \sum_{j=1}^{N} G\left(\frac{a_i - a_j}{h}, 2\boldsymbol{I}\right)(a_i - a_j) \tag{2}$$

This *information force* at each point is backpropagated into the MLP in the same way as with the MSE algorithm.

THE EEM ALGORITHM AND ITS OPTIMIZATION

In order to make neural network classification we use the information-theoretic concepts, applying an entropy approach to the classification task, using, as cost function, the entropy minimization of the error between the output of the network and the desired targets: the EEM algorithm.

The error entropy minimization approach, introduced by Erdogmus and Principe (2002) in time series prediction, states that Renyi's Quadratic Entropy of the error, with pdf approximated by Parzen window with Gaussian kernel, has minima along the line where the error is constant over the whole data set. Also the global minimum of this entropy is achieved when the pdf of the error is a Dirac delta function.

In classification problems we proved (Santos et al., 2004) a more strict result than simply the equality of the errors. As a matter of fact, we proved that by imposing some conditions to the output range and target values, the EEM algorithm drives all errors towards zero. Those conditions consist in a relation between the set of the output of the neural network and the set of the desired targets. In an unidimensional case the targets should be defined as $t \in \{-p, p\}$ and the output of the network as $y \in [-p, p]$.

The gradient of Renyi's Quadratic Entropy of the Error is back-propagated into the MLP in the same way as with the MSE algorithm. The updating of the neural network weights is performed using $\Delta w = \pm\eta \partial V / \partial w$. The choice of the learning rate η is one of the most important aspects in the implementation of the EEM algorithm. We will see in the next section how the variation of the learning rate along the training process can yield good results.

We started the optimization of EEM algorithm by trying to make the kernel smoothing parameter (kernel window size) h variable along the training process, namely proportional to the error variance. This strategy was based on the fact that, as we approach the optimal solution, the errors tend to zero (m-tuples of zeros) and so, it makes sense to decrease h since the points are all near. The entropy and the subsequent *information force* depends on the values of h (smaller h originates higher entropies and information forces), and that could be opposite to our objective of minimization of the entropy of the error. However, if, in each instance of the algorithm, we minimize the entropy function we can, at least theoreticaly, get an optimal solution. The problem in the variablility of h is that, in the proximity of the minimum training error the algorithm is very unstable and looses the capability of convergence.

In the next optimization phase of the EEM algorithm we used a variable learning rate and a fixed smoothing parameter h.

The variability of the learning rate follows a simple but efective rule. If the entropy of the error decreases between two consecutive epochs of the training process then the algorithm produces an increase in the learning rate parameter. Similarly, if the entropy of the error increases between two consecutive epochs then the algorithm produces a decrease in the learning rate parameter and, furthermore, it restarts the update step.

The rule for learning rate variability is:

$$\eta^{(n)} = \begin{cases} \eta^{(n-1)}.u & \text{if } H_{R2}^{(n)} < H_{R2}^{(n-1)} \\ \eta^{(n-1)}.d & \text{if } H_{R2}^{(n)} > H_{R2}^{(n-1)} \end{cases} \tag{3}$$

where $\eta^{(n)}$ and $H_{R2}^{(n)}$ are the learning rate and the Renyi's Quadratic entropy of the error in nth iteration, respectively, and u and d are the increasing and decreasing factors.

We performed several experiments in order to find good values for u and d. We used a bi-dimentional data set (Jacobs(1991)), with 608 data points, 4 classes, consisting of two separable groups of two classes each. The two classes in each group are non separable.

In Fig. 1 we show the training phases with fixed learning rate, FLR, (doted lines) and with variable learning rate, VLR, (solid lines), of two experiments that have produced the least classification errors. The use of VLR produces a continuos decreasing entropy curve and a minimum training error is achieved.

In Table 1 we present the results of the experiments made with diferent values for u and d. The column (*restart*) indicates the number of times that the algorithm restarts the update step. These experiments suggest that, if the algorithm produces an increase on the entropy then the learning rate should be decreased by a considerable factor. Based in the several tests that we performed and in the fact that our errors are allways limited to a restrict set, due to the conditions mentioned in (Santos et al., 2004), we recommend a value around 0.2 for d and around 1.2 for u. However this issue deserves further extensive tests with multidimentional errors to support this recommendation. The solid line in Fig. 1 represents a case with $d = 0.2$ and $u = 1.2$.

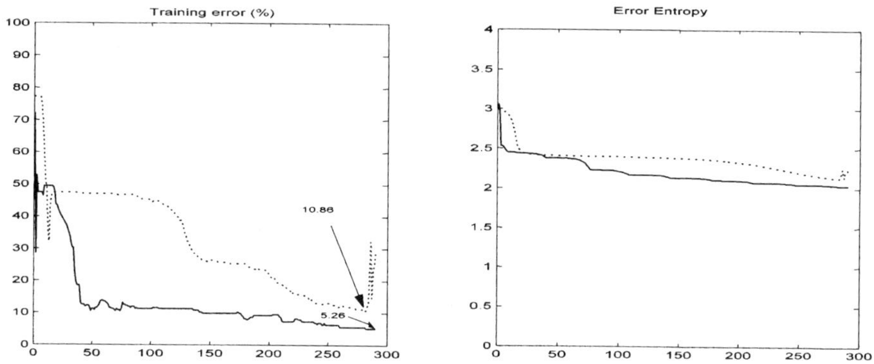

Fig. 1 - Two best results for FLR (doted) and VLR (solid)

Table 1 - Results for the variable learning rate

u	d	*restart*	Training Error
1.2	0.2	36	5.26
1.2	0.4	65	5.26
1.2	0.6	112	5.59
1.2	0.8	256	5.92
1.4	0.2	64	5.59
1.4	0.4	115	5.26
1.4	0.6	197	24.34
1.4	0.8	465	5.59

u	d	*restart*	Training Error
1.6	0.2	90	5.59
1.6	0.4	154	5.26
1.6	0.6	279	5.59
1.6	0.8	640	5.26
1.8	0.2	112	5.59
1.8	0.4	193	5.59
1.8	0.6	352	5.59
1.8	0.8	801	5.26

EEM-VLR VERSUS MSE-VLR

We made a first experiment, using multilayer perceptrons (MLP), to show the application of the Error Entropy Minimization with Variable Learning Rate (EEM-VLR) algorithm to data classification and compare it with Mean Square Error with Variable Learning Rate (MSE-VLR) algorithm.

In this experiment we used the data set described in the previous section. Several MLP's with 2 inputs, n neurons in the hidden layer and 2 outputs (2:n:2), were trained and tested 40 times, 300 epochs, using the EEM-VLR and also the MSE-VLR. We made n vary from 3 to 18. Each time, half of the data set was randomly chosen for training and the other half for testing. Then the data sets were used with inverted roles (the original training set became the test set and the original test set became the training set). The results of this experiment are shown in Table 2.

Table 2 – Classification errors for EEM-VLR and MSE-VLR

	Number of neurons in hidden layer																
	3	4	5	6	7	8	9	10	11	12	13	14	15	16	17	18	
EEM-VLR	9.68	**8,18**	8.54	8.73	9.22	8.67	9.03	8.77	9.90	9.30	10.16	10.01	10.14	11.50	10.72	12.68	Mean
	3.31	2.30	2.81	2.51	4.60	2.60	2.51	1.88	3.55	2.56	2.83	2.50	2.16	5.54	1.94	4.47	Std
MSE-VLR	24.46	17.49	15.86	13.80	14.35	12.29	12.46	11.95	11.34	10.67	9.44	9.46	8.61	9.22	9.77	10.61	Mean
	9.84	9.10	8.61	7.61	8.26	6.58	7.48	6.64	6.66	6.01	3.84	3.63	1.30	3.48	4.97	6.18	Std

We see in Table 2 that EEM-VLR algorithm produces better results comparing to MSE-VLR algorithm. Only for larger values of the number of neurons in the hidden layer the MSE-VLR algorithm produces better results. However this could be due to overfitting. We also see that similar results are achieved with less complex MLP's in the EEM-VLR algorithm (Fig. 2). This sugests that, with EEM-VLR, we need less complex neural nerworks, compared to MSE, in order to solve a particular classification problem.

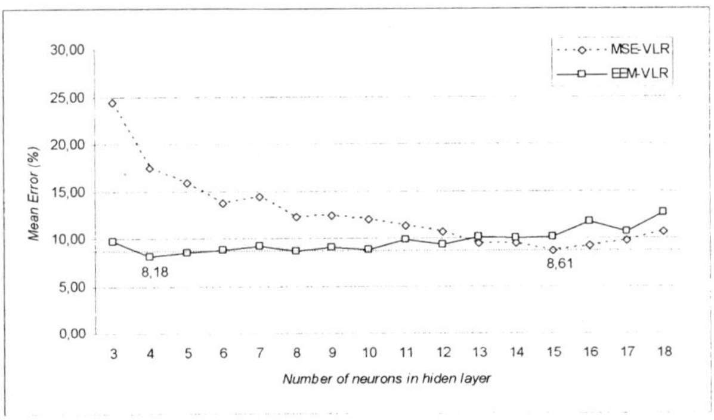

Fig. 2 - Classification mean error between EEM-VLR and MSE-VLR algorithms

Two more experiments were made applying the two algorithms in real data sets. These data sets are publicly available (*diabetes* can be found in Marques de Sá (2003) and *wine* can be found in the UCI repository of machine learning databases, http://www.ics.uci.edu/~mlearn/MLRepository.html. Table 3 contains a summary of the characteristics of these data sets.

Table 3 - The data sets used in second experiments

Data set	N. points	N. Features	N. Classes
Diabetes	768	8	2
Wine	178	13	3

Several MLP's were trained and tested 10 times, 120 epochs, with d=0.2 and u=1.2. Each time, half of the data sets were randomly chosen for training and the other half for testing. Then the data sets were used with inverted roles. The results of this experiments are shown in Table 4. Again, the best results (bold), in this three classification problems, were achieved with the EEM-VLR algorithm.

Table 4 – Classification errors for the EEM-VLR and the MSE-VLR algorithms.

		Number of neurons in hidden layer							
		4	5	6	7	8	9	10	
Diabetes	EEM-VLR		23,8	24,1	24,1	23,9	*24,3*	**23,6**	Mean
			1,04	1,33	0,9	0,71	1,42	0,86	Std
	MSE-VLR		25,1	24,7	24,4	23,9	24	24,1	Mean
			1,8	1,8	1,06	1,18	0,95	1,2	Std
Wine	EEM-VLR	**1,94**	2,5	2,47	*2,44*	2,16	2,22	2,31	Mean
		0,72	1,01	1,2	1	0,92	0,83	0,51	Std
	MSE-VLR	3,03	3,2	3,06	2,39	2,92	2,5	2,95	Mean
		1,08	1,83	1,43	1,5	1,07	1,35	1,29	Std

CONCLUSIONS

In this paper we present an improved version of the EEM algorithm, using a variable learning rate parameter, which we call the EEM-VLR algorithm. This algorithm shows a very good performance achieving good results in classification problems when compared to MSE-VLR algorithm.

Despite the fact that the results using variable smoothing parameter h were not satisfactory we think that, this issue deserves further investigation, namely on how to combine the two variable factores, η and h in order to produce an even more efficient algorithm.

REFERENCES

Erdogmus D. and Principe J., 2002, "An Error-Entropy Minimization Algorithm for Supervised Training of Nonlinear Adaptive Systems", Trans. On Signal Processing, Vol. 50, No. 7, pp. 1780-1786.

Jacobs, R., Jordan, M., Nowlan, S. and Hinton, G., 1991, "Adaptive mixtures of local experts", Neural Computation, pp.79-87.

Marques de Sá, J., 2003, Applied statistics using SPSS, STATISTICA and MATLAB, Springer.

Principe J., Fisher J. and Xu D., 1998, "Information-Theoretic Learning", Computational NeuroEngineering Laboratory, University of Florida, Florida.

Renyi A., 1976, "Some Fundamental Questions of Information Theory", Selected Papers of Alfred Renyi, Vol. 2, pp. 526-552.

Santos J., Alexandre L. and Marques de Sá J.,2004, "Neural network Classification using Error Entropy Minimization", submitted to the Int. Conf. on Recent Advances in Soft Computing, Nottingham, United Kingdom.

Silva, F. and Almeida, L., 1990, "Speeding up Backpropagation", Advanced Neural Computers, Eckmiller R. (Editor), pp. 151-158.

Xu D. and Principe J., 1999, "Training MLPs layer-by-layer with the information potential", Intl. Joint Conf. on Neural Networks, pp.1716-1720.

PERFORMANCE SENSITIVITY ANALYSIS OF THE R-K CLASS ESTIMATOR COMMITTEE (RKC)

DANAIPONG CHETCHOTSAK
Dept. of Industrial Engineering,
Faculty of Engineering,
Khon Kaen University,
Khon Kaen, 40002, Thailand

JANET M. TWOMEY
Dept. of Industrial and
Manufacturing Engineering,
Wichita State University,
Wichita, KS 67260, USA.

ABSTRACT

This paper studies the performance of a committee network formed using the r-k class estimator (RKC). RKC introduced by Chetchotsak and Twomey (2002 & 2004) was proposed to deal with multicollinearity problems among the networks in the committee under sparse data conditions. By properly adjusting the tuning parameters, e.g., the number of principal components (r) and the biased term (k), multicollinearity effects could be reduced and thus the committee could perform robustly. However, performance sensitivity of RKC due to parameter selection has not been analyzed and also RKC' s performance under non-sparse data conditions was not reported. This paper therefore studies the effects of parameter selection (r and k) and how well RKC performs under sparse and non-sparse data cases. Here, multilayer perceptrons trained by the backpropagation algorithm are used as a committee member and are trained to approximate a complex nonlinear function. Our results suggest that there is a possibility that RKC' s performance could be optimized by appropriately adjusting r and k. In addition, the results show that RKC performs well under both sparse and non-sparse data cases when compared to the simple bootstrap committee.

INTRODUCTION

Performance of the r-k class estimator committee (RKC) is analyzed in this paper. RKC was first introduced by Chetchotsak and Twomey (2002 & 2004). It was proposed to improve the generalization capability of the bootstrap committee under sparse data conditions. The results revealed that by adjusting the tuning parameters, e.g., the number of principal components (r) and the biased term (k), multicollinearity effects could be reduced and thus the committee could perform robustly. Nevertheless, Chetchotsak and Twomey (2002) did not analyze the effects of tuning parameter selection on RKC's performance. Moreover, they did not study the algorithm's performance under non sparse data conditions. This paper therefore studies performance sensitivity of RKC with respect to a change in value of r and k. Also we will demonstrate how well RKC performs with the non sparse data cases.

BACKGROUND

Several methods have been proposed to improve neural network performance. One of the most popular approaches is to use committee networks. The concept of committee networks is to combine several networks which have different expertise into a single model. Many papers have shown that the committees perform better than a single neural network (see Parmanto and Munro, 1996; Lam, 1999; Siriphala, 2000; Hashem, 1997;

Perrone and Cooper, 1993; Krogh and Vedelsby, 1995; and Merz and Pazzani, 1999). The committee network model may be expressed in a mathematical form as

$$\hat{f}(\mathbf{X}) = \sum_{i=1}^{m} \alpha_i f_i(\mathbf{T}, \mathbf{x}) \tag{1}$$

where $\hat{f}(\mathbf{x})$ is the committee's output, $f_i(\mathbf{T}, \mathbf{x})$ is the output of network i (based on the input $\mathbf{x}$), and α_i is the combination weights. Here, the networks are trained using the training set $\mathbf{T}$, where $\mathbf{T} = \{(\mathbf{x}_1, y_1), (\mathbf{x}_2, y_2), ..., (\mathbf{x}_n, y_n)\}$.

Chetchotsak and Twomey (2002 & 2004) used committee networks to improve regression estimates under sparse data condition. The committee is formed using a set of bootstrap networks and the r-k class estimator (RK) is used as a linear combiner to combine all the useful information from the networks in the committee. Here, the bootstrap networks are used because we want to encourage each committee member to be uncorrelated and RK are used for two reasons: (1) to encourage good networks to perform a task and (2) to reduce multicollinearity effects among the networks. Next Section describes the RKC algorithm.

R-K COMMITTEE

To be brief, the concept of the r-k class estimator is not explained here, but the reader may be referred to Bay and Parker (1984) and Chetchotsak and Twomey (2002). Let $\mathbf{f}(\mathbf{T}, \mathbf{x})$ be the vector of a neural network's outputs where the network trained by the training set $\mathbf{T}$ gives the output based on the input vector $\mathbf{x}$. And let $\mathbf{Z} = [\mathbf{f}_1(\mathbf{T}^{*1}, \mathbf{x}) \;\; \mathbf{f}_2(\mathbf{T}^{*2}, \mathbf{x}) \;\; \cdots \;\; \mathbf{f}_B(\mathbf{T}^{*B}, \mathbf{x})] = [\mathbf{z}_1 \;\; \mathbf{z}_2 \;\; \cdots \;\; \mathbf{z}_B]$, where $\mathbf{T}^{*i}$, $i = 1,2,..,B$ is a bootstrap training set produced from $\mathbf{T}$ (see the bootstrap procedures in Parmanto *et. al.*, 1996) and $\mathbf{f}_i(\mathbf{T}^{*j}, \mathbf{x}) = \mathbf{z}_j = \left(f_i(\mathbf{T}^{*i}, \mathbf{x}_1) \ldots f_i(\mathbf{T}^{*i}, \mathbf{x}_l) \ldots f_i(\mathbf{T}^{*i}, \mathbf{x}_n)\right)$, $i = 1,2,....,B$ is a column vector of the output produced by bootstrap network i, which is trained using $\mathbf{T}^{*i}$ and gives an output based on the vector $\mathbf{x}$. Let $\tilde{\mathbf{Z}}$ be the standardized matrix in such a way that $\tilde{\mathbf{Z}}'\tilde{\mathbf{Z}}$ is the correlation matrix of $\mathbf{Z}$. RKC is formed using the algorithms described in Tables 1.

Here, RKC's performance depends on r (the number of principal components remained) and k. If $r = p$ and $k > 0$, the committee will become ridge regression committee (RRC). And if $1 \le r \le 20$ and $k = 0$, the algorithm is called principal component committee (PCRC). Chetchotsak and Twomey (2004) proposed an algorithm namely the minimum error estimate method (MEE) to tune the parameters r and k (See Table 2). The algorithm is based on the concept that the committee's performance is maximized by tuning the parameters to minimize the committee's error estimate ($\widehat{Err}(r,k)$). They reported that only RRC and RKC used in conjunction with the MEE algorithm performed well under sparse data conditions.

According to Chetchotsak and Twomey (2004), the MEE algorithm determines r for RRC through the golden section search (Press *et al.*, 1986). For RKC, the MEE algorithm determines r and k as follows.

First set $k = 0$ and determine r by

$$\begin{aligned} &\max \quad r \\ &\text{s.t.} \quad \overline{VIF} \le 1 \end{aligned} \tag{2}$$

Here, $\overline{VIF}$ is the average variance inflation factor (VIF), which is computed from the diagonal elements of the matrix

$$\mathbf{E}_r(\mathbf{\Lambda}_r^{-1} + k\mathbf{I})^{-1}\mathbf{\Lambda}_r(\mathbf{\Lambda}_r + k\mathbf{I})^{-1}\mathbf{E}_r^{'}, \tag{3}$$

where $\mathbf{\Lambda}_r = \mathbf{E}_r^{'}\widetilde{\mathbf{Z}}^{'}\widetilde{\mathbf{Z}}\mathbf{E}_r$. Next, we search for k using the golden search to minimize $\hat{Err}(k)$.

By doing this we may introduce a large amount of bias into the model since some useful principal components are deleted and thus causing the error to increase. RKC then may not yield proper results. There may be a possibility that we can choose r and k to optimize RKC's performance. In this paper, we analyze performance sensitivity of RKC with respect to various values of r. To be specific, we observe RKC's performance when we delete the principal components one by one. Once a single principal component is deleted, k is determined using the golden section search through the MEE algorithm.

EXPERIMENTAL METHOD

RKC's performance is tested using a nonlinear function approximation problem as below:

$$y = 0.05x^3 - 0.2x^2 - 3x + 20 + \eta, \tag{4}$$

where η indicates noise level and $-10 \le x \le 10$. In this experiment, two levels of noise are used: (1) noise-free and (2) noisy conditions. For the noisy condition, $\eta \sim N[0, 0.15]$. The sample size used to train the networks is chosen to be 100 (randomly generated) and a test set of 5,000 is used to test the committee's performance. To remove dependency on sampling of the training data, this experiment is replicated, say 100 times. Here, multilayer perceptrons (MLPs) trained by the backpropagation algorithm is used as a committee member and the number of committee members is chosen to be 20 according to the results reported by Siriphala (2000). For the sake of comparison, performance of the bootstrap committee fused using the simple average (SAVGC) is also recorded.

The committee's performance is measured in terms of a prediction error (MSE) and the bias and variance decomposition. According to Geman *et al.* (1992), the prediction error can be decomposed into bias and variance which are expressed in an empirical form for this problem as

$$\begin{aligned} MSE &= \frac{1}{5000}\sum_{i=1}^{50000}\left(\overline{\hat{f}}(\mathbf{T}^k,\mathbf{x}_i) - y_i\right)^2 \\ &+ \frac{1}{100}\sum_{k=1}^{100}\left(\frac{1}{5000}\sum_{i=1}^{50000}\left(\hat{f}(\mathbf{T}^k,\mathbf{x}_i) - \overline{\hat{f}}(\mathbf{T}^k,\mathbf{x}_i)\right)^2\right) \end{aligned} \tag{5}$$

where $\overline{\hat{f}}(\mathbf{T}^k,\mathbf{x}_i) = \sum_{k=1}^{100}\hat{f}(\mathbf{T}^k,\mathbf{x}_i)$. The first term is referred to as bias and the second term is the variance. For a prediction model, having large bias implies that the network gives an incorrect model, but having large variance indicates that the network gives unstable predictions; that is changes in training sets lead to a significant change in the prediction value (Geman *et al.*, 1992). An algorithm will perform well if it has ability to balance both bias and variance. This experiment therefore will help us to see whether or not RKC has such ability.

RESULTS

Figures 1 and 2 show the experimental results. Figure 1 which illustrates the noise-free results reveals that when r is in between 6 to 20, RKC's performance is stable and yield reasonable results. The average MSE of RKC is approximately 0.0002 which is significantly less than that of SAVGC (0.0042). When $r < 6$, we eliminate too many principal components and introduce a large amount of bias into the committee's model. As a result, the MSE considerably increase when $r < 6$.

Figure 2 show the result of the noisy data. The Figure reveals that RKC's performance is almost insensitive to a change in values of r. But there is a small difference; that is when r increases, the bias component slightly decreases but the variance portion slightly increases. This as a result, causes the total error to slightly decrease when r increases. Here, RKC still gives reasonable results. Its MSE is approximately in the neighborhoods of 0.0083 whereas SAVGC's MSE is reported as 0.0085.

From theses results, it is clear that RKC used in conjunction with the MEE method works well in both noisy and noise-free conditions. Moreover, using large r gives us more benefit than using small r since the bias component is smaller, where as the variance portion is almost constant across r values. In fact, using $r = 20$ (keeping all components) yield a reasonably small MSE and therefore is recommended since we do not have to worry if too much bias is added in to the committee's model. It should be noted that when $r = 20$, RKC will become RRC. Using $r = 20$ will not cause multicollinearity problems since we have k play an important role to remove multicollinearity and balance bias-variance. Our experiment also reveals that RKC can also apply to a problem with smaller sample sizes.

CONCLUSIONS

This paper studies the performance of the committee network formed using the r-k class estimator. When used in conjunction with the minimum error estimate (MEE) algorithm to adjust the tuning parameters, the committee performs well under both sparse and non-sparse data conditions with and without the presence of noise in the data. Furthermore, the results show that the committee's performance is highly dependent on the number of principal components retained (r). The results of bias-variance analysis illustrate that if r is too small, the bias portion will be large since some useful information is deleted, causing the total error to be large. The results also suggest that retaining all the principal components will also give reasonably results since the parameter k will play an important role in balancing bias and variance under all kinds of data conditions.

ACKNOWLEDGEMENTS

The authors would like to thank God for wisdom and guidance—"So give me the wisdom I need to rule your people with justice and to know the difference between good and evil.....," (1King 3:9). We also want to acknowledge the support of the Faculty of Engineering, Khon Kaen University, Thailand.

REFERENCES

Baye, M. R. and Parker, D. F., 1984, "Combining Ridge and Principal Component Regression: A Money Demand Illustration," *Communications in Statistics*, Vol. 13(2), pp. 197-205.

Chetchotsak, D. and Twomey, J.M., 2002, "Improving Generalization Capability of Neural Networks under Conditions of Sparse Data: A New Committee Formation Approach," in C.H. Dagli *et.al.* (Eds.), Intelligent Engineering Systems through Artificial Neural Networks, Vol. 12, New York, NY.: ASME Press.

Chetchotsak, D. and Twomey, J. M., 2004, "Improving Committee Networks' Performance under Sparse Data Conditions: The Biased Regression and Bootstrap Error Estimation Approaches," *Working Paper.*

Geman, S., Bienenstock, E., and Doursat, R., 1992, "Neural Networks and the Bias/Variance Dilemma," *Neural Computation*, Vol. 4, pp. 1-58.

Hashem, S., 1997, "Optimal Linear Combinations of Neural Networks," *Neural Networks*, Vol. 10 (4), pp. 599-614.

Krongh, A. and Vedelsby, J., 1995, "Neural Network Ensembles, Cross Validation, and Active Learning," *Advance in Neural Information Processing Systems*, Vol. 7, pp. 1-8.

Lam, S. S.Y., 1999, "Improved Prediction and Validation Using Resampled Neural Networks: Committee Networks and Hybrid Validation", Ph.D. Thesis, Department of Industrial Engineering, University of Pittsburgh.

Merz, C. J. and Pazzani, M. J., 1999, "A Principal Components Approach to Combining Regression Estimates," *Machine Learning*, Vol. 36, pp.9-32.

Parmanto, B., Munro, P.W., and Doyle, H.R., 1996, "Reducing Variance of Committee Prediction with Resampling Techniques," *Connection Science*, Vol. 8, (3 & 4), pp., 405-425.

Perrone, M.P. & Cooper, L.N., 1993, "When Neural Networks Disagree: Ensemble Methods for Hybrid Neural Networks. In R.J. Mammone (Ed.), *Artificial Neural Networks for Speech and Vision*. London, UK: Chapman & Hall.

Press, W.H., Flannery, B.P., Teukolsky, S.A., & Vetterling, W.T., 1986, *Numerical Recipes: The Art of Scientific Computing*, Cambridge, UK: Cambridge University Press.

Siriphala, P., 2000, "Controlling Artificial Neural Networks Overtraining When Data is Scarce", Ph.D. Thesis, Department of Industrial and Manufacturing Engineering, Wichita State University.

Table 1. The RKC Algorithm

i. Determine k and r, where $k \geq 0$ and $1 \leq r \leq p$.

ii. $\boldsymbol{\beta} = \mathbf{E}_r(\mathbf{E}_r'\tilde{\mathbf{Z}}'\tilde{\mathbf{Z}}\mathbf{E}_r + k\mathbf{I})^{-1}\mathbf{E}_r'\tilde{\mathbf{Z}}'\tilde{\mathbf{y}}$, $\mathbf{E}_r$ is the eigenvector.

iii. $(\alpha_i) = \dfrac{(\beta_i)}{s_{\mathbf{z}_i}\sqrt{n-1}}$, and $(\alpha_0) = \overline{y} - \sum_{i=1}^{B}(\alpha_i)\overline{z_i}$, $i = 1,.....B$,

($\overline{z_i}$ and $s_{\mathbf{z}_i}$ are the mean and standard deviation of column vector $\mathbf{z}_i$, $i = 1,.....B$)

iv. $\hat{f}(\mathbf{x}_l) = (\alpha_0) + \sum_{i=1}^{B}(\alpha_i)f_i(\mathbf{T}^{i*},\mathbf{x}_l)$, $l = 1,...,n$.

Table 2. The MEE Algorithm

i. Receive $\hat{f}(\mathbf{x})$ from the RKC algorithm.

ii. Use the bootstrap method to resample data in matrix $\mathbf{Z}$ where the number of bootstrap samples is B. This produces $\mathbf{Z}^{*1},\mathbf{Z}^{*2},...,\mathbf{Z}^{*j},...,\mathbf{Z}^{*B}$,

iii. Form committees based on $\mathbf{Z}^{*1},\mathbf{Z}^{*2},...,\mathbf{Z}^{*j},...,\mathbf{Z}^{*B}$. This should return the weights $(\alpha_0)_j$, $(\alpha_i)_j$, and $\hat{f}_j(\mathbf{x})$, $j = 1,...,B$.

Table 2. (Cont'd)

iv. $\hat{f}_j(\mathbf{x}_l) = (\alpha_0)_j + \sum_{i=1}^{B} (\alpha_i)_j (z_i)_l$, $j = 1,\ldots,B$, $l = 1,\ldots,n$

$\hat{f}_j(\mathbf{Z}_l^{*j}) = (\alpha_0)_j + \sum_{i=1}^{B} (\alpha_i)_j (z_i^{*j})_l$, $j = 1,\ldots,B$, $l = 1,\ldots,n$.

iv. Compute the error estimate based on the bootstrap method:

$$\hat{E}rr(k,r) = \frac{1}{n}\sum_{l=1}^{n}\left(y_l - \hat{f}(\mathbf{x}_l)\right)^2 + \frac{1}{B}\sum_{j=1}^{B}\left(\frac{1}{n}\sum_{l=1}^{n}\left(y_l - \hat{f}_j(\mathbf{x}_l)\right)^2 - \frac{1}{n}\sum_{l=1}^{n}\left(y_l^{*j} - \hat{f}_j(\mathbf{Z}_l^{*j})\right)^2\right).$$

v. Return $\arg\min \hat{E}rr(k,r), k \geq 0, 1 \leq r \leq B$.

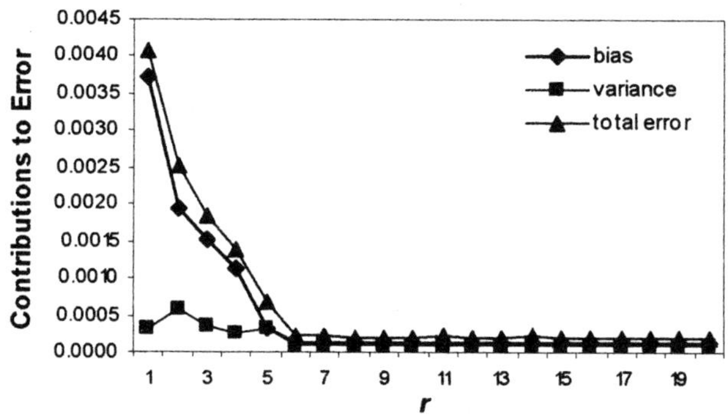

Figure1 Results in Terms of Bias-Variance Decomposition with respect to r : The Noise-free Data Case

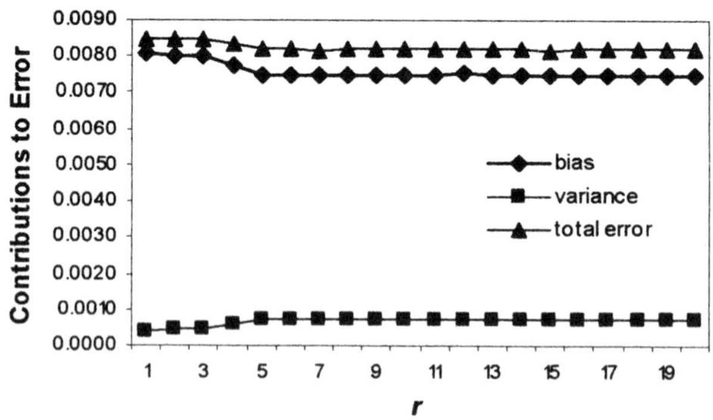

Figure 2 Results in Terms of Bias-Variance Decomposition with respect to r : The Noisy Data Case

A VARIABLE STRUCTURE LEARNING ALGORITHM FOR MULTILAYER PERCEPTRONS

KARL MATHIA
Newport Corp.
750 National Court, Richmond, California 94804
kmathia@newport.com

ABSTRACT
Choosing the 'best' neural network structure for a given problem is often a difficult task. A data-driven, automated design method has therefore been an appealing concept for years, and research resulted in network pruning as well as constructive algorithms. The Variable Structure Learning (VSL) algorithm proposed here is a fully automatic structure learning algorithm for Multilayer Perceptrons. VSL attempts to converge to the minimum complexity network for a given problem by combining both network construction and pruning concepts. A normalized and continuously monitored learning metric enables structure convergence and avoids the scaling problem.

INTRODUCTION

A common challenge with artificial neural networks (ANNs) is to chose a sufficiently complex network structure for learning a desired mapping, e.g. for function approximation, classification, etc., where 'network complexity' refers to network parameters such as the number of layers and neurons, as well as the connection pattern between layers. An ANN designed too small may not be able to learn a mapping as represented by the training data, while excess network complexity can result in overfitting and poor generalization [2]. *A Priori* knowledge about the desired mapping can point to a 'good' initial ANN structure [5][6], but may not be available.

Data-driven, automated structure learning is therefore an appealing network design concept, and past research resulted in several network pruning and network construction algorithms. See, for example, [1][3][4][8][10]. Simulations of variable structure ANNs demonstrated superior learning performance over fixed structure ANNs [7]. Based on similar ideas, the Variable Structure Learning (VSL) algorithm proposed here is a fully automatic structure learning algorithm for Multilayer Perceptrons, a popular feedforward ANN. The error backpropagation algorithm [9], which per se is not a structure learning algorithm, is utilized for weight training between structural changes.

Unlike other algorithms, VSL combines both network construction and pruning methods while maintaining a continuously decreasing learning metric (mean squared error). This is possible by adding neurons without 'forgetting' already learned knowledge. The normalized and decreasing learning metric, monitored after every learning epoch, supports the objective to converge to a small (ideally the minimum complexity) structure for learning a given problem. It also also avoids the well-known scaling problem via a unified treatment of different problem complexities.

STRUCTURE LEARNING FRAMEWORK

An artificial neural network is uniquely specified by a 4-tuple of network parameters $\Psi = \{W, n, g, G\}$ [3][4]:

- directed connectivity graph, G
- number of hidden neurons, q
- transfer function of the hidden neurons, g
- connection weights, W.

Note that more than one tuple (Ψ_m, Ψ_n,...) can implement the same ANN function or mapping. The network parameters in Ψ are available as free variables for neural network learning. Adjusting the connection weights in a fixed network structure is most common, while structure learning usually refers to adjusting the directed connectivity graph and the number of hidden neurons. Constructive algorithms 'grow' an ANN, i.e. increase network complexity, while pruning algorithms 'shrink' it, i.e. decrease network complexity.

The goal of MLP training for regression problems is to approximate an unknown mapping or function, represented by data, via an iterative, supervised learning process. Let $f_\Psi \in \Re^{mxn}$ be the function implemented by an ANN with network parameters. During learning one or more parameters are adjusted, resulting in a series of tuples Ψ_k, $k=1,2,..,K$, and associated ANNs

$$f_{\Psi_1}, f_{\Psi_2}, \ldots, f_{\Psi_K}. \tag{1}$$

The learning process is terminated after K iterations when a success criterion $\|f_{des} - f_\Psi\| \leq \varepsilon$ is satisfied, i.e. after the learning process converged to a prespecified limit ε. Although the unknown, desired function $f_{des} \in \Re^{m \times n}$ is only represented by experimental data, the distance $\|.\|$ can be estimated from the data. The mean squared error (MSE) in Equation 6 below between

$$d = f_{des}(x) \text{ and.} \tag{2}$$

$$y = f_\Psi(x) \tag{3}$$

is a common estimate, where $x \in \Re^m$ is the ANN input and $y,d \in \Re^n$ represent the actual and desired ANN output, respectively.

VARIABLE STRUCTURE LEARNING

Variable Structure Learning (VSL) combines both constructive and pruning methods. It adds and trains hidden neurons to an initially small ANN until a prespecified success criterion is satisfied. The network size is then minimized by successively pruning the 'least significant' hidden neurons while maintaining that success criterion. Here the well-known multilayer perceptron (MLP) and the error backpropagation (EBP) algorithm are used to demonstrate how VSL extends an established neural network learning algorithm to a structure learning algorithm. The VSL concept is also intended for enhancing and extending other ANN architectures and weight training algorithms.

Network Parameters and Learning Variables. Learning variables (here: VSL variables) are free network parameters which are adjusted during training in order to achieve a given learning objective. Many ANN learning algorithms, like EBP, adjust only the connection weights. VSL trains both the connection weights and the number of hidden neurons.

Directed Connectivity Graph. The directed connectivity graph G defines how all input, output, and hidden neurons are interconnected. The pruning of connection weights is one example of structure learning. Here G is not considered an independent VSL variable. Rather, G is a consequence of the number of neurons in the fully connected hidden layer. It was shown that one hidden layer (Figure 1) is sufficient for a universal approximator [11].

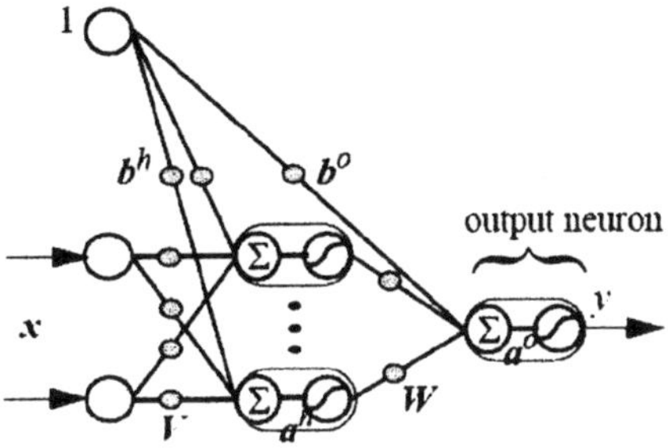

Figure 1. MLP with one hidden layer.

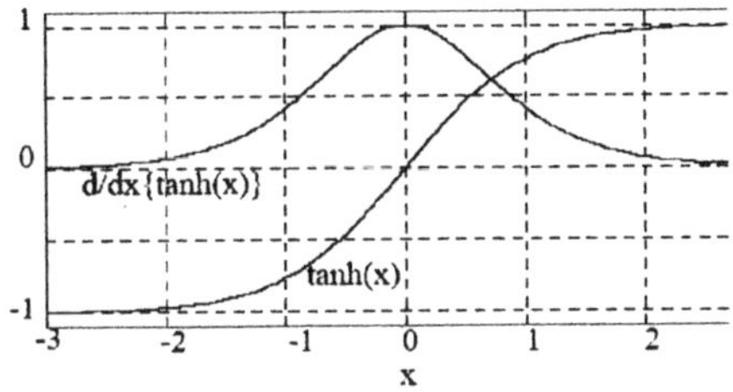

Figure 2. Hyperbolic tangent.

Number of Hidden Neurons. The number of hidden neurons is a VSL variable, while the number of input and output neurons are fixed and dictated by the data being approximated. VSL begins with one hidden neuron and adds or prunes fully connected neurons as needed. Of course, any available *a priori* knowledge about the unknown function can be used to specify the initial MLP.

Transfer Function of Hidden Neurons. Here the transfer function from activation value to neuron output is not a VSL variable and remains unchanged. For pruning the 'least significant' hidden neuron, i.e. the neuron with the smallest weight values, it is convenient to identify that neuron by the smallest contribution to the overall MLP mapping. A small neuron output in response to a small input is achieved using a transfer function with $g(0)=0$. Thus the hyperbolic tangent (Figure 2) replaces the common sigmoid with $g(0)=0.5$:

$$\tanh(x) = \frac{\sinh(x)}{\cosh(x)} = \frac{e^{x} - e^{-x}}{e^{x} + e^{-x}} = \frac{1 - e^{-2x}}{1 - e^{-2x}}. \tag{4}$$

$$\frac{d}{dx}\tanh(x) = \frac{d}{dx}\left\{\frac{1 - e^{-2x}}{1 + e^{-2x}}\right\} = [\mathrm{sech}(x)]^{2}. \tag{5}$$

*Connection Weights **W**.* The connection weights of neurons are probably the most common learning variable for ANNs. The VSL algorithm trains the weights of hidden and output neurons using EBP. Weight and structure updates occur sequentially and are independent (Figure 3), so a different weight training algorithm could also be utilized.

Learning Metric for Structure Learning. A critical element of the VSL algorithm is the learning metric, which is continuously decreasing if the entire training set is used for batch training [2]. Its decreasing and normalized profile, representing learning error and learning 'time scale' (Figure 3) provides the information for

- deciding if and when adding or pruning neurons (evaluate learning),
- convergence of both weight and structure (when to terminate VSL),
- avoiding the well-known scaling problem (unified treatment of problems with different complexities).

The VSL and EBP learning metric is the well-known mean squared error (MSE) between desired output vector and actual ANN output vector taken over n output neurons,

$$E = \frac{1}{n} e^{T} e = \frac{1}{n} (d - y)^{T} (d - y). \qquad (6)$$

The MSE is normalized with respect to the initial (maximum) error E_{max} and monitored after every k-th epoch:

$$\bar{E}_k = \frac{E_k}{E_{max}} = \frac{E_k}{E_1}, \ \bar{E}_k \in [0, 1]. \qquad (7)$$

E_{max} is obtained after the first EBP iteration. Normalization allows to specify the success criteria, the minimum error E_{min}, as a percentage of the initial error. For similar reasons it is also convenient to normalize the epoch number with respect to the maximum number of epochs, k_{max}, specified by the user:

$$\bar{k} = \frac{k}{k_{max}}, \ \bar{k} \in [0, 1]. \qquad (8)$$

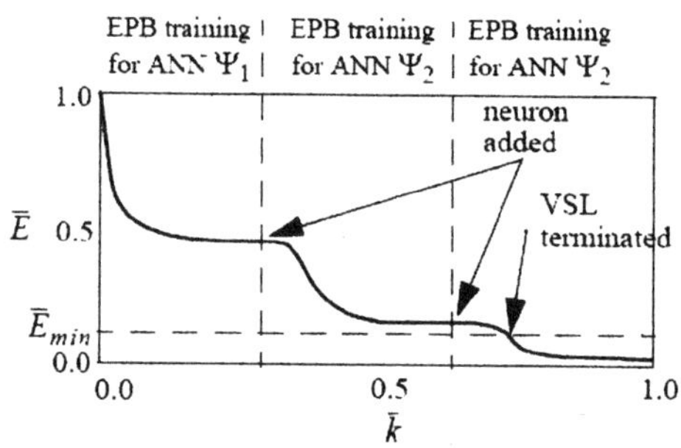

Figure 3. Example of a VSL metric.

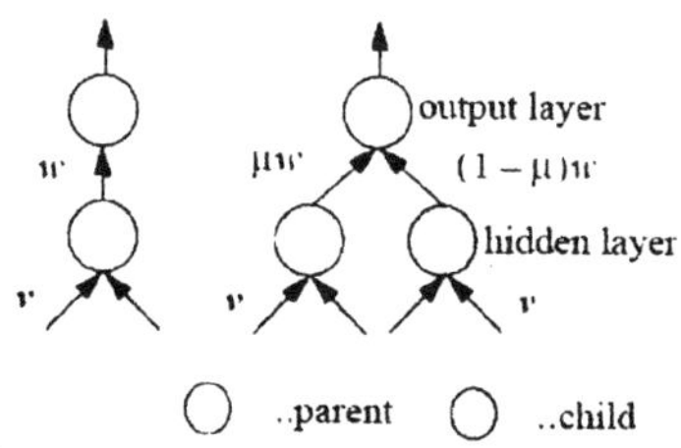

Figure 4. Adding a neuron.

Rules for Structure Learning. The VSL rules, based on the VSL metric and its rate of change $d\bar{E}/d\bar{k}$, determine when to add or prune hidden neurons. For the remainder of the paper the notation used is E and k without 'bar'.

- Rule 1: the constructive phase is in progress if E is greater than E_{min} **and** decreasing,

  $$E > E_{min} \text{ and } \Delta E / \Delta k < 0. \qquad (9)$$

  Action: continue weight training.
- Rule 2: the ANN structure is insufficient or weight training is stuck in a local minimum if E converges to a value greater than E_{min},

  $$E > E_{min} \text{ and } \Delta E / \Delta k \to 0. \qquad (10)$$

Action: add neuron to hidden layer.

- Rule 3: constructive VSL phase is successful if E drops below the desired minimum value E_{min}:

$$E < E_{min}. \tag{11}$$

Action: terminate constructive VSL phase; initiate VSL pruning phase.

- Rule 4: the pruning phase is in progress if

$$E < E_{min}. \tag{12}$$

Action: prune the least significant neuron; re-train all weights.

- Rule 5: the pruning phase is completed when E increases to

$$E > E_{min}. \tag{13}$$

Action: restore last ANN with $E < E_{min}$ and terminate VSL.

The initial VSL parameters are the initial structure and VSL limits:

- Initial ANN structure (number of hidden neurons), default is $q=1$.
- Maximum admissible number of learning epochs, k_{max}.
- Success criterion, E_{min}.
- Epoch size P for EBP learning.

The VSL algorithm determines all other parameters.

Adding Hidden Neurons. Neurons are added per Rule 2 by splitting off a 'child' neuron from a 'parent' neuron. The child inherits the connection weights such that the current ANN mapping does not change, i.e. the child is a *clone* of the parent with exception of its output weight:

$$\text{Parent: } \{(\mathbf{v}, \boldsymbol{b}^h), \mu w\} \tag{14}$$

$$\text{Child: } \{(\mathbf{v}, \boldsymbol{b}^h), (1-\mu)w\}. \tag{15}$$

with $0 < \mu < 1$. The vector of input weights $\boldsymbol{v}$ is cloned, while the sum of the parent's and child's output weight is equivalent to the parent's original output weight (Figure 4). Note that, although the network parameters change ($\Psi_k \neq \Psi_{k+1}$), the associated ANN mappings do not: $\boldsymbol{f}_{\Psi k} = \boldsymbol{f}_{\Psi k+1}$.

Pruning Hidden Neurons. Hidden neurons are pruned per Rule 4. The 'least significant' hidden neuron, i.e. with the smallest weights, is pruned, i.e.

$$\min_{hidden\ neurons} \{\|\mathbf{v}\|_1 \cdot \|\mathbf{w}\|_1\}. \tag{16}$$

All other weights in the MLP remain unchanged and weight training resumes. The pruning process is repeated until the VSL metric returns to $E > E_{min}$. In this case $\boldsymbol{f}_{\Psi k}$, the ANN at iteration k, is replaced with the previously saved $\boldsymbol{f}_{\Psi k-1}$, the final ANN. The learning process is completed and VSL is terminated. Pruning an insignificant neuron usually has little impact on the ANN mapping, and re-training is fast and computationally inexpensive.

x_1	x_2	y
0	0	0
0	1	1
1	0	1
1	1	0

Table 1: XOR truth table.

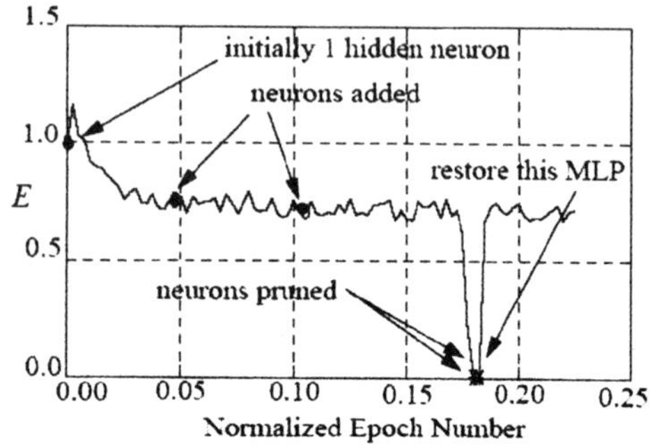

Figure 5. XOR problem: VSL metric for pattern training (not batch training).

EXAMPLES

The VSL algorithm was implemented in Matlab and tested using three function approximation problems and one classification problem.

XOR Problem. The purpose of this simple benchmark test was to verify that VSL converges to the minimum ANN structure possible. For the XOR problem this structure is well known: two hidden neurons. The truth table for the XOR problem is given in Table 1, with inputs x_1 and x_2, and output y.

The XOR problem received remarkable attention after Minsky and Papert published 'Percpetrons' in 1969. The authors showed that a single perceptron *cannot* learn the XOR problem, due to a lack of linear separability of the 0's and 1's in the x_1/x_2-plane. It was not until the 1980's when it was discovered that an MLP with two hidden neurons, i.e. a 2-2-1 structure [2], can perform that task. The VSL algorithm converges to exactly this structure after six VSL iterations, as is shown in Figure 5 (VSL metric) and Figure 6.

Strain Prediction for a Titanium Workpiece. The goal for the MLP was used to predict the strain on a workpiece of titanium, based on the workpiece size, i.e. width, thickness, and volume. Other inputs are temperature, the allowable ultimate strain, and the measured strain rate. Therefore a six-to-one mapping was to approximated. The training set contained 25 I/O vectors (Figure 7). The VSL algorithm converged to two hidden neurons, which is a surprisingly small network size. Intuitively suggested MLPs had up to two hidden layers and over 20 neurons, e.g. a 6-15-5-1 structure. This result demonstrates one of the potential benefits of structure learning: avoiding oversized neural network architectures. The learning curve is shown in Figure 8. In response to the initially flat MSE the VSL algorithm adds four neurons. It is then determined that, once the problem is learned, only two neurons are sufficient.

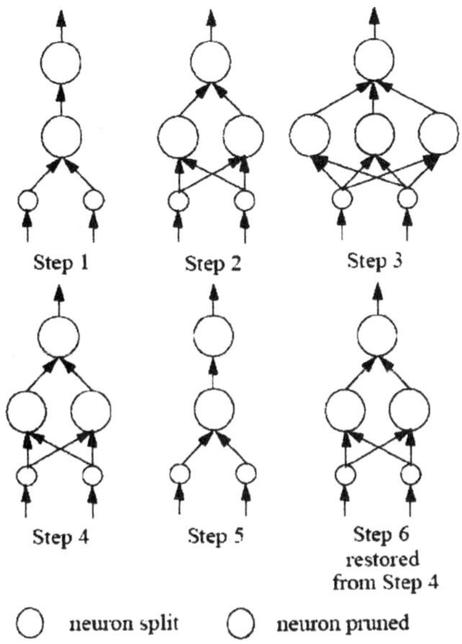

Figure 6. XOR problem: MLP structure during VSL.

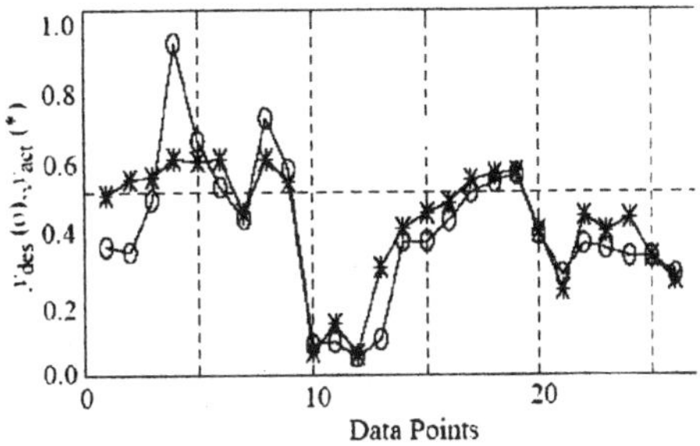

Figure 7. Titanium problem: desired (o) and learned mapping (*).

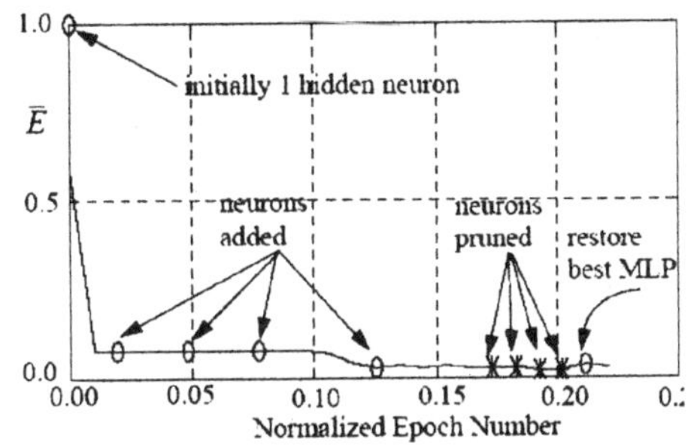

Figure 8. VSL for the Titanium problem: normalized squared error.

Classification Problem: Non-Destructive Evaluation, NDE. The non-destruction evaluation of composite materials is represented as a a classification problem. A laser beam created a heat shockwave within the material. The time history of the reflected shockwave contains information about invisible damages within the material. The 16-point Fourier transform of 776 recorded signals was associated with different classes (damaged, not damaged, etc.), resulting in 776 16-to-3 mappings. The learning curve is shown in Figure 9. The changing structure during the VSL process is illustrated in Figure 10. The VSL algorithm converged to an MLP with two neurons. Intuitively a larger MLP might have been chosen by a human designer.

CONCLUSIONS

Variable Structure Learning, a data-driven, automated design method for Multilayer Perceptrons, was introduced. It was shown that VSL automates the process of choosing a 'good' (ideal: minimum complexity) neural network structure for a given problem. VSL starts with a small initial network and adds and prunes artificial neurons based on a success criteria monitored during the learning process. The VSL algorithm was tested with different sets of data, and it was shown that it potentially converges to the smallest structure possible. Further research will include generalization tests and comparison with other structure learning algorithms.

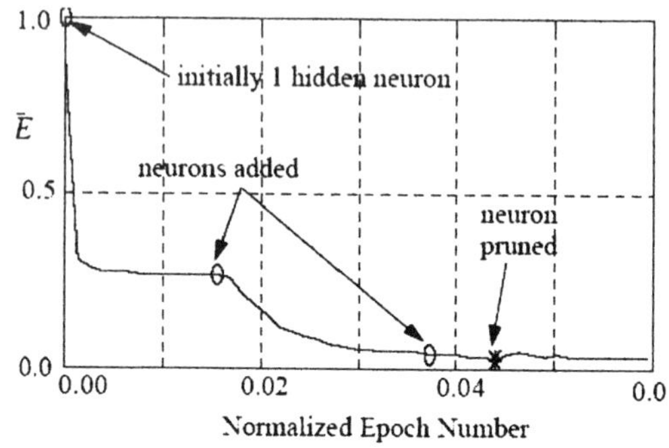

Figure 9. VSL for the NDE problem: normalized squared output error.

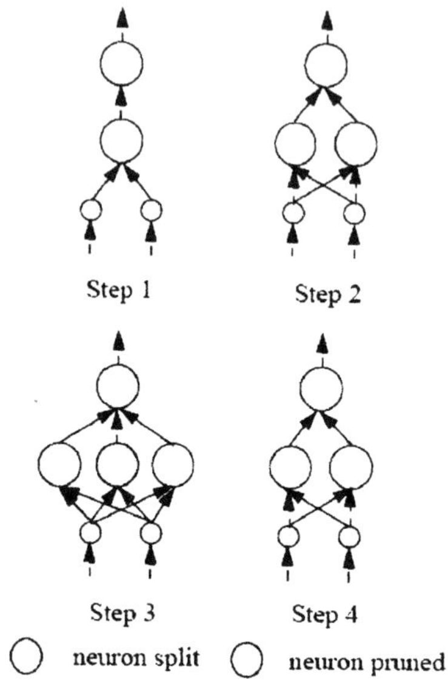

Figure 10. VSL for the NDE problem: MLP during learning.

REFERENCES

[1] F.L. Luo, Applied Neural Networks for Signal Processing, Cambridge Univ. Press, Cambridge, Mass., 1999.

[1] T. Ash, "Dynamic Node Creation in Backpropagation Networks," *Connection Science*, Vol. 1, No. 4, pp. 365-375, 1989.

[2] S. Haykin, *Neural Networks - A Comprehensive Foundation*, IEEE Press/Macmillan College, New York, 1994.

[3] T.Y. Kwok and D.Y. Yeung, "Objective Functions for Training New Hidden Units in Constructive Neural Networks," *IEEE Trans. Neural Networks*, 8(5), pp. 1131-1148, Sep 1997.

[4] T.Y. Kwok and D.Y. Yeung, "Constructive Algorithms for Structure Learning in Feedforward Neural Networks for Regression Problems," IEEE Trans. Neural Networks, 8(3), pp. 630-645, May 1997.

[5] G.G. Lendaris and K. Mathia, "Using A Priori Knowledge to Prestructure ANNs", *Australian Journal of Intelligent Information Processing Systems,* Vol. 1, No. 1, pp. 25-30, May 1994.

[6] G.G. Lendaris, M. Zwick, and K. Mathia, "On Matching Network Structure to Problem Domain Structure", *Proc. World Cong. Neural Networks '93*, Portland, Oregon, pp. 488-493, July 1993.

[7] B.Y. Pearce, "Implementation of a Variable Structure Neural Network," Masters Thesis, University of Alabama, Auburn, March 2001.

[8] Reed R., "Pruning Algorithms - A Survey," *IEEE Transactions on Neural Networks*, Vol. 4, No. 5, pp. 740-747, 1993.

[9] Werbos P.J., "Beyond regression: New Tools for Prediction and Analysis in the Behavioral Sciences," Ph.D. Thesis, Harvard University, Cambridge, Mass, 1974.

[10] Y. Zhao and C.G. Atkeson, "Some Approximation Properties of Projection Pursuit Learning Networks," in *Advances in Neural Information Processing Systems 4*, J.E. Moody, S.J. Hanson, and R.P. Lippmann, Eds., pp.936-943, Morgan Kaufman, San Mateo, CA, 1992.

[11] T.C. Lee, *Structure Level Adaptation for Artificial Neural Networks*, Kluwer Academic Publishers, Norwell, Massachusetts, 1991.

UNSUPERVISED LEARNING OF MIXTURES ON LARGE SPACES WITH INTEGRATED FEATURE AND COMPONENT SELECTION

MICHAEL W. GRAHAM
The Pennsylvania State University
Department of Electrical Engineering
University Park, Pennsylvania 16802

DAVID J. MILLER
The Pennsylvania State University
Department of Electrical Engineering
University Park, Pennsylvania 16802

ABSTRACT
The availability of very high dimensional data sets (such as text documents) has inspired extensions of unsupervised clustering methods for these large feature spaces. These works, however, often fail to address two pervasive problems that can prove unusually difficult in this setting—selecting the "correct" number of clusters and determining the subsets of features truly representative of these clusters. To address this, we propose special structured mixture models which allow for parsimonious model choices. To search over the (vast) space of model structures, we propose an efficient joint optimization strategy based on a generalized expectation-maximization (GEM) algorithm that minimizes the Bayesian Information Criterion at each candidate model order. For a subset of the Reuters-21578 data set, the multinomial version of our model—learned without labeled examples, without knowledge of the true number of topics and without feature preprocessing—compares quite favorably with a supervised naïve Bayes classifier.

INTRODUCTION

There exist several methods for estimating the number of components in a mixture model. One standard approach is to choose the model that minimizes a principled criterion function. A common choice is the Bayesian Information Criterion (BIC), written as:

$$BIC = \frac{N_p}{2}\log N - \log L(\chi \mid \theta) \tag{1}$$

with N_p the number of free parameters in the model, N the data set length and $L(\chi \mid \theta)$ the likelihood of the data given the model (Schwarz, 1978). While use of this criterion often gives reasonable order estimates for low-dimensional data, there are *serious* difficulties in its (direct) application to high-dimensional data. In the text domain, for example, the commonly used naïve Bayes "bag of words" mixture requires a component-specific parameter for *every* unique feature (i.e., word). Such a model might consist of hundreds of components, each with thousands to tens of thousands of parameters. In this case, the model penalty term within (1) dominates. The BIC cost is thus generally *strictly increasing* with increasing model order, with the BIC-"optimal" model the (obviously incorrect) one with a single component.

One could argue that the failure of BIC on text means we should discard it as the criterion in favor of a cost that penalizes complex models less severely. In this work, however, we show that BIC can be used quite effectively on text and that the phenomenon described above is mainly attributable to the (quite) limited set of model fitness/complexity tradeoffs in standard mixtures. To expand on this, note that BIC is a theoretically grounded criterion (Schwarz, 1978) that does capture the fundamental tradeoff between data representation (the log-likelihood) and model complexity (the penalty term). In principle then, using BIC, one could hope to find mixtures that achieve a reasonable tradeoff between fitness and model parsimony. Unfortunately, *for a fixed feature space,* standard naïve Bayes mixtures have only a single degree of freedom—the number of components—by which to explore this tradeoff.

Alternatively, we propose a structured generalization of standard naïve Bayes mixtures which offers a much richer set of fitness/complexity tradeoffs by allowing the "sharing" of parameters between components. Components in our model are offered the choice of representing a given feature using a component-specific distribution or a "tied" distribution, i.e. one also used (shared) by some other components. The complexity cost of models within this framework (including standard naïve Bayes mixtures as a special case) is thus determined by *both* the number of components and the number of unique parameters used by each component to explain the data. It is thus made possible to learn parsimonious (in terms of BIC cost) models having *many* components. A key aspect of this approach is (effectively) the use of a different (non-tied) feature space for each component.

A related approach can be found in (Law, Figueiredo & Jain, 2002), which introduced an extra "universal" model, used to explain (and hence effectively remove) irrelevant features. The main differences from our approach are that (Law et al.): 1) forms a soft, rather than a hard feature space partition; 2) forms the *same* (soft) partition for each component, whereas we learn *component-specific* feature partitions; 3) only considers dimensions < 30 and it is unclear this method scales up to large spaces such as text. Model selection for text was considered in (Vaithyanathan & Dom, 1999). As in the work just mentioned, the learned feature partition was common to all components. The authors were less than sanguine about explicit optimization of BIC, to jointly choose the space partition and the number of components. Thus, they applied a "wrapper" approach, using a Bayesian integrated likelihood to evaluate candidate models. While (Vaithyanathan & Dom, 1999) was not hopeful about direct optimization of BIC for the (huge) text space, we next propose just such a method. This paper will demonstrate that, for a suitably defined mixture model, integrated learning and model selection to minimize BIC on huge spaces *can* be practically achieved and yields quite reasonable estimates of the number of components. Moreover, the effectiveness of this approach is (to our mind) somewhat surprising – our method, which learns without labeled examples and even without knowledge of the number of true topics, achieves (test set) classification accuracy on the *Reuters* domain only modestly worse than naïve Bayes *supervised* classification. In the following sections, our integrated learning and model selection technique is developed. In section 4, experiments on the *Reuters* domain are reported.

OBJECTIVE FUNCTION

Finite mixtures of multinomial distributions have been shown effective for document modeling tasks (e.g. McCallum & Nigam, 1998). Consider a text database with N unique documents and D unique words. Each document can be represented by a feature vector $\underline{x}_i = \{x_{i1}, x_{i2}, \ldots, x_{iD}\}$ with x_{ik} the number of times the kth word occurs in document i. According to the multinomial PMF, the probability of generating document i (with length L_i) using an M-component mixture is given by:

$$P[\underline{x}_i] = \sum_{j=1}^{M} \alpha_j \left[L_i! \cdot \prod_{k=1}^{D} \left(\frac{1}{x_{ik}!} p_{jk}^{x_{ik}} \right) \right] \qquad (2)$$

Here, the $\{\alpha_j\}$ are nonnegative component masses and the $\{p_{jk}\}$ are nonnegative multinomial parameters. Equation (2) is subject to the constraints:

$$\sum_{k=1}^{D} p_{jk} = 1 \quad \forall j \qquad and \qquad \sum_{j=1}^{M} \alpha_j = 1 \tag{3}$$

We construct a structured variant of (2) that allows the *sharing* of multinomial parameters between components. This mixture is given by (ignoring constants):

$$P[\underline{x}_i] = \sum_{j=1}^{M} \left[\alpha_j \prod_{k=1}^{D} \left(p_{jk}^{v_{jk}} p_{\phi k}^{(1-v_{jk})} \right)^{x_{ik}} \right] \quad where \sum_{k=1}^{D} \left(v_{jk} p_{jk} + (1 - v_{jk}) p_{\phi k} \right) = 1 \, \forall j \tag{4}$$

Here, v_{jk} is a binary-valued "switch" parameter. It equals 0 if component j uses a shared parameter for feature k and 1 otherwise. The $\{p_{\varphi k}\}$ are the shared multinomial parameters. They are initially (globally) estimated using:

$$p_{\phi k} = \frac{\sum_{i=1}^{N} x_{ik}}{\sum_{i=1}^{N} \sum_{k'=1}^{D} x_{ik'}} \quad \text{which satisfies}: \sum_{k=1}^{D} p_{\phi k} = 1 \tag{5}$$

The BIC cost for this model (and the objective function for our learning algorithm) is therefore:

$$BIC = CC(\{v_{jk}\}) - \sum_{i=1}^{N} \log \left[\sum_{j=1}^{M} \left(\alpha_j \cdot \prod_{k=1}^{D} \left((v_{jk} \cdot p_{jk} + (1 - v_{jk}) \cdot p_{\phi k})^{x_{ik}} \right) \right) \right] \tag{6}$$

subject to the constraints in (4). Here, $CC(\{v_{jk}\})$ represents the BIC model penalty term for our mixture. We first simply write down an expression for this penalty, subsequently explaining its constituents:

$$CC(\{v_{jk}\}) = \frac{M-1}{2} \log N + \frac{D}{2} \log N + \sum_{j=1}^{M} \sum_{k=1}^{D} \frac{v_{jk}}{2} \log N + \sum_{k=1}^{D} F(\mathbf{v_k}) \cdot M \log 2 \tag{7}$$

$$\text{where} \quad F(\mathbf{v_k}) = \begin{cases} 1; & if \ \sum_{j=1}^{M} v_{jk} > 0 \\ 0; & otherwise \end{cases} \quad \text{and} \quad \mathbf{v_k} \equiv \{v_{jk}, j = 1,2,\ldots, M\} \tag{8}$$

The first term in (7) is the BIC cost for the M component masses. The second term is the cost for the D shared parameters. Critically, we note that this is a constant for all model orders. It thus has no effect on model selection and is safely ignored in the final objective function. The third term is the cost for component-specific parameters. This term penalizes using a component-specific parameter in favor of the shared parameter. The final term is the cost for the $\{v_{jk}\}$ switches. We note, significantly, that as (8) expresses, this cost is not incurred for a feature deemed uninformative by *all* components.

LEARNING ALGORITHM

We seek to minimize the BIC cost in (6) with respect to the $\{\alpha_j\}$, $\{p_{jk}\}$, $\{p_{\varphi k}\}$, $\{v_{jk}\}$, and the number of components M subject to the constraints in (4). Our overall optimization method is a *model order reduction procedure*, one which repeatedly applies a learning algorithm (detailed shortly) for minimizing (6) given a *fixed* number of components. We first initialize our model with $M=M_{max}$, chosen to over-estimate the true number of clusters. We then minimize the BIC cost for this M_{max} component model. Next, we delete the least-massive component and rerun our learning algorithm to retune the remaining $M_{max} - 1$ components. This procedure is repeated, reducing the model size all the way down to a single component. The slected model (with associated order) is then simply the model in this sequence with the smallest BIC cost.

For a given number of components, we minimize the BIC cost in (6) using a generalized version of the Expectation-Maximization (GEM) algorithm (Meng & van Dyk, 1997). Use of this approach is attractive because of its guaranteed monotonic descent in the penalized log-likelihood. The optimization, however, is complicated by the constraint in (4), whose satisfaction depends on the values chosen for the $\{p_{jk}\}$, $\{p_{\varphi k}\}$ *and* $\{v_{jk}\}$. We can, however, develop an efficient method for *jointly* optimizing the parameters based on a sequence of GEM iterations, each consisting of: i.) a standard E-step; ii.) an M-step for updating the component masses; iii.) a joint optimization step over the $\{p_{jk}\}$ and $\{v_{jk}\}$. We also minimize (6) with respect to the shared $\{p_{\varphi k}\}$ parameters. In this case, we are forced to use gradient descent to perform this minimization, as there is no closed-form update for these parameters within the GEM framework.

E-Step

We treat the component of origin for each point as the *hidden data* values within EM. The expected hidden data, based on the current model parameters are the probabilities:

$$P[Z_i = j|\underline{x}_i] = \frac{P[Z_i = j]\cdot P[\underline{x}_i|Z_i = j]}{P[\underline{x}_i]} = \frac{\alpha_j \cdot \prod_{k=1}^{D}\left(P[x_{ik}|Z_i = j]^{v_{jk}} \cdot P[x_{ik}]^{(1-v_{jk})}\right)}{\sum_{r=1}^{M}\alpha_r \cdot \prod_{k=1}^{D}\left(P[x_{ik}|Z_i = r]^{v_{rk}} \cdot P[x_{ik}]^{(1-v_{rk})}\right)} \quad (9)$$

M-Step

Given the probabilities calculated in (9), the expected value of the complete-data BIC cost is:

$$E[BIC] = CC(\{v_{jk}\}) - \sum_{i=1}^{N}\sum_{j=1}^{M}\left[P[Z_i = j|\underline{x}_i]\cdot\left(\log\alpha_j + \sum_{k=1}^{D}\left(v_{jk}x_{ik}\log p_{jk} + (1-v_{jk})x_{ik}\log p_{\phi k}\right)\right)\right] \quad (10)$$

By constraining the sum of the component masses to one and setting partial derivatives equal to zero, we get the M-step mass update:

$$\alpha_j = \frac{1}{N}\cdot\sum_{i=1}^{N}P[Z_i = j|\underline{x}_i] \quad (11)$$

Jointly Optimizing $\{p_{jk}\}$ and $\{v_{jk}\}$

To develop an effective joint learning procedure for the $\{p_{jk}\}$ and $\{v_{jk}\}$, we apply constraint (4) to (10) and construct the following Lagrangian:

$$L = E[BIC] - \sum_{j=1}^{M}\mu_j\sum_{k=1}^{D}\left[v_{jk}(p_{\phi k} - p_{jk})\right] \quad (12)$$

Here, μ_j is the Lagrange multiplier for the constraint on component j's multinomial parameters. Our notation will be simplified if we also define the quantity:

$$\bar{x}_{jk} \equiv \sum_{i=1}^{N}\left(P[Z_i = j|\underline{x}_i]\cdot x_{ik}\right) \quad (13)$$

This is the expected number of occurrences of the kth feature "explained by" component j. Setting the derivative of (12) with respect to p_{jk} equal to zero and solving, we find the optimal estimate of p_{jk} to be:

$$p_{jk} = v_{jk}\frac{\bar{x}_{jk}}{\mu_j} \quad (14)$$

Summing both sides of (23) over all k for which $v_{jk} = 1$ and applying our constraint, we may solve for the Lagrange multiplier:

$$\mu_j = \frac{\sum_{k=1}^{D}(\bar{x}_{jk}\cdot v_{jk})}{\sum_{k=1}^{D}(p_{\phi k}\cdot v_{jk})} \quad (15)$$

Taking (14) and (15) together and recognizing $\{\bar{x}_{jk}\}$ and $\{p_{\varphi k}\}$ as constants, we see that the form of the optimal estimate for p_{jk} (which minimizes (10) while satisfying the constraints in (4)) is *completely determined* by the current state of *all* switches associated with component j. Thus, if we plug (14) and (15) into (10), we get a function that only depends on the $\{v_{jk}\}$ and which, for *any* choice of $\{v_{jk}\}$, is guaranteed to satisfy the constraints (4) while *implicitly* using the optimal $\{p_{jk}\}$. Specifically, we get:

$$E[BIC] = CC(\{v_{jk}\}) - \sum_{i=1}^{N}\sum_{j=1}^{M}\left[P[Z_i = j|\underline{x}_i]\cdot\left(\log\alpha_j + \sum_{k=1}^{D}\begin{pmatrix} v_{jk}x_{ik}(\log\bar{x}_{jk} - \log\mu_j) \\ + (1 - v_{jk})x_{ik}\log p_{\phi k}\end{pmatrix}\right)\right] \quad (16)$$

We have, thus, converted the *constrained* optimization of (10) over $\{v_{jk}\}$ and $\{p_{jk}\}$ into the *unconstrained* optimization of (16) over only the $\{v_{jk}\}$. Note that since the optimal $\{p_{jk}\}$ are implicitly determined by our choice for $\{v_{jk}\}$ we do not need to explicitly compute them during the $\{v_{jk}\}$ optimization—they can be computed via (14) and (15) once we have determined our final $\{v_{jk}\}$ configuration. Unfortunately, recognizing the μ_j as a function of *all* $\{v_{jk}\}$ associated with component j, we cannot immediately determine the $\{v_{jk}\}$ configuration that globally minimizes (16). We can, however, determine the optimal configuration of switches associated with feature k (represented by the set $\mathbf{v_k}$) given fixed values for all other switches (i.e. with $\mathbf{v_{k'}}$ held fixed $\forall k' \neq k$). Specifically, we can minimize (16) over $\mathbf{v_k}$ by first tentatively choosing (for each of the M switches associated with feature k) $v_{jk} = 1$ only if:

$$\frac{1}{2}\log N - \bar{x}_{jk}\left(\log\bar{x}_{jk} - \log\mu_j^{(v_{jk}=1)}\right) + \sum_{k'=1:k'\neq k}^{D}\left(\bar{x}_{jk'}v_{jk'}\log\mu_j^{(v_{jk}=1)}\right)$$
$$< -\bar{x}_{jk}\log p_{\phi k} + \sum_{k'=1:k'\neq k}^{D}\left(\bar{x}_{jk'}v_{jk'}\log\mu_j^{(v_{jk}=0)}\right) \quad (17)$$

In (17), the superscript on μ_j indicates that the value of the Lagrange multiplier is a function of the value chosen for v_{jk}. The condition in (17) effectively optimizes (16) with respect to $\mathbf{v_k}$ assuming the (M log 2) cost (in equation (7)) of transmitting the switches associated with $\mathbf{v_k}$ is always incurred. However, this cost is *not incurred* if all $v_{jk} \in \mathbf{v_k}$ are equal to zero. We therefore must still decide between allowing the v_{jk} to maintain their tentative positions determined by (17) or switching them *all* to zero. To minimize (16), we let $\mathbf{v_k}$ maintain its current configuration if and only if:

$$M\log 2 + \sum_{j=1:v_{jk}=1}^{M}\left[\frac{1}{2}\log N - \bar{x}_{jk}v_{jk}\left(\log\bar{x}_{jk} - \log\mu_j^{(v_{jk}=1)}\right) + \sum_{k'=1:k'\neq k}^{D}\bar{x}_{jk'}v_{jk'}\log\mu_j^{(v_{jk}=1)}\right]$$
$$< \sum_{j=1:v_{jk}=1}^{M}\left[-\bar{x}_{jk}\log p_{\phi k} + \sum_{k'=1:k'\neq k}^{D}\bar{x}_{jk'}v_{jk'}\log\mu_j^{(v_{jk}=0)}\right] \quad (18)$$

Conditions (17) and (18) yield the optimal configuration of switches in the set $\mathbf{v_k}$ *with all other switches held fixed.* It is necessary to sequentially apply these conditions in a cycle over all the features to determine a complete switch configuration. These updates (sequential with respect to features, batch with respect to the components) can be repeated until *all* v_{jk} remain constant through a cycle, or a predetermined number of cycles is reached. It should be noted here that these updates are not guaranteed to achieve a global minimum $\{v_{jk}\}$ configuration. They are, however, non-increasing in BIC and their effectiveness is supported by the empirical results presented in the next section.

EXPERIMENTAL RESULTS

We experimented on a subset of the Reuters-21578 data set (Lewis, 1999). Since the goal of any document clustering algorithm is to produce a solution with a high degree of topic "purity" with respect to the (assumed ground truth) labeling of the corpus, we compared our model against a *supervised* naïve Bayes classifier. Note that the supervised classifier addresses an easier problem since it has knowledge of the number of classes and labeled examples of each. Our method, on the other hand, estimates the topics (and their number) in an *unsupervised* fashion, as outlined in the previous section.

To ensure unambiguous results, only *Reuters* documents with *a single label* were included. The final corpus consisted of 1,942 documents from 22 topics, randomly split into training and test sets of equal size. After stemming and stoplist removal, the feature set consisted of 10,326 unique words. The supervised naïve Bayes classifier was initialized with 22 components and trained by maximum likelihood estimation (along the lines of McCallum & Nigam (1999)), using the 971 training documents. Its performance on the test set was then evaluated using the percentage of correctly classified test set documents based on a maximum likelihood decision rule.

The unsupervised clustering model was learned for five different random initializations on the same training set, using the algorithm described above. We chose M_{max} = 100 and initially set all v_{jk} equal to 1. Initial cluster membership was determined using the k-means algorithm with a cosine similarity measure. The starting k-means cluster centers were randomly chosen from among the training data. The BIC cost at each model order for a *single* representative initialization is shown in Fig. 1, with the minimum at M = 25. The classification results, summarized in Table 1, show that the proposed model, learned on an unlabeled training set without even knowledge of how many classes are present, compares favorably with a well-known *supervised* classifier.

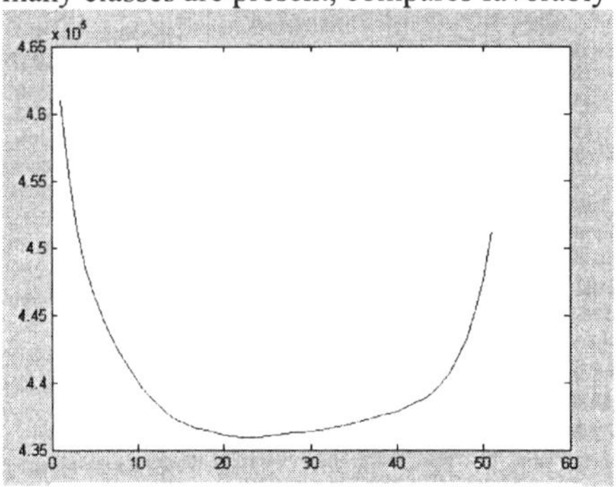

Figure 1: BIC cost vs. model order

Table 1: Comparison of proposed method and supervised naïve Bayes classifier on 22-topic Reuters domain

	Number of Components	Test Set Classification Accuracy
Supervised NB Classifier	22 (ground truth)	0.812
Unsupervised Proposed Model	27.2 +/- 3.3	0.738 +/- 0.021

ACKNOWLEDGEMENTS

This work was his work was supported in part by National Science Foundation Award IIS-0082214 and by a DoD graduate fellowship.

REFERENCES

Figueiredo, M. A. T., & Jain, A. K. (2002) Unsupervised learning of finite mixture models. *IEEE Transactions on Pattern Analysis and Machine Intelligence*, 24, 381-392=6.

Lewis, D. D. (1999) Reuters-21578 text categorization test collection distribution 1.0

Law, M.H., Jain, A. K., & Figueiredo, M. A. T. (2002). Feature selection in mixture-based clustering. *Advances in Neural Information Processing Systems 15* Cambridge: Sebastian Thrun.

McCallum, A, & Nigam, K. (1999). A comparison of event models in Naïve Bayes text classification. *AAAI-98 Workshop on Learning for Text Classification.*

Meng, X. L., & van Dyk, D. (1997) The EM algorithm – an old folk-song sung to a fast new tune. *Journal of the Royal Statistical Society Series B*, 59, 511-567.

Schwarz, G. (1978) Estimating the dimension of a model. *The Annals of Statistics*. 6, 461-464.

Vaithyanathan, S., & Dom, B. (1999) Model selection in unsupervised learning with applications to document clustering. *Proceedings of the 16th International Conference on Machine Learning* (pp. 433-443) San Francisco: Morgan Kaufmann.

A DESIGN METHOD FOR REPETITIVE LEARNING CONTROLLERS FOR TIME-DELAY SYSTEMS

KOU YAMADA
Department of Mechanical System Engineering, Gunma University
1-5-1 Tenjincho, Kiryu, Japan

KEIJI SATOH
Department of Mechanical System Engineering, Gunma University
1-5-1 Tenjincho, Kiryu, Japan

TOORU ARAKAWA
Department of Mechanical System Engineering, Gunma University
1-5-1 Tenjincho, Kiryu, Japan

ABSTRACT
In this paper, we propose a simple design method for repetitive learning control systems for time-delay systems using the parameterization approach. That is, we clarify the parameterization of all stabilizing repetitive learning controllers for time-delay systems. The basic idea obtaining the parameterization of all stabilizing repetitive learning controllers for time-delay systems is very simple. If a repetitive learning controller stabilizes the plant, then the repetitive learning controller must be included in the class of all stabilizing controllers for the plant. The parameterization of all stabilizing controllers for the plant was obtained by Youla et al. and Vidyasagar. Stabilizing repetitive learning controllers for time-delay systems can be designed using the free parameter in the parameterization by Youla et al. and Vidyasagar. Using this, we obtain the parameterization of all stabilizing repetitive learning controllers for time-delay systems.

Introduction

We examine the parameterization of all stabilizing repetitive learning controllers for time-delay systems. The parameterization of all stabilizing repetitive learning controllers was studied by Hara and Yamamoto (1986). Hara and Yamamoto(1986) state that because the sufficient condition for stability of a repetitive learning control system is decided as an H_∞ norm problem, the parameterization for repetitive learning control systems is given by resolution into the Nevanlinna-Pick interpolation problem. Katoh and Funahashi (1996) gave the parameterization of all repetitive learning controllers for minimum phase systems by solving the Bezout equation exactly. Katoh and Funahashi(1996) state that because the parameterization is not given based on the sufficient stability condition the repetitive learning control system is internally stable, this result is important in the sense that class of repetitive learning controllers is more extensive than the class of repetitive learning controllers given by Hara and Yamamoto(1986). However, the parameterization of Katoh and Funahashi(1996) has some remaining difficulties. Yamada and Okuyama (2000) gave the parameterization of all stabilizing repetitive learning controllers for minimum phase systems. However, the parameterization of all stabilizing repetitive learning controllers for time-delay systems has not been considered.

In this paper, we propose the parameterization of all stabilizing repetitive learning controllers for time-delay systems. The basic idea for obtaining the parameterization of all stabilizing repetitive learning controllers for time-delay systems is very simple. If a repetitive learning controller stabilizes the plant, then the repetitive learning controller must be included in the class of all stabilizing controllers for the plant. The parameterization of all stabilizing controllers for the plant was obtained by Youla et al. (1976) and Vidyasagar(1985). The parameterization of all stabilizing controllers includes a free parameter, which is stable. That is, stabilizing repetitive learning controllers for time-delay systems can be designed using the free parameter in the parameterization of Youla et al. (1976) and Vidyasagar(1985). Using this, we obtain the parameterization of all stabilizing repetitive learning controllers for time-delay systems.

Problem formulation

Consider the unity feedback system

$$\left\{ \begin{array}{ll} y & = G(s)e^{-sL}u \\ u & = C(s)(r-y) \end{array} \right. , \tag{1}$$

where $G(s)e^{-sL}$ is the plant with input time-delay $L > 0$, $C(s) \in R(s)$ is the controller, $y \in R$ is the output, $u \in R$ is the control input. $r \in R$ is the periodic reference input with period T satisfying

$$r(t+T) = r(t) \ \ (\forall t \geq 0). \tag{2}$$

Yamamoto and Hara (1987)state that even if the plant $G(s)$ has a periodic disturbance with period T and uncertainty in order for the output y to follow the periodic reference input r with period T with small steady state error, the controller $C(s)$ must be

$$C(s) = C_1(s) + C_2(s)C_r(s), \tag{3}$$

where $C_1(s) \in R(s)$, $C_2(s) \in R(s) \neq 0$, $C_r(s)$ is an internal model of the periodic reference input with period T

$$C_r(s) = \frac{q(s)e^{-s(\bar{T}-L)}}{1-q(s)e^{-sT}}, \tag{4}$$

$q(s)$ is strictly proper low pass filter satisfying $q(0) = 1$ and $\bar{T} \geq L$.

Under these assumptions, the problem considered in this paper is to obtain the parameterization of all stabilizing repetitive learning controllers for the plant $G(s)e^{-sL}$.

The parameterization

In this section, we give the parameterization of all stabilizing repetitive learning controllers $C(s)$ for the plant $G(s)e^{-sL}$.

The parameterization of all stabilizing repetitive learning controllers $C(s)$ for the plant $G(s)e^{-sL}$ is summarized by the following theorem.

Theorem 1 *The controller $C(s)$ stabilizes the control system in Eq.(1) and works as the repetitive learning controllers, that is, $C(s)$ is Eq.(3), and $C_1(s)$ and $C_2(s)$ in Eq.(3) are rational functions if and only if the controller $C(s)$ is*

$$C(s) = \frac{\tilde{X}(s) + D(s)Q(s)}{\tilde{Y}(s) - N(s)Q(s)} e^{sL}, \tag{5}$$

where $N(s) \in RH_\infty$ and $D(s) \in RH_\infty$ are coprime factors of $G(s)$ on RH_∞ satisfying

$$G(s) = N(s)D^{-1}(s) = \tilde{D}^{-1}(s)\tilde{N}(s), \tag{6}$$

$Q(s)$ is

$$\begin{aligned} &Q(s) \\ &= \frac{Q_{n1}(s) + Q_{n2}(s)e^{-sL} + Q_{n3}(s)e^{-sT} + Q_{n4}(s)e^{-s(T+L)} + Q_{n5}(s)e^{-s\bar{T}}}{Q_{d1}(s) + Q_{d2}(s)e^{-sL} + Q_{d3}(s)e^{-sT} + Q_{d4}(s)e^{-s(T+L)} + Q_{d5}(s)e^{-s\bar{T}}}, \end{aligned} \tag{7}$$

and $Q_{ni}(s)(i = 1, \ldots, 5)$ and $Q_{di}(s)(i = 1, \ldots, 5)$ are any RH_∞ functions satisfying

$$-\frac{\tilde{Y}(0)Q_{d3}(0) - N(0)Q_{n3}(0)}{\tilde{Y}(0)Q_{d1}(0) - N(0)Q_{n1}(0)} = 1, \tag{8}$$

$$\tilde{X}(s)Q_{d1}(s) + D(s)Q_{n1}(s) = 0, \tag{9}$$

$$\tilde{Y}(s)Q_{d2}(s) - N(s)Q_{n2}(s) = 0, \tag{10}$$

$$\tilde{X}(s)Q_{d3}(s) + D(s)Q_{n3}(s) = 0, \tag{11}$$

$$\tilde{Y}(s)Q_{d4}(s) - N(s)Q_{n4}(s) = 0, \tag{12}$$

$$\tilde{Y}(s)Q_{d5}(s) - N(s)Q_{n5}(s) = 0, \tag{13}$$

$$\begin{aligned} &\tilde{X}(s)Q_{d4}(s) + D(s)Q_{n4}(s) \\ &= \frac{\left(\tilde{X}(s)Q_{d2}(s) + D(s)Q_{n2}(s)\right)\left(\tilde{Y}(s)Q_{d3}(s) - N(s)Q_{n3}(s)\right)}{\tilde{Y}(s)Q_{d1}(s) - N(s)Q_{n1}(s)} \end{aligned} \tag{14}$$

and

$$\frac{\tilde{X}(s)Q_{d5}(s) + D(s)Q_{n5}(s)}{\tilde{Y}(s)Q_{d3}(s) - N(s)Q_{n3}(s)} \neq 0. \tag{15}$$

$\tilde{X}(s)$ and $\tilde{Y}(s)$ are RH_∞ functions satisfying

$$\begin{bmatrix} Y(s) & X(s) \\ -\tilde{N}(s) & \tilde{D}(s) \end{bmatrix} \begin{bmatrix} D(s) & -\tilde{X}(s) \\ N(s) & \tilde{Y}(s) \end{bmatrix} = I. \tag{16}$$

Proof of Theorem 1 requires following lemma and theorem.

Lemma 1 *Unity feedback control system*

$$\begin{cases} y &= G(s)u \\ u &= -C(s)y \end{cases} \tag{17}$$

is internally stable if and only if the controller $C(s)$ *is*

$$C(s) = \frac{\tilde{X}(s) + D(s)Q(s)}{\tilde{Y}(s) - N(s)Q(s)}, \tag{18}$$

where $N(s) \in RH_\infty$ *and* $D(s) \in RH_\infty$ *is coprime factors of* $G(s)$ *on* RH_∞ *satisfying*

$$G(s) = N(s)D^{-1}(s) = \tilde{D}^{-1}(s)\tilde{N}(s). \tag{19}$$

$\tilde{X}(s)$ *and* $\tilde{Y}(s)$ *are* RH_∞ *function satisfying*

$$\begin{bmatrix} Y(s) & X(s) \\ -\tilde{N}(s) & \tilde{D}(s) \end{bmatrix} \begin{bmatrix} D(s) & -\tilde{X}(s) \\ N(s) & \tilde{Y}(s) \end{bmatrix} = I. \tag{20}$$

$Q(s)$ *is any asymptotically stable function (Vidyasagar, 1985).*

Theorem 2 *Assume that* $C_1(s)$, $C_2(s)$ *in Eq.(3) and* $q(s)$ *in Eq.(4) are rational functions. The controller* $C(s)$ *in Eq.(3) stabilizes the plant* $G(s)e^{-sL}$ *if and only if the controller* $\hat{C}(s) = C(s)e^{-sL}$ *stabilizes* $G(s)$.

(Proof) Proof is obvious, Because $C_1(s)$, $C_2(s)$ in Eq.(3) and $q(s)$ in Eq.(4) are rational functions. ∎

Using Lemma 1 and Theorem 2, we show the proof of Theorem 1.
(Proof) From Theorem 2, the parameterization of all stabilizing controllers $C(s)$ for the plant $G(s)e^{-sL}$ is equivalent to that for all stabilizing controllers $\hat{C}(s) = C(s)e^{-sL}$ for $G(s)$.

First, necessity is proved. That is, we show that if $C(s)$, written as Eq.(3), stabilizes $G(s)e^{-sL}$, then the controller $C(s) = \hat{C}(s)e^{sL}$ and the free parameter $Q(s)$ are given by Eq.(5) and Eq.(7), respectively.

From Lemma 1, the parameterization of all stabilizing controllers $\hat{C}(s)$ for the plant $G(s)$ is

$$\hat{C}(s) = C(s)e^{-sL} = \frac{\tilde{X}(s) + D(s)Q(s)}{\tilde{Y}(s) - N(s)Q(s)}. \tag{21}$$

This equation is equivalent to Eq.(5). Next, we show that if the controller $\hat{C}(s) = C(s)e^{-sL}$ stabilizes $G(s)$, then the free parameter $Q(s)$ in Eq.(5) is given by Eq.(7). Substituting $C(s)$ in Eq.(3) into Eq.(5), we have

$$Q(s) = \frac{Q_{n1}(s) + Q_{n2}(s)e^{-sL} + Q_{n3}(s)e^{-sT} + Q_{n4}(s)e^{-s(T+L)} + Q_{n5}(s)e^{-s\bar{T}}}{Q_{d1}(s) + Q_{d2}(s)e^{-sL} + Q_{d3}(s)e^{-sT} + Q_{d4}(s)e^{-s(T+L)} + Q_{d5}(s)e^{-s\bar{T}}}, \tag{22}$$

where

$$Q_{n1}(s) = -\tilde{X}(s)C_{1d}(s)C_{2d}(s)q_d(s) \in RH_\infty, \tag{23}$$

$$Q_{n2}(s) = \tilde{Y}(s)C_{1n}(s)C_{2d}(s)q_d(s) \in RH_\infty, \tag{24}$$

$$Q_{n3}(s) = \tilde{X}(s)C_{1d}(s)C_{2d}(s)q_n(s) \in RH_\infty, \tag{25}$$

$$Q_{n4}(s) = -\tilde{Y}(s)C_{1n}(s)C_{2d}(s)q_n(s) \in RH_\infty \tag{26}$$

$$Q_{n5}(s) = \tilde{Y}(s)C_{1d}(s)C_{2n}(s)q_n(s) \in RH_\infty \tag{27}$$

$$Q_{d1}(s) = D(s)C_{1d}(s)C_{2d}(s)q_d(s) \in RH_\infty, \tag{28}$$

$$Q_{d2}(s) = N(s)C_{1n}(s)C_{2d}(s)q_d(s) \in RH_\infty, \tag{29}$$

$$Q_{d3}(s) = -D(s)C_{1d}(s)C_{2d}(s)q_n(s) \in RH_\infty, \tag{30}$$

$$Q_{d4}(s) = -N(s)C_{1n}(s)C_{2d}(s)q_n(s) \in RH_\infty \tag{31}$$

and

$$Q_{d5}(s) = N(s)C_{1d}(s)C_{2n}(s)q_n(s) \in RH_\infty. \tag{32}$$

$C_{1n}(s)$, $C_{1d}(s)$, $C_{2n}(s)$, $C_{2d}(s)$, $q_n(s)$ and $q_d(s)$ are coprime factors of $C_1(s)$, $C_2(s)$ and $q(s)$ on RH_∞ satisfying

$$C_1(s) = \frac{C_{1n}(s)}{C_{1d}(s)}, \quad C_2(s) = \frac{C_{2n}(s)}{C_{2d}(s)}, \quad q(s) = \frac{q_n(s)}{q_d(s)}. \tag{33}$$

From these equations, we have proved that if the controller $C(s)$, written as Eq.(3), stabilizes the control system in Eq.(1) then the free parameter $Q(s)$ in Eq.(5) is given by Eq.(7). From simple manipulation and Eq.(23)~Eq.(32), we can easily confirm that Eq.(9)~ Eq.(15) are satisfied. Therefore, necessity has been shown.

Next sufficiency is proved. That is, we show that under the assumption of Eq.(9)~Eq.(15) if the free parameter $Q(s)$ is given by Eq.(7) the controller $C(s)$ is given by Eq.(3). Substituting Eq.(7) into Eq.(5), we have

$$C(s) \quad = \quad C_1(s) + C_2(s)\frac{q(s)e^{-s(\bar{T}-L)}}{1-q(s)e^{-sT}}, \tag{34}$$

where $C_1(s)$, $C_2(s)$ and $q(s)$ are denoted by

$$C_1(s) = \frac{\tilde{X}(s)Q_{d2}(s) + D(s)Q_{n2}(s)}{\tilde{Y}(s)Q_{d1}(s) - N(s)Q_{n1}(s)}, \tag{35}$$

$$C_2(s) = -\frac{\tilde{X}(s)Q_{d5}(s) + D(s)Q_{n5}(s)}{\tilde{Y}(s)Q_{d3}(s) - N(s)Q_{n3}(s)} \tag{36}$$

and

$$q(s) = -\frac{\tilde{Y}(s)Q_{d3}(s) - N(s)Q_{n3}(s)}{\tilde{Y}(s)Q_{d1}(s) - N(s)Q_{n1}(s)}, \tag{37}$$

respectively. From Eq.(37) and the assumption in Eq.(8), $q(0) = 1$. In addition, from Eq.(36) and Eq.(15), $C_2(s)$ in Eq.(3) satisfies $C_2(s) \neq 0$. This imply that $C(s)$ in Eq.(5) works as a modified repetitive learning controller.

We have, therefore, proved Theorem 1. ∎

Using the result in this paper, if $Q_{ni}(s)(i = 1, \ldots, 5)$ and $Q_{di}(s)(i = 1, \ldots, 5)$ are selected using Neural Networks, we can obtain high performance stable repetitive learning controllers for time-delay systems.

Conclusion

In this paper, we propose the parameterization of all stabilizing repetitive learning controllers for time-delay systems. This research was partially supported by the Saneyoshi Scholarship Foundation.

References

S. Hara and Y. Yamamoto: Stability of Multivariable Repetitive Control Systems - Stability Condition and Class of Stabilizing Controllers, Trans. of the Society of Instrument and Control Engineers, Vol.22, No.12, pp.1256-1261, (1986)

H. Katoh and Y. Funahashi: A Design Method of Repetitive Controllers, Trans. of the Society of Instrument and Control Engineers, Vol.32, No.12, pp.1601-1605, (1996)

K. Yamada, and T. Okuyama: A parameterization of all stabilizing repetitive controllers for linear minimum phase systems, Trans. of the Society of Instrument and Control Engineers, Vol.36, No.4, pp.328-334, (2000)

M. Vidyasagar: Control System Synthesis - A factorization approach -, MIT Press, (1985)

Y. Yamamoto and S. Hara: The Internal Model Principle and Stabilizability of Repetitive Control System, Trans. of the Society of Instrument and Control Engineers, Vol.22, No.8, pp.830-834, (1987)

D.C. Youla, H. Jabr and J.J. Bongiorno: Modern Wiener-Hopf design of optimal controllers. Part I, IEEE Trans. on Automatic Control, AC-21, pp.3-13, (1976)

LEARNING IMAGE-BASED LANDMARKS FOR WAYFINDING USING NEURAL NETWORKS

JEREMY D. DRYSDALE **DAMIAN M. LYONS**
Robotics and Computer Vision Laboratory
Fordham University
Bronx, New York

ABSTRACT
In this paper we address the problem of automatically selecting and predicting landmarks for use in wayfinding on a mobile robot. Our constraints for wayfinding landmarks are that we be able to uniquely recognize the landmark from a visual image and be able to tell whether the landmark is growing nearer or farther away. We employ back-propagation to teach a multilayer neural network to predict the *image location* and appearance of future landmarks based on the appearance and *image location* of currently visible landmarks.
We employ a hybrid reactive/deliberative architecture (Arkin, 2000). The reactive component collects candidate landmark feature measurements while the robot explores its (previously unknown) environment. For the deliberative component, we use a neural network running on a Beowulf cluster to process the large amount of data being collected from camera. We describe our architecture and algorithm in detail and present data gathered using our Pioneer DX2 robot to learn wayfinding landmarks.

1.0 INTRODUCTION

A robot traversing unknown terrain needs to have a method to find its way back. For example a Search & Rescue robot (Jacoff, Messina, Evans, 2000) winding through a complicated rubble field looking for victims or other targets needs to have a way to return the target to base for medical help or backup. Clearly an a-priori map of a rubble field would not be available. One approach could be to construct a detailed geometric map of the area as the robot moves. This approach has many advantages but has several practical problems. The geometric features of a rubble field are less easy to define than indoor or outdoor natural terrain; and the landscape may be ephemeral – changing rapidly due to weather, or due to local rubble motion, or even due to motion of the robot. An alternative approach is to learn qualitative features of the landscape.

When the robot is in an area it doesn't know, it becomes necessary for it to identify and learn a useful set of landmarks in its surroundings, so that it can return through the area. Throughout this learning process the robot must identify potential landmarks based on sensory information, learn where those landmarks are, and then be able to predict, with reasonable accuracy, where to expect to sense the next landmark.

Insects appear to employ a "visual snapshot" concept of landmark navigation (Bianco, Zelinksy, Lenrer, 2000) and we are inspired by this in our purely image based representation and prediction approach. In this paper we will present an approach to landmark identification and learning. We employ a multilayer neural network to learn to predict expected image landmark locations based on the image locations of current landmarks. Because we expect landmark learning to be an ongoing, data-intensive background computation, we also propose a novel landmark learning architecture based on the hybrid reactive/deliberative architecture (Arkin, 2000) consisting of reactive landmark identification & prediction coupled to a concurrent and separate landmark learning system running on a 15 node Beowulf Cluster.

2.0 LITERATURE REVIEW

Bayesian landmark learning (Thrun, 1997) for robot localization involves the use of recursive Bayesian estimation to accurately locate features of the environment around the robot so that the robot's position and orientation with respect to the environment can be calculated. In (Thrun, 1997) the network was trained to minimize sensory extraction errors so it was better able to extract landmarks in the future. Previous work done to solve the problem of learning landmarks for wayfinding include using edge density to determine what is a candidate for a landmark (Sim and Dudek, 1999). High edge density tended to mean that there was furniture or a wall, something that would make a good landmark present. The candidates were then grouped by which candidates corresponded to similar visual regions of the environment.

In (Mata and Armingol, 2002), a pattern search engine was used to learn the patterns of the landmarks. Patterns were 2-D images containing odd but distinct shapes, symbols, text or a combination of a few of these. This worked well with landmarks that contained text, because the text created the patterns that were picked up by the system.

For our application, we expect that landmarks may modify their appearance and location while the robot is active. We would like therefore to have a more qualitative concept of landmark, while retaining the ability to use the landmark to guide wayfinding. One interesting piece of work was the studying of insects and how they were able to learn landmarks (Bianco, Zelinksy, Lenrer, 2000). One such method was the Turn-Back-and-Look method used by bees. When observing the behavior of bees it was discovered that whenever a bee finds itself in an unfamiliar place, it turns around and views the landscape behind it. In this manner it is able to analyze where it has been and teach itself how where it is relates to what it already knows. This is similar to how we designed our system, it stores what landmarks it has seen previously, and where they are. It can use this information to get an idea of where the new landmarks it is seeing are.

In (Wellington and Stentz, 2004), a neural network is used to learn the terrain of the land as viewed from a camera mounted on a tractor. This work employs a grid overlayed on the camera view. Features can be observed and calculated for each cell in the grid, thus allowing for easy comparison between areas of an image. We will also adopt this approach for landmark feature calculations.

3.0 IDENTIFYING VISUAL LANDMARKS

To identify visual landmarks we took as input a visual image as collected by the X10 camera mounted on the Pioneer robot, which was divided into a grid. This way, feature measurement could take place on it, and be evaluated by analyzing the features on particular grid squares and how they compared with the same features in the surrounding grid squares. The features calculated for each grid square were normalized average color and intensity where *i* and *j* refer to individual pixel coordinates within the grid square:

$$r_n = \frac{256 * r}{r+g+b} \quad g_n = \frac{256 * g}{r+g+b} \quad Y = \frac{r+g+b+1}{3} \tag{1}$$

$$\frac{\sum_{i=0}^{xPixSize}\sum_{j=0}^{yPixSize} r_n}{xPixSize * yPixSize} \quad \frac{\sum_{i=0}^{xPixSize}\sum_{j=0}^{yPixSize} g_n}{xPixSize * yPixSize} \quad \frac{\sum_{i=0}^{xPixSize}\sum_{j=0}^{yPixSize} Y}{xPixSize * yPixSize} \tag{2}$$

and standard deviation:

$$\frac{\Sigma(r_n - r_{navg})^2}{(xPixSize \cdot yPixSize) - 1} \qquad \frac{\Sigma(g_n - g_{navg})^2}{(xPixSize \cdot yPixSize) - 1} \tag{3}$$

A good landmark is one in which the standard deviation of the average color between grid squares is fairly low. When this is the case, it signifies that the landmark is large enough to cover multiple grid squares, and the color is contiguous enough such that there isn't too much difference.

A good landmark can be represented mathematically. If both the average normalized red and average normalized green fall within one standard deviation of the averages of an adjacent grid square, the adjacent squares are considered to be good landmarks.

A bad landmark is one in which the standard deviation of the average color is high. When this is the case it can signify a few things. One of which is that the landmark does not span multiple grid squares. This is not a good landmark because you cannot distinguish it from other aspects of the image easily. Another thing it can signify is a massive change in coloration. This tends to not be a good landmark because typically massive color changes indicate smaller objects around one another, which are difficult to see from a distance.

4.0 LEARNING LANDMARKS

The neural network contains six (6) inputs, six (6) outputs, and six (6) hidden nodes. The function of this neural network is to take in the landmark information, and predict where the next landmark will appear. This neural network uses a standard backpropagation algorithm (Fausett, 1994).

The input to the neural network is information about the closest landmark to the robot. This information is the center Cartesian x and y grid coordinate of the landmark, the normalized average red value, the normalized average green value, the number of grid squares the landmark takes up, and the change in the number of grid squares since the last image was observed. The output of the neural network is the same information, except for the predicted landmark.

Because of the massive amount of data the robot will be taking in and processing, the landmark prediction will be extremely data intensive and always active – as long as the robot is active, data is being collected and analyzed. Because of this, we used a Beowulf cluster.

We plan to implement a system that will allow the robot to communicate with the Beowulf cluster through an open socket. The PC will send the Beowulf the data collected by the robot. The Beowulf cluster will receive this data and feed it through the neural network. Once this is complete, the Beowulf cluster will send the PC the information on the predicted landmark.

Currently the Beowulf cluster is being used to train the neural network. The training data is copied by hand to the Beowulf, and after the training is complete, the weights data is copied by hand again to the PC controlling the robot.

5.0 EXPERIMENTAL METHOD

We began by creating a small course Fig. 1 for the Pioneer robot to traverse so that it could gather learning data to train the network. The images collected by the camera were divided into a grid, so that the robot could use the grid squares as spatial coordinates. As the robot traversed the course it gathered information on landmark locations, their average colors, their sizes, and the difference in size between the current and previous images. This data was outputted to a file for use at a later time.

The Pioneer robot is outfitted with two sonar arrays, each containing eight (8) sonar for a total of sixteen (16). The camera mounted on the front is an X10 Wireless Camera, Model #VR36A. There is a wireless modem mounted on the back of the Pioneer for wireless connectivity. It is an ACT0106 Lo-speed Serial Ethernet device.

There were three training landmarks that were used. The first of which was an orange box containing black writing and a green image of a computer hardware card of length 12" and width 10" and height 1.5". The second was a dark blue bound notebook of length 11", and width 8.75" and height 0.5". The third was a silver Aibo robotic dog standing on all fours of length 10" and width 6" and height 11". These landmarks were positioned at alternating points on either side of the robot starting from the left approximately two (2) feet apart.

As the robot traversed its data gathering course the camera image was displayed on the screen containing where it thought all landmarks where. This was accomplished by outlining the grid squares containing the landmarks in green.

A three layer neural network was built next containing six (6) nodes in the hidden layer. This network was trained on the data gathered from the robots traversal of the course. The learning part of the network took place on a sixteen (16) node Beowulf cluster and the weights data was exported back to the PC containing the robotics code for testing. A backpropagation algorithm was implemented to learn the weights.

Now that the network was built and trained, the testing process could begin. There were four testing cases that took place on the network: forward landmark recognition, reverse landmark recognition, arbitrary start forward landmark recognition and arbitrary start reverse landmark recognition:

Forward landmark recognition testing was done by traversing the robot through the course in the same direction as the training. Reverse landmark recognition testing was done by traversing the robot through the course in the reverse direction as the training. Arbitrary start forward landmark recognition was done by placing the robot in an arbitrary location on the course, and traversing it through in the same direction as the training. Arbitrary start reverse landmark recognition was done by placing the robot in an arbitrary location on the course, and traversing it through in the reverse direction as the training.

In all cases, the neural network took as input the landmark closest to the robot, and the output was the location and size of the next landmark. The predicted landmark was displayed on the screen by outlining the grid squares containing the predicted location of the landmark in red Fig. 2.

6.0 RESULTS

The results of all the testing cases were good. The standard of error was calculated using the formula:

$$(\text{predicted}_x - \text{actual}_x)^2 + (\text{predicted}_y - \text{actual}_y)^2 + (\text{predicted}_{size} - \text{actual}_{size})^2 \qquad (4)$$

The results of the forward landmark recognition testing were good. The neural network was able to pinpoint the y-axis location of the next landmark 38% of the time. Outside of this it was able to predict within three grid squares 62% of the time. It was able to pinpoint the x-axis location 45% of the time. Outside of this it was able to predict within three grid squares 16% of the time. The neural network was able to pinpoint the size of the next landmark 21% of the time. Outside of this it was able to predict within three grid squares of the size 45% of the time. Figure 3 shows that the exact landmark location was predicted 12% of the time.

The results of the reverse landmark recognition testing were also good. The neural network was able to pinpoint the y-axis location of the next landmark 33% of the time. Outside of this it was able to predict within two grid squares the other 67% of the time. It was able to pinpoint the x-axis location of the next landmark 40% of the time. Outside of this, it was able to predict within three grid squares 20% of the time. The neural network was able to pinpoint the size of the next landmark 12% of the time. Outside of this it was able to predict within three grid squares of the size 52% of the time. Figure 4 shows that the exact landmark location was predicted 5% of the time.

The results of the arbitrary start location forward landmark recognition testing were the best of all the tests performed for overall accuracy. The neural network was able to pinpoint the y-axis location 24% of the time. Outside of this it was able to predict within two grid squares the other 76% of the time. It was able to pinpoint the x-axis location 57% of the time. Outside of this it was able to predict within three grid squares 34% of the time. The neural network was able to pinpoint the size of the next landmark 19% of the time. Outside of this it was able to predict within three grid squares the size 62% of the time. Figure 5 shows that the exact landmark location was predicted 10% of the time.

The results of the arbitrary start location reverse landmark recognition testing were also very good. The neural network was able to pinpoint the y-axis location 29% of the time. Outside of this it was able to predict within two grid squares the other 71% of the time. It was able to pinpoint the x-axis location 33% of the time. Outside of this it was able to predict within three grid squares 24% of the time. The neural network was able to pinpoint the size of the next landmark 5% of the time. Outside of this it was able to predict within the three grid squares the size 43% of the time. Figure 6 shows that the exact landmark location was predicted 14% of the time.

7.0 CONCLUSIONS

This paper has presented a method for learning to predict image-based landmarks for wayfinding using a multilayer neural network. The method was evaluated by creating a training course, collecting training data, and using that data to train the neural network to predict landmarks.

The experimental results indicate that this is a very feasible method of predicting landmarks. Current experiments have shown good results, but with a few outlying results. One approach to address improve performance would be to train the network on more landmark data. Our goal is to construct a system that continually learns landmark positions and locations.

The landmarks used in this example were fairly simple. Our goal was to apply this qualitative, image-based approach to landmark recognition in a Search and Rescue application. Our next step is to use landmarks that are more representative of that application.

To increase performance, a Beowulf cluster can also be used not only to learn the appropriate weights for the neural network, but also to predict the next landmark location. A socket can be opened between the PC running the robot and the Beowulf cluster, thus allowing transmission of data between components.

Finally, this work has just used visual information. However, we believe that a combination of sonar and visual information would be more useful for representing and predicting the kind of landmarks we expect to see in our application.

Figure 1: Course

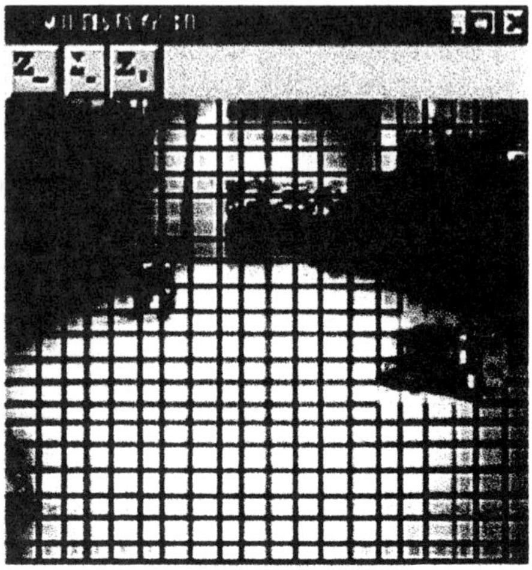

Figure 2: Landmark Prediction

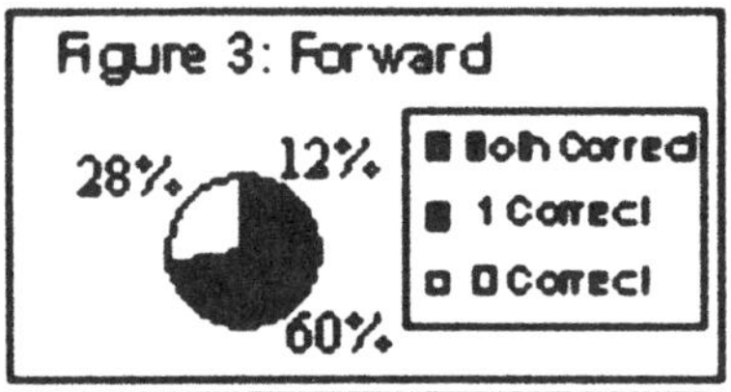

Figure 3: Forward

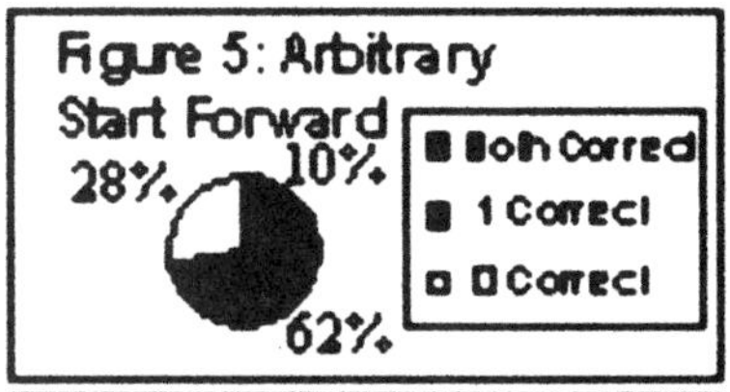

Figure 5: Arbitrary Start Forward

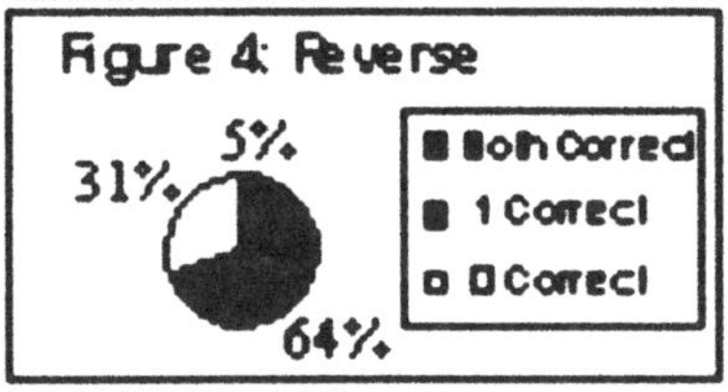

Figure 4: Reverse

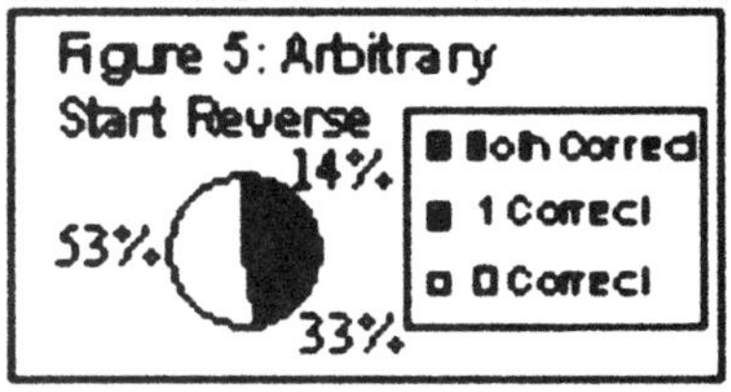

Figure 5: Arbitrary Start Reverse

8.0 REFERENCES

Olson, *Landmark Selection for Terrain Matching*, IEEE Int. Conf. On Robotics and Automation, San Francisco, CA, 2000

Arkin, *Behavior-Based Robotics*, MIT Press, Cambridge, MA, 2000

Sim and Dudek, *Learning Visual Landmarks for Pose Estimation*, Centre for Intelligent Machines, McGill University, Montreal, Canada, 1999

Mata and Armingol, *Learning Visual Landmarks for Mobile Robot Navigation*, Division of Systems Engineering and Automation, Madrid, Spain, 2002

Bianco, Zelinksy, Lehrer, *Visual Landmark Learning*, Verona, Italy; Canberra, Australia; Zurich, Switzerland, 2000

Thrun, *Bayesian Landmark Learning for Mobile Robot Localization*, Computer Science Department and Robotics Institute, Carnegie Mellon University, Pittsburgh, PA, 1997

Wellington and Stentz, *Online Adaptive Rough-Terrain Navigation in Vegetation*, Robotics Institute, Carnegie Mellon University, Pittsburgh, PA, 2004

Fausett, *Fundamentals of Neural Networks*, Prentice-Hall, Englewood Cliffs, NJ, 1994

Jacoff, Messina, Evans, *A Standard Test Course for Urban Search and Rescue Robots*, Performance Metrics for Intelligent Systems Workshop, 2000

TRANSFERRING SKILLS TO A SIMULATED ROBOT

MOHAMMAD H. SALAH
ECE Department, Clemson University, Clemson, SC 29634
msalah@ces.clemson.edu

ANDREW L. KUN
ECE Department, University of New Hampshire, Durham, NH 03824
andrew.kun@unh.edu

ABSTRACT:
A skill transfer and improvement framework was designed and implemented to transfer skills to a simulated robot without the help of a robotics expert. A skill expert first learns to perform the desired task by maneuvering the robot and giving actuator commands using the keyboard. The framework is then used to transfer the expert's skills to the robot by teaching the robot's controller to perform the skill. CMAC neural networks are responsible for learning skills. Learning is accomplished using imitation of the demonstrated movements that are mapped to a set of primitives. After transferring a skill, the expert can give advice to the controller to improve the robot's performance.

INTRODUCTION

The problem tackled in this research is how to transfer a skill from a skill expert to a robot. A skill expert is a person who possesses the skill to perform a task but is not a robotics expert. With today's technology we need robotics experts to program robots to perform some specific task. Consequently, a skill expert who is not a robotics expert cannot easily transfer skills to a robot.

Our first hypothesis is that an adaptive learning controller [1] can be used to implement the skill transfer. Adaptive control will allow adaptation to variations in the environment of the robot. The second hypothesis says that the learning controller can be based on the idea of cloning [1]. Cloning is also called learning by example, or imitation learning by researchers [2-4]. Cloning design allows imitating the skill(s) demonstrated by an expert. The third hypothesis proposes that the expert first needs to learn how to execute the skill by maneuvering the robot (controlling the robot's actuators) while observing the feedback from the robot's sensors. Then the expert should provide the imitation controller with pairs of state inputs (functions of sensor readings) and desired actuator outputs. The fourth hypothesis proposes that all robot skills should be described using action primitives, where primitives describe simple robot motions taking into account interactions with the environment. All skills should be described as concatenated primitives, where combined primitives represent skills. The fifth hypothesis deals with improving the performance of the imitation controller. The human expert can let the controller execute a skill and then give an advice to the controller on how to improve the performance of the skill. This advice can be advice about desired outcomes and advice about the state space variables.

Our research is constrained to robots with a small number of degrees of freedom interacting with a small number of static objects. Thus we will consider a two dimensional (2D) model of a truck with a trailer, a parking spot, and obstacles. The technique of transferring skills will handle some of the kinematics of the robot and it will not handle any dynamics.

BACKGROUND

Daxwanger et al. have presented an approach to acquire and transfer an experienced driver's skills to an automatic parking controller [5] using an artificial neural network and fuzzy network-based controller. Skill transfer for an experimental space robot was implemented at the German Aerospace Center (DLR) [6]. As Schaal points out in [3], imitation learning of skills can be implemented by learning a control policy directly from a task expert or by building a new policy from observations of a behavior. In our system the teacher will control and move the robot directly based on the feedback obtained from the robot sensors. This means that the teacher's states and actions will all be known and observable. Schaal defines movement primitives as "sequences of action that accomplish a goal-directed behavior." The idea of motion primitives comes from studies that suggest the existence of force-field motor primitives in the spine. Studies on frogs and rats showed that these primitives are vector-additive, and can encode a large number of motor behaviors [7]. Mosemann and Wahl define a skill primitive as a 6-tuple that includes the movement to be performed, the set of sensors to observe the primitive execution, and the goals for sensor readings at the beginning and end of the primitive [8]. In this paper, we define motion primitives similarly to the definition of Mosemann and Wahl.

PRIMITIVE-BASED CONTROL

We will consider primitives as the basic units that describe any kind of motion. Primitives will describe our truck motions in terms of actuator commands and sensor feedback. We will define a primitive as:

$$P = < commands, transformation, stimuli, goals, references > \qquad (1)$$

The *commands* element of the primitive represents the actuator commands that will result in the desired robot motion. The state input is created based on the outputs of relevant sensors and reference values provided by the expert as shown in Fig. 1 that shows a view of our primitive-based control architecture.

In this control architecture, the expert will select a primitive for execution from a set of stored primitives. Then the *stimuli*, *transformation*, *goals* and *references* elements of the selected primitive will be retrieved.

The *references* element makes the primitives independent of absolute locations in the state space. The *stimuli* element of the primitive provides information about which sensors are relevant. The *commands* element in the primitive P specifies the set of actuators that should be activated in order to execute the motion. The *transformation* element determines actuator commands based on the state of the robot (input). The sensor outputs associated with the references in turn can determine the robot's state. Once the state of the robot is quantified, actuator activation can be controlled by the transformation element of the primitive P.

Fig. 1 introduces the idea that the performance of the *transformation* element of a primitive can be adaptively learned as well as improved. Every group of actuators in the commands element of the primitive has an associated error. The *goals* element of the primitive specifies these functions. The transformation is adaptively changed to minimize the errors.

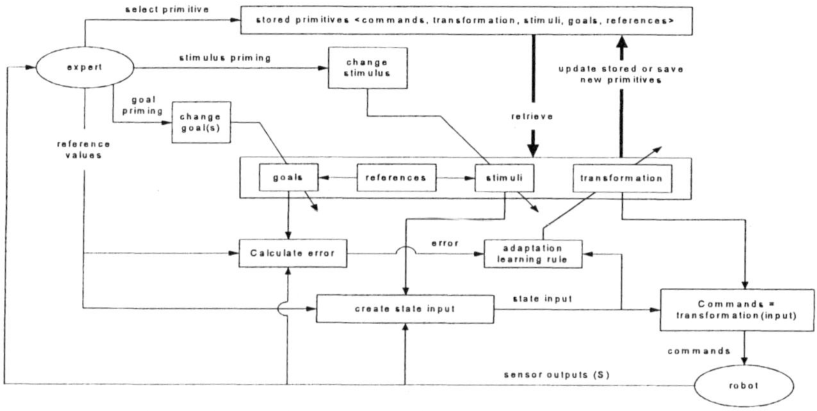

Fig. 1 *A view of a primitive-based control architecture*

SKILL EXPERT ADVICE

Adaptation allows improving the *transformation* element of primitives. However, when a primitive is executed, the skill expert may realize that training the *transformation* element using the existing goals does not improve the performance as desired. Fig. 1 shows a system that allows changing the *goals* element. In this system the expert can retrieve a stored primitive and can then initiate goal and/or stimuli priming. Goal/Stimuli priming refers to adding, removing or changing one or more of the goal/stimuli functions. Stimulus priming is needed if the primitive's state space has to be modified by the expert.

PRIMITIVE-BASED MOTION DESCRIPTION OF A TRUCK

The expert can create different combinations, sequentially, of three basic primitives to describe the desired path or skill to be transferred. For the sake of simplicity, we predefine three basic primitives as follows:

- Primitive 1 which is "Go_Straight." It is implemented just on the truck, with the trailer following. This primitive is implemented when the angle of the front wheels of the truck are aligned with the angle of the truck itself.
- Primitive 2 which is "Make_A_Right_Turn." The front wheels of the truck turn right by 20°, and the truck moves forward with the trailer following. This angle is the angle between the truck's angle and the front wheels' angle.
- Primitive 3 which is "Make_A_Left_Turn." It is the same as primitive 2 but executes a left turn.

The argument values of the primitive equation change depending on the type of primitive to be executed. According to equation (1), our basic primitives are:

$P_1 = < GF, T\#, Sgn(CDSR - RV), G, RV >$ where:

***P_1*:** "Go_Straight" primitive.
***GF*:** Actuator command of going forward.
***T#*:** Transformation number.
***CDSR*:** Current distance sensor reading.
***G*:** Goal that relies on (current distance sensor reading – reference value).
***RV*:** Reference value (either certain value or previous distance sensor reading).
Sgn: Sign of the difference.

$P_2 = < GF \cup TR, T\#, (RV - TOAS), G, RV >$ where:

***P_2*:** "Make_A_Right_Turn" primitive.
***TR*:** Actuator commands of turning the wheels right.
***TOAS*:** Truck's orientation angle sensor.

$P_3 = < GF \cup TL, T\#, (TOAS - RV), G, RV >$ where:

***TL*:** Actuator command of turning the wheels left.

The parallel activation operator, $\cup$, indicates that the actuators are activated concurrently. Fig. 2 depicts an example of how we can execute the basic primitives by determining the *stimuli*, *goals* and *references* elements.

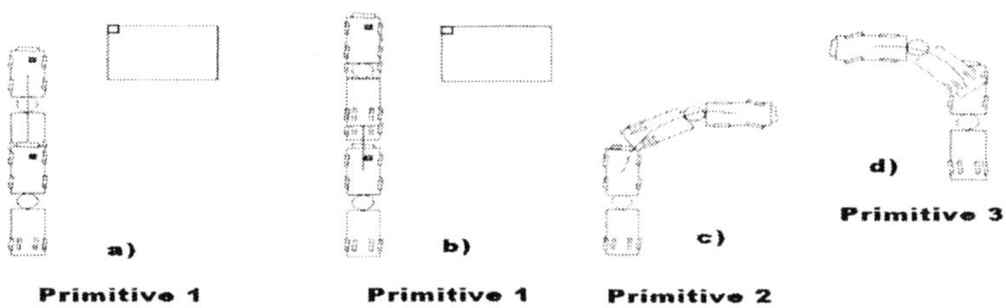

Fig. 2 *Primitives 1, 2, and 3*

In panel a) of Fig. 2 we use a distance sensor to measure the distance from a location on the truck to a corner of the obstacle (the upper left corner in this example). In this example our reference is a specific distance *d* between the sensor and the corner. Our goal is to minimize the difference between the distance sensor reading and the reference value. In panel b), our goal is to obtain the minimum distance to the same corner while keeping the current truck heading. In order to minimize this distance we observe the sign of the difference between the current and past distance sensor readings. When the sign of this difference changes, it can be said that the truck has reached the minimum distance to the corner. The reference value is the last distance reading. For panel c) of Fig. 2, a right turn is executed. The sensor that measures the truck's angle is activated and the reference value is adjusted to be 0°. The goal is to minimize the difference between the angle of the truck and the reference value. Panel d) of Fig. 2 is the same as panel c) except the sign of the angles change.

SIMULATION RESULTS

Fig. 3 shows an example of a skill to be transferred to the truck.

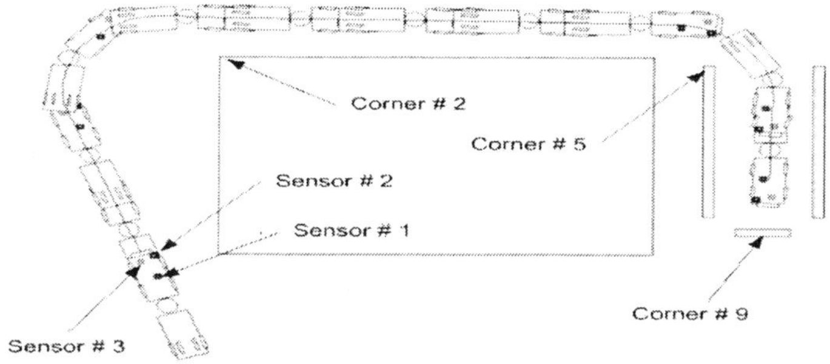

Fig. 3 *Skill to be transferred to the truck*

The expert will try to reach the parking spot by making a big turn around the obstacle. This skill can be divided into five primitives in the order: P_1, P_2, P_1, P_2, and then P_1. Next, the expert has to let the truck's controller learn how to implement these primitives. The learning will be done by the CMAC Neural Networks (NNs) [9] located in the imitation-learning controller. The CMAC NNs represents the transformation element defined in equation (1). After learning, the expert has to combine these two learned primitives to accomplish the skill sought. The truck's controller will learn how to execute the primitives sequentially according to the primitive. Our controller will perform correctly even if the truck's position or angle changes (within limits) compared to Fig. 3. The truck follows the same order of basic primitives and makes turns as desired.

Fig. 4 depicts a situation where a new obstacle (red circle) is added to the environment and set in the path of the truck. In this case, an advice can be made by changing the state input to get desired outcomes in order to overcome a variation in the truck's environment. This could be done by adding a sensor to the sensors installed on the truck to measure the distance from the truck's position to the center of the new obstacle. In our implementation, the advice requires adding a CMAC NN to prevent the truck from moving over it.

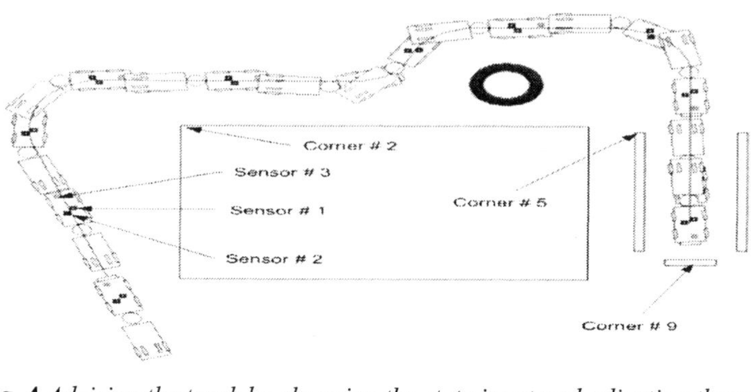

Fig. 4 *Advising the truck by changing the state input and adjusting the path*

Under some circumstances, giving advice will not solve the problem (variations in the environment) encountered by the truck. In this case, a new combination of primitives (a new skill) is needed.

CONCLUSION

In this paper we proposed a machine-learning framework that allows a layperson to transfer skills to a simulated robot. The elements that make up this imitation technology are adaptation, imitation-based learning and primitives that describe the truck's motion. Skill transfers are performed using imitation where the demonstrated movements are mapped to a set of primitives to implement novel skills. Creating a similar framework to transfer skills to physical robots could have a tremendous effect on our everyday lives that would be similar to the effect that software applications for PCs had on our society.

ACKNOWLEDGMENT

This research was funded in part by the University of New Hampshire.

REFERENCES

[1] P. J. Werbos, "*Neurocontrollers,*" in J. G. Webster (ed.) Wiley encyclopedia of electrical and electronics engineering, John Wiley, 1999, pp. 350-366.

[2] M. Mataric, "*Sensory-motor primitives as a basis for imitation: linking perception to action and biology to robotics,*" in C. Nehaniv and K. Dautenhahn (eds.) Imitation in Animals and Artifacts, MIT Press, 2001.

[3] S. Schaal, "*Is imitation learning the route to humanoid robots?,*" Trends in Cognitive Sciences, vol. 3, no. 6, pp. 233-242, 1999.

[4] A. Ude, C. Man, M. Riley, and C. G. Atkeson, "*Automatic generation of kinematic models for the conversion of human motion capture data into humanoid robot motion,*" First IEEE-RAS International Conference in Humanoid Robots, Cambridge, MA, 2000.

[5] W. A. Daxwanger and G. K. Schmidt, "*Skill-based visual parking control using neural and fuzzy networks,*" IEEE International Conference on Systems, Man and Cybernetics, 1995, 'Intelligent Systems for the 21st Century', vol. 2, no. 1695-1664, Vancouver, BC , Canada.

[6] B. Brunner, G. Hirzinger, K. Landzettel, and J. Heindl, "*Multi-sensory shared autonomy and tele-sensor-programming - key issues in the space robot technology experiment ROTEX,*" IEEE/RSJ International Conference on Intelligent Robots and Systems (IROS), Yokoham, Japan.

[7] F. A. Mussa-Ivaldi and E. Bizzi, "*Motor learning through the combination of primitives,*" Philosophical Transactions of the Royal Society of London: Biological Sciences, vol. 355, no. 1404, pp. 1755-1769, 2000.

[8] H. Mosemann and F. M. Wahl, "*Automatic decomposition of planned assembly sequences into skill primitives,*" IEEE Transactions on Robotics and Automation, vol. 17, no. 5, pp. 709-718, 2001.

[9] J. S. Albus, "A new approach to manipulator control: the Cerebellar Model Articulation Controller (CMAC)," Trans. of ASME, Journal of Dynamic Systems, Measurement, and Control, vol. 97 pp. 220-227, Sep 1975.

A TORNADO DETECTION ALGORITHM USING EMPIRICAL ORTHOGONAL FUNCTIONS

PRASHANT KAKANI
School of Computer Science, University of Oklahoma, Norman, OK

S. LAKSHMIVARAHAN
School of Computer Science, University of Oklahoma, Norman, OK

MICHAEL B. RICHMAN
School of Meteorology, University of Oklahoma, Norman, OK

ABSTRACT
A new class of discriminant function based on the empirical orthogonal functions (EOF) which achieves over 95% probability of detection is described. A comparison of this method with other existing methods is also provided.

1. INTRODUCTION

Beginning about thirty years ago, interest in using radar to detect severe weather became practical (Grey et al., 1975). During this period, great strides have been made in the detection and issuance of warning to the public, of the approaching tornadic thunderstorms. Two vital components in this success story are (i) the development and deployment of weather radar networks covering the continental United States, culminating in the Weather Surveillance Radar 1988 Doppler (WSR-88D) and (ii) various severe weather algorithms to post-process the output of the weather radar.

In this regard, one of the algorithms widely deployed is the mesocyclone detection algorithm (MDA), developed by the National Severe Storms Laboratory (NSSL). Comprehensive accounts of the development, use and accuracy of MDA is contained in Stumpf, et al. (1998).

Since the WSR-88D has three native variables as output (reflectivity, velocity and spectrum width), in principle, the MDA can generate features of the underlying thunderstorm at multiple elevation and azimuth angles based on any of the native variables and combinations. In practice, spectrum width is rarely used, owing to problems in the values output. This leaves velocity based and reflectivity based features to be interpreted. Marzban and Stumpf (1996) using a subset of 23 velocity based features from the MDA develop an **artificial neural network** (ANN) based classification system to discriminate between tornadic and non-tornadic cases with considerable success. This approach defines intrinsically a nonlinear surface in the 23-dimensional feature space that divides it into two half spaces with points in one-half denoting tornadoes and those in the other non-tornadoes. Recently, Trafalis, et al. (2003) report a new class of discriminant functions based on the support vector machines (SVM) and the minimax probability machines (MPM). They also provide a comparison of the performance of the approaches based on ANN, SVM and MPM.

The challenge of developing a "good" detection and forecast system depends on ample lead-time for tornado warnings while avoiding failing to issue a warning for tornadoes that occur. Simultaneously, the forecast system must avoid issuing warnings for tornadoes that fail to materialize. In order to accomplish this, a forecast system must accurately **discriminate** circulations that become tornadic from those that do not. Various forecast evaluation statistics have been developed to define such a "good" forecast. One of the common features of many of the detection algorithms currently in operational use is that while the **probability of detection** of tornadoes (POD) is quite high, the **false alarm rate** (FAR) is also very high. Since too many false alarm can lead to the classic "cry wolf" skepticism and the subsequent apathy to warnings, a continuing challenge is to improve the overall quality of the forecast products, namely to achieve very high POD and low FAR, among others. This work was motivated by the desire to understand the reasons for higher values of false alarm rate.

This paper consists of two parts. In the first part, we, for the first time, quantify the underlying probability distributions of the 23 velocity-based MDA features used in a discriminant analysis by fitting a gamma distribution. While gamma provides a good fit of the histograms, it turns out that the gamma distribution for each of the features exhibit large overlap between tornadic and non-tornadic cases. This overlap underscores the challenge and the difficulty in the discrimination process. Secondly, we derive a linear transformation of the underlying data set using the **empirical orthogonal functions** (EOF) which are the orthogonal system of eigenvectors of the second moment matrix of the raw data. By projecting the data set onto the new co-ordinate system spanned by the EOF, we obtain a transformed data set with the following properties: (1) the new set of features are (geometrically) orthogonal, (2) while the transformation is information lossless, over 95% of the underlying information is concentrated in the first three features, and (3) the histograms of the transformed data exhibit better separation between tornadic and non-tornadic cases. These properties directly lead to a new discriminant rule that has the highest POD hither to be achieved.

To our knowledge, Nestlerode and Richman (2003) were the first to describe the statistical properties of the MDA features by computing their histograms and the correlation structure. They used the principal component analysis (PCA) to transform the data set from a highly correlated set of features to a smaller number of uncorrelated ones. Within this PCA framework, they required over nine features to explain 90% of the underlying variance. However, in the present context, by using EOF we could obtain nearly 95% of the information using only three features. This data reduction from 23 to 3 features leads to a considerable simplification in the discriminant rule and saving in the computational cost.

The mathematical basis linear transformation using EOF is described in Section 2. The new discriminant function, its performance and a comparison with the existing methods are described in Section 3. A summary is provided in Section 4.

2. LINEAR TRANSFORMATION OF THE DATA BASED ON THE EOF

Let X denote the $M \times N$ data matrix with $M > N$. Define the $N \times N$ second moment matrix S given by $S = (X^T X)/M$ (2.1)

Assuming that X is of **full rank**, it can be verified that S is a **symmetric and positive definite** (SPD) matrix. Let (v_i, λ_i) for i =1,2,..N be the eigenvector – eigenvalue pair for the matrix S. Then

$$S v_i = v_i \lambda_i \text{ for } i = 1, 2, N \qquad (2.2)$$

where it is assumed without loss of generality that $\lambda_1 \geq \lambda_2 \geq \lambda_3 ... \geq \lambda_n > 0$. Let V be the $N \times N$ matrix of eigenvectors of S and Λ be the diagonal matrix of eigenvalues. Then (2.2) can be succinctly written as $S\,V = V\Lambda$. Since S is SPD, it can be verified that the columns of V are orthonormal (Bellman (1995)), that is, $V^T = V^{-1}$ and $V V^T = I$ and S can be rewritten as $S = V \Lambda V^T$.

It follows from the above development that the columns of V constitute a **new orthonormal basis** for the N dimensional feature space. The idea of the linear transformation we are seeking is to obtain a representation of the old data matrix X in the new co-ordinate system defined by the columns of V. This representation is given by a $M \times N$ matrix Z where $Z = XV$. To get a sense of this representation, recall that $Z_{ij} = X_{i*} V_{*j}$ that is, the $(i, j)^{th}$ element of Z is the inner product of the ith row, X_{i*} of X with the jth column, V_{*j} of V. Since the latter column is a unit vector, this value Z_{ij} denotes the projection of the ith object (represented by X_{i*}) onto the jth co-ordinate dimension (represented by V_{*j}) in the new co-ordinate system. Since V is an orthonormal matrix, it can be verified that the columns of Z are geometrically orthogonal.

One challenge in eigen analysis is to determine the number of basis vectors associated with signal to retain. There are a number of techniques available, mostly based on the magnitude of the eigenvectors. A smaller number are based on eigenvector spacing (Richman, 1986).

$$\text{Define } \lambda(i, j) = \sum_{k=i}^{j} \lambda_k \quad if \quad j \geq i$$

$$= 0 \text{ otherwise}$$

Thus the ratio $\lambda(1:K)/\lambda(1:N)$ denotes the amount of "information" carried by the first K eigenvalues. The idea of data reduction relates to choosing the least value of K such that $\frac{\lambda(1:K)}{\lambda(1:N)} \geq \alpha$ (2.3)

for some pre-specified threshold α (typical value is α = 0.90). This in turn implies that the $M \times K$ matrix Z containing only the first K columns of Z contains at least 100α % of the information in the matrix X. The distinct advantage of working with Z is that it has only K $(< N)$ features each of which is geometrically orthogonal with the other. While such a test is considered useful, it is important to assess the closeness of adjacent eigenvalues to avoid intermixing of the information in adjacent eigenvectors. If two eigenvalues are separated by more than $\lambda_i * (1/M)^{1/2}$ from λ_{i+1}, then it is said to be well separated.

3. DATA ANALYSIS

The data analysis is done in two phases – the **training** phase and the **evaluation** phase.

A. Training phase: The goal of this phase is to derive a discriminant rule based on the data set with **known** classification. To this end, we first divide X_t into two parts; let X_{t1} be a $M \times N$ matrix, consisting of the first M rows of X_t and X_{t2} a $(M_t - M)\times N$ matrix with the rest of the rows in X_t. Similarly, let X_{n1} be a $M \times N$ matrix, consisting of the first M rows of X_n and X_{n2} a $(M_n - M)\times N$ matrix with the rest of the rows in X_n. The values of the parameters used in our analysis are: $t1 = n1 = M = 1{,}500$; $N = 23$, $M_t = 2{,}259$ and $M_n = 63{,}116$.

By way of applying the linear transformation described above, we first computed $S_{t1} = 1/M\ (X_{t1}^T X_{t1})$ and $S_{n1} = 1/M\ (X_{n1}^T X_{n1})$ and their respective (V_{t1}, Λ_{t1}) and (V_{n1}, Λ_{n1}) matrices using the standard procedures in MATLAB. The transformed matrices $Z_{t1} = X_{t1}V_{t1}$ and $Z_{n1} = X_{n1}V_{n1}$ are then obtained. Choosing the threshold $\alpha = 0.90$ in (2.3) it turns out that we can obtain 95% for the tornadic and non- tornadic cases by having $K = 3$, that is, the first three components. Moreover, for $K = 3$, the eigenvalue spacing between the third and fourth eigenvalues is sufficient to avoid intermixing.

Using the value $K = 3$, we then extracted $\overline{Z_{t1}}$ and $\overline{Z_{n1}}$ which are $M \times 3$ matrices. The histograms of the columns of these matrices are quite interesting in the sense that they reveal the separability between the tornadic and non-tornadic data.

Based on these histograms, we then extracted a simple discriminant rule which may be stated as follows. Let y be a row vector with 23 components denoting an input event.

Step 1: First compute the projections p_1, p_2 and p_3 of y onto the first three columns (corresponding to the three largest eigenvalues) of V_t. Similarly let q_1, q_2 and q_3 be the projections of y onto the first three columns of V_n

Step2:IF $\{(p_1 \geq\ 10000)\,AND\ (q_2 \leq\ 2500)\,AND$
$((p_3 < -1500)\ OR\ (p_3 > 1000))\}$

THEN Y is a tornado ELSE Y is a non-tornado.

B. Evaluation phase: This phase uses the data from the matrices X_{t2} and X_{n2}. First we picked a set of 200 tornadic cases at random from X_{t2} and 10,000 non-tornadic cases at random from X_{n2} to give a mix of 10,200 cases with only 2% tornadoes. We then applied the above decision rule on this data set and created a contingency table (Wilks (1995), Doswell (1990))

		OBSERVATION T	NT
PREDICTION	T	193 Hits (a)	3277 False Alarms (b)
	NT	7 Misses (c)	6723 Correct Negatives (d)

Table 1: A Typical Contingency Table for 2% tornadoes

Based on this table, we then computed the following standard measures of forecast evaluation (Wilks (1995)) - Probability of detection, False Alarm rate, Accuracy, Critical Success Index, Probability of False Detection, Bias and Heidke's Skill.

The entries in above table are random since their values depend on the chosen random sample. To reduce this inherent randomness, we repeated the above mix with 2% of tornadoes ten times with different random samples of 10,200 numbers and obtained the average and the standard deviations of each of these measures. We then repeated the above experiment by increasing the percentage of tornadoes from 2 to 22 in steps of 4. The graph showing the average and the $\pm\sigma$ error bands for each of these measures is given in Table 2. It is readily seen that the average value of POD is always above 95% which is far superior to every other method applied to this same data set. By way of comparing our result with the existing results (Trafalis et. al (2003)), we have plotted all the known results along side our results, for details refer to kakani et.al (2004).

Table 2 - Forecast Eval Indices with their Avg values and standard errors

%	POD	FAR	CSI	Accur	Bias	POFD	H.Skill
2	0.96 *0.018*	0.94 *0.003*	0.05 *0.003*	0.68 *0.017*	17.00 *0.920*	0.32 *0.018*	0.07 *0.005*
6	0.96 *0.011*	0.86 *0.021*	0.13 *0.021*	0.63 *0.064*	7.45 *1.133*	0.38 *0.068*	0.14 *0.038*
10	0.97 *0.015*	0.78 *0.035*	0.20 *0.034*	0.65 *0.067*	4.73 *0.753*	0.37 *0.074*	0.22 *0.058*
14	0.96 0.018	0.67 *0.083*	0.32 *0.082*	0.73 *0.085*	3.10 *0.679*	0.29 *0.096*	0.36 *0.117*
18	0.97 *0.017*	0.61 *0.110*	0.38 *0.108*	0.74 *0.102*	2.63 *0.665*	0.30 *0.120*	0.42 *0.150*
22	0.96 *0.016*	0.54 *0.145*	0.44 *0.142*	0.75 *0.111*	2.28 *0.613*	0.29 *0.135*	0.47 *0.180*

Several observations are in order. The new discriminant function based on the EOF has the highest POD compared to all the other methods.

The variation of these forecast indices with the increasing percentage of tornadoes for this linear method based on EOF is quantitatively very similar to those obtained using ANN which in general defines a non-linear surface of separation. The Accuracy is not strongly affected by the percentage of tornadoes used. It compares well to linear discriminant analysis. The Bias is very high at a low percentage of tornadoes and this decreases as the percentage of tornadoes increases. This conveys the high false alarm rate at low percentages of tornadoes and qualitatively similar in structure to the ANN. The two measures of overall goodness of forecast, CSI and Heidke Skill, show a fairly low skill at low percentages of tornadoes with improving skill as the percentage of tornadoes increases. At about 20%, the results are almost as high as the ANN is. Taken collectively, these forecast evaluations suggest that a well-constructed linear discriminator is almost as accurate as an ANN for the purpose of discriminating circulations that became tornadic from those that did not. Additionally, they provide a baseline to determine improvement for newer techniques, such as SVM and MPM.

4. CONCLUSION

The following is a summary of the key results reported in this paper. We have shown that there is a large overlap in the conditional distribution of the raw data (output of the radar) relating to the 23 features considered in this analysis. This clearly brings out the intrinsic difficulty of the problem of discriminating between tornadoes and non-tornadoes. This new rule achieves over 95% POD which is the highest among all the known methods.

Methodologically, our approach provides a simple, linear baseline analysis using which, other non-linear methods can be judged. Our future efforts will concentrate on expanding the initial set of 23 features to include other relevant output of the radar and examine their incremental power for discrimination especially to reduce FAR.

REFERENCES

R. Bellman (1995), *Introduction to Matrix Analysis*, SIAM, Philadelphia.

C.A. Doswell III, R. Davies-Jones, and D.Keller (1990), On summary measures of skill in rare event forecasting based on contingency tables. *Weather and Forecasting*, **5**, 576-585.

G.R. Gray, R.J. Serafin, D. Atlas, R.E. Rinehart, and J.J. Boyajian, (1975), Real-Time Color Doppler Radar Display. *Bulletin of the American Meteorological Society*,**56,** 580–588.

P. Kakani, S. Lakshmivarahan and M. Richman (2004) " A Tornado Detection Algorithm using Empirical Orthogonal Functions", Technical Report, School of Computer Science, University of Oklahoma, Norman, OK.

C. Marzban, and G.J. Stumpf, (1996), A Neural Network for Tornado Prediction Based on Doppler Radar-Derived Attributes, *Journal of Applied Meteorology*, **35**, 617-626.

C.M. Nestlerode and M.B.Richman (2003), "Analysis of Mesocyclone Detection Algorithm Attributes to Increase Tornado Detection". *REU-Final Project Report*, School of Meteorology, University of Oklahoma, Norman, OK 73019.

J.C. Platt, (1999), Fast Training of Support Vector Machines using Sequential Minimal Optimization, *Advances in Kernel Methods – Support Vector Learning*, B. Scholkopf, C. Burges, and A. Smola, eds., MIT Press.

M.B. Richman, (1986). Rotation of principal components, International J. of Climatology, 6, 293-335.

G.J. Stumpf, A. Witt, E.D. Mitchell, P.L. Spencer, J.T. Johnson, Michael. D. Eilts, K.W. Thomas, and D.W. Burgess (1998), The National Severe Storms Laboratory Mesocyclone Detection Algorithm for the WSR-88D*, *Weather and Forecasting,* **13**, 304-326.

T.B.Trafalis, B.Santosa and M.B. Richman (2003), Tornado Detection with Kernel-Based Methods. ",*Intelligent Engineering Systems Through Artificial Neural Networks*, (C.H. Dagli, A.L. Buczak, J. Ghosh, M.J. Embrechts, O. Ersoy, and S.W. Kercel, eds.), ASME Press, **13,** 677-682.

D.S. Wilks,(1995), *Statistical Methods in Atmospheric Sciences*. Academic Press, London.

IDENTIFICATION OF THE RADIAL BASIS FUNCTION NETWORKS BY USING THE MULTI-LAYERED GMDH-TYPE NEURAL NETWORK ALGORITHM

TADASHI KONDO
School of Health Sciences,
The University of Tokushima,
Tokushima 770-8509, Japan

ABHIJIT S. PANDYA
Computer Sciences & Engineering,
Florida Atlantic University,
Boca Raton, FL33431,U.S.A.

ABSTRACT

In this study, the multi-layered GMDH(Group Method of Data Handling)-type neural network algorithm with radial basis functions is proposed. This algorithm can generate optimum radial basis function type neural network architectures fitting the complexity of nonlinear system so as to minimize the error criterion defined as PSS (Prediction Sum of Squares) or AIC (Akaike's Information Criterion). The multi-layered GMDH-type neural networks are organized by using the heuristic self-organization method and have abilities of self-selecting the number of layers, the number of neurons in the hidden layers and the useful input variables. Therefore, it is very easy to find out the optimum neural network architectures fitting the complexity of nonlinear system by using the multi-layered GMDH-type neural network algorithm.

INTRODUCTION

The GMDH-type neural networks and their applications have been proposed in our early works (Kondo 1998, Kondo, Pandya and Zurada 1999a and Kondo, Pandya and Zurada 1999b). The GMDH-type neural networks can automatically organize the neural network architecture by using the heuristic self-organization method (Ivakhnenko 1970) and they can also determine structural parameters such as the number of layers, the number of neurons in the hidden layers and the useful input variables. These structural parameters are automatically determined so as to minimize the error criterion defined as PSS (Allen 1974) or AIC (Akaike 1974).

In this study, the multi-layered GMDH-type neural network algorithm with radial basis functions is proposed. The multi-layered GMDH-type neural network algorithm with radial basis functions is a revised algorithm based on the conventional GMDH-type neural networks. The resulting neural network is then applied to the identification problem of the complex nonlinear system, and the results are compared with those obtained by the GMDH algorithm and the conventional radial basis function type neural networks.

THE MULTI-LAYERED GMDH-TYPE NEURAL NETWORK ALGORITHM WITH RADIAL BASIS FUNCTIONS

The multi-layered GMDH-type neural networks with radial basis functions have a common feedforward multi-layered architecture. This neural networks are organized by using the heuristic self-organization method. But this algorithm does not need the separation of the original data into the training and test sets because PSS and AIC can be used instead of test errors. So all the data are used as the training data.

PSS is described by the following equation:

$$PSS = \sum_{\alpha=1}^{n} (\phi_\alpha - y_\alpha^*)^2 \tag{1}$$

where

$$y_\alpha^* = b_{0\alpha} + b_{1\alpha}x_{i\alpha} + b_{2\alpha}x_{j\alpha} + b_{3\alpha}x_{i\alpha}x_{j\alpha} + b_{4\alpha}x_{i\alpha}^2 + b_{5\alpha}x_{j\alpha}^2, \quad \alpha=1,2,\ldots,n \tag{2}$$

n is the number of training data, ϕ_α is the α-th observed value for the output variable, $x_{i\alpha}$ is the α-th observed value for the input variable x_i and y_α^* is the α-th estimated value obtained by the linear regression analysis of all the data except the α-th datum. In order to compute PSS of Eq. (1), the linear regression analysis must be repeated n times, and the amount of computation increases in the number of data. But PSS of Eq. (1) can be reduced as follows,

$$PSS = \sum_{\alpha=1}^{n} \left((\phi_\alpha - y_\alpha)/(1 - \mathbf{x}_\alpha^{\mathrm{T}}(\mathrm{X}^{\mathrm{T}}\mathrm{X})^{-1}\mathbf{x}_\alpha) \right)^2 \tag{3}$$

where

$$y_\alpha = b_0 + b_1x_{i\alpha} + b_2x_{j\alpha} + b_3x_{i\alpha}x_{j\alpha} + b_4x_{i\alpha}^2 + b_5x_{j\alpha}^2, \tag{4}$$

$$\mathbf{x}_\alpha^T = [1,\ x_{i\alpha},\ x_{j\alpha},\ x_{i\alpha}x_{j\alpha},\ x_{i\alpha}^2,\ x_{j\alpha}^2], \quad \alpha=1,2,\ldots,n \tag{5}$$

$$\mathrm{X}^{\mathrm{T}} = [\ \mathbf{x}_1,\ \mathbf{x}_2,\ \ldots,\ \mathbf{x}_n\ ] \tag{6}$$

y_α is the α-th estimated value obtained by the linear regression analysis of all the data. With this procedure, we need not repeat the regression analysis n times. In the multi-layered GMDH-type neural network algorithm, Eq.(4) is called as the partial description of the nonlinear system.

In the multi-layered GMDH-type neural network algorithm, we can also use the error criterion defined as AIC to organize the optimum network architecture.

AIC is described by the following equations:

$$AIC = n\ \log_e S_m^2 + 2(m+1) + C \tag{7}$$

$$S_m^2 = \sum_{\alpha=1}^{n} (\phi_\alpha - y_\alpha)^2 / n \tag{8}$$

$$y_\alpha = b_0 + b_1x_{i\alpha} + b_2x_{j\alpha} + b_3x_{i\alpha}x_{j\alpha} + b_4x_{i\alpha}^2 + b_5x_{j\alpha}^2 \qquad \alpha=1,2,\ldots,n \tag{9}$$

Here, m is the number of terms in Eq.(9), n is the number of training data and C is a constant.

The procedures for determining the architecture of the multi-layered GMDH-type neural networks with radial basis functions conform to the following:

(1) The first layer

$$u_j = x_j \quad (j=1,2,\ldots,p) \tag{10}$$

where x_j $(j=1,2,\ldots,p)$ are the input variables of the system, and p is the number of input variables. In the first layer, the output variables are equal to the input variables.

(2) The second layer

Many combination of r input variables are generated. For each combination, the neuron architectures are automatically selected from the following neurons so as to minimize PSS or AIC value.

i) The first type neuron

Σ: (Nonlinear function)

$$z_k = w_1u_i + w_2u_j + w_3u_iu_j + w_4u_i^2 + w_5u_j^2 + w_6u_i^3 + w_7u_i^2u_j + w_8u_iu_j^2 + w_9u_j^3 - w_0\theta_1 \tag{11}$$

f : (Nonlinear function)

$$y_k = exp\ (-z_k^2) \quad (12)$$

Here, $\theta_1 = 1$ and $w_i\ (i=0,1,2,\ldots,9)$ are the weights between the first and second layer. The value of r, which is the number of input variables u in each neuron, is set to two for the first type neuron.

ii) The second type neuron

Σ: (Linear function)

$$z_k = w_1u_1 + w_2u_2 + w_3u_3 + \cdots + w_ru_r - w_0\theta_1 \ \ (r<p) \quad (13)$$

f : (Nonlinear function)

$$y_k = exp\ (-z_k^2) \quad (14)$$

Here, $\theta_1 = 1$ and $w_i\ (i=0,1,2,\ldots,r)$ are the weights between the first and second layer. The value of r, which is the number of input variables u in each neuron, is set to be greater than two and smaller than p for the second type neuron. Here p is the number of input variables x_i $(i=1,2,\ldots,p)$.

The optimum neuron architecture for each combination is selected from the first and the second type neuronal architectures. The weights $w_i\ (i=0,1,2,\ldots)$ are estimated by the stepwise regression analysis using PSS or AIC.

Only useful variables in Eq.(11) and Eq.(13) are selected by the stepwise regression analysis using PSS or AIC and the optimum neuronal architectures are organized by the selected useful variables.

From these generated neurons, the L neurons which minimize PSS or AIC value are selected. The output variables y_k of L selected neurons are set to the input variables of the neurons in the third layer.

(3) The third and succeeding layers

In the third and succeeding layers, the same computation of the second layer is iterated until PSS or AIC value of L neurons stop decreasing. When iterative computation is terminated, the neural network architectures are produced by the selected neurons in each layer.

By using these procedures, the multi-layered GMDH-type neural networks with radial basis functions can be organized.

APPLICATION TO THE NONLINEAR SYSTEM IDENTIFICATION

The nonlinear system is assumed to be described by the following equations:

$$\phi = f_1(x_1, x_2, x_3) / f_2(x_1, x_2, x_3) + \varepsilon \quad (15)$$

$$f_1(x_1, x_2, x_3) = 1.0 + 2.0\, x_1^2 x_2 + 3.0\, x_2^2 x_3 \quad (16)$$

$$f_2(x_1, x, x_3) = 1.0 + 2.0exp(x_1) + 3.0exp(x_1x_2) + 4.0exp(x_3) \quad (17)$$

Here, ϕ is the output variable and $x_1 \sim x_3$ are the input variables and ε is the Gaussian white noise which is N(0, 0.005^2). An additional input, x_4, is added as the input variable of the neural networks in order to check that the multi-layered GMDH-type neural networks can detect and eliminate useless input variables. The neural networks are organized by using twenty training data. Twenty other data are used to check the prediction and generalization ability.

The identification results obtained by using the multi-layered GMDH-type neural networks with radial basis functions

In both cases of AIC and PSS criterion, the same architecture of the radial basis function type neural networks was identified by the multi-layered GMDH-type neural network algorithm. The identification results of the multi-layered GMDH-type neural networks are shown as follows:

(1) Input variables.

Four input variables were used, but the useless input variable x_4 was automatically eliminated.

(2) Number of selected neurons in each layer.

Four neurons were selected in each hidden layer.

(3) Variation of AIC.

The variation of AIC is shown in Fig.1. AIC values converged at the fourth layer.

(4) Variation of PSS criterion.

The variation of PSS is shown in Fig.2. PSS values also converged at the fourth layer.

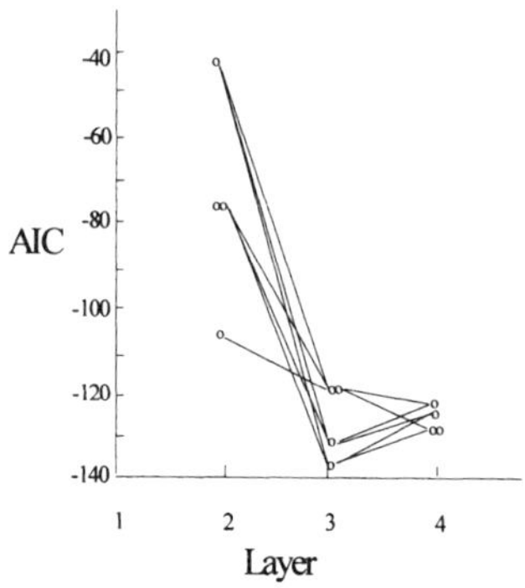

Fig.1 Variation of AIC in the multi-layered GMDH-type neural networks

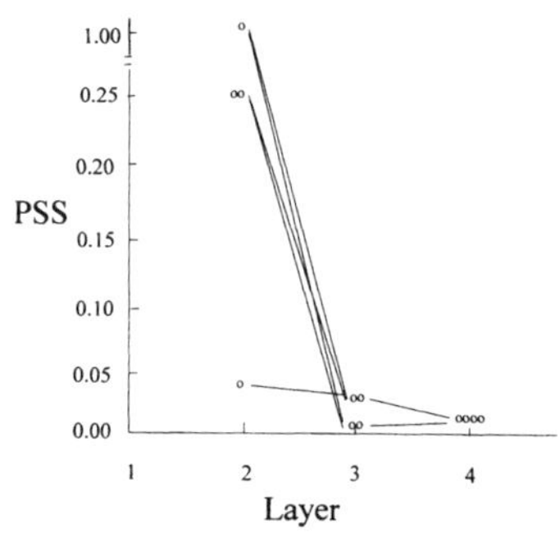

Fig.2 Variation of PSS in the multi-layered GMDH-type neural networks

(5) Architecture of the neural networks.

The calculation of the multi-layered GMDH-type neural networks was terminated at the fourth layer and the neurons of the third layer had minimum AIC and PSS values. Therefore, three layered neural network architecture was organized. The first layer is the input layer and the second layer is the hidden layer and the third layer is the output layer.

(6) Estimation accuracy.

The estimation accuracy was evaluated by using the following equation:

$$J_1 = \sum_{i=1}^{20} |\phi_i - \phi_i^*| / 20 \qquad (18)$$

where ϕ_i $(i = 1,2,\cdots,20)$ were the actual values with the Gaussian white noise ε and ϕ_i^* $(i=1,2,\cdots,20)$ were the estimated values by the multi-layered GMDH-type neural networks. ϕ_i $(i = 1,2,\cdots,20)$ ware used to organize the multi-layered GMDH-type neural networks. The value of J_1 is shown in Table1. In this table, Multi GMDH-NN shows the multi-layered GMDH-type neural networks and GMDH shows the GMDH networks and conventional RBF-NN shows the conventional radial basis function type neural networks.

(7) Prediction accuracy.

The prediction accuracy was evaluated by using the following equation:

$$J_2 = \sum_{i=21}^{40} |\phi_i - \phi_i^*| / 20 \qquad (19)$$

where ϕ_i $(i = 21, 22, \cdots, 40)$ were the actual values with the Gaussian white noise ε and ϕ_i^* $(i = 21, 22, \cdots, 40)$ were the predicted values by the multi-layered GMDH-type neural networks. ϕ_i $(i = 21, 22, \cdots, 40)$ were not used to organize the multi-layered GMDH-type neural networks and were used to check the generalization ability. The value of J_2 is shown in Table1 and is very small. From this prediction result, we can see that the multi-layered GMDH-type neural networks do not overfit the training data and have good generalization ability.

Table 1 Identification results of three methods

Method	J1	J2	Layer
Multi GMDH-NN (PSS)	0.00928	0.01075	3
Multi GMDH-NN (AIC)	0.00928	0.01075	3
GMDH (PSS)	0.04094	0.03829	5
GMDH (AIC)	0.03991	0.04526	4
Conventional RBF-NN	0.03282	0.03071	3

(8) Estimated and predicted values.

The estimated and predicted values of ϕ by the multi-layered GMDH-type neural networks are shown in Fig.3. We can see that the estimated and predicted values are very accurate.

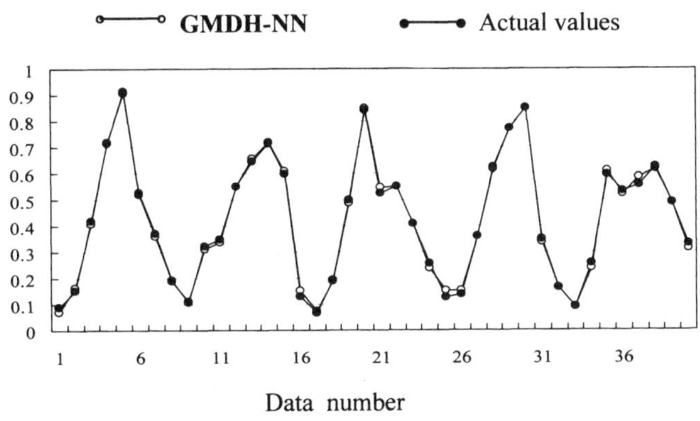

Fig.3 Estimated and predicted values by the multi-layered GMDH-type neural networks

The identification results obtained by the GMDH algorithm.

The architectures of the polynomial type networks identified by the GMDH algorithm using AIC ware different from those identified by the GMDH algorithm using PSS criterion.

In the case of the GMDH algorithm using AIC, the GMDH calculation converged at the fourth layer and the neurons of the fourth layer had the minimum AIC value. Therefore, four layered polynomial type networks were organized.

In the case of the GMDH algorithm using PSS, the GMDH calculation converged at the fifth layer and the neurons of the fifth layer had the minimum PSS value. Therefore, five layered polynomial type networks were organized.

The estimation accuracy was evaluated by using Eq.(18) and the prediction accuracy was evaluated by using Eq.(19). The values of J_1 and J_2 are shown in Table1.

The identification results of the conventional RBF neural networks.

In the conventional radial basis function type neural networks, the neural network was developed as a three layered architecture. Four input variables were used in the input layer and twenty neurons were used in the hidden layer. The weights of the neural networks were estimated by using the regression method. The estimation accuracy was evaluated by using Eq.(18) and the prediction accuracy was evaluated by using Eq.(19). The values of J_1 and J_2 are shown in Table1

From these identification results, both estimation and prediction errors (J_1 and J_2) of the multi-layered GMDH-type neural networks were the smallest of the three identified models and the estimated and predicted values of ϕ by the multi-layered GMDH-type neural networks are very accurate.

CONCLUSION

In this study, the multi-layered GMDH-type neural network algorithm with radial basis functions was proposed. This algorithm can automatically organize the multi-layered radial basis function type neural network architecture fitting the complexity of the nonlinear system by using the heuristic self-organization method. It is very easy to apply this algorithm to the identification problem of the practical complex nonlinear system because the structural parameters such as the number of layers, the number of neurons in the hidden layers and the useful input variables are automatically determined so as to minimize PSS or AIC. This algorithm was applied to the nonlinear system identification problem and it was shown that this algorithm was a very useful method.

REFERENCES

Akaike H., 1974, " A new look at the statistical model identification", *IEEE Trans. Automatic Control*, Vol.AC-19, No.6, pp.716-723.

Allen D.M., 1974, " The relationship between variable selection and data augmentation and a method for prediction" , *Technometrics,* Vol. 16, No.1, pp.125-127.

Ivakhnenko A.G., 1970, " Heuristic self-organization in problems of engineering cybernetics", *Automatica*, Vo.6, No.2, pp.207-219.

Kondo T, 1998, "GMDH neural network algorithm using the heuristic self-organization method and its application to the pattern identification problem", *Proc. of the 37th SICE Annual Conference*, pp.1143-1148.

Kondo T, Pandya A.S., Zurada J.M., 1999a, "GMDH-type neural networks with a feedback loop and their application to nonlinear system identification", *Intelligent Engineering Systems through Artificial Neural Networks*, ASME Press, Vol.9, pp.117-124.

Kondo T., Pandya A.S.and Zurada J.M., 1999b, "Logistic GMDH-type neural networks and their application to the identification of the X-ray film characteristic curve", *Proceeding of IEEE international conference on systems, man and cybernetics*, Vol.1, pp.437-442.

A COMPARISON OF MACHINE LEARNING APPROACHES TO PROMOTER RECOGNITION AND PCR PRIMER DESIGN

JAWAD AZIM and STEFAN C. KREMER
Dept. of Computing and Information Science, University of Guelph
Guelph, ON N1G 2W1, CANADA {skremer|jazim}@uoguelph.ca

ABSTRACT
This paper looks at a number of approaches to recognizing genetic sequences that have been proposed in the literature and compares their performance on two different DNA datasets. Specifically, we compare genetic algorithms, formal grammar induction and several artificial neural network approaches to sequential pattern recognition. The problems we study are PCR primer design and promoter recognition. In a field where many new approaches are developed extremely frequently, this is the first objective comparison of these techniques on these problems. It thus provides a critical review of the in-practice effectiveness of these particular approaches and a point of comparison for future approaches.

1 INTRODUCTION

This paper is organized as follows. In Section 2 we introduce the problem of identifying specific DNA sub-sequences, called "promoters", that serve as the starting points for RNA synthesis and subsequently protein manufacture. Then, in Section 3, we talk about the process of using PCR primers for DNA amplification and the problem of designing effective primers. After these motivating sections, we turn our attention to machine learning approaches to sequence classification in Section 4. Next, in Section 5 we perform some experiments applying the machine learning techniques to the two bio-sequence problems. We present some conclusions and directions for future research in the last section.

2 PROMOTERS

The underlying operational components of almost all metabolic processes are proteins. These proteins are manufactured from RNA templates which serve as blueprints. The RNA, in turn, is synthesized from DNA in a process called transcription. RNA synthesis is initiated by the enzyme known as RNA polymerase which binds to a specific region of the DNA called a promoter. For *E. Coli* bacteria, the promoter is marked by two common patterns that indicate the start of RNA transcription. The typical patterns, called consensus sequences, are referred to as the -35 and -10 regions. That is, -35 and -10 bases upstream of the transcription start location. In the majority of cases, the consensus sequences are separated by a spacer of length 17 bases whereas the -10 region and the transcription start site are separated by a spacer of length 7 bases but sometimes the separations are 16 and 6 bases respectively. Additionally, while the sequences typically consist of the patterns "TTGACA" and 'TTAACT" in some cases other sequences (e.g. "TTCCAA" and "TATCT") occur instead.

Our machine learning problem, in this case, is to try and classify DNA sequences as promoters or non-promoter instances given that we have available a set of promoters that has already been tested and classified experimentally using methods from the biological literature. A data set containing DNA promoter sequences has been compiled by (Hershberg et al., 2001) for the *E. Coli* bacteria. The database (Hershberg et al., 2001) contains 468 promoter sequences, each of which is 65 bases in length. Since the data set contains no examples of non-promoter sequences for the *E. Coli* bacteria. By non-promoter sequence examples of the *E. Coli* we mean DNA sequences of the *E. Coli* bacteria, we have located another data set which contains examples of non-promoter *E. Coli* sequences from the machine learning data repository at the University of California at Irvine. The data set is composed of 53 promoter and 53 non-promoter instance respectively. Since it is not sufficient to have only 53 non-promoter sequences in our data set versus 468 promoters, (following (Ma and Wang, 1999)) we concatenated all 53 non-promoter instances into one very long sequence and randomly selected 465 sequences of length 65. Therefore, in total, our data set which we will call the "Promoter Set", contains 933 sequences with a 50%-50% distribution.

3 PCR PRIMER DESIGN

The Polymerase Chain Reaction (PCR) is a technique used in molecular genetics in order to copy/amplify specific DNA fragments so they can be more easily identified and analysed. This technique has had many applications in areas such as diagnostics, molecular evolution, forensics and genetic engineering (Lo, 1997). The copying of a DNA sequence is initiated by a pair of small DNA strands, called primers, which initiate transcription of the sequence from each end. There exist several primer picking programs such as the Primer 3 program from the NCSA Biology Workbench. In order for the reaction to proceed efficiently, the two primers must roughly have the same melting temperature; must not anneal in more than one place on the target DNA; must not anneal to one another themselves, or other instances of themselves. In this paper, we will assume that a candidate primer sequence can take on any of three labels: amplify correctly, fail to amplify or amplify multiple targets.

Our task is to identify whether a DNA sequence would make an effective primer. We have available a set of primers that has already been classified and tested within the context of a project. This problem has been tackled by (Ashlock et al., 2002) where finite state machines were trained to classify PCR primers using a genetic algorithm. The data set used in (Ashlock et al., 2002) is that of the *Zea mays* (corn) and contains a total of 1390 primer sequences of length 17-25 bases. Of the 1390 sequences, 880 are classified as "good primers", 86 as "multiple primers" and 424 as "bad primers". We will call the data set containing the sequences the "Primer Set".

4 MACHINE LEARNING FOR BIO-SEQUENCE CLASSIFICATION

Due to the availability of high-throughput sequences analysers, there has recently been an explosion in the amount of genetic data available in on-line repositories. As the volume of bioinformatic data grows at an exponential rate, the challenge of analysing the data and extracting useful information at a similar speed becomes more and more difficult. A number of machine learning approaches have been proposed to analyse and process the volumes of data in an automated fashion (Baldi and Soren, 2001). One of the most common analysis tasks is the classification of biological sequences such as DNA into meaningful categories. In the machine learning community, a number of approaches have been developed for classifying inherently sequential data. These approaches must meet the following criteria: they must be able to classify sequences of varying lengths, and they must be able to classify sequences based on shift-invariant properties of the sequence.

4.1 RECURRENT NEURAL NETWORKS

Recurrent Neural Networks (RNNs) are artificial neural networks (ANNs) with recurrent, time-delayed connections. These special connections afford a kind of short-term memory in that node activations at a given time (called context) can influence the same or other activations at a later time. This short-term memory is in sharp contrast to the long-term memory usually found in the form of connection weights. While the former varies quickly within a few input presentations, the latter is only adapted during the training processes and changes much more slowly. A large number of RNNs have been proposed. For a detailed review see (Kolen and Kremer, 2001). In this paper we will focus on only 3 architectures.

Stornetta *et al.*, 1988. In this architecture, the input layer acts as both an input and a context layer by making the input units "capacitive", i.e., the input layer is fed by the external input as well as the previous input to the network. The architecture consists of three different layers (Figure 1(a)). where all the layers are fully connected to one another. Values of successive input/context nodes are computed according to the following Equation: $X_{i+1} = \alpha I_{i+1} + dX_i$ where, X_i is the value computed by an input node at time t_i, I_i is the input signal to the same node at the same time step, α is the fixed input amplitude and d is the fixed decay rate. The standard back-propagation algorithm can be used to train the network.

Mozer, 1989. This network consists of four different layers: an input layer, a context layer, a hidden layer and an output layer. Figure 1(b) contains a diagram of the architecture All layers are fully connected to one another and there exist self-recurrent connections within the context layer. In this case, as opposed to Stornetta, the recurrent connections are trainable. Hence, the standard back-propagation algorithm cannot be used to train this network. Instead, Mozer introduces a special learning algorithm called focused back-propagation the details of which can be found in the original publication.

Elman, 1990. This architecture is known as the Simple Recurrent Network (SRN). The SRN is composed of four different layers: an input layer, a context layer, a hidden layer and an output layer. Figure 1(c) contains a diagram of the architecture. There exist one-to-one recurrent connections from the hidden layer to the context layer with fixed weight set equal to one. Both the input and context units are used to activate the hidden units and then the hidden units feed forward to activate the output units (Elman, 1990). It should be noted here that Elman's training method assumes that the gradient of the activations of the context units with respect to the network weights is zero and hence uses the standard back propagation algorithm for training, even though the values of the context units do actually depend on the weights within the network.

4.2 GRAMMAR INDUCTION ALGORITHMS

Computer scientists and linguistic theorists have been using grammars and automata for many decades to represent strings of discrete symbols. Grammar Induction (GI) refers to the process of identifying an unknown grammar from a set of example strings. Recently there has been much development in this area, particularly focussed on the induction of finite-state automata (or equivalently regular expressions). In particular, a number of recent publications have addressed the issue of inducing random finite state automata from small sets of example strings. A comprehensive survey is found in (Cicchello and Kremer, 2003).

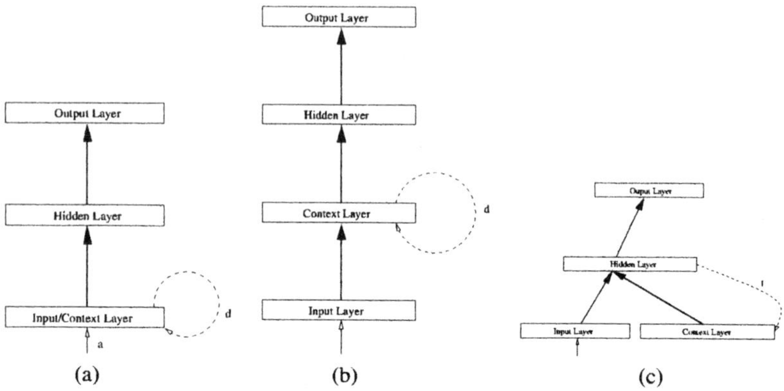

Figure 1: **Three architectures investigated.** Thick bold arrows represent full connectivity. (a) Architecture and figure adapted from (Stornetta et al., 1988). Dotted arrow represents one-to-one recurrent connections with fixed weight *d*. (b) Architecture and figure adapted from (Mozer, 1989). Dotted arrows represents one-to-one recurrent connections with trainable weights *d*. (c) Architecture and figure adapted from (Elman, 1990). Dotted arrow represents one-to-one recurrent connections with fixed weight 1.

While these algorithms have been very successful in inducing large random automata, this paper presents the first results of applying these approaches to a real-world problem.

TraxBar (Trakhtenbrot and Barzdin, 1973). This algorithm laid the foundation for the algorithms which were developed after it including the TBW-EDSM algorithm which we will dscribe in the next sub-section. TraxBar is guaranteed to produce a Moore-Minimized FSA, in polynomial time, given that it has the complete data set of a given language (Cicchello and Kremer, 2002). First, the set of training strings is converted into an augment prefix tree acceptor. This representation places the start of each string at the root node and then forms a tree with each symbol of the string on a tree branch. The algorithm then proceeds as follows:

- Consider the root of the APTA as a unique node and append it to the current empty list of unique nodes.
- While visiting each successive node (λ) of the APTA in breadth-first order, compare the sub-tree rooted at λ with the sub-tree rooted at each node in the unique nodes list.
- If λ is pairwise distinguishable from each node in the unique list, append λ to the end of the list.
- Otherwise, disconnect λ from the APTA by redirecting all transitions leading to λ to point to the first node encountered from the list of unique nodes with which λ is indistinguishable.

TraxBar-Windowed Evidence Driven State Merging (TBW-EDSM) This algorithm is an extension of the original TraxBar approach, where instead of always selecting the nodes to merge in breadth-first order, multiple merge candidates chosen from a window are examined and evaluated. The best of the candidates is then selected for merging and the process continues.

- for i in 1, ..., t

- Merge only the ith pair of indistinguishable nodes that in encountered with the breadth-first traversal of the APTA.
- For the remainder of the induction process evaluate all the nodes within a window of candidates using a simple heuristic and select the best for merging.
- Select the best results for all i.

where t is the total number of merge pairs that are to be used as the alternative first merge.

4.3 GENETIC ALGORITHMS

Our final approach to tackling our biological sequences is based on a recent study in rule induction by Ashlock *et al.* (Ashlock et al., 2002) employs a genetic algorithm to evolve FSA in order to classify PCR primers as good/bad primers.

The algorithm uses a FSA as its representation where a given FSA is composed of 64 states. The FSA uses the bases of a primer sequence (A, C, G and T) for its transitions as it is fed a sequence. In this case, the states of the FSA can take on any of the following three labels: + (good primer), - (bad primer) and ? (don't know). That is, if a FSA is fed a primer sequence and by the time it reaches the last base in the sequence it is at a state labeled + then the sequence is classified as a primer that does work, if it is at a state labeled '-' then the sequence is classified as a primer that does not work and if it is at a state labeled ? then the sequence could not be classified. Such labels allow the FSA to function as a classifier (Ashlock et al., 2002).

Ashlock *et al.* (Ashlock et al., 2002) measured the fitness of a given FSA as the FSA is driven by a primer. After the the training process is completed, primers are fed to the FSA with the highest fitness. The FSA then classifies a given primer by keeping track of how many +, -, or ? states it saw. If the majority of state labels were +, then the primer is classified as good, if the majority of state labels were -, then the primer is classified as bad and if the majority of labels encountered is ? then the primer is classified as unknown.

The following is a summary of the evolutionary computation method as proposed by Ashlock *et al.* (Ashlock et al., 2002). It discusses several features of the genetic algorithm that were used such as, the population size, the selection criteria, the breeding criteria and the mutation criteria.

- A population of 600 FSAs is evolved for 100 generations.
- The selection criteria is based on a size 4 tournament selection.
- The selected chromosomes (this is a string representation of a FSA) are subjected to 2-point crossover.
- During mutation, the initial state of the FSA is modified 10% of the time, a new transition for a randomly selected state is done 30% of the time and a state label is modefied 60% of the time.

5 RESULTS

Results are presented in Table 1. We examined performance: (a) using all the data as both training and test sets, and (b) using 90% of the data, selected randomly, for testing and the reamining 10% for training. Results presented are the average of 10 independent trials in each case.

6 CONCLUSION

In this paper, we applied six different machine learning methods to two DNA sequence classification problems. Our findings show that while many of the methods can easily obtain high performance on the training data, getting comparable performance on an unseen test set is no small feat. Our results suggest that the grammar induction and genetic algorithm approaches are more prone to overfitting the training data and performing poorly on the test data than the neural network approaches. We hope that the results presented here will form a starting point for other comparisons of machine learning problems for these and other biological sequences. A more detailed analysis can be found in (Azim, 2004).

ACKNOWLEDGEMENTS

Prof. Kremer is funded by grants from the NSERC, CFI, ORDCF and OIT.

REFERENCES

Ashlock, D., Wittrock, A., and Wen, T.-J. (2002). Training finite state machines to improve PCR primer design. *In Proc. of the 2002 Congress on Evolutionary Computation CEC2002*, pages 13–18.

Azim, J. (2004). Machine learning approaches to artificial and DNA language recongition. Master's thesis, CIS, University of Guelph.

Baldi, P. and Soren, B. (2001). *Bioinformatics: The Machine Learning Approach*. MIT Press.

Cicchello, O. and Kremer, S. C. (2002). Beyond EDSM. In *In Proc. of the International Colloquium on Grammatical Inference*, pages 37–48.

Cicchello, O. and Kremer, S. C. (2003). Inducing grammars from sparse data sets: A survey of algorithms and results. *Journal of Machine Learning Research*.

Elman, J. L. (1990). Finding structure in time. *Cognitive Science*.

Hershberg, R., Bejerano, G., Zavaleta, A. S., and Margalit, H. (2001). An updated database of Escherichia Coli mRNA promoters with experimentally indentified transcriptional start sites. *Nucleic Acids Research*, 29:277–00. Available on-line at `http://bioinfo.md.huji.ac.il/marg/`.

Kolen, J. F. and Kremer, S. C. (2001). *A Field Guide to Dynamical Recurrent Networks*. IEEE Press.

Lo, T. (1997). Detection and identification of Actinobacillus Pleuropaneumoniae Serotype 5 by multiplex polymearse chain reaction. Master's thesis, Virginia Polytechnic Institute and State University.

Ma, Q. and Wang, J. (1999). Recognizing promoters in dna using bayesian neural networks.

Mozer, M. C. (1989). A focused backpropagation algorithm for temporal pattern recognition. *Complex Systems*, 3:349–381.

Stornetta, W., Hogg, T., and Huberman, B. (1988). A dynamical approach to temporal pattern processing. In *Neural Information Processing Systems*, pages 750–759.

Trakhtenbrot, B. A. and Barzdin, Y. M. (1973). *Finite Automata Behavior and Synthesis*. North-Holland Publishing Company.

(a) Performance on training data:

	Stornetta	**Elman**	**Mozer**	**Traxbar**	**TBW-EDSM**	**EC**
Promoters	81.1%	50.4%	58.4%	100.0%	100.0%	-
Primers	67.3%	63.3%	63.3%	98.4%	98.4%	71.5%

(b) Performance on unseen test data:

	Stornetta	**Elman**	**Mozer**	**Traxbar**	**TBW-EDSM**	**EC**
Promoters	78.9%	55.6%	54.8%	65.6%	74.5	-
Primers	60.8%	62.6%	62.6%	48.2%	42.5%	55.9%

Table 1: Summary of results.

COLLISION AVOIDANCE FOR MULTI-AGV BY LEARNING COLLISION

MASASHI FURUKAWA
Asahikawa National College of Technology
ASAHIKAWA, JAPAN

MICHIKO WATANABE
Asahikawa National College of Technology
ASAHIKAWA, JAPAN

MASAHIRO KINOSHITA
Hokkaido Institute of Technology
SAPPRO, JAPAN

KATSUMI HAMA
Hakodate National College of Technology
HAKODATE, JAPAN

TAKASHI KAWAKAMI
Hokkaido Institute of Technology
SAPPRO, JAPAN

NORIHIKO TAKATORI
Rakuno Gakuen University
EBETSU, JAPAN

KEITARO NARUSE
Aizu University
AIZU, JAPAN

YUKINORI KAKAZU
Hokkaido University
SAPPORO, JAPAN

ABSTRACT

This paper represents a new collision avoidance method, which is based on reinforcement learning for multi-AGV. In order to realize the collision avoidance among multi-AGV, at first, multi-AGV learns how to make collision. Q-learning is employed to multi-AGV for acquiring their collision course knowledge. Then, multi-AGV oppositely makes use of this knowledge to avoid their collision. The reason why an indirect decision way is adopted is that pursuing other AGV is easier than avoiding one by learning. Numerical experiments are attempted in case when two to six AGVs meet at the same place. Results verify that all AGVs can stray out their course to avoid collisions among multi-AGV and return to their own courses.

INTRODUCTION

An intelligent material handling system is an important sub-system to contribute the production system. Especially, an automatically guided vehicle (AGV) plays a central role in the intelligent material handling system, because it has a high degree of freedom to move on a factory floor.

There are several researches on the autonomous AGV navigation problem (Beaufrere B. and Zeghloul S. (1995), Canny J. (1989), Kaihara T., Fujii S. and Kunimasa S. (1998)),

Watanabe M., Furukawa M. and Kakazu Y. (2000)). These researches only pay attention on collision avoidance. The proposed method in this study deals with the problem for chasing and catching a moving object instead of directly dealing with the collision avoidance problem. Namely, we propose an indirect approach to the collision avoidance problem.

An Advantage for the indirect approach is as follows. A region including collision courses among multi-AGV is smaller than one excluding the collision courses, because there are many possible courses to avoid collisions. Once AGV can learn the collision course against other AGV, it has only to avoid the collision courses. Therefore, avoiding collision courses is easily accomplished by unselecting acquired collision knowledge.

In the followings, at first, AGVs' collision problem and its inverse problem are formulated.Then, AGVs are defined as learning automaton. After that Chapter 4 shows results of numerical experiments are shown and finally concluding remarks are described.

AGVS COLLISION AVOIDANCE PROBLEM

Let A and B define two AGVs, respectively. Also, let $a(t)$ and $b(t)$ define actions of two AGVs, A and B at instance t, respectively. When V represents a set of possible actions of AGV, actions of two AGVs are $a(t),\ b(t) \in V$. The possible actions of AGV are, for example, acceleration, velocities, and steering angles of AGV, which usually determine moving directions of AGV. Let $R_A(a(t))$ and $R_B(b(t))$ be sensing regions determined by actions $a(t)$ and $b(t)$ at instance t, respectively. The AGVs' collision avoidance problem is formulated as follows.

$$\begin{aligned}&\text{Find } [a(T), a(T+1), \cdots, a(T+N)]\\ &\text{such that } R_A(a(T+i)) \cap R_B(b(T+i)) = \phi \quad (i = 1, 2, \ldots N)\end{aligned} \tag{1}$$

where T is a current time, and N is the instance counted forward from the current time T.

On the other hand, a collision problem is described as

$$\begin{aligned}&\text{Find } [a^*(T), a^*(T+1), \cdots, a^*(T+N)]\\ &\text{such that } R_A(a(T+i)) \cap R_B(b(T+i)) \neq \phi \quad (i = 1, 2, \ldots N)\end{aligned} \tag{2}$$

From two above formulations, it becomes possible to write

$$a(T+i) = \mathrm{V} - a^*(T+i) \quad (i = 1, 2, \ldots, n) \tag{3}$$

As a result, it is possible to think that a collision problem is an inverse problem of a collision avoidance problem.

MODELLING AGVS AS LEARNING AUTOMATON

In order to model multi-AGV, an agent concept is introduced. Namely, multi-AGV is modeled as the agents by automaton.

Preconditions

The following preconditions are assumed to model AGV as an agent.

(1) AGV has five sensors ahead of AGV itself. Each sensor recognizes an object (other AGV) in a limited sector area as shown in Fig. 1.

(2) Each sector area is divided into three areas depending on a distance measured from the sensor, namely a close area, middle one, and far one.

(3) The sensor recognizes the object moving within one of the divided area.

Automaton model

AGV is represented as an automaton. The automaton is usually defined by quintuple as (S, I, O, F, G), where S, I, O, F, and G represent a state, an input, an output, a state transition function, and an output function, respectively. Let a set of multi-AGV be defined by

$$A = \{A_i : i = 1, 2, \cdots, n\} \tag{4}$$

where n is the number of AGVs. Then, each vehicle is defined in the form of the automaton as follows;

$$A_i = (I_i, O_i, S_i, F_i, G_i) \tag{5}$$

where I_i, O_i, S_i, F_i, and G_i represent an input, output, state, state transition function, and output function, respectively. As far as not misunderstanding a suffix, the suffix i is removed from each entity in A_i in the followed discussion. Each entity is illustrated as follows.

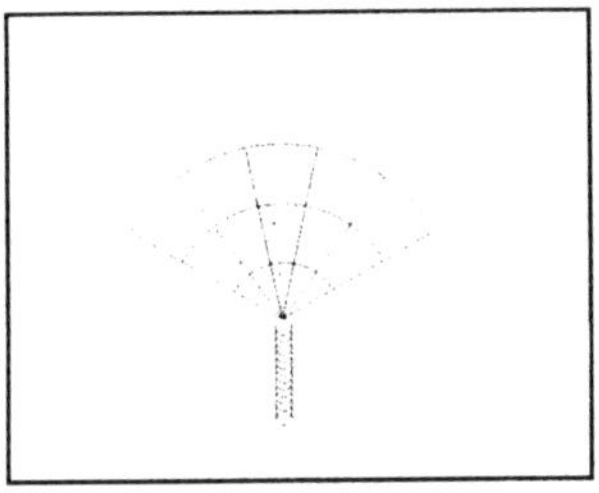

Fig. 1 Sensed area divided into fifteen regions

Input The input I is represented by a set of $p(t)$ and $d(t)$ and is defined by

$$I = \{\mathbf{p}(t), \mathbf{d}(t)\} \tag{6}$$

where $\boldsymbol{p}(t)=[p_j(t): j=1,2,\ldots,15]$ and $\boldsymbol{d}(t)=[d_j(t): j=1,2,\ldots,5]$. An element of $\boldsymbol{p}(t)$ means that

$$p_j(t) = \begin{cases} 0 \ : \ \text{other AGV exists in the } j^{\text{th}} \text{ sensor area} \\ 1 \ : \ \text{no AGV exists in the } j^{\text{th}} \text{ sensor area} \end{cases} \tag{7}$$

at an instant time t, and $\boldsymbol{d}(t)$ means that

$$d_j(t) = j \text{ (AGV is currently driving towards the } j^{\text{th}} \text{ sensed area)} \tag{8}$$

at an instant time t.

Output The output O is represented by a set of AGV driving directions (actions) and is defined as

$$O = \{\mathbf{a}\}, \ \mathbf{a} = [a_1, a_2, a_3, a_4, a_5]\,. \tag{9}$$

where a_1, a_2, a_3, a_4, and a_5 mean AGV driving directions, "turn hard-left", "turn left", "go forward", "turn right", and "turn hard-right", respectively.

State The state S is defined by a time series of sensed information from the instant time t-k to the current time t as

$$S = (I(t), I(t-1), \cdots, I(t-k)) \tag{10}$$

where k+1 becomes the number state elements.

Transition and output function When Q-learning is applied to AGV as an agent model, Q-value represents a state-action transition function F and r becomes a reward value from the environment for a pair set of the state $s(t)$ and the action $a(t)$. A combination of $s(t)$, $a(t)$, and Q($s(t)$,$a(t)$) makes a tableau as shown in the Eq. (11).

$$Q(s(t+1), a(t+1)) = (1-\alpha)Q(s(t), a(t)) + \alpha\{r + \max_{a(t)\in\mathbf{a}} Q(s(t+1), a(t+1))\} \tag{11}$$

where α is so called a learning ratio. This tableau is so call Q-table. A reward r(t) is set as the Eq. (12).

$$r(t)=\begin{cases}\text{a possitive value: the AGV moves closer to other AGV}\\ \text{a negative value : the AGV moves away from other AGV}\end{cases} \qquad (12)$$

where $r(t)$ is a direct reward from the environment. Also, a bucket brigade algorithm is introduced to distribute a reward to Q-value for a pair set of the past states and selected actions. This procedure is performed by

$$r(t-l)=\tau^{l}r(t),\ l=1,2,\cdots,k \text{ where } 0<\tau<1 \qquad (13)$$

In order to select the action at an instant time t+1, the action selector G is used. The following procedure is introduced as the action selector

$$a_j = \underset{a_j\in \mathbf{a}}{\mathbf{arg\ prob}}\ \frac{\exp(s(t+1),a_j)/T_{mp}}{\sum_j \exp(s(t+1),a_j)/T_{mp}}. \qquad (14)$$

where T_{mp} is a computational temperature.

NUMERICAL SIMULATION

Simulation is performed as numerical experiments in a virtual filed.

Learning for chasing and catching a moving object

At first, learning for chasing and catching a moving object is examined. Fig. 2 shows three snapshots in learning as a pre-experiment. In those pictures, sensor regions are drawn in front of AGV in the shape of sectors. Parameters for learning are shown in Table 1.

Table 1 Parameter values used for experiments

Parameter items	Parameter value
A simulation field size	200x200 (cells)
An initial Q-Value	2
A learning ratio α	0.3
A discounted ratio γ	0.8
A successful reward r_1	0.08
A failure reward r_2	-0.04
Learning times a cycle	200
Learning cycle times	20000

After the pre-experiment, the proposed method is applied to the following three cases for chasing and catching a moving object.

[I] The moving object is crossing ahead of AGV.

[II] The moving object is coming close to AGV.

[III] The moving object is driving away from the AGV.

Learning for three cases is alternatively done. In this experiment, the maximum number of AGV trial (movement) for one learning cycle is two hundreds. If the trial number reaches two hundreds, two AGVs are reset to the starting location, again. Fig. 3~5 shows simulation results after learning. Twenty thousand cycles are required for learning. This experiment verifies that the proposed method successfully learns how to chase and catch the moving object. Fig.6 shows a collision avoidance experiment not to use the acquired knowledge on purpose for chasing and catching a moving object.

Collision avoidance by learning collision

In above experiments, it is conformed that learning collision realizes learning collision avoidance. However, it is observed that learning does not proceed to acquiring collision knowledge in pre-experiments if multi-AGV equal to and more than three AGVs are set in the same field. Therefore, the sensors are implemented with all AGVs.

Figure 7 (a)~(i) show collision and collision avoidance aspects on three to six AGVs after learning. The same learning parameters are used in the previous experiments except that a learning cycle time is set to thirty thousand.

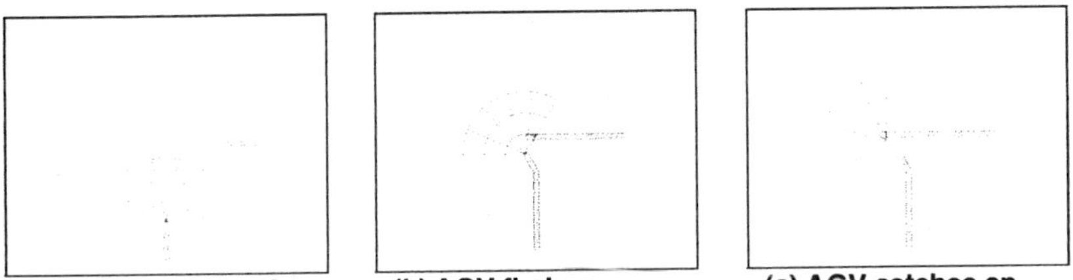

AGV drives upward (b) AGV find an object (c) AGV catches an object

Fig. 2 Snapshots in simulation for chasing and catching a moving object. AGV has a sector-like sensor

Fig. 3 Collision simulation in the case I

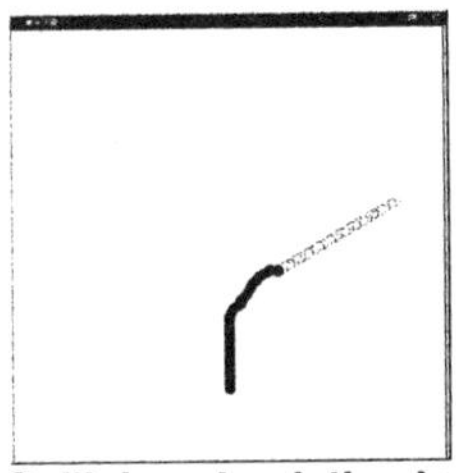

Fig. 4 Collision simulation in case of case II

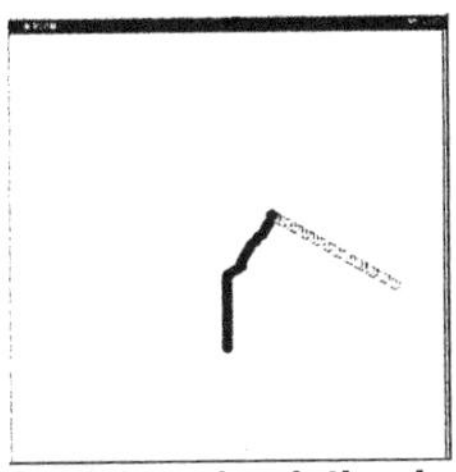

Fig. 5 Collision simulation in case of case III

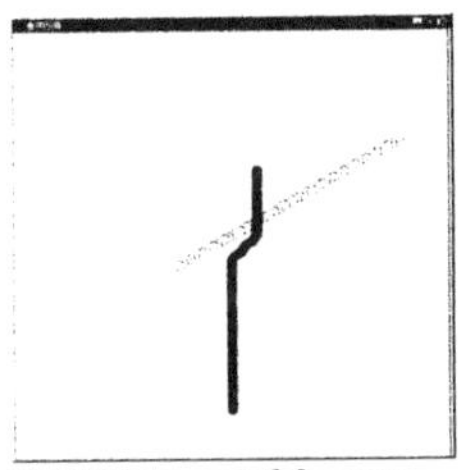

Fig. 6 Collision avoidance between two AGVs

CONCLUSION

A new collision avoidance method is proposed for autonomous AGV driving. The proposed method does not directly deal with the collision avoidance problem, but it indirectly deals with the problem, namely a collision problem. The driving knowledge is acquired by use of Q-learning to successfully conquer the collision problem. Through numerical experiments, the following is verified that AGV entirely predicts other AGV behavior to make a collision within sensor areas by use of Q-learning and that the proposed method realizes collision avoidance among multiple AGVs.

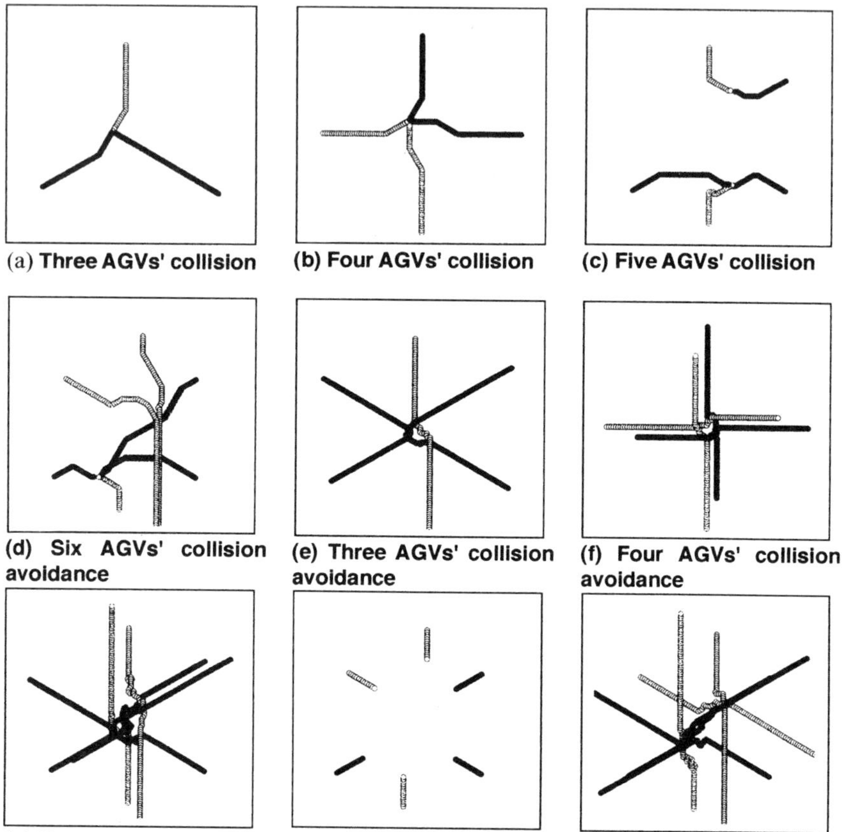

(a) Three AGVs' collision (b) Four AGVs' collision (c) Five AGVs' collision

(d) Six AGVs' collision avoidance (e) Three AGVs' collision avoidance (f) Four AGVs' collision avoidance

(g) Five AGVs' collision (h) Six AGVs' collision avoidance at the almost initial positions (i) Five AGVs' collision avoidance after driving

Fig. 7 Multi-AGV collision and collision avoidance

REFERENCES

Beaufrere B. and Zeghloul S., 1995), "A Mobil Robot Navigation Method Using a Fuzzy Logic Approach", Robotica, Vol. 13, pp. 437-448

Canny J., 1989, "Constructive Roadmaps of Semi-Algebraic Sets I: Completeness", Geometric Reasoning edited by D. Kapur and J.L. Mundy, Cambridge, MA, A Bradford Book, pp. 204-222

Kaihara T., Fujii S. and Kunimasa S., 1998, "An Evolutionary self-organization Scheduling using Coordinated Autonomous Work Agents", Proc. Of Japan-USA Symposium on Flexible Automation, III, pp. 1375-1381

Kawakami S. and Kakazu Y., 1993. "A Study on the Autonomous Robot Navigation by Use of the Classifier Systems", Transactions of the Japan Society of Mechanical Engineers -C-, Vol. 59, No. 564, Sept., pp. 2339-2345

Watanabe M., Furukawa M. and Kakazu Y., 2000, "INTELLIGENT AGV DRIVING TOWARD AN AUTONOMOUS DECENTRALIZED MANUFACTURING SYSYTEM", Proc. of FAIM'00, Vol. II, pp. 161-170

A COMPARISON OF 2 NEURAL FUSION MODELS USING AN OPTIMIZATION FRAMEWORK TO ASSESS REJECTION AND ROC THRESHOLDS FOR CORRELATED TEMPORAL DATA

TREVOR I. LAINE
Department of Operational Sciences
Air Force Institute of Technology
Wright-Patterson AFB, Ohio 45433

KENNETH W. BAUER, JR.
Department of Operational Sciences
Air Force Institute of Technology
Wright-Patterson AFB, Ohio 45433

Abstract

In many pattern recognition applications, significant costs can be associated with various decision options. Often, a minimum acceptable level of confidence is required prior to making an actionable decision. One way to increase decision confidence is to allow non-declaration or rejection, followed by fusion of data obtained from new sources or through time. Numerous methods have been published to obtain optimal decision rules if class prevalence and decision costs are known. This paper applies a novel mathematical framework to optimize multiple decision thresholds subject to decision maker preferences, without use of explicit costs. The decision variables include rejection thresholds to specify non-declaration regions and ROC thresholds to explore true positive and false positive classification rates. Optimization identifies thresholds compliant with decision maker constraints, and is partially visualized by a 3D ROC surface. This optimization framework is applied to 2 RNN models fusing multiple looks of generated temporal data. We vary the RNN input, as either a salient subset or all available input features. All data have significant levels of correlation within temporal looks and between some features. The objective function assesses temporal system effectiveness and a secondary measure of system robustness is proposed.

1. INTRODUCTION

The purpose of this paper is to present the concepts of our methodology, to optimize ROC and rejection thresholds, for a two class problem subject to non-declarations. As introduced in [13] this novel methodology is formulated to optimize a decision maker's primary objective, while constrained by other key performance preferences. This technique may help determine optimal parameter settings and may be useful for evaluation and comparison of different classifiers. While the proposed methodology is applicable to many decisions with high-stake consequences, our research focus is military Automatic Target Recognition (ATR). We consider an ATR scenario to identify enemy targets, in which the most substantial cost of incorrect declarations leads to friendly-fire. By performing this research insight may be gained for ATR systems or other decision processes, where a "Non-declaration," triggers subsequent collection and fusion of new data. In section 2, we provide a brief background for ATR, ROC analysis and rejection. Section 3 presents an overview of the optimization strategy. Section 4 provides an illustrative experiment and results. Finally, Section 5 provides a summary of our findings and recommendations for further research.

2. BACKGROUND FOR ATR, ROC & REJECTION

Many classification problems can be modeled at the top-level using 2-classes, whereby either the desired class is present or not. For example, an ATR system may declare an unknown object as "Target" or "Non-target," where "Target" includes enemy assets and "Non-Target" includes clutter, neutral or friendly forces. Yet, before a target is declared and engaged, the USAF requires a minimum level of confidence [5]. Consequently, an ATR system forcing 2 decision labels is inadequate. A minimum of 3 output classes, including "Target," "Non-target" and "No-declaration" is required when class confidence is low. Intelligence fusion is identified as a guiding principle to increase confidence for combat identification [5]. Current literature indicates data fusion as an emerging area of research for both DoD and non-DoD applications, where better estimates of an unknown state can be obtained by combining information derived from multiple sources [9]. ROC curve analysis is a common evaluation tool for ATR systems and has been extensively applied to many dichotomous decision problems [19],[20]. A typical ROC curve illustrates the estimated feasible range of false positive, P_{FP}, vs. true positive, P_{TP}, detection probabilities. A ROC curve, f, can be generated by varying a threshold, θ, over its range,Θ, as: $f = f(\theta) = \{P_{FP}(\theta), P_{TP}(\theta) | \theta \in \Theta\}$.

While ROC analysis is a standard tool for ATR evaluation [1], an operational ATR system should, at a minimum, provide 2 output labels plus a "reject" option. A rejection parameter establishes a region where samples considered too difficult to classify [4] are declared "Unknown." By varying rejection parameters, a family of ROC curves associated with different rejection criteria can be generated. By rejecting more samples, an improvement in P_{FP} & P_{TP} may be observed for the associated ROC curves [13]. Some rejection research [4],[6],[8] present a Bayes optimal classification strategy to determine classification and rejection rules by minimizing a Loss function. A Loss function may include costs of rejection, correct and incorrect decisions. Equivalent units are used for cost values and the prior probabilities of class membership are needed. However, since ATR systems are likely to operate in a variety of conditions, the expected prior probability of Targets to Non-Targets may vary greatly [17]. Further, costs of "Non-declarations" that initiate ATR re-looks may be difficult to place in comparable cost units to false positive target IDs, which may lead to friendly fire. Thus, a Loss function may not be appropriate to determine ATR decision rules, and an alternative measure is sought.

Some extensions of ROC analysis include more than 2 classes [10],[15], yet do not address rejection. A reject option is presented in [21] to generate a family of ROC curves via two thresholds. Rejection assessment is then accomplished through analysis of numerous confusion matrices, which may be partially summarized by ROC curves. Sadowski [18] discusses "horizontal" and "vertical" analysis of confusion matrices for ATR systems, and a general discussion of ATR evaluation is found in [17]. A sample 2-class confusion matrix (*CM*) with a "No declaration" option is presented as Table 1, with a row for each true class and a column for each model label. Engineers tend to perform "horizontal" analysis, independent of class membership prior probabilities. In contrast, warfighters are predominately concerned with ATR output labels [18]. "Vertical" analysis of *CM*s yield error estimates from the number of declarations, as seen in Table 2. Estimated values are obtained from the *CM* cell counts associated with the tested prior probabilities of classes. The critical error rate of labeling a Friend a "Target" is E_{CR}, and the non-critical error rate of labeling a Target a "Friend" is E_{NC}, with lost opportunity to deny the enemy. Equivalently, the error metrics may be calculated as conditional probabilities using Bayes' rule with prior probabilities of class membership (P_T and P_F). Assuming all objects belong to one of the true classes, the probability of declaration, P_{Dec}, can be used as a performance measure of the "Unknown" declarations. The probability of rejecting a sample is related as: $P_{Rej} = 1 - P_{Dec}$. Table 2 summarizes probability estimates associated with horizontal analysis of each row, and vertical analysis metrics in terms of the confusion matrix cells, *CM*(row, column) from Table 1.

Table 1. Sample confusion matrix with rejection (typically unique values for each threshold, θ).

True Classes	Classifier "Labels": *"Target"*	*"Friend"*	*"No declaration"*	**Totals**
Target	# Targets labeled *"Target"*	# Targets labeled *"Friend"*	# Targets labeled *"Unknown"*	**# Targets evaluated**
Friend	# Friends labeled *"Target"*	# Friends labeled *"Friend"*	# Friends labeled *"Unknown"*	**# Friends evaluated**

Table 2. Typical performance measures associated with a confusion matrix (*CM*) calculated form the cells, denoted as *CM*(row, col), obtained from the confusion matrix in Table 1.

True Classes	Classifier "Labels": *"Target" | declaration*	*"Friend" | declaration*	*"No declaration"*
Target	$P_{TP} = \frac{CM(1,1)}{CM(1,1)+CM(1,2)}$	$P_{FN} = 1 - P_{TP} = \frac{CM(1,2)}{CM(1,1)+CM(1,2)}$	$P_{UT} = \frac{CM(1,3)}{CM(1,4)}$
Friend	$P_{FP} = \frac{CM(2,1)}{CM(2,1)+CM(2,2)}$	$P_{TN} = 1 - P_{FA} = \frac{CM(2,2)}{CM(2,1)+CM(2,2)}$	$P_{UF} = \frac{CM(2,3)}{CM(2,4)}$
Vertical error & reject metrics	$E_{CR} = \frac{CM(2,1)}{CM(1,1)+CM(2,1)}$ $E_{CR} = \frac{P_F P_{FP}}{P_F P_{FP} + P_T P_{TP}}$	$E_{NC} = \frac{CM(1,2)}{CM(1,2)+(2,2)}$ $E_{NC} = \frac{P_T P_{FN}}{P_F P_{TN} + P_T P_{FN}}$	$P_{Rej} = \frac{CM(1,3)+CM(2,3)}{CM(1,4)+CM(2,4)}$ $P_{Dec} = 1 - P_{Rej}$

3. OPTIMIZATION STRATEGY

Optimization is performed to obtain a desirable objective, such as maximizing the True Positive declaration Rate, $TPR(\boldsymbol{\theta})$, subject to meeting other desired constraints. To facilitate optimization, a continuous *a posterior* class-membership estimate is required from the ATR system for each data observation. Optimal declaration and ROC thresholds can be obtained by solving:

$$\arg\max_{\boldsymbol{\theta}\in\boldsymbol{\Theta}} TPR(\boldsymbol{\theta}) \quad \text{i.e. maximize the True Positive Rate} = P_{TP}(\boldsymbol{\theta})/\mathrm{E}(\mathrm{L}(\boldsymbol{\theta})) \qquad (1)$$

$$\begin{aligned} \text{s.t.} \quad & E_{CR}(\boldsymbol{\theta}) < \Pi_1 && \text{to limit potential friendly fire} \\ & E_{NC}(\boldsymbol{\theta}) < \Pi_2 && \text{to limit lost opportunities to engage the enemy} \\ & P_{Ref}(\boldsymbol{\theta}) < \Pi_3 && \text{to limit non-declarations} \end{aligned}$$

Performance metrics are defined in Table 2, and each Π_i is set at a tolerable limit < 1. The expected number of looks is $\mathrm{E}(\mathrm{L}(\boldsymbol{\theta}))$, and $\boldsymbol{\Theta} = \{\boldsymbol{\theta}: \boldsymbol{\theta} = (\theta_l, \theta_u)^T \in \Re^2 \ni 0 \le \theta_l \le \theta_u \le 1\}$ will be refined in the following discussion. By expanding the 3D trajectory presented in [2] our proposed 3D ROC surface, extends a ROC curve by adding a measure to show performance when difficult to classify objects are rejected. For a given finite data set, a 3D ROC surface, S, is a function of $\boldsymbol{\theta}$ represented in 3-space by estimated probabilities. The three probabilities are functions of $\boldsymbol{\theta} = (\theta_l, \theta_u)^T$. A 3D ROC surface, S, is generated empirically by varying $\boldsymbol{\theta}$ over its entire range, $\boldsymbol{\Theta}$:

$$S = s(\boldsymbol{\theta}) = \{(P_{TP}(\boldsymbol{\theta}), P_{FP}(\boldsymbol{\theta}), P_{Dec}(\boldsymbol{\theta})) \mid \boldsymbol{\theta} \in \boldsymbol{\Theta}\}. \qquad (2)$$

Rejection should improve ATR performance by only declaring those objects with high likelihood of class membership. Classification can be delayed until additional data are obtained and sequential analysis is performed. The 3D ROC surface may be a useful tool for understanding tradeoffs between P_{TP}, P_{FP} & P_{Dec}. For this investigation, we chose $\boldsymbol{\theta}$ to include the size or width of the rejection zone along with a ROC threshold. To illustrate use of a variable rejection region we study a 2-class detection problem with class 1 "Targets" and class 2 "Friends." Let o_1 & o_2 be estimated class posterior probabilities, such that: $o_1 + o_2 = 1$. Thus, decisions can be based on o_1:

$$class = \{\, class\ 1 \text{ if } o_1 > \theta_u,\ class\ 2 \text{ if } o_1 < \theta_l, \text{ and } reject \text{ if } \theta_l \le o_1 \le \theta_u \,\} \qquad (3)$$

where θ_l and θ_u are upper and lower thresholds calculated from the ROC threshold, θ_r, and the rejection or declaration width, θ_d, as $\theta_l = \theta_r$ and $\theta_u = \theta_r + \theta_d$. To generate a 3D ROC surface, we vary θ_d from 0 (no rejections) to some upper limit ($\theta_d \le 1.0$ for probability scores) and θ_r from 0 to $1 - \theta_d$. This facilitates evaluation of the ATR classification rule decision trade-space and generation of a ROC surface as a function of the two thresholds.

4. EXPERIMENT AND RESULTS

In this paper we present a designed experiment between two ATR systems allowed to obtain up to 10 looks of "Target" or "Friend" class satellite data. The objective is to identify a maximum number of enemy targets with a limited sensing resource, constrained by allowable errors. Data were generated to model the signatures collected for 2 geosynchronous satellite types processed by a Johnson filter, and observed through time. The real data included the magnitude, corrected for distance, in red and blue frequency bands, with temporal trends associated with the rotation of the earth, reflection from the sun and other atmospheric effects. Three features were generated from a known parabolic "red" signature corrupted with 3 levels of noise. Similarly, 3 features were generated from a decreasing logarithmic "blue" signature. Since the data were generated as continuous functions of time with noise added, autocorrelation was statistically significant, as was crosscorrelation between variables derived from the same "color". Two "noise" features were constructed with no difference between classes. No feature provided linear separation of classes. The data generation resulted in 8 input features across 10 time units for each satellite target under investigation.

Since a strong temporal component may be hypothesized for an ATR system processing multiple looks in close spatial-temporal proximity, a neural fusion model was sought with the capability to fuse input features with a single architecture for any number of re-looks. An Elman RNN [7] was selected since it includes internal feedback and the ability to model temporal patterns without restrictions on the structure of input data correlation or number of temporal samples obtained [11]. To explicitly model temporal patterns, the Elman RNN hidden layer outputs are included as context nodes to be used as additional network input for the next data observation. The RNN's input features consisted of either all 8 input features or a parsimonious subset of 3 features, as determined in [12]. The reduced features were determined using both a Signal-to-Noise weight based saliency measure [3] and an output error based saliency measure [14]. The reduced features included "red" & "blue" features with low noise plus "blue" with medium noise. Using the Neural Net Toolbox in Matlab 6.1, RNNs were initialized with 8 hidden and 2 output nodes with hyperbolic tangent and sigmoid transfer functions. Desired outputs were 0.9 and 0.1 for correct and incorrect classes. All networks were trained using gradient descent with momentum and adaptive learning for a maximum of 2500 epochs. Data sets included 10 sequences of each class, with 200 total observations. 20 sets were generated for training, training-test and validation. Training data was used to calculate error and update weights, training-test data facilitated stopping training before over-fitting, and validation data was held independent to assess generalization. The RNN weights associated with the minimum training-test set MSE were retained as the ATR fusion model.

The fusion strategy attempts to maximize target declarations per time, subject to constraints as outlined in Eq. 2. The tth ATR score for a target is the estimated probability of class membership obtained from the outputs of a trained RNN using the current input exemplar and the previous t-1 input features. For example, if the 2nd observation is "Undeclared" a 3rd observation is obtained as RNN input and updated posteriors are obtained. Updates continue until a declaration is made or the 10th observation is left undeclared. Twenty RNN outputs are combined, yielding 400 data sequences to generate each ROC curve. Thirty training and test set ROC curves are presented in each subplot of Fig. 1. Each was generated as a function of 30 uniformly spaced ROC thresholds, repeated for 30 different declaration thresholds. The benefit of additional looks is illustrated by comparing the single lowest ROC curve associated with only 1 observation and no rejection, to the other curves. In general, the ROC curves with larger rejection regions converge toward the upper NW plot corner, indicative of improved performance. To determine feasible and optimal thresholds, $TPR(\boldsymbol{\theta})$ was maximized with Eq. 2 constraints at $\Pi_1 = 0.05$, $\Pi_2 = 0.20$ and $\Pi_3 = 0.30$. Fig. 2 adds $P_{Rej}(\boldsymbol{\theta})$ to the ROC curves from Fig. 1 to generate surfaces and help visualize the impact of rejection on the ROC curves. Feasible points, meeting all decision maker constraints, are identified by the dark circles in Figs. 1, 2 & 3. The optimal thresholds and performance parameters are identified in Table 3, along with performance and threshold values for other excursions of target to friend prior ratios. The P_T:P_F excursions were performed primarily to obtain additional feasible points. In general, increasing target density provided a means to increase feasible points and thus, compare classifiers with respect to the objective function or compare robustness as the percentage of feasible thresholds.

The pattern of fewer feasible points from training, to test, to validation sets was similar to RNN behavior observed with a forced 2-class decision using the same data with a winner-take-all declaration rule [12]. In addition to generating the 3D ROC surfaces in Fig. 2, similar plots were examined for the RNN using 3 input features with differing priors. At both P_T:P_F = 1:1 & 4:1 about

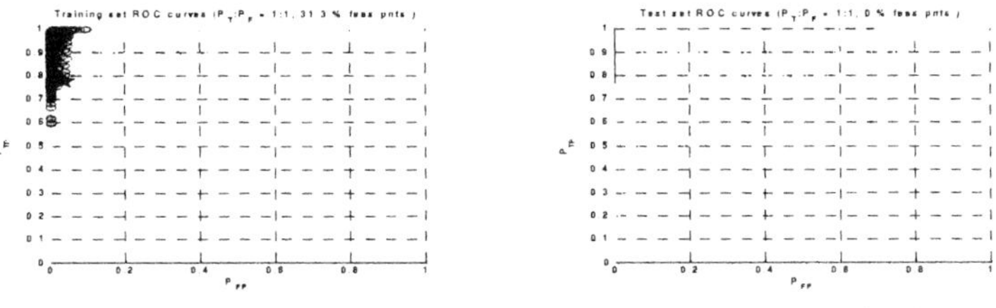

Fig. 1. An RNN with 8 input features is assessed to generate one ROC curve for 30 uniform ROC thresholds for each of 30 uniform declaration thresholds. With P_T:P_F = 1:1, the left plot is for training data, and the right plot, without feasible points, is for test data. An "o" indicates feasible $\boldsymbol{\theta}$, and a "star" is for the optimal $TPR(\boldsymbol{\theta}) = 0.61$.

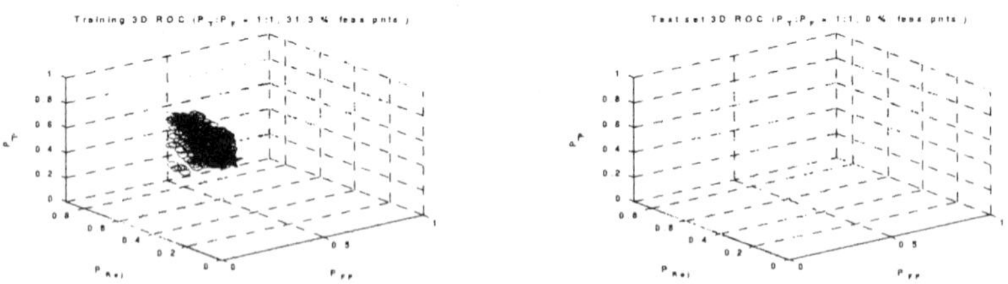

Fig. 2. Thirty ROC curves generated as in Fig. 1, but now connected across P_{Rej} values. With equal priors, the feasible points appear densely around a "knee" in the training set ROC surface, yet are predominately conservative.

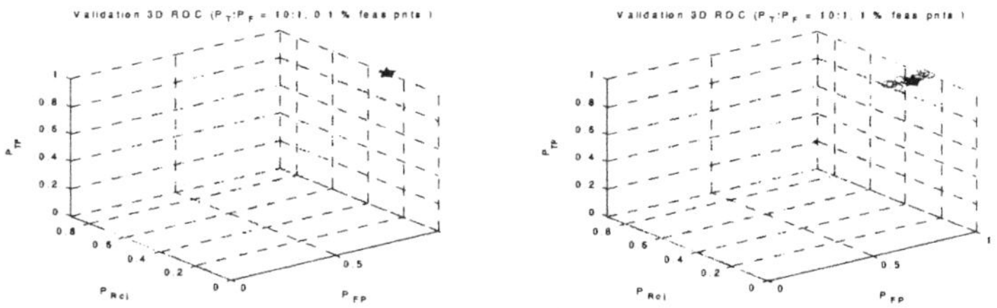

Fig. 3. ROC surfaces from Validation data using an RNN trained using 8 features on the left and 3 on the right for P_T:P_F = 10:1. With additional feasible points, the reduced feature set appears to generalize better. The optimal $TPR(\boldsymbol{\theta})$ is denoted with very aggressive ROC thresholds that classify most objects as "Targets" with $P_{FP} \cong 1$.

4% of the training data thresholds resulted in feasible points as compared to about 20-30% of the 8 feature model. Evaluation of the test data yielded no feasible points. A new prior ratio of P_T:P_F = 10:1 was assessed for the test data and is included in Table 3.

Analysis of the independent validation set showed significant performance degradation in both RNN fusion models. With P_T:P_F = 4:1, no feasible operating points were obtained for either feature set, indicative of poor model generalization outside of the training and test data. Validation data were then optimized in target rich environments with P_T:P_F = 10:1 (Fig. 3) and P_T:P_F = 20:1, with optimal thresholds aggressively labeling most of the declared data "targets." Differences in training and test set data, using either max $TPR(\boldsymbol{\theta})$ or the percentage of feasible operating thresholds, indicate using all 8 features may be preferred to the subset. Yet, both feature sets failed to generalize well to an external validation set with no feasible points when P_T:P_F = 4:1. Further performance evaluation of the validation sets for P_T:P_F = 10:1 and P_T:P_F = 20:1 resulted in minimal differences between use of either feature set. These results are comparable with those obtained by [12], where forced declaration was analyzed after each look and no statistical difference could be declared for either data set. Similarly, steady degradation was observed between training, test, and validation sets, and the apparent differences between complete and reduced feature sets diminished. Thus, for classification of data independent of the RNN training algorithm, use of the reduced feature set appears reasonable. In addition, a reduced feature set may be more efficient for ATR in terms of requiring less data to be collected and processed in near real-time. Overall, additional measures should be explored for the optimization framework to help identify a preferred model when neither yields feasible thresholds compliant with the levied decision maker constraints and desired priors.

Table 3. Optimal thresholds to maximize True Positive target ID's per number of looks and associated performance measures for Training (TR), Test (TE) and Validation (VA) data sets.

feats	*data*	P_T:P_F	P_{TP}	P_{FP}	E_{CR}	E_{NC}	P_{Dec}	P_{Rej}	θ_I	θ_{II}	*ID/time*	*max TPR*	*% Feas*
8	TR	1:01	78%	4%	4.9%	19%	100%	18%	0.52	0.70	0.79	0.61	29.30%
3	TR	1:01	78%	4%	4.9%	18%	92%	48%	0.35	0.83	0.27	0.21	4.80%
8	TE	1:01	---	---	---	---	---	---	---	---	---	---	0%
3	TE	1:01	---	---	---	---	---	---	---	---	---	---	0%
8	TR	4:01	96%	18%	4.5%	16%	100%	30%	0.21	0.51	0.54	0.51	20.30%
3	TR	4:01	97%	27%	4.8%	16%	84%	42%	0.17	0.59	0.25	0.25	3.70%
8	TE	4:01	97%	31%	4.8%	20%	75%	66%	0.07	0.73	0.20	0.19	0.50%
3	TE	4:01	---	---	---	---	---	---	---	---	---	---	0%
8	TE	10:01	100%	59%	4.1%	15%	83%	51%	0.05	0.56	0.25	0.25	1.40%
3	TE	10:01	100%	100%	4.9%	0%	75%	51%	0.00	0.51	0.24	0.24	0.30%
8	VA	10:01	100%	100%	4.7%	0%	71%	54%	0.00	0.54	0.22	0.22	0.10%
3	VA	10:01	100%	91%	5.0%	0%	75%	51%	0.03	0.54	0.23	0.23	0.90%
8	VA	20:01	100%	100%	4.8%	0%	100%	0%	0.00	0.00	1.00	1.00	2.00%
3	VA	20:01	100%	97%	4.6%	0%	100%	0%	0.07	0.07	1.00	1.00	6.90%

5. SUMMARY & CONCLUSION

In this paper we presented our optimization strategy for rejection and ROC thresholds to maximize a preferred objective while constrained by other requirements. To visualize some key performance relations, a 3D ROC surface was presented. An objective function to maximize TP's per time was selected; yet, further investigation is required to properly refine the objective function as may be preferred by an ATR system user. One advantage of our optimization methodology is development of acceptable constraints vs. quantifying difficult misclassification costs, leading to feasible regions in addition to optimal points. The percentage of feasible operating thresholds may help measure a system's robustness and only gives credit to acceptable portions of a ROC curve. This may be useful for comparison of systems desired to perform across untested operating conditions with potential deviations from the training data [16]. This optimization framework may also be easily expanded to include additional constraints, and objective function revision can reflect different goals, such as minimizing the critical error, E_{CR}, or maximizing a certain class of ID, etc.

While a generated fusion scenario is presented, this methodology may be extended to incorporate more observations or fusion of multiple sensors or ATR systems; provided continuous valued output scores for each class are obtained. Further research may extend classes, search for optimal thresholds for each sensor look, or use different fusion models. In general, this formulation and framework has the potential to be a helpful tool for ATR assessment when P_{TP} & P_{FP} are not sufficient to evaluate competing classifiers. Yet, when no feasible points are obtained, additional metrics are needed to facilitate assessment. Evaluation in a target rich environment favoring one system may not remain valid across sparse target environments, with conservative/aggressive action varying by situation. In general, we view this optimization framework as a significant step to assist evaluation of ATR systems. This approach may yield insight of ATR systems performing real-time data fusion to operate within acceptable error rates. The optimization framework can also be used to identify binding decision-maker constraints, and sensitivity analysis may point to areas of valuable system improvement. Overall, a decision maker's primary objective, subject to constraints, is established in a flexible framework with both the warfighter's "vertical" concerns of ATR declaration labels and the engineer's "horizontal" view of classification by known class type.

ACKNOWLEDGEMENTS

This research is jointly sponsored by ACC/DR and AFOSR under grant #NMIPR045203616. The views expressed in this paper are those of the authors and do not reflect official policy or position of the United States Air Force, Department of Defense, or United States Government.

REFERENCES

1. S.G. Alsing, *The Evaluation of Competing Classifiers*, Dissertation, Air Force Institute of Tech., OH, 2000.

2. S.G. Alsing, E. P. Blasch and K.W. Bauer, Jr., "Three-dimensional receiver operating characteristic trajectory concepts for the evaluation of target recognition algorithms faced with the unknown target detection problem," Proc. of SPIE Vol. 3718, pp. 449-458, Apr 1999.

3. K.W. Bauer, S.G. Alsing, and K.A. Greene, "Feature screening using signal to-noise ratios", Neurocomputing, Vol 31, Mar 2000, pp. 29-44.

4. C.K. Chow, "On optimum rejection error and reject tradeoff," IEEE Trans. on Inf. Theory, pp. 41-46, 1970.

5. Department of the Air Force (DAF), Air Warfare. AFDD2-1, Washington, D.C., HQ USAF, 2000.

6. P.A. Devijver and J. Kittler, Pattern Recognition - a Statistical Approach, Prentice-Hall Int'l, London, 1982.

7. J.L. Elman, "Finding structure in time," Cognitive Science, Vol 14, 1990, pp. 179-211.

8. G. Fumera, F. Roli and G. Giorgio, "Reject option with multiple thresholds," Pattern Recognition, 33, pp. 2099-2101, 2000.

9. D.L. Hall and J. Llinas (eds.) *Handbook of Multisensor Data Fusion,* CRC Press, New York, 2001.

10. D.J. Hand and R.J. Till, "A simple generalisation of the area under the ROC curve for multiple class classification problems," Machine Learning, Vol 45, pp. 171 – 186, 2001.

11. J.F. Kolen and S.C. Kremer (eds.) *A Field Guide to Dynamical Recurrent Networks*, IEEE Press. NY, 2001.

12. T.I. Laine and K.W. Bauer, "Feature Selection Assessment and Comparison using Two Saliency Measures in an ERNN," Proc. Int'l Joint Conf. on Neural Nets, IEEE Press, pp. 2807-2812, 2003.

13. T.I. Laine and K.W. Bauer, "A mathematical framework for the optimization of rejection and ROC thresholds in the fusion of correlated sensor data," Proc. of SPIE, Vol 5434, pp. 37-48, 2004.

14. J. Moody, "Forecasting the economy with neural networks: a survey of challenges and solutions," Neural Networks: tricks of the trade, Orr & Muller (ed.). Springer. NY, 1998, pp. 348-371.

15. D. Mossman, "Three-way ROCs," Medical Decision Making, Vol 19, pp.78-89, 1999.

16. T.D. Ross, L.A. Westerkamp, E.G. Zelnio and T.J. Burns, "Extensibility and other model-based ATR evaluation concepts," Proc. of SPIE, Vol. 3070, pp. 213-222, 1997.

17. T.D. Ross, L.A. Westerkamp, R.L. Dilsavor and J.C. Mossing, "Performance measures for summarizing confusion matrices – the AFRL COMPASE approach," Proc. of SPIE, Vol. 4727, pp. 310-321, 2002.

18. C. Sadowski, "Measuring Combat Identification," presentation, 69th MORS Symposium, MD, June 2001.

19. J.A. Swets, *Signal Detection and Recognition by Human Observers*, Wiley & Sons, Inc., NY, 1964.

20. J.A. Swets, R.M. Dawes and J. Monahan, "Psychological science can improve diagnostic decisions," Psychological Science in the Public Interest, Vol. 1, pp. 1-26, May 2000.

21. T. Varner, "ACE TestJig Evaluation Metrics," Jacobs Sverdrup WP, AFRL COMPASE Center, OH, 2002.

PART II: ARTIFICIAL LIFE

ADVANCES IN EVOLUTIONARY AGENT LEARNING

ANNA L. BUCZAK, DAVID G. COOPER, MARTIN O. HOFMANN
Lockheed Martin Advanced Technology Laboratories
Cherry Hill, New Jersey
{abuczak, dcooper, mhofmann}@atl.lmco.com

ABSTRACT
This paper describes a novel methodology for software agent learning. Evolutionary Platform for Agent Learning (EPAL) creates both subtle and drastic changes to agent behavior. Subtle changes arise from learning task parameters. Drastic changes emerge from learning improved workflows containing new programming constructs and tasks. EPAL presents a general approach to agent learning, based on an extension to Genetic Programming that we developed. This approach is suitable for learning by any agent whose behavior can be represented as a workflow that can be further decomposed into building blocks, such as operators, tasks, and parameters. This paper describes a real-world problem that our agents learned to solve that is similar to problems encountered in Navy Fleet Battle Experiment-Juliet. Several sets of results are presented, showing increasing learning capabilities of our agents.

1. INTELLIGENT AGENTS AND LEARNING

Learning plays a fundamental role in most human activities. Humans learn from their experiences, both successes and mistakes. Babies learn to walk and talk, adults learn foreign languages, new skills and concepts. Learning seems to be the fundamental property that allows humans to adapt to changes in the environment and to be successful. The skill of learning is of dynamic nature in humans who continuously acquire and modify representations of the world [Sun, 2001]. On the other hand, artificial systems such as software agents are usually static. For software agents to work properly, humans need to envision all contingencies and code them at the agent development time. Most agents react the same way to similar external stimuli, even when the previous reaction failed. Our goal is for the agent to learn different behavior in response to those stimuli. If software agents could "just" learn from their successes and mistakes, they would be more rapidly deployable and agent systems would have a longer life span. However developing a general learning method for software agents is a difficult proposition. Several attempts have been made in the past such as "conscious learning" mechanism [Ramamurthy, 1998], ABLE agents [Bigus, 2002], layered learning approach [Stone, 1998]. Our method differs from the ones proposed in the literature since it is capable of learning completely new agent behaviors by using Genetic Programming.

2. EXTENDABLE MOBILE AGENT ARCHITECTURE

Lockheed Martin Advanced Technology Laboratories (ATL) developed the Extendable Mobile Agent Architecture (EMAA). EMAA is used in about two dozen projects covering a full range of intelligent systems, including information management for time-sensitive strike [Hofmann, 2001], situation awareness for small military units, and executing user requests entered via spoken language dialogue. Starting with the Domain Adaptive Information System, experimentation with prototypes in military exercises has guided our research and development towards the adaptable EMAA architecture. EMAA was used in the U.S. Navy Fleet Battle Experiment (FBE) series as a human aiding tool. From these experiments, an Interoperable Intelligent Agent Toolkit (I2AT) was created under DARPA Control of Agent Based Systems (CoABS) funding to allow people to construct agent systems without coding the agents from scratch, but by generating a workflow of tasks and parameters in a graphical fashion.

EMAA agents are designed with a workflow model for agent construction. An EMAA agent's workflow (Fig. 1) is a list of tasks, linked by execution paths that can be conditional or unconditional. Each task can take a certain number of task dependant parameters. The workflow architecture enables a new approach to agent development called agent composition, characterized by configuring and assembling elementary agent tasks into work flows. Typical tasks include queries to relational databases, retrieval of content from Web pages, reading and sending e-mail, etc. Key features have been added to EMAA that support agent learning. The goal of EMAA's new learning capability is allowing agents to adapt to the environment in which they operate.

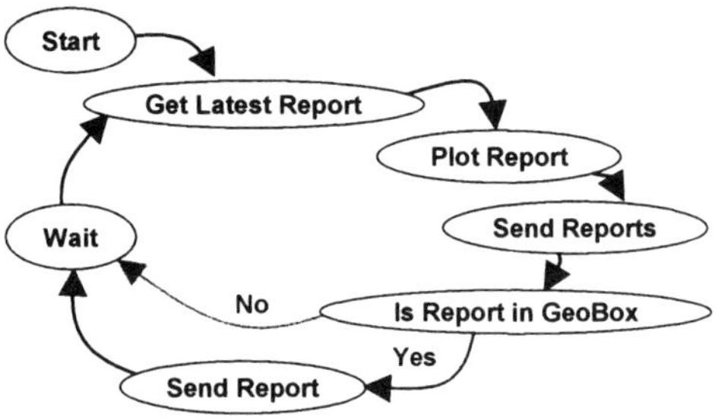

Fig. 1. Example of an EMAA Agent Workflow.

3. EVOLUTIONARY PLATFORM FOR AGENT LEARNING

Our approach to agent learning is based on Genetic Programming (GP). John Koza invented GP as a means of program synthesis by genetically breeding a population of computer programs using the principles of Darwinian evolution [Koza, 1993]. The basic operators of reproduction, crossover and mutation operate on individuals in the population and a fitness function describes how good a given individual is. In GP each individual is represented as a tree. In our approach (Fig. 2) GP evolves an agent workflow instead of directly evolving a computer program. The first step is to represent agent workflows in a GP tree form (these workflows are used in the initial population). GP individuals are translated from a tree format into a workflow, using their jar file descriptions from I2AT toolkit. The Activity Graph is then used to instantiate a composable agent, which is injected into the simulated system. Fitness is collected while the agent is run in the simulated environment.

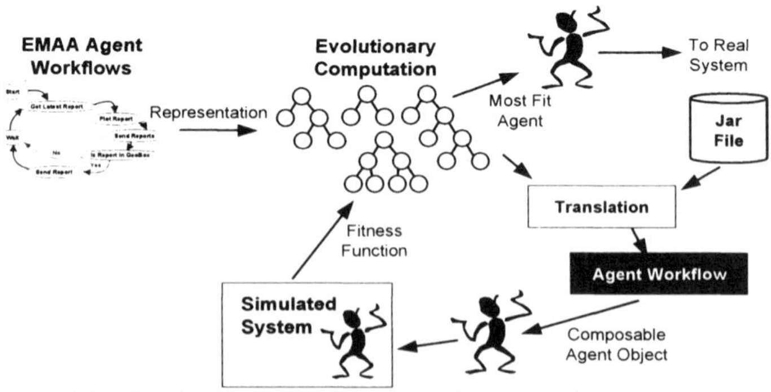

Fig. 2. Evolutionary Platform for Agent Learning.

GP operators work on agents' genetic material to generate new agents that have learned to overcome certain problems in their environment. Once the agents have learned, the most fit are injected into the real system and take the place of their parents who did not know how to overcome the problems. The method proposed is a general method that can generate completely new agent workflows, as well as related workflows but with new parameters. Augmenting an agent's workflow is synonymous with changing the agent's behavior.

In order to use GP for agent learning, several extensions to standard GP had to be developed. These extensions include: a novel GP tree representation that instead of two types of nodes has three node types (operators, tasks, task parameters), and restricted crossover and mutation operators that are guaranteed to produce legal offspring(s) from legal parent(s). The special mutation operators introduced include parameter mutation, task mutation, and operator mutation. The details of the representation and the new operators are described in our previous publication [Buczak, 2003].

Our GP implementation is based on Evolutionary Computation in Java (ECJ). ECJ [ECJ] is a flexible genetic algorithm and genetic programming freeware. Its source code is readily available which allowed us to make modifications necessary for agent learning.

4. FLEET BATTLE EXPERIMENTS: A REAL WORLD LEARNING SCENARIO

The scenario that we are using to demonstrate our agents' learning capabilities is similar to a real problem encountered in Fleet Battle Experiment-Juliet (FBE-J). In our scenario agents transmit vehicles' track information over a network and plot all the reports. Those track reports are coming from two vehicles: a fast vehicle moving at 100 knots and a slow vehicle moving at 10 knots. As message arrival rates increase, the network bandwidth becomes insufficient to transmit all messages, message queues grow and delivery delays grow. A solution to the problem encountered, suggested by a SPAWAR expert, was to exploit the differences in message urgency, i.e. match the rate of sending track updates to the urgency of the message. This typically means that slow moving tracks can be sent less frequently than fast moving tracks. Another possible solution would be to reduce the scope of the updates i.e. send updates in a smaller area of interest (smaller GeoBox).

The overarching goal for agents is to improve the network latency. One way agents can achieve this goal is to discriminate between fast and slow moving vehicles and to skip a number of slow reports. The appropriate ratio for filtering is proportionate to the ratio of the vehicle speeds (1:10). We make discrimination and filtering tasks available for EPAL with the filtering task parameterized by the number of messages to skip. We also make a GeoBox task available so that agents can choose a second way of filtering.

5. PARAMETER LEARNING

5.1 Experiment Description

The goal of the first EPAL test was to show parameter learning. This is a simpler form of learning where all agents in the initial population have the right workflow but none of them has the right task parameters. As such, the goal is to maximize the agent's fitness by adjusting the task parameters without changing the agent's workflow. In the parameter learning only parameter mutation was used (with probability 100%).

An important part of GP is the fitness of an individual. Our ultimate goal is to make agents learn everything, similarly to what humans do. Consequently we do not want to give too much guidance to the GP individuals. The fitness criteria we used to evaluate the agents during learning: all fast reports should be displayed; and, slow reports should be displayed at the ratio between the average speed of the slow reports and the speed of the fast reports. This fitness is collected when the agent is executed, counting the number of slow and fast reports displayed. This is done realistically, and when the network slows down the number of fast and slow reports read and displayed by the agent changes.

In the experiments three experimental settings were varied: type of selection, maximum number of mutations per individual, and existence/absence of user guidance. The type of selection refers to the tournament or roulette wheel selection for choosing GP individuals for the next generation. The maximum number of mutations per individual specifies the number of times mutation will be called per individual (2 or 3). There is a 100% probability of the first parameter mutation, a 50% probability that there is a second mutation, and (in the case of 3 mutations) a 25% probability that there is a third mutation.

The existence/absence of user guidance specifies whether each parameter can undergo mutation (no guidance - undirected) or specifies which parameters can be mutated (user guidance - directed). In order to better explain it, let's look at Fig. 3 where the circles around the parameters indicate the way they can be mutated during learning. In case of undirected experiment, all the parameters in any type of circle can be mutated. In case of user directed experiment, only the parameters that are in solid line circles can undergo mutation. Since during mutation a new value is chosen at random from a set of legal values for a given parameter, there is always a non-zero probability that the same value will be chosen i.e. the parameter will not change (for most of the parameters this probability is very low).

For Parameter Learning we performed four sets of experiments. The first experiment uses tournament selection, a maximum of 2 mutations per agent, and no user guidance. The second experiment uses tournament selection, a maximum of 3 mutations per agent, and no user guidance. The third experiment uses tournament selection, a maximum of 2

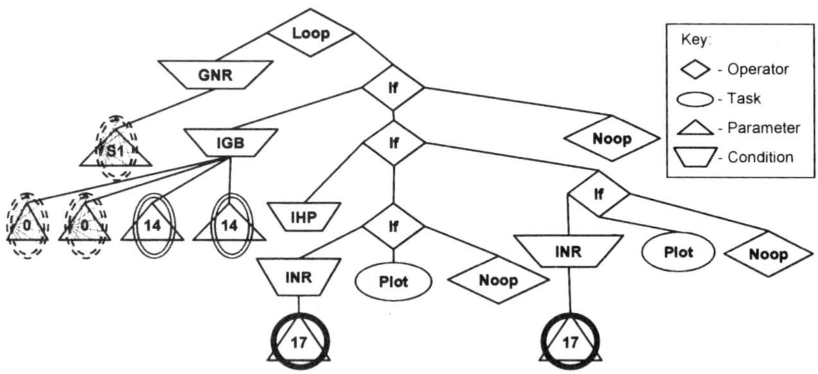

Fig. 3. The tree of the initial agent in parameter learning. The tree is read from the top down and left to right. GNR = Get Next Report, IGB = Is in GeoBox, IHP = Is High Priority, INR = Is Nth Report. In this case:

```
while (getNextReportFrom ("Sensor 1") {
GeoBox geoBox = new GeoBox(0,0,14,14);
if (geoBox.isInside(report) { if  (isHighPriority(report)) {
   fastCounter++;if((fastCounter modulo 17) == 0) {Plot(report);}
  } else { // report is low priority
   slowCounter++; if((slowCounter modulo 17) == 0) {Plot(report);}}}}
```

mutations per agent, and uses guidance. The fourth experiment performs roulette wheel selection, a maximum of 2 mutations per agent, and uses guidance. Each experiment was repeated several times (at least 32), and minimum, maximum, and mean generation number for finding the best agent were recorded. All the runs used a population of 50 GP trees. In the experiments the filtering values (under INR node on Fig. 3) are integers that can range from 1 to 100. The latitude length and longitude length (under IGB node) are rational numbers from 1.0 to 20.0, and all other parameters can assume only one value.

5.2 Results

Table 1 shows the results of the four experiments described in the previous section. EPAL was able to find the best agent in all the runs, regardless of the number of mutations used, type of selection, and whether user direction was given. The best results were obtained for experiment 3; on average only 11.03 generations were needed to find the optimal agent, and the maximum number of generations needed was the smallest of all experiments (32). This experiment uses user direction. User directed experiments (3 and 4) give better results than the undirected experiments—the reason being that the search space is smaller since only 2 parameters can be mutated instead of 7. A very large improvement occurs when the maximum of 3 mutations is used instead of the maximum of 2 (experiment 2 vs. experiment 1): on average 14.35 generations are needed, instead of 24.76. Experiment 2 results were very close to experiment 4 results, even though the search space was so much larger. This shows the power of performing more mutations on the agent. The best agent found in parameter learning experiments has the same workflow as on Fig. 3 but the parameters of two INR tasks are set to 1 and 10, thus it performs the prefect filtering.

Table 1. The results for parameter learning.

	Experiment 1	Experiment 2	Experiment 3	Experiment 4
Ave number generations	24.76	14.35	11.03	13.94
Std deviation	4.99	1.044	0.59	0.55
Number runs	33	66	106	32
% runs best agent found	100%	100%	100%	100%
Min number generations	6	1	1	2
Max number generations	96	44	32	35

6. WORKFLOW LEARNING

6.1 Experiment Description

Workflow learning is a more difficult form of learning, since the agents do not have the right workflow, or the right parameters. When performing this type of learning, EPAL needs to generate new elements in the workflows, add new tasks and programming constructs, remove other tasks and programming constructs, and adjust the task parameters. Hence, workflow learning generates new agent behaviors. For this experiment the probabilities of different operations were as follows: reproduction - 0.25, crossover - 0.1, parameter mutation - 0.2, task mutation - 0.4 and operator mutation - 0.05. The fitness function is the same as in case of parameter learning.

In FBE-J, the agents had the workflow shown in Fig. 4. Those agents were getting reports from a sensor, and sending them if those reports fell inside a Geo Box. They did not perform any filtering of reports based on priority.

We used a population of 50 GP individuals with 50% of initial population with random workflows and 50% with skeleton workflows as the one on Fig. 4. None of the

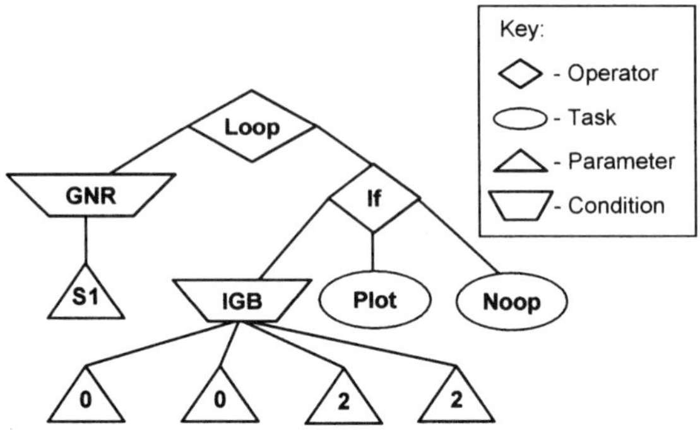

Figure 4. Best agent in generation 0 of workflow learning experiments. GNR = Get Next Report, IGB = In GeoBox:

```
while (getNextReportFrom ("Sensor 1") {
geoBox = new GeoBox(0,0,2,2);
if (geoBox.isInside(report) {Plot(report);} }
```

skeleton agents perform the filtering needed to satisfy the requirements. In order to be a fit agent, slow and fast re-ports need to be differentiated, and the slow reports need to be filtered. The tasks needed for this are "Is High Priority" task and "Is Nth Report" task.

6.2 Experiment 1 Results

In our first experiment, the input was very regular: fast and slow reports were always interleaved (fast, slow, fast, etc.) and the two vehicles' x, y positions stayed the same during the tests. This experiment was run about 10 times, and the "best agent" was found on average in 84 generations. EPAL found many solutions that exploited the ordering of the slow and fast reports, an example is shown in Fig. 5. In the lower right part of the tree, the check for the 18th report (INR) is outside of checking if the report is high priority (IHP). This means that the agent is filtering every 18th report, and if the reports are interleaved, it is equivalent to plotting every 9th of slow reports (ratio 1:9). However should the reports come in a different order, the filtering done by the agent won't be acceptable. This means that the agent is taking advantage of the interleaved nature of fast and slow reports. To counter these effects, we designed a second experiment.

6.3 Experiment 2 Results

Our goal in the second experiment was to make the learning conditions for agents more

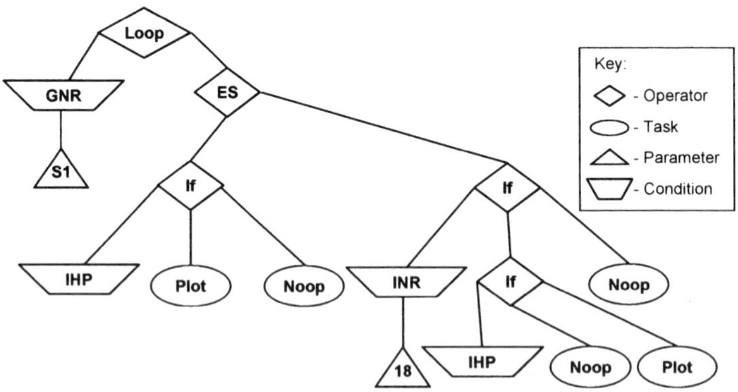

Figure 5. Best agent from one run of Experiment 1. GNR = Get Next Report, IGB = In GeoBox, IHP = Is High Priority, INR = Is Nth Report:

```
while (getNextReportFrom ("Sensor 1") {
if  (isHighPriority(report)) {Plot(report);}  counter++;
if((counter modulo 18) == 0) {if  (not(isHighPriority(report))) {Plot(report);}} }
```

realistic. The first real-world modification was that slow and fast reports could come in any order, with the probability of getting a slow or a fast report set at 0.5. The second modification was for the values in sensor reports themselves (describing x, y positions) not to be constants but to be provided by a sensor model interfacing with a Joint Semi Automated Forces (JSAF) simulator.

These changes led to very noisy fitness values, meaning that the fitness would significantly change for the same agent from generation to generation (depending on the order of slow and fast reports that the agent was scored on). To alleviate this problem, we modified EPAL to evaluate each agent three times on three random sequences of reports and additionally to compute an average fitness value based on all evaluations that the agent performed so far. If an agent survives many generations, the average fitness would be based on more evaluations, and would be less likely to have a good value due to idiosyncrasies with one set of sensor inputs. By using the realistic sensor data, the exact ratio of 10:100 knots in the speed of the slow to fast targets did not hold anymore. Moreover this ratio was not constant, varying between 9 and 10, and it was rarely an integer. Those changes made the learning problem much more difficult, albeit realistic.

EPAL learning was conducted for 400 generations. The experiment was run four times due to the length of each run. One run is discussed here. In generation 0 the best agent had the workflow of Fig. 4. Small improvements are made in consecutive generations. At around generation 117 EPAL creates an agent with the right workflow, but the filtering ratio is 1:7 instead of 1 to 9 or 10. By generation 337, the best agent in the run was found (Fig. 6) with a ratio of 1:8. It performs a loop in which it gets the next sensor report (GNR), checks if the report is high priority (IHP), if yes it plots the report. If the report is not high priority it checks if the report is in GeoBox (IGB - will always evaluate to true in this case). If it is, it plots every 8th report (INR), and does nothing with other reports. In other words this agent plots all fast reports and every 8th of slow reports.

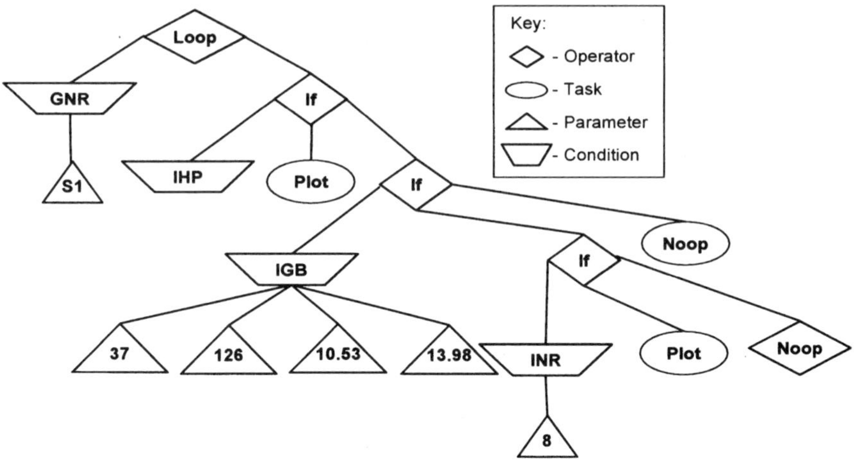

Fig. 6. Experiment 2, Best Agent of one run found in generation 337.

```
while (getNextReportFrom ("Sensor 1") {
if (isHighPriority(report)) {Plot(report);}
else { GeoBox geoBox = new GeoBox(37,126,10.53,13.98);
   if (geoBox.isInside(report) { slowCounter++;if((slowCounter modulo 8) == 0) {
     Plot(report);}}}}
```

By comparing the initial agent (Fig. 4) with the final one (Fig. 6), it is apparent how different the workflows are. The tasks added (in the right location) were IHP and INR. Comparing the workflow of the best agent from this run with the workflow that we made for parameter learning, notice that the filter (If, INR) for high priority reports is missing in the learned workflow. This makes sense since the problem requires no High Priority (fast) reports being filtered. The other difference is that the GeoBox is only utilized for slow reports. This didn't make a difference since the GeoBox is so large that it does not exclude any reports.

The overall results of workflow learning are very encouraging. Our agents were able to learn the new desired behavior on average in 350 generations. They did that even though the fitness function was noisy and constructed in such a way as not to suggest how to solve the problem. Very often the resulting workflows had many parts that were never executed: we developed a pruning algorithm that removes those parts.

7. CONCLUSIONS

EPAL is a framework for software agents to automatically learn how to better perform in their environment. The learning methodology we developed for intelligent agents is revolutionary. It has a capability to generate and discover completely new behaviors as well as adapt existing behaviors by changing task parameters. EPAL is a general framework for intelligent agent learning that can be used for any intelligent software agents as long as they are described by a workflow that can be further decomposed into simple building blocks. The uniqueness of EPAL comes from its ability to generate real software agents that can be executed in real military/other scenarios. To our knowledge the solution we formulated is the first platform in which real software agents can learn from their experience to perform standard tasks better. In the future, as we augment the set of tasks that agents can build their workflows from, agents should be able to "learn anything", similarly to what humans do.

8. REFERENCES

Bigus, J.P., Schlosnagle, D.A., Pilgrim, J.R., Mills III, W.N., Diao, Y., 2002, "ABLE: A Toolkit for Building Multiagent Autonomic Systems," *IBM Systems Journal*, Vol. 41, No. 3.

Buczak, A.L., Cooper, D.G., Hofmann, M.O., (2003), "Evolutionary Platform for Agent Learning", Intelligent Engineering Systems Through Artificial Neural Networks, eds. C.H. Dagli, A.L. Buczak, J. Ghosh, M.J. Embrechts, O. Ersoy, Vol. 13., pp. 201-206, ASME Press, New York.

ECJ, www.cs.umd.edu/projects/plus/ec/ecj/.

Hofmann, M.O., Chacón, D., Mayer, G., Whitebread, K.R., Hendler, J., 2001, "CAST Agents: Network-Centric Fires Unleashed," *Proceedings of the 2001 National Fire Control Symposium*, Lihue, HI, August 12-30.

Koza, J., 1993, "Genetic Programming – On the Programming of Computers by Means of Natural Selection," Cambridge, Massachusetts, MIT Press.

Ramamurthy, U., Bogner, M., Franklin, S., 1998, "Conscious Learning in an Adaptive Software Agent," *Proceedings of Second Asia Pacific Conference on Simulated Evolution and Learning*, Canberra, Australia.

Stone, P., 1998, "Layered Learning in Multi-Agent Systems," PhD Thesis, CMU.

Sun, R., Merrill and E., Peterson, T., 2001, "From implicit to Explicit Knowledge: A Bottom-up Model of Skill Learning," *Cognitive Science*, Vol. 25, No. 2, pp. 203-244.

AN ANT-LIKE HEURISTIC FOR CONSTRUCTING HIGH-QUALITY STEINER TREES

XIAOPING YU
Dept. of Computing and Information Science, University of Guelph, Guelph, Ontario, Canada N1G 2W1

GARY GREWAL
Dept. of Computing and Information Science, University of Guelph, Guelph, Ontario, Canada N1G 2W1

CHARLIE OBIMBO
Dept. of Computing and Information Science, University of Guelph, Guelph, Ontario, Canada N1G 2W1

ABSTRACT

The Steiner tree Problem in a Graph (SPG) is an NP-hard problem with numerous practical applications. In this paper, we present an algorithm, called Trail-based Shrubbery, for solving the SPG and discuss its application to multicast communication. In this algorithm, Steiner trees are constructed stochastically much like "shrubs" grow in a garden. Resembling an Ant Colony Optimization (ACO) algorithm, pheromone trails are accumulated on the edges used in the construction of the Steiner trees, with the goal of identifying and combing important paths in the graph for construction of even better trees. We evaluate the performance of Trail-based Shrubbery by running simulations with a large number of benchmarks from SteinLib [1]. Our results show that Trail-based Shrubbery generates higher quality Steiner trees in shorter run time than the very popular Shortest-Path Heuristic (SPH).

1. INTRODUCTION

In this paper a new algorithm for the *Steiner tree Problem in a Graph (SPG)* is presented. Given a weighted graph $G = (V,E)$ and designated subset of vertices, called terminals T, $(T \subseteq V)$, the problem is to find a minimum-cost tree that spans the terminal vertices, using zero or more intermediate non-terminals.

The SPG often arises in network design and wiring layout problems. For example, given a set of sites that must be connected by cables as cheaply as possible; the minimum Steiner tree represents the best way to connect them. Our primary motivation for solving the SPG comes from the need to efficiently create multicast trees to support group communication. A common solution to point-to-multipoint or multicast communications is to connect the members of the communicating group who share a single Steiner (or multicast) tree. The link cost of the Steiner tree may represent relative bandwidth consumption, expected delay, or even the monetary cost of using the link. Especially important is the fact that multicast communication is often highly dynamic, with members joining and leaving the group over time. Thus, the algorithm used to construct the Steiner tree must also be able to modify or improve the current structure of the tree in a timely, efficient manner.

Our algorithm, called *Trail-based Shrubbery*, is a hybrid algorithm that combines an effective heuristic for growing good Steiner trees, which we call

Stochastic Shrubbery, with concepts from *Ant-Colony Optimization (ACO)* [3,4]. In a traditional ACO approach to the SPG, Ants would likely start from each terminal forming paths. These paths would be weighted with pheromone etc. and combined to form a new tree. Unfortunately, having ants find good quality trees is difficult for challenging problem instances. Therefore, we propose here to replace the traditional concept of an ant with the Shrubbery algorithm to produce the initial pool of candidate trees required by ACO.

The basic idea of Trail-based Shrubbery is to grow separate partial trees to form a final Steiner tree. It can construct a Steiner tree from scratch or can begin with a partially formed tree. The ability to start with a partially constructed tree is extremely useful in dynamic or faulty applications, where the structure of the tree may have to be quickly altered to respond to changes in the network. In general, Trail-based Shrubbery allows a vertex (member) to join or leave the tree (group) at any time *without the need to re-compute the entire tree*; reapplication of Trail-based Shrubbery is sufficient to rejoin the disconnected parts of the tree.

2. STOCHASTIC SHRUBBERY

Before presenting the Trail-based Shrubbery algorithm, we present the general idea of Stochastic Shrubbery (SS). SS begins the construction of a Steiner tree by simultaneously growing separate trees rooted at every terminal. Each tree is called a "*shrub*" which initially consists of a single terminal vertex, its root, and each shrub belongs to a unique grove. These shrubs grow towards each other in a coordinated manner. Whenever nearby shrubs touch each other for the first time, they join the same "*grove*". Their connecting paths are merged into a "*hedge*" within the grove. A hedge is a tree (in a graph) that connects all roots (terminals) belonging to the same grove. Eventually all the shrubs become connected and belong to a single grove. Each "dangling" branch is pruned, and the remaining hedge is a Steiner tree.

The key idea in this heuristic is that the selection of the next edge for shrub growth is performed probabilistically. Each edge is associated with a value, called a *complex weight*, based on some rule (the specific rule for Trail-based Shrubbery will be discussed in the next section). The probability of an adjacent edge being chosen by a shrub is proportional to its complex weight. Therefore, by running Stochastic Shrubbery multiple times, a pool of candidate trees can be generated for the ACO algorithm in place of the traditional ants.

3. TRAIL-BASED SHRUBBERY

Trail-based Shrubbery is an ant-like version of Stochastic Shrubbery. The pheromone trail plays an important role in the proportional selection of next edge for shrub growth. In this algorithm, the complex weight of an edge e_{ij} (used to determine the probability of this edge being chosen for shrub growth), is a combination of two aspects: the visibility (denoted as η_{ij}) and the density of the pheromone trail (denoted τ_{ij}). Here, the visibility of an edge is defined as the inverse of root-distance of the destination vertex v_j, which is the cost of the path by which vertex v_j was reached from the root of the shrub. It is fixed during the execution of the algorithm. However, the density of the pheromone trail changes during the process. Let $\tau_{ij}(t)$ denote the function returning the density of pheromone trail of e_{ij} at the t-th iteration. The function $f_{ij}^{a}(t)$ denoting the complex weight of a candidate edge e_{ij} with respect to shrub S_a at the t-th iteration is as follows.

$f_{ij}^{a}(t) = [\tau_{ij}(t)]^{\alpha} \cdot [\eta_{ij}]^{\beta}$, where $\eta_{ij} = \frac{1}{d_j^a}$. Parameters α and β are adopted for adjusting the relative importance of the visibility and the pheromone trail. The probability for candidate edge e_{ij} being chosen by S_a at the t-th iteration is:

$$p_{ij}^{a}(t) = \frac{f_{ij}^{a}(t)}{\sum_{e_{uv} \in S_a^c} f_{uv}^{a}(t)} = \frac{[\tau_{ij}(t)]^{\alpha} \cdot [\eta_{ij}]^{\beta}}{\sum_{e_{uv} \in S_a^c} [\tau_{uv}(t)]^{\alpha} \cdot [\eta_{uv}]^{\beta}}, \text{ where } \eta_{ij} = \frac{1}{d_j^a}.$$

Solutions representing lower cost trees in the pool are reinforced with higher amounts of pheromone, so they are more likely to be used again to produce the next pool of high-quality trees. In this way, a positive feedback loop is formed guiding the search towards better solutions.

3.1 AN EXAMPLE

An example is provided in Fig. 1 to illustrate the proportional selection of the next edge for shrub growth. The original graph is presented in Fig. 1(a). The edge costs are shown beside the edges with the amount of pheromone shown in parentheses. Fig. 1(b) shows the status of the three shrubs after each shrub has grown by one edge. The range of a shrub is identified by a shaded area. As can be seen from Fig. 1(c), Shrub 6 and Shrub 7 have touched each other and joined the same grove. A hedge, which is part of the final tree, is formed between them represented by solid lines. At this stage, there are three candidate edges for Shrub 1, which are represented by dashed lines. Three Steiner trees that can consequently be formed with different probabilities are shown in Fig. 1(d)-(f). The probabilities shown are evaluated setting both α and β to 1. Note that more Steiner trees can be formed as shrub growth in the early stages can be different than that shown in this case.

3.2 THE TRAIL-BASED SHRUBBERY ALGORITHM

A detailed description of Trail-based Shrubbery is presented in Fig. 2. Variables t and *count* (line 1) are used to record the number of cycles, and the number of consecutive cycles for which no improved tree has been found. H^+ and L^+ are used for keeping the best Steiner tree ever found and the cost of the tree. Initially, a small amount τ_0 of pheromone is deposited on each edge (line 3).

Lines 7 to 18 contain the pseudo code for constructing a Steiner tree. It searches for the edge e_{ij} from the elected edge set E_E whose weight w_{ij} extends the shrub S_a to which v_i belongs by the *smallest* root-distance among the elected edges (line 18). If the vertex that edge e_{ij} meets (v_j) does not already belong to a shrub, the original shrub (S_a) expands to include both the new edge and vertex (line 10). If, however, the connecting vertex v_j was found to be part of another shrub S_b, two possibilities exist. Either v_i and v_j belong to shrubs in different

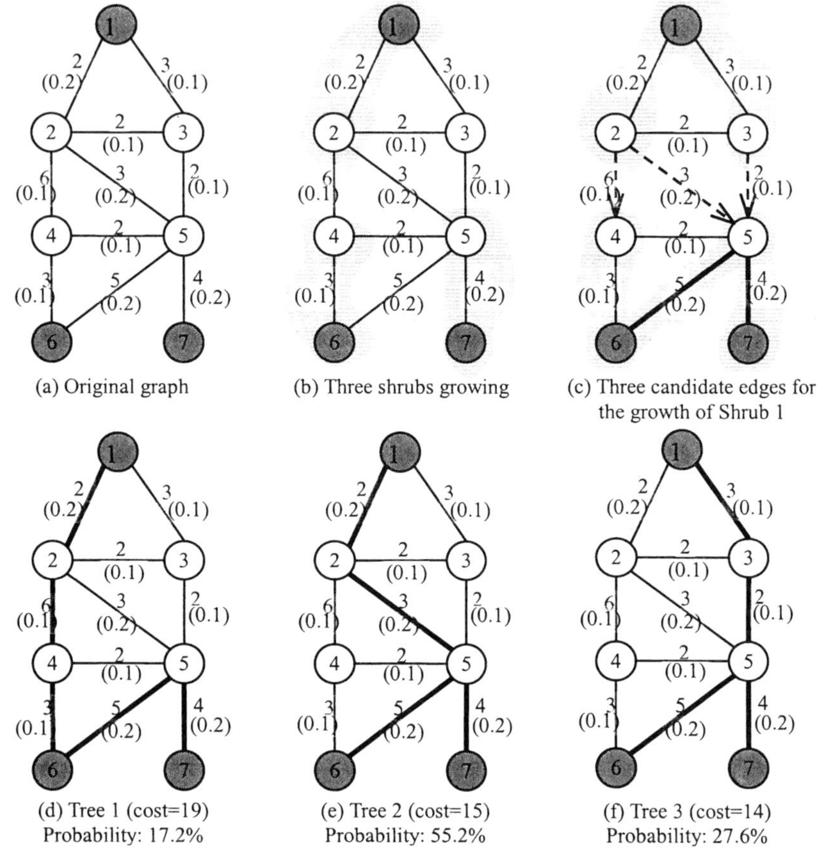

Figure 1: *An example for shrub growth in Trail-based Shrubbery*

groves, or to shrubs in the same grove. The former case implies that the edge (e_{ij}) has caused two groves (G_a and G_b) to meet for the first time. Both groves will merge to form a single grove, and their respective hedges will be connected by a new hedge segment (line 12). The latter case implies that both shrubs (S_a and S_b) are already connected by a hedge, the edge in question (e_{ij}) is not eligible for further consideration.

Inclusion of vertex v_j brings more candidate edges to the candidate edge set S_a^c. A new candidate edge (e_{uv}) is selected probabilistically (line 16), the edge is removed from candidate edge set and added to elected edge set E_E for next shrub growth (line 17).

When a new pool of Steiner trees has been constructed, the pheromone trail of each edge is updated based on the cost of the tours that use this edge (lines 27 to 31). The pheromone trail of each edge also evaporates by a small percentage (ρ). The cycle of generating a pool of Steiner trees and updating the pheromone trails repeats until no better Steiner trees can be found for a preset number (MAX_COUNT) of cycles, or all trees in the pool become identical.

set $t = 0; count = 0; H^+ = \{\}; L^+ = MAX\_VALUE$

For every edge e_{ij} **do**

$\tau_{ij}(t) = \tau_0$

End For

Do

For $k = 1$ to q **do** **/* k trees in a pool */**

Do

Let e_{ij} satisfy $e_{ij} \in E_E$ and $\forall T, \min_{i,j}(d_i^a + w_{ij} : v_i \in S_a, v_j \notin S_a)$

If $v_j \notin S_b, \forall b \in T$

add v_j and e_{ij} to S_a; $P_{aj} = P_{ai} \cup \{e_{ij}\}$

Else If $v_i \in G_a$ and $v_j \in G_b, \forall a \in T, \forall b \in T, a \neq b$

$G_a = G_a \cup G_b;\ H_a = H_a \cup H_b \cup P_{bj} \cup \{e_{ij}\}$

End If

$S_a^c = S_a^c \cap \overline{\{e_{uv} : v_u \in G_a, v_v \in G_a\}} \cup \{e_{jk} : v_j \in G_a, v_k \notin G_a\}$

select edge e_{uv} from S_a^c with probability :

$$p_{uv}^k(t) = \frac{[\tau_{uv}(t)]^\alpha \cdot [\eta_{uv}]^\beta}{\sum_{e_{xy} \in S_a^c} [\tau_{xy}(t)]^\alpha \cdot [\eta_{xy}]^\beta}, \text{ where } \eta_{xy} = \frac{1}{d_y^a}, v_x \in G_a, v_y \notin G_a$$

$S_a^c = S_a^c \cap \overline{\{e_{uv}\}};\ E_E = E_E \cap \overline{\{e_{ij}\}} \cup \{e_{uv}\}$

Until G_a contains all m terminals

$L^k = weight(H_a);\ H^k = H_a$ **/* place the tree in the pool */**

End For

If $L^+ > \min\{L^k : k = 1 \text{ to } q\}$ **/* record the lowest cost tree from the pool */**

$H^+ = H^i, L^+ = L^i$, where $L^i = \min\{L^k : k = 1 \text{ to } q\}$

$count = 0$

Else

$count{+}{+}$

End If

For every edge e_{ij} do **/* update pheromone trails */**

$\tau_{ij}(t) \leftarrow (1-\rho) \cdot \tau_{ij}(t) + \Delta\tau_{ij}(t)$ where

$$\Delta\tau_{ij}(t) = \sum_{k=1}^{q} \Delta\tau_{ij}^k(t), \text{ and } \Delta\tau_{ij}^k(t) = \begin{cases} \tau_o \cdot L^+ / L^k(t), & \text{if } e_{ij} \in H^k(t); \\ 0 & \text{otherwise.} \end{cases}$$

$\tau_{ij}(t+1) = \tau_{ij}(t)$

End For

Until $count > MAX\_COUNT$ or all trees in the pool are identical

Figure 2: *The Trail-based Shrubbery algorithm*

4. RESULTS FOR TRAIL-BASED SHRUBBERY

Our algorithm was tested using 58 instances from sets B, C, and D from the SteinLib repository[1]. Each series contains randomly generated instances, ranging in size from 50 vertices and 500 edges to 1000 vertices and 25000 edges. Edge weights are taken from a uniform distribution in the interval [1,10].

Instance	Trail-based Shrubbery		Shortest-Path Heuristic	
	Avg. Time (s)	Avg. Gap (%)	Avg. Time (s)	Avg. Gap (%)
B (18)	0.04	2.06	0.00	2.4
C (20)	1.69	2.09	1.78	4.3
D (20)	4.48	5.17	13.99	5.2

Table 1: *Computational results for Trail-based Shrubbery, Shrubbery and SPH*

In Tab. 1, we report the problem set and the number of problem instances in each set (in parenthesis) in column 1. In columns 2 and 3 we present the computation time in seconds and the average percentage gap with respect to the optimal value for Trail-based Shrubbery. Similar results are presented in columns 3 and 4 for the well-known Shortest-Path Heuristic (SPH) developed by Takahashi and Matsuyama [2]. Table 1 shows that Trail-based Shrubbery generates higher quality trees (with lower percentage gaps with respect to optimums) than SPH, and it requires less run time than SPH.

5. CONCLUSIONS

Trail-based Shrubbery, a new heuristic for solving the Steiner tree problem in a graph was presented, and its relevance to multicast communication was discussed. As a pool is used to record multiple Steiner trees for cooperatively exploring better solutions, this algorithm has the flexibility to provide multiple solutions based on the application requirements.

A centralized-version of Trail-based Shrubbery was presented. However, the distributed nature of Trail-based Shrubbery enables it to be implemented in a parallel processing system with just minor modifications. Using 58 problem instances from SteinLib repository[1], it was empirically shown that, on average, Trail-based Shrubbery outperformed the popular heuristic, SPH [2], with respect to both solution quality and run time.

6. REFERENCES

[1] K. Voss, A. Martin, and T. Koch, "SteinLib Testdata Library", online document at http://elib.zib.de/steinlib/steinlib.html

[2] H. Takahashi and A. Matsuyama, "An Approximate Solution for the Steiner Problem in Graphs", Math. Japonica, Vol.24, pp.573-577, 1980

[3] M. Dorigo, V. Maniezzo, A. Colorni, "The Ant System: Optimization by a colony of cooperating agents", IEEE Transactions on Systems, Man, and Cybernetics-Part B, Vol. 26, No.1, pp.1-13, 1996

[4] T. Vincent, M. Nicolas, T. Fabrice, L. Daniel, "An Ant Colony Optimization algorithm to solve a 2-machine bicriteria workshop scheduling problem", European Journal of Operational Research, vol. 142, pp. 250-257, 2002

RULE GENERATION FOR CLASSIFICATION BY ANT COLONY OPTIMIZATION

THOMAS HOLLY
Computer Science Department
The University of Texas at Tyler
Tyler, TX 75799
Email: tfholly@yahoo.com

ARUN KULKARNI
Computer Science Department
The University of Texas at Tyler
Tyler, TX 75799
Email: Arun_kulkarni@UTTyler.edu

ABSTRACT
Ant Colony Optimization (ACO) is an exciting model, which can solve a variety of optimization problems, based on observing the cooperative behavior of social insects such as ants. Recently, it has been adapted to the generation of an ordered set of IF-THEN rules, producing categorical classification of unknown input data. The purpose of this paper is to confirm the usefulness of the new application of the Ant Colonization Algorithm to generation of classification rules. This new classification model presents certain advantages similar to those attributed to statistical methods and neural networks, i.e. resistance to noise and attribute interaction, as well as the ability to produce simple rules, useful in the real world. We have implemented the in Visual Basic. We have analyzed six public data sets, mostly in the medical domain.

INTRODUCTION

Overview of Ant Colony Algorithms

The concept of an Ant System was first introduced by Dorigo et al. (Dorigo, 1996). The paradigm is that of a system that is versatile, robust and population-based, as are genetic algorithms. It involves a search for optimum or near-optimum solutions to an optimization problem by using a population of simple agents, with specifically defined simple abilities. Working together, they can solve complex problems. The agents cooperate through indirect communication, and the entire colony can draw on the experience gained by individual agents. The only way agents (ants) communicate is through a pheromone trail they deposit as they travel over an area. Future ants that happen on that area will be more likely to travel down that path, with a probability proportional to the level of pheromone.

Ants looking for food are exhibiting foraging behavior. Since the goal is finding sources of food, it is desirable to find the shortest or near-shortest path to that food source. This is an optimum solution for the ants. An ant bases its direction of travel on pheromone levels. If the ant does not detect any pheromone, or the pheromone in all directions is equal, the ant will essentially go in a random direction initially. If by chance, an ant finds a short path to the food, the pheromone will accumulate along that path more quickly than others, because an ant going a certain average speed can complete more trips in a given time. Because a certain amount of evaporation of pheromone also occurs per unit of time, unused or rarely used paths will lose any pheromone they may have acquired. But short (more optimum) paths will be reinforced by future ants' pheromone trails faster than evaporation can occur. That is because, given a choice of a number of different directions to go, an ant will choose that with the greater pheromone most often. There is still random chance involved, but the ants will probabilistically prefer this direction. This self-reinforcing mechanism is known as a positive feedback loop or autocatalytic behavior. That is, if an ant follows a certain path, it is somewhat more likely that other ants will follow the same path. After a number of ants follow that path, it becomes very likely that even more ants will do so. When nearly all ants follow the same path, this is what is called convergence. It can be observed in the ant trails of real ant colonies.

Modeling Ant Systems by Computer

By observing the behavior of actual ants and other social insects, researchers began to understand their behavior as a kind of "swarm intelligence" (Crichton, 2002), which just means that individually simplistic creatures can, working together, solve a complex optimization problem, for the benefit of the entire colony. This type of behavior is actively being mimicked in computer science with a variety of models and algorithms. The Ant System concept can be used effectively to solve a number of the classical optimization problems, such as the Traveling Salesman, Quadratic Assignment Problem, Job Shop Scheduling, and network routing (Dorigo, et al., 1996).

Although real ants get from one point to another point through all intervening locations, it becomes necessary to define all the adjacent states (locations) possible for an artificial ant to visit. These locations are problem specific but they must store some kind of local information the ant can use to make a decision. This is the amount of pheromone at a particular place. An ant determines the amount of pheromone at a particular place and time (and leaves some by being present for a unit of time).

Dorigo et al. (1999) discussed the similarities of the ACO system with other systems for solving problems or searching for solutions. Each ant can be considered an individual, parallel, probabilistic "experiment" which searches the solution space. Certain transmitted knowledge between the ants (pheromone level) allows them to avoid parts of the search space less likely to produce good solutions. In addition, there are similarities between ACO and neural networks. Both systems learn. In the case of ACO, the system learns by accumulating pheromone trails in frequently visited locations. On the other hand, neural networks learn by reinforcing connection strengths along frequently used synaptic connections. Finally, both ACO and evolutionary computation (genetic algorithms) use a population-based approach. In evolutionary computing, all the knowledge is stored in the genome of the current population, whereas in the ant system, the knowledge gained in the past is remembered by the pheromone distribution.

METHODOLOGY

Description of the Ant Miner System

The algorithm outputs an ordered set of rules for classification in the form of IF-THEN rules, more specifically IF <conditions> THEN <class>. The <conditions> antecedent part of the rule consists of a set of one or more terms, joined with the logical operator AND. The <class> portion following the antecedent is the consequent, or decision of the rule. The terms in the antecedent are triples consisting of form <attribute = value>. The form of the rules and the fact that both algorithms output an ordered set, make the Ant-Miner algorithm comparable to CN2 (Clark and Niblett, 1989). The algorithm is shown in Figure 1. We have implemented the newest version of the Ant System algorithm (Parpinelli, et al., 2002). Note that every iteration of the Repeat-Until loop represents a single ant, which builds a complete rule (a candidate solution). After the rule is built, there is an increase of the pheromone of all the terms contained in the rule. Future ants will make use of this information and will be more likely to repeat rules of past ants, which were of high quality. There are four user-input parameters, which control the program. These are:

A) Number of ants (No_of_ants): the maximum number of iterations the Repeat-Until loop of the algorithm will perform. Since each creates a rule, this is the maximum number of rules created for the current training set.
B) Minimum number of cases per rule (Min_cases_per_rule): During the construction phase, a term cannot be added to the current partial rule if this would make the number of covered cases fall below this number. The algorithm thereby excludes possible solutions, which cover very few cases.
C) Maximum number of uncovered cases in the training set (Max_uncovered_cases): The point at which rule discovery will stop. Each iteration of the While Loop reduces the size of the training set and the number of cases will eventually fall below this number.
D) The number of rules to test convergence (No_rules_converg): The alternative stopping condition for the Repeat-Until loop is if this number of identical rules is produced in sequence by the ants.

```
Training Set = All Training Cases
Initialize Discovered Rule List
While (Training_Set > Max_uncovered_cases)
        t = 1; j = 1;  Initialize Pheromone Trails
     Repeat
           Construction of rule
           Pruning of rule
           Updating of pheromone
       If (the current rule is the same as the last ant's rule) then
           j = j + 1  Else  j = 1 End if
           t = t + 1
     Until (t >= No_of_ants)  OR (j >= No_rules_converg)
   Add best rule, R_best discovered by this population of ants to Discovered Rule List
   Remove those cases covered by R_best from Training Set
End While
```

Figure 1. Ant Miner Algorithm

By having this second test, one does not have to continue producing candidate solutions after there is a high degree of certainty the solutions have been optimized. When you have reached the limit of the ants available (t >= No_of_ants) or repeatedly generated the identical rule a certain number of times (j >= No_rules_converg), the best rule constructed to that point is output. So, a number of ants (a population of ants) have produced a high-quality solution, which is added to the discovered rule list. At this point, the training set is modified by removing all cases correctly matching this best rule, and the process begins again with a new population of ants.

IMPLEMENTATION

We implemented the Ant Miner algorithm using Visual Basic 6.0. We chose Visual Basic 6.0 because we wanted to program in an environment which can easily handle comparisons of the string data type and through which interfacing with a Microsoft Access database is simple using the gateway Microsoft's ADO and SQL. The result has lower performance than a program written in C, but is an object-oriented, visually appealing program useful as a teaching tool. During execution, the program interacts with a Microsoft Access database (*.mdb), in particular with a table named DataSetTraining, which represents the Training Set . The name of each column in the table is assumed to be the attribute name. All data (every value in every field for a record) is assumed to be categorical, i.e. not a continuous value. Values are treated as strings by the program. Values may be integers (i.e. a domain of 1, 2, 3, 4, 5, or 6), but they are also treated as "1", "2", etc. The important point is there must be a limited number of discrete values in the domain (there are an infinite number of continuous values).

Algorithm Overview

The rule discovery process consists of three steps. They are a) rule construction, b) pruning, and c) pheromone updating. These steps are described below.

Step 1: The process of rule construction deals with adding terms to the rule. Terms are added to the rule, one at a time, based on the probability calculations as shown in Equation (1) until one of two stopping criteria is met A) adding any other term will cause the number of covered cases to be less than the minimum number of cases per rule or B) all attributes are already part of the current rule.

$$P_{ij} = \frac{\eta_{ij} \cdot \tau_{ij}(t)}{\sum_{i=1}^{a} \chi_i \cdot \sum_{j=1}^{b_i} \left(\eta_{ij} \cdot \tau_{ij}(t)\right)} \tag{1}$$

where P_{ij} is the probability of the term$_{ij}$, η_{ij} is the problem dependent heuristic function value for term$_{ij}$ and is given by Equation (2). $\tau_{ij}(t)$ is the pheromone value for term$_{ij}$ for iteration t, χ_i is a constant has value 1 if the attribute has not yet has been used and 0 otherwise, a represents the total number of attributes, and b_i is the number of possible values for attribute i.

$$\eta_{ij} = \frac{\log_2 k - H\left(W \mid A_i = V_{ij}\right)}{\sum_{i=1}^{a} \chi_i \cdot \sum_{j=1}^{b_i} \left(\log_2 k - H\left(W \mid A_i = V_{ij}\right)\right)} \tag{2}$$

where $H\left(W \mid A_i = V_{ij}\right)$ is the entropy for term $< A_i = V_{ij} >$ and is given by Equation (3)

$$H\left(W \mid A_i = V_{ij}\right) = -\sum_{w=1}^{k} \left(P\left(w \mid A_i = V_{ij}\right) \cdot \log_2 P\left(w \mid A_i = V_{ij}\right)\right) \tag{3}$$

Both $H\left(W \mid A_i = V_{ij}\right)$, the entropy for a particular term $< A_i = V_{ij} >$, and η_{ij}, its heuristic value, are measures of the amount of information associated with this term in the dataset. The heuristic value is a normalized representation appropriate to the Ant Miner model. A high entropy value indicates uniform distribution of classes (therefore low predictive power) and a low value indicates the opposite. This value must vary within the range $0 \leq H\left(W \mid A_i = V_{ij}\right) \leq \log_2 k$.

Step 2. This deals with pruning. Terms are removed and replaced one at a time noting the improvement in quality. The term that gave the minimum improvement is removed permanently. This is repeated until further pruning will no longer improve the quality of the rule or only one term remains. The quality (*Q*) is defined as a product of *sensitivity* and *specificity*.

Step 3. A critical part of the ACO algorithm is the pheromone updating. All possible terms' pheromone values were initially set according Equation (4).

$$\tau_{ij}\left(t=0\right) = 1 \Big/ \sum_{i=0}^{a} b_i \qquad (4)$$

Where $\tau_{ij}\left(t\right)$ is the pheromone value for term$_{ij}$ for iteration *t*, *a* represents the total number of attributes, and b_i is the number of possible values for attribute *i*. The pheromone values of the terms found in the current rule are increased in proportion to the quality using Equation (5)

$$\tau_{ij}\left(t+1\right) = \tau_{ij}\left(t\right) + \tau_{ij}\left(t\right)Q \qquad (5)$$

Pheromone evaporation is simulated by normalization. All terms' pheromone values are reduced by dividing each τ_{ij} by the sum of all. The order in which the rules appear in the list matters in an algorithm such as Ant Miner. For each unknown case to be classified, the rules are scanned and the first rule that covers the sample is applied. The class predicted by the rule becomes the class assigned to the case. If none of the listed rules covers the case, the majority class of the remaining records in the training set is applied. To determine the accuracy of a rule, the predicted class is compared to the actual class, which must be known. The accuracy of the algorithm's set of rules was determined in two ways for each of six publicly available medical datasets: A) Using the entire dataset as the training set, and reclassifying all cases from the same dataset, B) using 10% of the records as a validation set to test the rules produced by the remaining 90%

RESULTS

The implemented program was run on six publicly available datasets from the UCI Machine Learning Repository (http://www.ics.uci.edu/~mlearn/MLRepository.html), and rule outputs and predictive accuracies were obtained. The Ljubljana Breast Cancer and Tic-Tac-Toe datasets are the only ones of the six that have all categorical attributes. To discretize the continuous attributes of the other four data sets, we used discretization parameters supplied by Parpinelli (Parpinelli et al., 2002).

As expected, the predictive accuracies in the cross-validation scenario were comparable to that using the full training set, sometimes slightly higher or lower due to the small number of validation samples represented by 10% of the dataset, and also compared favorably to the results previously published (Parpinelli et al., 2002). It is possible the relatively poor results obtained for the Hepatitis and Dermatology data sets were due to errors in the discretization or to the use of different parameters. The predictive accuracy and rule simplicity results are shown in Table 1 and 2, respectively.

Data Set	Full Training Set	90% Tr. Set, 10% Val. Set
Ljubljana Breast Cancer	78.7	82.14
Wisconsin Breast Cancer	96.5	97.06
Tic-Tac-Toe	72.87	70.8
Dermatology	80.02	91.7
Hepatitis	51.2	56.25
Cleveland Heart Disease	56.4	63.33

Table 1-Predictive Accuracy Results

Data Set	No. of Rules	Terms/Rule
Ljubljana Breast Cancer	7	1.286
Wisconsin Breast Cancer	6	1.83
Tic-Tac-Toe	9	1.3
Dermatology	6	2.8
Hepatitis	5	2.0
Cleveland Heart Disease	14	2.36

Table 2-Rule Simplicity Results

REFERENCES

Clark, P. and Niblett, T., 1989. The CN2 Induction Algorithm. *Machine Learning Journal*, vol. 3, pp. 261-283.

Dorigo et al., 1996. The Ant System, Optimization by a colony of cooperating agents. *IEEE Transactions on Systems, man and Cybernetics,* vol. 26, pp. 1-13.

Dorigo, M. and Gambardella, L., 1999. Ant Algorithms for Discrete Optimization. *Artificial Life* , vol. 5, pp. 137-172.

Crichton, M., 2002. *Prey*. New York, NY: Harper Collins.

Parpinelli, R., Lopes, H. and Freitas, A., 2002. Data Mining With an Ant Colony Optimization Program. *IEEE Transactions on evolutionary Computing*., vol. 6, pp. 321-322.

EVOLVING INTELLIGENT AGENTS FOR FIRST RESPONDER TRAINING SIMULATION

ALEX J. BERRY, DANIEL R. TAURITZ, MICHAEL G. HILGERS
ajberry@umr.edu; tauritzd@umr.edu; hilgers@umr.edu
Computer Science
University of Missouri – Rolla
Rolla, Missouri

ABSTRACT Many training simulations can benefit from increased levels of reality obtained through the use of intelligent autonomous agents. The optimization of multiple interacting agent programs is an open research problem. Evolutionary Algorithms allow for an efficient directed stochastic search of the (near) infinite space of all possible agent programs. This paper describes a proof-of-concept experiment for evolving autonomous agents in a first responder training simulation employing genetic programming. There are three types of agents (friendly, neutral, and hostile) operating interactively in a two dimensional environment. Each of the agent types has its own goals to enhance or reduce the hostility of the environment, which are correlated to a fitness value. The results show that genetic programming can successfully be employed to optimize the agent programs . With further work, agents should be able to operate in a virtual world to train first responders.

INTRODUCTION

Since 9/11, the need to train first responders has increased drastically. In a joint venture between several UMR labs and consulting firms with funding from the Tank-automotive and Armaments Command, we have begun the task of developing a system to train first responders in a virtual reality environment.

Training First Responders

A system called FiRSTE (First Responder Simulation and Training Environment) is being developed at UMR as the virtual reality training platform for first responders. Our focus is on chemical events that occur inside of populated buildings. It is very important that the responders in training feel like they are in a real event to increase their response to the environment (Leu et al, 2003; Tichon et al, 2003).

Typical Training Event. Training a First Responder typically begins with the premise that either a Hazardous Materials (HAZMAT) or Weapon of Mass Destruction (WMD) event has occured. The appropriate officials are notified and a first responder team arrives at the site. Upon arrival, the incident commander establishes a command post that will act as a starting and ending point for the first responder teams. The responders are sent in the building in groups of two to sweep the building. During this survey, they will look for casualties, locate the deceased, identify the contamination source in the building, and provided assistance to victims as needed. The person or persons responsible for the toxic release may still be present in the building. The responders will also attempt to mitigate the spill to stop it from spreading further. This can be done by throwing a blanket over a spill or turning off a gas canister. Once the responder has finished surveying the building or is running low on air, the team reports to decontamination at the command post.

Issues in Virtual Training. Three main issues existed when attempting to increase the reality of training exercises. First was dispersing the chemical throughout the building using a pre-computed fluid dynamics model (Misra et. al, 2003). The second was to create realistic models of the sensors that first responders use to detect the chemicals and place them in the virtual world (Berry and Hilgers, 2003). The final issue that we faced was to put autonomous agents in the environment with which the first responder may interact. This paper is a proof of concept of this part of training.

Background

Work done by Thomas Haynes describes an approach to evolving agents in a hostile environment (Haynes and Wainwright, 1995). Haynes simulated simple agents in a hostile environment using genetic programming techniques to evolve behaviors in the environment. The emphasis of his approach was evolving an agent that could operate on a randomly generated grid. This project extends some of this work.

Genetic Programming

Genetic Programming is an Evolutionary Computing (EC) technique where the individuals in the population typically represent executable computer programs (Koza, 1990; Langdon, 1995). The individuals in the population are parse trees that consist of terminals and non-terminals. Two types of trees are implemented for this project: traditional LISP style decision trees and expression trees.

METHODOLOGY

The project consists of three elements: the map generator, the agents, and the genetic programs. Each of these was approached with different techniques to combine the whole project as one system.

Map Generator

The map generator is used to generate grids for performing the experiments and is also used as the memory storage device for the agents. For this iteration of the project, randomly generated maps were generated with a parameter called *wall weight*, (p_{wall}). This parameter represents the percentage of the building that will be filled with walls.

Agents

Three types of agents operate on the map with different goals and abilities: friendly, neutral, and hostile. These agents operate based off of a generic agent base class. For this proof of concept, the first responder and victim agents were the primary focus. The basic operations of the first responder-the friendly agent-are to identify victims and hazards at the location and, if possible, to remove potential hazards. In the developed environment all of these goals were simulated. The first responders identified living victims and helped to remove them from the building. When a deceased victim or a potential hazard is found the first responder remembered the location, in essence notifying the commander. The responder can attempt to mitigate the trap at its own risk. First responders could interact with other first responders in the environment, this simulated radio contact.

The neutral, or victim, agents moved undirected in the environment in a "panicky" state. They had only one goal: trying to escape the building. When the victim agent encountered a first responder, the victim escaped the building and transferred its knowledge of the building to the first responder. This transfer of knowledge was blurred to simulate the real effects of how a victim would remember the environment.

The terrorist, or hostile, agent existed to cause mayhem in the environment. The terrorist agents were able to set traps that had timed detonation. When the traps detonated, they affected the surrounding cells in the grid, killing all agents in those cells.

The Evolutionary Process

The first responder agents were evolved to explore the large search space of possible states in order to find agents that are adept in the goal emphasized in its fitness function.

Individual Representation. Each individual consisted of a collection of expression and decision trees. The expression trees contain logical operators and terminals associated with the map. The logic operators used are XOR, AND, OR, and NOT. The terminals and their meanings are shown in Table 1. "S" represents some location on that map. Figure 1 shows a random expression tree instance that evaluates to true when there is a terrorist or trap at location S, but not a victim.

The decision trees consist of expression trees, an operator, and terminals. The decision tree is built around the *if-then-else*, or IFTE, operation. The IF evaluates on an expression tree and the THEN and ELSE can be terminals or further decision trees. The terminals associated with the decision tree are listed in Table 2; a manually generated action tree has been illustrated in Figure 2. The terminals were developed so that they could be easily adapted to the evolution of hostile and other agents.

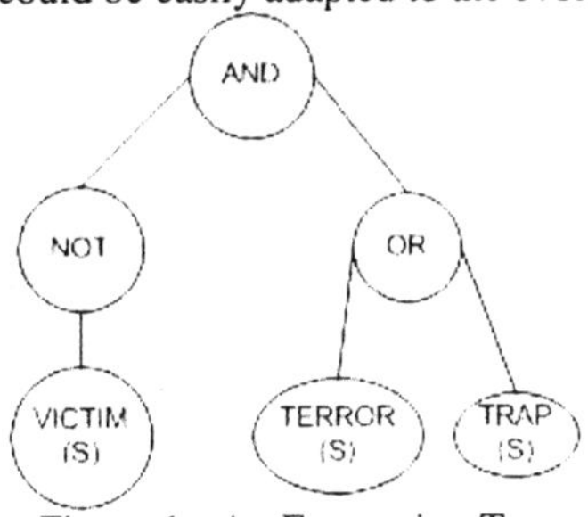

Figure 1 - An Expression Tree

Table 1 – Terminals for Expression Trees

Terminal	Meaning
VICTIM(S)	Victim at Location S?
TRAP(S)	Trap at Location S?
VALIM(S)	Moving to S a valid move?
FIRSTR(S)	First Responder at Location S?
TERROR(S)	Terrorist at Location S?

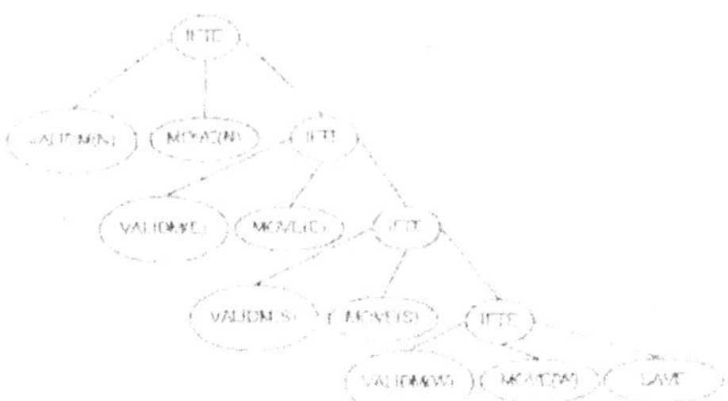
Figure 2 - A Decision Tree

Table 2 – Terminals for Decision Trees

Terminal	Meaning
MOVE(S)	Move to Location S.
SAVE(S)	Save victim(s) at S.
KILL(S)	Trap Terrorist at S.
PRTRAP(S)	Remove Trap S.

Initialization. The population was initialized using either randomly or manually generated trees.

Evaluation. Every generation the agents were evaluated in the form of running a simulation with the agents multiple times. The simulation was run multiple times to counteract the effects of the initial random placements giving an average fitness that were more representative of the individual. Each agent entered the environment differently:

the victim and terrorist agents were randomly placed in the grid while the responder agents entered through "doors" on the side of the map. The terrorists continued to set traps, victims moved randomly, and the first responders surveyed the area. After the collection of simulations had finished, the agents were evaluated on their performance, which was used as the fitness for competition. Fitness for a first responder was based on the weighted sum of the number of victims rescued, length of survival time, number of terrorists caught, number of traps diffused, and the amount of the map explored. The lower bound of the fitness function is zero and the upper bound is dependent on several stochastic values (number of traps placed, exploration path) and deterministic values (the size of the map and the number of agents in the simulation).

Selection. Selection was a simple rank-based selection. The trees are sorted based on their calculated fitness. Since the populations are small, around ten, the best two or three individuals were used to generate the children.

Reproduction. Reproduction consisted of two operators: crossover and mutation. Only one was performed at a time due to the destructive nature of these operators when using GP. A parameter is used to control the rate that each is used. Crossover replaced a sub-tree of one individual with a similar size sub-tree from another. Mutation replaced a sub-tree in one individual with a randomly generated tree of similar size. When either of these operations was used, expression trees can only replace expression trees and decision trees can only replace decision trees.

Competition. Elitist-deterministic competition is used for this project. The individuals with the highest fitness values from the simulation were kept and used for the production of the next generation of individuals.

EXPERIMENTS AND RESULTS

Many different experiments were needed to optimize the 25 relevant parameters of this evolutionary process. While exploring the parameters, it was found that the crossover versus mutation rate had interesting effects based on its value.

Experimental Setup

For the experiments, all three agent types were used. While not evolving, the terror and victim agents were still active in the environment. The weights for the fitness function of the first responder were set to emphasize the amount of the map explored and the number of victims that were rescued, the most important factors for the friendly agents. In this case, the number of cells in the map that were explored and the number of victims helped had the highest multipliers. The map size was set to a 50 by 43 square grid. With this limit, the maximum fitness that is achievable is 20,000. Two thousand would be a good individual, an agent that explored 1/8th of the map, helped several victims, and mitigated several traps can achieve this fitness value.

Results

The first experiments run were done to get a baseline for the parameter values. To start with parameter values were chosen based on knowledge of the problem, knowledge of GPs, and some random values. The initial results were not good. Occasionally, exceptions with fitnesses up to 1000 were seen, but did not last long. Figure 3 shows a graph of the fitnesses versus number of generations for a sample of the early experiments. The fitness values can increase and decrease drastically since agents' actions were affected by other agents in the environment. Two parameters were increased for the next trials in order to explore the problem. The crossover versus mutation chance was raised to an 80% chance in favor of crossover. The map was also set to regenerate every five generations so that agents could improve on a given map before the next was explored. This run resulted in a lower average fitness of about 250, but more individuals reached above a fitness of 1400. Figure 4 shows a sample output from this run. Since this change produced promising results, the crossover versus mutation chance was further explored.

The crossover versus mutation chance was next run set to 0 (pure mutation) and 1 (pure crossover). While it was set to zero, no reasonable results were observed. When the parameter was set to 1, good results started to appear, only to be hindered by limitation of the computing environment. Figure 5 shows the output from this run. There is little change in the data for the first 4750 generations, but suddenly between generations 4750 and 4810 intelligence starts to emerge. Upon exploration it was found that the program was halted due to excessive memory usage. The best individual from this run had a depth of 60 and 3,354,136 nodes. This experiment was run again with the RNG unseeded to see if the same results would occur. This time the signficant increase in magnitude occured at 100 generations, and again a giant tree was produced that obtained the highest fitness. Table 3 shows the tree node count, tree depth, and fitness for the best individuals at the ends of all of these trials. This seems to indicate that crossover is more important than mutation in this environment. More runs were done with different initial random seeds to see if this held. It was found that other runs produced good results with a high number of nodes and depth, often in less than 100 generations.

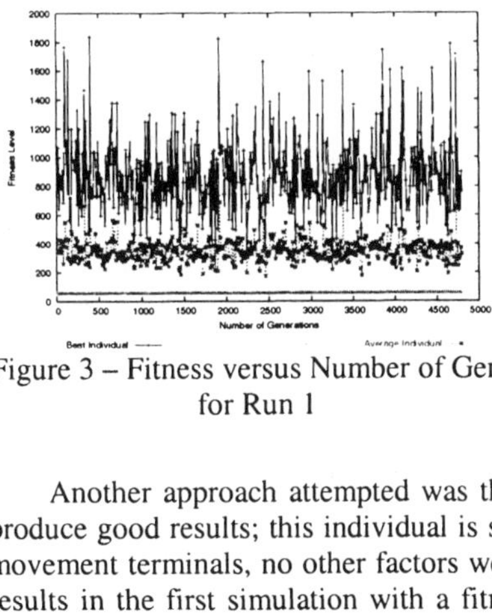

Figure 3 – Fitness versus Number of Gens. for Run 1

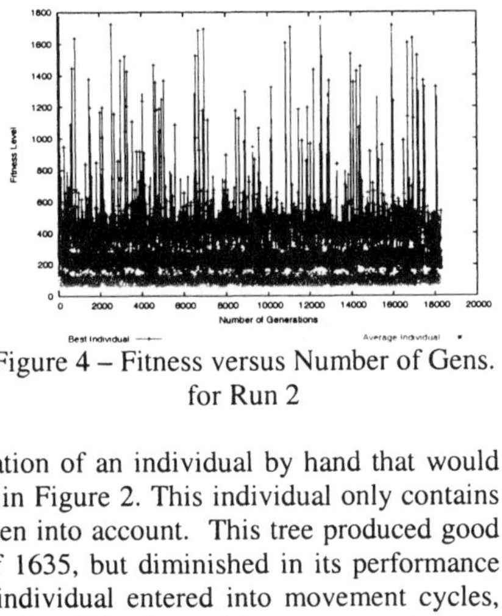

Figure 4 – Fitness versus Number of Gens. for Run 2

Another approach attempted was the creation of an individual by hand that would produce good results; this individual is shown in Figure 2. This individual only contains movement terminals, no other factors were taken into account. This tree produced good results in the first simulation with a fitness of 1635, but diminished in its performance after that. Later it was discovered that this individual entered into movement cycles, where it looped along the same path countinuously. This showed that more usage of the agent's memory is needed to produce good results.

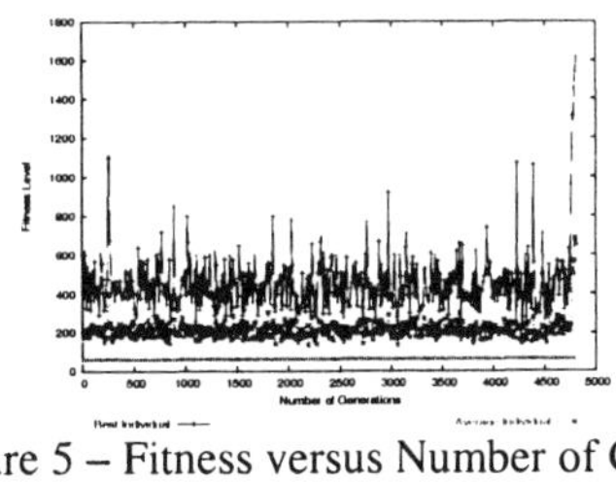
Figure 5 – Fitness versus Number of Gens. for Run 3

Table 3 – Summary of Results for Runs

Run	Tree Depth	Number of Nodes	Fitness
1	5	21	757
2	14	315	535
3	60	3,354,136	1615
4	53	2,864,677	1105

CONCLUSIONS

First responder training is becoming more important in our world with today's terrorist threats. Currently, the Virtual Environment and Object Modeling (VEnOM) Labs is working on a virtual reality software suite to train first responders to meet this need. One of the features that is needed for advanced training is autonomous agents in the VR environment. This research showed that it is possible to evolve intelligent agents to operate in a hostile environment. The three agent types (friendly, neutral, and hostile) were put into a grid world where they interacted. It was found that these genetic agents have very complex genetic programs that help them explore the world. It has also been shown that the crossover operator is better for reproduction than the mutation operator. The use of a hand generated agent showed the importance of using the agent's memory to influence how it explores the map. The use of GP to evolve agents in a hostile environment has proved successful in this research. With further exploration and development of new operators, it is conceivable to produce agents suitable for virtual reality training meeting Homeland Security needs

Future Work

Later, an approach to building maps that look like real floor plans will be used; these maps will correspond with the maps that the real first responders are exploring. Experiments involving the co-evolution of hostile and friendly will be performed in order to develop counter agents.

Acknowledgements

Terry Lambert at Battelle for all of his help with information about training first responders. This work was funded by the U.S. Army's Tank-Automotive and Armaments Command (TACOM, grand #DAAE07-02-C-L068).

REFERENCES

A.J. Berry and M.G. Hilgers. Modeling First Responder Emergency Sensors for Virtual Training. In M.H. Hamza, editor, Proceedings of the 15th IASTED Modeling and Simulation Conference, pages 234-239, Anaheim, CA, USA, 2004. ACTA Press.

Thomas D. Haynes and Roger L. Wainwright. A simulation of adaptive agents in hostile environment. In K. M. George, Janice H. Carroll, Ed Deaton, Dave Oppenheim, and Jim Hightower, editors, Proceedings of the 1995 ACM Symposium on Applied Computing, pages 318-323, Nashville, USA, 1995. ACM Press.

John R. Koza. Genetically breeding populations of computer programs to solve problems in artificial intelligence. In Proceedings of the Second International Conference on Tools for AI, Herndon, Virginia, USA, pages 819-827. IEEE Computer Society Press, Los Alamitos, CA, USA, 6-9 1990.

William B. Langdon and Adil Qureshi. Genetic programming - computers using "natural selection" to generate programs. Technical Report RN/95/76, Gower Street, London WC1E 6BT, UK, 1995.

M.C. Leu, M.G. Hilgers, S. Agarwal, R.H. Hall, T. Lambert, R. Albright, and K. Nebel. Training in virtual environments for first responders. In Proceedings of the ASEE Midwest Section Meeting, 2003.

A. Misra, A. Decker, B. Barker, and M.G. Hilgers. Modeling chemical events within complex buildings for first responder virtual training. In M.H. Hamza, editor, Proceedings of the 15th IASTED Modeling and Simulation Conference, pages 240-245, Anaheim, CA, USA, 2004. ACTA Press.

J. Tichon, R.H. Hall, M.G. Hilgers, M. Leu, and S. Agarwal. Education and training in virtual environments for disaster management. In Proceedings of the World Conference on Educational Multimedia, Hypermedia, and Telecommunications, pages 1191-1194, 2003.

A. J. Berry. Evolving Agents in a Hostile Environment. Technical Report. http://web.umr.edu/~tauritzd/courses/cs401/fs2003/project/Berry.pdf. December 2003

SMART CONTROLL FOR COLLECTIVE AGENTS

MASAHIRO KINOSHITA
Hokkaido Institute of Technology

MAKOTO OYA
Hokkaido University

TAKASHI KAWAKAMI
Hokkaido Institute of Technology

MICHIKO WATANABE
Asahikawa National College of Technology

MASASHI FURUKAWA
Asahikawa National College of Technology

ICHIKO KINJO
Hokkaido University

YUKINORI KAKAZU
Hokkaido University

ABSTRACT
Recent advances in a multi-agent system are standing on the basis how to treat several agents from a viewpoint of the agent approach. This paper proposes a new concept "Smart Control for Collective Agents" and a new methodology "Adaptive Strategic Mechanism for Collective Agents" from a viewpoint of adaptation in natural. Then, they are applied to a various kind of collective agents' problems. The smart control means that the collective agents explore their proper strategy through the adaptation under dynamic and ill-known environments, and that each agent makes an autonomous decision under the explored strategy as if he/she has intelligence. Based on the smart control, some behavior patterns for the collective agents emerge and they are controlled to be adaptable for the environments. The collective agents can often be considered as a mobile multi-robot in a robotics field. However, the proposed concept and methodology are applicable to other engineering field such as an information network, a social behavior, and so on. In order to verify the proposed concept and methodology concretely, several examples are shown.

INTRODUCTION

In this paper, we consider the smart control for collective agent and the adaptive strategic mechanism model for collective agents from a viewpoint of adaptation. Adaptive systems have been introduced by Holland[1)] as open systems make think much of interactions between the systems and the environment. Much effort has been expended to solve multi-agent tasks and autonomous decentralized tasks. However, many of further researches lack of a viewpoint of adaptation and a viewpoint of whole of the systems. We focus a kind of multi-agent systems are constructed by collective agents that emerge collective patterns take into consideration of adaptive systems. Practical studies have just recently been appeared to the problem of the controlling and emerging collective patterns for collective agents by those in different fields, namely robotics, distributed artificial intelligence and artificial life. In the robotics field, many efforts have been addressed to multi-agent systems, where a robot is regarded as an agent. Kawakami, Kinoshita and Kakazu[2)] and their subsequent works solved the problem of coordinating multiple homogeneous and heterogeneous mobile robotic units utilize the common knowledge, and demonstrated their results applied to the navigation problem. In the distributed artificial intelligence, interactions between multi-agents were mainly concerned. Namely, the distributed artificial intelligence has focused on the negotiation and coordination problem of multi-agents under given environments. Because the essential problem of the multi-agent system in the distributed artificial intelligence did not exist in applying the knowledge-based system but solving the sorting algorithm, approaches to the problem varied from applying heuristic search to adopting a decision theory. In the artificial life field, bottom-up modeling of various complex systems has been focused on. Simulations of colonies by emotional agents are referred in Naruse[3)]. In this way, the points of interest of collective agent are how to control collective agents as a whole, how and when make patterns by collective agents and how obtain collective behaviors caused by interaction between collective agents and the environment.

COLLECTIVE AGENT MODEL

We termed "collective agent" that was the system whose elements have decision-making mechanisms autonomously to generate patterns. As a result, collective patterns are formed by the whole of collective agents as a whole of systems. And we consider the adaptive strategic mechanism that is the feature to determine the adaptive strategy in order to adapt to the dynamically changeable environment. We describe collective agent system as follows;

$$CAS = (CA, E) \tag{1}$$

where CA is collective agent, and E denotes an environment.

$$CA = (\Sigma, \Omega, B, M) \tag{2}$$

Collective agent is represented by an adaptive plan Σ, a set of selected plans Ω, a set of collective patterns B and environmental measurement M. An adaptive plan determines selected plan that generates collective patterns, taking account of measurement from environment E.

$$\Sigma : \Omega \times M \to \Omega \tag{3}$$

In other words, Σ is a strategy selector and Ω is a strategy function. Also, μ is the evaluation function.

$$M = \mu(\Omega) \tag{4}$$

Figure 1 shows the overview of the adaptive system model for collective agent. At first, initial collective pattern $B(0)$ is given, and the adaptive plan chooses selected plan $\Omega(1)$ using the measurement by environment. This selected plan $\Omega(1)$ generates next collective pattern $B(1)$. Subsequently, the adaptive plan selects the selected plans $\Omega(2), \Omega(3)$ and collective patterns $B(2), B(3)$. In this way, the selected plan carries out the transition of the patterns make better use of the feedback from the environment. The evaluations of selected plan by the environment $\mu(\Omega(2)), \mu(\Omega(3))$ become inputs for the system in the next step.

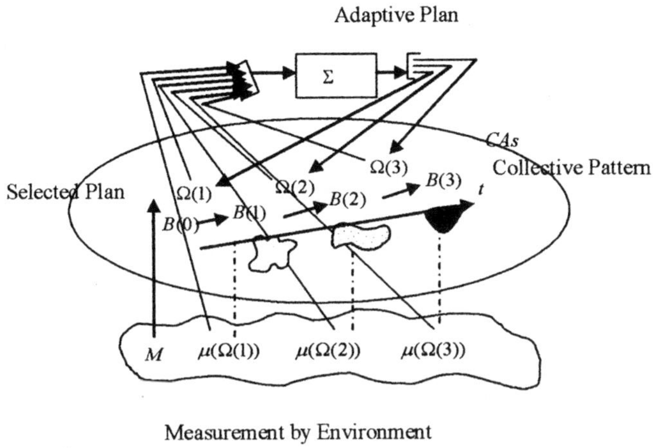

Figure 1 Adaptive Plan, Selected Plan, Collective Pattern and Measurement

ACQUISITION OF THE ADAPTOVE STRATEGIC KNOWLEDGE

In engineering, the warehouse problem in the future faculty is typically similar with collective behavior. However, this kind of factory is not reality at the present yet. Okino[4)] proposed the Bionic Manufacturing Systems with flexible adaptive mechanism for the future manufacturing systems. In this system, the machines, crates, cargoes, sometimes, AGV(Automatically Gained Vehicle) can move around free-space in the faculty autonomously. This type of manufacturing system can adapt the changing the environment getting rid of the stiffness of the system. Such being the case, the scheme to control collective agents is motivated by multiple robotics. Specifically, we are interested in the patterns formed by multiple robots. For this purpose we consider strategy function Ω in adaptive systems to generate the patterns. Some selected plans $\Omega = \{\Omega_1, \Omega_2, \cdots, \Omega_a\}$ are prepared in advance, and they are selected by the system for obtaining the feasible collective patterns adaptively. Difficulties of selection the selected plan are "when change the plan" and "which plan is adequate". For this problem, we utilized the strength map in classifier system that characteristics are several reward systems available and capability of adjusting a dynamical changeable environment. Therefore adaptive switching mechanisms that can select the set of hierarchical sub plans $\Omega_i = \{\omega_{i1}, \omega_{i2}, \cdots, \omega_{ib}\}$ are introduced. Consequently the adaptive plan Σ selects the set of sub plans by adaptive switching mechanism using the strength map. More concretely, the time t of switching is decided by the time when the strength value is becoming higher than the threshold value. The problem treated in this paper is removing the mobile robot from the container. In this time, the mobs of the mobile robots form the collective pattern B . Here, methods of acquisition of the adaptive strategic knowledge of collective agents based on the classifier system are introduced. Relationship between the collective agents system and the classifier system is shown in Table 1.

CAS	CS
Adaptive Plan Σ	Learning Classifier System
Selected plan **Ω**	Reward-System Strength-Map Strategy
Collective pattern **B**	Movement to target Position
Measurement **M**	Steps for task accomplishment

Table 1 A relationship between collective agent system and classifier system

In this table, adaptive system is the structure of classifier system itself. The selected plan is constructed by some mechanism in the classifier system. Namely, reward-system, strength-map and strategy are utilized for deciding the selected plan. A set of agents are construct of the collective patterns while agents behave in the environment. For example, the initial configuration of agents, the middle of configuration of movement and the final configuration of agents are units of the collective patterns. Thus, from the viewpoint of objective problem, such as navigation problem, the positions of agents in Euclidean space are important factors of collective patterns.

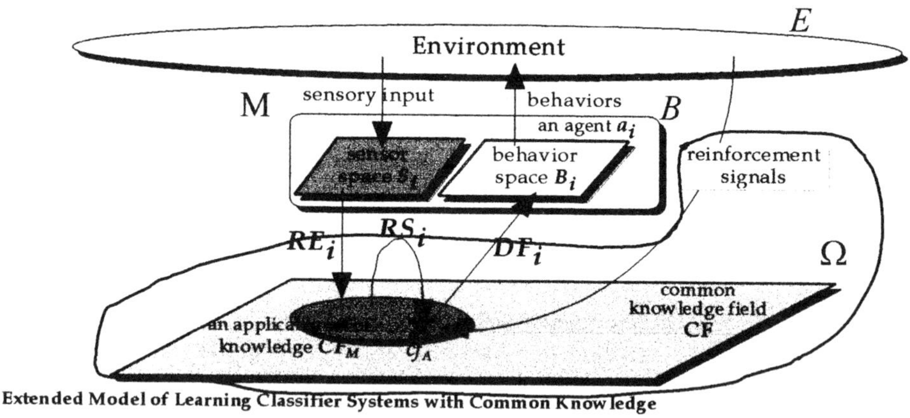

Figure 2 A structure of the classifier system with the collective agents system

In this section, construction of adaptive strategy that utilizes the rule-base system and the performance system is described. Figure 2 shows an overview of the classifier system. The rule-base system plays as reactive rule and the position of strength for storing in classifier is decided by the rule-base. Therefore, if only one classifier is prepared for all collective agents, we can construct a common knowledge as a strength map in the classifier system. The value of strength is decided by the performance system using by reward system. Such as mechanism which can perform the reactive system deciding position and value for storing strength is realized as the selected plan Ω. Thus, the strength map and the reward system constitute the selected plan Ω. For embody the collective agent system, a concrete problem which termed "Removing Problem" is introduced. In this problem, we treat a 2-dimensional mobile robot that shaped circular and rectangular as a collective agent. The purpose of the problem is all of the agents removing from the container. For realization of the adaptive system for collective agents, it is necessary to verify what kind of reward system is adequate.

COMPUTER SIMULATIONS

Based on the proposed method, the agent removal simulator is constructed and some computational experiments are carried out. Our one of major objective is realization of the adaptive system utilizes the classifier system and avoiding deadlocks under the condition of the autonomous behavior of the agents. The number of classifier rules is fixed to 47200. The initial population of classifiers is generalized randomly, and every strength value of initial classifiers is set equivalently. First, to determine the effective reinforcement scheme, we performed primary experiments using the simple and same agents (homogeneous collective circle agents), and all of the agents are able to attain the goal position. That is, there are no agents which dimensions are large enough compare with the width of the exit of the container. Figure 3 shows learning curves, x-axis represents learning times and y-axis represents the steps achieving tasks. For instance, in the left panel, the learning is stopped at time 62, in the right panel, the learning is succeeded when the adaptive switching adopted. Figure 4 shows the trajectories of 55 agents with the adaptive switching mechanism when the learning was succeeded. In this figure, avoiding the deadlock phenomena was appeared and we can see the all of agents could remove from the container adaptively.

CONCLUTION

We proposed adaptive systems for agents which we termed the collective agents and suggested that an adaptive strategic mechanism using a classifier system as a selected plan. The collective behaviors appeared while the agents were moving in order to adapt to the environment. This simple simulation should be followed up by more complicated simulations, with further research to investigate more efficient solutions.

REFERENCES

[1] Holland, J.H., Adaptation in Natural and Artificial System, University of Michigan Press, Ann Arbor, Michigan, 1975.

[2] Takashi Kawakami, Masahiro Kinoshita, Yukinori Kakazu, Collective Robots Navigation by Reinforcement Learning Mechanisms with Common Knowledge Field --An Approach for Heterogeneous-Agent Systems--, International Symposium on Flexible Automation and Intelligent Manufacturing, 2000

[3] Keitaro Naruse, Satoshi Kawai, Hiroshi Yokoi, Yukinori Kakazu, "Group Formation of Agents with Two-dimensional Inner State and One-to-one Subjective Evaluation", 2003 IEEE International Symposium on Computational Intelligence in Robotics and Automation, 2003.

[4] Norio Okino, Bionic Manufacturing System(in Japanese), Asakura-Publishment, 1993.

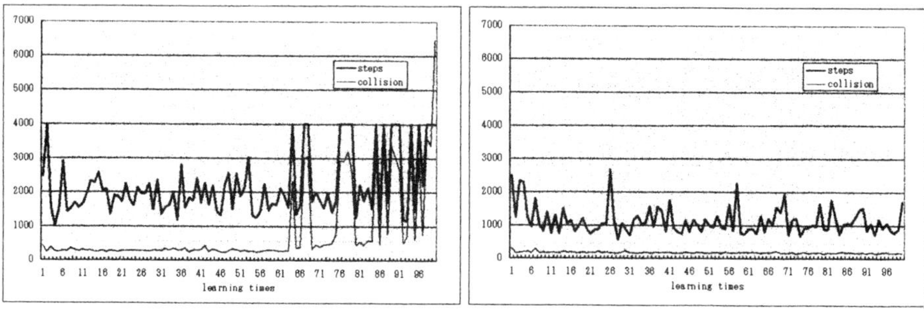

Figure 3 Learning curves

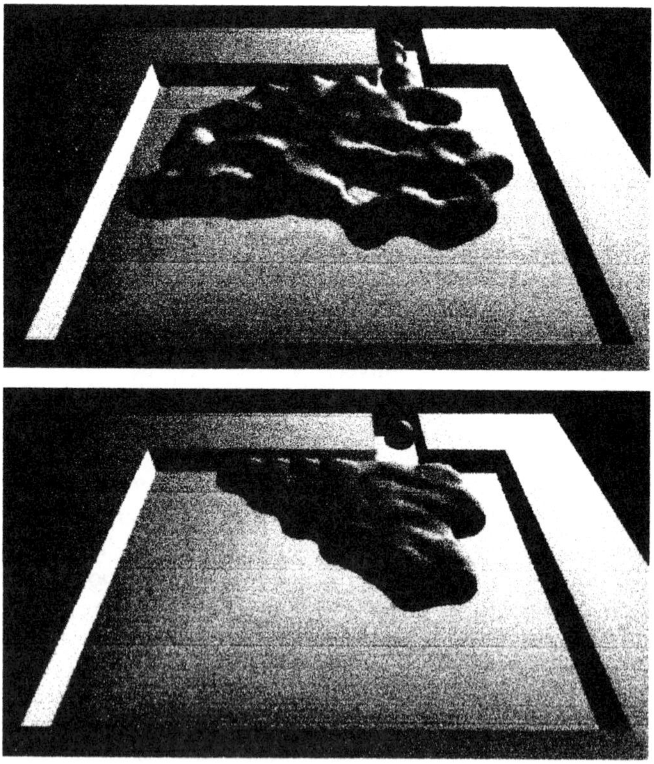

Figure 4 Generated patterns in collective agents system

AGGRERATION AND DISTRIBUTION OF SOCIAL AGENTS

KEITARO NARUSE
University of Aizu, Japan

MASAHIRO KINOSHITA
Hokkaido Institute of Technology, Japan

MASASHI FURUKAWA
Asahikawa National College of Technology, Japan

RYUICHI OKA
University of Aizu, Japan

ABSTRACT
The objective of this paper is to present a control method of self-organized formation such as aggregation and distribution of agents in a non-metric space. In this paper, the self-organization is regarded as finding multiple solutions simultaneously in a multi-modal function in a discrete space. For the search problem, we introduce the concept of the particle swarm optimization (PSO). However, it has been known PSO converges too much to a single solution. We solve the problem by giving social structure to the agents. We investigate and discuss how the social structure affects to the self-organization of the agents as well as the search ability. Computational experiments are conducted and the results show that the proposed agent system can find a good solution while the aggregation and distribution can be controlled by a parameter.

INTRODUCTION

As the growth of World Wide Web and associated services, a huge amount of information becomes available potentially. However, we cannot fully utilize them, because we do not know where information we want are located in. One of the ways to find it is to search in the whole Web, but it requires a vast computational costs. So, it is desired a search engine which searches it in a promising area extensively while it puts a little effort to the other areas for expecting to find them by chance. In other words, it is to control aggregation and distribution of search engine focuses, or it is called agents in this paper, according to the relevance of the information we want.

The objective of this paper is to present a control method of self-organized formation such as aggregation and distribution of agents in the Web space. As one of the characteristics of the Web space, a distance with respect to the relevance of the information is difficult to be defined; each of the Web pages is linked to other pages with a hyperlink, which does not relate to the relevance of contents directly, although some relation can be expected. Therefore, the agents suffer from the self-organization in the non-metric space.

In this paper, we regard the information search in the Web space as an optimal solution search problem. Then, the self-organization in the Web space turns to finding multiple solutions simultaneously in a multi-modal function in a discrete space. For the search problem, we introduce the concept of the particle swarm optimization (PSO). It is a multiple-point-simultaneous-search algorithm. However, PSO converges too much to a single solution.

We solve the convergence problem by giving social structure to the agents;

the agents are divided into several groups. In each of the groups, the agents cooperate to find a good solution. Among the groups, they sometime compete, cooperate, or ignore the other group depending on pre-determined relationship. By the social structure, we attempt to realize the self-organization of the agents.

In this paper, we investigate and discuss how the social relationship affects to the aggregation and distribution of the agents as well as the search ability of the agent system. We carried out the computational experiments and the results show that the proposed agent system can find a good solution while the aggregation and distribution can be controlled by a parameter.

PARTICLE SWARM OPTIMIZATION

Particle Swarm Optimization (PSO) is one of the evolutionary computation methods developed by Kennedy and Eberhart (1995, 2001). In PSO, potential solutions, called particles, are flown through a problem space by following current optimal particles.

The update of the particles is accomplished by the following equations. Equation (1) calculates a new velocity for each particle based on its pervious velocity (V_{id}), the particle's location at which the best fitness so far has been achieved (p_{id}), and the best particle among the neighbors (p_{nd}) at which the best fitness has been achieved so far. Equation (2) updates each particle's position in a solution space. The two random numbers are randomly generated (ϕ_1 and ϕ_2), and c_1 and c_2 are learning factors. The inertia weight is provided for improving performance.

$$V_{id}(t+1) = wV_{id}(t) + c_1\phi_1(p_{id} - x_{id}(t)) + c_2\phi_2(p_{nd} - x_{id}(t)) \quad (1)$$

$$x_{id}(t+1) = x(t) + V_{id}(t+1) \quad (2)$$

The neighborhood means connection between the particles determined before the evolution starts; it does not mean a small area in the solution space around the particle. In the following, the neighbor size of three is considered, which includes the particle itself and two adjacent particles. Figure 1 illustrates the particle connection and velocity in PSO. The number in the circles means ID of each particle, and t represents a time instance. The number below the circles shows the fitness value of each particle.

Compared with genetic algorithms (GAs), the information sharing mechanism in PSO is significantly different. In GAs, chromosomes share information with each other. So the whole population moves like a group towards an optimal area. In PSO, only the best solution in the neighbor gives out the information to the others. It is a one-way information sharing mechanism. The evolution only looks for the best solution. All the particles tend to converge to the best solution.

PROPOSED AGENT SYSTEM

For realizing the self-organized aggregation and distribution of the agents, first, it should be described where and how much the agents are aggregated and distributed. In this paper, it is given as function representation and the agents stay at an optimal point of the function. That is, if the agents should be aggregated, it is given as a uni-modal function and they are concentrated at an optimal point. On the other hand, if they should be distributed, it is given as a constant function. Furthermore, if they are requested to make several small groups, it is given as a multi-modal function in which each peak of the function corresponds to a location of each group. One of the advantages of the function representation is that it can represent a time-dependent landscape as well as restrictions and constraints among the agents.

It has been known that PSO outperforms the simple genetic algorithm with respect to the search speed and ability. However, it converges to a single solution. In this paper, to solve the convergence problem, we introduce social structure to the agents (Naruse 2003a, 2003b). The agents are divided into several groups. In each of the groups, the agents cooperate to find a good solution. Among the groups, they sometime compete, cooperate, or ignore the other group depending on pre-determined relationship. By the social structure, we attempt to realize the self-organization of the agents.

Suppose the agent i belongs to the group I. The velocity of the agent is defined as follows:

$$\begin{aligned} V_i(t+1) &= wV_i(t) + c_1\phi_1(p_i - x_i(t)) + c_2\phi_2(p^I{}_n - x_i(t)) \\ &\quad - c_3\phi_3 \sum_J (p^J{}_n - x_i(t)) \end{aligned} , \qquad (3)$$

where $p^I{}_n$ and $p^J{}_n$ are the best agent is the group I and J, respectively. c_3 is a coefficient of the effect from the other groups, and the agent moves closer to the group if it is a positive value, the agent moves away from the group if it is a negative value, and the agent ignores the group if it is zero. The range of c_3 is $[-1,1]$. ϕ_3 is a random number as well as ϕ_1 and ϕ_2. Figure 2 illustrates the social structure and connection among the agents. The green circles represent the best agents in each group.

With this dynamics, each group independently searches for a good solution, receiving the effect from the other groups. If c_3 is a negative value, each of the groups is expected to converge to a different peak, because it moves away from the other groups. On the other hand, if c_3 is a positive value, all of the groups get closer, so they are expected to converge to a single peak. Therefore, the proposed agent system can aggregate and distribute the agents by the landscape of the function. In addition, the agent system can do the same thing with the parameter of c_3. It is verified with computational simulations in the next section.

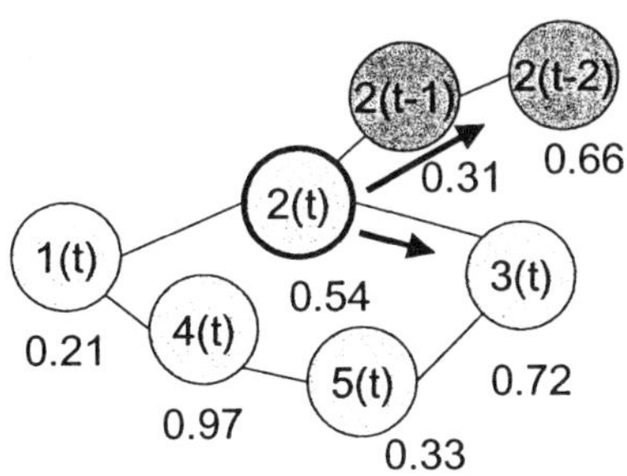

Figure 1: Particle connection and velocoity in Particle Swarm Optimization.

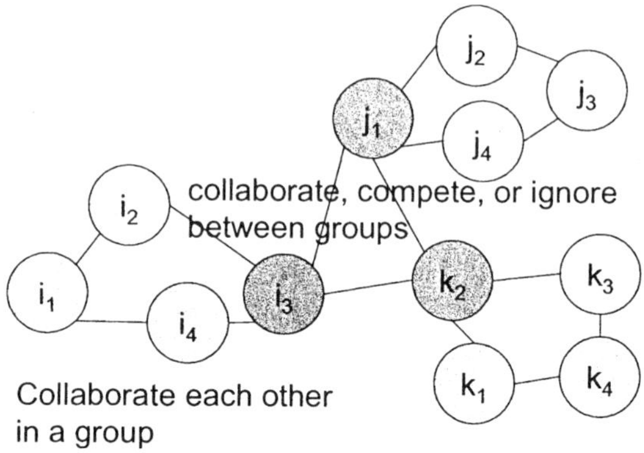

Figure 2: Social structure of the proposed agent system.

COMPUTATIONAL EXPERIMENTS

In this paper, as an instance of multi-modal functions, the modified version of DeJong F_5, as shown in the following equations.

$$F_5(x,y)=\sum_{j=1}^{25}\frac{1}{kj+(x-ax_j)^6+(y-ay_j)^6} \tag{4}$$

$$\begin{aligned} ax_j =[&-32,-16,0,16,32,-32,-16,0,16,32,-32,-16,0,16,32,\\ &-32,-16,0,16,32,-32,-16,0,16,32] \end{aligned} \tag{5}$$

$$\begin{aligned} ay_j =[&-32,-32,-32,-32,-32,-16,-16,-16,-16,-16,0,0,0,0,0,\\ &16,16,16,16,16,32,32,32,32,32] \end{aligned} \tag{6}$$

The function is represented as a function of two variables, x and y. However, in an actual search process, they are encoded into 17 bit strings, respectively. The range of them is [-65.535, 65.536] and the resolution is 0.001. Therefore, each agent searches for a good solution in a 34-dimensional binary space.

The original DeJong function is often employed for a benchmark of evolutionary computation. The peaks of the modified function can be changed by a value of k, while the one of the original F_5 is scaled from 1 to 0. Figure 3 shows the landscape of the original DeJong function, which corresponds to k=1 in the modified function.

We have conducted computational simulations with 100 agents: The agents are divided into 25 groups, and each group contains four agents. The group effect parameter c_3 is changed from -0.10 to 0.10 with the step of 0.01. A hundred independent runs with a hundred generations are performed in each case. The average of the hundred runs is plotted in the following graphs.

Figure 2 and 3 shows the changes of the peak occupied ratio in the case of k=0 which represents all of the peaks have a same value of 1.0, and k=1 which represents the original function as shown in Figure 1, respectively. The peak occupied ratio means how many peaks are found and attained in the last generation among the 25 peaks of the function. The high peak occupied ratio represents the agents are distributed, and the low one does they are aggregated.

Comparing Figure 4 with Figure 5, as the height of the peaks decreases, the peak occupied ratio decreases. It means that the proposed agent system distribute the agent groups according to the landscape of the function. From Figure 4 and 5, we can see the peak occupied ratio decreases as c_3 gets higher when it is a positive value. However, it does not change so much when c_3 is a negative value.

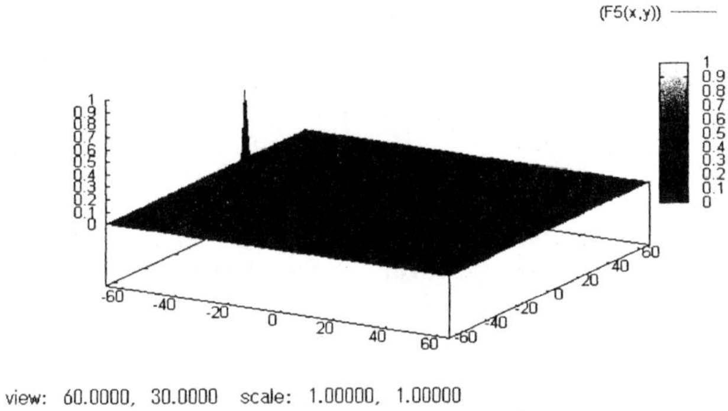

Figure 3: DeJong F_5 function.

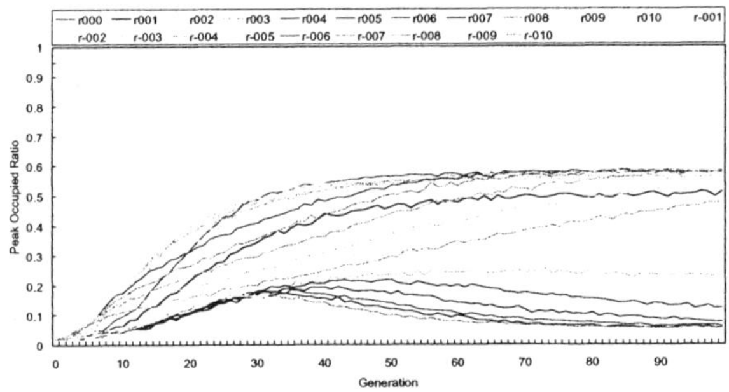

Figure 4: Peak occupied ratio in the case of k=0.

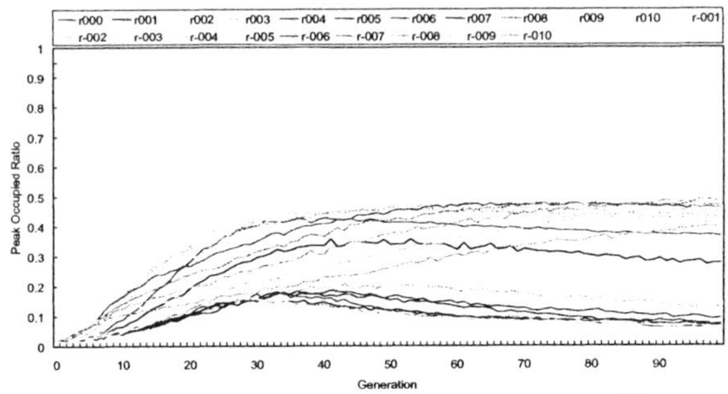

Figure 5: Peak occupied ratio in the case of k=1.

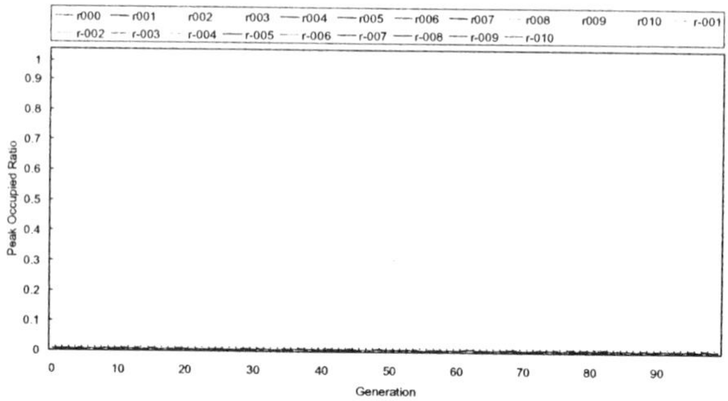

Figure 6: Peak occupied ratio in the flat function.

Figure 6 shows the peak occupied ratio in the flat function $f=0$ as reference. In this case, the agents are distributed across the space. From these results, it means that the propose agent system works well for aggregation of the agents, but not so good for the distribution. It is one of the future work.

CONCLUSION

The objective of this paper was to present a control method of self-organized formation such as aggregation and distribution of agents. The self-organization was regarded as the search problem in this paper, and the concept of the particle swarm optimization (PSO) was introduced.

We have solved the convergence problem of PSO by giving social structure to the agents; the agents are divided into several groups. In each of the groups, the agents cooperate to find a good solution. Among the groups, they sometime compete, cooperate, or ignore the other group depending on pre-determined relationship.

We carried out the computational experiments and the results show that the proposed agent system can find a good solution while the aggregation and distribution can be controlled by a parameter.

ACKNOWLEDGEMENT

This research was partially supported by the Ministry of Education, Science, Sports and Culture, Grant-in-Aid for Exploratory Research, 16650041, 2004.

REFERENCES

Kennedy, J. and Eberhart, R. C., 1995, "Particle swarm optimization," Proc. of IEEE International Conference on Neural Networks IV, pp. 1942-1948.

Kennedy, J. and Eberhart, R. C., 2001, "Swarm intelligence," Morgan Kafumann Publishers.

Naruse, K., Kinoshita, M., Yokoi, H. and Kakazu, Y., 2003a, "Group Formation of Agents with Two-dimensional Inner State and One-to-one Subjective Evaluation", Proc. of the fifth IEEE International Symposium on Computational Intelligence in Robotics and Automation (CIRA2003), CD-ROM.

Naruse, K. Kinoshita, M., Yokoi, H., Kakazu, Y., 2003b, "Group formation of emotion agents", Intelligent Engineering System Through Artificial Neural Networks, vol. 13, pp. 213-218, ASME Press.

AGENT TALK IN NEURAL NETWORKS

SHIGEKI SUGIYAMA
University of Gifu, 1-1 Yanagido, Gifu City, Gifu 501-1193, Japan. E-Mail: shigeki1@cc.gifu-u.ac.jp

ABSTRACT

In this paper, the following things will be discussed and studied:

(1) What is a basic mechanism of human's and the living creatures' brains or a brain like function in a sense of a general processing mechanism on a stimulation from the outside world.

(2) Study the basic and primitive level of mechanism of brain function, and generalize it for making a basic brain function model by using a neural network.

(3) By using the results studied above, studies on an artificial semantic knowledge base, which makes it possible to communicate among agents.

THE BASIC MECHANISM OF BRAIN

Now we have much study on human's and the living creatures' although it is still far from the adequate. However, we are able to have some general functional views towards them.

(1) We know that the function of human brain is basically quite similar to the other living creatures' brains, referred to the chapter I of [2].

(2) It is true to say that those living creatures' brains are one of fostering organisms uniquely developed for sustaining the many situations of surviving in the livings by various kinds of performances. And so, it can be said that;

"A brain is a kind of functional organism (processor) to act against a stimulation from the external world or from an internal world of brain in order to adjust themselves to the world or to an internal world of brain." So the Brain Mechanism is able to be described in Sets of vector as follows.

BRAIN MECHANISM = {S, **P** | S = (the stimulations in vector),
P = (the action performances in vector) } ----- (1)

Inside the Brains, Brain Mechanism is trying to find the optimized solution to the stimulation for sustaining *the living* (**L**: the living in vector) as mentioned above. So the Brain Behaviour is also able to be described as follows, as well.

THE WHOLE WORLD {W} = **{W1>=W2>=**...>=**Wn}**
W1 = **{ΣKNOWLEDGE,ΣENVIRONMENT}**, **W2** = **{ΣKNOWLEDGE,ΣENVIRONMENT}**, etc., **Wn** = **{ΣKNOWLEDGE,ΣENVIRONMENT}**, **{KNOWLEDGE}** = **{WORD, FUNCTION, TOPOLOGY}**, **{ENVIRONMENT}** = **{MATTER, TOPOLOGY}**, **{WORD}** = {S+V+O+C, S+V+O, S+V+C, etc.} **{FUNCTION}** = {any **FUNCTION**}, **{MATTER}** = {any **MATTER**} **{TOPOLOGY}** = **{ROUTE, CONNECTION}**, **{ROUTE}** = **{Vertical Relationship}**, **{CONNECTION}** = **{Lateral Relationship}**, etc.

And, for example, a sentence consists of SVOC or other forms with words and these words make possible to correspond with **BPNN INPUT**. Each **BPNN** has a relationship with **Fnn** within **Wn** as below, referred to [4][5]. So, in general, we can say that the whole world **{W}** can be expressed in the form as shown below.

THE WHOLE WORLD {W} = **{ W1>=W2>=**...>=**Wn}**, ----- (8)
where **Wn>={F1n=BPNN1n,...,Fnn=BPNNnn}**.

KNOWLEDGE BEHAVIOUR

From the above discussions and studies, we can conclude in a quite broad and primitive meaning for a brain behaviour that;

"***the Brain Behaviour in the basic and primitive mechanism is a kind of performance to find the optimized equilibrium situation in behaviour against the stimulations for sustaining the livings.***"

In the same way, we can say that;

"the Knowledge Behaviour is a kind of performance to find an equilibrium situation for OUTPUT to INPUT."

As for the things considered above and the things mentioned in [3], we are able to accept the following things as a fact that happens in the nature of the Knowledge Behaviour of the brain.

(1) All knowledge behaviour or action converges onto towards some kind of system equilibrium, (2) Saturated knowledge of system equilibrium remains unchanged, (3) Unstable knowledge of system unbalance tends to change.

Here considers about a method of finding any kind of suitable **OUTPUT** to **INPUT** by seeing a change in a knowledge base chain.

For each **INPUT**, it is true to say that **Fnn (BPNNnn)** likely produces **OUTPUT** that might be *relevant* or *irrelevant* to each **INPUT**. And here is interested in a method to find a *relevant* **BPNNnn** series. When **BPNN1n** has an input from the world, the output information goes to interaction and form a certain knowledge structure. In another words, **F** and **E** work one another with some kind of collaboration. Within the collaboration, only necessary **F** and **E** are excited about/by for working in order to get a desired behaviour in a brain activity.

KNOWLEDGE DESCRIPTION IN GENERAL

When we think about a knowledge of "Getting A Target", for example, it consists of a ***Target Kind*** and its ***Method*** to get. So **K** may be able to be further described as follows.

K = {F, E}, ----- (5)

where **F = {Method={M}}, E = {Target={T}}, M = {car, bicycle, bus, train, on foot,** ... }, **T = {building, sea, house, ball, cat,** ... }, **car = {small, sedan, sport type, for a special purpose,** ... }, **building = {small, medium, tall, little, huge, red,** ... }, etc.

This may go on and on until the stage of the smallest unit can appear for each. And in the same way, we know intuitively that any knowledge;

Any Knowledge (K) = {F, E},

is able to be described and extended in the same sort of series (**M**, **T**) as shown above. So we can have

K = {F, E} = {{F1, E1}>={F2, E2}>=...>={Fn, En}}.

And also, this method of series description can be expanded to any kinds of system including a living creature in the world as shown below.

THE WHOLE WORLD = {W}, ----- (6)

{W} = {W1>=W2>=...>=Wn}, where **n** is an integer. ----- (7)

Let each Set of **Wn** lie in a certain **Layer** and let the connexion (or compound) between **Layers** be combined by Graph Theory. Inside each **Layer**, let **Wn** consist of Subsets that consist of subworlds and let the connexion (or compound) among the Subsets be also combined by Graph Theory, too.

KNOWLEDGE ACTION AND STRUCTURE IN GENERAL

We can say the following things about a knowledge action when we think about a brain of living creatures, referred to [3].

(1) Every knowledge elects some other kinds of knowledge,

(2) In every action of knowledge, there is a sharing and an interchange,

(3) All action is occasioned within/by a certain world **Wn** in a brain,

(4) Many kinds of **Wn** in each **Layer** are associated with one another.

From the above facts, and by using Equation (7), it is possible to restate the whole world as follows.

SAp is mapped into **SBq** that is the set of relevant knowledge. It is defined as below.

$$\Phi i(x): Sap \rightarrow SBq, \ i=1,\ldots,m.$$

Each element of **x** consists of a primitive data of each stimulation from the World. If the performance is not satisfied, the mapping is done to the next most relevant knowledge as shown below.

$$\Phi i(x): Sap \rightarrow SBr, \ i=1,\ldots,m.$$

In this way, the **Agents** will be able to find the most appropriate performance to the stimulus.

3. Present Situation In Knowledge Description And Knowledge Behaviour

There are some computational mechanical interpreters and artificial intelligences that are able to treat semantics. The computational mechanical interpreters are generally just one by one a sentence translation oriented processor that can only treat a sentence processing, and no relationship with another sentences can be created with in a semantic meaning (**IS-A** link, referred to [3]). And Artificial Intelligences (AI) are possible to solve some kinds of problems in a very restricted atmosphere intelligently but they need a lot of pre-processes before inputting an information for the AI systems, referred to [4]. This occurs out of two reasons;

(1) Lack of understanding in *a structural matter* about an intelligence of knowledge, (2) Lack of understanding in *a functional matter* about an intelligence of knowledge. So in the next chapters, ***a structural matter of knowledge description*** and ***a functional matter of knowledge behaviour*** are studied by introducing a brand new idea of Semantic Transformation into Knowledge Base.

KNOWLEDGE IN GENERAL

When we think about **KNOWLEDGE**, it will be a knowledge of words, a knowledge of making a cake, a knowledge of solving a problem, or a knowledge of getting a target, etc. It is a tangible or intangible formulated matter (**element**) or thought (**factor**) as an existence but we cannot see the knowledge itself. All that we can only see is the phenomenon of a knowledge behaviour in an action. So we can at least say that these various kinds of knowledge will consist of various **factors** and **elements** in those action or interactions as shown below.

$$\textbf{KNOWLEDGE (K)} = \{\textbf{Factor}=\{\textbf{F}\}, \textbf{Element}=\{\textbf{E}\}\} \quad \text{----- (4)}$$

When we see a living creature's brain including a human brain, it is true to say that these **F** and **E** are related with each other in an action or an

BRAIN BEHAVIOUR = **{S, P | P = (S, L)}** ----- (2)

So here, we can conclude in a quite broad and primitive meaning about a brain that;

"***The Brain Behaviour in the basic and primitive mechanism of brain is a kind of performance to find the optimized behaviour against the stimulations for sustaining the livings.***"

BASIC MODEL FOR BRAIN BEHAVIOUR

1. Brain Behaviour in Communication

In Equations (1) and (2), we can say that the Brain Behaviour (**BB**) is mostly related with and is to find ***something between*** S and **L** for finding an optimised performance **P**. In the living creatures, a brain consists of many sections that will take some functional parts in the performance. And the parts ***communicate*** with other necessary or related parts for finding an optimised response in the performance. (In the field of Artificial Intelligence, The Part is described as Agent, too.) Here, this phenomenon is called as *for* ***Something Between*** as ***Communication***. So by extending the above idea, Equation (2) can be rewritten as follows.

L = S * C ----- (3)

where **L**: a performance in living, **S**: a stimulation, **C**: a communication, *: certain function.

2. Communication Mechanism

Here studies about a Communication Mechanism (**C**) between Agents in general. The whole world and the agents that we are thinking about are generalized as follows. The Whole World consists of Agent and World, and it can be written as

WHOLE WORLD = {**AGENT**, **World**},

where **AGENT** = {**A, B, C, ...**}, **World** = {**W1, W2, ... , Wn**}.

World stimulates **Agent** and **Agent** performs against the stimulus as follows each other.

AGENT ←→ World

Agent performances occur within **Agent** as follows, because each **Agent** consists of Parts for each.

If **AGENT** = {**A**, **B**}, then

{**A**} = {**A**| **SA1>=SA2>=**...**>=SAn**},

{**B**} = {**B**| **SB1>=SB2>=**...**>=SBn**}.

And by the performances of agent talk, the **Agents** try to find the best response to stimulus from the World. The agent talk is basically done by the information mapping as shown below.

BPNN2n and then tries to find the most correlated **BPNN2n** pair. And this output information goes onto the next **BPNN3n** if it is necessary to find the most correlated next **BPNN3n**. And the same kind of procedure shown above will go on and on until it gets a satisfied **OUTPUT**.

For finding the most correlated **BPNNnn**, here introduces the partial deviation factor about each **Fnn** on **BPNNnn** as follows.

$$\frac{\partial \mathbf{Fnn}}{\partial \mathbf{BPNNnn}} = \delta \mathbf{Fnn} \qquad \text{----- (9)}$$

Let the above fraction define δ**Fnn** and we redefine it as a correlation factor as shown below.

CRFnn = 1/δ**Fnn**, where **CRF**: CorRelation Factor. ----- (10)

As δ**Fnn** is "1" when it is the maximum value, so we can have the following relation. **CRFnn** >= 1. ----- (11)

For the system behaviour in an action, we can say the following things. (1) From the behaviour of single **Fnn**, it cannot be always said that the most correlated **Fnn** (**CRF** near to 1) has the ability to produce the most appropriate **OUTPUT**. (2) We know that there is a case that larger values of **CRFnn** can contribute to produce a suitable **OUTPUT**. And so, when a system wants to produce the most appropriate **OUTPUT**, it needs to have Set of family of Σ**Fpn** that are properly correlated with **INPUT**. So it is necessary to find a *boundary* that includes properly correlated Σ**Fpn**. That is to say, **Fnn** family has to have a boundary condition by the value **CRF**.

So, here studies on a boundary condition. From the above discussions, it can see that the Boundary Condition (**BC**) for each **Fnn** within **Wn** is determined by a certain **CRF** value because of its correlated nature. If we let define a certain **BC** value as θ, we are able to configure a system behaviour of the system as shown below according to the **BC** value θ. ∞>**CRFtrivial>=**θ, : Within this boundary, the another target world **Wn** must be searched and be found across one **Fpq/Wn+1** or another. θ>**CRFappropriate>=**1, : Within this boundary, the system takes an action for getting an appropriate (an optimized) output to the input by using appropriated family of Σ**Fpn**.

By using the above method, elements of **Fnn** are divided into two categories; one is Set of group for appropriate **OUTPUT**s and another is Set of group for trivial **OUTPUT**s. For this categorization, **CRF** value can be used as the boundary condition in order to find Set of group for appropriate **OUTPUT**s. And by this way, it makes possible to find series of related **Fnn** groups' chain. By this way, it made possible to find an appropriate **OUTPUTtoINPUT**.

So from the above study, we can see that semantic **INPUT** is transformed into Knowledge Base, and also that this method makes it possible for the artificial semantic knowledge base to communicate among agents within series of related knowledge **Fnn** groups' chain.

CONCLUSION

Through the examinations and discussions in this paper, the following results have been given;

(1) Understanding in *a structural matter* about an intelligence of knowledge has been shown structurally,

(2) Understanding in *a functional matter* about an intelligence of knowledge has been shown functionally,

(3) Basic idea of Agent Talk for communication mechanism has been introduced,

(4) Generalized mechanism of communication in dynamic behavior of Agent has been introduced, which makes possible for the artificial semantic knowledge base to communicate among agents.

REFERENCES

[1] M.A. Arbib, "The Brain as Network of Neurons", The Metaphorical Brain2, New York: Wiley-Interscience, 1989.

[2] Floyd E. Bloom, Arlyne Lazerson, Laura Hofstadter, "BRAIN, MIND, AND BEHAVIOR", Educational Broadcasting Corp., 1985.

[3] James A. Anderson, "Introduction to Neural Networks", Cambridge, MA:MIT Press, 1989.

[4] Jeffrey L. Elman, "Learning and development in neural networks: The importance of stating small, Cognition, 48, 1993.

[5] Shigeki Sugiyama, "Semantic and Logic Theories in Neuron Networks", IEEE International Conference on system, Man and Cybernetics proceedings, October 2-5, 1994.

THE QUANTUM PERTURBATION MODEL OF ORGANIZATIONS

W.F. LAWLESS
Paine College
1235 15th Street
Augusta, GA 30901-3182
lawlessw@mail.paine.edu
homepage.mac.com/lawlessw

Margo Bergman
Penn State Worthington
Scranton, Dumore, PA 18512,
mwb12@psu.edu,
www.personal.psu.edu/mwb12

Jorge Louçã
University of Lisbon
Laboratory of Agent
Modelling
(LabMag)
Jorge.L@iscte.pt

ABSTRACT

Integrating individual and organizational theory, the major unsolved problem in social psychology, is key to the autonomy of future multi-agent system (MAS) missions. Multiple Predators or other MAS's will not be able to interact like humans to solve problems autonomously without rationalizing the shift from individual to MAS. This problem resists solution primarily because theories of the social interaction have until now been based primarily on the individual rational perspective; e.g., maximizing individual utility in game theory. In contrast, we have made progress on a mathematics of social interaction with Bohr's conjugate factors of action (Δa) and belief uncertainty (ΔK) for a group naturally constrained to process the information, I, generated by opponents entangled with neutral decision-makers. We have made extensions to argument and organizational theory and now to perturbations.

INTRODUCTION

Axtell (2002) questioned whether the orders of magnitude separating the atomic and social levels precluded applying quantum theory to the social interaction. However, the dual nature of the human interaction (observation and action) led Bohr (1955) to believe that it did apply. The inability to validate game theory has led to the development of quantum game theory (e.g., Eisert et al., 1999), although it has also not been validated. Our quantum perturbation model (QPM) is meant to better model social reality to serve as a tool to study the dual nature of social interaction and individual cognition (Louça, 2003).

The key contribution from quantum game theory portrays agents in an interaction as "entangled" simultaneously as they rotate through different energy, E, states (Lawless & Grayson, 2004b). Entanglement allows participants an infinity of "adjustments" that transform the game theory given matrix of values to become what the social game theorist Kelley (1992) called an unknowable, unpredictable "effective" matrix, what we call random rotations from social forces. Feynman (1996) showed that quantum-mechanical states could transform from the action of operators. And Deutsch (1989) showed that a superposition of mixed quantum states could be explored simultaneously in parallel computations more powerful than digital ones. From this brief overview of our research, the fitness of solutions driven by operators increases with the N adopting the solutions, a crucial link to control theory (May, 2001, p. 172).

We have proposed for interactions the following bistable interdependence:

$$\Delta v \Delta K \approx \Delta E \Delta t \geq c \qquad (1,2)$$

with ΔK as observer beliefs and Δv as action uncertainty ($v = \Delta K/\Delta t$; $\Delta K = I$, and $I = -\sum_x p(x) \log_2 p(x)$), and ΔE as energy and Δt as time uncertainty (Lawless et al., 2000). Based on the Penrose model (Hagan et al., 2002), if neurons across the brain can be modeled as entangled, and if c is Planck's constant, h, then $\Delta E \Delta t = \Delta(h\,\omega/2\pi)\Delta t \geq h/2\pi$ reduces to $\Delta\omega\Delta t \geq 1$. Choosing ω as gamma waves associated with object awareness at about 40 Hz gives a reasonable minimum Δt of 25 ms (Crick & Koch, 1998). But from our perspective, the primary reasons to apply quantum mathematics to the social interaction and organizations are the relationship of K and perturbations.

THE MEASUREMENT PROBLEM

Tajfel (1970) experimentally established that even random human groups automatically create "in-group" and "out-group" K beliefs. Schama (1995) recognized that "social memory" is enacted as a series of competing history beliefs between groups. These findings make no sense from an individual rational perspective. However, if human interactions are bistable (Equation 1), measurement collapses the bistable K into classical I, precluding the reconstruction of the original bistable state. By collapsing into individual histories that cannot recreate the interaction, the measurement problem at the human social level is analogous to the atomic level (Zeilinger, 1999), alone justifying the quantum model for social interaction or competing social organizations. Measuring or polling the members of a group forces them to respond as individuals, but then summing the individual data does not reconstitute the group (Levine & Moreland, 1998). For example, a survey in 1991 (Slovic et al., 2001, pp. 102-3) led to the prediction that the negative images associated with a nuclear waste repository at Yucca Mountain would significantly harm the Las Vegas economy by reducing tourism; but with the repository construction still underway, ten years later the authors admitted that tourism continued to make Las Vegas the fastest growing community in the U.S.

Now assume that organizational structures are bistable and seek a minimum E state, in both physical space and I space. The bistable potential E surface (E^{PES}) of an organization represents the function, hierarchy and geo-cultural-intellectual differences across a group, organization, or society (Sallach, 2002):

$$E^{PES}(x,y) = \min_{z,R\text{-}org} E^{TOT}(x,y,z,R_{org}) \qquad (3)$$

A recruit moves across the bistable E surfaces of an organization, R_{org}, where E^{TOT} is the ground state and PES the minimum total E along the z coordinate of the organizational hierarchy until reaching an E minima. The growth rate of organization, P, is contingent on available E (Lawless & Grayson, 2004a):

$$\Gamma_P = n_R n_M\, v\, \sigma_{RM} \exp(-\Delta A/k_B T). \qquad (4)$$

where n_R and n_M are the numbers of targeted outsiders (R) and organization members (M) interacting together (e.g., recruits with members or potential clients with marketers); K flow, v, is the rate of change of I in the interaction; σ_{RM} is the interaction cross-section area between agents interacting like coupled harmonic oscillators but under the influence of bistable differences between the vocal, brain, or interaction frequencies of outsiders, ω_R and members, ω_M, where ω_R is the driver that transforms an organization, increasing rapidly (resonance) from a random exploration that converges socio-psychologically as frequencies "match"; i.e., $\sigma_{RM} = f(\omega_M{}^4/(\omega_R{}^2 - \omega_M^2)^2)$; $exp(\bullet)$ is the probability that sufficient free E, ΔA, is available to overcome the barriers to an interaction--the more ΔA required for an activity, the less likely it occurs; k_B is Boltzman's constant and T temperature, $T = (\partial E/\partial K)_V$, for a constant volume, V; k_BT represents the average distribution of emotional activity directed at the target interaction; e.g., all things being equal, the greater the average excitement generated by a new product or idea, the lower the barrier to the interaction.

Frequency, ω, provides other information. If the average distance between agents in an MAS implies organizational wave length, λ (where $\lambda = f(1/\omega)$), the more cooperation among agents, systems, and humans, the less I density and more K homogeneity (e.g., fewer of Schama's competing beliefs), with the likelihood K remains localized as inversely proportional to an organization's success (Arrow, 1962). The converse occurs under perturbations from competition, reproducing the well-established finding that organizations under threat become physically closer; i.e., a threat to an organization increases E, reducing λ. The more well-organized an organization like a city that is attacked, the more likely it pulls together versus a disorganized organization (Glaeser, 1996); e.g.,, the stock price of the comparatively well-run Dutch/Shell Group fell after news that it revised downward its oil and gas reserves then quickly recovered, but the $32 price for US Airways stock has fallen and stayed around $5 with news that it was under competitive assault from Southwest Airlines.

But why does a group stick together? The advantages to an individual of joining a group are reduced E expenditures in exchange for membership: social loafing (Latane, 1981); enhanced skills from audience effects (Zajonc, 1998); better health from greater interaction density (House et al., 1988) and protected belief systems (Rosenblatt et al., 1990). (To address the notion of social influences in an organization or between organizations, we are considering a community matrix of bistable interpersonal influences for a collective belief, $K = [k_{11}\ k_{12}\ ...\ k_{nn}]$, where k_{xy} represents the belief influence of agent x over agent y or organization-1 over organization-2; e.g., bistability may result in coupled Kolmogorov relations between the actions of Prigogine's ants and Louça's cognitive map of social influences among the agents of an organization).

PERTURBATIONS AND KNOWLEDGE

In that K is often hidden, perturbations become the prime reason to apply the quantum model to organizations. Under traditional models of organizations, perturbations are disturbances that agents resolve or avoid (Nowak & Sigmund, 2004). In the ideal world of traditional theory, disturbances are to be controlled by increasing cooperation (Axelrod, 1984). In contrast, we have found an increase in social welfare with an increase in competition (i.e., the more competitive a nation, the more scientific wealth, better health among its citizens, and less corruption associated with it; in Lawless & Grayson, 2004a), allowing us to envision that perturbations from competition provide a valuable source of I with the power to transform it into K (Figure 1), a radically different view of organizations. In essence, perturbations between two organizations raise their E

levels and those of their entangled neutral witnesses, who while in a state of superposition choose the winner (Lawless & Grayson, 2004b). As organizations randomly explore for maximum competitive advantage, they drive entangled neutral witnesses across the fitness landscape of potential solutions.

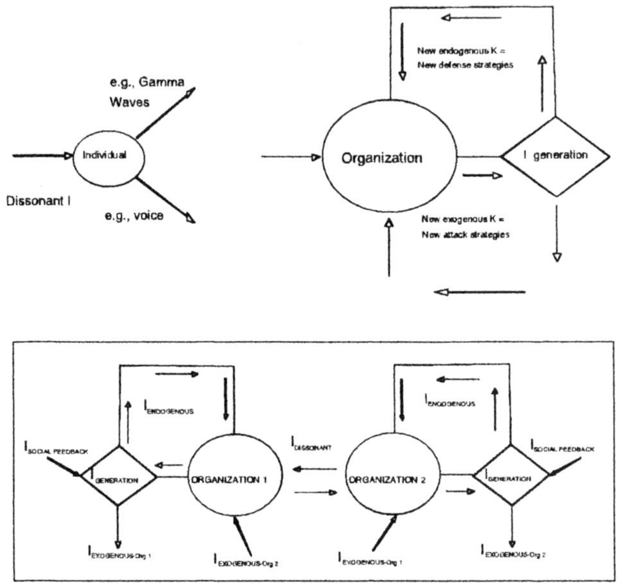

Fig. 1 (upper left). Based on Picard's liquid model of emotion, we have found for an individual a significant difference between normal and angry vocal E (Lawless & Grayson, 2004a); Penrose has established a similar effect with gamma waves in the brain (Hagan et al., 2002). **Fig. 1 (upper right).** After a perturbation sufficient to elevate an organization to an excited state, an organization's goal is to innovate, merge or adopt new technology to defend itself (e.g., the 2004 offer to merge with eMachines by Gateway to offset its declining computer sales and better compete with Dell and H-P). Conversely, using exogenous feedback, a competitor's goal is to devise new strategies to defeat the organization. In general, the more efficient, quicker respondent determines which organization wins and evolves (Chagnon, 1988); e.g., in 2003 in the war with Iraq, coalition decision-making and implementation of those decisions occurred faster than Iraq's Defense Forces, causing the latter to panic (i.e., in engineering control theory late feedback is destabilizing; in May, 2001, p. 5). **Fig. 1 (bottom).** Our revised model of game and quantum game theory (Lawless & Grayson, 2004b) has general applications among competing groups such as businesses, churches, politicians, etc. The interdependent flow of dissonant I between Organizations 1 and 2 produces belief uncertainties (ΔK) in the exact state of the competitors (e.g., deception or bluffing). Perfect resolution implies truth. But truth obtained by driving ΔK to zero has limits. Per Lewin (1951), how an organization behaves must also be determined (i.e., Δv), but a K of behavior in turn also has limits. Specifically, an interdependence exists between Δv and ΔK that limits the truth produced, making it embedded (i.e., $K = f(x)$). The result is Equations (1,2; see Figure 2).

Organization inertia, j, is key to perturbations (Lawless & Grayson, 2004a). As an example, Robert Hutchings, Chair, National Intelligence Council (www.cia.gov/nic/speeches), noted that an underestimate by the National Intelligence Estimate of Iraq weapons for the 1991 war may have led to overestimates in the 2003 war. Figure 1 also illustrates that mergers arise from perturbations: Should organizational inertia cause its execution of technology to falter, as in the case of AT&T Wireless in early 2004, it becomes the prey or acquired organization instead of the predator. Unlike game and quantum game theory, by including social feedback and inertia, competition significantly improves social welfare with power accruing to the winning organization (Lawless & Grayson, 2004a); e.g., Southwest Airlines is significantly reducing air fares for consumers in the Northeast, but as a consequence of its low-airfares policy, has grown to twice the value of all six U.S. airlines larger than it combined (ATA, 2002); also, as businesses move East in the newly expanded European Union, the power of unions has weakened, leading to changes that could revolutionize labor relations in Europe with flexible labor rules and enhanced European competitiveness (online.wsj.com); and last year the traditional hard-line IG Metall union lost its fight for a 38 hr work week, its first strike failure in 49 years; yet it is currently considering a 40 hr work week at Damiler-Chrysler in Stuttgart. Finally, social feedback has similar uncertainty limitations (see Figure 2), motivating the reduction of action and observation uncertainties with perturbations, accounting for a market economy as a series of institutionalized perturbations (e.g., Lawless & Castelao, 2001).

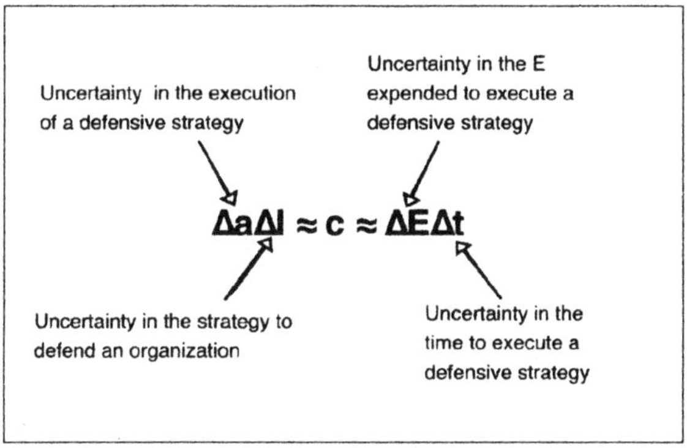

Figure 2. The measurement problem from the perspective of a merger target (parallel uncertainty relations exist for the acquiring organization). Measuring an interdependent or bistable phenomenon such as a human organization produces classical *I* that cannot recreate the original phenomenon. For example, **Strategy**: after AT&T Wireless put itself on the auction block and Cingular made the first offer, AT&T Wireless did not know whether bids would be received from other players such as Vodaphone, or how much more would be offered; **Execution**: Cingular expected that AT&T Wireless would execute its strategy by choosing the best bid by the deadline it had set, an expectation that turned out to be incorrect; ***E* of Acquisition**: AT&T Wireless did not know whether Cingular or Vodaphone would increase their bids to an amount it considered sufficient; **Cycle Period**: while the bidders believed incorrectly that the deadline was firmly established, AT&T Wireless was uncertain of the time between the bids that would be offered.

CONCLUSIONS

We have begun to illustrate the difference between traditional and bistable models. The basic assumption in the traditional model is that events to be modeled are of sufficient strength and clarity to locate an organization in either the strategy or execution of a takeover. In contrast, by permitting social entities to be in a superposition of both states simultaneously, generating constructive and destructive interferences, the bistable model breaks with the traditional methodological individual perspective to become the first theory of a group that is not equal to the sum of the components of the group (Von Neumann was well aware of this issue; see Von Neumann & Morgenstern, 1953, p. 148). Next we plan to explore the implications as well as a tensor model of Figure 2, the related community matrix of cognitive influences, and the Fourier model of May.

ACKNOWLEDGEMENTS: The lead author thanks J.A. Ballas, Information Technology Division, Naval Research Lab, Washington, DC, where most of this research was conducted with funds from the Office of Naval Research through an ASEE grant.

REFERENCES

Arrow, K. J. (1962). Economic welfare and the allocation of resources for invention. The rate and direction of inventive activity. R. Nelson. Princeton University Press.

ATA (2002). Cost of air travel, www.airlines.org/public/home/default1.asp.

Axelrod, R. (1984), The evol. of cooperation, Basic.

Axtell, R. (2002). Personal communication.

Benardete, S. (2002), The argument of the action: Essays on Grk poetry and philos., U. Chicago.

Bohr, N., Ed. (1955). Science and unity knowledge. Doubleday.

Chagnon, N. A. (1988). "Life histories, blood revenge, and warfare in tribal populations." Science **239**: 985-992.

Crick, F., & Koch, C. (1998). "Consciousness and neuroscience." Cerebral Cortex **8**: 97-107.

Deutsch, D., (1989). Proc Royal Society **Ser. A, 425**: 73.

Eisert, J., Wilkens, M., & Lewenstein, M. (1999). "Quantum games." PRL, **83**(15): 3077-3080.

Feynman, R. (1996). Feynman lectures on computation. New Yåork, Addison-Wesley.

Glaeser, E. L. (1996). "Why economists still like cities." City Journal **6(2)**.

Hagan, S., Hameroff, S.R., & Tuszynski, J.A. (2002). Physical Review E **65**: 061901-1, 11.

House, J. S., Landis & Umberson (1988). "Social relationships and healthq." Science **241**: 540.

Kelley, H.H. (1992). Lewin, situations, and interdependence. J Social Issues, 47, 211-233.

Latane, B. (1981), The psychology of social impact, American Psychologist, 36, 343-356.

Lawless, W. F. (2004). DOE's policy of consensus seeking versus truth seeking. Proc WM'04..

Lawless, W.F., Castelao & Abubucker (2000), In Tessier et al., Conflicting agents, Kluwer.

Lawless, W.F. & Castelao, T. (2001), Univ Dec. Center, IEEE Techn. Soc., 20(2), 6-17.

Lawless, W. F., & Grayson, J.M. (2004a). Agent mediated knowledge management. L. van Elst, V. Dignum, & A. Abecker (Eds.), pp. 143-161, Springe..

Lawless, W. F., & Grayson, J.M. (2004b). A conjugate model of organizations, autonomy, and control. AAAI Spring Symposium, Stanford University, AAAI Press.

Levine, J.M. and Moreland, R.L. (1998), In Gilbert et al., Hdbk Soc Psych, pp. 415-469, McGraw.

Louça, J. (2003). Representing emergent socio-cultural phenomena, NAACSOS Conference, Carnegie Mellon University, Pittsburgh.

May, R. M. (1973). Stability and complexity in model ecosystems, Princeton University Press.

Nowak, M. A. & Sigmund, K. (2004). Science **303**: 793-799.

Rosenblatt, et al.,. (1990). J Personality Social Psychology **57**: 681-690.

Sallach, D. (2002). Modeling emotional dynamics: Currency versus fields. unpublished, U. Chicago.

Schama, S. (1995). Landscape and memory. New York, Random House.

Slovic, et al.,. (2001). Perceived risk. Risk, Media and Stigma. J. Flynn, et al.. Earthscan.

Tajfel, H. (1970). "Experiments in intergroup discrimination." Scientific American **223(2)**: 96-102.

Von Neumann, J., and Morgenstern, O. (1953). Theory of games and economic behavior. Princeton, Princeton University Press.

Zajonc, R. B. (1998). Emotion. Handbook Social Psychology. Gilbert et al.,. Boston, McGraw-Hill.

Zeilinger, A. (1999), Experiment and foundations of quantum physics, RMP, 71: S288

ROBOT BRAINS: EXPERIMENTS IN IMPLEMENTING A-BRAINS ON SMALL MOBILE ROBOTS

DANIEL P. STORMONT
Department of Electrical and Computer Engineering
Utah State University
Logan, Utah
stormont@cc.usu.edu

HUGO DE GARIS
Department of Computer Science
Utah State University
Logan, Utah

ABSTRACT

Genetic Networks (GenNets) are a biologically-inspired approach to developing artificial brains (a-brains) for use in intelligent machinery. One application of these a-brains is in mobile robots, which need artificial intelligence to be able to operate autonomously in the unstructured environment that is our everyday world. This paper discusses a planned series of experiments to test the feasibility of implementing an a-brain on a mobile robot. The mobile robots are two small, commercially available robot chassis' equipped with color CCD cameras. One of the robots uses a microcontroller for its a-brain implementation, while the other uses a field-programmable gate array (FPGA). The details of the design and implementation are discussed, along with conclusions and plans for future work.

INTRODUCTION

In his PhD dissertation, de Garis (1992) introduced the concept of the genetic network (GenNet); essentially, a combination of genetic algorithms for the weights between neurons and a fully-connected neural network. For this project, we were interested in applying the theoretical and simulation results de Garis achieved with GenNets to an autonomous mobile robot application tracking a brightly-colored ball using a color charge-coupled device (CCD) camera. An illustration of this is supplied in Figure 1. This series of experiments will explore two different tracking problems and two different approaches to implementing the GenNets. The two tracking problems are to track the ball in the x-axis (left to right) and in the x- and y-axes (left, right, forward, and backward). The two approaches to implementing the GenNets are a software implementation using a subset of Java on a microcontroller and a hardware implementation on a Field Programmable Gate Array (FPGA) using the VHSIC Hardware Description Language (VHDL). The ball tracking application is not a particularly novel or difficult one, but it serves as a mechanism for evaluating the usefulness of GenNets in a real-time implementation for an autonomous mobile robot, helping to validate deGaris' (1992) simulation results through a "real-world" robotics application. This series of experiments will also provide a useful stepping stone to more advanced applications, as discussed in the future work section of this paper.

Figure 1. The mobile robot using the CCD color camera to track a red ball.

GENETIC NETWORKS (GENNETS)

GenNets are fully-connected neural networks, meaning each neuron is connected to every other neuron in the network, including itself. There are no specific layers, e.g., there is not a specific input layer, hidden middle layer, and output layer. Any neuron in the network can be an input neuron and any neuron can be an output neuron, although the inputs and outputs are usually specified in advance. There is also no required number of neurons, although a minimum network would have as many neurons as there are external inputs and outputs for the network. An artificial brain (a-brain) can be created with one or many GenNets. If there are multiple networks connected together, their connections are specified by an inter-module signaling interface (IMSI) that specifies which outputs of one network are connected to which inputs of another network.

The genetic portion of a GenNet is the genetic algorithm used to evolve the weights for the internal inputs to a neuron. Each input to a neuron that is an output from another neuron is multiplied by a weight, typically between 0 and 1. The sum of the weighted inputs and an unweighted (multiplied by 1) external input, if any, makes up the total input to the neuron. These weights are usually represented with a binary string that indicates the fractional value of the weight. In other words, each bit in the genetic chromosome that represents the weight stands for a multiple of two raised to a negative power equal to the bit position. The genetic algorithms can use mutation (where the value of a bit is flipped if a random number is greater than a mutation threshold value) and/or crossover (where the remainder of two randomly selected chromosomes are switched at a given point, again if a random number exceeds the crossover threshold value). Figure 2 shows a GenNet neuron. In the figure, each neuron has an identification number, *i*; internal inputs from all of the neurons in the network (including itself), *S1...SN*; corresponding weights, *W1i...WNi*; one external input (which is optional), *Ei*; a product of the inputs and weights, *ACTIVNi*; and an output, *Si = f(ACTIVNi)*.

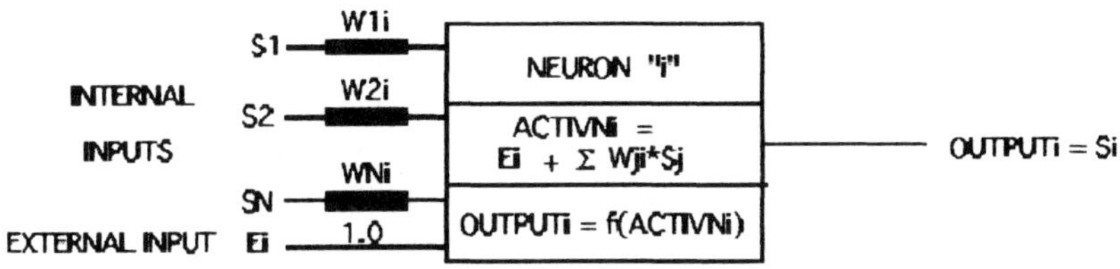

Figure 2. A GenNet neuron. (de Garis, 1992)

MOBILE ROBOTS

The robots used for this project are based on the Boe-Bot chassis sold by Parallax, Inc. The Boe-Bot is a two-wheeled, differential drive robot powered by modified hobby servo motors. One robot is controlled by a Javelin Stamp, also from Parallax. The Javelin Stamp has the same form factor and pinout as the Basic Stamp microcontroller, but it is programmed in a subset of the Java language instead of the PBasic language used by the Basic Stamp. It also has a much larger memory space than the Basic Stamp (32 Kbytes of RAM for the Javelin Stamp versus 2 Kbytes of EEPROM and 32 bytes of RAM for a Basic Stamp 2). This means much more memory is available to the program for variable and data storage – essential for GenNet applications. The second robot is controlled by a Cyclone field programmable gate array (FPGA) manufacutred by Altera. The FPGA allows a GenNet hardware design to be created using the VHSIC Hardware Description Language (VHDL). Both robots are equipped with a CMUcam color charge-coupled device (CCD) camera. The CMUcam is useful for robot applications because it has a microcontroller built in to pre-process the raw video. The available modes are selectable via a serial interface and the processed video attributes are returned via a serial interface. The processed video used for this project is the middle mass mode, where the camera returns an x and y value for the center of an object being tracked. Figure 3 shows the format of the message from the CMUcam and Figure 1 shows the Javelin-based Boe-Bot used for this project.

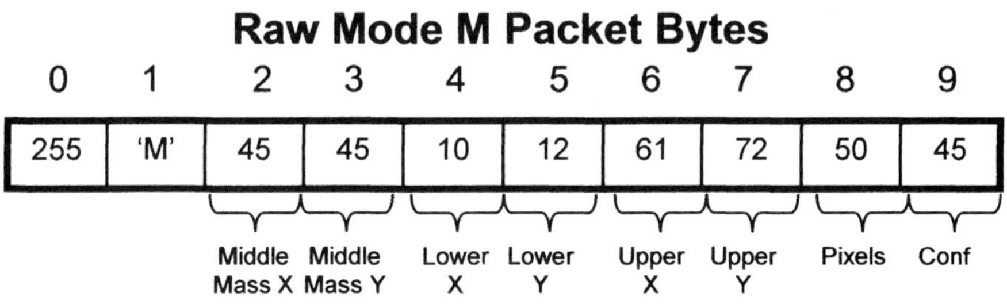

Figure 3. CMUcam message format. The bytes used for this project are the *middle mass x* and *middle mass y* bytes.

DESIGN CONSTRAINTS

The GenNets described by de Garis used floating point values for the inputs and the weights. Each input value is between 0.0 and 1.0, weights connecting neurons in the networks are between -1.0 and 1.0, and the output values are between 0.0 and 1.0. The chromosomes for de Garis' GenNets used a binary representation for the bits to the right of the binary point, which are then converted to floating point values as weights in the neural network before the new outputs are calculated. The problem is that the Javelin Stamp and the FPGA being used for this project don't have floating point units, thus a design that only uses binary or integer values had to be developed.

Fortunately, the inputs and outputs of the GenNet for this application are well defined. The inputs to the GenNet come from the CMUcam. As shown in Figure 3, the CMUcam indicates the x position of the center of a detected mass with a byte of data, which is equivalent to an integer value between 0 and 255. The center position of the camera is typically indicated by an integer value of 45. Thus, a one byte integer value can be supplied as the x-axis input to the selected input neuron of the GenNet. The same is true for the y axis.

Similar to the inputs, the outputs of the GenNet need to correlate to a pulse width between 1 ms and 2 ms for the pulse coded modulation (PCM) used to control the modified hobby servo motors. A value of 1 ms equals full speed rotation in one direction for the motor and a value of 2 ms equals full speed rotation in the other direction. A value of 1.5 ms equals the stopped position for the motor. The waveform for the PCM is shown in Figure 4. The selection of the pulse width is made by an integer value between 115 (for a 1 ms pulse) to 230 (for a 2 ms pulse). So, the output for each motor can be a one-byte integer value from the neurons selected as the output neurons for the left and right servo motors.

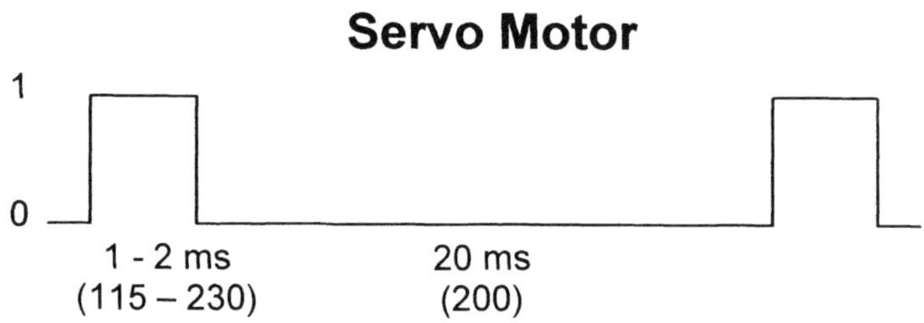

Figure 4. Pulse-Coded Modulation (PCM) for the modified servo motors with the integer number equivalents used by the Javelin Stamp.

Because of the constraints just listed, the GenNet was designed with an integer input for the middle mass x byte and the middle mass y byte and an integer output for the left servo motor and the right servo motor. Each of the weights associated with the connections between the neurons was an integer value between -256 and 255 (a 16-bit word length variable). A string of these integer values would make up a single chromosome for the genetic algorithm. To keep the output from any neuron within the required output range, the function de Garis used was a sigmoid function to ensure that the output would be no greater than 1.0. For this application, the output function had to be modified as follows:

$$O_j = \left(\sum w_{ij} s_i + I_j\right) \text{mod}\, 115 + 115$$

where O_j is the output if the jth neuron, w_{ij} is the weight of the connection from neuron i to neuron j, s_i is the output of neuron i (which is equal to O_i), and I_j is the external input (if any) to neuron j. The modulus of the sum by the floor of the output (115) is taken and then 115 is added to the modulus to yield an output between 115 and 230.

Memory constraints dictated minimizing the numbers of neurons since the number of connections (and the number of bits needed to represent them) grow exponentially with the number of neurons. Thus, a somewhat arbitrary decision was made to build a GenNet with seven neurons, where two of the neurons are selected as input neurons and two are selected as output neurons. The diagram of the GenNet is shown in Figure 5. For the evolution of the GenNet weights, a population size of four chromosomes was selected, again to keep the memory requirements down. The most fit chromosome and the second most fit chromosome (as determined by evaluating the GenNet output versus the fitness function) from any given generation of chromosomes would be retained, while the other two would be replaced by copies of the two fittest chromosomes. Then, all but the elite chromosome would be subject to mutation.

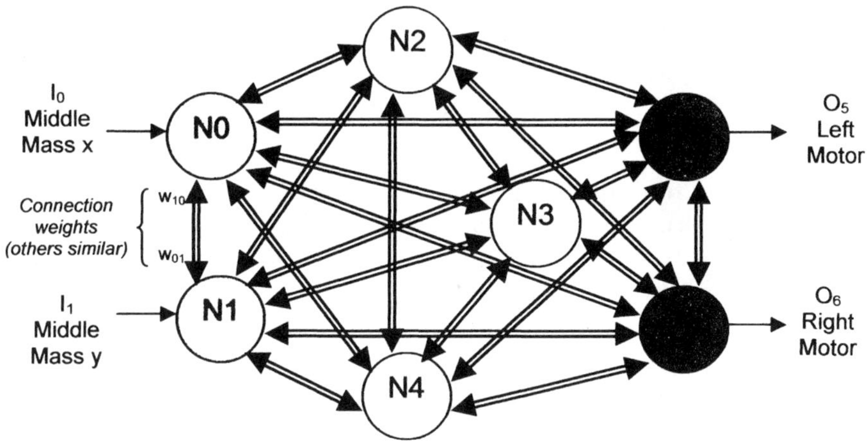

Figure 5. The design of the GenNet used for this project.

PROJECT PHASES

The project is planned for three phases, from the simplest to the most complex. The first two phases use the Javelin Stamp. The third phase uses the FPGA for a custom hardware implementation created in VHDL.

PHASE 1 – SOFTWARE IMPLEMENTATION FOR X-AXIS TRACKING

The first phase software implementation uses only the *middle mass x* byte for the input to allow the robot to track the ball in a lateral direction, meaning the GenNet only has six neurons since the *middle mass y* input neuron is unnecessary. de Garis (1992) described a method for generating a variable frequency generator that is well suited to the x-axis tracking problem. Using this method, the GenNet can be trained to associate an input of 0 with a maximum backward velocity on the right motor and a maximum forward velocity on the left motor (a right turn), an input of 45 with both motors stopped, and an input of 255 with a left turn. The training could be done through repeated iterations on the robot, using simulated inputs and no motor outputs. Once trained, the GenNet weights could be used to drive the motors with input from the camera with the expectation that intermediate input values would result in intermediate output values. This implementation is currently being developed on the Javelin-based Boe-Bot.

PHASE 2 – SOFTWARE IMPLEMENTATION FOR X-AXIS AND Y-AXIS TRACKING

The second phase of the project builds upon the phase 1 GenNet by adding a second input for the camera's y axis. This neuron receives the *middle mass y* byte from the CMUcam. This increases the number of training points from three to nine and produces forward and reverse motion in addition to left and right turns to keep the ball centered in front of the camera lens. This implementation will be developed once the phase 1 testing is complete.

PHASE 3 – HARDWARE IMPLEMENTATION USING VHDL

The final phase is to convert the software implementation of phase 2 into a specialized hardware implementation by programming the Altera FPGA with the GenNet design from phase 2 in VHDL.

RESULTS

This first phase of the project is currently in work. The implementation on the Javelin Stamp has been more difficult than anticipated because of issues unrelated to the GenNet, such as serial communications with the CMUCam.

CONCLUSIONS AND FUTURE WORK

This effort is a prelude to a more ambitious project to develop a GenNet-controlled robot to identify unexploded ordnance, such as bomblets from cluster bomb units (CBUs) and return them to a disposal area for disarming. This application would have obvious benefits in war zones.

REFERENCES

de Garis, H. (1992). *Genetic Programming: GenNets, Artificial Nervous Systems, Artificial Embryos.* PhD thesis, Brussels University, Brussels, Belgium.

PART III: EVOLUTIONARY PROGRAMMING

MULTI-DEME PLANNED TOURNAMENT SELECTION

DANIEL A. ASHLOCK
Department of Mathematics
Iowa State University

KENNETH M. BRYDEN
Department of Mechanical Engineering
Iowa State University

DOUGLAS MCCORKLE
Department of Mechanical Engineering
Iowa State University

ABSTRACT
Tournament selection is a model of evolution that permits an adjustable fitness gradient via choice of tournament size. Typically tournaments are chosen at random. This study is the second in a series that explores potential advantages of various techniques for non-random selection of tournaments. Planned tournament selection can be used to restrict or enhance the rate of spread of currently best genes, may be used to create island-like models of evolution, and enables an efficient parallel schedule for fitness evaluation. The type of planned tournament that is advantageous depends strongly on the character of the problem being solved. More complex versions of the technique that permit multi-deme algorithms with variable fitness functions are explored here. We demonstrate an impact of the use of multi-deme planned tournament selection. For problems that scale efficiently, running the problem at different sizes in different demes reduced time to solution. In a problem that scales inefficiently, multi-deme planned tournament selection is shown not to be superior to a baseline algorithm.

INTRODUCTION

Any evolutionary computation system requires a method of selecting members of a population to breed and also a means of placing children back into the population. Tournament selection (Blickle and Thiele, 1995) performs both these tasks in a simple manner. A *tournament* is a small group of population members from which good structures are selected to breed and bad structures are selected for removal to make way for the results of that breeding. When an evolutionary computation system uses crossover, two parents are required for a mating event. In *single* tournament selection, a mating event involves a single tournament from which two good individuals are drawn. *Double* tournament selection chooses two parents by selecting a tournament for each. Selection of those to be deleted may be done by selecting the worst two fitnesses within a single tournament, by selecting the worst fitness in each tournament in double tournament selection, or by employing some other selection method. This plethora of related techniques are all called tournament selection. The different types of tournament selection can have a profound effect on evolutionary algorithm behavior. The size of tournament is correctly recognized as a critical parameter. Small tournaments represent soft selection with superior genes given a modestly greater weight. Large tournaments represent a harsh type of selection.

Planned tournament selection (PTS) is any tournament selection scheme in which the individual tournaments are planned rather than chosen at random. There are a number of reasons to use planned tournament selection. Island genetic algorithms (Whitley et al., 1997) and graph based evolutionary algorithms (Ashlock et al., 1999; Bryden et al., 2003) are both examples of schemes where performance can be enhanced by restricting the flow of information by limiting potential mate choice with a form of geography. Planned tournament selection can create such restrictions. In addition, if tournaments are known in advance then the work of performing fitness evaluations can be sent to available processors in an efficient fashion. Finally, planned tournaments permit us to create multi-deme evolutionary algorithms with distinct fitness functions in distinct portions of the virtual world in which the evolutionary algorithm takes place. When using *multi-deme planned tournament selection* (MD-PTS) two of these issues must be addressed.

Deme Compatibility

In an MD-PTS algorithm, structures being evaluated by different fitness functions will be mixed. This creates boundary issues and requires the algorithm design make sure that structures evaluated with one fitness function can contribute in a sub-population (deme) being evaluated by another fitness function. This study gives positive and negative examples using the PORS (positive) and North Wall Builder (negative) test problems.

Mixing Rates

Even when different demes are compatible, there is a question of the amount of communication between demes that is the most advantageous. In this study we will only treat very low rates of inter-deme mixing. This is the simplest case and we will leave other cases for other studies.

PROBLEM DESCRIPTIONS

The two test problems that form the positive and negative example sets are three different cases of the PORS (Ashlock et al., 2004) problem and the North Wall Builder (Ashlock and Lathrop, 2004) problem. Detailed descriptions of the problems follow.

Plus-one-recall-store

The plus-one-recall-store (PORS) problem is described in detail in (Ashlock and Lathrop, 1998). It is a type of maximum problem within the domain of genetic programming (Koza, 1992; Kinnear, 1994; Banzhaf et al., 1998) with a small operation set and a calculator-style memory. The goal of the test problem, called the PORS efficient node use problem, is to find parse trees that, when executed, generate the largest integer result possible given a fixed maximum number of parse tree nodes. The language has two operations, integer addition and a store operation that places its argument in an external memory location. The language also has two terminals, the integer 1 and recall from an external memory. The difficulty of the PORS efficient node use problem varies strongly according to the congruence class (*mod* 3) of the number of nodes permitted. In this study all three congruence classes are explored, using smaller problems within a congruence class (*mod* 3) as additional demes that enhance algorithm performance. Crossover is performed by the usual subtree exchange (Koza, 1992). Mutation is performed by replacing a subtree picked uniformly at random with a new random subtree of the same size for each new tree produced. For the PORS experiments a local elite roulette mating is used.

(+ (Sto (+ (+ (Sto (+ (Sto (+ (+ 1 1) 1)) Rcl)) Rcl) Rcl)) Rcl)

Figure 1: An optimal PORS tree located by a GBEA with graph C_{512} for $n = 16$ nodes shown in LISP-like notation.

North Wall Builder

This grid robot task is somewhat similar to Terllers Tartarus task (Teller, 1994). The board used has odd side length, 5, 7, and 9 in this study, and is shown in its initial form in Figure 2. The robot may move forward or turn left or right in each time step, being permitted 6n**2 such moves where n is the board side length. The robot may push a single box ahead of it but not two and a box pushed off the edge of the board vanishes. Attempting to leave the board ends the robot's evaluation early. If the square containing the box is unoccupied another box is placed there. After the robot is done moving the number of squares not under or south of a wall is subtracted from the total size of the board to compute the robot's fitness. A perfect solution is thus a wall along the north side of the board. The robot is allowed to know the state of the squares adjacent to it, 0=empty, 1=box, 2=edge. These values are fed into the GP-Automaton controller's sensor inputs.

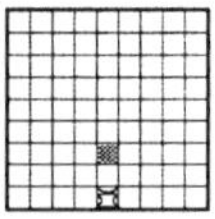

Figure 2: Initial configuration for the 9x9 north wall builder (NWB) task.

GP-Automata

GP-Automata are a hybrid representation incorporating genetic programming parse trees (reference Koza). A finite state machine is augmented by adding parse trees called deciders to each state. This permits the finite state machines to deal with large numbers of inputs and to incorporate complex data abstractions to drive their states. The crossover and mutation operators for GP-Automata are as in (Ashlock, 2004). In the GP-Automata used in this study (Fig. 3), deciders will process eight environmental variables, representing the contents of grid squares adjacent to the constructor, reducing them to a single bit of information, the parity of an integer. The transition and response functions thus have two choices at each state. The next state and response are given in the form **action → newstate.** The actions that the GP-Automata returns are from the set {0, 1, 2, 3}. These are interpreted as 0 - turn left, 1 - turn right, 2 - try to advance, and 3 - think. A *think* action produced no action in the virtual world and the simulation software makes the transition to the next state of the GP-Automata immediately. If eight think actions are executed in a row without producing a left, right, or advance, the constructor stands still for one time step. This wastes time and so is a *defacto* fitness penalty. Past work with GP-Automata appears in (Ashlock, 1997; Ashlock and Richter, 1997; Richter et al., 1998).

Start: →1			
	If Even	If Odd	Deciders
0	0→22	1→13	(ITE x_5 (~ -2) (x_1))
1	2→14	2→10	(ITE (~1) (Com x_7) (~x_6)
2	2→23	0→16	(~ (ITE x_4 x_2 (Odd x_8)))
3	1→13	3→23	(Com x_6)
4	1→22	3→21	(Com (Odd (<=x_6 (Odd x_2))))
5	3→1	3→5	(> (Com x_7) (>=x_4 x_3))
6	2→14	1→19	(Odd (+ 1 (+x_1 x_2)))
7	2→6	2→7	(Odd (ITE x_6 x_6 (Odd x_5)))
8	2→21	3→23	(= (Com x_6) x_4)
9	0→1	3→10	(~ (ITE x_4 x_7 (~x_4)))
10	0→0	0→17	(<> (ITE x_6 x_3 -1) x_2)
11	1→9	2→23	(<=x_3 (>=x_5 (Odd x_4)))
12	1→17	1→20	(<> (~x_2) (>x_5 (~x_5)))
13	0→16	2→7	(Com x_6)
14	2→16	1→20	(Odd (-x_5 (-x_7 x_7)))
15	1→19	0→2	(ITE x_7 (~x_7) (Com x_8))
16	1→7	0→21	(min x_2 (ITE x_1 x_2 x_4))
17	2→20	3→22	(<x_5) (Com (min x_6 x_2)))
18	0→23	0→11	(Com (<x_1 (<x_6 x_7)))
19	3→13	3→8	(- (Odd x_7) (+x_3 x_3))
20	2→4	1→4	(Com (+ (=x_4 x_6) x_7))
21	0→19	3→14	(~x_7)
22	1→11	3→4	(~x_5)
23	3→9	1→7	(ITE x_6 x_5 (<>x_5 x_1))

Figure 3: An example of a GP-Automata with integer valued deciders. This example was evolved for the table-top variant of the NWB task and received a fitness of 55.

	Arity	Semantics
I	0	Ephemeral integer constant
x_i	0	Input (sensor terminal)
~	1	Integer negation
Com	1	Computes 1-x
Odd	1	Predicate for oddness*
+	2	Integer addition
–	2	Integer subtraction
=	2	Equality*
>	2	Greater than*
<	2	Less than*
>=	2	Greater than or equal to*
<=	2	Less than or equal to*
Max	2	returns maximum of arguments
Min	2	returns minimum of arguments
ITE	3	If-then-else; if first argument** then return the second argument otherwise return the third argument

*returns 1 for true, zero for false
**all nonzero values are considered true
Figure 4: Operations and terminals of the integer valued parse tree language used in deciders.

EXPERIMENTAL DESIGN

For this study, 10,000 populations were run for each of the previously described problems. This allowed error estimation of mean time to solution for each problem to be run with 95% confidence intervals. Each population will be run for population sizes 256, 512, and 1024. Cyclic tournament selection was used within each deme and as a baseline for comparison of performance of MD-PTS. Cyclic tournament selection places the population in a circular array and then moves the tournaments in a cycle about the circle. It creates a very slow flow of information within a population. This is because demes are used to allow blocks to evolve on a subset of the problem to allow building blocks to be assembled as the population evolves and the demes run successively.

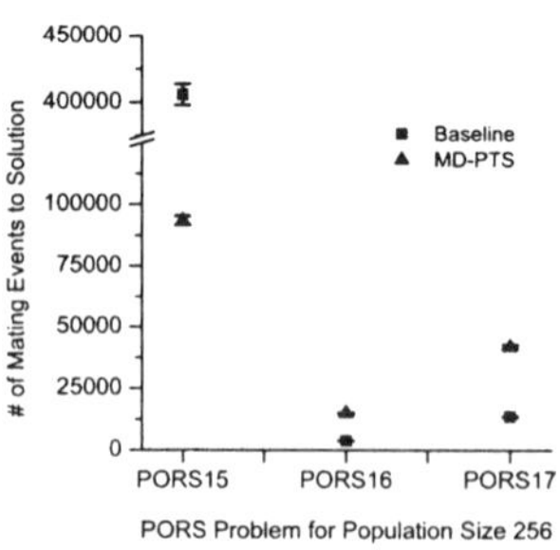

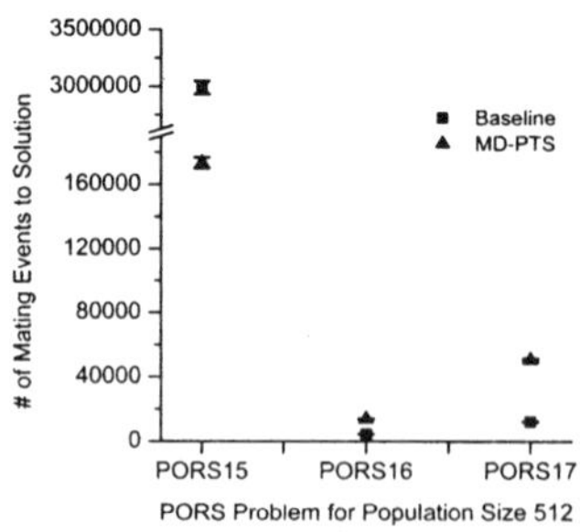

Figures 5 Figure6
Number of Mating Events to Solution versus Population Size for PORS.

For the NWB problem different values of *k* were used as the demes for MD-PTS. For the PORS problems the following schemes were used for each deme. For each problem there are four demes specified, each solving a different PORS problem. One deme is always the problem under investigation (i.e. PORS 15, PORS 16, or PORS 17). For PORS 15 each deme solves one of the following problems PORS 15, PORS 12, PORS 9, or PORS 6. For PORS 16 each deme solves one of the following problems PORS 16, PORS 13, PORS 10, or PORS 7. For PORS 17 each deme solves one of the following problems PORS 17, PORS 14, PORS 11, or PORS 8.

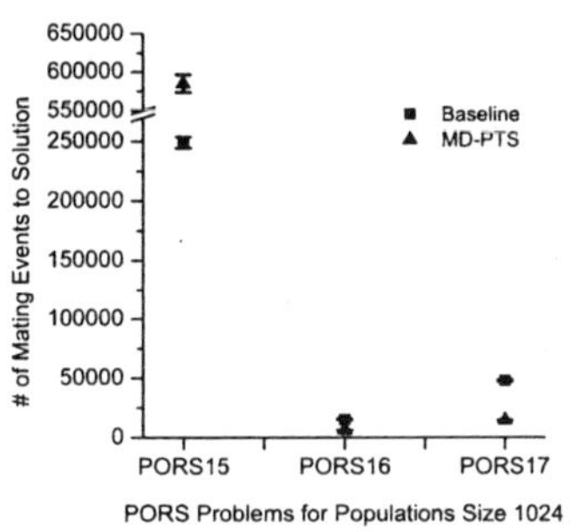

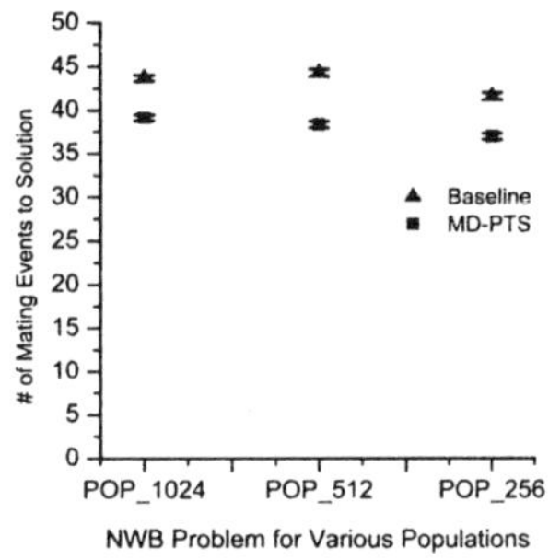

Figure 7 Figure 8

Number of Mating Events to Solution versus Population Size for PORS and NWB.

RESULTS

It can be seen from Figure 6-7 that MD-PTS is beneficial and results in a significant amount of reduction in computational time for the algorithm in PORS 15 and is not useful in the remaining PORS problems and the NWB problem. This illustrates that MD-PTS can be a significant enhancement to an evolutionary algorithm if implemented on a building block problems such as PORS 15 problems.

It can be seen that the PORS 15 problem is an ideal case for MD-PTS. The solution to the PORS 15 is comprised of blocks consisting of solutions for PORS12, PORS 9, and PORS 6. This results in sub-solutions to be developed in the demes and then assembled in the final deme in a more efficient manner than in the baseline algorithm. For the PORS 16 and PORS 17 problem two factors remove the impact of MD-PTS at a low mixing rate. First, there are more, and more complex, building blocks in these to versions of the PORS problem and so the ability of the demes with smaller tree sizes to contribute exactly the needed building blocks to larger tree sizes is reduced. Second, PORS 15 is far an away the hardest problem. The increased time to solution leaves more time for building blocks to be assembled and passed on.

With the NWB problem MD-PTS provides no computational savings (Figure 8). This is the result of the NWB problem not exhibiting building block properties. The NWB problem exhibits better solution speed under the baseline algorithm.

CONCLUSIONS AND FUTURE WORK

The MD-PTS technique yielded substantial time savings on the hardest of the four problems, PORS 15. The fitness landscape of PORS 15 has numerous local optima, constructed from building blocks useful for solving the PORS 16 and PORS 17 problem. It also contains a unique optimal solution that uses a fundamental building block, a three node tree fragment that multiplies by two, four times. Discovering and assembling four copies of this fundamental building block is what yields the difficulty of the PORS 15 problem. The other problem cases assemble a smaller number of building blocks from a more diverse collection of available building blocks.

The NWB problem is included as a control. Prior expectation was that multi-deme technique would show inferior performance on this problem. A correct solution to the problem for a smaller board size is not a bad solution for a larger board size, but it is not a terribly good one either. A correct solution for a larger board size dies instantly on a smaller board. Thus the flow of information from smaller board size demes to larger is not to helpful while the flow in the other direction will rapidly become non-existent.

The effect of more rapid inter-deme mixing and the location of more example of "natural" problems for MD-PTS is the logical next step in this research. The problem performed in this study suggest that back-flow of building blocks from partial solutions to harder cases of the problem may be a critical feature in MD-PTS compatibility of problems.

REFERENCES

Ashlock, D., 1997, "GP-Automata for Dividing the Dollar," *GP 97,* pp. 18-26, Cambridge: MIT Press.

Ashlock, D., Bryden, K., and Corns, S., 2004, "On Taxonomy of Evolutionary Computation Problems," *Proceedings of the 2004 Congress on Evolutionary Computation,* Portland, Oregon.

Ashlock, D., and Lathrop, J., 2004, "Building a Wall," program induction, *Proceedings of the 2004 Congress on Evolutionary Computation,* Portland, Oregon.

Ashlock, D., and Lathrop, J. I., 1998, "A Fully Characterized Test Suite for Genetic Programming," *Evolutionary Programming VII,* pp. 537-546, New York: Springer-Verlag.

Ashlock, D., and Richter, C., 1997, "The Effect of Splitting Populations on Bidding Strategies," *GP 97,* pp. 27-34, Cambridge: MIT Press.

Ashlock, D., Walker, J., and Smucker, M., 1999, "Graph Based Evolutionary Algorithms," *Proceedings of the 1999 Congress on Evolutionary Computation,* pp. 1362-1368, San Francisco: Morgan Kaufmann.

Ashlock, D., Willson, S., and Leahy, N., "Coevolution and Tartarus", *Proceedings of the 2004 Congress on Evolutionary Computation*, pp 1618-1624, IEEE Press.

Banzhaf, W., Nordin, P., Keller, R. E., and Francone, F. D., 1998, *Genetic Programming: An Introduction,* San Francisco: Morgan Kaufmann.

Blickle, T., and Tiele, L., 1995, "A Mathematical Analysis of Tournament Selection," *Proceedings of the Sixth International Conference on Genetic Algorithms,* ed. Larry Esehlman, pp. 9-16, San Francisco: Morgan Kaufmann.

Bryden, K. M., Ashlock, D. A., and Corns, S. M., 2003, "Graph Based Evolutionary Algorithms," submitted to *IEEE Transactions on Evolutionary Computation.*

Kinnear, K., 1994, *Advances in Genetic Programming,* Cambridge: MIT Press.

Koza, J. R., 1992, *Genetic Programming,* Cambridge: MIT Press.

Richter, C., Ashlock, D., and Sheble, G., 1998, "Effects of Tree Size and State Number on GP-Automata Bidding Strategies," *GP 98,* pp. 329-337, Cambridge: MIT Press.

Whitley, D., Rana, S. B., and Heckendorn, R. B., 1997, "Island Model Genetic Algorithms and Linearly Separable Problems," *Evolutionary computing, AISB Workshop,* pp. 109-125.

Advances in Ordered Greed

Peter G. Anderson,
pga@cs.rit.edu
Computer Science Department,
Rochester Institute of Technology,
Rochester, New York 146223

Dan Ashlock,
danwell@iastate.edu
Mathematics Department,
Iowa State University,
Ames, Iowa, 50011

Abstract

Ordered Greed is a form of genetic algorithm that uses a population of permutations whose fitnesses depend on their use as the orders in which parts of a problem are solved.

We have developed and investigate two new crossover operators specifically for ordered greed. The first uses the standard combinatorial mathematics notion of permutations' signatures, which are a list of numbers that specify a permutation, but for which the usual bit-string notions of substring-swapping crossovers apply. The second form of crossover works with permutations directly, merging two parents, as in a riffle shuffle, and extracting two children from the merged list consisting of the lists of first or second instances of each value. We compare the new methods with each other and with the well-known PMX

1 Ordered Greed (OG)

Greedy algorithms are heuristic approaches to finding solutions to combinatorial optimization problems. *Greedy* generally indicates that the problem is solved incrementally, choosing an optimum assignment at each stage, with no look-ahead and no backtracking. The simplest example of a greedy algorithm that is always successful is change making, expressing a given amount of money in, say American or Euro currency; namely, iterative reduce the outstanding amount using the largest possible coin. Another typical example is the *sequential algorithm* for graph coloring [3]: select an ordering of the vertices of the graph to be colored, $\{v_0, v_1, \cdots, v_{N-1}\}$, then color each vertex in order, using the first available color for each vertex (that is, so no edge's two end points are assigned the same color). Notice that an ordered set of colors is required.

This algorithm is very unlikely to color a graph using anywhere near the minimum number of colors (the graph's chromatic number), but it does achieve a valid coloring rapidly. However, a coloring using the minimum possible number of colors is clearly the result of this algorithm, if a suitable permutation is used. In fact there are a large number of suitable permutations. Take a coloring of a graph that is a witness to the chromatics number (an optimal coloring). Order the colors used. Now present the vertices to OG so that all vertices with a lower color are before those with a higher color. The greedy algorithm will then exactly reproduce the optimal coloring. We then see that for a given optimal coloring there are as many permutations that reproduce that coloring as the product of the factorials of the sizes of the monochrome sets of vertices. The space of permutations is huge, with a large but sparse subset of good ones. This is the type of search problem modern metaheuristics are applied to.

OG uses a genetic algorithm with a population of permutations. It assigns a fitness to each permutation according to the quality of the answer the greedy algorithm yields using that permutation. For the problem of coloring the vertices of a planar graph, a permutation's fitness could be the number of vertices successfully colored using just the first four colors.

A standard problem we use for testing OG is the classical N-Queens problem: place N chess Queens on an $N \times N$ board so that no two attack each other (no two Queens may occupy the same row, column, or diagonal). This is a rather easy instance of the Maximum Independent Set problem (MIS), but, unlike MIS, N-Queens is not NP-complete (contrary to what we might read on the Internet); see, for instance [4]. The OG approach to solving the N-Queens problem is to use a given N-permutation to specify the *order of the rows* into which we place the Queens. If we have an ordering of the chess board rows, $\{r_0, r_1, \cdots, r_{N-1}\}$, we place the first Queen in the far left position of row r_0, and continue, for each i, place a Queen in row r_i as far left as possible (i.e., greedily) avoiding attacking any previously placed Queens.

The OG approach to finding Queens solutions makes the solutions much denser in the search space of permutations that the obvious alternative—namely working with the space of N-permutations, each of which solves the N-rooks problem, and assigning a fitness to be the number of unattacked Queens. For example, when we solve the classical 8-Queens problem with OG, we find a perfect solution early in the initial population: 3 4 1 5 7 0 6 2. The solution, expressed as list of (row,column) pairs is: (3,0), (4,1), (1,2), (5,4), (7,3), (0,5), (6,7), (2,6). In 20,000 trials of the 64-Queens problem, using the permutation as the queen's placements, we achieved an average fitness of 39/64. Using the permutation to specify the row order of queens' placements, we achieved an average fitness of 61/64.

In addition to graph coloring and N-Queens, OG may be applied to whole host of other problems, such as: sports tournament scheduling, bin packing, traveling salesman, polyomino puzzles, satisfiability, scheduling faculty teaching assignments, and so on. We recommend that the following principle be observed:

> **The OG Principle:** *Prove that at least one optimal solution does, in fact, follow from the greedy algorithm with at least one permutation.*

1.1 Our steady-state GA

For the experiments reported in the present paper, our GA takes a steady-state form. Namely, a population is initialized with random individuals. Their fitnesses are computed. Then, we iteratively select two parents using two 2-element tournaments. The tournament winners are crossed over to create two new children, the children are subject to mutation then fitness evaluation. The new children replace the two tournament losers in the population. The process continues until an individual with a desired fitness appears or the number of permitted fitness evaluations occurs.

A mutation rate of p means that every element of a given individual is subject to re-randomization (for a list of values, such as a signature) or a random transposition (for a permutation) with probability p.

2 Permutation Crossovers for OG

A genetic algorithm with a population of permutations (or representatives of permutations, as we will see below) requires a crossover technique that tends to preserve and bring together the desirable properties ("schema") of parents into their children. The specific desirable property of a permutation, from the point of view of OG, is that some given items preceed others. Two of the three permutation crossover techniques given by Goldberg [2], partially-matched crossover (PMX) and cycle crossover (CX), preserve much of the absolute position of elements. The third method, ordered crossover (OX) preserves some orderings as well as absolute positions of elements.

We use PMX as one of the crossover techniques in the present investigation as well as two novel techniques. All three are described below.

2.1 Partially matched crossover (PMX)

Our implementation of PMX is the following. Initialize two children to be identical to their two parents. Denote these permutations by $\{a_0, a_1, \cdots, a_{N-1}\}$ and $\{b_0, b_1, \cdots, b_{N-1}\}$. Then the following is repeated $N/4$ times: select a random position k, $0 \leq k < N$, and interchange the values of a_k and b_k at all places they occur in the two children. This has the effect of modifying up to half of the positions in the two new individuals.

2.2 Signature representations and crossover

A permutation's signature is a list of integers $\{s_0, s_1, \cdots, s_{N-1}\}$ satisfying

$$0 \leq s_k < N - k, \text{ for all } k$$

Clearly, there are $N!$ signatures—they are equinumerous with permutations. A signature, s, may be converted into a permutation, p, by the following pseudo-code snippet:

```
for ( k = 0; k < N; k++ ) p[k] = k;
for ( k = 0; k < N; k++ ) interchange p[k] and p[k+s[k]];
```

The above code represents a one-to-one onto transformation of the set of signatures to the set of permutations. (A less straightforward, yet still $\mathcal{O}(N)$ procedure, can transform permutations into signatures. This is a student exercise.)

Signatures are particularly convenient for permutation-based genetic algorithms, because: (i) signatures are very easy to generate randomly, (ii) signatures are easy to mutate, and (iii) the bit-string (or small alphabet) crossover techniques, one-point, two-point, and uniform crossover can apply directly to signatures.

2.3 Merging crossover (MOX)

To form permutation children from parents using MOX, first randomly merge the two parents into a $2N$-element list, L (this operation is similar to a riffle shuffle of cards). The first instance of each value in L gives the ordering of elements for the first child, and the second instance gives the second child. For example, let $p_1 = \{ 3\ 9\ 0\ 1\ 2\ 4\ 6\ 8\ 7\ 5 \}$ and $p_2 = \{ 2\ 6\ 7\ 1\ 4\ 8\ 0\ 3\ 5\ 9 \}$ be the two parent permutations. One merging of p_1 and p_2

gives $L = \{ \mathbf{2}\ \mathbf{3}\ 6\ 7\ 1\ \mathbf{4}\ \mathbf{9}\ \mathbf{0}\ 8\ 0\ \mathbf{1}\ \mathbf{2}\ 3\ \mathbf{4}\ \mathbf{6}\ 5\ \mathbf{8}\ \mathbf{7}\ \mathbf{5}\ 9 \}$ (the elements from p_1 are shown in bold). From L, we extract the children $c_1 = \{ 2\ \mathbf{3}\ 6\ 7\ 1\ 4\ \mathbf{9}\ \mathbf{0}\ 8\ 5 \}$ and $c_2 = \{ 0\ \mathbf{1}\ \mathbf{2}\ 3\ \mathbf{4}\ \mathbf{6}\ \mathbf{8}\ \mathbf{7}\ \mathbf{5}\ 9 \}$ (the p_1 contribution is still shown in bold).

The intermediate list, L, is not needed, except conceptually. All we need is a one-element buffer, X, that is filled from the initial elements of the two parents, treated as queues, with the parents chosen at random. Then X is appended to the first child, if X is not already present, otherwise it is appended to the second child.

OG operates by seeking good precedence orders among permutation elements. Let "$a \prec b$" denote that "a precedes b" in a given permutation. We believe that MOX is particularly suitable for OG because of the following property: if $a \prec b$ in both parents, then $a \prec b$ in both children produced by MOX. This is illustrated in the MOX example above: $1 \prec 4$ in both parents and in both children. In case $a \prec b$ in one parent and $b \prec a$ in the other, then both children can have $a \prec b$, or both can have $b \prec a$, or the two children can be mixed.

It is easy to come up with examples for all of the other mentioned permutation crossover operations (plus Ordered Crossover (OX) and Cycle Crossover (CX) [2]) in which the property of $a \prec b$ in both parents is not preserved for both children.

In the following section, we describe a simple experiment that illustrates some of the power of MOX.

3 Evens precede odds

Following Goldberg's simple illustration problem [2] of a genetic algorithm search for a bit string with as many 1's as possible, we propose a permutation based genetic algorithm to search for a permutation in which all the even entries precede all the odd entries. As with Goldberg's problem, this is not to be taken seriously, but as representative of some aspects of the heuristic technique in question, and as a place-holder for the serious problems to follow.

An experiment in which the fitness counted the number of correct parity values in the desired half of the string showed us clearly that another fitness measure was called for—one that was able to assign finer partial credit and allow desired solutions to exert a pull on the search procedure. The fitness measure we found that does this works as follows: starting at the left end of the string, with subscript positions $k < \frac{N}{2}$ (where we want the even values to migrate), if a value has the correct parity, it contributes $\frac{N}{2} - k$ to the fitness. Positions with subscript $k > \frac{N}{2}$ with the desired (odd) parity contribute $1 + k - \frac{N}{2}$ to the fitness. The fitness of a perfect individual is therefore $\frac{N}{2}(\frac{N}{2} + 1)$.

We tested several crossover techniques for this problem, running each choice 100 times with different random seeds (provided by the Linux builtin `$RANDOM`), with the results shown in Table 3. For these runs we used permutations of length 100, a population size of 100, and a mutation rate of 0.001. The permutation crossover MOX is a clear winner.

xover	min	Q1	median	Q3	max
MOX	3,769	5,647	6,392	7,347	11,028
PMX	5,239	17,069	30,012	59,263	–
1 Pt.	15,824	31,325	44,534	70,175	–
2 Pt.	12,514	29,298	45,928	68,969	–
Unif.	8,648	23,764	38,847	61,547	–

Table 1: The number of fitness evaluations needed to solve the "evens preceed odds" for five crossover techniques. 100 attempts were made for each crossover. We report the minimum first quartile, median, third quartile, and maximum number of fitness evaluations. The entry "–" indicates the maximum value is over 100,000, at which point the process was stopped.

xover	min	Q1	median	Q3	max
MOX	162	974	1,444	2,049	5,005
PMX	184	988	1,722	2,573	7,862
1 Pt.	128	766	1,144	1,627	29,706
2 Pt.	30	763	1,142	1,726	10,885
Unif.	204	1,079	1,551	2,539	25,423

Table 2: The number of fitness evaluations needed to solve the 500-Queens problem for five crossover techniques.

4 Testing with 500 Queens

We performed a similar experiment on the 500-Queens problem using the same GA parameters as those for "evens precedes odds" with results shown in Table 4. Here, MOX did well, but the signature representation did well also. We consider MOX the winner based on the maximum values.

5 Generating & Coloring Planar Graphs

5.1 Two Types of Planar Graphs

For the present study, we considered two types of Hamiltonian planar graphs: (1) triangulations of a disk with all vertices on the boundary and (2) the union of two graphs of type (1), with the vertices identified. Both types are planar, hence four-colorable: type (1) graphs are a triangulation of a disk, hence planar; type (2) graphs are triangulations of two disks with their boundaries identified, hence they are graphs on a sphere, hence planar. Type (1) graphs are also three-colorable by the following algorithm. First, locate any triangle and color its vertices. Then locate triangles with two of the three vertices already colored and color the third vertex. This illustrates a successful application of the sequential algorithm. However, if the sequential algorithm is given an unfortunate permutation of vertices, many more colors will be needed. We have an example of a type (1) graph with

25 vertices for which one permutation yielded a coloring with five colors.

5.2 The Experiments

We generated 190 random graphs of each type with N vertices, $11 \leq N \leq 200$, and attempted to color them minimally, with three or four colors, with 21 attempts for each graph. The genetic algorithm used permutation representation for individuals with MOX crossover, a population size of 20, and a mutation rate of 0.01. We allowed a maximum of 100,000 fitness evaluations.

5.3 The Results

Type (1) graphs proved harder to color than type (2):

$11 \leq N \leq 30$	all trials succeeded
$31 \leq N \leq 64$	most trials succeeded
$65 \leq N \leq 110$	fewer than half succeeded
$111 \leq N \leq 200$	all trials failed

Every type (2) was four-colored a least once:

$11 \leq N \leq 50$	all trials succeeded
$59 \leq N \leq 171$	most trials succeeded
$172 \leq N \leq 200$	fewer than half succeeded

Type (1) graphs, of course, have unique three-colorings, up to color permutations. A coloring algorithm that first colors the more constrained vertices will succeed with these graphs, but that is a topic for a subsequent investigation.

References

[1] Peter G. Anderson. Ordered greed, II: Graph coloring. In *Proceedings of the International NAISO Congress on Information Science Innovations, Dubai, U. A. E.* Natural and Artificial Intellingent Systems Organization, 2001.

[2] David Goldberg. *Genetic Algorithms in Search, Optimization and Machine Learning.* Addison-Wesley, 1989.

[3] Marek Kubale. *Introduction to computational complexity and algorithmic graph theory.* Gdańskie Towarzystwo Naukowe, Gdańsk, 1998.

[4] R. Sosic and J. Gu. A polynomial time algorithm for the N-queens problem. *SIGART Bulletin*, 1(3):7–11, October 1990.

APPLICATION OF COMPETITIVE CO-EVOLUTION ALGORITHM WITH DIRECTION OF EVOLUTIONAL PROCESSES TO TSUME-GO GAME

MAKOTO OSHIMA
Information Engineering
University of Ryukyus
mako10@eva.ie.u-ryukyu.ac.jp

KOJI YAMADA
Information Engineering
University of Ryukyus
koji@ie.u-ryukyu.ac.jp

SATOSHI ENDO
Information Engineering
University of Ryukyus
endo@ie.u-ryukyu.ac.jp

MOEKO NEROME
Department of Regional Economics
And Environmental Policy
Okinawa International University
nerome@okiu.ac.jp

ABSTRACT

Tsume-go is life and death problem in Igo-game, which is most difficult board game in the field of AI by reason of the huge search space. In this paper, we introduced an improvement way of competitive co-evolution algorithm with a direction of evolutional processes to solve the game effectively (to deal with the huge space more effectively). We have achieved it by through following three phases. On the first phase, relative local information on the board is recorded. On the second phase, a relationship between local information and the fitness of individual, then connectivity strength is calculated, and the mining a set of the parameters which have stronger connectivity to a fitness value than the remaining parameters from local information. Final phase restricts to search a solution, which has a strong connection with such parameter-set. We apply the proposal method to the Tsume-go game in order to investigate its effectiveness. Furthermore, we analyze the process of the predictability method. In the simulation results, our method has acquired the directivity strategies and shown a better performance than a conventional method.

1. INTRODUCTION

We pick up the Igo-game as the object of study problem. An initiative and a passive move, each player try to improve until make it to optimum solution by learning from the other. Igo-game and co-evolution system are very similar in the point of the interactions of two populations.Thus co-evolution algorithm can be used for the acquisition problem of the Igo-game strategy. And it is useful to the research of their schemes for each other. In this study, initiative strategies set to population$_i$(P_i) and passive strategies set to population$_p$(P_p). We aim at getting the optimum strategy by interactions of P_i and P_p in co-evolution. In this paper, we explain the method of the coding which enables use of co-evolution algorithm at strategy acquisition of Igo-game. And we proposed effective solution in Igo-game. We focus on or direction for evolutional process to resolve the problem. Assuming that GA has an appropriate evolutionary direction, it can avoid the waste search domain, and we then can get a cutting down of computation time.

2. COMPETITIVE CO-EVOLUTION ALGORITHM AND ITS DRAWBACKS

A fitness for each individual is determined by competitions with other population in co-evolution algorithm. The strategy estimation is specified by the opponent. Available solutions and comparative assessments can be gained by competitions between two populations. Therefore cross populations advance each evolution each other by repeating a generational evolution.

However an expanse of search domain causes an unbalance of each evolutional speed and cooperation by increase of search time and local solutions in GA. It would cause the dead end of Competitive Co-evolution when the worst. Consequently, we aim at reduction of convergence time by escape from the local solution with the direction of evolution process.

In this paper, we explain the Competitive Co-evolution algorithm with direction estimation method to escape from local optimum.

3. THE COMPETITIVE CO-EVOLUTION ALGORITHM WITH DIRECTION DEFINITION METHOD

The way of how to define an appropriate direction, which goes further search, can be gained from the evolution process itself.

Selecting of the evolutional indicator and applying of it (shown in Figure1)

(1) In processes of the conventional GA cycle, individual information for offspring and its fitness are recorded together.

(2) Calculating the relationship between individual fitness and its local information (=a part of gene loci, the set of parameters). A set of the parameters which have best connectivity to fitness is mined from individual information and selected as an evolutional indicator.

(3) Renewal of a generation is carried out using the indicator calculated in (2). And individuals which have high value in the same portion with the mined parameters are selected, and anthers are rejected.

With that, waste searches are reduced, and GA gets short convergence time, therefore this function generates a direction of evolution in the GA cycle.

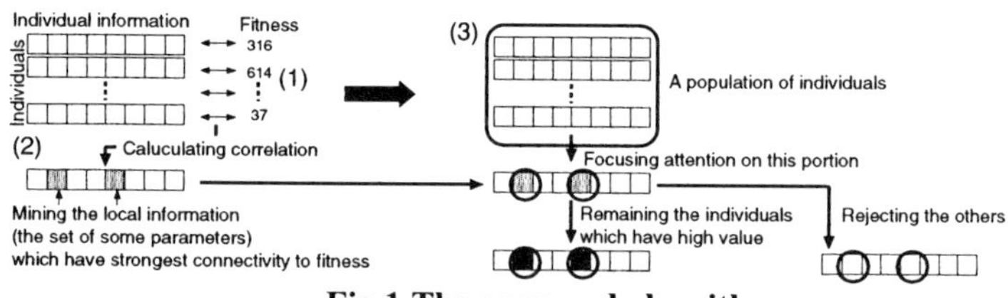

Fig 1 The proposed algorithm

4. APPLICATION OF PROPOSED ALGORITHM INTO TSUME-GO

In this study, we apply our method to Tsume-go problem. The goal of Tsume-go is composed of optimum strategies in all aspect. A search domain grows with a largeness of a go-board, therefore the trial times getting the optimum solution increase endlessly. The size of a board is 9*9. The number of the possible moves per aspect of affairs is 81. The following possible moves to each the aspect of affairs are 81. When possible moves are considered to third aspect of affairs, there are 531441 kinds of strategies. We discuss an efficient directional search by analyzing transition of the process of getting optimum solutions. And it aims at the verification of the proposed method effects on this large search domain problem.

4.1 Tsume-go problem

Tsume-go game is puzzle for one player. The role of initiative player and a passive move player is managed alone. An initiative player and a passive move player place one stone of the ones stones alternately on fixed points of a go-board. (Generally, the initiative player use black stones and passive move player use white stones.)Ultimately, goals of Tsume-go are divided into two cases by a problem situation. The first one is "survive oneself" another is "conquer the enemy". In this instance, we pick up the later problem "conquer the enemy".

4.2 Tsume-go model

An individual: an individual consists of a series of strategies.

A strategy: a strategy consists of an array, which is a set of applicable moves on a phase.

P_1: P_1 is a set of initiative (black stone) individuals.

P_2: P_2 is a set of passive move (white stone) individuals.

A cording of individual: one strategy is composed of array of stone moves in priority. Each gene in one strategy denotes a unique number on the board. (The number of possible patterns are 9*9= 81.).

Figure2 shows the cording of Tsume-go strategy. 0th to 80th genetic locus arrays indicate the priority of action in first move (black stones). Each gene indicates a point on the board, where the player wants to place it on.

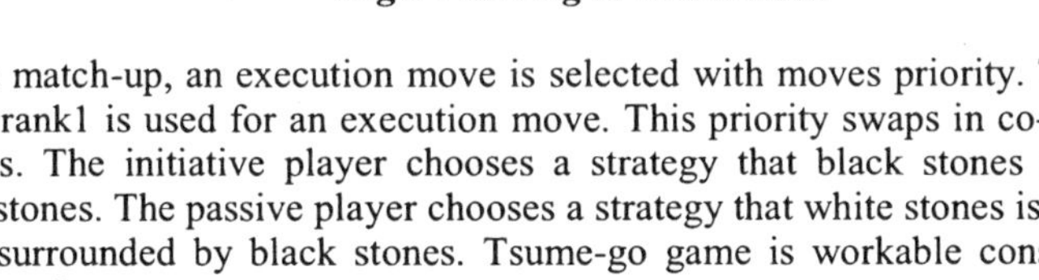

Fig 2 Cording of individuals

In match-up, an execution move is selected with moves priority. The value of the rank1 is used for an execution move. This priority swaps in co-evolution process. The initiative player chooses a strategy that black stones surrounds white stones. The passive player chooses a strategy that white stones is made not to be surrounded by black stones. Tsume-go game is workable constantly by these cording.

4.3 The implementation of propose algorithm

We calculate a correlation for the gene between the locus and its fitness by least squares method. Especially, we pretreat an individual into the relative information. On the problem of Tsume-go, we set up that each gene loci has circumbasal information by making its value into the header. It shows the situation of the circumference information on a go board. It consists of an array of the parameters of the local situation. We mine the evolutional indicator from this circumbasals information.

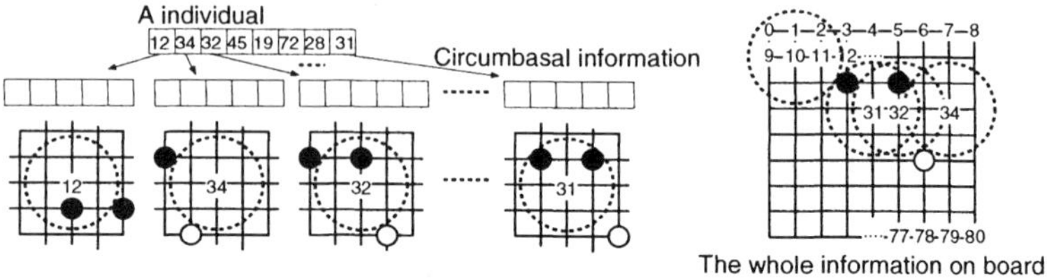

Fig 3 The circumbasals information

(1) Estimation of the correlation by least-squares method

The circumbasals are consisting of the array that indicates a condition of the circumbasals of the focused point.

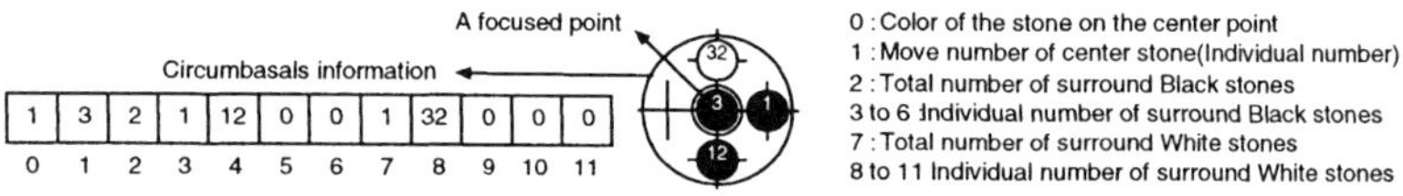

Fig 4 An example of genetic information

The relationship between the gene locus (or the combination of loci) and the fitness values are calculated by least-squares method. The distance between values of liner graph which is calculated form the actual value and the actual values (The actual values are individuals fitness actually calculated in the experiment which was preceded) is recorded. That is, the distance is the residual error. The gene locus with the smallest residual error is decided on the evolutional indicator. (In this paper, the strength of relationship of individual (i) is called as $D_{(i)}$.)

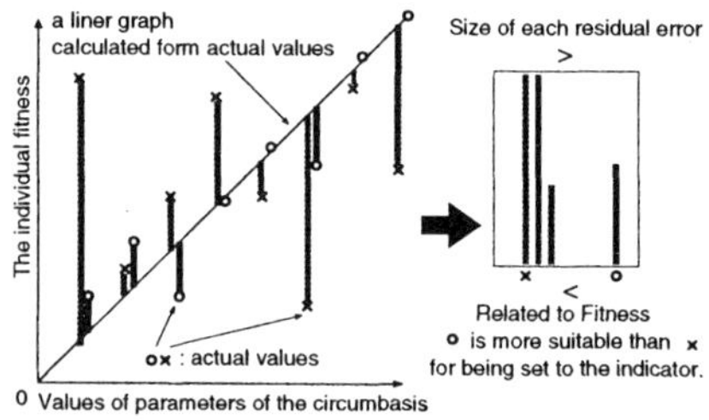

Fig 5 Distance between value of liner graph and actual value

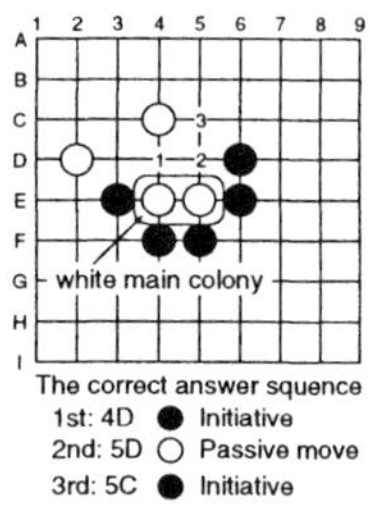

Fig 6 Three moves problem

(2) The fitness

We set up $D_{(i)}$ as the strength of the individual-(i) fitness by using the indicator.

$D_{(i)}$ = (The value which individual-(i) has in the position of the indicator) / (Maximum value which the parameter chosen as the indicator can take)

$(0 <= D_{(i)} <= 1)$ (1)

In order to reflect "$D_{(i)}$" in to a fitness for the individual, the fitness function is formulated to the application of the proposed algorithm.

The fitness of passive move strategies of individual-(i) is described as $F_{i\,(i)}$.

$F_{i\,(i)}$ = {(liberties of white stones)-(liberties of black stones)
+ (the average size of white colonies)
+ (liberties of the main colony) + (main colony size)} * $D_{(i)}$ (2)

Initiative is described as $F_{p\,(i)}$. $F_{p\,(i)} = -F_{i\,(i)}$ (3)

Note, "Liberty" is calculated as the number of vacant space surrounding remarkable point. The main colony is the most important group of stones. Assuming that the opponent takes off the main colony, this player loses the game.

4.4 GA-operators

The GA-operator accepts the coding of individual.

(1) One point cross over
(2) Mutation: the gene selected with a random order swaps other gene in the same chromosome.

4.5 Problem setting

In this experiment, we deal with three moves problem on Tsume-go problem. The dealt problem is shown in Figure6. In this case, the group of 4E and 5E stones is the white main colony. The correct sequence is 4D(black),5D(white),5C(black).

The parameters of this co-evolution are shown in table1

Table1 Parameter of this co-evolution

Population size	16
Sampling	10
Cross over rate	20%
Mutation rate	20%
Terminal generation for GA	10* T

T is generation number of Co-evolution

Table2 Transition of the average of trial times

Method	Indicator	Residual (deviation)	Generation size	Distribution (ratio)
No direction	-	-	341.1	35432(30.9)
Direction0	1st locus	16.2(57.4)	341.0	34972(30.6)
Direction1	2nd and 7th	7.7(49.4)	197.5	2204(1.9)
Direction2	7th locus	1.9(43.4)	139.2	1143(1.0)

"Distribution" is Distributions of Generation size.

4.6 The experimental result and prospect

We analyze the process of Competitive Co-evolution with the conclusion of the experimental graph, and discuss the difference between the conventional co-evolution and proposed method. In Figure7, a vertical axis shows fitness and a horizontal axis shows generation size. The superior line shows P_2 fitness. The lower lines show P_1 fitness. When two lines cross, It means that acquisition of the optimal solution in the set up of this fitness.

(1) Difference of generation sizes by the indicator

Table2 shows a result about indicators and its effect on generation sizes. There are the three patterns of genetic locus (or the combination of loci), which selected evolutional indicator, and these data. The indicators with little residual error tend to reduce the generation size.

(2) The distribution and variance of the generation size

Figure8 illustrates clearly that our algorithm tends a reduction tendency, which decrease the distribution.

The distribution of conventional method and the proposed method are shown in Figure10. And the difference in each distribution is shown to Table2.

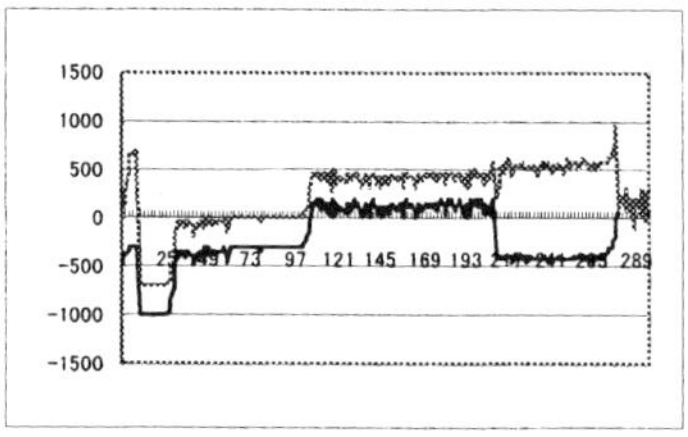

Fig 7 Fitness transitions of individual

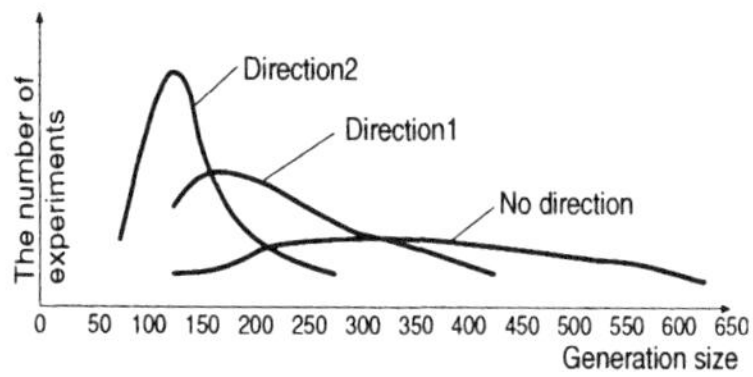

Fig 8 Distribution graph of generation sizes

In proposed method, a distributed value decreases according to reduction in residual error of indictor.

In consequence of proposed method, the generation size and the distributed value are decreasing compared with the conventional method.

5. CONCLUSIONS

In this paper, we described about "Application of Competitive Co-evolution Algorithm with Direction of Evolutional Processes to Tsume-go Games". Sorting of individuals is performed by using the evolutional indicator. This function induces the direction in evolutional processes. The indicator is given from the relationship between fitness and genetic locus. The relationships are calculated by least squares method. In this experiment, we applied to Tsume-go problem to investigate the system behavior, and its showed better validity than the conventional method. It is shown that the possibility of this algorithm functioned effectively to the problem of wide range solution space in Igo-game.

REFERENCES

[Hillis 1991] W.D. Hillis: Co-evolution parasites improve simulated evolution as an optimization procedure, Artificial Life II, Addition Wesley, pp.313-323(1991).

[Nerome 1997] M. Nerome, K. Yamada, S. Endo and H. Miyagi: Competitive Co-evolution Model on the Acquisition of Game Strategy, Lecture Notes in Artificial Intelligence, Springer, pp224-231(1997).

[Futuyma 1983] Futuyma, D.J. And D. Jablonski: Co evolution, Sinauer (1983).

A Taxonomy of Evolutionary Computation Problems

Dan Ashlock[1], *danwell@iastate.edu*
Kenneth M. Bryden[2], *kmbryden@iastate.edu*
Steven Corns[2], *scorns@iastate.edu*
Stephen J. Willson[1], *swillson@iastate.edu*
1Mathematics Department,
2Mechanical Engineering Department,
Iowa State University, Ames, IA, 50011

Abstract

Taxonomy is the practice of classifying members of a group based on their measurable characteristics. In evolutionary computation the problem of telling when two problems are similar is both challenging and important. Collections of test problems for evolutionary computation are common but means of resolving the diversity and quality of collections of test problems are scarce. This paper presents such a technique. A standard phylogenetic algorithm, hierarchical clustering, is used to build a taxonomic tree or cladogram of a set of problems from normalized average time-to-solution data for the problems using a graph based evolutionary algorithm for 26 different graphs. The resulting provides an estimate of how different the different problems are. Based on these results it is argued that the technique given here can be used to provide an objective, automatic, extensible classification tool for any collection of evolutionary problems.

1 Introduction

A *taxonomy* is a hierarchical classification of a set. Linnaeus established the first definite hierarchy used to classify living organisms. Constructing trees to find and visualize relationships among members of a group is a process with more general application. Hierarchical clustering can produced a tree-structured classification of any set of data given only a similarity measure on members of the set and some sort of averaging procedure for members of the set. In this study we will extract a set of measurements or *taxonomic characters* from a collection of test problems and use hierarchical clustering to produce a cladogram that classifies the problems as more and less similar. Hierarchical clustering starts with the members of a set, thought of as singleton subsets. It then joins the closest pair and replaces them with their union or average.

This paper presents a source of taxonomic characters that are computable for any evolutionary computation problem that has a detectable solution or end point. A type of evolutionary algorithm, *graph based evolutionary algorithms* are used to obtain the taxonomic characters. This type of evolutionary algorithm takes a geographical structure encoded as a combinatorial graph and uses it to restrict mating choice. Past work on GBEAs appear in [Ashlock et al., 1999, Bryden et al., 2003a]. The time-to-solution for a problem varies in a complex manner with the choice of graph. This complexity is the source of the taxonomic characters used. They are the normalized mean solution times for the problem on each of a variety of graphs.

2 Graphs Used

We assume some familiarity with graph theory [West, 1996]. In this paper a graph used to constrain mating in a population will be called the *population structure.* The general strategy is to use the graph to specify the geography on which a population lives, permitting mating only between neighbors, and finding graphs that preserve diversity without hindering progress that follows from heterogeneous crossover. The only nonstandard, non-random graph used in this paper is the graph Z which is described in full in [Ashlock et al., 1999]. Table 1 lists the graphs used in this study including the standard Petersen, toroidal, cycle, hypercube, and complete graphs. The random graphs used are not standard and so some description is required.

Definition 1 *An* edge move *is performed as follows. Two edges* $\{a, b\}$ *and* $\{c, d\}$ *are found that have the property that none of* $\{a, c\}$, $\{a, d\}$, $\{b, c\}$, *or* $\{b, d\}$ *are themselves edges. The edges* $\{a, b\}$ *and* $\{c, d\}$ *are deleted from the graph, and the edges* $\{a, c\}$ *and* $\{b, d\}$ *are added. Notice that edge moves preserve the regularity of a graph if it is regular.*

Definition 2 *We generate* random regular *graphs by the following algorithm. Start with a regular graph and then repeatedly perform 3,000 edge moves on vertices selected uniformly at random from those that are valid for edge moves. These graphs are denoted* $R(n, k, i)$ *where* n *is the number of vertices,* k *is the regular degree, and* $i = 1, 2, 3$ *is the instance of the graph in this study.*

Definition 3 *We generate random toroidal graphs as follows. A set of 512 points are placed onto the unit torus (unit square wrapped at the edges), and edges are created between those at distance* 0.07 *or less from one another. These graphs are denoted* $R(r, i)$, *where* $r = 0.07$ *is the radius for edge creation, and* $i = 1, 2, 3$ *is the instance of the graph in this study.*

Graph	Reg.	Diam.	Mean Degree	Graph	Reg.	Diam.	Mean Degree
C_{512}	2	256	2	$R(512, 9, i)$	9	4	9
H_9	9	9	9	$R(0.07, i)$	n/a	16-20	7.445
K_{512}	511	1	511	$T_{16,32}$	4	24	4
$P_{256,1}$	3	129	3	$T_{4,128}$	4	66	4
$P_{256,17}$	3	18	3	$T_{8,64}$	4	36	4
$P_{256,3}$	3	46	3	Z	4	19	4
$P_{256,7}$	3	22	3	$RBT(512, 3)$	3,1	16	1.996
$R(512, 3, i)$	3	10-11	3	$RBT(512, 4)$	4,1	11	1.996
$R(512, 4, i)$	4	7-8	4	$RBT(510, 5)$	5,1	9	1.996

Table 1: Graphs used together with their regularity, diameter, and mean degree.

3 Graph based evolutionary algorithm

This section defines a graph based evolutionary algorithm (GBEA) as it is used in this study. Assume that a graph G has been chosen as a population structure. One individual is placed on each vertex of G. A steady state evolutionary algorithm [Whitley, 1989] is used. Picking who breeds and deciding if the new individual replaces the individual on v are together called the *local mating rule* of the GBEA. In this research the local mating rule will pick a first vertex at random and then pick neighbors with Roulette selection. A single new individual is generated and replaces the individual selected at random if the new individual is more fit. This is called *local elite roulette mating.* One problem, one-max, has the child replace the parent absolutely rather than only if it is better. This modification yields a harder problem (the elite one-max is too easy to yield useful data). In each GBEA mutation is performed on the new individual before it replaces the individual on the randomly selected vertex.

4 The problems used

A suite of 22 test problems is used. Some 5,000 simulations were performed for all the test problems for each of the graphs except for differential equation solution where 10,000 simulations were performed to obtain better resolution. The number of mating events required to find a correct solution to the problem were saved. For each graph and problem the mean number of mating events to solution were normalized to the range [0,1] to yield the taxonomic characters.

String Problems
The one-max problem [Ashlock, 2004] uses a string of 20 bits for a chromosome. The fitness of a string is its weight (number of 1's in the string). Two-point crossover and single bit-flip mutation were used. The self-avoiding walk (SAW) problem uses a string over the alphabet $\{up, down, left, right\}$ as its chromosome and is judged on its ability to visit each square of an $N \times M$ grid once. The cases the SAW problem used are given in Figure 1. The SAW problem is discussed at some length in Chapter 2 of [Ashlock, 2004].

Real variable problems
We use DeJong's classic five functions[Whitley et al., 1996] as well as the Griewangk function[Whitley et al., 1996] in 3-7 dimensions. In this case the gene is a binary string with groups of twelve bits representing each real variable. Mutation is a probabilistic mutation with a probability of $\frac{1}{gene\ length}$ of flipping each bit. Two point crossover is used.

Genetic programming problems
We used four genetic programming problems. Three were version of the plus-one-recall-store efficient node use problem (PORS) problem, described in detail in [Ashlock, 2004]. The fourth was a differential equation solution problem described in subsequently. PORS is a type of maximum problem within the domain of genetic programming [Banzhaf et al., 1998] with a small operation set and a calculator-style memory. The goal of the test problem, called the *PORS efficient node use problem*, is to find parse trees that, when executed, generate the largest integer result possible given a fixed maximum number of parse tree nodes.

Solving differential equations is a standard genetic programming problem. In addition to solving a differential equation within a GBEA, we also modify the usual GP technique by extracting the derivatives needed to compute fitness symbolically. This method and a description of the details of the genetic programming system and fitness function used are given more completely in [Bryden et al., 2003b].

We solve the differential equation

$$y'' - 5y' + 6y = 0 \tag{1}$$

a simple homogeneous equation with a two dimensional solution space,

$$y = Ae^{2t} + Be^{3t}. \tag{2}$$

5 The Taxonomic Technique

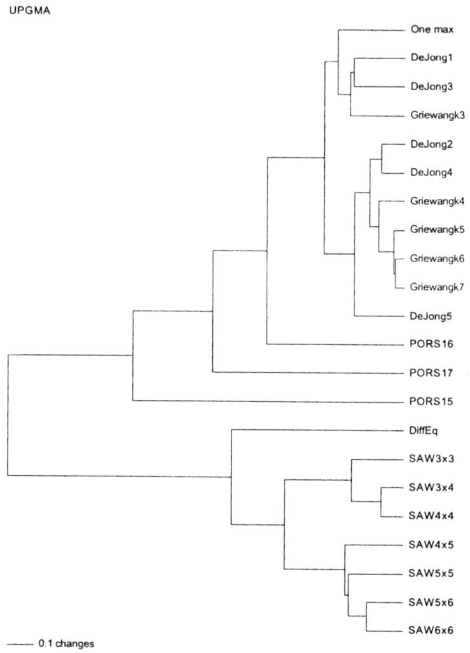

Figure 1: The problem taxonomy obtained by UPGMA. Horizontal distances represent the degree to which problems differ from one another while vertical distances have no taxonomic meaning, serving only to permit layout of the tree.

For each of the 22 problems P a real vector $m(P)$ with 26 entries corresponding to the 26 graphs was obtained. The entry $m(P, G)$ of $m(P)$ corresponding to graph G was the normalized mean number of mating events required to solve problem P on graph G. The linear normalization was set so that the solution of P on the graph G which required the largest mean number of mating events among the 26 different graphs received the score $m(P, G) = 1$, while the graph G which required the smallest mean number of mating events received the score $m(P, G) = 0$. For each pair of problems P and Q, the Euclidean distance $d(P, Q)$ between the vectors $m(P)$ and $m(Q)$ was then computed by the formula

$$d(P, Q) = \sqrt{\sum_{i=1}^{26}[m(P, G_i) - m(Q, G_i)]^2}.$$

We interpreted $d(P, Q)$ as the distance between the problems P and Q. In order to describe the taxonomic relationships among the 22 problems, we then found the "UPGMA" tree.

UPGMA is a clustering method commonly used to transform distance data into a tree. It received attention in [Sneath and Sokal, 1973], and a good recent description may be found in [Swofford et al., 1996]. It is especially reliable if the distances have a uniform meaning. Our normalization of the numbers $m(P, G)$ had the effect of making the widely different rates of convergence comparable, so that we think that the inferred distances are appropriate for analysis by UPGMA.

UPGMA is an acronym for "Unweighted Pair Group Method with Arithmetic mean." Given a collection of taxa and distance d_{ij} between taxa i and j, the method first links the two taxa x and y that are least distant. The taxa x and y are merged into a new unit z. For all taxa i other than x and y, a new distance d_{iz} is computed as the average of d_{ix} and d_{iy}, and it is noted that the new taxon z really represents the average of 2 original taxa. Henceforth, x and y are ignored, and the procedure is repeated to find the next pair of taxa that are least distant. When two taxa u and v are combined into a new taxon w, the new distance d_{iw} is the average of d_{iu} and d_{iv}, weighted according to the number of original taxa in u and v respectively. It is noted that w contains all the original taxa in both u and v. The procedure ends when the last two taxa are merged.

The UPGMA tree T was computed using the standard software package PAUP*[Swofford, 2002]. T is shown in Figure 1. Horizontal distances are proportional to the edge lengths, while vertical distances are arbitrary and selected for legibility. Problems separated by a small horizontal distance (such as Griewangk5, 6, and 7) should be regarded as very similar. The separation of widely separated problems should be regarded as significant.

6 Discussion

Figure 1 shows a very reasonable taxonomy for the problems used. The instances of the Griewangk function and the various DeJong's problems group together exhibiting only modest separation. Recall that horizontal difference corresponds to the degree to which the problems behave differently. The SAW problems formed a "clade" in the problem classification in much the same manner as the numerical test problems but exhibit more difference in their behavior from one another. Unlike the Griewangk function the SAW problems did not grow more similar as the dimension increased. It is interesting to note that the very easy (low mean time to solution) differential equation problem groups with the much harder SAW problems. The three PORS functions are taxonomically more similar to numerical problems than any other. Their position in the tree with long branch lengths shows they are quite different from all the other problems tried and also more different from one another than the SAW or numerical problems. This result is in accord with the mathematical analysis on the PORS problems given in [Ashlock and Lathrop, 1998].

7 Conclusions

The technique presented here can and should be extended to other problems, possibly adding other taxonomic characters. It achieved a plausible and informative taxonomy of the problems used. The study presented here is an opportunistic one, built on research initially performed to study the impact of GBEAs on a fairly broad set of problems. The taxonomy has some immediate and obvious uses. A smaller number of cases of the SAW problem could be used, likewise the numerical problems could be winnowed. The three cases of the PORS problem used behave very differently under the probe of normalized time to solution. The easy problems (SAW 3x3, differential equation solution) as well as the trivial one-max problem serve as useful reference points. A problem that is taxonomically near to one-max, for example, is best solved with a plain genetic algorithm.

References

[Ashlock, 2004] Ashlock, D. (2004). *Optimization and Modeling with Evolutionary Computation.* Springer-Verlag, New York.

[Ashlock and Lathrop, 1998] Ashlock, D. and Lathrop, J. I. (1998). A fully characterized test suite for genetic programming. In *Evolutionary Programming VII*, pages 537–546, New York. Springer-Verlag.

[Ashlock et al., 1999] Ashlock, D., Walker, J., and Smucker, M. (1999). Graph based genetic algorithms. In *Proceedings of the 1999 Congress on Evolutionary Computation*, pages 1362–1368, San Francisco. Morgan Kaufmann.

[Banzhaf et al., 1998] Banzhaf, W., Nordin, P., Keller, R. E., and Francone, F. D. (1998). *Genetic Programming : An Introduction.* Morgan Kaufmann, San Francisco.

[Bryden et al., 2003a] Bryden, K. M., Ashlock, D. A., McCorkle, D. S., and Urban, G. L. (2003a). Optimization of heat transfer utilizing graph based evolutionary algorithms. *International Journal of Heat and Fluid Flow*, 24(2):267–277.

[Bryden et al., 2003b] Bryden, K. M., Kirstukas, S., and Ashlock, D. (2003b). A hybrid genetic programming approach for analytical solution of differential equations. to appear: International Journal of Smart Engineering System Design.

[Sneath and Sokal, 1973] Sneath, P. A. and Sokal, R. R. (1973). *Numerical Taxonomy; the Principles and Practice of Numerical Classification.* W.H. Freeman, San Francisco.

[Swofford et al., 1996] Swofford, D., Olsen, G., Waddell, P., and D.M.Hillis (1996). Phylogenetic inference. In Hillis, D., Moritz, C., and Mable, B., editors, *Molecular Systematics, second edition.* Sinauer, Sunderland, MA.

[Swofford, 2002] Swofford, D. L. (2002). PAUP*. phylogenetic analysis using parsimony (*and other methods). version 4. Sinauer Associates, Sunderland, Massachusetts.

[West, 1996] West, D. B. (1996). *Introduction to Graph Theory.* Prentice Hall, Upper Saddle River, NJ 07458.

[Whitley, 1989] Whitley, D. (1989). The genitor algorithm and selection pressure: why rank based allocation of reproductive trials is best. In *Proceedings of the 3rd ICGA*, pages 116–121. Morgan Kaufmann.

[Whitley et al., 1996] Whitley, D., Mathias, K., and Dzubera, R. J. (1996). Evaluating evolutionary algorithms. *Artificial Intelligence*, 85:245–276.

A GENETIC PROGRAMMING TECHNIQUE FOR SOLVING SYSTEMS OF DIFFERENTIAL EQUATIONS

STEVEN J. KIRSTUKAS
Dept of Mechanical Engineering
Iowa State University

KENNETH M. BRYDEN
Dept of Mechanical Engineering
Iowa State University

DANIEL A. ASHLOCK
Department of Mathematics
Iowa State University

ABSTRACT

The solution of differential equations is a topic of great interest to modelers of physical phenomenon. Popular numerical solution techniques such as the finite difference method provide solutions of sufficient accuracy but at a great time cost for large-scale problems. Current advances in Virtual Reality (VR) make it possible to envision that VR could be a new and interesting environment for engineering design. But for engineering design to operate in the required interactive manner, great advances need to occur in rapidly solving the differential equations that govern material behavior. Our method uses genetic programming techniques to find analytical functions that satisfy a given system of differential equations. The method employs automatically computed analytical derivatives of the candidate solution functions for higher accuracy and faster solution convergence.

INTRODUCTION

Solving differential equations is a topic of significant interest in technical disciplines ranging from engineering to ecology. One of the applications given by Koza in his seminal genetic programming series (1992, 1994, 1999) was the solution of differential equations. Genetic programming allows the computer to try to create a program to solve a particular problem. In the application of genetic programming to differential equations, the resulting computer program is the solution function to the differential equation. Expressions that comprise the solution functions are generated from a stock of available operators, variables, and constants.

In Koza's work, candidate solutions to a given differential equation were evaluated using numerically approximated derivatives. Diver (1993) and Burgess (1999) also used numerical differentiation in evaluating candidate solutions in a genetic programming scheme. Since derivative approximations decrease in accuracy as the distance between the points is increased, numerical errors build up quickly in a code that needs to run rapidly and hence somewhat limits the utility of the solution technique.

In this paper, our previously presented work on single differential equations (2002) is extended to systems of differential equations. We have fourteen function operations available to enable the precise specification of a wide range of functions. When performing the fitness evaluation, we use analytical evaluations of the derivatives of the candidate solution functions. By addressing the challenges caused by numerical approximations of derivatives, Koza's work can be generalized to higher order equations and higher dimensional spaces. This feature enables the method to locate analytical solutions to many differential equations. These solutions provide approximate analytical solutions of the same accuracy as traditional finite difference and finite element techniques and in some cases provide the exact analytical solution. However, the analytical solution approach provides a significant advantage in rapid reanalysis of the problem when the boundary conditions, initial conditions, or material properties change.

Potential applications of these techniques include evolutionary optimization of an engineering design problem or virtual engineering design in which the design engineer can probe the solution space, change parameters, and compute the result in real time. In both cases the engineer needs to be able to vary the design parameters (e.g., boundary conditions, material properties, and physical characteristics) and compute the result rapidly. Currently, these applications are generally based on engineering approximations and response surfaces. However, the construction of response surfaces from high fidelity models is time-consuming and restricts the search space. By creating analytical solutions that can rapidly incorporate changes in material properties, boundary conditions, and physical characteristics, this technique can permit direct interaction with a high fidelity model.

METHODOLOGY

To successfully use genetic programming techniques to solve differential equations, three parts are needed. These are: 1) a means to represent candidate functions, 2) a method to evaluate the fitness of a given candidate solution function, and 3) a process to generate new candidate solution functions that ultimately satisfy the differential equation and any specified boundary or initial conditions.

We use prefix-based LISP-like expressions to represent candidate functions. Using this notation, a candidate equation could be expressed as

(sqr (+ (exp X) (cos 0.6395))). (1)

In standard algebraic notation this is

$$(e^x + cos\,(0.6395)\,)^2. \tag{2}$$

The candidate solution functions can also be diagrammed as parse trees comprising a linked set of leaf and operation nodes. Leaf nodes are the terminal nodes on a given branch of the tree and consist of real constants and independent variables. Operation nodes are the non-terminal nodes of the tree and can be subdivided into those that act on a single subtree (unary operations) or those that act on two subtrees (binary operations). The allowable operations (Table 1) all have analytically defined derivatives and most of them exist everywhere. These operations permit the analytical expression of many equations. In Table 1 the unary timesby operator (×) is mathematically redundant to normal binary multiplication (*) involving a real constant. That is, the operation (× 5.6 X1) is mathematically identical to the expression (* 5.6 X1). Our motive for incorporating the timesby operator is related to the operation of evolutionary algorithms as search algorithms. The timesby operator increases the probability of locating the correct real constant because it has just two nodes in the parse tree. Thus it more effectively allows for adjustable multiplicative scaling—a critical parameter-fitting issue in solving differential equations, particularly for nonhomogeneous and nonlinear differential equations.

Node Class	Node Contents/Purpose	Node Symbol
leaf node	ephemeral real constant	e.g., 3.14159
	independent variable	X1, X2,..., X255
	symbolic constants	C0, C1,..., C255
unary operation	negation	~
	sine function	sin
	cosine function	cos
	arctangent function	atan
	exponential function	exp
	natural log function (of $\lvert x \rvert$)	log
	square function	sqr
	timesby (scale by constant)	×
	hyperbolic sine	sinh
	hyperbolic cosine	cosh
	differentiation operator (READ-ONLY)	dXi, with i=1,2,3,...
binary operation	addition	+
	subtraction	–
	multiplication	*
	division	/

Table 1. Nodes in the differential parse tree genetic programming environment.

A system of *m* differential equations typically contains *m* unknown functions. The algorithm begins with the generation of a population of 1600 candidate solutions for each of the unknown functions. These are represented as randomly initialized parse trees, each containing six nodes, with 50% of the leaf nodes populated by ephemeral real constants and the remaining 50% of the leaf nodes populated by independent variables.

With each differential equation in a given system of differential equations algebraically manipulated into a form equal to zero, the fitness of a set of candidate solution functions in a given system of differential equations is determined by evaluating the squared deviation from zero, summed over a set of *n* evaluation points for each of the *m* differential equations. For a single variable differential equation, this sampling takes place on 100 equally spaced points in the interval of interest. A large fitness value (10^{12}) is assigned to "not a number" results that occur in the numerical evaluation of a parse tree (such as a division by zero).

Derivatives appearing in the differential equation are handled by a partial differentiation method that produces a new parse tree that represents the analytical derivative. In the evaluation of a candidate solution function, the derivative chain rule is recursively applied to the original parse tree as necessary to generate the differentiated parse tree. This analytical representation of the differential equation allows for exact evaluation of the fitness function without resorting to numerical differentiation.

Once fitness has been assessed for all sets of parse trees, creation of new sets of candidate solutions (a new generation) is performed with single tournament selection of size four. In this model of evolution, the population of solution sets is shuffled into randomly selected groups of four. The two best (lowest squared error) members of each group of four are copied over the two worst members. With 50% probability, the copies undergo subtree crossover as described by Koza (1992). If their size exceeds the maximum permissible number of nodes (20), the tree is chopped by splitting the function at the root node into two subtrees, and one subtree would be randomly retained and its size would be reevaluated. Chopping is done iteratively until the size of the resulting tree meets the preset maximum size constraint. Each of the new trees also undergoes subtree mutation with 50% probability and constant mutation with 50% probability. Subtree mutation replaces a subtree selected uniformly at random with a new random subtree of the same size. Constant mutation selects a real constant leaf or timesby (scale-by-constant) node and adds a Gaussian random variable with a mean of zero and a standard deviation of 0.2 to the constant. These mutation probabilities are implemented independently, and a given new parse tree may undergo one, both, or neither.

As the algorithm runs, mutations and crossover events can cause the representations of the generated candidate functions to become unwieldy even when they represent rather simple functions. The raw parse tree representations are retained to provide good genetic stock for future generations of candidate solutions (Banzhaf et al., 1998). But prior to numerically evaluating the functions over the evaluation points, the raw representations are reduced to simpler representations. The simplification step scans the parse tree for common patterns and recursively simplifies the parse tree structure where possible. Thus the 12-node expression,

(* 0.512337 (* (* (sqr (exp X1)) (+ -0.552804 -0.345021)) (exp X1))), (3)

can be replaced by the easier to evaluate and understand 4-node expression,

(× -0.459989 (exp (× 3 X1))). (4)

The system rapidly discovered that functions such as $f(x) = 0$ were low-error solutions for many differential equations. To exclude these functions and functions that were near–zero over most of the sample domain, an internal filter was placed in the fitness evaluation function. Additionally, user-set constraints can also be specified at run-time to preclude functions with a zero first derivative, zero second derivative, etc.

The evolutionary process is repeated until the fitness of the most fit solution set is smaller than the preset tolerance for stopping (e.g., 0.001) or when the maximum number of generations has been exceeded. The process is then repeated a number of times to increase the probability that all solution sets are found (when multiple solution sets exist).

RESULTS

Proof of concept: A single second-order differential equation expressed as a system of two first-order differential equations

Consider the single second-order nonlinear differential equation,

$$f_1''f_1 - f_1'x = 0. \tag{5}$$

A solution to this equation is $f_1 = x^2$. Alternatively, the differential equation can be expressed as a set of two first-order differential equations,

$$f_2'f_1 - f_2 x = 0, \tag{6}$$

and

$$f_2 = f_1'. \tag{7}$$

Expressed this way, the expected solutions are $f_1 = x^2$ and $f_2 = 2x$. The fact that a single second-order differential equation can be expressed as a system of two first-order differential equations provides an ideal environment to extend, test, and compare our existing solution methodology to an expanded methodology that allows for the simultaneous solution of multiple differential equations.

Solution of the single differential equation

Because inspection reveals that the trivial solution, f_1 = constant, solves the differential equation, a user-defined filter condition was specified in the parameter file to reject functions that are constant with respect to x. In fifty attempts to find the solution, fifty solution functions were found that reduced the objective function to an acceptably low value. The solutions varied in their grammatical structure; however, after the automatic cleaning operation, forty-eight of the fifty solutions were reduced to exactly,

$$\text{(sqr X1)}. \tag{8}$$

The remaining two functions differed only by the addition of a very small number or the multiplication by a factor very close to unity. Thus, within acceptable numerical tolerances, the technique found the expected analytical solution in fifty of fifty attempts. The solution was most often found in the initial population of 1600 candidate solution functions: the mean number of generations to solution was 0.06 and the maximum number of generations to solution was 1.

Solution of the system of differential equations

Inspection reveals that a trivial solution set, f_1 = constant and $f_2 = 0$, solves the system of differential equations, so two user-defined filter conditions were specified in the parameter file to reject f_1 functions that are constant with respect to x and to reject f_2 functions that are equal to zero for all x. In 50 attempts to find the solution, 46 sets of functions that reduced the objective function to an acceptably low value were found. As with the single differential equation, the raw solutions varied in their grammatical structure, but reduced to the expected solutions after the automatic cleaning operation.

The primary difference between the solution of the single differential equation and the equivalent set of differential equations involves solution time. Compared to the single differential equation solution, the system solution was quite a challenge: the mean number of generations to solution was 27.67 and the maximum number of generations to solution was 80.

A second system of differential equations

Suppose that we have the following system of differential equations,

$$f_2' - f_1' - x f_2 + x e^x - e^x = 0 \tag{9}$$

$$x f_2' - f_1 - x e^x = 0. \tag{10}$$

User-defined filter conditions were specified to reject functions that are constant with respect to x. In 50 attempts to find the solution, 23 solution functions were found that reduced the objective function to an acceptably low value. The mean number of generations to solution was 171 and the maximum number of generations to solution was 404. As is typical, the raw solutions varied in their grammatical structure. After the automatic cleaning operation, the set of acceptable solutions reduced to

f_1	f_2	**Number of occurrences**
(* X1 (cos X1))	(+ (exp X1) (sin X1))	10
(× C (* X1 (cos X1)))	(+ (exp X1) (× C (sin X1)))	6†
(× -D (* X1 (sin X1)))	(+ (exp X1) (× D (cos X1)))	7†

†The constant C assumed real values -0.218, 0.303, -0.236, 0.353, -0.480, and -1.000. The constant D assumed real values 0.371, 0.375, -0.283, -0.290, 0.257, -1.000, and -0.287.

Note that the first solution set above is just a special case of the second solution set with C = 1.0. It is listed separately because it was found so often. Its 4-node and 5-node solution function set was considerably easier to find than the second (or third) set which required one more timesby node in each equation, and furthermore, the timesby constants had to equal one another.

CONCLUSIONS

An evolutionary strategy for obtaining an analytical solution for a system of differential equations has been presented and demonstrated. In this strategy the fitness evaluation is performed using analytical derivatives of the candidate solution functions. The method does not seem hindered by nonlinearity but scalability issues are a concern; the solution of a coupled system of differential equations is considerably more involved than simultaneously solving an uncoupled set of differential equations. At present we are experimenting with larger systems of equations to enable this method to be applied to a wide range of engineering problems.

Potential applications of these techniques include evolutionary optimization of an engineering design problem or virtual engineering design in which the design engineer can probe the solution space, and the resulting effects can be computed in real time. In both cases the engineer needs to be able to vary the design parameters (e.g., boundary conditions, material properties, and physical characteristics) and compute the result rapidly. Currently, these applications are generally based on engineering approximations and response surfaces. However, the construction of response surfaces from high fidelity models is time consuming and restricts the search space. By creating analytical solutions that can rapidly incorporate changes in material properties, boundary conditions, and physical characteristics, this technique can permit direct interaction with a high fidelity model.

ACKNOWLEDGMENTS

This work was funded in part by a grant from the U. S. Department of Energy, Office of Industrial Technology and the U. S. Department of Energy, National Energy Technology Laboratory.

REFERENCES

Banzhaf, W., Nordin, P., Keller, R. E., and Francone, F. D., 1998, *Genetic Programming: An Introduction: On the Automatic Evolution of Computer Programs and Its Applications,* San Francisco: Morgan Kaufmann.

Burgess, G., 1999, "Finding Approximate Analytic Solutions to Differential Equations Using Genetic Programming," Technical Report DSTO-TR-0838, Surveillance Systems Division, Defence Science and Technology Organisation, Australia.

Diver, D. A., 1993, "Applications of Genetic Algorithms to the Solution of Ordinary Differential Equations," *Journal of Physics A: Mathematical and General,* Vol. 26, pp. 3503-3513.

Kirstukas, S. J., Bryden, K. M., and Ashlock, D. A., 2002, "Evolving Solutions of Differential Equations Utilizing Analytical Derivatives," *Intelligent Engineering Systems through Artificial Neural Networks,* Vol. 12, pp. 275-280.

Koza, J. R., 1992, *Genetic Programming,* Cambridge: The MIT Press.

Koza, J. R., 1994, *Genetic Programming II,* Cambridge: The MIT Press.

Koza, J. R., 1999, *Genetic Programming III,* San Francisco: Morgan Kaufmann.

A NEW METHOD SOLVING A LARGE SCALE OF TSP BASED ON CONNECTIONISM

MASASHI FURUKAWA
Asahikawa National College
of Technology
ASAHIKAWA, JAPAN

Yusuke Matsumura
Asahikawa National College
of Technology
ASAHIKAWA, JAPAN

MICHIKO WATANABE
Asahikawa National College
of Technology
ASAHIKAWA, JAPAN

ABSTRACT

The traveling salesman problem (TSP) is one of the most difficult problems, which appear in a various type of industrial scheduling problem. The more the number of cities increases, the more it becomes difficult to solve the problem. This paper proposes a new solving method of a large scale of the TSP based on the principle of the self-organizing map (SOM). Although SOM is known to be capable of solving TSP, it is not applicable to the practical TSP. This is because SOM refers to city coordinates and assign their synapses to the coordinates. The new method indirectly adopts the principle of SOM. It does not refer to the city coordinates but costs between two cities, and determines the order of cities. The new method is applied to a large scale of TSP to examine its efficiency by numerical experiments. Results show that the proposed method obtains fine solutions.

INTRODUCTION

The traveling salesman problem (TSP) is the problem to find out the city order for the salesman, where he must visit all cities only once with minimum tour costs. Many solving methods have been studied such as the iterative nearest path method, the branch and bound method and the soft computing methods.

The soft computing methods include the neural network-based and the evolutionary computation-based methods. Two methods, Boltzmann model method (Nakano. K. (1990)) and the self-organizing map (SOM) (Kohonen. T. (1995)), are well-known as a neural network-based method. Because the Boltzmann model needs $(n-1)!$ synapses for n neurons, which represent n cities, this method is unpractical to solve a large scale of TSP. SOM only needs $2n$ synapses for n neurons.

As typical evolutionary computation methods, there is the genetic algorithm (GA) (Grefenstette. J., Gopal. R. et. Al. (1985)) and the immune algorithm (IA) (Toma. S., Endo. K., Yamada, K. (1997)). They are recognized as a powerful tool to efficiently find out the practical approximated solutions. However, the more the number of cities increases, the more the computation time increases.

The procedural method has been proposed instead of the search methods, recently. It is so-called m-step 2opt method (MS2O) (http,TSP-JAPAN). MS2O finds out the approximated tour faster than any other search methods. However, the MS2O is affected by the initial random tour and it often remains the long path.

In this research, the dominance of SOM is discussed, based on experimental results in comparison of SOM, GA, IA, and MS2O. After that, a new method, which is capable of applying to the general TSP, is proposed by use of SOM principle, because SOM is not applied to the general TSP. Finally, numerical experiments verify that the proposed new method can deal with a large scale of TSP.

COMPARISON OF SOM, GA, IA, AND MS2O

Outlook on the methods solving TSP

Solving TSP by SOM Let $J=\{j;\, j=1,2,\ldots,r\}$ be a set of neuron and $I=\{i;\, i=1,2,\ldots,n\}$ be a set of input signals. SOM's algorithm is based on the learning process expressed under below.

$$\mathbf{w}_j(t+1)=\mathbf{w}_j(t)+h_c(t)(\mathbf{x}_i(t)-\mathbf{w}_j(t)) \tag{1}$$

and

$$c=\underset{j}{\operatorname{argmin}}\{|\mathbf{x}_i-\mathbf{w}_j|\} \tag{2}$$

where $\mathbf{w}_j$ is a synopsis vector, $\mathbf{x}_i$ is an input vector, $i \in N_c$, N_c is a sub-set of neighborhood neurons of c, $N_c \in J$, and $h_c(t)(<1)$ is a learning parameter.
The SOM algorithm solving TSP is referred to (Kohonen , 1995).

Genetic Algorithms solving TSP GA proposed by J. Grefensette (Grefenstette, J., Gopal, R., B. Rosmatia, and Gucht, D.V., 1985) and its two variations are examined. This algorithm is so-named simple GA (SGA). GA, to which the inversion operation is added, is named IGA in this issue. It is possible to normalize fitness functions from 0 to 1 by $1/N$. This GA is named NGA.

Immune Algorithm solving TSP This algorithm resembles GA, but memory and suppression mechanisms are added to GA. The suppression mechanism excludes the solutions appeared in the GA similar to ones stored in the memories (Toma. S., Endo. K., Yamada, K. (1997)).

m-step 2opt Method Let $P=\{P_t : t=1,2,\ldots,n\}$, $\overline{P_tP_{t+1}}$ and $\phi(P_t,P_{t+1})$ be a set of city locations, a path from the city t to the followed city $t+1$ and its path cost, respectively. This algorithm is described as follows.

(1) A random round tour is generated. A set of city locations is set to $P=\{P_t : t=1,2,\ldots,n\}$. $t=0$

(2) Replace t with $t+1$. Obtain $\phi(P_t,P_{t+1})$, $\phi(P_{t+2+m},P_{t+3+m})$, $\phi(P_t,P_{t+2+m})$, and $\phi(P_{t+1},P_{t+3+m})$ for $\overline{P_tP_{t+1}}$, $\overline{P_{t+2+m}P_{t+3+m}}$, $\overline{P_tP_{t+2+m}}$, and $\overline{P_{t+1}P_{t+3+m}}$, respectively.

(3) Calculate C_{prev} and C_{next} as follows.

$C_{prev}=\phi(P_t,P_{t+1})+\phi(P_{t+2+m},P_{t+3+m})$ and $C_{next}=\phi(P_t,P_{t+2+m})+\phi(P_{t+1},P_{t+3+m})$.

(4) If $C_{prev}>C_{next}$, replace the paths $\overline{P_tP_{t+1}}$ and $\overline{P_{t+2+m}P_{t+3+m}}$ with the paths $\overline{P_tP_{t+2+m}}$ and $\overline{P_{t+1}P_{t+3+m}}$, respectively, reverse the sub-tour paths as $\overline{P_{t+1+m}P_{t+m}}$, $\overline{P_{t+m}P_{t-1+m}}$, ..., $\overline{P_{t+3}P_{t+2}}$. Go back to (2).

Comparison of GAs, IA, SOM and MS2O

SGA, IGA, NGA, IA, SOM and MS2O are compared by numerical experiments. The 150 cities problem referred to TSPLIB (http, TSPLIB) is used as a test function. Each method is computed for measuring its accuracy ten times. The accuracy is defined by the ratio of the obtained round tour cost to the optimal tour cost. As seen in Fig. 1, it becomes obvious that SOM reaches the approximated solution with the highest accuracy.

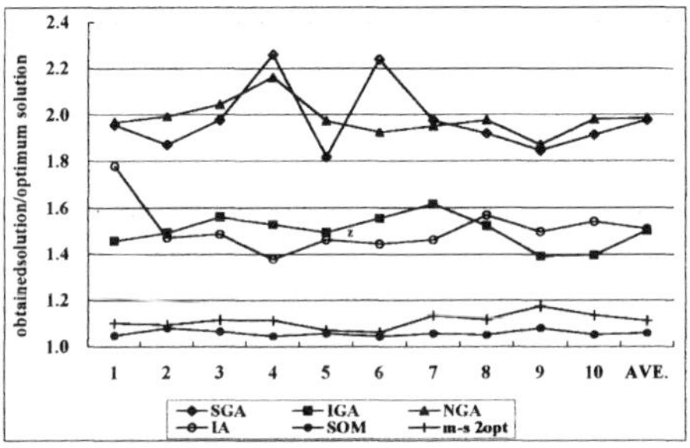

Fig. 1 Comparison of six algorithms

A NEW METHOD SOLVING TSP BASED ON THE SOM PRINCIPLE

Applying a SOM Principle to TSP

When TSP appears in an engineering field, SOM is not able to apply the practical TSP directly, because the cost between two cities is defined by criteria.

A learning principle of SOM is that neurons with similar synapses are gathered together in a local area. As a result of self-organizing, the neurons with the similar synapses are clustered into groups. Therefore, a new method proposes the local clustering method in a local area neurons randomly selected.

Let $\phi(\mathbf{w}_i, \mathbf{w}_j)$ be a cost between two neurons i and j corresponding two cities. A clustering method approximately realizes the following relations in the local area neurons after self-organizing.

$$|\mathbf{w}_i - \mathbf{w}_j| < |\mathbf{w}_i - \mathbf{w}_k| \Leftrightarrow \phi(\mathbf{w}_i, \mathbf{w}_j) < \phi(\mathbf{w}_i, \mathbf{w}_k) \quad (3)$$

The relation (3) shows that clustering neurons can be realized by sorting the neurons (cities) based on the cost $\phi(\mathbf{w}_i, \mathbf{w}_j)$ $(i, j = 1, 2, ..., n)$. Thus, the new algorithm based on the SOM principle is composed as follows.

(1) A round tour for a set of city $P = \{P_i;\ i = 1, 2, ..., n\}$ is generated at random. Set $t = 0$.

(2) Replace t with $t+1$. Select the city P_c at random and determine a set of neighborhood cities N_c, where

$$N_c = \{P_{c-d(t)/2}, P_{c-d(t)/2+1}, ..., P_{c-1}, P_c, P_{c+1}, ..., P_{c+d(t)/2-1}, P_{c+d(t)/2}\}.$$

(3) Exchange the city order in the round tour so as to satisfy $\phi(P_c, P_j) < \phi(P_c, P_k)$ where $P_j, P_k \in N_c$.

(4) If $t = T$, terminate the procedure. Otherwise, go back to the step (2).

Instead of using synapses to express the cost $\phi(\mathbf{w}_i, \mathbf{w}_j)$, a set of city $P = \{P_i;\ i = 1, 2, ..., n\}$ is used to express the cost $\phi(P_i, P_j)$ in the above algorithm.

Sorting Methods

The sorting methods are not materialized in the previous section. In this section, three sorting methods are proposed. It is assumed that a sub-tour in N_c is connected in the order

$$N_c = [P_{c-d(t)/2}, P_{c-(d(t)/2-1)}, \ldots, P_c, P_{c+1}, P_{c+2}, \ldots, P_{c+(d(t)/2-1)}, P_{c+d(t)/2}]$$

Simple Exchange Method (SEM)

(1) Set $node = 0$, and $term = d(t) - 1$.
(2) Set $\delta = 0$ and $k = node$.
(3) Replace k with $k+1$.
(4) Replace δ with $\delta + 1$.
(5) If $mod(\delta, 2) = 1$, set $i = k$. Otherwise set $i = -k$.
(6) Calculate C_{prev} and C_{next} as follows.

$$C_{prev} = \phi(P_{c-1}, P_c) + \phi(P_c, P_{c+1}) + \sum_{j=0}^{i-3} \phi(P_{c+j+1}, P_{c+j+2})$$
$$+\phi(P_{c+i-1}, P_{c+i}) + \phi(P_{c+i}, P_{c+i+1})$$
$$C_{next} = \phi(P_{c-1}, P_{c+i}) + \phi(P_{c+i}, P_{c+1}) + \sum_{j=0}^{i-3} \phi(P_{c+j+1}, P_{c+j+2})$$
$$+\phi(P_{c+i-1}, P_c) + \phi(P_c, P_{c+i+1})$$

(7) If $C_{prev} > C_{next}$, exchange P_c with P_{c+i} in the sub-tour of N_c.
(8) If $\delta = term$, terminate the procedure.
(9) If $mod(k, 2) = 0$, go back to the step (3). Otherwise go back to the step (2).

In the above procedure, $mod(.,2)$ is a mode function with the base number 2 and $d(t)$ is a number of cities in N_c

Inverse Exchange Method (IEM) In SEM, exchange the step (1), (6), and (8) to (1)', (6)' and (8)' described below.

(1)' Set $node = 1$, and $term = d(t)$.
(6)' Calculate C_{prev} and C_{next} as follows.

$$C_{prev} = \phi(P_c, P_{c+1}) + \sum_{j=0}^{i-2} \phi(P_{c+j+1}, P_{c+j+2}) + \phi(P_{c+i}, P_{c+i+1})$$
$$C_{next} = \phi(P_c, P_{c+i}) + \sum_{j=0}^{i-2} \phi(P_{c+i-j}, P_{c+i-j-1}) + \phi(P_{c+1}, P_{c+i+1})$$

(8)' If $\delta = term$, terminate the procedure.

Smoothing Method (SM)

(1) Set $i = 0$ and $j = 2$.
(2) Calculate C_{prev} and C_{next} as follows.

$$C_{prev} = \phi(P_{c-d(t)/2+i}, P_{c-d(t)/2+i+1}) + \sum_{k=1}^{j-1} \phi(P_{c-d(t)/2+i+k}, P_{c-d(t)/2+k+1})$$
$$+\phi(P_{c-d(t)/2+i+j}, P_{c-d(t)/2+i+j+1})$$
$$C_{next} = \phi(P_{c-d(t)/2+i}, P_{c-d(t)/2+i+j}) + \sum_{k=1}^{j-1} \phi(P_{c-d(t)/2+i+(k-1)}, P_{c-d(t)/2+k-1})$$
$$+\phi(P_{c-d(t)/2+i+1}, P_{c-d(t)/2+i+j})$$

(3) If $C_{prev} > C_{next}$, exchange $P_{c-d(t)/2+i+1}$ with $P_{c-d(t)/2+i+j}$ in the sub-tour of N_c, then reverse the order of the cities from $P_{c-d(t)/2+i+1}$ to $P_{c-d(t)/2+i+j-1}$.
(4) If $j = d(t) - i - 2$, go to the step (5). Otherwise, replace j with $j+1$ and go back to the step (2).

(5) If $i = d(t) - i - 2$, terminate the procedure. Otherwise, replace i with $i+1$, set $j = 2$, and go back to the step (2).

4.NUMERICAL EXPERIMENTS

Numeric experiments

Numerical experiments are executed using test functions. As a sorting method, SEM, IEM and SM are probabilistically selected and their probabilistic ratio is 1:1:2.

150 cities problem in TSPLIB Figure 2 shows one of the round tour results obtained by the proposed method, applied to the 150 cities in TSPLIB. Fig. 3 shows the obtained accuracies for three methods, and their averaged accuracies for ten times. Table 1 shows Their averaged computation time (Pentium4 (2.26Ghz)) for ten times. As a result, it becomes clear that the accuracy and computation speed of the proposed method compares to SOM, and that the proposed method reaches an excellent solution.

4900 square lattices arrangement problem TSP, in which 4900 cities are arranged on the lattice points of a square, is tested by the proposed method. Fig. 4 shows the initial obtained solutions.

Problem usa13509 in TSPLIB TSP, which is referred in TSPLIB known as usa13509, is tested by the proposed method. This problem includes 13509 cities. A result is shown in Fig. 5, in which a fine solution is obtained by the proposed method. Table 2 shows an averaged accuracy of solutions and an averaged ratio of solutions to the optimal solutions, when numerical experiments are executed ten times. As a result, these experiments verify that the proposed method is capable of solving a large scale of TSP with the high speed.

Problem pla33810 in TSPLIB TSP, which is referred in TSPLIB known as pla33810, is tested by the proposed method. This problem includes 33810 cities. A result is shown in Fig. 6. Table 2 shows an averaged accuracy of solutions and an averaged ratio of solutions to the optimal solutions as well as usa13509, when numerical experiments are executed ten times. It is impossible to find out the method solving this problem so far by PC.

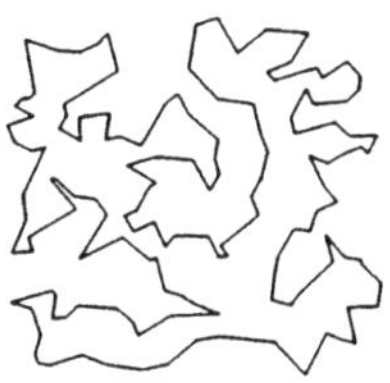

Fig. 2 An obtained solution by the proposed method for 150 cities problem (TSPLIB[8] 150cities)

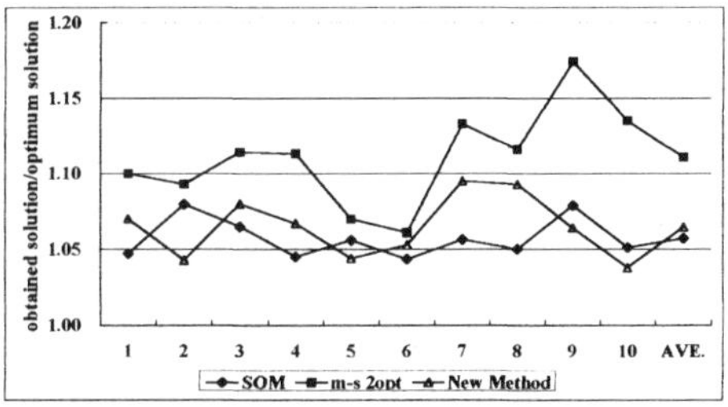

Fig. 3 Comparison of three algorithms

Table 1 Comparison of seven algorithms

Methods	SGA	IGA	NGA	IA	SOM	m-s 2opt	A New Method
Time(sec)	145.2	148.6	141.9	618.8	1.72	4.38	0.079
Ratio	1.977	1.501	1.985	1.509	1.057	1.111	1.065

(a) An initial solution

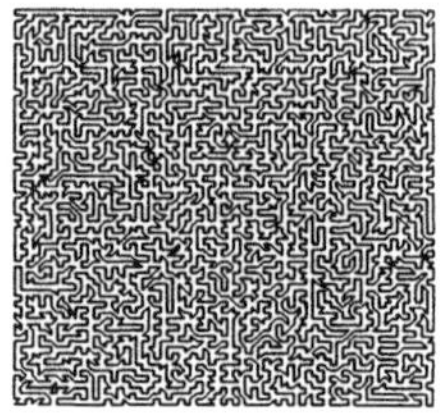

(b) An obtained solution

Fig. 4 Solutions obtained by the proposed method applied to the 500 cities problem, where cities are located on the points of lattices in a square

Table 2 Computation time and accuracy

Problems	usa13509	pla33810
Time(min)	3.716	24.17
Ratio	1.124	1.127

Fig. 5 An obtained solution by the proposed method applied to the usa13509 problem

Fig. 6 An obtained solution by the proposed method applied to the pla33810 problem

CONCLUDING REMARLS

The newly proposed method is applied to some test problems, including in TSPLIB, so as to examine its performance. Numerical experiments prove that the proposed method solves TSP with the high accuracy and speed.

REFERENCES

Nakano, K. et. al., Nurocomputing (in Japanese), Corona publishing company, 1990, pp.148-161

Kohonen , T., Self-Organizing Maps, Spring-Verlag, Berlin, 1995

Grefenstette, J., Gopal, R., B. Rosmatia, and Gucht, D.V., Genetic Algorithms for the Traveling Salesman Problem, Proc. of International Conference of Genetic Algorithms and Their Applications, Lawrence Erlbaum, Hillsdale, NJ, 1985, pp. 160-168.

Toma, S., Endo K, Yamada, K., Application of immunity algorithm to *n*TSP, Proc. of 55th Annual conference on Japan of Society Information Processing, Vol. 2, 1997, pp. 453-454

Youssef, H., Interactive Computer Algorithm with Application in Engineering, IEEE Computer Society, 1999,

TSP-JPN, http://pagetest.hp.infoseek.co.jp/m-s2-opt/m-s2-opt-frame.html/

TSPLIB, http://www.iwr.uni-heidelberg.de /groups /comopt /software /TSPLIB95/

PRESENTING A LARGE AUDIENCE INTERACTIVE MULTIMEDIA PERFORMANCE DRIVEN BY A CIRCULAR LINDENMAYER SYSTEM

AARON N. BRYDEN
Department of Computer Engineering
Iowa State University

KRIS A. BRYDEN
Department of Music
Iowa State University

DANIEL A. ASHLOCK
Department of Mathematics
Iowa State University

ABSTRACT

This paper presents a system for allowing a large audience to control an interactive multimedia performance that includes musical output. Each member of the audience uses a sign with 2 sides, each side representing an opposing direction the content of the piece could move toward. These inputs, which are seen and counted using a primitive computer vision system, are fed into a system that determines how the music should be generated. The music is generated using a variant of Lindenmayer systems called a circular Lindenmayer system (CL-system) in which the rule set can be changed as the output string is read. Additionally, the rule set and interpretation of the Lindenmayer system used is optimized for aesthetic value and coherency with a genetic algorithm. The audience input is used to determine which percentage of the string replacements the competing rules should be based on. This enables the audience to interactively drive the performance based on evolution of the Lindenmayer system.

BACKGROUND

L-systems (Lindenmayer systems) have been used to create geometrical objects such as fractals and models of realistic looking plants or other biological organisms or systems and to generate music (Prusinkiewiecz 1989). L-systems rewrite character strings in parallel to produce a longer, more complex string that in some way resembles the initial string. A set of rules renders the initial string—the axiom—into a longer, more complex string.

An L-System interpreter then renders the resulting string into an object. L-systems that render simple models of plants and geometrical objects such as fractals use graphical *turtles* as the interpreter. The turtle responds to commands represented by symbols to go in a specified direction (turn angle) and distance. The turtle can be commanded to go forward with or without drawing. For example, the symbol **F** could mean go forward one incremental unit, a + could mean go to the left 90°, and the symbol – could mean go to the right 90°. Given these interpretations, the string **FF+F-FF** would result in the path shown in Figure 1 with a turtle starting in the down direction. In this simple graph the turtle goes forward two units, then turns to the left and goes one unit. Finally it turns to the right and goes forward three units.

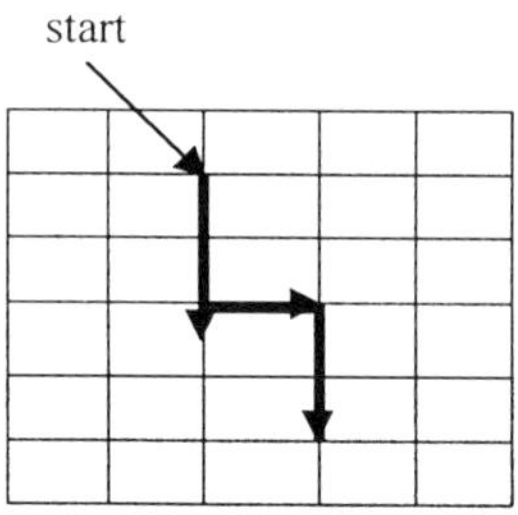

Figure 1: A simple turtle graph based on the string **FF+F-FFF**.

This application is unique in that it uses a variant of Lindenmayer systems, a CL-system (circular L-system), to enable the system to create musical output from a stream of real-time data input. This CL-system will incorporate an evolutionary algorithm that optimizes its rule set to produce music that is aesthetically pleasing to listen to. For the demonstration of the system described in this paper, a large audience provides the input data by holding up signs, choosing to show either the front or the back. Each side represents competing music composition rules. A computer vision system calculates percentages of each side, which are used for the data input to the CL-system, thus enabling the audience to interactively drive the multimedia performance.

CL-SYSTEMS

CL-systems are particularly useful for dealing with a real-time stream of data input because the user does not have to wait for a long process of iterations to finish. Unlike L-systems in which the user must specify the number of iterations before proceeding and then wait for completion before obtaining the results, a CL-system enables the user to obtain the rendered object as the data is being processed. Similar to traditional L-systems, a CL-system consists of an axiom and rules for rewriting the string. However, a CL-system also includes a deletion process, which is the core difference of a CL-system from a traditional L-system. In a traditional L-system the number of iterations is unlimited because it continuously replaces the current symbol according to the rewriting rules, causing the resulting L-string to grow infinitely. Using the deletion rule, the application will delete the sub string that has already been processed and interpreted, thus resulting in an L-string that grows only as long as is necessary to interpret the real-time input of data. As each of these sub strings are deleted, the newly generated string is added to the end of the stack. The implementation of a CL-system can be divided into the following steps:

Initialization

Initialize the axiom and the rewriting rules, which consist of an arbitrary string of alphabetic characters, as in a traditional L-system. The length of the L-string before deletion takes place depends on the application. The process of deletion will be explained in more detail in the "Deletion" section below.

Generation

The generation of a new L-string in a CL-system is the same as in a traditional L-system. However, instead of replacing the L-string, in a CL-system the newly generated string is simply added to the end. This may seem to diverge from the rewriting principle of L-systems, but because old sub strings are deleted continuously, the generation of new L-strings will still have the same characteristics as in the traditional L-System.

Deletion

The key component to the CL-system is to synchronize the generation and deletion process within the application according to the interpretation process. The deletion should achieve the goal of continuously producing L-strings according to the real-time input data. As the L-string is being interpreted into output, the CL-system will shorten the L-string while the generation continues. Two methods have been tried thus far. One method is to delete the already interpreted L-string after a fixed amount of time. In another method first choose a fixed length of string based on the application's interpretation method for producing the L-string. When the string reaches that fixed length, the part of the L-string that has already been interpreted will then be deleted. After deleting this part of the L-string, there are enough symbols in the remaining L-string for future production.

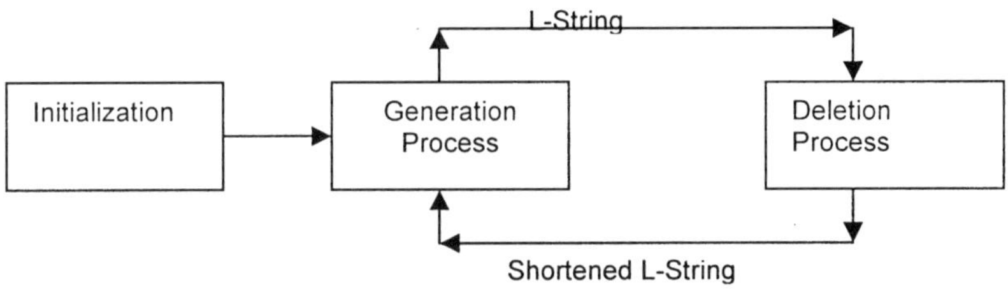

Figure 2. CL-system process flow diagram.

AUDITORIUM SYSTEM FOR GATHERING THE DATA

The system for interacting with the audience is designed with cost effectiveness and transportability in mind while allowing the system to interact with potentially large audiences. With these factors in mind, an image recognition system was chosen as the method for interacting with the audience. The primary reason for this is the ability to scale the system to virtually any size audience efficiently by simply moving the camera farther away from the audience and buying more cameras. Other methods, such as providing each member of the audience with a wireless keypad, are exponentially more expensive after a certain audience size is reached due to technological constraints of the systems available. Using image recognition guarantees that in the worst case one simply has to buy more computers and more cameras to keep up with audience size. This system was created inexpensively using a low cost PC of around $400 and available digital cameras that are used for recording instruction in a classroom. Additionally, this system can use a low cost camera such as a USB web cam or a digital camera capable of taking pictures at the command of the computer it is connected to. The input from the audience consists of one dual sided colored sign per audience member. A picture of an audience holding these signs can be found in Figure 3.

Figure 3

An audience member interacts with the system by holding up the sign and choosing whether to display the red side or the green side.

SYSTEM ARCHITECTURE

The system is built using the Microsoft .NET platform to build the system because this platform has the ability to rapidly develop an interactive GUI application without a lot of work as well as the existence of readily available libraries that work with this platform for both producing MIDI music and for grabbing images from a variety of camera types with the same interface. The libraries used consist of the MidiShare library and the OpenCV library. The languages used for this application are managed C++/C# and native C++. Managed C++/C# is used for the GUI part of the system and native C++ for the rest. The system has three threads running at once. The purpose of the primary thread is to run the interactive GUI and to periodically run the L-system code. The purposes of the two other threads are to manage the timing of MIDI events and to retrieve and process the image data.

PROCESSING THE IMAGE DATA

The algorithm for processing the image data relies primarily on counting the number of pixels of each sign color and applying appropriate weights based on where they are in the image. The colors bright pink and bright fluorescent green were chosen for the signs that would stand out in most digital cameras and would not be commonly used in people's clothing or other objects. The system requires two kinds of calibration: one to determine how to best compensate for the camera parameters and the shape of the room, and the other to determine what colors are in the range of colors on the signs in the given lighting conditions as well as the amount of noise present. The system calibrates the camera parameters by determining how much smaller or larger than a given object size a sign would be if it was placed at that location in the image. To achieve this, the system allows the user to interactively draw triangles onto the user interface on top of the triangles held by the audience shown in a preview of the camera output. To calibrate color the user obtains background level (without any color) and 100% saturation to determine minimum and maximum thresholds.

USING THE SYSTEM TO CREATE MUSICAL OUTPUT

After receiving input from the audience, the CL-system creates musical output. First an initial string and an initial state are put into the system. This initial string is the basis for replacement in the L-system. The initial state is a musical motive. As the system takes in data at periodic intervals (every three seconds in the test case), several events occur. When the data comes in from the image recognition system, it picks a specific set of replacement rules for the CL-system from a pool of rules specified by the user or created using an evolutionary algorithm. This interpreter then drives the music. After this sub string has been processed and interpreted, it is deleted.

INTERPRETER FOR THE MUSICAL OUTPUT

To produce the music component of the system, a musical motive is specified as the initial state of the system. The interpreter looks at the output string of the CL-system to decide if various musical parameters should increase, decrease, or stay the same. These musical parameters use MIDI values and are rendered using the open source MidiShare software on a Windows platform.

MIDI (Musical Instrument Digital Interface) is a protocol language that sends and receives information to and from a set of instruments on how sounds should be produced. The language consists of a series of binary bytes, beginning with a status byte that specifies Note-on. This is followed by a series of data bytes, each of which include directions to produce a specified result within one musical parameter such as pitch, instrument sound, dynamics (called "velocity" in MIDI protocol), reverb (giving a sense of the performance space), pitch bend, and duration. A MIDI instrument such as a keyboard or onboard sound card renders the results into sound.

The musical parameters incorporated into the system include the following:

- Transposition of individual pitches
- Velocity, specifying the loudness or softness of the music
- Attack rhythm; that is, the space between individual notes
- Duration of individual notes
- Tempo, that is, how many beats are occurring in a given amount of time. In music this is usually denoted as the number of times the duration of the beat occurs in one minute. For example, if a quarter note is the beat, and the composer wanted 120 quarter notes in a minute, the tempo would be written as quarter note =120.

RESULTS

Thus far, we have developed a system that uses data from a live audience in real-time to pick the interpreter. The audience interaction system is generally accurate within 5% of the values specified by the audience. The reason for this level of performance rather than being 100% accurate is because of audience members holding their signs at varying heights and the noise inherent in the electronics. In the test set up a random generator generates numbers every three seconds, using a MIDI-share timer. The rules it picks come from a set specifying musical duration, whether pitches should move up or down by a certain number of half steps, tempo, attack rhythm, (space between attack points), and velocity.

FUTURE WORK

At the current time to produce music that is aesthetically pleasing, we plan to use a genetic algorithm to produce the set of CL-system replacement rules and the initial string for the CL-system. In order to achieve this, the following principles to guide the choice of replacement rules will be used (Bryden et al, 2002):

- Varying degrees of intensity to give the music a sense of motion
- Using multiple quantifiable parameters outlined above to create variety to hold the listener's interest and concentration and to increase options for producing varying degrees of intensity
- Producing recognizable musical events. This approach transforms and moves around in time pre-composed motives to provide the music with a sense of coherency. Transforming the motive could include transposing the motive up or down a specific number of half steps, playing it in reverse order, or inverting it. For example, Figure 4a and b illustrate the process of inversion. To invert the input motive in Figure 4a, each successive melodic interval of the inverted motive moves in the opposite direction as its coresponding interval in the input motive. Thus, the ascending opening perfect fifth from C to G in Figure 4a becomes a descending perfect fifth from C to F in 4b and so on.

Figure 4a. Input motive.

Figure 4b. Inversion of the input motive.

To ensure that the audience has meaningful control over the direction of the music, two possible sets of replacement rules will be evolved, one that results in music that is consonant, mellifluous, and pleasant sounding and one that results in more ominous, dissonant and complex sounding music. For the first replacement rule set, the system will evolve rules that result in a sense of lower degrees of intensity. These rules will control quantifiable musical parameters to create diatonic (within a specified scale) sonorities, smooth melodic lines, predictable rhythmic patterns, moderate to slow tempos, and mellow timbres. For the second replacement rule set, the system will evolve rules that result in a sense of higher degrees of intensity, controlling quantifiable musical parameters that will create dissonant, nondiatonic chromatic sonorities, unpredictable rhythmic patterns, quick tempos, and rough timbres.

Additionally, there are several ways to extend the capabilities of the system. One way could be to implement a system that would allow the audience to grade the system on whether or not the audience is enjoying the performance and then adapt it to what the audience likes. Another possible extension would be to add a visual component to the interactive performance. This could be accomplished by either using the music to drive interactive visuals or by generating interactive visuals using CL-systems in the same way as the musical system.

REFERENCES

Ashlock, D. A., and Bryden, K. M., 2004, "Evolutionary Control of L-system Interpretation," 2004 IEEE Congress on Evolutionary Computation, Portland, Oregon.

Bryden, K. A., Meinert, K., Ashlock, D. A., and Bryden, K. M., 2002, "Transforming Data into Music Using Fractal Algorithms," *Intelligent Engineering Systems Through Artificial Neural Networks,* Vol. 12, pp. 665-670.

Prusinkiewicz, P., Hanan, J., 1989, *Lindenmayer Systems, Fractals, and Plants,* Vol. 79 of *Lecture Notes in Biomathematics,* New York: Springer-Verlag.

CONFORMATION ANALYSIS USING EVOLUTIONARY APPROACH

ALEKSANDER WAWER
Polish-Japanese Institute of
Information Technology
Koszykowa 86, 02-008 Warsaw,
Poland

FRANCISZEK SEREDYNSKI
University of Podlasie
Computer Science Department
Sienkiewicza 51, 08-110 Siedlce,
Poland
and
Polish-Japanese Institute of
Information Technology
Koszykowa 86, 02-008 Warsaw,
Poland

PASCAL BOUVRY
Faculty of Sciences, Technology
and Communication,
University of Luxembourg,
Luxembourg

ABSTRACT
In this article, a new evolutionary algorithm is designed, implemented and evaluated for the field of conformational analysis, field of pharmacy related to discovery and design of new drugs. The goal is to find the best possible spatial configuration of a molecule, which corresponds to finding its energy minimum by rotation of torsion angles. After fine tuning the algorithm for simple molecules, the approach is evaluated for the more complex case of Vitamine E.

1. INTRODUCTION

The competition on elaborating new and better drugs is very intense. Spatial configuration has a fundamental influence on biological and chemical properties of any molecule and therefore is of a great importance in the search of the most effective drugs. The scope of this paper is to describe and evaluate the use of evolutionary algorithms as a tool for conformational analysis. Conformational analysis studies the influence of spatial arrangement (conformation) on molecular energy. The paper is organized as follows: The coming section describes the problem, next, the third section provides a description of the design of implemented evolutionary mechanisms and the fine-tuning of the algorithm parameters. Section 4 presents the results of experiments, conducted with the previously established parameters on a complex molecule of vitamine E. The last section contains conclusions.

2. CONFORMATIONAL ANALYSIS

Each different spatial arrangement of a molecule, known as a conformation, is defined by the arrangement of its atoms in space, which can be interconverted by rotation about single bonds. Conformational analysis is a search through conformational space for optimal configurations in terms of global energy.

Differentiation of spatial structure is possible by means of changing lengths of bonds between atoms, values of valence angles or torsion angles. As valence angles and lengths of bonds require relatively high energy in order to change, it is different torsion angles that make conformations differ.

A torsion angle is a spatial angle between two planes, the first being defined through atoms 1,2,3 and the second through atoms 2,3,4, of the four-atoms sequence 1,2,3,4. Computation of molecular energy for a set of torsion angle values is called single-point, as it refers to a given point on energy hypersurface. Detailed description of the theory behind energy calculations is beyond the scope of this article and may be found in adequate literature [3]. Conformational analysis belongs to NP-hard problems. Indeed, finding an optimal configuration depends exponentially on the number of torsion angles (see,Fig 1 for a case of 2 torsion angles). In the case of many biological molecules there exists numerous local energy minima.
The literature reveals various approaches to the problem of conformational analysis including, e.g., Monte Carlo methods [5], random and tree-based search algorithms [3].

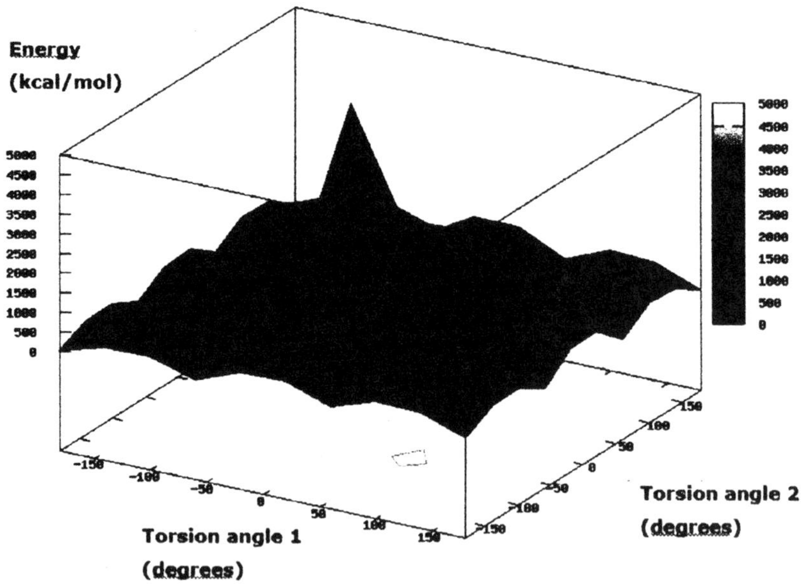

1. Energy surface defined by 2 torsion angles

3. GENETIC ALGORITHMS FOR CONFORMATIONAL ANALYSIS

The use of genetic algorithms [2] for conformational analysis has been described in [1]. Authors used binary coding of torsion angles, molecule described by Cartesian coordinates and exponential modification of fitness function.

3.1. Designing Evolutionary Searching Process

3.1.1. Individual

We decided to define individuals the same way than Brodmeier and Pretsch [1], i.e. an individual is composed of a set of values of torsion angles. The approach presented in this paper is based on a real value (i.e. $\in$ □) encoding for the chromosome representation.

3.1.2. Fitness Function

Molecular energy, obtained from single-bond computations, served as the basis of the fitness function. While Brodmeier and Pretsch used an exponential version of fitness function, we decided to implement an approach described by Michalewicz [4].

$$fi(x_i^t) = 1.05max^t - E(x_i^t)$$

where x_i^t is an ith individual from population t, $E(x_i^t)$ its energy, max^t is the highest energy among individuals from population t. Increasing the maximum energy by 5% protects from assigning zero values to the weakest individuals.

3.1.3. Genetic Operators

The classical operators *selection*, *cross-over* and *mutation* were applied to the population of individuals.

The accuracy of the following three variants of the *selection* operator was evaluated: proportional, tournament and ranking selection. In case of proportional selection, the probability of selecting an individual x to the next generation pr(x) is equal to $pr(x) = \dfrac{fi(x)}{F}$ where F stands for a sum of fit values for the whole generation and fi(x) for the fitness of individual x. Tournament selection is based on the idea of selecting for next generation, the best individuals from sub-sets of individuals. The most important parameter here is the size of such a set (tournament size). Ranking selection allows for selecting individuals using a set of weights, which are adjusted to individuals according to their order of fitness value. Probability of selection is equal to

$pr(x) = \frac{r(x)^k}{S_r}$ where r(x) is a rank of an individual, k is a parameter and S_r is a sum of rank values for the whole generation.

We similarly evaluated three mechanisms of cross-over.

In uniform cross-over, for every i^{th} torsion angle of the child, its value is copied from i^{th} angle from a fixed set of parents with equal probability. In averaging cross-over, value of each torsion angle in the child is equal to $Y_i = X_i^1 + E_{0,1}(X_i^2 - X_i^1)$ where X_i^1 and X_i^2 are values of ith angle of two parents, and $E_{0,1}$ is a random value. In case of one-point cross-over, every child is a combination of chromosomes of exactly two parents. Each part of the child's chromosome comes from a different parent; lengths of both parts are selected in a random way.

Finally three different mechanisms of mutation were evaluated: uniform, non-uniform and normal distribution based. Uniform mutation is the simplest: mutated angle is changed to any possible value with equal probability. Non-uniform mutation presents a more complex behavior. The range of possible values of a mutated angle is shrinking (in a linear way) with every generation. At the end, the algorithm only scans neighborhoods of the best individuals.

3.2. Fine-tuning of the evolutionary algorithm

In order to fine-tune the algorithm parameters, we conducted series of five experiments with every major combination of parameters. During each experiment, all remaining parameters were constant to measure the influence of the examined parameter. In order to perform a fast evaluation of the various parameters we used a simple molecule with four torsion angles, a derivative of butyl. The exact name of this molecule is 2-[4-[4-2-phirymidynyl-1-piperaynyl]butyl]-4-phenyl-hexahydro-1H,3H-pirydo[1,2c]pirymidyno-1,3-dion.

The aim of conducted experiments was to fine-tune the parameters of the GA. Results show that the best values of examined parameters are tournament selection, the size of tournament 4, one-point cross-over, probability of cross-over equal 0.3, mutation based on a normal distribution (gauss) or non-uniform mutation, and probability of mutation 0.05. We used a population size of 30 individuals.

4. EXPERIMENTAL RESULTS

In this section, we would like to present the results of an experiment, conducted with previously established, optimal values of algorithm parameters. The analyzed molecule has 17 torsion angles and is known as vitamine E.

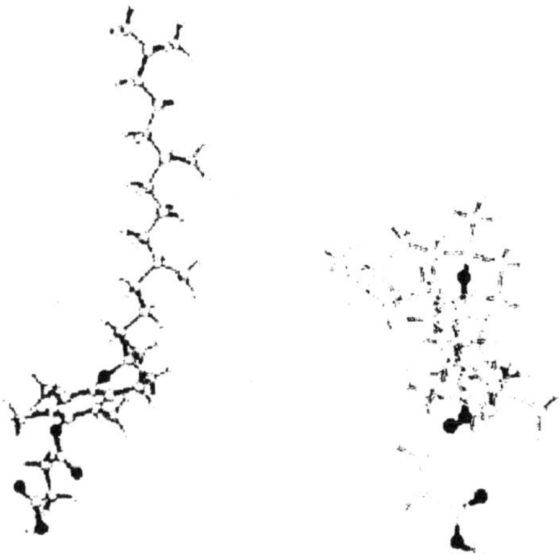

2. Left: 1st generation, energy = 17.5920 kcal/mol ; Right: 10th generation, energy = -5.4945 kcal/mol

The molecule used as an input (cf Figure 2 left) for computations has an energy as high as 17 kcal/mol and an expanded chain of molecules, called its *tail*.
The best individual in 10th generation (cf Figure 2 right) has the *tail* mostly convoluted.
In 50th generation (cf Figure 3), the molecule looks spherical, its energy reached a minimum of -7.4 kcal/mol (cf Figure 4). The overall results can therefore be described as satisfying and promising.

3. 50th generation, energy = -7.4026 kcal/mol

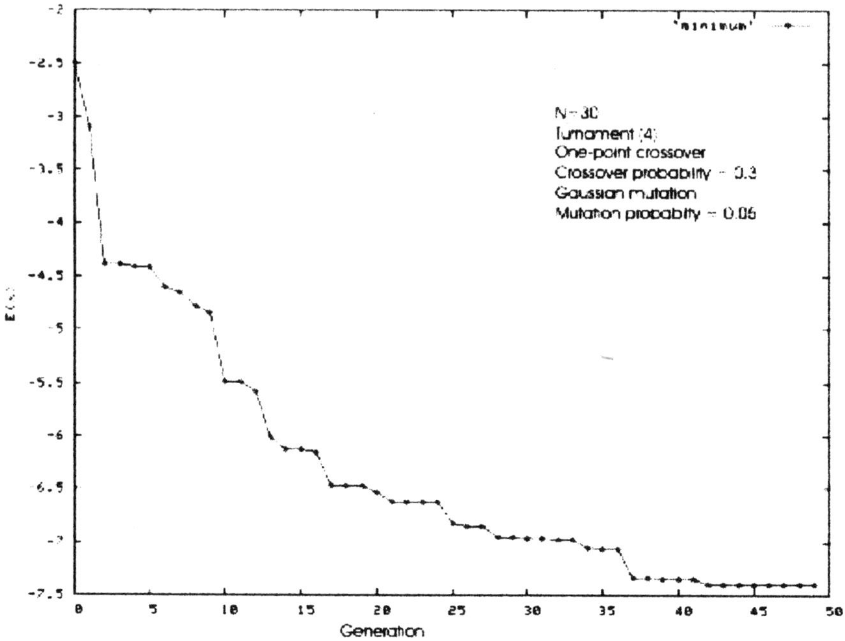

4. Results for the Vitamine E

5. CONCLUSIONS

We introduced an original way of applying evolutionary computing to conformational analysis. A study on fine-tuning the algorithm parameters has been provided. Finally the first experimental results on Vitamine E molecule have illustrated the performances of our algorithm.

BIBLIOGRAPHY

[1] Brodmeier D., Pretsch E., *Application of Genetic Algorhitms in Molecular Modeling*, Journal of Computational Chemistry, Vol. 15, No. 6, 1994

[2] Goldberg D. E., *Genetic Algorithms in Search, Optimization and Machine Learning*, Reading, Mass 1989

[3] Leach A., *Molecular Modelling: Principles and Applications*, Harlow & London, 2001

[4] Michalewicz Z., *Genetic Algorithms + data structures = evolutionary programs*, SpringerVerlag, 1996

[5] Guida W., Bohacek R., Erion M., *Probing the Conformational Space Available to Inhibitors in the Thermolysin Active Site Using Monte Carlo/Energy Minimization Techniques*, Journal of Computational Chemistry, Vol. 13, No. 2, 1992

ACCELERATION OF A PROCEDURE TO GENERATE FRACTAL CURVES OF A GIVEN DIMENSION THROUGH THE PROBABILISTIC CHARACTERIZATION OF EXECUTION TIME

MANUEL CEBRIAN
Manuel.Cebrian@ii.uam.es
Escuela Politécnica Superior
Universidad Autónoma de Madrid

ALFONSO ORTEGA
Alfonso.Ortega@ii.uam.es
Escuela Politécnica Superior
Universidad Autónoma de Madrid

MANUEL ALFONSECA
Manuel.Alfonseca@ii.uam.es
Escuela Politécnica Superior
Universidad Autónoma de Madrid

ABSTRACT
In a previous work [Ortega *et al.* 03], the authors have described the use of grammatical evolution to automatically generate L Systems (LS) representing fractal curves with a pre-determined fractal dimension. The experiments presented in this paper prove that the efficiency of this procedure is variable, with very different execution times for different executions with the same fractal dimension target. The paper shows that the probabilistic distribution of execution times belongs to a well-known family of random variables: heavy-tailed distributions. This analysis explains the erratic performance of the algorithm and suggests the use of a technique that corrects this variability and improves the efficiency about one order of magnitude.
Acknowledgements: *This paper has been sponsored by the Spanish Ministry of Science and Technology, project numbers TIC2001-0685-C02-01 and TIC 2002-01948.*

INTRODUCTION

Our procedure to generate fractal curves with a required dimension consists of three parts: a) representation of fractals by means of L Systems (LS); b) computation of the fractal dimension from the grammar; c) application of a grammar-evolution based genetic algorithm to get a grammar representing a fractal with the required dimension.

LS provide a powerful tool to represent fractals in the class of recursive transformations. The iterator may be represented by means of production rules, while the initiator corresponds to the axiom. The fractal curve is generated by the sequence of words derived from the axiom, by means of a *representation scheme: vector graphics or turtle graphics*. In a previous work [Alfonseca and Ortega 01] we have described an algorithm that estimates the fractal dimension of a non-trivial set of these fractals from their equivalent LS by means of symbolic manipulation, without the need of graphical procedures.

In [Ortega *et al.* 03] we applied Grammar Evolution (GE) [O'Neill and Ryan 2001] to obtain the LS equivalent to a fractal with the required dimension. The proposed procedure has a clear biological inspiration acting on three different levels: a genotype (a vector of integers) an intermediate level, equivalent to proteins (LS) and a phenotype (the fractal curve). See Figure 1.

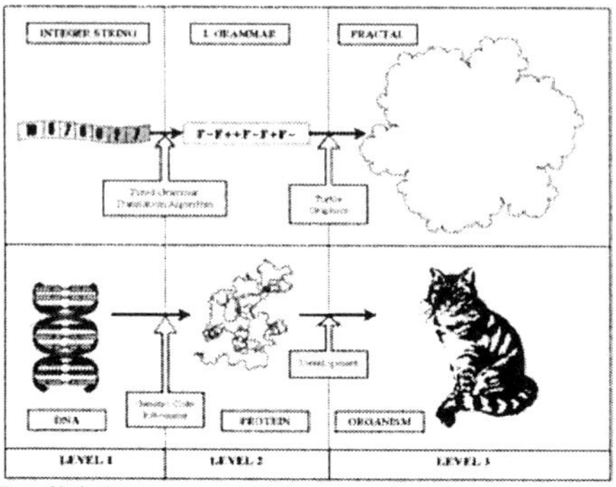

Figure 1. Parallels between our GE approach and biological evolution.

Finding by hand one fractal of a given dimension is easy. Our algorithm, however, generates an arbitrary number of different fractals with a required dimension, though with a widely varying efficiency [Ortega *et al.* 03]. Sometimes the objective is reached in the first generation. For less standard dimensions, the number of generations required is usually large, sometimes extremely large. Moreover, the standard deviation of the number of generations required (in separate execution runs, starting with different random seeds) is very large (see Table 1). This means that the performance of our implementation is very variable and may be quite low.

Table 1. Number of generations to reach the target in a set of GE tests.

Dimension	Angle	# tests	# generations to reach target
1.1	60	4	119 to 72122
1.2	45	8	188 to 11173
1.3	45	9	50 to 18627
1.25	60	15	1 to 2422
1.2618595...	60	4	1 to 2
1.4	60	10	33 to 1912
1.5	45	11	52 to 11138
1.6	45	5	275 to 3944
1.7	60	8	18 to 1221
1.8	60	13	69 to 3659
2	45	5	1

In the current work, we consider the random variable G_{dim} (the number of generations needed to generate a fractal with dimension *dim*). We show that G_{dim} belongs to a well-known class of moment-less distributions (they have infinite average and variance): the class of heavy-tailed (HT) distributions. This is the reason of the great deviation in execution times and of the loss in performance. First we present a few experimental evidences that gave rise to this study. Then we apply existing techniques, described in the statistical literature, to test our hypothesis that G_{dim} is HT. Finally, we will modify our algorithm by introducing *re-starts* in the executions, thus reducing significantly the variance and increasing the performance of the algorithm about one order of magnitude.

HT DISTRIBUTIONS

HT distribution have asymptotic tails of the Pareto-Lévy form:

$$P\{X > x\} \sim C.x^{-\alpha},\ x > 0 \tag{1}$$

where α is a constant (For HT distributions, $0 < \alpha < 2$). In our case, X is G_{dim} and x is a positive numeric value (a number of generations). In this way, $P\{G_{\mathrm{dim}} > x\}$ is interpreted as the probability that the algorithm requires more than x generations to get its goal. The symbol C in the expression is a normalizing constant to make $P\{0 < G_{\mathrm{dim}} \leq \infty\} = 1$.

We can compare this *polynomic* decay of probability with that of a standard normal curve, which is *exponential*:

$$P\{X > x\} \sim \frac{1}{x\sqrt{2\pi}} e^{-x^2/2} \tag{2}$$

Constant α is called *stability index*, and determines the existence of the distribution moments, since it is possible to prove that:

$$\alpha = \sup\left\{b > 0 : E\left|X^b\right| < \infty\right\} \tag{3}$$

This means that moments with exponent less than α are finite, while those greater or equal to α are infinite. The average is the moment with exponent one, thus if $\alpha \leq 1$ the random variable X has no average (it is infinite) or higher order moments (such as variance). The variance is a function of the moment with exponent two, thus if $1 < \alpha < 2$ random variable X does have an average, but not a variance. For a detailed treatment of the previous considerations, see [Samorodnitsky *et al.* 94, Zolotarev 86].

EXPERIMENTAL EVIDENCE

In this section we show experimental evidence that distribution G_{dim} is HT. This implies that the probability of extremely large execution times is very large in comparison with what would happen with a standard distribution.

First we observe the behavior of a few statistics for several values of *dim*. Then we show a Table that proves that the standard deviations of G_{dim} are greater than their averages (HT distributions have no standard deviation (nor average, in some cases), so when we mention these statistic measurements, they are assumed to refer to the sample).

Table 2. Summary of averages and standard deviations for several target dimensions, computed with a sample of 1000 experiments.

	1.3	**1.5**	**1.8**
Mean	1919	1560	2815
standard deviation	1898	1660	1866

This algorithmic phenomenon is atypical, and evidences that execution time depends strongly on the random seed. This behavior is typical of HT distributions. We have mentioned that HT distributions usually have no variance, (it is infinite). A way to test this is by checking its convergence speed.

Figure 2 shows the convergence of the variance of the sample for several values of *dim*. We observe that the sample variance has a strong fluctuation in all dimensions and does not converge when the size of the sample is increased, or at least it converges much more slowly than a normal distribution. This increases our suspicion that our data have an infinite variance.

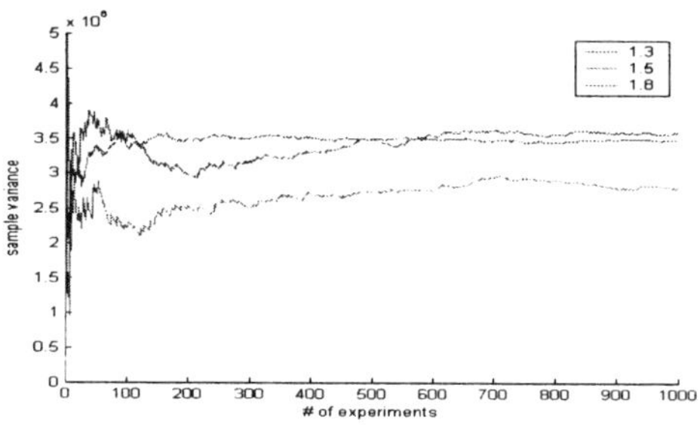

Figure 2. Variance for dim, showing its slow speed of convergence.

To complete our visual evidence, Figure 3 shows the cumulative probabilities for several values of *dim*. Looking also at Table 2, we observe that the probability that an execution takes longer than five times its standard deviation is over 10%, which implies that executions much longer than the average have a probability far higher than what would be expected for standard distributions.

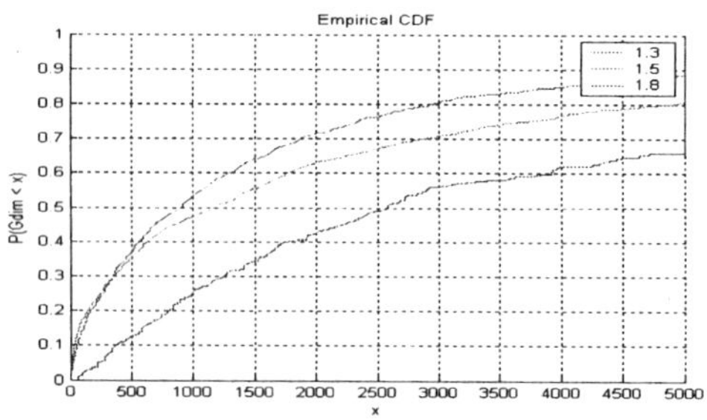

Figure 3. Empirical cumulative density function for several dimensions on samples with size 1000. After 5000 generations the execution was stopped.

ESTIMATION OF THE INDEX OF STABILITY

Once convinced experimentally that G_{dim} is a HT distribution, we estimate its *stability index* α using Hall's method [Hall 1982], a maximum likelihood estimator. Let $X_{n,1} \le X_{n,2} \le \ldots \le X_{n,n}$ be the ordered values (numbers of generations) in n experiments. Let $r < n$ be a truncation value used to take into account only the extreme observations. We get the following estimator:

Hall also determined the optimal value of r, but it is a function of unknown parameters of the distribution, therefore in practice values in the range $\left[n/4,\ n/3\right]$ are used. Table 3 shows our estimations of the stability indexes for the extreme values of the recommended interval and helps to give strength to our hypothesis: even testing the extreme values in the range, we still obtain values of $\alpha < 2$ in every case, which is consistent with the definition. Almost all these values are less than 1, which means that G_{dim} neither has a finite average.

Table 3. Estimation using Hall's method of the stability index of the distribution. The sample size used was 1000.

	***n*/3**	***n*/4**
1.3	0.626	0.511
1.5	0.917	0.800
1.8	1.078	0.854

EXPLOITING HT BEHAVIOUR

In HT distributions, events very far from the average have non-negligible probability and therefore should be taken into account. Since G_{dim} is HT, extremely long executions could happen. Even more important: the fact that execution has taken up to now a high number of generations (with respect to the average) gives no assurance that the end is near, however much we wait.

Looking at Figure 3, we can also reach the conclusion that the probability of executions below the average is great (over 50%). From both these two ideas we can deduce that we shouldn't be too patient with long executions, as there is a high probability of finding a short execution if we try again. This is done by choosing a threshold U in the number of generations; once it has been crossed, the algorithm is *re-started.* The new execution is different from the previous one, as it will use a different sequence of random numbers.

The optimal value for U can be determined if the distribution is known in analytical form, but in our case we only have experimental data and we have determined it empirically. To do this, we have repeated the experiments with different threshold values.

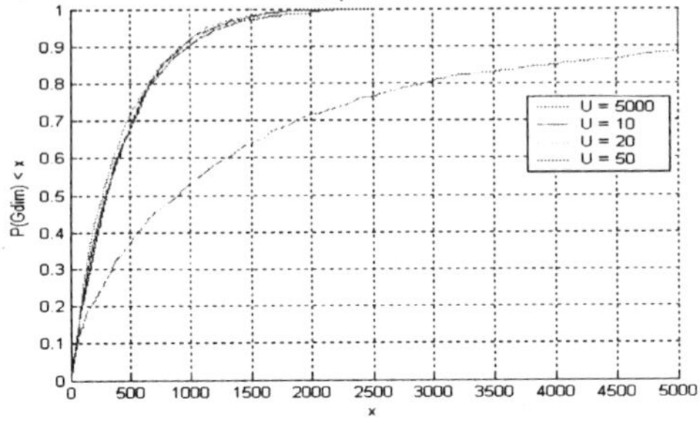

Figure 4. Cumulated density functions for several values of the threshold, with 1.5 fractal dimension goal. The HT nature disappears for low values of U.

In Figure 4 one can see that, for $U = 5000$, over 10% executions have not finished after 5000 generations. For $U = 10$, however, 90% executions are ended in less than 1000 generations. If we compute the *stability index* α for $U = 10$, we find it in the interval [2.01, 2.35], always greater than two, which proves empirically that the random variable G_{dim} is no longer HT.

Analyzing the 1.3 fractal dimension experiment, we find that the average number of generations for $U = 5$ is 228, while the average without re-starts (i.e. with a re-start threshold of 5000) is 1919, which means an improvement of about one order of magnitude in the execution time. We also saw that all the executions end before 1200 generations, which entails a big variance improvement (213 versus 1898 when measuring standard deviations).

CONCLUSIONS AND FUTURE RESEARCH

This paper presents a technique based on a probabilistic analysis to increase the performance and reduce the variance of an algorithm based on GE. The technique described transforms a HT random variable into another with standard distribution, by introducing filters that eliminate the heavy events (executions) and only allow the lighter ones. This technique may be used in different fields, whenever a similar probabilistic behavior of the execution time is detected.

At this point we are interested in finding the formal base that explains the HT properties of the random variable representing the execution time. We want to find if this behavior is something typical of the combinatorial problems explored by GE. [Mandelbrot 60] suggests that a HT behavior indicates that the search space is *self-similar*, independently of the search algorithm.

We intend to test whether the fact that our variable is HT depends on the topology of the search space for the problem under analysis, or is a consequence of its having been explored with GE. More work is needed for this: we must find problems solved by means of grammatical evolution that may be solved with other techniques, and study their execution time. In this way, we would add some formalism to this new branch in the family of genetic algorithms.

REFERENCES

M. Alfonseca and A. Ortega, "Determination of Fractal Dimensions from Equivalent L Systems", *IBM J. Res. & Dev.* 45, No. 6, 797– 805 (2001).

Hall, P.: On some simple estimates of an exponent of regular variation, *J. Roy. Statist. Soc.* 44 (1982), 37–42.

Mandelbrot, Benoit, B. (1960). The Pareto-Lévy law and the distribution of income. *International Economic Review* 1, 79–106.

M. O'Neill and C. Ryan, "Grammatical Evolution", *IEEE Trans. Evolutionary Computation* 5, No. 4, 349 –358 (2001).

A.Ortega, A.Abu Dalhoum, M.Alfonseca: Grammatical evolution to design fractal curves with a given dimension, *IBM Journal of Research and Development*, Vol. 47:4, p. 483-493, Jul. 2003.

M. O'Neill and C. Ryan, "Grammatical Evolution: Evolutionary Automatic Programming in an Arbitrary Language", Kluwer Academic Publishers, 2003, ISBN 1-4020-7444-1.

Samorodnitsky, Gennady and Taqqu, Murad S. (1994). Stable Non-Gaussian Random Processes: Stochastic Models with In-finite Variance, *Chapman and Hall*, New York.

Zolotarev, V.: One-Dimensional Stable Distributions, Transl. Math. Monographs 65, *Amer. Math. Soc.*, 1986. Translation from the original 1983 Russian ed.

Evolutionary Control of Bracketed L-system Interpretation

Dan Ashlock
Mathematics
Iowa State University

Kenneth M. Bryden
Mechanical Engineering
Iowa State University

Stephen Patrick Gent
Mechanical Engineering
Iowa State University

Abstract

An L-system or Lindenmayer system consists of a grammar together with an interpreter. The grammar contains an axiom which the grammar expands into a long, complex string. The interpreter renders the string into an object. The first use of L-systems was to provide morphological models of plants. In this exploratory initial study we use an evolutionary algorithm to perform parameter setting for an L-system interpreter. The interpreter is a graphics turtle with a stack. For a given L-system the evolutionary algorithm adjusts the turtle's parameter to cause it to drive in a constrained area of the Cartesian plane. Multiple L-systems and planar regions are given. The system manages to compensate for different L-system grammars and tune parameters to efficiently stay within the given regions.

1 Introduction

An *L-system* or *Lindenmayer system* [Lindenmayer, 1968] [Prusinkiewicz et al., 1990], consists of two parts. The first is a grammar consisting of an axiom and a collection of replacement rules. The L-system creates a sequence of strings starting with the axiom by applying these rules. This application is called an *expansion*. Rules are applied simultaneously to every character in a string to generate the next string. An example of such a grammar, together with the first two expansions beyond the axiom, is given in Figure 1. In this example rules are shown for every character that appears. It is standard to only give those rules that change a character. Thus only the first rule, $A \rightarrow A[+A][-A]$, would be shown. In the remainder of the paper trivial rules will not be displayed.

Axiom:
A
Rules:
A $\rightarrow$ **A[+A][-A]**

Expansions:
(0)**A**
(1)**A[+A][-A]**
(2)**A[+A][-A][+A[+A][-A]][-A[+A][-A]]**

Figure 1: An L system grammar and the first two resulting strings.Characters for which no rule is given are taken to themselves.

The second part of an L-system is the *interpreter*. The interpreter is used to transform the strings generated by an L-system into some object of interest. Lindenmayer's original application for the system named after him was as a family of computational models of plants. Simple models of plants and the work presented here both use graphical *turtles* as their interpreter. The characters within strings generated by an L-system are used as directions for turning and drawing by the turtle. In the example given in Figure 1 typical interpretations for each character are given in Table 1. If these interpretations are applied to the fifth expansion of the L-system grammar given in Figure 1 the tree shown in Figure 2 is obtained.

Character	Interpretation
A	Draw in the current direction.
+	Make a small left turn.
-	Make a small right turn.
[,]	Push, Pop turtle position and heading on a stack.

Table 1: A set of interpretations for the characters of the L-system given in Figure 1

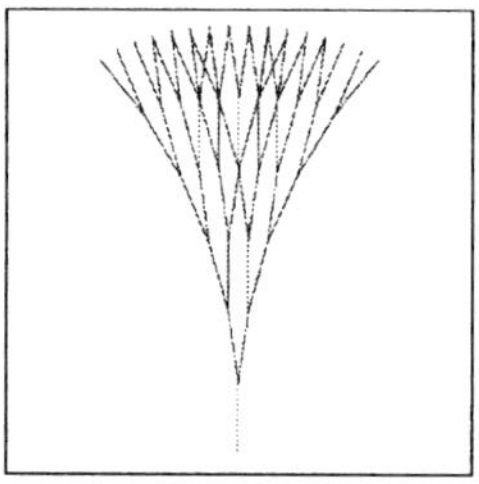

Figure 2: An interpretation of a bracketed L-system with a graphic turtle.

L-systems are typically hand designed to allow the interpreter to yield a desired appearance. The hand design touches on both the L-system's grammar and interpreter. This is probably due to the difficulty of writing an adequate fitness function to capture the notion of "plantlike" or even "beautiful" that is the typical goal of an L-system. Human-in-the-loop evolution has been performed [McCormack, 1993] to create interesting L-systems. In this study simple L-systems system interpreters will be evolved for bracketed L-systems. The goal is to cause a graphics turtle to draw within a restricted area of the plane called the *drawing arena.* The L-system interpreter selection via evolution will be a completely automatic process. An application of evolving an L-system grammar appears in [Miller et al., 1989, Kitano, 1990] where the L-system provided the connection topology of an artificial neural net. This particular system works on the grammar of the L-system rather than the parameters of the interpreter.

Evolvable Interpreters

A graphics turtle may be given commands to turn and advance with or without drawing. The turtle used in this study will always draw when it advances. There will be up to two angles available for turning and up two distances available for advancing. In order to make drawings that are not simply line drawings *brackets* are also used. The brackets come in matched pairs. An opening bracket pushes the state of the graphics turtle, position and heading, onto a stack. The closing bracket pops the same stack. An evolutionary algorithm is used to select the angle and distance parameters for the interpreter thus controlling where the interpreter draws. A set of parameters for a turtle based L-system interpreter is called a *turtle controller.*

The task of controlling where a turtle draws for a given L-system is one for which it is far easier to create a fitness function. A given turtle is rewarded for drawing within the drawing arena. Results are presented for 3 drawing arenas. These drawing arenas, together with interpretations of three L-systems described subsequently, are given in Figure 3. The goal of evolution is to have the turtle draw in the shaded areas.

2 Evolutionary Algorithm Design

The evolvable turtles used in this study will use the symbol set given in Table 2.

Character	Interpretation
R,S	Draw in the current direction an evolvable number of units. Initialized uniformly in the range 0 to 0.1.
θ,σ	Make a turn. Initialized in the range 0 to $\frac{\pi}{2}$.
[,]	Push,Pop turtle position and heading on a stack.

Table 2: Symbols used in the evolvable L-system and their interpretations or initial values.

The only difficult part of the system for evolving turtle controllers is the design of a fitness function. If the goal is to constrain the turtle to draw within a planar region by selecting a small number of turn angle and advance distance parameters for the turtle then there are several conflicting constraints. First, the turtle must be encouraged to move. A fitness function that rewards command executions within the specified area would also encourage the evolution of near-immobility within the drawing arena. Second, the turtle must be encouraged not to move outside of the drawing arena. Third, the penalties for moving outside of the arena must not be so harsh as to prevent progress. These constraints were identified by the process of evolving turtle controllers with fitness functions that violated those constraints. An ideal fitness function to address all these constraints is to compute the distance drawn within the drawing arena. This encourages motion and does not reward drawing outside the arena. Immobile turtles are granted nil fitness and turtles that drive wildly across the boundaries receive lower fitness evaluations.

The *k-approximate driving fitness* for a turtle controller executing a fixed string of commands in relation to a given drawing arena is computed as follows. Each time the turtle advances, the line segment of that advance is divided into k sub-segments. The turtle's fitness is increased by the length of each sub-segment that has both ends in the drawing arena. The fitness is the sum of sub-segment lengths with both ends in the arena over the execution of a given string of n turtle commands. Also, as k increases this function converges to distance driven within the drawing arena. As k increases the speed of fitness evaluation also drops. The parameter k thus permits the user to pick a point in the space of trade-offs between speed and good approximations of the amount of drawing the turtle did inside a given arena.

In an initial population there is often a large number of essentially worthless structures. A common type of unfit turtle controller is one that drives not only outside of the drawing arena but off into the Cartesian plane outside the unit square. To give evolution a push in the correct direction, each turtle commands that is executed and leaves the turtle outside the drawing arena yields a fitness penalty of 0.1, subtracted from the k-approximate driving fitness. The evolutionary runs in this study use $k = 4$. The penalized 4-approximate driving fitness will be referred to as simply "fitness" hereafter.

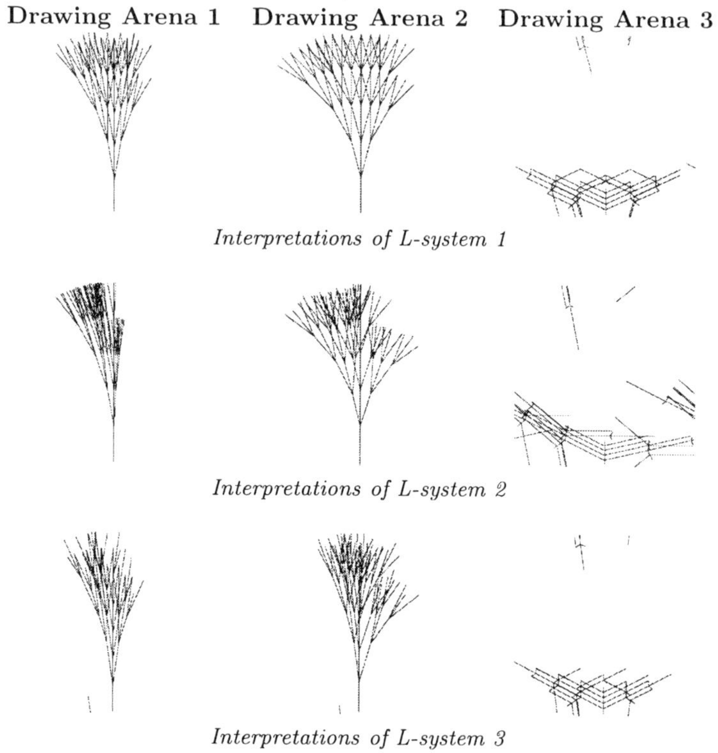

Figure 3: A typical interpretation by an evolved interpreter is shown for each of the three drawing arenas and three L-systems.

The evolutionary algorithm used operates on a population of 120 turtle controllers. The four parameters are treated as atomic objects and stored as machine reals in an array. The algorithm is steady state using single tournament selection with a tournament size of seven. The algorithm performs 48,000 mating events each time it is run. A single point crossover operator is used. A single parameter is mutated after crossover in each new controller. Mutation consists of multiplying the parameter by a number of the form e^X where X is uniformly distributed in the range $[-0.1, 0.1]$. The number of mating events was chosen in a preliminary study in which fitness appeared to plateau in most runs by mating event 10,000. The crossover operator is appropriate for the small genome size. The unusual mutation operator is chosen to permit mutation to operate by scaling the system.

3 Experiments Performed

A set of 400 evolutionary runs were performed for all nine combinations of the three drawing arenas with each of the three L-systems given in Table 3. To create the string of turtle commands, the successive expansions of the L-system were computed, starting with the axiom, until the length of the string equaled or exceeded 400 characters. The first 400 characters were then used as a fixed set of commands to the turtle with only the interpretation of those commands varying via choice of the parameters R, S, σ, and θ. The number 400 is large enough to capture the behavior of the turtle controller without being so long as to excessively slow fitness evaluation. The evolutionary algorithm searched for turn angles and advance lengths that yielded the highest fitness for a given string of turtle commands. The most fit turtle controller from each run was saved. The population mean, standard deviation, and maximum fitness were saved every 120 mating events to permit tracking of the behavior of evolution.

L1:	L2:	L3:
Axiom:	**Axiom:**	**Axiom:**
R	R	R
Nontrivial rules:	**Nontrivial rules:**	**Nontrivial rules:**
$R \rightarrow R\,[\theta S\sigma]\,[R]\,[\sigma S\theta]$	$R \rightarrow R\,[\theta S\sigma]\,[R]\,[R]\,[\sigma S\theta]$	$R \rightarrow R\,[\theta S\sigma]\,[R]\,[\sigma S\theta]$
$S \rightarrow S\,[\theta R\sigma]\,[S]\,[\sigma R\theta]$	$S \rightarrow S\,[\theta R\sigma]\,[S]\,[\sigma R\theta]$	$S \rightarrow S\,[\theta R\sigma]\,[S]\,[S]\,[\sigma R\theta]$

Table 3: The L-systems used in this study. The symbols θ and σ denote turn angles while R and S denote distances to advance.

4 Results

The behavior of the fitness traces for individual runs was typical for an evolutionary algorithm performing parameter optimization. Most runs exhibited a sharp initial increase in fitness followed by modest fitness increase and long static epochs. In all nine sets of evolutionary runs there was substantial success in constraining the turtle to operate inside the driving arena. In all cases solutions could be scaled to fit completely inside the drawing arena but such scaling would lower the fitness. The fitness function slightly emphasizes the importance of total distance traveled over that of staying in bounds. More than 90% of each set of runs found a fitness, and a drawing, that were quite similar to the best fitness and its associated drawing. For drawing arenas one and two, the common result was a full, bushy drawing extending both left and right. For the third drawing arena it was similar to the drawing given in in the upper right panel of Figure 3.

5 Discussion

As a target for evolutionary computation, parameter setting for L-systems appears to be a relatively straightforward task. This is somewhat at odds with the researcher's initial intuition. The four parameters of the tested L-systems are each used a large number of times and their effects are stacked upon one another. A small parameter change can thus have a very large effect of the shape of the final drawing, sending one up against the edges of the drawing arena outside of it. On the other hand, if a given L-system is well inside the drawing arena, the parameters may be reset a good deal and either increased fitness (for R and S) or little change (for θ and σ) will result. The fitness landscape thus has something of the character of an elliptical four-dimensional crater with a steep cliff outside the crater walls.

The picture drawn by a turtle does depend continuously on the angular and radial parameters. The picture also scales directly as the radial parameter. This means that the fitness landscape, at least if the sampling number k is large, depends continuously on the parameter values. For a given choice of angle(s), variation of the radius scales the drawing. Given that the turtle starts within the drawing arena this means that the algorithm can always optimize the radius to fit the drawing within the arena. This perhaps explains the relatively smooth functioning of the system.

Figure 4: Three members of an initial random population for **L1** on drawing arena two.

Figure 4 shows examples of members of the initial population. All examples have fitnesses below 15% of the maximum fitness. These random members of an initial population can be compared to the best-of-run solutions depicted in example 3 to give a sense of the degree to which the evolutionary algorithm is improving the quality of L-system interpretation.

One unexpected result in the current study is that bracketed L-systems seem to be easier to control than those without brackets. Results analogous to those presented here for non-bracketed L-systems may be found in [Ashlock and Bryden, 2004]. The diversity of local optima was higher in the non-bracketed L-systems and maximum fitness took longer to achieve. This result is somewhat at odds with the intuition that an interpreter that has a stack available to it is more computationally complex than one that does not. In this case the added computational complexity available to the interpreter in a bracketed L-system appear to have smoothed the fitness landscape.

References

[Ashlock and Bryden, 2004] Ashlock, D. and Bryden, K. (2004). Evolutionary control of L-system interpretation. to appear in the Proceedings of the 2004 Congress on Evolutionary Computation.

[Kitano, 1990] Kitano, H. (1990). Designing neural networks using genetic algorithms with graph generation system. *Complex Systems*, 4:461–476.

[Lindenmayer, 1968] Lindenmayer, A. (1968). Mathematical models for cellular interaction in development, parts i and ii. *Journal of Theoretical Biology*, 18:280–315.

[McCormack, 1993] McCormack, J. P. (1993). Interactive evolution of L-system grammars for computer graphics modelling. In Green, D. G. and Bossomaier, T., editors, *Complex Systems: from biology to computation*, pages 118–130. ISO Press, Amsterdam.

[Miller et al., 1989] Miller, G. F., Todd, P. M., and Hegde, S. U. (1989). Designing neural networks using genetic algorithms. In *Proceedings of the 3rd Inernational Conference on Genetic Algorithms.*, pages 379–384, San Mateo, CA. Morgan Kaufmann.

[Prusinkiewicz et al., 1990] Prusinkiewicz, P., Lindenmayer, A., and Hanan, J. S. (1990). *The algorithmic beauty of plants.* Springer-Verlag, New York.

HIERARCHICAL GENETIC ALGORITHMS FOR TOPOLOGY OPTIMIZATION IN FUZZY CONTROL SYSTEMS

OSCAR CASTILLO, FEVRIER VALDEZ, PATRICIA MELIN
Department of Computer Science
Tijuana Institute of Technology
Tijuana, México

ABSTRACT
We describe in this paper the use of hierarchical genetic algorithms for fuzzy system optimization in intelligent control. In particular, we consider the problem of optimizing the number of rules and membership functions using an evolutionary approach. The hierarchical genetic algorithm enables the optimization of the fuzzy system design for a particular application. We illustrate the approach with the case of intelligent control in a medical application. Simulation results show that we are able to find an optimal set of rules and membership functions for the fuzzy control system.

INTRODUCTION

We describe in this paper the application of a Hierarchical Genetic Algorithm (HGA) for fuzzy system optimization (Man et al., 1999). In particular, we consider the problem of finding the optimal set of rules and membership functions for a specific application (Yen and Langari, 1999). The HGA is used to search for this optimal set of rules and membership functions, according to the data about the problem. We consider, as an illustration, the case of a fuzzy system for intelligent control.

Fuzzy systems are capable of handling complex, non-linear and sometimes mathematically intangible dynamic systems using simple solutions (Jang et al., 1997). Very often, fuzzy systems may provide a better performance than conventional non-fuzzy approaches with less development cost (Procyk and Mamdani, 1979). However, to obtain an optimal set of fuzzy membership functions and rules is not an easy task. It requires time, experience and skills of the designer for the tedious fuzzy tuning exercise. In principle, there is no general rule or method for the fuzzy logic set-up, although a heuristic and iterative procedure for modifying the membership functions to improve performance has been proposed. Recently, many researchers have considered a number of intelligent schemes for the task of tuning the fuzzy system. The noticeable Neural Network (NN) approach (Jang and Sun, 1995) and the Genetic Algorithm (GA) approach (Homaifar and McCormick, 1995) to optimize either the membership functions or rules, have become a trend for fuzzy logic system development.

The HGA approach differs from the other techniques in that it has the ability to reach an optimal set of membership functions and rules without a known fuzzy system topology (Tang et al., 1998). During the optimization phase, the membership functions need not be fixed. Throughout the genetic operations (Holland, 1975), a reduced fuzzy system including the number of membership functions and fuzzy rules will be generated. The HGA approach has a number of advantages:

1) An optimal and the least number of membership functions and rules are obtained
2) No pre-fixed fuzzy structure is necessary, and
3) Simpler implementing procedures and less cost are involved.

We consider in this paper the case of automatic anesthesia control in human patients for testing the optimized fuzzy controller. We did have, as a reference, the best fuzzy controller that was developed for the automatic anesthesia control (Karr and Gentry,

1993), and we consider the optimization of this controller using the HGA approach (Castillo and Melin, 2001, 2003). After applying the genetic algorithm the number of fuzzy rules was reduced from 12 to 9 with a similar performance of the fuzzy controller (Lozano 2003). Of course, the parameters of the membership functions were also tuned by the genetic algorithm. We did compare the simulation results of the optimized fuzzy controllers obtained with the HGA against the best fuzzy controller that was obtained previously with expert knowledge, and control is achieved in a similar fashion.

EVOLUTION OF FUZZY SYSTEMS

Ever since the very first introduction of the fundamental concept of fuzzy logic by Zadeh in 1973, its use in engineering disciplines has been widely studied. Its main attraction undoubtedly lies in the unique characteristics that fuzzy logic systems possess. They are capable of handling complex, non-linear dynamic systems using simple solutions. Very often, fuzzy systems provide a better performance than conventional non-fuzzy approaches with less development cost. However, to obtain an optimal set of fuzzy membership functions and rules is not an easy task. It requires time, experience, and skills of the operator for the tedious fuzzy tuning exercise. In principle, there is no general rule or method for the fuzzy logic set-up. Recently, many researchers have considered a number of intelligent techniques for the task of tuning the fuzzy set.

Here, another innovative scheme is described (Tang et al., 1998). This approach has the ability to reach an optimal set of membership functions and rules without a known overall fuzzy set topology. The conceptual idea of this approach is to have an automatic and intelligent scheme to tune the membership functions and rules, in which the conventional closed loop fuzzy control strategy remains unchanged, as indicated in Fig. 1.

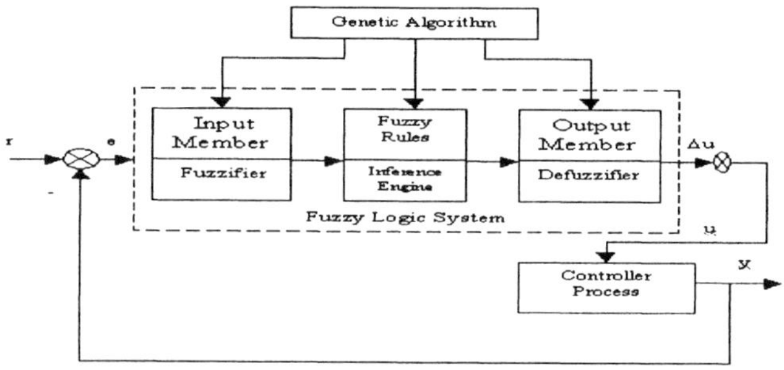

Fig. 1 Genetic algorithm for a fuzzy control system.

In this case, the chromosome of a particular system is shown in Fig. 2. The chromosome consists of two types of genes, the control genes and parameter genes. The control genes, in the form of bits, determine the membership function activation, whereas the parameter genes are in the form of real numbers to represent the membership functions.

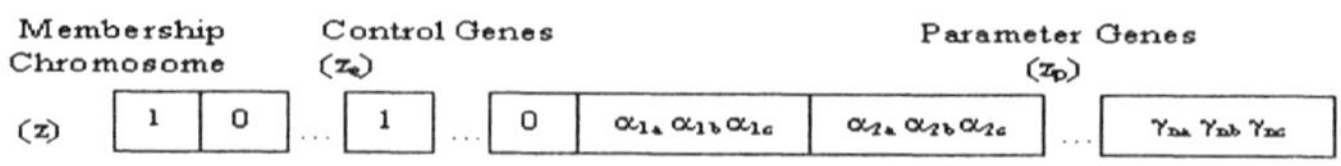

Fig. 2 Chromosome structure for the fuzzy system.

To obtain a complete design for the fuzzy control system, an appropriate set of fuzzy rules is required to ensure system performance. At this point it should be stressed that the introduction of the control genes is done to govern the number of fuzzy subsets in the system.

Once the formulation of the chromosome has been set for the fuzzy membership functions and rules, the genetic operation cycle can be performed. This cycle of operation for the fuzzy control system optimization using a genetic algorithm is illustrated in Fig. 3.

There are two population pools, one for storing the membership chromosomes and the other for storing the fuzzy rule chromosomes. We can see this in Figure 3 as the membership population and fuzzy rule population, respectively. Considering that there are various types of gene structure, a number of different genetic operations can be used. For the crossover operation, a one-point crossover is applied separately for both the control and parameter genes of the membership chromosomes within certain operation rates. There is no crossover operation for fuzzy rule chromosomes since only one suitable rule set can be assisted.

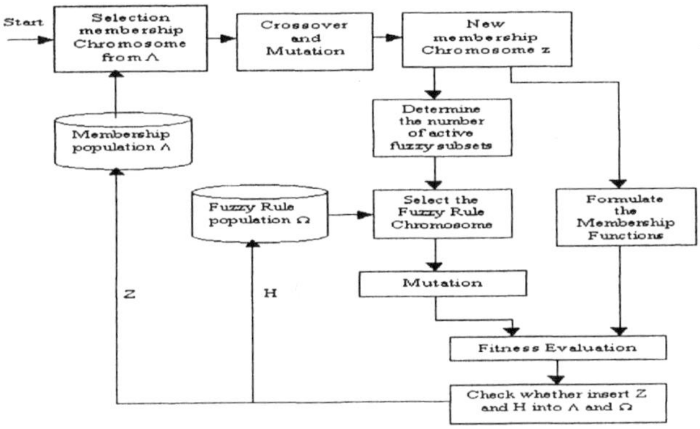

Fig. 3 Genetic cycle for fuzzy system optimization.

Bit mutation is applied for the control genes of the membership chromosome. Each bit of the control gene is flipped if a probability test is satisfied (a randomly generated number is smaller than a predefined rate). As for the parameter genes, which are real number represented, random mutation is applied. The complete genetic cycle continues until some termination criteria, for example, meeting the design specification or number of generation reaching a predefined value are fulfilled.

The fitness function can be defined in this case as follows:

$$f_i = \Sigma \mid y(k) - r(k) \mid \qquad (1)$$

where Σ indicates the sum for all the data points in the training set, and y(k) represents the real output of the fuzzy system and r(k) is the reference output. This fitness value measures how well the fuzzy system is approximating the real data of the problem.

APPLICATION TO INTELLIGENT CONTROL

We consider the case of controlling the anesthesia given to a patient as the problem for finding the optimal fuzzy system for control (Lozano 2003). The complete implementation was done in the MATLAB programming language. The fuzzy systems were build automatically by using the Fuzzy Logic Toolbox, and genetic algorithm was coded directly in the MATLAB language. The fuzzy systems for control are the individuals used in the genetic algorithm, and these are evaluated by comparing them to the ideal control given by the experts. In other words, we compare the performance of the fuzzy systems that are generated by the genetic algorithm, against the ideal control system given by the experts in this application. We give more details below.

The main task of the anesthesist, during and operation, is to control anesthesia concentration. In any case, anesthesia concentration can't be measured directly. For this reason, the anesthesist uses indirect information, like the heartbeat, pressure, and motor activity. The anesthesia concentration is controlled using a medicine, which can be given by a shot or by a mix of gases. We consider here the use of isoflurance, which is usually given in a concentration of 0 to 2% with oxygen. In figure 4 we show a block diagram of the controller.

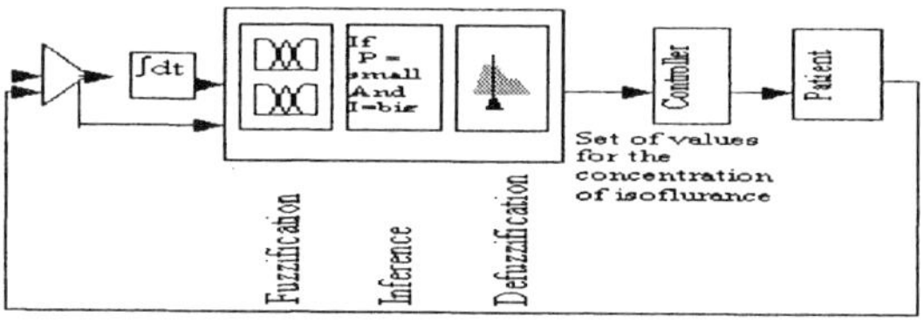

Fig. 4 Architecture of the fuzzy control system.

The air that is exhaled by the patient contains a specific concentration of isoflurance, and it is re-circulated to the patient. As consequence, we can measure isoflurance concentration on the inhaled and exhaled air by the patient, to estimate isoflurance concentration on the patient's blood. From the control engineering point of view, the task by the anesthesist is to maintain anesthesia concentration between the high level W (threshold to wake up) and the low level E (threshold to success). These levels are difficult to be determine in a changing environment and also are dependent on the patient's condition. For this reason, it is important to automate this anesthesia control, to perform this task more efficiently and accurately, and also to free the anesthesist from this time consuming job. The anesthesist can then concentrate in doing other task during operation of a patient.

The first automated system for anesthesia control was developed using a PID controller in the 60's. However, this system was not very successful due to the non-linear nature of the problem of anesthesia control. After this first attempt, adaptive control was proposed to automate anesthesia control, but robustness was the problem in this case. For these reasons, fuzzy logic was proposed for solving this problem. An additional advantage of fuzzy control is that we can use in the rules the same vocabulary as the medical doctors use. The fuzzy control system can also be easily interpreted by the anesthesists.

The fuzzy system is defined as follows:

1) Input variables: Blood pressure and Error
2) Output variable: Isoflurance concentration
3) Nine fuzzy if-then rules of the optimized system, which is the base for comparison
4) 12 fuzzy if-then rules of an initial system to begin the optimization cycle of the genetic algorithm.

The linguistic values used in the fuzzy rules are the following:
PB = Positive Big, PS = Positive Small, ZERO = zero, NB =Negative Big, NS = Negative Small
We show below a sample set of fuzzy rules that are used in the fuzzy inference system that is represented in the genetic algorithm for optimization.

if Blood pressure is NB and error is NB then conc_isoflurance is PS
if Blood pressures is PS then conc_isoflurance is NS

if Blood pressure is NB then conc_isoflurance is PB
if Blood pressure is PB then conc_isoflurance is NB
if Blood pressure is ZERO and error is ZERO then conc_isoflurance is ZERO
if Blood pressure is ZERO and error is PS then conc_isoflurance is NS
if Blood pressure is ZERO and error is NS then conc_isoflurance is PS
if error is NB then conc_isoflurance is PB
if error is PB then conc_isoflurance is NB
if error is PS then conc_isoflurance is NS
if Blood pressure is NS and error is ZERO then conc_isoflurance is NB
if Blood pressure is PS and error is ZERO then conc_isoflurance is PS.

The general characteristics of the genetic algorithm that are the following:
NIND = 40; % Number of individuals in each subpopulation.
MAXGEN = 300; % Maximum number of generations allowed.
GGAP = .6; %"Generational gap", which is the percentage from the complete population of new individuals generated in each generation.
PRECI = 120; % Precision of binary representations.
SelCh = select('rws', Chrom, FitnV, GGAP); % Roulette wheel method for selecting the indivuals participating in the genetic operations.
SelCh = recombin('xovmp',SelCh,0.7); % Multi-point crossover as recombination method for the selected individuals.
ObjV = FuncionObjDifuso120_555(Chrom, sdifuso); Objective function is given by the error between the performance of the ideal control system given by the experts and the fuzzy control system given by the genetic algorithm.

In Table 1 we show the chromosome representation, which has 120 binary positions. These positions are divided in two parts, the first one indicates the number of rules of the fuzzy inference system, and the second one is divided again into fuzzy rules to indicate which membership functions are active or inactive for the corresponding rule.

Table 1 Binary Chromosome Representation.

Bit assigned	Representation
1 a 12	Which rule is active or inactive
13 a 21	Membership functions active or inactive of rule 1
22 a 30	Membership functions active or inactive of rule 2
...	Membership functions active or inactive of rule...
112 a 120	Membership functions active or inactive of rule 12

SIMULATION RESULTS

We describe in this section the simulation results that were achieved using the hierarchical genetic algorithm for the optimization of the fuzzy control system, for the case of anesthesia control. The genetic algorithm is able to evolve the topology of the fuzzy system for the particular application. We used 300 generations of 40 individuals each to achieve the minimum error. The value of the minimum error achieved with this particular fuzzy logic controller was of 0.0064064, which is considered a small number in this application.

In Fig. 5 we show the simulation results of the fuzzy logic controller produced by the genetic algorithm after evolution. We used a sinusoidal input signal with unit amplitude and a frequency of 2 radians/second, with a transfer function of [1/(0.5s +1)]. In this figure we can appreciate the comparison of the outputs of both the ideal controller (1) and the fuzzy controller optimized by the genetic algorithm (2). From this figure it is clear that both controllers are very similar and as a consequence we can conclude that the genetic algorithm was able to optimize the performance of the fuzzy logic controller.

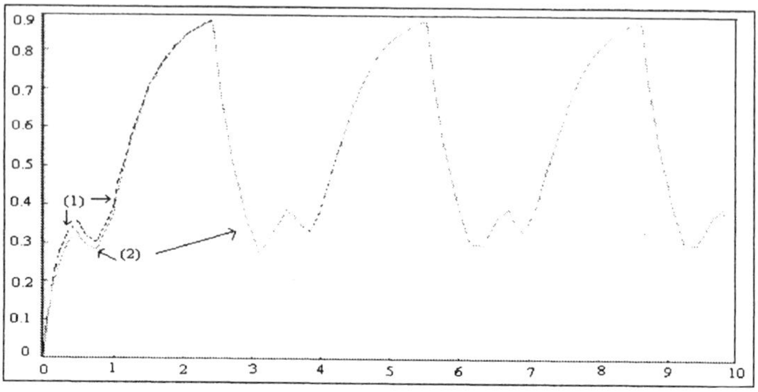

Fig. 5 Comparison between outputs of the ideal controller (1) and the fuzzy controller produced with the HGA (2).

CONCLUSIONS

We consider in this paper the case of automatic anesthesia control in human patients for testing the optimized fuzzy controller. We did have, as a reference, the best fuzzy controller that was developed for the automatic anesthesia control, and we consider the optimization of this controller using the HGA approach. After applying the genetic algorithm the number of fuzzy rules was reduced from 12 to 9 with a similar performance of the fuzzy controller. Of course, the parameters of the membership functions were also tuned by the genetic algorithm. We did compare the simulation results of the optimized fuzzy controllers obtained with the HGA against the best fuzzy controller that was obtained previously with expert knowledge, and control is achieved in a similar fashion. Since simulation results are similar, and the number of rules was reduced, we can conclude that the HGA approach is a good alternative for designing fuzzy systems.

REFERENCES

K.F. Man, K.S. Tang, and S. Kwong, 1999, *Genetic Algorithms: Concepts and Designs*, Springer Verlag.

J. Yen, and R. Langari, 1999, *Fuzzy Logic: intelligence, control and information*, Prentice Hall, Inc.

J.-S. R. Jang, C.-T. Sun, and E. Mizutani, 1997, *Neuro-fuzzy and Soft Computing, A computational approach to learning and machine intelligence*, Prentice Hall, Upper Saddle River, NJ.

T.J. Procyk and E.M. Mamdani, 1979, "A linguistic self-organizing process controller" *Automatica*, vol. 15, no. 1, pp 15-30.

J.-S. R. Jang and C.-T. Sun, 1995 "Neurofuzzy fuzzy modeling and control", *Proc. IEEE*, vol. 83, pp. 378-406.

A. Homaifar and E. McCormick, 1995, "Simultaneous design of membership functions and rule sets for fuzzy controllers using genetic algorithms", *IEEE Trans. Fuzzy Systems*, vol. 3, pp. 129-139.

K.-S. Tang, K.-F. Man, Z.-F. Liu and S.Kwong, 1998, "Minimal fuzzy memberships and rules using hierarchical genetic algorithms", *IEEE Trans. on Industrial Electronics*, vol. 45, no. 1.

J. Holland, 1975, *Adaptation in natural and artificial systems,* University of Michigan Press.

C.L. Karr and E.J. Gentry, 1993, "Fuzzy control of pH using genetic algorithms", *IEEE Trans. Fuzzy Systems*, vol. 1, pp. 46-53.

A. Lozano, 2003, "Optimización de un Sistema de Control Difuso por medio de algoritmos genéticos jerarquicos", Thesis, Dept. of Computer Science, Tijuana Institute of Technology, Mexico.

O. Castillo and P. Melin, 2001, *Soft Computing for Control of Non-Linear Dynamical Systems*, Springer-Verlag, Heidelberg, Germany.

O. Castillo and P. Melin, 2003, *Soft Computing and Fractal Theory for Intelligent Manufacturing*, Springer-Verlag, Heidelberg, Germany.

FINGERPRINT RECOGNITION USING THE FUZZY SUGENO INTEGRAL FOR RESPONSE INTEGRATION IN MODULAR NEURAL NETWORKS

PATRICIA MELIN, DIANA BRAVO, OSCAR CASTILLO
Dept. of Computer Science, Tijuana Institute of Technology
Tijuana, Mexico

ABSTRACT

We describe in this paper a new approach for pattern recognition using modular neural networks with a fuzzy logic method for response integration. We proposed a new architecture for modular neural networks for achieving pattern recognition in the particular case of human fingerprints. Also, the method for achieving response integration is based on the fuzzy Sugeno integral. Response integration is required to combine the outputs of all the modules in the modular network. We have applied the new approach for fingerprint recognition with a real database of fingerprints from students of our institution.

INTRODUCTION

Response integration methods for modular neural networks that have been studied, to the moment, do not solve well real recognition problems with large sets of data or in other cases reduce the final output to the result of only one module. Also, in the particular case of fingerprint recognition, methods of weighted statistical average do not work well due to the nature of the fingerprint recognition problem. For these reasons, a new approach for fingerprint recognition using modular neural networks and fuzzy integration of responses was proposed in this paper.

The basic idea of the new approach is to divide a human fingerprint in to three different regions: the top, the middle and the bottom. Each of these regions is assigned to one module of the neural network. In this way, the modular neural network has three different modules, one for each of the regions of the human fingerprint. At the end, the final decision of fingerprint recognition is done by an integration module, which has to take into account the results of each of the modules. In our approach, the integration module uses the fuzzy Sugeno integral to combine the outputs of the three modules. The fuzzy Sugeno integral allows the integration of responses from the three modules of the top, middle and bottom of a human specific fingerprint. Other approaches in the literature use other types of integration modules, like voting methods, majority methods, and neural networks (Albrecht, 1996) (Lu and Ito, 1998). The new approach for fingerprint recognition was tested with a database of students and professors from our institution. This database was collected at our institution using a special scanner.

MODULAR NEURAL NETWORKS

There exists a lot of neural network architectures in the literature that work well when the number of inputs is relatively small, but when the complexity of the problem grows or the number of inputs increases, their performance decreases very quickly. For this reason, there has been work in compensating in some way the problems in learning of a single neural network over high dimensional spaces (Castillo and Melin, 2001).

In the work by (Sharkey, 1998), the use of multiple neural systems (Multi-Nets) is described. It is claimed that multi-nets have better performance or even solve problems that monolithic neural networks are not able to solve. It is also claimed that multi-nets or modular systems have also the advantage of being easier to understand or modify, if necessary (Fu et al., 2001).

In the literature there is also mention of the terms "ensemble" and "modular" for this type of neural network (Boers and Kuiper, 1992). The term "ensemble" is used when a redundant set of neural networks is utilized, as described in (Hansen and Salomon, 1990). In this case, each of the neural networks is redundant because it is providing a solution for the same task (Smith and Johansen, 1997), as it is shown in Fig. 1. On the other hand, in the modular approach, one task or problem is decompose in subtasks, and the complete solution requires the contribution of the modules (Ronco, 1995), as it is shown in Fig. 2.

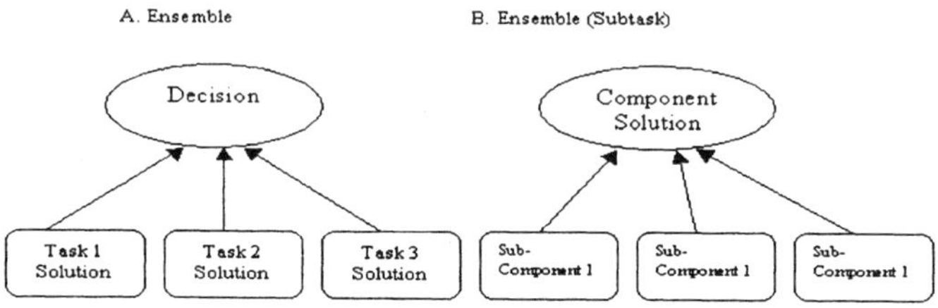

Fig. 1. Ensembles for one task and subtask.

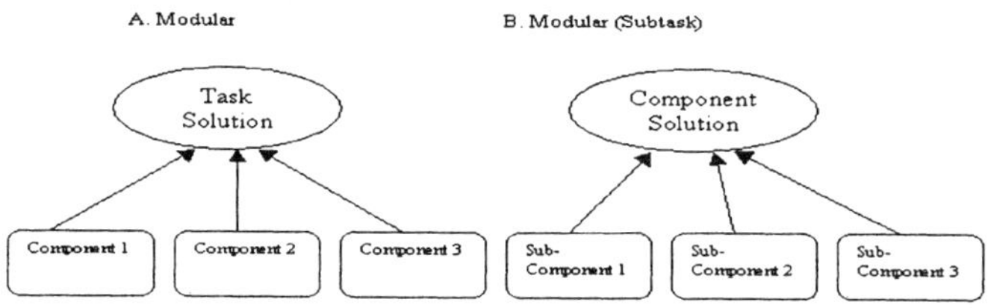

Fig. 2 Modular approach for task and subtask.

METHODS FOR RESPONSE INTEGRATION

The importance of this part of the architecture for pattern recognition is due to the high dimensionality of this type of problems. As a consequence in pattern recognition is good alternative to consider a modular approach. This has the advantage of reducing the time required of learning and it also increases accuracy. In our case, we consider dividing the images of a human fingerprint in three different regions, and applying a modular structure for achieving pattern recognition.

In the literature we can find several methods for response integration, that have been researched extensively, which in many cases are based on statistical decision methods. We will mention briefly some of these methods of response integration, in particular de ones based on fuzzy logic. The idea of using this type of methods is that the final decision takes into account all of the different kind of information available about the human face. In particular, we consider aggregation operators, and the fuzzy Sugeno integral (Sugeno, 1974).

Yager mentions in his work (Yager, 1999), that fuzzy measures for the aggregation criteria of two important classes of problems. In the first type of problems, we have a set $Z=\{z_1,z_2,\ldots,z_n\}$ of objects, and it is desired to select one or more of these objects based on the satisfaction of certain criteria. In this case, for each $z_i \in Z$, it is evaluated $D(z_i)=G(A_i(z_i),\ldots,A_j(z_i))$, and then an object or objects are selected based on the value of G. The problems that fall within this structure are the multi-criteria decision problems, search in databases and retrieving of documents.

In the second type of problems, we have a set $G=\{G_1,G_2,\ldots,G_q\}$ of aggregation functions and object z. Here, each G_k corresponds to different possible identifications of object z, and our goal is to find out the correct identification of z. For achieving this, for each aggregation function G, we obtain a result for each z, Dk(z)=Gk(A1(z), A2(z), … ,An(z)). Then we associate to z the identification corresponding to the larger value of the aggregation function.

A typical example of this type of problems is pattern recognition. Where A_j corresponds to the attributes and $A_j(z)$ measures the compatibility of z with the attribute. Medical applications and fault diagnosis fall into this type of problems. In diagnostic problems, the A_j corresponds to symptoms associated with a particular fault, and G_k captures the relations between these faults.

Fuzzy integrals can be viewed as non-linear functions defined with respect to fuzzy measures. In particular, the "gλ-fuzzy measure" introduced by (Sugeno, 1974) can be used to define fuzzy integrals. The ability of fuzzy integrals to combine the results of multiple information sources has been mentioned in previous works.

Definition 1. A function of sets $g{:}2^x\text{-}(0.1)$ is called a fuzzy measure if:

1) $g(0)=0 \quad g(x)=1$
2) $g(A)\leq g(B)$ if $A\subset B$
3) if $\{A_i\}i^{\alpha}=1$ is a sequence of increments of the measurable set then

$$\lim_{i\to\infty} g(A_i) = g(\lim_{i\to\infty} A_i) \tag{1}$$

From the above it can be deduced that g is not necessarily additive, this property is replaced by the additive property of the conventional measure.

From the general definition of the fuzzy measure, Sugeno introduced what is called "gλ-fuzzy measure", which satisfies the following additive property: For every A, $B \subset X$ and $A \cap B = \theta$,

$$g(A \cup B) = g(A) + g(B) + \lambda\, g(A)g(B), \tag{2}$$

for some value of $\lambda>-1$.

This property says that the measure of the union of two disjunct sets can be obtained directly from the individual measures. Using the concept of fuzzy measures, Sugeno developed the concept of fuzzy integrals, which are non-linear functions defined with respect to fuzzy measures like the gλ-fuzzy measure.

Definition 2 let X be a finite set and $h{:}X\to[0,1]$ be a fuzzy subset of X, the fuzzy integral over X of function h with respect to the fuzzy measure g is defined in the following way,

$$h(x) \circ g(x) = \max_{E\subseteq X} [\min(\min_{x\in E} h(x), g(E))] \tag{3}$$

$$= \sup_{\alpha\in[0,1]} [\min(\alpha, g(h_\alpha))]$$

where h_α is the level set α of h,

$$h_\alpha = \{ x \mid h(x) \geq \alpha \}. \tag{4}$$

We will explain in more detail the above definition: h(x) measures the degree to which concept h is satisfied by x. The term $\min(h_x)$ measures the degree to which concept h is satisfied by all the elements in E. The value g(E) is the degree to which the subset of objects E satifies the concept measure by g. As a consequence, the obtained value of comparing these two quantities in terms of operator min indicates the degree to which E satifies both criteria g and $\min(h_x)$. Finally, operator max takes the greatest of these terms. One can interpret fuzzy integrals as finding the maximum degree of similarity between the objective and expected value.

PROPOSED ARCHITECTURE AND RESULTS

In the experiments performed in this research work, we used 50 fingerprints that were taken with a scanner from students and professors of our Institution (Quezada, 2004). The images were taken in such a way that they had 198 pixels wide and 200 pixels high, with a resolution of 300x300 ppi, and with a color representation of a gray scale, some of these images are shown in Fig. 3. In addition to the training data (50 fingerprints) we did use 10 images that were obtained by applying noise in a random fashion, which was increased from 10 to 100%.

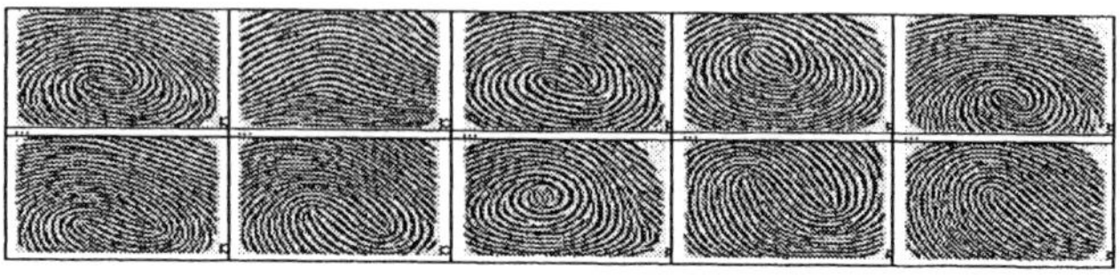

Fig. 3 Sample Images Used for Training.

The architecture proposed in this work consist of three main modules, in which each of them in turn consists of a set of neural networks trained with the same data, which provides the modular architecture shown in Fig. 4.

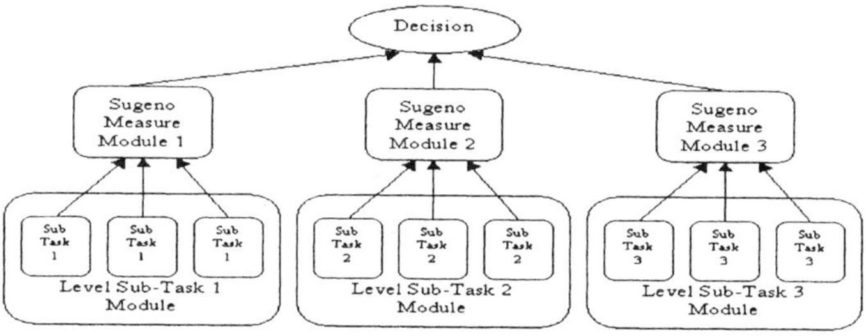

Fig. 4 Final Proposed Architecture.

The input to the modular system is a complete photograph. For performing the neural network training, the images of the human fingerprints were divided in three different regions. The first region consists of the area on top, which corresponds to Sub Task 1. The second region consists of the area on the middle, which corresponds to Sub Task 2. The third region consists of the area on the bottom, which corresponds to Sub Task 3. An example of this image division is shown in Fig. 5.

Fig. 5 Example of Image Division.

As output to the system we have an image that corresponds to the complete image that was originally given as input to the modular system, we show in Fig. 6 an example of this.

Description of the Integration Module

The integration modules performs its task in two phases. In the first phase, it obtains two matrices. The first matrix, called h, of dimension 3x3, stores the larger index values resulting from the competition for each of the members of the modules. The second matrix , called I, also of dimension 3x3, stores the image number corresponding to the particular index.

Once the first phase is finished, the second phase is initiated, in which the decision is obtained. Before making a decision, if there is consensus in the three modules, we can proceed to give the final decision, if there isn't consensus then we have search in matrix g to find the larger index values and then calculate the Sugeno fuzzy measures for each of the modules, using the following formula,

$$g(M_i) = h(A) + h(B) + \lambda\, h(A)\, h(B) \quad (5)$$

Where λ is equal to 1. Once we have these measures, we select the largest one to show the corresponding image.

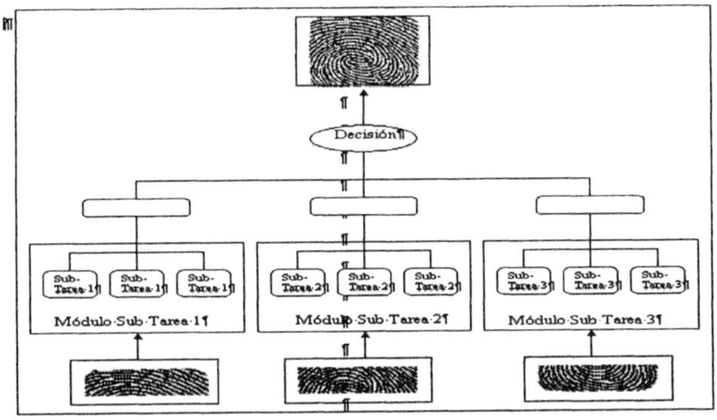

Fig. 6 Final architecture showing inputs and outputs.

Summary of Results

We describe in this section the experimental results obtained with the proposed approach using the 50 images as training data. We show in Fig. 7 a plot relating the percentage of recognition against the number of examples used in the experiments.

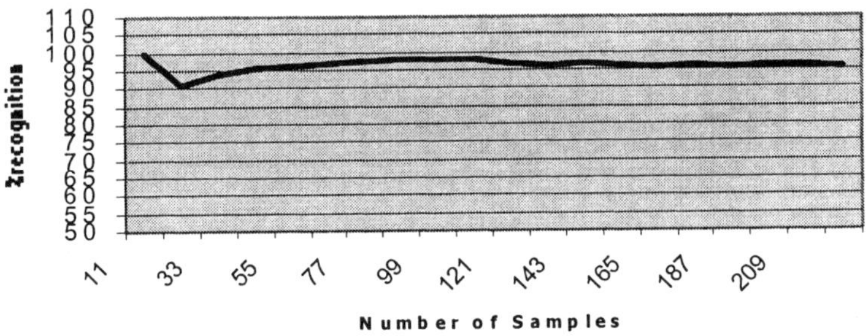

Fig. 7 Relation between recognition and number examples

In addition to the results presented before, we also compared the performance of the modular approach, against the performance of a monolithic neural network approach. The conclusion of this comparison was that for this type of input data, the monolithic approach is not feasible, since not only training time is larger, also the recognition is too small for real-world use. We show in Fig. 8 a plot showing this comparison but now in a graphical fashion.

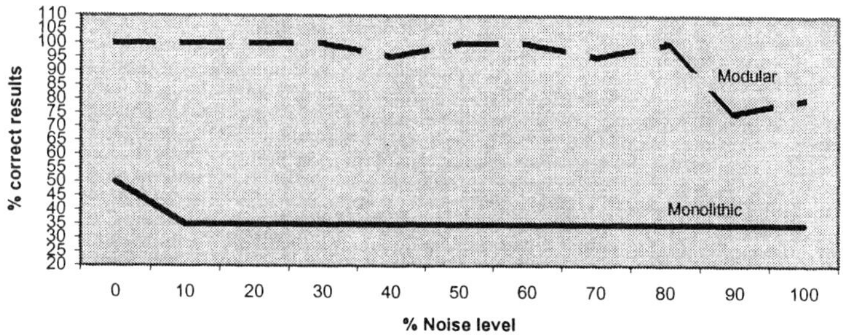

Fig. 8 Comparison between the modular and monolithic approach.

CONCLUSIONS

We showed in this paper the experimental results obtained with the proposed modular approach. In fact, we did achieve a 98.9% recognition rate on the testing data, even with an 80% level of applied noise. For the case of 100% level of applied noise, we did achieve a 96.4 % recognition rate on the testing data. The testing data included 10 images for each fingerprint in the training data. These 10 images were obtained by applying noise in a random fashion, increasing the level of noise from 10 to 100 %, to the training data. We also have to notice that it was achieved a 96.7 % of average reliability with our modular approach. These percentage values were obtained by averaging. In light of the results of our proposed modular approach, we have to notice that using the modular approach for human fingerprint pattern recognition is a good alternative with respect to existing methods, in particular, monolithic, gating or voting methods.

REFERENCES

A.J.C. Sharkey, Combining Artificial Neural Nets: Ensemble and Modular Multi-Nets Systems, Ed. Springer-Verlag, New York, 1998.

L. K. Hansen and P. Salomon. Neural Network Ensembles, IEEE Transactions on Pattern Analysis and Machine Intelligence, 1990.

S. Albrecht, A Modular Neural Network Architecture with Additional Generalization Abilities for High Dimensional Input Vectors, 1996.

Hsin-Chia Fu, Yen-Po Lee, Cheng-Chin Chiang and Hsiao-Tien Pao. Divide-and-Conquer Learning and Modular Perceptron Networks in IEEE Transaction on Neural Networks, vol. 12, 2001.

Egbert J.W. Boers and Herman Kuiper. Biological Metaphors and the Design of Modular Artificial Neural Networks. Departments of Computer Science and Experimental and Theoretical Psychology at Leid University, the Netherlands. 1992.

E. Ronco and P. Gawthrop. Modular neural networks: A State of the Art. Technical Report, Center for System and Control. University of Glasgow, Glasgow, UK, 1995.

B. Lu and M. Ito. Task Decomposition and module combination based on class relations: modular neural network for pattern classification. Technical Report, Nagoya Japan, 1998.

R. Murray-Smith and T. A. Johansen. Multiple Model Approaches to Modeling and Control. Taylor and Francis, 1997.

M Sugeno. Theory of fuzzy integrals and its application, Doctoral Thesis, Tokyo Institute of Technology, 1974.

R. R. Yager. Criteria Aggregations Functions Using Fuzzy Measures and the Choquet Integral, International Journal of Fuzzy Systems, Vol. 1, No. 2, December 1999.

A. Quezada, Reconocimiento de Huellas Digitales Utilizando Redes Neuronales Modulares y Algoritmos Geneticos. Thesis of Computer Science, Tijuana Institute of Technology, 2004.

O. Castillo and P. Melin, Soft Computing for Control of Non-Linear Dynamical Systems. Springer-Verlag, Heidelberg, Germany, 2001.

USING GENETIC ALGORITHM AND FUZZY LOGIC FOR THE IMPROVEMENT OF LOAD BALANCING IN SECONDARY NETWORKS

ANA BARBARA KNOLSEISEN
SÉRGIO F. MAYERLE
JORGE COELHO
MAURICIO SPERANDIO

UFSC – Federal University of Santa Catarina
LabPlan - Electrical Systems Planning Laboratory
Trindade - Florianópolis - SC - Brazil
P.O. Box: 476 CEP 88040-900

ABSTRACT

This work will present a model for reconfiguration of secondary distribution networks with a focus on balancing load between phases, achieved by selecting acceptable solutions from a intersection of fuzzy sets. These acceptable solutions then form an initial population for a genetic algorithm find the optimal alternative through a fitness function. The redistribution of load implies in transferring loads from one branch of the system to another, with a minimum set of actuation. For that, the chromosomes are allowed permutations between phases for each kind of consumer. The problem of balance will be characterized through a multi-objective focus, and its efficiency is assessed in a real system scheme.

INTRODUCTION

A balanced operation of the distribution system reduces probabilities of overload, however, the unbalance is an inherent characteristic of radial systems, caused mainly by the presence of unbalanced load [1].

The reconfiguration of distribution systems seeking balancing can be achieved, for instance, by means of load redistribution among feeder phases. The redistribution of load implies in transferring loads from one branch of the system to another, achieving an improvement in the operational condition of the system as a whole. The decision in favor of the best configuration, which should consider technical as well as economic factors, is usually a process that demands computational techniques, which has grown in the last few years [3, 4, 5, 6, 7, 8]. In [9] was presented a method where the problem of balance is characterized through a mono-objective focus and the model uses genetic algorithm to achieve the balancing. The theoretical background of genetic algorithms may be understood as a process of "intelligent" probabilistic search, which could be applied in a series of combinatory optimization problems [10].

In this work the model for the load balancing of secondary distribution networks is based on load transfer between networks phases, with a minimum set of actuation, achieved by selecting acceptable solutions from a intersection of fuzzy sets. These previous results then form a initial population for a genetic algorithm find the optimal alternative through a fitness function.

MODEL FOR THE BALANCING IN SECONDARY NETWORKS

The topology of low voltage networks may be defined by a graph $G=(N,A)$, where N is the set of nodes in the network, and A is the set of arcs, which connect these nodes. We say that $(i,j)\in A$ is a path of the network if between pair of nodes (i,j) there is a physical connection. In a general way, these networks present themselves as branches rooted in a node s, where the transformer is located. The model of balancing may be described as follows:

$$Max \quad z=f(\boldsymbol{V},\boldsymbol{I},\boldsymbol{Pl}) \qquad (1)$$

$$s.a: \quad V_i^k - V_j^k = R_{ij}^k \cdot I_{ij}^k \qquad \forall\, k\in K, \forall\,(i,j)\in A \qquad (2)$$

$$I_{ij}^k = \sum_{(j,m)\in A} I_{jm}^k + \sum_n \sum_\ell \frac{P_{n,j}^\ell}{V_j^k}\cdot x_{n,j}^{k\ell} \qquad \forall\, k\in K, \forall\,(i,j)\in A \qquad (3)$$

$$Pl_{ij}^k = R_{ij}^k \cdot \left(I_{ij}^k\right)^2 \qquad \forall\, k\in K, \forall\,(i,j)\in A \qquad (4)$$

$$V_s^k = V_{trafo} \qquad \forall\, k\in K \qquad (5)$$

$$\sum_k x_{n,j}^{k\ell} = 1 \qquad \forall n,j,\ell \qquad (6)$$

$$x_{n,j}^{k\ell}\in\{0,1\} \qquad \forall k,\ell,n,j \qquad (7)$$

where, $V=(V_j^k)$ is the voltage vector whose element V_j^k represents the voltage in the k phase on the $j\in N$ node; $\boldsymbol{I}=(I_{ij}^k)$ is the current vector whose element I_{ij}^k represents phase k current in the path $(i,j)\in A$; $\boldsymbol{Pl}=(Pl_{ij}^k)$ is the losses vector whose element Pl_{ij}^k represents loss; R_{ij}^k impedance in the k phase of the path $(i,j)\in A$; V_{trafo} is the reference voltage applied on the transformer; $P_{n,j}^\ell$ the power demanded by the lth phase of the nth consumer connected to the $j\in N$ node; $\boldsymbol{x}=(x_{n,j}^{k\ell})$ the binary variable vector, where $x_{n,j}^{k\ell}=1$ if the phase l actual load in the nth consumer connected to the $j\in N$ node should be allocated in the k phase; $x_{n,j}^{k\ell}=0$ otherwise.

In this model, Eq. (1) defines the objective to be maximized that characterizes the degree of adequacy of the solution. The restrictions Eq. (2), Eq. (3) and Eq. (4) define, respectively, voltage drop, current and electrical losses in each phase and path of the network, while Eq. (5) determines initial voltage condition applied on the transformer. The restrictions Eq. (6) and Eq. (7) ensure all loads to be allocated on one phase only, at the node in which the respective consumer should be connected.

The model is typically combinatory and non-linear, its resolution depends uniquely on the determination of the binary variable vector $\boldsymbol{x}=\left(x_{n,j}^{kl}\right)$, whose value allows us to determine all other variables in the model and, as a consequence, the merit function used.

MERIT FUNCTION FOR SOLUTION ASSESSMENT

Solution Adequate Criteria

Consider the set of viable solutions, defined by Eq. (6) and Eq. (7):

$$S_0 = \left\{ \boldsymbol{x} \mid \sum_k x_{n,j}^{k\ell} = 1, \forall n, j, \ell;\ x_{n,j}^{k\ell} \in \{0,1\} \right\} \tag{8}$$

In order to be considered adequate, a solution $\boldsymbol{x} \in S_0$ should satisfy some additional criteria:

Relative Voltage Drop:

$$S_1 = \left\{ \boldsymbol{x} \mid \frac{V_{trafo} - V_i^k}{V_{trafo}} \le \eta,\quad \forall k, i \in N \right\}$$

Transformer Loading:

$$S_2 = \left\{ \boldsymbol{x} \mid \frac{\sum_{(s,j)\in A} I_{sj}^k}{I_{trafo}} \le 1,\quad \forall k \right\}$$

Unbalance of Transformer

$$S_3 = \left\{ \boldsymbol{x} \mid \frac{I_{ij}^k}{I_{ij}^{\max}} \le 1,\quad \forall k, (i,j) \in A \right\}$$

Relative Electrical Loss

$$S_4 = \left\{ \boldsymbol{x} \mid \frac{\sum_k \sum_{(i,j)\in A} Pl_{ij}^k}{\sum_k \sum_n \sum_j P_{n,j}^k} \le \Delta \right\}$$

Maximum Number of Phase Transfer

$$S_5 = \left\{ \boldsymbol{x} \mid \frac{\sum_{k\ne\ell} x_{n,j}^{k\ell}}{\sum x_{n,j}^{k\ell}} \le \varepsilon \right\}$$

Pertinence Function

Although there may be norms that define acceptable limits to other adequacy criteria, it is reasonable to consider that, the closer to the limits the function is, the less adequate it will be. In this sense, the set of adequate solutions will be analyzed by *fuzzy sets*, through the pertinence functions. The set S_0 presents a precise definition, represented by the following pertinence function:

$$\mu_{S_0}(\boldsymbol{x}) = \begin{cases} 1 & \text{if } \sum_k x_{n,j}^{k\ell} = 1, \forall n, j, \ell;\ x_{n,j}^{k\ell} \in \{0,1\} \\ 0 & \text{otherwise} \end{cases} \tag{9}$$

Considering the need to satisfy all criterion simultaneously, and the pertinence function related to this intersection set as:

$$\mu_{S_0 \cap S_1 \cap S_2 \cap S_3 \cap S_4 \cap S_5}(\boldsymbol{x}) = \min\left(\mu_{S_0}(\boldsymbol{x}), \ldots, \mu_{S_5}(\boldsymbol{x})\right) \tag{10}$$

Thus, the search for the best solution to the problem consists in finding a vector $\boldsymbol{x}^* = \left(x_{n,j}^{kl}\right)$, so that:

$$\mu_{S_0 \cap S_1 \cap S_2 \cap S_3 \cap S_4 \cap S_5}(\boldsymbol{x}^*) = \max_{\boldsymbol{x}} \mu_{S_0 \cap S_1 \cap S_2 \cap S_3 \cap S_4 \cap S_5}(\boldsymbol{x}) \tag{11}$$

GENETIC ALGORITHM FOR THE SEARCH OF AN EFFICIENT SOLUTION

Structure of the Chromosome

For the problem in question, the determining characteristic of the solution is the indication of the phase switch scheme to be adopted for each consumer (Fig. 1). From an algebraic standpoint, each scheme may be represented as a permutation matrix (Fig. 1), which defines the values of the binary variables $x_{n,j}^{k\ell}$ associated to each consumer, in each node. In this matrix, the columns (ℓ) represent the present phases in the load scheme, while the lines (k)indicate the new phases of these loads. Considering the schemes of phase transfer to three-phase consumer presented, the following matrixes are produced.

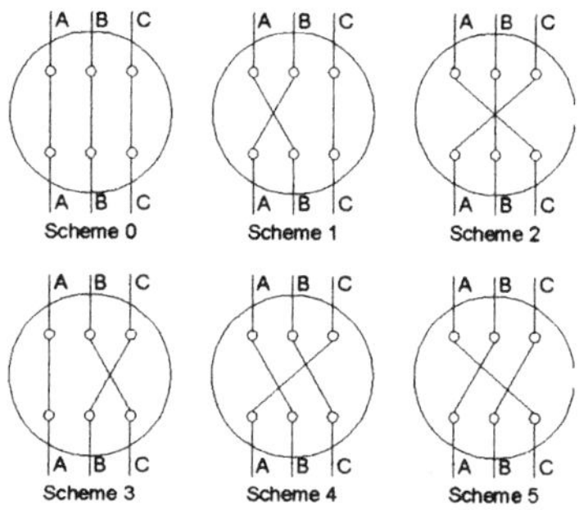

$$Scheme\ 0 \equiv \begin{bmatrix} 1 & 0 & 0 \\ 0 & 1 & 0 \\ 0 & 0 & 1 \end{bmatrix} \qquad Scheme\ 1 \equiv \begin{bmatrix} 0 & 1 & 0 \\ 1 & 0 & 0 \\ 0 & 0 & 1 \end{bmatrix}$$

$$Scheme\ 2 \equiv \begin{bmatrix} 0 & 0 & 1 \\ 0 & 1 & 0 \\ 1 & 0 & 0 \end{bmatrix} \qquad Scheme\ 3 \equiv \begin{bmatrix} 1 & 0 & 0 \\ 0 & 0 & 1 \\ 0 & 1 & 0 \end{bmatrix}$$

$$Scheme\ 4 \equiv \begin{bmatrix} 0 & 1 & 0 \\ 0 & 0 & 1 \\ 1 & 0 & 0 \end{bmatrix} \qquad Scheme\ 5 \equiv \begin{bmatrix} 0 & 0 & 1 \\ 1 & 0 & 0 \\ 0 & 1 & 0 \end{bmatrix}$$

Fig. 1: Possible schemes of phase transfer to three-phase consumers and matrixes that represent the permutation schemes for three-phase consumers.

All the permutation schemes, ensure satisfaction of the restrictions Eq. (6) and Eq. (7), as a consequence, for solutions formed with these schemes, we have $\mu_{S_0}(\boldsymbol{x}) = 1$. A vector may identify a fully viable solution to the balancing problem where each element represents the scheme to be adopted for a given consumer.

Fitness Evaluation

When all solution criteria are considered, the measure of fitness adopted is the value of the pertinence function presented in Eq. (12). Thus, for each solution $\mathbf{x}$ generated by the algorithm, the greater the level of *fitness*:

$$\begin{aligned} &Max \quad \mu = \min\left(\mu_{S_1}(\boldsymbol{x}), \mu_{S_2}(\boldsymbol{x}), \mu_{S_3}(\boldsymbol{x}), \mu_{S_4}(\boldsymbol{x}), \mu_{S_5}(\boldsymbol{x})\right) \\ &s.a. \quad x \in S_0 \end{aligned} \tag{12}$$

Considering that we wish to find a solution which maximizes this function, the measure should be considered in such a way that, the greater its value, the greater the ability of the individuals to adapt to their environment.

Natural Selection Process

The fitness is used in the algorithm to order the p individuals during the search process. The order is established so that $f_1 \geq f_2 \geq \ldots \geq f_p$. Thus, the first individual of the population presents the best *fitness*, while the last one presents the worst fitness, and will be replaced if a descendant is found. In the process of selection, a uniform probability distribution was considered.

Process of Reproduction

In this work the *single point crossover* is considered, since it has presented excellent results, which consists in choosing a random sectioning point in the structure of the ancestral chromosomes, and combining the left section of an ancestor with the right section of another ancestor. This operation allows two new descendants to be generated for each pair of ancestors selected.

Mutation Process

Through the operator of the mutation, the information which has been eliminated by the reproduction process, or which did not belong to the population, may be introduced along a number of generations. In the method, the mutation of an individual occurs at a constant rate, in random fashion, and consists in the switch of a gene swap by values different from those inherited.

NUMERICAL RESULTS

The sketch (Fig. 2) represents the geo-referenced shape of a secondary distribution network, in the south of Santa Catarina, under the jurisdiction of CELESC, distribution utility in the state. Such network will be the object of study in this article. Each node (post) of the network indicates where the consumer is located, and the node where the blue triangle is located indicates the position of the transformer. The load of the network is shown in [9]. Nominal voltage is 220V.

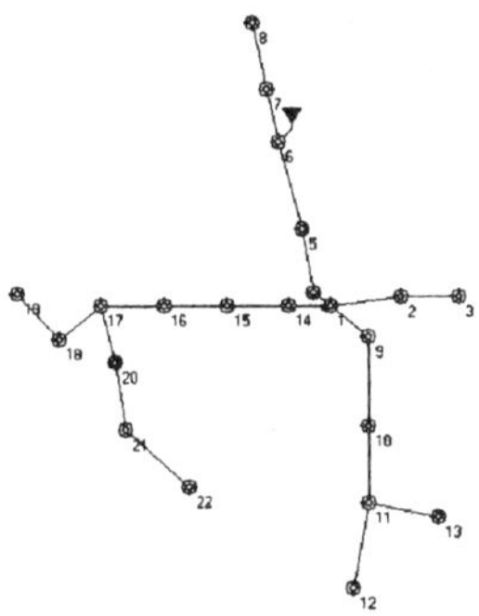

Fig. 2: Sketch of the distribution network in study.

Table 1 presents the voltage in the critical point (point number 12) in each phase, before and after balancing, as well as transformer unbalance and the biggest drop between critical points.

Table 1: Unbalance of Transformer and Voltage Drop.

	Before Balancing			**After Balancing**		
Voltage on critical point (V)	V_A	V_B	V_C	V_A	V_B	V_C
	202.85	206.71	208.58	204.62	207.34	205.16
Transformer unbalance (%)	11.7			1.1		
Voltage drop on critical point (%)	12.2			11.4		
Voltage drop on critical point (V)	28.1			26.4		

The genetic parameters used in the process of network balancing are: size of population=1000, mutation rate=0.01 and convergence precision=0.1, and the legal limit voltage in Brazil is 200.2V.

The analysis of the data after balancing shows a significant balance among voltage values in each phase. In relation to the voltage drop at the critical point there was an improvement (from 202.85 to 204.62), with a greater distance from the minimum legal limit and was noticed also an improvement in transformer unbalance (from 11.7% to 1.1%).

CONCLUSIONS

The model proposed for improving load balance in secondary networks, which seeks balance through reconfiguration of load connections, ensures improvement of distribution utility service quality due to the minimization of voltage drops along the main feeder.

It was shown, by means of the results presented, that the multi-objective approach obtain a significant balance among voltage values in each phase, an improvement in relation to the point with the greatest voltage drop, and a significant improvement in transformer unbalance, important for the balance of the system as a whole, and which also helps in the allocation of new consumers.

REFERENCES

[1] Silva, J.R.K.; Bezerra, U.H.. "A Model for Unbalanced Power Flow in Radial Energy Distribution Systems (in Portuguese)," in *XI Congresso Brasileiro de Automática,* São Paulo, Brazil, pp. 899-904, Set. 1996.

[2] Carvalho, P.M.S. et al."Distribution Network Expansion Planning Under Uncertainty: A Hedging Algorithm in an Evolutionary Approach," *IEEE Trans. Power Delivery*, vol. 15, pp. 412-416, Jan. 2000.

[3] Baran, M.E.; Wu, F.F. "Networks Reconfiguration in Distribution Systems for Loss Reduction and Load Balancing," *IEEE Trans. Power Delivery*, vol. 4, pp. 1401-1407, 1989.

[4] Wang, J.C.; Chiang, H.D.; Darling, G.R. "An Efficient Algorithm for Real Time Network Reconfiguration in Large Scale Unbalanced Distribution Systems," *IEEE Trans. Power Systems*, vol. 11, pp. 511-517, Feb. 1996.

[5] Kashen, M.A.; Ganapathy, V.; Jasmon, G. B. "Network Reconfiguration for Load Balancing in Distribution Networks," *IEE Proc Gener Transm Distrib*, vol. 146, pp. 563-567, 1999.

[6] Chen, T.H.; Cherng, J.T. "Optimal Phase Arrangement of Distribution Transformers Connected to a Primary Feeder for System Unbalanced Improvement and Loss Reduction Using a Genetic Algorithm," *IEEE Trans. Power Systems*, vol. 15, pp. 994-1000, Aug. 2000.

[7] Roytelman, I.et al. "Multi-Objective Feeder Reconfiguration by Distribution Management System," *IEEE Trans. Power Systems*, vol. 11, pp. 661-666, May 1996.

[8] Knolseisen, A.B. et al. "A Model for the Improvement of Load Balancing in Secondary Networks." IEEE Bologna PowerTech Conference, Bolonha, Itália, Jun. 2003.

[9] Coelho, J. et al. "Um Sistema de Apoio à Decisão Multicritério para o Balanceamento de Cargas em Redes Secundárias de Distribuição de Energia Elétrica." V SBQEE – Seminário Brasileiro sobre Qualidade de Energia Elétrica, Aracaju, SE, Ago. 2003.

[10] Davis, L. *Handbook of Genetic Algorithms*, New York: Van Nostrand Reinhold, 1991.

RANGE OPERATOR ENABLED GENETIC ALGORITHMS FOR HYPERSPECTRAL ANALYSIS

BRIAN L STEWARD
Iowa State University
Agric. and Biosystems Engineering
Ames, Iowa

DANIEL A ASHLOCK
Iowa State University
Mathematics
Ames, Iowa

STEVE M SHANER
Iowa State University
Computer Science
Ames, Iowa

ROBERT P EWING
Iowa State University
Agronomy
Ames, Iowa

AMY L KALEITA
Iowa State University
Agric. and Biosystems Engineering
Ames, Iowa

ABSTRACT
A novel genetic algorithm was developed using mathematical operations on spectral ranges to explore spectral range/operator space and to better identify useful relationships between spectral data and reference parameters. Each gene specified the starting wavelength and length of a spectral range, and an associated mathematical range operator; individuals contained multiple genes. Partial least squares (PLS) regression was used to develop models predicting reference variables from the range operations. Two data sets were investigated: (1) reflectance spectra from corn plant canopies, with proportion of plants starting to shed pollen as reference data, and (2) near infrared transmittance spectra from bulk corn kernels, with protein content as reference data. PLS models developed using the spectral range/operator framework had higher fitness than conventional full-spectrum PLS models for the canopy data, and similar fitness for the kernel data set. The range/operator framework enabled identification of those spectral range/mathematical operator combinations with the most predictive capability, which may have utility in sensor and algorithm design and in developing breeding stock for other algorithms.

INTRODUCTION

The interest in hyperspectral or spectroscopic sensing for agricultural applications comes from the hope that the resulting high dimensional data will lead to new understanding that was not attainable using only broad spectral sensors. However, with the availability of high spectral resolution sensing technology comes the problem of how to extract meaningful relationships from such overwhelming quantities of data. One approach has been to use conventional linear methods such as principal component analysis (PCA) or partial least squares (PLS) to relate linear combinations of spectral bands to independent physical variables of interest. These "soft modeling" approaches are powerful but limited, because they (a) apply only linear relationships between spectral variables, (b) incorporate little or no domain knowledge or physical first principles into the analysis (Martens and Martens, 2001), and (c) treat each channel as independent, rather than using information implicitly embedded in the structure of the spectrum.

A second approach uses domain knowledge to calculate indices using simple mathematical operations consisting of ratios, differences, and sums such as the Normalized Difference Vegetation Index (NDVI; Rouse et al., 1973). Furthermore, numerous studies have addressed the utility of derivative approaches to remote sensing data analysis (Demetriades-Shah et al., 1990; Clevers et al., 2002). With increasing numbers of spectral variables, the number of possible operational combinations can be prohibitive.

Evolutionary computation, and specifically the subset called genetic algorithms, are adaptive search methods that deal powerfully with difficult search problems without getting stuck in local extremes in the search space (Goldberg, 1989). Evolutionary computation has only rarely been used in spectral analysis. Tang et al. (2000) used a genetic algorithm (GA) to identify a region in color space for vegetation segmentation in field images. Rauss et al. (2000) used genetic programming (GP) to develop a classification algorithm for an image with 28 spectral bands. Burman (1997, 1999) used evolutionary computation methods to perform automatic object detection and recognition in hyperspectral images. Yao and Tian (2003) used a GA to select hyperspectral bands to include in a principal components transformation for information extraction. The few studies that have used evolutionary computation in spectral analysis have focused on linear combinations of the original data. To our knowledge, no studies to date have used evolutionary computation on spectral range operators such as slope.

The objective of this research was to use genetic algorithms to search the space of spectral ranges and operators to (a) determine the utility of range operators in hyperspectral data analysis, and (b) find those spectral regions with the greatest predictive capacity with respect to the reference variable.

MATERIALS

Two data sets were used for this work: (1) 63 visible and near infrared (NIR) reflectance spectra (321 wavebands from 397 to 902 nm) from corn canopies, collected in support of research to predict corn pollination, and (2) 920 NIR transmittance spectra (104 wavebands from 850 to 1048 nm) from bulk samples of corn kernel to be used for constituent analysis. An independent data set consisting of 429 samples of bulk kernel transmittance spectra was also available. Reference data for the canopy spectra were in-situ observations at 1- or 2-day intervals of the proportion of the crop at anthesis (pollen shed commenced). Reference data for the kernel spectra were protein measurement determined through standard reference chemistry methods. In both cases the spectra were converted to absorbance data.

METHODS

The range/operator-enabled genetic algorithm (ROE-GA) was developed in Matlab script (The Mathworks, Natick, MA) to search the space of possible spectral ranges in combination with several basic mathematical range operators. Features extracted in the form of the multiple range operators were used as inputs into PLS, which was used to calibrate a model for predicting associated reference variables. Cross validation was performed using multivariate analysis algorithms in PLS Toolbox (Eigenvector Research, Manson, WA), yielding the standard error of cross validation (SECV) as the fitness for the GA.

Each chromosone consisted of genes comprised of three numbers representing (a) the spectral starting point, (b) the length of the range and (c) a code for the operator. Six simple range operators were used: mean, median, maximum, minimum, variance, and slope (determined from a regression line fit to the spectral data over the range). In order to determine whether individual range operators could lead to relatively lower SECV models, a reduced version of the ROE-GA was also run, using a single fixed operator specified by the user. In this reduced case, only the starting point and length of the ranges were adjusted through evolution.

The population was sorted by fitness, and the less fit half of the population was discarded. The upper half was then replicated to form a new lower half, and children were formed using double point crossover. Each child was selected for mutation, and one to three genes were randomly selected for mutation in which either the starting point, length of range, or operator was mutated

The fitness for an individual was its SECV as calculated through a PLS cross-validation procedure (PLS Toolbox, Eigenvalue Research). The ROE-GA stopped when either 200 generations had passed, or more than one half of the population contained duplicate individuals

In order to get baseline full-spectrum calibration model performance, calibration models were developed using PLS operating on the full spectral data with no preprocessing. Cross validation was accomplished using random segment selection in which the data was divided into five segments. Each segment was predicted using a calibration model calculated from the remaining four segments. This five segment cross-validation was repeated ten times. Model performance was measured using standard error of cross validation (SECV). The minimum SECV across full spectral models with 1 to 20 latent variables was used as a measure of model performance.

RESULTS

The full spectrum PLS models resulted in SECV of 4.3% and 0.33% respectively for the canopy-begin pollen shed and the bulk corn kernel-protein calibration models (Table 1). The relative performance determinant (AACC, 1999; RPD; standard deviation of reference/SECV) for the canopy-begin pollen shed model was 3.52, indicating that the model has potential for quantitative prediction since model SECV was less than 30 percent of the variation in the the reference data. For the kernel transmittance data set, the RPD of the model was 5.2, again indicating good predictive ability.

When the fixed operator ROE-GA was applied to the data sets, the SECV for the top 20 models decreased substantially for the canopy model to a range of 0.5 to 1.4% across all operators (Table 1). Given the small number of samples in this dataset, most likely the lowered SECV is evidence of overfitting. SECV did not typically reach a minimum within the 20 latent variables. For protein calibration models, SECV increased over that of the full spectrum model to a range of 0.48 % to 1.32%. The variable operator ROE-GA had SECV of 0.8%

Table 1. SECV from full spectra PLS models and the best 20 models from each ROE-GA run. Mean range length from each ROE-GA run also included.

Algorithm	Range operator	Canopy – Begin Pollen Shed Model		Kernel – Protein Model	
		SECV (%)	Mean Range Length	SECV (%)	Mean Range Length
Full Spectrum PLS	NA	4.3	NA	0.33	NA
ROE-GA Fixed Operator	Mean	0.9	18.6	0.48	20.6
	Median	0.8	20.5	0.49	12.2
	Maximum	0.9	21.2	0.49	13.5
	Minimum	0.9	21.4	0.52	11.3
	Variance	1.4	17.9	1.32	16.2
	Slope	0.5	17.7	0.48	14.9
ROE-GA Var. Oper.	NA	0.8	20.7	0.36	20.5

and 0.36% respectively for canopy and kernel models, showing similar or better performance as the full spectrum model.

For the kernel-protein model, the test data set was used to compare predictive performance of the GA-derived models with the full-spectrum PLS model. Calibration models were developed for the extracted features specified by each individual in the five populations resulting from the variable operator ROE-GA. Then using the test set, protein was predicted and SEP (standard error of prediction) was calculated. SEP was 0.61 for a full-spectrum PLS model with 14 latent variables. The GA-extracted range operator feature models had SEPs that ranged from 14.5 to 0.40. Thus even though some cases had poor performance, GA-extracted range operator feature models were generally able to explain a substantial amount of variability (Figure 1), and in several cases their SEP was lower than that of the full spectrum model.

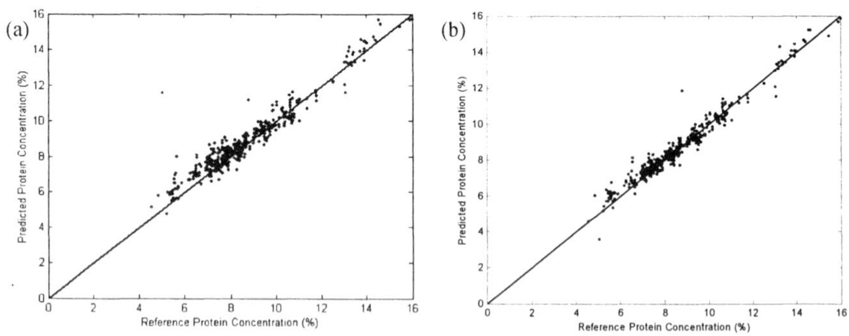

Figure 1. Predicted protein concentration against reference protein concentration using (a) full spectrum PLS model and (b) GA-extracted feature model.

The mean number of spectral variable selections for each operator was used as intensity of a gray scale and showed how ranges of the spectrum were selected by ROE-GA for both data sets (Figure 2). In the case of the canopy models, the region from about 600 to 670 nm was rarely selected by any operator, indicating little relevant information in this region. However, in the red edge region (750-850 nm), wavebands were heavily preferred by mean, median, variance, and slope operators. The slope operator, for example, tended to use ranges from 700 to about 802 nm, with very little selection of other ranges. Slope also only used very narrow bands in the red edge range.

For the kernel models, each of the operators except minimum and median had ranges with high frequency of selection, and often these ranges were different from one operator to another. This shows that certain ranges may have information that can be accessed better by one specific operator and not accessed well by others.

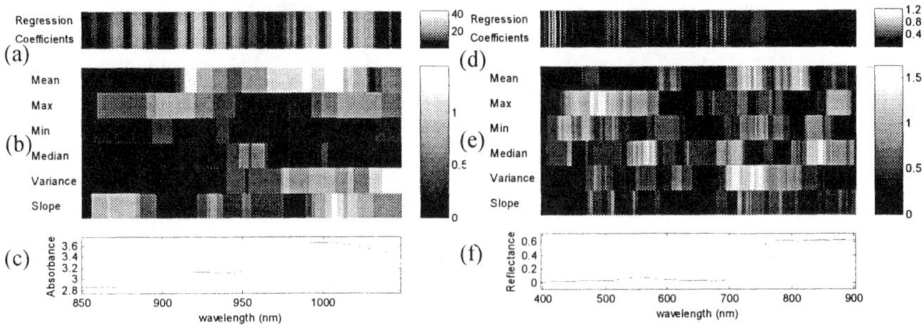

Figure 2. The absolute value of regression coefficients from full spectra PLS calibration models for (a) using bulk corn kernel transmittance (c) used to predict percent protein and (d) using corn canopy reflectance (e) used to predict percentage of plants beginning to shed pollen. Mean number of times a variable was selected, (b) and (e), by a range operator from unique model populations of from ROE-GA algorithm.

CONCLUSIONS

This work shows that a collection of a few simple range operators are sufficient to discover useful feature sets. When these features are used to develop PLS models, the models exhibit performance in cross-validation similar or exceeding that of full spectrum models. Another useful outcome is the association of particular operators with spectral ranges, which may prove useful in understanding how spectral ranges are associated with reference variables of interest.

While we have applied this representation to two hyperspectral modeling problems, the technique has far broader potential application. Any problem involving large noisy data sets that need to be modeled could conceivably benefit from the techniques used here.

ACKNOWLEDGEMENTS

This research of the Iowa Agriculture and Home Economics Experiment Station, Ames, Iowa, Project No. 3612, was supported by Hatch Act and State of Iowa funds, the Iowa State University Special Research Initiation Grant Program, and the Iowa Space Grant Consortium. Special thanks to M. E. Westgate, J. L. Hatfield, and the National Soil Tilth Laboratory for the corn canopy reflectance data, and to the ISU Grain Quality Laboratory for the corn kernel transmittance data.

REFERENCES

AACC, 1999, "AACC method 39-00: Near-infrared methods: Guidelines for model development and maintenance." In *Approved Methods of the American Association of Cereal Chemists*, 10th ed, AACC, St. Paul, Minn.

Burman, J. A., 1997, "Non-literal pattern recognition method for hyperspectral imagery exploitation using evolutionary computing methods," *In Imaging spectrometry III, SPIE Proceedings,* Bellingham, WA., Vol. 3118, pp. 250-261.

Burman, J. A., 1999, "Hybrid pattern recognition method using evolutionary computing techniques applied to the exploitation of hyperspectral imagery and medical spectral data," *In Image and signal processing for remote sensing V: SPIE proceedings*, Bellingham, WA, Vol. 3781, pp. 348-357.

Clevers, J. G., S. M. De Jong, G. F. Epema, F. D. Van Der Meer, W. H. Bakker, A. K. Skidmore, and K. H. Scholte, 2002, "Derivation of the red edge index using the MERIS standard band setting," *International Journal of Remote Sensing,* Vol. 23, pp. 3169-3184.

Demetriades-Shah, T. H., M. D. Steven, and J. A. Clark, 1990, "High resolution derivative spectra in remote sensing," *Remote Sensing of Environment,* Vol. 33, pp. 55-64.

Goldberg, D. E., 1989, "Sizing populations for serial and parallel genetic algorithms." In *Proc. 3rd Int. Conference on Genetic Algorithms*, Morgan Kaufman, San Mateo, Calif, pp. 70-79.

Martens, H. and M. Martens, 2001, *Multivariate Analysis of Quality*, John Wiley, New York.

Rauss, P. J., J. M. Daida, and S. Chaudhary, 2000, "Classification of spectral imagery using genetic programming," *Proc. of the Genetic and Evolutionary Computation Conference,* July 10-12, Las Vegas, NV, Morgan Kaufmann Publishers, San Francisco.

Rouse, J. W., R. H. Haas, J. A. Schell, and D. W. Deering, 1973, "Monitoring vegetation systems in the Great Plains with ERTS," *Proceedings, 3rd ERTS Symposium*, Vol 1, pp. 48-62.

Tang, L., L. F. Tian, and B. L. Steward, 2000, "Color image segmentation with genetic algorithm for in-field weed sensing," *Transactions of the ASAE,* Vol. 43, pp. 1019-1027.

Yao, H. and Tian, L., 2003, "A genetic algorithm-based selective principal component analysis (ga-spca) method for high dimensional data feature extraction." *IEEE Transactions on Geoscience and Remote Sensing,* Vol. 41, pp. 1469 -1478.

A MIXER APPROACH FOR MULTIPLE CRITERIA SINGLE MACHINE SCHEDULING BY USING GENETIC ALGORITHMS

GÜRSEL A. SÜER(*), JOEL SANTOS(**), RAMON VAZQUEZ (**), SATYAJIT CHAKRAVARTY(*), DAVID ALLARD(*)

(*) Industrial and Manufacturing Systems Engineering
Ohio University
Athens, Ohio 45701, USA

(**) Electrical and Computer Engineering
University of Puerto Rico-Mayaguez
Mayaguez, Puerto Rico 00681, USA

ABSTRACT

This paper focuses on deterministic single machine scheduling with nonzero ready times. The objective is to sequence the jobs such that both maximum tardiness (T_{max}) and number of tardy jobs (n_T) are minimized. However, no preference is established between n_T and T_{max} and we aim to find non-dominated solutions. The proposed approach has two main elements: 1) Individual Population Evolvers (IPEs) and 2) Population Mixer (PM). IPEs focus on optimizing the designated performance measure while PM mixes solutions to improve both measures. The experimentation performed shows that mixing both populations at the MIXER improve the set of non-dominated solutions when the total number of solutions kept constant. The MIXER approach results were compared with the Optimal Pareto Frontier in 10-job category and finally the proposed approach was compared with another multi-objective Genetic Algorithm Approach. The results show that the MIXER approach performed very well in both comparisons.

1. INTRODUCTION

This paper focuses on deterministic single machine scheduling with nonzero ready times. The objective is to sequence the jobs such that both maximum tardiness (T_{max}) and number of tardy jobs (n_T) are minimized. However, no preference is established between n_T and T_{max} and we aim to find non-dominated solutions. The maximum tardiness measures the worst value of tardiness, i.e. $T_{max} = \max(T_i)$. On the other hand, tardiness for job (i) is given as $T_i = \max(0, c_i - d_i)$ where c_i is the completion time, d_i is the due date. The Earliest Due Date (EDD) rule finds the optimal solution in the case of zero ready times. When there are non-zero ready times, there are two cases to be considered; 1) preemption allowed, 2) preemption not allowed. In the former case, a job currently processed is removed from the machine if its due date is greater than the due date of a new arriving job. Once a job is completed, all available jobs are checked and the one with the Earliest Due Date is assigned. In this case, the EDD rule is applied as a dispatching rule (MEDD) and it finds the optimal solution (Jackson [6]). However, when preemption is not allowed, the scheduling task gets more complex. If the next job in the sequence has ready time lower than machine available time, it is assigned to the machine right away. On the other hand, if the ready time of the next job in the sequence is greater than machine available time, then there are two possible strategies: 2a) keep the machine idle until the job becomes available (Delay Strategy), or 2b) keep the machine busy by assigning the first available job in the sequence (Non-delay Strategy). What makes this problem even more complex is that the delay and non-delay strategies can be defined for each job independently. This problem is known as NP-hard and some branch-and-bound procedures have been suggested for similar problems. In this paper, we focus on 'preemption-not-allowed' case.

The second performance measure considered in this paper is minimizing the number of tardy jobs. A job is considered tardy when its completion time is greater than its due date ($c_i > d_i$). All zero ready time version has been solved by Moore[7] in an optimal fashion. The authors are not aware of any study reporting "preemption allowed" version when there are non-zero ready times. As in T_{max} problem, Delay and Nondelay strategies are both applicable for n_T problem as well when preemption is not allowed.

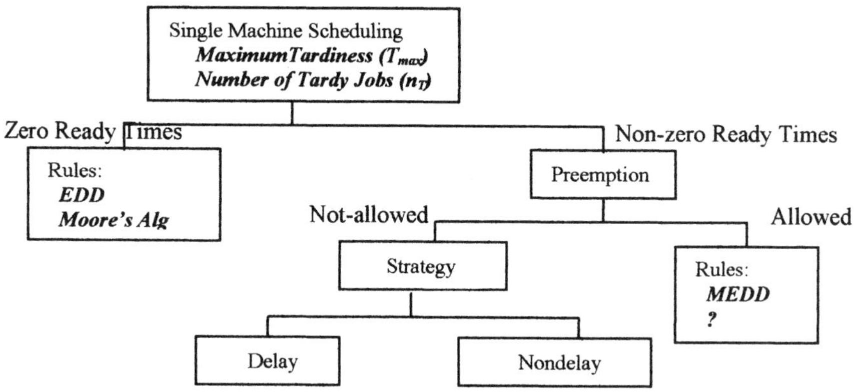

Figure 1. Summary of Single Machine Scheduling Problems wrt n_T and T_{max}

2. LITERATURE REVIEW

Fonseca and Fleming [3], Horn [4], and Tamaki, Kita and Kobayashi [12] have been surveying the application of GA to multi-objective optimization. Many fitness assignment mechanisms have been proposed, starting with Schaffer [10] with the Vector-Evaluated Genetic Algorithm (VEGA) approach to solve multi-objective problems. Horn, Nafpliotis and Goldberg [5] proposed the Pareto Tournament Method, which is a niched version of the Pareto Ranking-Based Approach. Murata, Ishibushi and Tanaka [8] suggested a Random-Weight Approach in order to create a statistically uniform selection pressure toward the Pareto Frontier, while Cheng and Gen [1] proposed an Adaptive-Weight Approach also to create selection pressure, but toward a specific "ideal point." Osyczka and Kundu [9] worked on multi-criteria optimization problems and proposed a Distance Method to assign fitness values according to its distance to the Pareto Solutions obtained in the previous generation.

3. PROPOSED MIXER APPROACH

In this section, the proposed mixer approach is explained briefly. The details of individual evolvers can be found in Süer et.al. [11] where minimizing average flow time is targeted in the case of non-zero ready times.

3.1 General Methodology

This study deals with multiple performance measures. The proposed approach has two main elements: 1) Individual Population Evolvers (IPEs) and 2) Population Mixer. IPEs focus on optimizing the designated performance measure while Population Mixer considers solutions coming from individual performance evolvers and try to find non-dominated solutions. IPEs work simultaneously and then feed the Population Mixer. The function of the Mixer is to "mix" the solutions that come from the independent evolvers in a "Genetic way," meaning that mixing is achieved by using customized GA operators. Later, selected solutions from the Mixer are fed back to IPEs for further improvement with respect to their designated performance measure after being exposed to solutions that consider other performance measures in the Mixer. This complete cycle is referred to as a "run". This process is repeated several items as defined by the user (number of runs). A graphical representation of the relations between the independent population evolvers and the Mixer are shown in Figure 2.

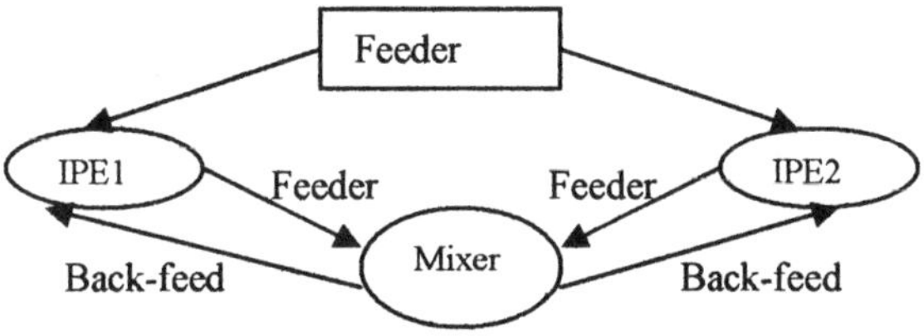

Figure 2. The Proposed Mixer Approach

3.2 Feeding, Mating, Back-Feeding Operators

For the mixer, additional GA operators were needed in addition to the operators used for IPEs. In this section, these operators are briefly defined.

3.2.1 Feed Operator

An adaptive feeding strategy is used. In this strategy, each population is assigned a *feeding probability* based on their respective percents of improvement. The higher the improvement with respect to a performance, the lower the feeding probability for that evolver in the next run. The Mixer is fed by selecting a population randomly based on its respective feeding probability, and then selecting a chromosome randomly, based on the chromosome's reproduction probability.

3.2.2 Mating Operator

Pairs to be mated in the MIXER are selected randomly.

3.2.3 Back-Feed Operator

The IPEs are fed with randomly selected chromosomes from the Mixer.

4. EXPERIMENTS AND RESULTS

In this section, experiments performed and the results obtained are discussed.

4.1 The Impact of Mixer

Various experimentations have been performed to i) find the best Mixer settings for various scenarios ii) test the effectiveness of the Mixer strategy in finding non-dominated solutions. A randomly generated 30-job problem has been used in the experimentation. The mutation probability for Individual Population Evolvers (IPE) and Mixer is .01. The population size for IPEs is 50. The delay and nondelay strategies are assigned randomly to each gene in individual population evolvers. IPE_1 focuses on minimizing n_T whereas IPE_2 targets minimizing T_{max}. Two different Mixer population sizes (50,100) and 6 different Mixer generation levels (10,25,50,100,200 and 500) have been tested in the experimentation. As a result, a total of 37 different cases have been generated. Four major scenarios have been generated such that the total number of generations of evolvers remains 1200 as shown in Table 1.

Senario	# gen	# runs	Total # gen
I	1200	0	1200
II	600	1	1200
III	400	2	1200
IV	300	3	1200

Table 1. Four Scenarios Generated

4.1.1 Results of Scenarios

In scenario I, each IPE evolves its population for 1200 generations, with no Mixer intervention. In scenario II, the results show that case (500,50) produced the best results. In scenario III, no single case dominated in terms of frequency of finding the overall non-dominated solutions. Cases (10,100), (200,50) and (500,50) are among the better ones. Finally, in scenario IV, even though no single case dominated, several cases produced acceptable frequencies. Interestingly, case (500,50) produced the lowest maximum variation and second lowest average variation.

4.1.2 Comparison of Scenarios

The summary of the entire experimentation is given in Figure 3. It is important to note that the sets in which the Mixer intervened produced better results. The scenarios (400, 3) and (300,4) continued to result in newer non-dominated solutions.

4.2 Consistency Test

The consistency test was conducted by running 10 identical experiments and then comparing results for each run. The parameters for this experiment have been set at IPE as (600,2), and at Mixer as (500,50). While the highest coefficient of variation is 0.0812, the average is only 0.0432 (can be considered as consistent).

4.3 Comparison with Optimal Pareto Frontier

In this section, the pareto frontier obtained using the proposed approach was compared with the optimal pareto frontier derived from the permutation schedules. The problem size was restricted to 10-job problems. We found the optimal solution in each of 5 problems using 0-run, 1-run, 2-run, and 3-run combinations.

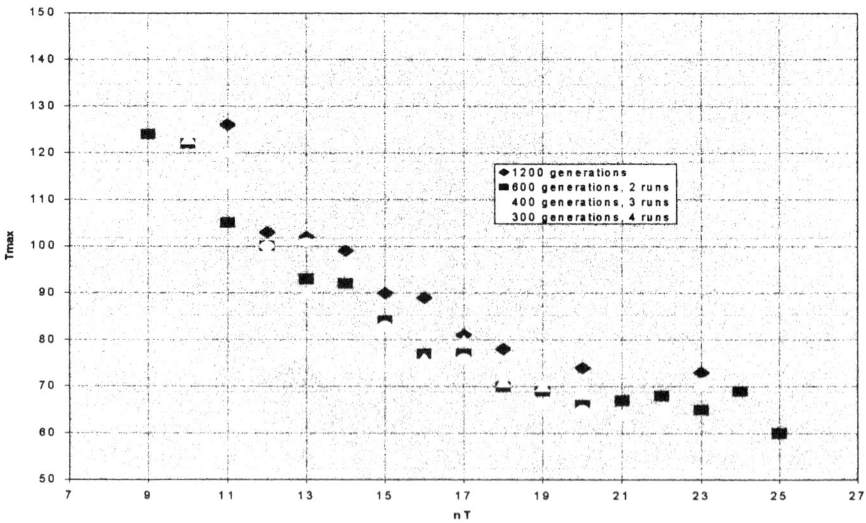

Figure 3. Global Non-Dominated Solutions

4.4 Comparison with Another Approach

In this section, the proposed approach was compared with the GA-based multi-objective optimization approach given by Cochran-Horng-Fowler [2]. The same parameters were used in both approaches to be consistent in the analysis. Five 50-job problems were generated randomly. The results are summarized in Tables 2a and 2b. Only 5 instances CHF produced better results than MIXER (bolded) with respect to at least one case of MIXER. Therefore, we can easily conclude that the MIXER approach dominated CHF in these problems. This experimentation also confirmed the results we have obtained in 4.1 where as the number of runs increased newer non-dominated solutions were obtained. The distribution of non-dominated solutions (underlined) across the number of runs is 16, 10, 13 and 6, for 1-run, 2-run, 3-run and 4-run cases, respectively. Another observation is that the MIXER approach produced wider range of pareto values than CHF method.

	Problem 1					Problem 2					Problem 3				
	CHF	1R	2R	3R	4R	CHF	1R	2R	3R	4R	CHF	1R	2R	3R	4R
nT	Tmax														
20															
21												392	426		
22			406									352	363	341	
23		394	392	372			360		400	378	402	293	323	313	353
24		348	376	327	362		345	374	351	326	**329**	290	304	303	337
25	394	336	338		353	350	339	334	325	333	321	283		278	309
26	361	328	306	319	339		314	319	306	307	306				295
27	325	312	296	295	318	332	311	284	304	300	302	266	283		282
28	306	299			298	**290**	292	273	274	226	281	258	271	269	260
29		286	289								279	257	247		
30		279	283	288	289		266		270	282				255	
31	302				271	277	265	264	264	274	271	254	243	250	
32	286	265	271	279				255		266		249			
33	281		261	256	265				262	261	258	243			
34	265	258					258		254	253					258
35				251					253					249	
36		259			260		262	250	250						
37		255			254			249							
38								246							
39								237							

Table 2a. CHF vs. Mixer Results (Problems 1,2,3)

	Problem 4					Problem 5				
	CHF	1-R	2-R	3-R	4-R	CHF	1-R	2-R	3-R	4-R
nT	Tmax									
13							379	346	322	387
14							361	315	315	373
15						400	318	267	296	351
16						356	311	258	268	296
17						311	284		275	261
18						-	250	268	247	
19						304	229	238	233	230
20		402				281	216	217	224	
21		323	281	319	321	256	214	208	210	229
22		253	257	297	283	**248**		205	-	195
23	331	-	-	265	260	246	200		198	
24	288	248	-	-	-	229				178
25		228	234	251	259	-	195		191	
26	269	-	-	-	239	-				
27	257	-	231	222	-	217		192		198
28	254	221	227	-	231	-				
29	242	-	215	224	-	203				176
30	**226**	218		-	229					
31	**224**	203		-	232					
32				-	216					
33				223						

Table 2b. CHF vs. Mixer Results (Problems 4,5)

5. CONCLUSIONS AND FUTURE WORK

The analysis in this study showed that the MIXER approach is feasible approach to deal with multiple performance measures. GA continued to find better instances as the number of runs increased. Since more runs mean different populations mix more often, this increased the chances to get better solutions with respect to both measures. However, there is decreasing benefit as the number runs increases. We recommend the user to try different number of runs as opposed to choosing only value and experiment with it. In 10-job category, MIXER found the optimal pareto frontier in each case. In 50-job category, the proposed approach outperformed the CHF approach.

We expect to continue experimentation with this approach and develop alternative strategies for feeding, mating and back-feeding operators.

References

1. Cheng, R. and Gen, M., An adaptive superplane approach for multiple objective optimization problems, Technical Report, Ashikaga Institute of Technology, 1998.
2. Cochran, J.K.,, Horng, S., Fowler, J.W., A multi-population genetic algorithm to solve multi-objective scheduling problem for parallel machines. Computers and Operations Research, Vol. 30, p. 1087-1102, 2003.
3. Fonseca, C. and Fleming, P., *An overview of evolutionary algorithms in multiobjective optimization*, Evolutionary Computation, vol. 3, no. I, pp. 1-16, 1995.
4. Horn, J., "Multicriterion decision making", in Bäck, T., Fogel, D., and Michalewicz Z., editors, *Handbook of Evolutionary Computation*, pp. 517-522, Oxford University Press, NY, 1997.
5. Horn, J., Nafpliotis, N. and Goldberg, D., A niched Pareto genetic algorithm for multiobjective optimization, in Fogel, D., editor, *Proceedings of the First IEEE Conference on Evolutionary Computation*, pp. 82-87, IEEE Press, Piscataway, NJ, 1994.
6. Jackson, J.R., Scheduling a Production Line to Minimize Maximum Tardiness. Research Report 43, Management Science Research Project, University of California, Los Angeles.
7. Moore, J.M., An n-Job, *One Machine Sequencing Algorithm for Minimizing the Number of Late Jobs*, Management Science, Vol.15, pp.102-109, 1968.
8. Murata, T., Ishibuchi, H., and Tanaka, H., *Multiobjective genetic algorithm and its application to flowshop scheduling*, Computers and Industrial Engineering, vol. 30, no. 4, pp. 957-968, 1996.
9. Osyczka, A., Kundu, S., A modified distance method for multicriterion optimization using genetic algorithm, *Computers and Industrial Engineering*, vol. 30, no. 4, pp. 871-882, 1996.
10. Schaffer, J., Multiple objective optimization with vector evaluated genetic algorithms, in Grefenstete, J. J., editor, *Proceedings of the First International Conference on Genetic Algorithms*, pp. 93-100, Lawrence Erlbaum Associates, Hillsdale, NJ, 1987.
11. Süer, G. A., Vazquez, R. and Santos, J., *Evolutionary Programming for Minimizing the Average Flow Time in the Presence of Non-zero Ready Times*, International Journal of Computers and Industrial Engineering, Vol. 45, pp.331-344, 2003.
12. Tamaki, H., Kita, H. and Kobayashi, S., "Multiobjective optimization by genetic algorithms: a review", in Fogel, D., editor, *Proceedings of the IEEE International Conference on Evolutionary Computation*, pp. 517-522, IEEE Press, Piscataway, NJ, 1996.

EVOLUTIONARY COMPUTATION APPLIED TO MELODY GENERATION

MATT D. JOHNSON
Computer Science Department
University of Missouri-Rolla
Rolla, Missouri

DANIEL R. TAURITZ
Computer Science Department
University of Missouri-Rolla
Rolla, Missouri

RALPH W. WILKERSON
Computer Science Department
University of Missouri-Rolla
Rolla, Missouri

ABSTRACT
One of the major goals in the field of computer generated music is capturing the intangible human perception which determines whether or not a melody is "good." Human perception of music is extremely difficult to encode in a computer because doing so requires modeling human experiences which combine to form an individual's perception. Modeling perception is even more difficult when one considers that every person on earth has a unique vantage point. A solution employed by many researchers in the field is selecting one genre of music and building models from "good" selections in that style of music.

The principal goal of this research is to determine whether a tree based music model can be used in an evolutionary algorithm fitness function to rate computer generated melodies. Well-known examples of church hymnody were employed in the construction of our music model. The results presented show that tree based music models are effective music critics when combined with application specific genetic operators.

INTRODUCTION

In recent years, personal computers have become tools used to store and typeset sheet music. There is currently research underway which will hopefully lead to computer applications that are capable of generating and arranging music as well as a human being can.

This paper presents an evolutionary algorithm which generates melodies in the traditional style of church hymnody. The resulting melodies are well suited for most soprano vocalists. Alto, tenor, and bass parts are generated to accompany the melody using CAVM, a tool that automatically adds voice parts to an existing melody (Johnson, Wilkerson, 2001).

RESEARCH METHODOLOGY

The decision to use an evolutionary algorithm to generate a melody is driven by one main factor—complexity. An average soprano vocalist can sing eighteen different pitches. There are 9 note durations typically found in church hymnody: whole, dotted half, half, dotted quarter, quarter, dotted eighth, eighth, dotted sixteenth, and sixteenth. The number of notes found in a typical hymn ranges from roughly 20 to 60 (40 on average). Given this information, the number of potential melodies is approximately $2.4 * 10^{88}$.

Reduction of the search space is desireable to make the problem more manageable. This is done by acting on two observations. First, most melodies stay within the key of the musical piece. Second, the range of most melodies does not exceed one octave. By constraining the melody to notes within one key and one octave, the number of pitches drops from 18 to 8. For completeness, a rest is included as a pitch, making the number of pitches 9. This makes the approximate number of potential melodies $2.18 * 10^{76}$.

This is still a daunting number of melodies, but it is significantly smaller than the unrestricted case. Additionally, the restrictions placed on the melody will automatically produce a more pleasing sound, because notes outside the key will not occur.

Problem Representation

The note is the building block of music. Therefore, the cornerstone of the representation is a *Note* structure. The structure consists of a scale degree and a duration. A complete melody consists of an array of notes.

A class called *Individual* is responsible for storing the melody. In addition to the melody, an *Individual* also contains the following functions: Initialize, Crossover, GetFitness (two versions), ForceBeats, ChangeOneNoteDegree, ChangeOneNoteLength, and Mutate. These functions are used throughout the evolutionary process, and will be explained in later sections.

The controlling class is named *Population*. The *Population* class directs the evolutionary process and stores all the individuals in an AVL tree based on the fitness of that *Individual.*

Evolutionary Cycle

The evolutionary cycle used starts with an initialization and evalutation. Then the algorithm will perform the following steps until a terminating condition has been reached: Select two parents, Reproduction, Mutate the children, Correct the rhytm of the children, Evaluation, Competition.

Initialize and Evaluate the Population. The size of the population is encoded in the *Population* class and is set at fifty individuals. For every member of the population, *Population* will instantiate an *Individual* and call the *Individual::Initialize* function. The *Individual::Initialize* function will decide the length of the melody (from 20 to 60 notes) and then generate that number of notes; each note has a randomly generated scale degree and duration. The *Individual::ForceBeats* function is called after *Individual::Initialize* is called. Each *Individual* is then stored in the AVL Tree based on its fitness.

Terminating Condition. A population will evolve until 100,000 generations has been reached, or until the best individual in the population has a fitness of at least 30. (The 30 cutoff applies when using Fitness 1 only.)

Selection of Parents. Since the individuals are stored in an AVL Tree based on their fitness, implementation of rank based selection is straight forward. The tree is traversed starting with the most fit individual, proceeding toward the least fit individual. At any point along the traversal, the current individual has a twenty percent chance of being selected (forty percent with Fitness 2). Traversal will continue through the tree, giving every individual along the way the same chance of selection when it is visited, until one is finally selected. If the traversal fails to select an individual, the most fit individual in the tree will be used. Once an individual is selected, the traversal starts over and a second parent is selected using the same criteria. It is possible that the same individual will be selected both times.

Reproduction. Reproduction is essentially crossover between the two children, who at this point are just copies of their parents. One child will call its *Individual::Crossover* function. The *Crossover* function takes as an argument another *Individual*, which is the second child. To facilitate the discussion of reproduction, the following terminology will be used:

- *this_melody*: The melody contained in the *Individual* whose *Crossover* function is currently executing.
- *in_melody*: The melody contained in the *Individual* who was passed into the *Crossover* function.
- *temp_melody*: A temporary melody created inside the *Crossover* function.

The *Crossover* function will randomly select a scale degree and use it as a crossover point. The length of *temp_melody* will be either the length of *this_melody* or *in_melody*, whichever is shorter. The melody *temp_melody* is created by copying notes from *this_melody* until the crossover point is hit. Then *in_melody* will be scanned for the crossover point. If the crossover point is not found, then *temp_melody* becomes a copy of *this_melody*, although it may be shorter. If the crossover point is found, then starting with this crossover point in *in_melody*, notes will be copied from *in_melody* to *temp_melody* until another crossover point is encountered. The algorithm will at this point switch back to *this_melody* for another section of notes. Thus, *temp_melody* is created by adding subsequences of notes from the other two melodies until the melody is full. At the end of *Individual::Crossover*, *this_melody* is reassigned to be the same as *temp_melody*. (See Figure 1.)

Mutation. Every child that is created is subjected to three mutation operators: *ChangeOneNoteLength*, *ChangeOneNoteDegree*, and *Mutate*. ChangeOneNoteLength randomly selects a note in the melody. Then, it either decreases or increases the integer which represents the note duration. ChangeOneNoteDegree operates in exactly the same manner, except it modifies the scale degree instead of the note duration. The Mutate function will choose one of the following five actions with equal probability:

- Change the first note in the melody to the tonic (scale degree one) note.
- Change the last note in the melody to the tonic note.
- Call ChangeOneNoteLength.
- Call ChangeOneNoteDegree.
- Do nothing.

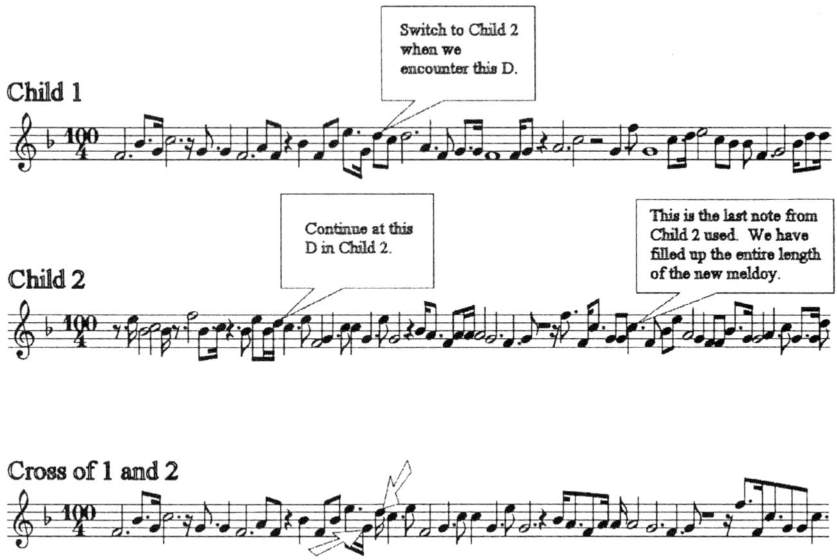

Figure 1: Reproduction Crossover.

Rhythm Correction. During the developmental stages of this project, the observation was made that the rhythm patterns in the melodies were exceptionally difficult and unusual. To correct this problem, a deterministic function called *ForceBeats* was introduced. A description of this function is available in the full length version of this paper (*http://web.umr.edu/~matt/research/EC_MelodyGeneration.pdf*).

Evaluation and Competition. Every generation, two individuals are born, and two individuals die. The two individuals created are evaluated and then stored in the tree based on their fitness. Then the two least fit individuals in the tree are terminated.

Fitness

Two different fitness functions were developed to evaluate the melodies generated. We refer to the first one developed as Fitness 1. This method is a straight forward approach which seeks to optimize melody generation by selecting melodies which have characteristics deemed to be "good." While this function performs well, it quickly peaks and generates "Johnny one note" types of melodies. Fitness function 2 was written in an effort to find a fitness function which will continue to improve the melody over time. The following paragraphs describe both of these fitness functions in detail.

Fitness 1. Fitness function 1 uses a "Fitness Loop," which cycles through every note in the melody, checking the relationship of the current note with the note which follows it. As the melody is evaluated, the fitness function keeps a running total of "fitness points." Characteristics such as stepwise movement and jumps of a third, fourth, or fifth, are all rewarded with positive fitness points. Characteristics such as large jumps or drastic changes in rhythm make the melody more difficult to sing; when these changes are found a negative number is added to the total fitness.

Results with Fitness 1. In the early stages of development, the melodies generated were quite disappointing. However, after fine tuning the fitness function, juggling parameters, and deterministically correcting rhythm patterns, many of the resulting melodies are quite nice. While we did experience some success with Fitness 1, its performance peaks and then begins a down hill trend toward boring melodies which typically consists of the same note repeatedly. Thus, we developed Fitness 2.

Fitness 2. The second fitness function is centered around a model built from existing "good" melodies. The concept for this model was inspired by (Dubnov, et al, 2003). Construction begins by reading a file which contains a number of melodies from the same genre. In this case, we selected eighteen melodies from The Ames Hymn Collection (*http://junior.apk.net/~bmames/hymnsjs.htm*). As the notes are read in, nodes containing two consecutive notes are created and added to a tree. Thus, a melody containing N notes will produce N - 1 nodes in the tree. However, every node in the tree must be unique. When an attempt to insert a duplicate node is made, a counter in the existing node will be incremented; no other change to the data structure will occur at that time. The result is a tree whose nodes are all unique. Each node stores a sequence of two notes that occurred in a known melody, as well as a count of the number of times that sequence of two notes was found.

Once the melody model is constructed, it will be used by the second fitness function through the duration of the evolutionary process. The second fitness function is listed in Algorithm 1.

Results with Fitness 2. Fitness 2 is far superior to Fitness 1. The main reason for this is that the function will continue to improve the quality of the melodies as the population evolves. By basing the fitness on how closely a melody matches known melodies (according to the metric described above), we are able to capture some of the features in existing tunes that the human ear appreciates. Additionally, this approach is expandable to any style of music. Very little genre specific knowledge is required to implement Fitness 2. In the future, we hope to use this concept to generate music in a number of different musical styles.

CONCLUSIONS

At the beginning of this project, we set out to develop an evolutionary algorithmic approach to melody generation. Research in the field provided inspiration and ideas from which to start. We learned from (Santo, et al, 2000), (Papadopoulos,Wiggins), and (Wiggins, et al, 1998) that rule based systems can be used to generate melodies with moderate success. Using ideas from these papers, we wrote our own rule based fitness function and verified that this idea works.

In an effort to attain even better results, we looked to the machine learning example presented in (Dubnov, et al, 2003), which led us to develop a simple tree based music model. This approach works even better than the rule based system. In addition, it is very expandable. Thus, we conclude that a tree based music model is indeed an effective music critic.

```
Build a tree model of this melody
Set fitness to zero
for(currNode = firstNode to lastNode)
{
   if(currNode exists in the melody model)
   {
      hitDiff = the difference between the percent occurrence of
                currNode in this melody and the melody model
      if(hitDiff > 0)
         Add hitDiff to fitness
   }
   else
   {
      currNode did not occur in the melody model, so add a large
      value to fitness
   }
}
if(fitness > 0)
   return 1 / (fitness * 1000)
else
   return the largest number possible
```

Algorithm 1: Fitness Function 2.

ACKNOWLEDGEMENTS

Special thanks to Kay Johnson, director of bands at Crocker High School, Crocker Missouri, for critiquing generated music melodies.

All music shown in this document was typeset by Lilypond. *http://lilypond.org/web*

A C++ AVL tree template written by Walt Karas was used in this project. This template is available in the public domain.

GNMIDI was used to process midi files. *http://www.gnmidi.com*

REFERENCES

Dubnov, S., Assayag, G., Lartillot, O., and Bejerano, G. "Using Machine-Learning Methods for Musical Style Modeling," *Computer* 36, 10 (2003), pp. 73-80.

Johnson, M. D., and Wilkerson, R. W. "Computerized Arrangement of Vocal Music," *Intelligent Engineering Systems Through Artificial Neural Networks Volume II*, (2001), pp.1025-1030

Papadopoulos, G., and Wiggins, G. "A genetic algorithm for the generation of jazz melodies."

Santos, A., Arcay, B., Dorado, J., Romero, J., and Rodriguez, J. "Evolutionary computation systems for musical composition." *Proceedings of Acoustics and Music: Theory and Applications* (2000). Vol 1, pp 97-102.

Wiggins, G., Papadopoulos G., Phon-Amnuaisuk, S. and Tuson, A. "Evolutionary Methods for Musical Composition." *Proceedings of the CASY98 Workshop on Anticipation, Music & Cognition* (1998).

IMAGE DITHERING AS N-QUEENS PROBLEM

PAUL M. WHEELER
Computer Science Department
Rochester Institute of Technology
Rochester, NY

VLADIMIR MISIC
Computer Science Department
Rochester Institute of Technology
Rochester, NY

MATT MORSE
Computer Science Department
Rochester Institute of Technology
Rochester, NY

PETER G. ANDERSON
Computer Science Department
Rochester Institute of Technology
Rochester, NY

ABSTRACT
N-Queens is one of the most well know problems that can be solved using genetic algorithms. The goal of this paper is to show how a modification of the basic N-Queens problem can be used to find an optimal distribution of any number of points in a given area, thus generating an even, stochastic diffusion pattern for any gray level. The nature of N-Queens solutions to minimize the number of queens on the same row, or column results in a distribution that has a low occurrence of artifacts that are easily detected by the human eye. As with N-Queens it is relatively simple to apply genetic algorithms to this problem. Using greedy algorithms and intelligent mutation and crossover, an optimal solution can be found in a very small number of generations.

INTRODUCTION

Traditional half-toning is done through one of several different algorithms for distributing points in some ordered or pseudo-random way to give the appearance of the correct gray level. However, ordered dithering methods tend to result in obvious patterns which can be visually displeasing, and make the fact that the image is in duotone more apparent (Ulichney, 2000). Another method called stochastic dithering based on a *blue noise* mask properties, results in a much more visually pleasing dithering, and can be calculated just as easily as the traditional methods (Mitsa, 1991). Stochastic dithering is based on "point comparison," meaning that each pixel of the original image is compared with the corresponding pixel of the halftone mask, and the result is either black or white, depending on whether the original pixel is darker or lighter than the halftone mask respectively (Yu, 1998).

The focus of this paper is an alternative method for generating masks, also called threshold arrays, for stochastic dithering. It is not our intention to find a method that is better than existing methods, but instead to show that Genetics Algorithms (GA) can be applied to the problem in such a way that the solution could easily be modified to create other noise patterns, and be applied to other applications. The ideal halftone mask is evenly distributed, random, and does not contain patterns that are easily picked up by the human visual system. Typically Blue-Noise masks are generated starting with a randomly generated white noise mask, by repetitively swapping points between light and dark areas until a "good" mask is found. Several metrics exist for measuring the quality of a mask, including radial frequency, and average distance between the nearest-neighboring minority-pixels (Misic 2003). The method we propose uses a GA to evolve an optimal solution, based on the quality of distribution, and the rate of occurrence of visually recognizable artifacts.

N-QUEENS AND ORDERED GREED

The goal of the traditional N-Queens problem is to place N non-attacking queens on an $N \times N$ chessboard. The search space for this problem is extremely large, but it can be significantly reduced by using a simple heuristic, also called a "greedy algorithm". The simplest way of doing this is to reduce the encoding of solutions to a permutation from 1 to N, where the value at position in the permutation represents the horizontal position of the queen in the corresponding row. This reduces the search space significantly because it eliminates any positioning that has two queens on the same row, but the space is still large, and the results for a genetic algorithm using this approach are only slightly better than random search.

A better approach, called *ordered greed*, is to interpret the same permutation as the order in which the queens are to be placed on the board, and place each queen in the leftmost non-attacking position. This shrinks the search space to a manageable size, and genetic algorithms are very effective using this approach (Anderson 2000).

PERMUTATION ENCODING

Using a permutation for the encoding of the solution introduces complications for the genetic algorithm. Permutations must contain one of each number in their range, and no repetitions. Therefore simple mutation and crossover will not generate valid solutions in most cases. There is a representation of the permutation, however, which does not have these drawbacks, called a *signature*. A permutation is generated by creating a number sequence and performing a series of random swap operations. A signature is simply a way of recording those swap operations. The value S_i where i goes from 0 to N-1 of each position in a signature represents a swap between the corresponding position i in the number sequence and the position $i+S_i$. Signatures can undergo simple single- or double- point crossover without corruption since the rules restricting each value are not dependant on the other values in the signature. Mutation is similarly simple, and is performed by incrementing a value, taking the modulus with respect to the length, N, and subtracting one.

MULTI-OBJECTIVE GENETIC ALGORITHMS

A problem that involves the optimization of multiple independent parameters is called a multi-objective problem. Generating optimal halftone masks involves the optimization of multiple parameters, one being the evenness of distribution, and the second being the occurrence of artifacts. There are several ways to either optimize multiple parameters, or combine them into a single parameter, including Pareto optimality, or using a vector of weights to combine the parameters (Goldberg, 1989).

(a) (b)

Figure 1. The resulting halftone masks (a) least fit from first generation (b) most fit after 50 generations

GENERATING HALFTONE MASKS

The applicability of the N-Queens problem to generating dithering (halftone) masks lies in the elimination of visual artifacts. The N-Queens problem prohibits any two queens from ever being placed on the same horizontal, vertical, or diagonal line. By modifying these rules slightly to make them less restrictive and taking distance to the nearest neighbor into account, we can use the same techniques as used for the N-Queens problem to generate a "good" halftone mask (Fig. 1). The first change to the rules involves limiting the range of attack of each queen, allowing some queens to technically lie on the same line, so long as they are far enough apart. Secondly, instead of placing the each queen at the left-most non-attacked position, they will be placed at an optimal distance from the other queens on the board. Lastly the fitness function must be modified to measure both the number of attacking queens and the evenness of distribution. The results of such a genetic algorithm appilied to the population of 50 masks, after approximately 10-50 generations appear to converge toward a good dithering mask, for a fixed gray level g (Fig. 2).

This method can then be applied iteratively on the same board, adding another N queens with each iteration (and not moving previously placed queens), until the entire board is full. Each group of queens added at one time represents a value in the threshold array, with the first being the lowest.

GENOME ENCODING

Each genome representing a halftone mask is made up for a set of permutations, one for each group of N pixels. Each permutation specifies the order in which pixels should be added to the mask. Each genome also contains two scalar values, one representing the optimal distance at which to place each pixel, and one representing the rate at which that distance decreases.

The genome is decoded by placing each pixel on the row specified by the permutation, at the point where it is closest to the optimal distance from any other pixel with a similar value, and at which the pixel is on attacking lines from the fewest other pixels with similar values.

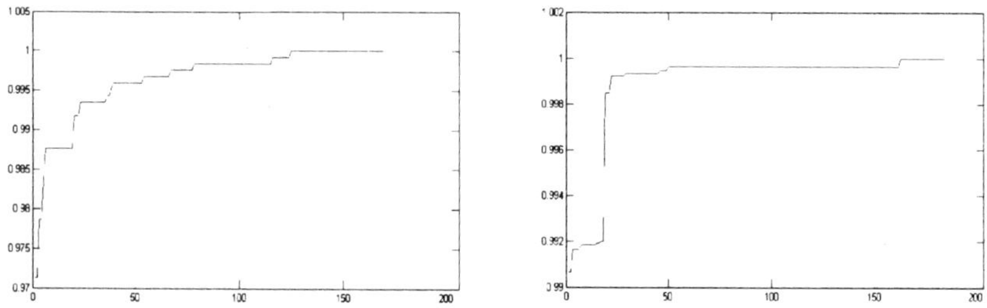

(a) (b)

Figure 2. Two fitness functions converge simultaneously (at different rates), as GA adjusts spatial distribution of queens: (a) distribution fit (Eq. 2), (b) distance fit (Eq. 3). The process is observed at the gray level *g=0.01* over 200 generations.

FITNESS FUNCTION

The fitness of a genome is represented by two vectors, one representing the error in distribution after each group of *N* pixels is added, and the second representing the number of attacks between pixels with similar values. When comparing the fitness of two genomes, for the purpose of selection, one genome is considered more fit than another if either both its vectors are more fit than the other, or one vector is significantly greater and the other is equal too, or only slightly less than the other genome's vector. Thus if one genome has significantly fewer attacks, but only slightly worse error in distribution than another genome, it will be considered better.

The fitness measure for distribution is implemented by dividing the board up into iteratively smaller sections and counting the error in the distribution of pixels in that section. The goal is to have approximately the same number of pixels (queens) in any given section. The fitness is represented by the vector:

$$(d_1, d_2, \ldots, d_N) \tag{1}$$

Where

$$d_i = \frac{\sum_{f=1}^{\log_2(N/2)} \sum_{x=1}^{N/2^f} \sum_{y=1}^{N/2^f} \left| count(x, y, 2^f, i) - 2^f \right|}{\sum_{f=0}^{\log_2(N/2)} 2^f} \tag{2}$$

The function *count(x-pos, y-pos, size, level)* represents the number of pixels at the specified level in the specified section.

The fitness measure for occurrence of artifacts is based on number of "attacks" between pixels, similar to the N-Queens problem. The number of attacks is then divided by N^2 to get the average number of attacks per square. Again, the fitness is represented by a vector, but the formula is different:

$$d_i = \sum_{x=1}^{N} \sum_{y=1}^{N} \frac{attacks(x, y, N / i, i)}{N^2} \tag{3}$$

The function *attacks(x-pos, y-pos, range, level)* represents the number of pixels of equal level lying on the same horizontal, vertical, or diagonal line as the specified position, within the specified range, and returns zero if the value at (x, y) is not equal to i.

These two equations could easily be modified to favor some other form of noise pattern (e.g. green noise). By adjusting the penalties given for the relative positioning of pixels and the evenness of distribution, similarly effective results could be obtained for an entirely different purpose.

RESULTS

While the results we have in no way been shown to be superior to other stochastic halftoning methods, it can be clearly seen that the results visually resemble Blue Noise Mask (Fig. 3), and the visual result of using our mask for halftoning is similar to the BNM (Fig. 4). It is conceivable that a different pair of fitness functions based on the same model would result in an even better Blue Noise mask.

CONCLUSIONS

This paper demonstrates the groundwork on which a more robust system for generating optimal noise distributions could be built. It has been demonstrated that, by making use of ordered greed in genome encoding, it is possible to apply genetic algorithms to a variety of noise or pattern generation problems. Additionally we have shown that solutions to two problems from different domains, namely N-Queens and image dithering, can easily be combined using genetic algorithms.

While the *N-queens* modification studied here was related to image dithering, there are a variety of other areas involving similar problems – for example: frequency-hop coding schemes used in radio transmissions and cellular telecommunications (Code Division Multiple Access - CDMA). We predict that even, random distributions evolved by a GA similar to the one used here could be used to evolve a time-frequency codes (masks) optimized to reduce signal interference and cross talk, as well as to increase security of data transmission. The future research will concentrate on this problem.

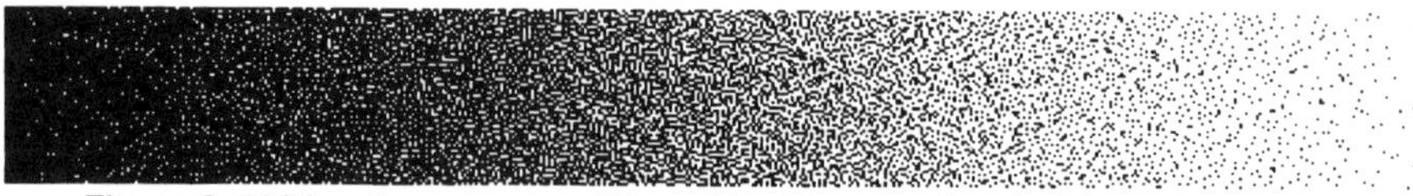

Figure 3. 128 level gray ramp, dithered by N-queen threshold matrix.

(a) (b) (c)

Figure 4. (a) 256 level grayscale, (b) 128 level "N-Queens" half-toned image, (c) Blue Noise Mask half-toned image. Images are half-toned in low resolution to make halftone texture visible.

REFERENCES

Yu, Q., and Parker, K. J., 1997, "Stochastic Screen Halftoning for Electronic Imaging Devices," Journal of Visual Communication and Image Representation, vol. 8, no. 4, pp. 423–440.

Ulichney, R., 2000, "A Review of Halftoning Techniques," SPIE Proceedings, vol. 3963., pp. 378-391.

Mitsa, T., and Parker, K. J., 1991, "Digital Halftoning Using a Blue Noise Mask," SPIE Proceedings, vol. 1452.

Misic, V., and Parker, K. J., 2003, "Morphological Characterization of Dithering Masks," Journal of Electronic Imaging, vol. 12, pp. 278-283.

Anderson, P. G., and Gustafson, G. T., 1999, "Ordered Greed," Proceedings of the ICSC Conference of Soft Computing, International Computer Science Conventions, 1999.

Goldberg, D. E., 1989, "Genetic Algorithms in Search, Optimization, and Machine Learning", Addison-Wesley, Boston, MA.

AUTONOMOUS ROBOT NAVIGATION USING A GENETIC ALGORITHM WITH AN EFFICIENT GENOTYPE STRUCTURE

ADITIA HERMANU
Vico Indonesia
Project Engineering Dept.
Jakarta, Indonesia

KAVEH ASHENAYI
University of Tulsa
Dept. of Electrical Engineering
Tulsa, Oklahoma

THEODORE W. MANIKAS
University of Tulsa
Dept. of Electrical Engineering
Tulsa, Oklahoma

ROGER L. WAINWRIGHT
University of Tulsa
Dept. of Mathematical & Computer Sciences
Tulsa, Oklahoma

ABSTRACT

The goal for real-time mobile robots is to travel the shortest path in minimal time while avoiding obstacles in a navigation environment. Autonomous navigation allows robots to plan this path without the need for human intervention. The path-planning problem has been shown to be NP-hard, thus this problem is often solved using heuristic optimization methods such as genetic algorithms. An important part of the genetic algorithm solution is the structure of the genotype that represents paths in the navigation environment. The genotype must represent a valid path, but still be simple to process by the genetic algorithm in order to reduce computational requirements. Unfortunately, many contemporary genetic path-planning algorithms use complex structures that require a significant amount of processing, which can affect the real-time response of the robot. This paper describes the development of a genotype structure that contains only the essential information for path planning, which allows for more efficient processing. A genetic algorithm using this structure was tested on a variety of simulated navigation spaces and was found to produce valid, obstacle-free paths for most cases.

INTRODUCTION

Mobile robots are desirable for operations such as bomb disposal or hazardous material management, which would be potentially dangerous for humans. An important task for the robot is autonomous navigation, where the robot travels between a starting point and a target point without the need for human intervention. While basic information may be available to the robot about the navigation area boundaries, unknown obstacles may exist within the navigation area. A path between the starting and target points that avoids collisions with obstacles is said to be *feasible* - this is a path that lies within free space. Thus, robot navigation methods need to solve the *path-planning problem*, which is to generate a feasible path and optimize this path with respect to certain criteria. The work presented here is part of a larger project to build an autonomous path-planning robot. This research is motivated by earlier work in this field of interest (Geisler and Manikas, 2002) by the same research team. This paper presents the research and simulation results of a genetic algorithm based path-planning software.

GENETIC ALGORITHM TECHNIQUES FOR ROBOT PATH PLANNING

Robot path planning is part of a larger class of problems pertaining to scheduling and routing, and is known to be NP-hard. Thus, a heuristic optimization approach is recommended as shown by Hwang (Hwang and Ahuja, 1992). One of these approaches is the use of genetic algorithms. A genetic algorithm (GA) is an evolutionary problem solving method, where the solution to a problem evolves after a number of iterations (Mitchell, 1996). A genetic algorithm starts with a population of individuals (*chromosomes*). Each individual represents a possible solution for a given problem. For robot navigation, an individual may represent a path between the starting and target points. Each individual is assigned a *fitness value*, based on how well the individual meets the problem objectives. Using these fitness values, individuals are selected to be *parents*. These parents form new individuals, or *offspring*, via *crossover* and *mutation*. Parent selection, crossover and mutation operations continue for several iterations (*generations*) until the algorithm converges to an optimal or near-optimal solution.

Various genetic algorithm methods have been applied to the robot navigation problem. One approach is to combine fuzzy logic with genetic algorithms (Arsene and Zalzala, 1999; Kubota et al., 1999; Pratihar et al., 1999). In this approach, the genotype structure represents fuzzy rules that guide the robot navigation, so the genetic algorithm evolves the best set of rules. While this approach can produce a feasible path through an uncertain environment, the genotype structure becomes very complex, as it needs to represent a variety of fuzzy rules. Another approach is to use genotype structures that represent local distance and direction, as opposed to representing an entire path (Cazangi and Figuieredo, 2002; Di Gesu et al., 2000; Gallardo et al., 1998; Vadakkepat et al., 2000). While these are simple to process and allow for faster real-time performance, the local viewpoint of these methods may not allow the robot to reach its target. Some methods have relatively simple genotype structures that can represent feasible paths, but require complex decoders and fitness functions (Hocaoglu and Sanderson, 2001; Sugihara and Smith, 1997; Xiao et al., 1997). This can also affect real-time response. Our research has focused on improving the genetic algorithm performance by developing a more efficient genotype structure.

Row-wise Structure

Previous research by our group used a row-wise navigation model (Geisler and Manikas, 2002). Given a navigation environment that is modeled by N rows, a path in that environment is represented by a genotype with N genes. Each gene position (locus) corresponds to a row index, while each gene value (allele) corresponds to a column index within that row. For example, assume that we have the chromosome {3,3,5,1,2,6}. This genotype represents a path that starts in row 1, column 3 (1,3) and ends at row 6, column 6 (6,6). The intermediate points on this path are (2,3), (3,5), (4,1), (5,2), respectively. Fig. 1 shows the navigation along this path in the world space, where point (1,1) is assumed to be at the top left corner.

The direction information of a chromosome represents the intermediate steps, or vertices, of a path. However, sending the robot on a straight line directly from the center of one vertex to the center of the next vertex would mean that the robot moves on a diagonal line across many adjacent cells. This will cause problems if any adjacent cells that the robot traverses from one row to the next have an obstacle. A better approach is to split the diagonal path segment into a horizontal segment and a vertical segment, which will allow the robot to circumvent obstacles. Therefore, we added a direction bit to the chromosome structure to indicate the first direction that the robot will turn to proceed to the next vertex.

Assume that we have a segment that starts in row 1, column 2 (denoted by (1,2)) and ends in row 2, column 5 (2,5). If the direction bit is 0 (Fig. 2a), then the path segment is split into a vertical segment from (1,2) to (2,2) and a horizontal segment from (2,2) to (2,5). However, if the direction bit is 1 (Fig. 2b), then the path segment is split into a horizontal segment from (1,2) to (1,5) and a vertical segment from (1,5) to (2,5).

The genetic algorithm using this genotype structure was tested on a set of simulated navigation environments. While this approach is simple, we discovered limitations with the row-wise model. The row-wise model assumes that each path-segment will start and end in consecutive rows. Unfortunately, this may not result in feasible paths for some world spaces.

Row and Column Structures

In order to address the limitations of our previous research involving only the row-wise genotype structure, we decided to incorporate more flexibility into the navigation model by allowing the orientation to be either row-wise or column-wise. For row-wise orientation, the robot is assumed to travel in consecutive rows from top to bottom, while for column-wise orientation, the robot is assumed to travel in consecutive columns from left to right. Thus, we modified the genotype structure by adding an orientation bit to each chromosome: 0 = column-wise, 1 = row-wise.

The row-wise orientation follows the same rules as our previous row-wise genotype structure. However, for a column-wise chromosome, each locus corresponds to a column index, while each allele corresponds to a row index. Fig. 3 shows the navigation for the column-wise chromosome {3,3,5,1,2,6}. This genotype represents a path that starts in row 3, column 1 (3,1), and travels along intermediate points (3,2), (5,3), (1,4), and (2,5) to reach its target point in row 6, column 6 (6,6).

For column-wise orientation, the direction bit is interpreted as follows: Assume that we have a column-wise path segment as shown in Fig. 4. The segment starts in row 2, column 1 (2,1) and ends in row 5, column 2 (5,2). If the direction bit is 1 (Fig. 4a), then the path segment is split into a vertical segment from (2,1) to (5,1), and a horizontal segment from (5,1) to (5,2). Conversely, if the direction bit is 0 (Fig. 4b), then the path segment is split into a horizontal segment from (2,1) to (2,2) and a vertical segment from (2,2) to (5,2).

GA ELEMENTS

The genetic algorithm parameters were experimentally determined. Crossover rate is 0.7, while mutation rate is 0.07. The population size is 50. Termination occurs if there is no improvement in the best path after 30 generations, or if a maximum of 800 paths have been generated. The fitness function weights are $w_l = w_t = 2$, $w_f = 3$. This penalizes infeasible steps, since we want our path to be obstacle free. Elitism was also used in order to keep the best individual (path) within a generation. If elitism is applied, the fittest chromosome path is copied to the offspring population without any changes.

Fitness Evaluation

Each chromosome represents a path in the world space. Recall that the goal for autonomous robot navigation is to determine the shortest feasible path and traverse this path in minimal time. A path is evaluated by examining its segments. The total path length is the sum of its segments. If a segment intersects an obstacle, then this is called an infeasible step. Thus, a path is obstacle-free only if all of its steps are feasible. Minimizing path length will minimize travel time; however, so will minimizing the number of turns required to traverse this path.

Given these criteria, our fitness function must consider the following fitness factors: feasibility, length, and number of turns. Equation (1) shows how to calculate the feasibility factor f_f. S is the number of infeasible steps in the chromosome, while S_{max} and S_{min} are the maximum and minimum number of infeasible steps for the population. The length factor f_l is calculated in a similar manner, as shown in Eq. (2), where L is the total length of the path segments. The number of turns factor f_t is also calculated in a similar manner, as shown in Eq. (3), where T is the total number of turns. Putting this all together, we get the fitness function f shown in Eq. (4). w_f, w_L and w_T are weights for feasibility, length, and number of terms, respectively. After the fitness value for all chromosomes in the population have been computed, Rank Selection (Mitchell, 1996) is used to determine the parent chromosomes that will be used for reproduction.

$$f_f = 1 - \frac{S - S_{\min}}{S_{\max} - S_{\min}} \tag{1}$$

$$f_l = 1 - \frac{L - L_{\min}}{L_{\max} - L_{\min}} \tag{2}$$

$$f_t = 1 - \frac{T - T_{\min}}{T_{\max} - T_{\min}} \tag{3}$$

$$f = 100 w_f f_f \frac{(w_l f_l + w_t f_t)}{w_l + w_t} \tag{4}$$

Crossover and Mutation

In our GA, two parent chromosomes are combined applying a single-cross-point, value encoding crossover. The crossover operator produces two offspring chromosomes with each crossover operation. This is achieved by using the gene information, which was not used to build the first offspring, in order to build a second chromosome.

For mutation, almost every operation that changes the order of genes within a chromosome or that changes a gene's value is a valid mutation operator. A random number is generated for each gene. If this number is less than the mutation rate, then the gene is mutated. If a gene is to be mutated, another random number between 1 and the total number of rows or columns in the search space is assigned to *location,* and a random direction, either 1 or 0, is assigned to *direction* and *orientation*.

SIMULATION RESULTS AND CONCLUSION

The genetic algorithm was applied to seven sample spaces to simulate the navigation process. These spaces vary in size and in obstacle configuration. Fifteen trials were run for each space. Table 1 shows the success rate for each data set comparing Geisler's approach (Geisler and Manikas, 2002) to our new approach. For each test set, our new GA had more success navigating the search space. Figure 5 shows examples of successful runs for test sets SPSet05, SPSet06, and SPSet07.

Our modification to the genotype structure to allow more options in path planning improves the success of robot navigation. While the success rate was high, there were still trials where our new GA failed to find a feasible path. We are currently exploring methods to combine row-wise and column-wise representations in the same genotype structure. Hopefully, this will improve the success rate of the navigation algorithm.

REFERENCES

Arsene, C. T. C., and Zalzala, A. M. S., 1999, "Control of Autonomous Robots Using Fuzzy Logic Controllers Tuned by Genetic Algorithms." *Proceedings of the 1999 Congress on Evolutionary Computation (CEC99)*, pp. 428-435.

Cazangi, R. R., and Figuieredo, M., 2002, "Simultaneous Emergence of Conflicting Basic Behaviors and Their Coordination in an Evolutionary Autonomous Navigation System." *Proc. 2002 IEEE Conf. on Evol. Comp. (CEC '02)*, pp. 466-471.

Di Gesu, V., Lenzitti, B., Lo Bosco, G., and Tegolo, D., 2000, "A distributed architecture for autonomous navigation of robots." *Proceedings Fifth IEEE International Workshop on Computer Architectures for Machine Perception, 2000.*, pp. 190 - 194.

Gallardo, D., Colomina, O., Florez, F., and Rizo, R., 1998, "A Genetic Algorithm for Robust Motion Planning." *11th Int. Conf. on Industrial and Engineering Applications of Artificial Intelligence and Expert Systems*, pp. 115-122.

Geisler, T., and Manikas, T. W., 2002, "Autonomous Robot Navigation System Using a Novel Value Encoded Genetic Algorithm." *45th IEEE Int. Midwest Symp. on Circuits and Systems*, Tulsa, OK, pp. 45-48.

Hocaoglu, C., and Sanderson, A. C. 2001, "Planning Multiple Paths with Evolutionary Speciation." *IEEE Trans. Evolutionary Computation*, Vol. 5, pp. 169-191.

Hwang, Y. K., and Ahuja, N. 1992, "Gross Motion Planning - A Survey." *ACM Computing Surveys*, Vol. 24, pp. 219-291.

Kubota, N., Morioka, T., Kojima, F., and Fukuda, T., 1999, "Perception-Based Genetic Algorithm for a Mobile Robot with Fuzzy Controllers." *Proceedings of the 1999 Congress on Evolutionary Computation (CEC99)*, pp. 397-404.

Mitchell, M., 1996, *An Introduction to Genetic Algorithms*, MIT Press.

Pratihar, D. K., Deb, K., and Ghosh, A., 1999, "Fuzzy-Genetic Algorithms and Mobile Robot Navigation Among Static Obstacles." *Proceedings of the 1999 Congress on Evolutionary Computation (CEC99)*, pp. 327-334.

Sugihara, K., and Smith, J., 1997, "Genetic Algorithms for Adaptive Motion Planning of an Autonomous Mobile Robot." *Proc. 1997 IEEE Int. Symp. Computational Intelligence in Robotics and Automation (CIRA '97)*, pp. 138-143.

Vadakkepat, P., Tan, K. C., and Ming-Liang, W., 2000, "Evolutionary Artificial Potential Fields and Their Application in Real Time Robot Path Planning." *Proc. 2000 Congress on Evolutionary Computation (CEC00)*, pp. 256-263.

Xiao, J., Michalewicz, Z., Zhang, L., and Trojanowski, K. 1997, "Adaptive Evolutionary Planner/Navigator for Mobile Robots." *IEEE Trans. Evolutionary Computation*, Vol. 1, pp. 18-28.

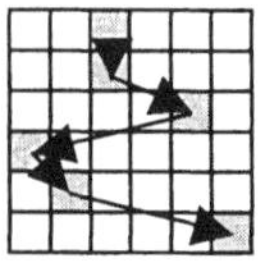

Figure 1. Row-wise navigation in world space.

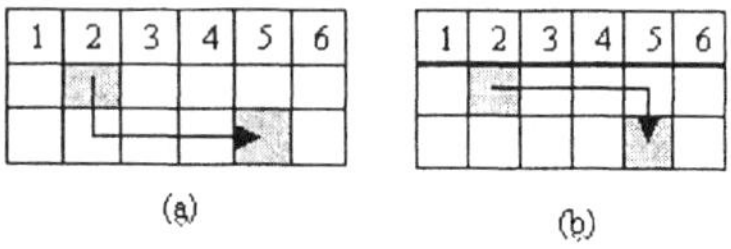

Figure 2. Navigation direction: (a) vertical first, (b) horizontal first.

Figure 3. Column-wise navigation in world space.

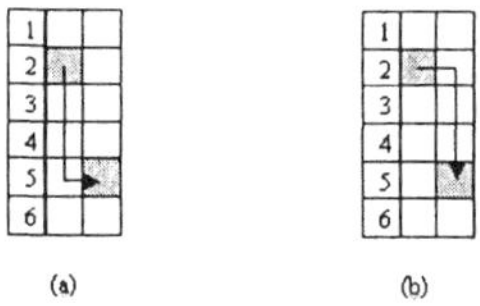

Figure 4. Column-wise direction: (a) vertical, (b) horizontal.

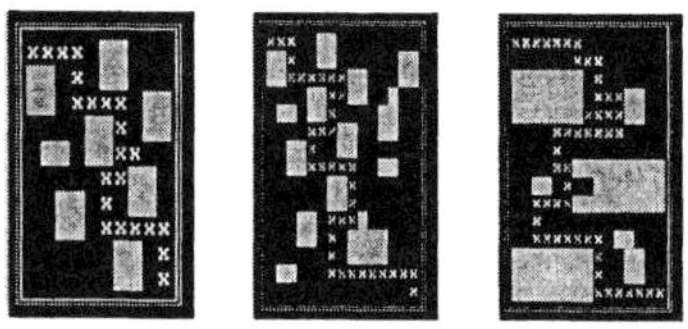

Figure 5. Navigation path examples for test sets (a) SPSet05, (b) SPSet06, (c) SPSet07.

Table 1. Comparison of methods.

Test Set	Success Rate (%)	
	Geisler's GA	Our new GA
SPSet01	0	87
SPSet02	47	100
SPSet03	73	87
SPSet04	87	100
SPSet05	53	80
SPSet06	0	93
SPSet07	0	100

PART IV: FUZZY SYSTEMS

ON THE RESEARCH OF FUZZY OPERATORS USING NORMALIZATION FUNCTIONS

SIMON L. PODVALNY
Voronezh State Technical University
Automatical & Computer Systems
Voronezh, Russia

TATYANA M. LEDENEVA
Voronezh State University
Mathematical Methods of Operation Research
Voronezh, Russia

IRINA A. CHERNIKOVA
The University of Akron
Associate Studies
Akron, USA

TATYANA N. NEDIKOVA
Voronezh State Technical University
Automatical & Computer Systems
Voronezh, Russia

ALEKSEJ V. GRIBOVSKIJ
Voronezh State University
Mathematical Methods of Operation Research
Voronezh, Russia

ABSTRACT

Definition of basic fuzzy operations is the fundamental problem of Fuzzy Set Theory. The purposeful approach to the forming of fuzzy operators has become a reality owing to the introduction of triangular norms, the wide class of which constitutes operators represented as quotients of two polynomials or, in a special case, as polynomials. In this paper we study several ways of generating such fuzzy operators based on the special normalization functions.

Processing of fuzzy information is one out of many paths of investigation in the modern information technology and a powerful tool for development of the intellectual information systems. The effectiveness of methods used for representing vagueness determines degree of the intellectuality of the information system. The use of fuzzy mathematics gives very good results when modeling the vagueness and uncertainty. The key problem of theory is the definition of the basic fuzzy operators. L. Zadeh (1965) proposed a fuzzy disjunction $G(x,y) = \max(x,y)$ and a fuzzy conjunction $F(x,y) = \min(x,y)$. The purposeful approach to the forming of fuzzy operators has become a reality owing to the introduction of triangular norms – T-norms and S-conorms. T-norm is a commutative, associative, non-decreasing in each argument, bounded operation T: $[0,1] \times [0,1] \to [0,1]$, $T(0,0) = 0$, $T(1, x) = x$ for any $x \in [0,1]$. S-conorm is defined as $S(x,y) = 1 - T(1 - x, 1 - y)$, hence $S(1,1) = 1$, $S(0, x) = x$.

T-norm and S-conorm can be interpreted as an extension of the classical ({0,1}) conjunction $\wedge$ and disjunction $\vee$ defined on the whole unit interval. The most widely used triangular norms are presented in Table 1 ($F_m(x, y)$, $G_m(x, y)$, $F_p(x, y)$ and $G_p(x, y)$ was introduced by Zadeh (1975) and $F_0(x, y)$, $G_{-1}(x, y)$, $F_\alpha(x, y)$ and $G_\beta(x, y)$ was introduced by Hamacher (1976)).

Table 1. Triangular norms

Conjunction operators (T)	Disjunction operators (S)
$F_m(x, y) = \max(x + y - 1, 0)$	$G_m(x, y) = \min(x + y, 1)$
$F_p(x, y) = xy$	$G_p(x, y) = x + y - xy$
$F_0(x, y) = \dfrac{xy}{x + y - xy}$, $F_0(0,0) = 0$	$G_{-1}(x,y) = \dfrac{x + y - 2xy}{1 - xy}$, $G_{-1}(1,1) = 1$
$F_\alpha(x,y) = \dfrac{xy}{\alpha + (1-\alpha)(x + y - xy)}$ $(\alpha > 0)$	$G_\beta(x,y) = \dfrac{(\beta - 1)xy + x + y}{1 + \beta xy}$ $(\beta > -1)$

Analysis of some properties of these operators shows (Ledeneva, 1997) that it is impossible to find representations of fuzzy conjunction and disjunction operators, which differ from already known (Table 1) in class of function

$$\Phi(x, y) = \frac{a_0 + a_1(x + y) + a_2 xy}{b_0 + b_1(x + y) + b_2 xy}.$$

The aim of this paper is to present some approaches for obtaining new types of fuzzy operations.

Let us consider normalization function

$$t(x_{min}, x, x_{max}) = \frac{x - x_{min}}{x_{max} - x_{min}}$$

where $x \in [x_{min}, x_{max}]$. Notice that normalization operators are the linear transformations of value x. Let $[x_{min}, x_{max}]$ be [0,1], then $t(0, x, y) = \frac{x}{y}$ – normalized value x on [0,y]; $t(x, y, 1) = \frac{x - y}{1 - y} = x \ominus y$ – normalized value x on $[y,1]$, where intervals $[0, y]$ and $[y,1]$ are termed *normalization intervals*.

If $x \ominus y = z$ then $x = y \oplus z$ where $\oplus$ denotes algebraic sum. Notice that Sugeno norms

$$DP_q(x, y) = \frac{xy}{\max(x, y, q)},\quad DP_q^*(x, y) = \frac{x + y - xy - \min(x, y, 1-q)}{\max(1-x, 1-y, q)}$$

were obtained using normalization functions. As T-norms model conjunction, S-conorms disjunction of fuzzy sets and $T(x, y) \le S(x, y)$, let us assume

$$T'(x,y) = \frac{T(x,y)}{S(x,y)};\quad S'(x,y) = \frac{S(x,y) - T(x,y)}{1 - T(x,y)}.$$

In order to use these expressions we obtained the ranking of fuzzy operators from the Table 1. Some results are given (Ledeneva, 1999):

For disjunction operators:

if $\beta \in (-1,0)$, then

$$G(x, y) \leq G_{-1}(x, y) \leq G_{\beta}(x, y) \leq G_{p}(x, y) \leq G_{m}(x, y) \leq 1; \tag{1}$$

if $\beta \to \infty$, then

$$G(x, y) \leq G_{p}(x, y) \leq G_{-1}(x, y) \leq G_{m}(x, y) \leq G_{\beta}(x, y) \leq 1. \tag{2}$$

For conjunction operators:

if $x + y - 1 < 0$, then

$$0 < F_{m}(x, y) \leq F_{\alpha}(x, y) < F_{0}(x, y) < F_{p}(x, y) \leq F(x, y); \tag{3}$$

if $x + y - 1 > 0$, then under conditions

$$\begin{cases} \alpha < \eta(x+y) \\ \eta(\alpha) > x \oplus y \end{cases} \text{or} \begin{cases} \alpha > \eta(x+y) \\ \eta(\alpha) < x \oplus y \end{cases},$$

where $\eta(x) = \dfrac{x}{x-1}$, we obtain

$$0 < F_{m}(x, y) \leq F_{\alpha}(x, y) < F_{0}(x, y) < F_{p}(x, y) \leq F(x, y). \tag{4}$$

Using ranging of fuzzy operators as a basis for normalization intervals forming new fuzzy operators can be obtained. But they can't be represented as $\Phi(x,y)$.

The surfaces of $T'(x, y)$ and $S'(x, y)$ for different $T(x, y)$ and $S(x, y)$ are shown on the Fig. 1. It's easy to show that $T'(x, y)$ and $S'(x, y)$ satisfy main properties of triangular norms such as associativity, commutativity, monotonicity and boundary conditions.

General representation of the main fuzzy operators can be obtained by using the generalized normalized difference $R^{t}(x, y) = \dfrac{y-x}{1-txy}$, and the generalized algebraic sum can be defined as $G^{t}(x, y) = x + y - txy$. If $n(x) = 1 - x$ and De Morgan Laws are hold true, we can define generalized algebraic product as

$$F^{t}(x, y) = (1-t)(x + y) + txy - (1-t).$$

Therefore, generalized division can be written in the form

$$D^{t}(x, y) = \frac{x-(1-t)y+(1-t)}{(1-t)+ty}.$$

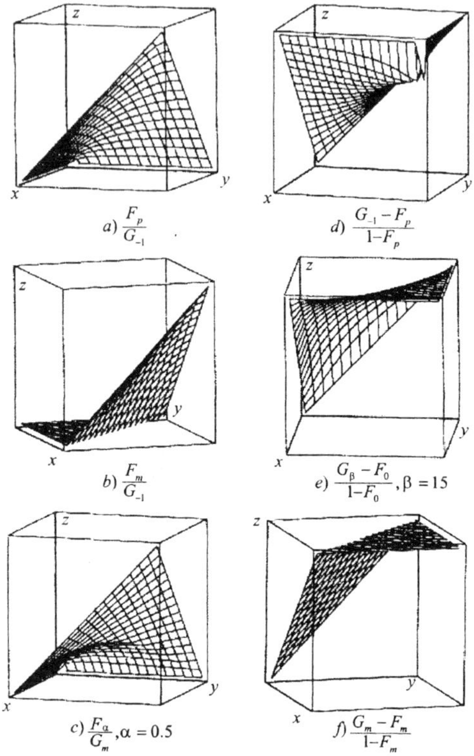

Fig.1. The surfaces of T'(*x*, *y*) and S'(*x*, *y*) for different T(*x*, *y*) and S(*x*, *y*)

We did computer research of these operators (Ledeneva, 1999). Consider $G^t(x, y) = x + y - txy$ when $t > 0$. Analysis of surface corresponding to $G^t(x, y)$ for different t and their comparison with properties of fuzzy operators allow to do following inferences:

(1) If $t \in (0,1)$, then it is necessary to use projection operator for preservation the properties of disjunction operators, that is:

$$G^t_*(x, y) = \min(1, x + y - txy).$$

The surface of $G^t_*(x,y)$ lies in unit cube; if $t = 1$, then $G^t(x, y) = G_p(x, y)$.

(2) If $t \in (1,2)$, then operation is not fuzzy logical operation since returning values in the cube corners are not congruent with values of the crisp logical operation.

(3) $G^t(x, y)$ corresponding to $t = 2$ and $G^t_{**}(x, y) = \max(0, x + y - txy)$ when $t \in (2, \infty)$ correspond to fuzzy nonequivalence function by definition. It may be used to evaluate degree of discrepancy for the sets elements.

Similarly, the research was done for $F^t(x, y)$:

(1) If $t = 0$, then $F_m(x, y)$ is obtained using a projection operator for $F^t(x, y)$; if $t \in (0,1)$, then it is necessary to use the operation

$$F^t_*(x, y) = \max(0, (1-t)(x+y) + txy - (1-t)),$$

the surface of which lies in unit cube; if $t = 1$, then $F^t(x, y) = F_p(x, y)$.

(2) If $t \in (1,2]$ the surface of $F^t(x, y)$ lies in unit cube, but it is a fuzzy logical operation only when $t = 2$: $F^2(x, y)$ is an equivalence function. Using this operation we can define the similarity operator on any set of elements. When $t > 2$, it is necessary to pass on operation

$$F^t_{**}(x, y) = \min(1, (1-t)(x+y) + txy - (1-t)).$$

Comparison of $F^t_{**}(x, y)$ properties with Boolean operations properties allows us to identify $F^t_{**}(x, y)$ as equivalence.

Notice that if we do the change of parameter $t = -\lambda$, then operators

$$G^t_*(x, y) = \min(1, x + y - txy),$$

$$F^t_*(x, y) = \max(0, (1-t)(x+y) + txy - (1-t))$$

become the Sugeno operators $S_\lambda(x, y)$ and $S_\lambda^*(x, y)$.

Regarding $G^t(x, y)$ and $F^t(x, y)$ operations as basic operations, we can define generalized operations for $G_{-1}(x, y)$, $G_\beta(x, y)$, $F_0(x, y)$, $F_\alpha(x, y)$ using their representation based on the normalization functions on different normalization intervals.

The definition of the notion of fuzzy implication is one of the most important problems of fuzzy modeling, since a fuzzy logic systems have been successfully applied to a variety of industrial processes and consumer products.

In Boolean logic an implication is defined as follow:

$$I(x, y) = x \rightarrow y = \bar{x} \vee y. \tag{5}$$

Generally, using S-conorm as a disjunction Eq. (5) can be written in the form:

$$I(x, y) = S(n(x), y), \tag{6}$$

where $n(x)$ – denotes the negotiation function, corresponding to given S-conorm.

Using the negotiation $n(x) = 1 - x$ and $S_t(x, y)$ yield the implication

$$I_t(x, y) = 1 - x + y - ty + txy.$$

$I_t(x, y)$ takes its maximum and minimum value on the bounds of the square $[0,1] \times [0,1]$. If $x = 1$ then $I_t(x, y) = y$ and arrives at maximum 1 when $y = 1$, and minimum 0 when $y = 0$. Similarly, from studying of the other three cases: $x = 0$, $y = 1$, $y = 0$ we obtain that when $t > 1$, $2 - t \leq I_t(x, y) \leq 1$, therefore, in order to bound operator's value area, $I_t(x, y)$ should be used in the form:

$$I_t(x, y) = \max(1 - x + y - ty + txy, 0).$$

When $t \leq 1$ and $0 \leq I_t(x, y) \leq 2 - t$, $I_t(x, y)$ takes the form:

$$I_t(x, y) = \min(1 - x + y - ty + txy, 1).$$

The shapes of surface of $I_t(x, y)$ for different t are shown on the Fig. 2.

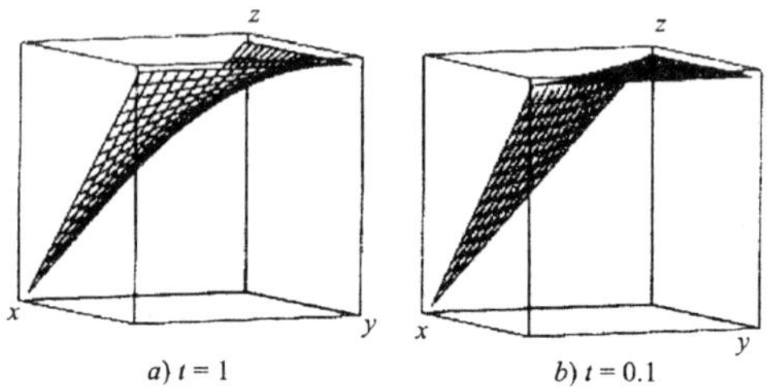

Fig.2. The surfaces of $I_t(x, y)$ for different t

CONCLUSIONS

This paper contains theoretical results concerning generating mathematical operators which can be used in modeling of semantics of AND/OR relationships in systems serving for knowledge processing. The main idea of the approach is applying of normalization functions (both well known and original) to triangular norms. The general normalization function $R^t(x, y)$ is particular interesting because it allows to obtain more general parametric representations of basic fuzzy operators. The following questions have been studied:

(1) Dependence between the parameter and the shape of surface.
(2) Dependence between the parameter and the semantics of operator (identification of the type of operator).

Notice that parametric operators are of the great practical interest because the modification of parameter values allows providing flexibility when working with vagueness and uncertainty, tuning up the mathematical instrument on informational environment of application. Selection of the operator should be done on the basis of operation properties and expert knowledge. Before using specific operator as a fuzzy operation, it is necessary to do the preliminary research in order to check if the operation properties and specific characters of application are well coordinated.

REFERENCES

Hamacher, H., 1976, "On Logical Connectives of Fuzzy Statements and Their Affiliated Truth Function," Proceedings, 3rd European Meeting Cybernetics and Systems Research, Viena.

Ledeneva, T.M., 1997, "On Some Aspects of a Representation of Fuzzy Operators as a Quotient of Two Polynomials," *News of Academies, Mathematics*, Vol. 11, pp. 33-40.

Ledeneva, T.M., 1999, "The Modeling of an Information Aggregation Process in the Purposeful Systems," Voronezh State Technical University, Voronezh, Russia.

Trillas, E., Alsina, C., and Valverde L., 1982, "Do We Need Max, Min and 1-j in Fuzzy Set Theory?" *Fuzzy Set and Possibility Theory: Recent Developments*, Pergamon Press, New York, USA, pp 275-297.

Zadeh, L., 1965, "Fuzzy Sets," *Information and Control*, Vol. 8, pp. 338-353.

Zadeh, L., 1975, "Calculus of Fuzzy Restrictions," Fuzzy Sets and their Applications to Cognitive and Decision Processes, edited by L. Zadeh, Academic Press, New York, pp. 1-39.

A STUDY OF ANTENNA-TO-ANTENNA COUPLING PREDICTION WITH FUZZY INFERENCE SYSTEM

Taymor S. Rashidi
The Boeing Co.
Canoga Park, CA
taymor.s.rashidi@boeing.com

Cihan H. Dagli
University of Missouri-Rolla, MO
dagli@umr.edu

ABSTRACT

This paper focuses on the study and application of the Fuzzy Inference System (FIS) to assist *predicting the Antenna-to-Antenna Coupled (AAC) electromagnetic interference (EMI)* at the frequency ranges of 30 MHz and 1710 MHz on a platform such as an aircraft. The FIS AAC prediction is brought about because of an exact prediction of AAC EMI on a platform has been somewhat difficult and complex by using the traditional analytical techniques. For this reason, using the FIS models with the Matlab to *predict* the AAC will be in the best interest of the engineering practice and provides practical results. The advantage of using the FIS method over the traditional analytical method for *predicting* the AAC is that the FIS method includes the uncertainty margins, which are: the antenna cabling-loss, the geodesics path loss, and the surface reflection over the airframe. This study demonstrates more favoring to the FIS method than the traditional method during systems engineering trade-offs study.

INTRODUCTION

A reliable prediction of the expected *antenna-to-antenna coupling* is a significant piece of information, and is required to make a final decision on the antenna placement on a platform. Most communication system engineers are keenly interested in an analytical guideline for predicting the antenna-to-antenna coupling before the antennas are to be installed on a platform.

Most traditional AAC modeling such as Aircraft inter-Antenna Propagation with Graphics and Uniform Geometrical Theory of Diffraction techniques are too complex to be validated by testing. There has been significant margin between the analytical and measured data. Examples that confirm the complexity and uncertainty of these traditional techniques have been shown by: Lin (1995), Foreman (1984, 1987 & 1991), Lesniakowski (1984), Bull (1990), Burnside (1998), Marhefka (1992), and Bull (1979). Therefore, the fuzzy logic application is relatively a better candidate for predicting the AAC. A Master thesis on the subject of the antenna-to-antenna coupling prediction with the fuzzy inference system is published by Rashidi (2004).

Fuzzy logic is a suitable means of heuristic processing of incomplete and otherwise imperfect data. So that the fuzzy logic algorithm and sets which are a generalization of conventional set theory was introduced by Zadeh (1965). In supporting of this paper, numerous fuzzy engineering applications have been reviewed that are published by Klir (1988), Dubios (1980), Zimmermann (1990), Kauffmann (1985) and Schmucker (1984). The antennas surveyed in this study are made by the Sensor System Inc (2000).

An intelligent engineering intuition and judgment to call the AAC margin is safe when the antenna isolation is greater than 40 dB and its fuzzy linguistic is "*desirable isolation*". This "*desirable isolation*" judgment is derived from the Military Standard 55680B (1991) that requires minimum 40 dB of isolation between the antennas.

CRISP AND FUZZY ANALYSIS

One of the crisp methods to estimate the AAC is by using the Friis transmission formula established by Friis (1946) and Skolnik (1962). The Friis transmission Eq. (1) requires two antennas to be in a far field of each other when meeting the criterion of Eq. (2), and their spacing was estimated by Paul (1987) to be $3\lambda_0$, where λ_0 is the antenna propagation wavelength.

$$AAC = G_t(\phi,\theta) + G_r(\phi,\theta) - 20Log[\frac{4\pi R f}{c}] \tag{1}$$

$$R_{far-field} \succ \frac{2D^2}{\lambda_0} \tag{2}$$

Where: G_t = the transmitting antenna gain; G_r = the receiving antenna gain; f = frequency (30 MHz to 1710 MHz); R = spacing between two antennas (0.1 meter to 5 meters); c = Speed of light; λ_o = Wavelength, and D = Maximum dimension of the antenna. The fuzzy area is revealed in Fig. 1 when the crisp and measured data is compared by Harris (1992).

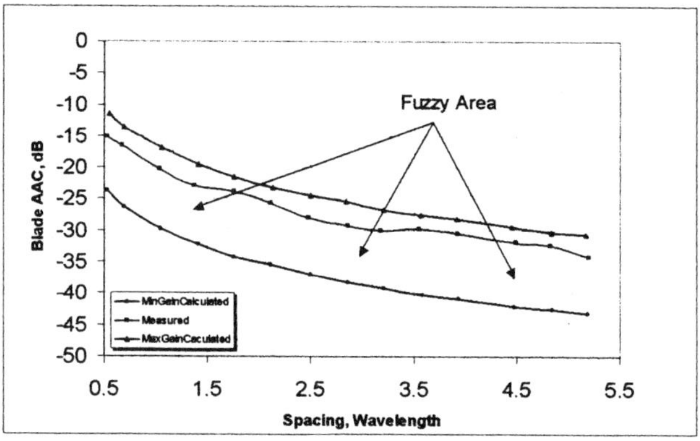

Figure 1. Blade antenna AAC measurements, crisp and the fuzzy area

Fuzzy analysis involves with defining fuzzy language such *as Low Gain, Average Gain,* and *High Gain*, and fuzzy rules, which there are several kinds of fuzzy rules described by Horikawa (1992), Koso (1992), and Lee (1993). The proper fuzzy rule for this application is the Mamdani-type (1976) as described in Eq. (3):

$$\begin{aligned} &If\ x_1\ is\ S_1, \quad and\ x_2\ is\ S_2, \cdots, x_i \quad is \quad S_i, \\ &then\ y_1\ is\ T_1, and\ y_2\ is\ T_2, \cdots, y_i \quad is \quad T_i \end{aligned} \tag{3}$$

Where, each y_i is the output variable whose value is inferred, each x_i is an input variable, and each S_i and T_i is a fuzzy set represented by a membership function. A general inference process used for the antenna coupling is derived from Ross (1995):

1. Fuzzification of the actual values of the input variables such as the antenna gains, operating frequency, and distance between two antennas is defined to be as triangle membership functions, which determine the degree of truth for each rule premise. The *Triangle* membership function is defined in Eq. (4).

$$f_{triangle}(x) = \begin{cases} 0, & if \ x < x_1 \\ 2\dfrac{x - x_1}{x_2 - x_1}, & if \ x_1 \le x \le \dfrac{x_2 + x_1}{2} \\ 2\dfrac{x_2 - x}{x_2 - x_1}, & if \ \dfrac{x_2 + x_1}{2} < x \le x_2 \\ 1, & if \ x > x_2 \end{cases} \tag{4}$$

2. The second step of the FIS developing process is the inference that deals with the truth-value for the premise of that each rule is computed, and applied to the conclusion part of each rule. When constructing the AAC FIS models guidelines, the "Min" inference method is used, that the output membership function is clipped off at a height corresponding to the rule premise's computed degree of truth (fuzzy logic *AND*).
3. In Composition, all output variables with fuzzy subsets are integrated to form a single fuzzy subset for each output variable. When constructing the AAC FIS models, the Max inference method is used. In using the Max composition, the integrated output fuzzy subset is built by taking the point-wise maximum over all of the fuzzy subsets assigned to variable by the inference rule (fuzzy logic OR).
4. Finally, the fuzzy output is converted to a crisp number that is called Defuzzification. There are many defuzzification methods available. For application of the AAC FIS models, the *Centroid method* calculates the variable value of the center of gravity of the membership function for the Fuzzy values, as described in Eq. (5).

$$y_o = \frac{\int y \max_i \mu_{B_1}(y)dy}{\int \max_i \mu_{B_1}(y)dy} \tag{5}$$

Where, y_o is the crisp value, y is the fuzzy variable, B is the universe of discourse, and μ is the fuzzy membership function.

THE AAC FUZZY MEMBERSHIP FUNCTION

The AAC membership functions are constructed by using of the extension principle with a known procedure of the DSW algorithm by Dong (1985) and Berkan (1997), which consists of the following steps:

1. Select a λ value, where $1 \geq \lambda \geq 0$
2. Find the input membership function(s) interval(s) in corresponding to the λ.
3. Compute the interval for the output membership function for the selected λ-cut level, and
4. Repeat steps 1-3 for different values of the λ to complete a λ-cut representation of the solution.

Since the antenna coupling is a real continues function, so that its fuzzy members are defined on the real line. The input fuzzy member functions include the frequency and the distance between two antennas, and the output is the antenna-to-antenna coupling. The system performance is observed based on two disjunctive rules of inference:

Rule 1: $IF\ f\ is\ A_{11}\ (Low\ Frequencey)\ and\ d\ is\ A_{12}\ (Close)$
$Then\ AAC\ is\ B_1\ (Average\ Coupling).$

Rule 2: $IF\ f\ is\ A_{21}\ (High\ Frequencey)\ or\ d\ is\ A_{22}\ (Very\ Close)$
$Then\ AAC\ is\ B_2\ (High\ Coupling).$

Subsequently, the above two rules are illustrated graphically in Fig. 2. For example, let *input(i)* = 1060MHz (frequency) and *input(j)* = 3.5 m (wavelength). The two inputs and one output are modeled as a delta function as illustrated below with a Mamdani implication.

$$\mu(f) = \delta(f - input\,(i)) = \begin{cases} 1, & f = input\,(i) \\ 0, & otherwise \end{cases} \qquad \mu(d) = \delta(d - input\,(j)) = \begin{cases} 1, & d = input\,(j) \\ 0, & otherwise \end{cases}$$

$$\mu_{B^k}(AAC) = \underbrace{\max}_{k}[\min[\mu^k_{A_1}(input\ (i)), \mu^k_{A_2}(input\ (j))]] \qquad k = 1, 2, \ldots r$$

Refering to Fig. 2., Rule 1 (A_{11}) is a linguistic dialog of "*low frequency*" input at 500 MHz, when antennas are "*close*" as much as 3.5 meters. Executing Rule 1, the AAC "*average coupling*" is the output. The "*average coupling*" is in the range of -10dB and -40dB. Similarly, Rule 2 (A_{12}) is a linguistic dialog of "*high frequency*" input at 1060 MHz when the antennas are "*very close*" as much as 2 meters. After Rule 2 is executed, the AAC "*high coupling*" is the output (B_1 & B_2). In this case, the "*high coupling*" range is between -10dB and -50 dB. A weighted average method is used to defuzzify the output, which convert the fuzzy value to a crisp value. The defuzzified or crisp value is calculated to be -24.64 dB, which don't meet the criteria of "*desirable isolation*" of -40 dB or less. Therefore, the recommendation will be to move the antennas apart until it meets the "*desirable isolation*".

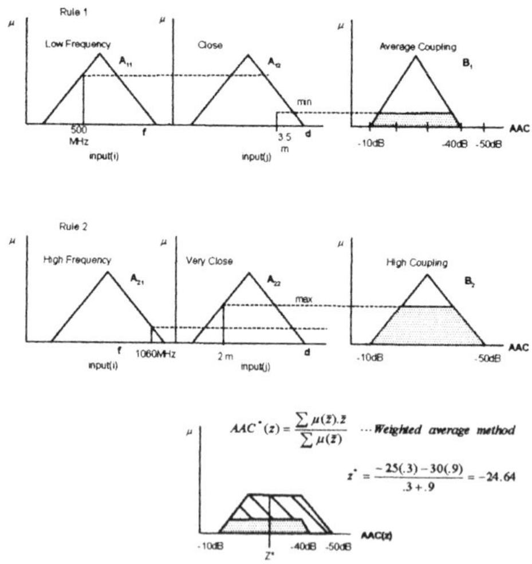

Figure 2. Graphical fuzzy inference illustration

TWO-INPUT AND ONE OUTPUT MODEL

The detailed two-input and one-output antenna fuzzy modeling system was published by Rashidi (2004). The two input are the frequency and the spacing between two antennas; and the output is the coupling between two antennas. There are *three types* of AAC FIS models built by using the Matlab. *Type A* is defined to be a *low gain antenna* (ranges: -6 to -2), *type* B is defined to be an *average gain antenna* (ranges: -2 to 2), and *type C* is defined to be a *high gain antenna* (ranges: 2 to 6). An example of type A Matlab model is shown in Fig. 3.

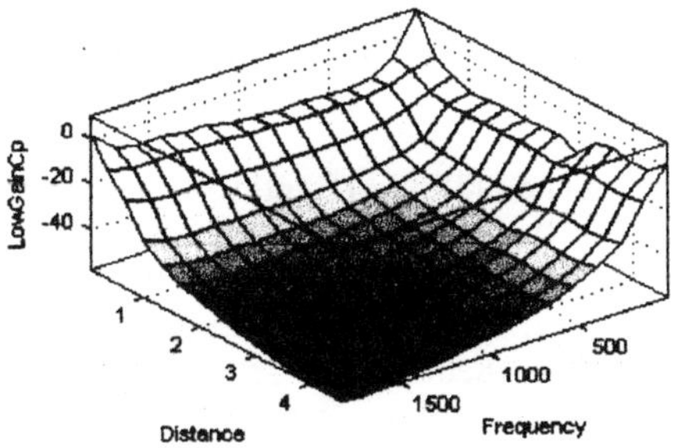

Figure 3. FIS AAC EMI of two input one output

The universe of discourse for this type is the frequency and spacing between two antennas. The crisp representation of this type can be in following form:

$$\chi_A(f,R) = \begin{cases} 1 & f,R \in A \\ 0 & f,R \notin A \end{cases}$$

Where set A contains crisp frequencies (f) and crisp distance between two antennas (R); their characteristic function is χ_A. For the given crisp set, its fuzzy function is derived as follows:

$$A = \{(f,R,\mu_A(f,R))\ \},\quad f,R \in C(f,R)$$

Where, μ is the membership function, and $(f,R,\chi_A(f,R))$ is a singleton. For the type A model, there are 15 frequency membership functions and 15 spacing membership function established, where the natural language specification is derived from Zadeh (1973). For example, *very close and high frequency*, which the adverbs *very* and *high* are part of the natural language, is selected for type A fuzzy modeling. Similarly, there is 15 antenna coupling membership function constructed.

THREE-INPUT AND ONE-OUTPUT MODEL

The 3 inputs and 1 output AAC FISS modeling is somewhat complex. The detailed fuzzy modeling was constructed by Rashidi (2004). The 3 input variables are the frequency, the antenna gain, and the spacing between two antennas; the output is the antenna coupling. Their linguistic variables are: *low frequency* (Lf: 30-510MHz), *average frequency* (Af: 630-110MHz), and *high frequency* (Hf: 1230-1710MHz), *low distance* (Ld: 0.1-1.3m), *average distance* (Ad: 1.6-2.8m), and *high distance* (Hd: 2-4.3), *low gain* (Lg: -4 to -1.6dB), *average gain* (Ag: -1 to 1.4dB), *high gain* (Hg:2 to 4.3dB), and *low coupling* (L-

AAC). At last, the linguistic variables for the antenna coupling are: *average coupling* (A-AAC), and *high coupling* (H-AAC). The most confident linguistic rule set that configures the fuzzy system for the AAC is defined as follows:

Rule (1): IF (Lf), (Ld), and (Lg); THEN the result is (H-AAC)

Rule (2): IF (Af), (Ad), and (Ag); THEN the result is (A-AAC)

Rule (3): IF (Lf), (Hd), and (Hg); THEN the result is (H-AAC)

Rule (4): IF (Lf), (Hd), and (Hg); THEN the result is (H-AAC)

Rule (5): IF (Hf), (Ld), and (Lg); THEN the result is (H-AAC)

VALIDATION

The antenna-to-antenna coupling prediction with the fuzzy inference system is validated by comparing the crisp, the test data and the fuzzy models, which was extensively described by Rashidi (2004). Only one of the examples is described herein. The antenna coupling between UHF/AM radio and Satcom radio on the MH-60 HAWK helicopter was measured by Harris (1992). The fuzzy model of the antenna coupling is anchored with measured data in the frequency ranges of 225-400 MHz. The maximum and minimum antenna gain select is 2.8 dB and –3.4 dB, respectivily. Table 1 illustrates the input fuzzy membership function and Table 2 is the names and parameters of the output fuzzy membership functions. Finaly, Table 3 shows the fuzzy rules and Fig. 4 is the result.

Table 1: Fuzzy frequency membership functions

Fm No.	Fm Name	Fm Type	Fm Parameter	Fm Range
1	Very low frequency	Triangle mf	206, 225, 273	208, 444
2	Low frequency	Triangle mf	215, 252, 303	208, 444
3	Average frequency	Triangle mf	253, 303, 353	208, 444
4	High frequency	Triangle mf	278, 352, 398	208, 444
5	Very high frequency	Triangle mf	352, 398, 444	208, 444

Table 2 Fuzzy AAC EMI membership function

Fm No.	Fm Name	Fm Type	Fm Parameter	Fm Range
1	High AAC EMI *	Triangle fm	-25, -24, -23	-38, -24
2	Average AAC EMI *	Triangle fm	-26, -25, -24	-38, -24
3	Less AAC EMI *	Triangle fm	-28, -26, -25	-38, -24
4	Very Less AAC EMI *	Triangle fm	-33, -28, -26	-38, -24
5	Acceptable AAC EMI **	Triangle fm	-38, -33, -28	-38, -24

Note: * Don't comply with the AAC isolation requirement
** Comply with the AAC isolation requirement

Table 3: Fuzzy rules for the antenna coupling model

Rule #	Rule for the AAC EMI FIS (Aircraft blade antenna)	Frequency	AAC
1	If (frequency is 1) then (AAC EMI is 2)	230	-25
2	If (frequency is 2) then (AAC EMI is 3)	252	-26
3	If (frequency is 3) then (AAC EMI is 1)	302	-24
4	If (frequency is 4) then (AAC EMI is 4)	352	-28
5	If (frequency is 5) then (AAC EMI is 5)	398	-33

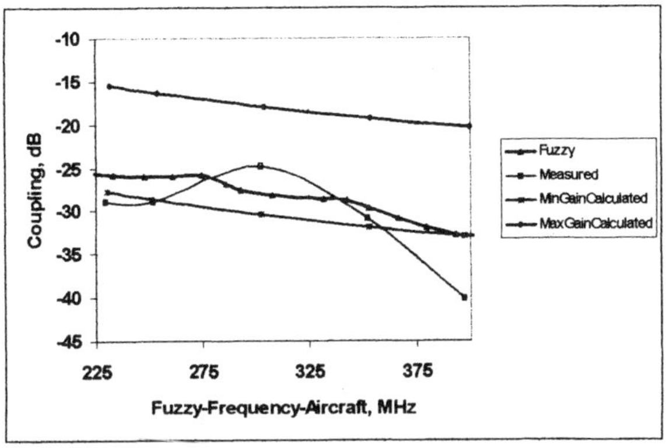

Figure 4. AAC EMI fuzzy, measured and calculated

CONCLUSIONS

This paper is primarily aimed at utilizing Fuzzy Inference System for executing an engineering analytical tool/guideline for predicting the Antenna-to-Antenna Coupled (AAC) on a platform such as an aircraft. Aircraft industries are required to perform an analytical modeling to predict potential antenna interference before the antenns are mounted on a platform. The fundamentals of Fuzzy logic and Fuzzy Inference System were introduced for developing 2-input-1-output and 3-inputs-1-output models. The models were anchored with the refrenced measured data. The challenging predicament which was to come up with an analytical tool to predict antenna-to-antenna coupling margin using fuzzy logic application is accomplished. Commercial electromagnetic software exist in the market for predicting the antenna coupling, but they are very costly, however; the AAC fuzzy analytical tool is an alternative method which it requires only the Matlab.

REFERENCES

Lin, J.L., Price, D.G., Chapman, W.O., 1995, "HF Antenna Coupling on the Boeing 767 AWACS," Boeing Defense and Space Group P.O.Box 3999, M/S 8H-10, Seattle, WA 98124, IEEE.

Foreman, T., 1991, "A Radar-to-Radar Interference Prediction Model," EG&G Washington Analytical Services Center, Inc., P.O.Box 552, 1900 Dahlgren Rd., Dahlgren, VA 22448, IEEE.

Foreman, T., 1987, "NATO Electromagnetic Compatibility Analysis Program Description and User's Guide," EG&G Washington Analytical Service Center, Inc., Technical Report: WASC TR 4H2-0002, Ch. 3, pp 1-16

Lesniakowski, T. and Maiuzzo, M., 1984, "Design Electronics Algorithm (DEEAL), Electromagnetic Compatibility Analysis Center (ECAC),"

Foeman, T., 1989, "Antenna Coupling Model for Radar Electromagnetic Compatibility Analysis," IEEE Transactions on Electromagnetic Compatibility, pp 85-87.

Bull, D.A., 1990, "Testing Civil Aircraft and Equipment to New External RF Evironmental Conditions," BRA Technology Ltd Center, N.J., REA Farunborogh Mod (PE) IEEE 7th International Conference on EMC 28-31 August.

Burnside, W.D. and Marhefka, R.J., 1988, "Antenna on aircraft ship, or any large, complex environment," in Antenna Handbook: Theory, Application, and Design, Y.T. Lo and S.W.Lee, Eds. New York: Van Nostrand Reinhold, ch. 20.

Marhefka, R.J., 1992, "Antenna on Complex Platform," IEEE, Vol. 80, No.1, pp204-208, January.

Bull, D.A. and Smithers, B.W., 1979, "Antenna-to-Antenna coupling in aircraft radio systems," Electrical Research Association Ltd., Leatherhead, Surry England.

Zadeh, L.A., 1965, "Fuzzy sets," Information and Control, vol. 8,pp.338-352.

Klir, G., Folger, G., and Folger, T., 1988, "Uncertainty and Information," Englewood Cliffs, NJ, Prentice-Hall.

Dubois, F. and Prade, H., 1980, "Fuzzy Sets and Systems: Theory and Applications," New York, Academic Press.

Zimmermann, H., 1990, "Fuzzy Set Theory and its Applications," 2nd Edition, Boston, Kluwer.

Kaufmann, A. and Gupta, M., 1985, "Introduction to Fuzzy Arithmetic: Theory and Applications," New York, Van Nostrand Reinhold.

Schmucker, K., 1984, "Fuzzy Sets, Natural Language and Computation," Rockville, MD, Computer Science Press.

MIL-A-55680B, 1991, " Military specification for Antennas,"

Sensor Systems Inc.,2000, "Aircraft Antennas," 8929 Fullbright Ave., Chatsworth, CA.

Friis, H. T., 1946, "A Note on a simple Transmission Formula," Proc., IRE, pp. 254-256.

Skolnik, M. I., 1962, "Radar Systems," Mc Graw-Hill, New York, 1962, Chapter 2.

Paul, C.R. and Nassar, S.A., 1987, "Introduction to Electromagnetic Fields," second edition, McGraw-Hill, NY.

Harris, J. C. and Levin, R. J., 1992, "Far-Field Techniques for Predicting Aircraft Antenna Coupling," Georgia Tech Research Institute, Electromagnetic Environmental Effects Laboratory, Atlanta, GA, IEEE.

Horikawa, S., Furuhashi, T., and Uchikawa, Y., 1992, "On fuzzy modeling using fuzzy neural networks with the back-propagation algorithm," IEEE Trans. Neural Networks, vol. 3, no. 5, pp. 801-806.

Koso, B., 1992, "Neural Networks and Fuzzy System: A Dynamical Systems Approach to Machine intelligence," Englewood Cliffs, NJ: Prentice Hall, p 449.

Lee, K.M., Kwak, D.H., and Lee-Kwang, H., 1993, "A fuzzy neural network for fuzzy inference and rule tuning," in Proc. First Asian Fuzzy System Symp., pp. 320-333.

Mamdani, E.H,1976, "Advances in linguistic synthesis of fuzzy controllers," Int. J. Man Mach. Stud., vol. 8, pp. 669-678.

Ross, T.J., 1995, "Fuzzy Logic with Engineering Application," pp. 152-178, McGraw-Hill, Inc.

Dong, W., Shah, H., and Wong, F., 1985, "Fuzzy computations in risk and decision analysis," Civ. Eng. Syst., vol. 2, pp. 201-208.

Berkan, R.C. and Trubatch, S. L., 1997, "Fuzzy Systems Design Principles Building Fuzzy IF-Then Rule Bases," IEEE press, NJ.

Zadeh, L., 1973, "Outline of a new approach to the Analysis of Complex Systems," IEEE Trans. On Sys., Man and Cyb. 3.

Rashidi, T.S., 2004, "A study of antenna-to-antenna coupling prediction with fuzzy inference system," MS thesis, University of Missouri-Rolla, Rolla, MO.

DOSAGE-FILM RESPONSE ANALYSIS WITH FUZZY LINEAR REGRESSION

YONGSHEN NI
Dept. of Electrical and Computer Engineering, University of Oklahoma

GEORGE THOMAS
Dept. of Radiological Sciences, University of Oklahoma Health Science Center

YUSHAN LI
Dept. of Electrical and Computer Engineering, University of Oklahoma

ROBERT CHU
Radiology Service, Veterans Affairs Medical Center, Oklahoma City

JOHN Y. CHEUNG
Dept. of Electrical and Computer Engineering, University of Oklahoma

ABSTRACT

Regression analysis is an important tool to characterize the relationship between a radiation exposure and film response. However, the classical method rarely describes the true relationship due to complex uncertainties existing in observation data and relationships. Therefore, in this paper we have developed a fuzzy linear regression based method to realize dosage-film response analysis which tries to manage those model error resultant uncertainties in a mathematical formulated way. This method has been applied to analyze the relationship between radiation exposure in interventional radiological procedures and GafChromic XR type R film response. Based upon the test results of four GafChromic XR Type R film images, it shows we could get better estimation by applying fuzzy modeling technique to this problem.

INTRODUCTION

Conventional regression analysis is based on probability theory; the most popular way to find the best regression coefficients is least square estimation which minimizes the sum of the squared differences between the measured values and the predicted values.

In least-squared method, the deviations between the observation and predicted value given by regression model are assumed to be due to randomness nature of the data which comes from measurement errors. Fuzzy linear regression (FLR) was proposed by Tanaka (1982) and his colleagues. In their regression method, the deviations are assumed to be due to fuzziness of the data which comes from model errors instead of measurement errors.

However, the deviation can result from both random error and fuzzy errors. Random error is clear, the fuzzy error appear because of using improper regression model due to lacking of available information or due to the vagueness nature of the data.

In this dosage-film response relationship study, a fuzzy linear regression based method is proposed which considers both random errors and modeling errors and tries to manage the complexity of uncertainty in a mathematical formulated way.

MATHEMATICAL MODEL

The errors may be resulting from the uncertainties in the values of the input and/or output as well as the fuzziness of the model parameters. In this study, some calibration patterns along with their corresponding dosages level are given as reference, our task is trying to figure out the relationship between the dosage and film response which is expressed as intensity of pixels. Observing the calibration pattern, it's apparent, although the dosage is crisp value; calibration patterns show a significant variation. This may be due to the film and to non-uniform nature of the radiation beam.

The membership function for the observed fuzzy intensity data can be formulated as the following non-symmetric triangular function:

$$Y_i = (y_i, e_i) \qquad (1)$$

Where y_i is the center of the output data (intensity of pixel in this paper) and e_{il}, e_{ir} are the left and right spreads of the fuzzy data respectively.

The estimated regression equation is

$$Y_i^* = (c_0, s_0) + (c_1, s_1) * x_{1i} + (c_2, s_2) * x_{2i} + \ldots + (c_n, s_n) * x_{np}, i = 1, 2, \ldots m \qquad (2)$$

Where m is the size of dataset, n is the number of independent variables. c is the center vector of regression coefficient, s is the spread vector of regression coefficient.

According to Zadeh's extension principle [2], the membership function $\mu_{Y^*}(y)$ of the estimated output variable Y* can be expressed as

$$\mu_{Y^*}(y) = \begin{cases} 1 - \dfrac{|y - x^T c|}{s^T |x|}, x \neq 0 \\ 0, x = 0, y \neq 0 \\ 1, x = 0, y = 0 \end{cases} \qquad (3)$$

Where T denotes vector transposition.

For this paper, we want to minimize the total fuzziness of regression coefficients. That is, we want to get most specific expression for sufficient good fit which is decided by the compatibility level between the observation and prediction.

In order to handle the fuzziness, Tanaka introduced this restriction [4][6]:

$y_i \subseteq [Y_i^*]_h$ Or $[Y_i]_h \subseteq [Y_i^*]_h$

Where the condition must hold for all data points at a specific possibility level h which is chosen by the decision maker. The decision maker could have the flexibility to estimate the reliability of the observation data such that he or she may give a high h for unreliable data and low h for reliable data. Usually high h value can reduce the error of center but result in wider estimation, low h value does the opposite thing.

Many fuzzy regression models have been developed by different people [3~13]. According to the situation in our study, fuzzy linear regression model can be represented in terms of the following linear programming problem:

Minimize $s_0 + \sum_{i=1}^{n} s_i x_{ij}$

$$\text{St.} \quad y_i - (1-h)*e_{il} \geq c^T x_i + (1-h)*s_l{}^T x_{ji}$$

$$y_i + (1-h)*e_{ir} \leq c^T x_i + (1-h)*s_r{}^T x_{ji}$$

$$s_i \geq 0 \qquad i=1,2\ldots,m \quad j=1,2,\ldots,n \qquad (4)$$

Where h is possibility level which locates in the interval [0 1], s is the spread vector of regression coefficient, c is the center vector of regression coefficient. Y is the center of observation vector; e is the spread of observation vector.

CASE STUDY

Increasing concern for the potentially high radiation dose in interventional radiological procedures has led to the use of radiochromic films in the imaging modality. The GafChromic XR-Type R Dosimetry film has been used in this study [1].

The x-ray photons incident on the film is assumed to be in a Poisson distribution. To be simple, in this paper we just use the average value to represent the intensity for each calibration pattern.

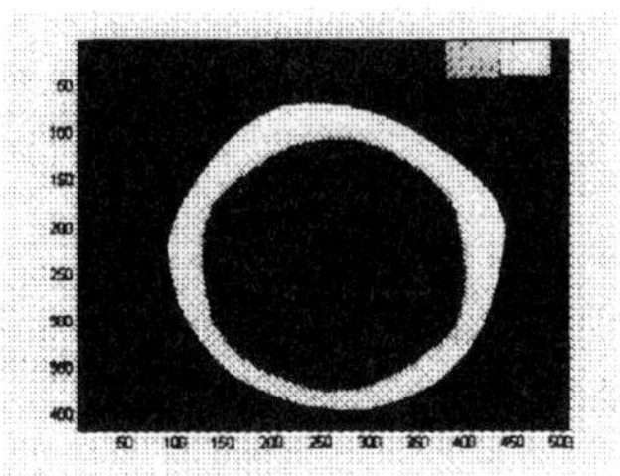

Fig. 1. film image illustration

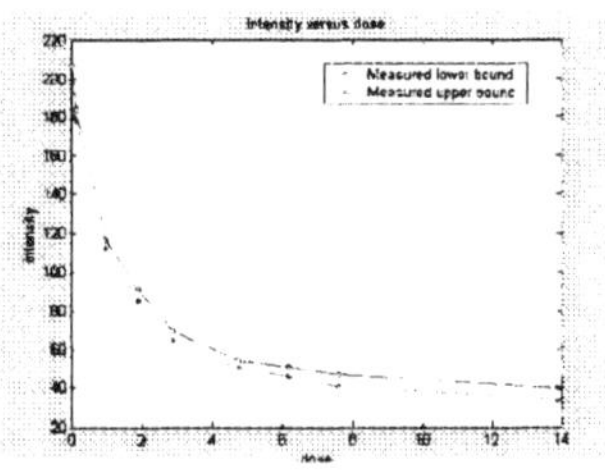

Fig. 2. dose-film response

To study the film response, an x-ray machine (Philips Optimus V5000, Philips Medical Sytems, Andover,MA) was used to create a calibration tablet. Pieces of the GafChromic film were exposed to different amounts of radiation with a maximum air kerma of 13.88Gy. This tablet was stored in a dark room under normal room temperature and humidity.

This created tablet was then scanned by a flatbed reflective-type scanner(Microtek ScanMaker 4800), as well as images with different dosage level. All we want to do is to estimate dosage level based on the image and calibration patterns. From Fig.2, it's clear the relationship between film response and dosage is a nonlinear relationship with one independent variable.

As we just discussed above, both randomness and fuzziness have to be considered in this process, so let's combine probability theory and possibility theory together in this study, and propose the following algorithm:

Step1: preprocessing each calibration pattern

Since calibration pattern is scanned with a black reference, It is possible that some lower pixel readings in the pattern are from the black reference itself instead of the film, we must take those pixels into account or it will severally distort the estimation since darker area means high dosage level.

Outliers have significant impact on the regression equation, it's important to remove them before we do regression analysis. Based on the intensity histogram for each calibration pattern, remove those points whose frequency count for less than 5% of total events.

Step2: Consider random errors

Determine the center of fuzzy regression coefficient by the least square method. In this study a polynomial curve fitting technique is used with order 4.

Step3: Consider fuzzy errors

Build fuzzy linear regression model to modify regression coefficient. Since only one independent variable appears in this equation, and all the other X_n terms are highly correlated with X term, we set spreads of those terms as zero.

By solving the linear programming problem, the lower limit and upper limit dosage-film response curves can be computed. The true dosage value is supposed to be in this estimated interval.

Step 4: compute dosage for each image using dose-film response curve

Step 5: Defuzzification

It can give decision-maker a clearer view about the dosage value.

Many defuzzification methods have been introduced and discussed in the literature. Of them the centroid method is the most famous one. This method weighs all the values with different possibility levels to form a single value. In our case, let X_{ic} and Y_{ic} be the defuzzified values of X_i and Y_i, we use the following formula [8]:

$$X_{ic} = \frac{\int_{-\infty}^{+\infty} x\mu(x)dx}{\int_{-\infty}^{+\infty} \mu(x)dx} = \frac{1}{3}(X_{il} + X_{im} + X_{ir}) \tag{5}$$

$$Y_{ic} = \frac{\int_{-\infty}^{+\infty} y\mu(y)dy}{\int_{-\infty}^{+\infty} \mu(y)dy} = \frac{1}{3}(Y_{il} + Y_{im} + Y_{ir}) \tag{6}$$

RESULTS

To test the validity of the proposed method, we got some scanned film images from University of Oklahoma health science center along with calibration patterns. Four images are randomly picked from those films.

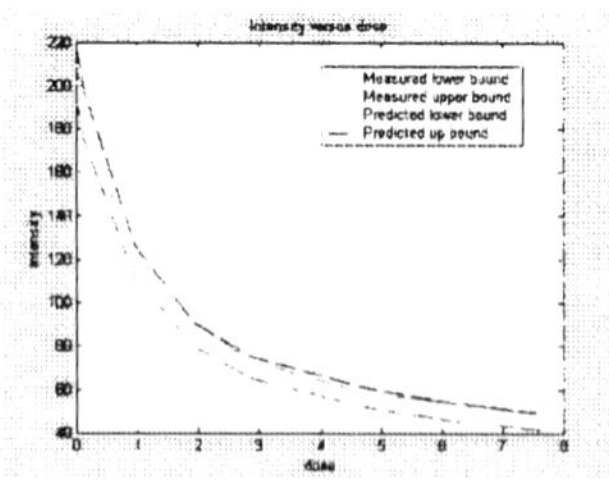

Fig. 3. Dosage- film response h=0

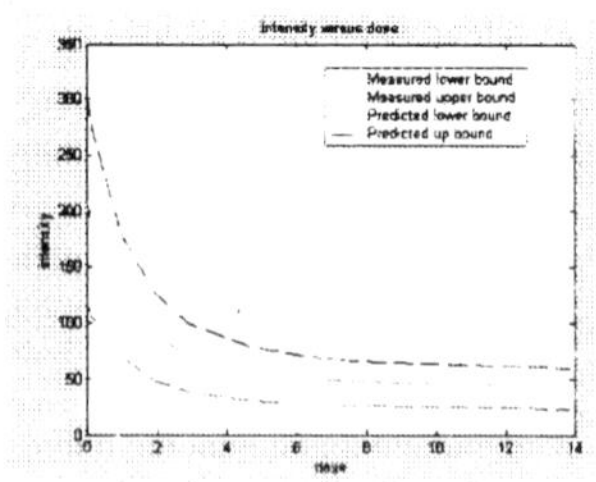

Fig. 4. Dosage-film response h=0.9

Figure 3 and Figure 4 describe the resultant dosage-film response for h equals to 0 and 0.9 respectively. As we can see, the estimation becomes fuzzier with the increasing of h. If the estimated interval is too wide, it will be hard to provide precise estimation for the decision maker, but if it's too narrow, some observations couldn't be covered in this interval, the decision maker will be too optimistic about the estimation. Thus an appropriate value is desired.

Finally we list the experiment result as the following table.

No.	Machine value	CLR	Error	FLR(h)	Error
1	79.3	86.20	8.7%	87.44 (0)	10.26%
2	584	763.83	30.79%	681.69 (0.9)	16.73%
3	748	929.95	24.32%	777.32(0.9)	3.92%
4	1124	1007.7	-10.35%	948.12 (0.5)	-15.65%

Table.1. Simulation results

Table 1 summarizes the experimental results of four test film images. If we only consider random errors of this process, the result are listed in column 3. Column 5 gives results which have considered both random errors and model errors. Observing figure 2, we find most data in calibration patterns focus on the dosage range 0~8 Gy; while there is almost no reference data between the range 8~14 Gy. So those pixels with value between 30 and 40 are unreliable in the computation and it's a major error source especially those data correspond to high dosage level. If the image has a large amount of unreliable data, model errors can not be ignored. So it's intuitively reasonable we should set a relatively bigger h for the dataset whose histogram has a large part of low pixels. Figure 5,6 are histograms of the two test images(No.1 and 2) in this study. We can see the No.1 image almost has no low value pixels except the black background. While the No. 2 image has low value pixels, that's why it needs high h value.

In No.1 and No.4 images, randomness phenomena dominates this process, fuzzy regression degrades the performance a little bit; while in No.2 and No.3 images, if only random errors are considered, unbearable errors will occur. Fuzzy regression improves the performance significantly. In general, Fuzzy regression generates a more steady result than the classical method for our case.

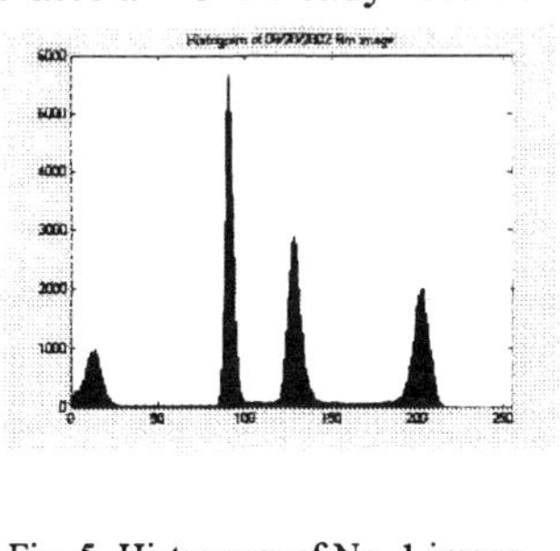

Fig. 5. Histogram of No. 1 image

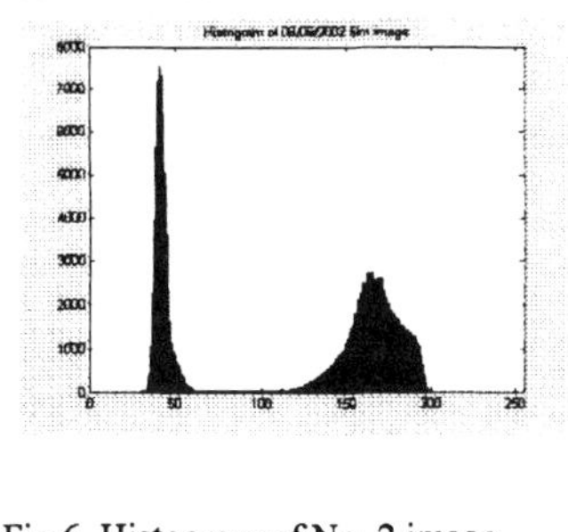

Fig.6. Histogram of No. 2 image

DISCUSSION

Both opportunity and challenge exist in applying fuzzy regression model to data analysis. It can take advantage of expert knowledge to improve the model which is hard to be implemented by classic probability theory, however, the decision about the possibility of a dataset is very flexible. If a bad decision has been made, the result won't improve much even gets worse in some cases. So it's still a research topic about how to make a good support system which can eliminate the random factor in decision making process as much as possible. It's now under development for our future research.

SUMMARY

Radiologists and scientists alike agree that radiation in large doses causes cancer; so it is a big concern in clinical radiological application area about how to estimate radiation dosage level a patient is exposed to. This paper proposed a method to estimate dosage level based on film image and calibration patterns. The method considers both random errors and fuzzy errors which exist inherently in this process. Random errors are handled by classical probability theory. Fuzzy linear regression is applied to fix up the model error. Four GafChromic XR Type R film images have been used to test this algorithm. Observing the results, we find combining fuzzy regression with classical regression together can give more steady and generally better estimation under the condition that the data possibility level h can be chosen wisely.

REFERENCE

[1] G. Thomas, R.Y.L.Chu, and Frank Rabe, 2003, "A study of GafChromic XR Type R film response with reflective-type densitometers and economical flatbed scanners", Journal of applied clinical medical physics, Vol. 4, No. 4.

[2] George J. Klir/Bo Yuan, 1995, "Fuzzy Sets and Fuzzy Logic". Englewood Cliffs, NJ:Prentice-Hall..

[3] Yun-His O. Chang, Bilal M. Ayyub, 2001, "Fuzzy regression methods- a comparative assessment", Fuzzy Sets and Systems 119, pp187-203.

[4] Hideo Tanaka, Haekwan Lee, 1997, "Fuzzy Linear Regression Combining Central Tendency and Possibilistic Properties", IEEE trans. on Fuzzy Systems.

[5] Rajan Alex, P.Z.Wang, 1998, "A New Resolution of Fuzzy Regression Analysis", IEEE Trans. On Fuzzy Systems.

[6] Hideo Tanaka, 1998, "Interval Regression Analysis by Quadratic Programming Approach", IEEE 1998 Trans. On Fuzzy Systems.

[7] Yun-Shiow Chen, 2001, "Outliers detection and confidence interval modification in fuzzy regression", Fuzzy Sets and Systems 119, pp259-272.

[8] Chiang Kao, Chin-Lu Chyu, 2002, "A fuzzy linear regression model with better explanatory power", Fuzzy Sets and Systems 126, pp401-409.

[9] Yun-His O.Chang, 2001, "Hybrid fuzzy least-squares regression analysis and its reliability measures", Fuzzy Sets and Systems 119, pp225-246.

[10] D.Savic and W.Pedrycz, 1991, "Evaluation of fuzzy linear regression models", Fuzzy Sets and Systems, vol.39,pp.51-63.

[11] E.S.Lee, P.T. Chang, 1994, "Fuzzy linear regression analysis with spread unconstrained in sign", Comp. Math. Appl. 28(4), pp 61-70.

[12] G. Peters, 1994, "Fuzzy linear regression with fuzzy intervals", Fuzzy Sets and Systems 63 pp45-55.

[13] A.Celmins, 1987, "Least squares model fitting to fuzzy vector data", Fuzzy Sets and Systems, vol.22, pp 245-269.

WEB SERVICE FOR TOURISM USING THE FUZZY RELATION INEQUALITY

ICHIKO KINJO
Graduate School of Engineering,
Hokkaido University

YUKINORI KAKAZU
Graduate School of Engineering,
Hokkaido University

MASAHIRO KINOSHITA
Hokkaido Institute of Technology

ABSTRACT

Recently, various information of tourism exists on Web and we can obtain the latest information from Web pages. In this paper, we propose a methodology for decision-making that used such tourism information. However, there is a problem of taking the labor in order to judge whether it is right result or not for multiple results, and effort to looking for the information which is needed. Then, in this paper, we propose a method of decision-making support system in web service. In making decision, the decision-maker often imposes certain qualifications on alternatives. For the vague evaluation items, the decision-maker may give his desire "At least they should satisfy my minimal requirements". To formulate the problem, we introduce the fuzzy relation inequality.

INTRODUCTION

Recently, the tourism information such as hotel and transportation etc. are provided in various media. Especially, large quantities of information exist on Web and we can obtain the latest information from Web pages. For example, when planning a travel, to arrange airline tickets or to reserve hotels are possible on Web, and we can obtain the information about hotels from Web and choose hotel from two or more hotels that is suitable for the purpose. However, there is a problem of taking the labor in order to judge whether it is right result or not for multiple results, and effort to looking for the information which is needed out of a lot of collected information. Then, in this paper, we propose a method of decision-making support system in web service. We analyze the contents of Web pages and make decisions using the value acquired from them. And decision-making is supported by preset the evaluation to the decision-maker.

In the decision-making problem, the decision-maker evaluates for some alternatives and makes decision based on the value of evaluation. However, the decision-maker often intends to evaluate each alternative by vague evaluation items. For the vague evaluation items, the decision-maker may give his desire "At least they should satisfy my minimal requirements". In this paper, we set the selecting condition of the decision-maker to vague evaluation items and propose a method for supporting that to decide the optimal alternatives under this condition.

DECISION-MAKING PROCESS

Here, we show below the decision-making process in the decision-making support system.

[step1] Acquire the fuzzy relation between vague evaluation items and observable items

The fuzzy relation expresses the relation between vague evaluation items and observable items by fuzzy numbers. The fuzzy relation is used for evaluating alternatives. Then, we acquire value of the fuzzy relation from information on Web. In the proposing method, it acquires value of the fuzzy relation by processing statistically to Web pages.

[step2] Set up the decision-maker's minimal requirements to vague evaluation items

For vague evaluation items, the decision-maker may give his desire "At least alternatives should satisfy my minimal requirements ". To formulate the problem, we introduce the fuzzy relation inequality.

[step3] •• Calculate "the degree of importance" using the fuzzy relation inequality

In order to calculate evaluation value of alternatives for vague evaluation items, "the degree of importance" for observable items is calculated using value of the decision-maker's requirements and the fuzzy relation.

[step4]•• Acquire evaluation value of alternatives for observable items

Evaluation value of alternatives for observable items is acquired from Web pages of each alternative.

[step5]•• Calculate matrix of "the degree of satisfaction" for alternatives

Matrix of "the degree of satisfaction" for alternatives is calculated using "the degree of importance" for observable items and evaluation value of alternatives for observable items.

[step6]•• Calculate evaluation value of alternatives for vague evaluation items

Evaluation value of alternatives for vague evaluation items is calculated using matrix of "the degree of satisfaction" and the fuzzy relation.

[step7]•• Evaluation of alternative

Evaluation of alternatives with some attribute is an important application in fuzzy theory. We utilize fuzzy measure and fuzzy integrals in evaluation alternatives.

[step8]•• Choice of alternative by the decision-maker

The decision-maker makes decision based on the synthetic evaluation value of alternatives presented by the decision-making support system.

DECISION-MAKING USING FUZZY RELATION INEQUALITY

In making decision, the decision-maker often imposes certain qualifications on alternatives. In most cases, the given qualifications are based on human's subjectivity and thus requirements are not sharply defined. For the problem, this paper proposes a fuzzy translation between vague requirements and criteria for evaluated alternatives. The fuzzy translation is formulated by fuzzy relation inequality, and the criteria on alternatives are obtained from the requirements, using the fuzzy backward reasoning. The resulting criteria are regarded as the weights of the evaluation items. The final aggregated score for each alternative is calculated by using fuzzy measure and fuzzy integrals. The effectiveness of the fuzzy relation inequality has been clarified in some experiment.

A set of vague evaluation items such as "quality of service", "delicacy of dish", or "good view" is represented by

$$X = \{x_1, x_2, \cdots, x_m\}$$

It is not easy to observe these items as crisp values even if we observe them for a long period. A set of observable items which have mutual relation with X is

$$Y = \{y_1, y_2, \cdots, y_n\}$$

Then, relation R between X and Y is defined by

$$R = \begin{array}{c} \\ x_1 \\ x_2 \\ \vdots \\ x_m \end{array} \begin{array}{c} \begin{array}{cccc} y_1 & y_2 & \cdots & y_n \end{array} \\ \begin{bmatrix} r_{11} & r_{12} & \cdots & r_{1n} \\ r_{21} & r_{22} & \cdots & r_{2n} \\ \vdots & \vdots & \ddots & \vdots \\ r_{m1} & r_{m2} & \cdots & r_{mn} \end{bmatrix} \end{array}$$

An element r_{ij} denotes the depth of relation between x_i and y_j. We suppose that the value of element is obtained from Web. Next, using a set of alternatives

$$C = \{c_1, c_2, \cdots, c_v\}$$

a matrix Q which gives evaluated values of alternatives for observable evaluation items Y is presented as

$$Q = \begin{array}{c} \\ c_1 \\ c_2 \\ \vdots \\ c_v \end{array} \begin{array}{c} \begin{array}{cccc} y_1 & y_2 & \cdots & y_n \end{array} \\ \begin{bmatrix} r_{11} & r_{12} & \cdots & r_{1n} \\ r_{21} & r_{22} & \cdots & r_{2n} \\ \vdots & \vdots & \ddots & \vdots \\ r_{v1} & r_{v2} & \cdots & r_{vn} \end{bmatrix} \end{array}$$

These vague evaluation items, observable items, fuzzy relation and evaluated values of alternatives for observable evaluation items are acquired from Web.

In making decision, the decision-maker may have some requirements "I want alternative such as ...". In this paper, set the decision-maker's selection conditions to vague evaluation items and consider the method of decision-making that decide the optimal alternatives under these conditions.

Let a set of requirements be L as

$$L = \{l_1, l_2, \cdots, l_h\}$$

Here, elements l_i are fuzzy linguistic items. If we assign fuzzy numbers to l_i, we can have a fuzzy requirement vector B. Then, the relation between "the degree of importance A" of observable evaluation items and "requirements B" of vague evaluation items is given by the fuzzy relation equation.

$$R \circ A = B \tag{1}$$

where

$$A = [a_1, a_2, \cdots, a_n]^T$$
$$B = [b_1, b_2, \cdots, b_m]^T$$

In this paper, as the requirement vector B denotes decision-maker's minimal requirements, the fuzzy relation equation in (1) is replaced with the fuzzy relation inequality such that

$$R \circ A \geq B \tag{2}$$

SOLUTION OF FUZZY RELATION INEQUALITY

Here, we describe the method of solving the fuzzy relation inequality used in decision-making. In this paper, method depending on algorithm that is quite different from the image that solves an inequality is avoided and we aim at deriving all solutions by using brief operation formula. In order to achieve this aim, the definition of the operator is important. Then, we propose the method of solving the fuzzy relation inequality by using composition.

$$\begin{bmatrix} r_{11} & r_{12} & \cdots & r_{1n} \\ r_{21} & r_{22} & \cdots & r_{2n} \\ \vdots & \vdots & \ddots & \vdots \\ r_{m1} & r_{m2} & \cdots & r_{mn} \end{bmatrix} \circ \begin{bmatrix} a_1 \\ a_2 \\ \vdots \\ a_n \end{bmatrix} \geq \begin{bmatrix} b_1 \\ b_2 \\ \vdots \\ b_m \end{bmatrix} \tag{3}$$

We pick up ith row of (3) as

$$\bigvee_j (r_{ij} \wedge a_j) \geq b_i \quad for \quad \forall i, \forall j \tag{4}$$

In order to hold Fuzzy relation inequality (4), at least one term of the left side of the inequality (4) satisfies

$$r_{ij} \wedge a_j \geq b_i \quad for \quad \exists j \tag{5}$$

and the other terms have to satisfy

$$r_{ij} \wedge a_j < b_i \quad for \quad \forall j' \neq j \tag{6}$$

We call r_{ij} which satisfies (5) "criterion element" and the rest "auxiliary element".

Criterion and Auxiliary

We consider the conditions for "criterion element" having solutions. In inequality (5), if we regard a_{ij} as variable and regard $r_{ij} \wedge a_j$ as a function, graph can be written about the following two kinds of cases.

( )• $r_{ij} \geq b_i$, ( )• $r_{ij} < b_i$

The solutions are

$$a_j = \begin{cases} r_{ij}^{*} \cup b_i^{*} & for \quad r_{ij} \geq b_i \\ r_{ij}^{\#} \cap b_i^{*} & for \quad r_{ij} < b_i \end{cases} \tag{7}$$

and we define it "criterion". where, e^{*}• $e^{\#}$• $e^{\#\#}$ are symbols which satisfy

$$e^{*} = [e \quad 1], \quad e^{\#} = [0 \quad e], \quad e^{\#\#} = [0 \quad e)$$

Similarly, we consider the conditions for "auxiliary element" having solutions.

$$a_j = \begin{cases} r_{ij}^{\#} \cap b_i^{\#\#} & for \quad r_{ij} \geq b_i \\ r_{ij}^{*} \cap b_i^{\#\#} & for \quad r_{ij} < b_i \end{cases} \tag{8}$$

And we define it "auxiliary".

u operation

The solutions are arranged, it will become as it is shown in Table 1.

Table 1. Criterion and auxiliary

	criterion	auxiliary
$r_{ij} \geq b_i$	$a_j = [b_i, \ 1]$	$a_{j'} = [0, \ b_i)$
$r_{ij} < b_i$	• •	$a_{j'} = [0, \ 1]$

Then, the "u" operation is defined as follows.

$$r_j \ u \ b = \begin{cases} [b, \ 1] \ (for \ r_{j=k} \geq b), \ [0, \ b) \ (for \ r_{j \neq k} \geq b) \\ \qquad\qquad\qquad\qquad [0, \ 1] \ \ (for \ r_{j \neq k} < b) \end{cases} \tag{9}$$

Finally, solution A for fuzzy inequality is derived as the product set of A_j. Thus,

$$a_j = \bigcap_i (r_{ij} \ u \ b_i) \tag{10}$$

From this,

$$\begin{bmatrix} a_1 \\ \vdots \\ a_j \\ \vdots \\ a_n \end{bmatrix} = \begin{bmatrix} r_{11} ub_1 \cap \cdots \cap r_{i1} ub_i \cap \cdots \cap r_{m1} ub_m \\ \vdots \\ r_{1j} ub_1 \cap \cdots \cap r_{ij} ub_i \cap \cdots \cap r_{mj} ub_m \\ \vdots \\ r_{1n} ub_1 \cap \cdots \cap r_{in} ub_i \cap \cdots \cap r_{mn} ub_m \end{bmatrix} \tag{11}$$

Then, if we define u operation as

$$r^T \bullet u\, b = \bigcap_i (r_{ij}\; u\; b_i) \tag{12}$$

thus,

$$[r_1, \quad r_2, \quad \cdots \quad r_m] \bullet u \begin{bmatrix} b_1 \\ b_2 \\ \bullet \vdots \\ b_m \end{bmatrix} \tag{13}$$

$$= (r_1 u b_1) \cap (r_2 u b_2) \cap \cdots \cap (r_m u b_m)$$

The equation (11) is rewritten as follows

$$\begin{bmatrix} a_1 \\ a_2 \\ \vdots \\ a_m \end{bmatrix} = \begin{bmatrix} r_{11} & r_{12} & \cdots & r_{1m} \\ r_{21} & r_{22} & \cdots & r_{2m} \\ \vdots & \vdots & \ddots & \vdots \\ r_{n1} & r_{n2} & \cdots & r_{nm} \end{bmatrix} \bullet u \begin{bmatrix} b_1 \\ b_2 \\ \bullet \vdots \\ b_n \end{bmatrix} \tag{14}$$

The solution of fuzzy relation inequality $R \circ A \geq B$ is

$$A = R^{-1} \bullet u\; B \tag{15}$$

where $R^{-1} = \{r_{ji}\}$.

CONCLUTION

In this paper, we proposed a methodology which supports decision-making in Web service that is method for effectively utilizing "knowledge resources" on Web. Then, the decision-making problem in which decision-maker imposes certain qualifications on alternatives was considered. This paper presented the method of supporting decision-maker who decide optimal alternative under this condition.

REFERENCES

Semantic Web, http://www.w3.org/2001/sw/

W3C Web-Ontology Working Group, http://www.w3.org/2001/sw/WebOnt/.

Miyagi, H., Fan, Y., and Yamashita, K., 2001, "Solution of Fuzzy Relation Equations using Composite Operators," The Institute of Electrical Engineers of Japan, Vol. 121-C, No. 4, pp.756-761

Han, S., and Sekiguchi, T., 1995, "Decision-Making of Person Perception by the Observed Quantities-Problem of the Perception and Personal Choice by the Extended Fuzzy Relation Equation," Japan Society for Fuzzy Theory and Systems, Vol. 7, pp. 1269-1277.

Sanchez, E., 1976, "Resolution of Composite Fuzzy Relation Equations," Information and Control, Vol. 30, pp. 38-48.

Miyagi, H., Fukumura, H., and Yamashita, K., 1998, "Solution of Fuzzy Relation Equations using the Rule of Exclusion," Japan Society for Fuzzy Theory and Systems, Vol. 10, pp. 168-175.

PART V: ADAPTIVE CONTROL

UNDERWATER VEHICLE MODEL IDENTIFICATION WITH THE AID OF NEURAL NETWORKS

PEPIJN W.J. VAN DE VEN, COLIN FLANAGAN
DANIEL TOAL, EDIN OMERDIC and WILLIAM LYONS
University of Limerick
Department of Electronic and Computer Engineering
Control and Instrumentation Systems Group
Limerick, Ireland

email: pepijn.vandeven@ul.ie, colin.flanagan@ul.ie, daniel.toal@ul.ie, edin.omerdic@ul.ie, william.lyons@ul.ie

ABSTRACT
In this paper the identification of underwater vehicle dynamics with the aid of neural networks is discussed. Due to the varying nature of the underwater environment it may prove impossible to use an offline identified model of the underwater craft together with disturbances due to wind, waves and current. Neural networks offer interesting possibilities as they can be used to update the model of the underwater craft during deployment. The literature mainly reports on neural networks used in parallel to the whole system model. Rather than using one neural network to approximate a functional representing the whole dynamics, in this article it is proposed to use several neural networks to represent certain model parameters. In this way better use of the model structure, of which detailed information is available, can be made. The advantages of this 'divide and conquer' approach are demonstrated.

INTRODUCTION

As described in Fossen (1994) a vehicle's six degrees of freedom rigid-body equations can be expressed as:

$$\mathbf{M}\dot{\boldsymbol{\nu}} + \mathbf{C}(\boldsymbol{\nu})\boldsymbol{\nu} + \mathbf{D}(\boldsymbol{\nu})\boldsymbol{\nu} + \mathbf{g}(\boldsymbol{\eta}) = \boldsymbol{\tau} \tag{1}$$
$$\dot{\boldsymbol{\eta}} = \mathbf{J}(\boldsymbol{\eta})\boldsymbol{\nu},$$

with

$\boldsymbol{\eta}$ = position and orientation of the vehicle in earth fixed frame
$\boldsymbol{\nu}$ = linear and angular velocity of the vehicle in body fixed frame
$\mathbf{M}$ = inertia matrix
$\mathbf{C}(\boldsymbol{\nu})$ = matrix consisting of Coriolis and centripetal terms
$\mathbf{D}(\boldsymbol{\nu})$ = matrix consisting of damping or drag terms
$\mathbf{g}(\boldsymbol{\eta})$ = vector of forces and moments due to gravitation
$\boldsymbol{\tau}$ = vector of control inputs

The matrix $\mathbf{J}(\boldsymbol{\eta})$ converts velocity in a body fixed frame, $\boldsymbol{\nu}$, to velocity in an earth fixed frame, $\dot{\boldsymbol{\eta}}$. A detailed derivation of these non-linear equations of motion can be found in Fossen (1994). Below a short summary is given.

In the matrix $\mathbf{M}$ two inertial components are accounted for,

$$\mathbf{M} = \mathbf{M}_{RB} + \mathbf{M}_{A}. \tag{2}$$

The rigid body inertial matrix, $\mathbf{M}_{RB}$, represents the mass and inertia terms. Added mass is accounted for by the matrix $\mathbf{M}_{A}$.

For the matrix $\mathbf{C}(\boldsymbol{\nu})$, a similar discourse can be held. Both the Coriolis and the centripetal forces are functions of the rigid body mass and added mass and the velocity, $\boldsymbol{\nu}$.

$$\mathbf{C}(\boldsymbol{\nu}) = \mathbf{C}_{RB}(\boldsymbol{\nu}) + \mathbf{C}_{A}(\boldsymbol{\nu}). \tag{3}$$

$\mathbf{C}_{RB}(\boldsymbol{\nu})$ accounts for rigid body while $\mathbf{C}_{A}(\boldsymbol{\nu})$ accounts for the added mass.

In the damping matrix, $\mathbf{D}(\boldsymbol{\nu})$, four terms are combined:

$$\mathbf{D}(\boldsymbol{\nu}) = \mathbf{D}_{P} + \mathbf{D}_{S}(\boldsymbol{\nu}) + \mathbf{D}_{W} + \mathbf{D}_{M}(\boldsymbol{\nu}), \tag{4}$$

where:

$\mathbf{D}_P$	=	potential damping
$\mathbf{D}_S(\boldsymbol{\nu})$	=	linear and quadratic skin friction
$\mathbf{D}_W$	=	wave drift damping
$\mathbf{D}_M(\boldsymbol{\nu})$	=	damping due to vortex shedding

In general it is difficult to identify the various parameters in Eq. 1. Some parameters can be identified analytically (e.g. rigid body mass), but other parameters, such as added mass and damping, will have to be approximated using (full) scale tests or numerical methods. Both methods are time consuming and expensive. Additionally it should be kept in mind that no online updating of model parameters is possible.

To circumvent these problems, in this paper it is proposed to use neural networks for the identification of the model parameters. Rather than using one neural network in parallel with a known part of the model, it is proposed to use several neural networks to represent individual parameters.

In the following section the above procedure is explained. Then the identification procedure is demonstrated using simulations and finally conclusions are drawn.

REAL-TIME LEARING OF MODEL PARAMETERS USING NEURAL NETWORKS

This section details an identification procedure aimed at extracting individual parameters using separate neural networks.

Initially data is collected to calculate the mass matrix. Although the mass matrix is constant, it is difficult to obtain the values of its elements straight from the measurements. One could take measurements for low speed ($\boldsymbol{\nu} << \dot{\boldsymbol{\nu}}$) as then all factors incorporating $\boldsymbol{\nu}$ can be neglected and Eq. 1 thus simply becomes:

$$\mathbf{M}\dot{\boldsymbol{\nu}} = \boldsymbol{\tau} - \mathbf{g}(\boldsymbol{\eta}) \tag{5}$$

In theory one can calculate the mass matrix, $\mathbf{M}$ from Eq. 5. However in practice it poses severe problems as the velocity $\boldsymbol{\nu}$ is seldom small enough to be negligible.

Neural networks offer an elegant solution to the aforementioned problem. To identify the mass matrix a neural network is trained to represent the full dynamics of the craft (as expressed in Eq. 1). Its inputs are $\boldsymbol{\tau}$, $\mathbf{g}(\boldsymbol{\eta})$ and $\boldsymbol{\nu}$ from which it will calculate $\dot{\boldsymbol{\nu}}$. As the six components of the input velocity need not be of the same magnitude, use can be made of six separate networks. Otherwise complications can occur due to the fact that neurons with small learning signals tend to learn slower. When a satisfactory representation of Eq. 1 has been achieved, the mass matrix is distilled by calculating the response of the neural network for a series of control inputs, $\boldsymbol{\tau}$, while the velocity inputs, $\boldsymbol{\nu}$, are kept close to zero. A convenient value for $\boldsymbol{\nu}$ is its mean value if this is close to zero. The neural network will thus yield the product of $\mathbf{M}^{-1} \cdot (\boldsymbol{\tau} - \mathbf{g}(\boldsymbol{\eta}))$. As $\boldsymbol{\tau}$ and $\mathbf{g}(\boldsymbol{\eta})$ are known, $\mathbf{M}$ can be calculated by using a standard least squares fitting algorithm to identify $\mathbf{M}^{-1}$ and invert this matrix consecutively.

Care should be taken that independent measurement data is obtained for all six degrees of freedom. If a degree of freedom is not, or insufficiently, excited the corresponding column in the mass matrix will consist of zeros or the estimates will be far off. It is thus of paramount importance to induce movement in all degrees of freedom. For underactuated craft (underactuated meaning that it is impossible to excite all degrees of freedom) it is impossible to excite all degrees of freedom through thruster or control surface actuation. Although most underwater vehicles are underactuated, it is, however, normally possible to obtain movement in all degrees of freedom due to cross coupling or through operator manoeuvers. The same issue holds for the measurements of the induced forces when a craft is underactuated. In these cases measurements of the restoring forces, induced due to gravity and buoyancy forces, play an important role. By manoeuvering the vehicle into certain attitudes a zero force in a certain degree of freedom can be prevented due to the restoring forces now having a component in this degree of freedom. It should be mentioned that, for this strategy to be applicable, the craft should not be neutrally buoyant.

After identification of the mass matrix, the Coriolis matrix, which is a function of the mass matrix, $\mathbf{M}$ and the velocity $\boldsymbol{\nu}$, can be calculated and identification of the damping matrix, $\mathbf{D}$, can be initiated. The used procedure has previously been reported in Van de Ven *et al.* (2004). In this procedure the damping is identified by measuring the difference in output between two systems: the real system or process plant model (ppm) with damping parameters and the control plant model (cpm) in which the damping matrix is not accounted for. The difference in output is thus solely due to the damping matrix. The dynamic equation for the ppm and cpm respectively can be written as:

$$\begin{aligned} \dot{\boldsymbol{\nu}}_{ppm} &= \mathbf{M}^{-1}[\boldsymbol{\tau} - \mathbf{C}(\boldsymbol{\nu}_{ppm})\boldsymbol{\nu}_{ppm} - \\ &\quad \mathbf{D}(\boldsymbol{\nu}_{ppm})\boldsymbol{\nu}_{ppm} - \mathbf{g}(\boldsymbol{\eta}_{ppm})], \qquad (6) \\ \dot{\boldsymbol{\nu}}_{cpm} &= \mathbf{M}^{-1}\left[\boldsymbol{\tau} - \mathbf{C}(\boldsymbol{\nu}_{cpm})\boldsymbol{\nu}_{cpm} - \mathbf{g}(\boldsymbol{\eta}_{cpm})\right]. \qquad (7) \end{aligned}$$

The ppm model is used to perform a simulation with inputs given by the operator. During the simulation one-step-ahead predictions are computed from the cpm model. At every time step one assumes both systems have the same state vector: $\boldsymbol{\nu}_{ppm} = \boldsymbol{\nu}_{cpm} = \boldsymbol{\nu}$. Substituting $\boldsymbol{\nu}$ for $\boldsymbol{\nu}_{ppm}$ and $\boldsymbol{\nu}_{cpm}$ in Eq. 6 and Eq. 7, the difference between Eq. 6 and Eq. 7 becomes the damping matrix $\boldsymbol{D}(\boldsymbol{\nu})$, multiplied by the state vector $\boldsymbol{\nu}$ and the inverse of the mass matrix, $\boldsymbol{M}^{-1}$. The product $\boldsymbol{D}(\boldsymbol{\nu})\boldsymbol{\nu}$ can thus be calculated as:

$$\mathbf{D}(\boldsymbol{\nu})\,\boldsymbol{\nu} = \mathbf{M}\left[\dot{\boldsymbol{\nu}}_{cpm} - \dot{\boldsymbol{\nu}}_{ppm}\right]. \tag{8}$$

Equation 8 will be used in the identification process in which neural networks are used to make an approximation of the damping as a function of the velocity. Six separate feedforward neural networks (one for each degree of freedom) are trained to map the velocity, $\boldsymbol{\nu}$, to the damping multiplied by the velocity, $\mathbf{D}(\boldsymbol{\nu}) \cdot \boldsymbol{\nu}$.

SIMULATION STUDY

In this section application of the identification strategy outlined in the previous section is described. Using a model of the UL in-house underwater vehicle, Tethra, simulations are performed during which the model parameters are identified. To ascertain that all degrees of freedom are excited, a human operator was used. This scenario was simulated in Matlab using the virtual-reality toolbox to make a realistic representation of a real-world situation. A human operator can control the vehicle in this virtual world during which data is recorded. Once enough data has been collected to perform identification, the parameter in question is estimated. As discussed a certain order should be used for identification:

1. First a normal matrix representation of the mass matrix is determined through the use of neural networks.
2. Then the Coriolis matrix, $\mathbf{C}$ can be determined from the estimate of the mass matrix, $\mathbf{M}$.
3. Using the estimates of $\mathbf{M}$ and $\mathbf{C}$, the damping matrix, $\mathbf{D}$ can be determined using Eq. 8.

During a 250 second initial period, information was gathered to identify the mass matrix. A sampling rate of 10 Hz is used. After 250 seconds the first neural network training stage was commenced. In this stage 6 neural networks with 12 inputs neurons, 10 neurons in one hidden layer with hyperbolic tangent activation function and 1 linear output neuron were used. After 50 epochs of training the process was stopped and extraction of the mass matrix was performed. All values for $\boldsymbol{\tau}$ used in the training process were fed into the neural network one by one, while $\boldsymbol{\nu}$ was kept constant at its mean value of $[0.030.0050.0050.00020.001 - 0.02]^T$. This is sufficiently small not to be of any influence. From the collected data, which represents the product of $\boldsymbol{\tau}$ and $\mathbf{M}^{-1}$, $\mathbf{M}^{-1}$ was calculated using a least squares fitting algorithm. Finally matrix inversion of $\mathbf{M}^{-1}$ yields:

$$\mathbf{M} = \begin{bmatrix} 231.86 & -.82 & .43 & -.35 & -52.48 & .07 \\ .40 & 236.00 & .33 & 51.49 & .16 & -1.66 \\ -.12 & .45 & 235.10 & .12 & 1.45 & -.01 \\ .09 & 51.85 & .07 & 53.13 & -.09 & .47 \\ -52.57 & .16 & 1.18 & -.06 & 95.68 & -.05 \\ .03 & -1.26 & -.11 & .58 & -.05 & 98.94 \end{bmatrix} \tag{9}$$

$$\mathbf{M} = \begin{bmatrix} 231.68 & 0 & 0 & 0 & -52.53 & 0 \\ 0 & 234.73 & 0 & 51.57 & 0 & -1.22 \\ 0 & 0 & 234.73 & 0 & 1.22 & 0 \\ 0 & 51.57 & 0 & 53.12 & -.11 & .56 \\ -52.53 & 0 & 1.22 & -.11 & 95.57 & 0 \\ 0 & -1.22 & 0 & .56 & 0 & 98.56 \end{bmatrix} \tag{10}$$

This compares well with the real mass matrix in Eq. 10.

During a consecutive 250 seconds the approximate for the mass matrix is used for identification of the damping matrix. The damping to be approximated is:

$$\mathbf{D} = \begin{bmatrix} 23.17 & 0 & 0 & 0 & 0 & 0 \\ 0 & 23.47 & 0 & -0.09 & 0 & 0 \\ 0 & 0 & 23.47 & 0 & 0 & 0 \\ 0 & -0.09 & 0 & 5.31 & -0.01 & 0.056 \\ 0 & 0 & 0 & 0 & 9.56 & 0 \\ 0 & 0 & 0 & 0.056 & 0 & 9.86 \end{bmatrix} + \begin{bmatrix} 20 & 0 & 0 & 0 & 0 & 0 \\ 0 & 20 & 0 & 0 & 0 & 0 \\ 0 & 0 & 20 & 0 & 0 & 0 \\ 0 & 0 & 0 & 5 & 0 & 0 \\ 0 & 0 & 0 & 0 & 10 & 0 \\ 0 & 0 & 0 & 0 & 0 & 10 \end{bmatrix} \cdot |\boldsymbol{\nu}| \tag{11}$$

Again proper identification will highly benefit from a complete data set. Complete in this sense means that, again, all degrees of freedom need be excited. But, as damping is a non-linear function of velocity, it is also important that training data is acquired for the full range of operating velocities. After data collection the collected data is split up in train and test data. As for identification of the mass matrix, 6 different networks are used to approximate the six components of $\mathbf{D} \cdot \boldsymbol{\nu}$. The 6 networks, with 12 inputs, 10 neurons in a hidden layer using a hyperbolic tangent activation function and 1 linear output neuron, were trained with the Levenberg-Marquardt training algorithm. After 50 cycles the mean squared error for all six networks was less than $2 \cdot 10^{-5}$.

Verification of the neural network approximation of the damping matrix was performed using the test data. As the product $\mathbf{D} \cdot \boldsymbol{\nu}$ is approximated rather than the damping matrix, **D**, the verification was performed as follows.

With the test data, the neural network estimates for $\mathbf{D}\cdot\boldsymbol{\nu}$ were calculated and stored. With a least squares fitting algorithm the matrix constants of a function:

$$\mathbf{D}_f = \left(\mathbf{C_1}^{6\times 6} + \mathbf{C_2}^{6\times 6} \cdot |\nu|\right) \boldsymbol{\nu} \approx \mathbf{D}(\boldsymbol{\nu}) \cdot \boldsymbol{\nu} \tag{12}$$

were approximated, resulting in:

$$\mathbf{C_1} = \begin{bmatrix} 23.17 & 0 & 0 & 0 & 0 & 0 \\ 0 & 23.47 & 0 & -0.10 & 0.01 & 0 \\ 0 & 0 & 23.47 & 0 & 0.04 & 0 \\ 0 & 0.09 & 0 & 5.31 & -0.01 & 0.06 \\ 0 & 0 & 0 & -0.01 & 9.56 & 0 \\ 0 & 0 & 0 & 0.06 & 0 & 9.86 \end{bmatrix} \tag{13}$$

$$\mathbf{C_2} = \begin{bmatrix} 20.00 & 0 & 0 & 0.07 & -0.05 & 0 \\ 0 & 20.00 & 0 & 0.02 & -0.05 & 0 \\ 0 & 0 & 20.00 & 0 & -0.45 & 0 \\ 0 & 0 & 0 & 5.00 & 0 & 0 \\ 0 & 0 & 0 & 0 & 10.00 & 0 \\ 0 & 0 & 0 & -0.01 & -0.011 & 10.00 \end{bmatrix}. \tag{14}$$

This compares very well with the used values for the linear ($\mathbf{C_1}$) and nonlinear ($\mathbf{C_2}$) damping matrices as shown in Eq. 11.

CONCLUSIONS

In this article the main parameters of the hydrodynamic model of an underwater vehicle, namely: mass, Coriolis and centripetal forces and damping were estimated using neural networks. The neural networks are used in two different ways. In case of identification of the mass matrix (from which the Coriolis matrix can be calculated), the neural networks were used to process raw measurement data such that the mass matrix can be approximated using a least squares fitting algorithm. The identified mass matrix was used to obtain data for a neural network that was then trained to represent the damping matrix. The results show that this approach leads to satisfactory approximations of both mass and damping.

ACKNOWLEDGEMENT

This work was supported by the Irish Research Council for Science, Engineering and Technology: funded by the National Development Plan.

References

Fossen, T.I. (1994). *Guidance and Control of Underwater Vehicles.* John Wiley & Sons.

Van de Ven, P., T. A. Johansen, A. J. Sørensen, C. Flanagan and D. Toal (2004). Neural network augmented identification of underwater vehicle models. In: *IFAC conference on Control Applications in Marine Systems, July 2004.* pp. 263–8.

Hierarchical Path-Planning with Feedback of a Trailer-Truck for Online Obstacle-Avoidance

Robert Woodley and Levent Acar
Department of Electrical and Computer Engineering and
Intelligent Systems Center
University of Missouri-Rolla

ABSTRACT:
A scale model of a tractor-trailer truck was developed as a testbed for control algorithms. The truck operates in autonomous or semi-autonomous modes. Our research focus has been in the autonomous control of vehicles using intelligent systems. For this document we have employed a multi-resolutional hierarchy to plan a path for the tractor-trailer truck. The hierarchy starts with a simple path then warps it around obstacles. The modular construction of the hierarchy will allow more intelligent agents to perform some of the tasks. The current system has a feedback loop in the hierarchy which allows it to handle some motion of the obstacles. The algorithm is fast enough to allow online adaptation of the path while the truck is moving.

1 Introduction

In our previous work, the truck has been used as a testbed in non-linear dynamics, neuro-control, and fuzzy logic control applications (Woodley, Han, and Acar, 1996; Woodley, 1997; Woodley and Acar, 1998b; Woodley and Acar, 1998a). Additional earlier work was presented in (Han and Acar, 1997; Antony and Acar, 1994; Woodley and Acar, 1999). Figure 1 shows the scale model.

The current control scheme utilizes a multi-resolutional hierarchy to solve the problem of creating the path and the ability to avoid obstacles. Preliminary results may be found in (Woodley and Acar, 2004). In a multi-resolutional hierarchy, each level has a complete picture of the control system to various levels of detail. The lowest level contains the actual control signals to the servos of the system, yet the amount of information is limited. Each level of the hierarchy knows how to complete the command given to it by the previous level. The top level sets the goal.

The hierarchy increases the ability of path-planning in two ways. First, each level has only a certain range of information to learn. Second, since the hierarchy is modular by nature, a problem at one level is likely to just require retraining of that level. This is also true for the case of changing environments.

Presently, each level of the hierarchy is a fixed algorithm rather than an intelligent agent. Much is known about the truck system and the environment we are currently using. Given this information, we developed each level's algorithm knowing what situations were likely. With the success we will show here, further intelligent agents will be developed to handle even larger classes of situations.

Figure 1: The scale model trailer-truck with all the components.

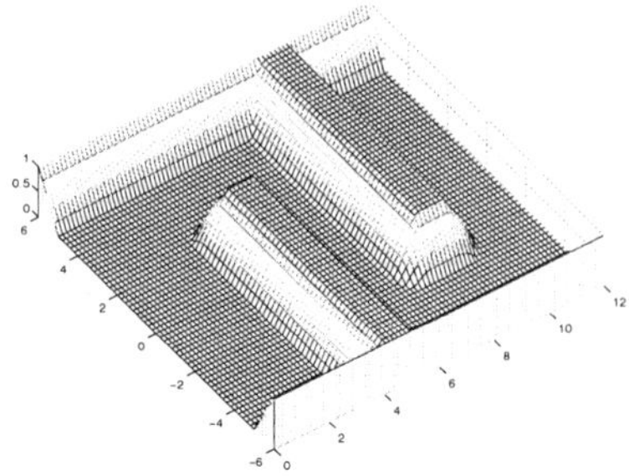

Figure 2: An example of an error-field map used by the obstacle avoidance level.

2 The Multi-Resolutional Hierarchy

The hierarchy we created has six levels as shown in Table 1. The top level, Level A, has the duty of determining if the target has been reached. Level B then adjusts the straight line path around any obstacle that the line crosses. Level C refines the path to eliminate any unnecessary turns from the path. Level D smooths the path so that any corner can then be navigated by the truck. Level E calculates the time steps between sample points, the velocity the truck will move, the angle profile of the trailer to follow the path, the angle profile of the cab to move the trailer, and the angle profile of the steering tires to move the cab. Level F contains a local feedback loop with the truck sensors to provide the signals to the truck actuators to follow the path and angle profiles. In addition, there is a feedback loop from Level C back to Level A. After each pass through the hierarchy, Level A is given the current, straight-line path that avoids obstacles.

In our previous work we trained a neural network using training vectors developed through the use of a path-planning algorithm developed by Rensselaer Polytechnic Institute (RPI) (Woodley and Acar, 1998a; Divelbiss, 1993). We showed how the approach we took improved upon work done by RPI and that it had advantages over other neural network and fuzzy logic implementations of the truck backing problem as found in (Nguyen and Widrow, 1989; Kosko, 1992). We learned that we only had to come up with a path that was somewhat close to being viable and the control system would follow it.

Level A has as its inputs the positions of known obstacles, the current position of the truck, and if any previous path has been calculated. The current position is used to generate the straight path. If the system has already generated a path, Level A can take that as the starting path to send to the other levels. If the obstacles are all still in the same location, the path will remain unchanged. If, however, an obstacle moves to a new location that intersects the existing path, the hierarchy will refine the path to avoid this obstacle.

Level B has the duty of creating straight line segments around obstacles. The obstacle locations are provided to Level B as well as the current path. The obstacle data are provided to Level B by means of an error map as shown in Figure 2.

Table 1: Level descriptions in the multi-resolutional hierarchy

Level	Action	Input	Output
A	Determine target Create initial path	Obstacle position Current position Current path	Obstacle position Current position Current path
B	Adjust path (around obstacles)	Current position Obstacle position Current path	Obstacle clearance path Obstacle position
C	Refine path (remove extra turns)	Obstacle position Obstacle clearance path	Refined path
D	Smooth path	Refined path	Smoothed path
E	Calculate movements	Smoothed path	Velocity profile Displacement profile Angle profiles
F	Control actuators (follows profiles)	Velocity profile Displacement profile Angle profiles	Steering voltage Drive voltage

The next two levels have much simpler functions, but more detail. Level C has the duty of removing unnecessary turns. The refined path generated by Level C is fed-back to Level A as the current good path. Level D takes the refined path and smooths the corners.

The dimensions, maximum velocity, and acceleration, as well as limits on the steering, are all known at level E. Level E knows what the time step size is from one path point to the next. From the time step data and the dynamics of the truck, a velocity profile is created along the path. Then the trailer, cab, and steering angles are calculated for the particular path point.

In previous work (Woodley and Acar, 2004) it was discovered that, for the trailer-truck system, the path given to the control loop need only be close to a realizable path for the controller to remain stable. Level F contains the linear controllers used on the truck. Each path position is applied to the linear controllers at a particular time. The controllers then compare the actual sensor data with desired path data to create the control signal to the actuators.

3 Simulation Results

Preliminary simulation results may be found in (Woodley and Acar, 2004), where we show how the system is able to generate near-viable paths from simple straight line initial paths. For this paper, we show how the system reacts to a moving object.

Figure 3 shows the initial path used and the output path generated. Figure 4 shows how the refined path generated by the previous pass through the hierarchy is used as the initial path for the next pass. Figure 5 shows that the obstacle is moved at a rate of 0.2 meters per iteration. Each iteration of the hierarchy takes only seconds, so the update to the path is performed online while the vehicle is moving. Figure 6 shows that the path warping continues as the obstacle moves. Figure 7 shows that the path can be warped even past the center line of the area.

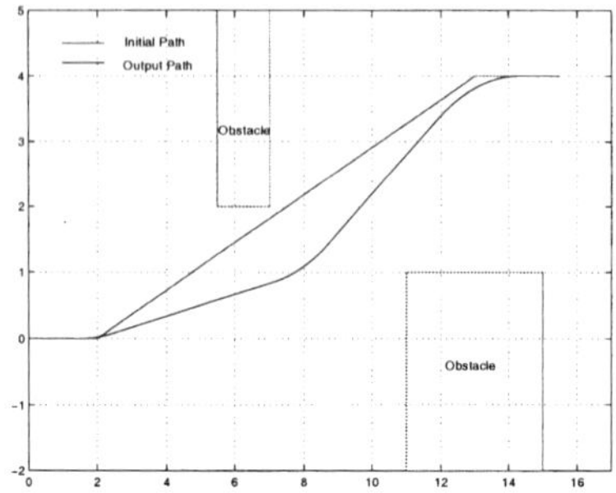

Figure 3: The initial path generated around the obstacle.

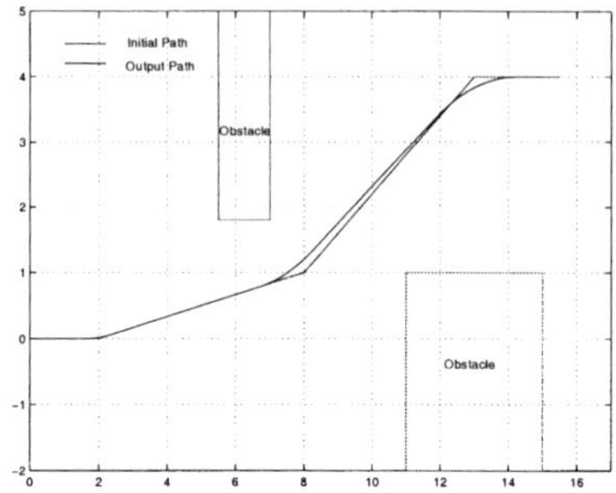

Figure 4: The previous path is used as the initial path which then warps to handle the obstacle motion.

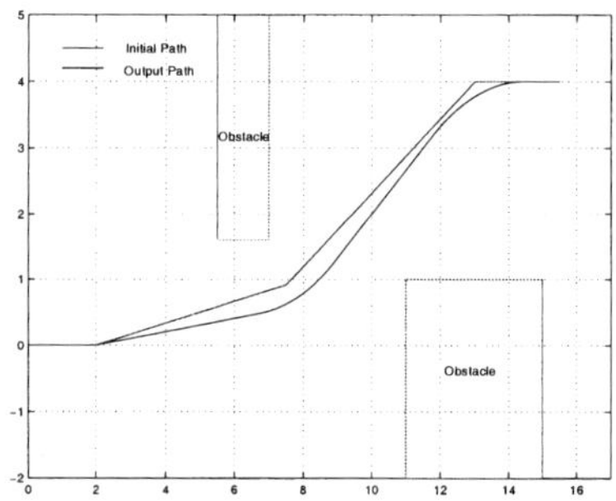

Figure 5: The obstacle is moved 0.2 meters at each step.

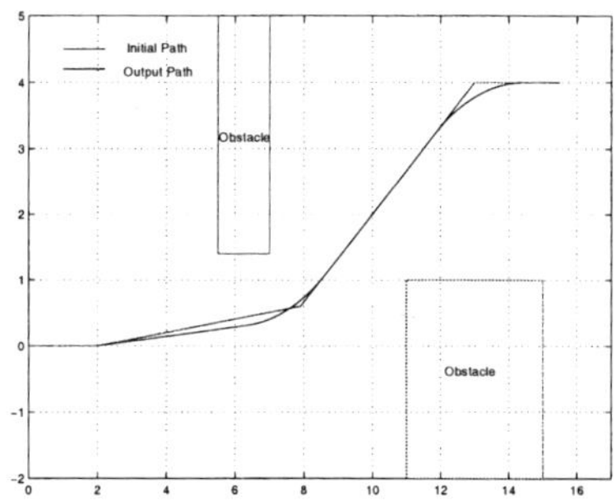

Figure 6: Each path is warped to move around the obstacle.

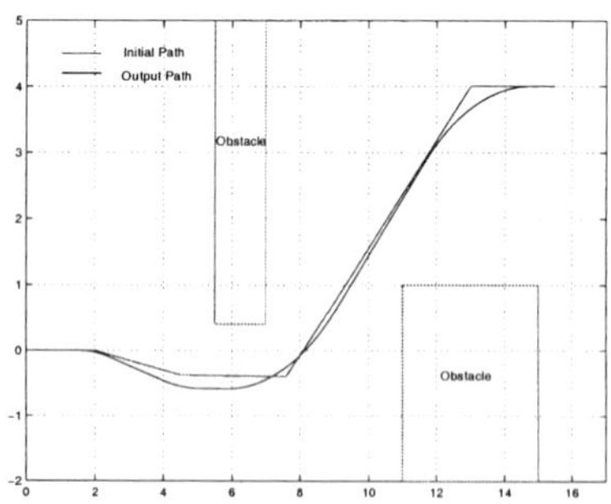

Figure 7: The path is able to continue to warp below the center line.

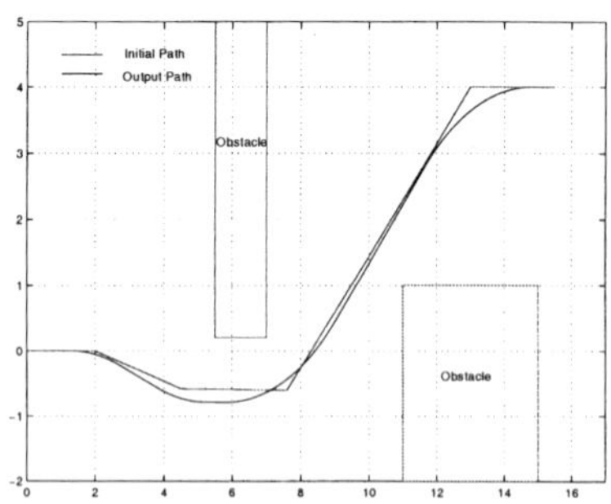

Figure 8: The path continues to warp away from the obstacle as it moves.

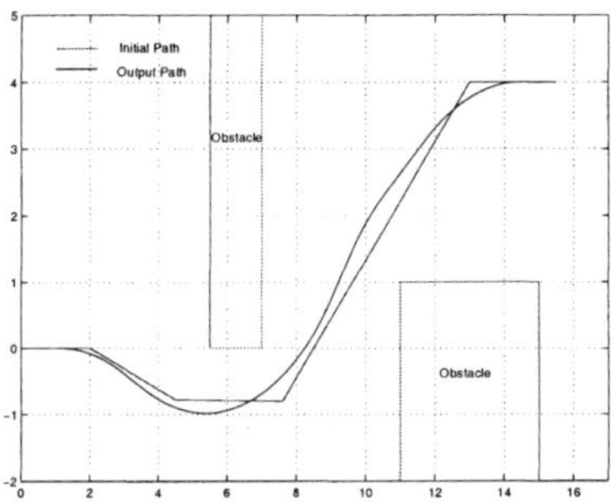

Figure 9: The path is able to to warp around additional objects as they contact the path.

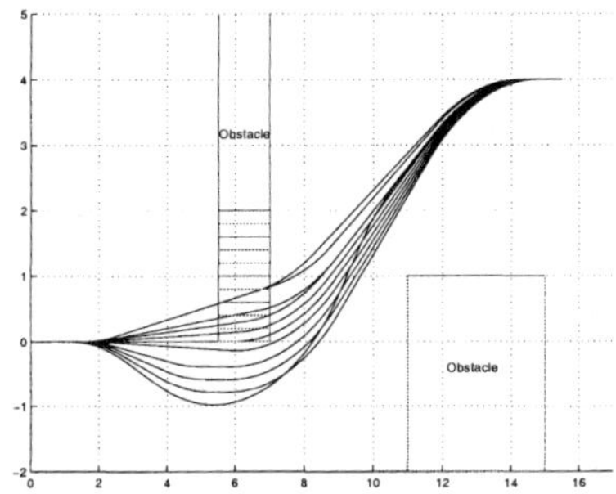

Figure 10: The progression of path changes shows how the system would react to a moving object.

Figure 8 shows how the path can continue to be warped as needed. Figure 9 shows that even if the warped path intersects an additional obstacle, the algorithm still finds a path around all the obstacles. Figure 10 shows the progression of paths as the obstacle moves. Provided the obstacle's motion doesn't cause a large change from the current path, the controllers will be able to move to the new path.

4 Conclusion

In this document we present a hierarchical, obstacle-avoidance path-planner for use on a scale model of a tractor-trailer truck. The scale model was previously developed for other intelligent system experiments.

The hierarchical approach helps to eliminate problems experienced in our previous work. The main advantage of the hierarchy is its modular construction. Small parts of the problem are able to be solved by the individual levels. The multi-resolutional aspect of the hierarchy is that each level has a complete picture of the situation to different degrees of detail and information.

The lowest levels have the most detail as to the actual motion of the truck, yet they lack the information about the goal or how to avoid obstacles. It is the job of the upper levels to provide the goal or any other difficult task. Since the problem is segmented, each task is much easier to solve. With just the simple algorithms we applied to the current system we are able to perform more difficult maneuvers, as well as in a much faster time, than we could with our previous neural network path-planning.

We have also added feedback to the system. By providing the top level of the hierarchy a good path that avoids obstacles, the system is able to refine the path for the case of a moving object. If nothing changes, the path remains unchanged. If an obstacle is detected, the algorithm recomputes a path around the obstacle.

We can now apply more robust intelligent agents in each level to try and improve the performance of the system. At present, the system is restricted to simple obstacles spaced a set distance apart. Given how this system is structured it will be easier to solve the problem of avoiding an obstacle. A system starting from scratch to solve the whole problem of path-planning, obstacle avoidance, and control of the truck will undoubtedly have a much more difficult time and take far longer to reach a solution than our system.

References

Antony, J. K. and Acar, L. (1994). Real-time nonlinear optimal control using neural networks. In *Proceedings of the 1994 American Control Conference*, Baltimore, Maryland, June-July.

Divelbiss, A. W. (1993). *Nonholonomic motion planning in the presence of obstacles.* Ph. D. thesis, Rensselaer Polytechnic Institute.

Han, T. and Acar, L. (1997). A neural network based approach for the identification and optimal control of a cantilever plate. In *Proceedings of the 1997 American Control Conference*, 1, Albuquerque, New Mexico, June, 232–236.

Kosko, B. (1992). *Neural networks and fuzzy systems: A dynamical approach to machine intelligence.* Prentice Hall, Inc.

Nguyen, D. and Widrow, B. (1989). The truck backer-upper: An example of self-learning in neural networks. In *Proceedings of 1989 IEEE International Joint Conference on Neural Networks*, 357–363.

Woodley, R. S. (1997). The identification and a neural network based control for a backward maneuvering trailer truck. Master's thesis, Department of Electrical Engineering, University of Missouri-Rolla, Rolla, Missouri.

Woodley, R. S. and Acar, L. (1998a). Neural network based control for a backward maneuvering trailer truck. In *Proceedings of the 37th IEEE Conference on Decision and Control*, 1611–1616. IEEE Press. CDC '98.

Woodley, R. S. and Acar, L. (1998b). Non-linear system control using path generating neural networks. In *Intelligent Engineering Systems Through Artificial Neural Networks*, 8, 599–604. New York, New York: ASME Press. Proceedings of the Artificial Neural Networks in Engineering (ANNIE '98).

Woodley, R. S. and Acar, L. (1999). A testbed system for nonlinear or intelligent control. In *Proceedings of the 1999 American Control Conference*, 3441–3445. IEEE Press. ACC '99.

Woodley, R. S. and Acar, L. (2004). Hierarchical path-planning with feedback of a trailer-truck for on-line obstacle-avoidance. In *Proceedings of the 2004 American Control Conference*, 1161–1166. IEEE Press. ACC 2004.

Woodley, R. S., Han, T., and Acar, L. (1996). A new control scheme applied to the trailer-truck backing-up problem. In *Intelligent Engineering Systems Through Artificial Neural Networks*, 6, 599–604. New York, New York: ASME Press. Proceedings of the Artificial Neural Networks in Engineering (ANNIE '96).

ROBUST STABILIZING CONTROLLERS FOR NONLINEAR SYSTEMS USING AN APPROXIMATE FEEDBACK LINEARIZATION

KOU YAMADA
Department of Mechanical System Engineering, Gunma University
1-5-1 Tenjincho, Kiryu, Japan

KOUJI NITTA
Department of Mechanical System Engineering, Gunma University
1-5-1 Tenjincho, Kiryu, Japan

TAKASHI OGIWARA
Department of Mechanical System Engineering, Gunma University
1-5-1 Tenjincho, Kiryu, Japan

ABSTRACT
In this paper, we propose a design method for robust stabilizing controllers of nonlinear systems to which exact linearization is not applicable. The feedback linearization problem is one of the most important control problems for nonlinear systems. Several papers on exact linearization methods have been published but these methods only apply to a limited class of nonlinear systems. Yamada and Yuzawa proposed a design method for an approximate linearization that can be applied to almost all nonlinear systems. However, their approximate linearization method does not guarantee stability of the closed control system, even without plant uncertainty. Furthermore, their method does not consider the stability of the closed control system when plant uncertainty is present. We expand the result of Yamada and Yuzawa, to propose a design method for stabilizing controllers of nonlinear systems with uncertain robustness.

Introduction

We describe a design method that robustly stabilizes controllers for nonlinear systems using approximate feedback linearization. The feedback linearization problem is a significant control problem for nonlinear systems (Isidori, 1989, Vidyasagar, 1993, Slotine and Li, 1991). There exists an approximate linearization method using a Taylor series approximation (Isidori, 1989, Vidyasagar, 1993, Slotine and Li, 1991) that is in general use. This method is effective for those nonlinear systems having a narrow range of action but is less effective for nonlinear systems with a wide range of action. Therefore, this method cannot be applied to robotic systems because, in general, robotic systems have a wide range of action. For robotic systems, exact feedback linearization using state feedback control is used (Isidori, 1989, Vidyasagar, 1993, Slotine and Li, 1991). Because this method does not use a Taylor approximation, it can be applied to nonlinear systems with a wide range of action. However, plants to which this method is applicable are restricted. For example, this method does not apply to a mobile robot. Isidori (1989) proposed exact linearization using nonlinear feedback control and coordinate transformation. This method is a powerful tool for nonlinear systems to which exact linearization using nonlinear feedback control cannot be applied. It has been shown that this method can readily be applied to nonlinear systems of the first and second order. However, it is difficult to apply to nonlinear systems of orders higher than the third. Yamada and Yuzawa (2002) proposed an approximate linearization method for nonlinear systems to which the exact approximate linearization method is not applicable. Because their method adopts an approximate feedback linearization approach, it does not guarantee the stability of the control system. In addition, when the nonlinear system has uncertainty, their method cannot be applied to the nonlinear system.

In this paper, we expand the result of Yamada and Yuzawa (2002) and propose a design method for robust stabilizing controllers of nonlinear systems with uncertainty. We adopt a three-step procedure to solve this problem. First, a state transformation matrix is determined such that the nominal nonlinear system is transformed approximately into the controllable canonical form. Then, the nonlinear system is divided into the controllable canonical representation section and the remainder. Second, the standard nonlinear feedback linearization method is used to transform the controllable canonical form into a linear system. Then the problem of designing robust stabilizing controllers is reduced to that of robust stabilizing controller design with structured uncertainty. Third, using a quadratic stabilization method, we design the robust stabilizing controllers.

Problem formulation

Consider the nonlinear system written as

$$\frac{dx}{dt} = (A(x) + \Delta(x))\,x + B(x)u, \tag{1}$$

where $x \in R^n$ is the state variable, $u \in R$ is the control input, $A(x)$ and $B(x)$ are analytic on x and $\Delta(x)$ is the uncertainty of the nonlinear system. Without loss of generality, the origin $x = 0$ is the equilibrium point. It is assumed that all the elements of $A(0)$ are finite and

$$\operatorname{rank}\begin{bmatrix} B(x) & A(x)B(x) & \cdots & A^{n-1}(x)B(x) \end{bmatrix} = n \tag{2}$$

holds in the neighborhood of $x = 0$.

The problem considered in this paper expands the result of Yamada and Yuzawa (2002) and proposes a design method for an approximate linearization method that guarantees the stability of the closed control system even if uncertainty, $\Delta(x)$, exists.

Robust stabilizing controller design

In this section, we propose a design method using approximate linearization that guarantees the stability of the closed control system even if uncertainty, $\Delta(x)$, exists. We adopt a three-step procedure to solve this problem. First, a state transformation matrix is determined, so that the nominal nonlinear system is approximately transformed into the controllable canonical form. Then, the nonlinear system is divided into the controllable canonical representation section and the remainder. Second, standard nonlinear feedback linearization is used to transform the controllable canonical form into a linear system. Then the problem of designing the robust stabilizing controller is reduced to that of robust stabilizing controller design with structured uncertainty. Third, using a quadratic stabilization method, we design the robust stabilizing controllers.

We select the coordinate transformation matrix written as

$$x = T(x)z. \tag{3}$$

Here $T(x)$ is denoted by

$$\begin{aligned} T(x) &= \begin{bmatrix} B(x) & A(x)B(x) & \cdots & A^{n-1}(x)B(x) \end{bmatrix} \\ & \begin{bmatrix} a_1(x) & a_2(x) & \cdots & a_{n-1}(x) & 1 \\ a_2(x) & & & 1 & \\ \vdots & & & & \\ a_{n-1}(x) & 1 & & & \\ 1 & & & & \mathbf{0} \end{bmatrix}, \end{aligned} \tag{4}$$

where

$$\det(sI - A(x)) = s^n + a_{n-1}(x)s^{n-1} + \cdots + a_0(x). \tag{5}$$

Applying Eq.(3) to the system in Eq.(1), we have

$$\begin{aligned} \frac{dz}{dt} &= \left(T^{-1}(x)A(x)T(x) + T^{-1}(x)\Delta(x)T(x) - T^{-1}(x)\frac{dT(x)}{dt} \right) z \\ &\quad + T^{-1}(x)B(x)u. \end{aligned} \tag{6}$$

The control input u is settled as

$$u = -\left(F_1(x) + F_2\right) z, \tag{7}$$

where $F_1(x)$ acts as the linearization feedback law to make $T^{-1}(x)A(x)T(x) - T^{-1}(x)B(x)F_1(x)$ a linear matrix and $F_2 \in R^{1\times n}$ acts as a robust stabilizing feedback law. According to Yamada and Yuzawa (2002), when $T(x)$ is selected using Eq.(4), $T^{-1}(x)A(x)T(x)$ and $T^{-1}(x)B(x)$ are written as

$$T^{-1}(x)A(x)T(x) = \begin{bmatrix} 0 & 1 & 0 & \cdots & 0 \\ \vdots & & \ddots & \ddots & \vdots \\ & & & & 0 \\ & & & & 1 \\ -a_0(x) & -a_1(x) & \cdots & & -a_{n-1}(x) \end{bmatrix} \in R^{n\times n} \tag{8}$$

and

$$T^{-1}(x)B(x) = \begin{bmatrix} 0 \\ \vdots \\ 0 \\ 1 \end{bmatrix} \in R^n, \tag{9}$$

respectively. Therefore $F_1(x)$ that makes $T^{-1}(x)A(x)T(x) - T^{-1}(x)B(x)F_1(x)$ a linear matrix is given by

$$F_1(x) = \begin{bmatrix} -a_0(x) & \cdots & -a_{n-1}(x) \end{bmatrix} \tag{10}$$

Then the control system in Eq.(6) is rewritten as

$$\frac{dz}{dt} = \left(A_z + \bar{\Delta}(z) - B_z F_2\right) z, \tag{11}$$

where

$$A_z = \begin{bmatrix} 0 & 1 & 0 & \cdots & 0 \\ \vdots & & \ddots & \ddots & \vdots \\ & & & & 0 \\ & & & & 1 \\ 0 & 0 & \cdots & & 0 \end{bmatrix} \in R^{n\times n}, \tag{12}$$

$$B_z = \begin{bmatrix} 0 \\ \vdots \\ 0 \\ 1 \end{bmatrix} \in R^n \tag{13}$$

and

$$\bar{\Delta}(z) = T^{-1}(x)\Delta(x)T(x) - T^{-1}(x)\frac{dT(x)}{dt}. \tag{14}$$

Rewrite $\bar{\Delta}(z)$ in Eq.(14) as

$$\bar{\Delta}(z) = D\hat{\Delta}(z)E \tag{15}$$

and

$$\left\|\hat{\Delta}(z)\right\| \leq 1, \tag{16}$$

where D and E are appropriate real coefficient matrices. Using Eq.(15), the control system in Eq.(11) is rewritten as

$$\frac{dz}{dt} = \left(A_z + D\hat{\Delta}(z)E - B_z F_2\right) z. \tag{17}$$

Then, the problem of designing a robust stabilizing controller is equivalent to finding F_2 to make $A_z + D\hat{\Delta}(z)E - B_z F_2$ stable, for all $\hat{\Delta}(z)$ satisfying Eq.(16). On F_2 to make $A_z + D\hat{\Delta}(z)E - B_z F_2$ stable the following theorem is satisfied.

Theorem 1 *For appropriate $\epsilon > 0$, $R > 0 \in R$ and $Q > 0 \in R^{n\times n}$, if*

$$A_z^T P + PA_z - \frac{1}{\epsilon}PB_z R^{-1}B_z^T P + PDD^T P + E^T E + \epsilon Q = 0 \tag{18}$$

has a solution $P > 0$, then F_2 written as

$$F_2 = \frac{\gamma}{2\epsilon}R^{-1}B_z^T P \ \ (\gamma \geq 1) \tag{19}$$

makes the control system in Eq.(17) exponentially stable.

(Proof) We show that if Eq.(18) has the solution $P > 0$ and F_2 is defined by Eq.(19), then the control system in Eq.(17) is exponentially stable. Consider the candidate Lyapunov function $V(z)$

$$V(z) = z^T P z. \tag{20}$$

$V(z)$ in Eq.(20) is obviously positive definite and satisfies

$$\lambda_{min}(P)\|z\|^2 \le z^T P z \le \lambda_{max}(P)\|z\|^2, \tag{21}$$

where $\lambda_{min}\{\cdot\}$ and $\lambda_{max}\{\cdot\}$ imply the smallest singular value of $\{\cdot\}$ and the largest singular value of $\{\cdot\}$, respectively. Using F_2 in Eq.(19), $\dot{V}(z)$ is written as

$$\dot{V}(z) = z^T\left(A_z^T P + P A_z - \frac{\gamma}{\epsilon} P B_z R^{-1} B_z^T P\right) z + 2z^T P D\hat{\Delta}(z) E z. \tag{22}$$

From $\gamma \ge 1$ and the assumption in Eq.(16),

$$\begin{aligned} 2z^T P D\hat{\Delta}(z)Ez &= z^T P D D^T P z + z^T E^T \hat{\Delta}^T(z)\hat{\Delta}(z) E z \\ &\quad - \left\| D^T P z - \hat{\Delta}(z) E z \right\|^2 \\ &\le z^T P D D^T P z + z^T E^T E z \end{aligned} \tag{23}$$

is satisfied. This equation yields

$$\begin{aligned} \dot{V}(z) &\le z^T\left(A_z^T P + P A_z - \frac{\gamma}{\epsilon} P B_z R^{-1} B_z^T P\right) + z^T P D D^T P z + z^T E^T E z \\ &\le z^T\left(A_z^T P + P A_z - \frac{1}{\epsilon} P B_z R^{-1} B_z^T P + P D D^T P + E^T E\right) z. \end{aligned} \tag{24}$$

Substituting Eq.(18) into Eq.(24), we have

$$\begin{aligned} \dot{V}(z) &\le -\epsilon z^T Q z \\ &\le -\epsilon \lambda_{min}(Q)\|z\|^2. \end{aligned} \tag{25}$$

From Eq.(21) and Eq.(25), if Eq.(18) has the solution $P > 0$ and F_2 is defined by Eq.(19), then the control system in Eq.(17) is exponentially stable.

∎

Remarks 1 *Yamada and Yuzawa (2002) considered that* $T^{-1}(x)\dfrac{dT(x)}{dt}z$ *in Eq.(6) is* 0. *Therefore, even if uncertainty in the plant does not exist, the method by Yamada and Yuzawa (2002) guarantees the stability of the closed control system. Using the result in Theorem 1, finding D and E satisfying*

$$T^{-1}(x)\frac{dT(x)}{dt} = D\hat{\Delta}(z)E \tag{26}$$

and

$$\left\|\hat{\Delta}(z)\right\| \le 1 \tag{27}$$

and obtaining the solution $P > 0$ *in Eq.(18), if* F_2 *is defined by Eq.(19), then the control system by Yamada and Yuzawa (2002) is exponentially stable.*

Remarks 2 *The existence of $P > 0$ in Eq.(18) is independent of the selection of Q and R.*

Remarks 3 *If Eq.(18) has the solution $P > 0$ for a ϵ^*, then for any $\epsilon \in (0, \epsilon^*)$ Eq.(18) has the solution $P > 0$.*

Using the result in Remarks 3, the procedure to design the controller satisfying Theorem 1 is summarized as:

Step 1) Select $Q > 0$, $R > 0$ and $\epsilon > 0$ in an appropriate manner.

Step 2) Obtain the solution P in Eq.(18) using the standard method. If P is positive definite, F_2 is defined by Eq.(19) and finish.

Step 3) If P is not positive definite, ϵ is reduced to half and return to Step 2).

Conclusion

By expanding the result of Yamada and Yuzawa (2002), we propose a design method for robust stabilizing controllers for nonlinear systems with uncertainty. We adopt a three-step procedure to solve this problem. First, a state transformation matrix is determined, such that the nominal nonlinear system is approximately transformed into the controllable canonical form. Then, the nonlinear system is divided into the controllable canonical representation section and the remainder. Second, the standard nonlinear feedback linearization method is used to transform the controllable canonical form into linear systems. Then the problem of designing the robust stabilizing controllers is reduced to that of robust stabilizing controller design with structured uncertainty. Third, using a quadratic stabilization method, we design the robust stabilizing controllers that guarantee that the closed control system is exponentially stable. Finally, a procedure to design the controller satisfying Theorem 1 is presented.

This research was supported by the Takayanagi Foundation for electronic science and technology.

References

A. Isidori: Nonlinear Control Systems (Third Edition), Springer-Verlag, New York (1989)

M. Vidyasagar: Nonlinear Systems Analysis, Prentice Hall, New Jersey (1993)

J.J.E. Slotine and W. Li: Applied Nonlinear Control, Prentice Hall, New Jersey (1991)

L.R. Hunt, R. Su and G. Meyer: Design for Multi-Input Nonlinear Systems, in R.W. Brockett et al. Eds., Differential Geometric Control Theory, Birkhauser(1982)

K. Yamada and A. Yuzawa: Approximate feedback linearization for nonlinear systems and its application to the ACROBOT, American Control Conference 2002, 1672/1677(2002)

ROBUST SERVO CONTROL FOR NONLINEAR SYSTEMS USING AN APPROXIMATE FEEDBACK LINEARIZATION

KOU YAMADA
Department of Mechanical System Engineering, Gunma University
1-5-1 Tenjincho, Kiryu, Japan
KOUJI NITTA
Department of Mechanical System Engineering, Gunma University
1-5-1 Tenjincho, Kiryu, Japan
TAKASHI OGIWARA
Department of Mechanical System Engineering, Gunma University
1-5-1 Tenjincho, Kiryu, Japan

ABSTRACT
In this paper, we propose a design method for robust servo control of nonlinear systems to which the exact linearization method is not applicable. The feedback linearization problem is one of the most important control problems for nonlinear systems. Several papers on exact linearization methods have been published, but these methods only apply to a limited class of nonlinear systems. Yamada and Yuzawa proposed a design method for an approximate linearization method that can be applied to almost all nonlinear systems. However their approximate linearization method applies to the regulator problem, that is, their method cannot be applied to the robust servo control problem. In this paper, we expand the result of Yamada and Yuzawa, to propose a design method for robust servo control for nonlinear systems where the exact linearization method cannot be applied.

Introduction

In this paper, we describe a design method for robust servo control of nonlinear systems where the exact linearization method cannot be applied. The feedback linearization problem is a significant control problem for nonlinear systems. There exists an approximate linearization method using a Taylor series approximation (Isidori, 1989, Vidyasagar, 1993, Slotine and Li, 1991) that is in general use. This method is effective for those nonlinear systems having a narrow range of action, but this method is less effective for nonlinear systems with a wide range of action. Therefore, this method cannot be applied to robotic systems because, in general, robotic systems have a wide range of action. For robotic systems, exact feedback linearization using state feedback control is used (Isidori, 1989, Vidyasagar, 1993, Slotine and Li, 1991). Because this method does not use a Taylor approximation, it can be applied to nonlinear systems with a wide range of action. However, plants to which this method is applicable are restricted. For example, this method does not apply to a mobile robot. Isidori proposed exact linearization using nonlinear feedback control and coordinate transformation (Isidori, 1989). This method is a powerful tool for nonlinear systems to which the exact linearization method using nonlinear feedback control cannot be applied. It has been shown that this method can easily be applied to nonlinear systems of first and second order, but it is difficult to apply to nonlinear systems of orders higher than the third. Yamada and Yuzawa (2002) propose an approximate linearization method for nonlinear systems for which the exact approximate linearization method is not applicable. However their approximate linearization method only applies to the regulator problem, that is, their method cannot be applied to the robust servo control problem. This paper aims to expand the result of Yamada and Yuzawa (2002), to propose a design method for robust servo control systems for nonlinear systems that cannot utilize the exact linearization method. We adopt a two-step procedure to solve the robust servo controller design problem. First, a state transformation matrix is derived such that the augmented nonlinear system is approximately transformed into the controllable canonical form. Second, a standard nonlinear linearization method is used to transform the controllable canonical form into a stable linear system.

Problem formulation

Consider the nonlinear system written as

$$\left\{ \begin{array}{rcl} \frac{dx}{dt} & = & A(x)x + B(x)u \\ y & = & C(x)x \end{array} \right. , \tag{1}$$

where $x \in R^n$ is the state variable, $u \in R$ is the control input, $y \in R$, and $A(x) \in R^{n\times n}(x)$, $B(x) \in R^n(x)$ and $C(x) \in R^{1\times n}(x)$ are analytic on x. Without loss of generality, the origin $x = 0$ is assumed to be the equilibrium point. It is assumed that all the elements of $A(0)$ are finite and

$$\text{rank} \left[\begin{array}{cccc} B(x) & A(x)B(x) & \cdots & A^{n-1}(x)B(x) \end{array} \right] = n \tag{2}$$

holds in the neighborhood of $x = 0$.

The problem considered in this paper expands the result of Yamada and Yuzawa (2002) and proposes a design method for control systems such that the output y of the system in Eq.(1) follows the reference input r, written as

$$r = C_r(sI - A_r)^{-1}B_r\hat{r}, \tag{3}$$

without steady state error, where $A_r \in R^{n_r \times n_r}$, $B_r \in R^{n_r}$, $C_r \in R^{1\times n_r}$ and $\hat{r} \in R$.

Robust servo controller design

In this section, we propose a design method for control systems such that the output y of the system in Eq.(1) follows the reference input r in Eq.(3) without steady state error using the approximate feedback linearization method of Yamada and Yuzawa (2002).

From the internal model principle described in Francis and Vidyasager (1983), for the output y to follow the reference input r, written as Eq.(3), without steady state error the controller must include all modes of the reference input, r. Therefore, the control input u is given by

$$u = -F(x)x(t) - K(x)x_r, \tag{4}$$

where

$$\frac{dx_r}{dt} = A_r x_r + B_r e, \quad e = r - y$$

and $x_r \in R^{n_r}$.

The control system of Eq.(1), including the control input u of Eq.(4) is rewritten as

$$\begin{cases} \frac{d\hat{x}}{dt} &= \hat{A}(x)\hat{x} + \hat{B}(x)u \\ y &= \hat{C}(x)\hat{x} \end{cases} \tag{5}$$

$$u = -\hat{F}(x)\hat{x}, \tag{6}$$

where $\hat{A}(x) = \begin{bmatrix} A(x) & 0 \\ -B_r C(x) & A_r \end{bmatrix}$, $\hat{B}(x) = \begin{bmatrix} B(x) \\ 0 \end{bmatrix}$, $\hat{C}(x) = \begin{bmatrix} C(x) & 0 \end{bmatrix}$, $\hat{x} = \begin{bmatrix} x \\ x_r \end{bmatrix}$ and

$$\hat{F}(x) = \begin{bmatrix} F(x) & K(x) \end{bmatrix}. \tag{7}$$

Next, we present a design method for $\hat{F}(x)$ to make $\hat{A}(x) - \hat{B}(x)\hat{F}(x)$ be an approximately linear matrix using the approximate feedback linearization of Yamada and Yuzawa (2002).

We adopt a two-step procedure to solve the approximate linearization. First, a state transformation matrix is determined such that the nonlinear system is approximately transformed into a controllable canonical form. Second, the standard nonlinear linearization method is used to transform the controllable canonical form into a linear system. We adopt the coordinate transformation matrix $T(x)$ written as

$$\hat{x} = T(x)z, \tag{8}$$

where $T(x)$ is denoted by

$$\begin{aligned} T(x) &= \begin{bmatrix} \hat{B}(x) & \hat{A}(x)\hat{B}(x) & \cdots & \hat{A}^{n+n_r-1}(x)\hat{B}(x) \end{bmatrix} \\ &\quad \begin{bmatrix} a_1(x) & a_2(x) & \cdots & a_{n+n_r-1}(x) & 1 \\ a_2(x) & & & 1 & \\ \vdots & & & & \\ a_{n+n_r-1}(x) & 1 & & & \\ 1 & & & & 0 \end{bmatrix}, \end{aligned} \tag{9}$$

$$\det\left(sI - \hat{A}(x)\right) = s^{n+n_r} + a_{n+n_r-1}(x)s^{n+n_r-1} + \cdots + a_0(x). \tag{10}$$

In addition, we adopt the following approximation written as

$$T^{-1}(x)\frac{dT(x)}{dt}T^{-1}(x)\hat{x} \simeq 0 \ \ \forall t, x, \tag{11}$$

that is, below it is assumed to satisfy Eq.(11).

Under the approximation of Eq.(11), applying Eq.(8) to the system in Eq.(5), requires

$$\det\left(T\left(x\right)\right) \neq 0, \tag{12}$$

to be satisfied. The system in Eq.(5) is written as

$$\left\{\begin{array}{rcl} \frac{dz}{dt} & = & T^{-1}(x)\hat{A}(x)T(x)z + T^{-1}(x)\hat{B}(x)u \\ & \equiv & A_z(x)z + B_z(x)u \\ y & = & \hat{C}(x)T(x)z \\ & \equiv & C_z(x)z \end{array}\right. , \tag{13}$$

where $A_z(x)$, $B_z(x)$ and $C_z(x)$ are denoted by

$$A_z(x) = \begin{bmatrix} 0 & 1 & 0 & \cdots & 0 \\ \vdots & & \ddots & \ddots & \vdots \\ & & & & 0 \\ & & & & 1 \\ -a_0(x) & -a_1(x) & \cdots & & -a_{n+n_r-1}(x) \end{bmatrix} \in R^{(n+n_r)\times(n+n_r)},$$

$$B_z(x) = \begin{bmatrix} 0 \\ \vdots \\ 0 \\ 1 \end{bmatrix} \in R^{n+n_r}, C_z(x) = \begin{bmatrix} C_{z1}(x) & \cdots & C_{z(n+n_r)}(x) \end{bmatrix} \in R^{1\times(n+n_r)},$$

respectively. For the system in Eq.(13), the control input u is defined by

$$u = -\begin{bmatrix} -a_0(x) + \lambda_0 & \cdots & -a_{n+n_r-1}(x) + \lambda_{n+n_r-1} \end{bmatrix} z. \tag{14}$$

When the control input u in Eq.(14) is applied to the nonlinear system in Eq.(13), the nonlinear system Eq.(13) becomes

$$\frac{dz}{dt} = \begin{bmatrix} 0 & 1 & 0 & \cdots & 0 \\ \vdots & & \ddots & \ddots & \vdots \\ & & & & 0 \\ & & & & 1 \\ -\lambda_0 & -\lambda_1 & \cdots & & -\lambda_{n+n_r-1} \end{bmatrix} z. \tag{15}$$

This is easily confirmed by using the same procedure as Yamada and Yuzawa (2002). This system is obviously a linear system. This implies that the similarity transformation in Eq.(8) and the nonlinear feedback control law in Eq.(14) make the nonlinear control system Eq.(13) linear. In addition, if $\lambda_i (i = 0, \ldots, n + n_r - 1)$ are selected such that all of the roots of

$$s^{n+n_r} + \lambda_{n+n_r-1}s^{n+n_r-1} + \cdots + \lambda_0 = 0 \tag{16}$$

are in the open left half plane, then the state equation in Eq.(15) is asymptotically stable.

From Eq.(14), Eq.(6) and Eq.(7), $F(x)$ and $K(x)$ are selected by

$$\begin{array}{rcl} \hat{F}(x) & = & \begin{bmatrix} F(x) & K(x) \end{bmatrix} \\ & = & \begin{bmatrix} -a_0(x) + \lambda_0 & \cdots & -a_{n+n_r-1}(x) + \lambda_{n+n_r-1} \end{bmatrix} T^{-1}(x). \end{array} \tag{17}$$

From the above discussion, the necessary and sufficient condition that the proposed method can be applied is obviously that $T(x)$, defined in Eq.(9), is nonsingular.

Numerical example

In this section, a numerical example illustrates the effectiveness of the proposed method. Consider the two-link planar robot in Figure 1 . Here,

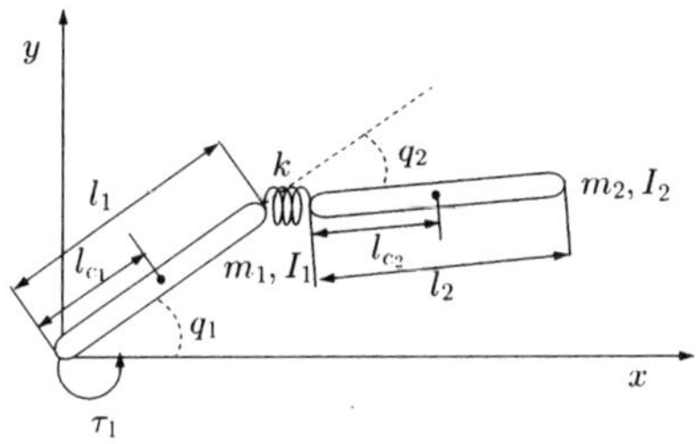

Figure 1: The two-link robot system

$m_i(i = 1,2)$ is the mass of link i, $l_i(i = 1,2)$ is the length of link i, $l_{c_i}(i = 1,2)$ is the distance to the center of link i, $I_i(i = 1,2)$ is the moment of inertia of link i about its centroid, g is the acceleration due to gravity, q_1 is the angle that link 1 makes with the horizontal, q_2 is the angle that link 2 makes with link 1, k is the stiffness of the spring and τ_1 is the torque applied on link 1. Let $\theta_j(j = 1,\dots,3)$

$$\theta_1 = m_1 l_{c_1}^2 + m_2 l_1^2 + I_1, \quad \theta_2 = m_2 l_{c_2}^2 + I_2, \quad \theta_3 = m_2 l_1 l_{c_2},$$

respectively. Using $\theta_j(j = 1,\dots,3)$, the dynamic equations of the system in Figure 1 are

$$\left\{ \begin{array}{lcl} \tau_1 & = & (\theta_1 + \theta_2 + 2\theta_3 \cos(q_2))\ddot{q}_1 + (\theta_2 + \theta_3 \cos(q_2))\ddot{q}_2 \\ & & -2\theta_3 \sin(q_2)\dot{q}_1\dot{q}_2 - \theta_3 \sin(q_2)\dot{q}_2^2 \\ 0 & = & \theta_2\ddot{q}_2 + (\theta_2 + \theta_3\cos(q_2))\ddot{q}_1 + \theta_3 \sin(q_2)\dot{q}_1^2 + kq_2, \end{array} \right. , \qquad (18)$$

where all parameters of the two-link planar robot in Eq.(18) are $\theta_1 = 0.0799$, $\theta_2 = 0.0244$, $\theta_3 = 0.0205$, $k = 1$ and $g = 9.8$. Let the state $x = [q_1(t), q_2(t), \dot{q}_1(t), \dot{q}_2(t)]^T$ and the output $y(t) = q_2(t)$. The equations in Eq.(18) are rewritten in the form of Eq.(1). Using the method described in the preceding section, we design the control system such that the output $y(t) = q_2(t)$ follows the reference input $r(t) = 0.5 \sin \omega t = 0.5 \sin \pi t$ in Eq.(3). That is, A_r, B_r, C_r in Eq.(3) are written as $A_r = \begin{bmatrix} 0 & 1 \\ -\omega^2 & 0 \end{bmatrix}$, $B_r = \begin{bmatrix} 0 \\ 1 \end{bmatrix}$ and $C_r = \begin{bmatrix} 0 & 0.5\omega \end{bmatrix}$. Using the method described above, the control input u is given by Eq.(14), where $\lambda_i(i = 0,\dots,5)$ are selected as $\lambda_0 = 464.453125$, $\lambda_1 = 918.43750$, $\lambda_2 = 777.4375$, $\lambda_3 = 362.500$, $\lambda_4 = 98.75$ and $\lambda_5 = 15$. For an initial state valuable $x(0) = [0, 0.1, 0, 0]^T$, the time response of $y(t) = q_2(t)$ is shown in Figure 2 . Here, the solid line shows

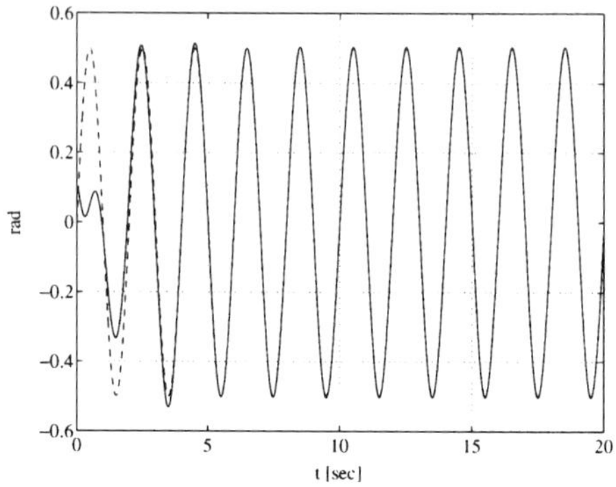

Figure 2: The time response of $y(t) = q_2(t)$

the response of $y(t) = q_2(t)$ and the dotted line shows the reference input $r(t) = 0.5 \sin \pi t$. Figure 2 shows that the output $y(t) = q_2(t)$ follows the reference input $r(t) = 0.5 \sin \pi t$ without steady state error.

Conclusion

By expanding the result of Yamada and Yuzawa (2002), we propose a design method for robust servo control for nonlinear systems where the exact linearization method is not applicable. If $\lambda_i (i = 0, \cdots, n+n_r-1)$ in Eq.(14) is selected using Neural Networks, we can design the nonlinear control system to have intelligences and linearity. This method does not make use of a Taylor approximation, as in conventional methods. It provides a wide stabilizable range for various nonlinear systems. This method is very simple and can be applied to almost all nonlinear systems.

References

A. Isidori: Nonlinear Control Systems (Third Edition), Springer-Verlag, New York (1989)

M. Vidyasagar: Nonlinear Systems Analysis, Prentice Hall, New Jersey (1993)

J.J.E. Slotine and W. Li: Applied Nonlinear Control, Prentice Hall, New Jersey (1991)

K. Yamada and A. Yuzawa: Approximate feedback linearization for nonlinear systems and its application to the ACROBOT, American Control Conference 2002, 1672/1677(2002)

B. Jakubczyk and W. Respondek: On linearization of control systems, Bull. Acad. Polonaise Sci. Ser. Sci. Math., 28,517/522(1980)

R. Su: On the Linear Equivalents of Nonlinear Systems, Systems and Control Letters, 2-1, 48/52(1982)

B. Francis and M. Vidyasager: Algebraic and topological aspects of the regulator problem for lumped linear systems, Automatica, 19, 87/90(1983)

A DESIGN METHOD FOR ADAPTIVE CONTROL SYSTEMS USING THE PARAMETERIZATION OF ALL STABILIZING CONTROLLERS FOR MINIMUM PHASE SYSTEMS

KOU YAMADA
Department of Mechanical System Engineering, Gunma University
1-5-1 Tenjincho, Kiryu, Japan

KEIJI SATOH
Department of Mechanical System Engineering, Gunma University
1-5-1 Tenjincho, Kiryu, Japan

NOBUAKI MATSUSHIMA
Department of Mechanical System Engineering, Gunma University
1-5-1 Tenjincho, Kiryu, Japan

ABSTRACT
In this paper, we describe a design method for adaptive control systems of minimum phase systems using the parameterization of all stabilizing controllers. The parameterization problem finds all stabilizing controllers. Glaria and Goodwin gave the parameterization of all stabilizing controllers for minimum phase systems. However, their parameterization has practical difficulties. Yamada overcame their problems and proposed the complete parameterization of all stabilizing controllers of minimum phase systems. In this paper, using the result by Yamada, we present new design method for adaptive control systems of minimum phase systems.

Introduction

In this paper, we examine a design method for adaptive control systems of minimum phase systems. In previous studies of control design methods, many arguments have been made under the assumption that the plant is of minimum phase, for example decoupling control (Falb and Wolovich,1967; Gilbert, 1969), model matching control, inverse systems (Yamada and Watanabe, 1992), model feedback control (T. Narikiyo and T. Izumi, 1991), simple adaptive control (Sobel, Kaufman and Mabius, 1982), model reference adaptive control (Narendra and Annaswamy, 1989). Almost all the above design methods adopt the idea such that all of zeroes of the plant are cancelled by the poles of the controller. To achieve internal stability conditions, all of zeroes of the plant must be in the open left half plane. That is, the plant is necessarily minimum phase. These methods use only one characteristic of the minimum phase, the minimum phase system has no zeroes in the closed right half plane. Other characteristics have not been used and clarified. Considering the control characteristics of minimum phase systems, it is natural to start discussion from the parameterization of all stabilizing controllers of minimum phase systems. The parameterization of all stabilizing controllers for the minimum phase systems was solved by Glaria and Goodwin (1994) and by Yamada (2001).

The purpose of this paper is to clarify the control structure for minimum phase systems using the parameterization of Glaria and Goodwin (1994) and Yamada (2001). In addition, we propose a design method for an adaptive control system using the control structure obtained. First, we clarify the control structure for the minimum phase systems using the parameterization of Glaria and Goodwin(1994) and Yamada(2001). It is shown that if the existence of the infinite gain loop is allowed, then we can design control system such that the control system stabilizes any minimum phase plant even if the coefficients of the plant are all unknown. That is, we can design an asymptotically stable control system even if the coefficients of the plant are all unknown. In some cases, the existence of the infinite gain loop is not allowed. When the existence of the infinite gain loop is not allowed, the control structure for the minimum phase system is given. Using this structure, we propose a design method for adaptive control systems.

Control structure for minimum phase systems

In this section, we summarize the parameterization of all stabilizing controllers for the minimum phase systems (Glaria and Goodwin, 1994, Yamada, 2001) and present new control structures for minimum phase systems.

Consider the unity feedback control system

$$\left\{ \begin{array}{lcl} y & = & G(s)u \\ u & = & -C(s)y \end{array} \right. . \tag{1}$$

Here, $G(s) \in R(s)$ is the single-input/single-output linear minimum phase system. That is, $G(s)$ has no zero in the closed right half plane. $C(s) \in R(s)$ is the controller, $y \in R$ is the output and $u \in R$ is the input. When $G(s)$ is biproper, that is, the degree of numerator of $G(s)$ is equal to that of denominator of $G(s)$, the necessary and sufficient condition that the control system in Eq.(1) is asymptotically stable is summarized by the following theorem.

Theorem 1 *If $G(s)$ is of minimum phase and biproper, then the proper controller $C(s)$ stabilizes the unity feedback control system Eq.(1) and all of the transfer function $(1+G(s)C(s))^{-1}$, $C(s)(1+G(s)C(s))^{-1}$, $G(s)(1+G(s)C(s))^{-1}$ and $G(s)C(s)(1+G(s)C(s))^{-1}$ are proper if and only if $C(s)$ can be written as*

$$C(s) = \frac{1}{Q(s)} - \frac{1}{G(s)} \left(\lim_{\omega \to \infty} (1 + G(j\omega)C(j\omega)) \neq 0 \right), \tag{2}$$

where $1/Q(s)$ is any minimum phase and biproper rational function (Glaria and Goodwin, 1994, Yamada, 2001).

By Theorem 1, the control structure to stabilize the minimum phase biproper system $G(s)$ is shown in Figure 1 . Figure 1 is rewritten by Figure 2 to hold u in Figure 1 to be equal to u in Figure 2 . It is interesting that when we construct the control system in Figure 2 , the dynamics of the plant $G(s)$ are not required. That is, the control structure in Figure 2 can always stabilize any minimum phase biproper plant $G(s)$ even if the coefficients of the plant $G(s)$ are all unknown.

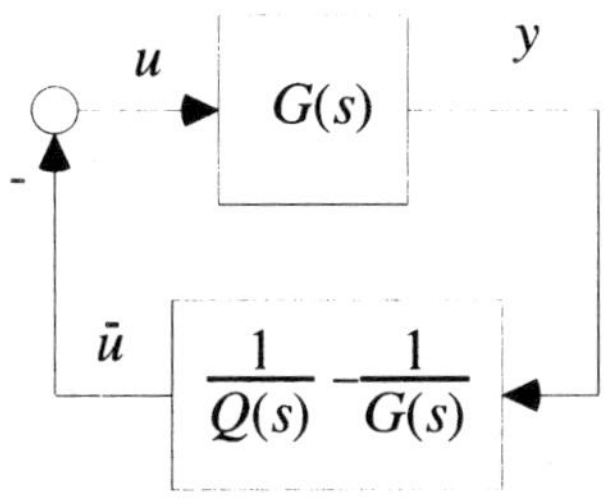

Figure 1: Control structure for the minimum phase biproper system

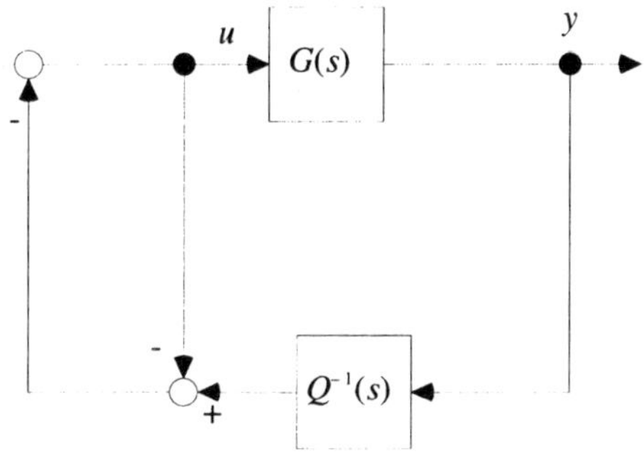

Figure 2: Similarity transformation of Fig.1

The control system in Figure 2 has infinite gain loop. In practice, infinite gain loop is not desirable or not allowed. In such cases, to stabilize the minimum phase system $G(s)$, it is necessary to do system identification or adaptation. When the infinite gain loop is not allowed, the control system in Figure 1 is rewritten as Figure 3 to hold u in Figure 1 to be equal to u in Figure 3 . Here, $Q_1(s) \in RH_\infty$ and $Q_2(s) \in RH_\infty$ satisfy

$$Q(s) = G(s)Q_1(s) + Q_2(s). \tag{3}$$

Any asymptotically stable $Q(s)$ can always be factorized as Eq.(3). The parameterization of all $Q_1(s)$ and $Q_2(s)$ may be written as

$$\begin{bmatrix} Q_1(s) \\ Q_2(s) \end{bmatrix} = \begin{bmatrix} 0 \\ Q(s) \end{bmatrix} + \begin{bmatrix} D(s) \\ -N(s) \end{bmatrix} L(s), \tag{4}$$

where, $L(s) \in RH_\infty$ is any rational function, $N(s) \in RH_\infty$ and $D(s) \in RH_\infty$ are coprime factors of $G(s)$ on RH_∞ satisfying $G(s) = N(s)/D(s)$.

In this section, we show that if the control system in Figure 2 is allowable, then we can design a control system such that the unity feedback control system in Eq.(1) is asymptotically stable. When the control system Figure 2 is not allowable, we can use the control structure in Figure 3 .

In the next section, we give a design method of adaptive control system using the control structure in Figure 3 .

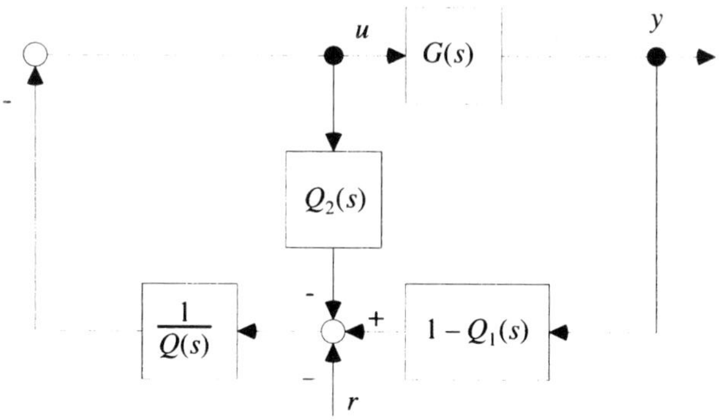

Figure 3: Control system for the biproper system

Model reference adaptive control

In this section, we propose a design method of adaptive control system using control structure described in the preceding section.

$G(s)$ is assumed to be biproper and of minimum phase. $G_m(s)$ denotes the reference model

$$y_m(t) = G_m(s)r(t), \quad G_m(s) = 1, \tag{5}$$

where $r(t)$ is the reference input, $y_m(t)$ is the output of the reference model. Without loss of generality, $r(t)$ is a bound and continuous signal, that is, $r(t)$ is differentiable.

The problem considered in this section is to design a control system to satisfy

$$\lim_{t\to\infty} (y(t) - y_m(t)) = 0 \tag{6}$$

and all of signals in the control system are bounded by the assumption that all coefficients of both numerator and denominator of $G(s)$ are unknown.

From Figure 3 and Eq.(4), the control input u is

$$\begin{aligned} u(t) &= -\frac{1}{Q(s)}\{(1 - Q_1(s))\,y(t) - Q_2(s)u(t)\} + \frac{1}{Q(s)}r(t) \\ &= \frac{L(s)D(s) - 1}{Q(s)}y(t) + \frac{Q(s) - L(s)N(s)}{Q(s)}u(t) + \frac{1}{Q(s)}r(t). \end{aligned} \tag{7}$$

Let $\omega_1(t)$ and $\omega_2(t)$

$$\omega_1(t) = \frac{1}{\lambda_1(s)}\begin{bmatrix} 1 \\ \vdots \\ s^{n+n_l} \end{bmatrix} y(t) \tag{8}$$

and

$$\omega_2(t) = \frac{1}{\lambda_2(s)}\begin{bmatrix} 1 \\ \vdots \\ s^{n+n_l+n_q} \end{bmatrix} u(t), \tag{9}$$

respectively. θ_1 and θ_2 are settled to satisfy

$$\theta_1\omega_1(t) = (L(s)D(s) - 1)\, y(t) \tag{10}$$

and

$$\theta_2\omega_2(t) = (Q(s) - L(s)N(s))\, u(t), \tag{11}$$

respectively. Here $\lambda_1(s)$ is polynomial of the denominator of $L(s)D(s)$, $\lambda_2(s)$ is polynomial of the denominator of $Q(s) - L(s)N(s)$, n_l is the degree of the denominator of $L(s)$, n_q is the degree of the denominator of $Q(s)$. Eq.(7) is rewritten as

$$u(t) \;=\; \frac{1}{Q(s)}\theta_1\omega_1(t) + \frac{1}{Q(s)}\theta_2\omega_2(t) + \frac{1}{Q(s)}r(t). \tag{12}$$

From the assumption that all of coefficients of the plant $G(s)$ are unknown, θ_1 and θ_2 are unknown parameters. Let the estimated values of θ_1 and θ_2 be denoted by $\hat{\theta}_1(t)$ and $\hat{\theta}_2(t)$, respectively. Then we have an adaptive control law

$$u(t) \;=\; \frac{1}{Q(s)}\hat{\theta}_1(t)\omega_1(t) + \frac{1}{Q(s)}\hat{\theta}_2(t)\omega_2(t) + \frac{1}{Q(s)}r(t). \tag{13}$$

Next, we describe an estimation law for θ_1 and θ_2. To produce an estimation law an estimation model for Eq.(13) is required. In control law Eq.(12), replacing $1/Q(s)r(t)$ with $1/Q(s)y(t)$ we have

$$y(t) = Q(s)u(t) - \theta_1\omega_1(t) - \theta_2\omega_2(t). \tag{14}$$

Let $\xi_1(t)$, $\xi_2(t)$ and $\nu(t)$ be $\xi_1(t) = \omega_1(t)$, $\xi_2(t) = \omega_2(t)$ and $\nu(t) = Q(s)u(t)$, respectively. Then Eq.(14) is

$$y(t) = \nu(t) - \theta_1\xi_1(t) - \theta_2\xi_2(t). \tag{15}$$

The error $e(t)$ between the output $y(t)$ and the output of the reference model $y_m(t)$ is

$$e(t) \;=\; y(t) - y_m(t) = \nu(t) - \theta_1\xi_1(t) - \theta_2\xi_2(t) - y_m(t). \tag{16}$$

To identify θ_1 and θ_2 in Eq.(16), the following method can be used. Let $\hat{e}(t)$ be estimation value of $e(t)$ Eq.(16). We have

$$\hat{e}(t) \;=\; \nu(t) - \hat{\theta}_1(t)\xi_1(t) - \hat{\theta}_2(t)\xi_2(t) - y_m(t). \tag{17}$$

The error $e_e(t)$ between $e(t)$ and $\hat{e}(t)$ is

$$e_e(t) \;=\; e(t) - \hat{e}(t) = \zeta_1(t)\xi_1(t) + \zeta_2(t)\xi_2(t) = \zeta(t)\xi(t), \tag{18}$$

where $\zeta(t) = \begin{bmatrix} \zeta_1(t) & \zeta_2(t) \end{bmatrix}$, $\xi(t) = \begin{bmatrix} \xi_1(t) \\ \xi_2(t) \end{bmatrix}$ and $\zeta_i(t) = \hat{\theta}_i(t) - \theta_i(i = 1,2)$. Eq.(18) is linear function of θ_1 and θ_2. We have adaptive law for Eq.(18) by

$$\dot{\hat{\theta}}(t) = -\frac{e_e(t)\Gamma\xi(t)}{\sigma + \xi^T(t)\xi(t)}, \tag{19}$$

where Γ is any positive definite diagonal matrices and $\sigma > 0$.

Thus, the proposed adaptive control law is summarizes as follows:

1. The parameter estimation law is given by Eq.(19).
2. The control law is given by Eq.(13).

Stability of the control system using the proposed adaptive control law is summarized by the following theorem.

Theorem 2 *$G(s)$ is assumed to be of minimum phase and biproper. If the control law is given by Eq.(13) and parameter estimation law is given by Eq.(19), then all signals in the feedback loop are bounded and Eq.(6) holds.*

(Proof is omitted due to space limitations.)

Using a similar procedure, we can design an adaptive control system for the minimum phase strictly proper system. The detail of the design method for an adaptive control system for a minimum phase system is omitted due to space limitations.

Conclusion

In this paper, we clarify the control structure for minimum phase systems and propose a design method for an adaptive control system using the control structure obtained.

References

E.G. Gilbert: The decoupling of multivariable systems by state feedback, SIAM J. on Control, 7, pp.50–64(1969)
J.J. Glaria and G.C. Goodwin: A parameterization for the class of all stabilizing controllers for linear minimum phase systems, Trans. on AC, 39, pp.433–434(1994)
K.S. Narendra and A.M. Annaswamy: Stable adaptive systems. Prentice Hall (1989)
K. Sobel, H. Kaufman and L. Mabius: Implicit adaptive control for a class of mimo systems, IEEE Trans. Aerospace and Electronic Systems, AES-18, pp.576–589(1982)
K. Yamada: A parameterization for the class of all proper stabilizing controllers for linear minimum phase systems, Preprints of the 9th IFAC/IFORS/IMACS/IFIP/ Symposium on Large Scale Systems: Theory and Applications, pp.578–583(2001)
K. Yamada and K. Watanabe: State space design method of filtered inverse systems, Trans. of the Society of Instrument and Control Engineers, 28, pp.923–930(1992) P.L. Falb and W.A. Wolovich: Decoupling in the design and synthesis of multivariable control systems, IEEE Trans. on AC, 12, pp.651–659(1967)
T. Narikiyo and T. Izumi: On model feedback control for robot manipulators, Journal of Dynamic Systems, Measurement, and Control, 113, pp.371–378(1991)

DEVELOPMENT OF AN AUTONOMOUS MOBILE ROBOT FOR RADIATION SOURCE DETECTION USING NEURAL NETWORKS

MANASH BURAGOHAIN
Department of Mechanical and Aerospace Engineering, University of Missouri – Rolla, USA

GANESH K VENAYAGAMOORTHY
Department of Electrical and Computer Engineering, University of Missouri – Rolla, USA

AKIRA TOKUHIRO
Department of Mining and Nuclear Engineering, University of Missouri – Rolla, USA

ABSTRACT

This paper presents the design of an autonomous mobile robot to map out the radiation sources on a contaminated surface. This involves simulation of a mobile robot with sensors and the radiation sources on a surface. The basic search criteria are dependent on the strength of the source and the distance it is from the robot. A neural network is developed to navigate the mobile robot to the radiation sources. This paper provides an alternative to human involvement in detection and identification of radiation contamination. Preliminary simulation results are promising and are presented in the paper.

INTRODUCTION

Considering a hypothetical situation such as an accident at a nuclear plant, a site of dirty bomb or Radiological Dispersal Device (RDD) [1] attack. There is a need for immediate identification and isolation of the radiation sources. It is a very hazardous task, at the same time neither it be neglected nor delayed. Traditionally humans did the task. There have been attempts to develop technologies which will reduce human involvement. One of the prominent among the many technologies proposed and developed consists of the class of remotely operated systems. Though remotely operated systems reduce the human involvement, it is seen by the industry as a very complicated and cost intensive technique. Also it is widely accepted that the factor of time and human exposure will be the critical parameters in developing any system for identification and the isolation of the radioactive sources in a situation of nuclear emergency. Because more swiftly a radiation source is identified the lesser time it will take to isolate it and thus reduces the chance of contaminating more areas. In a situation of nuclear emergency the amount of radiation dispersed cannot be determined or projected accurately [2] as during experiments performed under controlled conditions.

There have been efforts for radiation detection in an unstructured environment [3] and some using distributed system for surveillance in unstructured environments [4]. In the past decade, there has been considerable effort to develop autonomous robotic vehicles for random patrols, barrier assessment, intruder detection, reconnaissance and surveillance, building entry, target detection, building or terrain mapping, and explosives neutralization.

Mobile robotic platforms with the above capabilities will improve the ability to counter threats, limit risks to personnel, and reduce manpower requirements in hazardous environments. By increasing sensory "reach", giving the robots a significant degree of autonomy and it seeks to augment human capabilities, reduce exposure to risk, and present timely, relevant information to the user.

Similar initiatives to develop Unmanned Ground Vehicles for remote reconnaissance and surveillance have been reported in the literature. Sandia National Laboratories developed the Surveillance And Reconnaissance Ground Equipment (SARGE) [5] robotic vehicle for the US DoD. SARGE is a teleoperated robot for battlefield surveillance applications without computing power to support autonomous navigation or vision processing. SARGE was built around a Yamaha Breeze 4-wheel all-terrain vehicle.

In [6] an Autonomous Robot for Surveillance Key Applications (ARSKA) is presented. This UGV is built around a Honda TRX 350 all-terrain vehicle. ARSKA is equipped with ultrasonic sensors for contour following and obstacle avoidance. Two positioning systems have been used with the vehicle: an external optical measurement device called a tachymeter, and differential GPS (DGPS). ARSKA can be controlled using a ground station. The basic functions of the ground station are task preparation and monitoring and on-line telecontrol of the vehicle. ARSKA has been used to guard an Army storage area.

The focus of the above autonomous robotic surveillance and reconnaissance systems is the use of real time computing based on conventional algorithms to accomplish the task at hand. In this type of autonomous surveillance system, minimal supervised autonomy is achieved at the expense of costly and power-intensive sensors and high-bandwidth, bulky tele-operated command and control ground stations. In general, a high degree of autonomy requires considerable computing power. The path planning algorithms used generally require prior knowledge of free paths and obstacles in the environment, which are not always available. These deficiencies pose considerable challenges when such autonomous platforms are to be employed in applications or environments that they were not initially designed for.

In these single-platform surveillance systems, the principal cost is that of the computing and payload. However, if a intelligent computing technique such as neural network is employed, and limit the payload according to the specifics of the task, cheap intelligent autonomous mobile agents can be developed.

In this paper, the use of a feedforward neural network navigator for a robot for radiation source mapping is presented. The feedforward neural network structure is favourable for real time implementation on a field programmable gate array with less computational intensity and memory requirements.

MOBILE ROBOT AND SENSORS

The design of the robot is such that it is equipped with four radiation intensity sensors (1-4) in four cardinal directions as shown in figure 1. The sensors have a resolution of 180 degrees, which makes them effective towards radiation in front and not influenced by radiations behind them. The intensity of a radiation source measured by a sensor depends on its orientation with the sensor and also on the Euclidean distance between them.

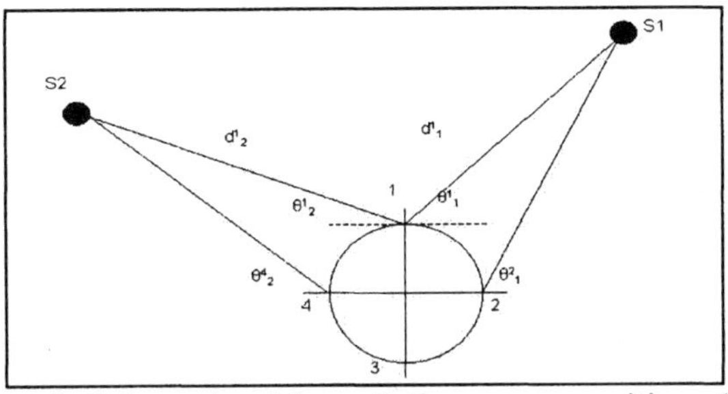

Figure 1: Schematic of the radiation sensor positions (1-4) and the orientations with two radiation sources (S1 and S2).

For the simulation of these radiation intensity sensors, they are modeled based on the formula given in (1a) and (1b) for sensor 1 and 2 respectively.

$$I_1 = \frac{S1}{(d_1^1)^2}\sin(\theta_1^1) + \frac{S2}{(d_2^1)^2}\sin(\theta_2^1) \tag{1a}$$

$$I_2 = \frac{S1}{(d_1^2)^2}\cos(\theta_1^2) \tag{1b}$$

Hence, (1a) and (1b) can be generalized as:

$$I_j = \sum_{i=1}^{n} \frac{Si}{(d_i^j)^2}\sin(\theta_i^j) \tag{2a}$$

for, $j = 1$ and 3.

$$I_j = \sum_{i=1}^{n} \frac{Si}{(d_i^j)^2}\cos(\theta_i^j) \tag{2b}$$

for, $j = 2$ and 4.

Where:

- j is sensor number.
- i is number of active sensor w.r.t. sensor j
- I is the intensity measured at the individual sensors
- Si is the absolute strength of the radiation source
- d is the Euclidean distance between the source and the sensor
- θ is the angle between the source beam and the sensor.

Random radiation sources are initialized in the field of activity. The robot with the four sensors starts with a initial step, gets the intensity feedback for all its sensors and orients itself and moves another step. The basic criteria for reorientation is such that the the robot moves towards the source, which emits the strongest signal. During the search process, the cardinality of the sensors remains intact, only the orientation with respect to the movement of the robots keeps updating according to the changes in the intensity fields. This approach is explained below.

As a convention, the numerals – 1, 2, 3 and 4 are replaced with the cardinal directions North, South, East and West respectively for denoting the sensors. The sensor strengths are recorded for the first step as N_1, S_1, E_1 and W_1 and for the nth step the strengths are N_n, S_n, E_n, W_n. The algorithm then proceeds towards calculating the potential gradient in the sensors on the basis of the strengths in two consecutives steps. This is illustrated in (3) below.

$$N_{grad} = \frac{N_{n+1} - N_n}{k},\ S_{grad} = \frac{S_{n+1} - S_n}{k},\ E_{grad} = \frac{E_{n+1} - E_n}{k},\ W_{grad} = \frac{W_{n+1} - W_n}{k} \qquad (3)$$

Where 'k' is the distance moved by the robot in a single step.

Based on the gradients and the actual strengths a "Decision Matrix" is generated for deciding the course of direction of the robot (Table 1).

Table 1: Decision matrix

	N_{grad}	S_{grad}	E_{grad}	W_{grad}
N_{grad}	0	*NS*	*NE*	*NW*
S_{grad}	*SN*	0	*SE*	*SW*
E_{grad}	*EN*	*ES*	0	*EW*
W_{grad}	*WN*	*WS*	*WE*	0

Where: $NS=SN= N_{grad}-S_{grad}$, $NE=EN= N_{grad}-E_{grad}$, and so on.

The decision on the direction of motion is based on a set of rules illustrated for the case where N_{grad} is the highest. In the matrix the values of *NS*, *NE*, *NW* are considered and the rules below are applied.

a. If *NE* is the lowest then move in the *N-E*
b. If *NW* is the lowest then move in the *N-W*
c. If $NE=NW$ and are the lowest then move in the *N*
d. If *NS* is the lowest AND $NE < NW$ OR $NE = SE$ then move in the *E*
e. If *NS* is the lowest AND $NE > NW$ OR $NW = SW$ then move in the *W*
f. If $NE = NW = SE = SW$ move in the direction highest of among $N_{n+1}=E_{n+1}=S_{n+1}=W_{n+1}$.

Similarly, a set of rules exist for cases where S_{grad}, W_{grad}, and S_{grad} are the highest.

As can be seen, the method described above for locating the sources involves a great deal of compuation. And to incorporate it into a real unit, and embedding the whole program into a hardware is not viable when we need to develop a low cost, miniature autonomous mobile radiation detection unit. Therefore, in this paper the alternative design based on a neural network to overcome the computational burden and provide a nonlinear path for the detection unit is presented.

NEURAL NETWORK NAVIGATOR

A feedfoward neural network [7] shown in figure 2 is trained with backpropagation for the mobile robot navigation.

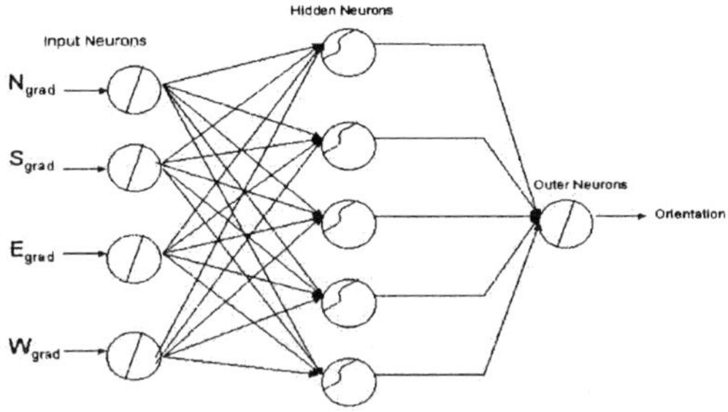

Figure 2: The feedforward neural network architecture implemented for estimating the orientation of the robot.

The inputs to the neural network are the intensity gradients recorded by the four radiation intensity sensors, and the output is the orientation of the robot corresponding to input set of intensity gradients. The feedforward neural network has linear neurons in the input and output layer, and five sigmoidal neurons in the hidden layer. A trained network having a sufficient accuracy can predict the path of the robot that was obtained using the conventional method (non-neural network). For training the neural network, data is generated using the conventional algorithm at this stage.

RESULTS

The results obtained with the conventional algorithm is denoted in the diagrams below as 'Actual'. The results obtained with the neural network is denoted as 'NN based'. Figure 3 shows the path of the robot taken to locate the five radiation sources of equal intensity when they are both located in a single quadrant.

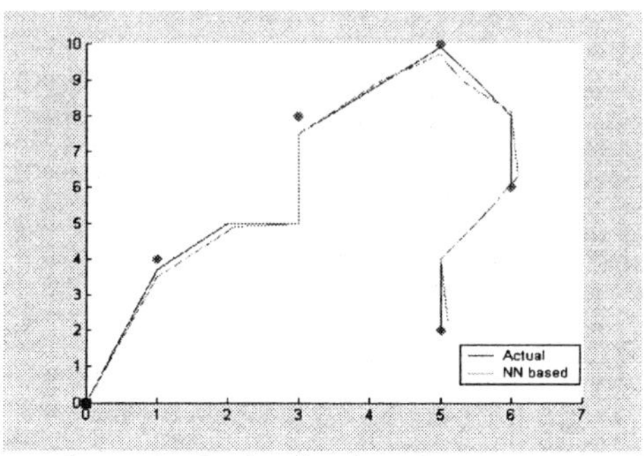

Figure 3: This shows the path obtained using the conventional method and with the neural network method.

Figure 4 shows the path taken by the robot for locating the same five radiation sources but now placed in all the four quadrants. In both the cases , it is clear the neural network has learned the conventional algorithm but can locate the sources much faster than the conventional algorithm which requires more time to calculate the orientation at each instant.

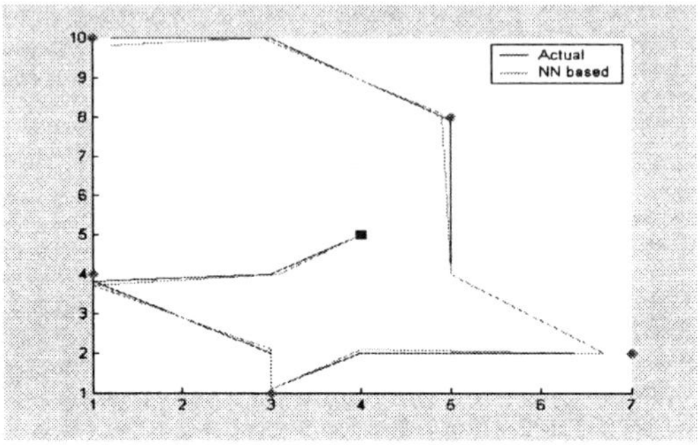

Figure 4: This shows the path obtained using the conventional method and with the neural network method when the sources in the adjacent quadrants.

CONCLUSIONS

It have been shown that a feedfoward neural network can be successfully trained to locate radiation sources randomly spread out in a field or building. The accuracy achieved is comparable to the conventional method but at the same time the computation involved using the neural network (4×5×1) is noticeably small compared to that taken by the conventional algorithm.

Future work involves the development of the above system for radiation sources of varying intensity and an environment with obstacles. It is anticipated that some form of reinforcement learning will be used. The next step is implementing the simulated system into an actual robotic system with actual radiation intensity sensors using a digital programmable platform.

REFERENCES

[1] U.S. Nuclear Regulatory Commission, “Fact Sheet on Dirty Bombs,” http://www.nrc.gov/reading-rm/doc-collections/fact-sheets/dirty-bombs.html , 04/30/2004.

[2] Center for Disease Control and Prevention, “Dirty Bombs - Dangers of a dirty bomb,” http://www.bt.cdc.gov/radiation/dirtybombs.asp , 04/30/2004.

[3] Ron Fulbright and Larry M. Stephens, "SWAMI: An Autonomous Mobile Robot for Inspection of Nuclear Waste Storage Facilities”. Autonomous Robots, vol. 2., 1995, pp. 225-235.

[4] John M. Dolan, Ashitey Trebi-Ollennu, Alvaro Soto and Pradeep Khosla, “Distributed Tactical Surveillance with ATVs”. SPIE (the International Society for Optical Engineering), Proceedings on Unmanned Ground Vehicle Technology (AeroSense '99), Vol. 3693, April, 1999, pp. 192-199

[5] J. Bryan Pletta and John Sackos, “An Advanced Unmanned Vehicle for Remote Applications” Sandia National Laboratories Report, 1998.

[6] Schönberg, T., Ojala, M., Koskimäki, E., Suomela, J. & Halme, A., “A small Scaled Autonomous Test Vehicle for Developing Autonomous Off-Road Applications”, International Conference on Machine Automation, Tampere, Finalnd, 1994, pp. 143-157

[7] Andries P. Engelbrecht, “Computational Intelligence: An Introduction”, John Wiley, 2002. ISBN: 0-470-84870-7

A PERCEPTION-BASED APPROACH TOWARD ROBOT CONTROL BY NATURAL LANGUAGE

MASOUD GHAFFARI
Center for Robotics Research
University of Cincinnati
Cincinnati, Ohio

SOUMA M. ALHAJ ALI
Industrial Engineering Department
Hashemite University
Zerka, Jordan

ERNEST L. HALL
Center for Robotics Research
University of Cincinnati
Cincinnati, Ohio

ABSTRACT

Mobile robot navigation is an active area of research with many potential military and civilian applications. Yet, there are many unsolved problems which probably either need a breakthrough in the current theories or a completely new approach for the solution. Extraordinary abilities of humans in doing these tasks without any measurement have inspired many researchers. One of these abilities is the ability of processing words instead of numbers. The purpose of this paper is to survey different applications of natural language for robot control and to propose a perception-based model.

INTRODUCTION

The problem of autonomous navigation in unknown environments is very difficult, and calls for sophisticated sensing strategies and control architectures (Oriolo, Ulivi, & Vendittelli, 1996). Most of methods have been basically realized by combining algorithms acquired by human. How can we realize the capability of acquiring algorithms automatically like the human brain? This problem is very difficult to solve (Kubota, Morioka, Kojima, & Fukuda, 2001).

Artificial intelligence, psychology, biology, neuroscience, linguistics, and many other fields try to get insights into what is called human intelligence. This includes being able to model the world, plan and predict events, learn, make decisions, as well as many other abilities.

In many real world applications it is not possible to have previous data about the course and predict the dynamic environment. One example is driving a car in a city. That is a place that human perception shows its extra ordinary capability.

The classical AI methodology has two important assumptions: the ability to represent hierarchical structure by abstraction, and the use of "strong" knowledge that utilizes explicit representational assertions about the world (Boden, 1995). The assumption was that knowledge and knowledge representation are central to intelligence, and that robotics was no exception. Perhaps these were the result of studying human-level intelligence and not lower live forms of creatures.

LITERATURE REVIEW

ROBOT (Harris, 1977) and SHRDLU (Winograd, 1972) were among the first attempts for natural language communication with robots (Harris, 1977; Romano, Camacho, Ortega, & Bonilla, 2000; Winograd, 1972). However, both of them used simulated robots and not real ones. SHRDLU allows the user to command a robot that moves in a world made of blocks. Selfridge and Vannoy (1986) present a natural language interface to an assembly robot which allows the user to talk with the system in order to recognize the shapes of objects and put them together to make a more complex component. The knowledge base consists of a set of if-then rules (Selfridge & Vannoy, 1986).

Some natural language interfaces include both written and spoken forms of natural language. The users of SAM (Brwon et al., 1992) can use a telephone or a keyboard to command the robot. The robot was a manipulator arm with six axes and a gripper. The user can introduce a description of the objects. This description will later be used to command the robot to perform actions with them (Brown, Buntschuh, & Wilpon, 1992; Romano et al., 2000).

Most of these robots can run a very specific and limited plan. This is a common feature in the majority of systems designed for natural language communication with robots (Romano et al., 2000).

Uncertainty representation is an important point to consider. Initial works mainly focused on probabilistic methods where Bayesian probabilities were used to represent partial beliefs (Elfes, 1987; Gasos & Rosetti, 1999). These approaches cannot distinguish between lack of information and uncertain information, and a probability assignment to a proposition automatically implies an assignment also to its negation (Tirumalai, Schunck, & Jain, 1995). Dempster-Shafer used the theory of evidential reasoning (Kim & Swain, 1995) and fuzzy logic have been used as alternatives (Gasos & Rosetti, 1999; Saffiotti & Wesley, 1996).

Fuzzy logic based approaches uses different types of behavior using fuzzy reasoning rather than simply inhibiting some types of behavior according to an assigned priority. As a result, unstable oscillations between different types of behavior can be avoided (Li, Ma, & Wahl, 1997).

HUMAN PERCEPTION

Perception is the name given for the process of the organization, interpretation and the explanation of the data reaches to the brain from the sense organs. The data reaching at the sense organs have no importance without perception. The senses have to be perceived, in other words explained. We can only decide what kind of a reaction we are going to give to the senses only after perception.

Perception is a vital part of human reasoning. Human do a variety of physical and mental tasks without any measurements and computations. Some examples of these activities are driving in traffic, parking a car, cooking a meal, playing an instrument and summarizing a story. In fact, the capability to perform these tasks is based on the brain's ability to manipulate perceptions, perceptions of time, distance, force, direction, speed, shape, color, likelihood, intent, truth and other attributes of physical and mental objects (Zadeh, 1999).

The literature on perception is huge, including thousands of papers and books in the areas of psychology, linguistics, philosophy, brain science, and many others (Carruthers & Chamberlain, 2000). And yet, what is not in existence is a theory in which perceptions are treated as objects of computation. Such a theory is needed to make it possible to conceive, design, and construct systems which have a much higher machine intelligence than those we have today (Zadeh, 1999).

APPLICATIONS OF NATURAL LANGUAGE CONTROL

In practical products, applications of natural language perception-based control might be implemented differently. One application might be object identification. Range sensors such as laser, ultrasonic, and stereovision, the most commonly used sensors in robot navigation, only provide information about the existence of objects in some given positions of space. Many applications require identifying the type of objects that have been detected to make the appropriate decision by the robot, considering the fact that the object identification problem has not been solved for many real world situations (Gasos, 2001).

For example an unmanned combat vehicle may face a variety of environments. If the object recognition algorithm tries to match the description of the detected object with all possible objects, the search would be huge and probably unpractical. But, if a user describes the more probable objects that might be found in a certain mission, object identification would be much easier.

Natural language also can be used for industrial robot programming especially when users are inexperienced and don't know about computer programming. It can replace the current teach pending modules which still use a keyboard interface. Another potential application of natural language perception-based control is in Ergonomics.

Ergonomics studies the human-machine interaction and tries to find a more user friendly interface for man machine communication. Human made systems are getting more complex and sophisticated everyday. At the same time human operators have to interact to and control these systems. They get information from the system status and they perform proper actions. It is possible to reduce complexity of interaction by designing automated systems and by designing an adequate interface between the operator and the system. Design of a friendly interface which decreases complexity of interaction and allows the operators to act in a simple and quick way in every kind of situation is important (Romano et al., 2000).

Probably it is not unrealistic to predict a time that design software packages like AutoCAD™ are able to design modules by recognizing the verbal description of system from the designer. Combination of such a system with the traditional interfaces could change the human design's ability tremendously. The software industry already is moving in that direction. Now, there are voice recognition word processors and in many packages menu commands can be run by voice.

PROPOSED FRAMEWORK

Most of research on verbal communication with robots has mainly focused on issuing commands, like activating pre-programmed procedures using a limited vocabulary (Lauria, Bugmanna, Kyriacou, & Klein, 2002). They directly convert the voice commands to measurement without computing on perceptions. The focus of this approach is on mimicking human perception and some degree of computation on perception.

Information which is conveyed by propositions drawn from a natural language will be said to be perception-based (Zadeh, 2002). Natural language perception-based control (NLPC) can be defined as "*perceiving information about the dynamic environment by interpreting the natural language and reacting accordingly*".

In the NLPC, perceptions are not dealt with directly. Instead, NLPC deals with the descriptions of perceptions expressed in the natural language. Therefore, propositions in a natural language play the role of surrogates of perceptions. In this way, manipulation of perceptions is reduced to a familiar process, manipulation of propositions expressed in a natural language (Zadeh, 1999). Table 1 compares measurement-based and perception-based information.

Table 1. Comparison of measurement and perception-based information

Information	**Data**	**Example**
Measurement-based	Numerical	There is a obstacle 20.2 feet away
Perception-based	Linguistic	There is a ramp in front

The problem is how to compute on perceptions and use it for robot control. To be realistic, the proposed framework applies some assumptions to restrict the scope of model.

- Natural language processing is limited to simple propositions related to the robot navigation.
- The robot will work on the semi-supervised mode by receiving the feedback from the environment. Full autonomous mode of work, which includes replacing of the operator by sensory systems, is not in the domain of this research.
- Less precision, which is an intrinsic part of perception, in exchange to the lower cost and complexity of sensory system, is accepted.

An experiment of proposed framework was implemented and tested by the authors (Ghaffari et al., 2004). The robot control was implemented in two phases. The first phase is the instructional mode. The commands was given to the robot and robot followed the instructions based what operator perceives. Table 2 shows some examples of these commands.

The second mode is the declarative mode. In this mode the environment was described to the robot with simple propositions. The robot should make its movement decisions based on what is described to it. Propositions are limited to what is expected in the Intelligent Ground Vehicle Competition (IGVC) course. Table 3 gives an idea about some of these propositions.

Table 2. Example of instructional control commands

What	Where	How much
MOVE	LEFT	A LITTLE
MOVE	FORWARD	UNTIL SEE OBSTACLE/LINE DISAPEAR
GO TO	OBSTACLE	UNTIL VERY CLOSE/CLOSE
FOLLOW	KNOWN ROUTE	UNTIL it is DEFFERNT
LOOK	from RIGHT CAMERA	UNTIL SEE A LINE/OBSTACLE
CONTINUE	in AUTOMODE	
STOP		

What makes these two modes of control different is different between traditional language based robot control and the perception based control. The first mode is based on issuing commands. In this case it is not difficult to covert voice commands to computer instructions. In contrast, the second mode of control calls for more sophisticated algorithms. This mode is closer to human communication and it is a place that perception-based control shows its advantages.

Table 3. Examples of propositions in the declarative mode

Proposition	Possible action
There is an obstacle in the front left	Move a little bit to right
Left line is disappearing	Switch to the right camera for line following
The obstacle is very close in front	Make a big turn
There is a obstacle in front close to the left line	Turn to right and then left

MODEL VALIDATION

The IGVC course was used as a test bed for model validation. In the navigation challenge of this contest there are white lines to follow, which sometimes disappear, and barrels to avoid. This course declared to the system by an operator and the robot was supposed to navigate through the path.

CONCLUSIONS

New efforts have been made that pay more attention to computation of words, and perceptions carried out by natural language. Among many disciplines who study human brain abilities probably fuzzy logic and its new trend, computational theory of perceptions, have closer ties to engineering and practical applications. This research provided a survey of current technology and a framework for perception-based natural language control of robots. Further description and design details of the test robot is explained in (Ghaffari et al., 2004).

REFERENCES

Boden, M., 1995, "AI's Half-Century," *AI Magazine,* Vol. 16, 2, pp. 69-99.

Brown, M. K., Buntschuh, B. M., & Wilpon, J. G. ,1992, "A perceptive spoken language understanding robot," *IEEE Transactions on Systems, Man and Cybernetics*, Vol. 22, 6, pp. 1390-1402.

Carruthers, P., & Chamberlain, A., 2000, "Evolution and the human mind, modularity, language and meta-cognition," Cambridge: Cambridge University.

Elfes, A., 1987, "Sonar-based real world mapping and navigation," *IEEE Journal of Robotics and Automation*, Vol. 3, pp. 249-265.

Gasos, J., 2001, "Integrating linguistic descriptions and sensor observations for the navigation of autonomous robots," In D. Driankov & A. Saffiotti (Eds.), *Fuzzy logic Techniques for autonomous vehicle navigation,* Vol. 61, pp. 313-339. New York: Physica-Verlag.

Gasos, J., & Rosetti, A., 1999, "Uncertainty representation for mobile robots: Perception, modeling and navigation in unknown environments," *Fuzzy Sets and System,* Vol. 107, pp. 1-24.

Ghaffari, M., Alhaj Ali, S. M., Murthy, V., Liao, X., Gaylor, J., & Hall, E. L., 2004, "Design of an Unmanned Ground Vehicle, Bearcat III, Theory and Practice," *Journal of Robotic Systems,* Vol. 21, 9.

Harris, L. R. ,1977, "ROBOT: a high performance natural language processor for data base query," *ACM SIGART Newsletter,* Vol. 61, pp. 39-40.

Kim, H., & Swain, P., 1995, "Evidential reasoning approach to multi source data classification in remote sensing," *IEEE Transactions on Systems, Man and Cybernetics,* Vol. 25, 8, pp. 1257-1265.

Kubota, N., Morioka, T., Kojima, F., & Fukuda, T., 2001, "Learning of mobile robots using perception-based genetic algorithm," *Measurement,* Vol. 29, pp. 237-248.

Lauria, S., Bugmanna, G., Kyriacou, T., & Klein, E., 2002, "Mobile robot programming using natural language," *Robotics and Autonomous Systems*, Vol. 38, 171-181.

Li, W., Ma, C., Wahl, F. M.,1997, "A neuro-fuzzy system architecture for behavior-based control of a mobile robot in unknown environments," *Fuzzy Sets and System,* Vol. 87, pp. 133-140.

Oriolo, G., Ulivi, G., & Vendittelli, M., 1996, "Fuzzy Maps: A New Tool for Mobile Robot Perception and Planning," *Journal of Robotic Systems,* Vol. 14, 3, pp. 179-197.

Romano, J. M. G., Camacho, E. F., Ortega, J. G., & Bonilla, M. T. , 2000, "A generic natural language interface for task planning application to a mobile robot," *Contrōl Engineering Practice,* Vol. 8, pp. 1119-1133.

Saffiotti, A., Wesley, L., 1996, "Perception-based self localization using fuzzy locations," In L. Dorst (Ed.), *Reasoning with Uncertainty in Robotics, Lecture Notes in Artificial Intelligence,* pp. 368-385, Berlin: Springer.

Selfridge, M., Vannoy, W. , 1986, "A natural language interface to a robot assembly system," *IEEE Journal of Robotics and Automation,* Vol. 2, 3, pp. 167-171.

Tirumalai, A., Schunck, B., Jain, R., 1995, "Evidential reasoning for building environment maps," *IEEE Transactions on Systems, Man and Cybernetics,* Vol. 25,1, pp. 10-20.

Winograd, T., 1972, *Understanding natural language.* New York: Academic Press.

Zadeh, L. A., 1999, *A new direction in fuzzy logic-toward automation of reasoning with perceptions.* presented at the Fuzzy Systems, IEEE International.

Zadeh, L. A., 2002, "Toward a perception-based theory of probabilistic reasoning with imprecise probabilities," *Journal of Statistical Planning and Inference,* Vol. 105, pp. 233-264.

USING A DIGITAL CONTROLLER FOR A NEURAL NETWORK AUTONOMOUS NAVIGATION SYSTEM FOR A WHEELED MOBILE ROBOT

SOUMA M. ALHAJ ALI
Industrial Engineering Department
The Hashemite University
B. O. Box: 150459, Zerka 13115
Jordan

MASOUD GHAFFARI
Center for Robotics Research
University of Cincinnati
Cincinnati, OH 45221-0072

ERNEST L. HALL
Center for Robotics Research
University of Cincinnati
Cincinnati, OH 45221-0072

ABSTRACT

This paper presents the development of a PD digital motion controller for the autonomous navigation of a wheeled mobile robot (WMR) in an outdoor environment. The controller selects the suitable control torques so that the WMR will follow a desired path that was produced from a navigation algorithm. The navigation algorithm was developed using a feed forward multi-layer neural network. Software was developed to simulate the performance and efficiency of the controller. The simulation shows that the tracking error did not exceed .05 using a 20 msec sample period. The significance of this work is in using the digital controller in a new application which would facilitate the use of WMR in numerous applications including defense, industrial, and medical robots.

INTRODUCTION

Different controllers had been developed for the motion control of robot manipulators; however, not until recently has there been an interest in moving the robot itself, not only its manipulators (Alhaj Ali, 2003).

A computed torque control scheme for Cartesian velocity control of WMRs has been developed by Rajagopalan and Barakat (1997). Zhang and Hirschorn (1997) presented a discontinuous stabilizing controller for WMRs with nonholonomic constraints where the state of the robot asymptotically converges to the target configuration with a smooth trajectory. Koh and Cho (1999) formulate a path tracking problem for a mobile robot to follow a virtual target vehicle that is moved exactly along the path with specified velocity. A dynamic modeling for a tracking controller for a differentially steered mobile robot that is subject to wheel slip and external loads was employed by Zhang, et al. (2003).

A solution for the trajectory tracking problem for a WMR in the presence of disturbances that violate the nonholonomic constraint was proposed based on discrete-time sliding mode control (Alhaj Ali, 2003, Corradini and Orlando, 2002, Corradini, et al., 2002).

Wu, et al. (2001) investigated an electromagnetic approach for path guidance of a mobile-robot-based automatic transport service system with a PD control algorithm. An adaptive robust controller was proposed for the global tracking problem for the dynamic of the non-holonomic systems with unknown dynamics (Dong, et al., 1999).

This paper presents the development of a digital controller for WMR navigation in unstructured outdoor environments; the controller selects suitable control torques for the motors, which causes the robot to follow the desired path from the navigation algorithm. The navigation algorithm was developed using a feedforward neural network with five layers; the network was trained using the quasi-Newton backpropagation algorithm. For further details on the navigation algorithm please refer to (Alhaj Ali, 2003).

A dynamic simulation was conducted from a framework developed by Lewis, et al. (1999). The Lewis framework was formulated for a trajectory of robot manipulators. However, this paper is oriented toward robot navigation. Thus, the Lewis framework was adjusted, as needed, to control the robot path, instead of the manipulators trajectories (Alhaj Ali, 2003).

Simulation software permitting easy investigation of alternative architectures was developed by using MATLAB and C++. The simulation used the Bearcat III dynamic model developed in (Alhaj Ali, 2003).

DIGITAL CONTROLLER

Due to the rapid advances in digital control theory, the availability of high performance low-cost microprocessors, and digital signal processors, digital control systems have gained popularity and importance in industry. However, stability and sampling period selection are important factors to consider (Kuo, 1992).

The objective of a motion controller is to move the robot according to the desired motion trajectory $q_d(t)$. The actual motion trajectory is defined as $q(t)$. The tracking error, in this case, can be defined as Lewis, et al. (1999):

$$e(t) = q_d(t) - q(t) \tag{1}$$

The Brunovsky canonical form can be developed by differentiating $e(t)$ twice and writing it in the terms of the state x (Lewis, et al., 1999, Alhaj Ali, 2003):

$$\frac{d}{dt}\begin{bmatrix} e \\ \dot{e} \end{bmatrix} = \begin{bmatrix} 0 & I \\ 0 & 0 \end{bmatrix}\begin{bmatrix} e \\ \dot{e} \end{bmatrix} + \begin{bmatrix} 0 \\ I \end{bmatrix} u \tag{2}$$

where:

$$u \equiv \ddot{q}_d + M^{-1}(q)(N(q,\dot{q}) - \tau)$$

$x = \begin{bmatrix} e^T \\ \dot{e}^T \end{bmatrix}$, $M(q)$: is the inertia matrix in the WMR dynamic model;

$N(q,\dot{q})$: are all the nonlinear terms in the WMR dynamic model.

To develop the controller, a linear system design procedure is used to select the feedback control signal $u(t)$, which stabilizes the tracking error equation. Then the torques needed for the motors are computed by using the inverse of the dynamic equation for the WMR (Lewis, et al., 1999, Alhaj Ali, 2003):

$$\tau = M(q)(\ddot{q}_d - u) + N(q,\dot{q}) \tag{3}$$

Eq. (3) represents a nonlinear feedback control law, which guarantees tracking the desired motion trajectory $q_d(t)$. It is termed feedback linearization, based on computing the motor torques making the nonlinear dynamic systems

A PD feedback for $u(t)$, with a derivative gain matrix K_v and a proportional gain matrix K_p, produces the PD CT controller, where the motor torques equal (Lewis, et al., 1999):

$$\tau = M(q)(\ddot{q}_d + K_v\dot{e} + K_p e) + N(q,\dot{q}) \tag{4}$$

which has the tracking error dynamics $\ddot{e} = -K_v\dot{e} - K_p e$

The PD digital controller output can be calculated by using the following equation (Lewis, et al., 1999, Alhaj Ali, 2003):

$$\tau_\varepsilon = M(q_\varepsilon)(\ddot{q}_{d\varepsilon} + K_\upsilon\dot{e}_\varepsilon + K_p e_\varepsilon) + N(q_\varepsilon,\dot{q}_\varepsilon) \tag{5}$$

The control input can be calculated only at certain sample times, $t_\varepsilon = \varepsilon T$, where T is the sample period, and ε is the integer value.

Care should be taken with some of the problems inherent to digital controllers, such as stability, actuator saturation, and antiwindup (Lewis, et al., 1999).

SIMULATION OF THE DIGITAL CONTROLLER FOR THE WMR

Simulation software for the digital controller of WMR was developed, as follows, using Eq. 5 and the WMR dynamics that was developed in (Alhaj Ali, 2003), the WMR parameters are according to a three wheels WMR called Bearcat III (Alhaj Ali, 2003).

The simulation was developed as follows (Alhaj Ali, 2003):

- The controller input is only updated at times εT.
- The controller computes the first control output by using the initial robot dynamics state values. The integrator then holds this value for its calculations over one sample time.
- For the next sample period, the final robot dynamics state values are assigned as the new initial robot dynamics state values. The integrator holds this value for its calculations over this sample time period, etc.

RESULTS

Different controller parameters and different trajectories were tried and the results discussed below:

Case I: In the first experiment, the following simulation parameters were used:
Desired trajectory: $q_{d1}(t) = 0.1\sin t$, $q_{d2}(t) = 0.1\cos t$, $q_{d3}(t) = 0.1\sin t$.

Controller parameters: k_p =2, k_v =0, sample period=20 msec.

The tracking errors for this case were in the range of -0.8-0.2. The actual motion trajectories are smooth, but far from the desired motion trajectories.
Case II: To study the effect of increasing the derivative gain, another experiment was conducted, with the following simulation parameters:
Desired trajectory: $q_{d1}(t) = 0.01\sin t$, $q_{d2}(t) = 0.01\cos t$, $q_{d3}(t) = 0.01\sin t$.

Controller parameters: k_p =2, k_v =1, sample period=20 msec.

The results are shown in Figs. 1-2. As shown in Fig. 1, the tracking errors were very small in this experiment. The tracking errors for x and θ are almost zero. For y, the tracking error oscillates between 0.000 and -0.025. The actual motion trajectories are smooth and match the desired motion trajectories for x and θ. For y, the actual motion trajectory is also smooth, but higher than the desired motion trajectory.

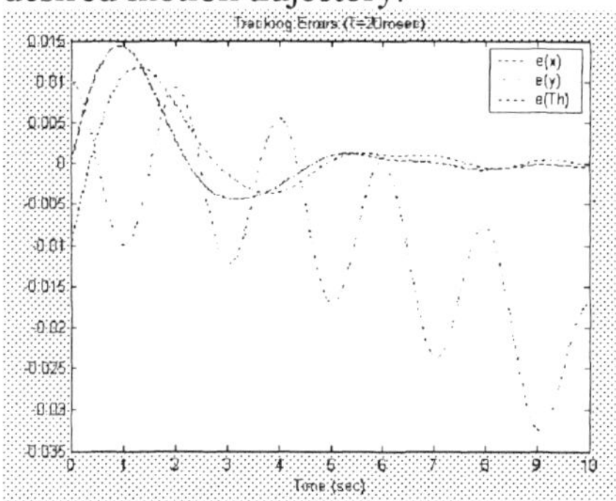

Figure 1: Tracking errors for case II (Alhaj Ali, 2003).

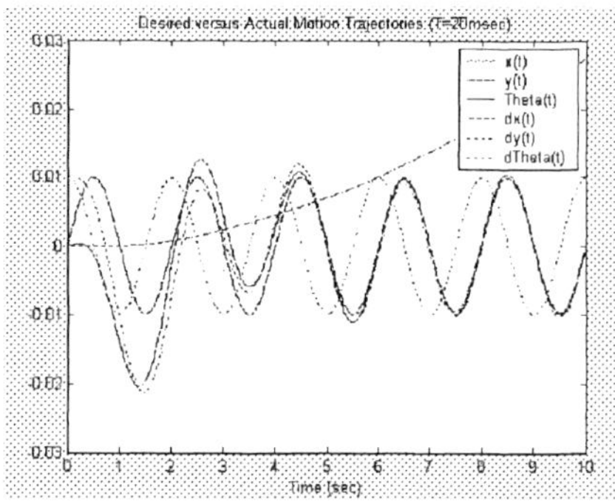

Figure 2: Desired versus actual motion trajectories for case II (Alhaj Ali, 2003).

Further increasing the derivative gain, k_v, from 1 to 100 does not improve the results.
Case III: To study the effect of the different amplitudes for the desired motion trajectories, another experiment was conducted with the following simulation parameters:
Desired trajectory: $q_{d1}(t) = 0.001\sin t$, $q_{d2}(t) = 0.001\cos t$, $q_{d3}(t) = 0.001\sin t$.

Controller parameters: k_p =2, k_v =1, sample period=20 msec.

The results are shown in Figs. 3-4. As shown in Fig. 3, the tracking errors were very small in this experiment. The actual motion trajectories are smooth and match the desired motion trajectories for x and θ. For y, the actual motion trajectory is equal to zero. This result is interesting, since it shows that even the amplitudes of the desired motion trajectory have an effect on the tracking errors.

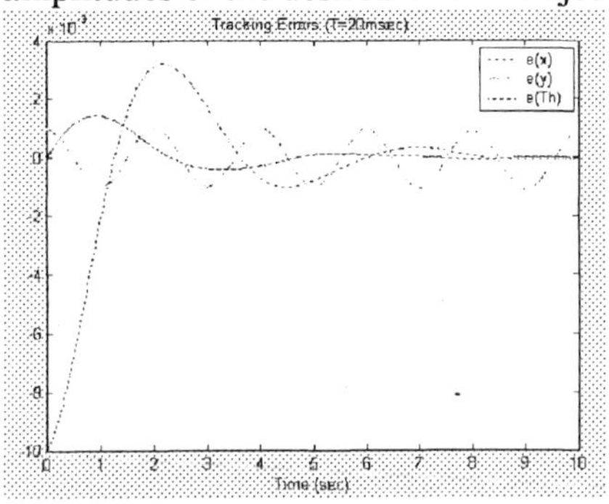

Figure 3: Tracking errors for case III (Alhaj Ali, 2003).

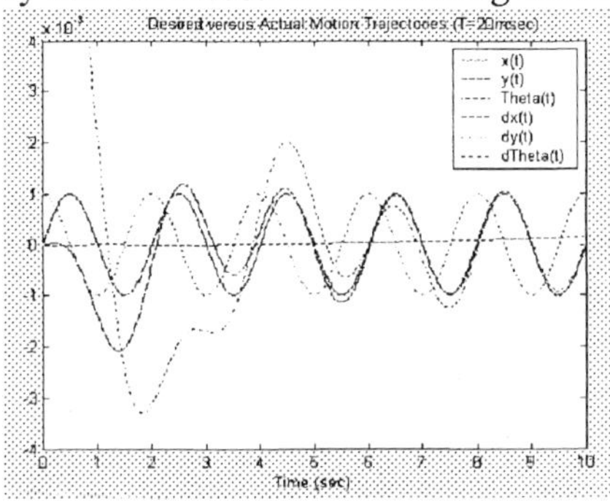

Figure 4: Desired versus actual motion trajectories for case III (Alhaj Ali, 2003).

Case IV: To study the effect of different desired motion trajectories, another experiment was conducted, with the following simulation parameters:

Desired trajectory: $q_{d1}(t) = 0.0005t^2$, $q_{d2}(t) = 0.0005t^2 + .008t$, $q_{d3}(t) = 0.01\sin t$.

Controller parameters: k_p =2, k_v =1, sample period=20 msec.

As shown in Fig. 5, the tracking errors are almost zero for x and θ. For y, the tracking error increases from 0 to 0.045.

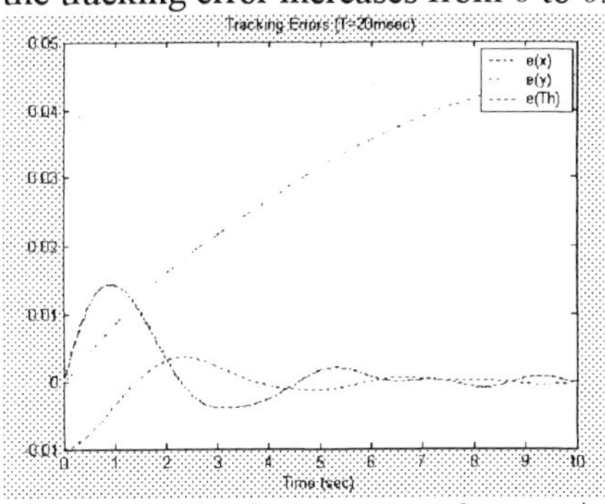

Figure 5: Tracking errors for case IV(Alhaj Ali, 2003).

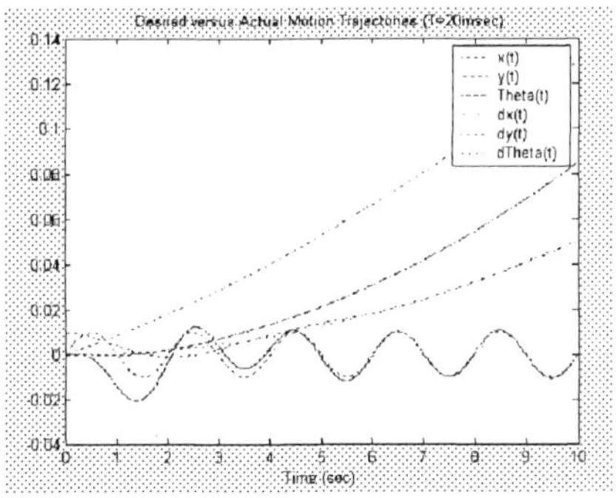

Figure 6: Case IV desired versus actual motion trajectories (Alhaj Ali, 2003).

Case V: To study the effect of increasing the proportional gain, another experiment was conducted, with k_p =50, k_v =1, the results shows that the tracking error the tracking error for y is reduced, however, for x and θ the tracking errors are still small but exhibit more oscillations compared to the previous case.

Further increasing the proportional gain to 100 makes the system unstable, the tracking errors are very high, and the actual motion trajectories are very far from those desired.

CONCLUSIONS

This paper presents the development of a digital controller for WMR autonomous navigation in an outdoor environment. The controller was tested under various control parameters and motion trajectories. Simulation results shows that gain matrices needs to be small positive numbers. $k_p=2$ and $k_v=1$ are the best controller parameters. Increasing the value of k_v does not improve results. However, increasing the value of k_p does, provided its value does not exceed 50.

Comparing the performance of the digital controller with the PD and PID computed-torque controllers that were used for the same application show that the digital controller provides the best results. Hence, its use is recommended for WMR autonomous navigation.

REFERENCES

Alhaj Ali, S. M., 2003, "Technologies for Autonomous Navigation in Unstructured Outdoor Environments." Cincinnati, OH: University of Cincinnati.

Corradini, M. L., Leo, T., and Orlando, G., 2002, "Experimental testing of a discrete-time sliding mode controller for trajectory tracking of a wheeled mobile robot in the presence of skidding effects," *Journal of Robotic Systems*, Vol. 19, Issue 4, pp. 177-188.

Corradini, M. L., and Orlando, G., 2002, "Control of mobile robots with uncertainties in the dynamical model: a discrete time sliding mode approach with experimental results," *Control Engineering Practice*, Vol. 10, Issue 1, pp. 23-34.

Dong, W., Liang Xu, W., and Huo, W., 1999, "Trajectory tracking control of dynamic non-holonomic systems with unknown dynamics," *International Journal of Robust and Nonlinear Control*, Vol. 9, Issue 13, pp. 905-922.

Koh, K. C., and Cho, H. S., 1999, "A smooth path tracking algorithm for wheeled mobile robots with dynamic constraints," *Journal of Intelligent and Robotic Systems*, Vol. 24, Issue 4, pp. 367-385.

Kuo, B. C., 1992, Digital Control Systems. 2nd ed., Ft. Worth: Saunders College Publishing, pp. 1-3.

Lewis, F. L., Jagannathan, S., and Yesildirek, A., 1999, Neural Network Control of Robot Manipulators and Nonlinear Systems. Padstow, UK: Taylor and Francis Ltd, T. J. International Ltd, pp. 147-167.

Rajagopalan, R., and Barakat, N., 1997, "Velocity control of wheeled mobile robots using computed torque control and its performance for a differentially driven robot," *Journal of Robotic Systems*, Vol. 14, Issue 4, pp. 325-340.

Wu, S.-F., Mei, J.-S., and Niu, P.-Y., 2001, "Path guidance and control of a guided wheeled mobile robot," *Control Engineering Practice*, Vol. 9, Issue 1, pp. 97-105.

Zhang, M., and Hirschorn, R. M., 1997, "Discontinuous feedback stabilization of nonholonomic wheeled mobile robots," *Dynamics and Control*, Vol. 7, Issue 2, pp. 155-169.

Zhang, Y., Chung, J. H., and Velinsky, S. A., 2003, "Variable structure control of a differentially steered wheeled mobile robot," *Journal of Intelligent and Robotic Systems*, Vol. 36, Issue 3, pp. 301-314.

A DESIGN METHOD FOR PI CONTROL FOR MINIMUM PHASE TIME-DELAY SYSTEMS

KOU YAMADA
Department of Mechanical System Engineering, Gunma University
1-5-1 Tenjincho, Kiryu, Japan

KEIJI SATOH
Department of Mechanical System Engineering, Gunma University
1-5-1 Tenjincho, Kiryu, Japan

ZHENG HAI-RONG
Department of Mechanical System Engineering, Gunma University
1-5-1 Tenjincho, Kiryu, Japan

NOBUAKI MATSUSHIMA
Department of Mechanical System Engineering, Gunma University
1-5-1 Tenjincho, Kiryu, Japan

ABSTRACT
In this paper, we propose a design method for a PI controller for minimum phase time-delay plants using the parameterization of all causal stabilizing controllers for linear minimum phase time-delay plants. The PI controller is the most widely used controller in industrial applications, but no method has been proposed to guarantee the stability of the PI control system for plants with time-delay. In this paper, we propose a design method for PI/PID controllers for minimum phase time-delay plants such that the stability of the control system is guaranteed.

Introduction

In this paper, we examine a design method for proportional-integral (PI) controllers for minimum phase time-delay plants. PI control is a control system for which the controller includes a proportional gain and integral of the error (Minorsky, 1922, Callender et al., 1936, Astrom and Hagglund, 1955). The PI controller structure is the most widely used controller in industrial applications (Astrom and Hagglund, 1955). The controller has two tuning parameters, which are often tuned by trial and error (Ziegler and Nichols, 1942, Astrom and Hagglund, 1955). Several papers on PI tuning methods have been published and used industrially (Ziegler and Nichols, 1942, Astrom and Hagglund, 1955). However, no method has been proposed to guarantee the stability of the PI control system for time-delay plants.

In this paper, we propose a method to design PI controllers for minimum phase time-delay plants such that the PI control system is asymptotically stable. In order to design PI controller, we fuse the concepts of the parameterization of all stabilizing controllers for minimum phase time-delay plants (Yamada and Okuyama, 2000) and model driven control (Kimura, 2000). First, the problem considered in this paper is described. Next, we propose a design method for PI controller for time-delay plants such that the stability of PI control system is guaranteed. Finally, expanding this result, we present a design method for the proportional-integral-differential (PID) controller for minimum phase time-delay plants such that the stability of the PID control system is guaranteed.

Problem formulation

Consider the control system written as

$$\begin{cases} y = G(s)e^{-sT}u \\ u = C(s)(r-y) \end{cases}, \tag{1}$$

where $G(s)e^{-sT}$ is the single-input/single-output minimum phase time-delay plant, that is, $G(s)e^{-sT}$ has no zero in the closed right half plane, $G(s) \in R(s)$ and $T > 0$ is a time-delay. In addition, $G(s)$ is assumed to be strictly proper. $C(s) \in R$ is the controller, $u \in R$ is the control input, $y \in R$ is the output and $r \in R$ is the reference input.

When the controller $C(s)$ is given by

$$C(s) = a_P + \frac{a_I}{s}, \tag{2}$$

then the controller $C(s)$ is called a PI controller, where $a_P \in R$ and $a_I \in R$. a_P and a_I are determined such that the control system in Eq.(1) has desirable control characteristics, such as its steady state and transient characteristics. Using the PI controller in Eq.(2), the transfer function from r to y in Eq.(1) is written as

$$y = \frac{G(s)e^{-sT}\left(a_P + \frac{a_I}{s}\right)}{1 + G(s)e^{-sT}\left(a_P + \frac{a_I}{s}\right)} r. \tag{3}$$

Clearly if a_P and a_I are settled at random, the stability of the control system in Eq.(1) is not guaranteed. In addition, no design method for the PI controller has been proposed such that the stability of control system in Eq.(1) is guaranteed.

The problem considered in this paper is to propose a design method for the PI controller such that the stability of the control system in Eq.(1) is guaranteed. We propose a design method for PI controller combining the parameterization of all stabilizing controllers for minimum phase time-delay plants (Yamada and Okuyama, 2000) and model driven control systems (Kimura, 2000). In the next section, we describe the design method for PI controller using this combination.

PI control

In this section, we propose a design method for the PI controller $C(s)$ of a time-delay plant $G(s)e^{-sT}$ such that the stability of the control system in Eq.(1) is guaranteed.

From Yamada and Okuyama (2000), the parameterization of all stabilizing controllers for $G(s)e^{-sT}$ is given by

$$C(s) = \frac{C_f(s)}{1 + C_f(s)K(s)} \quad \left(\lim_{\omega\to\infty}(1 + C_f(j\omega)K(j\omega)) \neq 0\right). \tag{4}$$

Here $K(s) \in H_\infty$ is any bicausal function that makes $G(s)e^{-sT} + K(s)$ of minimum phase. $C_f(s)$ is denoted by

$$C_f(s) = \frac{1}{Q(s)} - \frac{1}{G(s)e^{-sT} + K(s)} \tag{5}$$

and $Q(s)$ is any non-zero asymptotically stable bicausal function. $K(s) \in H_\infty$ is selected satisfying

$$K(0) = 0 \tag{6}$$

from the class of bicausal functions to make $G(s)e^{-sT} + K(s)$ of minimum phase. That $K(s)$ satisfying Eq.(6) exists is proved as follows.

Theorem 1 *If $G(s)$ is of minimum phase, there exists $K(s)$ that satisfies the following conditions:*

1. *$G(s)e^{-sT} + K(s)$ is of minimum phase.*
2. *$K(s) \in H_\infty$ is a bicausal function.*
3. *$K(0) = 0$.*

(Proof) Let $\bar{K}(s) \in H_\infty$ and $A(s) = \frac{s}{s+\alpha}$, where $\alpha > 0$. $G(s)e^{-sT}/A(s) + \bar{K}(s)$ may be rewritten as

$$\frac{G(s)e^{-sT}}{A(s)} + \bar{K}(s) = \frac{N(s)e^{-sT} + \bar{K}(s)A(s)D(s)}{A(s)D(s)}, \tag{7}$$

where $N(s)$ and $D(s)$ are any right coprime factorization of $G(s)$ on RH_∞ given by

$$G(s) = D^{-1}(s)N(s). \tag{8}$$

Theorem 1 is proved by showing that $\bar{K}(s) \in H_\infty$ exists such that $N(s)e^{-sT} + \bar{K}(s)A(s)D(s) \in \mathcal{U}$. This is equivalent to the interpolation problem satisfying

$$\frac{\mathrm{d}^j}{\mathrm{d}s^j}U(s_i) = \frac{\mathrm{d}^j}{\mathrm{d}s^j}\left\{N(s_i)e^{-s_iT}\right\} (j = 0, \ldots, m_i - 1, i = 1, \ldots, l), \tag{9}$$

where $U(s)$ is defined by

$$U(s) = N(s)e^{-sT} + \bar{K}(s)A(s)D(s), \tag{10}$$

$s_1, \cdots, s_l$ are distinct zeroes of $A(s)D(s)$ on the positive real axis and $m_1, \cdots, m_l$ are the corresponding multiplicities. Because $G(s)e^{-sT}$ is of minimum phase, $N(s)e^{-sT}$ is also of minimum phase. This implies that all of $N(s_i)e^{-s_iT}$ are the same sign. From the result by Vidyasagar (1985) there exists $U(s) \in \mathcal{U}$ such that Eq.(9) holds. From Eq.(10), $\bar{K}(s)$ is

$$\bar{K}(s) = \frac{U(s) - N(s)e^{-sT}}{A(s)D(s)}. \tag{11}$$

Using $U(s)$ satisfying Eq.(9), $\bar{K}(s)$ written as Eq.(11) is included in H_∞.

Next, we show that there exists $\bar{K}(s)$ which is bicausal. That is, it is shown that if $U(s) \in \mathcal{U}$ exist such that Eq.(9) is satisfied then $\bar{K}(s)$ is bicausal. Because $U(s)$ is included in $\mathcal{U}$, both $A(s) \in RH_\infty$ and $D(s)\ inRH_\infty$ are biproper and $N(s)$ is strictly proper, $\bar{K}(s)$ in Eq.(11) is bicausal.

The remaining proof of this theorem is to show that when $K(s)$ is defined by

$$K(s) = A(s)\bar{K}(s), \tag{12}$$

then $K(s)$ is included in H_∞, a bicausal function and satisfying $K(0) = 0$. The fact that $K(s)$ is bicausal is obvious because both $A(s)$ is biproper and $\bar{K}(s)$ is bicausal. Clearly $K(s) \in H_\infty$ because $\bar{K}(s) \in H_\infty$ and $A(s) \in RH_\infty$. Because $\bar{K}(s) \in H_\infty$ and $A(0) = 0$, $K(s)$ written as Eq.(12) satisfies $K(0) = 0$. This completes the proof of Theorem 1. ∎

The parameterization of all stabilizing controllers in Eq.(5) for $G(s)e^{-sT}$, $G(s)e^{-sT} + K(s)$ is considered a bicausal model of $G(s)e^{-sT}$ because $G(s)e^{-sT} + K(s)$ takes the characteristics of $G(s)e^{-sT}$, such as the poles of $G(s)e^{-sT}$ and the minimum phase characteristics. The model driven control of Kimura (2000) improves the control performance using a model of the plant. Using model feedback control and the parameterization of all stabilizing controllers for $G(s)e^{-sT}$, we propose a design method for PI controller for time-delay plant $G(s)e^{-sT}$ such that the stability of the control system in Eq.(1) is guaranteed. To design the PI controller using model driven control, $Q(s)$ in Eq.(5) of the controller $C(s)$ in Eq.(4) is designed as

$$\frac{1}{Q(s)} = a_P + \frac{a_I}{s}. \tag{13}$$

From the above, $Q(s)$ must be a bicausal asymptotically stable function. It is obvious that the necessary and sufficient condition for $Q(s)$ in Eq.(13) to be bicausal is

$$a_P \neq 0. \tag{14}$$

The necessary and sufficient condition that $Q(s)$ in Eq.(13) is asymptotically stable is summarized by following theorem.

Theorem 2 *The necessary and sufficient condition that $Q(s)$ is asymptotically stable is that a_P and a_I are satisfied*

$$a_P > 0, \qquad a_I > 0 \tag{15}$$

or

$$a_P < 0, \qquad a_I < 0. \tag{16}$$

(Proof) From Eq.(13), $Q(s)$ is rewritten as

$$Q(s) = \frac{s}{a_P s + a_I}. \tag{17}$$

From this equation, it is obvious that the necessary and sufficient condition that $Q(s)$ is included in RH_∞ is satisfied by Eq.(15) or Eq.(16). We have therefore proved the theorem. ∎

Next, we show the role of a_P and a_I in Eq.(13) are equivalent to that of conventional PI parameters (a_P and a_I) in Eq.(2). First, the role of a_P in Eq.(13) and that of a_P in Eq.(2) are considered. $C(s)$ in Eq.(2) satisfies

$$\lim_{s \to 0} sC(s) = a_I. \tag{18}$$

This implies that when a_I is increased the influence of the integrator is greater. Conversely when a_I is decreased the influence of the integrator is decreased. On the other hand, the proposed PI controller in Eq.(4) satisfies

$$\lim_{s\to 0} sC(s) \quad = \quad \frac{1}{\dfrac{1}{a_I}+k}, \quad \left(k=\lim_{s\to 0}\frac{K(s)}{s}=\text{const.}\right). \tag{19}$$

This implies that when a_I is increased the influence of the integrator is greater. Conversely when a_I is decreased the influence of the integrator is decreased. Therefore, the role of a_I in the proposed PI controller in Eq.(4) is equivalent to that of a_I in the conventional PI controller in Eq.(2).

Next, we consider the role of a_P in Eq.(4) in Eq.(2). To clarify the role of a_P, let $a_I = 0$. The conventional PI controller $C(s)$ in Eq.(2) satisfies

$$\lim_{s\to 0} C(s) = a_P. \tag{20}$$

This implies that when a_P is increased the influence of the proportional is greater. Conversely when a_P is decreased, then the influence of the proportional is decreased. On the other hand, the proposed PI controller in Eq.(4) satisfies

$$\lim_{s\to 0} C(s) = a_P - \frac{1}{G(0)}. \tag{21}$$

This implies that when a_P is increased the influence of the proportional is greater. Conversely when a_P is decreased, then the influence of the proportional decreases. Therefore, the role of a_P in the proposed PI controller in Eq.(4) is equivalent to that of a_I in the conventional PI controller in Eq.(2).

Therefore, we can design the PI control system such that the stability of the control system is guaranteed.

PID control

This section expands the result in the preceding section to a design method for a PID controller $C(s)$ for time-delay plant $G(s)e^{-sT}$ such that the stability of the control system in Eq.(1) is guaranteed.

In order to design the PID controller using the concept of model driven control, $Q(s)$ in Eq.(5) of the controller $C(s)$ in Eq.(4) is designed as

$$\frac{1}{Q(s)} = a_P + \frac{a_I}{s} + \frac{a_D s + \alpha}{1+\tau s}, \tag{22}$$

where $\alpha = 1/G(0)$, $\tau > 0$ and $a_D \in R$. From the discussion in the preceding section, $Q(s)$ must be a bicausal asymptotically stable function. It is obvious that the necessary and sufficient condition that $Q(s)$ in Eq.(22) is bicausal is

$$a_P\tau + a_D \neq 0. \tag{23}$$

The necessary and sufficient condition that $Q(s)$ in Eq.(13) be included in RH_∞ is as summarized by the following theorem.

Theorem 3 *The necessary and sufficient condition that $Q(s)$ is asymptotically stable is that a_P, a_I and a_D are satisfied by*

$$a_I > 0, a_P + a_I\tau + \alpha > 0, a_P\tau + a_D > 0 \tag{24}$$

or

$$a_I < 0, a_P + a_I\tau + \alpha < 0, a_P\tau + a_D < 0 \tag{25}$$

(Proof) By simple manipulation, this theorem is obvious. ∎

By simple manipulation, we can find that when $Q(s)$ is selected by Eq.(22), then the role of a_P, a_I and a_D in Eq.(22) are equivalent to conventional PID parameters.

Conclusion

We propose a design method for PI and PID controllers for minimum phase time-delay plants such that the PI or PID control system is asymptotically stable. This research was partially supported by the Saneyoshi Scholarship Foundation.

References

N. Minorsky: Directional stability of automatically steered bodies, J. Amer. Coc., Naval Engineers, 42-2, pp.280-309(1922)
A. Callender, D.R. Hartree and A. Porter: Time-lag in a control system, Phil. Trans. Roy. Soc. London, A235-756(1932)
J.G.Zieglae and N.B. Nichols: Optimum settings for automatic controllers, Trans. ASME, 64, pp.759-768(1942)
K. Astrom and T. Hagglund: PID controllers: Theory design, and tuning, Instrument Society of America, North Carolina(1995)
K. Yamada and T. Okuyama: A parameterization for the class of all stabilizing controller for linear minimum phase time-delay systems, Proceedings of the 3rd Asian Control Conference, pp.1293-1298(2000)
H.Kimura: Is the Model a Good Controller? Perspectives on Brain Motor Control,CDC(2000)
M. Vidyasagar: Control System Synthesis–A factorization approach–, MIT Press, (1985)

FUZZY LOGIC CONTROL USING PLC'S

PAUL BAUER
ECE Department
South Dakota School of Mines & Technology, Rapid City
South Dakota 57701

MYCHAL HOFFMAN
ECE Department
South Dakota School of Mines & Technology, Rapid City
South Dakota 57701

MADHAVI CHUNDRU
ECE Department
South Dakota School of Mines & Technology, Rapid City
South Dakota 57701

DR. ABUL R. HASAN
ECE Department
South Dakota School of Mines & Technology, Rapid City
South Dakota 57701

ABSTRACT
This paper presents a preliminary study of the implementation of fuzzy control using a programmable logic controller (PLC). The study uses a thermal system to demonstrate that a process can be controlled using fuzzy logic implemented in a simple PLC without the need for built-in fuzzy logic instructions or specialized expert control-system software and computers. The study involves building a physical system (plant), designing the control system, and implementing the fuzzy controller in PLC program code. A Mamdani fuzzy control model with symmetrical triangular membership functions and the weighted-average defuzzification method is used (Barriga, et al. 2000). Results of the controller performance before and after tuning are presented

INTRODUCTION

PLC's play an important role in machine and process-control of commercial and industrial control system applications. PLC's range in capability from less than 16 discrete Inputs/Outputs (I/O) up to and exceeding 1000's of discrete and analog I/O signals. One drawback with current PLC-based control systems is that few PLC manufacturers provide commands in their program instruction-set for implementing complex and/or non-linear process control loops.

In large control system applications PLC's are used to connect hundreds of analog and discrete I/O signals while personal computers (PC's) are used to provide a human-machine interface (HMI), data collection, and to run expert-system software for analyzing and calculating complicated control algorithms. Expert-systems typically use, but are not limited to, Fuzzy Logic, Neural Networks, Batch Processing and Statistical Process Control. The PLC becomes an extension of the PC, performing logic operations and providing an interface between PC's and actual process signals.

Unfortunately some processes, while very complicated, are not large enough to justify the expense of sophisticated control system architectures. Expert-system software alone can cost over $50,000.00. In these situations the control engineer is challenged to find ways to control a complex process using conventional control equipment. The purpose of this paper is to demonstrate that fuzzy control can be implemented in even a simple PLC so that the dependency on complicated and expensive expert-control systems can be avoided.

PHYSICAL SYSTEM

The physical system (plant) used is modeled after a classic thermal system (Phillips & Nagle 1995, and Cengel & Boles 1998). The plant consists of a $0.1m^3$ box constructed of 1/4" plywood, a heat source, and a stirring-fan and valve (damper) to allow rapid cooling of the system. The controller consists of a PLC, a temperature sensor, and a variable power supply to control the heat source. Discrete PLC outputs are used to control the fan and damper.

The heat source is three 250-watt strip-heaters controlled by a 220VAC variable power supply. The power supply is a variable frequency drive (VFD) normally used in variable speed AC motor control. There is no significance to the power supply chosen except that it provides a constant volts/hertz ratio and is easy to control through a 4-20mA current loop. The heater elements are resistive devices so the varying frequency component has little affect on element impedance and total heat output.

PLC relay-contact outputs are used to switch the fan on and off and to open and close the damper. The PLC is an Allen-Bradley SLC500™ with one kilobyte of memory and a 2-slot expansion chassis to accommodate a thermocouple input module and an analog output module. The temperature sensor is a Type J thermocouple connected to the PLC's thermocouple input module. Figure 1. illustrates the control system components.

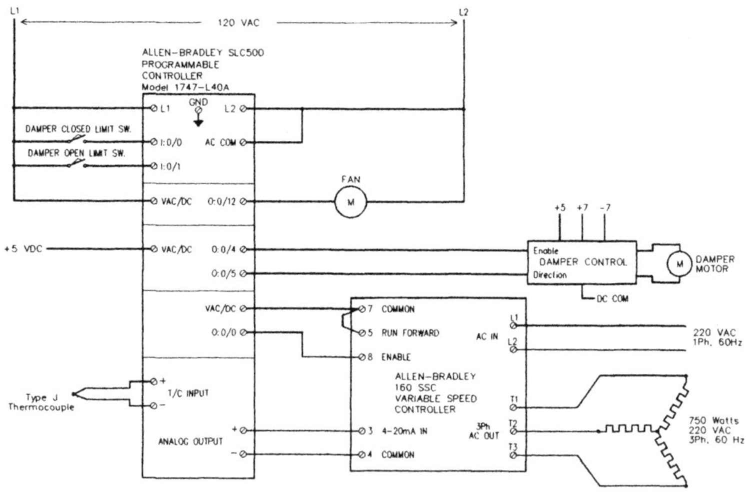

Figure 1: Temperature Control System Schematic

The plant can be modeled by two first-order transfer functions each describing the two states of the system depending on whether it is heating up or cooling down respectively. Either equation can represent the plant in the closed-loop system shown in Fig. 2. Conventional methods could be used to develop a PID compensator based on the transfer functions previously derived. However, two separate compensators may be required because of the two separate system states. Fortunately, substituting a fuzzy controller into the compensator block of the closed-loop system allows us to develop a controller without knowledge of the system state equations or transfer functions. Only knowledge of the plant behavior is required to implement fuzzy logic control (Ying 2000). This will be the topic of the remainder of this paper.

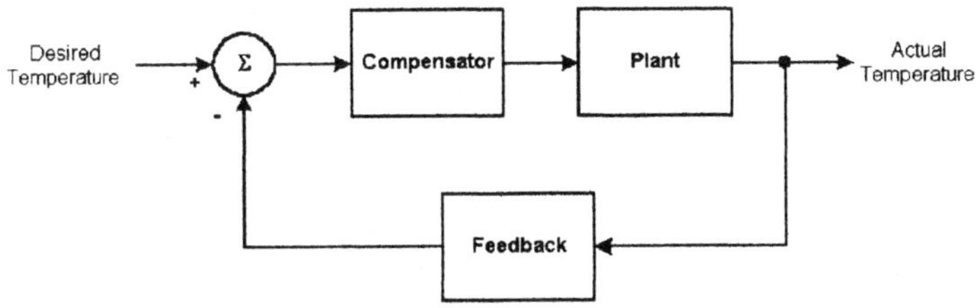

Figure 2: Closed-loop Control System

3. CONTROLLER DESIGN

Fuzzy controller designed involves fuzzifying the system inputs, determining the fuzzy rules, and defuzzifying the fuzzy outputs into a single, crisp output that can be used to control a device. In this application triangular membership functions are used because they are easy to implement in a PLC.

The two input signals to the fuzzy controller are Percent-Error and Sum-of-Errors. The output signal controls the variable power supply, which regulates the power output of the heater elements. Once the input signals are defined fuzzy sets for input signals are then developed. The rule table is initially filled-in by considering the extreme cases such as the center and corner conditions of the table and then filling-in the remainder of the table assuming a linear system requiring a symmetrical controller response. Adjustments are made to the fuzzy rules during the tuning phase of the controller design.

Table 1: Fuzzy Controller Rule Matrix

		PERCENT ERROR						
		NH	NM	NS	Z	PS	PM	PH
SUM OF ERRORS	LN	OFF	OFF	OFF	OFF	Low	Low	Med_Low
	N	OFF	OFF	OFF	OFF	Low	Med_Low	Medium
	Z	OFF	OFF	OFF	OFF	Med_Low	Medium	Med_High
	P	OFF	Low	Med_Low	Med_Low	Medium	Med_High	High
	LP	Low	Med_Low	Medium	Med_High	Med_High	High	High

In a PLC implementation the fuzzy sets must be stored numerically in the PLC's memory (data table) and the degree of memberships are interpolated from the membership functions through a series of math calculations just as they are in a PC. For example, consider the Negative Small membership function which has three co-ordinates A, B, and C, can describe this triangular membership function as shown in Fig. 3. below.

The values of these coordinates (A = -66, B = -33, and C = 0) are stored in the PLC's data table under the variable names NS_A, NS_B, and NS_C. If the Percent-Error signal falls within the limits of the Negative Small membership function then the degree of membership will be interpolated as follows:

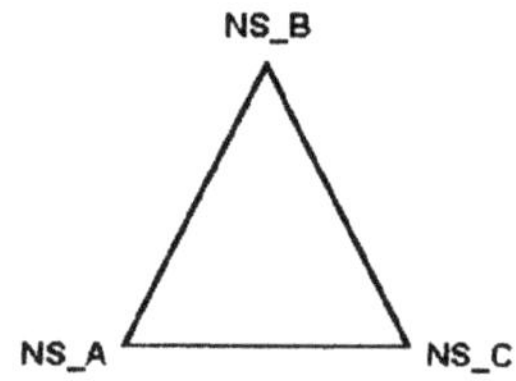

Figure 3: Negative-Small Membership Function from the Percent-Error Fuzzy Set

For NS_B < Percent-Error ≤ NS_A, $$y = \frac{NS\_A - \%Error}{NS\_A - NS\_B}$$ (Eq. 1)

For NS_B ≤ Percent-Error ≤ NS_C, $$y = \frac{NS\_C - \%Error}{NS\_C - NS\_B}$$ (Eq. 2)

Where, y is the degree of membership from 0 to 1.

The coordinate values for all membership functions are stored in the PLC data table. Controller tuning is performed by adjusting these values, which effectively changes the shape of the membership function and the range of values included. Table 2 illustrates a typical data table array for the Percent-Error input signal:

Table 2: PLC Data Table Array for Percent-Error Fuzzy Set

	A	B	C	Σ1	Σ2	R
NH	-100	-100	-66	num	den	Inter
NM	-100	-66	-33	num	den	Inter
NS	-66	-33	0	num	den	Inter
Z	-33	0	33	num	den	Inter
PS	0	33	66	num	den	Inter
PM	33	66	100	num	den	Inter
PH	66	100	100	num	den	Inter

In Table 2 columns A, B, and C store the defining coordinates of the Percent-Error fuzzy set. Column Σ1 holds the numerator and Σ2 holds the denominator of equations 9 and 10, and column R stores the interpolated result of these equations.

Referring back to Table 1, assume that the Percent-Error input signal falls within the Positive Small membership function limits while the Sum-of-Errors signal falls within the Positive membership function limits. This combination results in the controller's Medium output membership function, corresponding to fuzzy rule 28, to be activated. Figure 4. is a typical example of PLC ladder logic program used to calculate the degree of membership of the Medium output membership function.

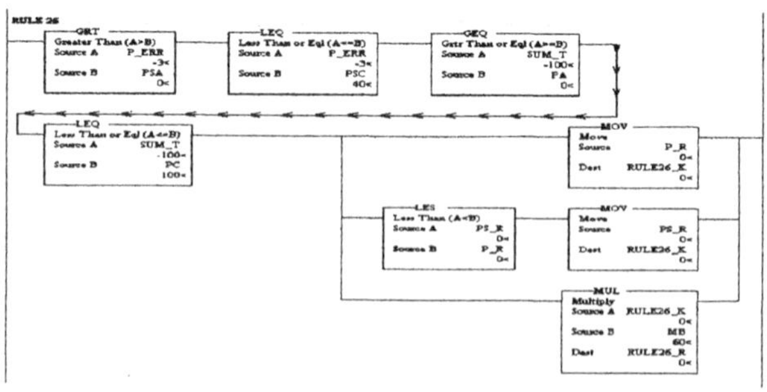

Figure 4: Example of PLC Ladder Logic Programming

This rung of ladder logic is read as follows: "If Percent-Error is greater than the Positive Small minimum value, and less than or equal to the Positive Small maximum value, and if the Sum-of-Errors is greater than or equal to the Positive minimum value and less than or equal to the Positive maximum value, then find and store the minimum degree of membership and calculate the degree of membership of the Medium Output membership function." This entire statement constitutes the expression for fuzzy rule 26. Normally there are multiple output membership functions activated for a given set of input conditions. The final defuzzified crisp output is then calculated using the minimum weighted average method.

CONSTRAINTS

Design constraints were encountered due to the limited capability of the SLC500™. One constraint is that this controller model does not have floating point capability. This means all values and calculations must be done in whole numbers. The maximum integer range for the controller is +/-32767. This limitation resulted in several design problems.

First the thermocouple input-module is capable of 0.1-degree temperature resolution. A 100.0-degree temperature appears in memory as a value of 1000. However multiplying, dividing and summing numbers of this magnitude can quickly exceed the maximum integer values. The simplest way to circumvent this problem is to set the thermocouple input-module to 1-degree resolution. By doing this we are accepting the poor resolution in exchange for reducing the magnitude of the temperature measurements and avoiding exceeding the maximum limits.

Second, when calculating the degree of membership fractional numbers are always encountered. To maintain the precision of these values percentages must be represented as whole numbers within the controller. In the SLC500™ any division that returns a fractional answer will be returned as either 0 (<.5) or a 1 (>= .5). To avoid this the numerator must be multiplied by 100 first, before the division takes place. The same considerations must be made when summing or multiplying large lists of numbers.

TESTING

Controller performance data is required in order to make adjustments to signal gains, fuzzy sets, and fuzzy rules. Knowledge of the plant being controlled is also essential to tuning a fuzzy controller for optimal performance. During the initial test a desired temperature (setpoint) well above the box's ambient temperature was entered into the controller. Once the system reached a steady state, another setpoint that was below the original setpoint and above the box initial temperature was entered. This allowed for the testing of the controller when the set point was above and below the current temperature. Figure 5(a) is a graph of the system response based on the initial fuzzy sets and fuzzy rules. The temperature is in degrees Celsius and the stair-step effect is the result of the 1-degree resolution from the thermocouple input-module. As the graph shows the response time of the controller is very slow (approximately 4 minutes) and a 5-degree overshoot occurred. Cooling of the system is much responsive and had no overshoot.

After adjustments to the fuzzy sets and fuzzy rules were made the performance was improved considerably as shown in Fig. 5(b). It can be seen that system response time has been reduced, overshoot has been eliminated, and steady-state oscillation has been improved considerably.

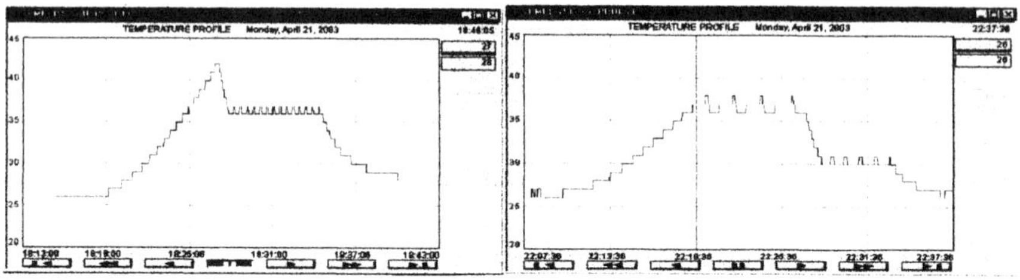

(a) (b)

Figure 5: System Response for the Plant; (a) Untuned, (b) Tuned

CONCLUSIONS

This paper briefly discussed the reasons and advantages of implementing fuzzy logic control using a PLC. The physical system (plant) used to demonstrate the principles presented in the paper were described. The fuzzy controller design procedure was outlined and examples were given to illustrate the design process. Constraints created by the limitations of the PLC chosen were discussed. These constraints could be avoided by selecting a higher level PLC that supports floating point data types and has more memory. Despite these constraints, fuzzy control of the thermal system was successfully implemented and good performance was achieved with only slight adjustments and tuning of the initial control system.

The study presented here has proven that fuzzy control using PLC's is a viable and cost effective solution for small scale but complicated control applications.

REFERENCES

I. Baturone, A. Barriga, S. Sanchez-Solano, C.J. Jimenez-Fernandez, and D.R. Lopez, *Microelectronic Design of Fuzzy Logic-Based Systems*, CRC Press, Boca Raton, 2000.

Charles L. Phillips, and H. Troy Nagle, *Digital Control System Analysis and Design*, 3rd Edition, Prentice Hall, New Jersey, 1995.

Yunas A. Cengel, and Michael A. Boles, *Thermodynamics: An Engineering Approach*, 3rd Edition, McGraw-Hill, Boston, 1998.

Hao Ying, *Fuzzy Control and Modeling: Analytical Foundations and Applications*, IEEE Press, New York, 2000.

ADAPTIVE NEURO-FUZZY CONTROL OF A SPRING-MASS-DAMPER SYSTEM

RAJAB CHALLOO, PARIKSHIT S. MEHENDALE, SHUHUI LI
Dept. of EE/CS, MSC 192
Texas A&M University-Kingsville
Kingsville, Texas 78363

SELAHATTIN OZCELIK, ROBERT A. MCLAUCHLAN
DEPT. OF ME/IE, MSC 191
Texas A&M University-Kingsville
Kingsville, Texas 78363

ABSTRACT

This research work addresses the problem of position control of a linear, single-input-single-output spring-mass-damper system. In this work an '*Adaptive Neuro-Fuzzy Inference System*' is used to implement position control. Fuzzy logic and neural networks are complementary technologies. As a part of the research work a controller as mentioned above was designed for the "*Three Degrees of Freedom Spring-Mass-Damper System*". The simulation results were then compared with the actual implementation of this *Adaptive Neuro-Fuzzy Controller* on a real-time system. These results proved to be satisfactory, and the performance of the proposed design was thus validated.

INTRODUCTION

An '*Adaptive Neuro-Fuzzy Inference System*' is used to implement position control for the system shown in Figure 1. The Input can be applied only to mass1.Output can be measured from all the three masses. This poses a challenge for position control of mass2 and mass3 as signal cannot be directly applied to them but can only be transmitted.

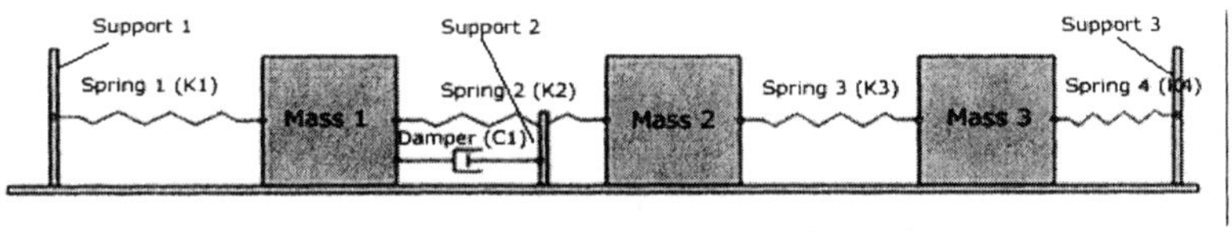

Fig 1 System under consideration

An overall block diagram of the various components of the proposed system is shown in Figure 2.

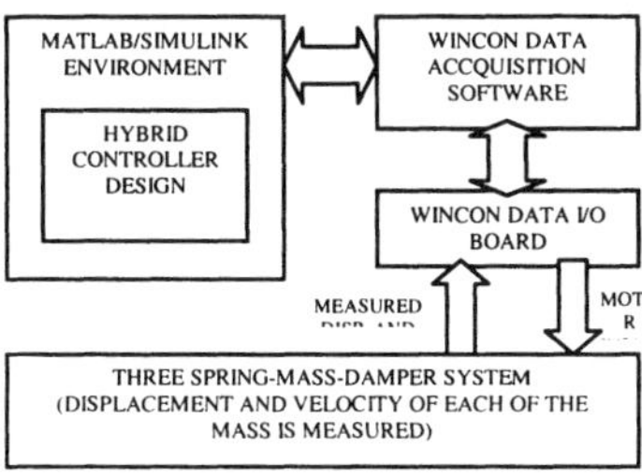

Fig 2 Overall block diagram of proposed system

General comparison between Fuzzy and Neural systems

Fuzzy systems and neural networks are both *numerical model-free* estimators and dynamical systems. They both have the ability to improve the intelligence of systems working in uncertain, imprecise, and noisy environments. Integrated system can *learn* and *adapt.* They learn new associations, new patterns, and new functional dependencies. The two technologies can be merged into three categories:

1. Neural fuzzy system: the use of neural networks as tools in fuzzy model.
2. Fuzzy neural networks: fuzzification of conventional neural network model.
3. Fuzzy-neural hybrid system: incorporating fuzzy technologies and neural networks into hybrid systems.

In the first approach, aim at providing fuzzy systems with the kind of automatic tuning methods typical of neural networks but without altering their functionality (e.g. fuzzification, defuzzification, inference engine, and fuzzy logic base). In neural fuzzy system, neural networks are used in augmenting numerical processing of fuzzy sets, such as membership function elicitation and realization of mapping between fuzzy set that is utilized as fuzzy rules. Since neural fuzzy systems are inherently fuzzy logic systems, they are mostly used in control application.

In the second approach, fuzzy neural networks retain the basic properties and architectures of neural networks and simply "fuzzify" some of their elements. In fuzzy neural networks, a crisp neuron can become fuzzy and the response of the neuron to its lower-layer activation signal can be of a fuzzy relation type rather then a sigmoid type.

Finally, in the third approach, both fuzzy techniques and neural networks play a key role in the hybrid system. They do their own job in serving different functions in the system. We have concentrated on the Adaptive-Network-based Fuzzy Inference System (ANFIS) in this category which is by embedding the fuzzy inference system into the framework of adaptive networks.

PRACTICAL IMLEMENTATION AND RESULTS

The experimental set-up consists of the hardware and the software. Here, the mass-spring-damper system manufactured by Educational Control Products (ECP) is used. The hardware part of the experiment uses the above mentioned system, servo amplifier, MultiQ-3 data acquisition card, and the I/O (terminal) board. The software part consists of Wincon software with Matlab/Simulink. The Wincon software has Real-Time Workshop, VC++ and Wincon Server and Client. The block diagram of the experimental set-up is shown in Figure 3.

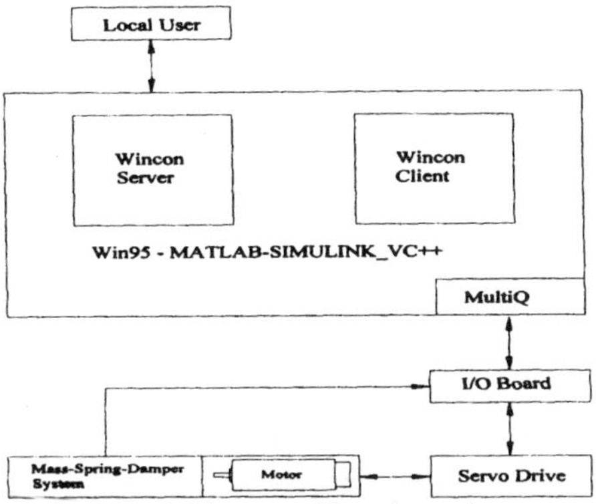

Fig 3 Block Diagram of Experimental set-up

The system is an electromechanical apparatus, which consists of the rectilinear mechanism, its actuator and sensors. It features a brushless DC motor, a precision rack and pinion drive, high-resolution encoders, adjustable mass carriages, and reconfigurable system type. The mechanism consists of three mass carriages, which are interconnected by bi-directional springs. The mass suspension is anti-friction ball bearing types with approximate ±3-cm of available travel. The linear drive is comprised of a gear rack suspended on an anti-friction carriage and pinion coupled to the brushless servo motor shaft. The optical encoders are provided to measure the position of the mass carriages via a cable and pulley arrangement. Springs of various stiffness can be attached between the mass carriages or the base plate. In order to check the position of the mass carriages physically, scales are also provided. Changing the number of brass weights (500g each) can change the inertia of the system. For safety purposes travel limit stops are also provided. The actuator used in the plant to generate the required force is a brushless motor. In any motor, to provide continuous torque, the current must be successively altered or switched depending upon the absolute position of the rotor. In DC brushless motor, a rotor-positioning sensor is used and commutation is done electronically by using the rectangular commutation also known as Hall-effect. The experimental set-up consists of a 4-pole, 3-phase star-wound brushless motor with Hall-effect commutation. Three sensors are positioned on the stator. The sensed magnetic field switches between the adjacent north/south poles as the rotor rotates. This switching sequence is used to direct the commanded motor current to the individual winding phases. A simple electronic logic circuit is used for the generation of the switching steps. Analog high bandwidth proportional plus integral current feedback loops are then used on two of the three phases to assure almost instantaneous response of the actual winding current following any change in the current. The third phase does not require a current feedback loop because the current in third phase is the negative of the sum of the current in the other two phases. The logic sequencer and the PI feedback is provided by the servo drive used in the set-up.

A servo amplifier is used to drive the motor. The servo amplifier is manufactured by Advanced Motion Controls (model B12A6). The amplifier is capable of providing 6A of continuous current. It requires a single unregulated power supply of 20-80V. The amplifier can be used to adjust the current limit, loop gain, input gain and offset. The amplifier can be operated in three modes depending upon the application. DIP switches are used to configure the circuit board for particular type of application. In the current mode, the motor produces a torque output proportional to the input reference signal from the controller. So, depending upon the position error the controller can produce a signal, which in turn can produce a torque to drive the error to zero. In order to achieve this, for this experiment, the amplifier is operated in the current mode. The following table gives the range of the different system parameters:

PARAMETER	RANGE
Ml(kg)	0-2
M2(kg)	0-2
M3(kg)	0-2
Kl(N/m)	175
K2(N/m)	450
K3(N/m)	800
K4(N/m)	800

Table 1 System Parameter Range

Wincon is a real-time Windows 95/98/NT application that runs SIMULINK generated code using Real-Time Workshop on a PC. Wincon consists of a client and a server referred to as Wincon Client and Wincon Server .

The results obtained during the implementation of adaptive neuro-fuzzy controller on the mass spring damper system are as follows. High gains are required for the physical ideal system performance since the actuating motor is not only used to actuate the system for the desired transient and steady state response but also to overcome the inertia and the restoring forces of the coupling springs. Due to the physical limitations of the system, the experiments were carried out with much smaller magnitudes of reference signals than the ones considered in the simulation.

Parameter	Case1	Case2	Case3
M1(kg)	1	0.5	1.5
M2(kg)	1	0.5	1.5
M3(kg)	1	0.5	1.5
K1(N/m)	450	175	800
K2(N/m)	800	450	800
K3(N/m)	800	800	175
K4(n/m)	175	800	450

Table 2 Values of plant parameters for the experiment

Position control of Mass1: Here, the implementation of ANFIS for the position control of Mass1 is considered. As discussed earlier, in the practical implementation, the actuating force is applied by the brushless motor to mass1. The position of mass1, which is obtained from the encoder, is feedback to the real-time system through the I/O board. The position of mass2 and mass3 are obtained from encoder 2 and encoder 3.

Figures 4, 5 and 6 give the positions of mass1, mass2 and mass3 for the three cases considered. In all three cases the mass which is being controlled is mass1. It is observed that positions of mass2 and mass3 show a stable response irrespective of the change in the stiffness of the springs. Figure 7 shows the error signal for all the three masses considered. The signal reduces to zero and remains there, once the required position of 0.013m is achieved. This error signal represents the variation of the actual position of the masses from the set-point. Figure 7 shows the error in position of masses in all three cases.

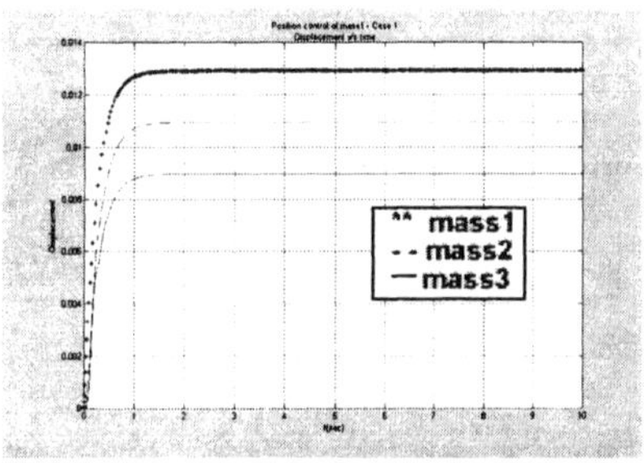

Fig 4 Position control of mass1-case 1

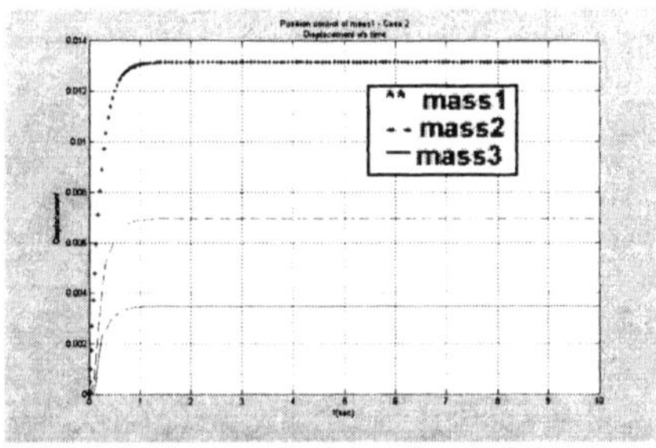

Fig 5 Position control of mass1-case 2

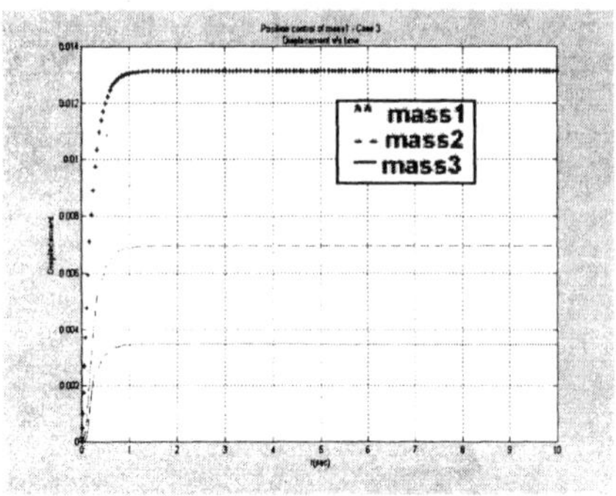

Fig 6 Position control of mass1-case 3

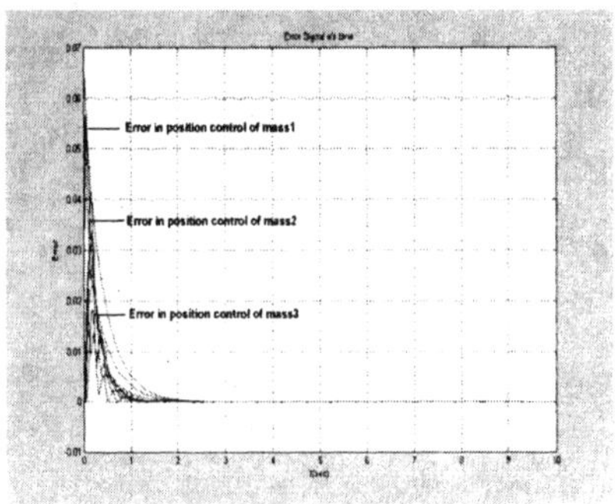

Fig 7 Error signal v/s time for Mass1,2,&3

CONCLUSIONS

Position control of a mass-spring damper system with three degrees of freedom, poses a great challenge as it not only involves control of the position of the masses but also suppression of vibrations in the system. The goal of this work was to implement an Adaptive Neuro-Fuzzy Controller for the position control of the masses. The controller was designed for this system and the implementation was successful. As seen from the results obtained from the simulations, the desired output response was obtained in each case. It was observed that even when the parameters associated with the system like the stiffness of the springs or the mass were changed the response obtained was stable. The Adaptive Neuro-Fuzzy Inference System was thus, found to be capable of handling parametric variations and changes in the system configuration. The controller was also implemented on an actual mass-spring-damper system and the experiments were carried out using real-time system. The main objective of the implementation was to validate the simulation results and its ability to cope with unknown plant parameters. The response obtained when compared to the simulation results was found to be valid. As compared to other work done on the same system using different controller, we can safely conclude that the response obtained by the implementation of the ANFIS was found to be much more consistent and accurate. This work would hold a great relevance in today's world with the ever increasing need for intelligent adaptive control solutions. The same controller (ANFIS) would find a lot of applications in implementing control solutions for various electro-mechanical and real-time systems. It would be a good exercise to implement this intelligent control scheme on other similar systems and check for the reliability and versatility of this logic.

REFERENCES

Ayoubi M. (1995). Neuro-fuzzy Structure For Rule Generation And Application in The Fault Diagnosis of Technical Processes, Proc. American Control Conference, Washington, 2757-2761

Babuska R. (1998).Fuzzy Modeling for Control, Kluwer Academic publishers, Boston.

Kazuo Tanaka and Tak Niimura, "An Introduction to Fuzzy Logic for Practical Applications", Springer Verlag, November, 1996. ISBN: 0387948074

Bhalerao A. (1999). Direct Model Reference adaptive Control of A Multi Degree of Freedom Spring-Mass-Damper System, Texas A&M University-Kingsville (1999).

Closed loop fault diagnosis based on a non-linear process model and automatic fuzzy rule generation, Proc. of IFAC symposium on fault detection, supervision and safety for technical process safeprocess'97, The University of Hull, UK.

Dexter A. L. (1995). Fuzzy model based fault diagnosis, IEEE Proc. Control Theory Appl., vol. 142 (6), pp. 545-550.

Gustafson D. E. and Kessel W. C. (1979). Fuzzy clustering with a fuzzy covariance matrix, in Proc. IEEE Conf. Decision Contr., San Diego, CA, pp 761-766.

Hauptmann W. and Heesche K. (1995). A neural net topology for bidirectional fuzzy – neuro transformation, Proc. of IEEE Int. Conf. on fuzzy systems, vol. **3.** March 20-24, 1995, Yokohama, Japan.

Palade U. and Mizumoto I., (1992), Simplified adaptive model output for plants with modeled dynamics. Int. Journal of Control, pp. 61-80

Jang J. S. R. (1993). ANFIS: Adaptive network based fuzzy inference system, IEEE Transactions on Systems, Man, and Cybernetics, vol. 23(3), pp. 665-684.

Jang J.S. and Sun R. (1995). Neuro-fuzzy modeling and control. Proc. IEEE. Vol. 83(3), pp. 378-405.

Jang J. S. R (1994). Structure determination in fuzzy modeling: a fuzzy CART approach. In Proceedings of IEEE International Conf. On Fuzzy Systems, Orlando, Florida, June 1994.

NEURO EMISSION CONTROLLER FOR MINIMIZING CYCLIC DISPERSION IN SPARK IGNITION ENGINES WITH EGR LEVELS

P. HE, H. BUI, S. JAGANNATHAN
The University of Missouri –Rolla
Dept. of Electrical and Computer Engineering
Rolla, MO 65409, USA

B. KAUL, J. DRALLMEIER
The University of Missouri –Rolla
Dept. of Mechanical and Aerospace Engineering
Rolla, MO 65409, USA

ABSTRACT
Past literature (Inoue et al., 1993) has indicated that a significant amount of NO_x can be reduced by operating a spark ignition (SI) engine at the stoichiometric condition with high exhaust gas recirculation (EGR) levels. However, the problem has been the engine instability due to cyclic dispersion in heat release (Sutton and Drallmeier, 2000). A novel neural network (NN) controller is developed to reduce the cyclic dispersion in heat release in SI engines with high levels of EGR when the engine dynamics are unknown. The NN controller can also be used to minimize engine emissions at extreme lean condition, where similar complex cyclic dynamics are observed.

INTRODUCTION

Lean combustion and high levels of exhaust gas recirculation (EGR) control can be used to decrease the total amount of emissions and to minimize the fuel consumption. Several literatures (He and Jagannathan, 2003, and Inoue et al., 1993) have studied the lean combustion control technology. However, few EGR control results have been reported due to the complex unknown engine dynamics and the cyclic dispersion in heat release, which causes significant engine performance deterioration (Sutton and Drallmeier, 2000).

In this paper, a direct adaptive neural network (NN) controller is proposed for stable operation of the SI engine with high EGR levels at stoichiometric condition. The designed controller learns the unknown engine dynamics by using two NNs and reduces the cyclic dispersion by minimizing variations in equivalence ratio. Equivalence ratio variations is reduced by 1) keeping the mass of both air and fuel bounded close to their target values by an adaptive backstepping approach; and 2) keeping the variations of injected EGR as small as possible by a separately controlled EGR control loop.

BACKGROUND

We developed a mathematical representation for spark ignition (SI) engines operation with EGR levels, which has a striking resemblance with experimental data (Sutton and Drallmeier, 2000). This model is expressed as

$$a(k+1) = F(k)\cdot\left[a(k) - R\cdot CE(k)\cdot m(k) + r_{O_2}(k) + r_{N_2}(k)\right] + (1-F(k))\cdot AF(k) + d_1'(k), \tag{1}$$

$$m(k+1) = m(k)\cdot(1-CE(k))\cdot F(k) + (1-F(k))\cdot(MF(k) + \delta MF(k)) + d_2'(k), \tag{2}$$

$$i(k+1) = F(k)\cdot(i(k) + EGR(k)) + F(k)\cdot\left(r_{CO_2}(k) + r_{H_2O}(k) + r_{N_2}(k)\right), \tag{3}$$

where

$$\varphi(k)=R\cdot\frac{m(k)}{a(k)}\cdot\left(1-\gamma\frac{i(k)+EGR(k)}{(m(k)+a(k)+i(k)+EGR(k))}\right), \tag{4}$$

$$CE(k)=\frac{1}{1+100^{-(\varphi(k)-\varphi_m)/(\varphi_u-\varphi_l)}}\ \varphi_m=\frac{\varphi_u+\varphi_l}{2}, \tag{5}$$

$$Q(k)=m(k)\cdot CE(k), \tag{6}$$

$$r_{H_2O}(k)=\gamma_{H_2O}\cdot m(k)\cdot CE(k), \tag{7}$$

$$r_{O_2}(k)=\gamma_{O_2}\cdot m(k)\cdot CE(k), \tag{8}$$

$$r_{N_2}(k)=\gamma_{N_2}\cdot R\cdot m(k)\cdot CE(k), \tag{9}$$

$$r_{CO_2}(k)=\gamma_{CO_2}\cdot m(k)\cdot CE(k), \tag{10}$$

where *m(k)*, *a(k)*, $i(k)$, and $EGR(k)$ are the mass of fuel, air, inert gas, and EGR into the cylinder before *kth* burn, respectively, $MF(k)$ and $AF(k)$ are the mass of fresh fuel and air fed per cycle, respectively, $\delta\,MF(k)$ is the small changes in mass of fresh fuel per cycle, $F(k)$ is the fraction of cylinder gas remaining, R is the stoichiometric air- fuel ratio, *CE(k)* is the combustion efficiency, $\varphi(k)$ is the equivalence ratio, $Q(k)$ is the heat release in the *kth* cycle, $\varphi_m,\varphi_l,\varphi_u$ are system parameters, $r_{H_2O}(k)$, $r_{O_2}(k)$, $r_{N_2}(k)$, and $r_{CO_2}(k)$ are mass of water, oxygen, nitrogen, and carbon oxygen in cylinder respectively, γ_{H_2O}, γ_{O_2}, γ_{N_2}, and γ_{CO_2} are constant parameters associated with water, oxygen, nitrogen, and carbon oxygen respectively, γ is a constant, $d_1'(k)$ and $d_2'(k)$ are unknown but bounded disturbances. From the above equations, it is clear that the dynamics are highly nonlinear with combustion efficiency $CE(k)$ and residual gas fraction $F(k)$ being unknown.

NN CONTROLLER DESIGN

The overall goal is to minimize the cyclic dispersion, i.e., to minimize the heat release variations with high EGR levels, without needing to know the dynamics of SI engines. The control objective is accomplished by keeping both fuel *m(k)* and combustion ratio *CE(k)* held constant (see Eq. (6)). In other words, the main objective is to reduce the variations in the equivalence ratio $\varphi(k)$ since constant equivalence ratio $\varphi(k)$ could result in a constant *CE(k)* (see Eq. (5)). From Eq. (4), this can be realized with a separately controlled EGR system and by keeping both mass of air and fuel tightly bounded to their respective targets. By doing so, inert gas in Eq. (3) will automatically evolve to a stable value since Eq. (3) is a stable linear system with $F(k)$ being always less than 1 and $r_{H_2O}(k)$, $r_{N_2}(k)$, and $r_{CO_2}(k)$ are kept constant with small variations. Once the amount of air, fuel, EGR and inert gas is controlled precisely, the equivalence ratio in Eq. (4) is held constant. This implies that the combustion efficiency variations in Eq. (5) are minimized. So the variations in heat release are reduced.

We will focus on controlling the air and fuel. A virtual control signal is designed to control the air intake system and the actual control input is selected to control the fuel intake system using a backstepping approach. When the total fuel and air are tightly controlled, the equivalence ratio and the heat release variations are reduced, and the engine can operate smoothly with high EGR levels.

A. Controller Design

Step 1: State space model of the system.

Let us denote

$$x_1(k)=a(k),\ x_2(k)=m(k),\ x_3(k)=i(k). \tag{11}$$

Let us choose small changes of the injected fresh fuel as the control variable

$$\delta\, MF(k)=u(k). \tag{12}$$

Substituting Eq. (11) and (12) into Eq. (1) through (3) results in

$$x_1(k+1)=F(k)\cdot\lfloor x_1(k)-R\cdot CE(k)\cdot x_2(k)+r_{O_2}(k)+r_{N_2}(k)\rfloor+(1-F(k))\cdot AF(k)+d_1'(k) \tag{13}$$

$$x_2(k+1)=x_2(k)\cdot(1-CE(k))\cdot F(k)+(1-F(k))\cdot MF(k)+(1-F(k))\cdot u(k)+d_2'(k), \tag{14}$$

$$x_3(k+1)=F(k)\cdot x_3(k)+F(k)\cdot(EGR(k)+(r_{CO_2}(k)+r_{H_2O}(k)+r_{N_2}(k))). \tag{15}$$

Once states $x_1(k)$ and $x_2(k)$ are controlled tightly bounded to their respective target values, Eq. (15) can be viewed a stable system with variations in terms of $F(k)\cdot(EGR(k)+(r_{CO_2}(k)+r_{H_2O}(k)+r_{N_2}(k)))$. So in the controller design, we do not consider Eq. (15). Assigning

$$f_1(k)=F(k)\cdot(x_1(k)+r_{O_2}(k)+r_{N_2}(k))+(1-F(k))\cdot AF(k), \tag{16}$$

$$g_1(k)=-F(k)\cdot R\cdot CE(k), \tag{17}$$

$$f_2(k)=x_2(k)\cdot(1-CE(k))\cdot F(k)+(1-F(k))\cdot MF(k), \tag{18}$$

$$g_2(k)=1-F(k). \tag{19}$$

Then system Eq. (13) and (14) becomes

$$x_1(k+1)=f_1(k)+g_1(k)x_2(k)+d_1'(k), \tag{20}$$

$$x_2(k+1)=f_2(k)+g_2(k)u(k)+d_2'(k). \tag{21}$$

Since the residual gas fraction $F(k)$ and combustion efficiency $CE(k)$ are typically unknown beforehand, $f_1(k)$, $g_1(k)$, $f_2(k)$, and $g_2(k)$ are unknown. Here, NNs are employed to approximate these nonlinear functions.

Step 2: Virtual controller design.

Assumption 1: Since $g_i(k), i=1,2$ are smooth functions, they are bounded within the compact subset S, whose bounds are $g_{1M}>|g_1(k)|>0$ and $g_{2M}>|g_2(k)|>0$, respectively, where $g_{1M}\in R^+$ and $g_{2M}\in R^+$.

Define the error between actual and desired air as

$$e_1(k)=x_1(k)-X_{1d}, \tag{22}$$

where X_{1d} is the desired constant value of the mass of the air. Hence Eq. (22) is rewritten as

$$e_1(k+1)=x_1(k+1)-X_{1d}=f_1(k)+g_1(k)x_2(k)-X_{1d}+d_1'(k). \tag{23}$$

By viewing $x_2(k)$ as a virtual control input to Eq. (23), there exists a desired virtual control input given by

$$x_{2d}(k) = g_1^{-1}(k)(-f_1(k) + X_{1d}) + l_1 e_1(k). \tag{24}$$

where $l_1 \in R$ is a design constant, such that the error, $e_1(k)$, is bounded.

Since $f_1(k)$ and $g_1(k)$ are unknown, $x_{2d}(k)$ cannot be implemented in practice. From Eq. (24), the unknown part $(1/g_1(k))(-f_1(k) + X_{1d})$ is a smooth function of $x_1(k), x_2(k), x_3(k)$ and X_{1d}. By utilizing NN to approximate the unknown part in Eq. (24), $x_{2d}(k)$ can be expressed as

$$x_{2d}(k) = w_1^T \phi(v_1^T z_1(k)) + \varepsilon_1(z_1(k)) + l_1 e_1(k), \tag{25}$$

where

$$z_1(k) = [x_1(k), x_2(k), x_3(k), X_{1d}]^T, \tag{26}$$

is the input to the first NN, $w_1 \in R^{n_1}$ and $v_1 \in R^{4 \times n_1}$ represent the matrix of target weights of the output layer and hidden respectively, n_1 is the number of hidden layer node, $\phi_1(\cdot) \in R^{n_1}$ is the activation function vector, and $\varepsilon_1(z_1(k)) \in R$ is the NN reconstruction error. It is demonstrated by Igelnik and Pao (1995) that, if the hidden layer weight, v_1, is chosen initially at random and kept constant and the number of hidden layer nodes is sufficiently large, the NN reconstruction error $\varepsilon_1(z_1(k))$ can be made arbitrarily small since the activation function forms a basis.

Consequently, the virtual control input, $\hat{x}_{2d}(k)$, is taken as

$$\hat{x}_{2d}(k) = \hat{w}_1^T(k)\phi(v_1^T z_1(k)) + l_1 e_1(k) = \hat{w}_1^T(k)\phi(k) + l_1 e_1(k), \tag{27}$$

where $\hat{w}_1(k) \in R^{n_1}$ is the actual weights of the output layer to be tuned. The hidden layer weight, v_1, is randomly chosen initially and kept constant. For convenience, $\phi(v_1^T z_1(k))$ is written as $\phi(k)$. Let the weights estimation error be

$$\tilde{w}_1(k) = \hat{w}_1(k) - w_1. \tag{28}$$

Define the system error between $x_2(k)$ and $\hat{x}_{2d}(k)$ as

$$e_2(k) = x_2(k) - \hat{x}_{2d}(k). \tag{29}$$

Equation (23) becomes

$$\begin{aligned} e_1(k+1) &= f_1(k) + g_1(k)(e_2(k) + \hat{x}_{2d}(k)) - X_{1d} + d_1'(k), \\ &= g_1(k)(l_1 e_1(k) + e_2(k) + \zeta_1(k) + d_1(k)), \end{aligned} \tag{30}$$

where

$$\zeta_1(k) = \tilde{w}_1^T(k)\phi(k), \text{ and } d_1(k) = d_1'(k)/g_1(k) - \varepsilon_1(z_1(k)). \tag{31}$$

Step 3: Design of the control input *u(k)*

Writing the error in the total mass of fuel in the cylinder from Eq. (21) as

$$e_2(k+1) = x_2(k+1) - \hat{x}_{2d}(k+1) = f_2(k) + g_2(k)u(k) - \hat{x}_{2d}(k+1) + d_2'(k). \tag{32}$$

Similarly, choosing the desired control input by using the second NN as

$$u_d(k) = (1/g_2(k))(-f_2(k) + \hat{x}_{2d}(k+1)) + l_2 e_2(k) = w_2^T(k)\sigma(v_2^T z_2(k)) + \varepsilon_2(z_2(k)) + l_2 e_2(k). \tag{33}$$

where the input to the second NN, $z_2(k) \in R^6$, is taken as

$$z_2(k) = [z_1^T(k), e_1(k), e_2(k)]^T, \tag{34}$$

Assumption 2: The NN reconstruction errors $\varepsilon_1(z_1(k))$ and $\varepsilon_2(z_2(k))$ are bounded over the compact set S by ε_{1m} and ε_{2m}, respectively.

The actual control input is selected as

$$u(k) = \hat{w}_2^T(k)\sigma(k) + l_2 e_2(k), \tag{35}$$

where $\hat{w}_2(k) \in R^{n_2}$ represents actual weights of the output layer.

Substituting Eq. (33) and (35) into Eq. (32) yields

$$e_2(k+1) = g_2(k)(l_2 e_2(k) + \zeta_2(k) + d_2(k)). \tag{36}$$

where

$$\tilde{w}_2(k) = \hat{w}_2(k) - w_2,\ \zeta_2(k) = \tilde{w}_2^T(k)\sigma(k), \text{ and } d_2(k) = d_2'(k)/g_2(k) - \varepsilon_2(z_2(k)). \tag{37}$$

In order to ensure the stability of the closed loop system, suitable NN weight updating rules are necessary and they are presented next.

B. Closed Loop System Stability Analysis

Assumption 3: Both the ideal weights and the activation functions for all NNs are bounded by known positive values so that

$$\|w_1\| \le w_{1\max},\ \|w_2\| \le w_{2\max},\ \|\phi(\cdot)\| \le \phi_{\max} \text{ and } \|\sigma(\cdot)\| \le \sigma_{\max}. \tag{38}$$

Theorem 1: Consider the system given by Eq. (20) and (21). Assume that the Assumptions 1 through 3 hold. Take the first NN weight tuning as

$$\hat{w}_1(k+1) = \hat{w}_1(k) - \alpha_1 \phi(k)(\hat{w}_1^T(k)\phi(k) + l_1 e_1(k)). \tag{39}$$

with the second NN weight tuning be provided by

$$\hat{w}_2(k+1) = \hat{w}_2(k) - \frac{\alpha_2}{l_2}\sigma(k)(\hat{w}_2^T(k)\sigma(k) + l_2 e_2(k)). \tag{40}$$

where $\alpha_1 \in R, \alpha_2 \in R$ are NN learning rates, $l_1 \in R$ and $l_2 \in R$ are controller gains. The errors $e_1(k)$ and $e_2(k)$, the NN weights estimates, $\hat{w}_1(k)$ and $\hat{w}_2(k)$ are bounded provided the design parameters are selected as:

$$\text{(a) } 0 < \alpha_1 \|\phi(\cdot)\|^2 < 1, \tag{41}$$

$$\text{(b) } 0 < \alpha_2 \|\sigma(\cdot)\|^2 < l_2, \tag{42}$$

$$\text{(c) } 0 < |l_1| < 1/(\sqrt{12}g_{1M}), \tag{43}$$

$$\text{(d) } 0 < l_2 < \left(-1 + \sqrt{(4 + g_{2M}^2)}\right)/(6g_{2M}). \tag{44}$$

Moreover, the equivalence ratio error is bounded; hence the actual equivalence ratio is also bounded. The heat release dispersion is reduced.

Proof: Due to space consideration, it is omitted here. ■

SIMULATION

The simulation parameters are selected as the following: 10000 cycles are considered at equivalence ratio of 1 with variation of 1%, R =14.6, F = 0.15, mass of new air = 9.1295, $\phi_u = 0.82$, $\phi_l = 0.79$, molecular weight of fuel = 114, molecular weight of EGR=30.4, molecular weight of air = 28.84, total gas mole in cylinder = 0.5, and ratio of hydrogen/carbon for fuel = 1.87. Initial conditions for all residues including air, fuel and inert are selected to be equal 0. The desired mass of air is taken as $X_{1d} = 9.0123$ and the desired mass of fuel is calculated as $X_{2d} = 0.6173$. The gains of controllers are selected as $l_1 = l_2 = 0.1$, respectively. Both NNs are configured to possess 15 nodes in the hidden layer. The learning rate is selected as $\alpha_1 = 0.01$ and $\alpha_2 = 0.001$. The initial weights are selected uniformly within an interval of [0, 1] and all the activation functions are selected as hyperbolic tangent sigmoid functions.

A 21.2% EGR level (with variation of 0.004) is fed back into the intake in order to simulate the effectiveness of proposed controller. The plots below are a pair of return maps of heat release with and without control. Results indicate that with the proposed NN controller, the dispersion in heat release is reduced. Future effort involves further reducing the cyclic dispersion at high EGR levels.

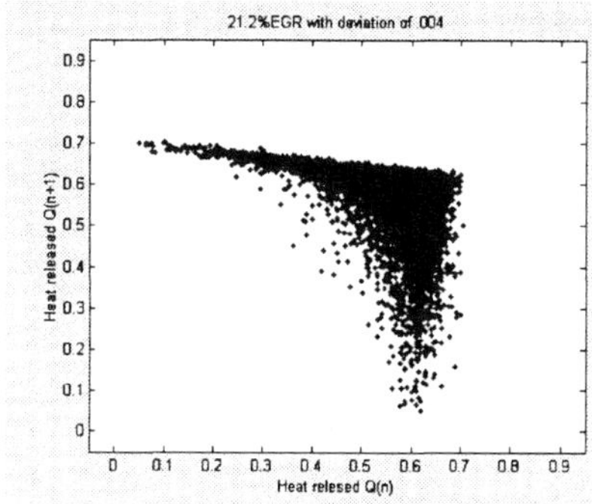

Fig. 1. Cyclic dispersion without control.

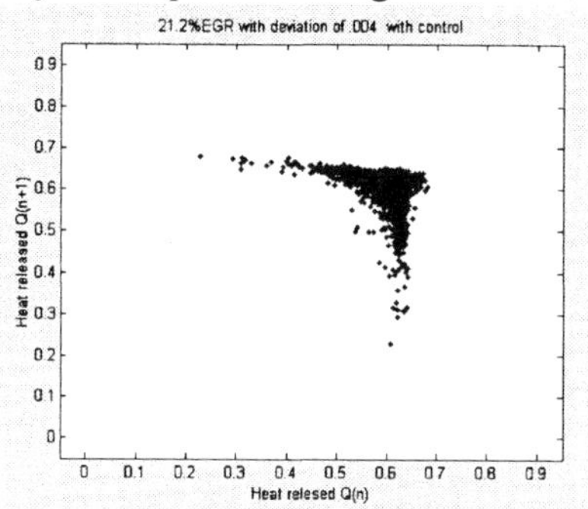

Fig. 2. Cyclic dispersion with control.

CONCLUSIONS

A novel NN controller scheme is presented to reduce the cyclic dispersion in engine combustion with high EGR levels. Future work will involve reducing cyclic dispersion at high EGR levels and simultaneously minimizing emissions while achieving drivability and fuel efficiency.

ACKNOWLEDGMENTS

The authors would like to thank the support by the NSF under Grant ECS #0327877.

REFERENCES

He, P. and Jagannathan, S., 2003, "Neuro emission controller for minimizing cyclic dispersion in spark ignition engines", in *Proc. Int. Joint Conf. Neural Networks*, Vol. 2, pp. 1535–1540.

Igelnik, B., and Pao, Y. H., 1995, "Stochastic choice of basis functions in adaptive function approximation and the functional-link net," *IEEE Trans. Neural Networks*, Vol. 6, pp. 1320-1329.

Inoue, T., Matsushita, S., Nakanishi, K., and Okano, H. 1993, "Toyota lean combustion system-The third generation system," *SAE* 930873.

Sutton, R. W., and Drallmeier, J. A., 2000, "Development of nonlinear cyclic dispersion in spark ignition engines under the influence of high levels of EGR", *Proceedings of the Central States Section of the Combustion Institute*, pp. 175-180.

SINGLE PHASE FLUID FLOW CLASSIFICATION VIA NEURAL NETWORKS & SUPPORT VECTOR MACHINE

THEODORE B. TRAFALIS
OLUTAYO OLADUNNI
School of Industrial Engineering
University of Oklahoma
202 West Boyd, Room 124
Norman, OK 73019
ttrafalis@ou.edu; tayo@ou.edu

ABSTRACT
The main objective of this paper is to apply Support Vector Machine (SVM) and Neural Networks (NNs) classifiers to characterize the flow pattern of a non-Newtonian fluid. This approach is achieved by simulating the Reynolds number equation through SVM and NNs. Classification of fluid flow patterns can be seen as a machine learning problem where the inputs are vectors of length 6 with attributes that represent the parameters which determine the fluid flow in the annulus/pipe. SVM classifiers can play an important role in the control/monitor of fluid flow, because the algorithm can be easily implemented in the design of an automated system that will provide real-time control of the fluid flow. The algorithm constructs separating hyperplanes, where the weights of the hyperplane represent a scaled level of importance for each parameter. Preliminary results show that the most accurate model favors the SVM polynomial and radial basis kernel function model.

INTRODUCTION

In a physical process the objective is usually to study the process for changes in physical state, and it's usually performed using quantitative analysis of numerical models. In some cases quantitative analysis is not always feasible and this is usually due to the high complexity of the models. Sometimes quantitative models are feasible but not necessary.

It would be unwise to try to solve all problems with SVM as this would lead to very complex problems, regardless of some parameters being defined by a measurement method that is defined in terms of qualitative operations. This draws out the need to understand possible relationships between different types of methodologies. SVM for a physical state will be characterized by variables which take on continuous and/or categorical values, and perform a mapping of the variables in a feature space. Classification is done in this feature space making use of a hyperplane in the decision surface. Then a decision function is used for determining the physical state. Since SVM involves changes in state, the problem is how to determine this decision function. The SVM model, developed by Vapnik (1995) has gained popularity in solving classification and regression problems due its success in various disciplines such as time series prediction (Trafalis et. al., 2002) and finance (Trafalis and Ince, 2000).

The idea of developing a model for predictive control of drilling dynamic systems similar to the flow pattern classification for non-static well conditions is not a new concept. Dashevskiy et al. (1999) proposed a NN model for real-time monitoring bottom-hole assemblies (BHA) and drill bit dynamic behavior. We can draw on the similarities; flow pattern is connected to drilling dynamics because flow pattern identification involves the monitoring of patterns and fluid flow behavior in a dynamic well, as well as estimating the pressures at various points of a non-static well. The dynamic nature of the problem makes it a drilling dynamic candidate with respect to flow pattern behavior.

Flow pattern classification is also a part of mud and cement planning, which ultimately is under well planning. To draw a connection, flow pattern provides information on how to determine pressures for the initial circulation of fluid in the well. In some cases, the pressure required to initiate circulation in the annulus may be much higher than pressure required in sustaining circulation at the desired flow rate, the difference of the pressures accounts for the pressure drop. To estimate that pressure drop flow pattern information is necessary. There are several references for the NN approaches in well planning; such include the work of Sadiq and Nashawi (2000), who proposed a NN model for predicting formation fracture gradients using depth, overburden pressure gradient and Poisson's ratio. Sultan and Al-Kaabi (2002) also proposed a NN model for determining well test interpretation model which is essential to the reservoir plans of well planning. An interesting application is the work of Bilgesu et al. (2000) who used NN's for drill bit selection. Several networks were developed using 10 attributes and as much as 489 different bit types, making it a large scale multi-class problem.

This paper models a physical process as a classification problem using SVM and neural networks approach (learning algorithms) with emphasis on the fluid flow pattern in a wellbore. Both algorithms define a decision surface with the aid of a decision function that identifies two states (laminar and turbulent flow).

SUPPORT VECTOR MACHINE CLASSIFICATION

SVM avoids overfitting by maximizing the margin between two classes of training data. The formulation can be written as follows in its primal form (Gunn, 1998; Mangasarian; Scholokpf, 2002; and Vapnik, 1995):

$$\min_{w,b} \left\{ \frac{1}{2}\|w\|^2 + C\sum_{i=1}^{l}\xi_i \mid y_i(wx_i + b) + \xi_i \geq 1,\ \xi_i \geq 0 \quad i = 1,\ldots,l \right\} \tag{1}$$

where $\|w\|^2$ is the 2-norm of the weight vector. ξ_i is a non-negative slack that measures the degree of violation of the constraints and also used to reduce the sum of distance of separation errors especially when the data is linearly inseparable. C is a constant, the regularization parameter that controls the trade-off between minimizing training error and minimizing the norm of the weight vector (generalization ability); it can also represent the knowledge of noise on the data. C is to be chosen by the user and a larger value corresponds to a higher penalty to the errors with less generalization ability and can result in a complex model, while a smaller one corresponds to fewer penalties with a higher generalization ability and can result in a less complex model.
With the introduction of positive Lagrange multipliers α_i, to the constraints in the primal form we can formulate the dual problem below:

$$\max_{\alpha} w(\alpha) = \max_{\alpha} \left\{ \sum_{i=1}^{l}\alpha_i - \frac{1}{2}\sum_{i=1}^{l}\sum_{j=1}^{l}\alpha_i\alpha_j y_i y_j \langle x_i, x_j \rangle \mid \sum_{i=1}^{l}\alpha_i y_i = 0,\ 0 \leq \alpha_i \leq C, \quad i = 1,\ldots,l \right\} \tag{2}$$

The decision function is given by

$$f(x) = sign\left(\sum_{i=1}^{l} \alpha_i y_i \langle x_i, x_j \rangle + b\right) \tag{3}$$

The solution is then given by $w = \sum_i \alpha_i y_i x_i$. The free coefficient b can be derived from $\alpha_i(y_i(w.x_i + b) - 1) = 0$, for any i such that α_i is not zero.

The input vectors of the SVM can be transformed into a higher dimensional feature space using a (kernel function) $k(x_i, x_j)$. The inner product can be expressed by the kernel function (Scholokopf, 2002): $k : \Re^d \times \Re^d \rightarrow \Re : k(x_1, x_2) = \langle \phi(x_1), \phi(x_2) \rangle$. This function can be viewed as determining the similarity or distance between the input vectors in the feature space.

So we can replace $\langle x_i, x \rangle$ in the dual problem by the kernel function $k(x_i, x)$.

The kernel functions used in this study are the polynomial and Gaussian RBF kernel given as:

$k(x_i, x) = (x_i^T x + 1)^P$, p is the degree of polynomial for the polynomial kernel function.

$k(x_i, x) = \exp(-\|x_i - x\|^2 / 2\sigma^2)$, σ is the spread for the Gaussian RBF kernel function.

NEURAL NETWORKS (NNs)

One of the most popular neural net models is the feed-forward neural network and the associated back-propagation training algorithm (FFBP) (Tang and Fishwick, 1993). In a feed forward neural network, the neurons (i.e., processing units) are usually arranged in layers, denoted by *I* * *H* * *O*, where *I, H* and *O* represent the number of inputs, the number of hidden units, and the number of output units respectively. The input units pass on the input vector x. The units in the hidden layer and output layer are processing units. Each processing unit has an activation function. For this paper the activation function is the hyperbolic-tangent sigmoid function given below

$$f(x) = \frac{e^x - e^{-x}}{e^x + e^{-x}}. \tag{4}$$

Usually, the output net of the neuron obtained by summing the weighted inputs is passed through an activation function, *f(x)*, to get a final output, y

$$net = \sum_{i=1}^{I} w_i x_i + b, \qquad y = f(net) = f\left(\sum_{i=1}^{I} w_i x_i + b\right) \tag{5}$$

where x is the input, w are the weights and b is the bias, which determines the location of the activation on the x axis. A feed forward neural net works by training the network with known samples, it's an iterative procedure whereby, a random sample of x is drawn from the training set and fed into the network through the input layer. The network computes an output vector based on the hidden layer output and compares it with the desired output, which is part of the training data set.

FLOW PATTERN DATASET

Our dataset consists of 92 instances/datapoints, which were obtained from several fields in Oklahoma. There are 2 classes (laminar or turbulent) and 6 variables as attributes namely, flow rate, density, viscosity, borehole diameter, drill collar diameter and mud type. The flow pattern data is based on a Bingham plastic model (pseudoplastic) (Bourgoyne, 1991). The dataset was normalized using a sigmoidal function to reduce the

data, thus making computation easy. The function transforms input data non-linearly into the range -1 to 1.
Each input variable is normalized using the formula given below:

$$x' = \frac{1-e^{-\alpha}}{1+e^{-\alpha}}, \qquad \alpha = \frac{\bar{x}_i - \mu_i}{\sigma_i}, \tag{6}$$

Where x' = normalized input, x = original input, σ = standard deviation of input, μ = mean of the original input, α = Zscore, and i = index of input.

Each input variable was normalized using the equation. This normalization process was applied to the whole data including the training and testing sets. The dataset where divided up as follows; 60% of the whole data was used as training data, while the remaining 40% was used as testing data. The data was cross-validated to obtain ten runs to facilitate comparison and draw conclusions. All classification analysis was implemented using the SVM routines in MATLAB (Gunn, 1998) as well as the NNs routines in MATLAB (MATLAB, 1994-2003).

DISCUSSION OF RESULTS

Ten runs were trained and tested to obtain the error rates so as to determine the accuracy of the SVM and NN model. The kernels used are Polynomial kernel (Poly) with p = 2 and Gaussian Radial Basis kernel (rbf) with σ = 1 for the SVM, while a **6*26*1** architecture was used for the NNs model. The kernel parameters were selected based on trial and error and the 26 hidden units for NNs were adopted by taking the average of the number of support vectors for SVM rbf for the 10 runs. The summary statistics of the learning algorithms and mean classification results for 10 runs are given in Tables 1 & 2 respectively. Following is the discussion of results obtained using the remaining 40% of the data that were not seen by the learning algorithms.

Figure 1 shows the comparison of the mean error rate for the learning algorithms with their respective tradeoff cost. The results show good agreements with the data; the model provides a good generalization classifier capable of characterizing the flow pattern of the fluid in the annulus opposite the drill collar. The models produced mean error rates ranging from 5% - 10%, with the smallest error belonging to the SVM rbf kernel with C = 100.

Figure 2 shows the plot of test data of SVM mean error rates. It was necessary to see how the tradeoff cost affects the model accuracy. Results indicate that the classification accuracy is dependent on the tradeoff cost (Tables 1 & 2). While there are no apparent differences in the error rates for the polynomial kernel for the value of C of interest, it does not suggest that all C values are optimal. From Table 2, the margin (0.7791) favors C = 1. This seems ideal because it reduces the chances of having a misclassified point. The errors of the rbf kernel do show differences. Specifically, as C increases the errors rates appear to be decreasing, and this happens because more emphasis is placed on minimizing the misclassification error, thereby producing small training/misclassification error.

A significant test was performed to see how the learning model depends on the mud type attribute. So the model was run without the mud type. The results were also favorable with a 90% success rate; however the inclusion of the mud type improves the model by 5%. This suggests that an omission of the mud type attribute can decrease the accuracy of the model.

CONCLUSION

The single phase fluid flow pattern in annulus has been formulated as a machine learning problem and solved using the novel learning machines SVM and NNs. The study results show that the SVM model has a 95% success rate in simulating the Reynolds number equation for classification of fluid flow pattern.

The predictive capabilities of SVM model is a good direction in the development and improvement of a drilling dynamics automated system. The model strengths provide a good approximation for the Reynolds equation and accurate simulation of the non linear patterns through the observation of the fluid flow behavior. It has been demonstrated that the SVM model is feasible for the classification of the fluid flow type. Real drilling data were used to reveal its feasibility and it provided a qualitative classification of the fluid flow behavior. However, a more extensive analysis would be to observe and gather data for the entire period of the drilling operation. Then train the data for a particular drilling operation and validate with other drilling operational data, preferably from the same reservoir and then use the weights in making decisions regarding future operations.

The SVM approach can be applied to determine the flow pattern of fluids with different rheology using the same approach. The fluid modeled in this paper is a non-Newtonian fluid, pseudoplastic model (Bingham plastic) with 2 flow patterns, the same concept can be applied to a Newtonian or non-Newtonian fluid with 3 flow patterns (laminar, transition and turbulent) using a multi-classification SVM model. This is the subject of a forthcoming paper.

Since the SVM was successful at simulating the Reynolds equation, one can go a step further to estimate the pressure drop in the annulus using support vector regression.

REFERENCE

Ayeni, K.B., 2003, *Drilling Fluid Hydraulics Simulator with emphasis on Rheological Models*, "Master Thesis", University of Oklahoma, chapter 2, May 2003.

Bared, S.G., 1990, *The New Reynolds Number and the Estimated Drilling Rate under High Gravitations*, SPE 21630.

Bilgesu, H.I., Al-Rashidi, A.F., Aminian, K., and Ameri, S., 2000, *A New Approach for Drill Bit Selection*, SPE 65618, October 2000.

Bourgoyne, A.T. Jr., 1991, Chenevert, M.E., Millheim, K.K., and Young, F.S. Jr., *Applied Drilling Engineering*, SPE Textbook Series Vol. 2, Richardson, TX, pp. 137 – 144.

Dashevskiy, D., Dubinski, V., and Macpherson, J.D., 1999, *Application of Neural Networks for Predictive Control in Drilling Dynamics*, SPE 56442, October 1999.

Gunn, S.T., 1998, *Support Vector Machine for Classification and Regression*, Technical Report, Department of Electronic and Computer Science, University of Southampton.

Joshi, S.D., 1991, *Horizontal Well Technology*, Pennwell Publishing Co., Tulsa, Oklahoma, chapter 10.

Kokar, M.M., 1987, *Critical hypersurfaces and the quantity space.* In Proceedings, AAAI-87, Sixth National Conference on Artificial Intelligence, AAAI, pp 616-620.

Mangasarian, O.L. *Data Mining via Support Vector Machines*, Computer Science Department, University of Wisconsin. [olvi@cs.wisc.edu].

MATLAB. User's Guide, 1994-2003, The Math-Works, Inc., Natwick, MA 01760, http://www.mathworks.com.

Mir Asif Sultan and Abdulaziz U. Al-Kaabi, 2002, *Application of Neural Network to the Determination of Well-Test Interpretation Model for Horizontal Wells*, SPE 77878, October.

Sadiq, T., and Nashawi, I.S., 2000, *Using Neural Networks for Prediction of Formation Fracture Gradient.* SPE/Petroleum Society of CIM 65463, November 2000.

Scholokopf, B., 2002, *Statistical Learning and Kernel Method.* Technical Report MSR-TR-2000-23, Microsoft Research Ltd., Microsoft Corporation.

Tang, Z., and Fishwick, P.A., 1993, "Feedforward Neural Nets as Models for Time Series Forecasting", *ORSA Journal of Computing*.

Trafalis, T.B., M. Richman, and B. Santosa, 2002, "Prediction of Rainfal from WSR-88R Radar using Support Vector Regression", ASME Press, *Book* Published of Collection: C.H. Dagli, A.L. Buczak, J. Ghosh, M.J. Embrechts, O. Ersoy, and S.W. Kercel, *Intelligent Engineering Systems Through Artificial Neural Networks*, Vol. 12 (pp 639-644). (Novel Smart Engineering System Design Award)

Trafalis, T.B. and Ince, H., 2000, "Support Vector Machine for Regression and Applications to Financial Forecasting", *IEEE-INNS-ENNS International Joint Conference on Neural Networks*, Como, Italy, July 24-27, 2000.

Vapnik, V., 1995, *The Nature of Statistical Learning Theory*. Springer-Verlag, New York.

Table 1. Summary statistics of the machine learning methods for 10 runs

	Accuracy						
	SVM poly, C=1	SVM poly, C=10	SVM poly, C=100	SVM rbf, C=1	SVM rbf, C=10	SVM rbf, C=100	NN FFBP
Max	100%	100%	100%	100%	100%	100%	100%
Mean	95%	95%	95%	90%	93%	95%	90%
Min	72%	69%	69%	58%	64%	64%	72%

Table 2. Mean classification result for 10 runs

	SVM						NN
	poly, p = 2			rbf, σ = 1			FFBP
	C=1	C=10	C=100	C=1	C=10	C=100	
Test error rate	0.0500	0.0500	0.0500	0.1000	0.0694	0.0472	0.0972
Test accuracy rate	0.9500	0.9500	0.9500	0.9000	0.9306	0.9528	0.9028
Margin	0.7791	0.4506	0.2917	0.6102	0.2887	0.1703	-
Learning rate	-	-	-	-	-	-	0.3
Momentum constant	-	-	-	-	-	-	0.6

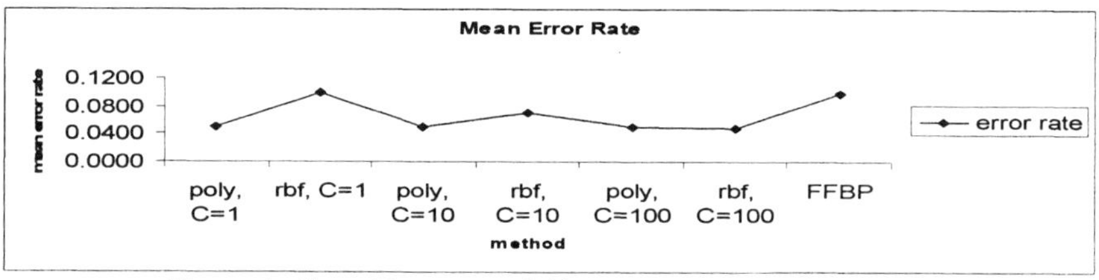

Figure 1. Mean Error rate of 10 runs on varying algorithms

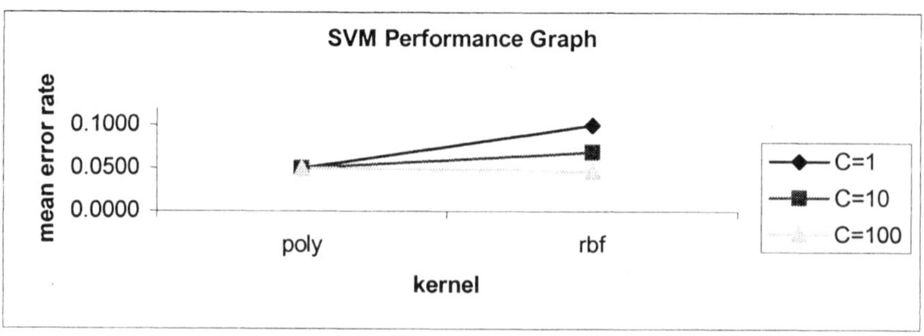

Figure 2. Mean Error rate on Tradeoff cost (C)

USING EVOLUTIONARY DATA SEGREGATION TECHNIQUES TO REDUCE THE COMPUTATION TIME NEEDED TO DESIGN PIPING FLOW USING CFD

PETER E. JOHNSON, PH.D.
Department of
Mechanical Engineering
Valparaiso University
Valparaiso, Indiana

KENNETH M. BRYDEN, PH.D.
Department of
Mechanical Engineering
Iowa State University
Ames, Iowa

DANIEL A. ASHLOCK, PH.D.
Department of
Mathematics and Statistics
University of Guelph
Guelph, Ontario, Canada

ABSTRACT
Analyzing fluid flow using computational fluid dynamics (CFD) is most often performed in the later stages of product development due to the lengthy turnaround times involved (up to three weeks to obtain an adequate solution). To reduce this time, an evolutionary technique has been utilized. AMoEBA, the Adaptive Modeling by Evolving Blocks Algorithm, has been used to automatically segregate a CFD flowfield and to place different solution methods in the resulting sub-regions. A substantial reduction in the turnaround time of a CFD model is achieved by assigning minimal cost solvers to regions with simple flow dynamics. The physical system being modeled is flow through a 90° elbow. The long-term goal is for the algorithm to develop a segregation scheme that can be used in a virtual engineering design tool. The results show an improvement in the speed of the multi-solver when compared with a single model solution with no significant loss of accuracy.

KEYWORDS
Main: General Engineering Applications
Other Keywords: Binary Tree, Engineering Applications, Evolutionary Algorithm, Fitness Function, Genetic Algorithm, Genetic Programming, Optimization

INTRODUCTION
Virtual reality is being used in a variety of engineering applications due to its ability to present three-dimensional (3-D), complex data and information in an intuitive and interactive manner. Similarly, the steady rise in computational power has increased the demand for high-fidelity modeling in engineering communities. By combining virtual reality and high-fidelity modeling a virtual engineering platform is created in which the user can interact directly with individual virtual components in the same manner as they would with a real prototype. Furthermore, as a design tool, this platform could enable changes to be made to a component and the response to be calculated with sufficient accuracy for an engineer to understand the answer. Unfortunately, numerical models are usually very large and require significant compute times. Often, CFD analysts create models that solve the Navier-Stokes equations on as many as 10 million nodes. Although simplifications exist for these equations, they are not generally used for large complex flows. Combining these simplifications into a multi-solver computational technique will allow each zone to receive the minimum attention and fidelity it requires to efficiently

produce a solution that is within a known level of accuracy. The difficulty in creating such a technique is in the application: how does one decide which areas require complex models and in which can simplified models be used?

Before the digital computer, computations were performed manually, and therefore, a minimal number of calculations were essential. Engineers developed methods for combining analytical solutions through similarity techniques (Rosenhead, 1963). For example, engineers in the 1940s and 1950s combined inviscid flow equations with boundary layer equations to model flat plate boundary layer problems. Flow over an airplane wing is a natural progression from this flat plate example because it also can be divided into a boundary layer and the outer, inviscid flow. These techniques, known as zonal methods, are mostly used in high-speed flows where the placement of the solvers is based on knowledge of the flowfield (Wuthrich, et al., 1996). Multi-solver techniques for more complicated flows are also being studied (Anderson and Kozlak, 2002; Niksa, et al., 2002) but, they, too, require user intuition for the solver placements.

This paper presents the Adaptive Modeling by Evolving Blocks Algorithm (AMoEBA) (Ashlock, et al., sub.; Ashlock, et al., 2002; Johnson, 2003; Johnson, et al., 2003; Johnson, et al., 2001), an evolutionary technique for automatically generating a segregated domain and placing solvers in the resulting sub-regions.

PROBLEM DESCRIPTION

Applications of AMoEBA have included the geometric decomposition of an arbitrarily generated diffusion data set (Ashlock, et al., sub.; Ashlock, et al., 2002); the segregation and solver assignment for a multi-solver solution of a laminar, steady-state, fully-developed pipe flow problem; and the material placement for an inverse heat conduction problem (Johnson, et al., 2003). The main goal of AMoEBA in its current setting is to create a multi-solver scheme that can be used to recalculate a flowfield as quickly as possible within a known level of accuracy. To accomplish this, AMoEBA segregates the flowfield and assigns different solution methods to the sub-regions. Accuracy is determined by the abilities of the solver networks to match the outlet velocity profile to an exit profile from a single model solution. Speed is a major priority in the algorithm because a CFD data set must be calculated for every structure in the population.

The goal of this research is to minimize the fluctuations in the exit velocity profile of a 90°-pipe elbow. The diameter of the pipe is 0.5 m with 5.0 m straight sections before and after the elbow. The radius of curvature of the elbow is 5.0 m giving a total axial centerline length of 17.85 m (5 m + 7.85 m + 5 m). The inlet velocity for this problem is a uniform flow of 1.0 m/s. This is a precursor to the larger goal of designing pipe systems that minimize the uneven flow distributions that occur due to elbows. The goal is to use AMoEBA to determine the best segregation scheme that can reproduce the exit profile accurately in a shorter period of time than using a single model. In this case, the accuracy throughout the entire pipe is of less concern than the accuracy at the exit, therefore, the fitness function is based on the outlet velocity profile of the candidate solutions.

AMOEBA DESCRIPTION

The AMoEBA algorithm evolves candidate multi-solver segregation schemes through the use of a generational evolutionary algorithm. The details of the parent selection, crossover and mutation strategies, replacement, etc. can be found in (Johnson, 2003). The key differences from other implementations of AMoEBA (Ashlock, et al., sub.; Ashlock, et al., 2002; Johnson, 2003; Johnson, et al., 2003; Johnson, et al., 2001) are the fitness function and the solvers assigned to the multi-solver schemes. The data segregation and solver assignments for each creature in the evolutionary algorithm are encoded into a binary tree, or segregation tree. Nodes are defined by a floating-point value describing the location of a partition. These partitions are only made in the straight inlet and exit portions of the pipe. It was decided that placing segregations in the elbow section would not be beneficial to the goal of the problem. The straight sections are mapped to the range [0, 1], with 0 as the pipe exit and 1 as the inlet (Fig. 1). The terminal leaves are integers that assign solvers to the corresponding region defined by traversing the tree to that particular leaf. In the example (Fig. 1), the top node defines a partition that is placed 10% of the way across the entire domain [0, 1]. Solver 1 is placed in the upper region, and the lower region, defined by the right node, is further divided. This division is placed 55% of the way through the remaining segregation with Solver 2 placed in the upper/left region. The remaining portion of the pipe is divided in a 65%-35% split with Solvers 1 and 3 placed in the remaining two sub-regions, respectively.

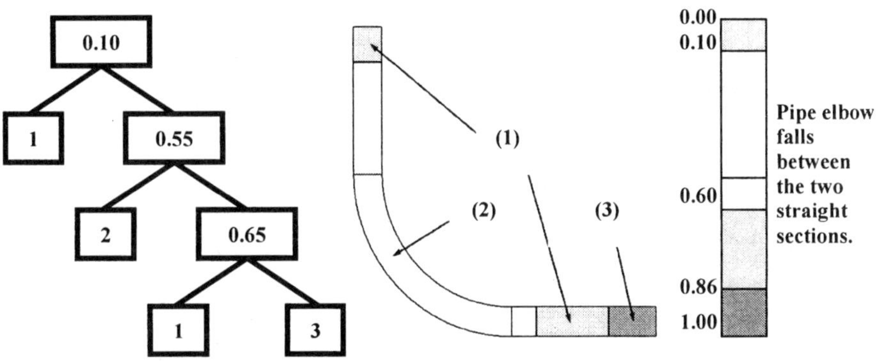

Fig. 1. A data segregation tree, the resulting segregation scheme which places Solvers 1, 2, and 3 in the resulting partitions, and the computational domain mapped to the range [0, 1].

The fitness function is calculated by a percentage error at the exit plane of the pipe. The absolute value of the difference in the axial velocity between the candidate and "exact", single model solutions is first weighted by the fractional area of the cell, then summed over each cell in the cross-sectional area of the exit. The resulting value is normalized by the average axial velocity through the pipe to yield an area-weighted per cell average of the error in the candidate solution (Eq. 1).

$$Error = \frac{\sum_{i=0}^{N} \frac{A_i \left| u_i - u_i' \right|}{A_{tot}}}{\overline{u}} \tag{1}$$

where A_i is the area of cell i, A_{tot} is the total area of the exit plane, u_i is the axial velocity in cell i of the single model "exact" solution, u_i' is the axial velocity in cell i of the candidate case, and $\overline{u}$ is the average velocity through the pipe.

A secondary fitness is also used. During each calculation of the candidate solver networks, the time spent on each iteration of each solver is summed to give the total time spent on that structure. This does not include the time spent on creating the grid and transferring the information from the solvers to the boundaries. These time costs are overhead for having more than one solver and are excluded from the total time for each network during a comparison. At the coarse AMoEBA-grid level, this overhead is of the same order as the flowfield calculations. Because of this, the speedup associated with using multiple solvers is lost unless the overhead is removed from the total time. At a fine-grid level, multi-solvers reduce the time to solution significantly because the overhead is of a much lower order than the flowfield calculation time. Since the goal is to find a multi-solver to be used at the fine-grid levels, the speedup will be retained when the evolved scheme is later implemented.

Although implementing two different fitness functions into the same algorithm can be challenging, this demonstration lends itself to a simple solution. The multi-solvers must be accurate to a certain degree, but it is more important to understand their accuracy and to know how this accuracy translates to different grid sizes, geometries, etc. For this reason, an initial limit was used for the accuracy criterion. When comparing two structures, their accuracy to the "exact" data set is first measured. If both are within 5%, for example, their solution times are then compared. The algorithm continues until a structure is found that meets the accuracy criterion within a set time limit. Based on preliminary studies, 5% error and 100 seconds were chosen as the two fitness criteria.

A variety of solution methods are provided for AMoEBA to assign to each partition. These include a high Reynolds number k-ε solver; a k-ε RNG (renormalized group theory) solver; and two constant turbulent viscosity solvers. A CFD software program applies these solvers. A final solution technique directly transfers information from the inlet to the outlet of the segregation. Although this solver is the least accurate of the solvers used, it is very quick (no grid/geometry is necessary), and, can significantly reduce the time to solution for a network of solvers.

RESULTS

AMoEBA found eight segregation schemes for the elbow flow problem starting from seven different random populations of structures. Each case was run until the stopping criteria of 5% error and 100 seconds were reached. Case 1 was allowed to run beyond the stopping criteria to determine if any interesting structures could be found after reaching the 100-second criterion. Thirty-two generations after reaching the stopping criteria, a faster solution was found. This second scheme has also been analyzed.

Every segregation scheme found by AMoEBA utilized the inlet-to-outlet mapping solver for the entrance to the elbow. This shows there is only a slight difference at the exit of the domain when the placement of the inlet is moved closer to the elbow itself. Five of the eight solutions found placed the inlet within three cells of the elbow which resulted in less than 1.5% error of the single model solution.

Grid Size Study Results

This study compares the accuracy of the schemes on different grid sizes to show that schemes found by AMoEBA translate to finer meshing schemes. Three more grid sizes were analyzed: 18,000 cells (20 radial, five angular, 180 axial), 36,000 cells (20×5×360), and 72,000 cells (20×5×720). This test is important in determining if AMoEBA is an effective algorithm since most CFD analyses use much larger grid sizes than that used by AMoEBA. The accuracy and the times to solution for the schemes are compared. For accuracy, the cell-to-cell comparison used by AMoEBA is calculated to determine the error at the exit profile from a single k-ε RNG model case of the same size.

As expected, the schemes on the coarse grid (1800 cells) were not faster than a single model. At the next level (18,000 cells), the fastest schemes (~13-14 min.) converged in approximately the same order of time as the single model solution (11 min.) while all others were slower. Significant improvement came at the finest two grid sizes studied. On the 36,000-cell grid, five of the eight schemes were slightly faster than the single model solution; and on the 72,000-cell grid, every scheme was faster, with the fastest converging 30% faster than the single case and the slowest at 5% faster.

The accuracies of the different schemes on the different grid sizes range from 0.34% to 1.68%. These errors are reasonable and well within the 5% limit chosen. The largest disparity between errors for the different grid sizes for one scheme was only 1.09%, and this was an improvement (Case 1b went from 1.68% at 1800 cells to 0.59% at 18,000 cells). The errors in the segregated results are not dramatically increasing for the different grid sizes which shows that the grid size does not adversely affect the results of the AMoEBA segregation schemes.

Elbow Angle Study Results

For the AMoEBA-created multi-solvers to be used effectively, they must be accurate and fast when changes are made to the geometry. To study these effects, the segregation schemes were applied to six different angles of the pipe elbow. Since the AMoEBA segregation schemes are based on a 90° elbow, angles of 75°, 60°, 45°, 30°, and 15° were also analyzed. For each of these cases, the accuracy of the segregated solutions has been compared to a single k-ε RNG model results. The grid sizes of these elbows vary but each is comparable in cell size to the 72,000-cell grid used on the 90° elbow. The total times were also recorded and have been included in the comparison (Table 1).

Table 1. Accuracy and times to solution for the angle study performed on the eight different segregation schemes found by AMoEBA.

	15°		30°		45°		60°		75°	
Case	% Error	Time [h]:[m]	% Error	Time	% Error	Time	% Error	Time	% Error	Time
1a	6.47	0:30	5.51	0:37	3.39	0:46	1.52	0:55	1.07	1:05
1b	2.43	0:43	1.85	0:54	0.87	1:03	0.66	1:18	0.84	1:26
2	1.59	0:41	1.19	0:50	0.56	0:56	0.42	1:05	0.53	1:18
3	1.46	0:47	1.20	0:53	0.72	1:02	0.57	1:12	0.69	1:25
4	5.07	0:28	4.18	0:37	2.33	0:46	0.93	0:55	0.73	1:11
5	6.97	0:22	6.11	0:30	3.67	0:41	1.56	0:49	0.80	1:00
6	5.00	0:30	4.13	0:38	2.37	0:51	0.93	0:56	0.66	1:09
7	6.10	0:26	5.08	0:35	3.14	0:47	1.33	0:54	0.91	1:07
Single	-	0:56	-	1:01	-	1:15	-	1:28	-	1:33

For each segregation scheme, the time to reach convergence on the different angles was less than the time to solve the single model solution. Case 5 was the fastest for each angle, reaching convergence 59.6%, 49.8%, 45.5%, 44.0%, and 35.7% faster than the single model for the 15°, 30°, 45°, 60°, and 75° elbows, respectively. However, the error of the solution from the Case 5 scheme on the 45°, 30°, and 15° elbows increased as the departure from the 90° case increased (3.67%, 6.11%, and 6.97% errors). For these same three angles, the faster segregation schemes (Cases 1a, 4, 6, and 7) performed similarly to Case 5. Although the faster schemes obtained errors greater than the 5% value chosen initially, this does not mean the schemes are unacceptable. The 5% error criterion was chosen arbitrarily. It does not correspond to any physical law of the system. The reason for the study is to understand the level of accuracy that is maintained by the AMoEBA segregation schemes when geometry changes are made. In this case, using the fastest scheme (Case 5), an engineer can be confident that any changes made to the pipe angle will result in a solution with a reasonable amount of error. The grid study and angle study help to provide an understanding of this level of accuracy.

CONCLUSIONS AND FUTURE WORK

The evolving segregation trees of AMoEBA are capable of partitioning a CFD flowfield and assigning the proper solution methods in the segregated regions. The grid study showed that the segregated solutions were within a reasonable amount of error for the three different grid sizes studied, and as the grid size was increased, these schemes became faster than using a single model solution. The changing angle study pointed out that not all of the AMoEBA segregation schemes were accurate for all angles in the study, but those that were within the error limit improved the time to solution. The decreased compute times with reasonable and known degree of error illustrate the effectiveness of the multi-solver technique as well as the abilities of AMoEBA in automatically locating segregation schemes that perform well at the grid sizes chosen.

REFERENCES

Anderson, D. K. and Kozlak, M. J., "Leveraging Physical and Computation Flow Modeling Techniques in the Optimization of Commercial Selective Catalytic Reduction System Designs," *Proceedings of the 2002 International Joint Power Generation Conference*, 2002.

Ashlock, D. A., Bryden, K. M., Johnson, P. E., and McCorkle, D. S., "Diversity Control of a Data Segregation Routine Using Graph Based Evolutionary Algorithms," submitted to the *International Journal of Smart Engineering System Design*.

Ashlock, D. A., Bryden, K. M., Johnson, P. E., and McCorkle, D. S., "Improving Data Segregation with a Graph Based Evolutionary Algorithm," *Intelligent Engineering Systems Through Artificial Neural Networks*, Proceedings of the Artificial Neural Networks in Engineering Conference (ANNIE 2002), ASME Press, 2002, pp. 417-422.

Johnson, P. E., "AMoEBA: The Adaptive Modeling by Evolving Blocks Algorithm," Doctor of Philosophy Dissertation, Iowa State University, 2003.

Johnson, P. E., Bryden, K. M., and Ashlock, D. A., "Solution of a 2-D Inverse Heat Conduction Problem Using Evolutionary Data Segregation Techniques," *Intelligent Engineering Systems Through Artificial Neural Networks*, Proceedings of the Artificial Neural Networks in Engineering Conference (ANNIE 2003), ASME Press, 2003, pp. 315-320.

Johnson, P. E., Bryden, K. M., Ashlock, D. A., and Vasquez, E., "Evolving Cooperative Partial Functions for Data Summary," *Intelligent Engineering Systems Through Artificial Neural Networks*, Proceedings of the Artificial Neural Networks in Engineering Conference (ANNIE 2001), ASME Press, 2001, pp. 405-410.

Niksa, S., Liu, G., Felix, L. G., and Vann Bush, P., "Advanced CFD Post-Processing for Pulverized Fuel Flame Structure and Emissions," *Proceedings of the 2002 International Joint Power Generation Conference*, 2002.

Rosenhead, L., ed., *Laminar Boundary Layers*, Oxford University Press, Oxford, England, 1963.

Wuthrich, S., Sawley, M. L., and Perruchoud, G., "The Coupled Euler/Boundary Layer Method as a Design Tool for Hypersonic Re-entry Vehicles," *Zeitschrift fuer Flugwissenschaften und Weltraumforschung/Journal of Flight Sciences and Space Research*, 20(3):137-144, 1996.

VOICE ACTIVITY DETECTION USING RADIAL BASIS FUNCTION

HONG-IK KIM SUNG-KWON PARK

Division of Electrical and Communication Engineering, Hanyang University, Seoul, Korea

ABSTRACT

This paper proposes a Voice Activity Detection (VAD) algorithm using Radial Basis Function (RBF) network. The k-means clustering and Least Mean Square (LMS) algorithm are used to update the RBF hidden layer nonlinear functions and output layer weights over the duration of speech. The inputs for RBF network are the three parameters a Code Excited Linear Prediction (CELP) coder, which works stably under various background noise levels. The RBF network output is compared to threshold to determine whether the voice or silence period. The experimental results show that the proposed VAD algorithm achieves better performance than G.729 Annex B at any noise level.

INTRODUCTION

Voice Activity Detection (VAD) is defined as the process of detecting voice and silence periods during speech. VAD is required in automatic speech recognition applications such as Discontinuous Transmission (DTX). DTX is transmitted only during the voice period of conversation. If silence periods are detected, the transmitter is turned off. Therefore, DTX increases the system capacity and reduces the radiated power emission through discontinuous transmission. VAD algorithms are also useful in other application such as speech coding, hands-free telephony, and echo cancellation (Tanrikulu et al., 1997). For these applications, VAD applications need robustness in the VAD decision to varying speech features and varying background noise. It is clear from VAD applications that accurate detection of the boundaries of the voiced and silenced segments is necessary in most speech processing applications. VAD does not only reduce the mean speech coding rate by suppressing transmission during the silent periods, but also enables recycling the use of bandwidth to improve the transmission efficiency.

Several VAD algorithms have been designed for specific coders such as LPE-LTP in GSM, CS-ACELP in the G.729, QCELP speech coders in the IS-95 standard, and EVRC in the IS-127. These VADs are utilized for several different types of coders in mobile communication. If a VAD can be adapted for a coder, it would entail reduction of the cost of developing VAD as well as the communication terminal cost.

In the last few years, various types of different approaches to neural network VAD have been proposed, because neural network can accomplish the classification function for VAD algorithms. Multi Layer Perception (MLP) VAD shows much better performance than G.729 Annex B (IKEDO, 1998). MLP VAD works stably under at any background noise level. But the learning speed of MLP network is slow and there is a local minimum problem in the process of clustering. MLP VAD has weakness under varying characteristics of speech and background noise signal because learning parameters are not updated adaptively.

In order to overcome these problems mentioned above, this paper has proposed a Gaussian basis Radial Basis Function (RBF) for VAD. RBF network learning is much faster than MLP. RBF network does not have the local minimum problem in the process of clustering. The most time consuming process in VAD using Gaussian basis RBF is the fast searching of the centers and weights in implementation. The k-means clustering algorithm and the Lest Mean Square (LMS) algorithm are used to update the optimal centers and weights continuously over the speech duration. These algorithms find centers and weights, which may change adaptively under varying speech feature condition. The inputs for the RBF VAD are three parameters, which are basically used by CELP (Code Excited Linear Prediction) which operates stably under high level background noise (IKEDO, 1998). The short time power, the zero-order most likelihood parameter, and the pitch period difference parameters are applied for the RBF VAD decision. By using the CELP coder parameters, the RBF-VAD will be able to adapt easily for any CELP based coder, and background noise does not heavily influence the output of the RBF.

BASIC STRUCTURE OF RBF-VAD

The RBF network is a two-layered processing structure where the output layer nodes form a linear combination of the outputs of the basis functions. Fig.1 shows a block diagram of the RBF VAD system. The hidden layer consists of an array of computing nodes. The nonlinear functions in the hidden layer produce a localized response to input stimulus. It means that the hidden layer produces a significant nonzero response only when the input falls within a small localized region of the input space. The hidden layer consists of an array of computing units. Each unit contains a parameter vector called a center, and the unit calculates a squared distance between the center and the network input vector. The squared distance is then divided by a parameter called a width and the result is passed through the nonlinear function. The nonlinear function Φ is chosen as the Gaussian basis function Eq. (1).

$$\Phi(x) = \exp\left(-\frac{(x-c)^2}{\rho^2}\right), \tag{1}$$

where c is the center and ρ is the width of the unit.

The closer the input is to the center of the cluster, the larger the response of the node. The node output is identical for all input that lie in a fixed redial distance from the center. The output layer is a linear combiner with a set of connection weights, w. The overall response of the RBF network is y

$$y(X) = \sum_{i=1}^{n} w_i \Phi(\|X - c_i\|^2 / \rho_i), \tag{2}$$

where n is the number of the computing units, X is the input, c_i is the ith coordinate of the RBF center, and w_i is the ith weight.

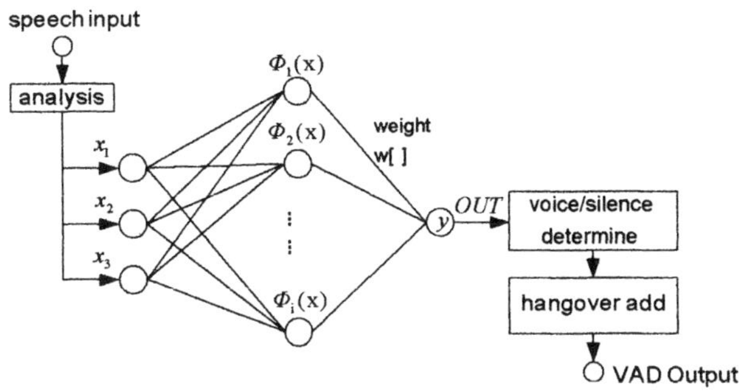

Fig. 1 Basic structure of propose RBF-VAD

The hidden layer can be trained using any unsupervised data clustering algorithm. The most commonly used competitive learning algorithm is the k-means clustering algorithm. It has been used for processing the input data of complicated classification tasks in RBF networks (Moody and Darken, 1989). The output layer nodes compute the linear combination of the first layer outputs with the connection weights as shown in Fig. 1. The output layer is trained using the LMS algorithm.

The k-means clustering algorithm and LMS algorithm are used to update the RBF network parameter continuously over the speech duration. These algorithms make RBF network parameters possible to change adaptively under varying speech character condition.

The output layer combines all hidden layer outputs with the connection weights. In this paper, the RBF network output node uses the bipolar sigmoid function as shown in Eq. (3) because this equation normalizes the output value between 0 and 1. It is useful in deciding the current speech either a voiced or a silent period.

$$OUT = \frac{1}{1 + e^{-IN}} \tag{3}$$

Here, IN is the sum of the hidden layer output with the connection weights and OUT is the output of the RBF network. The output of the RBF value is used for detecting either a voiced or a silent period

SPEECH ANALYSIS PARAMETERS EXTRACTION

The three parameters were used as the input variables for RBF network. These are the short time average power parameter, the zero-order most likelihood parameter and the pitch period difference parameter. These parameters are widely used by CELP based coder, which works stably under a high background noise level (IKEDO, 1998). In a voiced period, the short time average power is high, the zero-order most likelihood parameter is high, and the pitch is stable. On the other hand, these parameters show completely opposite characteristics in silent periods. The parameters are used in RBF network training and the output of the RBF network is compared to a threshold to determine if the speech period is either voiced or silent.

The short-time average power parameter is defined as the logarithm value of the zero-order autocorrelation function. The short-time average power parameter is computed as follows

$$E = 10\log[\frac{1}{N}\sum_{n=m-N+1}^{m} s_w^2(n)] \tag{4}$$

where the speech frame is $s_w(n)$ with length N. The short-time average power, E is small at silence and is high during voiced periods.

The zero-order most likelihood parameter measure is generated as the logarithm sum of the squares of the linear prediction coefficients (LPC) as shown below.

$$F = \log \sum_{i=0}^{p} \alpha_i^2 \tag{5}$$

where p is the linear prediction order and α_i is LPC. This parameter is known as the distance between the voiced and the unvoiced flat spectral envelop.

The pitch period difference parameter measure is generated as the normalized maximum autocorrelation. This is related with the pitch stability. The pitch period difference parameter is defined as

$$P = \max\left[\frac{\log \sum_{t=0}^{N-1}\{r(t)r(t-\tau)\}}{\log \sum_{t=0}^{N-1}\{r(t)r(t)\}}\right] \tag{6}$$

where $20 \le \tau \le 160$ and $r(t)$ is the linear prediction error signal in time t. Also, time $t = 0$ means the beginning part of the analysis.

RBF-VAD ALGORITHM

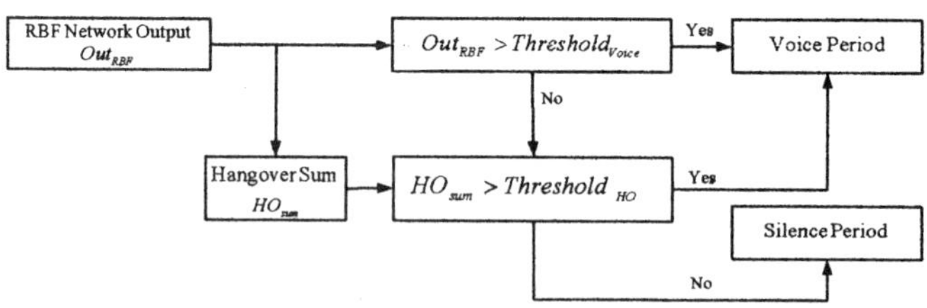

Fig. 2. The flow chart of the proposed RBF-VAD decision algorithm

A flow chart of the proposed RBF VAD algorithm is shown in Fig.2. If the output of RBF network OUT_{RBF} is larger than voice threshold $Threshold_{Voice}$, it is determined as a voice period. However, in order to more precisely detect voice periods, if RBF network output becomes less than voice threshold $Threshold_{Voice}$, it is not immediately determined as silence. Instead, it will be determined as silence when the sum of hangover duration output HO_{SUM} is less than hangover threshold $Threshold_{HO}$. The transition from voice to silence period is controlled by duration of the hangover. It helps reduce the classified errors in voice periods. A hangover is transition delay for determining silence period after voice period. This is compensated for silence period transition error in voice period.

The larger the threshold value is, the less the error occurs in transition from a silence period to a voice period. However more error occurs in transition from a voice to a silence period. Therefore the threshold is decided considering this trade off relation. A hangover is transition delay for determining silence period after voice period, because of compensate transition error.

SIMULATION

The speech is sampled at the rate of 8 kHz, the total sample length is 40,000 and each sample is quantized by 16 bits. The input speech level is from -24 dBov to -40 dBov. The average input speech level was -30dBov. For testing noise environment, Gaussian random noise is added to speech. The noise levels are -63, -58, -53, and -48 dBov. The speech analysis window is the Hamming window whose size is 10 *ms*. The linear prediction order is 10.

The hangover frames reduces the classified errors in voice. However, the error on silence increases slightly. When using hangover frames, the hangover duration must be pre-determined. Fig.3 is the distribution on the error rate for different lengths of the hangover. Here, the voice threshold is 0.54, and the hangover threshold is 3.7. As a result, the most efficient hsangover length is from 5 to 6. In every experiment, it will be set as 6.

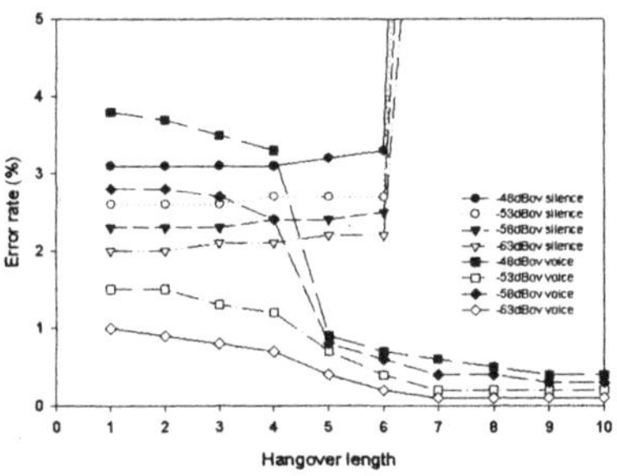

Fig. 3. Influence of hangover frame length

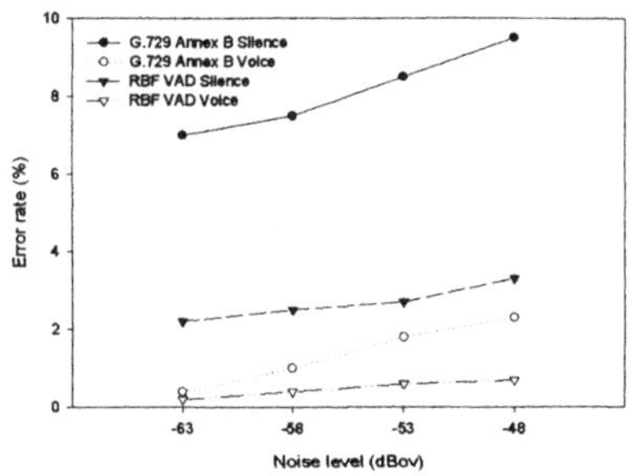

Fig. 4. Performance comparison between the proposed RBF-VAD and the G.729 Annex B

Fig. 4 shows the decision error rates of the proposed RBF-VAD and G.729 Annex B (Benyassine et al., 1997). As mentioned previously, both the k-means clustering algorithm and the LMS algorithm are used to update RBF VAD network parameter continuously. The proposed RBF-VAD demonstrated better performance than G.729 Annex B at any noise levels. Moreover noise level does not heavily influence of the proposed RBF VAD.

The complexity of the algorithm is also an essential factor. Because of the low complexity inherited in RBF and the CELP input parameters, the proposed algorithm has lower complexity than G.729 Annex B. However, the continuous update process of RBF network parameters has high complexity than G.729 Annex B.

CONCLUSIONS

A new VAD algorithm using RBF is proposed in this paper and the new VAD algorithm effectiveness is validated. Because of the nature characteristics of RBF, learning speed is very high and local minima problem is out of consideration. The k-means clustering algorithm and the LMS algorithm are used to update RBF VAD network parameters continuously over the speech duration. These simulation results show that the RBF-VAD gracefully functions under the varying condition of speech features. By using the CELP coder parameters for the RBF VAD input, it will be able to adapt easily for any CELP based coder under various background noise levels.

The performance of RBF-VAD is compared to G.729 Annex B. The results show that RBF-VAD achieves better performance than G.729 Annex B at any noise level and demonstrates moreover stable performance at any noise level. The proposed VAD algorithm can be practical for mobile and portable wireless systems because it shows good robustness against heavy noise and simplicity in implementation.

REFERENCES

Dong Enqing, Liu Guizhong, Zhou Yatong and Zhang Xiaodi, 2002, "Applying support vector machines to voice activity detection," Signal Processing, 2002 6th International Conference on , Vol.2 , pp.26-30.

Jotaro IKEDO, 1998, "Voice Activity Detection using Neural Network," IEICE TRANS. COMMUN. VOL. E81-B, NO.12, pp.2509-2513.

D.R. Hush, B.G. Horne, 1993, "Progress in Supervised Neural Networks: What's New Since Lippmann?" IEEE Signal Processing Magazine, pp.8-39.

J. Moody and C.J. Darken, 1989, "Fast learning in network of locally turned processing units," Neural Computation,vol.1, pp.281-294.

A. Benyassine, E. Shlomot, and H-Y Su, 1997, " ITU-T recommendation G.729 Annex B : A silence compression scheme for use with G.729 optimized for V.70 digital simultaneous voice and data application," IEEE Commun. Mag., vol.35, no.9, pp.64-73.

O. Tanrikulu, B. Baykal, A. G. Constantinides, and J. A. Chambers, 1997, "Critically sampled sub-band acoustic echo cancellers based on IIR and FIR filter banks," IEEE Trans. Signal Proccessing, Vol.45, pp.901–912.

PART VI: DATA MINING

Multiclass Procedure for Minimax Probability Machine

Budi Santosa and Theodore B. Trafalis

School of Industrial Engineering
University of Oklahoma
202 West Boyd, Room 124, Norman, OK 73019
E-mails: bsant@ou.edu & ttrafalis@ou.edu

ABSTRACT
In this paper, multiclass procedures for minimax probability machine(MPM)are developed. The procedures follow one-against-all (OAA) and one-against-one (OAO) approaches. Both multiclass approaches of MPM are tested on publicly accessible data, Iris, Balance Scale and Dermatology data. The generalization errors of the multiclass MPM are investigated. Comparison between OAA and OAO in terms of computing time is also provided. The results are compared to multiclass support vector machine (SVM). The results show that for the Iris data, multiclass MPM performance is comparable to multiclass SVM. For the Balance Scale and Dermatology data, multiclass SVM outperforms the multiclass MPM.

1. Introduction

Minimax probability machine (MPM) is a new technique that works by seeking the best classifier that minimizes the maximum probability of misclassification error in a binary problem. In (Lanckriet et al., 2002), a robust MPM to predict the class of new observations in binary class problems was developed. The optimization problem of MPM can be formulated as an unconstrained second order conic programming problem. The problem then can be solved with an iterative procedure to find the best classifier. Trafalis et al. (2003) shows that the MPM performance is comparable to SVM in the case of tornado detection with two classes. Motivated by the facts that in real applications the classification tasks include both binary and multiclass problems, this paper extends the MPM for multiclass classification problems. Section 2 describes the basic idea of SVM. In section 3, explanations about the basic idea and the mathematical formulation of MPM are given. Section 4 provides the procedures of multiclass SVM. In section 5, the extension of the models into multiclass cases are described. In section 6, the implementation and the results are presented. Some discussion is presented in section 7.

2. Support Vector Machines (SVM)

A well known method learning algorithm that finds an optimal classifier between two sets of points is the so called Support Vector Machines algorithm (Vapnik, 1995). The mathematical formulation of the SVM optimization problem is given as

$$\min \frac{1}{2}||w||^2 + C\sum_{i=1}^{\ell} t_i \tag{1}$$

$$\text{Subject to}$$

$$y_i(wx+b)+t_i \geq 1$$

$$t_i \geq 0$$

The dual solution to the problem (1) is explained in (Vapnik, 1995).

3. Minimax Probability Machines (MPM)

The MPM approach was introduced by Lanckriet et al. (2002) as depicted in Figure 1. The objective of this approach is that the problem of binary classification is solved by minimizing the maximum probability of misclassification of the future data points. The problem can be defined as follows. Let x and y denote random vectors in a binary class, with means and covariance matrices given by $(\overline{x}, \Sigma_x)$ and $(\overline{y}, \Sigma_y)$ respectively, where $x, \overline{x}, y, \overline{y} \in \Re^n$ and $\Sigma_x, \Sigma_y \in \Re^{nxn}$ and both are symmetric and positive semidefinite. Then, a hyperplane $H(a, b) = \{z | a^T z = b\}$, where $a \in \Re^n \{0\}$ and $b \in \Re$ which separates the two classes of points with maximal probability with respect to all distributions having these mean and covariance matrices is determined. Mathematically the resulting optimization problem can be formulated as:

$$\max_{\alpha, a \neq 0, b} \alpha \tag{2}$$

$$\text{Subject to}$$

$$\inf_{x \sim (\overline{x}, \Sigma_x)} Pr\left\{a^T x \geq b\right\} \geq \alpha$$

$$\inf_{y \sim (\overline{y}, \Sigma_y)} Pr\left\{a^T y \leq b\right\} \geq \alpha$$

After some manipulations by exploiting the powerful theorem by Popescue and Bertsimas Popescue and Bertsimas (2001) that states that:

$$\sup_{y \sim (\overline{y}, \Sigma_y)} Pr\left\{y \in S\right\} = \frac{1}{1 + d^2}, \tag{3}$$

with $d^2 = \inf_{y \in S} (y - \overline{y}) \Sigma_y^{-1} (y - \overline{y})$,
the above problem can be simplified as (Lanckriet et al., 2002):

$$\min_{\alpha} \left\| \Sigma_x^{\frac{1}{2}} a \right\|_2 + \left\| \Sigma_y^{\frac{1}{2}} a \right\|_2 \tag{4}$$

$$\text{Subject to}$$

$$a^T (\overline{x} - \overline{y}) = 1.$$

The value of b can be set as

$$b_* = a_*^T \bar{x} - \kappa_* \left\| \Sigma_x a \right\|, \tag{5}$$

where $\kappa(\alpha) = \sqrt{\frac{\alpha}{1-\alpha}}$ and a_*, κ_* are the optimal parameters.

The robustness of this approach is realized by providing the estimation of mean and covariance of each class of the data. It is assumed that the mean and covariance matrix of each class are only known within some specified set. In particular, it is assumed that $(\bar{x}, \sigma_x) \in X$, where X is a subset of $\Re^n \times S_n^+$, and S_n^+ is the set of $n \times n$ symmetric, positive semidefinite matrices. Likewise a set of Y, similar to X, is describing uncertainty of the mean and covariance matrix of the random variable y. The robust version of MPM is formulated as:

$$\max_{\alpha, a \neq 0, b} \alpha \tag{6}$$

$$\text{Subject to}$$

$$\inf_{x \sim (\overline{x}, \Sigma_x)} Pr\left\{a^T x \geq b\right\} \geq \alpha \forall (\bar{x}, \sigma_x) \in X$$

$$\inf_{y \sim (\overline{y}, \Sigma_y)} Pr\left\{a^T y \leq b\right\} \geq \alpha \forall (\bar{y}, \sigma_y) \in Y$$

In the case of nonlinear separability, the kernel method is used by mapping all the data into a higher dimensional feature space. In the feature space, we want to find a hyperplane $H(a,b) = \{\varphi(z)|a^T\varphi(z) = b\}$ that corresponds to the linear decision boundary $D(a,b) = \{z \in \Re^n|a^T\varphi(z) = b\}$ in the input space $\Re^n$ $(a \in \Re^n\{0\}$ and $b \in \Re)$.

4. Multi-Class Support Vector Machine

Currently there are two main approaches for multiclass SVM. One is by constructing and combining several binary classifiers and the other one is by directly considering all data in one optimization formulation. The first approach where several binary classifiers are constructed and combined includes two methods: One-against-all (OAA) and One-against-one (OAO)(Hsu and Lin, 2002). One of research utilizing the second approach is proposed in (Weston and Watkins, 1998).

4.1 One-against-all (OAA) Method

The OAA method, for the k-class classification problem, is based on the construction of k classifiers where k is the number of classes. We denote our classifier as ρ. In this method, ρ^i is trained with all of the examples in the ith class with positive labels(+1) and all other examples with negative labels(-1). Given ℓ training data $(x_1, y_1)...(x_\ell, y_\ell)$ where $x_i \in R^n, i = 1, 2..\ell$ and $y_i \in S = 1..k$ is the class of x_i, the ith classifier solves the following optimization problem (Hsu and Lin, 2002):

$$\min_{w^i,b^i,t^i} \frac{1}{2}(w_i)^T w_i + C\sum_{j=1}^{\ell} t_j^i \tag{7}$$

$$\text{Subject to}$$

$$w^i\varphi(x_j) + b^i \geq 1 - t_j^i,\ if\ y_j = i$$

$$w^i\varphi(x_j) + b^i \leq -1 + t_j^i,\ if\ y_j \neq i$$

$$t_j \geq 0, j = 1..\ell$$

After solving (7), there are k decision functions $w^1\varphi(x)+b^1, w^2\varphi(x)+b^2...w^k\varphi(x)+b^k$. Then, the class of point x is determined by the largest value of the decision function:

$$j = class\ of\ x = arg\ \max_{i=1..k}\ w^i\varphi(x) + b^i, wherej \in S \tag{8}$$

4.2 One-against-one (OAO) Method

This method constructs $k(k-1)/2$ classifiers where each one is trained on data from two classes. For example, if we have a three-class classification problem we have to construct 3 classifiers: ρ^{12}, ρ^{13} and ρ^{23}. When we train ρ^{12}, all points from class 1 are labeled with +1 and all points from class 2 are labeled with -1. For training data from ith and jth classes, we solve the following binary classification problem (Hsu and Lin, 2002):

$$\min_{w^{ij},b^{ij},t^{ij}} \frac{1}{2}(w^{ij})^T w^{ij} + C\sum_r t_r^{ij} \tag{9}$$

$$\text{Subject to}$$

$$w^{ij}\varphi(x_r) + b^{ij} + t_r^{ij} \geq 1,\ if\ y_r = i$$

$$w^{ij}\varphi(x_r) + b^{ij} - t_r^{ij} \leq 1,\ if\ y_r = j$$

$$t_r^{ij} \geq 0$$

After all classifiers $k(k-1)/2$ are constructed, max-vote strategy is used. Based on this strategy, for classifier ρ^{ij}, if the sign of a new point x is in the ith class, then the vote for ith class is added by one. Otherwise, the vote for the jth class is increased by one. We repeat this step for all classifiers. Then, we predict x as being in the class with the largest vote. In the case of two classes where we have identical votes, we select the one with the smallest index.

5. Multiclass MPM

In section 3, we have discussed MPM binary classification where the labels $t = \{t_1, .., t_m\} \subseteq \{\pm 1\}^m$. In this section, the discussion will be extended to the case where the label $t = \{t_1, .., t_m\} \subseteq \{1, .., k\}^m$, where k is the number of classes. Hereby, we adopt the approach where we construct and combine several binary classifiers (Hsu and Lin, 2002). Therefore as discussed previously there are two procedures: One-against-all (OAA) and One-against-one (OAO) (Hsu and Lin, 2002). We will develop multiclass MPM based on these two procedures.

5.1 One-against-all (OAA) Method

As explained in section 4.1, by this methods, for k-class classification problem, we construct k classifiers where k is the number of classes. Now suppose we are given m training data $(x_1, y_1), .., (x_m, y_m)$ where $x_i \in R^n, i = 1, 2.., m$ and $t_i \in S = 1, .., k$ is the class of x_i, the ith classifier solves the following MPM optimization problem (Hsu and Lin, 2002)

$$\max_{\alpha^i, a^i \neq 0, b^i} \alpha^i \tag{10}$$

$$\text{Subject to}$$

$$\inf_{x_j \sim (\overline{x}_j, \Sigma_{x_j})} Pr\left\{ {a^i}^T x_j \geq b^i \right\} \geq \alpha^i, if\ t_j = i$$

$$\inf_{y_j \sim (\overline{y}_j, \Sigma_{y_j})} Pr\left\{ {a^i}^T y_j \leq b^i \right\} \geq \alpha^i, if\ t_j \neq i$$

At each iteration, we solve a binary classification problem where X represents the data set from one class and Y represents all the data from the other classes. After solving (10), there are k decision functions ${a^1}^T z - b^1, {a^2}^T z - b^2, .., {a^k}^T z - b^k$. Then, the class of point x is determined by the largest value of the decision function:

$$j = class\ of\ x = \arg \max_{i=1..k} {a^i}^T z - b^i, where\ j \in S \tag{11}$$

5.2 One-against-one (OAO) Method

As explained in section 4.2, this method constructs $k(k-1)/2$ classifiers where each one is trained on data from two classes. For training data from ith and jth classes, we solve the following feasibility -approach binary classification problem (Hsu and Lin, 2002):

$$\max_{\alpha^{ij}, a^{ij} \neq 0, b^{ij}} \alpha^{ij} \tag{12}$$

$$\text{Subject to}$$

$$\inf_{x_r \sim (\overline{x}_r, \Sigma_{x_r})} Pr\left\{ {a^{ij}}^T x_j \geq b^{ij} \right\} \geq \alpha^{ij},\ if\ t_r = i$$

$$\inf_{y_r \sim (\overline{y}_r, \Sigma_{y_r})} Pr\left\{ {a^{ij}}^T y_j \geq b^{ij} \right\} \geq \alpha^{ij},\ if\ t_r = j$$

6. Implementation and Results

In our implementation, we observe the generalization error for MPM and SVM for both approaches, OAA and OAO respectively. Additionally, we also investigate the computing time to compare the speed of OAA and OAO. We test the algorithms or three data sets: Iris, Balance Scale and Dermatology data (Blake and Merz, 1998). Iris data consists of 150 data points with 3 classes. The experiments are done by using polynomial kernel with degree 2 for both procedures: OAA and OAO. For the first data, three different training and testing samples are choosen randomly. Each training sample consists of 100 data and each testing sample consists of 50 data. Balance Scale data consists of 625 data with 3 classes. Dermatology data consist of 358 observations with 6 classes. For these two data sets, the ratio for training and testing is 70:30. The results of the experiments are presented in Tables 1and 2. In Table 2, we show both the missclassification error in terms of percentage and the computing time (CPU time) in terms of seconds. For the Iris data since the testing sample is small, the computing time is not significantly different between OAA and OAO.

7. Discussion

Based on the results presented Tables 1 and 2, we can make some discussions about solving multiclass classification problems. In terms of computing time, one-against-one (OAO) is better than one-against-all (OAA). In other words, we can conclude that solving a large number of small binary problems is better than solving a small number of large binary problems. As shown in Table 2, the computing times for OAO are decreased significanly compared to OAA. In the case where the number of classes is large, OAO is preferred in terms of computing time. For MPM, OAA is more effective than OAO in terms of generalization error. Whereas, for SVM, OAO is preferred for both generalization error and computing time. Table 1 shows that multiclass MPM is comparable to multiclass SVM. Table 2 confirm that multiclass SVM is better than multiclass MPM in terms of generalization error. However the above results are preliminary. Comparing the above two methods on more data sets will provide us a better feeling about the multiclass MPM and SVM performances.

References

Blake, C. and Merz, C., 1998, "UCI repository of machine learning databases", Http://www.ics.uci.edu/~mlearn/MLRepository.html.

Hsu, C.-W. and Lin, C.-J., 2002, "A comparison of methods for multi-class support vector machines", *IEEE Transactions on Neural Networks*, 13, 415–425.

Lanckriet, G., Ghaoui, L. E., Bhattacharyya, C., and Jordan, M., 2002, "A robust minimax approach to classification", *Journal of Machine Learning Research*, 3, 555–582.

Popescue, I. and Bertsimas, D., 2001, *Optimal Inequalities in Probability Theory: A Convex Optimization Approach*, Tech. rep., INSEAD, Technical Report TM62.

Trafalis, T. B., Santosa, B., and Richman, M. B., 2003, "Tornado detection with kernel-based methods", *Intelligent Engineering Systems Through Artificial Neural Networks 13*, (eds.) Dagli, C., Buczak, A., Ghosh, J., Embrechts, M., O.Ersoy, and Kerc, S., ASME Press, pp. 677–682.

Vapnik, V., 1995, *The Nature of Statistical Learning Theory*, Springer Verlag.

Weston, J. and Watkins, C., 1998, "Support vector machines for multi-class pattern recognition", *Proceeding of the Seventh European Symposium on Articial Neural Networks ICANN'97.*

Table 1: Misclassification error(%) using OAA and OAO approaches on Iris data

Method	Approach	Sample			Average
		1	2	3	
Multi-MPM	OAA	1	2	2	1.67
	OAO	0	1	3	1.33
Multi-SVM	OAA	1	3	2	2
	OAO	1	3	1	1.67

Table 2: Misclassification error(%) and computing time (second) using OAA and OAO approaches on Balance Scale and Dermatology Data

Data	Method	Approach	Sample			Average error(CPU time)
			1	2	3	
Balance Scale Data	Multi MPM	OAA	6.95(97.2)	9.09(130.3)	6.95(97.3)	7(108.26)
		OAO	8.02(40.4)	5.35(41.7)	8.02(40.7)	7.13(40.93)
	Multi SVM	OAA	0(48)	0.53(66.4)	0(45.7)	0.18(53.36)
		OAO	0(20.9)	0(28.8)	0(21.4)	0(23.7)
Derma-tology data	Multi MPM	OAA	14.95(96.7)	18.69(94.6)	9.35(100.9)	14.33(97.4)
		OAO	21.50(12.4)	16.82(12.4)	6.54(12.8)	14.95(12.5)
	Multi SVM	OAA	4.67(310.6)	4.67(294.1)	7.48(332.7)	5.61(312.5)
		OAO	5.61(14.7)	2.80(15.3)	7.48(15.9)	5.30(15.3)

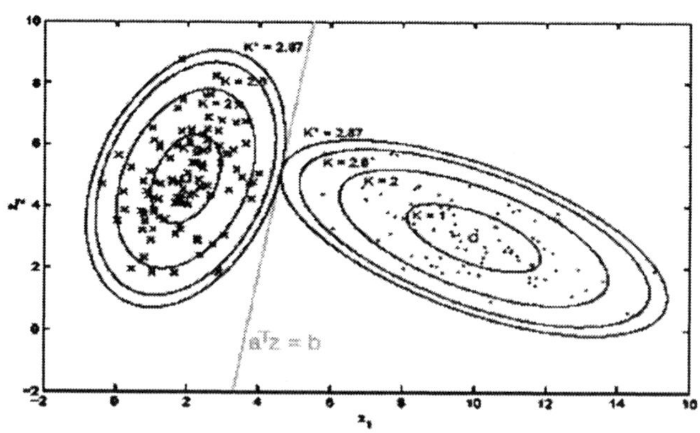

Figure 1: MPM classifier for binary-class classification problem

TEXT CLASSIFICATION WITH LEAST SQUARE SUPPORT VECTOR MACHINES AND LATENT SEMANTIC INDEXING

Satarupa Banerjee
Villanova University
CIS Department
Villanova, PA

Chia-Jiu Wang
University of Colorado
ECE Department
Colorado Springs, CO

Vikramjit Mitra
Worcester Polytechnic
Institute, EE Department
Worcester, MA

Abstract

This paper proposes a Least Square Support Vector Machine (LS-SVM) with Latent Semantic Indexing (LSI) which supports text classification of noisy document titles according to different given categories. Thc system's potential will be demonstrated with a 91229-word corpus from University of Denver's Penrose Library catalogue. The precision rate of the proposed system is found to be over 99.9%. The final classifier is an array of LS-SVM with Gaussian Radial Basis Function (GRBF) kernel, which uses the probabilistic coefficients generated by the Latent Semantic Indexing algorithm for classification of the text titles. These coefficients are also used to generate the confidence factors for the inference engine, which presents the final decision. The comparison between the conventional linear SVM based classifiers and Neural Network based classifying agents shows that the LS-SVM with LSI based classifying agents improves text categorization performance significantly and holds a lot of potential for developing robust learning based agents for text classification.

INTRODUCTION

Technology has motivated text documents to be available in electronic form. The World Wide Web itself contains a huge amount of documents, conference materials, publications, and journals available in electronic form. These materials along with others result in enormous amount of information, which are easily accessible but lack organization. The lack of organization of materials in the Internet necessitates a growing interest in assisting people to manage the huge amount of information. Organized search, browsing, information routing, filtering, objectionable material identification, junk mail, topic identification etc, are the central issues in current information management. This necessitates sophisticated learning agents that are capable of classifying relevant information and increases text organization. Initial work in the field of Internet agents has used manual or simple encoding techniques [1], Linear SVMs and Neural Network [2] based intelligent agents for information retrieval.

Text Classification (TC) is a technique that assigns texts to some predefined categories based on their content. The key issues in TC are feature coding and classifier design. Feature extraction is a method of document encoding; that automatically construct internal representations of documents. This paper is motivated to organize the materials available in a library, which has both electronic materials as well as physical documents. A library cataloging systems usually stores the entire information regarding a material, which results in higher storage space requirement.

This paper presents an analysis of learning agents based on Support Vector Machines (SVM). In particular Least Square Support Vector Machine (LS-SVM) with Latent Semantic Indexing (LSI) algorithm for feature extraction will be explored. Furthermore the details of the internal structure of the classifying agent along with the results obtained from our research are presented. The results claim the potential of using LS-SVMs as the intelligent classifying and search agents for semantic text classification.

LATENT SEMANTIC INDEXING

Latent Semantic Indexing (LSI) [3, 4, 5, 6] is a text classification and document indexing technique that generates a vector model of semantics based on word co-occurrences.

LSI [5,6] extracts the underlying semantic structure of a word corpus by estimating the most significant statistical factors in the weighted word space. It considers documents that have many words in common to be semantically close and those with few words in common to be semantically distant. This method emulates human knowledge to classify and categorize a document collection based on its content. LSI search agents look at similarity values it has calculated for every content word, and returns the documents that it thinks best fit the query [4]. This makes LSI successful where a plain keyword search will fail if there is no exact match. LSI preprocesses the text corpus by purging all the extraneous words from a document [4, 5], leaving only content words likely to have semantic meaning. This way it eliminates those words that introduces noise to the decision making task.

LSI algorithm generates a matrix representation of the corpus, with rows corresponding to words in the vocabulary and columns to the documents. Each value in this matrix is a weighted frequency of the corresponding term in the corresponding document, which reduces the influence of frequently occurring term [7]. The matrix thus generated is a large sparse one, which is then reduced to a compressed matrix based on Singular Value Decomposition (SVD) technique as follows: R = UPV where matrix R is decomposed into a matrix of reduced rank U, a diagonal matrix of singular values P and a document matrix V. The row vector of matrix U and the column vector of matrix V are the projections of word vectors and document vectors into singular value space.

SUPPORT VECTOR MACHINES

The most general form of Support Vector Classification is to separate two classes by a function, which is induced from available examples [8]. The main goal of this classifier is to find an optimal separating hyperplane that maximizes the separation margin or the distance between it and the nearest data point of each class.

In the case where a linear boundary is inappropriate the SVM can map the input vector, $\mathbf{x}$, into a high dimensional feature space, $\mathbf{z}$ [8]. The idea of kernel function is to enable operations to be performed in the input space rather than the potentially high dimensional feature space. To enable operations to be performed in the input space rather than the potentially high dimensional feature space, the idea of a kernel function is used. With the kernel function, the inner product does not need to be evaluated in the feature space, which provides a way of addressing the curse of dimensionality. The theory of Reproducing Kernel Hilbert Space (RKHS) [16] claims that an inner product in feature space has an equivalent Kernel in input space,

$$K(\mathbf{x}, \mathbf{x}') = \langle \phi(\mathbf{x}), \phi(\mathbf{x}') \rangle \tag{1}$$

provided that Mercer conditions are hold. The feature vector $\phi(\mathbf{x})$ corresponds the input vector $\mathbf{x}$. The Gaussian Radial Basis Function GRBF) has received significant attention and its form is given by

$$K(\mathbf{x}, \mathbf{x}') = \exp(-\| \mathbf{x}-\mathbf{x}' \| / 2\sigma^2) \tag{2}$$

Classical techniques using RBFs employ some method of determining a subset of centers; typically a method of clustering is employed to select a subset of centers [8]. The most attractive feature of SVM is its implicit selection process, with each support vectors contributing on local Gaussian functions, centered at that data point. By further consideration it is possible to select the global basis function width using the SRM principle.

Least Square - SVM

SVM is a powerful technique for solving problems in nonlinear classification, function estimation and density estimation, which had led to many recent developments in Kernel based learning methods [9,11,12,16,15]. Least Square Support Vector Machines (LS-SVM) are reformulations to standard SVMs [13,14]. LS-SVMs are closely related to regularization networks [10] and Gaussian processes but additionally emphasize and exploit primal-dual interpretations.

TEXT CLASSIFICATION

The Penrose library document collection contains real-world titles that are present in their cataloging system. All the titles in this word corpus belong to one or more of the six main categories: Engineering (**ENG**), Mathematics (**MTH**), Music (**MUS**), History (**HIS**), Economics and Management (**ECM**) and Literature and Arts (**LAR**). Table 1 shows example titles from the Corpus and their categories. 11892 titles were used for this experiment and each of them belongs to at least one of the above-mentioned categories. The total number of words used is 91229, with 12303 different words. The first 482 titles from each category, which is 2892 titles altogether, were used for training the LS-SVM module. The remaining 9000 titles were used for the testing purpose.

LSI is used to represent the title corpus as semantic significant vectors 'V', which determines the frequency of word occurrences in different semantic categories. Each word 'a' is represented with a vector $[V(a, b_1), V(a,b_2),\cdots, V(a, b_n)]$, where b_i represents a certain semantic category. A value $V(a, b_i)$ is computed for each dimension of the semantic vector as the normalized frequency of occurrences of word 'a' in semantic category b_i divided by the normalized frequency of occurrences of word 'a' in the Corpus. Hence, the vectors V represent the plausibility of a word 'a' occurring in a particular semantic category 'b'. These vectors 'V' for each word 'a' together form the matrix R, which is a large sparse matrix due to the large number of words. R is then reduced to a compressed matrix based on Singular Value Decomposition (SVD) technique, which generates the LSI coefficients; these coefficients are then fed to the SVM module.

Table 1. Example titles from the Corpus and their Categories

Semantic Category	Title
Engineering (ENG)	Randomized algorithms for analysis and control of uncertain systems Applications in time-frequency signal processing Nano electro-mechanics in engineering and biology
Mathematics (MTH)	Stochastic processes with applications to finance; Practical extrapolation methods; Solving polynomial equation systems
Music (MUS)	Unplayed melodies; The music of European nationalism; Elements of music
History (HIS)	A history of the Osage people A history of modern Germany since 1815 Shivaji: Hindu King in Islamic India
Economics and Management (ECM)	The economics of self-employment and entrepreneurship Ownership and governance of enterprises The new knowledge management.
Literature and Arts (LAR)	Rethinking social realism: African American art and literature, 1930-1953 Teaching and learning about multicultural literature Literary texts and the arts: interdisciplinary perspectives

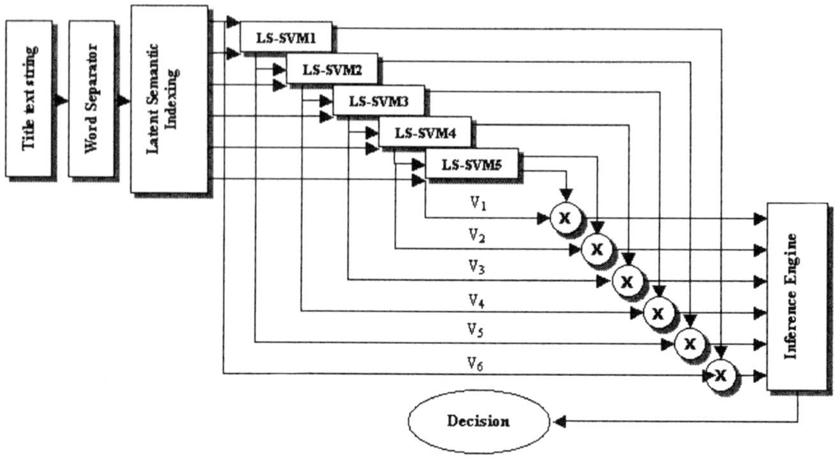

Figure1. Block Diagram of the LS-SVM text classifier

From the model depicted in Figure 1, it can be observed that at the beginning, the system starts with a text string. The word separator module separates each word from that string and feeds them one by one to the LSI module. LSI purges most of the extraneous words that has no semantic meaning and hence contributes little or nothing towards semantic categorization. Then LSI uses a stemming algorithm named 'Porter Stemmer' to remove common endings from the words. These words are further processed by the LSI algorithm and finally generate the LSI coefficients, which are fed to five LS-SVM modules. Each of the first four LS-SVM module, classifies between one category and the rest, where as the last one classifies between two categories. The conclusions drawn by the LS-SVMs are then multiplied with the LSI coefficients [V_1, V_2, V_3, V_4, V_5, V_6], which are used as confidence factors (*CF*) to increase the accuracy of the Inference Engine (IE).

Table 2. Rule Base for the Decision Logic

Vectors / Categories	A1	A2	A3	A4	A5	A6
ENG	$0.5 \leq A1$	$A2 < 0.5$	$A3 < 0.5$	$A4 < 0.5$	$A5 < 0.5$	$A6 < 0.5$
MTH	$A1 < 0.5$	$0.5 \leq A2$	$A3 < 0.5$	$A4 < 0.5$	$A5 < 0.5$	$A6 < 0.5$
MUS	$A1 < 0.5$	$A2 < 0.5$	$0.5 \leq A3$	$A4 < 0.5$	$A5 < 0.5$	$A6 < 0.5$
HIS	$A1 < 0.5$	$A2 < 0.5$	$A3 < 0.5$	$0.5 \leq A4$	$A5 < 0.5$	$A6 < 0.5$
ECM	$A1 < 0.5$	$A2 < 0.5$	$A3 < 0.5$	$A4 < 0.5$	$0.5 \leq A5$	$A6 < 0.5$
LAR	$A1 < 0.5$	$A2 < 0.5$	$A3 < 0.5$	$A4 < 0.5$	$A5 < 0.5$	$0.5 \leq A6$

The IE has a Decision Logic that uses a rule-based algorithm. It accepts a vector of 6 values [A_1, A_2, A_3, A_4, A_5, A_6] obtained by the product of the SVM decisions and the confidence factors. It uses this vector to make the final judgment. The rule base is given in Table 2. It should be noted that the rule base in Table 2 gives inferences only for a limited number of cases, as certain cases might arise where more than one member of the vector, A, have values ≥0.5. In such a case the decision will comprise all the weighted categories, corresponding to which the vectors are ≥0.5. In the practical research we have incorporated all the possible combination of vector A for which the values are ≥0.5.

SIMULATION RESULTS

In this study a 6-input 1-output system is considered, the six inputs corresponding to the 6 LSI coefficients generated after processing the text titles, where each coefficient gives the membership value of that word to a certain category. The test results are presented below in Table 3 and Table 4.

Table 3 depicts the accuracy for text classification in different categories, whereas Table 4 depicts the different stages of the classifying module. The first group of 6 columns in Table 4 presents the data obtained from the product of the SVM decision with the confidence factors (*CF*), the next group of 6 columns gives the decision logic output based on the rule base given in Table 4 ad the last column gives the final decision presented by the Inference Engine.

Table 3 Results using LS-SVM for text classification

Category	**Training Set (%)**	**Test Set** (%)
ENG	100.0	100.0
MTH	100.0	100.0
HIS	100.0	99.8
MUS	100.0	99.9
ECM	100.0	100.0
LAR	99.7	99.6
All Titles	99.95	99.90

Table 4. Different stages of the text classification module

Test Category	**LS-SVM (x C.F) Output**						**Decision Logic Output**						**Inference**
	ENG	**MTH**	**HIS**	**MUS**	**ECM**	**LAR**	**ENG**	**MTH**	**HIS**	**MUS**	**ECM**	**LAR**	
ENG	1.0	0.0	0.0	0.0	0.0	0.0	1.0	0.0	0.0	0.0	0.0	0.0	**ENG**
	0.7	0.0	0.2	0.0	0.0	0.0	1.0	0.0	0.0	0.0	0.0	0.0	**ENG**
MTH	0.0	1.0	0.0	0.0	0.0	0.0	0.0	1.0	0.0	0.0	0.0	0.0	**MTH**
	0.0	0.9	0.0	0.0	0.0	0.0	0.0	1.0	0.0	0.0	0.0	0.0	**MTH**
HIS	0.0	0.0	0.9	0.0	0.0	0.0	0.0	0.0	1.0	0.0	0.0	0.0	**HIS**
	0.0	0.0	0.9	0.0	0.0	0.1	0.0	0.0	1.0	0.0	0.0	0.0	**HIS**
MUS	0.0	0.0	0.0	0.7	0.0	0.3	0.0	0.0	0.0	1.0	0.0	0.0	**MUS**
	0.0	0.2	0.1	0.8	0.0	0.0	0.0	0.0	0.0	1.0	0.0	0.0	**MUS**
ECM	0.0	0.0	0.0	0.0	0.9	0.0	0.0	0.0	0.0	0.0	1.0	0.0	**ECM**
	0.0	0.1	0.0	0.0	0.9	0.0	0.0	0.0	0.0	0.0	1.0	0.0	**ECM**
LAR	0.0	0.0	0.0	0.2	0.0	0.7	0.0	0.0	0.0	0.0	0.0	1.0	**LAR**
	0.0	0.0	0.2	0.0	0.0	0.8	0.0	0.0	0.0	0.0	0.0	1.0	**LAR**

As evident from Table 4, the decision logic based on a rule base makes a wise estimation of the SVM outputs, based on which the Inference engine selects the category to which a specific string of word belongs. The output of the system is thus the final decision presented by the Inference engine. In case of a multi-class problem, the IE will present the weighted decision of both the classes.

CONCLUSIONS

We have described a LSI based LS-SVM module, for text classification. With a set of 91,229 word corpus the precision rate were fairly high with 99.93% accuracy in classifying the titles. Previous works on text classification have implemented neural networks and linear SVMs, where Recurrent Neural Networks and Linear SVMs showed an accuracy of 93.05% [2] and 97% respectively. The precision rate of the proposed system clearly outperforms the previous models. Prior to our research, LS-SVMs with GRBF kernel and LSI technique has not been designed and implemented for a high scale task of text categorization. The robustness of the proposed system enables it to classify noisy text titles with a high degree of precision. Future research should be devoted to explore SVMs with other possible kernel functions or Neuro-SVM based hybrid models that might act as a better classifying agent. Future direction should also address to increase the number of categories to observe the robustness and predictive accuracy of the system.

REFERENCES

[1] Schuetze H., Hull D. A., and Pedersen J. O., (1995) "A comparison of classifiers and document representations for the routing problem", Proceedings of the Special Interest Group on Information Retrieval,

[2] Wermter S., Arevian G. and Panchev C. (1999) "Recurrent Neural Network Learning for Text Routing", ICANN.

[3] Foltz, P. W., Kintsch, W., and Landauer, T. K., (1998) "The Measurement of Textual Coherence with Latent Semantic Analysis", Discourse Processes, 25, pp. 285-307.

[4] Foltz, P. W., (1990) "Using Latent Semantic Indexing for Information Filtering". In R. B. Allen (Ed.) Proc. of the Conference on Office Information Systems, Cambridge, MA, pp. 40-47.

[5] Landauer, T. K., Foltz, P. W., and Laham, D. (1998) "Introduction to Latent Semantic Analysis", Discourse Processes, 25, pp. 259-284.

[6] Landauer, T. K. and Dumais, S. T. (1997) "Solution to Plato's Problem: The Latent Semantic Analysis Theory of Acquisition, Induction ", Psychological Review, 104 (2), pp.211-240.

[7] Bellegarda R., (1998) "A Multi-Span Language Modeling Framework for Large Vocabulary Speech Recognition," IEEE Trans. Speech and Audio processing pp. 456-467, Sep., 1998.

[8] Gunn S. R. (1998) "Support Vector Machines for Classification and Regression", Technical Report, Department of Electronics and Computer Science, University of Southampton.

[9] Cristianini N., Shawe-Taylor J. (2000), "An Introduction to Support Vector Machines", Cambridge University Press.

[10] Evgeniou T., Pontil M., Poggio T. (2000), "Regularization networks and Support Vector Machines," Advances in Computational Mathematics, 13(1), 1-50.

[11] Schölkopf B., Burges C., Smola A. (1998), "Advances in Kernel Methods – Support Vector Learning", MIT press.

[12] Schölkopf B., Smola A. J., Müller K.-R. (1998), "Nonlinear component analysis as a kernel eigen value problem", Neural Computation, 10, 1299-1319.

[13] Suykens J.A.K., Vandewalle J. (1999), "Least square support vector machine classifiers", Neural Processing Letters, 9(3), 293-300.

[14] Van Gestel T., Suykens J., Baesens B., Viaene S., Vanthienen J., Dedene G. , De Moor B., Vandewalle J. (2001), "Benchmarking least square support vector machine classifiers" Machine Learning, in press.

[15] Vapnik V. (1995), "The Nature of Statistical Learning Theory", Springer-Verlag, New York.

[16] Vapnik V. (1998), "Statistical Learning Theory", John Wiley, New York.

STRUCTURING SEMANTICALLY DISTRIBUTED HOMOGENEOUS AND HETEROGENEOUS DATA SITES

MEHMED KANTARDZIC **PEDRAM SADEGHIAN**

Computer Engineering Computer Science
University of Louisville
Louisville, KY

ABSTRACT
The purpose of this paper is to introduce an efficient methodology based on fractal theory to analyze semantically distributed data. The analysis can be helpful in deriving accurate data mining models that correctly reflect the semantics of distributed data sites, and help in avoiding inappropriate summarization of the data. Although the methodology operates on distributed homogeneous data sets, it can also work with certain heterogeneous data sets that can be transformed into homogeneous data sets without a reduction in their intrinsic dimensionality. We tested our methodology on real world data sets, and showed that the proposed approach discovers differences in the semantics of both distributed homogeneous and heterogeneous data sites.

INTRODUCTION

Several different approaches to distributed data mining have been proposed (Ashrafi et al., 2002, and Turinsky and Grossman, 2000). However, many of the techniques are not taking into account a very important type of error, which we term the *semantically-caused-error,* that may be introduced during the modeling process. It is caused by the "forced" integration of skewed distributed data sets with different statistical characteristics into one integrated data set represented by a unique, integrated model (Kantardzic and Badia, 2003). Since hidden semantics of a data site could influence the theoretical distribution of the data, it is erroneous to assume that there will always exist an integrated model, which is the best model for the given data sets spread over multiple sites. In many distributed data mining applications this integrated and "best model" does not adequately reflect the semantics of the distributed data. One can find a centralized model by forcing integration process in any of the available methodologies, but the model will not reflect the semantics of the distributed data sites (Kantardzic and Badia, 2003, and Wirth et al., 2001).

Our approach starts with the assumption that each geographically distributed data site may have its own semantic, and similarity in the semantics of two or more data sites may be expressed through the similarity in:

1. Statistical distribution of the attribute values of the data sets at the sites.
2. Local data mining models at the sites.

Comparison of data sites should be performed in two steps: on a data level, and on a level of local mining models. While the first level is independent of the applied data mining methodology, the second level has to introduce specific similarity measures for different data mining models. In this paper we are developing and discussing a methodology for data level analysis. Specifically, we are developing the Distributed Similarity Matrix (DSM) algorithm for statistical analysis of distributed homogeneous and heterogeneous data sets, where similarity in data distribution is based on fractal theory. The analysis reveals important information about the statistical distribution of the attribute values of each data set located at each geographically distributed site. This information can be helpful in deriving accurate data mining models that correctly reflect the semantics of the distributed data sites, and help in avoiding inappropriate summarization of the data.

THE CORRELATION FRACTAL DIMENSION AND THE CROSS-VALUE

By embedding a n-dimensional data set in an n-dimensional grid with cell sides of size r, the frequency with which data points fall into the i-th cell, C_i, can be computed. Let N(r) be $\Sigma_i C_i^2$, then the plot of N(r) for different values of r in a log-log scale is called the box-counting plot. The linear slope of this plot is the estimation of the *correlation fractal dimension* (FD) for the given data set, *A* (Traina et al., 2000).

$$FD(A)= d(\log(\Sigma_i C_i^2)) / d(\log(r)) \quad (1)$$

Based on the same fractal theory principles, we can analyze similarity between two n-dimensional data sets, *A* and *B*. For this purpose, a new parameter called the *cross-function* (CF) is introduced (Traina et al., 2001). Consider an n-dimensional grid with cell sides of size r and let $C_{A,i}$ be the number of points from data set *A* in the i-th cell. Similarly let $C_{B,i}$ be the number of points from data set *B* in the i-th cell. The cross-function is defined as follows:

$$CF(A,B) = \Sigma C_{A,i} * C_{B,i} \quad (2)$$

The *cross–value* (CV) of two data sets in the same n-dimensional space is the linear slope of the plot of the cross-function versus r in a log-log scale.

$$CV(A,B) = d(\log(\Sigma C_{A,i} * C_{B,i})) / d(\log(r)) \quad (3)$$

STRUCTURING SEMANTICALLY DISTRIBUTED DATA SITES

Suppose that we want to analyze the relation between two distributed homogenous data sets, *A* and *B*. Our Distributed Similarity Matrix (DSM) methodology is based on the calculation of the correlation fractal dimension of each data set and the cross-value of the two data sets. These three elements build the elementary Distributed Similarity Matrix (DSM) represented in Table 1.

	A	*B*
A	FD(*A*)	CV(*A*, *B*)
B		FD(*B*)

Table 1: 2 × 2 Distributed Similarity Matrix (DSM)

The following rules may be applied to analyze similarity of distributed data sets *A* and *B* in our methodology (Traina, et al., 2001):

Rule 1: If the fractal dimension values of data sets *A* and *B* and the cross-value of *A* and *B* are close values,

$$FD(A) \approx FD(B) \approx CV(A,B),$$

then the data sets *A* and *B* are statistically similar and their origins are from the same distribution. They may be combined during the modeling process if their local mining models are also close.

Rule 2: If the fractal dimension values of data sets *A* and *B* are close, but the cross-value is much larger than either of the fractal dimensions,

$$(FD(A) \approx FD(B)) << CV(A,B),$$

then data sets *A* and *B* are not from the same statistical distribution, and their local data models should not be combined. Therefore, any fusion of mining models has to be performed very carefully even if they are similar.

The DSM algorithm consists of three phases (Sadeghian and Kantardzic, 2004):

1. **Data Normalization** - Data normalization is often necessary to avoid undesirable scaling effects and is the first step in the DSM algorithm. In order to perform the normalization process, *global* minimum and maximum value for each attribute are found by considering all sites. These values are sent to the local sites in order to perform distributed, local normalization using global minimum and maximum values. As a result, distributed data are normalized globally without transferring large data sets through the network.
2. **Site Oriented Fractal Dimension** - After all the distributed data sets have been normalized, the fractal dimension of the distributed data sets is calculated at each site using the box counting algorithm described in Eq. (1). In our approach, we store the cell count structure as a representation of each data site. This is accomplished by giving an integer ID to each cell that has at least one point in it, with the side of size r. In our implementation, we save the ID of the cell followed by the count of points in the cell.
3. **Cross-Value Computation** - After the fractal dimension together with the corresponding stored cell count structure is prepared for each distributed site, they are collected at a central site. It is at this site where the cross-value of the data sets will be calculated based on the local cell count structures without transferring the actual data sets from the local sites. The DSM algorithm will use the fractal dimensions for all sites and cross-values between distributed sites to build a DSM.

TRANSFORMATION OF HETEROGENEOUS DATA SETS INTO HOMOGENEOUS DATA SETS

The DSM algorithm takes as input distributed homogeneous data sets (i.e. all sites have the same schema, but each site has information on different entities). However if the distributed data sets are heterogeneous (i.e. different sites storing data for different set of attributes with some common attributes among sites) it is often still possible to operate on them. The basic idea is to convert *n* heterogeneous data sets into *n* homogeneous data sets by discarding their uncommon attributes. The new homogeneous data sets will be representative of the original data sets as long as the discarded attributes did not account for a significant part of the intrinsic dimensionality (as measured by the FD) of the individual data sets. The Transforming Heterogeneous Data Sets to Homogeneous Data Sets (THH) algorithm described in Figure 1 can be used to test the feasibility of transforming *n* heterogeneous distributed data sets into *n* homogeneous distributed data sets. After the homogeneous data sets are produced, they can be analyzed using the DSM algorithm that was presented earlier.

For each data set located at a distributed site X:
1. Compute the FD.
2. If the Ceil (FD) > number of common attributes of all data sets, do not proceed with this data set.
3. Otherwise, eliminate attributes it does not have in common with all other data sets.
4. Recalculate the FD.
5. If the FD of the homogeneous version of the data set is not significantly different than the FD of the original heterogeneous data set, it is a good approximation.

Figure 1: The THH algorithm

EXPERIMENTAL RESULTS AND DISCUSSION

In this section, we will first demonstrate how to determine the feasibility of transforming distributed heterogeneous data into homogeneous data required by the DSM algorithm. Later, we use real world homogeneous data sets to show how analysis of the DSM can lead to the discovery of the structure of the semantically distributed data sets.

Analysis of Distributed Heterogeneous Data Sites

In the first example, there are two distributed heterogeneous data sets taken from the Forest Cover Type domain derived from the UCI Knowledge Discovery in Databases Archives. The first data set, *For1*, has 4 attributes (elevation, aspect, slope, and horizontal distance to hydrology) and the second data set, *For2*, has 5 attributes (elevation, aspect, slope, Hillshade_9am, and Hillshade_Noon). Both have 10,000 records each and they share 3 attributes (elevation, aspect, slope). As the results in Table 2 a) show, the 3-D homogeneous data sets resulting from the THH algorithm are a good approximation of the original data sets, since discarding the extra dimensions did not significantly reduce the intrinsic dimensionality (FD) of either data set.

The next example involves two distributed 5-D heterogeneous data sets, *Alb1* and *Alb2*, from the Albalone domain, derived from the UCI Machine Learning Repository. Each data set has 2088 records. Both data sets have in common three attributes (length, height, and whole weight). *Alb 1* has the additional attributes of diameter and shucked weight. *Alb2* has the additional attributes of viscera weight and shell weight. Although the FD of either heterogeneous data set is less than the number of the common attributes (3),

Table 2 b) shows that the value of the fractal dimension of either of the 3-D homogeneous data set is significantly less than the respective 5-D heterogeneous data set. This means that the extra uncommon dimensions accounted for a significant amount of the value of the FD in both cases. Therefore, these 3-D homogeneous data sets may not be a sufficient representation for the original data sets.

	FD of 4-D/5-D Heterogeneous Data	FD of 3-D Homogeneous Data
For1	2.12	2.09
For2	2.09	2.08

a) Successful Transformation

	FD of 5-D/5-D Heterogeneous Data	FD of 3-D Homogeneous Data
Alb1	2.03	1.70
Alb2	1.97	1.70

b) Unsuccessful Transformation

Table 2: Experiments with the THH algorithm

Structuring Distributed Homogeneous Data Sites

When there are *n* distributed homogeneous data sets available or *n* heterogeneous data sets that can be transformed into homogeneous data sets with the THH algorithm, where $n \geq 2$, it is possible to apply the DSM algorithm and structure the data sites. An example using data from Forest Cover Type domain is presented here to demonstrate the results obtained by the methodology. There are four 3-dimensional homogeneous data sets (elevation, aspect, and slope) from this domain geographically distributed at four different data sites. *F-1* and *F-2* data sets, with 14,695 records each, have a semantic distribution such that records in the data set have small values for attribute 1 (i.e. elevation < 2856 meters). Data sets *F-3* and *F-4*, each with 18,072 records, don't have this restriction for their records, and they come from the same initial statistical distribution. The DSM is shown in Figure 2 a) and the representation of the proposed structure for the distributed data sites is shown in Figure 2 b).

	F-1	F-2	F-3	F-4
F-1	*1.84*	*2.20*	*27.98*	*27.98*
F-2		*1.73*	*27.98*	*27.98*
F-3			*1.89*	*2.18*
F-4				*1.74*

a) The DSM

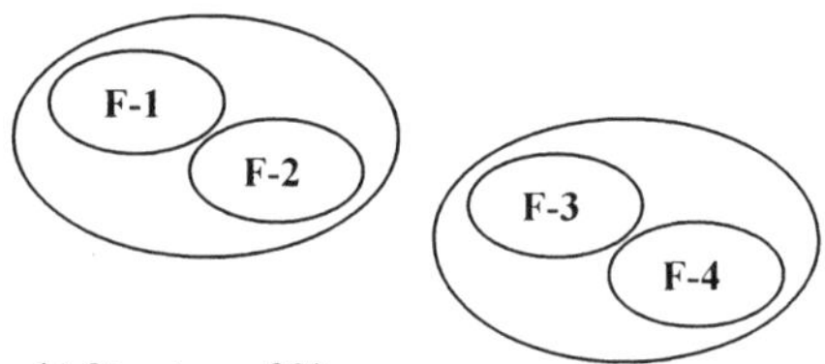

b) Structure of Sites

Figure 2: Data set *F-1* and *F-2* come from one semantic distribution, while *F-3* and *F-4* come from another.

Using Rule 1, it can be concluded that *F-1* and *F-2* come from the same semantic distribution since the fractal dimension (1.84 and 1.73, respectively) of the two data sets are similar and in turn they are also close to their cross-value (2.20). Similarly, we can conclude that *F-3* and *F-4* are from the same semantic distribution for the same reason. Notice how the cross-value (27.98) of any two data sets that don't come from the same semantic distribution is much higher than the fractal dimension of either data set (i.e. Rule #2). This allows us to cluster data sets that come from the same semantic distribution. In this example, *F-1* and *F-2* come from the same semantic distribution and form one cluster, while *F-3* and *F-4* come from another semantic distribution and form the other cluster.

CONCLUSIONS

In this paper we developed a methodology based on fractal theory to determine if distributed data is statistically similar or disjoint, and whether the data sets should or should not be combined in the data mining process. Data sites are often heterogeneous in nature. Therefore, we developed a method for testing the feasibility of transforming *n* heterogeneous data sets into *n* representative homogeneous data sets required for our methodology. In the next phase, we will combine our methodology as an initial step with distributed data mining algorithms (i.e. association rules, clustering, etc.) to obtain better insight into the semantics of distributed sites.

ACKNOWLEDGMENTS

This research has been supported by the Kentucky Science and Engineering Foundation under grant No. 148-502-03-56.

REFERENCES

Ashrafi, M. Z., Taniar, D., and Smith, K. A., 2002, "Data Mining Architecture for Distributed Environment," *Applied Parallel Computing, Lecture Notes in Computer Science,*2346, pp. 27-38.

Kantardzic, M. and Badia, A., 2003, "A Data Mining Framework for Semantically Distributed Databases," *Proceedings, IASTED International Conference on Artificial Intelligence and Soft Computing - ASC 2003*, Banff, Canada.

Sadeghian, P. and Kantardzic, M., 2004, "Structure Discovery in Semantically Distributed Data Sites: The Fractal Dimension Approach," *Proceedings, 8th World Multi-Conference on Systemics, Cybernetics and Informatics*, Orlando, Florida.

Traina, A., Traina, C., Papadimitriou, S., and Faloutsos, C., 2001, "Tri-Plots: Scalable Tools for Multidimensional Data Mining," *Proceedings, 7th ACM SIGKDD International Conference on Knowledge Discovery and Data Mining - KDD-2001*, San Francisco, CA, pp. 184-193.

Traina, C., Traina, A., Wu, L., and Faloutsos, C., 2000, "Fast Feature Selection Using Fractal Dimension," *Proceedings, 15th Brazilian Database Symposium,*João Pessoa - PA - Brazil, pp. 158-171.

Turinsky, A. L. and Grossman, R. L., 2000, "A Framework for Finding Distributed Data Mining Strategies that are Intermediate Between Centralized Strategies and In-Place Strategies," *Proceedings, 6th ACM SIGKDD International Conference on Knowledge Discovery and Data Mining - KDD-2000,* Boston, MA.

Wirth, R., Borth, M., and Hipp, J., 2001, "When Distribution is Part of the Semantics: A New Problem Class for Distributed Knowledge Discovery,"*Proceedings, PKDD 2001 Workshop on Ubiquitous Data Mining for Mobile and Distributed Environments,*Freiburg, Germany, pp. 56-64.

Abalone Data Set, *UCI Machine Learning Repository* [http://www.ics.uci.edu/~mlearn/MLSummary.html]

Forest CoverType Data Set, *UCI KDD Archive* [http://kdd.ics.uci.edu/databases/covertype/covertype.html]

INTRODUCTION TO STRUCTURAL HMM AND ITS APPLICATION IN PATTERN CLASSIFICATION

D. BOUCHAFFRA (Senior Member IEEE), J. TAN
Department of Computer Science & Engineering
131 Dodge Hall, Oakland University
Rochester, MI, 48309, USA
Phone: (248) 370-2242
{bouchaff, jtan}@oakland.edu

ABSTRACT
The classification of complex patterns remains a challenging problem in the pattern recognition community. In this paper we propose a classification paradigm that merges statistics with syntax in a seamless way. This novel approach called "Structural HMM"(SHMM) extends traditional HMM by incorporating syntax with statistics within a single probabilistic framework. We have applied SHMM in order to data mine customers' preferences for automotive designs. The results reported shows that SHMM's outperform traditional hidden Markov model classifiers.

INTRODUCTION

Human perception of objects contains roughly two types of relationships: the *classification* relationship, by which a human *generalizes* experience, and the *componential* relationship, by which we *organize* the whole made up of many parts that seems to be an inherent quality of all things. Therefore, statistics and structure are always driving humans in a decision problem in pattern recognition (PR). Unfortunately, for most practical problems, this *purely statistical* approach is not feasible. The reason is that a pattern contains some *relational information* from which it is difficult and sometimes impossible to derive an appropriate feature vector. *Therefore, the analytical approaches which process the patterns only on a quantitative basis but ignore the inter-relationships between components quite often fails.* Several approaches have been attempted in order to capture the structural relationship between observations. They are "syntactical pattern recognition" [Fu1982], "Bayesian belief networks" (BBN's) [Heckerman1995], and traditional "hidden Markov model" paradigm [Rabiner1993]. However, they all have the weak points that they either consider syntactic or statistical relationships, but not both at the same time. The thrust in this paper is to combine statistics with syntax in a seamless way so that we will be capable to optimally represent complex patterns. We propose a novel paradigm that we called *structural hidden Markov model* (SHMM) that merges statistical and syntactical data together in a single probabilistic framework. We extract structural information from sequences of observations viewed as input strings to be derived by a grammar. The structural information are conclusions (or variables of a grammar) that accept the input strings (sequences of observations). Because our world is full of complex patterns, we believe that the concept of SHMM opens a new door for understanding and unfolding these structures. In this research statistics and syntax as complementary, they do not compete in the pattern representation phase.

THE CONCEPT OF STRUCTURAL HMM

In this section, we introduce a mathematical description of the SHMM concept that goes beyond the traditional hidden Markov model since it emphasizes the structure (or syntax) of the visible sequence of observation.

In traditional HMM's, the visible observations are assumed to be *state conditionally independent*. Let $O = (o_1 o_2 \ldots o_T)$ be the observation sequence of length T and $q = (q_1 q_2 \ldots q_T)$ be the state sequence where q_1 is the initial state. Given a model λ, we can write:

$$P(O \mid \lambda) = \sum_{all\ q} P(O, q \mid \lambda), \text{ and } P(O, q \mid \lambda) = P(O \mid q, \lambda) \times P(q \mid \lambda).$$

Using state conditional independence, we obtain: $P(O \mid q, \lambda) = \prod_{t=1}^{T} P(o_t \mid q_t, \lambda)$.

However, there are several scenarios where the conditional independence assumption doesn't hold. For example, while standard HMM's perform well in recognizing amino acids and consequent construction of proteins from the first level structure of DNA sequences [Krogh1994], they are inadequate for predicting the secondary structure of a protein. Therefore, there is a need to balance the loss incurred by this state conditional independence assumption. Our idea is to consider the sequence of visible observations as input to a grammar. The sequence of observations is viewed as an input string to a grammar, and a conclusion (or a head) is computed given this string.

Each observation sequence O is not only one sequence in which all observations are conditionally independent, but a sequence that is divided into a series of s subsequences $O_i = (o_{i_1} o_{i_2} \ldots o_{i_{r_i}})$ $(1 \leq i \leq s)$. The observations in a subsequence are related in the sense that they represent evidences o_i that contribute to the production of a conclusion $\mathbf{C}_j = f_G(o_{i_1}, o_{i_2}, \ldots, o_{i_{r_i}})$, $(1 \leq j \leq L)$, where f_G is the derivation in the grammar that accepts the input string $o_{i_1}, o_{i_2}, \ldots, o_{i_{r_i}}$ and L is the number of conclusions. The whole sequence of observations can be written directly as:

$$O = (o_{1_1} \cdots o_{1_{r_1}}, C_1, o_{2_1} \cdots o_{2_{r_2}}, C_2, \cdots, o_{s_1} \cdots o_{s_{r_s}} C_s) = (O_1 C_1 O_2 C_2 \cdots O_s C_s).$$

where r_1 is the number of observations in subsequence O_1 and r_2 is the number of observations in subsequence O_2, etc. We consider the overall observation sequence O as a sequence of O_i with their corresponding conclusions C_j.

A sequence of visible observations is the input string presented to the grammar, the organization of the symbols in this sequence O_i produces a conclusion C_j with a certain probability $P(C_j \mid O_i)$. The higher the complexity of the pattern, the higher the number of conclusions needed to describe the structure of this pattern. Each conclusion C_i interacts with another conclusion C_j with some transition probability values $P(C_j \mid C_i)$. Therefore, we can define a Structural HMM as:

Definition 01 *A structural hidden Markov model is a quintuple* $\lambda = (\pi, \mathcal{A}, \mathcal{B}, \mathcal{C}, \mathcal{D})$, *where: (i),* π *is the initial state probability vector; (ii),* $\mathcal{A}$ *is the state transition probability matrix; (iii),* $\mathcal{B}$ *is the state conditional probability matrix of the visible observations; (iv),* $\mathcal{C}$ *is the posterior probability matrix of a conclusion given a sequence of observations; (v),* $\mathcal{D}$ *is the conclusion transition probability matrix.*

A SHMM is characterized by the following elements:

- **N**, the number of states in the model. We label the individual states as $1, 2, \ldots,$ N, and denote the state at time t as q_t.
- **M**, the number of distinct observations in one state. We use a symbol to represent each observation o_i, and the set of symbols is denoted as $V = \{v_1, v_2, \ldots, v_M\}$.
- π, the initial state distribution, $\pi = \{\pi_i\}$, where $\pi_i = P(q_1 = i)$ and $1 \leq i \leq N$.
- $\mathcal{A}$, the state transition probability distribution matrix, $A = \{a_{ij}\}$, where $a_{ij} = P(q_{t+1} = j \mid q_t = i)$ and $1 \leq i, j \leq N$, $\sum_j a_{ij} = 1$.
- $\mathcal{B}$, the state conditional probability matrix of observations, $B = \{b_j(k) = P(o_k \mid q_j)\}$.
- **F**, the number of distinct conclusions. We use a symbol to represent each conclusion, and the set of conclusions is denoted as $U = \{u_1, u_2, \ldots, u_F\}$.

- $\mathcal{C}$ is the posterior probability matrix of a conclusion given its corresponding observation sequence, $\mathcal{C} = P(C_j \mid O_i) = c_i(j)$. For each particular input string O_i, we have: $\sum_{All\ j} c_i(j) = 1$. A particular application requires a particular grammar G_h in which a conclusion C_i is assigned to O_i via a rule R_k which is written as: $G_h : C_i \overset{R_k}{\Longleftarrow} (o_{i_1}, o_{i_2}, \ldots, o_{i_t})$, k is the number of rules in the grammar G_h. Since we are using a stochastic context free grammar, there is only one conclusion (the most likely) that is assigned to a subsequence of observations.
- $\mathcal{D}$, the conclusion transition probability matrix. $D = \{d_{ij}\}$, where $d_{ij} = P(C_{t+1} = j \mid C_t = i)$, $\sum_j d_{ij} = 1, 1 \leq i, j \leq F$.

Figure 1 depicts a representation of a structural hidden Markov model

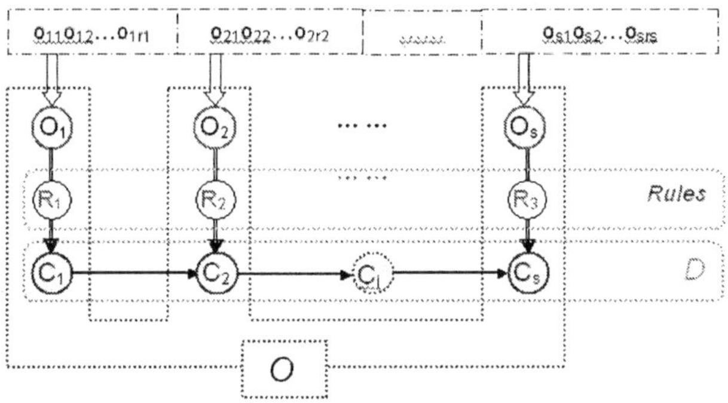

Fig. 1. A graphical representation of a structural hidden Markov model.

PROBLEMS ASSIGNED TO A STRUCTURAL HMM

There are four problems that are assigned to a SHMM:
(i) Probability evaluation, (ii) Statistical decoding, (iii) Structural decoding, and (iv) Parameter estimation.

PROBABILITY EVALUATION

The evaluation problem in SHMM consists of computing:

$$P(O \mid \lambda) = P(O_1C_1, O_2C_2, \ldots, O_sC_s \mid \lambda)$$

$$= \prod_{i=1}^{s} [P(C_i \mid O_iC_{i-1}O_{i-1} \ldots C_2O_2C_1O_1\lambda)P(O_i \mid C_{i-1}O_{i-1} \ldots C_2O_2C_1O_1\lambda)] .$$

We assume that the conclusion C_i depends only on the observation sequence O_i and the preceding conclusion C_{i-1}. Therefore, we have:

$$P(O \mid \lambda) = \prod_{i=1}^{s} [P(C_i \mid O_iC_{i-1}\lambda) \times P(O_i \mid C_{i-1}O_{i-1} \ldots C_2O_2C_1O_1\lambda)] .$$

Because O_i depends only on C_i, we obtain: $P(O \mid \lambda) = \prod_{i=1}^{s} [P(C_i \mid O_i, C_{i-1}, \lambda) \times P(O_i \mid \lambda)]$.
Now we have to focus on the term $P(C_i \mid O_iC_{i-1})$ which is the most challenging term for estimation. However, we know that: $P(C_i \mid O_iC_{i-1}) = \frac{P(O_i|C_iC_{i-1}) \times P(C_i|C_{i-1})}{P(O_i|C_{i-1})}$. Given the fact that the conclusion C_i is the only conclusion that might produce O_i, therefore we can write this conditional independence as: $P(O_i \mid C_iC_{i-1}) = P(O_i \mid C_i)$. Using Bayes'

rule, we obtain: $P(O \mid \lambda) = \prod_{i=1}^{s} \frac{[P(C_i \mid O_i\lambda)P(C_i \mid C_{i-1}, \lambda) \times P(O_i \mid \lambda)]}{P(C_i)}$.

Finally, this provides:

$$P(O|\lambda) = \prod_{i=1}^{s} \frac{c_i(i)}{P(C_i)} \times \sum_{q_1 \cdots q_T} \left[\pi_{q1} b_{q1}(o_1) a_{q1\,q2} \ldots a_{q(T-1)\,qT} b_{qT}(o_T) d_{C_1C_2} \cdot d_{C_{s-1}C_s}\right].$$

STATISTICAL DECODING

The statistical decoding problem consists of determining the optimal state sequence $q^* = \underset{q}{argmax}(P(O, q \mid \lambda))$ that best "explains" the sequence of observations . It can be computed using Viterbi algorithm as in traditional HMM's.

STRUCTURAL DECODING

The structural decoding problem consists of determining the optimal rule conclusion sequence

$\mathcal{C}^* =< C_1^* C_2^* \ldots C_t^* >$ such that: $\mathcal{C}^* = \underset{\mathcal{C}}{argmax}(P(O, \mathcal{C} \mid \lambda))$.

We define: $\delta_t(i) = \underset{\mathcal{C}}{max}\, P(O, C_1C_2 \ldots C_t = i \mid \lambda)$, that is, $\delta_t(i)$ is the highest probability along a single path, at time t, which accounts for the first t observations and ends in rule conclusion i. Then, we estimate the following by induction:

$$\delta_{t+1}(j) = \left[\underset{i}{max}\, \delta_t(i) d_{ik}\right] b_j(o_{t+1}).$$

Similarly, this can be computed using *Viterbi* algorithm. However, we estimate δ in each step *through conclusion transition probability matrix instead of state transition probability matrix.* This optimal sequence of conclusions describes the structural pattern piecewise.

PARAMETER ESTIMATION

The re-estimation phase of the parameters $\{\pi_i\}$, $\{a_{ij}\}$, $\{b_j(k)\}$ and $\{d_{ij}\}$ is conducted as in traditional HMM's [Rabiner1993], using the Baum-Welch optimization technique.

However, *the most difficult problem* is the estimation of $P(C_j \mid O_i)$. We need to construct a grammar G that enables the estimation of this term. Usually, it is the user who constructs an appropriate grammar based on personal knowledge and experience regarding a particular application. To construct such a grammar, a set of primitives is selected depending on the type of data involved in the application. *It is very important that the primitives provide a reasonable description of the patterns and the structural relations.* To derive a conclusion, we use "stochastic context-free grammar" [Jurafsky1995]. Similar to the decoding process, a Viterbi algorithm is used to find the best derivation.

Assume an incoming $x = O_i$ derives $S = C_j$, this can be illustrated as:

$$S = (C_j) \overset{R_1}{\Rightarrow} \alpha_1 \overset{R_2}{\Rightarrow} \alpha_2 \ldots \overset{R_t}{\Rightarrow} \alpha_t = x (= O_i)$$

where R_i are the production rules used in the productions, α_i $(1 \leq i \leq t)$ is the intermediate level of derivation and α_{i+1} is obtained from α_i using a rule that is related with the conclusion C_j in α_i. The production is performed with the probability $P(R_i)$ which is the probability of the production rule R_i being used in the production. Thus, in our model, $P(C_j \mid O_i)$ can be estimated as: $P(C_j \mid O_i) = P(R_1) \prod_{i=1}^{n-1} P(R_{i+1}|R_i)$.

Suppose C_j is the starting symbol of our grammar, o_i's are the terminal symbols, and we have only one production rule R_1 defined as $C_j \Longleftarrow O_i (= o_{i_1} o_{i_2} \ldots o_{i_r})$. Then we have the production procedure: $S \rightarrow C_j \overset{R_1}{\Longrightarrow} O_i \rightarrow o_{i_1} o_{i_2} \ldots o_{i_r}$.

Therefore, we have: $P(C_j \mid O_i) = P(R_i) = P(C_j \Longleftarrow o_{i_1} o_{i_2} \ldots o_{i_r})$.

APPLICATIONS: DATA MINING CUSTOMERS' PREFERENCES FOR AUTOMOTIVE DESIGNS

We have applied the concept of Structural Hidden Markov Model in order to mine customers' preferences for automotive designs. This data mining aids automotive design engineers in predicting customers' perceptions on particular car make's exterior contour before these cars are put into making. The purpose of this application is to build a computational method that helps engineers to improve their designs, speed up their job by releasing them from the tedious manual information processing, and eventually make cars that match the need of customers.

DATA COLLECTION

We collected 500 images of regular cars with their three exterior views (front, side and rear, i.e., 1500 images). A pre-processing phase of car images was performed in order to remove such influence of some features as color, lamp shapes, or tires. We then extracted the contours of the three views and presented them to 300 university students and ask them to give their opinions (adjectives expressing students' feelings of the car) on the three views separately. 300 students would probably give as much as 300 different opinions to one contour. We adopted the "simple majority voting" method to obtain a unique opinion that is assigned to a contour. Thus we obtained 1500 adjectives (some are identical) clustered with synonymy using the online lexical database WordNet [Fellbaum1998]. Each centroid of a cluster is called a *perception* which is a conclusion in the SHMM modeling. Conclusions are the customer's perceptions regarding the automotive contours and observations are standard 8-directions *chain code* string representing the contours. Therefore, we extracted the contour of "front (f)" and represented it as $O_f = (o_1 o_2 \ldots o_{r_f})$, where o_i's is the chain code string. The customer's opinion assigned to this view is represented by C_f, where C_f is the conclusion assigned to rule R_f that defines how the opinion of this view is obtained from the chain code description of its contour. We used the stochastic grammar to estimate the matrix C. The grammar G_c we used is defined as follows:
(1). The set of non-terminals V_N^c is {contour perceptions}.
(2). The set of terminals V_T^c is {0-8}, which is the chain code 8 directions.
(3). The set of production rules R^c is {"Perception of car contour" $\Longleftarrow$ "chain code description of that contour""},
(4). Q^c is set of probabilities of all rules in set P^c.
Thus, we defined a rule as: "$front\ is\ ordinary$" $\Longleftarrow$ "0200 ... 22220000".

TRAINING SHMM

Training a Structural HMM is an iterative process that seeks to maximize the probability that the SHMM accounts for the example sequences. To re-estimate $\{a_{ij}\}$, $\{b_j(k)\}$ and $\{d_{ij}\}$, we applied the Baum-Welch re-estimation algorithm. Table 1 show the transition probability matrix of 5 major conclusions. From the training data set, we generate 1000 rules and each rule is assigned a certain probability.

to / from	ugly	ordinary	nice	attractive	beautiful
ugly	.2100	.1053	.2105	.4211	.0526
ordinary	.0906	.2727	.2273	.2273	.1818
nice	.2603	.1304	.1304	.3043	.1739
attractive	.1532	.1795	.2564	.3846	.0256
beautiful	.0098	.3989	.1002	.4000	.0000

Table 1. Transition probability matrix $\mathcal{D}$ of 5 major conclusions estimated from the data set.

TESTING AND RESULTS

Once the SHMM for this application is built, we used the testing data set to evaluate the accuracy. Observation sequences are fed into the SHMM, then conclusions are predicted. If our predicted conclusion (or category) is C_p and the true conclusion obtained from survey is C_t, then our precision is defined as:

$$Precision = \sum \delta(C_p - C_t) / \mid input \quad patterns \mid$$

where $\delta(x-a)$ is the Kronecker symbol which is "1" if x=a, and "0" otherwise, the denominator $\mid input \quad patterns \mid$ represents the total number of patterns. We have compared the SHMM approach with the traditional Hidden Markov Model (HMM) classification technique. The training of both the SHMM and HMM were coded using MATLAB. Preliminary performance results are depicted in Table 2.

Precision (%) **Sample Size**	HMM	SHMM
100 cars	65.6	70.1
450 cars	72.5	83.4
500 cars	78.5	83.2

Table 2. Performances comparison between the HMM and the SHMM classifiers.

CONCLUSION AND FUTURE WORK

We have presented in this paper a novel modeling technique that merges syntactical and statistical information in a single probabilistic framework. Our approach relates visible observations through their contribution to a same conclusion (or consequence) of a syntactic rule. The SHMM concept represents a preliminary fusion between statistics and syntax. The automotive application shows that SHMM concept is promising since it has outperformed the traditional hidden Markov model classifier. However, this is an undergoing research, more data need to be collected, and comparisons with other classifiers are necessary in order to measure the real contribution of SHMM's. Our future work is twofold: (i), to use some other techniques to represent the visible observation sequences rather than chain codes; (ii), to apply SHMM's to other areas such as proteins identification and natural language processing where structure is prominent.

References

[Fellbaum1998] C. Fellbaum, "WordNet: an Electronic Lexical Database", Published by Bradford Book, 1998.

[Fu1982] K.S. Fu, "Syntactic Pattern Recognition and Applications", Prentice-Hall, Englewood Cliffs, N.J., 1982.

[Heckerman1995] D. Heckerman. "A Tutorial on Learning with Bayesian Networks", Technical Report MSR-TR-95-06, Microsoft Research, Redmond, Washington, 1995.

[Jurafsky1995] D. Jurafsky, C. Wooters, J. Segal, A. Stolcke, E. Fosler, G. Tajchman and N. Morgan, "Using a Stochastic Context-Free Grammar as a Language Model for Speech Recognition", In Proc. ICASSP'95 (pp. 189–192), 1995.

[Krogh1994] Krogh, A., M. Brown, I.S. Mian, K. Sjolander, and D. Haussler. "Hidden Markov Models in Computational Biology: Applications to Protein Modeling", J. Mol. Biol., Vol. 235, pp.1501-1531, 1994.

[Rabiner1993] L. Rabiner and B.H. Juang, "Fundamentals of Speech Recognition", Prentice Hall, 1993.

EXTENDING RELATIONAL OPERATIONS FOR CISET RELATIONAL DATABASE

PREMCHAND S. NAIR
Department of Mathematics and Computer Science
Creighton University
Omaha, NE 68116

ABSTRACT
The aim of this paper is to extend the traditional relational algebra operators into ciset relational operators. This in turn extends the relational database to ciset relational database. The ciset relational database has the capability to integrate both supporting and opposing evidences relating to the same fact. In particular, we prove the following results. Given two relations A and B, you may convert them to corresponding cisets. Performing a ciset operation and converting the result back to a relation is equivalent to applying the relational operation on A and B directly. Similarly, if you perform a relational operation first and then convert them to ciset relation it has the same effect as converting to ciset and then performing the ciset operation.

INTRODUCTION

Fuzzy theory holds that many things in life are matters of degree. A black and white photo is not just black and white; there are many levels of gray shades that can be observed in a typical picture. As an example, a pixel can have a brightness value between 0 and 1. The value 0 may correspond to black and the value 1 may correspond to white. In this case, every number between 0 and 1 corresponds to a certain gray level. Fuzzy theory has made significant contributions to many areas. In this paper we employ ciset (Nair, 2004), an extension of fuzzy sets to extend relational database to a ciset relational database that can integrate both supporting and opposing evidences relating to the same fact. For example, let us say one of the CIA members has informed the headquarters that Facility X in country ABC is used to produce biological weapons. This information is assigned a value 0.6. Later on, another source has informed the CIA headquarters that the facility is not used for the production of biological weapons. One possible solution is to keep this new information with a value assigned to it, say –0.3. However, in a relational database, the above two facts are not treated as two pieces of information regarding the same subject. In a relational database system they remain as two independent tuples. The aim of this work is to extend relational database so that we can integrate the supporting and the opposing facts based on the subject matter. In a ciset relational database there will be only one tuple with a confidence index (0.3, 0.6) assigned to it. Note that 0.3 indicates the degree of opposing evidence and 0.6 indicate the degree of supporting evidence.

Through out this paper, L stands for a complete distributive lattice under a partial order $\leq$. Let $\vee$ and $\wedge$ be the join and meet operations on L. Further, we use 0 and 1 to denote the 0 and 1 of the lattice L. Whenever we present an example to illustrate various concepts, we use unit interval [0, 1] under the partial order less than or equal to. Further, we shall use $\vee$ and $\wedge$ to represent the maximum and minimum operations on real numbers. Theory and various results on fuzzy sets can be found in (Mordeson and Nair, 1998). For results on relational database reader is encouraged to refer to any undergraduate text.

CISET

Let $\alpha, \beta \in L$. Then a pair $< \alpha, \beta >$ is called a confidence index α is the lower index and β the upper index. The confidence index $a_1 = < \alpha_1, \beta_1 >$ is said to be less than $a_2 = < \alpha_2, \beta_2 >$, denoted by $a_1 \prec a_2$, if $\alpha_1 \geq \alpha_2$ and $\beta_1 < \beta_2$ or $\alpha_1 > \alpha_2$ and $\beta_1 \leq \beta_2$. We define union, intersection, negation and difference as follows: $a_1 \cup a_2 = < \alpha_1 \wedge \alpha_2, \beta_1 \vee \beta_2 >$, $a_1 \cap a_2 = < \alpha_1 \vee \alpha_2, \beta_1 \wedge \beta_2 >$, $- a_1 = < \beta_1, \alpha_1 >$ and $a_1 - a_2 = a_1 \cap - a_2$. Observe that law of excluded middle and law of contradition do not hold. However, DeMorgan's Law holds.

Let S be a set. A confidence index set or ciset (pronounced as see-set) is a mapping F from the set S to the set of all confidence indexes. One can think of ciset F as a set in which each element has a confidence index; not a set membership. The upper index of an element x gives a confidence level for the fact that x is a member of the set S in the traditional sense; and the lower index of an element x gives a confidence level for the fact that x is not a member of the set S in the traditional sense. The basic set theoritic operations, union, intersection, complement and difference can be defined on cisets by pointwise using the union, intersection, negation and difference. For example, $F \cup G$ of two cisets F and G on a set S can be defined as $(F \cup G)(x) = F(x) \cup G(x)$, for all $x \in S$. We define Cartesian product of two cisets F on a set S and G on a set T as $(F \times G)(x,y) = F(x) \cap G(y)$, for all $x \in S$, $y \in T$. Observe that law of excluded middle and law of contradition do not hold. However, DeMorgan's Law holds.

Given a subset A of S, we use the symbol F_A to denote a ciset on S with the following property: $F_A(x) = <0, 1>$ for all $x \in A$ and $F_A(x) = <1, 0>$ for x not a member of A. Thus ciset is a generalization of set. Similarly if μ is a fuzzy set on S, we use the symbol F_μ to denote a ciset with the following property: $F_\mu(x) = <1 - \mu(x), \mu(x)>$ for all $x \in S$. Therefore ciset is a generalization of fuzzy set as well. For details see (Nair, 2004).

Theorem 1

Let A and B be subsets of a set S. Then

1. $F_A \cup F_B = F_{A \cup B}$,
2. $F_A \cap F_B = F_{A \cap B}$,
3. $F_A - F_B = F_{A-B}$,
4. $F_A \times F_B = F_{A \times B}$,
5. $-F_A = F_{A^c}$.

Theorem 2

Let μ and σ be fuzzy subsets of a set S. Then

1. $F_\mu \cup F_\sigma = F_{\mu \cup \sigma}$,
2. $F_\mu \cap F_\sigma = F_{\mu \cap \sigma}$,

3. $F_\mu \times F_\sigma = F_{\mu\times\sigma}$,
4. $-F_\mu = F_\mu{}^c$.

Given a ciset F on a set S, let F^s denote the set { $x \in S$ | upper index of x is 1}. Similarly, given a ciset F on S, let F^f denote the fuzzy { (x, u(F(x))) | $x \in S$}, where u(F(x)) is the upper index of x in the ciset F.

Theorem 3

Let A and B be subsets of a set S. Then

1. $(F_A \cup F_B)^s = A \cup B = (F_{A\cup B})^s$,
2. $(F_A \cap F_B)^s = A \cap B = (F_{A\cap B})^s$,
3. $(F_A - F_B)^s = A - B = (F_{A-B})^s$,
4. $(F_A \times F_B)^s = A \times B = (F_{A\times B})^s$,
5. $(-F_A)^s = A^c = (F_A{}^c)^s$.

Theorem 4

Let μ and σ be fuzzy subsets of a set S. Then

1. $(F_\mu \cup F_\sigma)^f = \mu \cup \sigma = (F_{\mu\cup\sigma})^f$,
2. $(F_\mu \cap F_\sigma)^f = \mu \cap \sigma = (F_{\mu\cap\sigma})^f$,
3. $(F_\mu \times F_\sigma)^f = \mu \times \sigma = (F_{\mu\times\sigma})^f$,
4. $(-F_\mu)^f = \mu^c = (F_\mu{}^c)^f$.

Theorem 3 states that given two subsets A and B of S, the five basic operations union, intersection, difference, Cartesian product and complement can either be computed in A or, you may compute their ciset equivelents, perform a corresponding ciset operation and convert the answer back to set. This result is very powerful. First, it demonstrates that our ciset operations are in fact true extensions of their counterparts in set. Secondly, this result also demonstrate that if two cisets are in fact sets, that is, every element has their lower index zero, then there is no need to compute the basic operations as cisets. Instead, you can perform the computaion as sets and convert them back to cisets. Theorem 4 states that similar results hold for fuzzy sets as well.

CISET RELATIONAL MODEL

A ciset relation is traditional relation that admits set of confidence indexes as domain and there may exist an attribute CI with the set of confidence indexes as the domain. As an example, consider the ciset relation given below.

FACULTY

FACID	FACNAME	DEPT	EVALUATION	CI
12312	John Smith	Marketing	<0.5,0.7>	<0, 1>
31807	Mary Lee	Mathematics	<0.4, 0.9>	<0.2, 0.9>
12674	Sandy DeWitt	Marketing	<0.1,0.8>	<0.3, 0.7>
56739	Bea Anthony	Accounting	<0.7,0.6>	<0.2, 0.9>

Table 1. Ciset relation FACULTY

The semantics of the second tuple is Mary Lee with faculty Id 31807 is a member of the Mathematics department and her teaching evaluation is rated as <0.4, 0.9>. The above fact has confidence index value <0.2, 0.9>. The semantics of other tuples is similar. Observe that all attributes of a tuple, other than CI qualifies the entity. However, the role of CI is quite different in the sense that CI qualifies the confidence index of the tuple itself.

A ciset relation do not explicitly store tuples with CI value <1, 0>. Therefore, tuples of the form (34287, Mark Molsen, Physis, <0, 0>, <1, 0>) are implicitly present in the FACULTY relation.

EXTENDING RELATIONAL ALGEBRA

Recall that a ciset relation do not store tuples with CI value <1, 0>. However, you need to take care of this fact during the computation. We begin our discussion with union, intersection and difference. In order to perform any one of the three operations, both ciset relations must be union compatible. That is, their attributes must match in number and domain. Let R and S be two union compatible ciset relations. Then union, intersection and difference of R and S are union compatible ciset relations obtained by combining the tuples in R and S as explained below.

Let RelR and RelS be two union compatible ciset relations on a ciset relational scheme $\{A_1, \ldots, A_n\}$. We use the term non-relational attributes to refer those attributes whose domain is the set of all confidence indexes. Let first k attributes of the ciset relational scheme $\{A_1, \ldots, A_n\}$ be relational attributes and let the rest of the attributes be non-relational attributes. Then each tuple of RelR and RelS can be represented as **(t, z(t))**, where **t** represents a vector of all relational attributes and **z(t)** represents a vector of all non-relational attributes.

We now proceed to formally define the ciset relational operator union. Let **(t, z(t))** be any tuple of RelR. If There exists no tuple of the form **(t, z'(t))** in RelS, then **(t, z(t))** is a member of RelR $\cup$ RelS. Similarly, let **(t, z(t))** be any tuple of RelS. If There exists no tuple of the form **(t, z'(t))** in RelR, then **(t, z(t))** is a member of RelR $\cup$ RelS. If there exists two tuples **(t, z(t))** and **(t, z'(t))** such that one of them is in RelR and the other is in RelS, then **(t, z(t)$\cup$z'(t))** is a member of RelR $\cup$ RelS. Here **z(t)$\cup$z'(t)** represents pointwise confidence index union of the vectors **z(t)** and **z'(t).** Note that tuples with identical relational attributes are combined by applying the union on each one of the attributes with confidence index as their domain.

The formal definition of the ciset relational operator intersection is as follows. Let **(t, z(t))** be any tuple of RelR. If There exists no tuple of the form **(t, z'(t))** in RelS, then **(t, z(t))** is not a member of RelR $\cap$ RelS. Similarly, let **(t, z(t))** be any tuple of RelS. If There exists no tuple of the form **(t, z'(t))** in RelR, then **(t, z(t))** is not a member of RelR $\cap$ RelS. If there exists two tuples **(t, z(t))** and **(t, z'(t))** such that one of them is in RelR and the other is in RelS, then **(t, z(t) $\cap$ z'(t))** is a member of RelR $\cap$ RelS. Here **z(t) $\cap$ z'(t)** represents pointwise confidence index intersection of the vectors **z(t)** and **z'(t).**

The formal definition of the ciset relational operator difference is as follows. Let **(t, z(t))** be any tuple of RelR. If There exists no tuple of the form **(t, z'(t))** in RelS, then **(t, z(t))** is a member of RelR – RelS. If there exists two tuples **(t, z(t))** and **(t, z'(t))** such that **(t, z(t))** is in RelR and the other is in RelS, then **(t, z(t) – z'(t))** is a member of RelR ∪ RelS. Here **z(t) – z'(t)** represents pointwise confidence index difference of the vectors **z(t)** and **z'(t).**

The select operation is extended by adding features that will allow the user to select a tuple based on the confidence index values. Similarly, project operation needs no additional treatment. The ciset project operation treats every attribute, including CI, identically.

The ciset relational Cartesian product is a direct extenstion of the ciset Cartesian product defined earlier. The formal definition of the ciset relational operator Cartesian product is as follows. Let **(t, z(t))** be a tuple of RelR and let **(s, z(s))** be a tuple of RelS. Then **(t, s, z(t) ∩ z(s))**, where **z(t) ∩ z'(t)** represents pointwise confidence index intersection of the vectors **z(t)** and **z'(t).**

Other relational operators join, equi-join, theta-join and divide can in fact be defined using union, intersection, difference, select, project and Cartesion product. We can make use of this fact. Thus to extend relational operators join, equi-join, theta-join and divide to corresponding ciset relational operators, we replace union, intersection, difference, select, project and Cartesion product by ciset operators. Due to Theorem 3, we have the following.

Theorem 5

Let RELA and RELB two relations. Let ⊗ stands for one of the binary operations : union, intersection, difference, Cartesian product, natural join, equi-join, theta-join and division. Further, let ⊕ stands for any one of the unary operations selection and project. Then we have the following:

1. $(F_{RELA} \otimes F_{RELB})^s = RELA \otimes RELB = (F_{RELA\otimes B})^s$,
2. $(\oplus F_{RELA})^s = (\oplus RELA) = \oplus (F_{RELA})^s$.

Theorem 5 states that given two relations RelA and RelB, there are two options for carrying out the relational algebra operators. In the first option, you may use the relational operators directly. In the second option, you may transform relations to ciset relations and the apply the ciset relational operators. Result is then converted to relations. Similarly, if we start with two ciset relations that are just relations represented as ciset relations by adding a CI attribute with all values <0, 1>, then there are two options as well. In the first option, you may use the ciset relational operators directly. In the second option, you may transform ciset relations to relations and the apply the relational operators. Result is then converted to ciset relations.

CONCLUSIONS

In this paper we have extended all relational operators to ciset relational operators. The extension has the following properties. Given two relations RelA and RelB, there are two options for carrying out the relational algebra operators. In the first option, you may use the relational operators directly. In the second option, you may transform relations to ciset relations and the apply the ciset relational operators. Result is then converted to relations. Similarly, if we start with two ciset relations that are just relations represented as ciset relations by adding a CI attribute with all values <0, 1>, then there are two options as well.

In the first option, you may use the ciset relational operators directly. In the second option, you may transform ciset relations to relations and the apply the relational operators. Result is then converted to ciset relations.

The operations mentioned in this paper can easily be implemented in any relational database that support objects. A ciset relational database captures the real world more accurately then the traditional database which essentially manages the supporting data only.

REFERENCES

Dubois, D. and Prade, H., 1980, *Fuzzy Sets and Systems: Theory and Applications, Mathematics in Science and Engineering,* Vol. 144, Academic Press, Inc., Orlando, Florida.

Kandel, A., 1986, *Fuzzy Mathematical Techniques with Applications*, Addison-Wesley Pub. Co.

Kaufmann, A., 1973, *Introduction to the Theory of Fuzzy Sets,* Vol. 1, Academic Press, Inc., Orlando, Florida.

Klir, G.J., 1989, "Probability - possibility conversion", In *Proc. Third IFSA Congress,* 408-411, Seattle.

Klir, G.J., 1990, "A principle of uncertainty and information invariance", *Intern. J. of General Systems,* 17 (2&3): 249-275.

Klir, G.J., 1994, "Multivalued logics versus modal logics: Alternative framework for uncertainty", In Wang, P.P., ed., *Advances in fuzzy theory and Technology,* 3-47, Duke Uni., Durham, N.C.

Klir, G.J. and Folger, T., 1988, *Fuzzy Sets, Uncertainty, and Information.* Prentice Hall, Englewood Cliffs, NJ.

Mordeson, J.N., and Nair, P.S., 1998, *Fuzzy Mathematics: An Introduction to for Engineers and Scientists, Studies in Fuzziness and Soft Computing,* Physica-Verlag, Heidelberg, Germany.

Mordeson, J.N., and Nair, P.S., 2000, *Fuzzy Graphs and Fuzzy Hypergraphs, Studies in Fuzziness and Soft Computing, Physica-Verlag, Heidelberg,* Germany.

Nair, P.S., 2004, "Ciset: A generalization of fuzzy sets", *In Proc. NAFIPS 2004,* 502-507, Banff, Canada.

Zimmermann, H.J., 1991, *Fuzzy Set Theory and Its Applications,* Second Edition, Kluwer Academic Publishers, Boston, Dordrecht/London.

L. A. Zadeh, 1965a, "Fuzzy Sets", *Inform. Control* 8: 338-353.

L. A. Zadeh, 1965b, "Fuzzy Sets and Systems", *Proc. Symp. System Theory,* Polytechnic Institute of Brooklyn, 29-37.

A HYBRID DECISION TREE AND NEURAL NETWORK TECHNIQUE FOR ENHANCING KNOWLEDGE DISCOVERY FROM INCOMPLETE SURVEY DATA

RONEN BECKER
School of Business Systems
Monash University
Australia 3800

VINCENT CS LEE
School of Business Systems
Monash University
Australia 3800

SUSAN E BEDINGFIELD
School of Business Systems
Monash University
Australia 3800

ABSTRACT
This research builds on the survey conducted by the Australian Vice Chancellors Committee into student finances. The largest currently available Australian dataset of student finances is explored using an intelligent data mining techniques to compare with the original findings which were based on a simple, statistical analysis. The computational power of classification trees is used to concisely summarize a very complex multi-attribute dataset in order to create a profile of a financially struggling student which will help highlight the attributes which need greater consideration in policy decision making. Rules are generated to highlight the hurdles financially struggling students are facing and are likely to face in the future. Given the limited research done into student poverty, this is one of the first attempts to explore it using an intelligent technique.

INTRODUCTION

Higher Education has long been a high priority in culturally and economically thriving societies. It is also the case that poverty has been an accepted stigma for many students. Society perceives student poverty almost as a rite of passage for becoming an adult. This has traditionally been based on the notion that 'doing it tough' for a few years means eventually coming out stronger. The paucity of solid research into student poverty has implied that it has not become an issue incorporated in to government policy decision-making. There is therefore a motivation to use currently existing data to explore the phenomena that is adversely affecting students' performance. One of the main aims of this paper is to bring this fast becoming student epidemic to the forefront of higher education policy making.

In 2000 a research paper titled 'Paying their way' was commissioned by the Australian Vice Chancellors Committee [1] with the aim of exploring the finances of 34,752 university students from universities across the nation. The findings of the report were acquired by the use of basic statistical techniques. Considering the size of the dataset, the knowledge attained by the AVCC was rather limited as a result of the unsophisticated data analysis. This provides us with a motivation to research student poverty by using the large dataset that was formed for 'Paying their way', using classification trees to mine through the dataset and generate rules for making predictions and create a profile of the dataset. The intention is to enhance the contribution of the AVCC findings.

Most specifically, this paper aims to create a more comprehensive research into student poverty by aiming to achieve the following goals:

- Create a profile of a financially struggling student using a hybrid intelligent methodology to concisely summarize a complex multi-attribute dataset and thus help highlight the attributes requiring greater consideration in policy decision making.
- Use classification trees to generate accurate predictions of the students who are likely to face financial stress at university.

AVCC SURVEY QUESTIONNAIRES AND ANALYSIS OF SURVEY RESULTS

The 34,752 responses of the 80,000 survey /questionnaires which were sent out in 2000 will be used as the dataset for this research. This dataset is the largest and most recent compilation of student finances in Australia and serves as currently one of the highest quality samples of the Australian student population. With a sound analysis of this dataset, further insight into student finances can be reached.

The questionnaires were designed by the AVCC according to predetermined areas of interest. 'Paying their way' was designed to explore all aspects of student finances not just poor students. Nonetheless the dataset has sufficient data for profiling 'the poor student'. The data consists of 65 Questions on the questionnaire broken down to 253 variables in the dataset. The dataset comprises 5 sections containing responses to questions relating to each of the following section headings: course enrolment details, income details, expenditure, student budgets for the year 2000 and personal details.

The Australian Vice Chancellors Committee (AVCC) [1] drew several conclusions in 'Paying their way'. Most of these conclusions had a similar sentiment – financial hardships and the extent to which full-time university students are engaging in longer hours of paid employment are having adverse effects on a student's academic progress.

PREVIOUS RESULTS AND THEIR LIMITATIONS FOR THE POLICY DECISION MAKER

Despite its important findings, the analysis failed to produce insightful discoveries into student poverty. This is not an indication of the quality of the report (which was received as a substantive study on student finances) but rather its aims, and its data discovery process. The dataset was used in a manner which creates findings by summarizing. The use of percentages to report on particular demographics highlights this. For example, "ten percent of students acquire a loan to be able to continue study". The fact that median, mean, standard deviation and statistical significance were used as the only tools of analysis limits the information discovery in the dataset. Summarizing as a form of reporting is a widely used and accepted. However, one of the goals of this report is to investigate the types of hurdles financially disadvantaged students face. This cannot be achieved by merely summarizing the dataset.

From the initial stages of the report there appeared to be a pre-perceived structuralized breakdown of the dataset by means of categorizing and sub-dividing it into areas of interest. As a means of putting together a report that covers a pre-decided scope (such as HECS, student income etc.) this approach is quite appropriate. However, given the magnitude of the data it is difficult to stipulate significant attributes. The analysis has been done on the basis of gender and mode of study (full time vs. part time). Alternatively, a breakdown of the dataset based on the actual merits of the attribute optimizes information discovery in the sense that it divides the data based on their actual relationships and the significance of the attributes. This approach was not taken by the AVCC.

METHODOLOGY

The steps adopted for achieving the goals specified were:

- Predict missing values in the dataset using a Neural network
- Create a profile of the dataset using classification trees
- Generate rules for prediction using cost files to encourage rule creation for small sub datasets

The See5 classification tree algorithm was used to mine the dataset [3]. However the existing missing value algorithm was replaced by a back-propagation algorithm to predict the missing data. Data collection by means of questionnaires and surveys is quite common in research involving student populations. The inherently ambiguous nature of this method of data collection results in attributes with missing values and/or misleading responses. Using a neural network classification tool many previously unused student records can now be salvaged. This can minimize the effects of missing or misleading responses. When making predictions it is important to have as much data available for training and testing as possible. Predicting missing values can in effect increase the available data. When looking at small subsets, such as students who suffer poverty, each record carries a lot of weight. Thus being able to accurately predict the missing values for a particular record which belongs to a small sub population can yield significant benefits.

Profiling is the process of understanding the dataset and its dimensions. By exploring the effects of the attributes on the demographics it can help produce statistics which can yield information that can potentially help in government decision making. The basis of profiling is to explore subsets which represent key groups by comparing them to the whole dataset. In other words it involves identifying problem groups, analysing them and comparing the results of the analysis to the whole dataset. This process will potentially generate information which one can identify as 'trouble spots'.

At times, the overall error rate can be quite low while the error rate for a particular class can be quite high. More importantly, the classifier can make too few predictions about a particular class. The cost file allows the user to 'force' See5 to make predictions. Although these predictions may not be highly accurate, they may still be of great use to the decision maker.

See5 constructs rules based on relationships that exist within the dataset. A five fold cross validation procedure was used to test the validity the rules derived. The prediction feature of decision trees is beneficial as rules give a more realistic idea of what poor students go through, rather than creating a breakdown of the data on predetermined attributes. Given that they can incorporate more than one attribute, it can help a policy maker identify cycles of adversity. Rules provide a context to some problems financially struggling students face. This can potentially lead to improved policy solutions.

RESULTS AND DISCUSSION

This research has shown (refer to Table 1) that neural networks are better at handling missing values than See 5. This is indicated by comparing the See 5 prediction error rates with no missing values, missing values predicted by See 5, and missing values predicted by back propagation network.

The fact that the neural network predictions resulted in a lower error rate on average for both all five training and test sets is a good indication that neural networks are better at handling missing values than See5.

Type of prediction	Average Error Rate (%)
No missing values	7.62
See 5 missing value prediction	9.16
Neural network missing value prediction	8.28

Table 1 Comparison of results for predicting missing values (average over 5 test sets)

In addition, the results show that neural networks can be used as a tool to predict missing values with high accuracy (with this particular dataset). Using a neural network have a significant affect on the dataset increasing the number of useable records in the dataset. Essentially no questionnaire is ignored and the dataset is more representative of all students who completed the survey.
Profiling was achieved by focusing on specific questions in the survey and using the alternative answers in those questions to focus on a subset of the students responding to the survey.
As an example, some characteristics of students who take out loans in order to continue studying are listed below.

- They were far more likely to receive government financial support (65.5% receiving government assistance) as compared with the average (39.02% of the whole dataset).
- Of those students who were employed 26.24% students represented by the subset claimed that their hours of work have a 'great deal' of impact on their performance at university and 47.38% said that they 'frequently' or 'sometimes' miss classes/lectures/tutorials due to needing to attend paid employment.

- In comparison, the whole dataset consisted of 17.06% of students claiming that their hours of work have a 'great deal' of impact their performance at university and 34.44% said that they 'frequently' or 'sometimes' miss classes/lectures/tutorials due to needing to attend paid employment.

At times See5 could not make predictions about small classes. In particular, when endeavouring to predict what kind of student 'sometimes' or 'frequently' missed classes/lectures/tutorials because he/she cannot afford childcare / after hours school care, See5 failed to do. The reason behind this limitation was that students with children make up a very small proportion of the dataset. See5 generates trees which yield the highest information levels, having very few records about a particular class is less likely to result in a high information level. As a result the classifier was more inclined to make predictions about classes that related to more cases. Costs are used as a means of associating a 'cost' to classification errors and thus'encourage' See5 to make predictions. For example, in an attempt to generate some findings about students who 'sometimes' missed classes/lectures/tutorials because they could not afford childcare / after hours school care, Question 53 (see Table 2) was used with cost files applied.

Class	Q53)Do you miss classes/lectures/tutorials because you cannot afford childcare / after hours school care?
1	NEVER miss classes/lectures/tutorials because he/she cannot afford childcare / after hours school care
2	RARELY miss classes/lectures/tutorials because he/she cannot afford childcare / after hours school care
3	SOMETIMES miss classes/lectures/tutorials because he/she cannot afford childcare / after hours school care
4	FREQUENTLY miss classes/lectures/tutorials because he/she cannot afford childcare / after hours school care

Table 2 Question 53 of the dataset

The decision tree that used a cost file had a higher error rate than the one which did not for test cases overall, as seen above. The real benefit of costs files is that more of class C is being classified correctly. Hence, cost files can be applied to encourage See5 to make prediction about classes which make up small proportions of the dataset.

Predictions

A complete review of the rules generated from the dataset is not possible in this discussion, however an example of the rules that are most relevant to a struggling student follows.

Rule:

IF: A student is receiving a student financial supplement from CentreLink

AND He/she pays all the study related costs themselves

AND English is the main language spoken at home

AND they 'frequently' miss tutorials because they cannot afford to travel to campus

THEN they are going to need to take a repayable loan in 2000 to enable them to continue their studies (67.2 % Confidence).

As evident in the rules generated using the classification trees, students who take out loans are more likely to:

- Have to meet start-up costs themselves.
- Have to move out of home for the primary reason of studying. A substantially larger proportion of students who take out loans had to move home/house for the primary reason of attending university with 31.20% as compared to 20.79% from the whole dataset.
- Be much less advantaged than the average student based under 10 different categories.

CONCLUSIONS AND SOME RECOMMENDATIONS FOR GOVERNMENT

Based on our findings it would be fair to suggest that the government need to look at a start up grant for students who have to move out of home and set up. This will at least allow for the often expensive transition phase into university such as paying a bond, buying books, while looking for a job in the demographic took up.

Additional to making predictions about the types of students who will need government aid in the future we are also able to highlight the areas of government policy which are working well and the areas that are not. For instance, a policy maker may use this approach to measure how equitable education system is for all students by balancing up the expenses of students who receive financial aid from the government with those students who do not.

Using Decision trees techniques more information and hence rules can be extracted from the same dataset as compared to the simple statistical analysis tools. This has been demonstrated in the additional findings given in the form of predictions and profiling.

Given the nature of surveys, with their ambiguities and subjectivity the dataset of student finances has many inconsistencies, which explains the relatively low confidence levels of some of the rules generated. By hybridizing decision trees with neural networks, the prediction errors can be reduced and other hidden knowledge can be discovered.

This paper has illustrated how an intelligent hybrid network can be used as a tool by government decision maker to identify student poverty and deficiencies in government policy.

REFERENCES

[1] Long, M., Hayden, M., *Paying their way*. 2001: Australian Vice Chancellors Committee, Australia.

[2] Negnevitsky, M., *Artificial Intelligence: A Guide to Intelligent Systems*. 2002: Pearson Education Limited, England.

[3] Quinlan J R *Programs for Machine Learning* California 1993: Morgan Kaufmann Publishers, California, USA.

DIRECT KERNEL PLS FOR SPECTRAL SOURCE IDENTIFICATION

Robert A. Bress (bressr@rpi.edu), **M. J. Embrechts, T. Repoff*, S. Sutherland****
Department of Decision Sciences and Engineering Systems
Rensselaer Polytechnic Institute
Troy, New York 12180-3590
*Applied Statistics Lab
General Electric Global Research Center
1 Research Circle
Niskayuna, NY 12309
**General Electric Infrastructure
205 Lowell St.
Wilmington, MA 01887-2941

ABSTRACT
Since the 1950's, academic and industrial institutions have used spectrometry to identify the composition of unknown substances. Spectrometers work by reading diffraction patterns of infrared light after it is passed through a substance. A peak matching or a stepwise regression algorithm is often used to determine the true identity of the substance in question by comparing the resulting spectrum to a library of known spectra. This paper introduces direct kernel partial least squares (DK-PLS) as a novel means for the classification of spectra where the library contains many classes (> 40). Direct kernel methods use a kernel transformation as a pre-processing step as a way to incorporate nonlinear relationships in the data prior to model building. Direct kernel PLS with a radial basis function (RBF) kernel is shown to have excellent classification accuracy and the ability to successfully classify mixed spectra.

INTRODUCTION

This paper introduces direct kernel PLS (DK-PLS) for the identification of compound mixtures from spectra. PLS [1-3] was first introduced in the mid seventies by Herman Wold, and is one of the methods of choice for chemometrics modeling. DK-PLS is a way to elegantly incorporate non-linearity into a PLS model by considering the kernel transform as a data transformation in the pre-processing stage. Hilbert first addressed the use of kernels in the early 1900's. A kernel can be defined as a matrix of similarity measures between either the data itself or with other data sets (e.g., [4]). The kernel matrix is symmetrical and each entry contains a similarity measurement between two data vectors.

Linear as well as nonlinear measures may be used for the kernel transform. The dot product is an example of a linear kernel. The Radial Basis Function (RBF) or Gaussian kernel is widely used as a nonlinear transformation in the literature and is the kernel function used in this study. This kernel is defined as a matrix where each kernel entry k_{ij} is defined as:

$$k_{ij} = e^{-\frac{\left\|\vec{x}_i - \vec{x}_j\right\|}{2\sigma^2}} \quad (1)$$

In this case, the kernel entry contains the square of the Euclidean distance (or two-norm) between data points. Since this measure is actually a dissimilarity, rather than a similarity, the negative exponential converts the dissimilarity measure to a nonlinear similarity measure. This exponential also contains a free parameter, σ, which is the Parzen window width for the RBF kernel. The appropriate value for σ is usually determined by an additional tuning (or hyper-tuning) on an external validation set.

Contrary to kernel PLS or K-PLS, introduced by Svante World [5] and reintroduced by Rosipal and Trejo [6], the kernel transformation in DK-PLS is applied in this study as a separate data transformation before applying a traditional partial least squares regression model.

IDENTIFICATION OF SPECTRA

Identification of chemical compounds from spectra can be challenging for a number of reasons. First, many substances may have similar spectra making them difficult to distinguish between. Secondly, there are many potential sources of measurement variability. These sources of variability include the spectrometer itself, and the temperature and humidity of the outside environment. Finally, different samples of the same substance can yield slightly different spectra readings.

Past work using kernel techniques on different types of spectra data has been reported in the literature. Some work using K-PLS on spectra for the identification of plastic substances was conducted by van den Broek et al [7]. Rosipal et al. use a Kernel Principal Component Analysis (K-PCA) as a technique for feature extraction in signal detection and de-noising applications [6, 8-9]. Detailed descriptions regarding PLS and K-PCA as a classification technique are given in [2-3, 10].

A more challenging problem associated with spectrometry involves the identification of mixtures of different substances. Often hazardous or illegal chemical substances are mixed with other substances thus disguising the spectrum one might be searching for. It is desirable not only identify the presence of different substances in a spectrum but also the percentage breakdown of how the substance is composed. This is generally done using a peak-matching algorithm that tends to be somewhat inaccurate. This paper describes the results obtained from the use of a multi-output KPLS algorithm as a novel means for mixed spectra identification. In this case, there is an output variable relating to each "pure" substance contained in the training library. The results from the KPLS algorithm are obtained in a format that is similar to the example in Table I. The prediction results are scaled relative to each other and a minimum threshold is set to note the actual presence of a substance in the spectra. For example if we set the minimum threshold at 0.05 then Test Spectrum #1 in Table 1 would be classified as Substance #1. We would estimate Test Spectrum #2 to be about a 50/50 mixture of Substance #1 and Substance #3.

Table I. Output for K-PLS classification

	Prediction Variables		
	Substance #1	**Substance #2**	**Substance #3**
Test Spectrum #1	0.93	0.04	0.03
Test Spectrum #2	0.45	0.04	0.51

The training set contains 190 spectra of different "pure" (i.e. non-mixture) substances. Actually, the dataset includes some commonly used pharmaceutical items that are composed of different substances however by "pure" we mean that the substances in the dataset are not made up of othebr sustances in that set. For each substance in the training set, there are five sample spectra. Figure 1 is an example of 5 spectra readings taken on the same substance. Clearly there is some variability in the readings due to conditions relating to the spectrometer. There is also a validation set consisting of some mixed and some pure substances.

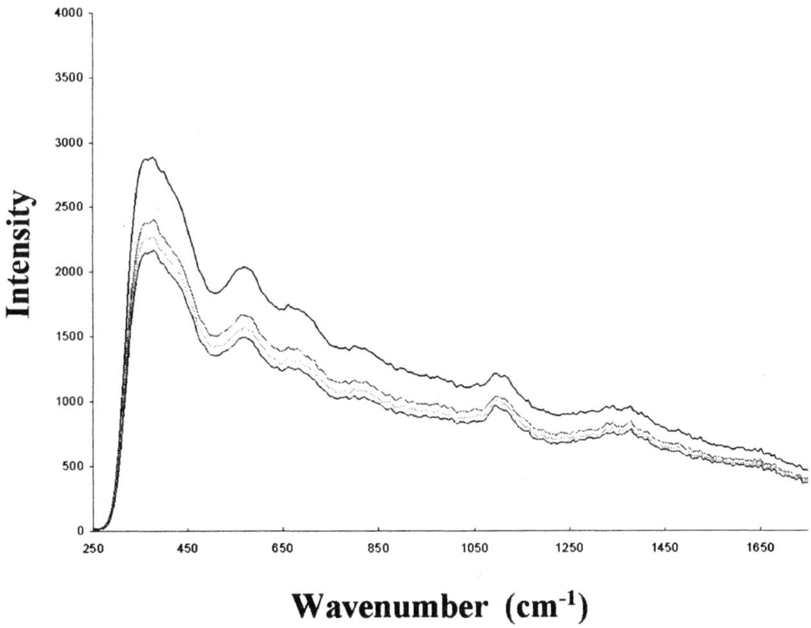

Figure1. Five spectral readings of substance X.

The validation set also contains pure substances not found in the training set. This is likely to occur with an industrial use of this machine since the library cannot be exhaustive.

The original data consists of 2048 measures of intensity at different wavelengths (actually wavenumbers which are equal to 1 divided by wavelength) for each substance. Each substance was originally measured at different (though similar) sets of wavelengths. In order to standardize the data, each spectrum was interpolated and scaled between wavenumbers of 101 cm^{-1} and 3000 cm^{-1}. These were chosen because all of the original spectra measurements were started and ended at or near these points. The data were then interpolated linearly between those points such that each spectrum was reduced to 256 points. We choose 256 points so wavelet transformations can be done as described later.

In order to maximize the classification performance of DK-PLS, further preprocessing is necessary. A per pattern (horizontal) normalization (or Mahalanobis scaling) is done whereby for each spectral data series, the mean is subtracted from the spectral data at each spectral point, and the result is divided by the standard deviation. Applying a second-order differencing allows us to transform the series such that it becomes stationary and thus serves to regularize the data. Furthermore, a Daubechies 8 wavelet transform was applied.

These transformations are applied consistently to the training library and the validation and test data. Following this, another normalization or Mahalanobis transform is applied but this time across attributes rather than data vectors. For each attribute in the validation or test set, we subtract by the mean as determined only from that attribute's data in the training set. Similarly, we divide by the standard deviation as determined from the training attributes. Finally, we apply the radial basis function kernel transformation to our data.

RESULTS AND ANALYSIS

For a preliminary analysis a system was trained for 79 classes and 950 sample spectra. The system was generally capable of correctly identifying single components for the test data in all cases. It was reasonably effective for indicating mixture data with the correct mixture ingredients if the minority compound in the mixtures would exceed a certain minimal threshold. Typical results are displayed in Figure 2.

CONCLUSIONS

Multi-output direct kernel PLS is a novel approach to classifying spectra. Even though PLS and kernel PLS are usually presented in a multiple output context, this capability has not been exploited for multi-class classification before. This approach is able to classify "pure" spectra accurately, and can also be used to identify mixture spectra. This technique requires often overlooked preprocessing in order to work well. Future work in this area should consider the effect of each

Mixture results for Test Sequence 1

Substance class # 11 has 100.00 percent (Library Sequence 5)

Mixture results for Test Sequence 2

Substance class # 57 has 100.00 percent (Library Sequence 8)

Mixture results for Test Sequence 3

Substance class # 57 has 55.30 percent (Library Sequence 5)

Substance class # 51 has 44.70 percent (Library Sequence 3)

Mixture results for Test Sequence 4

Substance class # 57 has 52.34 percent (Library Sequence 5)

Substance class # 51 has 47.66 percent (Library Sequence 9)

Figure 2. Typical results from K-PLS code for mixture spectra.

of these preprocessing steps when used in coordination because we have found that in some instances all may not be necessary. Direct kernel PLS is likely to be most valuable in cases where there may be excess sources of variability in the spectra readings. In these cases, DK-PLS serves as a more robust technique when compared to typical peak-matching algorithms. The results here illustrate how we are able to use direct kernels to model nonlinear problems while still using a linear technique such as PLS.

ACKNOWLEDGEMENT

The authors hereby acknowledge…

REFERENCES

[1] H. Wold, "Path Models with Latent Variables: The NIPALS Approach," in Balock, H. M., Ed., *Quantitative Sociology: International Perspectives on Mathematical and Statistical Model Building*, Academic Press, NY, pp. 307-357, 1975.

[2] S. Wold, M. Sjöström, and L. Erikson, "PLS-Regression: A Basic Tool of Chemometrics," *Chemometrics and Intelligent Laboratory Systems*, vol. 58, pp. 109-130, 2001.

[3] P. Geladi and B. R. Kowalski, "Partial Least-Squares Regression: A Tutorial," *Analytica Chimica Acta*, vol. 185, pp. 1-17, 1986.

[4] N. Cristianini and J. Shawe-Taylor, *An Introduction to Support Vector Machines and other Kernel-Based Learning Methods*: Cambridge Press, 2003.

[5] F. Lindgren, P. Geladi, and S. Wold [1993] "The Kernel Algorithm for PLS," *Journal of Chemometrics*, vol. 7, *pp.* 45-59.

[6] R. Rosipal and L. J. Trejo, "Kernel Partial Least Squares Regression in Reproducing Kernel Hilbert Space," *Journal of Machine Learning Research*, vol. 2, pp. 97-123, 2001.

[7] W. H. A. M. Van den Broek, E. P. P. A. Derks, E. W. Van den Ven, D. Wienke, P. Geladi, and L. M. C. Buydens, "Plastic Identification by Remote Sensing Spectroscopic NIR Imaging using Kernel Partial Least Squares (KPLS)," *Chemometrics and Intelligent Laboratory Systems*, vol. 35, 1996.

[8] R. Rosipal, M. Girolami, L. J. Trejo, and A. Cichocki, "Kernel PCA Feature Extraction and De-Noising in Non-Linear Regression," *Neural Computing and Applications*, vol. 10, 2001.

[9] R. Rosipal, M. Girolami, and L. Trejo, "Kernel PCA Feature Extraction of Event-Related Potentials for Human Signal Detection Performance," *Computing and Information Systems*, vol. 7, 2000.

[10] A. M. Jade, B. Srikanth, V. K. Jayaraman, B. D. Kulkarni, J. P. Jong, and L. Priya, "Feature Extraction and Denoising using Kernel PCA," *Chenical Engineering Science*, vol. 58, 2003.

COMPUTER INTRUSION DETECTION THROUGH PREDICTIVE MODELS

Paul F. Evangelista, Mark J. Embrechts
Department of Decision Sciences and Engineering Systems

Boleslaw K. Szymanski
Department of Computer Science

Rensselaer Polytechnic Institute
Troy, New York 12180

Abstract. Interrupting, corrupting, or destroying today's information systems is a real threat. Computer hackers are the nucleus of this threat. This article explores techniques to detect computer intruders based upon typical command usage of authentic users compared against non-authentic users, representing hackers. The hypothesis is that computing behavior of authentic users is somewhat unique and can be differentiated from others. In order to explore this hypothesis, several different variables that measure computing commands are created and utilized to perform predictive modeling to determine the presence or absence of a hacker. This is a classification problem that involves two known groups: intruders and non intruders. Techniques explored include predictive modeling through clustering and kernel partial least squares.

1 Introduction

Digital firms must augment preventive computer security measures by implementing intrusion detection systems (IDS) that monitor the network and detect fraudulent or unusual activity. Certain characteristics of computer IDS define their effectiveness. The typical measures of an IDS involve accuracy of detection, often expressed as a true positive rating and false positive rating. The overall effectiveness of an IDS can be shown on a receiver operating characteristic (ROC) curve, which plots the full range of a classification system's true positive and false positive rates. Typically, minimizing false positive alarms while maintaining an acceptable rate of true positives is paramount. Intrusion detection is inherently a statistical problem (DuMouchel et al. 2001). The problem involves collecting a sample of data, describing the data through statistical attributes, and then classifying the data based upon these attributes.

We have closely examined the work of Matthius Schonlau, a researcher with the Rand Corporation who is the creator of the dataset analyzed in this article. Schonlau's work includes analyzing unpopular commands, real time hypothesis testing, principal components regression, and structural zeroes(DuMouchel et al. 2001, DuMouchel and Schonlau 1998, DuMouchel and Schonlau 1999, Schonlau and Theus 2000, Schonlau and Theus 1998). Following the work of Schonlau provided a validity check of our new text mining programs written in Perl and provided a solid foundation of knowledge gained from his thorough analysis of the data.

Understanding the structure of the data is necessary before any programming or initial analysis can be conducted. The data set consists of 50 users with each user contributing a stream of 15,000 truncated UNIX commands. The user's data stream is further divided into blocks of 100 commands, thus creating 150 blocks of commands for each user. The first 50 blocks of data is training data only (contains no masquerading data), and the remaining 100 blocks of data contains masquerading data that appears based on a probability. Given that there are 50 users, this implies that in total there are 5,000 tuples of data in the non-intruded initial set and 10,000 tuples of data that potentially contain intrusion data. Since the true outcome of each of these subsequent 10,000 tuples is known, understand that there are only 231 intruded tuples. Only 2.31% of the data contains intruders, which makes this a very difficult and unbalanced classification problem.

The initial programming effort involved determining the data dictionary (list of every unique command), the frequency of the commands, and the popularity of the commands (number of users who use distinct command). In an effort to validate the programs, we compared our programming results with Schonlau's analysis (Schonlau and Theus 2000) and observed virtually identical results.

2 Method

After validating the Perl programs and developing a solid understanding of the dataset, new variables were necessary to create different techniques that accurately predict the presence or absence of an intruder. The machine learning approach involving these variables is fundamentally different from Schonlau's technique. These variables were created with the goal of developing a technique to measure the behavior of computer users in a manner that captures the differences between intruders and authentic users. The new variables and the prediction models involving these new variables work primarily with the latter 10,000 commands from each user. Therefore, with each user contributing 100 tuples of data for this section, there are a total of 5,000 tuples that we will examine. These new variables we are discussing measure the overall characteristics of the 100 commands contained within the tuple, and these variables can be seen in Table 1.

Table 1. Description of new variables

	Name of Variable	Description
1	% Unix	Percent of commands that are Unix
2	% Top 20	Fraction of commands that are within the top 20 most popular commands
3	% Internet	Fraction of commands that are internet/email commands
4	Average Uniqueness	Averages Uniqueness (number between .02 and .98) of commands in tuple
5	Average Frequency	Averages the frequency of each command in the tuple
6	% Foreign	Percent of commands never seen before
7	x_u value	x_u value from Schonlau's algorithm[8]; essentially provides an index that is based upon usage pattern of that particular user

Throughout this analysis we needed to separate the data into a training set and a testing set. The overall dataset contained 5000 tuples of data (50 users contributing 100 tuples of data each), and we randomly sequenced the tuples in order to prevent any effect due to the order. Secondly, we utilized the first 4000 random tuples for training and tested on the remaining 1000. This decision to split the data in such a way was arbitrary and simply based on the experience of the authors. Throughout the comparison of every technique, we maintained the same random order and split of the data in an effort to achieve consistent comparisons.

2.1 Clustering

Clustering is a technique commonly used for more than two groups or when the number of groups is unknown. However, due to the nature of clustering (determining a measure or method to separate groups), clustering can serve as an effective tool for discrimination. Initial clustering attempts using the K-means and Euclidean distances yielded poor results. We found that reducing dimensionality and utilizing Minkoski's equation for distance demonstrated promise. Through trial and error, we determined that the variable measuring the percent of internet commands and the x_u value from Schonlau's algorithm(Schonlau and Theus 2000) produced good separation between the groups. For each tuple of data in the test data, we measure Minkoski's distance to the centroid observed in the training data, and then the tuple is classified into the group that measures the closest(Johnson and Wichern 2002).

$$d(\mathbf{x}, \bar{\mathbf{x}}_{\mathbf{no\_int}}) = [\sum_{i=1}^{p} |x_i - \bar{x}_{no\_int}|^m]^{1/m} \tag{1}$$

$$d(\mathbf{x}, \bar{\mathbf{x}}_{\mathbf{int}}) = [\sum_{i=1}^{p} |x_i - \bar{x}_{int}|^m]^{1/m} \tag{2}$$

The above equations represent Minkoski's distance equation, where $\bar{x}_{int}$ represents the centroid of intrusion training data, and $\bar{x}_{no\_int}$ represents the centroid of non intrusion training data. p is the number of variables measured ($p = 2$ provided the best results).

It was important to collect a range of values for this classification tool in order to evaluate overall performance of the system. In order to obtain a range of confusion matrices, we introduced an offset value. Initially, if $d(\mathbf{x}, \bar{\mathbf{x}}_{\mathbf{int}})$ represents the distance between a test data point and the centroid of intrusion data, if $d(\mathbf{x}, \bar{\mathbf{x}}_{\mathbf{int}})$ was greater than $d(\mathbf{x}, \bar{\mathbf{x}}_{\mathbf{no\_int}})$ then the decision rule was to classify the point as a non intruder. However, by introducing an offset variable w, the new rule assigned a point as a non intruder if $d(\mathbf{x}, \bar{\mathbf{x}}_{\mathbf{no\_int}}) < d(\mathbf{x}, \bar{\mathbf{x}}_{\mathbf{no\_int}}) - w$, where w ranged from .2 to 1.2. This range of values for w produced an array of confusion matrices, again providing a method of plotting an ROC curve. The ROC curve for our clustering analysis with Minkoski's distance metric is shown in Figure 1.

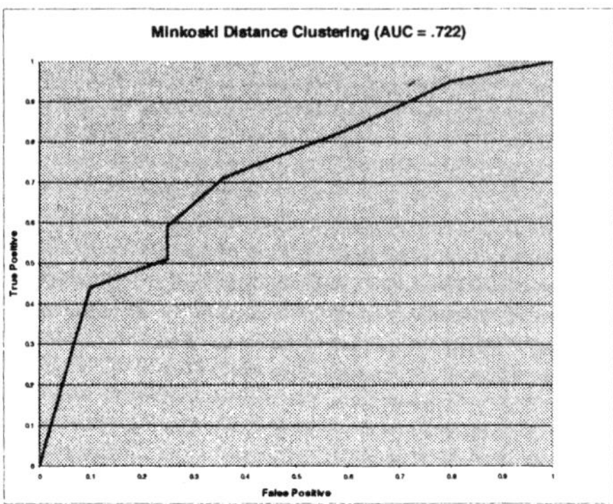

Figure 1. ROC Curve for Clustering with Minkoski's Distance Metric

The area under the curve is .722, which is a fair performance considering the unsupervised nature of prediction with clustering. Of particular interest in this ROC curve is the very steep slope for small values of the false positive representing a good IDS for low false positive values.

2.2 Determining Optimal Variable Combinations for K-PLS Prediction

The above analysis of these new variables provides insight into the relationship between the variables and the descriptive power of these variables. Exploring fundamental properties of the variables is an important first step.

The choice of learning machines is often complicated and data dependent. This analysis utilizes one learning machine for the sake of consistency - Rosipal's kernel partial least squares(Rosipal and Trejo 2001). This learning machine provided good results and remaining with one learning machine provides a consistent measure of comparison between preprocessing techniques and combinations of variables.

The most obvious method for prediction modeling given the set of new variables described is to simply represent each tuple of data with a combination of these seven variables. Let us call this the *seven feature model.* This is the initial approach. The file to be processed by the learning machine contained 5000 tuples of data, each containing 7 feature variables. **This *seven feature model* achieved exceptional results, with an AUC of .907.**

The technique tested next expands the details of the features in an attempt to improve the prediction. Each of the first six variables in the *seven feature model* is an average or percentage for the entire tuple of 100 commands considered. The seventh variable, Schonlau's x_u variable, represents a value which is a measure of the entire tuple. Therefore, each command can be represented by six different values, each value representing variables one through six. The result of this approach is a tuple of 601 features (the extra feature is Schonlau's x_u value). The results of this *601 feature model* were surprisingly not better than the seven feature model. The *601 feature model* was cumbersome because of its size, required much longer processing time, and did not predict as well. The best AUC achieved with the *601 feature model* was .77. We offer two explanations as to why this model did not predict as well:

1. Consider each variable as some type of random variable. The original *seven feature model* contained averages and percentages - a function of a summation of each variable for each command of the tuple of 100 commands. This average or percentage represents a statistic, and it is likely that these statistics are functions of sufficient statistics, which implies that regardless of how the observations are manipulated, further information regarding the true parameters of the underlying probability density functions that form these statistics cannot be obtained. Therefore, improvement is not an option if the variables calculated are already functions of sufficient statistics.

2. This file is too large and cumbersome for the KPLS learning machine. There is a curse of dimensionality. When the dimensionality grows too large, classification becomes very difficult because every tuple becomes equally dissimilar. Reduced and meaningful dimensions provide much more predictive power.

The evaluation of several more preprocessing techniques further supported the idea of poor performance with expanded variables that could be represented as some type of average or summation for an entire tuple. Additional preprocessing techniques evaluated eliminated Schonlau's x_u value in an effort to eliminate the effect of this index-type feature. These additional preprocessing techniques are described in the below table.

Table 2. Preprocessing Techniques and Results

Preprocessing Technique	Description of Variables	σ	AUC
no_xu_value	Six variables without Schonlau's x_u value	1	.829
Enhanced Features (a)	Same as no_xu_value plus an indicator for commands never seen from the user	3	.87
Enhanced Features (b)	Same as (a) except user number (integer between 1 and 50) included as a variable	1	**.917**
Rank Order	There are 635 distinct commands. Rank order from 1-635 based upon frequency. Now the tuple can be represented by a vector of 100 variables, with each feature being the number that represents the rank order of the command. The number 636 will represent any commands not seen in the training data.	1	.683
636feature	Utilize a vector of 636 variables for each tuple of data. Each position in the vector corresponds to the tuple's frequency of a distinct command, and position 636 will correspond to the frequency of foreign /never seen commands.	all values	.5

It is intentional that the new techniques discussed in this paper are not compared against Schonlau's techniques. Schonlau builds the statistics for his models from the first 5,000 authentic commands from each user; this is an unsupervised approach. He tests his techniques with the subsequent 10,000 commands. The techniques discussed in this paper focus on the subsequent 10,000 commands for each user and generally utilize a supervised approach. The techniques in this paper are not comparable with Schonlau's techniques; they are fundamentally different.

3 Results

The initial absence of Schonlau's x_u value created degraded performance as expected. Since the x_u value is an overall indicator of whether or not an intruder is present, it is a powerful predictor and hampers our clarity in determining the effectiveness of other variables. However, after improving our model by including two new variables, we recovered this degraded performance and improved even further. The two variables added to this preprocessing technique, commands never seen from the particular user (simply a 0 or 1 value) and the user number (integer between 1 and 50) provide an immense impact on the predictive power. This model titled *Enhanced Features (b)* achieved an AUC of .917 at $\sigma = 1$. It is likely that these two variables provide a personalization of each tuple, effectively providing a signature of each user that the learning machine identifies and uses to improve performance.

The other interesting thread of these results involves the continued poor performance of expanded preprocessing techniques that provide the learning machine with the raw data of each command as opposed to a summation or average. It is difficult to ascertain exactly why this phenomena occurs. During the discussion of the 601 feature model, we hypothesize that this degraded performance occurs because summations and averages are likely functions of sufficient statistics, and these sufficient statistics provide as much information as possible regarding the variable. The poor performance could also be an indicator that much noise and irrelevant data is digested by the learning machine, creating convoluted results.

4 Conclusions

The significance of research in this field expands well beyond the digital realm and computer intrusion detection. Intrusion detection is a security problem. This security could involve an airport, a national asset, vital infrastructure, or even the physical borders of our country. Every day Americans spend millions of dollars to secure their way of life, and this research presents innovative techniques to provide enhanced security. Although the vehicle of this research involves computer intrusion and hackers, these same techniques could be generalized to enhance the security of any important resource.

Acknowledgments

The authors would like to acknowledge Yongqiang Zhang and Joel Branch for their critical discussion and thoughts on this research.

References

DuMouchel, William, Wen-Hua Ju, Alan F. Karr, Matthius Schonlau, Martin Theus, and Yehuda Vardi [2001], "Computer Intrusion: Detecting Masquerade", Statistical Science, Vol. 16, No. 1, pp. 1-17.

DuMouchel, William and Matthius Schonlau [1998], "A Fast Computer Intrusion Detection Algorithm Based on Hypothesis Testing of Command Transition Probabilities", The Fourth International Conference of Knowledge Discovery and Data Mining, August 27-31, New York, pp. 189-193.

DuMouchel, William and Matthius Schonlau [1999], "A Comparison of Test Statistics for Computer Intrusion Detection Based on Principal Components Regression of Transition Probabilities", Proceedings of the 30th Symposium on the Interface: Computing Science and Statistics, pp. 404-413.

Embrechts, Mark J. [2003], $Analyze^{TM}$, Version 6.86, Rensselear Polytechnic Institute, Available from: http://www.rpi.edu/locker/82/001182/[Accessed 4 June 2004].

Fawcett, Tom and Foster Provost [2001] "Robust Classification for Imprecise Environments", Machine Learning Journal, Vol. 42(3), pp. 203-231.

Johnson, Richard A. and Dean W. Wichern [2002], Applied Multivariate Statistical Analysis, Fifth Edition, Prentice Hall.

Huseyin Cavusoglu, Birendra Mishra, and Srinivasan Raghunathan [2003] "Configuration of Intrusion Detection Systems", International Conference on Information Systems (ICIS), Seattle, December 2003.

Rosipal, Roman and Leonard J. Trejo [2001] "Kernel Partial Least Squares Regression in Reproducing Kernel Hilbert Space", Journal of Machine Learning Research, Vol. 2, pp. 97-123.

Schonlau, Matthius and Martin Theus [2000], "Detecting Masquerades in Intrusion Detection Based on Unpopular Commands", Information Processing Letters, Vol. 76, Issues1-2, pp. 33-38.

Schonlau, Matthius and Martin Theus [1998], "Intrusion Detection Based on Structural Zeroes", Statistical Computing & Graphics Newsletter, Vol. 9, No 1, pp. 12 - 17.

DATA MINING AGRICULTURAL DATA USING NEURAL NETWORKS

TYSON MCMILLAN
West Texas A&M University,
McNair Scholars Program
Canyon, Texas

RAJAN ALEX
West Texas A&M University
Department of CIS
Canyon, Texas

ABSTRACT
This paper analyzes agricultural data in order to discover patterns in the data, and to develop a model that predicts the selling price of beef cattle in Texas. We utilized a data mining method in neural networks known as back-propagation algorithm, and a computer program to implement the model. The variables needed for this model were chosen by interviewing experts who offered information pertinent to the agricultural process. Numerical data for the variables spans over five years. The relevance analysis will be performed using a statistical analysis method. After statistical analysis, the data for the statistically significant variables will serve as the input and output patterns needed for the neural network model.

INTRODUCTION

Today's beef cattle ranching is a complex process where individual animals are raised for being sold as beef in cattle auction centers. It would be very beneficial for cattle ranchers and feedlot operators to be able to predict the selling price of beef while the individual animals are being raised. This work seeks to acquire data and explore a selecting process by which the data related to the unit beef selling price can be transformed, reduced, and then modeled to predict the selling price. The prediction is the last part of this work. It is preceded by an appropriate relevance analysis. The relevance analysis attempts to identify factors that do not contribute to the prediction. These factors can then be deleted from further consideration. We discovered the initial set of factors that affect the unit beef selling price after interviewing experts in the field of agricultural business, and obtained the actual data needed for the analysis from various sources.

DATA COLLECTION PROCESS

The data collection process involves identifying the factors that affect beef price, and identifying the data that represents the factors. During this process, we interviewed experts in the field of agricultural business. We were interested, more specifically, in each individual expert's knowledge with respect to the beef cattle industry. The following 15 variables including the dependent variable were identified during the data collection process.

Y: Average monthly price received by Texas farmers for beef cattle (dollars per cwt) [1]
X_1: Average monthly price received by Texas farmers for calves (dollars per cwt) [1]
X_2: Average monthly price received by Texas farmers for corn (dollars per bushel) [1]
X_3: Average monthly price received by Texas farmers for wheat (dollars per bushel) [1]
X_4: Average monthly price received by Texas farmers for all hay—alfalfa hay plus other hay (dollars per ton) [1]
X_5: Average monthly price received by Texas farmers for sorghum (dollars per cwt) [1]
X_6: Average monthly price received by Texas farmers for cottonseed (dollars per ton) [1]
X_7: Monthly United States feeder and stocker cattle and calf price (dollars per cwt) [2]
X_8: Texas monthly supply of cattle on feed: number on feed by class, 1000+ capacity feedlots (per 1000 head) [1]
X_9: Monthly sales of livestock at Texas auction markets (per 1000 head) [1]
X_{10}: Monthly number of cattle slaughtered in Texas (per 1000 head) [1]
X_{11}: Monthly number of calves slaughtered in Texas (per 1000 head) [1]
X_{12}: Monthly Texas range and pasture condition [1, 3]
X_{13}: Palmer Drought Severity Index of all 10 Texas regions (inches) [4, 5,6]
X_{14}: Monthly precipitation totals of all 10 Texas regions (inches) [1, 7, 8]

Tables 2 and 3 give the regression analysis of the full model, and the correlation coefficient matrix for all the variables is given in Table 3.

Regression Statistics	
Multiple R	0.9149
R Square	0.8370
Adjusted R Square	0.7864
Standard Error	2.7086
Observations	60

Table 1-Summary Output

	df	SS	MS	F	p-value
Regression	14	1695.996674	121.1426196	16.512852	2.85613E-13
Residual	45	330.1318262	7.336262805		
Total	59	2026.1285			

Table 2-ANOVA

	Y	X_1	X_2	X_3	X_4	X_5	X_6	X_7	X_8	X_9	X_{10}	X_{11}	X_{12}	X_{13}	X_{14}
Y	1														
X1	0.860	1													
X2	-0.225	-0.380	1												
X3	-0.087	-0.337	0.800	1											
X4	-0.381	-0.438	0.034	0.117	1										
X5	-0.166	-0.344	0.878	0.823	0.124	1									
X6	-0.254	-0.312	-0.028	0.017	-0.209	-0.022	1								
X7	0.817	0.897	-0.407	-0.361	-0.508	-0.399	-0.094	1							
X8	0.447	0.464	-0.382	-0.384	-0.380	-0.253	0.300	0.645	1						
X9	-0.302	-0.296	-0.096	-0.138	0.190	-0.137	0.070	-0.147	-0.271	1					
X10	-0.184	-0.190	-0.002	-0.012	0.448	-0.064	-0.430	-0.273	-0.528	0.485	1				
X11	-0.221	-0.200	-0.051	-0.167	-0.142	-0.135	0.346	-0.120	0.047	0.284	-0.081	1			
X12	-0.105	-0.048	-0.029	-0.027	0.308	-0.104	-0.204	-0.017	-0.372	0.427	0.436	0.038	1		
X13	-0.034	-0.171	0.614	0.635	-0.190	0.640	0.150	-0.214	-0.165	-0.338	-0.237	-0.203	0.064	1	
X14	-0.242	-0.239	0.303	0.295	0.243	0.275	0.068	-0.319	-0.194	-0.066	0.184	0.157	0.208	0.394	1

Table 3-Correlation Coefficient Matrix

When the final step-down regression analysis was performed, the following summary output (Table 4), ANOVA (Table 5), and significant variables (Table 6) were achieved.

Regression Statistics	
Multiple R	0.8964
R Square	0.8035
Adjusted R Square	0.7930
Standard Error	2.6664
Observations	60

Table 4-Summary Output

	df	SS	MS	F	p-value
Regression	3	1627.974236	542.6580786	76.3243178	.93008E-20
Residual	56	398.1542642	7.109897576		
Total	59	2026.1285			

Table 5-ANOVA

	Coefficients	*Standard Error*	*t Stat*	*P-value*	*Lower 95%*	*Upper 95%*	*Lower 95.0%*	*Upper 95.0%*	***Partial F***
Intercept	9.77178	4.75066	2.05693	0.04436	0.25506	19.28850	0.25506	19.28850	4.23096
X1	0.33383	0.06701	4.98173	0.00001	0.19959	0.46807	0.19959	0.46807	24.81762
X3	2.90402	0.74161	3.91581	0.00025	1.41839	4.38965	1.41839	4.38965	15.33358
X7	0.21006	0.09251	2.27076	0.02703	0.02475	0.39537	0.02475	0.39537	5.15635

Table 6-Significant Variables

THE NEURAL NETWORK MODEL

The neural network model that uses the back-propagation algorithm is applied to the data for the significant variables that are obtained from the step-down regression analysis. The dependent variable values of the training phase of the algorithm are compared with the network's predicated value. The weights along the network's nodes are adjusted so that the future predications better approximate the actual values. The back-propagation algorithm used in this work is restated below [9]:

(1) Initialize the weights matrix $W^m = [w_{ij}^m]$ to random numbers between 0 and 1 for $m = 1,2,\cdots,M$. Each element of the weight matrix w_{ij}^m is the weight on the connection from node *j* in the layer *m*-1 to the node *i* in the layer *m*. Assume layer zero is the input layer and layer *M* is the output layer. There are *k* nodes in the input layer and there is one node in layer *M*, the output layer. Set the *Error* = 0.

(2) Set the next input vector to the input pattern denoted by $V^0 = (1, v_1^0, \cdots, v_k^0)^T$. The first component is set 1 so that w_{i0}^1 is the bias in layer I, for $i = 1,2,\cdots,k$.

(3) Take $v_0^m = 1$. Using the formula $h_i^m = \sum_j w_{ij}^m v_j^{m-1}$, compute $v_i^m = \phi(h_i^m), i \geq 1$, where $\phi(x) = \dfrac{1}{1+e^{-x}}$, and get the vectors $v^1, v^2 \cdots, v^M$. Since the output layer *M* has only one output, denote the single element vector v^M by O.

(4) Compute $Error = Error + \frac{1}{2}(T - O)^2$, where *T* is the target value for the input pattern, and *O* is as in step 3.

(5) Compute $\delta_i^M = \phi'(h_i^M)(T - O)$, $\phi'(x)$ denotes the derivative of $\phi(x)$. Compute δ^m for preceding layers using $\delta_i^{m-1} = \phi'(h_i^{m-1}) \sum_j w_{ji}^m \delta_j^m$, for $m = M, M-1, \cdots, 2$.

(6) Compute $\Delta w_{ij}^{m} = \eta \delta_{i}^{m} v_{j}^{m-1}$ and update the weights $w_{ij}^{m\,(new)} = w_{ij}^{m\,(old)} + \Delta w_{ij}^{m}$, $m = 1,2,\cdots,M$. Go to step 2 if there is a next pattern to be learned. If no more input patterns to be learned and the *Error* is greater than a desired minimum value, set the *Error* to zero and go to step 2 beginning with the first input; otherwise, go to the next step.

(7) When the *Error* is small enough, we say the network has "learned" the patterns. At this point, use steps 2 and 3 to predict the output for the next set of input that needs to be predicted.

COMPUTER IMPLEMENTATION OF ALGORITHM AND OUTPUT

We implemented the algorithm using a C++ program. The neural network architecture used 3 input nodes, 2 intermediate layers with 3 nodes in each layer, and a single output node. We utilized the first 53 observations for the significant variables in the data set as input patterns during the learning phase. The remaining observations were used for prediction after the learning phase. The learning rate was set to 0.085. The target error was within 0.0009.

Year	Month	Predicted Price (dollars per cwt)	Target Price (dollars per cwt)	Difference $\lvert Predicted\ Price - Target\ Price \rvert$
2001	June	$74.30	$75.00	$0.70
	July	$72.88	$73.10	$0.22
	August	$72.76	$72.50	$0.27
	September	$74.06	$71.80	$2.26
	October	$71.29	$66.80	$4.48
	November	$68.21	$64.60	$3.61
	December	$69.96	$66.50	$3.46

Table 7 – Predicted Price vs. Target Price

From Table 7, it is clear that the neural network's predicted price 'agrees' with the corresponding target price for the first three predictions. However, the predictions loose accuracy after the third prediction. Such results are highly expected for a large set of data with such a wide range of factors to be considered. The predictions decreased in accuracy as time increased.

CONCLUSIONS

When discussing the average monthly price received by Texas farmers for beef cattle (Y), the average monthly price received by Texas farmers for calves (X_1), the average monthly prices received by Texas farmers for wheat (X_3), and the monthly United States feeder and stocker cattle and calf price (X_7) have all proven to be statistically significant. It is interesting to note that variable X_1 achieved the largest partial F value of 24.82. This seems to suggest that the monthly price received by Texas farmers during the calf stage of beef cattle development is very pertinent to the current selling price of beef cattle. Variable X_3 came in second achieving a partial F value of 15.33. It is no surprise that wheat is among the statically significant variables since wheat is a major component of cattle feed. Variable X_7, which achieved a partial F of 5.16, is also no surprise. Feeder cattle and stocker cattle are important phases in the beef cattle life cycle.

The neural network's predicted values and target values are in close agreement for the first three predictions after the learning phase has been completed. However, the predictions loose accuracy after the first three predictions. Such results are highly expected. As with any prediction, the prediction itself usually decreases in accuracy as time increases. The accuracy of the prediction for the first 3 months alone makes this work worthwhile. The abilities and the complexities of neural networks reach far beyond this project, and have many other applications.

ACKNOWLEDGEMENTS

Our special thanks to Dr. Lal Almas of West Texas A&M University for his expertise and advice in the field of agricultural business. The authors also express their gratitude to Mr. Bob Lindsey, a farmer and rancher in town, for his expertise in the cattle industry.

REFERENCES

[1] Texas Department of Agriculture. Texas Agricultural Statistics 2001. Austin, TX: State of Texas, 2001.

[2] W. R. Kehoe. Cornell University Albert R. Mann Library. (n.d.). [Online]. USDA economics and statistics system. Available: http://jan.mannlib.cornell.edu/ Jun 14, 2003 [date accessed].

[3] J.F. Cadenhead, (personal communication), June 13, 2003.

[4] Robert Bradley, (personal communication), June 2 2003.

[5] National Oceanic and Atmospheric Administration. (1994 March). [Online]. Time bias corrected divisional temperature precipitation-drought index. Available FTP: ftp://ftp.ncdc.noaa.gov/pub/data/cirs/drought.README June 2, 2003 [date accessed]

[6] National Oceanic and Atmospheric Administration. (1994 March). [Online]. Drd964x.pdsi.txt. Available: ftp://ftp.ncdc.noaa.gov/pub/data/cirs/drd964x.pdsi.txt June 2, 2003 [date accessed]

[7] Texas Almanac 2000 – 2001. Dallas, TX: The Dallas Morning News, Inc., 1999.

[8] Texas Almanac 2002 – 2003. Dallas, TX: The Dallas Morning News, Inc., 2001.

[9] R. Roiger and M. Geatz. Data Mining a Tutorial-Based Primer. Upper Saddle River, NJ: Pearson Education Inc., 2003.

DISCOVERING CAUSES FOR FATAL CAR ACCIDENTS: A DISTANCE-BASED DATA MINING APPROACH

WAN HUANG
Department of Computer Science
SUNY College at Brockport
Brockport, New York, USA

HUI-CHUAN CHEN
Department of Computer Science
The University of Alabama
Tuscaloosa, Alabama, USA

DAVID CORDES
Department of Computer Science
The University of Alabama
Tuscaloosa, Alabama, USA

ABSTRACT

In this paper, a distance-based association rule extraction approach is introduced for discovering rules for fatal event, an event which is statistically improbable in the overall traffic safety dataset. Nevertheless, these fatal cases contain vital causal patterns in car accident analysis. This new approach is then used to discover causal patterns for fatal car accidents using 1998 traffic records of Baldwin County, Alabama. Comparing this approach with other data mining approaches shows that this method has better performance than traditional rule extraction methods in terms of both its efficiency and effectiveness for improbable yet critical events.

INTRODUCTION

In data mining tasks, it is not unusual to find that some events (or classes) are improbable (or scarce) in the given dataset when compared to the other events. One example is the case of a data mining benchmark problem supplied by Sentient Machine Research (The Insurance Company Benchmark, 2000), which used a data file that contained only 5% of caravan insurance policy holders, yet asked the question "who would be interested in buying a caravan insurance policy." The same situation occurs in the knowledge mining of fatal car accidents, where only 0.68% of all accident records are fatal cases).

A number of data mining methods assume that the training set contains roughly an equal number of instances in each class. As a result, these mining techniques either perform poorly or cannot be applied to an improbable class that has only a few instances in the training set. Targeting improbable yet critical events, we design a distance-based association rule extraction approach for discovering knowledge regarding the causality of fatal accidents from the car accident dataset. Our approach first reduces the dimension by selecting only relevant variables, and then uses a threshold clustering algorithm (Looney, 1997) to cluster the feature codes of each variable based on their similarity in the outcomes. A sequential coverage search algorithm (Mitchell, 1997) is then modified to facilitate the extraction of rules that describe the causes of fatality. The data to be mined were obtained from the CARE database, a software application developed at The University of Alabama. The selected dataset contained 1998 car accident records of Baldwin County, Alabama. This dataset held 3572 records, from which 3000 records were randomly selected to form the training set, and the remaining 572 records were used as the test set. Each record contains 220 variables and each variable contains between 2 and 500 different feature codes. A feature code may represent numeric or categorical data.

The rest of the paper is organized as follows. Section 2 gives a detailed description of the distance-based rule extraction approach by applying it to the knowledge discovery of fatal car accidents. Section 3 compares the new approach with existing traditional data mining methods. Section 4 then summarizes the results and concludes the paper.

DISTANCE-BASED ASSOCIATION RULE EXTRACTION

The proposed method consists of five stages: (1) Identify relevant variables that indicate accidents with a high severity, (2) Cluster each variable's feature codes based on their outcomes, (3) Develop a distance function that is based on conditional probabilities of occurrence for outcomes so that different feature code types can be transformed into a unified format; then calculate the distance based on the distance function, (4) Sort the transformed feature codes by increasing order of distance, and (5) Use a modified sequential coverage search to find association rules which cover all instances of fatalities in the training set. The details of this approach are discussed in the following subsections.

Relevant Variable Identification

The severity of the accident (variable V237 in the CARE system) was used as the target variable in this study. A value of ***3*** corresponds to a *fatal* accident, while a value of ***2*** corresponds to an accident with an *injury*, and a value of ***1*** indicates *property-damage* accidents. By referencing previous CARE reports (Brown, 1992-1997) and using two-way contingency tables and χ^2 tests, the number of causal variables was reduced to 37.

Code Clustering

The purpose of code clustering is to reduce feature dimension so as to save future computational time and search effort. The first stage of the algorithm simply generates a table of code frequency counts for each input variable. For a particular feature code, three primary counts were used, corresponding to the three possible outcomes, *i.e.*, the three values that the target variable V237 can take (*property-damage*, *injury*, *fatality*): (1) the number of instances with target=1 (property damage), (2) the number of instances with target=2 (injury), (3) the number of instances with target=3 (fatality). A given feature code can be represented by its frequency distribution among target outcomes. Codes with similar frequency distribution can be grouped into one cluster to represent one type of outcome distribution. A threshold clustering algorithm (Looney, 1997) was applied to group the codes of each variable X into four to six clusters. After clustering, each feature code is replaced by its corresponding cluster number.

Table 1 illustrates the clustering concept. Variable V077 stands for "Roadway Character," and originally had code values ranging from 1 to 8. After clustering, those 8 codes were grouped into 4 clusters based on the frequency distribution. Thus, V077 now has only 4 code values (1, 2, 3, and 4) rather than 8.

Table 1. Frequency distribution of variable V077

Variable name	Variable value	Target=1	Target=2	Target=3	Cluster
V077	1	1807	491	13	2
V077	2	186	78	2	3
V077	3	110	38	4	4
V077	4	9	6	2	1
V077	5	101	35	5	4
V077	6	25	16	1	1
V077	7	40	10	2	1
V077	8	1	0	1	1

Table 2. Conditional probabilities for input variable V077

X	C_i	P(Target=1|V077=C_i)	P(Target=2|V077=C_i)	P(Target=3|V077=C_i)	Distance
V077	1	0.70769	0.24615	0.04615	1.21295
V077	2	0.78191	0.21246	0.00563	1.28269
V077	3	0.69925	0.29323	0.00752	1.24898
V077	4	0.72014	0.24915	0.03072	1.23296

Distance Calculation and Code Sorting

To compare the significance of various contributive feature codes, we employed a distance function which is based on the conditional probabilities of the three outcomes, given that an input variable (feature) takes a particular code value. Since there were three possible outcomes (*property-damage*, *injury*, *fatality*), we used a 3-dimensional space, with each axis representing the conditional probability of one outcome. We then mapped an input feature code to a point in the *3*-D space. This is illustrated in Table 2. Input variable V077 has four feature codes. We computed their corresponding conditional probabilities as shown. Now each code of V077 can be associated with a coordinate vector (p_1, p_2, p_3), where p_1=P(Target=1|V077=C_i), p_2=P(Target=2|V077=C_i), p_3=P(Target=3|V077=C_i), for i = (1, 2, 3, 4). Therefore, each code C_i of V077 can be represented by a point in a 3-D space.

Similarly, we can represent any input feature code with a point in the same *3*-D space. By the definition of conditional probability, a point with coordinate vector (0, 0, 1) implies that only fatal outcomes occur for that feature code. Using the proximity concept, points that are close to point (0, 0, 1) have a greater tendency to cause a fatal outcome. Therefore, we calculated the Euclidean distance between any input point and the *fatality-occurred-only* point (0, 0, 1). We then sorted the feature codes by increasing order of distance. Feature codes that were more likely to be associated with fatalities were expected to quickly surface and dominate the upper part of the sorted feature code list.

Modified Sequential Coverage Search

The sequence of feature codes sorted in increasing order of distance represents a decreasing order of probability that these feature codes cause the fatality. Sequential coverage search (Mitchell, 1997) uses the sorted sequence to first find feature codes that contribute significantly to the fatality, then sequentially search through the remainder of the codes, identifying other potentially useful feature codes as needed.

With the original sequential coverage search, instances that were covered by the obtained rule are deleted from the training set after the rule is generated. The

> ***Algorithm***: Modified sequential coverage search to find *k*-variable association rules
>
> **Input**: Training set, Sorted feature code list, (*k-1*)-variable association rules
> **Output**: *k*-variable association rules
>
> **if** *k*=1 **then**
>   Use each feature code in the sorted feature code list as a candidate *1*-variable rule
> **else**
>   Combine each feature code in the sorted feature code list with the *k-1* feature codes in each (*k-1*)-variable association rule to form a candidate *k*-variable rule
> **end if**
> Find in the training set supporting cases* for this candidate *k*-variable rule
> **if** supporting case exists **then**
>   Add this candidate *k*-variable rule to the output rule list
> **end if**
> Mark all supporting cases found
> Continue **until** all fatal cases in the training set have been marked
>
> * We define *supporting case* as case with feature codes matching those in the candidate association rule and accident severity is fatal.

Figure 1. Modified sequential coverage search algorithm

search stops when all instances with the specified target outcome (*e.g.* the fatal class) have been covered by the generated rules. As a result, every instance belonging to the fatal class is counted even though it rarely occurs.

One problem with the original sequential coverage search algorithm is that when more feature codes are combined for rule generation, or multiple feature codes simultaneously caused the fatality, implementing feature code combinations becomes critical to the quality measure of the rules. This is due to the fact that instances corresponding to a new candidate rule may have already been deleted, since these instances also satisfied another rule that was generated earlier. In order to overcome this problem, a modified version of sequential coverage search was proposed, described in Fig. 1. In this modified search algorithm, instances that have been covered by the generated rules are marked but not deleted. Therefore, these instances can also be utilized by future rule generation. Supporting cases are found based on the entire training set, thus the order in which the rules are generated is no longer critical to the final rule set. This modified version can be easily extended to generate any *k*-variable rules to cover all fatal cases by combining the feature codes in each (*k-1*)-variable rule with all other feature codes.

An important contribution of the search algorithm is that it operates on a distance basis, which provides a sequence to direct the search. Thus we can ensure that the feature codes that are more important to the fatal class are considered by the rule generation process before other, less important, feature codes are considered. This differs from the *Apriori* algorithm (Agrawal and Srikant, 1994), where the large ***k***-itemset is generated without any guidance on which feature code should be considered first in order to extract rules for a particular class. The *Apriori* algorithm puts those improbable yet critical events at a disadvantage, since variables that may be significant to the improbable classes often do not have sufficient support to be included in the large ***k***-itemset, and are usually excluded from further rule generation in the first few stages.

Table 3. One-variable rules, modified sequential coverage search

No.	Rule	Accuracy
1	V064=2	6.90%
2	V077=4	3.64%
3	V077=1	3.57%
4	V038=3	3.26%
5	V032=3	3.13%
6	V033=2	2.70%

Table 4. One-variable rules, Apriori Algorithm (min. support=0.1)

No.	Rule	Accuracy
1	V010=1	4.29%
2	V038=3	3.26%
3	V033=2	2.70%
4	V016=2	2.68%
5	V040=3	2.66%
6	V090=4	2.61%

Table 5. One-variable rules, Apriori Algorithm (min. support=0.01)

No.	Rule	Accuracy
1	V064=2	6.90%
2	V010=1	4.29%
3	V077=4	3.64%
4	V077=1	3.57%
5	V038=3	3.26%
6	V032=3	3.13%

Table 6. Two-variable rules, modified sequential coverage search

No.	Rule	Accuracy
1	V064=2 and V077=1	50%
2	V064=2 and V077=4	33.33%
3	V064=2 and V079=5	33.33%
4	V038=2 and V077=1	33.33%
5	V032=3 and V077=4	25%
6	V040=3 and V064=2	25%

Table 7. Two-variable rules, Apriori Algorithm (min. support=0.1)

No.	Rule	Accuracy
1	V010=1 and V079=6	5%
2	V063=2 and V082=3	4.84%
3	V010=1 and V248=2	4.62%
4	V009=1 and V010=1	4.48%
5	V038=3 and V248=2	4.41%
6	V010=1 and V083=2	4.41%

Table 8. Two-variable rules, Apriori Algorithm (min. support=0.01)

No.	Rule	Accuracy
1	V028=2 and V037=5	25%
2	V040=3 and V064=2	25%
3	V016=2 and V064=2	22.22%
4	V007=2 and V064=2	20%
5	V038=3 and V077=4	18.18%
6	V068=3 and V077=1	16.67%

Table 9. Rules, C4.5 Algorithm

No.	Rule	Accuracy
1	V022=3 and V032=3 and V033=2 and V148=4	Did not fire on Test Set
2	V033=2 and V068=2 and V077=1 and V102=1	Did not fire on Test Set
3	V013=5 and V033=2 and V068=3 and V238=3 and V240=2	Did not fire on Test Set
4	V033=1 and V064=2 and V079=5 and V148=4 and V246=2	Did not fire on Test Set
5	V028=2 and V038=2 and V238=2	0.0

COMPUTATIONAL RESULTS AND COMPARISON

In order to measure the performance of the proposed approach, rules obtained from the training set were applied to the test set. The quality of a rule is defined in terms of the rule's degree of accuracy on the test set, which measures its generality (or applicability) to future unseen examples. First, one variable rules were generated. Table 3 shows the best six one-variable rules generated by the proposed modified sequential coverage search. In addition, one-variable rules generated by the *Apriori* Algorithm with different minimum support are tabulated in Table 4 and Table 5 respectively. Rule 1 in Table 3 means that 6.90% of accidents with V064 (Estimated Speed of Causal Driver) = 2 (over 70 MPH) are fatal cases. In other words, feature code "Estimated Speed of Causal Driver" "over 70 MPH" is the most important factor, based on rule 1. Rule 2 in Table 3 indicates that "Upgrade or Curve Level" "Roadway Character" is important. Although the accuracies of the one-variable rules obtained by the proposed algorithm are higher than those of the rules generated by the *Apriori* Algorithm, which are all higher than 0.68% of fatal cases in the dataset used for mining, they are still quite low. Given this, rules with multiple variables were sought to increase accuracy. The rules listed in Table 6 represent the best six two-variable rules generated by the modified sequential coverage search respectively. Rule 1 in Table 6 can be expressed as:

50% of accidents with V064=2 (accidents with Estimated speed of causal driver Over 70 MPH) and V077=1 (Roadway Character is Straight/Curve Hill Crest, or Curve Up/Down Grad) are fatal cases.

As a comparison with other rule generation methods, the two-variable rules generated by the *Apriori* Algorithm are listed in Tables 7 and 8, and the rules generated by the C4.5 decision tree algorithm (Quinlan, 1992) are shown in Table 9. It is noted that out of the 5 rules generated by C4.5, 4 did not fire on the test set, and the one rule that did fire was not a fatal case. Thus, the generality of this C4.5 rule set is quite poor. For the *Apriori* Algorithm, if the minimum support level is low, most of the variables that may be related to the target class could be included in the large ***k***-itemsets. To extract rules for dominant events, this minimum support level does not have to be very low. However, for improbable events, this is not the case. In order for the feature codes that are significant to the improbable event to be included in the large ***k***-itemset, the minimum support level has to be low because such feature codes have insufficient support. This fact is demonstrated in Tables 4 and 7, which list the rules generated by the *Apriori* Algorithm with minimum support = 0.1, and Tables 5 and 8, with minimum support = 0.01. It can be seen that by lowering the minimum support level, the *Apriori* algorithm did find the variables which were more significant to the target class. However, even with such a low minimum support level, the two-variable rules generated by the *Apriori* algorithm were still not as good as the rules generated by the modified sequential coverage search algorithm. On the other hand, lowering the minimum support level of the *Apriori* algorithm means increasing the number of variable combinations included in the large ***k***-itemset, which in turn increases the computational effort exponentially.

CONCLUSION

In this paper, we have presented a distance-based data mining approach for finding causal patterns in fatal car accidents by extracting association rules. When compared to the other approaches, we have shown that rules generated by this method have better prediction power and substantial improvements over existing data mining techniques.

REFERENCES

Agrawal R., and Srikant R., Fast Algorithms for Mining Association Rules, *Proceedings of International Conference on Very Large Data Base (VLDB)*, 487-499, Santiago, Chile, 1994.

Brown, D. Traffic Safety Reports. Department of Computer Science, *The University of Alabama. The CARE Official Web Site*. http://care.cs.ua.edu, 1992-1997.

Looney, C. G. *Pattern Recognition Using Neural Networks*. Oxford University Press, 1997.

Mitchell, T. M. *Machine Learning*. WCB McGraw-Hill, 1997.

Quinlan, J. R. *C4.5: Programs for Machine Learning*. San Francisco, Morgan Kaufmann, 1992.

The Insurance Company (TIC) Benchmark. http://www.liacs.nl/~putten/library/cc2000/, 2000.

BOUNDARY SAMPLING AND NEURAL NETWORK FOR WEB MINING APPLICATIONS

KAIRUI CHEN
SHUANG LIU
HUI-CHUAN CHEN
Department of Computer Science
The University of Alabama
Tuscaloosa, AL 35487

ABSTRACT

As internet sales and e-commerce are becoming more popular, the need to organize and adapt websites to customers' buying practices and the need to discover certain shopping habits of certain group of customers are growing. As a result, web mining is getting important for internet selling companies. In this paper, we introduce a novel approach that integrates data clustering, boundary sampling, neural network, and similarity measure to help web mining and also to improve mining performance. An internet dataset collected by Blue Martini Software from Gazelle.com is used to illustrate and test the proposed method. The performance of our proposed approach is better than conventional techniques available.

INTRODUCTION

Web mining is the process of discovering and analyzing useful information from the World Wide Web (Cooley et al., 1997). As internet sales and e-commerce are becoming more popular nowadays, the need to organize and adapt websites to shoppers' buying practices is becoming a vital part of web mining.

Web mining can be broadly categorized into three areas: web content mining, web structure mining, and web usage mining (Mulvenna et al., 2000). In this paper, we focus on web usage mining. As with any data mining test, data preparation and mining techniques used are very critical. Hence, data clustering, boundary sampling, neural network, and similarity measure coupled with entropy values are employed to ensure that the output generated by the web mining system is correct.

DATA PREPARATION AND TRANSFORMATION

The dataset we used is real world e-commerce data involving web click streams and purchase transactions collected by Blue Martini Software from Gazelle.com. In order to gain insight knowledge of the customers' buying behaviors, a neural network is used to learn the correct classification of user patterns. To illustrate the proposed approach in the web mining domain, we focused only on the task of identifying customers who spent \$12 or more on an average access session to the website. The data file has been preprocessed to reduce data dimensions by Lovell (Lovell et al., 2003). There are 1781 cases provided. 45 features were selected and each feature has less than or equal to 10 unique values. The feature values were represented by their relative frequencies (conditional probabilities) to target outcome. This representation shows the likelihood of each feature value corresponding to the interesting outcome. For example, in this paper, the interesting outcome is customers who spent over \$12 during their access sessions. The probability of spending over \$12 given the current feature value is computed. This representation also provides a unified way to handle different types of data.

When a neural network is used to solve a problem, it usually needs a training set which contains a set of inputs with the required output being described explicitly. The computational efforts often grow proportionally to its feature numbers and its training size. To effectively learn the information from training set, the size of training set should be scalable and the running time must be predictable and acceptable for practical use. In this paper, we focus on the selection of training set and the generalization performance. For the sake of illustration, we further reduce the problem dimensions to 14 features and limit the training data to be less than 100 cases. The remaining cases are used for testing the performance of the proposed approach on the unseen data.

NEURAL NETWORK APPROACH

1. Backpropagation Neural Network

We adopted a backpropagation network to learn the characteristics of customers who spent over $12 on an average visit to the site. Backpropagation network is a popular approach for modeling a complex decision system which may have a linear or non-linear decision function. The proposed backpropagation network is shown in figure 1. Each neuron in the input layer is responsible for receiving feature values of each case. Each of these data is multiplied by a weight value. The summed weighted inputs passed through an activation function which scales the output to a range of (0, 1) on the hidden layer. The results of activation function are then propagated to all of the neurons in the next layer. Eventually, the final results of the backpropagation network can be obtained from output nodes (Gupta et al., 2003).

2. Network Output

The outputs of the network represent customers' category. For our specific task, the feature labeled "spend over $12 per visit", which has a value of either "TRUE" or "FALSE", has been designated as the target feature. Therefore, two output nodes are used to indicate those two possible target categories. The output (1, 0) indicates target value equal to TRUE, and output (0, 1) means target value equal to FALSE. It is expected that an output value can not exactly reach desired output 1 or 0 in computation. An output value that is very close to designed value 1 (or 0) should be considered as 1 (or 0). Thus, the network output is considered correct if its activation is within a specified tolerance of the desired value. We call this tolerance α-cut (Gabrys et al., 2000 and Gupta et al., 1994). We apply the following function to the result of network output:

$$LC(x) = \begin{cases} 1 & \text{if } x >= \alpha \\ x & \text{if } \alpha < x < 1-\alpha \\ 0 & \text{if } x <= 1-\alpha \end{cases}$$

However, in the test phase, the real value between 0 and 1 generated by the network can be considered as the confidence in predicting corresponding target outcome (Cristinanini et al., 2000). The outputs which are not within the specified tolerance also provide some important information for classification. Therefore, in the test phase, a similarity analysis is employed to further recognition of its belonging despite its output values. We first view the output layer as a competitive layer, pick the node whose output is the largest (Cristinanini et al., 2000), and compute the sureness (S) of the given case belonging to the winner node category. A measure of "sureness (S)" was introduced by (Rizzo et al., 1994) to quantify the similarity of the TRUE or FALSE categorical outputs.

S is assessed by a scaled entropy measurement, defined as follows:

$$S = 1 - \frac{h}{h_{max}}$$

where h_{max} is the maximum possible entropy, which is equal to -0.5ln(0.5)-0.5ln(0.5) in the given dataset

h is the entropy at output layer and is defined as:

$$h = \sum (-y_i \ln y_i) \quad i = 1, 2$$

where y_i= output from the ith output node of the network.

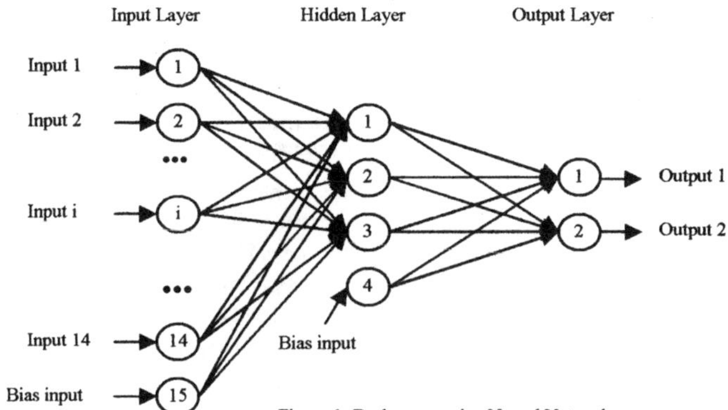

Figure 1: Backpropagation Neural Network

The algorithm is shown as follows:

a) If y1>y2 then X belongs to TRUE; if y1<y2 then X belongs to FALSE

b) Compute S for a given output vector.

c) If S>S* accept the result given in a); else reject the result in a).

3. Network learning

Learning in a neural network corresponds to determine weights for each arc in the network. We use generalized delta weight update rule for our network. The target function to be learned is defined over cases that can be described by a set of 14 feature values. The target function outputs are some real values between 0 and 1. The first problem faced by backpropagation is to select an appropriate training dataset. In this paper, we focus on two sampling techniques: random sampling and boundary sampling.

In random sampling, the number of training cases is predetermined. And these cases are chosen randomly from the whole dataset to train the network.

Boundary sampling seeks to generate a comparable, if not better, data sampling with fewer training cases. This is achieved by selecting training cases from only those designated as boundary clusters. In boundary sampling, we first need to cluster all the provided cases using a clustering algorithm. Clusters with only cases belong to a single outcome target value are called "pure" clusters. And those contain cases with different outcome target values all called "boundary" clusters as shown in Figure 2. Apparently, in a two target value situation like ours, if there is a boundary line that separates those cases belong to one target value from those cases belonging to the other target value, it should pass through the boundary clusters. Thus choosing the cases in the boundary cluster will be more efficient than choosing training cases randomly. K-means algorithm was employed to cluster those 1781 points in a 14 dimensional space into 20 clusters.

Figure 2 shows an example of a scatter graph for categorical data (class 1 and class 2) with two input features. The squares represent cases belonging to class 1 and the circles represent cases belonging to class 2. A well-defined nonlinear line is the boundary that separates the two classes. Figure 3 and 4 show the advantage of boundary sampling over random sampling. In Figure 3, random sampling is used for selecting training set. 6

points were randomly chosen to find the separator. The separator denoted by dashed lines found from random sampling varies and may be very different from the actual boundary. Whereas in figure 4, boundary sampling is used and only points in the boundary cluster are chosen. The separator found by the network is close to the actual boundary.

The termination condition for the weight updating has been a problem of backpropagation applications. Common strategy is either to continue training until the error on the training examples falls below some predetermined threshold, or to continue training until a predetermined number of training iterations is reached. In this paper, both stopping conditions are employed. A 95% correction on the training examples or 5000 iterations of updating whichever comes first will terminate the training.

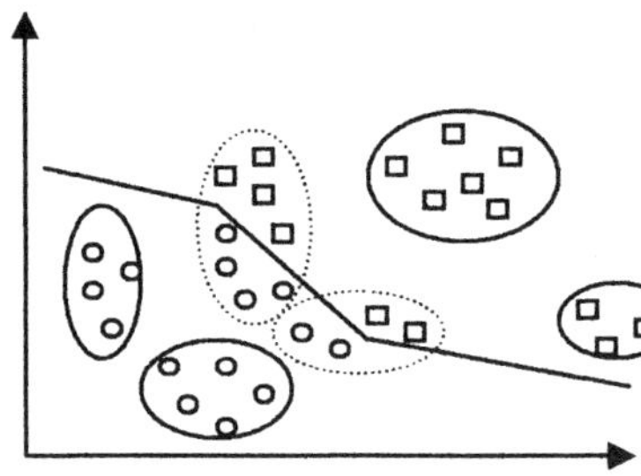

Figure 2: Boundary and Clusters

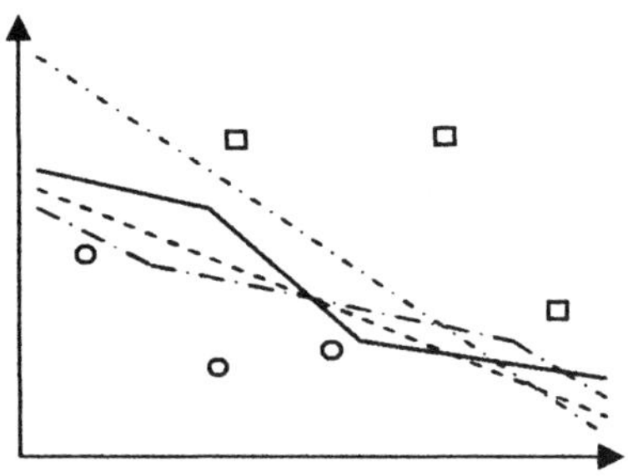

Figure 3: Random Sampling

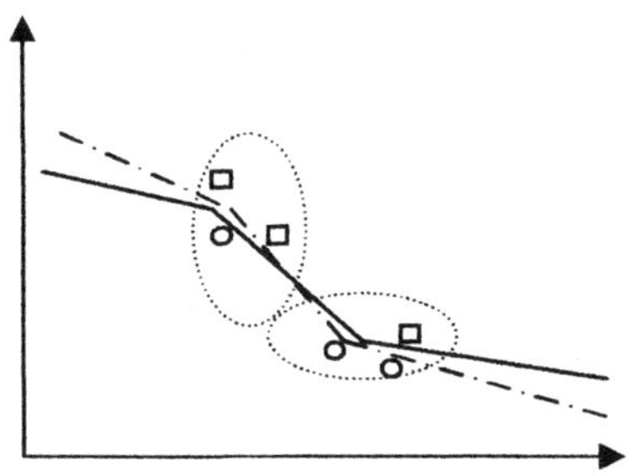

Figure 4: Boundary Sampling

EXPERIMENTAL RESULTS AND CONCLUSIONS

After a network is successfully trained, it is applied to an unseen dataset to make classification. The quality of the system performance is assessed in terms of the accuracy (percentage of correct classifications) in the test phase.

To test the performance of our proposed method, we first choose 70 training cases to train the backpropagation network. In the random sampling, each record is randomly selected from 1781 records. In the boundary sampling all 70 training cases are randomly picked up only among boundary clusters 4, 6, and 13. Due to randomness involved in sampling process, the accuracy measurements would slightly change in each experiment. Table 1 lists 10 experiments and the test accuracies measured from 1711 unseen cases. The accuracy of boundary sampling varies from 77.75% to 90.00%, while the accuracy of random sampling fluctuates from 47.94% to 90.81%. The average accuracies are 84% and 72% respectively. The variance for boundary sampling is 17.6 and much lower than the variance for random sampling which is 267.8. The overall computational results show that the network performance is more reliable and has higher accuracy when boundary sampling technique is used.

Table 1: Backpropagation accuracy with 70 training cases

Experiment No.	Boundary Sampling	Random Sampling
1	77.75	85.21
2	90.00	69.08
3	81.62	47.94
4	78.85	76.02
5	85.73	51.35
6	89.48	89.97
7	83.76	50.08
8	88.67	90.81
9	83.13	77.29
10	88.38	89.13
Average accuracy	84.74	72.68
Accuracy variance	17.6	267.8

To study the influence of similarity analysis, we evaluate the performance of the proposed method on several different levels of α and S* values. The resulting test accuracy values are listed in table 2 to table 5.

Table 2: Random Sampling with 70 training cases

	No S used	S = 0.3	S = 0.2	S = 0.1
α-cut=(0.9,0.1)	80.77%	82.75%	83.16%	83.22%
α-cut=(0.95, 0.05)*	77.38%	87.43%	87.49%	88.31%
α-cut=(0.99, 0.01)*	74.67%	88.13%	88.31%	88.60%

Table 3: Boundary Sampling with 70 training cases

	No S used	S = 0.3	S = 0.2	S = 0.1
α-cut = (0.9, 0.1)	88.89%	89.01%	89.48%	89.59%
α-cut=(0.95,0.05)*	90.23%	90.75%	90.94%	91.23%
α-cut = (0.99, 0.01)*	87.84%	90.35%	90.41%	90.53%

Table 4: Random Sampling with 50 training cases

	No S used	S = 0.3	S = 0.2	S = 0.1
α-cut=(0.9, 0.1)	82.26%	82.72%	83.59%	83.99%
α-cut=(0.95, 0.05)*	81.45%	83.53%	83.70%	83.93%
α-cut= (0.99, 0.01)*	79.54%	83.70%	83.70%	83.70%

Table 5: Boundary Sampling with 50 training cases

	No S used	S = 0.3	S = 0.2	S = 0.1
α-cut = (0.9, 0.1)	89.31%	89.60%	89.71%	90.12%
α-cut=(0.95,0.05)*	82.84%	90.29%	90.46%	90.52%
α-cut = (0.99, 0.01)*	80.76%	90.46%	90.52%	90.52%

* Training process did not converge within 5000 iterations

Comparing computational results given in table 2 to table 3 and table 4 to 5, it is noted that for every combination of α and *S* in these tables, the boundary sampling approach outperforms the random sampling. In some cases, boundary sampling approach even has an accuracy 13% higher than the random sampling. Furthermore, in each table when we apply S function to determine the output value, the accuracy gets further improved. For example in the case of random sampling with 70 training cases the S value of 0.1 improves the accuracy of α-cut (0.99, 0.01) from 74.67 percent to 88.60 percent as shown in table 2. The experiments show that S method can recognize the output category when the α-cut method gives up.

In this experiment, we choose three increasing α-cut values: (0.9, 0.1), (0.95, 0.05) and (0.99, 0.01). The higher α-cut value is, the more accurate boundary that the network draws will be. However, a high threshold of α-cut makes the training process hard to converge, thus degrading test accuracy. The tables show that if the α-cut values are chosen to be (0.95, 0.05) and (0.99, 0.01), training process did not converge to the specified α-cut tolerance within 5000 iterations, and the testing accuracy deteriorates. Hence, we can not choose too high α-cut value in the practical application.

The experiments also show that the backpropagation network can draw a good boundary for distinguish testing cases even if only 70 or 50 training cases are used for training. If we apply S to the output value with boundary sampling, the testing accuracy can be higher and reach 90.52 percent. This technique is quite promising for problems where training data are difficult to collect and cost of collecting data is high.

Based on the previous work, we increase the size of training set by adding some more cases including centers of pure clusters. The result of 100 training cases including cluster centers are listed in table 6 and 7.

Table 6: Random Sampling with 100 training cases

	No S used	S = 0.3	S = 0.2	S = 0.1
α-cut = (0.9, 0.1)	81.79%	83.40%	83.46%	83.58%
α-cut=(0.95, 0.05)	82.27%	83.93%	84.05%	84.05%
α-cut=(0.99,0.01)*	59.84%	84.05%	84.11%	84.23%

Table 7: Clustering Sampling with 100 training cases, containing cluster centers

	No S used	S = 0.3	S = 0.2	S = 0.1
α-cut=(0.9,0.1)	90.24%	90.48%	90.48%	90.89%
α-cut=(0.95,0.05)	85.18%	91.01%	91.01%	91.01%
α-cut=(0.99, 0.01)*	82.98%	91.01%	91.07%	91.13%

Boundary sampling containing cluster centers again outperforms in accuracy in every level of certainty index and α-cut. The highest accuracy value in table 7 is 91.13 percent, which is 7 percent better than the best performance of the random sampling in the same setup. Thus, the integration of boundary sampling, similarity analysis, α-cut tolerance and neural network performs efficient and effective knowledge discovery. It is not only appropriate for the web mining problem discussed here, but is also desirable for many mining problems where neural networks are employed.

REFERENCES

Cooley R., Mobasher B., and Srivastava J., "Web Mining: Information and Pattern Discovery on the World Wide Web", 8th IEEE Intl. Conf. on Tools with AI, 1997.

Cristinanini, Nello and Shawe-Taylor, John, "Introduction to Support Vector Machines and Other Kernel-based Learning Methods", Cambridge University Press, 2000.

Gabrys, B. and Bargiela, A., "General Fuzzy Min-Max Neural Network for Clustering and Classification", IEEE Trans. Neural Networks, Vol. 11, No.3, pp769-783, 2000.

Gupta, M. M., Jin, L., and Homma, N., "Static and Dynamic Neural Networks: From Fundamentals to Advanced Theory", Wiley-IEEE Press, 2003.

Gupta, M. M. and Rao, D.H., "On the Principle of Fuzzy Neural Networks," Fuzzy Sets Syst., Vol. 61, No.1, pp. 1-18, 1994.

Lovell, L. D., Chen, H. C., "A Data Reduction technique for Web Mining Applications", proceedings of ANNIE 2003 International Conference of Intelligent Engineering System, pp. 781-787.

Mulvenna, M.D., "Personalization on the Net Using Web Mining: A Collection of Articles", CACM Vol. 43, No. 8, pp122-125, 2000.

Rizzo, D. M., Dougherty D. E., "Characterization of Aquifer Properties using Artificial Neural Networks: Neural Kriging", Water Resource. Res., 30(2), pp483-497, 1994.

K-MEANS AND SOM, A CONCURRENT VALIDATION SCHEME FOR DATA MINING

MAURICIO SPERANDIO **JORGE COELHO**
Federal University of Santa Catarina
Electrical Systems Planning Research Laboratory (LabPlan)
Florianópolis - Brazil
sperandio@labplan.ufsc.br, coelho@labplan.ufsc.br

ABSTRACT
We present a concurrent validation scheme for clustering and data mining, where the knowledge discovery properties of the SOM (Self-Organizing Maps) are explored to determine a good k-means cluster number estimation, in order to visualize the k-means clusters over a trained map to compare and validate the result of both procedures. The SOM flexibility and visualization capacities are used to explore the results of a consolidated clustering algorithm like the k-means, and on the other hand, this method confirms the clustering presented by the neural map. An actual electricity consumer database is analyzed for feature extraction.

INTRODUCTION

Clustering methods are tools for exploratory data analysis in order to solve classification problems. The objective is to associate variable arguments (people, things, events, etc) in groups, or clusters, so that the similarity degree is large among members of a same group, and small among different groups. Then each group describes, in terms of the contained data, the class to which their members belong, and abstract one or more particular characteristics to denote them.

One of the most traditional clustering methods is the k-means, whose objective is to build a group of k groups starting from a mass of data, so that each unit belongs to just one group. It is a non-hierarchical method, so it doesn't establish any link between the grouped data.

The Self-Organizing Maps (SOM) are a category of Artificial Neural Networks, characterized by an unsupervised "learning" process, in which the data are disposed over a topologic plane (map) organized according to similarity (Kohonen, 2001).

Many authors used to compare these two methods, pointing out the advantages and disadvantages of each one. However it isn't common to use both of them together, to explore the best characteristics of each one. A work that used the idea of carrying out a competitive validation between the SOM and the k-means was presented in Coelho *et al.*(2002), but the methods didn't exchange information, and the objective was to forecast using a map trained with historical data.

In this paper a concurrent validation is presented, between those two different methods, to certify that the groups discovered are really coherent in their formation.

CONCURRENT VALIDATION

First, it is required to define the variables that will be part of the database, which is an important aspect and can demand studies such as factorial analysis, followed by procedures of clustering data with similar characteristics, knowledge discovery or subsequent classification.

In the proposed method, both procedures evaluate the same database, and the information is exchanged between the algorithms is carriewd out, at first, through the choice of the number of clusters to be formed by the k-means, based on the distance matrix of a trained map. Then, the data are labeled with the k-means defined groups and printed in the winning neuron in the map. The validation is made by verifying the k-means defined group that prevails in each neuron. As the map accomplishes a topologic organization, where neighboring neurons have a high degree of similarity, configurations of k-means defined groups that are dispersed over the map are not accepted. In case of not being satisfied with the disagreement among the algorithms, one can change the number of clusters (k), or resize the map, looking for the minimization of disagreements, quantization and topologic errors.

Therefore, at the end of the concurrent validation process, the defined clusters are consolidated by two algorithms, and furthermore, the visualization advantage that the SOM offers, showing the groups organization over the map, facilitates the borders identification, as well as the component maps, that show the contribution of each variable for the map formation.

A flowchart of this procedure is presented in Figure 1, showing the relationship among each stage, in which s some user intervention happens. First choice is map size, then, verifying the U-Mat (Ultsch and Siemon, 1990), the Smoothed Data Histogram (Pampalk *et al.*, 2002) and the Component Maps a number of groups for the k-means should be determined; hence, the validation process occurs, and the user evaluates the error report of crossing algorithms results to decide if he wants to change some parameter; if so, which one of them, the number k or the size of the map.

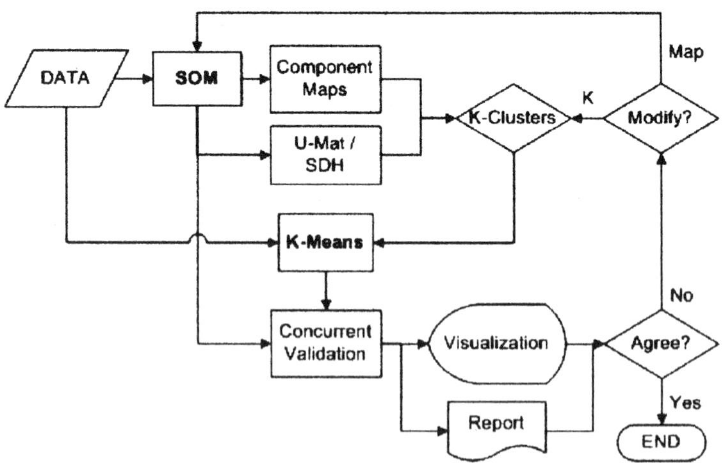

Figure 1. Concurrent Validation Flowchart (SOM x K-means).

The k-means and SOM algorithms were implemented in Matlab© by a group from the Neural Network Research Center of the University of Helsinki, and are available on the internet (SOM Toolbox), documented by Vesanto *et al.* (1999). That toolbox is a library of codes that explore the flexibility of previous functions of Matlab, especially graphics, for training and visualization of the maps, and other data that can be extracted from this powerful method.

Therefore the whole process presented in the flowchart of Figure 1 runs in the Matlab environment, in which the interface was developed, the algorithm to minimize the k-means error, the concurrent validation process, and adaptations were also made to visualize the k-means results over the map.

To start the clustering process it is necessary to define a size for the self-organizing map, and that decision can affect the number of choice groups for the k-means. As the intention is just to accomplish clustering, an option is to begin with a small map, with approximately one neuron for each four data inputs, which tends to form concise groups. However, small maps may have a larger intra-cluster dispersion. Then, larger maps should be inspected after the first validation. Scattered maps take shape with more neurons for each data vector, and too many empty neurons can hinder neuron association to form larger groups, but reveals relationships among variables that are not evident in the database. Big maps are necessary when one wants to use them for forecasting.

A good initial choice depends of the database characteristics. For instance, if the data tend to concentrate arround a particular value, a small map is enough to represent them. If they have a great dispersion in relation to the mean value, a big map characterizes them better. That initial estimation should be based in the descriptive analysis of the database variables that are being classified.

Concerning the process of concurrent validation, the two algorithms are independent, and the only information that is exchanged among them depends on the user decision when defining the k-means number of groups and the size of the self-organizing map. Even evaluating the error table reported during the process, one should be aware that, when increasing the number of groups, the intra-cluster dispersion is reduced, because less data will be allocated for each group, and when increasing the size of the map, the disagreement with the k-means decreases, because with more neurons there will be more space to allocate data, reducing border conflicts, which, except for few cases, are the main reason of divergences among the two clustering methods.

Even with big maps, such exceptions seem to be result of a larger sensibility of the SOM to the data variability, while the k-means is fastened to a defined number of groups by the user.

The SOM can point out a new cluster partition when k-means defined groups are disconnected in the map topology, in other words, empty neurons appear between data defined as being of a same group by the other algorithm. Another form of increasing group partition is verifying the component maps, which present each variable density over the map, and therefore, it can be expected that a group with a great participation of one variable exists, as well as another with a medium participation, and another in which such variable is not representative, and etc.

A REAL DATABASE CLUSTERING

Following the presented methodology, a study was accomplished to determine the clustering of a database with variables that define the characteristics of the electric power system from 260 municipal districts of the Santa Catarina state, in the south of Brazil.

Four variables were chosen to describe the system configuration, City-Substation distance, Number of Feeders, Feeder Interchange Capacity and Distribution Grid Length.

The initial map was 8x7 neurons, and after the training the distance matrix results were evaluated to determine an initial k-means number of clusters. This is done with the help of the U-Mat and the SDH figures. The first one shows the distance between each neuron in gray scale, and also plots the neurons size proportional to the amount of data associated to them. The SDH does something similar to this, but with a contour plot that indicates clustering regions.

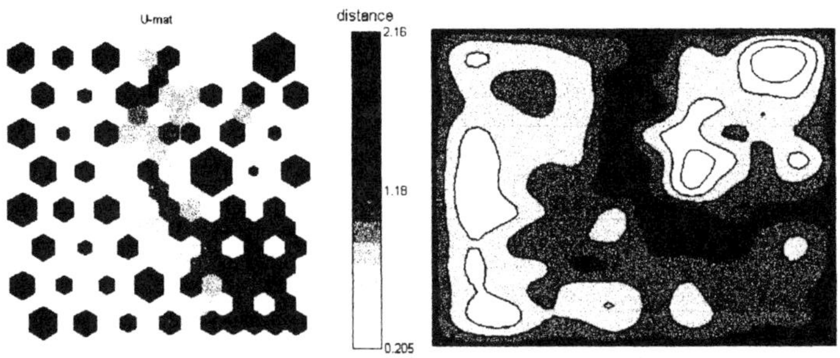

(a) (b)

Figure 2.: (a) U-mat with density; (b) Smoothed Data Histograms (SDH).

Evaluating the graphs presented in Figure 2, a division between two great groups can be quickly perceived, with an amount of small groups within them. Figure 2(a) shows an uniform distribution of the data among the neurons, due to the fact that in this database discrepant values almost don't exist.

The initial number of clusters estimated to be formed by the k-means was 8, however along the process it indicated an increase to 10, above that, the new groups only contained 2 or 3 elements, and didn't bring significant information. The map size was chosen according to the number of clusters and the validation error report, like showed in Table 1.

Table 1. Validation Errors Report for 10 clusters.

Map Size	Quantization Error	Topographic Error	Disagree	Linked
8x9	0,420	0,015	10	no
9x8	0,412	0,027	14	no
10x8	0,373	0,023	16	yes
8x10	0,393	0,012	10	no
10x9	0,353	0,019	9	no
10x10	0,341	0,019	6	yes
11x10	**0,319**	**0,038**	**4**	**yes**
12x11	0,294	0,012	7	no

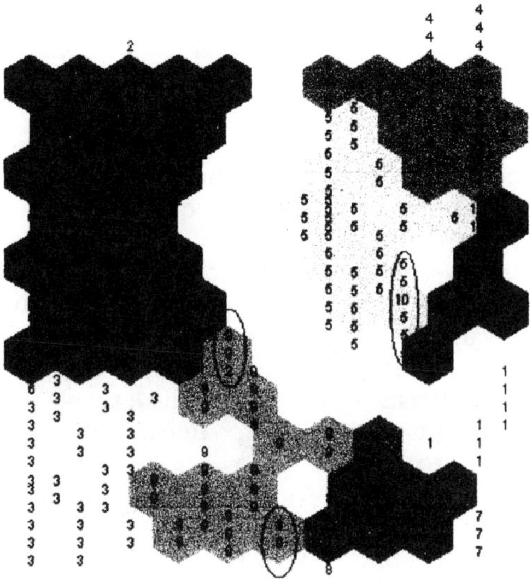

Figure 3. Best map with k-means group numbers.

Once the map configuration was determined (11x10 neurons, 10 clusters), we could observe the cluster distribution over it. Figure 3 shows the k-means cluster numbers over their winning neurons, the gray shades delimit clusters of neurons after the validation, and the ellipses emphasizes the four disagreeing data, where there are two border conflicts (6-2 and 10-5) and the others are actually a divergence among the algorithms (2-9 and 3-9). That divergent data are closer to the SOM validated cluster than to the k-means determined number.

The next figure shows the component maps that form Figure 3, and help in understanding each cluster characteristic. Each map represent only one variable, and the shades are its participation in each neuron.

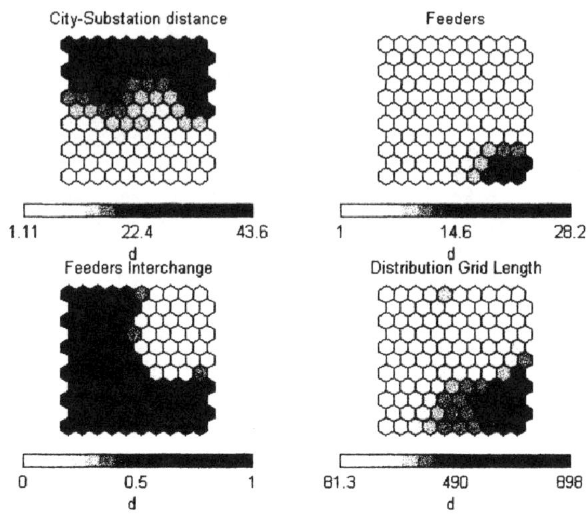

Figure 4. Four variables component maps .

The Feeder Interchange variable explains the division of the two larger groups presented in Figure 2, with or without this capability. There we can see that in the map area without Feeder Interchange (white), there are also neurons with larger City-Substantion Distance, and they still have only 1 Feeder. For the brazilian case, this is explained by the small Distribution Grid Length, in other words, neurons are associated with small municipal districts with small load. Consequently those districts should be the ones that have the worst supply continuity indexes.

After the electric system clustering, a cluster ranking was made based on their mean supply continuity indexes. The same cluster analysis was applied to electricity demand variables, and hence, the crossing of ranked clusters of demand and system attributes indicated municipal districts where the utility must apply system reinforcements to have adequate supply quality, or where the quality goal set by the regulatory body is too tight.

CONCLUSION

The presented validation scheme between the k-means statistical method and the Self-Organizing Maps (SOM) showed to be a flexible and reliable tool, because the best characteristics of both algorithms are explored .

The combination of the rigid and recognized k-means clustering, and the capacity of knowledge discovery and visualization of the SOM, allows one to look for the best group configuration to represent the attributes of the contained data, allowing border identification, as well as the most susceptible elements to group change. This is an important characteristic, because it makes rapid reclassifications possible, without running the algorithm again, by simply renumbering the desired border neuron.

This scheme also shows that the SOM is a good clustering tool, which used with appropriate knowledge could lead to excellent results. This work allowed an utility to argue with the brazilian energy regulatory body for suitable quality goals and adequate investment refund.

REFERENCES

Pampalk, E., Rauber, A., Merkl, D., 2002: Using Smoothed Data Histograms for Cluster Visualization in Self-Organizing Maps, *Proc. of the International Conference on Artificial Neural Networks*,.Springer Lecture Notes in Computer Science, Madrid, Spain.

Ultsch, A., Siemon, H.P, 1990: Kohonen's Self-Organizing Feature Maps for Exploratory Data Analisys, *Proc. Intern. Neural Networks*, pp: 305 – 308, Paris, France.

Kohonen, T., 2001, *Self-Organizing Maps*; Springer-Verlag, 3ª ed.

Vesanto, J., Himberg, J., Alhoniemi, E., Parhankangas, J., 1999: Self-Organizing Map in Matlab: the SOM Toolbox, *In Proc. of the Matlab DSP Conference*, pp: 35–40, Espoo, Finland.

Coelho, J., Gauche, E., Queiroz, H., Nassar, S.M., Ricardo,V.W., Lima, M., 2002: Influence of Weather Variables in Continuity Levels of Electrical Power Supply – An Analysis through Artificial Neural Networks, *Symposium of Specialists in Electric Operational Expansion Planning (SEPOPE),* Curitiba, Brazil.

Semantic Information Evolution

Hemant M. Joshi and Coskun Bayrak
Applied Science Department
University of Arkansas at Little Rock
{hmjoshi | cxbayrak@ualr.edu}

ABSTRACT

A librarian at Yale University, Mr. Rogers Rutherford says, "We're drowning in information and starving for knowledge" [9]. These quotes are very appropriate keeping in mind the rate at which World Wide Web is gathering information. It is essential to be able to make sense out of these huge piles of information. It is important to look at information from the point of view of its relevance, correlation and also form the point of view of its validity with respect to time. Semantic information will facilitate the correlation between two given concepts. The focus of the following paper is on some of the inherent intrinsic properties of information. The task of identifying any information with right context is very important. This paper deals with the concept of reference domains, which represents information as it evolves in our knowledge base.

BACKGROUND

Sherlock Holmes and Dr. Watson go on a camping trip, set up their tent, and fall asleep. Some hours later, Holmes wakes his faithful friend. "Watson, look up at the sky and tell me what you see." Watson replies, "I see millions of stars." "What does that tell you?" Watson ponders for a minute.

"Astronomically speaking, it tells me that there are millions of galaxies and potentially billions of planets. Astrologically, it tells me that Saturn is in Leo. Time wise, it appears to be approximately a quarter past three.

Theologically, it's evident the Lord is all-powerful and we are small and insignificant. Meteorologically, it seems we will have a beautiful day tomorrow. What does it tell you?" Holmes is silent for a moment, and then speaks. "Someone has stolen our tent"

The story is hilarious. What it highlights is how easy it is to complicate issues and then miss the most obvious things. Too much knowledge is no help unless it is supported by the wisdom to guide it to an effective conclusion.

More efficient searching for information has been a goal for the research community since the frequent use of the World Wide Web to find every possible answer needed. It is desired to look for information encompassing all possible areas for a given concept. The scope for information retrieval should not be confined to a particular field. This paper discusses the human-like cognitive abilities to retrieve information. Information is correlated with what is known and processed with respect to the given context. Concepts are more meaningful when they are expressed with the right context.

PROBLEM DEFINITION

Text has been the most prevalent method of representing information. Thus text pattern matching is the basis of information retrieval. Even though some progress has been made with techniques like latent semantic information and probabilistic latent semantic information, it is needed to look at information along with its context to make more intuitive judgment. Some of the techniques discussed in this paper are of utmost importance from the point of view of information representation. Information, if represented in the right context, makes more sense than text based searching.

Most of the top search engines [1-6] do a better job at matching text to the query. There is, however, limited semantics involved in this process. Same word might mean differently for different people. An Indonesian knows Java as one of the islands in

Indonesia, south of Borneo. A computer programmer knows Java as a programming language. Some coffee enthusiast would like to know about Java coffee. Most of the search engines including the popular ones do get the job done but fail to interpret and understand semantics of the same word java and its importance to various people. Google [2], [8] arguably the best search engine currently has pile of 3,307,998,701 web pages in it's database and search term Java results in 56600000 hits with none of the first 100 results about Java coffee or java islands. Google's highly acclaimed Page Rank technique along with some of the best search engine practices fails to take into account semantics or different meaning of the word Java. Effective representation is important to retrieve information by association, correlation, relevance and semantics.

PROPERTIES OF INFORMATION

Information in all its forms has some properties associated with it. These properties are inherent to the nature of information and do apply to all types of information.

1. **Temporal**: Information in its any form has temporal information associated with it. These temporal parameters talk about the validity of the information "from" and "to" date. Information is not created the day it is put on the web page but the day it is associated with. Some of the information may have unlimited validity [mostly facts] but still has temporal properties strongly associated with it.
2. **Semantics**: Semantic or meaning of the information is always a language issue, as it is dependent on the language it is expressed in. This is the reason why information processing should involve great deal of Natural Language Processing [7] as well. Semantic property also refers to the natural characteristics of different media to represent information. Considering the case of textual information, Natural Language Processing suggests that the most strongly correlated information is the one expressed in one single sentence. Information should be looked at from the context it was established in.

PREVIOUS WORK

The standard information representation and retrieval process includes parsing of web pages, removing (called as stemming [8]) unwanted or common words and remaining information is considered good to be indexed. This information is then ranked and indexed according to various algorithms. One of the most common and effective algorithm uses Term Frequency (TF) [14] and Inverse Document Frequency (IDF) [13] to determine weight of each term. When searched for the given term, documents that match certain threshold are listed as search results. The results produced by these systems are satisfactory but not intuitive from the point of view of context of information. Traditional lexical matching is more of pattern matching technique without any semantic involvement.

Latent semantic analysis (LSA) is the first step in the direction of semantic analysis of document space. There are known problems of mere lexical matching techniques and some of these are very well addressed in LSA technique. LSA expresses term by document matrix for the given document space and then tries reducing the dimensionality by employing Singular Value Decomposition (SVD) technique. The sparse matrix of term frequencies in the given document space is resolved and mapped to a semantic space where the query vector can be compared against each document to find cosine similarity. Performance is greatly improved with this SVD technique compared to original term document matrix [16].

Probabilistic LSA technique introduced by Thomas Hoffman [17] is a variant of LSA, which by forming aspect model represents data in latent probability space. Probabilistic LSA yields better results than traditional LSA model.

According to Thomas Landauer et. al [18], LSA even though better technique than lexical matching, lacks human cognitive abilities to intuitively understand correlations. It fails to take into account contextual information.

INTRODUCTION

The concept of semantic view of information is presented in this section. Following are the definitions of a few terms that are referred to in this paper.

- Information Domain(s) and sub-domains
  Information domains are those primary important word(s) in the text information, which represent given concept for its context established. Sub domains are synonyms and semantically similar meanings that constitute the entire information domain. Hierarchically sub domains are part of and belong to main domain that is encountered in the document space.
- Reference domains
  Various domains will attribute to the representation of information present in the given document space. If a document has two words that belong to different (sub) domains, in a single sentence, their strong correlation can easily be determined. Such (sub) domains will be combined to form a reference domain. In short, reference domains span across set of domains of information.
- Correlation and types of correlation
  Correlation is defined in terms of co-occurrence of two given terms occurring in the same document. Presence of these terms in a single document illustrates the correlation between them.
  Strong Correlation is said to exist if the two terms not only exist in the same document but also in a single sentence, as represented by reference domains.
  Weak correlation is more common and is handled by two terms occurring in a single document, not necessarily in a single sentence.
  No correlation exists in two given terms if they do not occur in a same document.
- Related Domains
  If two (sub) domains are (weakly/strongly) correlated in terms of their semantics, then they are considered as Related Domains. Reference domains are subset of related dataset as they represent only (positively) strong correlation. The three words term, domains and sub-domains can be used interchangeably. So strong, weak or no correlation, can be expressed in terms of two (sub) domains as well.
- Semantic Correlation among related domains
  As mentioned above, semantic correlations can be expressed between related domains. These relationships could be of strong, weak nature or no relation may exist semantically between two non-related domains.

INFORMATION CORRELATION AND ITS REPRESENTATION

Information correlation between two (sub) domains is represented by the qualitative correlation between the two. Consider domains d_i of elements. If there is a reference domain R such that there can be found an element of R ($r_{iq} \in R$), r_{jq} such that r_{jq} is either d_t itself or is in close vicinity of d_t. Then the qualitative correlation between d_i and d_t can be defined as:

$$Ci\ (d_t) = \begin{cases} 1 \\ 0 \end{cases} \tag{1}$$

Here the value of qualitative correlation is 1 if and only if d_t can be found in close vicinity of r_{jq} i.e. $r_{jq} - d_0 \leq d_t \leq r_{jq} + d_0$. Here d_0 is the shift interval for the depth till which references formed within reference domains can be persuaded. This factor can be standardized to be 1, which means 1 reference to outside domain from within actual reference domain is followed and is considered significant. On the other hand, value of correlation function Ci (d_i) is determined to be 0 if d_i cannot be found in given document space or in the close vicinity of reference domain element r_{jq}. The definition of Ci (d_i)

here indicates that for the given reference domain d_i, all the elements in that reference domain exhibit related domain property to establish relation with d_i.

SEMANTIC CORRELATION FUNCTION OF REFERENCE DOMAIN

Let there be m elements that are members of reference domain represented by d_i. In this case, Semantic Correlation Function of the entire domain d_i can be calculated by considering the qualitative correlation of each member with domain R_j. Because all the elements of domain d_i have same strong correlation to the term under consideration, the Semantic Correlation Function (SCF) for a given reference domain d_i is defined as follows:

$$SCF_i = \frac{m-1}{m}$$

where reference domain has m elements such that t = 1,2,3, ..., m, and, $0 < SCFi < 1$. Graph in Figure 1 represents relationship between number of elements in the reference domain and it's SCFi.

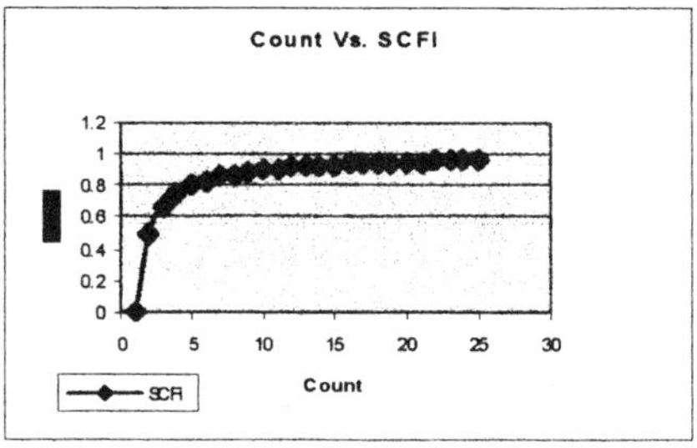

Figure 1: Relationship between number of elements in the reference domain and its SCFi

If count, m = 1 i.e. only one element is member of reference domain which is under consideration, then SCFi value is 0. As the number of words in the related domain increases, the SCFi value will be close to 1. In other words, SCFi is in direct proportion to the number of elements of reference domain that can be identified as related domains.

The relationship between correlation and number of outside references can be established if the number of outside references pointing to the given reference domain are considered. For any given count, once SCFi is obtained, correlation factor can be defined as:

$$Corr_i = \log_{10} (SCFi * (1+N)) \quad (2)$$

where N is the number of outside references for any given domain.

For any given number of elements in the domain, if the number of elements is kept steady and the number of outside references to that particular reference domain is increased, the value of correlation of the given domain increases linearly slightly as shown in graph of Figure 2. The increase is justified and the slight change in logarithmic function of correlation does correspond to the varying domain references that may be found in the given document space. The use of logarithmic function is suitable as there are a large number of outside domain references.

The affecting factor SCFi also plays a crucial role determining correlation factor for any given domain. The presence of 1 in the formula above ensures proper values even if there are no outside references to the given domain. Also it indicates that there is at least one reference (self referencing) to any domain at any given instance.

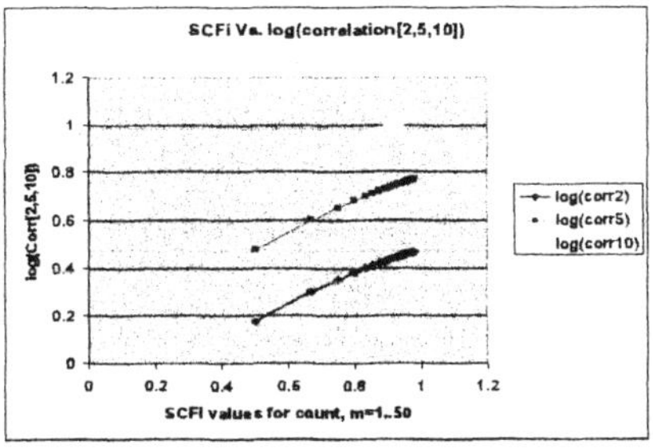

Figure 2: *SCF response to number of reference domain elements*

PROPERTIES

Some important aspects of above representation can be inferred. Dynamic shift interval or depth of reference, to related domain could be adjusted for tuning of related query results. In some cases, this parameter may be omitted to prevent any depth for related domain search. In this specific case, the qualitative correlation of information domains degenerates into fuzzy logic and d_0 becomes fuzzy logic interval.

Another evident interesting property is that for the same number of elements in two given domains, if number of outside references is more, the correlation value of that domain is higher. So correlation value is directly proportional to the number of outside references. Even though correlation value is directly proportional to number of outside references, it also is dependent on the SCFi value of the given domain.

These principles are applied to the document matrix method of information representation. The LSA technique is adopted to represent reference domains across the entire document space. Imagine a document space of about 500 documents, and around 2000 lines or sentences consisting of 5 word each making total of 10,000 terms. Lexical matching would identify and match any of these terms by their presence in text. No correlations can be established if the semantic aspect is not considered.

Instead of term document matrix of 10,000 x 500 size, the dimensionality is reduced by creating correlation factor matrix of reference domains and documents in the given document space. This matrix would be of considerably smaller size like 2000 x 500. The correlation factors for each reference domain correspond with respect to the given document. Singular Value Decomposition [19] to this matrix can be further applied to reduce dimension to represent data in truly semantic space. Even the query vector can be mapped to this same space. The cosine similarity between any given document vector and the query vector can be used as a measure to determine weather the particular document is similar or rather correlated to the query term. Local and global weights can be added to the equation (2) to further improve results.

An algorithm to find correlations semantically; employs LSA. The base matrix of reference domains vs. document can be split and reduced in dimensionality by using Singular Value Decomposition. The original matrix is represented by A here.

$$A = U * \sum * V^T$$

Here matrix A is of r reference domains and d documents, whereas Matrix U and V^T are of much smaller dimension. Both vectors U and V^T are orthogonal and vector $\sum$ consists of singular values. Original matrix is formed using equation (2) in this paper. Now the first selected k values of diagonal vector $\sum$ are used to reconstruct the original matrix. We form new matrix A_k such that,

$$A_k = U_k * \sum_k * V^T_k$$

The query vector can now be formulated. The query term defines the query vector. Querying approach looks for semantic context for the given query and forms a query reference domain. It is assumed that each reference domain has a potential to be a query result and minimum weight is given for that fact. As a result, query vector is formed of various reference domains correlation factors.

The query vector is then mapped to the semantic space of reduced dimensionality k as follows:

$$Q_k = Q^T * U_k * \sum_k^{-1}$$

Similarly all the document vectors can be individually mapped to semantic space as:

$$dj_k = dj_k^T * U_k * \sum_k^{-1}$$

where dj $\in$ D, document space. Now that query as well as every document is mapped to the semantic space, the cosine of angle between two vectors can be defined as:

$$sim(dj,Q) = cos\ \theta j = \frac{dj_k^T * Q_k}{\left\|dj_k^T\right\|_2 * \left\|Q_k\right\|_2}$$

Once the similarity has been established, correlated domains are identified and sorted for the closeness to the query vector.

The strength of this approach is in forming reference domains of synonyms and related contexts for the given terms. Information with its relevant context is preserved and mined for information retrieval. Also significant change can be achieved in terms of original matrix dimensionality. The term by document matrix has row dimension, which is much larger than original matrix of reference domain by document.

Information can be represented as it evolves in the document space. Once the correlation circle is complete, information keeps growing, seeking more and more correlation. Not all correlated concepts are strongly related in the reality but they are significantly represented the way human mind would try and correlate them. The context in which a particular concept is absorbed makes this approach establish newer correlations.

Test case environment was set up to analyze and implement concept correlation algorithm. The performance was tested in incremental fashion linearly increasing the size of the document space. Noise documents were also introduced to simulate real world scenario. Text as well as HTML documents were parsed and matched for dictionary meanings, synonyms. Figure 3 indicates the accuracy of the system developed to implement correlation algorithm.

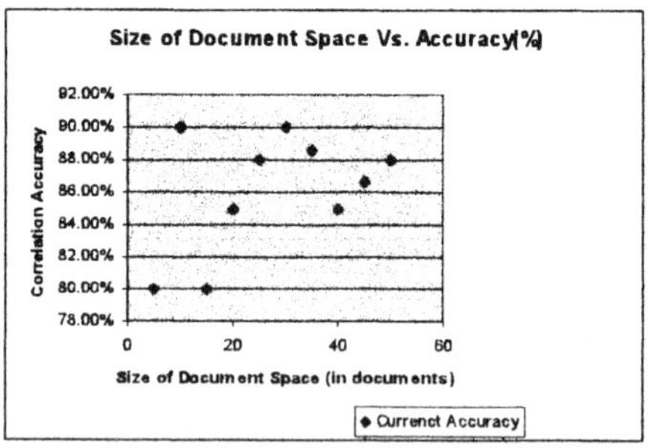

Figure 3: *Accuracy in finding correlations*

FUTURE WORK AND CONCLUSION

This paper shows the semantic relations between concepts that are strongly correlated. The established relationships should help determine relevant correlated information for the given query term. This technique can be used in conjunction with some of the existing techniques like LSA to reduce space and time complexity and to provide better and relevant search results.

Future work in this area will involve larger document space to form reference domains. Also the use of encyclopedia will help determine relevance and context of given concept in broader aspect. One key area of work can be devoted to understanding sentence boundaries in different languages. It will help improve this technique in various languages. Another key issue to be investigated is about temporal properties associated with information. These properties can help us associate information with its relevance and with respect to time features as well.

REFERENCES

[1] AltaVista web page search engine, http://www.altavista.com

[2] Google Search engine, http://www.google.com

[3] Vivisimo, cluster search engine, http://www.vivisimo.com

[4] Seeq search engine, http://www.seeq.com

[5] Kartoo, visual categorized search engine, http://www.kartoo.com

[6] Web page search engine, http://www.webcrawler.com

[7] Foundations of Statistical Natural Language processing, http://nlp.stanford.edu/fsnlp/

[8] Porter stemming algorithm, http://www.tartarus.org/~martin/PorterStemmer/

[9] Information drowning quote, http://www.bartleby.com/63/5/2605.html

[10] "Using Qualitative Hypotheses to Identify Inaccurate Data" By Qi Zhao and Toyoki Nishida, Journal of Artificial Intelligence Research 3, (1995) pp.119-145

[11] "Towards Semantic Web Mining" By Bettina Berendt, Andreas Hotho, and Gerd Stumme, ISWC 2002, LNCS 2342, pp. 264-278, http://citeseer.nj.nec.com/585344.html

[12] "The anatomy of a Large-Scale Hyper textual Web Search Engine" By Sergey Brin and Lawrence Page, http://www7.scu.edu.au/programme/fullpapers/1921/com1921.htm

[13] "Text categorization based on weighted inverse document frequency" By Tokenobu Tokenaga and Makoto Iwayama (1994), http://citeseer.nj.nec.com/tokunaga94text.html

[14] Term Frequency definition by search engine dictionary at http://www.searchenginedictionary.com/terms-term-frequency.shtml

[15] "Computing Iceberg Concept Lattices with TITANIC" By Gerd Stumme et. al (2002) at http://citeseer.ist.psu.edu/stumme02computing.html

[16] "Using Linear Algebra For Intelligent Information Retrieval" By Michael Berry et. al. at, Technical Report UT-CS-94-270, 1994 on the web at http://citeseer.nj.nec.com/berry95using.html

[17] "Unsupervised Learning by Probabilistic Latent Semantic Analysis" By Thomas Hoffman, Machine Learning, 42, 177-196, 2001 on the web at http://ai.uwaterloo.ca/~sjwang/cs886/hofmann.pdf

[18] "An introduction to Latent Semantic Analysis" By Thomas K. Landauer et.al, Discourse Processes, 25, 259-284 on the web at http://lsa.colorado.edu/papers/dp1.LSAintro.pdf

[19] "Learning Human-like knowledge by Singular Value Decomposition : A progress Report" By Thomas Lanauer, Darrell Laham and Peter Foltz, Artificial intelligence on the web at http://lsa.colorado.edu/papers/nips.pdf

[20] "The Theory Underlying Concept Maps and How To Construct Them" By Joseph D. Novak, Cornell University on the web at http://cmap.coginst.uwf.edu/info/

DEVELOPING INTELLIGENT INFORMATION SYSTEMS FOR GENOMIC DATA ANALYSIS

MARY QU-XUANYUAN YANG
School of Electrical and Computer Engineering, Purdue University.
West Lafayette, Indiana 47907 USA

JACK YONGSHENG YANG
School of Medicine, Indiana University Purdue University Indianapolis. Indianapolis, IN 46202

OKAN K. ERSOY
School of Electrical and Computer Engineering, Purdue University.
West Lafayette, Indiana 47907 USA
Contact: Professor Okan K. Ersoy
Fellow of IEEE and Fellow of OSA
ersoy@ecn.purdue.edu
purduexy@ecn.purdue.edu

ABSTRACT

In our attempt to understand structural and functional genomics, we must be able to develop automatic computational approaches. We demonstrate the efficiency of Ersoy's Support Vector Machine Trees by incorporate new biophysical and biochemical information in the development of intelligent integrated database with efficient feature selections in developing more robust learning algorithms using multi-stage decompositions of the feature space to transform the complex biological data mining problem into simpler subproblems that improve the generalization. Performance of our algorithm has been compared favorably with other machine learning algorithms such as traditional support vector machines and neural networks.

1. INTRODUCTION

With the advance of many biomedical technologies, the confederation of widely distributed databases creates problems because of unification, communication and validation difficulties. Sequence data, structural data and property data for a given set of proteins can be located in different databases with different interfaces and those databases do not communicate each other. In order to develop a seamless integration of multiple heterogeneous database that combines the datasets from Overhauser Effects enhanced experiments, NMR, X-ray crystallography and Circular Digestion Spectra etc, we are developing intelligent integrated database with queries processed by the mediators through multiple databases, each integrates environment interfaces with mediator through the wrapper, which acts as an intelligent proxy user on behalf of the mediator for retrieving and processing the data corresponding to the sub-queries from the database and passing it back to the mediator, which takes all data collected from all wrappers and integrates them. The mediator using medical and biological data model and ontology intelligently resolves inter-data dependencies and integrating the data. This enables us obtained more reliable data regarding much physical and biomedical prosperity of proteins that will be useful for our on-going research projects on alternative splicing and remote homolog dictations through computational intelligence.

It is estimated more than half of genes in eukaryotic species undergo alternative splicing. Currently, predication of alternative splicing is mainly using Express Sequence Tag (EST) data, hoping alternative splicing isoforms can be clustered and then can be mapped onto a genome. Such common approach does not use characteristics and function of the result proteins. We are developing a new efficient alternative splicing prediction using more protein characteristics, physical and biomedical information. After half century of the discoveries of Overhauser Effects, NMR and X-ray crystallography that determined many protein structures, A. Keith Dunker (Dunker et al. 1999-2004) introduced a new theory of Protein Trinity, that the central dogma of structural biology that amino acid sequence -> 3D structure -> protein function has been modified by Protein Trinity. Not all proteins fold into 3-D structure in native state in Nature. A protein lacks of 3-D structure in intrinsic state is called intrinsic unstructured/disordered protein (IUP) or protein disorder. With the advent of high-throughput genome sequencing technology, roughly a million protein sequences have been identified, but only about 24,000 structures had been determined. We need to bridge the gap between approximately one million sequences and 24,000 known structures. This paper demonstrates the practice of Ersoy's Support Vector Machine Tree algorithms using intelligent integrated database.

2. THE ALOGRITHM AND ERSOY'S SUPPORT VECTOR MACHINE TREE CLASSIFIER

The overall algorithm is to use our intelligent integrated database to extract features from structural and motional information for classification. It consists of three stages: the first stage is to obtain the useful features from our intelligent integrated database and perform the feature selections. The second stage partitions the feature space using Ersoy's Support Vector Machine Trees. As this stage is guided by support vector machines to partitioning the feature space recursively, it makes use of the class labels, and thus falls under the heading of supervised learning methods. The last stage then uses the tree as a classifier.

As with any classifier, the first step is to divide the data into a training set and a testing set. The root node initially contains all the training data. We then split the root node by defining a partition of the training data into two subsets; associated with each subset is a child node of the root node. Each of the child nodes is then recursively split until sufficient number of instances available of support vector machines. Such splitting of a node is guided by a support vector machine. As such type of trees was first invented by distinguished Professor Ersoy (Ersoy et al. 2002); it was named as Ersoy's Support Vector Machine Trees. Each of the left node contains ideally one dominant type of class and the right node contains the other dominant type of class. Once constructed, the Ersoy's Support Vector Machine Tree can be used as a classifier, which is defined by the tree structure. Any test instance can be mapped on the Ersoy's Support Vector Machine Tree and thus classifications can be given by several nodes on the tree. The overall classification was obtained by a majority voting scheme. Performance showed it outperformed traditional support vector machines, neural networks and other machine learning methods.

3 INTELLIGENT INTEGRATED DATABASE:

DNA micro-array technologies and genome sequencing technologies as well many other recent innovations have produced numerous databases. Today, generating biomedical data outstripped the speed to store and to analyze the resulting data in a timely manner. In facing avalanche of data, more efforts need to be made to standardizing the storage format, sharing, and publishing techniques. Our attempt is to provide an intelligent integrated database that facilitates the medical and biological discoveries by enhancing the interoperablilities among those data. We are generating a seamless integration of multiple heterogeneous information system beyond the limitations and boundaries of individual database. The system integrates multiple databases and consists of data model and ontology, mediator, wrapper, user interface and gene and protein network. The development of intelligent integrated data system provides better communication among databases, filter out incorrect and inaccurate data, and enhance data accessibility, retrieval, analysis, and more efficient learning from the combined data. Our system incorporates information from Protein Data Bank (PDB) and many other databases to obtain more useful features. We illustrate our feature generation and feature selection in the next section.

3. FEATURE GENERATION AND FEATURE SELECTION.

The algorithm is to use the intelligent integrated database to extract protein features from structural and motional information and combine feature selection into a classification algorithm based on Ersoy's Support Vector Machine Trees with majority voting schemes. We introduce a 9-gram encoding of amino acids based on the biophysical and biochemical proprieties of amino acids as illustrated below: gl = {C}, Cysteine remains strongly Cysteine during evolution; g2 = {M}, Hydrophobic, sulfur containing; g3 = {N, Q} Amides, polar; g4 = {D, E}, Acids, positive, polar; g5 = {S, T}, Alcohols; g6 = {P, A, G}, Aliphatic, small; g7 = {I, V, L}, Aliphatic; g8 = {F, Y, W}, Aromatic; g9 = {H, K, R}, Bases, charged. Let $g \subset$ { gl, g2, g3, g4, g5, g6, g7, g8, g9 }; The first set of feature vector of each position in the amino acid sequence is derived from a window which is the center at the position. The features contain first order statistics, regarding relative frequencies of a given gram in the feature window of given length. Therefore, we generated 9 features as illustrated below:

$$\mathbf{Pi}\,(g) = \frac{1}{k - k_0 + 1} \sum_{j=k_0}^{k} \delta_{x(j)g}$$

where, Pi (g) is the "probability" of 2-turple code at position i of the sequence, k and k_0 are defined below, where x (j) is the 2-turple code at the position j of the protein sequence. $\delta_{x(j)g} = \begin{cases} 1, & \text{if } x(j) = g \\ 0, & \text{otherwise} \end{cases}$

l : length of feature window. **L:** length of whole protein sequence
k_0 = min (1, i - (**l** - 1) / 2) and k = max (**L**, i + (**l** - 1) / 2)

The second order statistics of 2-turple code is calculated in the same window as before. This generates 9 x 9 = 81 features as:

given $S_{mn} = g_m g_n$

$g \subset \{ g1, g2, g3, g4, g5, g6, g7, g8, g9 \}$;

$$P_i(S_{mn}) = \frac{1}{k - k_0 + 1} \sum_{j=k_0}^{j=k-1} \delta_{x(j)g(m)} \delta_{x(j+1)g(n)}$$

where $P_i(S_{mn})$ is the second order statistics at position i and

$$\delta_{x(j)g(m)} \delta_{x(j+1)g(n)} = \begin{cases} 1, & \text{if } x(j) = g(m),\ x(j+1) = g(n) \\ 0, & \text{otherwise} \end{cases}$$

k and k_0 have the same definition as previous.

The next set of feature vector of each position of the amino acid in the protein sequence is derived similarly as above regarding relative frequencies of 20 amino acids in the feature window. Therefore, we generated additional 20 features. Similarly, we applied second order statistics, which gives 400 more features. We also use complexity in our features. According to the past research, most likely, disorder regions have low complexity patterns (Dunker et al 1999-2004). K2-entropy is used to measure the local complexity of amino acid sequence. Complex of each position in the sequence is calculated by the probabilities of 20 amino acids in the same feature window given before by:

$$Ci = -\sum_{n=1}^{20} P_i(a_n) \log_2 P_i(a_n)$$

In addition, we add the relative hydrophobicity of each amino acid, called hydropathy. The feature for hydropathy, Hi, is the average of hydropathy in the feature window.

$$Hi = \frac{1}{k - k_0 + 1} \sum_{j=k_0}^{k} Hydropathy(j)$$ where k, k_0 are defined same as before.

Final we add amino acid disorder propensities as our features.

We now generate at least 514 features, feature selection is necessary to speed up train process, especially for the supervised leaning algorithm. The result of train may not be convergent due to high dimensional input. The feature selection algorithm is based on distance measures. Assume two features: feature X, x is the value of feature X; and feature Y, y is the value of feature Y. Distance D(X) is the measurement how far the 2-class is separate by using feature X and distance D(Y) is the measurement how far the two class is separate by using feature Y. If D(X) > D(Y), then feature X is selected, since the interclass distance for feature X is larger than feature Y. Otherwise, feature Y is selected. This reduces feature space to an ideal size such as 59.

4 EXPERIMENTAL RESULTS

The process of evolution has resulted in the production of DNA sequences that encode proteins with specific functions. We construct our predicator using Ersoy's Support Vector Machine Trees by extracting useful feature information from the intelligent integrated database to obtain reliable structural and motional information. The software we developed is written in Microsoft Visual Studio.net C++ and is running under Windows XP Professional. Our classifier is performed by majority voting from the Ersoy's Support Vector Machine Tree on the tree structure. We set up a threshold as the boundary of class 1 and class 0. TP is denoted as true positive of class one that is above the threshold. TN is denoted as true negative of class 0 that is below the threshold. FP is denoted as false positive of class 1 but below the threshold. FN is denoted as false negative of class 0, but above threshold. Sensitivity is defined as TP / (TP + FN) which is True Positive Rate (TPR) and Specificity is defined as TN / (TN + FP) which is True Negative Rate (TNR). Average classification rate is arithmetic mean defined as (TPR+TNR) / 2, which is overall performance. Experimental results show our approach is better than SVMs in DISOPRED2 (Jones et al. 2003), neural networks in disEMBL (Linding et al. 2003) and propensity algorithm in Globplot (Linding et al. 2003) as reported in figures 1 and 2. For example protein 1ARU in PDB, our predicator gives 87.79% overall accuracy. True positive accuracy is 100%; true negative accuracy is 87.50%. Number of false positive is zero, which means there is no disorder amino acid that we fail to predict in this protein. Based on the comparisons, we outperform disEMBL, Globplot and DISOPRED2. The benchmark of our algorithm against others is given in the figure 1 and sample output is in figure 2.

5 CONCLUSIONS

Many protein crystallography data have large R-factors, which indicated the "solved" protein structures were not from protein crystals rather than from protein glasses. Missing coordinates of possible IUP region in the Protein Data Bank resulting from X-ray crystallography (more accurately should be called protein glass) data, indicate that IUPs are lacking of intrinsic 3-D structures, but do carry functions. Assessing protein functions based on structures from X-ray crystallography is inaccurate, while Overhauser Effects enhanced experiments may not solve structures of large proteins. The abilities of Ersoy's methods to overcome the limitations of other methods mean once our intelligent data system can be used; we may provide deeper insights into protein structural and functional relationships at genomic level and hereby deepen the understanding of Theory of Protein Trinity, which opens up new research in molecular biology.

The philosophy of support vector machines as used in DISOPRED2 is to transform original (low dimensional) data into higher dimensional space, hoping that inseparable original data may be separable in the high dimensional space. A support vector machine relies on a hyperplane in the transformed high dimensional space to separate the data and such hyperplane can not accommodate to the complexity of data if a real boundary to separate the data is not anything similar to a hyperplane in the transformed space as well. Therefore, support vector machine may still yield high misclassification rates. Ersoy's Support Vector Machine Trees overcome such deficiencies by majority voting schemes and pick up the outliers, thus tend to better accommodate the complexity of the type of data used.

protein	our classifier			GlobPlot(2.0)			DisEMBL(1.3)		
	TPR	TNR	AVG	TPR	TNR	AVG	TPR	TNR	AVG
Phosphoenolpyruvate Carboxykinase	0.75	0.95	0.85	0	0.91	0.46	0	1	0.5
Avian Sarcoma Virus Integrase Catalytic Core Domain	0.81	0.75	0.78	0	0.79	0.4	0	1	0.5
cyanide	1	0.88	0.94	1	0.85	0.92	1	0.94	0.97
Retinol-Binding Protein (Rbp) From Pig Plasma	0.86	0.99	0.93	0	0.83	0.42	0	0.95	0.48
Native Plasminogen Activator Inhibitor	1	0.7	0.85	1	0.78	0.89	0	1	0.5
D60S N-Terminal Lobe Human Lactoferrin	1	0.75	0.88	0.52	0.92	0.72	0	0.96	0.48
Calpain Domain VI With Calcium Bound	0.91	0.96	0.94	1	0.85	0.93	1	0.98	0.99
A Thermostable Serine Protease	0.78	0.77	0.77	0	0.78	0.39	0	1	0.55
Bovine Purine Nucleoside Phosphorylase Complexed	0.86	0.98	0.92	1	0.67	0.83	0	0.93	0.47
L-Fuculose 1-Phosphate Aldolase	1	0.98	0.99	1	0.83	0.92	0.88	1	0.94
N-Terminal Domain Of Sec18P	0.82	0.81	0.82	0.4	0.88	0.64	0.4	0.98	0.69

Fig 1.(above) Performance comparisons with GlobPlot & DisEMBL, Fig 2.(below) sample output

59 feature, 0.25 sequence similarity

PDB ID	Test Index	Test Sequence	Overal Accuracy	True positive	True Negative	Flase Postive	Flase Negative	True Disorder
1ARU	12	36th sequence	94.48%	100.00%	94.35%	0	19	8
1ASV	17	51th sequence	80.86%	81.25%	80.82%	3	28	16
1AYL	27	80th sequence	97.97%	87.50%	98.12%	1	10	8
1AZS	33	90th sequence	82.73%	93.33%	81.05%	2	36	30
1B27	40	107th sequence	83.33%	77.78%	83.95%	2	13	9
1B5T	54	141th sequence	80.73%	85.71%	80.60%	1	52	7
1B8G	63	162th sequence	75.52%	85.71%	75.36%	1	104	7
1BE3	75	201th sequence	73.12%	90.00%	72.32%	2	116	20
1BFE	81	213th sequence	73.95%	100.00%	71.82%	0	31	9
1BJ0	94	246th sequence	74.40%	85.71%	73.58%	2	51	14
1BJ1	95	247th sequence	79.22%	100.00%	77.98%	0	48	13
1A34	104	276th sequence	96.23%	91.67%	96.60%	1	5	12
1A52	111	295th sequence	73.26%	94.74%	71.55%	1	68	19
1BSX	135	356th sequence	79.23%	88.24%	78.60%	2	52	17
1BWP	141	381th sequence	73.82%	80.95%	73.11%	4	57	21
1BX0	142	385th sequence	72.61%	94.44%	71.28%	1	85	18
1BXS	144	392th sequence	74.45%	100.00%	74.09%	0	128	7
1BY3	146	396th sequence	72.27%	89.47%	71.80%	2	196	19
1BZC	151	407th sequence	71.65%	100.00%	69.46%	0	91	23
1C0M	153	415th sequence	70.17%	88.24%	68.78%	2	69	17
1C41	160	437th sequence	77.00%	97.06%	72.89%	1	45	34
1C8J	167	465th sequence	71.53%	85.71%	71.16%	2	154	14
1CDK	169	490th sequence	72.46%	100.00%	71.85%	0	114	9
1CEX	172	500th sequence	75.71%	100.00%	75.22%	0	85	7
1CF9	175	504th sequence	96.26%	87.50%	96.97%	2	6	16
1A7C	181	529th sequence	70.78%	92.31%	70.01%	2	218	26
1CTV	187	543th sequence	76.78%	85.71%	76.44%	2	86	14
1CJA	189	546th sequence	80.26%	81.82%	80.21%	2	74	11
1CK7	195	562th sequence	73.98%	100.00%	72.78%	0	89	15
1CKE	196	563th sequence	73.69%	100.00%	73.23%	0	166	11

ACKNOWLEDGEMENTS

We would like to thank Dr. A. Keith Dunker, Founder of Protein Trinity and Director of Indiana University School of Medicine, Center for Computational Biology and Bioinformatics, Indiana University Purdue University Indianapolis for his support and Dr. Albert W. Overhauser, discoverer of Overhauser Effects, Member of United States National Academy of Science and Stuart Distinguished Professor of Purdue University for his valuable discussion.

REFERENCE

[1] Dunker, A. Keith, Remero P. et al "Intelligent Data Analysis for Protein Disoder Predication" Artificial Intelligence Review 14, 447-484 (2000).

[2] Dunker A. Keith, P. Romero et al "Seq. complexity & disordered protein," Proteins 42 (2001).

[3] Dunker, A. Keith et al "Flavors of protein disorder" Proteins 52,573-84 (2003).

[4] Dunker A. Keith, P. Radivojac et al."Protein flexibility & intrin. disorder," Protein Sc.13 (2004).

[5] Linding R. et al. "Protein Disorder Prediction: Impl. Structural Proteomics" Structure 11, (2003)

[6] Linding R. et al. "GlobPlot: exploring protein seq. for globularity & disorder" NAR 31 (2003).

[7] Jones, D. et al."Prediction disorder. reg. in proteins from pos.spec.score matri"Proteins S6 (2003)

[8] Ersoy, Okan K and Chi, H. (2002) "Support Vector Machine Decision Trees with Rare Event Detection" International Journal of Smart Engineering System Design pp. 225-242

[9] Ersoy, Okan K, Choe W et al (2000)"Neural network schemes for detecting rare events in human genomic DNA" Bioinformatics Vol.16 no.12 pp 1062-72

[10] Yang, Jack, Mary Qu Yang and Okan K. Ersoy "Gene finding and Protein Function Determination using Protein Phylogenetic profiles and Computational Intelligence", Intelligent Engineering Systems through Artificial Neural Networks.Vol. 12, pp 733-740 (2002).

PART VII: PATTERN RECOGNITION

OBJECTS DETECTION AND RECOGNITION IN SCENE IMAGE USING NEURAL NETWORKS BASED ON VISUAL CHARACTERISTICS

SATORU ODO
Faculty of Humanities, Okinawa University, Okinawa, Japan

ABSTRACT

We propose a mouse-like function for estimating hand shape from input images with a monocular camera, with which a computer user feels no restraint or awkwardness. Our system involves conversion of sequential images from Cartesian coordinates to log-polar coordinates. Pulse Couple Neural Network (PCNN) is used to extract the hand region, because PCNN has superior segmentation ability. Recognition of the hand shape is carried out by the competitive neural network using higher order local autocorrelation features of log-polar Coordinate space. Mouse-like functions are realized with the hand shape and motion trajectory. Compared to conventional Cartesian coordinates, conversion to log-polar coordinates enables us to reduce image date and computation time, remove the variability by the scaling, and improve antinoise characteristics.

INTRODUCTION

Computer use is ubiquitous, with user needs for interfaces with better operability and natural handling. Pointing devices for use in such environments must not constrain the user spatially. In mobile environments, in particular, it is becoming difficult to install pointing devices based on direct contact by the user's finger or a stylus because of the reduced device surface area that comes with the trend in computer downsizing.

As a pointing device consists of a pointing mechanism and a switching mechanism, using the user's movements to realize these mechanisms should free the device from the limitations above.

Some types of pointing devices are available with contact sensors: such as the EMG control device, a leg operating device, three sensors combined system for the user's movement (Fukuda et. al., 2003), (Tsukada and Yasumura, 2002). Although high-speed, stable processing and high measurement precision can be achieved by direct placement of such sensors, along with the use of dedicated hardware, they tend to give the user a feeling of restraint or awkwardness in handling and are not always comfortable.

On the other hand, there is another type of pointing devices using non-contact sensors: ultrasonic waves sensor, multiple cameras system (Nonaka and Date, 1993), (Watanabe et. al., 2001). However, these systems require the use of special equipment, making them unsuitable for the general user.

Thus, a pointing device that the general user can use comfortably must be noncontact, be able to carry out real-time processing, allow free settings as to its installment or extra hardware, and be sufficiently compact and light-weight, and reasonably priced. In this study, we study a pointing device that does not impart a feeling of restraint or awkwardness, that estimates the user's hand shape and position from images captured by a monocular camera, a noncontact device.

The captured image is transformed from a Cartesian coordinate system to a log-polar system to reduce image data and computational cost. Higher order local autocorrelation features of the log-polar coordinate space were used to achieve robustness against background change and hand rotation. In addition to direct pointing, the ability to recognize gestures from the hand's motion trajectory was incorporated to achieve more comfortable user-computer interaction.

Gesture recognition is used to realize a mouse-like function based on hand-finger movements, specifically as a computer input device. Therefore, there are likely to be fewer erroneous operations when gesture recognition takes place only when the user actually intends to carry out an input operation, instead of having the computer recognize any arbitrary movement. For this reason, we had the user make an "enter" hand shape in front of the camera to turn on/off the mouse-like function.

SYSTEM CONFIGURATION

Gesture Recognition Algorithm

Each frame of time-series images captured by a stationary monocular camera is transformed into log-polar coordinate images using log-polar mapping (LPM) (Schwartz 1980). The advantages of LPM are that high resolution and a wide working field are obtained using relatively few pixels, while scaling invariance and rotational invariance against the center of transformation are realized. Furthermore, the smaller amount of image data can cut down on the computation time required for image processing. Its shortcoming, however, is unsuitability for dynamic visual processing when uneven sampling causes the image shape to change considerably with translation.

In the proposed system, a contour image is generated from the LPM image using pulse-coupled neural network and skin color information. For recognition of the hand shape, higher order local autocorrelation features are computed from the hand region extracted based on skin color information, and then used by a neural network that employs learning vector quantization. This procedure constitutes pointing. The hand region position is tracked for gesture recognition, so two hand operations ---- pointing and gesturing --- are executed consecutively. Mode selection between pointing and gesturing is done by the display of a preset hand shape.

Pulse-Coupled Neural Network

The PCNN is a digital simulation of the cat's visual cortex. It has a lot of good properties for image processing, pattern recognition (Eckhorn et. al., 1990).

A PCNN neuron contains two main compartments: the Feeding and Linking compartments. Each of these communicates with neighbouring neurons through the synaptic weights **M** and **W** respectively. Each retains its previous state but with a decay factor. Only the Feeding compartment receives the input stimulus, **S** . The values of these two compartments are determind by,

$$F_{ij}(n) = e^{-\alpha_F \sigma_n} F_{ij}(n-1) + S_{ij} + V_F \sum_{kl} M_{ijkl} Y_{kl}(n-1) \tag{1}$$

$$L_{ij}(n)=e^{-\alpha_L\sigma_n}L_{ij}(n-1)+V_L\sum_{kl}W_{ijkl}Y_{kl}(n-1) \tag{2}$$

where F_{ij} is the Feeding compartment of the i-th j-th neuron embedded in a 2D array of neurons, and L_{ij} is the corresponding Linking compartment $Y_{kl}^{'}s$ are the outputs of neurons from a previous iteration $(n-1)$. Both compartments have a memoryof the previous state, which decays in time by the exponent term. The constants V_F and V_L are normalising constants. If the receptivefields of $\mathbf{M}$ and $\mathbf{W}$ change then these constants are used to scale the resultant correlation to prevent saturation.

The state of these two compartments are combined in a second order fashion to create the internal state of the neuron, $\mathbf{U}$. The combination is controlled by the linking strength, β. The internal activity is calculated by,

$$U_{ij}(n)=F_{ij}(n)\left(1+\beta L_{ij}(n)\right) \tag{3}$$

The internal state of the neuron is compared to a dynamic threshold, θ, to produce the output, $\mathbf{Y}$, by

$$Y_{ij}(n)=\begin{cases}1 \ \textit{if}\ U_{ij}(n)>Q_{ij}(n)\\ 0 \ \textit{Otherwise}\end{cases} \tag{4}$$

The threshold is dynamic in that when the neuron fires ($Y>\theta$) the threshold then significantly increases its value. This value then decays until the neuron fires again. This process is described by,

$$\Theta_{ij}(n)=e^{-\alpha_\Theta\sigma_n}(n-1)+V_\theta Y_{ij}(n) \tag{5}$$

where V_θ is a large constant that is generally more than an order of magnitude greater than the average value of $\mathbf{U}$.

Log Polar Mapped Images

Coordinates $I(x,y)$ of the Cartesian image are assumed to form complex plane Z. A point on this complex plane is expressed by $z=x+iy$. Similarly, coordinates $L(p,q)$ of LPM are assumed to form complex plane W, on which a point is expressed by $w=p+iq$. LPM is then given by the following expression:

$$w=\log(z+\alpha) \tag{6}$$

where α is an offset to prevent singularity at the origin.

Original image I is decomposed by LPM into angular and radial components. Logarithmic sampling in the radial direction causes information at peripheral areas to be rough compared to the central area. High resolution is maintained in the center, while resolution decreases as the periphery is approached, so overall spatial information is captured roughly. The amount of data and hence processing time are thus drastically reduced.

The one-to-one correspondence between pixels on the original image and those on the LPM image must be computed to carry out LPM on the input image. While some methods achieve high-speed processing by installing hardware to execute LPM(Shimizu et. al., 1997), the present system employs software to carry out LPM to not burden the user.

Estimation of Hand Shape

Extraction of Hand Region

When using segmentation the method of accumulated response from the PCNN is used. When extracting the hand region from input image, skin color information is first used to select a region and skin color regions are labeled, then the region with the largest area is defined as the hand region. There are cases, however, when shadows may exist when extracting the skin color region from an image, because of the relative positions of the hand and room illumination, which causes the hand region to be incompletely extracted.

In the present system, the LPM image is scanned radially outward after extraction of the largest skin-color region to include the entire skin color region. Although some background noise is introduced, this ensures that there are no parts missing from the hand region. After edge enhancement of the image, higher order local autocorrelation features are extracted.

Computation of Higher Order Local Autocorrelation Features

Higher order local autocorrelation features are image features proposed by Otsu et al (1988). for image recognition and measurement. Among higher order autocorrelation functions, defined by Eq.(7), local ones are computed for pixels at the reference point and its vicinity.

$$x^N(a_1, a_2, \cdots, a_N) = \int f(r) f(r + a_1) \cdots f(r + a_N) dr \tag{7}$$

where $f(r)$ denotes the luminosity of pixels at position r, N the order, and $(a_1, a_2, \cdots, a_N)$ the direction of displacement.

Because the correlation between adjacent pixels is considered important when treating natural images, displacement directions are limited to a local region consisting of 3×3 pixels centered at reference point r, and higher order autocorrelation features up to the second order are obtained. Eliminating features that remain equivalent in translation, we obtain the 35 features. Each feature is computed by adding to all pixels the product of values of the corresponding pixels in the local pattern.

Learning by Learning Vector Quantization

The selection of LVQ is based on the following considerations: Hierarchical neural networks have such shortcomings as 1) recognition is treated as a black box, 2) causes of recognition error are difficult to establish, 3) learning requires considerable time, and 4) there is no well established methodology for determining the number of middle level neurons. In contrast, competitive neural networks consist of just two levels --- input and output, cluster classification is easily done even when the input has a high dimension, and causal explanations are easily found between input and output.

Several LVQ algorithms have been proposed including LVQ1 and its improved versions, LVQ2, LVQ3, and optimized learning rate LVQ1 (OLVQ1). OLVQ1 is LVQ1 in which coupling weight vectors are assigned learning rates. In this study, we use OLVQ1 for its fast learning.

Gesture Estimation

Since gesture recognition is used in the present system as a computer input device, there are likely to be fewer erroneous operations when gesture recognition takes place only when the user actually intends to carry out an input operation, rather than having the computer recognize arbitrary movement.

Therefore, the beginning or ending of gesturing is defined as the point when the user's hand shape matches a preregistered “enter key” gesture when hand movements are minimized, so the interval constitutes the gesturing period. Gestures are then matched by simple dynamic processing. It is normally considered difficult to precisely detect the moment when hand motion is minimized when estimating the gesturing period from a series of images. Our system achieves this by using the hand shape information, i.e., whether it agrees with a pre-registered shape, in addition to detection of minimal hand motion.
The trajectory vector obtained from the hand-finger trajectory tracked during the gesturing period is used as feature vector used in gesture estimation.

EXPERIMENT FOR EVALUATION

To realize mouse-like functions, the system must distinguish between “pointing'” the left and right mouse buttons. Together with the hand shape used as the “enter” key, the system must be able to recognize at least four classes. For the present system, the four hand shapes are used.

Based on a resolution of 360×240 pixels in the original image, we uesed LPM images with resolutions of 120×120 pixels, 60×60 pixels, 40×40 pixels, and 30×30 pixels, and analyzed the effects. Using a digital video camera (DVC), images were captured centered at the position of the user's raised hand and at a range so that the hand would fill the scene. Four users were asked to make the 4 hand postures, but slightly tilted either to the left or right. Captured images were transmitted to the PC at a 360×240 resolution via IEEE1394, 200 frames were captured per hand shape pattern per user to make a total of 3,200 frames (200 frames×4 users×4 hand shapes). The hand region was extracted from each image using a rectangular outer boundary frame and reduced in scale to obtain five differently sized hand images. These were then combined with a monochrome background image so the background center coincides with the centroid of the hand image, thus obtaining a total of 16,000 images (5 hand sizes×3,200 frames). Based on a reference size of 100%, which corresponds to the hand size when the user's upper body fills the camera image, hand images of 50%, 75%, 100%, 125%, and 150% were used.

Hold-out was used for training OLVQ1, where the entire sample set was divided into two subsets, one for training and the other for evaluation. The two sample sets were then interchanged and the average of the results taken to obtain a mutually calibrated recognition rate. A neural network trained with OLVQ1 was used to obtain recognition rates when the image was combined with the complex background.

As a result, We obtain an overall average recognition rate of 92.3%. Standard deviations are small, indicating that there is less dispersion in recognition rates caused by variations in hand shape. The results thus demonstrate the validity of the present system (Odo and Hoshino, 2004).

We then conducted an experiment using a software application that incorporated mouse functions based on the present method. A DVC was positioned to capture the user's hands from above at a distance of 120 cm so the captured image would consist of a rectangular area by 50 cm vertically and 70 cm horizontal.

The image captured by the DVC was transmitted via an IEEE1394 interface to a PC (Intel Pentium III 500 MHz). The experiment took place indoors under normal room illumination, with a 360 × 240 pixel image size, and 256 hues each for RGB. Prior to the experiment, the four basic perations of pointing, right click, left click, and mode switching were matched with hand shapes, and gestures were registered for the gesturing operation mode.

The results of hand shape recognition were displayed on the screen in the shape of a mouse cursor, which served to notify the user of the recognition results and enabled corrections easily whenever recognition failure took take. In this experiment, we were able to achieve satisfactory for practical use. However, it is a problem that this model takes somewhat a long time.

CONCLUSIONS

In this paper, we proposed a method to estimate hand gestures from input images obtained by a monocular camera, which as a noncontact sensor does not impart to the user a feeling of restraint or awkwardness. The sequential image is transformed from a Cartesian coordinate system to a log-polar coordinate system, Pulse Couple Neural Networks are used to extract the hand region. Hand shape is recognized by a neural network in which higher order local autocorrelation features in log-polar coordinate space are learned by OLVQ1. Aimed at realizing a comfortable user-computer interface, the system incorporates a pointing function to achieve direct operation and the ability to recognize symbolic signs from hand motion trajectories. Currently, it is a problem that this model takes somewhat a long time.

REFERENCES

Fukuda, O., Arita, J., and Tsuji, T., 2003 "An EMG-controlled omnidirectional pointing device using a HMM-based neural network," Proceedings of the IEEE International Joint Conference on Neural Networks, pp.3195-3200.

Tsukada, K., and Yasumura, M., 2002 "Ubi-Finger: Gesture Input Device for Mobile Use," Proceedings of APCHI 2002, vol.1, pp.388-400.

Nonaka, H., and Date, T., 1993 "Pointing device using supersonic position measurement," Transactions of the Society of Instrument and Control Engineers, vol.29, no.7, pp.735-744.

Watanabe, H., Hongo, H., Yasumoto, M., and Yamamoto, K., 2001 "Estimation of omni-directional pointing gestures using multiple cameras," The transactions of the institute of electrical engineers of Japan, vol.121, no.9, pp.1388-1394.

Schwartz, E.L., 1980 "Computational anatomy and functional architecture of striate cortex: a spatial mapping approach to perceptual coding," Vision Research, vol.20, no.8, pp.645-668.

Eckhorn, R., Reitboech, H.J., Arndt, M., Dicke, P., 1990 "Feature Linking via Synchronization among Distributed Assemblies: Simulations of Results from Cat Visual Corlez," Neural Comp, vol.2, pp293-307.

Shimizu, S., Suematsu, Y., and Yahata, S., 1997 "Wide-angle vision sensor with high-distortion lens (Detection of camera location and gaze direction based on the two-parallel-algorithm)," Journal of the Japan Society of Mechanical Engineers, Series C, pp.4257-4263, vol.63, no.616.

Otsu, N., and Kurita, T., 1988 "A new scheme for practical, fiexible and inteligent vision systems," Proc.IAPR Workshop on Computer Vision, pp.431-435.

Odo, S., and Hoshino, K., 2004, "Pointing device based on estimation of trajectory and shape of a human hand in a monocular image sequence," Journal of advanced computational intelligence and intelligent informatics, vol.8, no.2, pp.140-149.

DYNAMIC SCENE ANALYSIS USING QUALITATIVE MOTION DETECTION

GEORGE K. KNOPF AND PHILIP C. IGWE
Department of Mechanical & Materials Engineering,
Faculty of Engineering, The University of Western Ontario,
London, Ontario, Canada, N6A 5B9

ABSTRACT
Detection of moving objects by a mobile camera system is a complex problem because the velocity flow field captured by the imaging system arises from both camera motion and the movement of one or more objects through the unstructured environment. A motion detection algorithm that can deal with imprecise knowledge of the camera motion parameters is described in this paper. The technique is based on the notion that the full velocity calculated at each image point, for a camera moving through a rigid environment, will lie on a one-dimensional locus in the v_x -v_y velocity space. The algorithm is made more robust by introducing a fuzzy constraint region defined by approximate camera motion parameters and then mapping the computed normal velocities, as fuzzy singletons, onto the constraint support set. Finally, full velocity values are computed only in the regions of the image plane that violate the camera motion constraints.

INTRODUCTION

Dynamic vision involves the detection and identification of one or more objects that may be partially occluded, camouflaged or moving in an unstructured real-world environment. Most image-based motion analysis techniques employ sophisticated algorithms that attempt to accurately reconstruct *structure-from-motion* without any loss of information detail (Horne and Schunck 1981; Negel and Enkelmann 1986). Although it may be useful to recover complete information about both the camera motion and the structure of the environment from a sequence of images, the problem is often ill-conditioned and additional assumptions about both smoothness and rigidity must be made in order to obtain a unique solution. As a consequence, these solutions are very sensitive to small errors in the image flow thereby rendering them impractical for real world applications (Zhu 1997).

A number of qualitative approaches to interpreting visual motion have been proposed that do not require the explicit reconstruction of scene structure. Thompson *et al.* (1990) introduced the Epipolar method for movement detection based on the notion that in a rigid environment the projected velocity at any point in the image plane is constrained to lie on a 1D locus in velocity space whose parameters depend only on the camera (observer) motion. These Epipolar methods are dependent upon accurate information about both camera translation and rotation. Nelson (1991) applied the principles of the Epipolar method to a constraint ray filtering technique. The algorithm computes the minimal amount of information necessary to solve the task at hand, hence it is a computationally efficient method for detecting motion in the real world. Nelson and Aloismonos (1989) used a similar analysis method to solve the obstacle avoidance problem based on optical flow divergence.

This paper describes a pattern classification approach to detecting independently moving objects by a mobile camera system. The movement detection algorithm establishes a fuzzy constraint region based on approximate camera motion parameters and then maps the computed normal velocities from an image sequence, as fuzzy singletons, onto the constraint support set. The intersection between the fuzzy constraint region and singletons reflect the degree to which the normal velocity vectors belong to the image flow information produced by camera movement. Full velocity vectors are then computed only in the regions of the image plane that violate fuzzy camera constraints. Homogeneous regions in the image plane that violate the local constraints become points of fixation for advanced tracking and detailed scene analysis.

IMAGE FLOW AND CONSTRAINT-BASED MOTION DETECTION

A camera moving through a three-dimensional environment will generate a series of images that can be represented at any instant in time by a two-dimensional velocity field known as *image flow*. The full or "true" velocity $\boldsymbol{v}_{xy}$ at an image point (x, y) is the sum of the normal and tangential components,

$$\boldsymbol{v}_{xy} = v^n_{xy} + \boldsymbol{v}^t_{xy} \tag{1}$$

The normal velocity, $v^n_{xy} = (v^n_x, v^n_y)$ is parallel to the direction of the spatial gradient $\nabla I = (I_x, I_y)$, and is computed directly from the intensity derivatives using

$$v^n_x = -\frac{I_t I_x}{I_x^2 + I_y^2} \quad \text{and} \quad v^n_y = -\frac{I_t I_y}{I_x^2 + I_y^2}, \tag{2}$$

where (I_x, I_y, I_t) are the first-order spatial and temporal gradients of a time-varying image sequence. Underconstrained, the spatiotemporal gradients cannot be used to unambiguously estimate the full or "true" velocity on a local basis. The tangential component, $\boldsymbol{v}^t_{xy}$, is perpendicular to the direction of the spatial gradient ∇I. Iterative and global relaxation techniques must be employed to estimate the tangential velocity because of the *aperature problem*(Zhu 1997). All disambiguation methods, however, impose additional assumptions on the solution and significantly increase the computational complexity.

The projected velocity U_{xy} at image coordinate (x, y), arising from a camera system moving through a stationary environment, can be divided into rotation, R_{xy}, and translation components, T_{xy},

$$U_{xy} = R_{xy} + \alpha T_{xy} = \frac{1}{f}\begin{bmatrix} \omega_X\, xy - \omega_Y\,(f^2 + x^2) + \omega_Z\, yf \\ \omega_X (f^2 + y^2) - \omega_Y\, xy - \omega_Z\, xf \end{bmatrix} + \alpha \begin{bmatrix} -f V_X + V_Z\, x \\ -f V_Y + V_Z\, y \end{bmatrix} \tag{3}$$

where f is the focal length of the camera, $(\omega_X, \omega_Y, \omega_Z)$ are the camera's angular velocities, and (V_X, V_Y, V_Z) are the camera's translation velocities along the X, Y, and Z coordinate axes. The relationship between the motion parameters of a moving camera system $(\omega_X, \omega_Y, \omega_Z, V_X, V_Y, V_Z)$ is illustrated in Fig. 1. The parameter α is equal to $\frac{1}{Z}$, where Z is the distance from the center of projection to the world point. Although the lower bound of Z can theoretically range from 0 to $+\infty$, it is always greater than zero because of the physical nature of the mobile camera system.

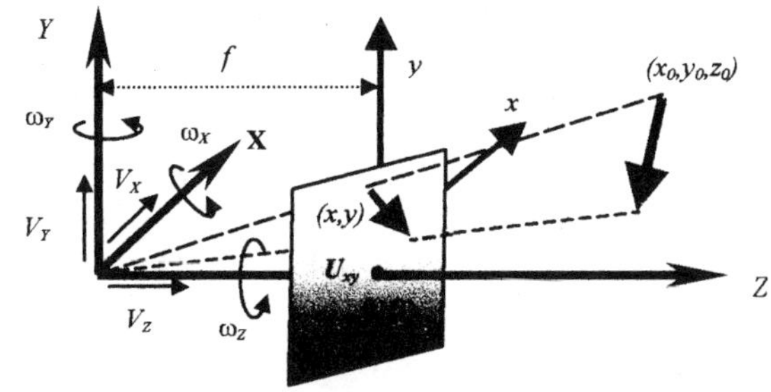

Figure 1. The angular and translation velocities of a camera moving with respect to a coordinate axes given at the center of projection.

Equation (3) represents a vector in 2D velocity space with an endpoint at R_{xy} and running parallel to T_{xy} as shown in Fig. 2. Since chords drawn from points on a circle to a third point on the circle meet at right angles, all normal velocity vectors v_{xy}^n associated with a true value of velocity U_{xy} will lie on a *constraint circle* that passes through the origin (Nelson 1991). The union of all circles generated by the points along the locus with endpoints R_{xy} and $R_{xy} + \alpha\ T_{xy}$ will generate a *constraint region* in the velocity space. If the camera motion is known at some instant in time, then the overall constraint region associated with that type of camera movement can be generated in the velocity space using the centers of the constraint sub-regions ($m_{R_{xy}}$, $m_{RT_{xy}}$).

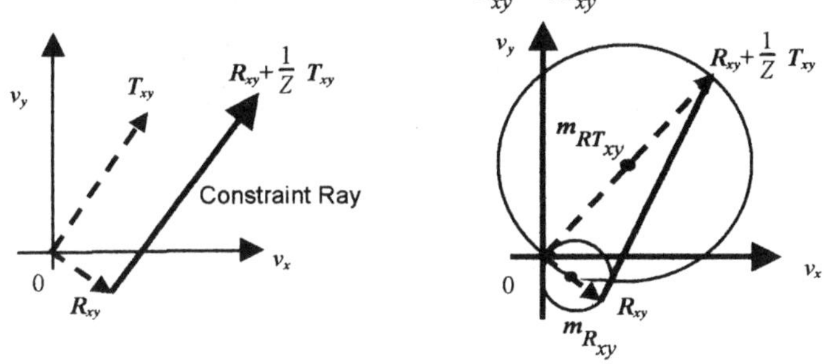

Figure 2. Constraint ray and region generated for camera movement.

QUALITATIVE MOTION DETECTION

For qualitative movement detection, the normal velocity vector computed using Eqn. (2) is mapped into the same velocity space as the projected camera velocity, and if this vector lies outside the constraint region it is "tagged" a point-of-interest. Approximate knowledge of camera movement can be used if the projected camera velocity U_{xy} is redefined as radial fuzzy sets with the support set given in the 2D velocity space (Knopf and Zhu 1997; Zhu 1997). The membership value $\mu_{U_{xy}}(v)$ is the degree to which the image flow velocity v belongs to the projected camera velocity U_{xy}. From experimental observations, it was determined that the maximum spread should be a function of pixel distance in the image plane.

If each projected velocity along the line segment with endpoints R_{xy} and $R_{xy} + \alpha T_{xy}$ is defined as a radial fuzzy set then the resultant constraint circles will exhibit a unique *confidence band.* The union of all the circles with graded boundaries will generate a new *fuzzy constraint region* in the velocity space (Fig. 3). Each fuzzy constraint sub-region can be modeled by the parameters representing the centroid and maximum spread of the fuzzy set.

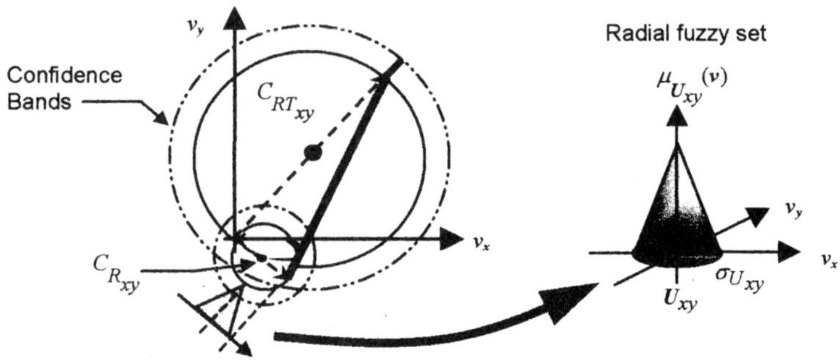

Figure 3. The confidence bands formed around the constraint circles due to a radial fuzzy set definition for the projected camera velocity.

The local constraint region at image location (*x,y*) for a camera system moving through a rigid environment is modeled as the *exclusive OR* (***XOR***) of the fuzzy constraint sub-regions ($C_{R_{xy}}, C_{RT_{xy}}$). In terms of membership to camera velocity, individual normal flow vectors v^n_{xy} are classified using

$$\mu_C\left(v^n_{xy}\right) = \mu_{C_R}\left(v^n_{xy}\right) \textbf{ XOR } \mu_{C_{RT}}\left(v^n_{xy}\right) \tag{4}$$

The degree with which the computed normal velocity at image location (*x*, *y*) violates the camera motion constraint is given by the complement of Eqn. (4),

$$\mu^{xy}_{\gamma} = 1 - \mu_{C_\gamma}\left(v^n_{xy}\right) \tag{5}$$

Since the image flow associated with an independently moving object is assumed to lie in a contiguous region of the image plane, any spatially isolated membership value can be treated as sporadic noise and removed using a fuzzy morphological filter. An accumulator array with fixed bin sizes is then used to generate a histogram of the full velocity vectors computed over all segmented regions. Since each moving object is assumed to be rigid, the full velocities associated with the object will "likely" fall into a common bin. Once all the velocity vectors have been categorized by the array the average relative "full" velocity and the regional centroid of the vectors located in each bin can be computed. The center of the identified region becomes the point of fixation for object tracking algorithm.

EXPERIMENTAL STUDY

The study required a CCD camera mounted on a manipulator arm, and a target fastened to a two-axis linear translation stage. The focal length of the camera lens was 7.5mm. Each captured image contained 512x400 pixels. The image plane coordinate scale was $S_x = 0.0128$ (mm/pixel) and $S_y = 0.0122$ (mm/pixel). The minimum distance from an object to the camera was assumed to be 300mm. All image sequences were pre-smoothed using a spatiotemporal Gaussian filter with a standard deviation of 1.5 pixels in space and 1.5 frames in time, sampled out to three standard deviations. The intensity derivatives for the central image were computed using the difference equations (Zhu 1997). The normal velocities for the central image were calculated at each image location. For the test, the camera was programmed to move slowly upward and forward into the scene with the camera motion parameters (0, 5.08, 5.08) mm/frame. Simultaneously, the target was programmed to translate from left-to-right at a speed of 2 mm/frame (Fig. 4).

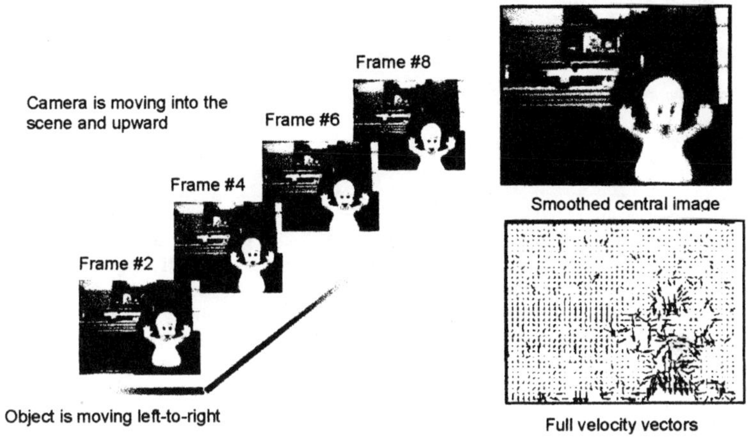

Figure 4. Image sequence generated by moving the camera up and forward.

Figure 5(a) shows the fuzzy membership image generated by applying a constraint region formed by using exact camera motion parameters and a fuzzy spread of zero ($\sigma_s = 0$). The regions of the image plane that violated the camera constraints are displayed as white intensities. The result of applying the region segmentation algorithm to the membership image is illustrated in Fig. 5(b). The "full" velocity vectors associated with these segmented regions are shown in Fig. 5(c).

(a) Fuzzy membership image. (b) Motion segmented region. (c) Velocity vectors.

Figure 5. Results for exact camera motion and a fuzzy spread of zero ($\sigma_s = 0$).

A second test was performed using *approximate* cameramotion parameters given by (1, 6, 6)mm/frame. The fuzzy spread parameter σ_s was set to 8. The fuzzy membership image is shown in Fig. 6(a) and result of applying the region segmentation algorithm is given by Fig. 6(b). The "full" velocity vectors associated with these two regions of interest are illustrated in Fig. 6(c). The estimated relative velocity of target #1 was determined to be (-0.005106, -0.056470) mm/frame centered at pixel location (361, 173), and for target #2 it was determined to be (-0.005740, -0.063333) mm/frame centered at pixel location (360, 306). Essentially, the velocity vectors associated with both regions fall within the same accumulator bin and, therefore they belong to the same object.

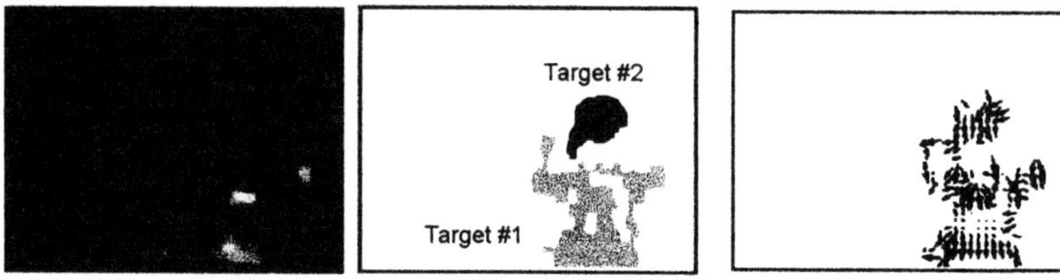

(a) Fuzzy membership image. (b) Motion segmented region. (c) Velocity vectors.

Figure 6. Results for approximate camera motion and a fuzzy spread > 0 (σ_s = 8).

CONCLUSIONS

The robust qualitative motion detection algorithm is based on the notion that the normal component of the image flow, due to a camera moving through a stationary environment, is constrained to lie within circular regions of the 2D velocity space. The normal velocity components generated by independent moving object are unlikely to fall within the constraint region. The introduction of constraint regions and normal flow information as radial fuzzy sets with graded membership enables the motion detection algorithm to tolerate uncertainty arising from measurement errors, incomplete knowledge of camera movement and minimizes the camera calibration requirements for real world applications. Future work involves studying the effect of errors in the rotational parameters and investigate higher-level scene analysis by applying linguistic variables and fuzzy reasoning to the motion detection information. For example, the estimated relative velocities of independently moving objects can be mapped into a linguistic domain such as "*target #1 is moving up and right a little bit*" and so on.

ACKNOWLEDGEMENTS

This work has been supported, in part, by the Natural Sciences and Engineering Research Council of Canada. The authors wish to acknowledge the early work and contributions of Ms. Shiping Zhu.

REFERENCES

Horn, B.K.P. and Schunck, B.G., "Determining optical flow", *Artificial Intelligence*, vol. 17, pp. 185-204, 1981.

Knopf, G.K., and Zhu, S., "Robust motion constraint technique for detecting moving targets", in *Real-Time Imaging*, D. Sinha (Eds.), SPIE Proceedings, vol. 3028, pp. 64 - 74, 1997.

Negel, H.H. and Enkelmann, W., " An investigation of smoothness constraints for the estimation of displacement vector fields from image sequences", *IEEE Trans. on Pattern Analysis and Machine Intell.*, vol. 8, pp. 565 - 593, 1986.

Nelson, R.C., " Qualitative detection of motion by a moving observer", *International Journal of Computer Vision*, vol. 7, no. 1, pp. 33 - 46, 1991.

Nelson, R.C. and Aloismonos, J., " Obstacle avoidance using flow field divergence", *IEEE Trans. on Pattern Analysis and Machine Intell.*, vol. 11, no. 10, pp. 1102 - 1106, 1989.

Thompson, W.B. and Pong, T.C., "Detecting moving objects", *Intern, J. Comput. Vision*, vol. 4, no.1, pp. 39 - 58, 1990.

Zhu, S., *Robust Detection of Object Movement by a Mobile Camera System*. M.E.Sc. Thesis, The University of Western Ontario, 1997.

A PARALLEL ARCHITECTURE FOR DETECTION OF UNDERWATER OBJECTS FROM LIDAR DATA

Vikramjit Mitra
Worcester Polytechnic Institute, EE Department
Worcester, MA

Chia-Jiu Wang
University of Colorado
ECE Department
Colorado Springs, CO

Satarupa Banerjee
Villanova University
CIS Department
Villanova, PA

ABSTRACT

This paper presents a parallel Neural Network architecture for classification of Light Detection And Ranging (LiDAR) data. Lidar data gives a sequence of laser backscatter intensity obtained from laser shots at various altitudes above the earth surface. The data can be categorized into three different classes: water-layer, bottom and fish. Two parallel neural architectures based on Multi-Layer Perceptrons (MLP) and Hybrid Radial Basis Function (HRBF) are presented in this paper. The LiDAR data is pre-filtered to remove high frequency noise and a segment of the sample is selected to extract features for classification. The data is transformed into frequency domain and feature segments are selected, that are encoded using Linear Predictive Coding and Polynomial Approximation. The coefficients thus generated are used as the input for the two branches of the parallel neural architecture and the decisions obtained from the two branches are multiplied and the result is fed to a rule-based Inference Engine (IE) that presents the final inference. The proposed structure well fits the Lidar data classification task due to the inherent classification efficiency of neural networks. Based on the results obtained and the simplicity of the proposed system, it is shown that the parallel Neural architecture based on Multilayer Perceptron hold a lot of potential and provides a greater prediction accuracy for LiDAR backscatter data classification.

INTRODUCTION

Biomass surveys are used as an important tool for fishery research and its use is increasing with full utilization of resources and increased accuracy. Aerial surveys using lidar technique were found to be a valuable supplement [1, 2] because of its high efficiency in classification of remote objects, high area coverage coupled with high spatial data density and rapid response. Detection of underwater fish population from lidar signals requires knowledge of the reflectivity of fish population. Researches performed by Squire et al., Krekova et al., Murphree et al. and Churnside et al claim a range of 5% to 50% of lidar reflectivity from under water fish schools. Lidar systems transmit and receive Laser beams at a high frequency and operate in the ultraviolet, visible and infrared region. The transmitted Laser beam interacts with and is changed by the target. Part of this beam is reflected and scattered back to the instrument receiver where it is analyzed. The change in the properties of the light enables to determine some properties of the target. Classification by Artificial Neural Network (ANN) is advantageous because of it's efficient classification, parallel computation potentials, high adaptivity and great error tolerance properties. This paper presents the result obtained from implementation of a parallel ANN architecture using Multi-Layer Perceptron (MLP) and Hybrid Radial Basis Function (HRBF) for classification of fish schools, clear water return and water bottom from airborne Lidar data. The Lidar backscatter pattern are preprocessed using signal processing techniques and the features thus extracted are used to train the ANNs. The airborne lidar data studied in this paper are obtained from National Oceanic and Atmospheric Administration (*NOAA*), Colorado.

LIDAR

A nonscanning, radiometric lidar, presented in Figure 1 is used, where the major components are the laser and beam control optics, the receiver optics, the detector and the data collection, processing and display computer. The system also has the capability to record aircraft position and altitude. The linearly polarized laser beam used in this research is frequency doubled, that produces *100mJ* of green light (*532nm*) in a *12ns* pulse at the rate of *30pulse/s*.

The receiver device uses a *17cm* diameter refracting telescope, where a polarizer is placed on the front to select either the copolarized or crosspolarized component. Previous researches claim that crosspolarized component produces the best contrast between fish and other small particle backscatter from water. It has also been found [3, 4] that the backscatter attenuation coefficient is lower at night than clear day light. The research presented in this paper is motivated to classify the signal backscatter with the most adverse settings; hence copolarized component used at day light is considered for classification. The grayscale image of the unprocessed lidar data is presented in Figure 2, where the vertical axis gives the depth, the horizontal axis gives the time along the flight track and the magnitude of the lidar backscatter is presented as the gray level. The dark band in Figure 2 represents the strong scattering region near the water surface. The backscatter characteristics presented in this paper are obtained by the plot of the logarithm of the lidar single pulse returns as a function of depth.

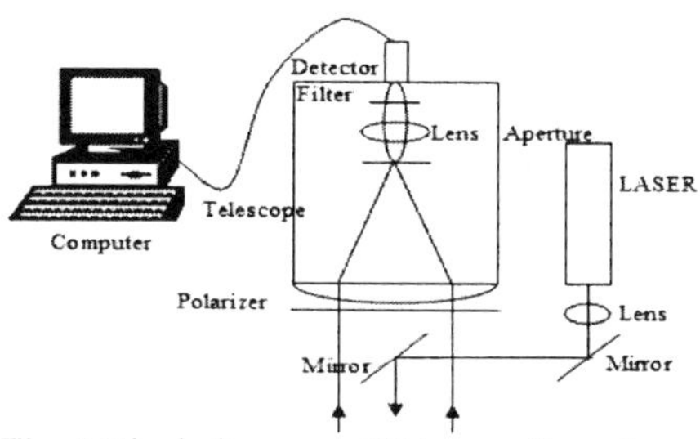

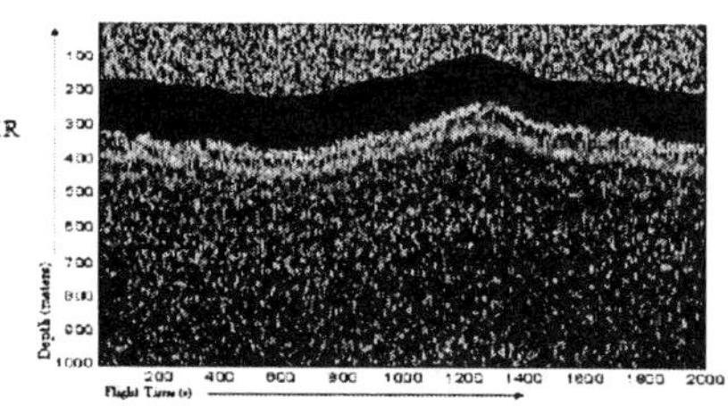

Fig. 1 Block diagram of lidar configuration . **Fig. 2** Raw data from the receiver

If there is absence of any underwater object, the lidar backscatter signal intensity is found to decay exponentially. There is a visible bump present on the exponentially decaying signal if the lidar pulse return from a school of fish. To recognize a visible bump in the lidar underwater return as a school of fish, it is necessary to monitor a succession of returns. Typically identical returns are obtained for five consecutive lidar pulses for a fish school [5].This approach may provide erroneous conclusions, since visible bumps can be present in more than five consecutive lidar returns for underwater objects like plankton layer. To increase the accuracy of prediction, a temporal knowledge about the possibility of fish school and plankton colony existance is strictly required. It is well known that a plankton population extends for a wider area, much larger than that of fish school. This would result in obtaining fish like lidar returns for a longer span (say, *N secs*) than possible from fish school. An estimate of a time limit is thus strictly required to classify between these two categories. From the lidar system specification we know, that each return corresponds to 33ms, hence the estimated time *N* (in seconds) can then be used as *N/0.033* samples (to the next possible integer value) to classify fish schools from plankton colonies, which is shown in the following rule base-

```
If (presence of visible bump below water level ≥ 5 consecutive
lidar return)
  { If( presence of visible bump below water level ≥ N/0.033
consecutive lidar return)
      Then (Class = Algae OR Class = Phytoplanktons)
    Else (Class = Fish)}
Else (Class = Other).
```

lidar frequency spectrum analysis

The change in the exponential decay of the lidar return is reflected in the frequency spectrum of the aforesaid three classes, i.e., water layer, bottom and underwater objects which are fishes in this study. Figure 3 shows the scaled overlaying frequency spectrum plots of the three cases. It is visibly distinct that the frequency spectrum differs from one another and this difference in pattern is used as input to the ANN based classifier proposed in this paper.

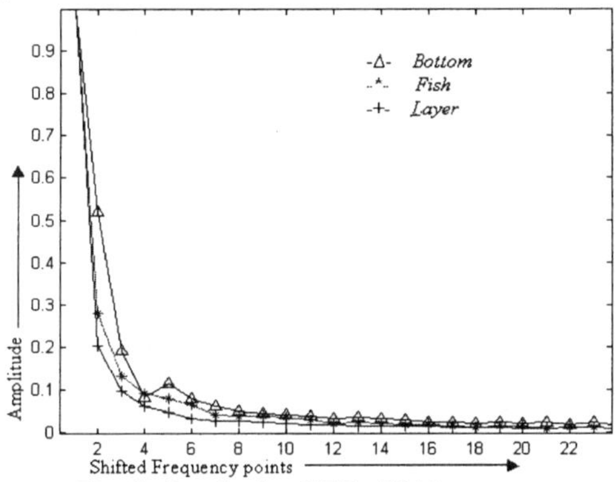

Fig. 3. Overlaying FFT of Lidar return.

DATA PREPROCESSING

The raw data obtained from NOAA is contaminated with high frequency noise, which is removed by the use of a Low Pass Butterworth Filter. From the lidar backscatters, it is evident that the lidar return before the water surface and after a certain depth below the water surface does not contain any information regarding underwater objects; hence those portions of lidar return are eliminated by selection of a window of the filtered signal. The window starts from the first peak obtained from the air-water interface and ends at the point where the signal backscatter intensity decays to 10^{-4} time its peak value. From several studies involving lidar data, it has been found that most of the information regarding underwater objects is obtained within this segment of data. The selected data window is transformed to frequency domain by the use of Fast Fourier Transform. As evident from the frequency plots of the lidar backscatter, the frequency spectrum is symmetric across the central frequency; hence only a half of the frequency points can be selected for the classification purpose. The data points close to the central peak are crucial for classification, as those sections have the presence/absence of the side lobes that helps us to distinguish between the different classes. Because of this, 15 points after the peak frequency value are selected and this window of frequency points are encoded by LPC Algorithm and Polynomial Approximation. The block diagram of the signal preprocessing is presented in Fig. 4.

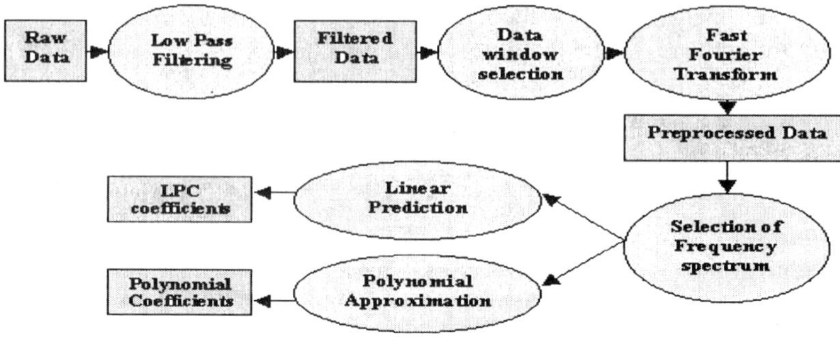

Fig. 4. Block Diagram of Data Preprocessor

Linear Predictive Coding (LPC) has been widely used specially in speech signal processing since its introduction in the late sixties. During the last three decades the number of available techniques have been growing rapidly. In linear prediction an estimate $\hat{s}(n)$ for a sample value $s(n)$ is given as a linear combination of previous sample values. There are many alternative ways to form a linear combination of signal history and use it to predict the next signal value. The most obvious way, a weighted sum of a finite number N of previous signal values, is typically utilized in coding applications. Traditionally LPC filter is assumed to be a conventional all-pole filter, and the optimal coefficients, are obtained from the celebrated Yule-Walker equations that obey a more general orthogonality principle of linear prediction. This system can be characterized by the following equations: $\hat{s}(n+1) = a_0\, s(n) + a_1\, s(n-1) + a_2\, s(n-2) + \ldots\ldots + a_N\, s(n-N)$
The polynomial curve fitting function requires a linear vector for modeling a system. It finds the coefficient of a polynomial $p(x)$ of degree 'n', that fits the data, $p(x(i))$ to $y(i)$ in a least square sense. The result p is a row vector of length '$n+1$' containing the polynomial coefficients in descending power. $p(x) = p_1 x^n + p_2 x^{n-1} + \ldots. + p_n x + p_{n+1}$
The polynomial coefficients [$p_1, p_2, \ldots. p_n$] are obtained in least square sense.

PROPOSED NEURAL BASED SYSTEM OVERVIEW

Artificial Neural Networks (ANN) are distributed, adaptive, generally nonlinear learning machines built from many different processing elements (PEs) [6]. Each PE receives connections from other PEs and/or itself. The interconnectivity defines the topology. The signals flowing through the connections are scaled by adjustable parameters called weights, w_{ij}. The PE's sum all these contributions and produce an output that is a nonlinear (static) function of the sum. The PE's outputs become either system outputs or are sent to the same or other PE's. Two types of ANN were considered in this research: Multi-Layered Perceptron (MLP) and Hybrid Radial Basis Function Networks (HRBF).
Radial Basis Function (RBF) networks are nonlinear hybrid networks. The RBF layer uses Gaussian transfer functions, rather than the standard sigmoid functions employed by MLPs. The centers and widths of the Gaussians are set by unsupervised learning rules, and supervised learning is applied to the output layer. RBF networks use Gaussian function to project the input space to an intermediary space where the classification is done with a hyperplane implemented as the weighted sum of the Gaussian PE outputs. These networks learn much faster than MLPs. MLPs are layered feed forward networks, trained with static back-propagation., which can have one or more hidden layers. These networks have been proved and found to be ideal for pattern classification and recognition applications. They are easy to use, and can approximate any input/output map. The key disadvantages are that they train slowly, and require lots of training data.

The polynomial coefficients and the LPC coefficients are used as the input to the two branches of the parallel neural architecture, presented in Fig. 5. MLP and HRBF based parallel neural architectures were considered in this research, with momentum learning (with a value of *0.7*). The networks were trained in supervised mode, with the desired outputs shown in Table 1. Five input one output ANNs are designed for each of the branches, where the inputs correspond to 5 LPC coefficients and 5 polynomial coefficients that were extracted from each frequency window. A dot product of the decisions of the two ANNs is obtained and the result is used as the input to the Inference Engine (IE).

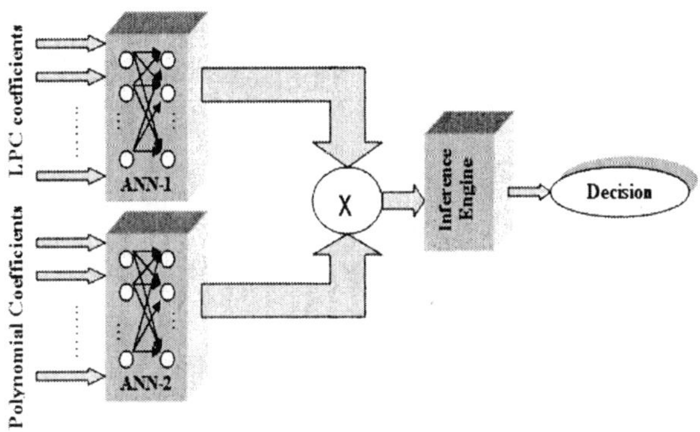

Fig. 5. Parallel Neural Architecture

Table 1. Desired output

Desired output	1	0.5	0
Implication	Fish	Layer	Bottom

Table 2 Decision boundary for Inference engine

	Decision boundary	
	Upper	Lower
Fish	< = 1.0	> 0.6
Layer	< = 0.6	> 0.2
Bottom	< = 0.2	> = 0.0

The ANN decisions are close to the desired output values but are not exactly it due to computation approximation. Because of this an Inference Engine is implemented, which has a rule based decision algorithm as shown in Table 2.

RESULTS AND DISCUSSIONS

In the first architecture a *2*-hidden layer HRBF neural network is considered, with *20* cluster centers and *25* PEs in each hidden layer, using Euclidean metric and conscience full competitive rule. The results thus obtained are presented in Table 3. The second architecture considers a *2*-hidden layer MLP each layer having *25* PEs, with sigmoid as transfer function. The result obtained from this architecture is presented in Table 4. *450* lidar return samples were considered in this research, where *150* samples are from each category. *330* samples (*110* samples from each category) were used to train the two ANNs and the remaining *120* samples (*40* samples from each category) were used to test the proposed system. Tables 3 and 4 depict the test result from 9 samples. The overall accuracy of the proposed system is found to be *99.8%*.

Table 3. Results from HRBF based ANN

Output				
ANN1	ANN2	Before IE	Desired	After IE
0.844	0.892	0.753617	1	1.0
0.819	0.896	0.734405	1	1.0
0.810	0.897	0.726921	1	1.0
0.130	0.129	0.016991	0	0.0
0.244	0.284	0.069398	0	0.0
0.103	0.123	0.012735	0	0.0
0.795	0.692	0.551133	0.5	0.5
0.507	0.717	0.364009	0.5	0.5
0.656	0.745	0.489841	0.5	0.5

Table 4. Results from MLP based ANN

Output				
ANN1	ANN2	Before IE	Desired	After IE
0.863	0.752	0.650085	1	1.0
0.861	0.772	0.665473	1	1.0
0.874	0.789	0.689831	1	1.0
0.323	0.176	0.057201	0	0.0
0.365	0.407	0.148924	0	0.0
0.336	0.121	0.040786	0	0.0
0.827	0.647	0.535724	0.5	0.5
0.638	0.567	0.362051	0.5	0.5
0.661	0.618	0.408758	0.5	0.5

CONCLUSIONS

Efficient on-the-fly classification of lidar returns is a major challenge for Biomass surveys and underwater object detection. This paper aims to present a solution to this problem. From the results it is evident that the parallel Neural Network architecture works efficiently in detecting the required classes from one another. The HRBF based system trained itself much faster than the MLP based system but was found to have lower prediction accuracy than MLP. MLP based system is found to project the output space much further from one another with distinct hyperplanes, that helped the Inference Engine to present the final decision with a higher accuracy. This research considers copolarized component of lidar return used at day light, which not only adds substantial noise to the system but also results in greater attenuation. Because of this the lidar returns for fish and water-layer were very close to each other and extracting features to distinguish between them was a major problem. Crosspolarized component used at night will result in much better detection accuracy and the system will be almost noise free, for which we may not need the low pass filter at the signal preprocessing stage. The Inference Engine presents the decision based on a hard coded rule base, which is not system specific. To make the inference process much more adaptive a Support Vector Machine based Inference Engine may be implemented, where complex hyperplanes can be generated to present the final decision with a higher accuracy. Due to lack of data and ignorance about the estimated time required to classify a fish school from other possible underwater objects, this research have assumed that the lidar underwater object returns are solely from fish school, hence future research should address the temporal aspect of lidar returns and implement an algorithm to make the final judgment based on it.

Acknowledgement: The authors would like to acknowledge NOAA for providing the real experimental data.

REFERENCES

[1] Sica R., 'Exploring the Atmosphere With Lidars', *University of Western Ontario, Department of Physics and Astronomy*, , © 1999 by Dr. R. J. Sica

[2] Arnold J.E., Kavaya M.J., 'LIDAR Tutorial', 1999, NASA.

[3] Churnside J.H. and McGillivary P.A., 'Optical properties of several Pacific fishes', *Applied Optics*. Vol. 30, pp. 2925-2927 (1991).

[4] Xiao R., Wilson R. and Carande R., 'Neural Network Classification with IFSAR and Multispectral Data Fusion' *IEEE Proc. of Geoscience and Remote Sensing Symposium*, Vol. 3, pp. 1327-1329, 1998.

[5] Churnside J.H., Wilson J.J., Tatarskii V.V., 'Airborne Lidar for Fisheries Application', *Journal of Optical Engineering*, Vol. 40(3), pp. 406-414, March 2001.

[6] Principe, Euliano and Lefebvre, *Neural and Adaptive Systems: Fundamentals through Simulations*, John Wiley & Sons, Inc. 2000.

RECONSTRUCTION OF VOLUMETRIC CAD MODELS USING 3D SOFM

GEORGE K. KNOPF AND PHILIP C. IGWE
Department of Mechanical & Materials Engineering,
Faculty of Engineering, The University of Western Ontario,
London, Ontario, Canada, N6A 5B9

ABSTRACT

Computer-aided design and engineering analysis requires geometric modeling tools that enable the designer to accurately create solid objects from measured, or user-entered, surface points. The automatic mesh generation technique introduced in this paper exploits the computational structure of a three-dimensional self-organizing feature map (SOFM) to create a hexahedral mesh from scattered surface data. The algorithm begins with a lattice of nodes that represent the vertices of regular six sided solid elements uniformly distributed in a mesh. The exterior nodes of the lattice are iteratively repositioned in the object space based on captured surface information whilst the interior nodes are pulled along by the neighborhood effect imposed by the SOFM adaptation algorithm. Throughout the shape transformation process the topology of the initial three-dimensional lattice remains unchanged. The performance of the proposed hexahedral mesh generator for volumetric model reconstruction is illustrated by producing a solid mesh of a hand carved wooden mask.

INTRODUCTION

Automated geometric modeling tools must have the capability to accurately create volumetric models of complex shapes from measured, or user-entered, surface points. The solid modellers approximate the shape of arbitrary freeform objects as a collection of primitive volumes such as cylinders, ellipsoids, spheres, cubes, or hexahedrons (Hoschek and Lasser 1993; Huang *et al* 2002, Maeda *et al* 2002; Maeda *et al* 2003; Ranjan and Fournier 1994). The method of volume reconstruction is largely dependent on the complexity of the object shape and the application domain. Typically, engineering applications exploit spatial occupancy enumeration or solid mesh generation techniques because these methodologies produce volumetric models that are more geometrically accurate.

Tetrahedron and hexahedron solid elements are often used for creating the meshes (Huang *et al* 2002, Maeda *et al* 2002; Maeda *et al* 2003). Although the algorithms for producing a tetrahedral mesh are easier to implement, the hexahedral meshes are more computationally efficient because fewer elements are required to represent the shape. It can take five tetrahedral elements to achieve the same geometric accuracy as a single hexahedral element. Furthermore, a valid mesh can only be generated if the angles in the tetrahedral elements are neither too obtuse nor too acute. Consequently, a model of a simple flat plate may inadvertently result in a large number of tetrahedral elements. To correct for many of the geometric errors that occur using tetrahedrons the designer must manually insert hexahedral elements and sub-meshes in certain regions of the volume model.

A variety of mesh generation techniques have been described in the literature for creating hexahedral meshes. In general, the process is not automatic and often very labour intensive because the designer must manually subdivide the model so that multiple meshes will optimally represent the object. One approach is based on a multiblock topology (Huang *et al* 2002). The designer must first partition the object geometry into multiple hexahedral blocks or "super-elements" within which an array of solid elements is produced. Each block is then further sub-divided into an array of elements whose size depends on the desired grid density. The major advantage of this multiblock mesh generation approach is that it produces a highly structured grid. Once the block topology is determined a variety of CAE software tools must be used to optimize the elements in the desired mesh.

An adaptive technique for automatically creating volumetric CAD models from acquired scattered surface points is briefly described in this paper. The hexahedral mesh of the underlying object is constructed using a self-organizing feature map (SOFM) with a three-dimensional lattice of uniformly distributed nodes. Self-organizing feature maps have been used extensively for a variety of pattern recognition and data compression applications (Kohonen 1997). The lattice structure of the map has also provided the basis of new algorithms for scientific visualization, scattered data interpolation, and three-dimensional object registration (Knopf and Sangole 2002; Knopf and Sangole 2004). In this context, the ordered lattice of the SOFM maintains the relative connections of neighboring nodes in the mesh as it geometrically into the desired shape, Fig. 1. The basic method of constructing a hexahedral mesh from surface data using the SOFM is described below. Experimental results are provided to illustrate the algorithms performance.

(a) Initial lattice. (b) Surface points. (c) Final mesh.

Figure 1. The basic structure of the original block lattice and the deformed shape after the corresponding nodes are repositioned by the self-organizing feature map (SOFM). Each cell in the mesh is a hexahedral element – a solid with six planar faces.

CONSTRUCTING A HEXAHEDRAL MESH USING A SOFM

The objective of this study is to automatically construct a volumetric model of an arbitrary freeform object from measured surface or boundary data. The volume model will be represented as a mesh of solid hexahedral elements. A hexahedron is a solid structure having six plane faces. A *regular hexahedron* is a cube with square faces. Each element is a cell bounded by faces where the vertices of the various hexahedral elements in the mesh are represented by the weight vectors assigned to the nodes in the three-dimensional lattice of the self-organizing feature map (Kohonen 1997). The lattice L is defined as a set of nodes $\{\mathbf{w}_{000}\ \ \mathbf{w}_{100}\ \ldots\ \mathbf{w}_{ijk}\ \ldots\ \mathbf{w}_{IJK}\}$ in the object space and information about the connectivity between the constituent nodes. To be well constructed the lattice must not have a vertex (or node) that lies on an edge that does not contain the vertex. Furthermore, all hexahedron cells are closed such that the faces of the cell do not form any holes. Finally, no two faces of a cell intersect (Figure 2). This final property ensures that the final lattice will not be a self-intersecting structure.

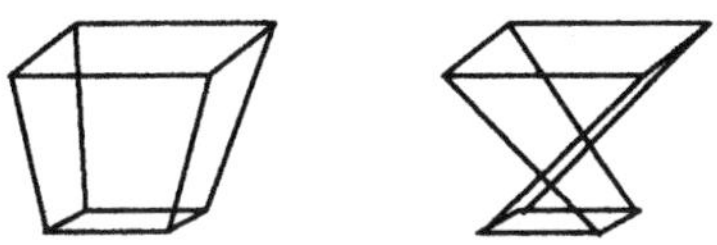

(a) Valid hexahedron. (b) Invalid hexahedron.

Figure 2. Comparison between a valid (a) and invalid (b) hexahedron cell in the lattice. The faces of the cell shown in (b) intersect and, therefore, it will result in a self-intersecting lattice.

During implementation the self-organizing feature map is initially given as a lattice of nodes distributed in a block structure, as shown in Figure 3, that encloses the measured surface points. Each surface point is provided by the vector $X^p = [\, x_1^p\, ,\ x_2^p\, ,\ x_3^p\,]$, where p = 1, 2, ... P, and P is the total number of coordinate data points used for mesh construction. The vector X^p corresponds to the (x, y, z) coordinates of a point in measurement space. The location of each lattice node in the object space is given by a weight vector w_{ijk}. The weight vector represents the position of a vertex of a hexahedral element in the mesh.

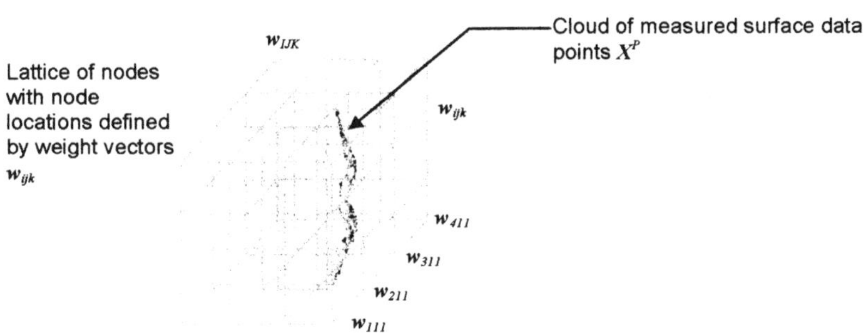

Figure 3. The initial values of the weights w_{ijk} for the lattice that encloses all coordinate data points.

The weight adaptation algorithm of the SOFM is designed such that the selected node, and all nodes residing in its neighbourhood are simultaneously updated. Thus, a node at location (i,j,k) in the lattice has an associated variable neighbourhood operator that covers an area of the map given by $(2NE_{ijk} + 1) \times (2\, NE_{ijk}+1) \times (NE_{ijk}+1)$ where NE_{ijk} is the decreasing neighbourhood radius in the i,j,k-directions, Figure 4. The size of the neighbourhood is decreased as training progresses until it contains only the winning unit. Under certain circumstances, the mesh generation technique will require an additional step that attempts to spread the nodes more evenly in the interior of the volume. On completion of the training process, the geometry mapped by the node weights represent the hexahedral mesh of the original object surface.

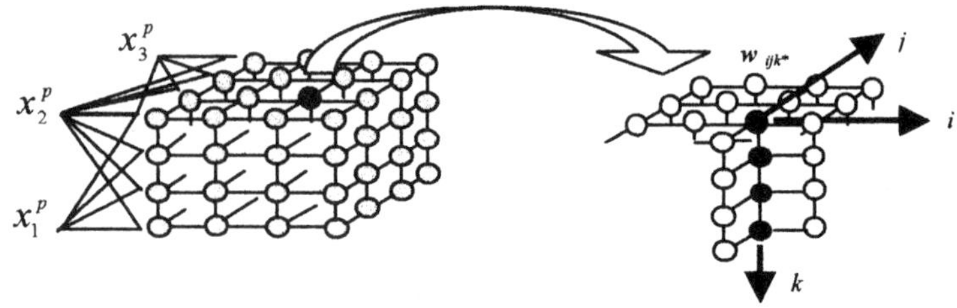

Figure 4. Basic structure of a SOFM used to create a hexahedral mesh model. The neighbourhood operator influences the interior nodes.

The various steps used to construct a hexahedral mesh from scattered surface data are as follows:

Step 0: Initialize the weights by assigning them to the node locations of a uniformly sampled mesh that encloses the measured surface data. Set the learning parameter, μ, size of initial neighbourhood operator, and the number of cycles, N_{cycle}, through the data.

Step 1: Randomly select a coordinate point X^p from the data set. For each selected coordinate point do Steps 2 – 5.

Step 2: Compute the error, $D^p_{i,j,k}$ between the input coordinate value and weight vectors for all exterior nodes in the lattice using the relationship

$$D^p_{i,j,k} = \Phi(u_{ijk}) \sum_{n=1}^{3} (x_n^p - w_{n,i,j,k})^2 \tag{1}$$

where $\Phi(u_{ijk})$ is a count-dependent non-decreasing function, x_n^p is the nth element of the input vector, $w_{n,i,j,k}$ is the weight from the nth input element to the $(i,j,k)^{th}$ node on the exterior of the SOFM lattice.

Step 3: Select the winning node w_{ijk^*} as the unit on the exterior of the lattice with the minimum distance $D^p_{i,j,k}$ from the selected sample point X^p.

Step 4: Update the weights to the winning node $(i,j,k)^*$ and all other nodes that reside within the specified neighbourhood of radius $\boldsymbol{NE}_{ijk}$ using

$$w_{ijk^*}(\text{new}) = w_{ijk^*}(\text{old}) + \alpha \left[X^p - w_{ijk^*}(\text{old}) \right] \tag{2a}$$

where $\alpha = \mu \left[1.0 - (\#_{\text{cycle}} / N_{cycle}) \right]$, (2b)

$\mu = 0.1$, and $\#_{\text{cycle}}$ is the number of cycles through the training data set.

Step 5: Reduce the radius of the topological neighbourhood based on the number of cycles through the training data set,

$$\boldsymbol{NE}_{ijk} = nint\left[7.0\left\{1.0 - (\#_{\text{cycle}} / N_{cycle})\right\}\right] \tag{3}$$

and $nint[..]$ is an operator that determines the nearest integer.

Step 6: Test the stopping condition. If the stopping condition is not satisfied then go to Step 1 and repeat the process.

The above SOFM algorithm may not spread the interior nodes so that they adequately fill the volume bounded by the surface nodes. This is the result of interior node clustering near the exterior nodes of the mesh. The problem is not significant if the number of nodes along one of the directions is small but can become pronounced if the lattice is comprised of many nodes in all three dimensions. An additional step is, therefore, required to shift the interior nodes throughout the volume without introducing invalid hexahedral cells that have intersecting faces. One simple approach is to reposition interior nodes based on regular incremental distances from two opposite surface points. The operation is straightforward because the node topology of the final mesh is the same as the initial mesh.

EXPERIMENTAL STUDY

The hexahedral mesh generation algorithm was tested using scanned surface data of a hand carved wooden mask. The data set for the test object contained 162,048 coordinate points as shown in Figure 5. The surface data was acquired from both the front and back of the wooden mask using a Cyberware Model 3030 head and face scanning system. Once captured the data set was reduced to 16,205 points in order to test the algorithm.

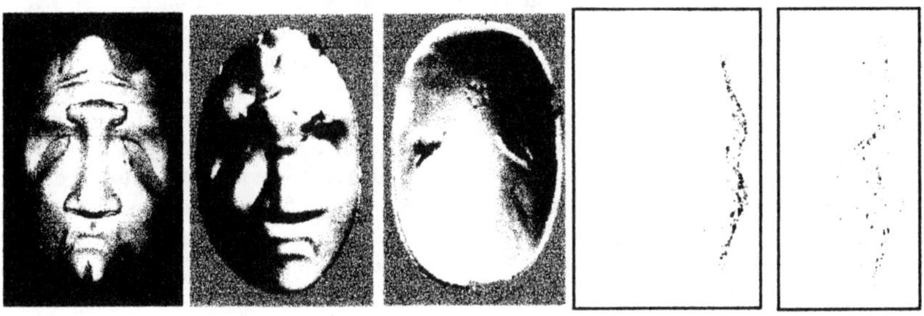

(a) Original object. (b) Range image of face and back. (c) Scattered surface data.

Figure 5. The hand carved wood mask and the range data used to train the SOFM for generating a volumetric mesh with hexahedral elements.

An initial 40x40x5 lattice used for constructing the hexahedral mesh of the mask. The final mesh was created using an initial region of influence of 15x15x8 units in the *i*,*j*, and *k*- directions. The maximum number of cycles through the captured data was set to N_{cycle} = 100 and the learning parameter was μ = 0.1. The final hexahedral mesh and facetted surface model for the 40x40x5 SOFM are illustrated in Figure 6. The greater density of exterior nodes increases surface detail. Selected hexagonal elements, or cells, from within the final mesh are displayed. The lighter lines in the figure show the edges of the solid elements in the interior of the volume.

The results show that solid hexahedral elements can be created from the SOFM lattice. In addition, the preliminary tests demonstrated some of the limitations imposed on the solution by this approach. Specifically, the algorithm could only create a hexahedral mesh that was topologically equivalent to the initial lattice. As well, the geometric accuracy of the resultant mesh is a function of the number of nodes in the lattice. Increasing the nodes will increase the computational time. Future investigations need to address the automatic addition of nodes in the lattice to improve geometric accuracy and the optimal filling-in of the volume bounded by the surface nodes.

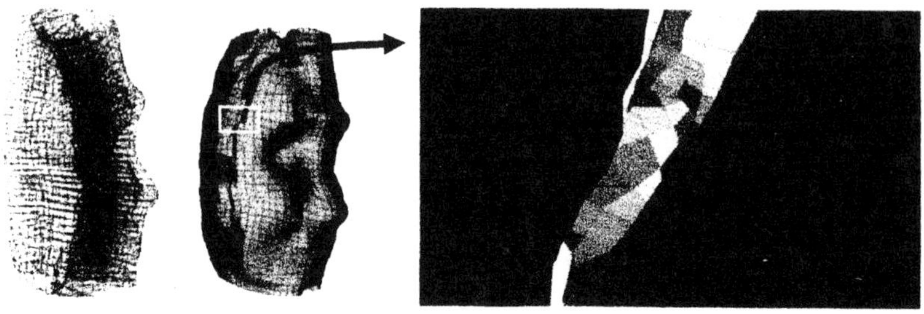

Figure 6. The final hexahedral mesh and facetted surface model for the 40x40x5 SOFM. Interior connections of selected hexagonal elements are shown.

CONCLUSIONS

Hexahedral mesh generation is a difficult problem for computer-aided design (CAD), computer-aided engineering analysis, and scientific visualization. Meshes comprised of hexahedral elements are more computationally efficient than tetrahedral or hybrid meshes. However, most hexahedral meshing algorithms involve a significant amount of manual correction. In this paper an algorithm was presented that used a 3D self-organizing feature map to automatically create a solid mesh based on captured boundary information. The neighbourhood operator of the SOFM algorithm ensured that topology of the original lattice did not change as the shape geometry was altered. The fixed node topology ensured that the mesh generator could always compute the connectivity between the constituent nodes. Furthermore, the iterative nature of the adjustments meant that individual cells in the volumetric model would not become self-intersecting and, therefore, all interior hexahedral elements remain valid cells.

ACKNOWLEDGEMENTS

This work has been supported, in part, by the Natural Sciences and Engineering Research Council of Canada.

REFERENCES

Hoschek J. and Lasser D., *Fundamentals of Computer Aided Geometric Design*. A.K. Peters Ltd.: Wellesley MA, 1993.

Huang, S., Shi, J., Maloo, S., and Steinhorsson, E., "Automatic generation of quadrilateral multi-block topology for FEA/CFD applications, *IEEE ICIT'02*, Bangkok Thailand, pp. 1300 – 1305, 2002.

Knopf, G.K. and Sangole, A., "Interpolating scattered data using 2-D self-organizing feature maps", *Journal of Graphical Models*, vol. 66, pp. 50 –69, 2004.

Knopf, G.K. and Sangole,A., "Registration of closed free-form surfaces using deformed spherical maps", *Intelligent Engineering Systems Through Artificial Neural Networks: Vol. 12*, C.H. Dagli et al (Eds.), ASME Press, pp. 583 – 588, 2002.

Kohonen, T., *Self-Organizing Maps*. Springer, New York, 1997.

Maeda, T., Noguchi,S, Yamashita, H., and Cingoski, V., "Automatic hexahedral mesh generation for FEM using shape recognition technique and tree method", *IEEE Trans. on Magnetics*, vol. 38, no. 2, pp. 417 – 420, 2002.

Maeda, T., Noguchi,S, Yamashita, H., and Cingoski, V., "Automatic hexahedral mesh generation for rotating machine", *IEEE Trans. on Magnetics*, vol. 40, no. 2, pp. 973 – 976, 2003.

Ranjan, V. and Fournier, A., "Volume models for volumetric data", *IEEE Computer*, pp. 28 – 36, July, 1994.

DYNAMIC DATA DRIVEN SUPPORT VECTOR MACHINES APPLIED TO TORNADO DETECTION

THEODORE B. TRAFALIS
BUDI SANTOSA
School of Industrial Engineering
University of Oklahoma
202 West Boyd, Suite 124,
Norman OK, 73019
405/325-4347
ttrafalis@ou.edu,bsant@ou.edu

MICHAEL B. RICHMAN
School of Meteorology
University of Oklahoma
1100 East Boyd, Suite 1310
Norman, OK 73019
405/325-1853
mrichman@ou.edu

ABSTRACT

In this research, Support Vector Machines (SVM) and Minimax Probability Machines (MPM), fueled by dynamically driven data, are applied for tornado detection. To detect tornadic circulations, the Weather Surveillance Radar 1998 Doppler (WSR-88D) is used. WSR-88D data stream in every six minutes and present a source for development of a dynamic data driven application system (DDDAS). The inputs to the SVM and MPM are from the National Severe Storms Laboratory's Mesocyclone Detection Algorithm (MDA). As each input varies, as a function of time, we investigate the behavior of the time signals before and the time of the tornado touch down to seek the dynamic pattern that gives rise to such storms. The results are compared to the performances of SVM and MPM using only information at the time of tornado touch down. Both SVM and MPM show better performance when information before tornado touch down is used.

1. INTRODUCTION

Detection of tornadoes with ample warning times has long been a goal of forecasters. With modern weather radar, high speed computing and advanced signal processing algorithms, steady progress has been made on increasing the average lead-time of such warnings. Despite this improvement, there is a strong need to push back the lead-time of warnings as far as possible to enhance public safety. Contemporaneously, there is a need to lower the false alarm rate, as a high rate can lead to the public ignoring warnings.

One of the severe weather detection algorithms created by the National Severe Storms Laboratory (NSSL) and used at the Weather Surveillance Radar 1998 Doppler (WSR-88D) is the Mesocyclone Detection Algorithm (MDA). This algorithm is designed to detect storm–scale circulations that are associated with regions of rotation in thunderstorms. The MDA is used by meteorologists as one input in their decision to issue tornado warnings. MDA utilizes the outputs of WSR-88D radar to detect tornadoes. Marzban and Stumpf (1996) showed that the performance of MDA is improved by post-processing with neural networks.

In a similar vein, this paper applies kernel-based methods, such as SVM and MPM, to detect tornado circulations by using the outputs of WSR-88D radar. The application of the kernel methods addresses the problem of nonlinearity of the data in the input space by mapping the data into a higher dimensional space where the problem becomes linearly separable. By exploiting the kernel method, it is possible to find nonlinear classifiers that separate the data into tornado and no tornado cases.

MPM is a new technique that works by seeking the best classifier that minimizes the maximum probability of misclassification error in a binary problem. The problem of minimax can be formulated as an unconstrained second order conic programming problem (Lanckriet et al., 2002) and can be solved with an iterative procedure to find the best classifier.

The paper is organized as follows. In section 2, the definition of the problem is provided. In section 3, description of the data is given. In section 4, the basics of the learning machines used and our methodology are discussed. In section 5, the experimental setting is described. Section 6 provides analysis of the results and, finally, section 7 concludes the paper.

2. PROBLEM STATEMENT

There are two classes of problems addressed in this research. One is physical (tornado detection) and the other is methodological (comparing SVM and MPM with varying time lags). The two are intimately entwined for the prediction of tornadoes. There are two challenges involved in tornado warnings from the meteorological viewpoint. The first one is tornado detection. Of those tornadoes that do occur, the number of tornados detected is smaller. The detection problem is obvious, as an efficient forecast system must detect as many of the pre-tornadic circulations as possible, due to the potential for loss of life. The second one is false alarms. The false alarm problem is insidious because it is possible to develop a system that always forecasts pre-tornadic circulations will become tornadic. However, if such forecasts do not verify, these are termed "false alarms" and have the potential to go unheeded by the public after a series of such forecasts. Accordingly, it is desirable to develop a statistical algorithm that will maximize detection and minimize false alarms.

Prediction of tornadoes is a difficult task owing to the small scale of their circulation and their rapid production in the atmosphere. They can form within minutes and disappear just as quickly. The best tool in the meteorologist's arsenal to remotely sense tornadoes is Doppler radar. However, present day operational radar takes approximately 6 minutes to complete one volume scan and the spatial resolution averages close to ¼ km for Doppler radar velocity. Many tornadoes and pre-tornadic circulations are smaller than that. Despite the challenges, lead times for tornadoes have increased from a few minutes (a decade ago) to approximately 11 minutes (with current radar), largely due to improvements in algorithms that use the radar data as inputs.

The second research problem is to develop an intelligent system that can generalize well with data that have a significant noise component. ANNs are considered robust classifiers in terms of input noise. However the resulting learning optimization problem is nonconvex. An alternative to ANN is SVM where the learning optimization problem is convex. More recent work by Lanckriet et al. (2002) has shown that MPM provides a classifier that is competitive with SVM.

3. DATA

The data used for this research are the outputs from WSR-88D radar. Trafalis et al. (2003) discuss the partitioning of these data into tornado and non-tornado cases. The predictor pool employed in the first portion of the study consists of 23 MDA attributes based on Doppler velocity data. These same attributes have been used successfully by Trafalis et al. (2003). The challenge here was to identify persistent circulations that evolve into tornadoes. The NSSL MDA has such information present as each circulation is assigned a unique identifier. The MDA data are processed to determine which radar the tornado reports came from and then are sorted sequentially by time to create sequences of observations. Only circulations that are non-tornadic and evolve into tornadoes can be used for the tornado detection part of the analysis. After examination of the number of such sequential observations associated with the same circulation, the most practical number of time steps to retain is three. Additionally, three time steps of nontornadic circulations are retained for the subsequent classifiers, as the goal is to develop an algorithm that can separate those circulations that evolve into tornadoes from those which remained as mesocyclones (a circulation that stays aloft). Although the MDA collects data on tornadoes impacting the conterminous United States, only those tornadoes impacting the Great Plains are selected, since the literature suggests that the dynamics of tornadoes in the eastern United States can be different from those in the center of the country (e.g., Hagemeyer and Schmocke, 1991; Giordano and Fritsch, 1991). There are 238 cases of three consecutive observations ending in a tornado selected. These are divided in half into training and testing data sets.

To improve the detection, three different predictor structures are used to detect a tornado touchdown (which is defined as time t). The first approach is dynamically data driven and uses all information of those 23 attributes at volume scans at times t-2, t-1 and t. Time t-2 indicates the observation at two volume scans prior to the tornado, whereas t-1 corresponds to the observation one volume scan prior to the tornado. The second approach uses information of the radar-derived attributes at times t-1 and t. In both experiments, since the data stream prior to the tornado is varying, this approach uses dynamically changing data. A third approach is non-dynamic and uses the single volume scan from the time the tornado is verified, at time t. This can serve as a baseline to determine if using dynamic data streams result in any improvement in the forecast of tornadoes.

The second portion of the study uses dynamic data driven application system (DDDAS) in a different manner by creating a vector of forecasts of a tornado/non-tornado based on the previous time step. This vector is incorporated into the SVM and MPM as a 24th attribute in the following time step (e.g., time t-2 generates a forecast vector that is used in the SVM/MPM for time step t-1).

4. METHODOLOGY

4.1 Support Vector Machines (SVM). Currently, SVM is a well-known method in data mining area as classification and function approximation tools. SVM usage and formulation can be found in Haykin (1999).

4.2 Minimax Probability Machines (MPM). The MPM approach was introduced by Lanckriet et al. (2002). The objective of this approach is that the problem of binary classification is solved by minimizing the maximum probability of misclassification of the future data points.

4.3 Forecast Evaluation Indices for Tornado Detection. In the detection paradigm, the forecast results are evaluated by using a suite of forecast evaluation indices based on a contingency table or a "confusion matrix" (Trafalis et al., 2003). The cell counts from the confusion matrix can be used to form forecast evaluation indices (Wilks, 1995). In this definition of the confusion matrix, there are several indices that can be defined to assess the 'goodness' of the forecast. These indices are defined and discussed in Trafalis et al. (2003).

5. EXPERIMENTS

In the experiments, the data are split into two sets: *training* and *testing*. The ratio between training and testing sets is 50:50. There are 100 different training samples that are randomly chosen from the data and 100 corresponding testing samples. SVM and MPM are trained with each training sample and tested on each corresponding testing sample. This is done for all training and testing samples. The performances of the two methods are computed based on the average of all testing samples.

In the first set of experiments, information expressed in the attributes' values at volume scans prior to time t are used to predict the output at time t. In the second portion of the study, the outputs from previous time (e.g., t-2 and t-1) are added to the 23 attributes at time t-1 and t to predict the output at time t. In this approach, when we are predicting the output at time t-1, the forecast output vector from t-2 is added to the 23 attributes at time t-1 (making 24 attributes). Therefore, we have one additional attribute. In addition, when we are predicting the output at time t, the output from t-1 is added to the 23 attributes at time t.

The SVM and MPM experiments were performed in the MATLAB environment. OSU SVM Classifier Matlab Toolbox by Jushui et al. is used to run experiments of SVM for classification.

6. RESULTS

The final results of the experiments are presented in Tables 1 and 2 and Figures 1a to 1d. Tables 1 and 2 are obtained after we process the confusion matrix for each time lag. Figures 1a through 1d show different aspects of the performance for each classification method for the aforementioned evaluation indices. Each graph describes the relation between a specific statistic and observations used for prediction at time t in the *testing* set for the two methods. The use of attributes' values at time t-2 to predict the output at time t is the least accurate across all of the evaluation indices. When time t-1 is dynamically added to t-2 to predict time t, the values of indices improve. The best results are shown for a dynamic data feed with t-2, t-1 and t. However, the relative improvement of t-2 through t-1 to t differs for the various indices and the levels of each index need to be interpreted to understand the behavior of the forecast system and allows comparison of SVM to MPM.

Figure 1a shows the POD for the two techniques at the various time sequences. For the t-2, t-1 and t time sequence, the best results are seen with all three time steps. While this is useful in a diagnostic sense, for forecasting the t-2, t-1 combination (to predict a tornado at time t) gives a detection of about 0.62 for SVM and 0.60 for MPM. The alternative sequence of t-1 and t is slightly less accurate for both the diagnostic (including time t) and prognostic (excluding time t) cases. The FAR values (Fig 1b) are interesting as they decrease steadily as the additional time steps are included. The results are considered to be desirable with values approaching 0.3 with multiple time steps. The SVM has a slight edge in low false alarms. Another way of examining the False Alarms is through POFD (Fig. 1c). In this case, the "no tornado" forecasts are isolated, thereby giving a fuller picture if compared with FAR. The POFD should be as close to zero as possible. In this study, the POFD values mimic the FAR values almost exactly. A summary evaluation index is Heidke skill. The Heidke skill provides information on how much of an improvement a forecast is compared to a random guess (or some other reference forecast). Those results (Fig. 1d) show a steady increase in skill as additional time steps are retained.

For the model with 24 attributes fed by dynamic data, the indices are somewhat lower (Tables 1 and 2). The SVM results are in line with the non-dynamic model with somewhat lower skill. The MPM results are slightly inferior to those given by SVM. The decrease in accuracy as the t-2 time step is omitted is similar between the two kernel methods.

7. SUMMARY AND CONCLUSIONS

Based on the performance improvement of all the methods when previous information before time t is used, we can conclude that the dynamic inclusion of data has a beneficial result on tornado prediction. As the lead-time to prediction increases, the accuracy of the forecast decreases. This is an expected result. The important finding is that there is skill available *at least* two radar volume scans prior to the tornado (approximately 12 minutes). Had there been ample cases with four successive observations, the skill at 18 minutes could have been assessed. In order to accomplish this, special data sets will need to be constructed. This is being investigated currently. The model with 24 dynamic fed attributes gave results similar but slightly inferior to the model with 23 dynamically fed attributes. It is possible that more optimal ways of including prior information in the next time step may improve the results further.

Acknowledgement: The present work has been partially supported by the NSF grant EIA-0205628.

References

Giordano, L.A. and J.M. Fritsch, 1991, "Strong tornadoes and flash-flood-producing rainstorms during the warm season in the Mid-Atlantic Region", *Weather and Forecasting*, 6, pp. 437–455.

Hagemeyer, B.C. and G.K. Schmocker, 1991, "Characteristics of East-Central Florida tornado environments", *Weather and Forecasting*, 6, pp. 499-514.

Haykin, S., 1999, *Neural Networks: A comprehensive Foundation*, 2nd edition, Prentice-Hall, Upper Saddle River, NJ.

Junshui, M., Y. Zhao, and S. Ahalt, "OSU SVM Classifier Matlab Toolbox", Available at http://eewww.eng.ohio-state.edu/~maj/osu_svm/

Lanckriet, G.R.G., El Ghaoui, L., Bhattacharyya, C., Jordan, M.I., 2002, "A Robust Minimax Approach to Classification", *Journal of Machine Learning Research*, 3, pp. 555-582.

Marzban, C. and Stumpf, G. J., 1996, "A Neural Network for Tornado Prediction Based on Doppler Radar-Derived Attributes", *Journal of Applied Meteorology*, 35, pp. 617-626.

Trafalis, T.B., B. Santosa, and M.B. Richman, 2003, "Tornado Detection with Kernel-based Methods", *Intelligent Engineering Systems Through Artificial Neural Networks*, (C.H. Dagli, A.L. Buczak, J. Ghosh, M. Embrechts, and O. Ersoy , Eds.), ASME Press, 13, pp. 677-682.

Wilks, D. S., 1995, *Statistical Methods in the Atmospheric Sciences*. Academic Press, London.

Table 1. Forecast evaluation indices using SVM and MPM for different time lags

	Time Lag											
	[t-2]		[t-2,t-1]		[t-2,t-1,t]		[t-1]		[t-1,t]		[t]	
	SVM	MPM	SVM	MPM	SVM	MPM	SVM	MPM	SVM	MPM	SVM	MPM
POD	0.642	0.569	0.620	0.582	0.652	0.582	0.591	0.512	0.645	0.618	0.634	0.582
FAR	0.364	0.419	0.357	0.441	0.304	0.441	0.408	0.437	0.338	0.360	0.369	0.441
POFD	0.362	0.406	0.340	0.453	0.281	0.453	0.402	0.392	0.326	0.344	0.366	0.453
Heidke's Skill	0.279	0.163	0.280	0.129	0.371	0.129	0.189	0.120	0.320	0.274	0.268	0.129

Table 2. Forecast evaluation indices using SVM and MPM by adding the output from previous time to the next consecutive time

	Time Lag			
	[t-2,t-1,t]		[t-1,t]	
	SVM	MPM	SVM	MPM
POD	0.638	0.566	0.588	0.510
FAR	0.361	0.415	0.405	0.431
POFD	0.356	0.397	0.396	0.382
Heidke's Skill	0.282	0.169	0.192	0.128

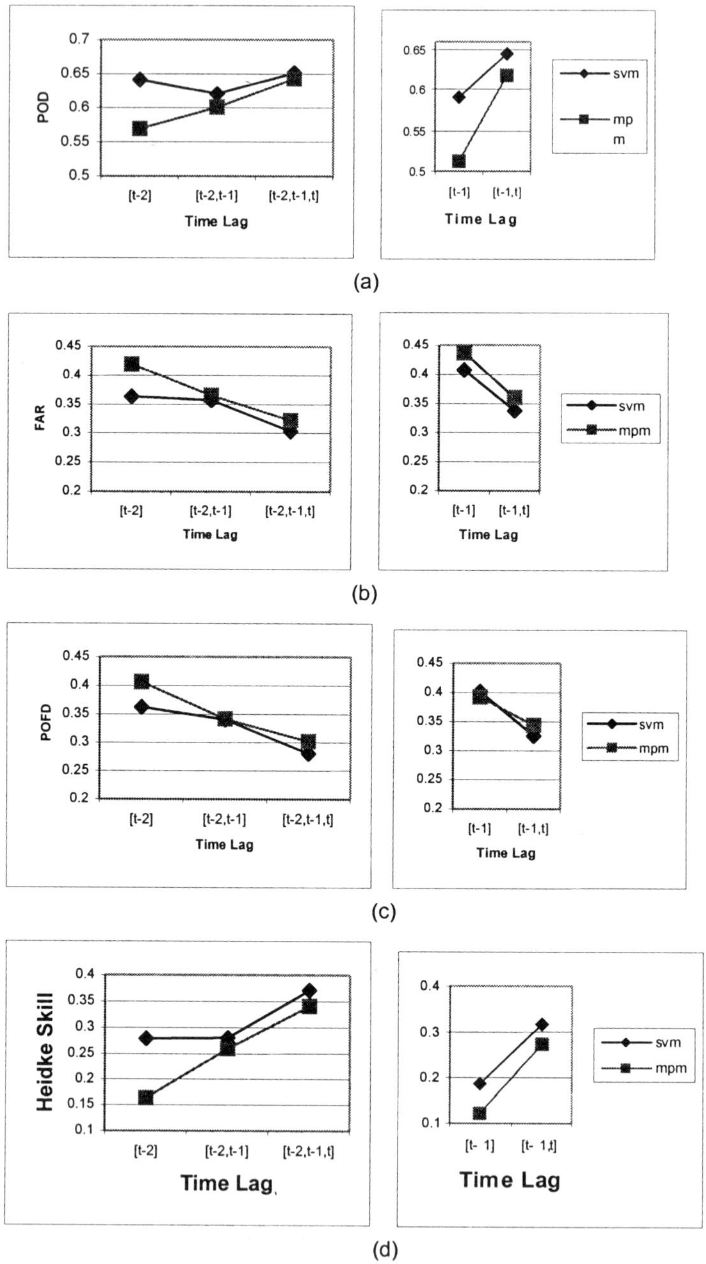

Figure 1. Forecast evaluation indices (a –d) of tornado detection at time t using three different predictors (left column) and two different predictors (right column). T he left column contains experiments from lags (t-2), (t-2, t-1) and (t-2, t-1, t), respectively. The right column contains experiments from lags (t-1) and (t-1, t), respectively.

FINGER LOOK FOR HIGH DEGREE INFORMATION SECURITY BASED ON NEURO-FUZZY METHODOLOGY

S. B. PATIL
Digital Micro Computing Lab.,
Dept. of Electronics & Telecomm.,
S. S. G. M. College of Engg.,
Shegaon-444203,
Dist. Buldhana (M.S), INDIA
E-mail: sbpatil@ssgmce.ac.in

R. D. KANPHADE
Digital Micro Computing Lab.,
Dept. of Electronics & Telecomm.,
S. S. G. M. College of Engg.,
Shegaon-444203,
Dist. Buldhana (M.S), INDIA
E-mail: rdkanphade@ssgmce.ac.in

ABSTRACT

Wherever authentication/identification is demanded, we believe biometrics identification is only the reliable identification. Among wide verity of biometrics applications to identify the persons, we worked on fingerprints and presented a fully automatic system which present true (genuine) personal identification and capable of identifying a person over a large database within no time. In our work we used hybrid fingerprint matching scheme. In this paper to speed up the matching process, a fast-automated feature based technique for fingerprint classification is presented.. In our novel approach we use neuro-fuzzy techniques to resolve the complexity involved in fingerprint processing.

INTRODUCTION

The traditional knowledge-based (Password or Personal Identification Number) and token-based (Passport, Driver license, and ID card) approaches are unable to satisfy the security requirements of our electronically interconnected information systems as an imposter can easily deceive them. The computer power has grown, so the idea that automated capture, measurement and identification of distinctive physiological or behavioral characteristics of human being could safeguard our identities and therefore our privacy and could also be used to fight crime. The technologies now being developed for this purpose have come to be labeled 'biometrics' because they apply statistical methods to biological observations and phenomena. Since biometric characteristics are distinctive, cannot be forgotten or lost, and the person to be authenticated needs to be physically present at the point of identification, biometrics is inherently more reliable and more capable than traditional knowledge-based and token-based techniques.

In this paper we have proposed a nuero-fuzzy based hybrid approach which uses *Reference points* i.e. core and deltas (classification), *Minutiae points* i.e. ridge ending and bifurcation and *Feature map* (finger code) for searching a claimed finger in the large database. Finger this way process can be used as a "*finger lock*" for any electronics access system. Following sections explains in detail all these three core concepts.

FINGERPRINT CLASSIFICATION

To reduce the search time and computational complexity, it is desirable to classify these fingerprints in an accurate and consistent manner such that the input fingerprint needs to be matched only with a subset of the fingerprints in the database. Fingerprint classification can be viewed as a coarse level matching of the fingerprints. We classify fingerprints into five classes, namely, *whorl* (*W*), *right loop* (*R*), *left loop* (*L*), *arch* (*A*), and *tented arch* (*T*) [5,7].

The novel system we proposed is capable of tolerating poor quality fingerprints. We used singular point (core and delta) and neural net based two-stage classifier proposed by *Jain et al* [5] with some modification in it. This hybrid approach is depicted in **Figure 1.** The main steps of our classification algorithm are as follows and details are given in the following sections:

1. In a scanned finger image, tessellate (sector) the major area using rectangular tessellation.
2. Compute the standard deviation of the component image in each sector to generate the feature vector (finger code) also find the directional map of each sector.
3. Feed the feature vectors to neural network based classifier.
4. From the directional map, compute the number of core and delta point points.
5. From the location of core and delta points in the fingerprint decide the class pattern.
6. Verify the result obtained from neural network based classifier and singular point classifier result to take the final decision

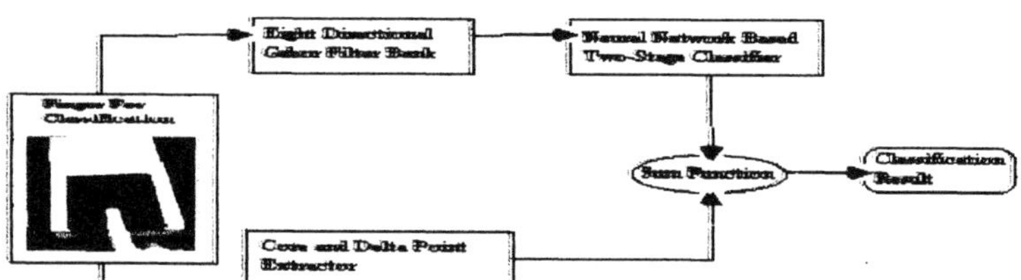

Figure 1: A novel approach for the fingerprint classification, which uses the finger code and core and delta point, position in a fingerprint.

COMPUTATION OF FEATURE VECTOR (FINGER CODE)

The category of a fingerprint is determined by its global ridge and furrow structures. A valid feature set for fingerprint classification should be able to capture this global information effectively. To compute the finger code we have followed, with some modification, the same algorithm proposed by *Jain et al.* [6,4]. Our algorithm includes following steps to compute the feature vector (finger code):

1. Decompose the input image into a set of component images.
2. Normalize each sector to remove the scanner noise [6].

3. Compute the standard deviation of gray level values in each sector to form the feature vector or the Finger code.

FINGERPRINT FILTERING USING GABOR FILTERS

Fingerprint images present a strong orientation tendency and have a well-defined spatial frequency in each local neighborhood that does not contain singular point(s). Gabor filters are band-pass filters which have both orientation-selective and frequency-selective properties and have optimal joint resolution in both spatial and frequency domains [1]. By applying properly tuned Gabor filters to a fingerprint image, the true ridge and furrow structures can be greatly accentuated [5,2]. These accentuated ridges and furrow structures constitute an efficient representation of a fingerprint image. An even symmetric Gabor filter has the following general form in the spatial domain:

$$G(x,y;f,\theta)=\exp\left[\frac{x'^2}{\delta_{x'}^{2}}+\frac{y'^2}{\delta_{y'}^{2}}\right]\cos(2\pi f x')$$

$$x'=x\sin\theta+y\cos\theta$$

$$y'=x\cos\theta-y\sin\theta$$

Where, f is the frequency of the sinusoidal plane wave along the direction θ from the x-axis, δ_x and δ_y specifies the Gaussian envelope along x and y-*axes*, respectively, which determine the bandwidth of the Gabor filter.

In the algorithm proposed by *jain et al.* [6,3] they convolved the finger image with four Gabor filters (θ = 0 °, 45°, 90°, and 135°) but in our experiment we have convolved each sector with a bank of eight Gabor filters (orientation angles 0, 22.5, 45, 67.5, 90, 112.5, 135°) to produce the eight component images. This will cover the complete semi circular rotation of the finger on the scanner and helps to capture more global information in a fingerprint image. The scheme is depicted in the **Figure 2.**

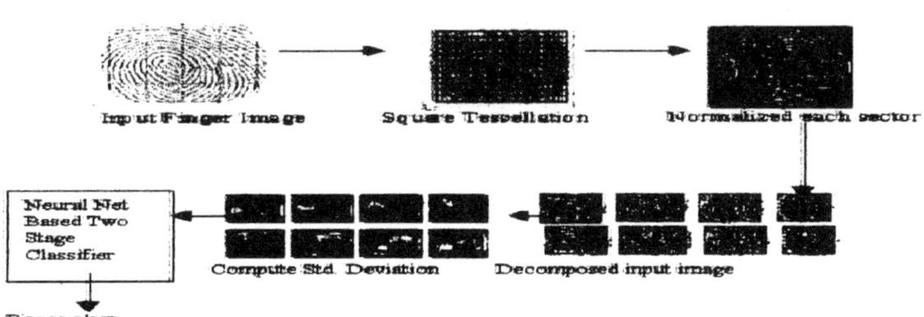

Figure2: Finger code computation using a bank of eight Gabor filters and this code is given to neural network based two-stage classifier to find out the finger class

Finger code

In each component filtered image, a local neighborhood with ridges and furrows that are parallel to the corresponding filter direction exhibits a higher variation, whereas a local neighborhood with ridges and furrows that are not parallel to the corresponding filter tends to be diminished resulting in a lower variation. The spatial distribution of the variations in local neighborhoods of the component images thus constitutes a characterization of the global ridge structures which is captured by the average absolute deviation of grayscale values from the mean (*AAD* features).

Let S_i be the ith sector of normalized image and C_{ideg} corresponding to deg (0° to 135°) rotation of S_i, a feature is the standard deviation defined as:

$$Vector = \sum_{i=1}^{n} C_{i\,deg} \quad (1)$$

$$Vector\_sum = \frac{Vector}{8} \quad (2)$$

Therefore, finger code is computed as:

$$Fingercode = \sum_{i=1}^{n} Vector\_sum \quad (3)$$

The same finger code so computed for the classification and be used for finger matching also as depicted in **Figure 6.**

Neural net based two-stage classifier

The same architecture (**Figure 3**) suggested by *Jain et al.* [5] used here. The top two categories can be retrieved from the *K*-NN classifier corresponding to the classes which have the highest and the second highest count among the *K* nearest neighbors, i.e., the first recall and the second recall. In the second stage of the classifier, 10 neural networks are trained to solve each of the 10 two-class problems. This neural network makes the final decision between these two classes. Here a multi layer feed-forward neural network is trained. The neural network has one hidden layer with 20 neurons, 8 input neurons (no. of sectors), and 5 output neurons corresponding to the five classes.

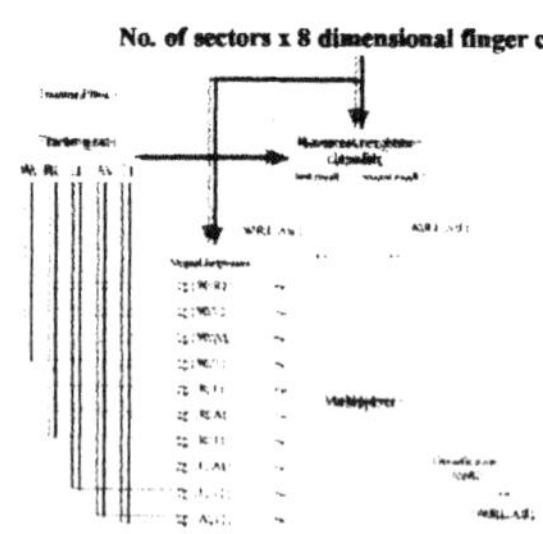

Figure 3: Neural network based two-stage classifier. This classifier uses finger code to classify the fingerprint. [5]

CLASSIFICATION BASED ON SINGULAR POINTS (CORE AND DELTAS)

From the singular point i.e. core and delta points we can classify the finger pattern. The basic algorithm to classify the finger patter as per Lasso classification (arch, tented arch, left loop, right loop and whorl). Algorithm is given below [7]:

1. If there are 0 delta or 0 core points, then the fingerprint is an arch.
2. If core and delta points are aligned in the vertical direction, then the fingerprint is an arch and if the length between the core and the delta point is less than 2.5 mm then it is tented arch.
3. If the core aligned right to delta point, then the fingerprint is a right loop.
4. If the core point aligned left to delta point, then the fingerprint is a left loop.

MINUTIAE EXTRACTION

Finger code technique suggested by *Jain et al* [5] does not work well on inferior quality fingerprints. There are number of distinct points, called minutiae, are available in the fingerprint which can be used for matching. We used on two i.e. ridge ending and ridge bifurcation because they are commonly available in all kinds of fingerprint images and easily detected. Here neuro-fuzzy technique used to extract the minutiae from a fingerprint.

Fuzzy logic approach

In our system we have use the fuzzy logic in detecting the valuable gray level pixel information from the fingerprint image. From the original scanned image, after normalization binary image is obtained. We have use 5x5-pixel window from the finger image to compute the average of 25 pixels. Then binary image is obtained as per the following definitions:

If $p_i < A_{vi}$ then the $p_i = 0$ and if the $p_i \geq A_{vi}$ then $p_i = 1$. Where, p_i is the i th pixel and A_{vi} is the gray value average of all 25 pixels in the image.

A 5x5-pixel test window is placed every point of the binary image. **Figure 4 a** shows the placement of test window. The average value (middle average) of the 25 pixels is then obtained. In addition, the average value (border average) of pixels within a 2-pixel border surrounding the test window is also obtained. These two averages form the linguistics variable of brightness as shown in **Figure 4b** For ridge endings detections, the first average determines the *DARK* full membership and second average determines the *BRIGHT* full membership. This is reversed for bifurcation detection.

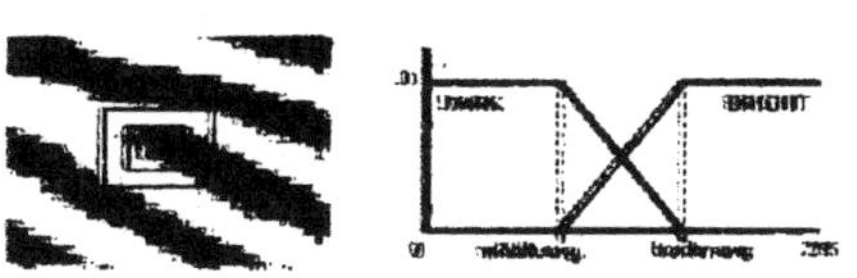

(a) (b)

Figure 4: a) placement of 5x5-test window on the binary image and b) Linguistics variable of brightness for ridge ending detection

Sets of 8 small windows (sub-windows) are used to gather the surrounding area information. These are of size 5x5 unlike the window size 1x5 chosen by *Sagar and Beng* [8]. To cater the uneven width of ridges and valleys, these 8 windows are shifted to all four direction (left, right, down and up) around the middle window (5x5). Using these fuzzy values of Bright and Dark fuzzy rules are modeled if a minutia is detected.

NEURAL NETWORK

The neural network as shown in **Figure 5** are 18x8x8x4 back propagation neural network [9]. Two nets (9x4x4x2) are used one for each minutiae detection i.e. ridge ending and ridge bifurcation. The algorithm is given below:

1) Select the size of neural network (in our case18x8x8x4), function for multiplication (*Sigmoid*) and error range.
2) Obtain the database of DARK and BRIGHT values of desired output in the neural network output layer and store it for comparison.
3) Apply input set of *DARK* and *BRIGHT* values obtained from fuzzification engine to the input layer of neural network.
4) Check the values of output layer whether it is '0' or '1'; count the number of iterations required to match with error.

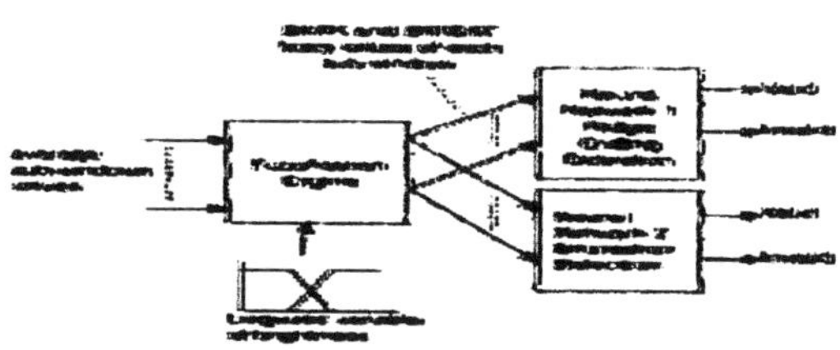

Figure 5: Neural network model with fuzzy values for the detection of minutiae: ridge ending and ridge bifurcation.[8]

HYBRID FINGERPRINT MATCHING SCHEME

The process of fingerprint matching depicted in **Figure 6** involves comparing a query fingerprint with a set of one or more template prints. Prior to the matching process, feature information is extracted from all the template images. The hybrid fingerprint matcher proposed here, utilizes three distinct features of the fingerprint image i.e. core and delta, finger code extraction and minutiae extraction: ridge ending and bifurcation. When a query image is presented, the matching proceeds as follows:

1) The query and template finger image is given to classifier.
2) Query and template finger class is matched.
3) The query and template finger image is given to a bank of 8-Gabor filter to extract the finger code.
4) The query and template finger codes are matched
5) The query and template minutiae features are extracted.
6) The minute set of query and template fingerprint is matched.

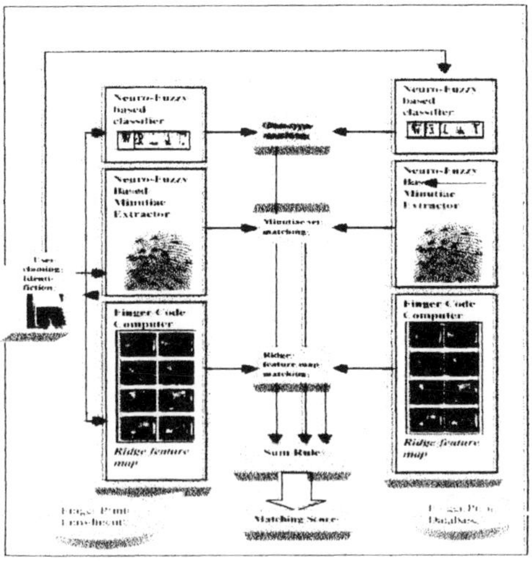

Figure 6: System architecture. Fingerprint enrollment and database contain class type, minutiae set and ridge feature map (finger code).

CONCLUSIONS

The hybrid system proposed here is fully automatic, fast processing and capable of handling poor quality of fingerprints. The system is designed taking all the problems of scaling, translation and rotation of fingerprint on the scanner. The system is capable of searching fingerprint over a large database.

REFERENCES

1. Daugman J. G., 1985, "Uncertainty Relation for Resolution in Space, Spatial Frequency, and Orientation Optimized by Two-Dimensional Visual Cortical Filters", J. Optical Soc. Amer. A, Vol. 2, pp. 1160-1169.
2. Hong L., and Jain A. K., 1998, "Classification of Fingerprint Images", Technical Report MSUCPS: TR98-18, Michigan State Univ.
3. Karu K., and Jain A. K., 1996, "Fingerprint Classification", Pattern Recognition, Vol. 29, No, 3, pp. 389-404.
4. Jain, A.K., Hong L., Pankani S., and Bolle R., 1997, "An Identity Authentication System Using Fingerprint", Proc.IEEE, Vol. 85, No. 9, pp. 365-1388.
5. Jain, A.K., Prabhakar Salil, and Hong Lin, 1999, "A Multichannel Approach to Fingerprint Classification", IEEE Transactions On Pattern Analysis and Machine Intellegence, Vol. 21, No. 4.
6. Jain, A.K., Prabhakar Salil, Hong Lin, and Pankani Sharath, 2000, "Filterbank-Based Fingerprint Matching", IEEE Transactions On Image Processing, Vol. 9, No. 5.
7. Meltem Ballen , Aygab Sajarath, and Brain L. Evans, " Fingerprint Classification Techniques Using Directional Images"
8. Sagar V. K. and Beng K. J., "Fingerprint Feature Extraction using Fuzzy Logic and Neural Networks", Technical Report.
9. Wilson C. L., Candela G. T., and Watson C. I., 1993, "Neural Network Fingerprint Classification', J. Artificial Neural Network, Vol. 1, No. 2, pp. 203-228.

REAL TIME FACE DETECTION IN VIDEO SEQUENCES IN COMPLEX BACKGROUND ENVIRONMENT

MING-JUNG SEOW
Department of Electrical and Computer Engineering
Old Dominion University, Norfolk, VA 23529

VIJAYAN K. ASARI
Department of Electrical and Computer Engineering
Old Dominion University, Norfolk, VA 23529

ABSTRACT

Ratio algorithm learns by minimizing the maximum distance of the statistical properties of the relative magnitudes of data at two neurons for all training patterns. The activation function of the network is determined by the statistical characteristics of the input patterns. The ratio algorithm has been applied for skin color modeling to do real time skin color classification. Experimental results show that the network can segment skin regions utilizing the skin model created from the ratio learning algorithm. Face detection is performed by using a multilayer feed-forward neural network trained with back-propagation learning algorithm in conjunction with a modular approach utilizing the distance based learning algorithm for reducing the structural complexity of the network in analyzing each frame of the video sequence. The performance of the new face detection technique is evaluated with real-time data of frame size 320×240 from video sequences captured using a surveillance camera. It is observed that the network can classify skin and non-skin regions effectively and the face regions can be detected in images with complex lighting and background environment.

INTRODUCTION

Face detection may seem like an easy task for humans, but computerized face detection system that detects faces from an image is a very challenging job due to large variations in facial appearance, head size, orientation and changes in background environment and lighting conditions (Rowley, Baluja, Kanade, 1998). Majority of the proposed methods use gray level images to detect faces in spite of the fact that most images used today are color images. As a consequence, most of these results are computationally intensive. To solve these problems, color based face detection has recently become a new direction for face detection. Color based face detection techniques first select the skin like regions from the image, and then detect the presence of facial features in these regions. Several approaches have been published and they all basically differ in the modeling of the skin color and in the nature of feature extraction methods. For example, in Garcia *et al* (1999), the face like regions are detected using quantized skin color region merging and wavelet packet analysis. This technique can detect faces with various sizes and different poses under minor illumination changes. However, it is also computationally expensive due to its segmentation algorithm and time-consuming wavelet packet analysis.

In color based face detection, the robustness of the skin color model is important for the overall success of face detection. In our previous work (Seow, Asari 2003a), we proposed a skin color model using ratio learning algorithm to perform skin segmentation. We extent this modeling concept to the face detection task in the proposed algorithm. We present a technique in which we use the skin color model to extract skin like regions from an image and distance based training algorithm (Seow, Asari, 2003b) trained with multilayer perceptron using backprobagation learning for face detection. We illustrate the efficiency of the proposed face detection method in image captured under complex background environment and lighting conditions.

SKIN COLOR MODELING

Using skin color as a feature for detecting, recognizing, and tracking a face region have many advantages because processing skin color is much faster than processing other features such as eyes, nose, and mouth. Under certain lighting conditions, color is orientation invariant. We have used the ratio learning algorithm for skin color modeling. The training set consists of 4,000 skin samples collected from a Sony EVI-D30 surveillance camera. Figure 1(a) shows the collected samples which include skins of people belonging to different races and skin-colors. The skin pixel distribution is plotted on a 3-D scatter plot and it is shown in Figure 1(b).

(a) Skin samples (b) 3-D scatter plot (RGB) of skin distribution

Figure 1: Skin samples and skin scatter plot

The collected skin samples are used for training the ratio learning algorithm using equation (7), which will be described in detail in the following section. Figure 2 shows the decision surfaces of the ratio rule. It can be seen that the ratio learning algorithm is able to encapsulate the data into skin regions with only the data from the skin samples.

Figure 2: Ratio memory

LEARNING MODEL

The relationship of a neuron with respect to another neuron can be described as

$$W_{ij}^{s} = b_i^s / a_j^s \tag{1}$$

for stimulus-response pair (a^s_j, b^s_i) and the resultant memory W^s_{ij}. This ratio finds the degree of similarity between each neuron with other neurons. Therefore, W^s can be written as

$$W^s = \begin{pmatrix} w_{11}^s & \cdots & w_{1N}^s \\ \vdots & \ddots & \vdots \\ w_{N1}^s & \cdots & w_{NN}^s \end{pmatrix} = \begin{pmatrix} b_1^s / a_1^s & \cdots & b_1^s / a_N^s \\ \vdots & \ddots & \vdots \\ b_N^s / a_1^s & \cdots & b_N^s / a_N^s \end{pmatrix} \tag{2}$$

To form a memory matrix W by combining W^s, we need to utilize statistical methods. The approach to this problem is to use the training samples to estimate the unknown probabilities and probability density, and then use resulting estimation as if they were the true values. To see how maximum-likelihood method applies to a specific case, we can reasonably assume that the values of b^s_i / a^s_j are drawn for a multivariate normal density with mean μ, although we do not know the exact value of these quantities. This knowledge simplifies the problem for estimating an unknown function as estimating the parameter μ. Let the log-likelihood of a single point b^s_i / a^s_j be

$$\ln\left[P(b_i^s / a_j^s \mid \mu)\right] = -\frac{1}{2}\ln(2\pi)^d |\Sigma| - \frac{1}{2}\left(b_i^s / a_j^s - \mu\right)^t \Sigma^{-1}\left(b_i^s / a_j^s - \mu\right) \tag{3}$$

where ? is the covariance matrix. We usually find the value of μ that maximizes $ln[\,P(b^s_i / a^s_j / \mu)\,]$ by differentiating it by the component μ and setting the result to zero

$$\nabla \ln\left[P(b_i^s / a_j^s \mid \mu)\right] = \Sigma^{-1}\left(b_i^s / a_j^s - \mu\right) \tag{4}$$

The maximum likelihood estimation for μ can be obtained by

$$\sum_{i=1}^{P} \Sigma^{-1}\left(b_i^s / a_j^s - \mu\right) = 0 \tag{5}$$

Multiplying (5) on left and right side by ? and rearranging, we obtain the maximum-likelihood estimation for μ as

$$\mu = \frac{1}{P}\sum_{s=1}^{P} b_i^s / a_j^s \tag{6}$$

Equation (6) shows that the maximum likelihood estimate for the unknown population mean is just the arithmetic average of the training samples. Figure 3 shows the weight graph illustrating the concept of training based on (6). A weight graph is a graphical representation of the relationship between the i th and j^{th} neurons for P patterns. The weight graph may help visualize the behavior of one neuron pair.

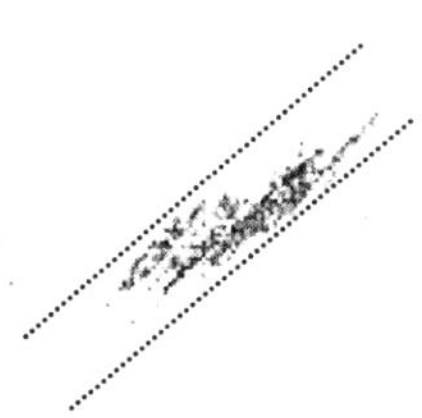

Figure 3: Weight graph describing the relationship of the ith neuron and the jth neuron

Based on the above theory, the memory matrix for the N neuron network can be obtained as

$$w_{ij} = \frac{1}{P}\sum_{s=1}^{P}\frac{x_i^s}{x_j^s} \quad for\ 1 \le i, j \le N \tag{7}$$

where $x_m \in \{1, 256\}$ can be the magnitude of the input at m^{th} neuron. The learning algorithm can be interpreted as the mean ratio between two neurons. The network architecture is a single layer fully connected recurrent neural network. The net output of the network can be computed as

$$Net_i = \frac{1}{N}\sum_{j=1}^{N} w_{ij}x_j \quad for\ 1 \le i \le N \tag{8}$$

where N is the number of neurons. The Net_i can be thresholded considering the region of distance of the weight components in the weight graph shown in Figure 3. That is, w_{ij} gives a linear approximation for all the points $x^s{}_i / x^s{}_j$. In order to preserve each pattern, we need to find the region where the threshold can preserve each pattern. The dashed line in Figure 3 is such a distance. Mathematically the threshold function can be represented as

$$o_i^{new} = f(Net_i) = \begin{cases} o_i^{old} & if winL_i \le Net_i - o_i^{old} \le winR_i \\ Net_i & otherwise \end{cases} \quad for\ 1 \le i \le N \tag{9}$$

where $winL_i$ and $winR_i$ are the window functions for thresholding. They can be expressed as

$$winL_i = \alpha \frac{1}{N}\sum_{j=1}^{N} Tl_{ij} \quad for\ 1 \le i \le N \tag{10}$$

$$winR_i = \alpha \frac{1}{N}\sum_{j=1}^{N} Tr_{ij} \quad for\ 1 \le i \le N \tag{11}$$

where a is a constant and $0 < a = 1$. Tl_{ij} and Tr_{ij} can be expressed as:

$$Tl_{ij} = Min\{(w_{ij}x_j^s - x_i^s) \quad for\ 1 \le s \le P\} \tag{12}$$

$$Tr_{ij} = Max\{(w_{ij}x_j^s - x_i^s) \quad for\ 1 \le s \le P\} \tag{13}$$

The window width between $winL_i$ and $winR_i$ decides if the o_i^{old} should be updated or not.

FACE DETECTION

The proposed face detection technique analyzes the skin regions for candidate faces in each skin-segmented image with a 20×20 mask, and generates an output ranging from 0 to 1, signifying the probability of presence of faces. Figure 4 shows the formulation of the input vectors from an image for the training of a 2-D multilayer neural network, employing distance based training algorithm presented in (Seow, Asari, 2002, 2003b).

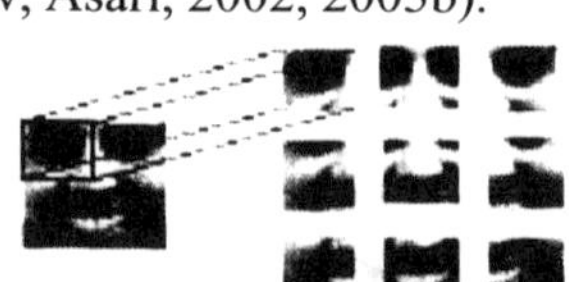

Figure 4: Formulation of the input vectors to the 2-D multilayer network from an image

Equations (14)-(15) describe such a structure after dividing the face image into 9 sub-regions.

$$D = \begin{cases} \eta & if \quad \eta = 1 \\ 0 & otherwise \end{cases} \tag{14}$$

$$\eta = Max\left\{\lambda \ at\left(\left\lfloor \frac{i-1}{n^{\lambda}} \right\rfloor = \left\lfloor \frac{k-1}{n^{\lambda}} \right\rfloor\right), \lambda \ at\left(\left\lfloor \frac{j-1}{m^{\lambda}} \right\rfloor = \left\lfloor \frac{k-1}{m^{\lambda}} \right\rfloor\right)\right\} \tag{15}$$

Probable face regions in the images are divided into 9 regions according to the scheme shown in the Figure 4. Nine different multilayer neural networks are used to decide the proximity of each of the 9 regions to a face region. The votes from all multilayer neural networks are used to decide if the probable face region is a face or non-face. To detect faces larger than the window size, the input image is repeatedly subsampled by a factor of 1.2, and a 20×20 neural network filter is used for scanning at each scale as it is described in (Rowley, Beluja, Kanada, 1998).

Segmented skin regions are scanned by a mask for detecting the faces by a scanning process shown in Figure 5. Each of the 9 regions obtained by using the mask on a pixel-by-pixel scan of the image is subjected to a threshold function to decide if it corresponds to a facial feature. The presence of 4 facial features in the regions is needed in order that it is detected as a face.

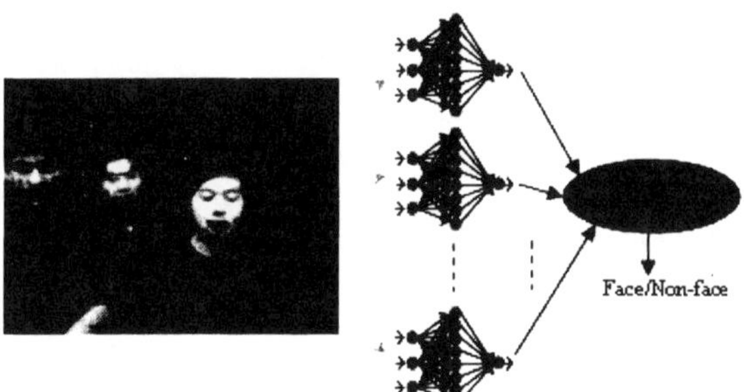

Figure 5: Illustration of the scanning process.

EXPERIMENTAL RESULT

In the first experiment, we tested the efficiency of the skin color model trained using the ratio learning algorithm. We applied the skin color model to a set of 100 images collected from the VLSI Systems Laboratory, which contain people from white to dark skins in different levels of background complexity and lighting conditions.

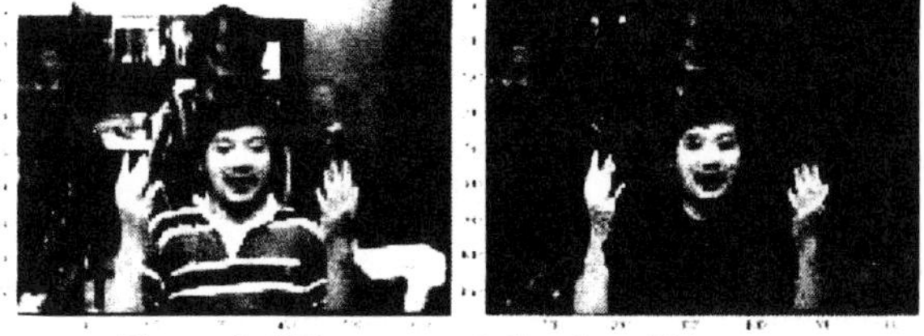

Figure 6: Skin segmentation for still image

Figure 6 shows a few examples of the results obtained in skin color detection. It can be observed that the ratio network can successfully distinguish skin regions of people belonging to different skin colors in complex lighting conditions.

Figure 7: Face detection in a video sequence

The speed and performance of the network are tested in a second experiment when it is applied to Sony EVI-D30 surveillance camera at 15 fps for 320×240 resolution images of 24-bit color. We created our training set for training the neural network based face detector by manually cropping 500 faces of size 20×20 from the images captured from the Sony surveillance camera. Figure 7 shows the image from the camera and the face detection results. It can be observed that the network is able to detect the face regions in all the frames in the video sequence.

CONCLUSIONS

A ratio rule based training algorithm suitable for skin color detection has been presented in this paper. The ratio rule learns by minimizing the maximum distance of the statistical properties of the relative magnitudes of two neurons. The threshold function has been represented by the statistical characteristics of the input patterns. Experimental results show that ratio learning can detect skin regions under complex background and lighting environment. Subsequent face detection is aided by multilayer perceptron trained using backpropagation-learning in conjunction with distance based learning algorithm. It can be observed from the experimental results that the proposed face detection system reduced the computation time considerably when compared to conventional techniques facilitating real-time applications.

REFERENCES

H. A. Rowley, S. Baluja, and T. Kanade, "Neural network-based face detection," IEEE Trans. Pattern Analysis and Machine Intelligence, vol. 20, no. 1, pp. 23-38, January 1998.

C. Garcia, and G. Tziritas, "Face detection using quantized skin color merged regions and wavelet packet analysis," IEEE Trans. Multimedia, vol. 1, no. 3, pp. 264-277, 1999

M. J. Seow and K. V. Asari, "Associative memory based on Ratio learning for real time skin region extraction," IEEE International Workshop on Applied Imagery and Pattern Recognition, AIPR - 2003, pp. 151-156, October 15 - 17, 2003a.

M. J. Seow and K. V. Asari, "High performance associative memory with distance based training algorithm for character recognition," Proc. IEEE International Joint Conference on Neural Networks – IJCNN 2003, pp. 1185-1188, July 2003b.

M. J. Seow and K. V. Asari, "Modular architecture for Hopfield network and distance based training algorithm for pattern association," Journal of Neural, Parallel and Scientific Computations, vol. 10, no. 4, pp. 371-386, December 2002.

SELF ORGANIZED FUZZY CLUSTERING

MIKA SATO-ILIC
Faculty of Systems and Information Engineering
University of Tsukuba
Tsukuba, Japan

ABSTRACT
This paper proposes a new fuzzy clustering method based on the idea of self-organized dissimilarity between two objects, while considering the degree of sharing of common properties of the pair of objects for the obtained fuzzy clusters. The dissimilarity changes dynamically in relation to the clustering structure; if the two objects have similar clustering structures then the dissimilarity is reduced. That is, the method is based on the idea that two similar objects have similar clustering structures. In addition, the clustering can obtain a result when objects are classified in a self-organized way. In order to show the performance of this method, several numerical examples are shown.

INTRODUCTION

Recently, the theories of self-organized techniques are well-known and many applications have proven their efficiency. The field of data analysis is not an exception, much research based on this idea have been proposed. This is especially true of, clustering methods which are important for the self organization based data analysis. (Kohonen, 1982, Van Hulle, 2000) Fuzzy clustering models are typical methods for obtaining the degree of belongingness of objects for the clusters. However, the conventional method is not adequate when the data has noise and complex structure, where the optimum solution (local minimum solution) is not suitable for the data.

This paper presents a new technique based on the idea that when the obtained degree of the objects for the same clusters are similar to each other, then the objects themselves are similar to each other, since the fuzzy clustering model is based on the measurement of the degree of common properties of objects for the fuzzy clusters. In this case, we use the difference of the estimated degree of belongingness for objects as the weights of the similarity among the objects. The process of iterations includes the following steps: fuzzy clustering model, estimating the degree of belongingness and the modification of the similarity among objects using the weights. Through these steps we will obtain the solution of the degree of belongingness of objects to clusters in a self organizing way.

GENERALIZED FUZZY CLUSTERING MODEL

The structure of an observed similarity is usually unknown and complicated, so various fuzzy clustering models are required to identify the latent structure of the similarity data. Therefore, we define a general class of fuzzy clustering models, so as to represent many different structures of a similarity data. (Sato and Sato, 1995) The merits of the fuzzy clustering models are: 1) the amount of computations necessary for the identification of the models are much fewer than in a hard clustering model, and 2) one can obtain a suitable fitness by using fewer of clusters. In the generalized clustering model, aggregation operators are used to define the degree of simultaneous belongingness of a pair of objects to a cluster. We present some required conditions for the aggregation operators. T-norms (Menger, 1942, Schweizer and Sklar, 1983) are concrete examples for satisfying these conditions.

Suppose that there exist K fuzzy clusters on a set of n objects, that is, the partition matrix $U = (u_{ik})$ is given. Let $\rho(u_{ik}, u_{jl})$ be a function which denotes a degree of simultaneous belongingness of a pair of objects i and j to clusters k and l, namely, a degree of sharing common properties. Then a general model for the similarity s_{ij} is defined as follows:

$$s_{ij} = \varphi(\rho_{ij}) + \varepsilon_{ij}, \tag{1}$$

$$\rho_{ij} = (\rho(u_{i1}, u_{j1}), \cdots, \rho(u_{i1}, u_{jK}), \cdots, \rho(u_{iK}, u_{j1}), \cdots, \rho(u_{iK}, u_{jK})).$$

To state simply, we assume that if all of $\rho(u_{ik}u_{jl})$ are multiplied by α, then the similarity is also multiplied by α. Therefore, the function φ itself must satisfy the condition "positively homogeneous of degree 1 in the ρ", that is,

$$\alpha\varphi(\rho_{ij}) = \varphi(\alpha\rho_{ij}), \quad \alpha > 0.$$

We consider the following function as a typical function of φ:

$$s_{ij} = \{\sum_{k=1}^{K} \rho^{r}(u_{ik}, u_{jk})\}^{\frac{1}{r}} + \varepsilon_{ij}, \quad 0 < r < +\infty. \tag{2}$$

We will deal with (2) ($r = 1$) hereafter. The degree ρ is assumed to satisfy the following conditions:

$$0 \leq \rho(u_{ik}, u_{jl}) \leq 1, \quad \rho(u_{ik}, 1) = u_{ik}, \quad \rho(u_{ik}, 0) = 0.$$

$$\rho(u_{ik}, u_{jl}) \leq \rho(u_{sk}, u_{tl}), \quad \text{whenever } u_{ik} \leq u_{sk}, \ u_{jl} \leq u_{tl}.$$

$$\rho(u_{ik}, u_{jl}) = \rho(u_{jl}, u_{ik}).$$

In particular, T-norms satisfy the above conditions.

In the case of $\rho(u_{ik}, u_{jl}) = u_{ik}u_{jl}$, (1) is represented as follows:

$$s_{ij} = \sum_{k=1}^{K} u_{ik}u_{jk} + \varepsilon_{ij}, \tag{3}$$

where u_{ik} is a fuzzy grade which represents the degree of belongingness of an object i to a cluster k, and satisfies the following condition:

$$u_{ik} \geq 0, \quad \sum_{k=1}^{K} u_{ik} = 1. \tag{4}$$

The product $u_{ik}u_{jk}$ is the degree of simultaneous belongingness of objects i and j to a cluster k. That is, the product denotes the degree of the sharing of common properties.

SIMILARITY BETWEEN CLUSTERS

If the observed similarity data is asymmetric, then the additive fuzzy clustering models in the previous section are not suitable. Let us extend the model (1) as:

$$s_{ij} = \sum_{k=1}^{K} \sum_{l=1}^{K} w_{kl}\rho(u_{ik}, u_{jl}) + \varepsilon_{ij}. \tag{5}$$

In this model, the weight w_{kl} is considered to be a quantity which shows the asymmetric similarity between a pair of clusters. That is, we assume that the asymmetry of the similarity between the objects is caused by the asymmetry of the similarity between the clusters.

In the case of $\rho(u_{ik}, u_{jl}) = u_{ik}u_{jl}$, (5) is represented as:

$$s_{ij} = \sum_{k=1}^{K}\sum_{l=1}^{K} w_{kl}u_{ik}u_{jl} + \varepsilon_{ij}. \tag{6}$$

If $k = l$, $u_{ik}, u_{jl} = 1$ and $w_{kl} > 1$, then the right hand side of (6) clearly exceeds 1.0. Hence we need at least the following condition

$$0 \leq w_{kl} \leq 1, \tag{7}$$

because $0 \leq s_{ij} \leq 1$. The method of fuzzy clustering based on this model is to find the partition matrix $U = (u_{ik})$ and $W = (w_{kl})$ which satisfy the conditions (4), (7) and have the best fitness for the model (6). Then we find U and W which minimize the following sum of square error η^2 under the conditions (4) and (7),

$$\eta^2 = \sum_{i \neq j = 1}^{n} (s_{ij} - \sum_{k=1}^{K}\sum_{l=1}^{K} w_{kl}u_{ik}u_{jl})^2. \tag{8}$$

If $U_{ij} = \sum_{k=1}^{K}\sum_{l=1}^{K} w_{kl}u_{ik}u_{jl}$, then (8) is

$$J \equiv \eta^2 = \sum_{i \neq j = 1}^{n} (s_{ij} - U_{ij})^2 \rightarrow \min$$

The descent vector is determined as follows:

$$\frac{\partial J}{\partial u_{ar}} = -4\sum_{i=1}^{n}(s_{ia} - U_{ia})u_{ir}, \quad a = 1, \cdots, n, \quad r = 1, \cdots, K. \tag{9}$$

$$\frac{\partial J}{\partial w_{bc}} = -2\sum_{i \neq j = 1}^{n} (s_{ij} - U_{ij})u_{ib}u_{jc}, \quad b, c = 1, \cdots, K. \tag{10}$$

The following method is used to find the solutions U and W.

(Step 1) Fix K, $2 \leq K < n$.

(Step 2) Initialize $U^{(0)} = (u_{ik}^{(0)})$, $(i = 1, \cdots, n;\ k = 1, \cdots, K)$, where $u_{ik}^{(0)}$ is generated by uniform pseudorandom numbers in the interval $[0, 1]$ and satisfy $\sum_{k=1}^{K} u_{ik}^{(0)} = 1$. Initialize $W^{(0)} = (w_{kl}^{(0)})$, $(k, l = 1, \cdots, K)$, where $0 \leq w_{kl}^{(0)} \leq 1$. And set the step number $l = 0$.

(Step 3) Set $l = l + 1$. Calculate the value of $\dfrac{\partial J}{\partial u_{ik}^{(l-1)}}$ by using (9) and $W^{(l-1)}$ obtained in Step 2. Find the optimal solution with respect to the direction of the descent vector by using the one dimensional direct search. That is update u_{ik} by using the next expression,

$$u_{ik}^{(l)} = u_{ik}^{(l-1)} - \lambda \left(\frac{\partial J}{\partial u_{ik}^{(l-1)}} \right),$$

where $\lambda > 0$ is step size.

(Step 4) Calculate the value of $\dfrac{\partial J}{\partial w_{kl}^{(l-1)}}$ by using (10) and $U^{(l)}$ obtained in Step 3. Find the optimal solution with respect to the direction of the descent vector by using the one dimensional direct search. That is update w_{kl} by using the next expression,

$$w_{kl}^{(l)} = w_{kl}^{(l-1)} - \lambda \left(\frac{\partial J}{\partial w_{kl}^{(l-1)}} \right),$$

where $\lambda > 0$ is step size.

(Step 5) Calculate the value of $\|U^{(l)} - U^{(l-1)}\|$ by using $u_{ik}^{(l)}$ and $w_{kl}^{(l)}$ obtained in Step 3 and Step 4, where $\| \cdot \|$ shows the norm of matrix.

(Step 6) If $\|U^{(l)} - U^{(l-1)}\| < \varepsilon$, then stop, otherwise go to Step 3.

SELF ORGANIZED FUZZY CLUSTERING

When we obtain the result of the degree of belongingness for the fuzzy clustering model using the above algorithm, there are times when we cannot obtain a suitable result because the solution is a local minimum solution. We present the new fuzzy clustering method using the result of the above fuzzy clustering.

The method consists of the following three steps:

(Step 1) Apply the similarity data for the model (6). If the similarity data is symmetric, then we can obtain the identical matrix for $W = (w_{kl})$. So, the model (6) is a generalized model of (3). Obtain the solution U and W.

(Step 2) Using the obtained U, recalculate the following similarity as:

$$\tilde{s}_{ij} = \frac{1}{\sum_{k=1}^{K} (u_{ik} - u_{jk})^2} s_{ij}, \quad i, j = 1, \cdots, n. \tag{11}$$

Using $\tilde{s}_{ij}$, go back to the step 1 and obtain the new result of $\tilde{U}$ and $\tilde{W}$.

(Step 3) Evaluate the fitness shown in (8) using $\tilde{U}$ and $\tilde{W}$ and compare with the fitness using U and W. Repeat from the step 1 to 3.

(11) shows that if objects i and j have a similar degree of belongingness for the obtained clusters, that is, if u_{ik} and u_{jk} are similar to each other, then the similarity between objects i and j becomes larger. So, this similarity is self organizing according to their degree of belongingness for the obtained clusters in each iteration.

Several numerical examples show better fitness and better results for the proposed method when compared with a single use of the fuzzy clustering model.

Figure 1 shows artificially created test data. In figure 1, the abscissa shows each variable and the ordinate shows the values for each variable. The solid lines show the objects o_1, o_2, o_3, and o_4 and the dotted lines show the objects o_5, o_6, o_7, and o_8. From this, we can see the similarity among objects o_1, o_2, o_3 and o_4 as well as the similarity among objects o_5, o_6, o_7 and o_8. The feature of this data is that the first group which consists of objects o_1, o_2, o_3, and o_4 has the property that values of variables v_1 is large and values of variables v_2 and v_3 are small. While, the other group has the opposite property.

The results are shown in table 1. This table shows the results of degree of belongingness of each object to clusters C_1 and C_2 using the conventional method shown in (6) and the proposed method. We determine the number of clusters as 2. From this table, we can see similarity between the two results and both of the results are adaptable considering the data feature shown in Figure 1. That is, we can obtain the two groups for both of the results. However, table 2 shows the results of the fitness shown in (8).

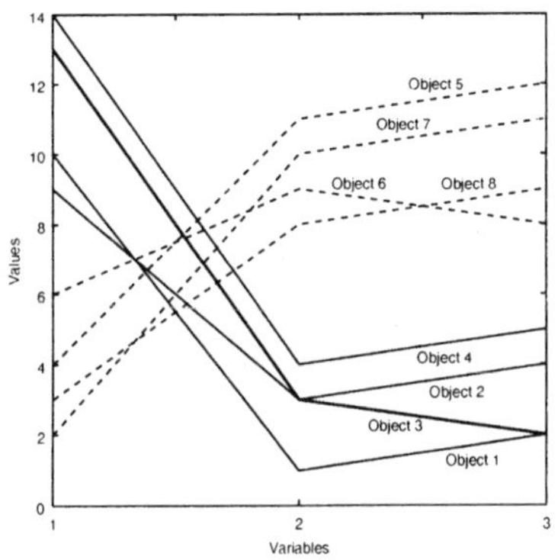

Figure 1 Artificial Data

From this, we can see that we obtain the better result for the use of the proposed method.

Table 1 Results using the Conventional Fuzzy Clustering Model and the Proposed Fuzzy Clustering Method

Clusters	Conventional Model C_1	Conventional Model C_2	Proposed Method C_1	Proposed Method C_2
o_1	0.90	0.10	1.00	0.00
o_2	0.76	0.24	0.99	0.01
o_3	0.96	0.04	1.00	0.00
o_4	0.85	0.15	1.00	0.00
o_5	0.03	0.97	0.00	1.00
o_6	0.29	0.71	0.01	0.99
o_7	0.00	1.00	0.00	1.00
o_8	0.17	0.83	0.00	1.00

Table 2 Comparison of the Fitness

	η^2	$\tilde{\eta}^2$
Fitness	0.29	0.02

$$\tilde{\eta}^2 = \sum_{i \neq j=1}^{n} (\tilde{s}_{ij} - \sum_{k=1}^{K}\sum_{l=1}^{K} \tilde{w}_{kl}\tilde{u}_{ik}\tilde{u}_{jl})^2$$

Next, we will show an example which used real observations. The data is landsat data which was observed over the Kushiro marsh-land. (NASDA) The value of the data shows the amount of reflected light from the ground with respect to 6 kinds of light for 75 pixels. We get data from mountain area, river area, and city area. The results are shown in figures 2 and 3. Figure 2 shows the result of conventional fuzzy clustering model shown in (6) and figure 3 is the result of the proposed method. In these figures, the abscissa shows each pixel and the ordinate shows the degree of belongingness for each cluster. We determine the number of clusters as 3. From these results, we can see that the result of the proposed method obtains a clear result when compared with the result shown in figure 2. Moreover, table 3 shows the comparison of the fitness for both the methods. From this table, we can see that we can obtain a better solution by using the proposed method.

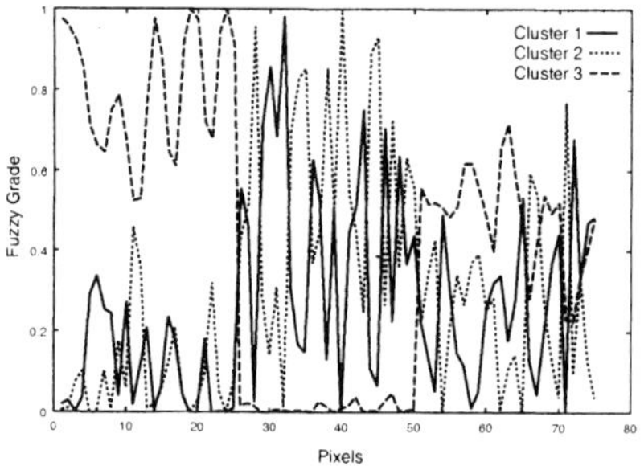

Figure 2 Result of Landsat Data using the Fuzzy Clustering Model

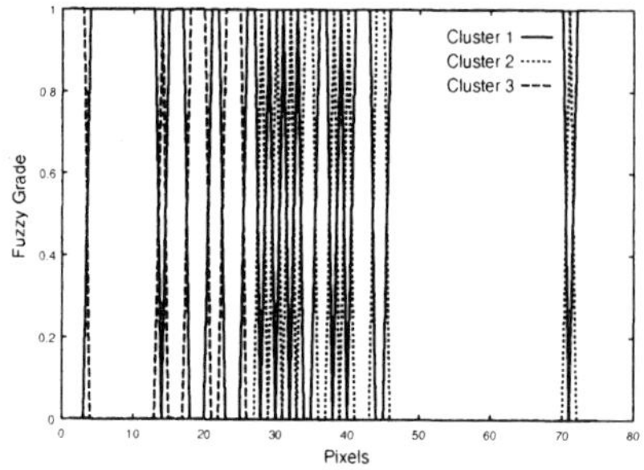

Figure 3 Result of Landsat Data using the Proposed Method

Table 3 Comparison of the Fitness

	η^2	$\tilde{\eta}^2$
Fitness	65.76	0.01

$$\tilde{\eta}^2 = \sum_{i \neq j=1}^{n} (\tilde{s}_{ij} - \sum_{k=1}^{K}\sum_{l=1}^{K} \tilde{w}_{kl}\tilde{u}_{ik}\tilde{u}_{jl})^2$$

CONCLUSION

This paper presents a new fuzzy clustering method in which self organized similarity using the result of fuzzy clustering is applied. That is, this method can controll the degree of belongingness of objects to clusters in each iteration step, according the classification situation under the assumption that similar objects have similar clustering situations.

REFERENCES

Kohonen, T., 1982, "Self-organized Formation of Topologically Correct Feature Maps", *Biol. Cybern.*, **43**, pp. 59-69.

Menger, K., 1942, "Statistical Metrics", *Proceedings of Nat. Acad. Sci.* USA, **28**, pp. 535-537.

Sato, M. and Sato, Y., 1995, "On a General Fuzzy Additive Clustering Model", *International Journal of Intelligent Automation and Soft Computing*, **1**, No. 4, pp. 439-448.

Schweizer, B. and Sklar, A., 1983, "*Probabilistic Metric Spaces*", North-Holland.

Van Hulle, M. M., 2000, "*Faithful Representations and Topographic Maps -From Distortion to Information based Self-Organization*", John Wiley & Sons.

NASDA, http://www.eorc.nasda.go.jp/.

ANALYSIS OF SURFACE EMG FOR SINGLE AND MULTI-FINGER MOTION RECOGNITION

WENWEI YU
Medical System Engineering Department, Chiba University, Japan
MASASHI FURUKAWA
Asahikawa National College of Technology, Japan
YUKINORI KAKAZU
Complex Engineering Department, Hokkaido University, Japan
RYU KATO
Complex Engineering Department, Hokkaido University, Japan
HIROSHI YOKOI
Precision Engineering Department, University of Tokyo, Japan

ABSTRACT
Our ultimate goal is to develop a natural Electromyogram (EMG) data-entry device that can also be used by forearm amputees. This gives rise to the necessity to analyze the activation patterns of finger muscles including extensor and flexors. Some results concerning the compartment characteristics of finger muscles have been reported, however, less study has discussed the possibility to distinguish the EMG patterns for single and multi-finger motions. In this study, we designed a series of experiment to investigate the finger muscle activation patterns during single and multi-finger extension and flexion. A cluster independency index was suggested to evaluate the possibility to classify between different finger patterns. A linear template-matching algorithm was further employed to match two-finger patterns to weighted sum of single finger patterns. Results showed that, single finger patterns could be distinguished with each other, and two-finger patterns could be expressed by weighted sum of patterns of correspondent single fingers.

INTRODUCTION

With the increased use of human-oriented mechatroinic devices, a high-efficiency human-computer interface (HCI) has been attracting much attention recently. Our ultimate goal is to develop a natural Electromyogram (EMG) data-entry device that can also be used by forearm amputees. This gives rise to the necessity to analyze the activation patterns of finger muscles including extensor and flexors. One may wonder that the anatomy (Nakamura, 1991) has already given the answers to the finger motion discrimination. But the fact is, the anatomical research reveals static musculo-skeletal structure. However, in order to complete one forearm action, multiple muscles should cooperate with each other, and unavoidably interact with each, which cannot be elucidated by anatomical research. Surface EMG supplies an uninvasive way to probe the muscles' function under moving condition, in turn gives a way to analyze and monitor the muscles function.

Surface EMG signals for forearm motion patterns were analyzed for the purpose of prosthetic hand control. Six to ten wrist and palm motion patterns, including wrist extension, flexion, open, grasp, pronation, supnation could be recognized through surface EMG analysis (Nishikawa, 2002)(Yu, 2002). However, few research efforts on finger muscle activation pattern analysis have been reported, except Fujiwara et al. employed the Independent Component Analysis (ICA) to analyze finger motion patterns (Fujiwara, 1999). However, the basic characteristics of activation patterns, as well as the relation between the single and multi-finger muscle activation patterns have not been discussed in that paper. Besides, the method is off-line and time-consuming and cannot adapt to human time-varying characteristics. One motivation of this research is to find if there exists some rules underlying the finger muscle activation patterns, and if they can be identified or not.

In the physiology and kinesiology research field, Danion et al. analyzed the surface EMG of multi-finger motion, in order to obtain the evidence for the notion of muscle compartments (Danion, 2002). However, their research was not from the viewpoint of signal processing and pattern recognition.

The purpose of this research was to investigate, 1) the feature extraction method suitable for the finger muscle EMG analysis, and the possibility to classify the EMG signals for finger motions, 2) the relationship between multi-finger EMG and single finger EMG patterns. If there exists linear or quasi-linear relationship between their EMG patterns, then the combinatorial problem when considering on-line recognition can be avoided.

METHOD

Devices

In order to investigate the basic characteristics of finger muscle activating patters, both finger bending angles and surface EMG signals are necessary. For that purpose, a potentiometer was used to obtain the finger-bending angle. Seven EMG electrodes (Model DE-02.3H, Delsys) were placed evenly around forearm within a belt zone 40-60mm distal to elbow joint. The amplifier was handmade. The A/D card used was CONTEC AD12-8 (PM) (input range –10V to +10V, resolution 12 bit). The sampling rate used for each channel was 1600Hz.

Procedure

Preprocessing: the EMG signals were smoothed using a moving average algorithm denoted in Eq. 1.

$$X_i(t) = \sum_{j=1-F} x_i(t) \Big/ F \qquad i = 1 - ch \qquad (1)$$

where, xi(t) is raw EMG signals, i denotes signal channel and F is a frame length for smoothing.

Data extraction: EMG data was extracted referring to the angular values. As illustrated in fig. 1, according to the angular data, EMG signals within a period of finger flexion, denoted by ①, was extracted. The extracted signals of all channels then were analyzed to decide the peak value among them. In the example shown in fig.2, the peak value appeared in channel 6. Using this peak point as a reference, 512 points before and after the point then were collected as the data to be analyzed. This data extraction was employed, because, the muscle activation is not necessarily consistent to the external movement.

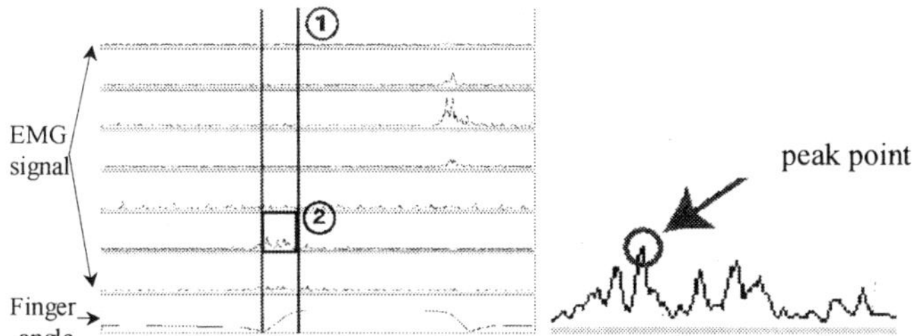

Figure 1. EMG data extraction referring to finger angle value

Feature extraction: Three feature extraction methods, moving averaged amplitude (see Eq. 2), standardized moving averaged amplitude (see Eq. 3), and power spectrum of the extracted data (see Eq. 4), were employed and compared.

$$Amp_{ik} = X_i(T_k) \qquad i = 1 - ch, k = 1 - pt\_num \tag{2}$$

where, *pt_num* means the number of feature point picked up from one channel. T_k can be decided by sampling the extracted data by a constant time-interval.

$$S\_Amp_{ik} = Amp_{ik} \Big/ \sum_{i=1-ch} Amp_{ik} \qquad i = 1 - ch, k = 1 - pt\_num \tag{3}$$

A fast Fourier transformation (FFT) was employed to get the power spectrum, which can be briefly expressed the following equation.

$$G\left(\frac{n}{N'\tau}\right) = \sum_{k=0}^{N'-1} \{\tau \cdot f(k\tau) e^{-i2\pi kn/N'}\} \tag{4}$$

where N' is the frame size for Fourier transformation, and τ is a time constant.

Data Analysis: Through trials of experiments, a constant number (N_{sample}) of samples for each finger were collected. They were compared and analyzed using the following techniques. 1) The correlation between the mean vector and feature vectors, and the standard deviation within each finger pattern cluster; 2) A cluster independency index; 3) a Kohonen self-organizing map (SOM) (Kohonen, 1997).

The basic consideration of cluster independency index is as follows: for two clusters A and B, if the distance between their cluster centers is expressed as *D(A,B)*, and the average and standard deviation values of the distances between cluster center and feature vectors are D_{ave} and D_{stdev}, respectively, then the Independency Index *CII(A,B)* was expressed by Eq. 5.

$$CII(A,B) = \frac{D_{ave}(A) + D_{ave}(B) + Dstdev(A) + Dstdev(B)}{D(A,B)} \tag{5}$$

Specific Setups for Two Experiments

The purpose of Experiment 1 is to collect the muscle activation patterns during single finger motion. The parameter for the data extraction and data processing were determined by experience and trial-and-error. Smoothing frame length F=50, the point number for amplitude and standardized amplitude comparison *pt_num*=1, the frame size for Fourier transformation N'=256, time constant τ=0.000625. For each finger motion, N_{sample} 60 samples were collected.

The purpose of Experiment 2 is to collect the muscle activation patterns during 2-finger motion. In the current stage, index-middle and middle-ring finger activation patterns were analyzed. In order to investigate the relationship between the single and multi-finger muscle activation patterns, a linear template matching method was employed.

For two single-finger muscle activation pattern clusters obtained in Experiment 1, if the mean feature vectors for two clusters are expressed by M_1, M_2, respectively, Eq.6 expresses the template for two-finger muscle activation .

$$M_{12} = xM_1 + yM_2 \qquad x + y = 2.0 \qquad 0 \le x \le 2{,}0 \le y \le 2 \quad (6)$$

When matching, a distance between a two-finger EMG pattern and all x, y combination cases for all the single-finger activation will be calculated. The combination with minimal distance is decided as the matched.

RESULTS AND DISCUSSION

Experiment 1

Table 1 shows the correlation between each cluster's feature vectors and its mean vector, for all finger cluster and all 3 features, that is, the amplitude, standardized amplitude and power spectrum. In all cases, the average value of correlation is large, and the standard deviation is small, so that, the mean vectors could be used as the representative vectors in all these cases.

Table 2 shows the CII value for each two mean vectors in 3 feature cases. From the definition of CII, a small CII value means two clusters could be clearly separated with each other. A CII value larger than 1 means that two clusters are likely to mix with each other. In the case that amplitude was used as the feature, except the index to ring finger clusters independency, the other clusters are comparably separable, denoted by small values of CII. In the case that standardized amplitude was used as the feature, index finger cluster are difficult to be discriminated from middle, ring, little finger clusters. Finally, in the case of that power spectrum was used as the feature, the CII values are large across all finger cluster pairs. Power spectrum is not suitable for the finger activation pattern discrimination.

Figure 2 shows the SOM of feature vectors in the case that amplitude, standardized amplitude as the features. They are obtained by selecting 5 feature vectors from each finger pattern cluster, and executing the Kohonen's algorithm.

Table 1. Correlation between each cluster's feature vectors and its mean vector: average and standard deviation

Feature	Statistics	Thumb	Index	Middle	Ring	Little
Amplitude	Average	0.9855	0.9849	0.9713	0.9889	0.9732
	Standard Dev.	0.0181	0.0191	0.0382	0.0118	0.0640
Standardized Amplitude	Average	0.9925	0.9939	0.9979	0.9912	0.9803
	Standard Dev.	0.0268	0.0060	0.0280	0.0113	0.0254
Power Spectrum	Average	0.9182	0.8718	0.9347	0.9014	0.9370
	Standard Dev.	0.0274	0.0496	0.0290	0.0394	0.0324

Table 2. CII values in the case that amplitude (A), standardized amplitude (SA), power spectrum (PA) were used as feature

	Thumb			**Index**			**Middle**			**Ring**			**Little**
	A	**SA**	**PA**	**A**	**SA**	**PA**	**A**	**SA**	**PA**	**A**	**SA**	**PA**	
Thumb													
Index	0.24	0.84	1.54										
Middle	0.30	0.80	1.25	0.38	1.37	1.93							
Ring	0.26	0.75	3.52	2.93	1.23	1.64	0.41	0.83	1.55				
Little	0.29	0.86	1.01	0.70	1.70	1.52	0.42	0.94	2.83	0.72	0.91	1.13	

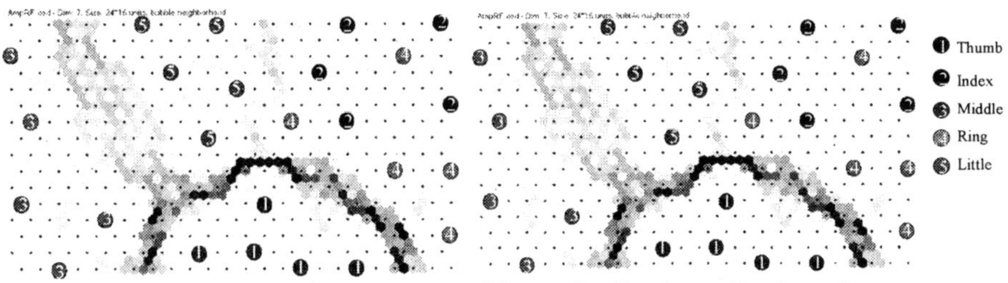

(a) amplitude as feature (b) standardized amplitude as feature

Figure 2. SOM of feature vectors

The pattern mixing of index and ring finger clusters revealed by CII value in Table 2 also appeared in fig. 2(a). That is, the feature vectors with mark ② and ④ are mixed in one big cluster. Note that, gray scale shading was used to represent the relative distances between neighboring codebook vectors (representative vectors). That is, if the average distance of neighboring codebook vectors is small, a light shade is used; and vice versa, dark shades represent large distance. The pattern mixing of index and middle, ring, little finger clusters revealed by CII value can also be confirmed in fig. 2(b).

Experiment 2

Index & Middle and Middle & Ring finger muscle activation patterns were recorded and matched to the templates made from single finger activation patterns. According to the results in experiment 1, amplitude was used as the feature to generate the templates and matching patterns. Table 3 shows the template matching results. As shown by Table 3, although 5 out of 30 two-finger patterns were matched to little & index finger template, 7 patterns were matched to index & index finger template, 18 patterns, 60% of all samples were matched to index & middle finger patterns. The details of the correct matching are shown in Table 4. Index finger muscles play a more important role in index & ring finger actions.

In the case of middle & ring finger pattern template matching, as shown by Table 3, although 9 out of 30 two-finger patterns were matched to index & middle finger template, 1 pattern was matched to middle & middle finger template, 20 patterns, 68% of all samples were matched to middle & ring finger patterns. The details of the correct matching are shown in Table 4. Middle finger muscles play a more important role in index & ring finger actions.

Table 3. Index & Middle(IM) and Middle & Ring(MR) finger patterns matched to single finger templates

	Thumb		Index		Middle		Ring		Little	
	IM	MR	IM	MR	IM	MR	IM	MR	IM	MR
Thumb	0	0	0	0	0	0	0	0	0	0
Index			7	0	18	9	0	0	5	0
Middle					0	1	0	20	0	0
Ring							0	0	0	0
Little									0	0

Table 4. Details of Index & Middle and Middle & Ring pattern matching

	9:1	8:2	7:3	6:4	5:5	4:6	3:7	2:8	1:9
Index & Middle	7	4	4	1	1	0	1	0	0
Middle & Ring	7	8	4	1	0	0	0	0	0

CONCLUSIONS

In this research, EMG signals and angular data during single and multi-finger motions were collected and analyzed. 3 feature extraction methods, amplitude of moving averaged data, standardized amplitude of moving averaged data and power spectrum, were compared. By using amplitude as the feature, finger muscle activation patterns can be discriminated with each other. Moreover, two-finger activation patterns could be matched to the linear sum of single finger activation patterns, by using a template-matching method.

However, at this stage, the finger muscle activation patterns under speed and force constraints, which are very important for an efficient data-input device, have not been studied sufficiently. This will be the next research theme. Moreover, in this research, the possibility of a finger motion classifier is investigated, but how to construct an efficient finger motion classifier should be studied and practiced.

REFERENCES

R. Nakamura, H. Saito, 1992, Fundamental Kinesiology, 4th edition, Ishiyaku Pbulishers INC.

D. Nishikawa, W. Yu, H. Yokoi, Y. Kakazu, 2002, On-Line Supervising Mechanism for Learning Data in Surface Electromyogram Motion Classifiers, Journal of Electronics and Communications in Japan, Vol. 33, No. 14, pp. 2634-2643,

W. Yu, H. Yamaguchi, M. Maruishi, H. Yokoi, Y. Mano, Y. Kakazu, 2002, EMG Automatic Switch for FES Control for Hemiplegics Using Artificial Neural Network, Robotics and Autonomous Systems (Elsevier), Vol. 40, Issue 2-3, pp. 213-224,

Y. Fujiwara, S. Maekawa, 1999, Finger Motion Classification by Independent Component Analysis of EMG data, MBE99-7, pp. 41-46,

F. Danion, S. Li, V. M. Zatsiorsky, M. L. Latash, 2002, Relations between Surface EMG of Extrinsic Flexors and Individual Finger Forces Support the Notion of Muscle Compartments, Eur. J. Appl. Physiol., pp. 185-188

T. Kohonen, 1997, Self-organizing maps, Springer-Verlag, New York

FACIAL EXPRESSIONS CLASSIFICATION USING LEARNING VECTOR QUANTISATION NETWORKS

NARENDRA K. CHENNAMSETTY
Department of Mechanical and Aerospace Engineering,
University of Missouri – Rolla, USA

GANESH K. VENAYAGAMOORTHY
Department of Electrical and Computer Engineering
University of Missouri – Rolla, USA

AKIRA TOKUHIRO
Department of Nuclear Engineering
University of Missouri – Rolla, USA

ABSTRACT

In this paper, an automatic facial expression recognition system is developed based on Gabor wavelet methodology and learning vector quantization networks (LVQs). Facial attributes from the frontal images are extracted in the form of feature vectors by evaluating the responses from a set of 18 complex Gabor filters at 34 fiducial points on face. The resultant high dimensional feature vectors are condensed by performing PCA and are classified into classes of expression using LVQs. Since the groups of feature vectors are non-linear separable, LVQ networks are chosen for classification instead of multilayer perceptron neural networks. In this paper, the optimum number of sub-groups, learning rate and other features of LVQ are determined to maximize the recognition accuracy of the system, using a set of designed experiments.

INTRODUCTION

Facial expressions provide vital clues about the emotional status of a person. Thus an automatic facial expression recognition system (FER) that can track the human expressions and correlate to the mood of the person can be used to detect the deception among humans and can be used in security related applications. The other applications of the automated facial expression recognition system include human behavior interpretation and human-computer interaction

Although a significant amount of research has been conducted in using face as a biometric, little work has been done in using the facial expressions for the same purpose. It has been demonstrated that the facial clues in conjunction with the other clues like body, voice, etc; provide indispensable information if a person is lying [3]. This is the motivation of the current work.

Typically an automated FER acquires an image or video from a camera and analyses them to determine the expression. Its functions can be categorized into three groups: face detection, facial feature extraction and correlation of the extracted features. Face detection is performed to determine the location and orientation of the face in the image which is necessary to normalize the images for same size and gray levels.

Facial feature extraction is done to generate an accurate facial representation in a low dimensional space (typically in form of a feature vector). Michael

Lyons et al [2] have demonstrated that a set of complex Gabor wavelet transforms can be successfully used for feature extraction and further proved that these transforms yield better recognition accuracy than the geometric co-ordinates of the facial landmarks. Zhang et al [6] has supported this by successfully building an automated expression recognition system based on Gabor-coding and a multi-layer perceptron.

Correlation of the extracted features to the expressions is typically done implicitly by classifying the feature vectors using neural networks. The commonly used multilayer perceptrons can only classify correctly if the classes of expression are linearly separable. LVQs are better suited for this purpose. Viresh Moonasar et al has demonstrated that the LVQ can be successfully implemented for the classification purposes by building an automatic speech recognition system based on them [7].

FEATURE EXTRACTION

Feature extraction is done by convolving the image I with a set of 2-D complex Gabor wavelet transforms [1, 2]. A 2-D Gabor kernel is a plane wave restricted by a Gaussian envelope defined by (1).

$$\psi_{\vec{k}}(\vec{x}) = \frac{\vec{k}^2}{\sigma^2}\exp(\frac{\vec{k}^2\vec{x}^2}{2\sigma^2})[\exp(i\vec{k}\vec{x}) - \exp(-\sigma^2)] \quad (1)$$

The oscillatory part of the wave is given by the first term in the square bracket and the second term compensates for the dc-value of the kernel to eliminate the effect of the intensity of image on the filter response. The wavelet is a combination of even and odd parts where the cosine type constitutes the even part and sine type constitutes the odd part. $\vec{k}$ is the wave vector which determines the wavelength and orientation of the $\psi_{\vec{k}}(\vec{x})$ (figure 1).

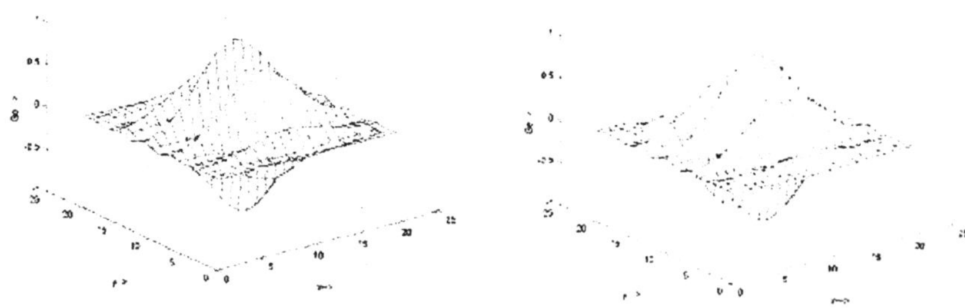

Figure 1: Even and odd Gabor wavelets with f = 2 and θ = 0 degree

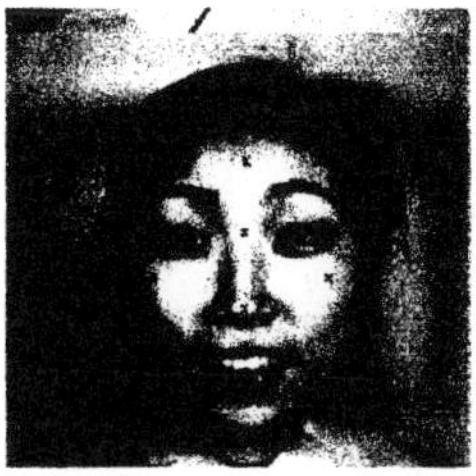

Figure 2: 34 feature points on the face used for the feature extraction

The convolution of the image with the Gabor filter is represented as follows where W is the convolution operator.

$$(WI)(\vec{k},\vec{x}_0) = \int \psi_{\vec{k}}(\vec{x}_0 - \vec{x}) I(\vec{x}) d^2 x \qquad (2)$$

Where, $k = \{\frac{\pi}{4}, \frac{\pi}{8}, \frac{\pi}{16}\}$ and $\theta = \{0, \frac{\pi}{6} \ldots, \pi\}$

We have selected 18 Gabor filters with wave vector of 3 magnitudes and 6 orientations as shown in (2). The response of these filters at 34 feature points on the face, selected as shown in the figure 2 , is combined to form a feature vector of size 612.This feature point selection scheme is similar to that of Michael Lyons group[2,6]

The high dimensionality of the feature vectors adversely effects the training time of the neural networks and therefore, the feature vector's size was reduced using Principal Component Analysis (PCA). Because there were fewer samples than the features, PCA was done by Singular Value Decomposition (SVD).

Database

JAFFE database was chosen for training and testing purposes. The database consists of 213 frontal images of 10 female expressers with 3 or 4 samples for each expression. The original images are scaled and cropped such that they have eyes at same position with a resolution of 256 x 256. Fear expression was excluded because people had trouble expressing it [2]. Figure 3 shows some of the sample pictures from the database.

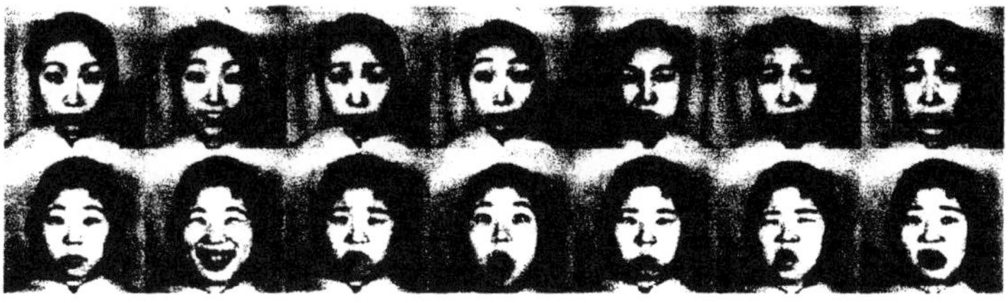

Figure 3: Sample images from the JAFFE database

CLASSIFICATION WITH LVQ NETWORKS

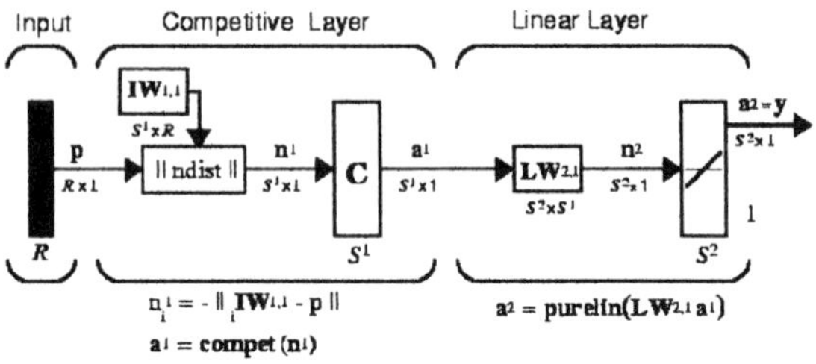

IW k,l: =input weight matrix
Where l= source layer
k=destination layer
LW k,l := layer weight matrix
$\mathbf{S^1}$:= sub classes
$\mathbf{S^2}$:= target classes
p := input vector of size R x 1
ά := learning rate

Figure 4: Architecture of the LVQ network

The architecture of the learning vector quantization (LVQ) network used for classification purposes is shown in figure 4 which consists of two layers: a competitive layer and a linear layer

Training of the competitive layer is done using the Kohonen's rule [8] which is briefly described here. The ||ndist|| function, shown in figure 4 calculates the negative Euclidean distances between input feature vector and rows of weight matrix and produces the **n** (S^1x1). The competitive layer's transfer function C classifies the **n** into one of the subgroups (48 subgroups). The winning neuron, i.e. the row vector of IW matrix corresponding to the most positive distance is updated according to the following rules:

$$ {}_{i^*}IW^{1,1}(q) = {}_{i^*}IW^{1,1}(q-1) + \alpha(p(q) - {}_{i^*}IW^{1,1}(q-1)) \tag{3} $$

if p is correctly classified or

$$ {}_{i^*}IW^{1,1}(q) = {}_{i^*}IW^{1,1}(q-1) - \alpha(p(q) - {}_{i^*}IW^{1,1}(q-1)) \tag{4} $$

if p is incorrectly classified.

The linear layer transforms the competitive layers classes into the 6 classes of expression: anger, distress happy, normal, sad and surprise. The simulation is carried out in MATLAB using the *newlvq* function. Training with 'learnlv1' and 'learnlv2' functions is performed.

Optimization of the LVQ training

To determine the optimal parameters of the LVQ a series of factorial experiments were conducted [4, 5] . Initially we have conducted two-level screening experiments [4, 5] in which the effects of subgroup size, training method, PCA, learning rate and epochs on the training accuracy were analyzed. The results of those experiments showed us that the subgroup size, PCA and training method had statistically significant effect on the training accuracy while epochs (500, 1000) and learning rate (0.01, 5) had negligible effect. The results are shown in figure 5.

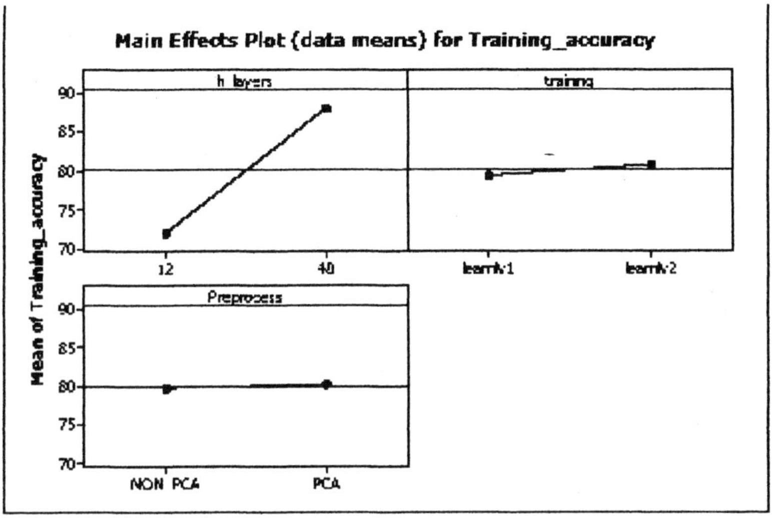

Figure 5: Average effects of subgroup size, PCA and training method

The effects of the aforementioned three important factors with a 2^3 factorial experiments were further analyzed and determined that on average the increasing subgroups from 12 to 48 increases the training accuracy by 16 % while PCA and training method contribute to a marginal increase (< 3%). However, PCA greatly reduced the training time.

Finally, a maximum training accuracy of 98.50% was achieved with the subgroup size of 48, the 'learnlv2' training method and by performing PCA on the input feature vectors.

RESULTS AND DISCUSSION

The performance of our facial expression recognition system was tested on the previously mentioned JAFFE database in completely randomized block design experiments [4, 5]. Due to limitations of the size of database(only 10 posers), testing was performed only on the trained set of images, so these results should not be compared with generalized testing done by other groups. Seven subjects were chosen with their 6 expressions (fear excluded) from the database for testing. The feature vectors of all these subjects were tested in a block with the order of the data completely randomized and replicated 5 times. The performance characteristic, average recognition accuracy defined as the ratio of the number of correct recognitions to the total number of feature vectors within a block was determined as about 92% at the optimal settings of LVQ.

The results of the test were also analyzed to determine the variation of recognition accuracy across people and expressions. Figure 6 shows that a very minor variance is present in recognition accuracy across people and their expressions.

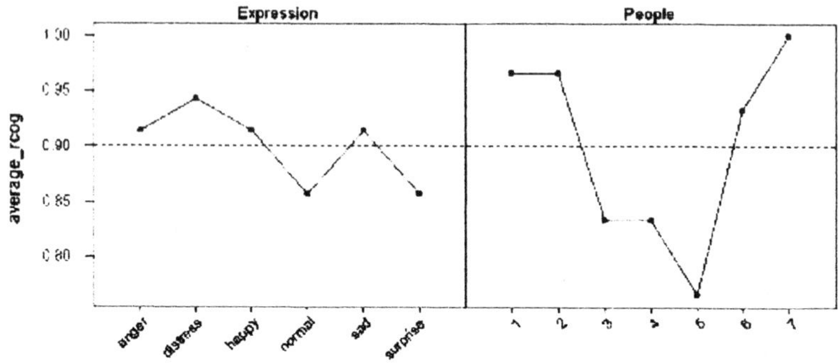

Figure 6: Effect of people and expressions on the recognition accuracy.

CONCLUSIONS

In this paper, the suitability of LVQ networks was investigated for facial expression recognition. The average recognition accuracy of 92% that was achieved while testing on trained set of images is comparable to the recognition accuracies achieved by Lyons [2] group using similar feature extraction method and multi-layer perceptron with 5 hidden layers. LVQ performance was optimal when subgroup size was set to 48, PCA was done to reduce the dimensionality of the feature vectors and second training method ('learnlv2') was used. The recognition accuracy of our system on the trained sets showed only minor variance across people and their expressions.

REFERENCES

[1] J. Daugman, "Complete discrete 2-D Gabor transforms by neural networks for image analysis and compression", *IEEE Transactions on Acoustic, Speech and Signal Processing,* 36(7):1169-1179, July 1988.

[2] M. Lyons, S. Akamatsu, M. Kamachi and J. Gyoba, "Coding Facial Expressions with Gabor wavelets", *Proceedings of third IEEE international conference on Automatic Face and Gesture Recognition,* pp: 200-205, April 1998.

[3] P. Ekman, *Telling Lies,* Oxford University Press, Inc. pp: 123 -161, 1997.

[4] D. Drain, *Handbook of Experimental Methods for Process Improvements,* International Thomson Publishing. pp: 110-278, 1997.

[5] D. C. Montgomery, *Design and analysis of experiments*, John Wiley & sons Inc, pp: 71-263.

[6] Z. Zhang, M. Lyons, S. Akamatsu, and M. Schuster, "Comparison between geometry based and Gabor wavelet based Facial Expression recognition using Multi-Layer perceptron", *Proceedings of third IEEE international conference on Automatic Face and Gesture Recognition, IEEE computer society,* pp: 454-479, April 1998.

[7] V. Moonasar V, G. K. Venayagamoorthy, "Automatic Speaker Recognition System using a Committee of Neural Networks – a DSP Based Hardware Implementation", *Proceedings of the Artificial Neural Networks in Engineering Conference ANNIE 2000,* St. Louis, USA, November 10-13, 2002, pp. 835 - 840.

[8] T. Kohonen, *Self Organization and Associative memory,* 2nd Edition, Berlin: Springer-Verlag, 1987.

AN INTELLIGENT INTERROGATION OF A FIBRE OPTIC BASED MULTIPOINT ULTRA VIOLET (UV) SENSOR.

W. B. LYONS
ECE Department,
University of Limerick
Castletroy, Limerick,
Ireland

C. FITZPATRICK
ECE Department,
University of Limerick
Castletroy, Limerick,
Ireland

P.W.J. VAN DE VEN
ECE Department,
University of Limerick
Castletroy, Limerick,
Ireland

C. FLANAGAN
ECE Department,
University of Limerick
Castletroy, Limerick,
Ireland

E. LEWIS
ECE Department,
University of Limerick
Castletroy, Limerick,
Ireland

H. EWALD
Infomatik & Elektrotech.
University of Rostock,
18051 ROSTOCK,
Germany.

ABSTRACT

This paper reports on further work involving the interrogation of a novel multi-point (3 sensors) luminescent-coated fibre. The sensor design is based around a 1mm core diameter polymer fibre which has had its cladding replaced with a phosphor doped epoxy that emits visible light when stimulated with ultra-violet (UV) radiation. Due to the use of phosphors with different emission wavelengths, the sensor is capable of distinguishing the location of UV exposure at multiple points along the fibre loop. In this investigation, the sensor has been interrogated further by exposure to various levels (4 distinct output levels) of UV radiation. The resulting output signals are complex in nature due to spectral cross coupling. Signal analysis has been carried out using Artificial Neural Network Pattern Recognition and the results of the analysis are presented.

INTRODUCTION

There are two common methods of disinfecting water, chlorine and ultra violet light. Chlorine has been the more traditional means of water sterilisation but recently ultra violet has become a more popular choice due to the numerous advantages which it offers over the chemical option.

Ultra violet light kills all viruses and bacteria in a few seconds including cryptosporidium which can exist in chlorinated water for up to forty minutes. In a recent study undertaken by the National Institute of Public Health of Norway it was reported that the chlorine treatment of water has been linked with some devastating diseases such as spina bifida, birth defects and urinary tract abnormalities. UV treatment is very attractive to the food processing industry as such a high power lamp in such a small size could be designed as a hand held device for sterilisation of the innards of carcasses which offers the advantage of not leaving any taste on the food [1].

In order to use a U.V. lamp for these applications it is necessary to install a reliable U.V. sensor to monitor for breakdowns which would otherwise go unnoticed due to the remote nature of the lamp. The U.S. Public Health Service published a policy stating the dosage requirement for drinking water should be approximately 16,000 μWs/cm^2 (micro watt seconds per square centimeter). This statement has formed the basis for a World Wide Standard [2]. The sensor would be used for active stabilisation via a feedback loop to guarantee these standards.

Optical Fibre Sensors techniques have proven useful for many applications including process monitoring e.g. pressure, temperature, pH, water coolant conditioning, and particle concentration. A typical process plant may require several measurements of a single parameter to be made simultaneously e.g. temperature at many locations inside a reactant vessel. A wide range of techniques exist and these have been widely reported [3,4] for measuring the above quantities at a single point. However, it is desirable in many applications to have the simultaneous measurement of such parameters made on a single fibre loop. This would mean that the sensors would not have to be addressed using individual fibres, light sources and detectors, but involves a single source and detector at the launching and receiving ends of the single fibre.

In the area of UV detection, an optical fibre sensor based detection technique offers significant advantages over conventional optoelectronic UV photodetectors. This is particularly the case if the UV source consists of a long tube where several such detectors would be necessary to monitor the output power, whereas, with an optical fibre-based sensing technique all that's required is for the length of the fibre sensor to be increased. This facilitates the measurement of optical power output distributed over relatively large lengths. Added advantages associated with an optical fibre sensor solution would be the adaptation for use in an aqueous environment as there are no electrical parts, which is in contrast with optoelectronic devices [5].

EXPERIMENTAL SET-UP

The quazi-distributed ultra violet sensor utilised in this investigation is based on previously reported design [6] developed in-house at the Optical Fibre Sensors Research Group at the University of Limerick, Ireland. The operation of the sensor is based on the generation of photoluminescence from incident ultra violet radiation detected within the cladding of the fibre.

The photoluminescent coating is achieved by removing the regular cladding from the fibre and replacing it with a phosphor doped epoxy. The phosphor is the photoluminescent agent, and an important design consideration is the overlap of its absorption spectrum with the ultra violet radiation being monitored in order to achieve maximum sensitivity. It has been shown that the intensity at the fibre's end is directly proportional to the intensity of the incident ultra violet radiation.

The multi-point configuration of this luminescent clad sensor is based not solely on the intensity received at the output of the fibre, but also on the spectral distribution. Coatings with the same absorption properties but different emission wavelengths are applied to different regions along the fibre. By monitoring the different peaks on the spectrum it is possible to gain information about localised areas of higher or lower ultra violet intensity.

A fluorescent ultra violet source (peak emission wavelength of 370nm) was used for stimulating the photoluminescent process in the cladding of the fibre sensor. Four different strength neutral density filters were used to deliver 4 distinct levels of UV power from the source. The experimental set-up is illustrated in Figure 1.

The Ocean optics spectrometer (S2000) was interfaced to a PC utilising National Instruments LabVIEW-based virtual instrument (VI) developed by the authors to facilitated a single point of operation for control of the spectrometer, the resulting data capture and associated signal pre-processing. The data output from this VI was subsequently made available for analysis by the artificial neural network which was implemented using Matlab.

The spectra received from the Spectrometer range from approximately 210 nm to 880nm. This spectral range is represented by a total of 2048 analogue voltage levels received from the CCD (Charged Coupled Device) detector within the spectrometer.

Figure 2 illustrates the typical distributed spectral output from the Spectrometer due to a full power UV exposure over the complete sensing regions of the fibre (red, green, and blue photoluminescent clad sections). The initial peak (on the far left) at 370nm is the wavelength peak associated with the ultra violet stimulation used. Part of this stimulation is scattered into the fibre's core and makes its way through the fibre and is detected. It is considered to be "optical noise". The second (456nm) and third (530) peaks are resultant from the emissions associated with the blue and green phosphors respectively. The red phosphor used in the sensor manufacture has a characteristic two peak emission spectra, which are illustrated by the forth and fifth peaks at 630nm and 710nm respectively.

RESULTS AND ANALYSIS

Numerous spectrometer readings were taken for each of the sensing stimulation conditions under test (7 in total; Red, Green, Blue, Red/Green, Red/Blue, Green/Blue, and Red/Green/Blue). Experimental results were obtained for each of the sensing conditions using four distinct UV exposure levels (25%, 50% 75% and 100%) at the various sensing locations. This was achieved utilising a combination of UV transmitting Neutral Density Filters and non-ultra violet transmitting tubing.

The data from the S2000 spectrometer was pre-processed in order to extract the features of interest and hence reduce the amount of input data required for the network. Feature extraction involved a two-step process: first, a windowing of the data trace was carried out in order to remove both the UV stimulated peak and the second red phosphor peak (the far left and far right peaks illustrated in Figure 2), and then the resulting trace was 'sampled' at every tenth point in order to further reduce the data set whilst still maintaining overall pattern integrity. An example selection of the resulting patterns (for all the sensing simulation conditions) used for ANN training and testing after feature extraction is illustrated in Figure 3. Each pattern is represented by a 72-point array.

The ANN consisted of a feed-forward three-layer network, with the number of input nodes representing the number of points required to represent the extracted feature from the sensors spectral response (in this case 72). Several methods were applied in order to train the ANN to perform the extraction of the relevant data. In the following these methods are briefly discussed and the test results are presented.

Classification of colour combination and sensor power levels

There are several possibilities for the output coding of both colour and power. As in [6] it is possible to use binary coding, thus using three bits for the colour coding and an additional two bits for power (7 colour patterns at 4 different power levels gives 28 possibilities which can be coded in 5 bits). The disadvantage of this first scenario is that a non-optimum classification rule is used. According to [7] optimum classification of binary output data is obtained when every class is represented by a separate output node and the input is classified to be belonging to class i if:

$$V_i(x) > V_j(x) \forall j \neq i$$

Where V is the value of the output node and x is the input vector to be classified. Rather than using the above classification, in simulation scenario 1 an output node is regarded to be a "1" in the coded output if the node's output value is higher than 0.75.

To be able to apply the optimum classification described above in the second simulation, in scenario 2 a neural network with two sets of output neurons is used. One set of 7 neurons is used for classification of colour and one set of 4 neurons is used for classification of power. No coding of the outputs is performed thus allowing for the optimum classification to be applied.

In the third scenario the classification of colour combinations and power is combined. This results in the following NN output configuration: 7 linear output neurons trained to give the power of the colour (combination) in fractions of 1, while all other neurons are trained to be 0. First the optimum classification is performed to obtain the colour (combination). Then the input power is extracted by comparing the found maximum value to table 1. Obviously for this method, the amplitude of the input data should be normalised to [0,1].

Table 1:

Power	Limits
25 %	$V_i(x) < 0.375$
50 %	$0.375 < V_i(x) < 0.625$
75 %	$0.625 < V_i(x) < 0.875$
100 %	$V_i(x) > 0.875$

Simulations:

Scenario 1: To obtain the 5-bit coded sensor output, a neural network with 72 inputs, 10 hidden neurons with hyperbolic tangent activation function, and 5 linear output neurons was used. Training was performed with a set of 4013 readings drawn randomly from a total set of 6020 readings. 2007 Measurements are thus reserved for verification purposes. After 25 epochs of training the mean square error had reduced $1*10^{-2}$. At this stage learning was stopped and the network was tested. With the training data, a classification error of zero was achieved. Both the colour and the power of the sensor signal were classified properly without a single error. However, for the verification data an unsatisfactory performance was obtained as shown in table 2.

Table 2:

	Colour [correct/total]	Power [correct/total]
Classification Data	4013/4013	3014/4013
Verification Data	2007/2007	1501/2007

Table 2 shows that the used coding has a considerable effect on the classification error.

Scenario 2: In order to be able to use the optimum classification as described in the previous section, the neural network is extended with 6 extra output neurons. Colour is classified using 7 neurons and the other 4 neurons are used for the classification of the 4 power levels. The colour combination of the input data is chosen to be colour *i* for which equation 1 holds. And the same classification criterion, used on the last 4 output neurons, is used for the classification of the power levels. After 25 epochs of training, the mean square error was less than $1*10^{-2}$. Table 3 shows the result of simulations, both with the training data and with the verification data.

Table 3:

	Colour [correct/total]	Power [correct/total]
Training Data	4013/4013	4013/4013
Verification Data	2007/2007	2007/2007

As expected the classification has improved considerably. For the used set, not a single classification error is present.

Scenario 3: The neural network from scenario 1 is extended with two output neurons in order to be able to represent each colour combination with one neuron. To classify the power levels, the neural network is trained to output the power level as a fraction of 1. Again 25 epochs of training were performed after which the mean square error was $1*10^{-2}$. Consecutively the network was tested, both with the training data and with the verification data. Table 4 lists results:

Table 4:

	Colour	Power
Training Data	4013/4013	4013/4013
Verification Data	2007/2007	2007/2007

From table 3 it can be seen that this kind of classification works perfectly on the set of data. It can be seen that in both scenario 2 and 3, a 100% correct classification has been obtained. This can be ascribed to Cover's theorem: due to casting the problem into a non-linear parameter space of higher dimensionality, the patterns become linearly separable and thus 100% correctness is achieved.

CONCLUSION

A novel multi-point (3 sensors) luminescent-coated fibre has been investigated and proven to be capable of detecting the presence of various levels of UV radiation at each of the three sensing points using a fibre optic spectrometer. The sensors were developed using a 1mm core diameter polycarbonate fibre where the cladding was removed in various sensing locations and replaced by different photoluminescent coatings. The length of the fibre was 15 cm, although longer and shorter lengths may be used as required.

Artificial neural networks were used to map the measured spectra to stimulations at the three measurement points along the fibre and the used power levels. Three different strategies were applied to the identification. First colour and power were coded using 5 bits. Then, in order to enable optimum classification, the neural network was extended to 11 outputs. In this network each of the 7 colour combinations and each power level has a separate output neuron. Finally power was coded by means of a fraction of 0.25, 0.50, 0.75 or 1 applied to 7 output neurons each representing 1 of 7 colour combinations. 5 Bit coding of all output states is advantageous as the sensor can easily be extended to contain more colours. However, an unsatisfactory classification performance was obtained. Both for the uncoded network and for the network with power coded as fractions, the classification was highly satisfactory. Future work will cover utilising more than three phosphors and the extension of the set of fractions to facilitate the use of e.g. 10 power levels.

ACKNOWLEDGMENTS

We wish to thank the "Irish Research Council for Science, Engineering and Technology" for the Government of Ireland Post-Doctoral Fellowship funding.

REFERENCES

[1] Fitzpatrick C., Lewis E., Al-Shamma'a A., Lucas J., Irish Signals and Systems Conference, 29th-30th June 2000, Dublin.

[2] Schafer T., "UV Radiation vs. Dirty Ballast", Photonics Spectra, May 2002, p 14.

[3] Udd E. "An overview of fiber-optic sensors", Rev. Sci. Instrum. 66 (8), August 1995.

[4] Kersey A. D. "A review of Recent Developments in Fiber Optic Sensor Technology". Optical Fiber Technology 2, 291-317 (1996)

[5] Fitzpatrick C., Lewis E., Al-Shamma'a A., Lucas J., Wismar Symposium on Automatic Control, 16th-17th September 1999, Wismar.

[6] C. Fitzpatrick, W.B. Lyons, C. Flanagan, E. Lewis., "A Novel Multi-Point Luminescent Coated Ultra Violet Fibre Sensor Utilising Pattern Recognition", *Proc. ANNIE 2003: Intelligent Engineering Systems Through Artificial Neural Networks*, **13**, pp 607-612, (2003)

[7] S. Haykin, "Neural Networks. A comprehensive foundation", Ch. 4.7, Prentice Hall International, 1999, New Jersey

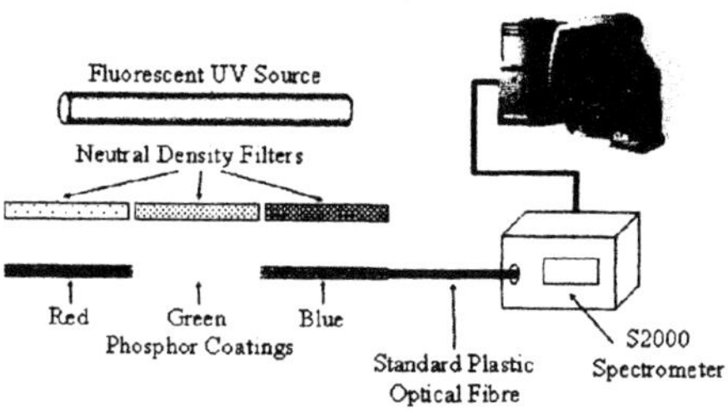

Figure 1: Experimental Setup

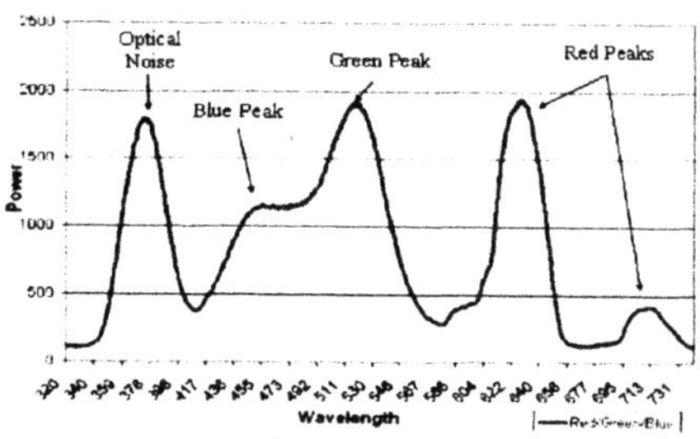

Figure 2: Spectral output showing UV exposure on the complete fibre sensor

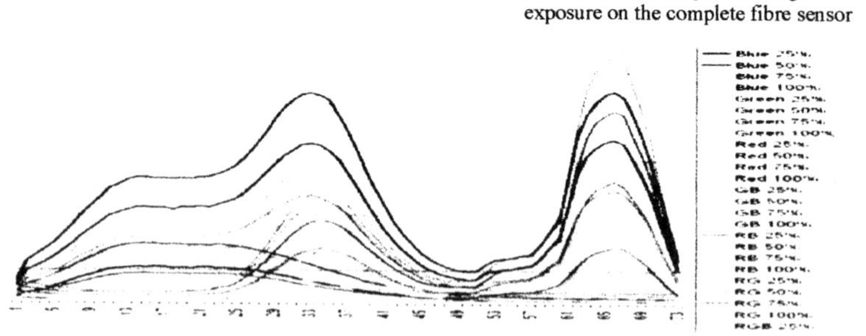

Figure 3: Training patterns for each of the exposure combinations.

A NOVEL CHART PATTERN RECOGNITION APPROACH: A CASE STUDY ON MODIFIED CUP WITH HANDLE

SANG C. SUH
Department of Computer Science
Texas A&M University - Commerce
Commerce, TX 75429-3011
sang_suh@tamu-commerce.edu

DAN LI & JINGMIAO GAO
Illinois Institute of Technology
3300 South Federal Street
Chicago, IL 60616
cs_danli@yahoo.com

ABSTRACT
Prediction of stock investment through stock analysis from historical patterns has drawn much attention from AI community. This paper brings a new insight into how to set criteria for stock patterns detections and how to select the acceptable candidates for prediction with more than 10,000 stocks in U.S. stock markets. We applied a naive efficient algorithm to do backward screening for acceptable chart patterns with the well-known pattern recognition method “Cup with Handle.” Our previous Intelligent Stock Selector System (ISSS), a rule-based intelligent system was optimized with Bezier Curve and statistics to achieve higher accuracy on stock pattern recognition and prediction. The main contribution of this research is to facilitate the design of pattern recognition modeling system for extensive forecasting and research purposes for both financial institutions and investment individuals.

Keywords: Expert Systems, Data Mining, Stock Analysis

MOTIVATION

Chart patern recognition has recently drawn very intensive research interests, especially in the area of financial time series forecasting. There have been many methodologies proposed and used for stock forecasting (DeLurgio, 1998). One notable among them is CAN SLIM methodology which combined both technical analysis and fundamental analysis (O’Neil, 2002). In this method, both technical and fundamental analysis are emphasized to identify some of the best stocks in a cycle. Main factors considered in the CAN SLIM methodology are current earnings, strong annual earning growth, new products, supply/demand, leading stocks, institutional sponsorship, and market direction (Bajkowski, 2003).

However, one inconvenient task for most successful investors is to manually screen stocks which meet all search criteria. For the serious investor using this system, a daily graph is a must at a minimum that provides detailed technical indexes and indicators with CAN SLIM criteria. Furthermore, one must still screen through hundreds of stocks daily to find stocks that have "set-up" and then monitor each of the selected stocks for days or weeks waiting for them to "break out" before buying. Visually screening is like a full time job which is too costly for most investors to perform. Equally important, the manual approach may miss many stocks as they break out and misses others which do not make it into publications (Rick Martinelli & Barry Hyman, 1998a,1998b, and 2001).

The motivation for our research is to provide efficient support for stock investment advisement to do backward screening for acceptable chart patterns from the huge database of more than 10,000 stocks that some of the data-download services provide. The acceptable stock candidates are selected by predefined rules or customization for investors to compare a number of selected stocks with criteria on stock indicators to make final investment decisions.

BACKGROUND

An Intelligent Stock Selector System (ISSS) was developed to perform technical and traditional analysis on stock data for predictive decision making. A raw time series data sequence of historic prices of stocks is given to a Pattern Recognition Filter (PRF) to get the technical analysis done based on some predefined or customized rules. Based on the result of the technical analysis, the final recommendation on candidate stock for investment is made by a Traditional Analysis Filter (TAF). The procedure for the PRF is shown in Figure 1. The expert system is used to recognize different patterns from time-series data sequence. The results of technical analysis are generated by PRF based on predefined criteria or customized criteria.

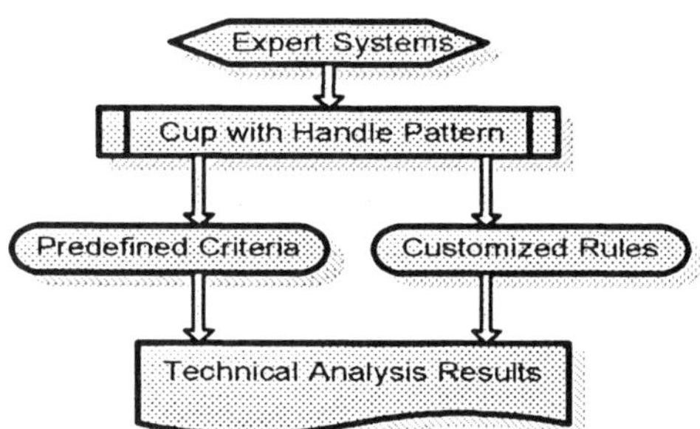

Figure 1. Pattern Recognition Filter (PRF) procedures

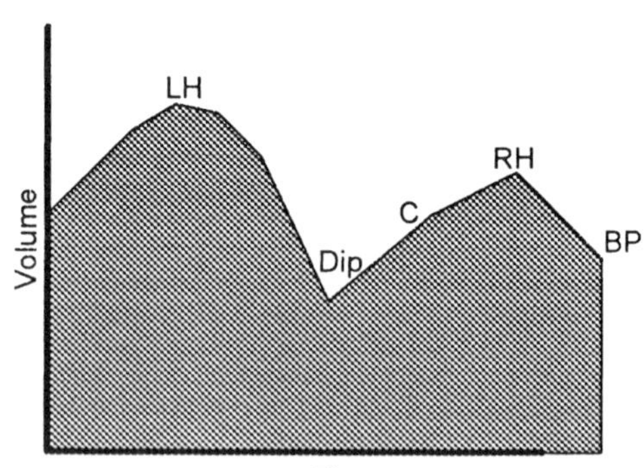

Figure 2. An Ideal "Cup with Handle"

In Pattern Recognition Filter (PRF) procedures, an ideal “cup with handle” looks like a cup with two handles aside as shown in Figure 2 above. In the figure, LH means left high point, RH right high point, Dip the lowest point, C construction, and BP buy points. Based on the ideal cup with handle structure, a pseudo code can be constructed for pattern recognition and prediction for stock analysis.

Bezier CURVE

Bezier curve was first developed and used at the Renault automobile company for a system for designing and manufacturing cars using free-form curves and surfaces in the mid-1960s. A computerized system named UNISURF provided a general mathematical framework for defining arbitrarily shaped curves and surfaces (Chang and Sederberg, 1997). It is a vector-valued Bernstein polynomial whose formular can be stated as follows:

$$P(t) = \sum_{i=0}^{n} B_i^n(t) P_i \text{ , } t \in [0,1] \tag{1}$$

,where each P_i is a control point.

$$B_i^n(t) = \binom{n}{i} x^k (1-x)^{n-k} = \frac{n}{1}\frac{(n-1)}{2}\cdots\frac{n-(k-1)}{k} x^k (1-x)^{n-k} \tag{2}$$

The curve (1) is called a Bezier curve of degree n and the polygon $P_0 P_1 \ldots P_n$ is called its control polygon. The Bezier curve is just the graph of a Bernstein polynomial (2), which is called the Bernstein basis polynomials of degree n. The Bernstein polynomials play a central role in the theory of free-form curves and surfaces. The two most obvious properties of the $B_i^n(t)$ are:

$$B_i^n(t) \geq 0 \text{ for } t \in [0,1] \text{ and } B_0^n(t) + B_1^n(t) + \ldots + B_n^n(t) = 1$$

,where $P(t)$ is a convex linear combination of $P_0, P_1, \ldots, P_n$. This means that the Bezier curve lies entirely in the convex hull of its control points. This is called the convex hull property of Bezier curves. Perhaps the most widespread use of Bezier curves is in the definition of font outlines. The characters on most printed pages that are typeset using a computer are defined using Bezier curves. In fact, every letter in newspaper or books contains dozens of Bezier curves too.

PROPOSED METHODOLOGY

The problems associated with chart pattern recognitions on arbitrary shape of curve for stock patterns are mani-fold. It is hard to compare and rank different stocks because they have different price ranges, scales, and volatiliteis. Besides the asymmetric behaviors affect the accuracy of pattern recognition. At certain point of the time series data sequence, one can only trace back to find certain pattern rather than look forward. From the viewpoint of investors, historical patterns are not as attractive as those near final breakout phase patterns since such a screening method as "cup with handle" is faster and more accurate in finding patterns from thousands of stocks. Although the general assumption is that the same pattern reoccurs under the same situation, the "cup with handle" pattern could even happen at the first time for a certain stock with different price ranges and volatilaties.

In the proposed study, the ISSS system is integrated with the Bezier curve by improving the handle pattern part in PRF procedures in Figure 1 as shown in

Figure 3. The idea is to use Simple Moving Average (SMA) method to smooth the volatile data, then use the Backward Screening Pattern Recognition Algorithm (BSPRA) algorithm to obtain three critical points (two cup tops and one bottom). In the Bezier curve phase, four mid points are further abstracted from the smoothed data and added to the three critical points as the input vectors to the Bezier curves. Through the application of the Bezier curve, the function of ideal "cup with handle" shape can be generated. Finally, the statistical correlation matrix is used to obtain the correlation coefficients by comparing the ideal function from Bezier curve with the original smoothed data sequence. If the correlation coefficient is large enough (greater than .85), then it can be concluded that the stock data shows a "cup with handle" pattern.

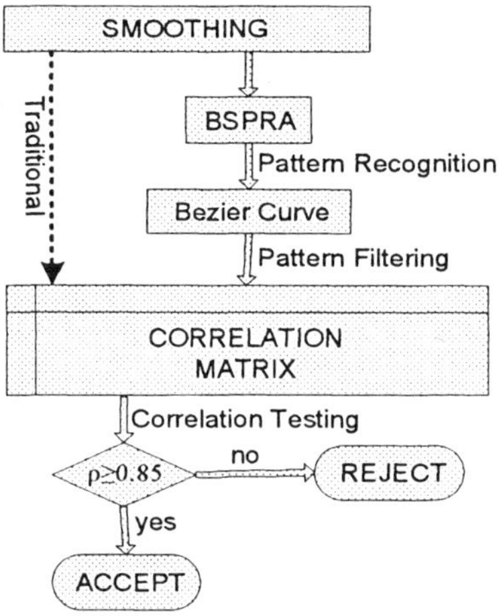

Figure 3. Modified Cup with Handle Pattern

EXPERIMENTAL RESULTS

During the testing phase with real world data, several experiments were made on several stocks with real world data. An example of Cisco stock on US market was chosen in this paper to show the effectiveness of the proposed approach. The historical data from the period January 2, 1997 to June 30, 1997 were collected with 125 observations on daily basis as shown in Figure 4 below.

After smoothing the original data, the size of the observations was reduced to 111 by using 15-day simple moving average methods (Suh et. al. 2003). Because of the breakout point, the observation size was further reduced to 104. Then by applying the BSPRA (Gao and Li, 2003), the 3 critical points and the 4 mid points were identified as the control points for Bezier Curve as shown in Figure 5 below. From the figure, one can see that the range of the control points is from observation 1 through observation 104. Therefore, the t in the formula (1) can be restricted within [0,1].

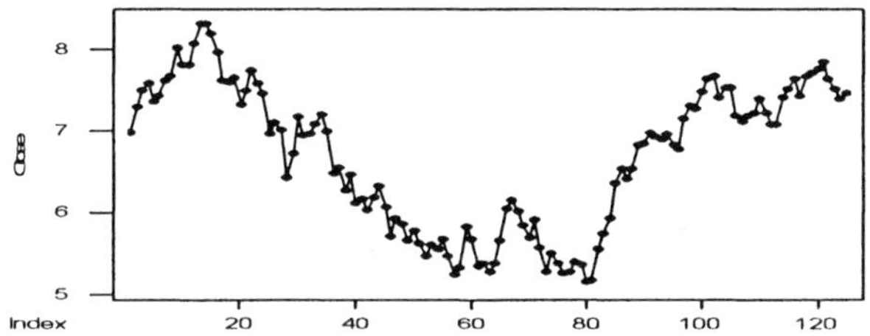

Figure 4. Time Series Plot on Cisco close price (1/2/97-6/30/97)

date	observations	close	critical points
22-Jan-97	1	7.73333	construction
31-Jan-97	8	7.84267	LH
18-Mar-97	39	5.932	
30-Apr-97	69	5.47533	Low
20-May-97	83	6.64867	
10-Jun-97	97	7.35667	RH
19-Jun-97	104	7.34867	before breakout

Figure 5. Control Points for Bezier Curve on Cisco Data

After applying those control points into Bezier Curve, we could generate an ideal "cup with handle". Then we used the Bezier Curve function to generate the perfect time series "cup with handle" data sequence. We compared this "ideal" one with the original smoothed time series as can be seen from Figure 6 below. Finally, we obtained the Pearson correlation coeffient of 0.942 with the p-value ≤ 0.001 to conclude that the Cisco close price in 1997 showed strong "cup with handle" pattern shape by applying all other criteria defined in CAN SLIM.

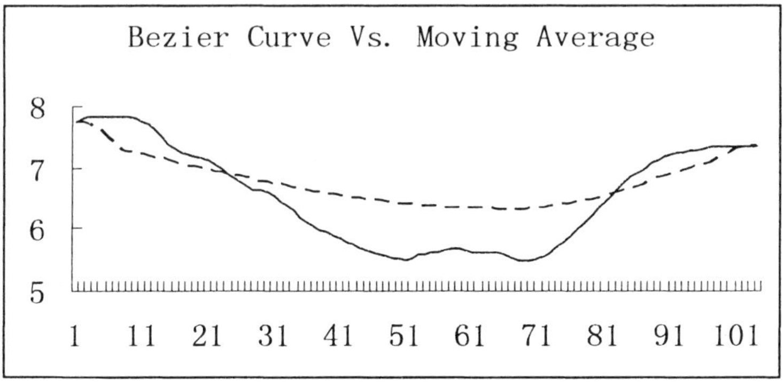

Figure 6. Bezier Curve versus Smoothed Time Series (Cisco Data)

CONCLUSION AND FUTURE WORK

In this paper, we showed how to achieve higher accuracy on user-defined stock pattern recognition. The Bezier curve method integrated with statistical analysis was used to extend the ISSS system for more efficient stock recognition and prediction. From the experimental analysis given in the previous section, we can conclude that the proposed method can indeed achieve more accurate and faster pattern reconition and prediction with "cup with handle" on user-defined stock.

In the modified "cup with handle" method, BSPRA was used to trace back to find critical points of cup handles, whereas Bezier curve was applied for recognition of arbitrary shaped pattern. In addition, SMA method was used for smoothing the volatilities of stock patterns integrated with correlation coefficient method to measure the accuracy of the results from the chart pattern recognition. Further study is currently being conducted to better qualify and quantify various stock and other financial time series pattern recognitions for all types of representatives including investment bankers, securities analysts, portfolio managers and other individuals.

ACKNOWLEDGEMENT

This project was supported in part by a research grant from Texas A&M University – Commerce (Grant #: 142001-20300). In addition, we would like to express our special thanks to Dr. Italo Simonelli for his timely feedback and suggestion on Bezier curve and statistical pattern recognitions.

REFERENCES

Gengzhe Chang and Thomas W. Sederberg, 1997, Over and Over Again, New Mathematical Library (NML), the Mathematical Association of America.

Jingmiao Gao and Dan Li, 2003, "An Empirical Study on Stock Pattern Recognition", Technical Report #04-03, Department of Computer Science, Texas A&M University-Commerce.

John Bajkowski, 2003, "*How To Use The CAN SLIM Approach To Screen For Growth Stocks*", AAII Journal

Rick Martinelli and Barry Hyman, 1998a, "Pattern Recognition in Time-Series", Technical Analysis of Stocks and Commodities

Rick Martinelli and Barry Hyman, 1998b, "Cup-With-Handle and the Computerized Approach", Technical Analysis of Stocks and Commodities

Rick Martinelli and Barry Hyman, 2001, "Trading within the Cup", Technical Analysis of Stocks and Commodities

Sang C. Suh, Sam I. Saffer, Dan Li, Jingmiao Gao, 2003, "*A New Insight into Prediction Modeling System*", proceedings of *the 7th World Conference on Integrated Design and Process Technology*, Society for Design and Process Science

Singh, S., 1999, "A Long Memory Pattern Modelling and Recognition System for Financial Forecasting", Pattern Analysis and Applications, vol. 2, issue 3, pp. 264-273.

Stephen A. DeLurgio, 1998, *"Forecasting Principles and Applications"*, International Editions, McGraw Hill

William J. O'Neil, 2000, "*24 Essential Lessons for Investment Success*", McGraw Hill

William J. O'Neil, 2002, "*How To Make Money In Stocks*", 3rd Edition, McGraw Hill

DETERMINING ORIENTATION OF EDGES AND COMPLEX FEATURES IN DIGITAL IMAGES VIA NEURAL NETWORK

William D. Braswell
Dept. of EE / CS, MSC 192
Texas A&M University-Kingsville
Kingsville, TX 78363

Rajab Challoo
Dept of EE / CS, MSC 192
Texas A&M University-Kingsville
Kingsville, TX 78363
r-challoo@tamuk.edu

ABSTRACT

Image segmentation is a fundamental process in the recognition of patterns in digital images, and is defined as the process by which objects in the image are isolated from other objects and the background. Once the segmentation has been performed, the objects thus isolated may be measured or classified by further processing. Segmentation may be accomplished in part by boundary tracking, a process by which one attempts to locate the boundaries that exist between objects by sequentially examining potential boundary pixels and determining the location of the next potential boundary pixel to be examined. Here we present a boundary tracking method in which a neural network is employed to determine successive potential boundary points.

INTRODUCTION

In the edge-based segmentation process, one attempts to isolate objects by locating regions in which a transition from one gray level to another occurs; this "edge" may represent the boundary between two objects. Other features such as "junctions" may be found where two edges converge, and these complex features may indicate the occlusion of one object by another object (Freeman, 1992).

Edge detection typically involves the application of some operator that will enhance the edges and subdue the large regions of relatively uniform intensity where no edge exists. However, analyzing these "edge-free" regions is computationally inefficient. The goal of boundary tracking, or tracing, is the reduction of this inefficient use of resources by analyzing only those parts of the image that contain the "useful" information; i.e., edges and junctions. Therefore, a means of confining processing to edges and other features is desirable.

The Sobel, Prewitt, Kirsch operators find direction of edges by convolving the same ROI (Region-Of-Interest) within the input image with multiple kernels, each of which is maximally sensitive to edges oriented in a particular direction

(Castleman, 1996). The edge direction is taken to be the direction that corresponds to the convolution kernel that yields the greatest output. The drawbacks of these operators are that they do not detect junctions or corners, and the outputs of these operators do not yield single-pixel-wide boundaries.

Steerable Filters (Freeman and Adelson, 1991, Freeman, 1992) are composed of quadrature-pair kernels based on directional derivatives of Gaussian functions. The output, taken as a linear combination of the quadrature pair, can detect edges of arbitrary oriention, as well as junctions and corners. However, the method is demanding from the standpoint of design of the kernels, and is computationally expensive as well. Furthermore, the technique is restricted to *determing* edge and junction orientation; it does not involve *doing* anything in particular with the information.

Crawford-Hines and Anderson (1997) have utilized neural networks to interactively assist in the initial segmentation of medical imagery by training a neural network to learn the characteristics of the contour being traced. However, their application is limited to simple edges and does not involve corner or junction features. Talu and Tatar (2003) describe an edge-tracing method similar to what we propose, but information on the specifics of their technique is not specified in their published paper.

Our approach involves application of a Difference-of-Gaussians convolution kernel at each pixel within an image ROI and employing a feedforward neural network to provide an $N-of-8$ output that is interpreted as the Boundary Direction Code described by Freeman (1961) and which designates the orientation (or orientations, in the case of complex features such as junctions) of the edge or feature relative to the current boundary point. This technique facilitates determination of the center of the next ROI to be examined and provides further information that may be utilized in the event such features as corners and junctions are located by the boundary tracking process.

DIFFERENCE-OF-GAUSSIANS CONVOLUTION KERNEL

Central to the edge detection scheme is the application of an operator that is sensitive to gray-level transitions and *not* sensitive to regions of uniform gray level intensity. A Difference-of-Gaussians convolution operator was chosen as the basis for the edge detection process. The Difference-of-Gaussians kernel, as described by Kronauer and Zeevi (1985) is given by the equation

$$g(x,y) = \frac{1}{2\pi\sigma_e^2} e^{-\left(\frac{x^2+y^2}{2\sigma_e^2}\right)} - \frac{1}{2\pi\sigma_i^2} e^{-\left(\frac{x^2+y^2}{2\sigma_i^2}\right)} \quad (1)$$

$$= G_e(x,y) - G_i(x,y) \quad (2)$$

where:

x,y: coordinates relative to kernel center at $(0,0)$
σ_e,σ_i: Standard Deviations of the excitatory and inhibitory Gaussian functions, respectively ($\sigma_i > \sigma_e$)

The fact that G_e and G_i are both scaled for unity integral over the x,y-plane implies that the integral of their difference is zero; hence, the Difference-of-Gaussians function does not respond to areas of relatively uniform intensity within the image. However,a digital or discrete implementation of the Difference-of-Gaussians necessitates that we truncate the impulse response at some point. In this case, the integral is taken over only a portion of the x,y plane. The integral over the x,y plane in this case is no longer unity, and therefore the kernel exhibits a finite nonzero response at zero frequency. Since it is required that $G_e - G_i \equiv 0$, each element of the discrete kernel can be compensated to make this true. Therefore, the modified Difference-of-Gaussians convolution kernel is

$$g(x,y) = G_e(xy) - G_i(x,y) - \frac{\sum_X \sum_Y G_e(x,y) - G_e(x,y)}{N_x \times N_y} \tag{3}$$

Convolving an $N \times N$ section of the image under analysis with the Difference-of-Gaussians kernel expressed in Eq. (3) yields a single output indicative of edge strength at that location within the image. Since only one output is obtained per convolution, it is necessary to apply the convolution operation at several locations in the immediate neighborhood; this neighborhood is referred to as the Region of Interest, or ROI, and is of size $M \times M$ (M odd) which corresponds to the number of units in the input layer of the neural network to be described.

If the center of the ROI happens to be located on an edge, one can observe that all portions of the ROI *not* on the edge have values very near zero, and that the edge is bounded on either side by parallel regions at which the Difference-of-Gaussians achieved maximum positive and negative response. These parallel regions of maximum response are indicative of the width of the edge; due to the fact that the Difference-of-Gaussians kernel functions in a manner similar to a second-derivative operator, the edge border will be positive on one side of the edge and negative on the other. In order to eliminate the possibility that the neural network will develop a "preference" for which edge border is positive and which is negative, the absolute value of all $N \times N$ convolutions within the ROI is taken. This results in an ROI image in which an edge is surrounded by two parallel regions or "ridges" of maximum filter output equidistant from the edge. It is at this stage that the ROI is used as input to the neural network.

DETERMINING FEATURE ORIENTATION VIA NEURAL NETWORK

Network Topology

A simple three-layer fully-connected feedforward neural network was employed to determine the next state of the boundary tracking unit. All networks have been trained via the standard Backpropagation Algorithm. The Stuttgart Neural Network Simulator (SNNS) is currently being employed for all aspects of neural network development in this project.

The input layer of the neural network consists of an $M \times M$ array representing the ROI of the input image under consideration. Two additional input units are provided to specify the previous position of the boundary tracking unit in terms of x,y coordinates relative to the current location; i.e., the possible values for each x or y are -1, 0, or $+1$, depending on the ROI input pattern in question.

The output layer consists of eight output units which are interpreted in terms of Boundary Direction Code (Freeman, 1961, Keyes and Winstanley, 2000, Li and Simske, 2002): each output unit corresponds to the direction of the next potential boundary point(s) relative to the boundary tracking unit's current position. It is possible for more than one output unit to be active in response to any given input pattern; this indicates that the boundary tracking unit is currently located at a junction of edges. This indicates that it is necessary to create additional boundary tracking units to follow these newly-discovered edges. It is also possible that no output units will be active; in this case the edge strength has deteriorated to the point that it is no longer identifiable.

At this time, sigmoid activation functions are employed for both hidden and output layer units, while identity functions are used for the input layer units. The ideal topology for the hidden layer has not been established.

Training Pattern Generation

A set of synthetic images, typical of what could be expected due to processing an ROI with the Difference-of-Gaussians kernel, was generated. These synthetic 13×13 images were constructed by drawing "ideal" versions of the expected output ROI in an image-editing program, then applying Gaussian blur with various standard deviations (to match σ_e in the Difference-of-Gaussians equation) to simulate the smoothing of the lowpass portion of the filter (See Fig. 1). The test images in question were of various types such as regular edges, "T" junctions, "L" junctions, "X" junctions, and "Y" junctions. The training set was then expanded by applying rotation in 45 degree increments so that edge primitives of various orientations could be obtained. Test images of size 13×13 were arbitrarily chosen as the largest ROI to be expected; smaller-sized test images could readily be extracted from these. This process yielded approximately 150 test images. Also, test images representing junctions have multiple "last position / next position" input / output mappings which expands the input test set to 376 patterns. XITE (X-based

Image processing Tools and Environment) was employed for all image-processing functions, while scripts written in the Python language and GNU BASH scripting languages converted the test images from their assembled the pattern set into a form suitable for use as an SNNS pattern file.

Figure 1. 13×13 pixel ROI "T"-type junction. *Left: ideal; Center: Gaussian blur with* $\sigma = 1.0$; *Right:* 3×3*-pixel ROI taken from the center 3 pixels of the* 13×13 *Gaussian-blurred ROI*

RESULTS, CONCLUSIONS, AND FUTURE WORK

At the present time, development has been limited to running training session on the neural network to determine feasibility of this scheme. A number of networks with 3×3 ROI input and output layers as previously described, and varying numbers of hidden layer units. While the 376-pattern training set is too large to provide a thoroughly detailed analysis of results in this paper, general results and observations will be discussed.

The network was trained for 200 epochs over the entire training set, with random presentation of input-output pairs. The network did learn correct mappings for all examples presented. One unexpected result occured in cases in which the 3×3 input pattern contained no active units due to the large size of the edge presented. In this case, the network should have no output units active. This was not accounted for in the generation of the SNNS pattern file; all outputs should have been specified to be zero but were not. Even though the input file erroneously specified that these patterns should have output units active, the network correctly (and unexpectedly) yields an output with no output units active.

The next phase of development and testing involves generating pattern sets taken from a real-world image and presenting these to the trained network.

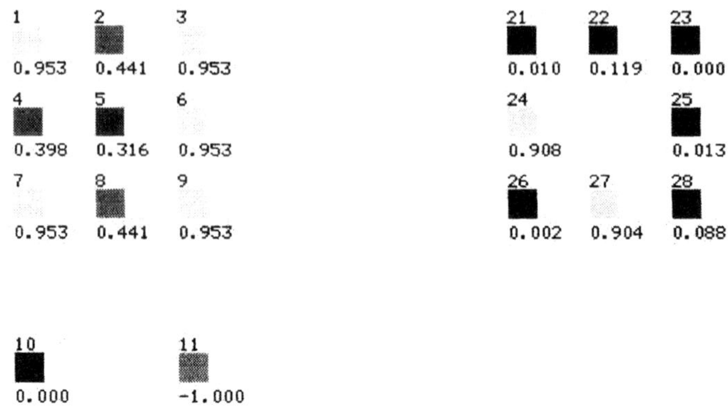

Figure 2. A screenshot from the SNNS simulator window. Left: Input layer showing unit numbers and activations for the 3×3 ROI of Fig 1. The two additional units below the 3×3 layer indicate that the previous position was $(x,y) = (0,-1)$, or Unit #2; Right: Output layer indicating that the next positions are to be $(x,y) = (-1,0)$ and $(x,y) = (0,+1)$ relative to current position (hidden layer not shown)

References

Castleman, K. R., 1996, 'Digital Image Processing", Prentice Hall, Englewood Cliffs, NJ., pp. 464-466

Crawford-Hines, S. and Anderson, C. W., 1997, 'Neural Nets in Boundary Tracing Tasks", *Proceedings of the IEEE Workshop on Neural Networks and Signal Processing*, pp. 207-215 .

Freeman, W. T. and Adelson, E. H., 1991, 'The Design and Use of Steerable Filters", *IEEE Transactions on Pattern Analysis and Machine Intelligence*, Vol. 13, pp. 891-906.

Freeman, W. T., 1992, 'Steerable Filters and Local Analysis of Image Structure", Ph. D. Thesis, Massachussets Institute of Technology, Cambridge, MA.

Freeman, H., 1961, 'On the Encoding of Arbitrary Geometric Confi gurations", *IRE Transactions on Electronic Computers*, Vol. EC-10, pp. 260-268.

Keyes, L. and Winstanley, A. C., 2000, "Applying Computer Vision Techniques to Topographic Objects", *International Archives of Photogrammetry and Remote Sensing*, Vol. 33(B3), pp. 480-487.

Kronauer, R.E. and Zeevi, Y.Y., 1985, 'Reorganization And Diversifi cation Of Signals In Vision", *IEEE Transactions on Systems, Man, and Cybernetics*, Vol. SMC-15, pp. 91-101.

Li, D. and Simske, S., 2002, 'Shape Retrieval With Flat Contour Segments", Technical Report HPL-2002-250, HP Laboratories, Palo Alto, CA.

Smith, S. M. and Brady, J. M., 1997, 'SUSAN - A New Approach to Low-Level Image Processing", *International Journal of Computer Vision*, Vol. 23(1), pp. 45-78.

Talu, F. and Tatar, Y., 2003, "A New Edge Tracing Method Developed for Object Recognition", *IJCI Proc. of Intl. XII. Turkish Symposium on Artificial Intelligence and Neural Networks*, Vol. 1, No. 1.

WOOD DEFECTS CLASSIFICATION USING FUZZY LOGIC

MARIO I. CHACON M.
DSP&Vision Lab
Chihuahua Institute of Technology
Chihuahua, Mexico

GRACIELA RAMIREZ A.
DSP&Vision Lab
Chihuahua Institute of Technology
Chihuahua, Mexico

ABSTRACT
This paper presents a fuzzy system to classify four types of wood defects. The defects are located on the surface of the wood and are known as knots. The features used by the classifier are derived from 2D Gabor filters. The features generated by the Gabor filters are analyzed by the incorporation method to select only the most discriminative features. The final features are used then to design a fuzzy classifier. The fuzzy classifier consists of nine inputs, seven rules, and four outputs. The performance of the classifier is of 89.28% of correct classification considering 140 defect samples. Results shown that the fuzzy classifier has a better performance than a human inspector who has a performance between 75% and 85% of correct classification.

INTRODUCTION

The price in the market of a board or a sheet of wood in the wood industry is related to the quality of the wood. Wood quality depends on the number of defects and their distribution found during inspection. The inspection is a subjective process achieved by a human inspector with a performance of 75% to 85% of correct classification. A human inspector during the inspection classifies the defects according to their appearance and texture. Based on this procedure the inspector determines the quality of the wood. If a vision system is designed to accomplish this inspection task, it must simulate the behavior of the human inspector to assure at least the same performance. The vision system would need a mathematical scheme for the classification stage able to simulate the behavior of the human inspector. It is known that fuzzy logic is a suitable scheme to perform the simulation of the human behavior under subjective tasks.

This paper presents a method based on fuzzy logic to classify four different types of defect named knots found on the surface of a wood sheet. The defects considered in this paper are encased, leaf, sound, and edge, (Kauppinen,1999), (Lampinen,1996,1995,1994). Figure1 shows some examples of these defects. The samples used, 140, were obtained from the University of Oulu, Finland. Several works using Artificial Neural Networks to try to solve this problem have been reported in the literature, (Kauppinen,1999), (Lampinen,1996). However, simulation of the human behavior to solve this problem has not been documented.

This work presents a fuzzy logic system to classify the four types of defects mentioned before. The contribution of the paper is to model in some level the behavior of a human inspector using the advantages of fuzzy logic systems. The paper is organized in the following sections; the feature extraction process, the design of the fuzzy system, and the results and conclusions.

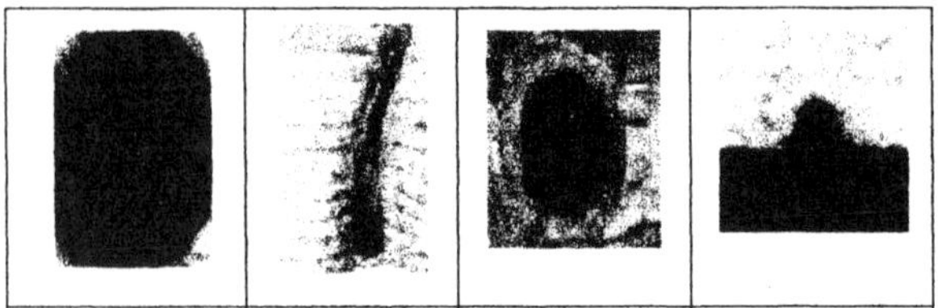

a) b) c) d)

Fig. 1 Defects a) encased, b) leaf, c) sound, d) edge.

FEATURE EXTRACTION

Geometric features like defect size, minimum rectangle, compactness, etc, have been used for machine vision systems to solve the knot defect classification problem. However, these systems have a poor performance, (Lampinen,1996). Geometric features have a big variance among the knots defects. Good features will be then, features that present invariance of defects characteristics. These kinds of features may be obtained with Gabor filters.

Gabor Filters

The features used to describe the knot defects must be invariant to rotation, translation and orientation. Gabor filters, GF, provide a form to obtain these kinds of features. GF have been used in image analysis, and they are derived from biological models, (Chengjun,2003). The kernels of the GF are similar to mammal cortical cells. Another advantage of the GF is that the filters can be defined to select features in a specific orientation and frequency.

The GF are 2D band pass filters. The GF are spatial sinusoids localized by a Gaussian window. The set of filters form a family or a filter bank. In this family each filter is a dilated, translated and rotated version of each other. The definition of the filters is given by

$$\psi(f,\theta,x,y)=\exp(i(f_x x+f_y y)-\frac{f^2(x^2+y^2)}{2\sigma^2}) \quad (1)$$

where $f_x = f\cos\theta$, $f_y = f\sin\theta$, $i=\sqrt{-1}$, x and y are the coordinates of the pixels in the image in the range $(-x/2, x/2)$ and $(-y/2, y/2)$. The central frequency of the band pass is f, the spatial orientation is θ, and σ represents the wide of the filter, in this work $\sigma = 1.5\pi$. Considering frequencies less than or equal to π, the frequencies of the filters were defined by

$$f_k = \frac{\pi}{\sqrt{2^k}} \qquad k = 2,3,4,5 \quad (2)$$

and the orientation by $\theta_t = \frac{\pi t}{8}, \quad t = 0,..,7$ (3)

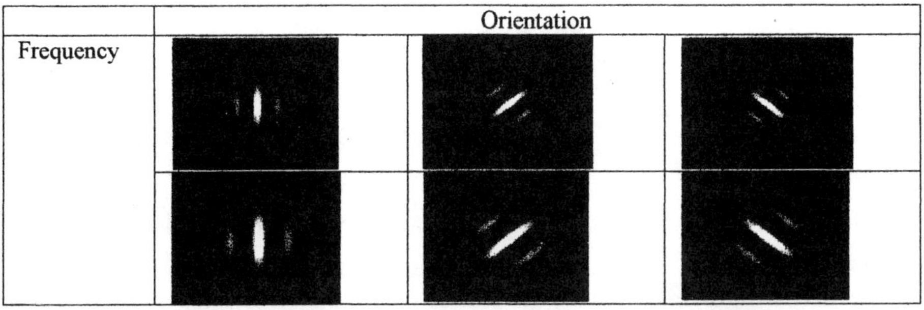

Fig. 2 Example of Gabor filters at different frequency and orientations.

Fig. 3 GF in the frequency domain, different frequencies same orientation.

where k determines the frequency band, resolution of the details obtained by the filter, and t specifies the directions of those frequencies. Some examples of the real part of the GF used are illustrated in Fig.2. Examples of GF in the frequency domain at different frequencies and same orientation are shown in Fig.3.

We can define the Gabor transform of an image, $I(x, y)$, as the convolution of $I(x, y)$ with the family of GF defined in Eq. (1). Using the convolution theorem of the Fourier transform we have

$$\Im\{O_{f,\theta}(x,y)\} = \Im\{I(x,y)\}\Im\{\psi_{f,\theta}(x,y)\} \tag{4}$$

and

$$O_{f,\theta}(x,y) = \Im^{-1}\{\Im\{I(x,y)\}\Im\{\psi_{f,\theta}(x,y)\}\} \tag{5}$$

where $O_{f,\theta}(x,y)$ is the filtered image with the GF $\psi_{f,\theta}(x,y)$, and f and θ are the frequency and orientation of the filter. The Gabor transform of the images was implemented in the frequency domain. Only the magnitude of the filters are used because it has been determined that it is robust and distortion tolerant in patter recognition tasks. The images $I(x,y)$ were normalized to 64x64 pixels, and their gray scale versions were used to improve the speed of the process.

A set of 32 filters were defined for the Gabor transformation, 8 orientations and 4 frequencies. When an image is convolved with this set of filters we obtain 32 filtered images of 64x64 pixels. Each of these images captures different information of the defect. This information corresponds to the frequency and orientation of the filter. The process to generate the feature vector is explained next. Consider the $O_{f,\theta}(x,y)$ images obtained form the image $I(x,y)$.

For $\theta = 1$ to 8

For $f = 1$ to 4

Take $O_{f,\theta}$ and generate a 4096x1vector, $V_{f,\theta}$, by concatenating the columns of $O_{f,\theta}(x,y)$

Generate a new vector of dimension 1024x1, $V_{f,\theta\downarrow}$, by subsampling by 4 the $V_{f,\theta}$ vector.

Use the 32 $V_{f,\theta\downarrow}$ vectors to generate the matrix, $M_{f,\theta\downarrow}$, of dimension 1024x32.

This matrix conveys information of the defect texture at different frequencies and orientations. In order to reduce the feature vector dimensionality represent each $V_{f,\theta\downarrow}$ of the $M_{f,\theta\downarrow}$ matrix by its mean and standard deviation. This step yields a reduced matrix with dimension 2x32. The complete process is illustrated in Fig.4.

The final step is to analyze the vector components to decide which ones provide better discrimination. Two methods were used to achieve this purpose, principal components analysis and the incorporation method. This second method gave better results than the first one, indicating that the best features are related to the filters, $\psi_{2,8}$, $\psi_{3,5}$, $\psi_{4,1}$, $\psi_{4,2}$, $\psi_{4,5}$, $\psi_{4,7}$, and $\psi_{4,8}$.

According to Lampinen (1996), gray level distribution of the defect represent also a good feature of the defect. Therefore, two new features were added to the feature vector, the mean and standard deviation of the original image. Thus, the final feature vector to represent a defect is defined by these two image features and the standard deviation of the selected GF.

$$X = \left\lfloor \mu_{I(x,y)}, \sigma_{I(x,y)}, \sigma_{\psi_{2,8}}, \sigma_{\psi_{3,5}}, \sigma_{\psi_{4,1}}, \sigma_{\psi_{4,2}}, \sigma_{\psi_{4,5}}, \sigma_{\psi_{4,7}}, \sigma_{\psi_{4,8}} \right\rfloor \tag{6}$$

FUZZY CLASSIFIER

The proposed fuzzy system to classify the defects uses the nine features of the vector X as the input to the system. The system is composed of seven rules to define the type of the defect. The defuzzification method is the mean of maximum. The fuzzy classifier was designed by considering 70 samples out of the 140 available. The shape of the fuzzy sets to represent each class was defined as follows.

For each one of the 9 inputs

Obtain the distribution of the samples for each class.

Generate the fuzzy set of each class accordingly to the shape of its distribution using Z, S and Pi functions.

Once the fuzzy sets have been defined a set of fuzzy rules are designed and the system is tested. If the error is too high the fuzzy set function of the class with more problems is adjusted. The process is repeated until the error is acceptable. The fuzzy rules are listed bellow

- If $\sigma_{I(x,y)}$, is *small* **or** $\mu_{I(x,y)}$ ***is medium then*** it's a ***sound*** defect
  $w = 0.5$

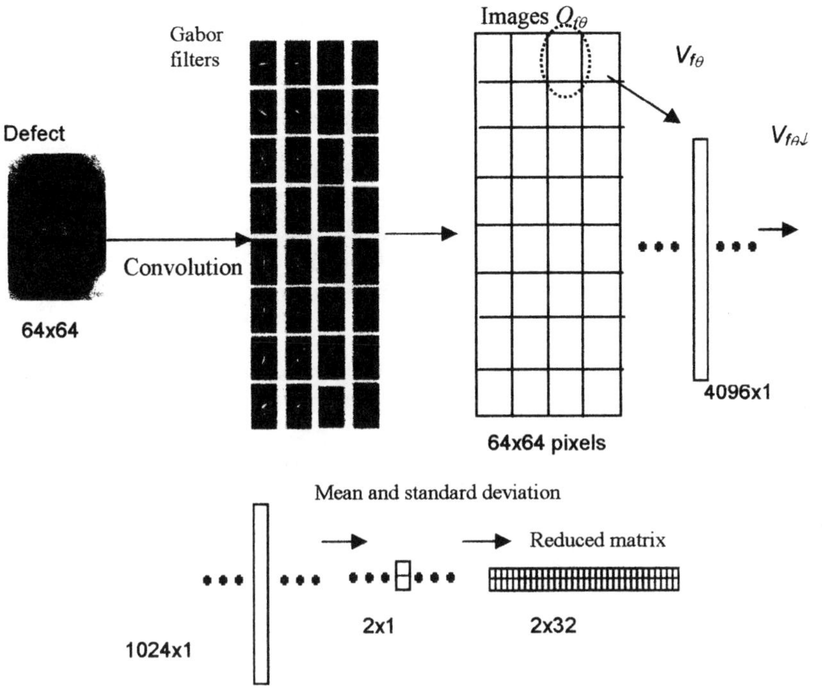

Fig. 4 Feature vector definition process.

-
- If $\sigma_{I(x,y)}$, *is medium* **or** $\mu_{I(x,y)}$ is *very small* **or** $\sigma_{\psi_{4,1}}$ *is medium* **or** $\sigma_{\psi_{4,2}}$ is *large* **or** $\sigma_{\psi_{4,5}}$ is small **or** $\sigma_{\psi_{4,7}}$ is *large* **or** $\sigma_{\psi_{4,8}}$ is *medium* ***then*** it's a ***encased*** defect $w = 0.4$
- If $\sigma_{\psi_{4,1}}$ is *very small* **and** $\sigma_{\psi_{4,2}}$ is *very small* **and** $\sigma_{\psi_{2,8}}$ is very small **then** it's a ***leaf*** defect $w = 1$
- If $\sigma_{\psi_{3,5}}$ is *medium* **and** $\sigma_{\psi_{4,5}}$ is *large* **then** it's a ***edge*** defect $w = 1$
- If $\sigma_{I(x,y)}$, is very small **or** $\mu_{I(x,y)}$ is large **then** it's a ***leaf*** defect $w = 0.5$
- If $\sigma_{I(x,y)}$, is small **and** $\mu_{I(x,y)}$ is medium **then** it's a ***sound*** defect $w = 1$
- If $\sigma_{I(x,y)}$, is large **and** $\sigma_{\psi_{3,5}}$ is medium then it's a ***edge*** defect $w = 1$

where w defines a weight assigned to each rule.

The four outputs of the system correspond to the four defects. The defuzzification method use in the classifier was the mean of maximum.

RESULTS AND CONCLUSIONS

Table 1 and 2 show the results obtained with the fuzzy classifier during the design and the verification stage. The results are shown using the confusion matrix. In the design the classifier had only 7 errors and 8 in the verification test. These errors generate a performance of correct classification of 90% in the design and 88.57% in the final test.

In conclusion we can comment that Gabor filters were able to capture discriminative features from the defects. Even the number of features were reduced significantly they still convey enough information to discriminate the four defect classes. The findings of this work also show that fuzzy systems are a suitable scheme to represent human behavior during inspection of wood defects. Although the inspection process seems to be complex it was modeled by only seven fuzzy rules yielding a better performance than a human inspector.

ACKNOWLEDGEMENT
The authors greatly appreciate the support from CONACYT under grant PFPN-03-29-05 to develop this research.

Table 1 Classifier results during design

	Sound	Encased	Edge	Leaf	Number of samples	Incorrect Classified
Sound	17	3	0	0	20	3
Encased	0	9	0	0	9	0
Edge	2	2	18	0	22	4
Leaf	0	0	0	19	19	0
Total Error						7

Table 2. 1 Classifier results final test

	Sound	Encased	Edge	Leaf	Number of samples	Incorrect classified
Sound	17	1	0	2	20	3
Encased	0	9	0	0	9	0
Edge	1	1	18	1	21	3
Leaf	2	0	0	18	20	2
Total Error						8

REFERENCES

Chengjun L., and Wechsler H.,2003, "Independent component analysis of Gabor features for face recognition," *IEEE Trans. Neural Networks*, Vol 14, pp 919-928.

Kauppinen H., Silven O. and Piirainen T.,1999, "Self Organizing Map based user interface for visual surface inspection," Proc. *11th Scandinavian Conference on Image Analysis*, Kangerlussuaq, Greenland, June, pp. 801-808.

Lampinen J. and Smolander S., "Self organizing feature extraction in recognition of wood surface defects and color images," *International Journal of Pattern Recognition and Artificial intelligence*, Vol. 10 No. 2, pp. 97-113.

Lampinen J., Smolander S., and Korhonen M.,1995," Word surface inspection system based on generis visual features," *International Conference on Artificial Neural Networks ICANN'95 Paris*, October 9-13.

Lampinen J. and Smolander S.,1994," Word defect recognition: A comparative study," Proc. of Workshop on Machine Vision in Advanced Production, 2.-3.6., Oulu, Finland.

Silven O., Niskanen M., and Kauppinen H.,2002, "Wood inspection with non-supervised clustering," *Machine Vision and Application*, vol.13,pp 275–285.

Tsoukalas L., and Robert E. Uhrig R.,1997,"Fuzzy and Neural Approaches in Engineering," *A Wiley-Interscience Publication*.

DETECTING ERRORS IN COTTON GRADING DATA USING BACK-PROPAGATION NEURAL NETWORKS

GENE BOGGESS
Department of Computer Science and Engineering, Mississippi State University
gboggess@cse.msstate.edu

XINTONG BI
Department of Computer Science and Engineering, Mississippi State University
xb7@cse.msstate.edu

GRETCHEN F. SASSENRATH
USDA-ARS APTRU, Stonevillle, MS
gsassenrath@msa-stoneville.ars.usda.gov

ABSTRACT
Back-propagation neural networks are powerful tools that have been applied to a variety of real-world problems, such as classification and categorization. Error detection can be regarded as classification and thus is also one of its applications. This project involves using back-propagation neural networks to detect erroneous entries in cotton fiber grading data from the USDA-ARS at Stoneville, Mississippi. The best results obtained yielded 98.89% accuracy on training, and about 94% accuracy in predicting erroneous entries in the testing data set.

INTRODUCTION

The price of cotton (*Gossypium* sps.) lint is determined by a process of calculation based on the values of a number of features of cotton These features are measured in a process termed "classing" after the cotton is harvested and ginned. The cotton lint characteristics are altered by pre-harvest factors, such as cultivar, environment, and crop age, as well as method of harvesting and ginning (Williford *et al.*, 1986; Anthony and Bragg, 1987; McAlister, 2001). The impact of harvest and ginning methods on quality of fiber parameters has recently been brought to the forefront as more studies are extrapolating research results to the production level. Due to time and size constraints, researchers commonly harvest and gin cotton on a smaller scale than do producers. These differences in harvest and ginning methods significantly alter the fiber properties, and hence the value of the cotton. These errors can directly affect the final buying price of the cotton, and thus affect the income of cotton farmers.

Cotton grown for research purposes often differ from cotton samples obtained from commercially-produced cotton. Research cotton samples are frequently harvested by hand, while commercially-grown cotton is harvested by machine. Cotton grown for research is often ginned using a small research gin, which does not perform any lint-cleaning or trash-removing steps. In contrast, a production-level gin employs additional processing steps to remove trash and leaves. Thus, even cotton grown in the same field may measure differently after harvesting and processing because of difference in harvesting and ginning methods (research vs. production methods). If a neural network can be trained to detect the differences in cotton data, it should also be possible to train a neural network to detect differences between research and production cotton data. Finally, it would be useful to be able to "translate" the results, that is, convert the quality parameters from those obtained by researchers to those obtained by producers. One key point to consider is that, in order to correctly represent fiber quality parameters from a research study into values that a producer would see, we want to translate a population of values. We do not want to replicate only the mean, but rather the range of values present in the sample.

This project is designed to detect "erroneous" entries in files containing cotton fiber data. For identical cotton lint samples, varying only in harvest and ginning methods, we separate the populations into "correct" samples that have been machine harvested and ginned on a system similar to that used by producers. These "production" samples are then used as the "correct" baseline against which the "erroneous" samples are compared. The "erroneous" samples are those collected either by machine or hand-picking, and ginned on the research gin. When an erroneous entry is detected, the program reports the location of the error so that an expert in cotton quality measurement can examine that entry in detail to verify the correctness of its features. If systematic data entries are detected it may be possible to deduce their cause and to correct the conditions that cause the errors. In this way, a grading of cotton quality more closely aligned with producer results may be achieved.

In phase 2 of this project, a neural network will be trained to detect differences between research and production cotton data. In phase 3, a neural network will be trained to translate from the results obtained by researchers to those obtained by producers.

The cotton samples for this experiment were harvested from plots at the United States Department of Agriculture, Agriculture Research Services (USDA-ARS) at Stoneville, Mississippi. Samples were either machine-harvested with a commercial cotton picker, or hand picked. The harvested samples were divided into lots, and ginned on either a large, production scale gin (micro-gin), or a small research scale gin. Because of size limitations, there was insufficient cotton fiber from the hand-harvested samples to run through the micro-gin. The hand-harvested samples were ginned only on the research gin.

Previous investigations into using neural networks for some types of classification tasks regarding cotton includes work done at the Southwestern Cotton Ginning Research Laboratory in New Mexico, where the spatial features of cotton fibers were examined by Siddaiah *et al.*, who used back-propagation neural networks to classify trash objects into their respective categories (Siddaiah et al., 1999). However, the experiment reported herein may be the first study in which back-propagation neural networks have been used to detect erroneous numerical entries in cotton fiber data.

METHODOLOGY

Artificial neural networks, especially back-propagation neural networks, have been applied widely in signal processing, pattern recognition, and image processing (Boggess, 1994). In this experiment, a back-propagation neural network is trained to detect erroneous data entries for ginned cotton.

Because we are interested in determining the cotton fiber properties comparable to that which a producer would find, we assign the machine-harvested, large-scale ginning cotton samples as the "correct" values. The same cotton, harvested by either machine or hand, and ginned on a small-scale research gin, then constitutes the "incorrect" data. In each entry of the data sets there are 9 variables, including 8 features, *color*, *staple*, *micronaire*, *extraneous matter*, *strength*, *leaf*, *uniformity*, and *discount value*, followed by a classification of the data item as correct/erroneous. A 1 or a 0 represents the correctness of that entry, with a "1" indicating that the whole entry is correct or expected to be correct and a "0" indicating that one feature in the entry is incorrect or is expected to be detected as incorrect. Both the training and test data sets are composed of 90 correct entries and 90 incorrect entries. The entries in the training set were shuffled before being fed to the network.

Hand-written code was used to obtain the results for this project. NevProp4 (Goodman and Harrell, 2003) was used to validate the results; its results were similar. The architecture of the back-propagation neural network used in this project is a standard back-propagation neural network with one input layer, one hidden layer and one output unit. There are 8 input units, plus one bias input. The number of hidden nodes is adjustable, and includes a bias unit. This network is fully connected in the sense that each input feature is connected to each hidden neuron (except the bias unit), and each hidden neuron is connected to the output neuron.

The initial weight on each of the connection was set to a random number ranging from –0.25 to 0.25. The input of the bias units is always set to 1. The activation function applied to the hidden neurons and the output neuron is the standard sigmoid-shaped logistic function. A "1" at the output unit indicates that the whole entry is correct or expected to be correct while the digit "0" indicates the whole entry is incorrect or expected to be detected as incorrect. The error is defined as the difference between expected output and actual output. The errors are propagated back through the network and the weight of each connection is changed according to a weight change function. The learning rate is set to 0.35. Momentum is used and is adjustable.

Two types of accuracy measurements were used to evaluate the performance of the trained network. One is averaged error, which is the sum of the errors divided by the total number of entries. Another measurement is the percentage of correct classifications. If the network is able to correctly classify 162 of 180 entries in test set, then the accuracy of the network on the test set is 90%. The same rule is applied to training accuracy. When the average error decreases, the accuracy of the network increases. However, under certain runs, a slight lower average error may be accompanied by a slightly lower accuracy percentage than a run with a slightly higher average error.

Preliminary explorations of the appropriate network parameters resulted in the selection of a hidden layer size of 8. These explorations also indicated that momentum should not be used.

INPUT ANALYSIS AND REPRESENTATION

The original data from the USDA-ARS were provided as two sets of data from three years 2001, and 2002. In each spreadsheet of year 2001 and year 2002, the data obtained from measuring micro-gin samples are listed before those obtained from research gin samples. Of the 120 rows of entries in the spreadsheets the first 30 are averaged summaries of data on 30 cotton samples collected that year, followed by 90 rows of un-averaged entries; This experiment only used the later 90 rows of entries. The first 18 columns are control variables and are labeled as Var1C, Var2C, ..., Var18C. The next 18 columns are the variables for which the values may or may not be correct, which are labeled as Var1T, Var2T, ... , Var18T. All the variables are labeled in such a way that Var1C corresponds to Var1T, Var2C corresponds to Var2T, and so on. The names of the first 12 variables are: *color, staple, micronaire, extraneous matter, strength, hvi color, color red, color blue, estimated average leaf, hvi trash, length, and uniformity.* The next five values are calculated from the preceding measured variables based on the discount price of the cotton (AMS Spot Cotton Quotation (USDA, 2003)): *CLS (color, leaf, staple) discount in mills, micronairee2, extran2, uniformity,* and *total discount in cents*. Of these, the last five values are the discount points calculated from the previous values, with the total discount being presented in cents (USDA, 2003). The numbers in the first 18 columns of C variables are obtained from measuring the bulk harvest, ginned on the micro-gin. The values in the following 18 columns of T variables are obtained from machine-harvest large samples, ginned on the research gin. The micro-gin is very close to a production-scale gin, differing only in size, so the results from the micro gin should be the "correct" values, or approximately what a producer would see. Consequently, the entries in the first 18 columns can be considered to be "correct". The correctness of the T variables is unknown. That is to say, it is not sure whether any given one of them is a correct entry or an incorrect entry.

Also provided by the USDA-ARS was a lookup table (based on the values recorded by the USDA-AMS Spot Cotton Quotations for the South Delta, (USDA, 2003)) that lists different ranks of cotton based on color and leaf values, in which the discount/premium points are given based on corresponding rank, plus another lookup table for calculating the discount/ premium points of each feature of cotton fiber.

In the original data, there are dependency relationships among the 18 features. Variable 13 depends on variable 1, variable 2, and variable 9. Variable 14 depends on variable 3, variable 15 depends on variable 5, variable 16 depends on variable 4 and variable 17 depends on variable 12. Variable 18 depends on variables 13, 14, 15, 16, and 17. Thus, we only need to be concerned with variables 1, 2, 3, 4, 5, 6, 7, 8, 9, 12, and 18. At the same time, since variables 6, 7, and 8 do not contribute to the calculation of variable 18 (the discount value) we only need to consider variables 1, 2, 3, 4, 5, 9, 12, and 18, which are c*olor*, *staple, micronaire*, *extraneous matter*, *strength*, *leaf*, *uniformity*, and *discount value.*

Decisions about the form in which to represent the data to the network are important; if an inappropriate data representational format is used, the network may not learn well, or may learn very slowly. Several experiments were performed to determine an appropriate form of data representation; as a result, a normalization function was applied to the original values of 7 variables (excluding discount value) so that the values range from 0.1 to 0.9.

Both training sets and test sets include two types of entries: correct entries and incorrect entries. The correct entries are those obtained from cotton samples ginned by the micro-gin. In the original data sets, the other part is unknown data obtained from measuring the samples ginned in the research gin. These data are unknown in the sense that their correctness is unknown; some may be correct and some may be incorrect. Therefore, it was necessary to generate *artificially incorrect* data.

The incorrect entries were obtained in the following way: the correct entries are copied and then one feature of each entry in the copy is artificially altered. In addition, the distribution of incorrect features remained even, so that there were the same number of errors on one feature as another. The *discount value* was not changed at all, so only 7 features values needed to be altered, with only one feature changed in each entry.

For example, if the *color* value in the correct entry was 42, it was randomly changed to, say, 62, keeping all the values of the other features untouched, and this whole entry was labeled as incorrect. The incorrect values of the changed features are made in such a way that this incorrect value must still be in the possible value ranges of that feature. For example, the possible value range for *leaf* is 1-8, so if a *leaf* feature needs to be changed and its old correct value is 5, the new incorrect value must be an integer between 1 and 8, excluding 5.

The training data sets were obtained from year 2001 data and the test sets were from year 2001 and 2002. In each sets, there are 180 entries with 90 entries correct and 90 entries incorrect. The training entries were randomly shuffled before being fed to the neural network

EXPERIMENTAL RESULTS AND ANALYSIS

The best training result yields a 0.0262 average error (98.89% accuracy) achieved at epoch 3500 by using the data of year 2001. The testing result achieved at this run is 0.0667 average error (93.89% accuracy) when test set is also taken from the set of year 2001 data. These results are generally repeatable. Slightly worse results have been obtained from the data for the year 2002.

Training on the data from one year and testing on the data from another year does not tend to produce good results. When 2001 data were used as the training set and 2002 data were used as a test set, the lowest average error varied from 0.3 to 0.35 (62% -77 % correct) achieved at 300 epochs. When 2002 data were used as the training set and 2001 data as the test set, the lowest average error varied from 0.38 to 0.4 (55% - 63 % correct) achieved at 1500 epochs. In the later case, the performance is unpredictable, in the sense that a very bad result, such as an average error of 0.61, may appear. Attempts to improve the results by using early stopping or increasing the number of hidden nodes were unsuccessful in this situation.

The use of momentum was found not to effectively help convergence. Under certain situations, momentum values of greater than 0.5 were found to be harmful, even if added only after a certain number of epochs. It may be the case that the use of momentum interferes with smooth convergence toward a solution and leads to unsettled performance.

If the input data is not normalized, poor results are obtained. Training results are about 0.5 average error or worse, whether trained for as little as 100 epochs or as many as 5000 epochs, with an average error on the test set of around 0.5 as well. When un-normalized data are used the network apparently needs to spend many more epochs adjusting its weights to reflect the relative influence of each specific input. This slows the learning process and does not produce satisfactory results.

A correctly trained network makes few errors, but it was observed that it tends to more frequently identify incorrect entries as correct ones than the other way around. It is suspected that the method for creating the incorrect data contributes to this phenomenon.

CONCLUSIONS

The results of using back-propagation neural network to detect erroneous entries in cotton fiber data sets are encouraging. The network is sensitive enough to achieve a 99% correct training result and 94% correct test result on training and test sets taken from data for the same year.

The technique of synthesizing the "incorrect" data seems creative and promising. It is important to determine a middle ground for synthesizing the "wrong" data for the training and test sets.

Finally, this application demonstrated the importance of normalization. When the inputs are scaled between 0.1 and 0.9, the network learns much more quickly, and substantially better results can be obtained.

REFERENCES

Anthony, W.S., and Bragg, C. K., 1987, "Response of cotton fiber length distribution to production and ginning practices." *Trans. ASAE*, 30:290-296.

Boggess, J. E., 1994, "Identification of Roads in Satellite Imagery Using Artificial Neural Networks: A Contextual Approach," *Proceedings of the World Congress on Neural Networks*, San Diego, CA, pp I-410 – I-415.

Goodman, P. H., and Harrell, Jr., F. E., 2003, *NevProp Manual with Introduction to Artificial Neural Network Theory*, http://brain.unr.edu/index.php (current 10 November 2003).

McAlister, III., D. D., 2001, "Gin process control and the resultant textile yarn and knit fabric quality," *Applied Engineering in Agriculture,* Vol. 17(6):761-764.

M. Siddaiah, M., Prasad, N. R., Lieberman, M. A., and Hughs, S .E., 1999, "Identification of Trash Types and Computation of Trash Content in Ginned Cotton Using Soft Computing Techniques," *42nd Midwest Symposium on Circuits and Systems*, August 1999, Vol. 1, pp. 547-550.

"USDA AMS Market News Reports - Cotton Reports," http://www.ams.usda.gov/cotton/mncs/index.htm (current 18 November 2003)

Williford, J.R., Meredith, W.R., Anthony, W.S. 1986, "Factors influencing yield and quality of Delta cotton." *Am Society of Ag Engineers, 1986 Winter Meeting*. Paper no. 86-1561.

AN INVESTIGATION OF THE EFFECTS OF CORRELATION AND AUTOCORRELATION ON CLASSIFIER FUSION AND OPTIMAL CLASSIFIER ENSEMBLES

NATHAN J. LEAP
Department of Operational Sciences
Air Force Institute of Technology
Wright-Patterson AFB Ohio

PAUL P. CLEMANS
Department of Operational Sciences
Air Force Institute of Technology
Wright-Patterson AFB Ohio

KENNETH W. BAUER, JR.
Department of Operational Sciences
Air Force Institute of Technology
Wright-Patterson AFB Ohio

MARK E. OXLEY
Department of Mathematics and Statistics
Air Force Institute of Technology
Wright-Patterson AFB Ohio

ABSTRACT

This paper extends the research found in Storm, Bauer, and Oxley, 2003. ISOC Fusion (Haspert, 2000), ROC "Within" Fusion (Oxley and Bauer, 2002), and Neural Fusion were the three classifier fusion techniques. In neural fusion, posterior probabilities from underlying classifiers are used as features in a Probabilistic Neural Network. We also contrasted the three fusion methods to a single, large classifier, a Generalized Regression Neural Network. Correlation was injected into the data set both within a feature set (autocorrelation) and across feature sets for a high dimensional two class problem. The fusion methods were then extended to three classifiers and a method is demonstrated that selects the optimal fusion ensemble.

INTRODUCTION

The Air Force does not give exact guidelines for fusion. Many fusion techniques assume that the classifier indications or their respective input data are statistically independent. Little is known about how these techniques perform in the presence of correlation (Willett, et al, 2000). Tumer and Ghosh (1996) derive expressions which quantify the effects of classifiers that are correlated by sharing a common feature set; meanwhile, Duin and Tax (2000) show results from combining classifiers correlated by both sharing a common feature set and different, possibly correlated, feature sets. Similarly, Hashem (1993) develops effects of linear combinations of neural networks. In this paper, the level of correlation is controlled both within and across a feature set. This feature set is input into different classifier fusion techniques, and the effects of the correlation are examined for all classifier fusion methods. This research compares four classifier fusion methods in the face of correlation and extends the research of Storm, Bauer, and Oxley (2003).

FUSION METHODS

Four methods of classifier fusion are used in this paper: Identification System Operating Characteristic (ISOC) Fusion, Receiver Operating Characteristic (ROC) "Within" OR Fusion, Probabilistic Neural Network (PNN) Fusion, and One Big Network (OBN) Fusion.

ISOC FUSION

The Identification System Operating Characteristic (ISOC) fusion method determines the optimal Boolean fusion rule with a set decision threshold through a novel algorithm under the assumption of statistical independence of the classifiers (Haspert, 2000). Extending the work in Haspert (2000), an algorithm is used to generate an improved ISOC curve.

ROC "WITHIN" OR FUSION

The ROC "Within" OR fusion method determines the optimal threshold sets from individual classifier ROC curves to form a fused ROC curve for a given Boolean rule, the logical OR rule, under the assumption of statistical independence (Oxley and Bauer, 2002).

PNN FUSION

The PNN Fusion method treats the posterior probabilities from the individual classifiers as features to a PNN and outputs an overall posterior probability of an exemplar being in a given class. PNN Fusion does not impose any independence assumptions on the classifiers.

ONE BIG NETWORK FUSION

The One Big Network model eliminates the individual classifiers and takes all features as inputs to a generalized regression neural network. OBN Fusion does not make any independence assumptions about the features.

CORRELATION

Multiple feature sets, each containing multiple features, are generated for experimentation. The first type of correlation considered is inter-correlation or the correlation between features in a given data set. The second type of correlation considered is intra-correlation or autocorrelation which is the correlation between observations in a single feature.

TWO PROBLEMS

In this paper we present two of a dozen such problem investigated in Leap (2004) and Clemans (2004). First, two classifiers are fused using four different fusion methods with a high sample size in the presence of both inter-correlation and autocorrelation. In the second problem, three classifiers are fused using three different fusion methods with low sample sizes in the presence of inter-correlation. Here the objective is to formulate and solve a mathematical programming problem to find the optimal fused classifier ensemble.

The first problem can be described as a TWO CLASSIFIER 8 FEATURE XOR AUTOCORRELATION situation. The specifics of this problem are given in Leap (2004). The  icon is associated with this problem in the results section. The second problem can be described as a THREE CLASSIFIER 6 FEATURE DOMINO NO AUTOCORRELATION situation. The specifics of this problem are given in Clemans (2004). The  icon is associated with this problem in the results section.

EXPERIMENTAL DESIGN

Three data sets are generated for each level of correlation $\rho \in \{0.0, 0.2, 0.4, 0.6, 0.8, 0.9\}$. The first data set is used to train the individual classifiers. Once the individual classifiers are trained, the second data set is used to validate the individual classifiers. Posterior probabilities are calculated from the second and third data sets for later use. In addition to being validation data for the individual classifiers, the second data set posterior probabilities are used to train the fusion methods. The posterior probabilities from the third data set are used to validate the fusion methods. All of the plots generated are results from the third data set.

THREE CLASSIFIER OPTIMAL ENSEMBLE / FUSION TECHNIQUE COMBINATION

The expected true positive classification rates are calculated for all ensemble / fusion technique combinations at the 0.1 false positive level. Two discrete prior distributions of the level of correlation, x = {0, 0.2, 0.4, 0.6, 0.8, 0.9} are studied:

$$\text{Uniform: } p(x) = \{0.167, 0.167, 0.167, 0.167, 0.167, 0.167\}$$

$$\text{Increasing: } p(x) = \{0.05, 0.09, 0.14, 0.19, 0.25, 0.28\}$$

The ensemble / fusion technique combination yielding the highest classification rate according to the optimality criterion of maximum expected true positive classification rate is then determined to be the best. A mathematical programming formulation of this situation is:

$$\underset{S \in R}{\text{ArgMax}} \; E_\rho(TP \mid S)$$

s.t.

$$FP(S) \leq 0.1$$

where

$$E_\rho(TP) = \sum_{i=1}^{6} (TP \mid \rho = x_i) * P(\rho = x_i)$$

Here R represents the set of all possible single classifier and classifier fusion ensembles. Note that ISOC, ROC, and PNN fusion techniques are applied to all classifier ensembles with 2 or more classifiers (can not fuse a single classifier).

CONCLUSIONS

TWO CLASSIFIER 8 FEATURE XOR AUTOCORRELATION CASE

Figure 1 shows four plots, one for each of the four fusion methods. They are the values of true positive for a false positive value of 0.1 on the averaged ROC curves (over five replications) with 1000 exemplars in each class. The true positive value is plotted against the level of inter-correlation. Each plot contains three lines, one for each of the three levels of autocorrelation.

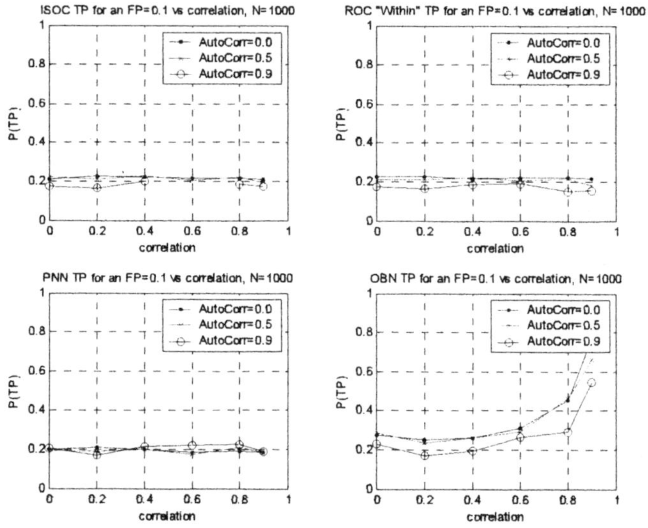

Figure 1: 8 feature XOR with autocorrelation case, N=1000.

In this problem the ISOC Fusion and ROC "Within" are very robust to correlation. Also, as autocorrelation increases from 0.0 to 0.5, there is no degradation in performance for the ISOC and ROC "Within." As the autocorrelation increases from 0.5 to 0.9, there is a drop in performance across all levels of correlation, but it is a small decrease for both ISOC and ROC "Within." The PNN seems to be robust to both types of correlation. The OBN seems to be affected by both types of correlation, but it always performs as well or better than the other three methods at all combinations of the two types of correlation. As with the first two methods, it seems there is little difference between an autocorrelation of 0.0 and 0.5, but there is a difference between an autocorrelation of 0.5 and 0.9. Also, there is an interesting pattern in performance for the OBN across levels of correlation for a given level of autocorrelation. The performance seems to decrease slightly at a correlation level of 0.2, but it increases as the geometry changes with the higher levels of correlation. The OBN continues to outperform the other methods, especially as the correlation level increases, in this type of problem; this can be explained through a geometric interpretation of the problem (see Leap (2004)).

THREE CLASSIFIER 6 FEATURE DOMINO NO AUTOCORRELATION

This experiment represents a case where two classifiers perform poorly and one classifier performs well. The only unusual finding is that the three-classifier PNN ensemble classification performance improves as the correlation increases (see Clemans (2004)).

The expected true positive classification rates, shown in Figure 2, show a variety of results across the ensembles. As expected, linear / quadratic fusion ensembles perform poorly. The ISOC ensembles which include the radial basis function classifier ignore the linear and quadratic classifiers. However, the three-classifier ISOC ensemble does not ignore the linear and quadratic classifiers. This is due to the fact that the radial basis function classifier performs poorly at points mid-way between sub-population centroids. The linear and quadratic classifiers perform relatively well at these points and they are included in the optimal ISOC rule. Unfortunately, the two classifiers perform poorly overall and the overall classification accuracy decreases. The ROC ensembles perform as expected. The fusion of poor classifiers with a good classifier causes the classification accuracy to decrease. When two poor classifiers are used, the classification accuracy drops even more.

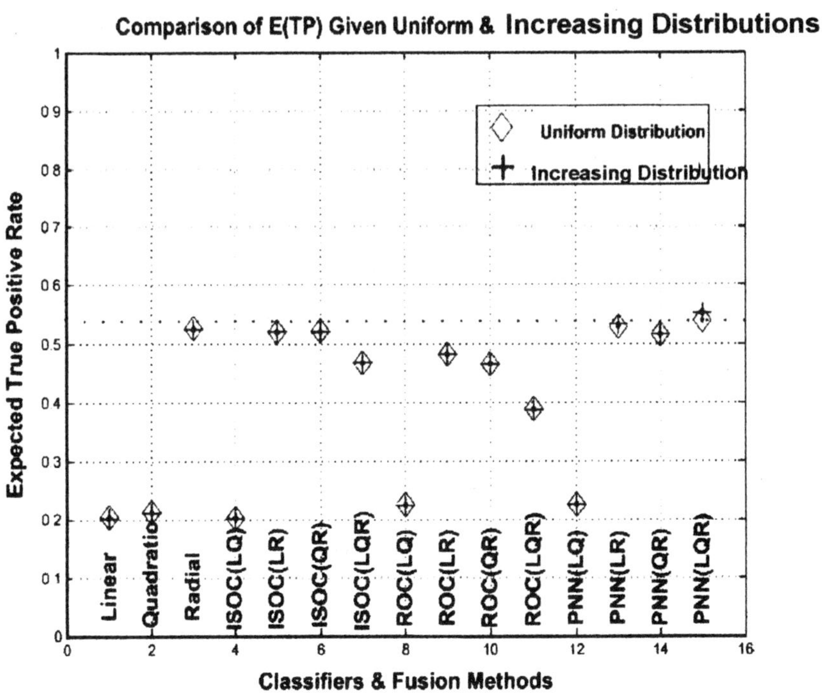

Figure 2: "Domino" Gaussian Expected True Positive Classification Rates

Finally, the PNN ensembles appear to overcome the poor classifiers' performance. This can be attributed to the classifiers making different types of errors in the regions mid-way between sub-population centroids. The PNN ensemble can adjust for these errors using the training data while the other methods can not.

CONCLUSIONS

Several conclusions can be drawn from the findings and analysis. In the two classifier problem, ISOC, ROC Within, and PNN are robust to correlation. Also, the OBN outperforms the other three methods at all levels of inter-correlation which is evidence that eliminating the individual classifiers is the better fusion technique. In the three classifier problem, the PNN is no longer robust to inter-correlation. PNN ensembles consistently outperformed the other fusion methods. Also, ROC "Within" fusion always performs no worse than the worst classifier. In these experiments, fusion does not yield large increases in classification accuracy above the single best classifier. It is useful because it mitigates the effects of poor classifiers. When a good classifier and a poor classifier are fused by any of methods studied here, the resulting classification accuracy is generally closer to the better classifier. Finally, in all problems that are investigated, the neural fusion methods, either PNN or OBN, outperform those methods that fuse based on Boolean rules.

REFERENCES

Clemans, Paul P, "An Investigation of the Optimal Sensor Ensemble For Sensor Fusion." Master's Thesis, Air Force Institute of Technology, Wright-Patterson AFB, OH, March 2004.

Duin, R.P.W. and Tax, D.M.J., "Experiments with combining Classifier Rules", Multiple Classifier Systems: *Proceedings of the First International Workshop*, MCS 2000, Cagliari, Italy, June 2000.

Hashem, S., Optimal Linear Combinations of Neural Networks. PhD thesis, School of Industrial Engineering, Purdue University, December 1993.

Haspert, J.K., "Optimum ID Sensor Fusion for Multiple Target Types." *IDA Document D2451*, 2000.

Laine, Trevor, "Relevant Background for the Research of Sensor Fusion as Applied to Automatic Target Detection/Recognition (ATD/R) in an Environment with Correlated Input Data." *Advanced Applications for ANNs Special Study*, 2003.

Leap, Nathan J, "An Investigation of the Effects of Correlation, Autocorrelation, and Sample Size in Classifier Fusion." Master's Thesis, Air Force Institute of Technology, Wright-Patterson AFB, OH, March 2004.

Oxley, M.E., and K. Bauer, "Classifier Fusion for Improved System Performance." *AFIT/ENS Working Document 02-02*, 2002.

Storm, Susan A. , Kenneth W. Bauer, Jr. and Mark E. Oxley "An Investigation of the Effects of Correlation in Classifier Fusion", Proceedings of the Artificial Neural networks in Engineering

AMERICAN SIGN LANGUAGE WORD RECOGNITION WITH A SENSORY GLOVE USING ARTIFICIAL NEURAL NETWORKS

CEMIL OZ, NEELESH N. SARAWATE ,and MING. C. LEU
Department of Mechanical and Aerospace Engineering,
University of Missouri-Rolla, Rolla, MO 65409

ABSTRACT
An American Sign Language (ASL) recognition system is being developed using artificial neural networks (ANN) to translate the ASL words into English. The system uses a sensory glove Cyberglove™ and a Flock of Birds® 3-D motion tracker to extract the gesture features. The finger joint angle data obtained from strain gages in the sensory glove defines the handshape while the data from the tracker describes the trajectory of hand movement. The data from these devices is processed by two neural networks, a velocity network and a word recognition network. Our goal is to continuously recognize ASL gestures using these devices in real time. We trained and tested our ANN model for 50 ASL words for different number of samples. Our test results show that the accuracy of recognition is 94 %.

1. INTRODUCTION

There are about two million deaf people in the United States. Some of them are born with hearing loss in both ears, while the others lose their hearing due to factors such as rubella, meningitis, and prolonged bouts of high fever. According to the National Center of Birth Defects and Developmental Disabilities, about one child out of every thousand is born deaf [1]. It is often very difficult for deaf people to interact with people outside the deaf community.

American Sign Language (ASL) is the main mode of communication for most deaf people in the United States. However, most people outside the deaf community do not understand ASL. If ASL can be translated automatically into English text and speech, it will be much easier for the deaf people to communicate with others. There are about 6000 signs in ASL to represent words, which consist of complex body movements. The signs are created by using the right hand, the left hand or both hands. Some signs also involve facial expressions.

Many researchers have studied ASL recognition and gesture recognition, but there are major difficulties due to the complexity of hand and body movements in ASL expressions. ASL recognition research can be categorized into three major classes: (i) computer vision based, (ii) data glove and motion sensor based, and (iii) a combination of these two methods. Computer vision based ASL recognition relies on image processing and feature extraction techniques for capturing and classifying body movement and handshape when a deaf person makes an ASL sign. On the other hand, data glove and motion tracker based ASL recognition methods use a special data glove and a motion tracker for detecting handshape and movement. The third method includes a combination of techniques from each of these two methods.

In parallel to the advancement in sensor and computer technology, some successful computer vision based ASL recognition systems have been developed [2,3,4,5,6,7,8,9].

There are also many studies in the area of glove and motion sensor based ASL recognition [10,11,12]. These studies are generally based on Artificial Neural Networks (ANN) [2,10,12,13], Hidden Markov Model (HMM) [3,4,6,7,9], and statistical methods [5,8]. Some recently published papers include the use of both methods, which are used together for ASL recognition [13].

In this paper, we present the design of an ASL word recognition system using ANN. The neural network for the word recognition is triggered using a velocity neural network. If the response of the velocity network is positive, then the data from the Cyberglove™ and Flock of Birds® is stored for every time cycle until the response of the velocity network becomes negative. We do not use all of this data for actual word recognition, but we choose the data at six time instants. The system is able to recognize a vocabulary of 50 ASL words successfully.

2. HARDWARE OF SYSTEM

Our primary physical connection to the world is through hands. We perform most of the everyday tasks with them, however we use constrained peripheral devices such as mouse, keyboard and joystick to work with a computer and computer controlled applications. Glove based input devices were designed to overcome this limitation [14]. The commercial devices, such as the VPL data glove and Mattel power glove, have led to an explosion of research and development projects using electronic glove interfaces to computer applications and computer controlled devices. These applications are virtual reality, video games, scientific visualization, puppetry, and gesture based control.

We use a right-hand Cyberglove™ (Figure 1) to retrieve the finger joint angle values for gesture features. The glove has 18 sensors which measure the bending angles at various positions and the frequency of data collection is up to 150 Hz. We have used 15 sensors of the glove; three sensors for the thumb, two sensors for each of the other four fingers, and four sensors between the fingers.

To track the position and orientation of the hand in 3-D space, the Flock of Birds® motion tracker (Figure 2) mounted on the hand wrist is used. The receiver is located in a DC pulsed magnetic field and its effective range is up to 8 feet around the transmitter. The measuring frequency is up to 144 Hz.

Open Inventor SDK (Software Development Kit) is used in the software development for the 3-D scene rendering and interactive programming. It is a high-level tool kit developed in OpenGL for graphic rendering and user interactions. We use the Microsoft® Speech SDK for the programming of speech synthesis.

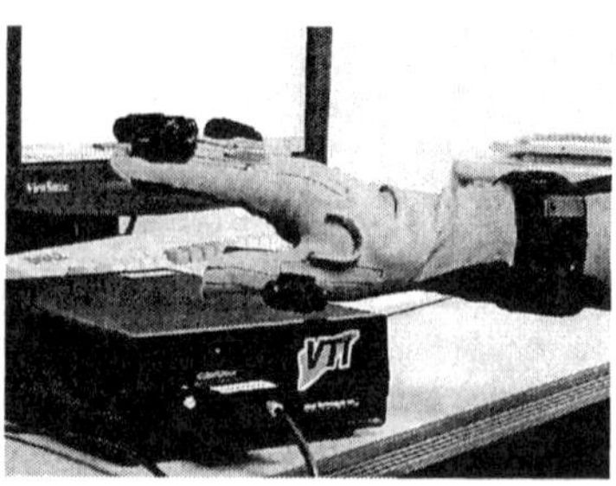

Figure1. Cyberglove™ with 18 sensors

Figure 2. Flock of birds® 3-D motion tracker

3. DATA COLLECTION FOR WORD RECOGNITION

Commonly used English words are represented by signs in ASL [15]. The signs are expressed by hand movement over a period of time. The data collected from the

Cyberglove^{TM} and Flock of Birds® acts as an input to the word recognition network. A velocity network is designed which classifies the hand movement at any time instant as 'moving' (1) or 'stopped' (0).

Figure 3 shows an example of the hand velocity profile during a typical signing movement. During the signing movement, the hand velocity can rise or drop momentarily due to momentary shaking and stopping of the hand. Hence, the use of a threshold value of velocity does not give a good solution for classification of hand movement. The ideal output for the shown velocity graph should be 1 from the time the first sudden change in velocity is seen till the time the velocity graph shows a series of low velocities. Thus, the velocity output should be calculated considering not only the instantaneous velocity value but also the history of previous velocities. Hence, after numerous trials, the input to the velocity neural network was selected as the 'summation of velocities during the previous five time instants'.

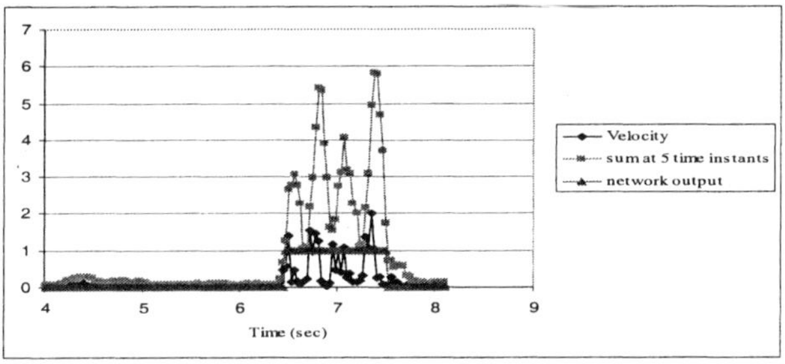

Figure 3. Velocity network performance for sign *BELL*

The two-stage velocity network has one input neuron, five hidden layer neurons, and two output neurons. The target vectors were manually created by studying the velocity graphs for different, randomly selected signs. Twenty training samples of different signs were sufficient to achieve the desired accuracy. The network was trained using the Levenberg-Marquardt algorithm. A hyperbolic tangent sigmoid function was used in both layers. The output of the network lies in the range of [-1, 1] which is converted to 0 or 1. The network continuously calculates the output using the stored data for the past five time instants, which gets updated at 33.33 Hz. Figure 3 shows the performance of the network for the sign *BELL*. As we can see, the network produces a continuous output of '1' during the actual signing period.

If the output of velocity network is 1, the 15 data elements from glove and 6 data elements from motion tracker are recorded in an array. This data is collected at a frequency of 33.33 Hz. No data is recorded if the output of the velocity network is zero. When the velocity network output changes from 1 to 0, the data recording for the given sign is completed, and the sign recognition phase starts. The data at six equally divided time instants is chosen from the recorded data, giving a total of 126 data elements. This creates a simple model, yet we have enough information. In our study, the signing time varied between 0.15-1.5 second. A virtual hand model in VRML displayed on the computer screen is updated at 33.33 Hz using the data gathered from the glove and motion tracker.

4. ARTIFICIAL NEURAL NETWORK MODEL

A backpropagation algorithm is used for training the ANN model. The basic structure and formulation of backpropagation is summarized here. Training a neural network involves computing weights so as to get an output response to the input within an error limit. The input and target vectors make up a training pair. The backpropagation algorithm includes the following steps [16]:

1- Select the first training pair and apply the input vector to the net.
2- Calculate the net output.
3- Compare the actual output with the corresponding target and find the error.
4- Modify the weights so as to reduce the error.

These steps are repeated until the error is within the accepted limits. In the step 2, output sets for test inputs are calculated. If they are the same within an error range as the expected sets, then it is considered as the net has learnt the problem, and the final weights are stored so that they can be reused when needed[17,18].

5. DESIGN OF ASL WORD RECOGNITION SYSTEM

Two of the ASL words used in the training set for the ANN are given in Table 1.

Table 1. Two words in American Sign Language [15]

ASL words	Definition
 Apple	(A chewing of the letter "A", for apple). The right "A" hand is held at the right cheek, with the thumb tip touching the cheek and palm facing out. In this position, the hand is swung over and back from the wrist several times, using the thumb as a pivot.
 Are	The right hand "R" position, palm facing left, is held at the lips, and the hand moves straight out and away from the lips.

A two-layer ANN is designed to recognize 50 words in ASL. The input to the network is the 126 data elements at six time instants recorded by the data collection algorithm. The proposed ANN, a multi-layer feedforward network, consists of 126 input neurons, 70 hidden neurons, and 50 output neurons and it is designed to recognize the isolated words in ASL. A Levenberg-Marquardt backpropagation algorithm is used for training. The ANN is trained and tested for two different data sets, single-user data and multi-user data. The output vector consists of 50 elements, the maximum of which corresponds to a word or sign.

The design of the recognition system is shown in figure 5. It consists of three parts: collection and selection of input data, trained network, and output decoding.

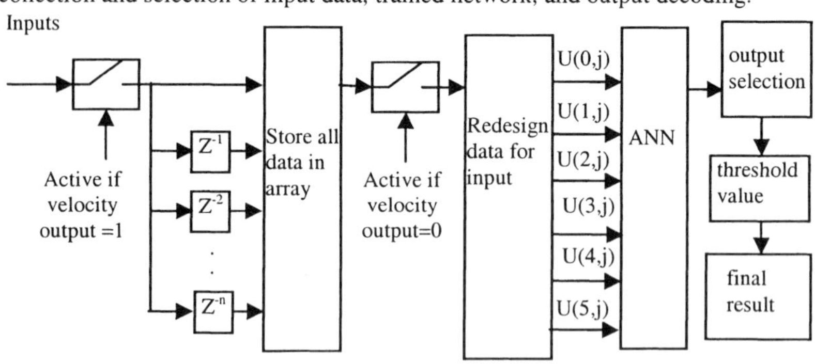

Figure 5. Block diagram of ASL word recognition system

The velocity network triggers the data recording function. The data gets recorded until the velocity network output becomes zero. As explained earlier, the data at six time instants is selected by the second box in Figure 5. U(i ,j) represents the filetered input, where i varies from 0 to5 corresponding to selected time instants and j varies from 1 to 21 corresponding to 21 inputs. This data of 126 elements is an input to the ANN. The two-layer word recognition network has 126 inputs, 70 hidden neurons and 50 output neurons. In the final part, the output selection block determines the maximum output of ANN, and then the threshold block checks if the maximum output value is acceptable or not. If it is acceptable, the corresponding index of the output vector is the recognized word. If it is not acceptable, the recognized word is considered to be out of the known ASL vocabulary. The recognized word is displayed on the screen using Open Inventor interface. Two of the ASL words recognized by our system are shown in Figure 6.

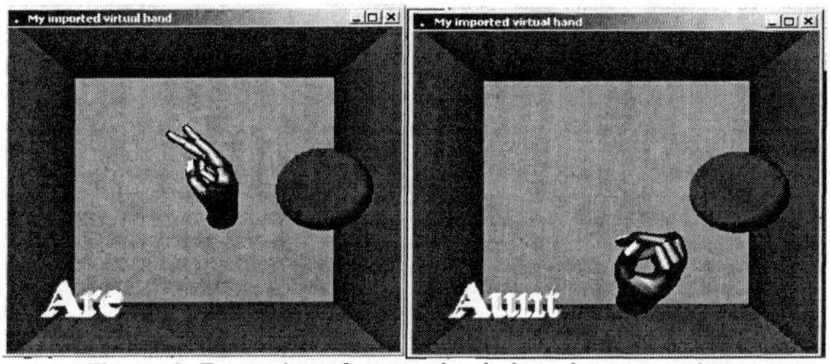

Figure 6. Examples of recognized signs by our system

6. TEST RESULTS

We tested the model with six data samples from single and multiple users i.e. we tested the network with 300 unknown words. In first case, the network missed 10 words and misrecognized 14. In second case, the network missed 13 words and misrecognized 12. Table 2 summarizes the test results.

Table 2. ANN model test results

	ANN trained by a single user	ANN trained by multiple users
Total test data	300 (6*50)	300 (6*50)
Missed	10	13
Misrecognized	14	12
Recognized	276	275

7. CONCLUSION

A real-time ASL word recognition system using a sensory glove based on ANN is presented. The system was trained and tested for single and multiple users for a vocabulary of 50 ASL words. Test results have shown that the proposed technique is capable of recognition in real time and the recognition accuracy of the system is 94 %. The finger bending angles vary from 0 to 256, the position data from the motion tracker changes from -88 cm to 88 cm, and the orientation data changes from $-\pi$ to π. Since all the data is normalized in the same scale, the effect of hand position and orientation is reduced. Also, out of 21 inputs, 15 inputs are from the glove and six from the motion tracker. Thus, the data from the glove is dominant in the total input data. Hence, the network accuracy is affected by the words which have similar hand positions but vary slightly in their position and orientation. For example, "around" and "always" have same overall action, but the Y position is slightly different. A better scaling system can overcome this problem. Some gestures in ASL use both hands. This problem can be overcome by using two datagloves and motion trackers, and applying the proposed model for recognition.

ACKNOWLEDGMENTS

This research is partially supported by a National Science Foundation award (DMI-0079404) and a Ford Foundation grant, as well as by the Intelligent Systems Center at the University of Missouri–Rolla

REFERENCES

[1] National Center of Birth defects and Developmental Disabilities home page, http://www.cdc.gov/ncbddd/bd/bdres.htm

[2] S. G. Wysoski, M. V. Lamar, S. Kuroyanagi, and A. Iwata, "A Rotation Invariant Approach on Static Gesture Recognition using Boundary Histograms and Neural networks", Proceeding of the 9th International conference on neural information processing (ICONIP'02), vol. 4, 2002, pp. 2137-2141.

[3] C. Vogler, and D. Metaxas, "ASL Recognition Based on a Coupling Between HMMs and 3D Motion Analysis", proceedings of sixth IEEE International Computer Vision Conference, January 1998, pp.363-369.

[4] G. Lalit, and M Suei, "Gesture-Based Interaction and Communication: Automated Classification of Hand Gesture Contours", IEEE Transactions on Systems, Man, and Cybernetics part c: Application and Reviews, vol. 31, no. 1, February 2001, pp. 114-120.

[5] M. H. Yang, and N. Ahuja, "Recognizing Hand Gestures using Motion Trajectories", IEEE, 1999, pp. 466-472.

[6] T. Stanner, and A. Pentland, "Real-Time American Sign Language Recognition from Video using Hidden Markov Models", Computer Vision International Symposium Proceeding, 1995, pp. 265-270.

[7] C. Vogler, and D. Metaxas, "Adapting Hidden Markov Models for ASL Recognition by using Three-Dimensional Computer Vision Methods", Proceeding of the IEEE International Conference on Systems, Man and Cybernetics, Orlando, 1997, pp.12-15.

[8] Y. Cui, and J. Weng, "A Learning-Based Prediction and Verification Segmentation Scheme for Hand Sign Image Sequence", IEEE transactions on Pattern Analysis and Machine Intelligence, vol. 21, no.8, August 1999, pp. 798-804.

[9] C. Vogler, and D. Metaxas, "Parallel Hidden Markov Models for American Sign Language Recognition", IEEE proceeding of International Computer Vision Conference, September 1999, pp. 116-122.

[10] M J. Allen, P. K. Asselin, and Richard Foulds, "American Sign Language Finger Spelling Recognition System", 29th Bioengineering Conference proceeding, IEEE, 2003, pp. 22-23.

[11] R. M. De Marco, and R. A. Foulds, "Data Recording and Analysis of American Sign Language", IEEE 29th proceeding of Bioengineering Conference, 2003, pp. 49-50.

[12] H. G. Wang, N. N. Sarawate, and M. C. Leu, "Recognition of American Sign Language Gestures with a Sensory Glove", Japan USA Symposium on Flexible Automation, Denver, CO, July 2004.

[13] L. K. Lee, S. Kim, and Y. K. Choi, M. H. Lee, "Recognition of Hand Gesture to Human-Computer Interaction", IEEE, 2000, pp. 2177-2122.

[14] D. J. Sturman, and D. Zelter, "A Survey of Glove-based Input", IEEE Computer and Applications, 1994, pp.30-39.

[15] M. L. A. Sternberg, "American Sign Language Dictionary (Revised Edition)", 1994, Harper Perennial, ISBN: 0-06-273275-7.

[16] R. P. Lippman, "An Introduction to Computing with Neural Nets", IEEE ASSP, 1987, pp.2-22.

[17] N. Abulafya, "Neural Networks for system Identification and Control", MSc Thesis, University of London, 1995.

[18] K. S. Narendra, "Adaptive Control Using Neural Networks", in Neural Networks for Control (W.T. Miller, R.S. Sutton, and P.J. Werbos, edds) 3 rd printing, 1992, MIT.

GENERALIZATION OF SUPPORT VECTOR MACHINES VERSUS NEURAL NETWORKS FOR PATTERN RECOGNITION

STEPHEN A. ZAHORIAN
Department of Electrical and
Computer Engineering
Old Dominion University
Norfolk, VA

MAME SALL
Department of Electrical and
Computer Engineering
Old Dominion University
Norfolk, VA

FANSHENG MENG
Department of Electrical and
Computer Engineering
Old Dominion University
Norfolk, VA

WEI WANG
Department of Electrical and
Computer Engineering
Old Dominion University
Norfolk, VA

ABSTRACT

One of the most fundamental issues in non-parametric statistical pattern recognition is the degree to which classifiers generalize from training data from which classifier parameters are learned to test data which has not been used in the training process. If multivariate probability density functions are known and are the same for both training and test data, it may be possible to determine the "optimum" classifier in terms of generalization. For the case of unknown density functions, a non-parametric classifier such as a multi-layer neural network may classify training data very well but may not generalize well to test data. One non-parametric classifier that is claimed to generalize well from training to test data is the support vector machine (SVM). In this paper, we compare neural networks (NNs) and SVMs both theoretically and experimentally from the point of view of generalization. For the examples investigated, no evidence is found to indicate better generalization for SVMs as compared to NNs.

INTRODUCTION

The most straightforward ways to improve generalization for NNs are to either decrease the size (total number of weights) of the networks or to increase the amount of training data. From our own past work (Zahorian, et al., 1998) with vowel classification for a speech training aid for the hearing impaired, the generalizability issue is illustrated with real data in Figure 1. In particular, the training and test classification accuracies are plotted as a function of training database size, for various size neural networks, for a fixed test database. In general, as the size of the training database increases, the accuracy of the classification of the training data decreases, whereas the accuracy of the classification of the test data (which ultimately is the only accuracy of importance) increases. With sufficient training data, the accuracy of classification for the test data matches that of the training data, implying good generalization. The amount of training data needed for the training and test data curves to match generally increases as the size of the neural network increases, but the performance level also increases with a larger network.

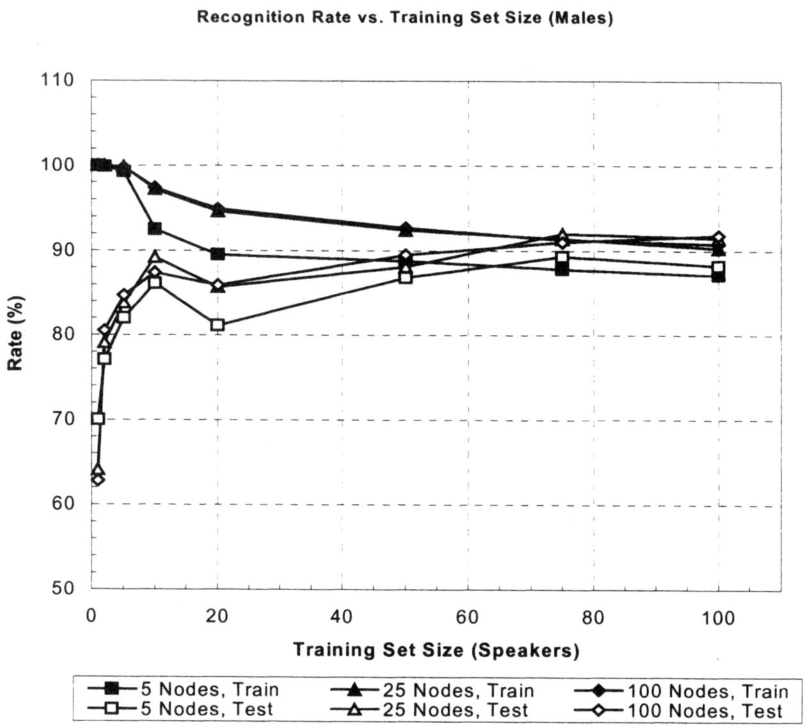

Figure 1. Recognition rates vs. training set size for neural networks with 5, 25 and 100 nodes in hidden the layer (male speakers)

Generalization based on larger database sizes or smaller networks are unsatisfactory for several reasons. Often it is not feasible or perhaps even possible to obtain sufficient training data for good generalization. The amount of training data needed increases exponentially with the complexity of the task (for example, a complete automatic speech recognition system versus a vowel classification system) and the number of features. The "curse of dimensionality" (Duda and Hart, 2001) is the well known effect that relates to classifier performance as the number of features is increased in the attempt to handle more complex tasks. The other method for improving generalization, reducing classifier size, is also not an appealing solution, since this generalization is usually obtained by decreasing performance on training data rather than improving performance on test data.
A more theoretical treatment of generalization is referred to as Bayesian regularization (Haykin, 1999). The essence of the idea is to that the "optimum" classifier is based on the minimization of an expression that involves one term based on empirical data (i.e., the training data) and another term which incorporates known constraints about the form of the solution. These two terms are weighted depending on the amount of training data available, and the known constraints on the solution. In practice, for the case of pattern recognition in high-dimensionality spaces, very little is generally known about the form

of the constraints on the solution. An implementation of Bayesian Regularization for the case of neural networks is given in Foresee and Hagan (1997).

Support Vector Machines (SVMs) are another non-parametric technique for pattern classification, and have been claimed to have superior generalization properties to neural networks. The basic idea of an SVM for pattern classification is to determine a classifier, which minimizes the empirical risk (that is, the training set error) and the confidence interval (which corresponds to the generalization or test set error). In the last few years, a significant amount of pattern recognition research has been performed with SVMs. Some of this research is summarized in *Proceedings of the First International Conference on Knowledge Discovery and Data Mining*, Menlo Park, CA, by Vapnik and Burges.

In the present paper, SVMs are compared with feedforward perceptron-like neural networks for pattern classification of both simulated and speech data. The simulated data consists of multivariate multi-mixture Gaussian data. The speech data consists of cepstral-like features used for automatic speaker recognition. In most of the evaluations, two-way classifiers were trained on one set of data and then evaluated on both the training data and on separate test data. Even with large speech data sets, it is possible to obtain 100% accuracy on training data with SVMs. However, test results obtained with SVM methods are typically about the same as those obtained with neural networks. Thus, at least in tests conducted to date, no evidence has been found for superior generalization of SVMs versus neural network classifiers.

SUPPORT VECTOR MACHINE

The support vector method is a recently developed technique, which is designed for efficient multidimensional function approximation. It has been introduced within the context of statistical learning theory and structural risk minimization. The SVM is a supervised machine learning approach. For pattern recognition problems, all the samples are tagged with +1 or -1 when training the SVM classification model. The objective of SVM is to predict the future test example, and to classify it into either the positive or negative group based on the sample knowledge.

In SVMs, the idea is to fix the empirical risk associated with architecture and then to use a method to minimize the generalization error. The primary advantage of SVMs as adaptive models for binary classification is that they provide a classifier with minimal VC (*Vapnik-Chervonenkis*) dimension, which implies low expected probability of generalization errors. SVMs can be used to classify linearly separable data and nonlinearly separable data. For the case where the training data is linearly separable, the objective of the SVM is to find an optimal hyperplane which separates the data without error and such that the distance between the hyperplane and the closest training points is maximal. For the nonlinearly separable case, SVMs can map thc input space to a high dimensional feature space. In this high dimensional feature space, linear classification can be performed.

In the high dimension space, it is not necessary to use the explicit input data to form the classifier. Instead, all that is needed is to use this inner product between the support vectors and the vectors of the feature space. Hence, by defining the kernel $K(\mathbf{s}_i, \mathbf{x}) = \mathbf{s}_i^T\mathbf{x}$, a nonlinear classifier can be obtained as:

$$f(x) = \mathrm{sgn}\left(\sum_{i=1}^{Ns} \alpha_i y_i \Phi(\mathbf{s}_i)\cdot\Phi(\mathbf{x}) + b\right) = \mathrm{sgn}\left(\sum_{i=1}^{Ns} \alpha_i y_i K(\mathbf{s}_i, \mathbf{x}) + b\right) \quad (1)$$

where the $\mathbf{s}_i$ are the support vectors, α_i' are Lagrange multipliers, Ns is number of support vectors and b is a real number.

EXPERIMENTAL EVALUATION

Two types of evaluations were conducted to compare the generalizations between NN classifiers and SVM classifiers. In one of these two class 2-D two-mixture Gaussian data was generated with a random number generator (from Matlab), and both SVM and NN were trained on one set of data, and evaluated on another set of data. For the second evaluation, classifiers were used to discriminate pairs of speakers from acoustic data.

Gaussian Mixture Separation

For these tests, samples were drawn from two Gaussian mixture populations. The populations were created to give reasonably good separation, but with some overlap between the two classes. NN and SVM classifiers were trained with 200 samples drawn from each population, and then tested with 800 independently drawn samples from each population. Results are depicted in figures 2 and 3, which depict cluster plots of the training data, and show decision boundaries for both the NN and SVM classifiers. For Figure 2, the SVM uses a polynomial function as the kernel set equal to 3. The NN has 1 hidden layer, with sigmoid nonlinearities, with 8 hidden nodes. For Figure 3, the kernel of the SVM uses the radial bases function set to 0.5, and the NN is the same type as for Figure 2, except the number of hidden nodes has been increased to 25.

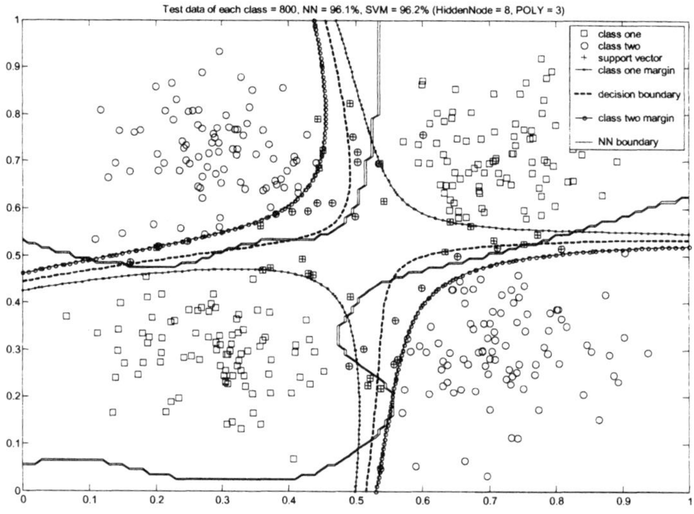

Figure 2. The decision boundaries of two classifiers. The kernel is selected with a level 3 polynomial function. The NN uses 1 hidden layer with 8 nodes.

For Figure 2, the decision boundaries obtained with the SVM and NN are nearly the same, and the test classification accuracy is also approximately the same for both classifiers (SVM = 96.1%, NN = 96.2%).

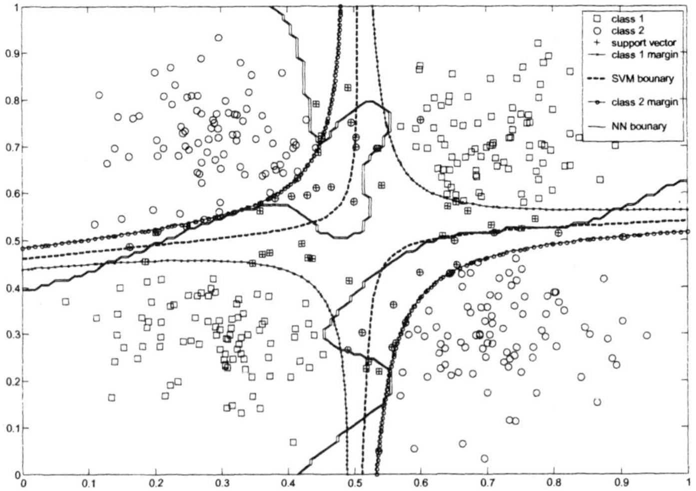

Figure 3. The decision boundaries of two classifiers. The kernel is selected with radial basis function with σ = 0.5. The NN uses 1 hidden layer with 25 nodes.

For Figure 3, the SVM boundaries are very similar to those obtained with other type of SVM used for Figure 2, but the NN boundaries are not very smooth, thus indicating "over fitting" of the large NN. Test classification results for the SVM are also somewhat higher for the SVM versus the NN, thus indicating somewhat better generalization. (SVM = 97.6%, NN = 95.2%) However, it should be noted that the NN boundaries were deliberately made too complex to indicate the potential for generalization problems; a smaller NN would have resulted in nearly identical boundaries as those obtained with the SVM, and thus similar generalization.

Automatic Speaker Identification

An example of a "real" pattern classification task is the automatic identification of a speaker using a sample of the speaker's voice. In our past work in this area, we have used a binary partitioned approach (BPP) (Mishra,2003), whereby N * (N-1) /2 elementary classifiers are trained to discriminate each pair of speakers in a population of N speakers. The outputs of the elementary classifiers can then be used to make N-way decisions about speaker identity. Any type of classifier can be used for each of the elementary classifiers, including NNs or SVMs.

In this paper, we summarize some sample results which illustrate the generalization of NNs and SVMs for speaker identification. In particular we looked at the performance of NNs and SVMs for the two-way classifications for all the speaker pairs in a population of 10 speakers (or 45 two-way classifiers total). For the experiments, 10 speakers from the TIMIT database were used, with each speaker producing 10 sentences. For the sample experiments, 6 sentences were used for training, and 4 sentences were used for testing. Features used were 29 Discrete Cosine Transform Coefficients (DCTCs) of the log magnitude spectrum computed for each frame. Typically, about 1800 feature vectors were used for training for each speaker, and about 1200 feature vectors were used for testing.

Two way neural network classifiers (29-25-2) were trained with backpropagation (400,000 network updates) for the case of NNs. Support Vector Machines with the Radial Basis Function kernel of radius $\sigma = 0.1$ were selected for the case of SVMs. This value of sigma was selected based since, after many runs; best test results were obtained with that value of σ. The neural network code was written in the speech lab at ODU, whereas the SVM experiments used a Matlab Toolbox developed by Gavin Cawley in November 2000. The toolbox implements Vapnik's Support Vector machine as described in (Vapnik,1995) and was first created to demonstrate the use of SVMs to distinguish between different species of iris. Both classifiers were trained for each of the 45 pairs of speakers. The training data results averaged 100% for all pairs for the SVMs while the neural network training results averaged approximately 95%. However, in both cases, the performance for test data was lower than for training data and nearly identical for the SVMs (81.68%) and for the NNs (80.85%).

Thus, these speaker identification tests do not indicate any significant differences in generalization between SVMS and NNs. Additionally, the configuration of the SVMs appeared to result in "memorization" of the training data (100% accuracy), and a very large number of weights in the classifier. Nevertheless, larger values of sigma for the SVM, which should have made the SVM boundaries smoother, resulted in lower test classification results.

CONCLUSIONS

The theory of support vector machine classifiers implies that SVM classifiers should have good generalization from training to test data. However, empirical testing comparing SVM and NN classifiers with two types of data did not indicate any significant advantage of SVMs in terms of generalization. Although SVMs do appear to form powerful classifiers, NNs appear to perform as well, and at a much lower computational burden both for training and evaluation.

REFERENCE

Burges C., 1998, "A Tutorial on Support Vector Machines for Pattern Recognition". Kluwer Academic Publishers.

Duda R., Hart P.& Stork D. 2001, "Pattern Classification (Second Edition)". A Wiley-Interscience Publication, John Wiley & Sons, Inc.

Foresee F. D., Hagan M.T, 1997: "Gauss-Newtonian Approximation to Bayesian Regularization" Proc. Inter. Joint Conf. Neural Networks, pp 1930-1935.

Haykin S., 1998, "Neural Networks: A Comprehensive Foundation (Second Edition)". Prentice Hall Press.

Mishra A., 2002, "Automatic Speaker Identification Using Reusable and Re-trainable Binary Partitioned Neural Networks", Master Thesis, Old Dominion University, Norfolk, VA.

Scholkopf B., 2001, "SVM and Kernel Methods." Tutorial given at the NIPS Conference.

Vapnik V.N., 1995, "The Nature of Statistical Learning Theory (Statistics for Engineering and Information Science)". Springer-Verlagm, New York.

Vapnik V.N., 1998, "Statistical Learning Theory (Second Edition)". A Wiley-Interscience Publication, John Wiley & Sons, Inc.

Zahorian, S. A., Zimmer, A. Dai, B. 1998 "Personal Computer Software Vowel Training Aid for the Hearing Impaired", International Conference on Acoustics, Speech, and Signal Processing, pp. VI-3625-3628.

PART VIII: CIVIL ENGINEERING

TRAFFIC PROFILING METHOD FOR SERVICE DEMAND ANALYSIS

KEN NISHIMATSU
NTT Service Integration Laboratories, Tokyo, JAPAN

AKIYA INOUE
NTT Service Integration Laboratories, Tokyo, JAPAN

TAKESHI KUROSAWA
NTT Service Integration Laboratories, Tokyo, JAPAN

ABSTRACT

This paper presents a traffic profiling method that enables us to understand service demand for various types of Internet services and telecommunications services. We have developed a scenario simulation framework for analyzing customer service choice behavior and service demand under assumed conditions. Our traffic profiling method is based on customer behavior models considering not only the decision process but also customer's character and preferences. Using survey data, we show an application example for Internet access line services.

1. INTRODUCTION

Internet service providers and telecommunication carriers have to plan investments in networks and systems considering customer needs and service demand. To determine service demand, service providers usually use measurement data such as traffic data. But these days, the telecommunications market is much more competitive, so they frequently change service specifications, such as service levels and prices, to get or keep customers. On the other hand, it is difficult for customers to know all of the service providers and all of their services. The decision-making factors and the decision process differ from customer to customer. Therefore, service choice is becoming a complicated and diversified process. Under these conditions, it is difficult to predict service demands on the basis of measurement data obtained in network management systems.

A new traffic profiling method is required to consider service choice behavior and usage patterns. We have developed a scenario simulation framework to analyze customer service choice behavior and service demand (Inoue et al., 2003a). This framework can be used to simulate scenarios under assumed conditions. It consists of customer behavior modeling, scenario simulation functions, and a learning process. We propose a new traffic profiling method based on customer behavior models considering not only the decision process but also customer characteristics and preferences. It is useful for various types of Internet and telecommunications services.

In this paper, we compare our method with related research. Next we explain the scenario simulation framework and traffic profiling method. Then, using survey data, we show an application example for Internet access line services. Finally we mention future studies and conclude this paper.

2. RELATED RESEARCH ABOUT SERVICE DEMAND ANALYSIS

In the telecommunication industry, service specifications such as charges and additional services change every month or week. If service providers had a methodology that could estimate demand for a service that had not yet begun and could evaluate the demand in an assumed scenario, it would be very useful in determining network and system investment planning. Conventional techniques such as time-series analysis are useful when market conditions are stationary, but there is no structure that can estimate the demands for unexpected situations. In a competitive environment, it is impossible to predict the service demand using aggregate data in which the past trend is shown. The real option method (Copeland and Antikarov, 2001) and scenario planning (Heijden, 1996) have been proposed as methods of evaluating a business model or strategy considering a future trend change. These ideas are very significant to risk management, and their viewpoint is similar to that of our method. However, their objectives are not to obtain a demand-forecasting result but to simulate scenarios under assumed conditions.

Furthermore, various services are offered on a carrier network. If a customer's purpose for using them changes, the traffic generating pattern will also change a lot. It is difficult to express a traffic generating pattern by a simple model as can be done for conventional telephone networks. We consider it is very important to understand the customer's behavior and to make a model of customers' service choice behaviors and usage patterns. Our method is useful for estimating the demand of an actual service or for a service that has not been put on the market yet and for simulating market share in an assumed scenario. We call this the framework for scenario simulation.

3. FRAMEWORK FOR SCENARIO SIMULATION

Figure 1 shows an overview of the framework for scenario simulation.

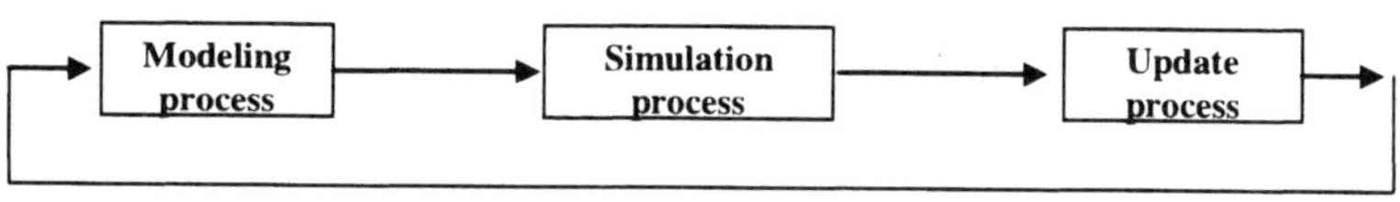

Figure 1: Framework for scenario simulation

(1) Modeling process for customer behavior

The attribute data about customer n is denoted by C_n. We define S_n as a subset of universal service set $S=\{1, 2, ..., j, ..., J\}$ defined for every customer. S_n includes all the selectable and known services on the basis of customer preferences and is expressed by

$$S_n = \{j \mid A_{jn} = 1 \ \wedge \ G(C_n, s_j)\}, \tag{1}$$

where $A_n = \{A_{1n}, A_{2n}, .., A_{jn}, .., A_{Jn}\}$ represents the environmental conditions, expressing limitations of the user's living environment and the area where service is offered. A_{in} equals 1 if alternative i is available to customer n; otherwise, it equals 0. The service specification of alternative j is denoted by s_j, where $s=\{s_1,..,s_J\}$. Function G is a *Boolean* function, which is true if customer n is aware of alternative j and is interested in it.

The choice result y_n is a vector defined as $y_n = \{ y_{jn} \mid j \in S_n \}$. Here, y_{jn} is a dummy variable that takes the value 1 if the alternative j is chosen by customer n from S_n and takes the value 0 otherwise. Then we make a customer behavior model that outputs probability $p_n(j)$ that customer n will choose alternative j, where p_n is a vector defined as $p_n = \{ p_n(j), \mid j \in S_n \}$. Discrete choice models

(Ben-Akiva and Lerman, 1987) (Inoue et al., 1990) are applied to determine the form of the customer behavior model.

$$p_n = F(s,\ S_n,\ C_n,\ y_n) \qquad (2)$$

Discrete Choice Theory

Each customer n $(=1 \ldots N)$ has a service choice set denoted by S_n. The utility U_{in} for customer n with respect to alternative i is defined. In random utility theory, U_{in} is a random variable composed of two parts:

$$U_{in} = V_{in} + \varepsilon_{in}. \qquad (3)$$

Here, V_{in} is called the systematic component of utility U_{in} and is assumed to be deterministic; ε_{in} is the random part and is called disturbance. The ε_{in} are independently and identically Gumbel distributed with a scale parameter μ, the probability that an alternative i in S_n chosen by customer n is given by:

$$\begin{aligned} p_n(i) &= p\ (U_{in} \geq U_{jn},\ \forall j \in S_n \wedge i \neq j) \\ &= p\ [V_{in} + \varepsilon_{in} \geq max\ (V_{jn} + \varepsilon_{jn}),\ j \in S_n] \\ &= \frac{e^{\mu V_{in}}}{\sum_{j \in S_n} e^{\mu V_{jn}}} \end{aligned} \qquad (4)$$

Generally, the positive scale parameter is normalized, so $\mu = 1$. $X_{in} = \{1, x_{in1}, x_{in2}, \ldots, x_{inK}\}$ are the variables that affect a user's selection and consist of customer attribute data or service specification attributes. V_{in} is usually expressed by a linear expression:

$$V_{in} = \beta X_{in} = \beta_0 + \beta_1 x_{in1} + \beta_2 x_{in2} + \ldots + \beta_K x_{inK}, \qquad (5)$$

where β_k $(k=1, 2, \cdots, K)$ is a coefficient denoting the weight for value x_{ink}, and β_0 is a constant related to the other attributes with the exception of x_{in1}, $x_{in2}, \ldots, x_{inK}$. These coefficients are estimated from a set of N samples. $\beta = \{\beta_0, \beta_1, \ldots, \beta_K\}$ is estimated by using maximum likelihood estimation.

(2) Simulation process

For a given scenario, the attribute of the service specifications s^* for which we want to evaluate demand and environment conditions A^*_n are defined $(s^* = \{s^*_1, s^*_2, \ldots, s^*_J\}$, $A^*_n = \{A^*_{1n}, A^*_{2n}, \ldots, A^*_{Jn}\})$. S^*_n is defined by Eq. (1). Service choice probabilities p^*_n for customer n are calculated by Eq. (6), and the choice results are aggregated to the total demands.

$$p^*_n = F(s^*,\ C_n,\ S^*_n,\ y_n). \qquad (6)$$

(3) Update process

Customer preferences and decision rules change frequently. In the update process, learning is important so that this process can respond to changes by analyzing a cause when an actual result differs greatly from a prediction. So scenario situations and the model parameters were evaluated and updated as the result of multiple simulation experiments. We have already proposed the concept of a learning mechanism to follow the changes. (Inoue et.al., 2003b)

3. TRAFFIC PROFILING METHOD FOR INTERNET ACCESS LINE SERVICES

A methodology of traffic profiling consists of two models: one for modeling service choice behaviors and the other for modeling usage patterns.
To simulate the traffic profiling using the framework, the following specifications have to be defined in the modeling process. There are five alternatives for Internet access line services (*IA*): dial-up (*DU*), *CATV*, *ADSL*, optical fiber (*OF*), and none. First, we explain the modeling of customer choice behavior for *IA*. This model can estimate *IA* market shares for an assumed scenario. Next, we describe the modeling of Internet usage time. This model is used to simulate changes in usage patterns, such as Internet usage time, if the *IA* market shares change in future.

Specifications of service choice behavior model

To simplify the problem, we assume that G is always true and $S_n = \{j \mid A_{jn} = 1\}$. The definition of F in Eq. (2) is transposed to the problem of defining a utility function for each alternative. The sensitivity to price or network speed changes depending on the customer's socioeconomic conditions, such as income, living environment, and experience level. Furthermore, the main decision-making factors differ for every customer. Therefore, we have to classify customers using not only socioeconomic conditions but also customer preferences. We developed the model in three stages, as shown below.

Model-1: Modeling using the service attribute variable of the alternatives

In this model, we assume that all of the customers have the same sensitivity to service attributes, such as price, network performance.

Model-2: Adding socioeconomic variables and experience level to Model-1

In order to classify users with different sensitivities to price and network speed, we add socioeconomic parameters (such as annual income) and also consider their level of experience in using broadband Internet or IP telephone (or Internet telephone) services.

Model-3: Adding customer preference variables to Model-2

We define five factors that customers consider when they choose a service from several alternatives: price, quality of service, optional services, customer-support, and compatibility with existing services (e.g., supporting existing email address). The weight of each factor is calculated by using AHP (Analytic Hierarchy Process) (Saaty, 1980) and the weight values are used to classify the customers into three segments: 1) those for whom price is the key factor in decision making, 2) those for whom quality of service is the key factor, and 3) others.

Specifications of usage pattern model

The target is to determine the distribution of usage patterns, such as usage time per day and the amount of traffic per unit time. Many factors affect the usage pattern. Using the information shown below, customers are classified and the distribution of usage pattern is measured for every classified group.

Internet access service: Usage patterns change with the fee structure and access speed.

Purpose of using the Internet: Traffic patterns generated by accessing web pages are different from those generated by streaming contents.

Customer characteristics: Usage patterns differ according to customer characteristics. For example, when they want information, some people search for it by themselves while others ask someone by telephone.

4. EVALUATION EXAMPLES

The evaluation results are shown in this section. We used market survey data. The number of samples N was 7590. Table 1 shows that adding customer attributes and preferences improved the accuracy of the customer choice behavior model. The main service attributes currently offered in the present market are shown in Table 2. Table 3 compares actual market shares of current services for the 7590 respondents with values estimated for four assumed scenarios. In scenario 1-1 *(SC1-1)*, the monthly charge for *OF* was set to 8000 yen and the other variables were set as in Table 2. The calculated share for *CATV* for *SC1-1* is significantly different from actual share. This is because *CATV* often bundles television, Internet access, and telephone services and the influence of this is not taken into account in the model. If it were, I think the model would agree well.

Scenario 1-2*(SC1-2)* is the same as *SC1-1*, except for the *OF* fee being 4000 yen. In scenario 2-1 *(SC2-1)*, $S_n=S$ is assumed in addition to the conditions of *SC1-1*. In scenario 2-2*(SC2-2)*, $S_n=S$ is assumed in addition to the conditions of *SC1-2*. The share of *OF* rapidly increased in *SC2-1* and *SC2-2*. This suggests that the share of *OF* will increase rapidly when customer interest in *OF* becomes high or when the service availability area

Table 1: Test results for model specifications

	Model-1	Model-2	Model-3
Number of coefficients	20	26	35
Null log likelihood: L(0)	-12215.6	-12215.6	-12215.6
Final log likelihood: L(*)	-7470.3	-7425.5	-7354.6
Likelihood ratio test	9490.7	9580.4	9722.1
Rho-squared (= 1- L(*) / L(0))	0.3885	0.3921	0.3979

Table 2: Values of service attribute parameters.

	Monthly charge (yen)	Setup cost (yen)	Upload speed (Mbps)	Download speed (Mbps)	IP telephone (available=1)
DU	2,500	0	0.056	0.056	0
ADSL	4,000	5,000	1	40	1
CATV	5,000	20,000	5	30	0
OF	4,000-10,000	20,000	100	100	1

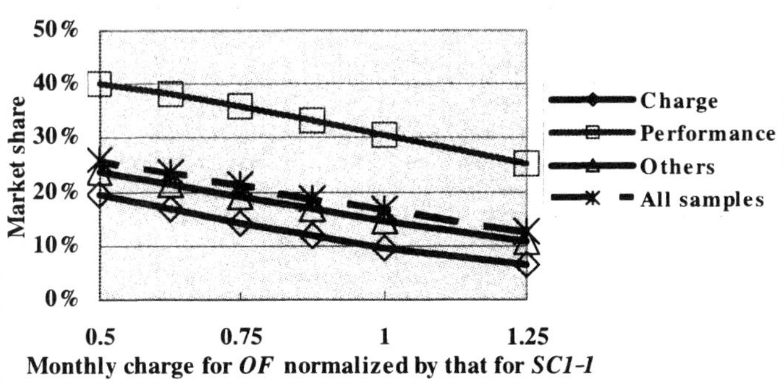

Figure 2: Share of *OF* according to customer preference.

Table 3: Estimated market share in assumed scenarios.

	Actual share	*SC 1-1*	*SC 1-2*	*SC 2-1*	*SC 2-2*
DU	9%	11%	10%	6%	4%
ADSL	45%	46%	41%	47%	28%
CATV	26%	19%	17%	17%	9%
OF	14%	17%	26%	27%	57%
NONE	6%	7%	6%	3%	2%

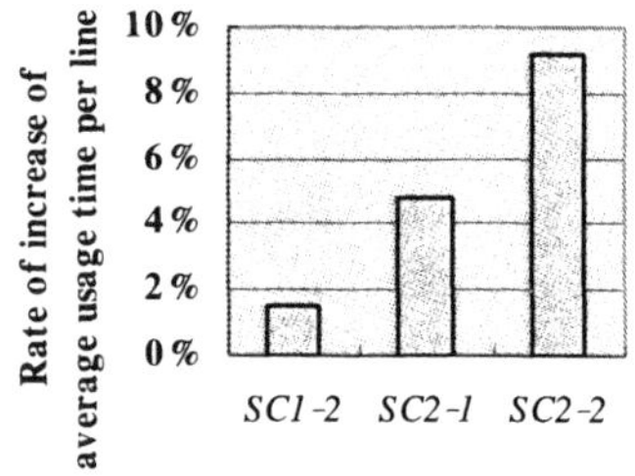

Figure 3: Internet usage time normalized by that for *SC1-1*

spreads. Figure 2 shows that segmentation based on customer preferences is useful in understanding market structures and there are strong possibilities that a customer will change to *OF* when the level of service attributes reaches a level that is acceptable to the customer. Figure 3 shows the average Internet usage time normalized by the time for *SC1-1*. These results show that this methodology is effective for evaluating service specifications and for investment planning in assumed scenarios.

5. CONCLUSION

Under competitive conditions, service providers need support tools to optimize service specifications and evaluate business strategies. It is very important to understand customer choice behavior and usage patterns. We proposed a traffic profiling method and a framework for scenario simulation using this traffic profiling method. We also showed an application example and evaluated the method. Our traffic profiling method is useful for analyzing the relationship between changes in service specifications and service demands. It is also meaningful to understand traffic generating patterns in assumed scenarios. The example models treated in this paper were very simple. In future, we will develop a model that is more realistic by including customer awareness and perception.

REFERENCES

Ben-Akiva, M. and Lerman, S. R., 1987, "*Discrete Choice Analysis*," MIT Press, MA, U.S.A.

Copeland, T. and Antikarov, V., 2001, "Real Options," *TEXERE LLC*, New York.

Kees van der Heijden, 1996, "SCENARIOS-The Art of Strategic Conversations," *John Wiley & Sons*.

Inoue, A. and Yamamoto, H., 1990, "Evaluation of New Telecommunications Services using Stated Preference Techniques," *IFIP International Conference Modeling the Innovation: Communications, Automation and Information Systems*, Rome, pp. 71-78.

Inoue, A., Takahashi, S., Nishimatsu, K., and Kawano, H., 2003a, "Service Demand Analysis Using Multi-Attribute Learning Mechanisms," *IEEE International Conference on Integration of Knowledge Intensive Multi-Agent Systems*.

Inoue, A., Nishimatsu, K., Takahashi, S., 2003b, "Multi-Attribute Learning Mechanism for Customer Satisfaction Assessment," *Intelligent Engineering Systems Through Artificial Neural Networks*, Vol. 13, pp.793-800

Saaty, T.L., 1980, "*The Analytic Hierarchy Process,*", McGraw-Hill.

PARALLEL GENETIC ALGORITHMS FOR ON-LINE TRAFFIC CONTROL PROBLEMS

HUI CHEN
Department of Civil and
Environmental Engineering
Michigan State University

GHASSAN ABU-LEBDEH
Department of Civil and
Environmental Engineering
Michigan State University

YACOUB "JACOB" NAJJAR
Department of Civil engineering
Kansas State University

ABSTRACT
This paper evaluates the computational advantages of Parallel Genetic Algorithms (PGAs) for optimizing dynamic roadway traffic control, and compares PGA performance to that of ordinary simple genetic algorithms (SGAs). PGAs were also applied to a standard GA-difficult, and a standard GA-easy problem. For all problems, significant speed-ups were realized but the exact magnitude varied considerably with problem difficulty and size. For GA "easy" problems, the magnitude of speed-up is approximately proportional to the number of subpopulations used. Advantages of PGAs are more pronounced for complex and difficult (deceptive) problems. The PGAs advantages mean more efficient and faster optimization for many applications in intelligent transportation systems (ITS).

INTRODUCTION

Advanced computation paradigms such as GAs are increasingly becoming an integral part of intelligent transportation systems (ITS). GAs have unique properties that make them particularly suited for applications in transportation systems including signal control, variable speed control, and traffic assignment and routing. However, GAs applications in transportation systems have not made use of recent advances in the field of Genetic-based computing.

Increasing demand on transportation systems and deployment of ITS technologies forced transportation agencies to seek the latest in computation and communication technologies to realize the full potential of modern transportation systems. For optimization, Evolutionary Computations, including GAs, offer uniqueness and power that make them an item of choice for certain classes of optimization problems. This paper is on how to make use of GAs in transportation more efficient.

BACKGROUND

There has been numerous applications of GAs in traffic control (Abu-Lebdeh and Benekohal, 2000; Duerr, 2000; Park et al.,2000). All of these applications have used Simple GAs (SGAs). However, SGAs may not be suitable for modern control optimization for three reasons: they are not easy to configure, they can be too slow to converge, and they have difficulty solving deceptive hard problems.

Recent advances in Evolutionary Computation can alleviate many of the shortcomings noted above. That promise coupled with the deployment of ITS-based systems forces us to look for alternatives and adopt efficient computation tools including newer generations of GAs. For on-line dynamic traffic control, the ability to produce efficient solutions quickly is a critical issue.

This paper presents an evaluation, and an attempt to quantify the computational merits (speed-ups) of PGAs for optimizing dynamic traffic control problems. To corroborate the results, the paper also tests and compares PGA and SGA performances on benchmark easy and difficult problems.

PROBLEM STATEMENT

SGAs are powerful but can be inefficient, especially for hard and large-scale combinatorial problems. This inefficacy can stem from one or more of the following three issues: 1) configuring the GA, 2) candidate solutions representation and/or stratification within the search space, and 3) GAs' sequential computation process.

With sequential computation, the evaluations are very time-consuming. Hence performing the many evaluations inherent in evolutionary search is sometimes impractical. This issue becomes particularly acute when the optimization solutions are needed in real time as, for example, in online traffic control. The problems attributed to sequential computation can be addressed by using parallel GAs (PGAs). However, we still do not, but need to know how the speed-up is related to the problem being solved. First, a brief note on PGAs.

PARALLEL GENETIC ALGORITHMS

There are three types of Parallel GA: 1) "Global Parallel" GAs, 2) Diffusion PGAs, and 3) Island PGAs. "Global Parallel" GAs uses multiple processors in parallel to evaluate the individuals in a single GA population. Diffusion PGAs and Island PGAs divide population(s) into some set of demes or subgroups which are treated separately. This paper deals with Island PGAs only.

In Island or Migration or Coarse-Grained PGAs, the population is divided into small clusters, each of which is treated as a separate breeding unit under the control of a conventional GA. The Island PGA does not operate globally on a single population. Occasionally, individuals from the various subpopulations (islands) are permitted to migrate to other islands, where they may subsequently mate with other members of that island

A notable advantage of Island PGAs is a reduction in takeover time by superior individuals. When a superior individual is found, a simple GA will tend to begin converging toward that individual, skewing all future searches. In contrast, until that individual or its descendants propagate through all the subpopulations of an Island PGA, search in the remaining islands goes on unaffected by that individual.

APPLICATION OF PGAs TO THREE PROBLEMS

For all three problems, the performance of the PGA was compared to that of an SGA. The comparison is based on the computation resources needed to reach the same or a closely comparable near-optimal solution. The PGA was used with different numbers of subpopulations, and for each number different population sizes were used. Different sizes of the traffic control problem were tested to see how the PGA performance changes with problem size.

Traffic Control Problem

The traffic problem used here is an adaptive-signal dynamic-speed control optimization problem where system output is to be maximized. It is structured as a discrete event time-varying dynamical system (see Abu-Lebdeh & Benekohal, 1997 and Abu-Lebdeh, 2002, for detailed formulation). The formulation is presented here only for the convenience of the reader. For each of the intersections, and over the entire control period (i.e., all cycles), the objective is to determine the best possible control. The definitions of the symbols used in the formulation are as follows:

s_i adjusted saturation flow rate per lane of approach i, veh/sec
$g_{(k)i}$ effective green time for arterial approach i during cycle k, sec.
$gc_{(k)i}$ effective green time for cross approach i during cycle k, sec.
$AV_{(k)i}$ arriving vehicles into approach i during cycle k, veh.
$q_{(k)i}$ length of queue on approach i at the beginning of cycle k, veh.
$d_{(k)i}$ mean departure rate from approach i during cycle k, veh/sec.

The control algorithm is to

$$\text{Maximize}(\sum_{k=1}^{n}\sum_{i=1}^{m} gc_{(k)i}d_{(k)i} +$$

$$\{j\times\sum_{k=1}^{n} \min[(q_{(k)j}+\frac{AV_{(k)j}}{g_{(k)j-1}}\times(g_{(k)j}-\frac{q_{(k)j}}{s_j}), AV_{(k)j}+q_{(k)j})]\}+\varpi+\omega)$$

where n is the number of cycles, m is the number of cross street approaches, and j is the number of arterial links. The first term of the objective function measures the output of crossing streets. The second term is the output of the arterial street as measured by the number of link-vehicles. ϖ and ω are adjustment terms for partial travel. The above function is maximized subject the following constraints on control and state variables (a complete list of constraints is in Abu-Lebdeh & Benekohal 1997 and Abu-Lebdeh, 2002):

$q_{(k+1)i}=q_{(k)i}+AV_{(K)i}-DV_{(k)i}$ (queue formation and dissipation models)

$g_{(k)i\,min} \leq g_{(k)i} \leq g_{(k)i\,max}$ (domain of green splits)

$Speed_{(k)i\,min} \leq Speed_{(k)i} \leq Speed_{(k)i\,max}$ (domain of speeds)

$Offsets_{(k)i} = f(\text{queue length}_{(k)i}, \text{space}_{(k)i}, \text{speed}_{(k)i})$

This is a combinatorial, highly constrained problem. The decision variables are green splits, offsets, and speeds. Speeds were allowed to vary between 17-45 km/hr. Phasing was not optimized. The algorithm was applied to a congested system of different sizes as will be described later. All links had two through lanes and ranged in length between 250 and 300 meters. A saturation flow rate of 1800 vehicles per lane per hour of green was used. Starting and stopping shockwave speeds were, respectively, 4.9 and 4.3 meter/second. The average effective vehicle length was assumed 7.6 meters.

Benchmark Difficult Problem

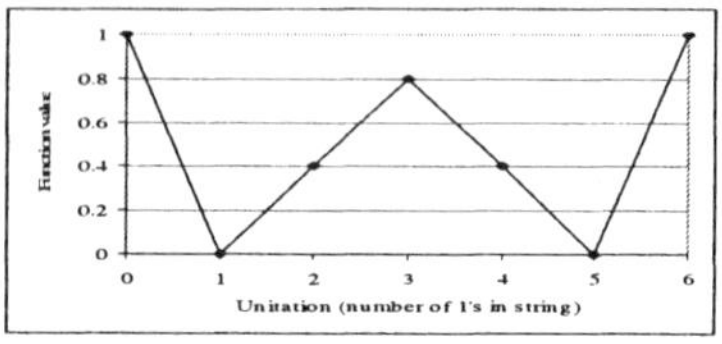

Figure 1: 6-bit bipolar function

The benchmark difficult problem uses the deceptive function described in Goldberg et al. (1989). The difficult problem is a 30-bit function constructed by concatenating five copies of the 6-bit bipolar function shown in Figure 1. The 30-bit function has over 5 million local optima and only 32 global optima.

Benchmark Easy Problem

The benchmark easy problem is that of maximizing a 30-bit one-max function as follows: Maximize $\sum_{i=1}^{n} x_i \qquad x_i \in \{0,1\}$

The one-max function counts the number of bits set to 1 in the string and uses that value as the fitness of the individual. This is a simple one global optimum that occurs when all string digits are 1s.

Results

Traffic System

The experiments were carried out on two traffic systems: a small system composed of five intersections and ten cycles, and a large system with ten intersections and twenty cycles. For each of the two systems, both SGA and PGA were allowed the same computation resources to optimize control. Elsewhere the solutions were shown to be "traffic sensible" using SGAs (Abu-Lebdeh, 2002). Only the computational side is presented here. Figure 2 shows the performance of the SGA, a PGA with four subpopulations (PGA-4) and PGA with eight subpopulations (PGA-8) in a typical run for the large system.

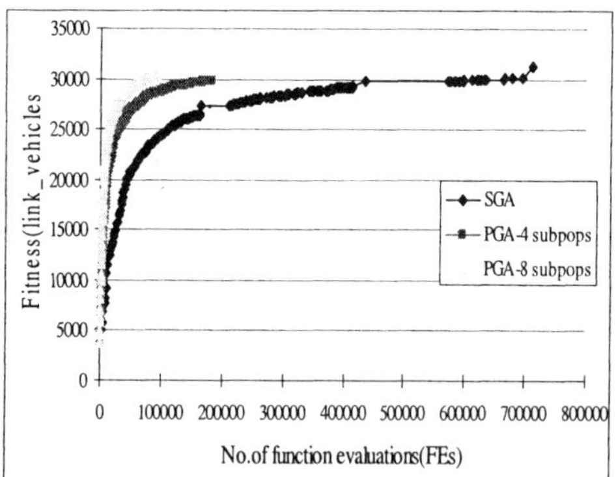

Fitness	SGA	PGA 4 subpop	PGA 8 subpop
10000	10714 (100%)	3477 (32%)	1104 (10%)
15000	26012 (100%)	6534 (25%)	2627 (10%)
18000	37834 (100%)	10286 (27%)	4351 (12%)
20000	44420 (100%)	11926 (27%)	5347 (12%)
23000	75123 (100%)	21769 (29%)	8973 (12%)
25000	112767 (100%)	31207 (28%)	13354 (12%)

Figure 2: Results for large traffic system

It is clear that the PGAs outperformed the SGA by a significant margin; the difference is largest in the early parts of the search where it is more critical for on-line control. Similar trends were observed for the small system. Of course, if enough time is given to the SGA it will eventually reach a comparable solution to the PGA. However, the point of using a PGA is to obtain high quality solutions in shorter time, as would be necessary for on-line traffic control optimization.

The numeric comparison of the performances of the SGA, PGA-4 and PGA-8 is shown in the table in Figure 2. The number of function evaluations (FE) needed to reach the shown fitness was noted for each of the three GAs. The number of generations needed for the SGA was used as a benchmark and was taken as 100%. Compared to the SGA, the PGA-4 needed only between 25 and 32% of the number of FE to reach the same fitness, while the PGA-8 needed only between 10 and 12% of the number of FE.

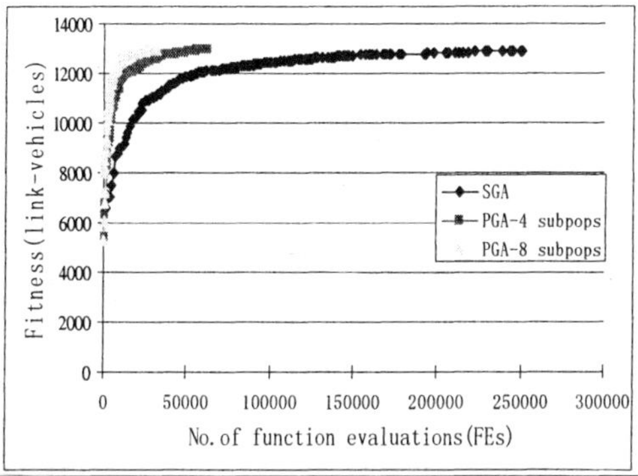

Fitness	SGA	PGA 4 subpop	PGA 8 subpop
8000	6517 (100%)	1792 (27%)	679 (10%)
9000	8490 (100%)	2778 (33%)	1335 (16%)
10000	12516 (100%)	4144 (33%)	2057 (16%)
11000	19847 (100%)	6170 (31%)	3597 (18%)
12000	38057 (100%)	10834 (28%)	7833 (21%)

Figure 3: Results for small system

Figure 3 shows results of the small system. Statistical tests were conducted and all mean fitnesses obtained by the different GAs were found to be statistically different.

The sensitivity of the results to the number of subpopulations is answered in part in the results shown in the tables. It is shown that doubling the number of subpopulations, while maintaining the same overall total number of individuals, cuts the number of FE needed by at least one-half. The impact of the number of subpopulations is more pronounced for the larger system.

Difficult Problem

The result of implementing PGAs on the difficult problem is shown in

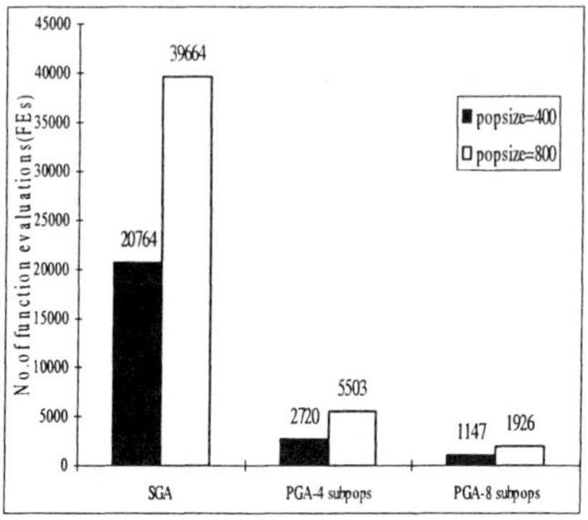

a. result of Bipolar function

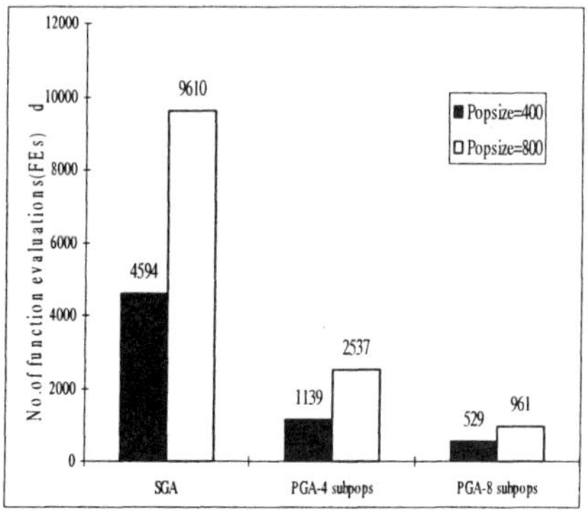

b. result of Onemax

Figure 4 Results of benchmark difficult and easy problems

Figure 4.a. An SGA, a PGA-4, and PGA-8 each with two population sizes (400 and 800) where used to find the first of the 32 global optima. The Figure shows the average number of FEs needed to reach the global optima. The PGA-4 used less than one seventh (1/7) of the FEs the SGA needed. Doubling the population size, however, reduced the effectiveness of the PGA. This is not surprising since there is an optimal population size given the size and complexity of the problem being optimized. In this work no attempt was made to determine the optimal population size. The PGA-8 outperformed the PGA-4 by more than two folds for both population sizes. And within the PGA-8, the lower population size outperformed the higher one although the difference is not as marked as in the case of the PGA-4.

Easy Problem

Figure 4.b summarizes the results of the experiments on the easy (one-max) problem. The PGA-4 used around ¼ of th the FEs the SGA needed to reach the global optima. Doubling the population size reduced the effectiveness of the PGA. This reaffirms the notion that optimal choice of different parameter values (as the population size) is necessary regardless of the type of GA used. The PGA-8 outperformed the PGA-4 by more than two folds, as was the case with the bipolar problem.

CONCLUSIONS

This paper demonstrates the advantages of using PGAs through experimentation on optimization problems of different sizes and degrees of complexity. A dynamic traffic control problem, a benchmark GA-easy problem, and benchmark GA-difficult problems were used. In all experiments performances of Simple GAs were used as reference point.

For all problems evaluated, significant savings in computation resources were realized when PGAs were used. The savings were related to the size and difficulty of the problem at hand. The results show that for the combinatorial dynamic traffic control, PGAs hold a great promise as they reduce computation time needed to reach near-optimal solutions by many-folds; at minimum, the computation time is reduced in direct proportion to the number of subpopulations. With such results, on-line optimization of such control problems seems feasible.

REFERENCES

Abu-Lebdeh, G. & Benekohal, R.F., 1997. Development of a Traffic Control and Queue Management Procedure for Oversaturated Arterials. In *Transportation Research Record 1603*, TRB, National Research Council, Washington, DC, pp. 119-127.

Abu-Lebdeh, G., 2002. Integrated Adaptive-signal Dynamic-speed Control of Signalized Arterials. In *Journal of Transportation Engineering, Vol 128, No 5*, pp. 447-451.

Duerr, P.A., 2000. Dynamic Right-of-Way for Transit Vehicles: Integrated Modeling Approach for Optimizing Signal Control on Mixed Traffic Arterials. In *Transportation Research Record 1731*, TRB, National Research Council, Washington, DC, 2000, 31-37.

Goldberg, D.E., 1989. Sizing Populations for Serial and Parallel Genetic Algorithms." *Proceedings of the 3rd Int'l Conference on Genetic Algorithms*, pp.70-79

Park, B., Messer, C.J. & Urbanik, T II, 2000. Enhanced Genetic Algorithm for Signal Time Optimization of Oversaturated Intersections. In *Transportation Research Record 1727*, Transportation Research Board, Washington, D.C, 2000, pp. 32-41.

CATEGORIZATION OF HIGHWAY TRAFFIC IN FLORIDA BY USING CONNECTIONIST APPROACH

VALERIAN KWIGIZILE Dept. of Civil Engineering

MAJURA SELEKWA Dept. of Mechanical Engineering

RENATUS MUSSA Dept. of Civil Engineering

Florida A&M University-Florida State University College of Engineering
Tallahassee, Florida

ABSTRACT

Highway traffic categorization data are required for designing and managing paved roads. Federal Highway Administration (FHWA) Office of Highway Planning requires states to furnish vehicle categories data. Most states use guidelines given by FHWA in "Scheme F", which specifies 13 vehicle categories depending on the number of axles and axle spacing. The process of automating these guidelines is hindered by the absence of a suitable logic to be used in digital computers. Florida Department of Transportation uses decision logic which implements the "IF-THEN" rules. Field evaluation of these systems revealed a high categorization error rate. This paper presents a connectionist approach that is based on Probabilistic Neural Networks (PNN) for vehicle categorization. It explains the design of the PNN for this purpose, selection and conditioning the training data and an approach for handling multi-category problems. Field results showed that the proposed approach reduced the overall error from 9.6% to 3.0%.

INTRODUCTION

Vehicle categorization data are required by agencies involved in any aspect of highway transportation. The data are used by the transportation departments and the state legislatures to determine and allocate the costs (e.g., between private autos and large commercial vehicles) associated with maintaining the country's extensive highway system and to prioritize the improvements that can be afforded (Lyles and Wyman, 1982). Other uses of categorization data include prediction and planning for commodity flows and freight movements, provision of design inputs relative to the current and predicted capacity of highways, analysis of alternative highway regulatory and investment policies, and developing weight enforcement strategies. Additionally, vehicle categorization data can be used in conducting environmental impact analysis, and reviewing accident records and mitigation strategies.

The vehicle categorization data are available in different format depending on their intended use; for example vehicle types, number of axles, vehicle length, and body type. The standards for collecting and analyzing vehicle categorization data vary countrywide. Truck type distributions are heavily affected by local economic activities, weight limits, and truck size specifications imposed by the states. Some trucks are designed to carry specific commodities; for example, coal trucks in Kentucky and Pennsylvania (FHWA, 2001). The Federal Highway Administration (FHWA) Office of Highway Planning requires states to furnish vehicle categorization data. To comply with this requirement, most states use guidelines provided by FHWA in "Scheme F" to categorize vehicles. This scheme is basically a visual categorization scheme based on the vehicle types. Appendix 1 outlines the details of "Scheme F" (FHWA, 2001). In the past, vehicle categorization could only be done visually by counting traffic stream. However, the visual categorization methods were expensive and prone to errors due to inconsistent concentration of the observers. As a result, automated classifiers were developed. To categorize vehicles, the automated classifiers use the information on number of axles and axle spacing detected by traffic sensors installed in the roadways. To assign a vehicle to one of the 13 categories in "Scheme F," a reference table implemented through a decision tree is required.

In Florida, different vendors supply the Florida Department of Transportation (FDOT) with vehicle categorization equipment. The reference table in each vendor's equipment is unique to that vendor. A comparison of vehicle categorization algorithms used by these vendors revealed discrepancies in the decision boundaries, a factor which might be contributing to errors in categorization of vehicles. In order to minimize errors, the FDOT decided to set common decision boundaries shown in Appendix 2 that could be used with any vendors' equipment. However, these decision boundaries were not optimally set and field evaluation of the table revealed a high rate of misclassifications. In this paper the application of a connectionist approach, such as Probabilistic Neural Networks (PNN), in optimizing the FDOT reference table for categorization of vehicles is proposed. The PNN uses observed patterns on the number of axles, axle spacing and vehicle weights categorize vehicles. The optimum decision boundaries for the reference table are derived from more accurately categorized vehicle data.

FDOT REFERENCE TABLE AND "SCHEME F"

The Federal Highway Administration issued guidelines for vehicle categorization in a form known as "Scheme F" (FHWA 2001); which classifies vehicles in 13 categories. "Scheme F", shown in Appendix 1, was developed by the Department of Transportation of the State of Maine (Wyman et al., 1985). In its basic form this scheme provides information that cannot be quantified in a way suitable for computer application. Therefore, it is in general difficult to automate the vehicle categorization process using the guidelines of "Scheme F" alone. Many software vendors have developed decision trees that are based on the number of axles and axle spacing. Appendix 2 shows such a decision tree used by FDOT. This reference table can be used to automate the vehicle classification process by using a set of linked "IF-THEN" rules. However, as is evident from the table, the margin between the categories is very thin and often has resulted in misclassifications. For example, while the second axle spacing for classes 4 and 6 are overlapping, the upper limit for the first axle spacing for class 6 is 23.0 ft while the lower limit for class 4 is 23.01 ft. The margin is therefore within 0.01 ft only. The objective of this research was, among other things, to develop a better way of automating vehicle classification process that satisfies the guidelines provided by "Scheme F". After an extensive evaluation of the problem and the available classification tools (Michie et al., 1994; Tsoukalas and Uhrig, 1997), a Probabilistic Neural Network (PNN) approach was chosen. The following section briefly describes the principles behind PNN.

PRINCIPLES OF PROBABILISTIC NEURAL NETWORKS

PNN (Specht, 1990a; Specht, 1990b) is a pattern classification network that is believed to provide a general method for pattern classification problems (Tsoukalas and Uhrig, 1997). PNN is a class of neural networks that combine some of the best attributes of statistical pattern recognition and feed-forward neural networks. Details of how this network works can be found in many standard textbooks, for example (Bose and Liang, 1996; Michie et al., 1994; Tsoukalas and Uhrig, 1997); however, a brief description of this network is given below.

Any pattern classifier places each observed vector of data $\mathbf{x}$ in one of the predefined classes c_i; $i = 1,2,\ldots n$ where n is the number of possible classes in which $\mathbf{x}$ can belong. The effectiveness of many classifiers is limited by the number of data elements that vector $\mathbf{x}$ can have and the number of possible classes n. The classical Bayes pattern classifier implements the Bayes conditional probability rule that the probability $P(c_i/\mathbf{x})$ of $\mathbf{x}$ being in class c_i is given by

$$P(c_i/\mathbf{x}) = \frac{P(\mathbf{x}/c_i)P(c_i)}{P(x)} \qquad \text{(i)}$$

where $P(\mathbf{x}/c_i)$ is the conditioned probability density function of $\mathbf{x}$ given set c_i, $P(c_j)$ is the probability of drawing data from class c_j and $P(x) = \sum_{j=1}^{n} P(\mathbf{x}/c_j)P(c_j)$. Vector $\mathbf{x}$ is said to belong to a particular class c_i if $P(c_i/\mathbf{x}) > P(c_j/\mathbf{x});\ \forall j = 1,2,\ldots,n.\ \ j \neq i.$

This classifier assumes that the probability density function of the population from which the data was drawn is known a priori; and this is one of the major limitations of implementing Bayes classifier. The PNN simplifies the Bayes classification procedure by using a training set for which the desired statistical information for implementing the Bayes classifier can be drawn. The desired probability density function for each class is approximated by using the Parzen windows approach (Parzen, 1962; Murthy, 1965; Murthy, 1966; Cacoullous, 1966). The Parzen windows method is a non-parametric procedure that synthesizes an estimate of a probability density function by superposition of a number of windows, replicas of a function (often the Gaussian). The Parzen windows classifier takes a classification decision after calculating the probability density function of each class using the given training examples. Input $\mathbf{x}$ is classified by the label corresponding to the maximum posterior. To classify an input **x** as being in class c_i, the multicategory classifier decision requires the following condition to be satisfied:

$$P(\mathbf{x}/c_i)P(c_i) > P(\mathbf{x}/c_j)P(c_j) \qquad \text{(ii)}$$

The decision regions for a Parzen window classifier depend upon the choice of window function (Duda et al., 2001). In particular, the PNN approximates the probability that vector **x** belongs to a particular class c_i as a sum of weighted Gaussian distributions centered at each training sample, i.e.,

$$P(\mathbf{x}/c_i) = \frac{1}{(2\pi)^{\frac{N}{2}}\sigma^N n_{t_i}} \sum_{j=1}^{n_{t_i}} \exp\left[-\frac{(\mathbf{x}-\mathbf{x}_j^i)^T(\mathbf{x}-\mathbf{x}_j^i)}{2\sigma^2}\right] \qquad \text{(iii)}$$

where $\mathbf{x}_j^i$ is the j-th training vector for the patterns in class i, σ is known as a smoothing factor which is approximately equal to the standard deviation of the Gaussian distribution of the population, N is the dimension of the input pattern, and n_{t_i} is the number of training patterns in class i. The single free parameter of this function is σ and the rest of the terms are determined directly from the training data. The smoothing factor defines the decision boundaries for the classes based on the training data. Nonlinear decision boundaries require the smoothing factor σ to be as small as possible since details of the probability density may be lost if the smoothing parameter is large. However, too small values of the smoothing factor σ can cause spiky approximation of the decision boundary hence failing to fairly represent it. An appropriate deviation is chosen by experiment during PNN training. In this work, the decision boundary was assumed to be highly nonlinear and σ was estimated as

$$\sigma = \frac{p}{\|\Sigma\|} \qquad \text{(iv)}$$

where p is the user selected value and $\|\Sigma\|$ is the Frobenius norm of a matrix formed by concatenating the standard deviation vectors for each training set; it corresponds to the maximum standard deviation in the training patterns. The value of p was selected through experimentation relative to some evaluation criterion, particularly the number of categorization errors during cross validation. As indicated in the formula, σ became automatically small when the training set had large variances, which called for nonlinear decision boundaries. Figure A shows the computational structure of the PNN.

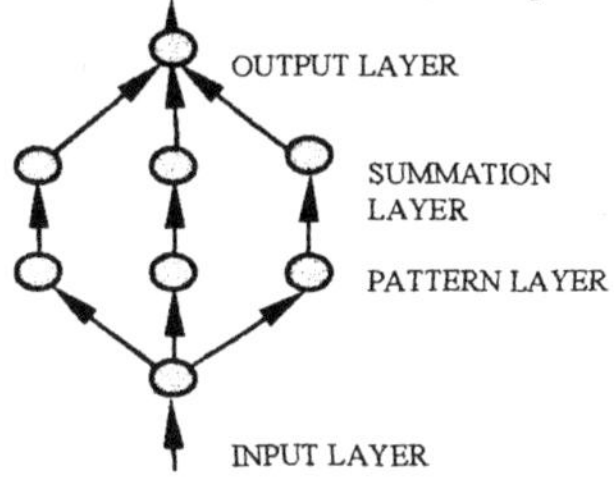

Figure A: Structure of PNN

The network is made up of four layers; an input layer, a pattern layer, a summation layer and an output layer. The input **x** to the network is a vector defined as

$$\mathbf{X} \stackrel{\Delta}{=} [x_1, x_2, x_3, \ldots x_p]^T. \qquad \text{(v)}$$

From the input layer, the input **x** is passed to each of the patterns in the pattern layer. For each class there are several pattern nodes made up of representative data for that class known as the training data. Each pattern computes the probability of data being in that pattern by using equation (iii). The probabilities from all representative pattern in each class are summed up in the summation layer to determine the overall probability of the given input **x** to be in each of the classes i represented by the patterns in the pattern layer. The output layer picks the class for which highest probability was obtained in the summation layer. The input is then classified to belong to this class. The effectiveness of the network in classifying input vectors depends highly on how the training patterns are chosen. The next section describes how the data were collected and how the training patterns for the vehicle classification problem were chosen.

DATA COLLECTION AND SELECTION OF TRAINING DATA SET

Field data were collected from different calibrated Weigh-In-Motion (WIM) sites along the major highways in the state of Florida. The WIM sites provided individual vehicle records that included the number of axles, axle spacing, vehicle length, and the overall vehicle weight. Video data were simultaneously collected at the same sites in order to establish ground truth data. Each monitored vehicle was visually classified and compared to field machine classification that implements the FDOT reference table. Misclassified vehicles were identified and recorded. Information for more than 3,300 vehicles was collected. Representative vehicles for each vehicle class were chosen from the data collected to form a training data set. Since the axle spacing for some vehicles were wider than for others, certain vehicle types were represented by more data than others. All vehicles were assumed to have 9 axles, which is the observed maximum number of axles. Vehicles with fewer axles were assumed to have additional fictitious axles so that the total number is 9; axle spacing for these fictitious axles were fixed to be 0 ft. Some of the classes span over a different number of axles; for example, class 3 and 5 cover vehicles with two to five axles depending on the number of axles per trailer. It is difficult to automatically classify the two axle vehicles in the same group as the four-axle vehicles. Because of this, such classes were broken down to simple subclasses and a total of 28 subclasses were defined based on the 13 predefined standard classes. Therefore, the PNN patterns were drawn to reflect these subclasses and the network was asked to categorize the vehicle into one of these 28 subclasses. The training patterns were chosen in such a way that the standard deviation was kept as minimum as possible. Classes that involved wider axle spacing range had more training patterns than those with narrow axle spacing range. In total, there were 325 training patterns; which is an average of about 12 patterns per subclass. Selection of training patterns was carefully done in order to pick the representative vehicles that would reflect all required vehicle characteristics in a class. Wide ranges of axle spacing values possible for a particular pattern were used.

COMPARATIVE PNN FIELD PERFORMANCE RESULTS

Field data collected were used to train and test the performance of the PNN as compared to methods that follow FDOT decision tree. Individual vehicle records were obtained from the WIM sites and video data were used as ground truth. The individual vehicle records contained the information on how vehicles were classified using the FDOT reference table. The PNN was initially supplied with data with only number of axles and axle spacing, which are the same features used with FDOT Table. In order to increase features for vehicle categorization, overall vehicle weight was included in the data and categorization using the PNN was redone. Table A shows the results that were obtained using the neural network method compared to those that are based on FDOT reference table. However, not all traffic monitoring sites are capable of recording vehicle weight; therefore, vehicle weight was only used to increase separability between vehicle categories in order to set the optimum axle spacing boundaries to be used at any traffic monitoring site. However, it is understood that for some vehicle classes, the data used was not sufficient to justify the superiority of the PNN; therefore more data is still being collected to increase the sample size for these classes. It is evident from the results that the PNN outperforms the FDOT decision tree based method. Inclusion of vehicle weight as a classification variable reduced the overall error from 9.6% to 3.0%. The results are being used in improving the axle spacing decision boundaries for FDOT reference table. Due to possibility of overlaps between vehicle axle spacings of different classes (for example classes 3 and 8), it may not be possible to completely eliminate misclassification. However, with optimum axle spacing decision boundaries, the classification error rate may be significantly decreased. The use of PNN provides an insight on how best the axle spacing decision boundaries can be set to reduce misclassifications.

Table A. Categorization Results and Comparison of Performance between PNN and FDOT Reference Table

Vehicle Class	Total Vehicles Observed	FDOT Table Performance		PNN Performance Weight Not Included		PNN Performance Weight Included	
		Total Misclassified	Percentage Misclassified	Total Misclassified	Percentage Misclassified	Total Misclassified	Percentage Misclassified
1	20	0	0.0%	0	0.0%	0	0.0%
2	669	37	5.5%	23	3.4%	11	1.6%
3	603	133	22.1%	83	13.8%	41	6.8%
4	57	11	19.3%	3	5.3%	0	0.0%
5	329	130	39.5%	92	28.0%	46	14.0%
6	112	5	4.5%	3	2.7%	0	0.0%
7	19	0	0.0%	0	0.0%	0	0.0%
8	214	1	0.5%	0	0.0%	0	0.0%
9	1116	2	0.2%	0	0.0%	0	0.0%
10	40	0	0.0%	0	0.0%	0	0.0%
11	81	0	0.0%	0	0.0%	0	0.0%
12	37	0	0.0%	0	0.0%	0	0.0%
13	12	0	0.0%	0	0.0%	0	0.0%
Total	**3309**	**319**	**9.6%**	**204**	**6.2%**	**98**	**3.0%**

CONCLUSIONS

The paper presented a connectionist approach for optimizing FDOT axle spacing reference table by using PNN. The PNN was used to estimate the maximum classification accuracy that can be achieved. The network accepts information about axle spacing and overall vehicle weight to determine the class to which a particular vehicle belongs. The performance of the PNN depends on both its design (i.e., selection of the smoothing factor (σ)) and selection of representative training patterns. The smoothing factor was selected as a function of the variances of the training patterns, and the pattern set for each class was chosen to have a sufficiently small variance and a mean that is sufficiently far from the mean of the pattern for the adjacent class. Performance results showed that the proposed connectionist approach outperforms the current FDOT axle spacing reference table based approach. The classification error was decreased from 9.6% to 6.2% when only axle spacing was used as a classification variable and from 9.6% to 3.0% when both axle spacing and vehicle weight were used as classification variables. Due to better performance showed through the connectionist approach, it is expected that after extensive field tests and validation, the FDOT may eventually consider adopting the approach as a classification method to replace the conventional approach.

REFERENCES

Bose, N. K.; and Liang P. 1996. *Neural Network Fundamentals with Graphs, Algorithms, and Applications.* McGraw-Hill, Inc. (USA).

Cacoullous, R. 1966. Estimation of a probability density. *Annals of the Institute of Statistical Mathematics (Tokyo)* 18(2):179–189.

Duda, O. R.; Hart, P. E.; and Stork, D. G. 2001. *Pattern Classification.* John Wiley & Sons, Inc. (USA).

Federal Highway Administration 2001. *Traffic Monitoring Guide, Section 4 : Vehicle Classification Monitoring.* Office of Highway Policy Information.

Lyles, R.W and Wyman, J. 1982. *Evaluation of Vehicle Classification Equipment.* Final Report for Contract No DOT-FH-61 C-00156 for U.S. Department of Transportation, FHWA, Office of Planning, Maine Department of Transportation.

Michie, D.; Spiegelhalter, D. J.; and Taylor, C. C. 1994. *Machine Learning, Neural and Statistical Classification.* Ellis Horwood.

Murthy, V. K. 1965. Estimation of a probability density. *Annals of Mathematical Statistics* 36:1027–1031.

Murthy, V. K. 1966. Nonparametric estimation of multivariate densities with applications. *In Multivariate Analysis*, 43–58. P. R. Krishnaiah, (Editor), New York: Academic.

Parzen, E. 1962. On estimation of a probability density function and mode. *Annals of Mathematical Statistics* 33:1065–1076.

Specht, D. F. 1990a. Probabilistic Neural Networks. *Neural Networks* 3(1):109–118.

Specht, D. F. 1990b. Probabilistic Neural Networks and the polynomial adaline as complementary techniques for classification. *IEEE Transactions on Neural Networks* 1(1):111–121.

Tsoukalas, L. H., and Uhrig, R. E. 1997. *Fuzzy and Neural Approaches in Enegineering.* John Willey.

Wyman, J. H.; Braley, G. A.; and Stephens, R. I. 1985. *Field Evaluation of FHWA Vehicle Classification Categories.* Final Report for Contract DTFH-71-80-54-ME-03 for U.S. Department of Transportation, FHWA, Office of Planning, Maine Department of Transportation.

Appendix 1: "Scheme F" Guidelines

Motorcycles (Optional) -- All two or three-wheeled motorized vehicles. Typical vehicles in this category have saddle type seats and are steered by handlebars rather than steering wheels. This category includes motorcycles, motor scooters, mopeds, motor-powered bicycles, and three-wheel motorcycles. This vehicle type may be reported at the option of the State.

Passenger Cars -- All sedans, coupes, and station wagons manufactured primarily for the purpose of carrying passengers and including those passenger cars pulling recreational or other light trailers.

Other Two-Axle, Four-Tire Single Unit Vehicles -- All two-axle, four-tire, vehicles, other than passenger cars. Included in this classification are pickups, panels, vans, and other vehicles such as campers, motor homes, ambulances, hearses, carryalls, and minibuses. Other two-axle, four-tire single-unit vehicles pulling recreational or other light trailers are included in this classification. *Because automatic vehicle classifiers have difficulty distinguishing class 3 from class 2, these two classes may be combined into class 2.*

Buses -- All vehicles manufactured as traditional passenger-carrying buses with two axles and six tires or three or more axles. This category includes only traditional buses (including school buses) functioning as passenger-carrying vehicles. Modified buses should be considered to be a truck and should be appropriately classified.

Two-Axle, Six-Tire, Single-Unit Trucks -- All vehicles on a single frame including trucks, camping and recreational vehicles, motor homes, etc., with two axles and dual rear wheels.

Three-Axle Single-Unit Trucks -- All vehicles on a single frame including trucks, camping and recreational vehicles, motor homes, etc., with three axles.

Four or More Axle Single-Unit Trucks -- All trucks on a single frame with four or more axles.

Four or Fewer Axle Single-Trailer Trucks -- All vehicles with four or fewer axles consisting of two units, one of which is a tractor or straight truck power unit.

Five-Axle Single-Trailer Trucks -- All five-axle vehicles consisting of two units, one of which is a tractor or straight truck power unit.

Six or More Axle Single-Trailer Trucks -- All vehicles with six or more axles consisting of two units, one of which is a tractor or straight truck power unit.

Five or fewer Axle Multi-Trailer Trucks -- All vehicles with five or fewer axles consisting of three or more units, one of which is a tractor or straight truck power unit.

Six-Axle Multi-Trailer Trucks -- All six-axle vehicles consisting of three or more units, one of which is a tractor or straight truck power unit.

Seven or More Axle Multi-Trailer Trucks -- All vehicles with seven or more axles consisting of three or more units, one of which is a tractor or straight truck power unit.

Appendix 2: FDOT Axle Spacing Reference Table

Veh.		Num.		Axle Spacing (ft)									Max.
Type	Class	Axles	Description	Ax.1-2	Ax.2-3	Ax.3-4	Ax.4-5	Ax.5-6	Ax.6-7	Ax.7-8	Ax.8-9	Weight	Length
1	1	2	Motorcycle	0.1-6.0								0.1 >	10
2	2	2	Auto, Pickup	6.01-10.0								1.0 >	22
3	3	2	Other (Limo, Van, RV)	10.01-13.30								1.0 >	26
10	4	2	Bus	23.01-40.00								12.0 >	45
20	5	2	2D	13.31-23.0								1.0 >	40
3	2	3	Auto W/1 Axle Trailer	6.01-10.0	6.0-25.0							1.0 >	32
7	3	3	Other W/1 Axle Trailer	10.01-13.30	6.0-25.0							1.0 >	60
11	4	3	Bus	23.01-40.0	0.1-6.0							12.0 >	52
	5	3	2D W/1 Axle Trailer	13.31-23.0	6.0-25.0							1.0 >	60
24	6	3	3 Axles	6.01-23.0	0.1-5.99							12.0 >	40
30	8	3	2S1, 21	6.01-23.0	11.0-40.0							12.0 >	75
4	2	4	Auto W/2 Axle Trailer	6.01-10.0	6.0-25.0	0.1-6.0						1.0 >	45
9	3	4	Other W/2 Axle Trailer	10.01-13.30	6.0-25.0	0.1-6.0						1.0 >	60
	5	4	2D W/2 Axle Trailer	13.31-23.0	6.0-25.0	0.1-6.0						1.0 >	60
28	7	4	4 Axles	6.01-23.0	0.1-6.0	0.1-13.0						12.0 >	45
34	8	4	3S1, 31	6.01-23.0	0.1-6.0	6.01-44.0						20.0 >	75
38	8	4	2S2	6.01-23.0	11.0-40.0	0.1-10.99						20.0 >	75
	3	5	Other W/3 Axle Trailer	10.01-13.30	6.0-25.0	0.1-6.0	0.1-6.0					1.0 >	60
	5	5	2D W/3 Axle Trailer	13.31-23.0	6.0-25.0	0.1-6.0	0.1-6.0					1.0 >	60
40	9	5	3S2	6.01-26.0	0.1-6.0	6.01-46.0	0.1-10.99					12.0 >	80
44	9	5	32	6.01-26.0	0.1-6.0	6.01-23.0	11.0-27.0					12.0 >	80
60	11	5	2S12	6.01-26.0	11.0-26.0	6.1-20.0	11.01-26.0					12.0 >	85
50	10	6	3S3, 33	6.01-26.0	0.1-6.0	0.1-46.0	0.1-11.0	0.1-11.0				12.0 >	85
70	12	6	3S12	6.01-26.0	0.1-6.0	11.01-26.0	6.01-24.0	11.01-26.0				12.0 >	110
54	10	7		6.01-16.70	0.1-6.0	13.3-40.0	0.1-13.3	0.1-13.3	0.1-13.3			12.0 >	85
80	13	7	2S23, 3S22, 3S13	1.0-45.0	1.0-45.0	1.0-45.0	1.0-45.0	1.0-45.0	1.0-45.0			12.0 >	110
84	13	8	3S23	1.0-45.0	1.0-45.0	1.0-45.0	1.0-45.0	1.0-45.0	1.0-45.0	1.0-45.0		12.0 >	120
90	13	9	PERMIT	1.0-45.0	1.0-45.0	1.0-45.0	1.0-45.0	1.0-45.0	1.0-45.0	1.0-45.0	1.0-45.0	12.0 >	120
	15		ERRORS OR UNCLASSIFIED VEHICLES NOT MEETING AXLE CONFIG. FOR CLASS 1 THROUGH 13										

USE OF ARTIFICIAL NEURAL NETWORKS FOR THE ANALYSIS AND DESIGN OF CONCRETE PAVEMENT SYSTEMS SERVING THE A380-800 AIRCRAFT

HALIL CEYLAN
E-mail: hceylan@iastate.edu

ALPER GUCLU
E-mail: alper@iastate.edu

Iowa State University of Science and Technology
Department of Civil, Construction, and Environmental Engineering
Ames, Iowa

ABSTRACT

This study focuses on the development and performance of a comprehensive artificial neural network (ANN) model for the analysis of jointed concrete slabs under simultaneous aircraft and temperature loading. Using the results from the ISLAB2000 finite element program, a backpropagation type comprehensive ANN model was trained for the different loading conditions of gear load only, temperature load only, and simultaneous aircraft and temperature loading cases. Special consideration has been given to the loading of a typical jointed slab assembly under the tri-tandem type gear of the new Airbus A380-800/800F aircraft. Comparing the ANN predictions to the ISLAB2000 solutions validated the performance of the ANN model. The use of an ANN-based analysis and design tool is deemed to be very effective for studying hundreds or thousands of "what if" scenarios for including the temperature effects in pavement analysis and design.

INTRODUCTION

Today's large aircraft with complex loading patterns, such as the two six-wheel tri-tandem and two dual-tandem new generation Airbus A380-800 gear loading, require detailed analysis in airport pavement design. The LEDFAA design approach currently used by the Federal Aviation Administration (FAA) employs an elastic layered program (ELP) for the analysis of rigid airfield pavements. Joints within a Portland Cement Concrete (PCC) pavement naturally conflict with the assumption of an infinite, semi-elastic halfspace concept utilized in ELPs. In addition, ELPs cannot be used to solve for the effects of varying climatic conditions, e.g., slab curling and warping. These restrictions further necessitate the use of finite element models for a more sophisticated pavement analysis and an improved airfield pavement design for new generation aircraft.

This paper mainly focuses on the development and performance of a comprehensive ANN model for the analysis of jointed concrete slabs under: (1) A380-800 tri-tandem gear loading, (2) temperature gradient loading, and (3) simultaneous aircraft and temperature loading. Because the new A380 gear is currently one of the most complex gear configurations, special consideration was given to loading a jointed slab assembly under the tri-tandem A380 aircraft gear. When compared to the actual ISLAB2000 (Khazanovich et al., 2000) analyses, the trained ANN model successfully predicted the maximum bending stresses and maximum vertical deflections. Most importantly, using the ANN model, the magnitudes of gear loading and temperature loading (curling) stresses could be individually predicted to contribute to the total maximum bending stress.

RIGID PAVEMENT THEORY AND THE ISLAB2000 FINITE ELEMENT MODEL

Jointed slab analysis was performed using a finite element program called ISLAB2000 which is based on the original ILLI-SLAB (Tabatabaie, 1977; and Tabatabaie and Barenberg, 1978 and 1980) finite element model. ILLI-SLAB model was developed at the University of Illinois in the late 1970s for the structural analysis of jointed concrete slabs consisting of one or two layers, with either a smooth interface or complete bonding between layers subjected to wheel and temperature loadings. Load transfer across joints/cracks can be provided by aggregate interlock or dowels or combinations of the two. The model employs the 4-noded, 12-dof rectangular plate bending elements (ACM or RPB 12). This model has been extensively tested by comparison of results with available theoretical solutions and results from experimental studies (Tabatabaie and Barenberg, 1980).

BACKPROPAGATION ARTIFICIAL NEURAL NETWORKS

A backpropagation type artificial neural network model was trained in this study with the results from the ISLAB2000 finite element program and was used as an analysis design tool for predicting stresses and deflections in jointed concrete airfield pavements. Backpropagation ANNs are very powerful and versatile networks that can be taught a mapping from one data space to another using example of the mapping to be learned. The term "backpropagation network" actually refers to a multi-layered, feed-forward neural network trained using an error backpropagation algorithm. The learning process performed by this algorithm is called "backpropagation learning" which is mainly an "error minimization technique" (Haykin, 1999; Hecht-Nielsen, 1990; and Werbos, 1974).

As with many ANNs, the connection weights in the backpropagation ANNs are initially selected at random. Inputs from the mapping examples are propagated forward through each layer of the network to emerge as outputs. The errors between those outputs and the correct answers are then propagated backwards through the network and the connection weights are individually adjusted to reduce the error. After many examples (training patterns) have been propagated through the network many times, the mapping function is learned with some specified error tolerance. This is called supervised learning because the network has to be shown the correct answers for it to learn. Backpropagation networks excel at data modeling with their superior function approximation capabilities (Haykin, 1999; and Meier and Tutumluer, 1998).

ISLAB2000 ANALYSIS OF CONCRETE SLABS

Concrete airfield pavements analyzed in this study were represented by a nine-slab assembly, each slab having dimensions of 7.62 m by 7.62 m (25 ft by 25 ft). Figure 1 depicts the geometry and analysis conditions of the pavement sections such as the constant slab size (L), standard tri-tandem A380 loading applied only on one quadrant of the middle slab, and the standard finite element mesh used. The elasticity modulus and the Poisson's ratio for the concrete slabs were set at 27,560 MPa (4,000 ksi) and 0.15, respectively. A total of 3,780 ISLAB2000 analyses were conducted with the nine-slab assembly by varying a number of design parameters used to generate a neural network training data file. Various loading locations (slab interior, corners and/or edges) and joint load transfer efficiencies (LTEs) chosen along x- and y- directions are tabulated in Table 1. The representative/realistic variations of field values of the slab thickness (h), moduli of subgrade reaction (k), and the linear temperature gradient (t_g) considered in the ISLAB2000 finite element analyses for a total of seven input design parameters are also given in Table 1. The standard tri-tandem gear loading consisted of a 209.7 kN (47,142 lb) wheel load approximated by a uniform pressure of 1,344 kPa (195 psi) applied over six rectangular areas of 0.156 m^2 (1.68 ft^2) each (see Figure 1).

TABLE 1. Values of the input parameters used in ISLAB2000 analyses

Location of the Airbus A380 Main Landing Gear	Slab thickness, h		Modulus of subgrade reaction, k		Load Transfer Efficiencies, LTEs		Temperature gradient, t_g	
					LTEx	LTEy		
x, y coordinates	mm	in.	MPa/m	psi /in.	%	%	°C /m	°F/in.
Corner	305	12	27	100	0	0	-65.6	-3.0
Interior	406	16	81	300	50	50	-43.7	-2.0
X-Edge	508	20	136	500	95	95	-21.9	-1.0
Y-Edge	610	24					0.0*	
							+21.9	+1.0
							+43.7	+2.0
							+65.6	+3.0

* Zero temperature gradient corresponds to the Airbus A380 gear loading case only

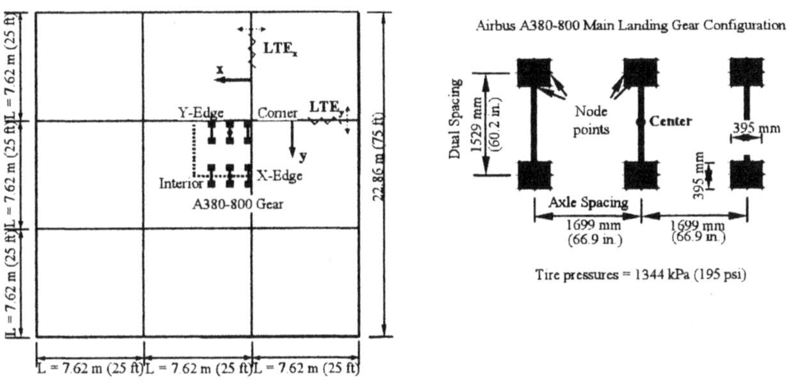

FIG 1. Geometry and analysis conditions for the six-slab concrete airfield pavement system

The ISLAB2000 analyses were performed in the following manner. For each ISLAB2000 run, the input variables for load location, h, k, LTEs, and tg were recorded along with the outputs (i.e., principal stresses, critical bending stresses and critical vertical deflections). A total of seven realistic through-the-slab-thickness linear temperature gradients between –65.6 °C/m (-3.0 °F/in.) and +65.6 °C/m (+3.0 °F/in.) were considered at 21.9 °C/m (1.0 °F/in.) increments (see Table 1). Only Westergaard loading locations (slab interior, corner, and two mid-span slab edges) were considered in the analyses since most of the critical pavement responses occur at these load locations. Because load transfer efficiency values change throughout the year depending on the joint openings caused by the expansion and contraction of the slabs under different climatic/temperature conditions, the LTEs were varied between 0 % and 95 %. Such correlations between LTEs and the air/pavement temperature values were studied by Foxworthy (1985) using the Falling Weight Deflectometer (FWD) results.A total of 3,780 ISLAB2000 analyses were conducted to represent a complete factorial of all the input values. 756 of these analyses correspond to the temperature gradient loading. 3,024 of ISLAB2000 analyses were for the simultaneous aircraft and temperature gradient loading, and the remaining 432 runs were made to study the effects of A380 gear loading.

After all the analyses were completed, an ISLAB2000 data file was formed comprising of the seven input design parameters and six outputs, two critical vertical deflections, two critical bending stresses, and two principal stresses.

A detailed analysis of the ISLAB2000 solutions showed that the critical stresses for the gear load only and the simultaneous gear and temperature loading cases generally occurred directly under one of the wheels except for the mid-span edge loading condition in which case the maximum stresses were found at the slab edges.

NEURAL NETWORK DESIGN AND TRAINING

To train a backpropagation type neural network with the results of the ISLAB2000 finite element analyses, a network architecture was required. Seven input variables (x, y, h, k, LTEx, LTEy, and t_g) constituted the network input layer. The six output variables for each loading case were the critical x- and y- bending stresses (σ_x-max and σ_y-max), two principal stresses (σ_p_bottom-max and σ_p_top-max) and the critical downward and upward vertical deflections (δ_D-max and δ_U-max). An ANN training data file was formed comprised of 3,024 rows and 25 columns with seven input parameters and eighteen output responses. This was done by carefully recording the six critical pavement responses for the three loading cases. About 10 % of the 3,024 ANN training data (300 cases) was reserved as an independent testing set to confirm the proper training and validate the performance of the trained ANN models. A network with two hidden layers was exclusively chosen for the ANN models trained in this study. Satisfactory results were obtained in the previous studies with these types of networks due to their ability to better facilitate the nonlinear functional mapping (Ceylan, 2002).

Six network architectures with two hidden layers were trained for predicting the critical pavement responses with 7 input nodes and 18 output nodes for 10,000 training epochs. Overall, the MSEs decreased as the networks grew in size with increasing number of neurons in the hidden layers. The testing MSEs for the two stresses and deflections were, in general, slightly lower than the training ones. The lowest training MSEs in the order of 5.5×10^{-7} (corresponding to a root mean squared error of 0.074 %) were obtained with the 7-60-60-18 architecture for both the maximum deflections and stresses (see Figure 2).

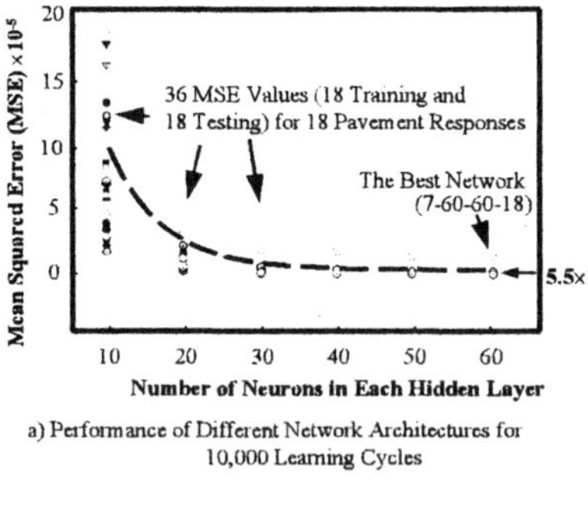

a) Performance of Different Network Architectures for 10,000 Learning Cycles

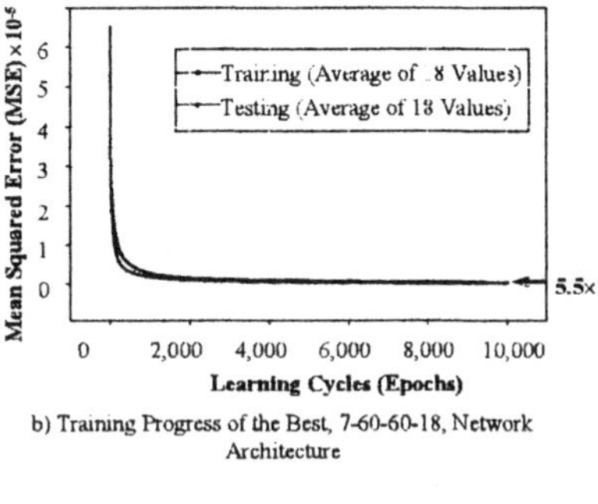

b) Training Progress of the Best, 7-60-60-18, Network Architecture

FIG 2. Artificial neural network training

PERFORMANCE OF THE TRAINED NEURAL NETWORK ARCHITECTURES

The 7-60-60-18 architecture was chosen as the best architecture for the ANN model based on its lowest training and testing MSEs. Figure 2b shows the training and testing MSE progress curves for the 7-60-60-18 network. Both the training and testing curves for each of the eighteen outputs are in the same order of magnitude thus depicting proper training. The almost constant MSEs obtained for the last 5,000 epochs (see Figure 2b) also provided a good indication of adequate training for this network.

TABLE 2. AAEs for different loading cases.

Loading Type	Deflections		Stresses		Principal Stresses	
	Downward Deflection	Upward Deflection	Bending Stress-X	Bending Stress-Y	Bottom of Slab	Top of Slab
A380 Gear Loading	0.12 %	0.20 %	2.78 %	2.70 %	0.14 %	0.32 %
Temperature Gradient Loading	0.23 %	0.84 %	2.53 %	1.76 %	0.28 %	0.39 %
Simultaneous Aircraft & Temperature Loading	0.27 %	1.32 %	2.64 %	3.20 %	0.30 %	0.60 %

Average absolute errors (AAEs) were calculated as sum of the individual absolute errors divided by the 300 testing patterns. The AAEs for each case are summarized in Table 2. Such very low AAEs are indicators of the superior function approximation ability of the trained ANN model. Figure 3 shows the prediction ability of the 7-60-60-18 network at 10,000 learning cycles for the simultaneous aircraft and temperature gradient loading case. All 300 testing data points fell on the line of equality indicates that the predicted critical ANN responses and the ISLAB2000 finite element results are in very good agreement.

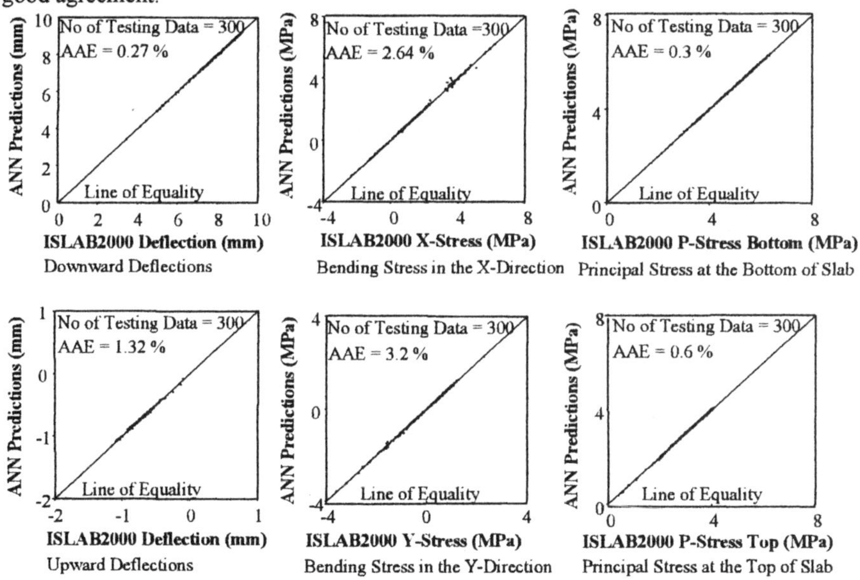

FIG3. Accuracy of the 7-60-60-18 network for predicting the critical pavement responses under the simultaneous aircraft and temperature loading

The prediction ability of the trained ANN model is very good even for the most complex simultaneous loading condition. Only the seven input design variables are entered and the trained ANN model accurately predicts the six types of critical pavement responses in less than a millisecond for all three cases. An overall AAE value of about 2.1 % was computed for all the eighteen pavement responses. The 7-60-60-18 ANN model is deemed to have achieved its goal by literally enabling quick predictions of the

ISLAB2000 stresses and deflections on the standard concrete slabs. The most important benefit of the ANN model is that it does not require any complicated and time-consuming finite element input file preparation for routine design applications. Applications of such an ANN-based design methodology has been demonstrated by Ceylan (2002) indicating how pavement engineers could use the ANN models as an essential tool for checking alternative design inputs ("what if" scenarios) with the inclusion of climatic effects.

CONCLUSIONS

Use of artificial neural networks (ANNs) as pavement analysis and design tools was demonstrated in this paper by analyzing concrete airfield pavements under the following three loading cases: (1) Airbus A380-800 new generation aircraft gear loading only, (2) climatic loading only, and most importantly, (3) simultaneous aircraft gear and climatic loading. For the three different loading cases, the ANN model predicted maximum bending stresses and deflections with an overall average absolute error of less than 2.1 %. The use of the ANN model also resulted in a simplification of the complicated finite element program input and output requirements. The most important analysis consideration for design, determining individually the critical pavement responses due to (1) gear loading (load-induced stress) and (2) climatic loading (curling stress) for their contributions to the total response, was successfully dealt with using the artificial neural networks. The trained ANN model conveniently predicted these critical pavement response contributions and also resulted in both a drastic reduction in computation time (about 0.3 million times faster than the finite element model) and a simplification of the complicated finite element program input and output requirements. It was demonstrated that ANNs are capable of successfully predicting the critical responses of a large scale nonlinear finite element model. Such ANN models provide invaluable help to pavement engineers for studying the effects of heavy loading new generation aircraft.

REFERENCES

Ceylan, H., 2002, "Analysis and design of concrete pavement systems using artificial neural networks." Ph.D. Dissertation, University of Illinois at Urbana-Champaign, December.

Foxworthy, P.T. (1985), Concepts for the Development of a Nondestructive Testing and Evaluation System for Rigid Airfield Pavements, Ph.D. Dissertation, University of Illinois, Urbana, IL

Haykin, S. (1999), Neural Networks: A Comprehensive Foundation. Prentice-Hall, Inc., New Jersey

Hecht-Nielsen, R. (1990), Neurocomputing. Addison-Wesley, New York.

Khazanovich, L., Yu, H. T., Rao, S., Galasova, K., Shats, E., and Jones, R. (2000). ISLAB2000 - Finite Element Analysis Program for Rigid and Composite Pavements, User's Guide, ERES Consultants, A Division of Applied Research Associates, Champaign, Illinois.

Meier, R. and E. Tutumluer (1998), "Uses of Artificial Neural Networks in the Mechanistic-Empirical Design of Flexible Pavements." Proceedings of the International Workshop on Artificial Intelligence and Mathematical Methods in Pavement and Geomechanical Engineering Systems, Florida International University, Florida, pp. 1-12.

Tabatabaie-Raissi, A.M. (1977), Structural Analysis of Concrete Pavement Joints, Ph.D. Dissertation, University of Illinois, Urbana, IL, USA.

Tabatabaie, A.M., and E.J. Barenberg (1978), "Finite-Element Analysis of Jointed or Cracked Concrete Pavements," In Transportation Research Record No. 671, TRB, National Research Council, Washington, D.C., USA, pp. 11-18.

Tabatabaie, A.M., and E.J. Barenberg (1980), "Structural Analysis of Concrete Pavement Systems," Journal of Transportation Engineering, ASCE, Vol. 106, No. TE5.

Werbos, P. (1974), Beyond Regression: New Tools for Prediction and Analysis in the Behavioral Sciences, Ph.D. Dissertation, Harvard University, MA, USA.

INVERSE NONLINEAR STRUCTURAL ANALYSIS UTILIZING NEURAL NETWORK

HASAN CHARKAS
Kansas State University, Manhattan, Kansas, US

HAYDER RASHEED
Kansas State University, Manhattan, Kansas, US

YACOUB NAJJAR
Kansas State University, Manhattan, Kansas, US

ABSTRACT

Conventional material modeling uses mathematical formulas to describe material behavior. These functions are not expected to exactly reproduce global experimental response. Furthermore, the increase in the material complexity results in an increase in the number of model parameters to be identified. Alternatively, the measured global response at specific domain or surface points can be used to guide the nonlinear structural analysis. By imposing the measured displacement at monitoring points onto the solution that uses an approximate material model, a set of improved stress-strain data points is generated. This data set is then used to develop an adaptively improved material model. Neural Networks are known to computationally capture physical phenomena by training the neuro-net to reproduce available data. Therefore, it is utilized as a suitable framework to accomplish the desired adaptive pattern recognition. The partially trained neural network is then used within an iterative non-linear structural analysis procedure in order to provide subsequent stress-strain information. As a result, the discrepancy between the measured and the predicted structural response at the monitoring points is iteratively minimized leading to suitably trained Neural Network. The applicability of the proposed approach is demonstrated by solving simple mechanical and structural systems

INTRODUCTION

Inverse problems have had a significant impact on various fields of science and engineering, and are attracting considerable attention of scientists and engineers. However, their applications in structural engineering are limited (Markiewicz 1998, Park et al. 1998, Sukhorukov 2000, Rikands et al. 2001 and Liu and Chen 2002)

Neural networks are massively parallel computational models, inspired by the human brain. Its powerful characteristics have lead to implementing it in all kinds of engineering applications. With the evolution of neural computing, new sets of inverse problems are introduced. These problems have the objective of extracting material models from global structural measurements. Two groups of researchers (Ghaboussi et al. 1998 and Shin and Pande 2000) have tried to use pre-defined global structural response in terms of load-displacement data at specific points to back-predict or extract the local stress-strain relationship. They formulated their procedures based on a combined finite element and neural network analysis. However, the solution strategies followed have resulted in different levels of success in convergence at different convergence rates. Since these studies were preliminary in nature, they did not rigorously address the relationship between the number and location of monitoring points and the complexity of stress field. Moreover, no attempts were made to systematically highlight convergence difficulties. Ghaboussi et al. (1998) used a dual load and displacement-control analysis to obtain sets of improved stress-strain data at each integration point for a certain load step. Then, they added these sets of data points to the neural network, which is trained up to this load step, for retraining. Afterwards, they repeated the prediction/training of this load step iteratively until the computed response, at the key monitored points, converges to the measured response. In this procedure, the stress-strain history states are considered in the training based on the complexity of the material model. The number of history states is unknown apriori. Therefore, they used an adhoc trial and error approach to determine how many history states are sufficient to model the underlying material behavior. As this procedure is applied to the following load steps, the neural network training changes the stress-strain results established in earlier steps, due to adding additional low stress-strain estimates at lightly stressed integration points. This requires repeating the entire procedure through a number of passes over all the load steps to improve convergence. Ghaboussi et al (1998) used a Conjugate Gradient Method to solve for the incremental displacements by minimizing the derivatives of the total potential energy. All these factors make this approach computationally expensive to implement. Therefore, no attempts were made to code this algorithm for comparison. Instead, the authors solved one of the examples reported by Ghaboussi et al. (1998) and qualitatively compared the efficiency of this approach relative to the present one.

Motivated by Ghaboussi et al.'s work, Shin and Pande (2000) attempted to develop a different solution strategy that alternates between analysis prediction and neural network training. They applied all load prediction-displacement correction steps in one pass without sub-step training or analysis iterations. This is believed to improve the efficiency of the algorithm at the expense of the quality of the neuronet predictions at lower strain levels. This is mainly due to the inclusion of the full range stress-strain data in a single session of static training. The algorithm also requires storing all sets of data at all integration points of all load steps for training. In addition, Shin and Pande (2000) developed a procedure to estimate the incremental constitutive matrix from the derivatives of the neural network weights.

Alternatively, the present approach is intended to develop a more robust and efficient solution strategy. By focusing on the highly stressed integration points and using a dual nonlinear analysis-dynamic training approach, an improved quality of the results can be obtained while reducing the extensive stress-strain data storage. Two examples are solved and useful comparisons and conclusions are highlighted

Description of the present procedure

The present approach provides a more rational formulation of the stiffness matrix and an extensive reduction in the data storage and training as well as less computational effort. The load increments are sequentially applied, in the predictive analysis, to solve for displacements using stiffness matrices based on the currently trained neural network

$$\Delta p = K_i^t \Delta u \qquad (1)$$

This yields sets of stress-strain data at the integration points. The current displacements predicted at the monitored points are not expected to match the calculated displacements for a partially trained network. Therefore, a corrective analysis is required to adjust the displacements at the monitoring points to match the measured values, at all load steps. This requires adjusting the strains at the selected integration points to reflect the effect of displacement correction at the constitutive level. The existing stress-adjusted strain sets, at the selected integration points, are expected to have an improved representation of the material model. It is observed that the highly stressed integration points have captured and experienced all possible stages of stresses, which would be diluted if lower stresses at comparable strains were added for training. The inclusion of highly stressed points is controlled by a user defined parameter α. This parameter typically ranges from 0.9-1. The integration point with maximum stress is identified first. Then, other integration points having stresses equal or above 90% of the maximum stress are included for training in case of $\alpha = 0.9$. For the other extreme case, $\alpha = 1$, only the maximum stressed integration point is considered in the training. This substantially reduces the data storage and provides more focused data sets for the neural network to learn. The learning process will be explained in detail below. The neural network model, in general, provides estimates for the tangent Young's modulus, Poisson's ratio and shear modulus, at different load levels, needed to form the stiffness matrix.

Dynamic neural network technique, depicted in Fig .1, is used within the framework of the conventional feedback propagation neural networks approach (Najjar 1999). Thus there are two sets of input neurons in the input layer, history units and current state units. During training, network outputs from the previous set (lags) are fed into network input layer as current-state units to predict outputs for future states. The dynamic nature of the feedback technique has the advantage of reproducing the trained data on its own from a given initial condition. Accordingly, the stress vector predicted at the *i*-th load increment is not only dependent on the strain of that increment but also is dependent on the predicted stress vector of the (*i-1*) increment. This guarantees continuity in the predicted curves

$$\sigma_i = NN(\varepsilon_i, \sigma_{i-1}) \tag{2}$$

The training is conducted after performing both the predictive and corrective analyses. This provides a set of stress-strain values for each load step for the number of the integration points considered as highly stressed points. The spectrum of the data variation is wide since it reflects the entire loading range. The present procedure proposes the use of dual networks to train the stress-strain data. The first network is used to train low stress-strain values to obtain good predictions without unfavorable dominance of the higher stress-strain values. The second network is used to capture the response of the higher stress strain levels. The coffiecients of the stiffness matrix of an element is calculated according to the following equation

$$K_i^t = \int_{vol} B^T E_i (NN\left(\sigma_i^{t-1}, \varepsilon_j^t\right)) B dv \tag{3}$$

APPLICATIONS

Shin and Pande's approach along with the present one are used to extract the material behavior of a simple mechanical model. Then, the present approach is used to solve the same nonlinear truss problem presented by Ghaboussi et al (1998) for the sake of comparison between the two approaches.

Example I: This example consists of ten rods of the same length 6-*in* connected to a 10-*in* rigid bar, which is subjected to an eccentric loading, Fig 2. It has two degrees of freedom and ten integration points. The material model used to generate the load-deflection response at a monitored point, in a nonlinear forward analysis is based on Ramborg-Osgood equation:

$$\varepsilon = \frac{\sigma}{E}\left[1 + \frac{3}{7}\left(\frac{\sigma}{\sigma_y}\right)^{n-1}\right] \tag{4}$$

where E = modulus of elasticity of the material =*29000 ksi*, n = the material hardening coefficient = *5* and σ_y = yielding stress = *10.39 ksi*. The material model in the inverse analysis is assumed to be unknown apriori and the objective is to extract it back by matching the generated load-deflection response at the monitoring point. The load deflection responses predicted by both approaches are shown in Figs. 3-4. Both approaches show quick convergence to the exact load-deflection curve. However, the present approach required less iterations, only three compared to four for that of Shin and Pande. The α parameter for the present approach is 1. Therefore, only one integration point was used in the training. In addition, a single network achieved the desired learning process. On the other hand, Approach I by Shin and Pande used data sets from all integration points for training. The material model prediction was achieved for the both approaches, Fig 5. However, as it is mentioned above the present procedure offered faster convergence rate at a small fraction of the data storage needed.

Example II: In this example the present approach is compared to the approach proposed by Ghaboussi et al. (1998). This comparison is accomplished by solving the same example presented by Ghaboussi et al. (1998). The example is a 2-D cantilever truss, shown in Fig. 6, consisting of 25 members. The simulated experimental data is obtained by carrying out a standard load control nonlinear structural analysis. The material model used in this analysis is a Ramberg-Osgood expression:

$$\varepsilon = \frac{\sigma}{E} + \frac{2\beta\sigma_y}{3E}\left(\frac{\sigma}{\sigma_y}\right)^n \tag{5}$$

The material properties are taken as E=8.69x10^3 ksi, β = 1.25, the initial yielding stress σ_y = 10.39 ksi and n = 5. The deflection is monitored at the upper right node of the truss, Fig. 6. The simulated nonlinear load-displacement curve is shown in Fig. 7. The advantage of the present procedure is that only highly stressed points are included in the training. Since the mode of deformation is the fundamental one, α is considered in this example equals to 1 as well. That is, only the integration point of the maximum axial stress is included in training. The learning of the behavior by the neural networks is performed through two separate networks. The lower 10% of the data points are trained in the first network and the remaining is trained in the second network. Fig. 7 shows load-deflection comparison between the monitored and the predicted curves from the present and Ghaboussi et al.'s (1998) approach. The present approach required three iterations to exactly predict the load-deflection compared to two passes with extensive sub-step local iterations/training by the other procedure. The data storage is approximately 1/p*25 less than what required for Ghaboussi et al (1998) procedure, where p number of load steps. Three training cycles were needed for the present approach compared to at least 3-4 training cycles for each load step of the other approach (assuming 3-4 iterations to converge). Ghaboussi et al.'s predictions achieved excellent agreement with the simulated data. However, the present approach is seen to be closer the actual simulated data, in general. This reflects the perfect prediction of the material model by the present approach, as shown in Fig. 8.

CONCLUSIONS

In this paper, different approaches to solve inverse problems are reviewed. an efficient algorithm is incorporated to inversely solve mechanical systems and structural problems by a combination of dynamic neural network and nonlinear structural analysis. The measured global response is used to guide the solution towards predicting the inherent material behavior. The proposed method is explained by solving a simple mechanical model and a truss problem. The results obtained show that the present approach yields faster convergence rate due to focusing the neuronet training on the highly stressed points. The use of dual networks enhanced the training and the reproduction of the low stress-strain sets. The present approach also has the potential to offer a more efficient data management when applied to larger problem. This will be further investigated in the future within the framework of 2-D finite element procedure.

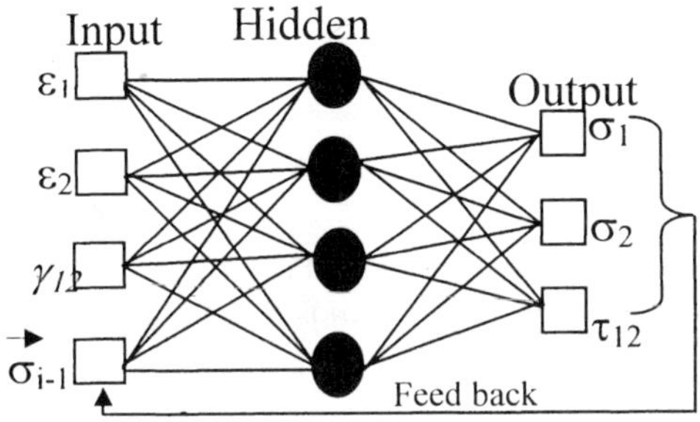

Fig. 1. Feed back neural network

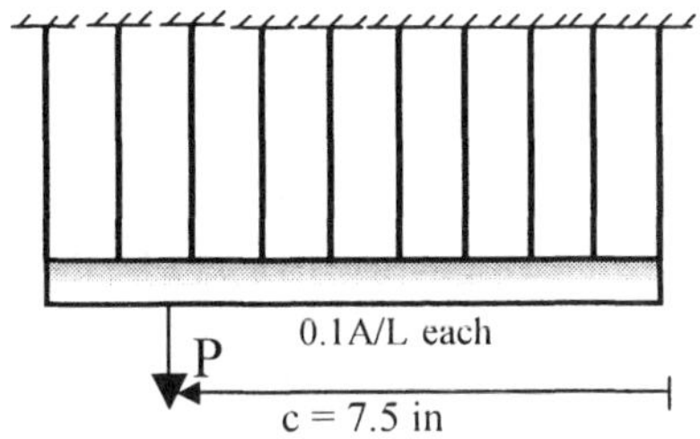

Fig. 2. Geometry of Example I.

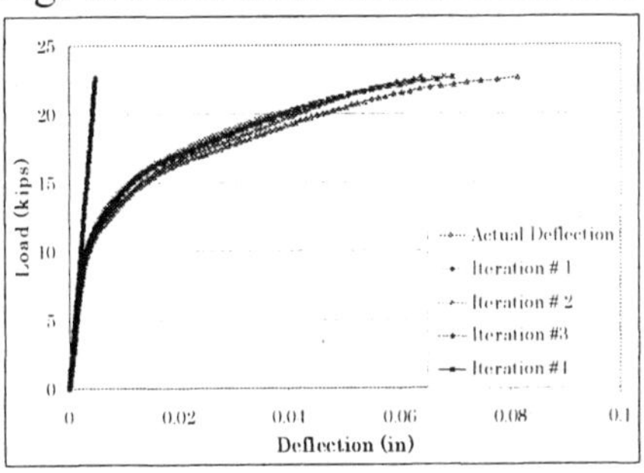

Fig. 3. Example I Prediction using Shin and Pande (2000) approach

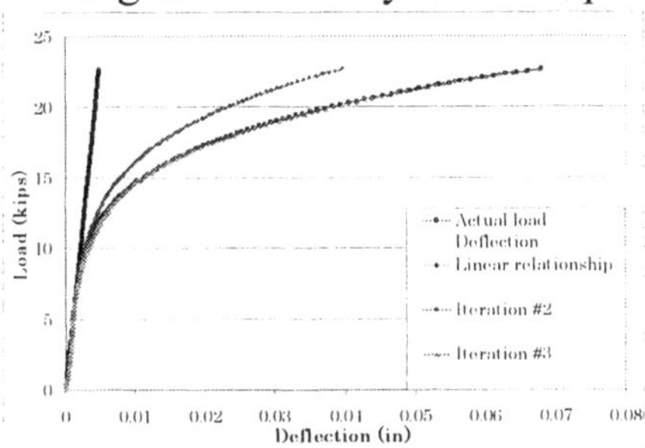

Fig. 4. Example I, Prediction using the present approach

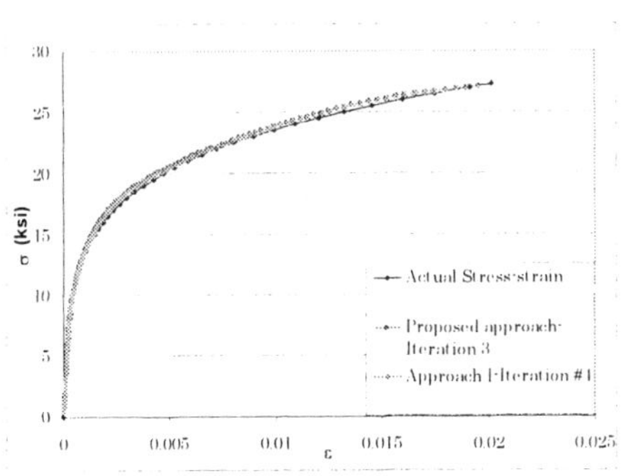

Fig. 5. Example I Prediction of stress-strain curve for both approaches.

L= 10 in, A=12 in for columns
L= 10 in, A= 4 in^2 for the diagonals and horizontals

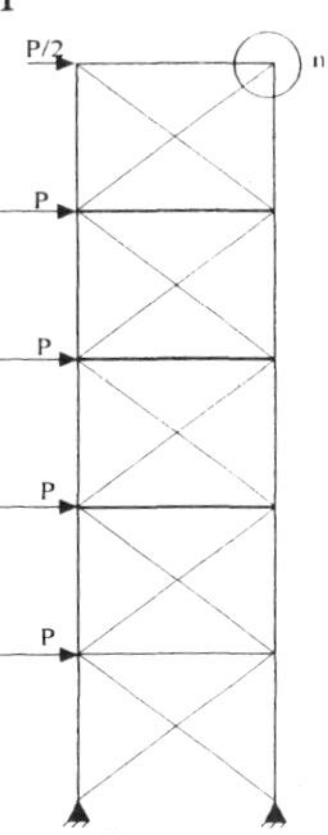

Fig. 6. Geometry of Example II.

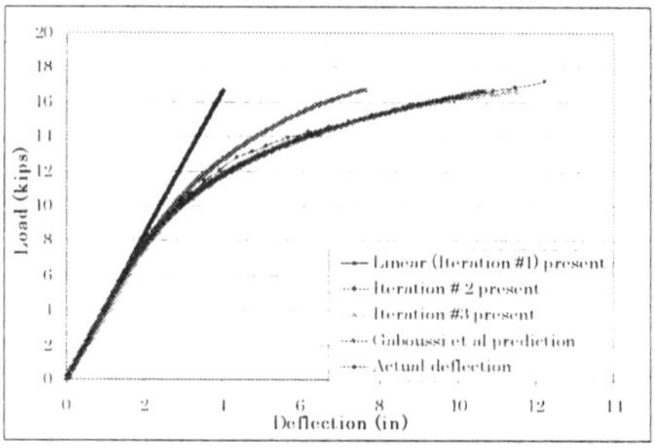

Fig. 7. Example II Prediction using Ghaboussi et al.'s approach and the present

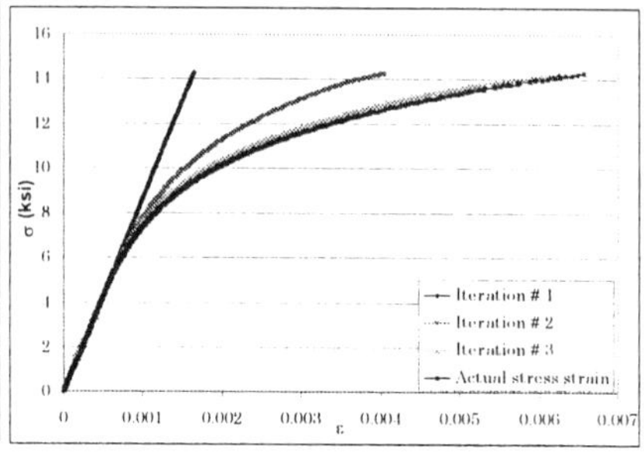

Fig. 8. Example II Prediction of stress-strain for the proposed approach and approach 1

ACKNOWLEDGMENTS

The authors would like to acknowledge the support of the National Science Foundation through its grant NSF-CMS0334391

REFERENCES

Markiewicz, E., Ducrocq, P. and Drazetic, P (1998), "Inverse Approach to Determine the Constitutive Model Parameters from Axial Crushing of Thin-Walled Square Tubes," International journal of Impact Engineering, 21(6) 433-449.

Park, K. C., Felippa, Carlos. A. "Flexibility-Based Inverse Problem Algorithm for Identification of Sub-structural and Joint Properties,' Computational Methods for Solution of Inverse Problems In Mechanics, ASME V228 11-22

Sukhorukov, I. V. (2000), "Inverse Problem of Reinforced Panels Forming," 5th Asia-Pacific Symposium on Advances in Engineering Plasticity and Its Applications, AEPA2000, Jun 12-Jun 16, 491-496

Rikards, R., Chate, A., and Gailis, G., (2001), "Identification of Elastic Properties of Laminates Based on Experiment Design," International Journal of Solids and Structures 38(30-31) Jun 8, 5097-5115

Liu, G. R. and Chen, S. C. (2002) "A Novel Technique for Inverse Identification of Distributed Stiffness Factor in Structures," Journal of Sound and Vibration 254(5), 823-835

Ghaboussi J, Pecknold, D., Zhang, M, and Haj-Ali R., (1998) "Auto-progressive Training of Neural Network Constitutive Models," International Journal For Numerical Methods in Engineering, 42, 105-126.

Shin. S. H. and Pande, G. N. (2000), "On Self-Learning Finite Element Codes Based on Monitored Response of Structures," Journal of Computers and Geotechnics, 27(3), 161-178.

Najjar, Y. M. (1999) *Quick Manual for TR-SEQ1*. Department of Civil Engineering, Kansas State University, Manhhatan, Kansas

CONSTITUTIVE MODELING OF ANGLE-PLY COMPOSITES USING COMBINED NEURAL NETWORKS-MECHANICS APPROACH

HASAN CHARKAS
Kansas State University, Manhattan, Kansas
YACOUB NAJJAR
Kansas State University, Manhattan, Kansas
HAYDER RASHEED
Kansas State University, Manhattan, Kansas

ABSTRACT
Standard constitutive modeling of fiber-reinforced polymer composite is based on uniaxial properties obtained from simple coupon testing. The nonlinear in-plane shear behavior is recognized long ago. Further research has shown that the multiaxial behavior affects the stress-strain relationship in the transverse direction and its coupling with in-plane shear response. In this study (0°, ±45°, ±75°) specimens were tested. The 0° results are used to directly obtain the fiber modulus and corresponding Poisson ratio. The ±45° plies are known to be dominant by in-plane shear behavior while the ±75° are expected to reflect the transverse behavior to a great extend. Nevertheless, the interaction of nonlinear transverse and in-plane shear response is recognized for both fiber orientation angles. In this paper, nonlinear classical lamination theory is used to assemble the ply stiffness for global tensile axial response in terms of the secant E_{22} and G_{12} values. A dual alternating inverse approach is devised to characterize the local nonlinear ε_{22}-σ_{22} and γ_{12}-τ_{12} curves using Neural Network training to capture the global experimental response. The trained models are used to predict the global response for other lay-ups.

INTRODUCTION

Fiber reinforced polymers (FRP) have been implemented in aerospace and mechanical engineering applications for around 50 years. However, their use in civil engineering infrastructure is still evolving. The linear elastic mechanical behavior of laminated composites is well discussed in textbooks (Barbero 1998). The nonlinear characterization of these composites is still a subject of interest. Efforts to model nonlinear behavior of composites existed since the 1970's. Hahn and Tsai (1973) assumed linear elastic behavior in the fiber and transverse directions and nonlinear in-plane shear response. Amijima and Adachi 1979 presented a method of predicting nonlinear stress-strain curves for unidirectional orthotropic plies. They restricted the analysis to in-plane shear nonlinearity as well. Schapery (1989) developed a work potential model to account for the effect of damage on the degradation of the transverse modulus of elasticity E_{22} and shear modulus G_{12}. Sicking (1992) applied this model to characterize unidirectional and angle-ply specimens. He concluded that the model predictions were very sensitive to small changes in E_{22} and G_{12}

This paper examines the nonlinear response of angle-ply laminates for the sake of extracting the complete in-plane nonlinear material response. This was facilitated by manufacturing several 12 in.x12 in. plates and conducting uniaxial tensile tests on 15 Carbon unidirectional and angle-ply specimens to measure their global mechanical properties (Charkas et al 2004). Neural networks are known to learn and reproduce available data. Therefore, they were implemented as a tool to recognize the pattern of the experimental measurements. After the neural networks are fully trained, they are used to generalize the behavior of the test data and reproduce it. These features made the neural networks suitable to obtain a unique global response of the 0°, ±45° and ±75° specimens. The neural network models, after training, are used to guide the inverse approach. The specimens were divided into three sets. The 0° coupons are used to obtain the constant E_{11} and ν_{12} values. The response of the ±45° and ±75° specimens is used to recover the nonlinear variation of E_{22} and G_{12} by following a dual alternating inverse approach.

In this paper, dynamic neural networks technique is used with in the framework of the back propagation neural network (Najjar 1999). Accordingly, two sets of input neurons are used, namely history units and current state units. During training, network outputs from previous set are fed into the network input layer as current state units to predict outputs for future states.. The stress prediction using neural networks can be expressed mathematically by

$$\sigma_i = NN(\varepsilon_i, \sigma_{i-1}) \tag{1}$$

Constitutive modeling by inverse approach:

The experimental measurements of the 0° specimens are used as the training data for neural networks to learn the behavior in the fiber direction. After training of the neural networks, the output is expected to be the generalized response needed to calculate the E_{11} modulus. The calculation of the E_{11} modulus is simply accomplished by finding the slope of the stress strain curve. Poisson's ratio is obtained similiarly by training the relation between the transverse strain and the axial strain. Accordingly, E_{11}= 16114755 psi, ν_{12} =0.364 are obtained from the first set of specimens.

The modulus of elasticity in the transverse direction E_{22} is usually obtained by conducting a tensile test on 90° specimens. This orientation was not prepared and tested under the experimental program that provided the data for this study. Instead, ±75° angle-ply specimens were used, which incorporates some multi-axial stress effects. Due to the coupling between the nonlinearities in E_{22} and G_{12}, an inverse approach is developed to calculate back the nonlinear variation of the transverse and in-plane shear moduli by simultaneously using the trained neural network curves of the ±45° and ±75° specimens. It is important to note that different specimens have slightly different dimensions, Table 1. Therefore, the experimental axial force-strain curves (N_x-ε_x) are normalized to get the effective $\overline{\sigma}_x$-ε_x data prior to training. The ±45° and ±75° specimens were separately trained and the neural networks were able to learn and store the knowledge in the connection weights. Each network was then used to reproduce the effective stress-strain curves. This is made prior to extracting the ply constitutive properties in the transverse and in-plane shear directions. Figs. 1-2 show the predicted curve using the neural networks versus the experimental measurements. These curves for the ±45° and ±75° specimens will be used in the dual inverse mechanics approach to guide the process of extracting the transverse and in-plane shear local responses.

Based on nonlinear lamination theory of a symmetric angle-ply laminate in direct tension, the secant applied load-in plane strain relationship is expressed as follows:

$$\begin{bmatrix} Nx \\ 0 \\ 0 \end{bmatrix} = \begin{bmatrix} A_{11s} & A_{12s} & 0 \\ A_{21s} & A_{22s} & 0 \\ 0 & 0 & A_{66s} \end{bmatrix} \begin{bmatrix} \varepsilon_x \\ \varepsilon_y \\ 0 \end{bmatrix} \tag{2}$$

where N_x = the applied tensile force, ε_x = the axial strain, ε_y = the transverse strain, $A_{ijs} = \sum_{k=1}^{n} (\overline{Q}_{ijs})_k\, t_k$, t_k = the thickness of each ply, $\overline{Q}_{ijs}$ = transformed in-plane constitutive coefficients in global coordinates (Barbero 1998). These are functions of the individual ply constitutive matrix elements in local coordinates $Q_{11}=E_{11}/\Delta$, $Q_{12s}= Q_{21s} = \nu_{12}E_{22s}/\Delta$, $Q_{22s}= E_{22s}/\Delta$, $Q_{66\,s}= G_{12\,s}$ and $\Delta = 1\text{-}\nu_{12}\nu_{21s}$

Solving for ε_y from equation (2) yields:

$$\varepsilon_y = \frac{-A_{21s}}{A_{22s}}\varepsilon_x \tag{3}$$

Thus, the axial force is related directly to the axial strain by the following:

$$N_x = \varepsilon_x \left[A_{11s} - \frac{A_{12s}^2}{A_{22s}} \right] \tag{4}$$

and the relevant A_{ijs} expressions become:

$$A_{11s} = \left[\frac{E_{11}^2 \cos^4\theta + 2\upsilon_{12}E_{11}E_{22s}\sin^2\theta\cos^2\theta + E_{11}E_{22s}\sin^4\theta}{E_{11} - \upsilon_{12}^2 E_{22s}} + 4G_{12s}\sin^2\theta\cos^2\theta \right] t \tag{5}$$

$$A_{22s} = \left[\frac{E_{11}^2 \sin^4\theta + 2\upsilon_{12}E_{11}E_{22s}\sin^2\theta\cos^2\theta + E_{11}E_{22s}\cos^4\theta}{E_{11} - \upsilon_{12}^2 E_{22s}} + 4G_{12s}\sin^2\theta\cos^2\theta \right] t \tag{6}$$

$$A_{12s} = \left[\frac{E_{11}(E_{11} + E_{22s})\sin^2\theta\cos^2\theta + \upsilon_{12}E_{11}E_{22s}(\sin^4\theta + \cos^4\theta)}{E_{11} - \upsilon_{12}^2 E_{22s}} - 4G_{12s}\sin^2\theta\cos^2\theta \right] t \tag{7}$$

where t = the total thickness of the laminate which is dropped from both sides of equation (4) to achieve consistency in the measured data that are independent of geometrical variations. As a result of the above formulation, the effective stress is related directly to the measured axial strain with E_{22s} and G_{12s} being the only independent unknowns. Accordingly, equation (4) is applied simultaneously to the trained neural network results of the ±45° and ±75° specimens to recover the two unknowns at common local ply strain levels.

$$\overline{\sigma}_{x(\pm45)} = \varepsilon_{x(\pm45)}\hat{a}_{(\pm45)}(E_{22s}, G_{12s}) = \varepsilon_{x(\pm45)}\left(a_{11s} - (a_{12s}^2 / a_{22s})\right) \tag{8}$$

$$\overline{\sigma}_{x(\pm75)} = \varepsilon_{x(\pm75)}\hat{a}_{(\pm75)}(E_{22s}, G_{12s}) = \varepsilon_{x(\pm75)}\left(a_{11s} - (a_{12s}^2 / a_{22s})\right) \tag{9}$$

where $a_{ij} = A_{ij} / t$. The proposed inverse approach is based on the fact that the ±45° laminates are known to capture the dominance of in plane shear response. On the other hand, the ±75° specimens are expected to reflect the transverse behavior to a great extent.

Description of the procedure:

It is evident that common levels of the axial strain ε_x or tensile effective stress do not correspond to the same levels of local strains (ε_{22}, γ_{12}). Accordingly, equations (8) and (9) cannot be solved simultaneously in any direct way. In the present procedure, the nonlinear in-plane shear curve and the nonlinear transverse ply response are extracted using a dual alternating inverse approach. This approach requires an assumed initial σ_{22}-

ε_{22} curve to recover an estimated nonlinear shear response from equation (8). This solution is expected to yield a good estimate since the results of the ±45° laminates are dominated by in-plane shear. Therefore, a constant E_{22} = 1500 msi is assumed in the first cycle (Carlsson and Gillespie 1989). For every level of $\bar{\sigma}_{x(\pm 45)}$ - $\varepsilon_{x(\pm 45)}$, the smallest positive root (G_{12s}) of equation (8) is determined. The corresponding local γ_{12} value in any ply of the laminate is computed using equation (3) along with standard strain transformation of ε_x and ε_y to ε_{11}, ε_{22}, γ_{12}, which are the axial strain, transverse strain and shear strain respectively in material or ply coordinates. The transverse strain is used to calculate a corresponding E_{22s} modulus from the latest ε_{22}-σ_{22} curve. If the substitution of this new secant value in equation (8) does not give back the measured load value (or effective stress value), seeking a new $G_{12}s$ is repeated until the convergence to the experimental measurement is attained.

Once a nonlinear τ_{12}-γ_{12} curve is recovered from the first cycle, it is used to calculate back an estimated nonlinear σ_{22}-ε_{22} curve from equation (9) in terms of E_{22s} following the same iterative procedure used in the prediction of G_{12s}. This dual alternating procedure is repeated until both curves converge. It is important to note that it took only one cycle for in-plane shear and two cycles for the transverse curve to converge in the present application, which is confirmed by the results of the following cycle, Figs 3-4.

Description of the forward analysis procedure

The obtained properties are used to calculate the response of any angle ply composite laminates through nonlinear analysis. The E_{11}, ν_{12} values are kept constant during the analysis while the transverse and in-plane shear strains are assumed to follow the predicted nonlinear curves, Figs 1-2. By gradually increasing the axial strain ε_x in each case, current secant values of E_{22s} and G_{12s} are used to determine the corresponding ε_y from equation (3), (6) and (7). The global strains are then transformed to get the local strains ε_{22} and γ_{12} through standard strain transformation. The latter values are used to update the E_{22s} and G_{12s} according to Figs. 3-4. The process is repeated iteratively for each axial strain step until convergence of axial force is achieved. The failure criterion used in the analysis is the well known strain criterion. The modes of failure are labeled S for in-plane shear failure and M for matrix extensive cracking. The complete effective axial stress-strain curves are re-computed and plotted in Fig. 6 for the ±45° and ±75° specimens respectively. The other orientation angles are divided into two sets and plotted in two different graphs for clarity. Different stacking angles are considered (±15°, ±30°, ±50°, ±55°, ±60°). Fig. 5 shows the response of the ±15° orientation. It is clear that the curve does not have a pronounced non-linearity. This is due to dominance of the fiber direction on the response. However, with the increase of fibers orientation angle, the non-linearity becomes more pronounced as in the case of ±30° laminates. The ±45° lay-up represents a pure shear case as it is reflected in the response shown in Fig. 6. For angles larger than 45, more strain is transferred to the transverse direction, which accordingly delays the in-plane shear failure. This provides more ductility as more axial strain to failure is engaged. The angle of optimum ductility could be investigated. It is worth mentioning that the simultaneous failure of matrix and shear failure is reached at ±55° orientation. The ductility is reduced with orientation angles larger than ±55° because of the yet larger strain values transferred to the transverse direction causing the matrix to assume failure first.

CONCLUSIONS

In this paper, neural networks were used to train the experimental data obtained from tensile tests of unidirectional and angle-ply coupons. Excellent agreement is obtained between the neural network predictions and the experimental results. An inverse dual alternating approach is used to extract the nonlinear transverse behavior and the in-plane shear curve from the global response learned by neural network of angle-ply laminates. Nonlinear classical lamination theory is adopted, along with the secant stiffness approach, to assemble the ply stiffness for global tensile response that guide the inverse approach. The analytical forward calculations using the predicted nonlinear ply curves are shown to recover back the global response results in perfect match with the measured experimental data. This re-confirms the accuracy of the constitutive model predictions. Furthermore, the extracted material model is used to analyze laminates with different orientation angles. The analysis showed that more ductility can be achieved by an optimum orientation which qualifies its introduction to infrastructure strengthening applications, where ductility is a major concern.

Table 1. Specimens' geometry

sp #	Fiber Orientation/ Stacking	t (in)	w (in)	sp #	Fiber Orientation/ Stacking	t (in)	w (in)	sp #	Fiber Orientation/ Stacking	t (in)	w (in)
1	$(0)_8$	0.053	1.032	6	$(\pm45)_{4s}$	0.056	1.03	11	$(\pm75)_{4s}$	0.053	1.03
2	$(0)_{16}$	0.098	1.04	7	$(\pm45)_{4s}$	0.053	0.91	12	$(\pm75)_{4s}$	0.053	1.03
3	$(0)_8$	0.055	1	8	$(\pm45)_{4s}$	0.056	1.04	13	$(\pm75)_{4s}$	0.053	1.03
4	$(0)_8$	0.049	1.027	9	$(\pm45)_{4s}$	0.053	1.03	14	$(\pm75)_{4s}$	0.053	1.03
5	$(0)_8$	0.055	1	10	$(\pm45)_{4s}$	0.053	1.02	15	$(\pm75)_{4s}$	0.053	1.03

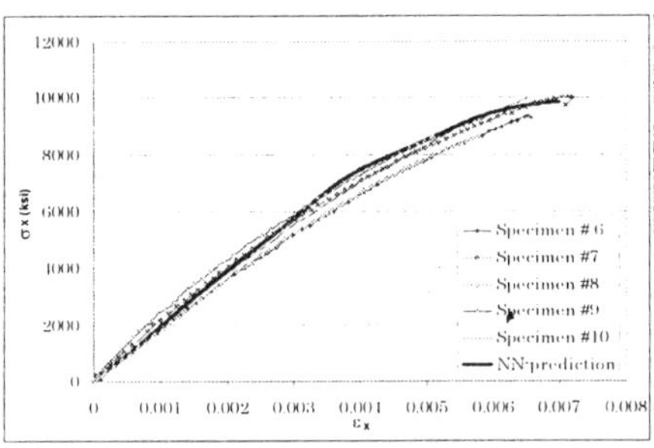

Fig. 1. ±45 NN prediction compared to experiment

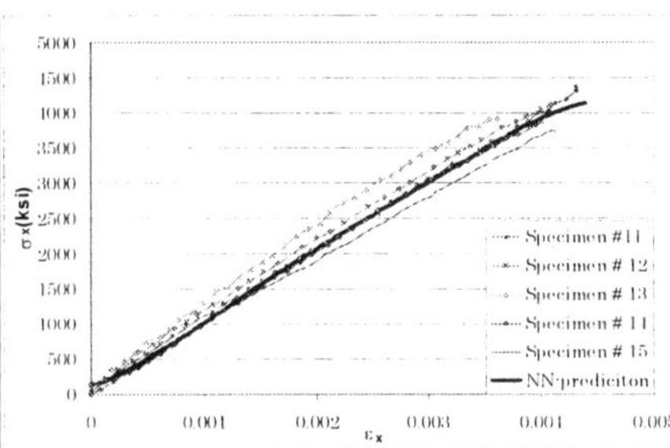

Fig. 2. ±75 NN prediction compared to experiment

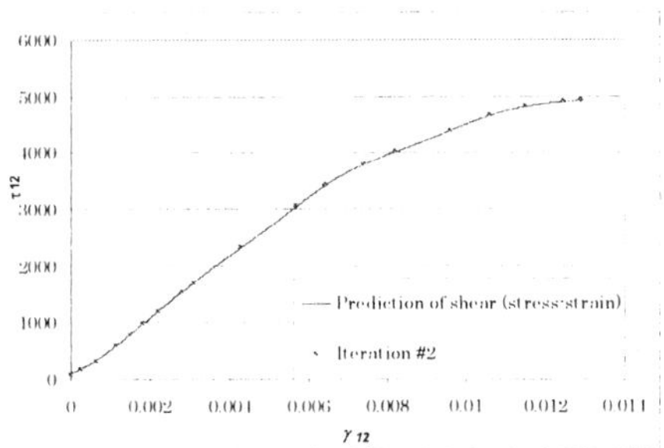

Fig. 3. Prediction of the γ_{12}-τ_{12} curve

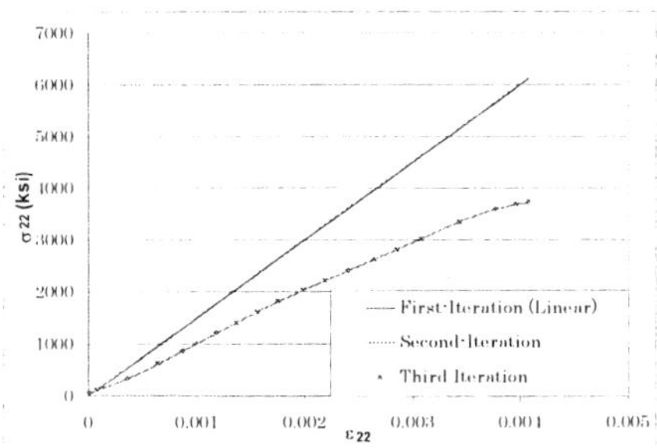

Fig. 4. Prediction of the ε_{22}-σ_{22} curve

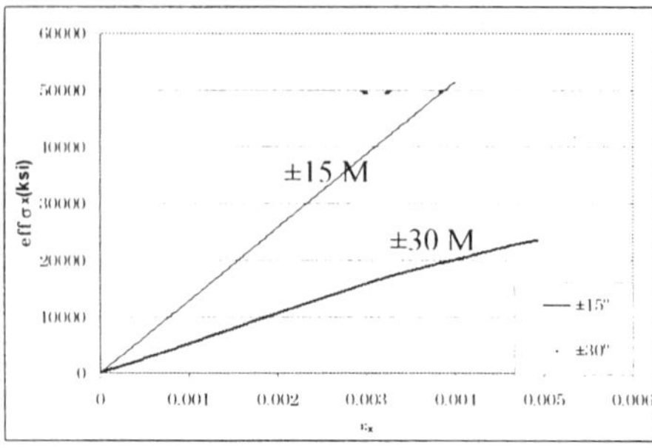

Fig. 5. Prediction of the effective stress strain curve ε_x- $\overline{\sigma_x}$

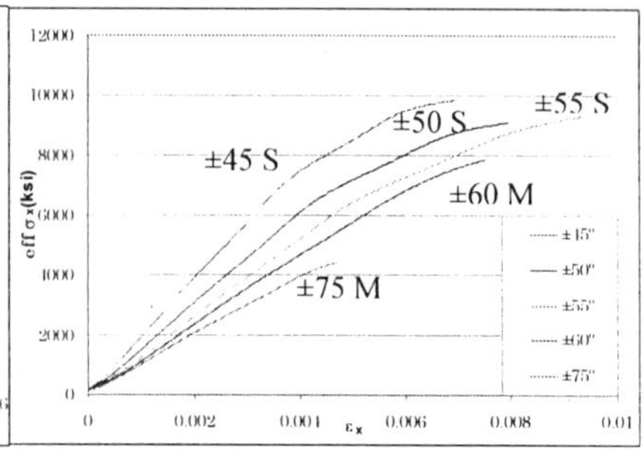

Fig. 6. Prediction of the effective stress strain curve ε_x- $\overline{\sigma_x}$ (±45, ±45, ±45, ±45, ±45)

ACKNOWLEDGMENTS

The authors would like to acknowledge the support of the National Science Foundation through its grant NSF-CMS0334391

REFERENCES

Amijima, S. and Adachi, T., (1979) "Nonlinar Stress-Strain Response of Laminated Composites," Journal of Composite Materials, Vol. 13, pp. 206-218.

Barbero, E. J. (1999), Introduction to Composite Materials Design, Taylor & Francis, Pennsylvania, USA, 336p.

Carlsson, L, A. and Gillespie, J, W. (1989) Delaware Composites Design Encyclopedia, Technomic Publishing Co., Lancaster, Pa., U.S.A, 150p.

Charkas, H, Rasheed, H., Elbella A., Lease, K. "Characterization of the Nonlinear Response of FRP Angle Ply Laminates," 17th Engineering Mechanics Conference, ASCE, June 14-16, University of Delaware, Newark.

Hahn, H. T. and Tsai, S. W. (1973). "Nonlinear Elastic Behavior of Unidirectional Composite Laminate," Journal of Composite Materials, Vol. 7, pp. 102-118.

Najjar 1999 add with pages.

Schapery, R. A. (1989), "Mechanical Characterization and Analysis of Inelastic Composite Laminates with Growing Damage, In: Mechanics of Composite Materials and Structures," ASME AMD-Vol. 100, pp. 1-9.

Sicking, D. L. (1992) "Mechanical Characterization of Nonlinear Laminated Composites with Transverse Crack Growth," Ph.D. Dissertation, Texas A&M University, Dec. 1992, 122p.

FAULT DIAGNOSIS IN ROTATING MECHANICAL SYSTEMS USING SELF-ORGANIZING MAPS

ABHINAV SAXENA
School of Electrical and Computer Engineering, Georgia Institute of Technology, Atlanta, Georgia

ASHRAF SAAD
School of Electrical and Computer Engineering, Georgia Institute of Technology, Savannah, Georgia

ABSTRACT

The power of Self-Organizing Maps (SOM) for the visualization of high-dimensional data has been well recognized over the past decade. They map nonlinear statistical relationships among different variables of a high dimensional input data on a low dimensional network, preserving most of the topographic relationships from the input space. This paper presents an SOM-based multi-sensor diagnostic system architecture for the condition monitoring of a bearing health. Bearings being an essential part of most of the rotating machinery their failure are one of the most common causes of machine breakdowns. Therefore a continuous monitoring of the bearing health is required and several sensors are often used for this purpose. Out of several sensors used, all do not respond to the fault in a similar fashion, and thus may or may not be indicative of a problem individually. A SOM based approach has been used to map the time series data produced by various sensors to map the process dynamics onto the network and a trajectory of system states showing the bearing health trend has been shown to warn of impending failure and/or shut down to prevent damage

INTRODUCTION

One of the most effective descriptions for complex industrial plants or machines is the state space representation. Such systems are monitored by measurements from a variety of sensors to identify the current system states. The number of such measurements increases fast with the complexity of the system, and typically the number of state variables in such representations exceeds the number of measurements by an order of magnitude. Furthermore the fact, that the relationship among different variables may not be completely linear, makes the analysis fairly complex. Particularly in the process of fault diagnosis, it is very important to identify a smaller set of system states that are characteristic of the general behavior of the system, and can be assessed from the measurements. Therefore the application of SOM in system health monitoring can be a suitable choice to accomplish this goal. SOM has the ability to map a high dimensional signal manifold on a low dimensional topographic feature map, with most of the topological relationships of the signal domain preserved (Kohonen, 1996a, 1996b). It aggregates clusters of input information from the raw data, and projects them on a much simpler two or three dimensional network, thereby contributing to relatively comprehensible visualizations.

The organization of the paper is as follows: Section I describes the basic SOM algorithm with a deeper insight of its capabilities, citing some applications. The roller bearing health monitoring context for fault diagnosis along with the methodology has been explained in section II. An approach based on SOM visualization has been suggested for health monitoring in section III. Section IV discusses the results thus obtained, followed by the conclusion from the study.

THE SOM ALGORITHM

Kohonen and Simula (1996) explain the SOM algorithm for engineering application context, and describe it as nonlinear, ordered and smooth mapping of high dimensional input data domain onto the elements of a regular, low-dimensional array. The algorithm can be implemented in the following manner.

An SOM array is defined in the final output dimension, usually 2-d or 3-d. The number of points/nodes in SOM array depends on the requirement to be able to best represent the input data vector set. For the original version of SOM algorithm, one needs to specify the size of the network in the beginning, however the Growing SOM implementation dynamically adjusts the array size at the time of training. Dittenbach *et al* (2000) discuss Growing Hierarchical SOM (GHSOM) architecture, where the training starts with a initial map size of 2x2 and further nodes are added/deleted until a predetermined criteria like the quantization error (QE) and the mean quantization error (MQE) have reached a predetermined threshold. However for simplicity the basic SOM algorithm has been presented here. Let the high dimensional input data be represented by a set $\{X_j\}$ of real vectors $\mathbf{x} = [x_{i1}, x_{i2}, x_{i3}, \ldots, x_{in}]^T \in \mathbb{R}^n$. A parametric real vector $\mathbf{m}_i = [\mu_{i1}, \mu_{i2}, \ldots, \mu_{in}]^T \in \mathbb{R}^n$ is associated with each element of SOM array. A decoder function is defined on the basis of distance $d(\mathbf{x},\mathbf{m}_i)$ between the input vector and the nodes of SOM, to define the image of the input vector on the map. Definition of $d(.)$ can be chosen based on the application, however the Euclidean distance measure is most widely used . The image is defined as the index of the node with minimum distance from the input vector.

$$c = \arg\min_i \{d(\mathbf{x}, \mathbf{m}_i)\} \tag{1}$$

The task is to define $\mathbf{m}_i$ such that the mapping is ordered and descriptive of the order of $\mathbf{x}$ using vector quantization, optimized $\mathbf{m}_i$,can be obtained. As a result a set of values $\{\mathbf{m}_i\}$ is obtained as the limit of convergence of the following sequence (Kohonen, 1996b):

$$m_i(t+1) = m_i(t) + \alpha(t)\delta_{ic}[x(t) - m_i(t)] \tag{2}$$

Where $\alpha(t)$ is the monotonically decreasing learning rate and δ_{ic} is the neighborhood function, which models elastic interconnections between the adjacent nodes. The learning in such elastic environment is shown schematically in Fig. 1.

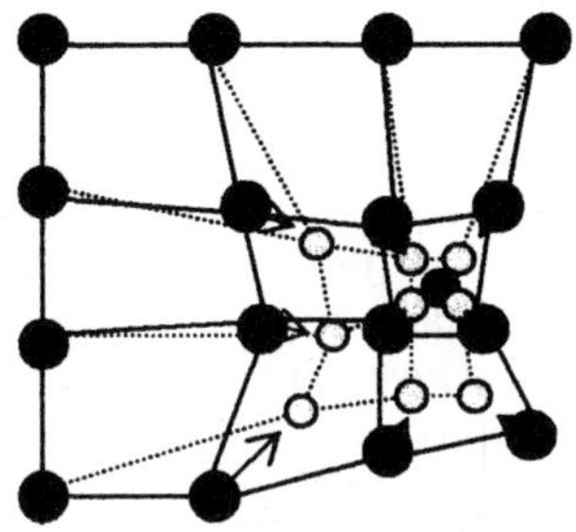

Figure1. Updating of $\mathbf{m}_i$ based on best matching unit (BMU) criteria. Red node represents current input vector, black and grey nodes represents $\mathbf{m}_i$ after successive updating.

This elastic nature of the map helps it self organize it into a shape that best represents the data. For example a neighborhood function can be defined as δ_{ic} = 1 if the distance between node c and node i is less than a specified radius, else δ_{ic} = 0, and all such nodes for which the neighborhood function is non zero are said to be the neighbors of node c and thus belong to N_c. Thus SOM equations reduce to:

$$m_i(t+1) = m_i(t) + \alpha(t)[x(t) - m_i(t)],\ i \in N_c(t) \tag{3}$$

$$m_i(t+1) = m_i(t),\ i \notin N_c(t) \tag{4}$$

Several variants of the basic SOM have been used for different applications based on different distance and neighborhood functions. Also the learning rate $\alpha(t)$ can be defined specific to the problem. Other methods to find $\mathbf{m}_i$ have been described in (Kohonen and Simula, 1996).

BEARING FAULT DIAGNOSIS

Rolling element bearings are common components to almost all forms of rotating machinery. Bearing failure is one of the foremost causes of breakdowns in such machinery. This breakdown, when unexpected, can be catastrophic, as in a helicopter main rotor bearing, or result in costly downtime, as in a process plant machine. Critical machines are therefore subjected to continuous condition monitoring for bearing health trending, to warn of impending failure, and/or to shut down a machine to prevent further damage. Several sensors can be used to obtain the signatures of the fault, but the vibration and acoustic sensors have been shown to be the most effective in most of the rotating machine parts. This study shows how the measurements obtained for a faulty bearing can be mapped to a two dimensional pictorial representation and state trajectory can be plotted to observe the system heading.

Eight channels of data corresponding to 8 different sensors (2 acoustic emission sensors (AE), and 6 accelerometers) were obtained for a faulty tapered roller bearing as shown in Fig.2. Sensors being of different kind and mounted at different locations were expected to respond differently to the faults. These sensors were attached to signal conditioners and programmable lowpass filter such that each had ground-isolated outputs. Groove defects were constructed with an Electrical Discharge Machine. Total 8 different grooves sizes were included in the study in addition to normal bearing. The groove geometries used in these tests have been described in (Billington 1997). All tests were run at a radial load of 14730 N and a rotational speed of 1400 RPM. The data was acquired as several snapshots of the time series for each case.

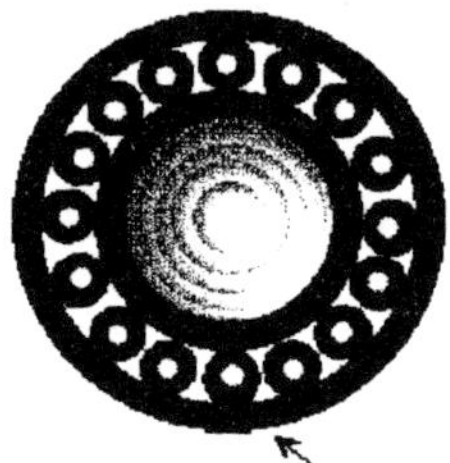

Figure2. Outer race defect in tapered roller bearing

SOM APPROACH FOR BEARING HEALTH MONITORING

As SOM algorithm is a nonlinear projection method, it efficiently maps different characteristic features into the clusters on the map, without any explicit modeling of the system. The feature selection is however very critical, and one of the most important factors in the success of modeling. In practical situations some measurement values may be missing, due to any of the many possible reasons, but such deficiencies in the data can be handled very well by SOM (Samad and Harp, 1992). Two approaches have been proposed in the literature for the application of SOM for fault diagnosis (Kohonen and Simula, 1996). First, as a supervised case when data corresponding to almost all the states, including faults, is available, secondly as the unsupervised case where only the non-faulty data is available. Whatever may be the choice of applicability, SOM shows its strengths. This paper presents the case of a supervised SOM, where the data corresponding to a particular fault in several stages has been used to train the SOM. This data gets mapped onto different regions on a 2D topographic map. Once the SOM network is ready, it is exposed to the actual data from the system under unknown state. The data points are mapped onto the network as they are sequentially fed to the map describing the current state of the system. A trajectory is drawn joining all the points to show, how and to which state the system is approaching next. This information can be used for fault diagnosis, and with few enhancements, also for making prognostic assessments towards the remaining useful life of system. Feature extraction was done using mainly two features, Kurtosis and the Curve length. Both provide statistical information about the nature of data, and were found to be reasonably good features for single shaft bearings. Kurtosis is the fourth moment about the mean normalized with variance as given by Eq (5):

$$K = \Sigma(x-\mu)^4 / N\sigma^4 \quad (5)$$

Where N is the number of sample points in the window used to calculate Kurtosis. The feature vectors are then fed to the SOM for training. To test the effectiveness of SOM, several snapshots of data corresponding to a fault evolution in a similar bearing were used. The points map to the nodes representing the similar state as the current input, and when plotted give trajectories showing the system advancement during fault evolution. All the implementation was done using SOM Matlab Toolbox (URL toolbox, 2003).

RESULTS AND DISCUSSIONS

As shown in Fig. 3, a 2D topographic map for each sensor was created, and nodes corresponding to different features mapped at different points. It can be seen that these sensors form about 3-4 different groups. Sensors number 1, 2 and 3 fall in one category, as they show similar behavior at similar positions. Sensors number 5, 6 and 7 fall in one group. However both acoustic sensors namely number 4 and number 8 do not match in response to any of the accelerometer groups. U-matrix (Fig. 5) shows a comprehensive mapping taking into account the feature values from all sensors collectively. Three groups can be easily identified. Group 1 consists of very closely scattered data points in the input space, and group 3 consists of relatively sparse data. Furthermore, Fig. 4 shows the system trajectory for data from sensor number 3. It can be clearly seen that the system started (marked as blue star) from a low feature value and approached towards high feature value suggesting the fault evolution. The shape of the trajectory remains the same on all maps. Since the data from different sensors map differently, depending upon how they perceive the change in the vibration signal, not all sensors are able to detect the fault in a similar fashion. Some sensors that did not detect fault can be recognized by the fact that even for small fault levels they show high feature values and for large faults they do not necessarily approach towards the high values. Moreover this idea can also be extended to the cases where the a priori information about the faults is not available. A suitable measure like quantization error can be defined, and if it increases beyond a certain bound for the new input vectors, an alarm can be raised to indicate that the system is approaching a faulty state. The SOM toolbox itself implements the growing SOM, and hence determines the number of nodes on the map based on the input vectors. It was observed that up to an extent increasing the size of network decreased both the quantization error and the topographic error, but beyond that both errors did not change much. For the illustrations in this paper a map size of 9x9 was used. An area of future research is to use hierarchical SOM models to discover if the data contains any inherent hierarchy.

CONCLUSIONS

It has been shown that SOMs can be used to detect faults in roller bearings, and can therefore prove to be a powerful tool for bearing health monitoring. This approach can be used for both supervised and unsupervised learning. User-friendly and fairly comprehensible visualizations are easy to monitor and also indicate which sensors respond to what faults, and under what conditions. A fault may be indicated by a collective response of several sensors, which may not be obvious just looking at the data using other diagnostic techniques

ACKNOWLEDGEMENTS

Authors would like to thank Woodroof School of Mechanical Engineering, and Intelligent Control Systems Loboratory at the School of Electrical and Computer Engineering, Georgia Instirute of Technology for the experimental data sets provided for the work.

REFERENCES

Ahola, J., Alhoniemi, E., Simula, O., "Monitoring Industrial Processes Using the Self-Organizing Map", Soft Computing Methods in Industrial Applications, SMCia/99 Proceedings of the 1999 IEEE Midnight-Sun Workshop on , June 1999, pp. 22 – 27

Billington,S. A., "Sensor and Machine Condition Effects in Roller Bearing Diagnostics" Master's Thesis, Department of Mechanical Engneering, Gerogia Institute of Technology, Atlanta, 1997

Deboeck,G., Kohonen,T.,Visual Explorartions in Finance with Self-Organizing Maps, Springer Finance, 1998

Dittenbach,.M, Merkl,D., Rauber, A., "Using Growing Hierarchical Self-Organizing Maps for Document Classification", ESANN'2000 proceedings – European Symposium on Artificial neural Networks, Bruges(Belgium), April 2000, pp. 7 – 12

Kohonen, T., Self-Organizing Maps, 2nd ed. Springer Series in Information Sciences.

Kohonen, T., "The Self-Organizing Map", Proceedings of the IEEE ,Vol. 78 , Issue: 9, Sept. 1990 pp. 1464 – 1480

Kohonen, T., "New Developments and Applicatons of Self-Organizing Maps", IEEE Transactions 1996a, pp. 164 – 171.

Kohonen, T., Simula, O., Oja, E., Simula, O., "Engineering Applications of the Self-Organizing Maps", Proceedings of the IEEE, Vol. 84, No. 10, October 1996b, pp. 1358 – 1384

Kohonen, T., "Analysis of Processes and Large Data Sets by a Self-Organizing Method", Intelligent Processing and Manufacturing of Materials, 1999. IPMM '99. Proceedings of the Second International Conference,Vol. 1 , July 1999 pp. 27 – 36

Samad,T., and Harp, S. A., "Self-Organization with Partial Data", Network: Computation in Neural Systems, May 1992, 3(2), pp. 205-212

Simula, O., Kangas, J., "Process Monitoring and Visualization using Self-Organization Maps", pp. 371- 382

Simula, O., Vesanto, J., Vasara, P., "Analysis of Industrial Systems Using the Self-Organizing Map, Knowledge-Based Intelligent Electronic Systems, 1998. Proceedings KES '98. 1998 Second International Conference, vol.1, April 1998 pp. 61 – 68

URL: SOM Toolbox http://www.cis.hut.fi/projects/somtoolbox/, last updated: August 2003

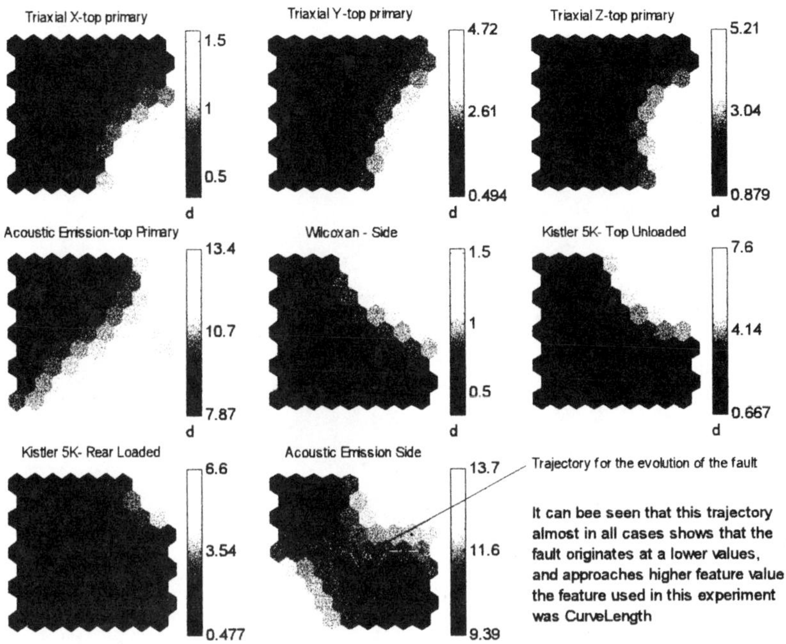

Figure3. Shown above are the eight different SOM planes corresponding to eight sensors. Different sensors perceive vibrations differently, and therefore for the same evolving defect, they organize themselves differently in the topographic plane.

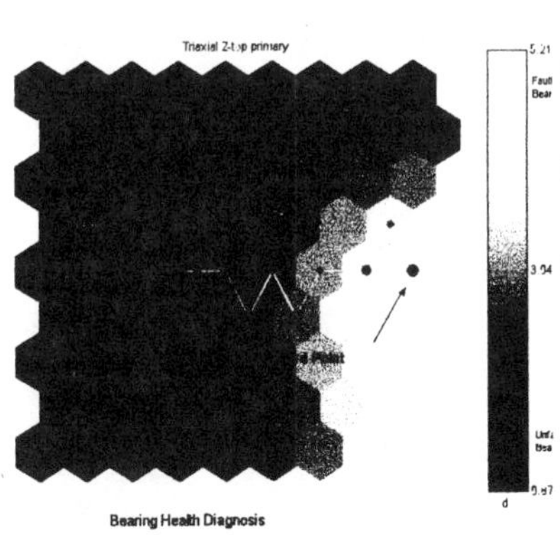

Figure4. Detailed view of accelerometer (z-axis) response (mounted on the top of the housing). This accelerometer nicely captures most of the states in the evolution of the fault, and thus the trajectory clearly seems to approach lighter (faulty) region, as time progresses.

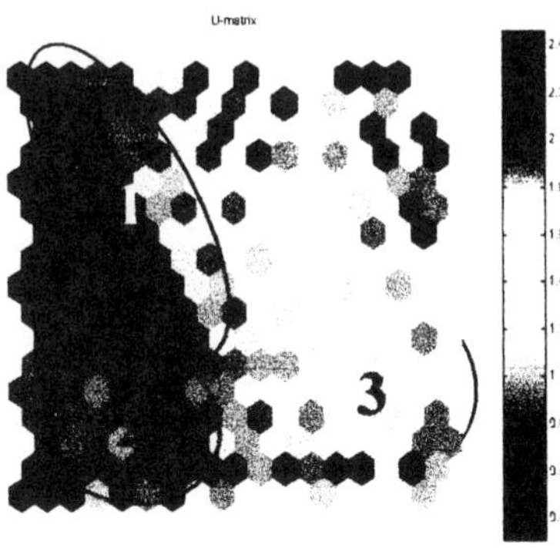

Figure5. U-Matrix shows overall dispersion of data, taking into account the information from all sensors. Three different clusters can be very clearly seen.

PART IX: FINANCIAL ENGINEERING

FINANCIAL FORECASTING USING A NEURAL NETWORK TRAINED WITH THE MACD TECHNICAL INDICATOR

VINCE OVLIA AND DAVID ENKE
Engineering Management Department
Laboratory for Investment and Financial Engineering
Center for Intelligent Systems
University of Missouri – Rolla
Rolla, MO 65409-0370

ABSTRACT
This research studied the use of neural networks in financial forecasting using the MACD technical indicator. Specifically, a backpropagation neural network was trained with four inputs: closing price, volume, MACD, and signal line. Moving windows were used for each input to the network. The optimal moving window size for each input was found. Also, output threshold levels were applied to the output of the network. The results were examined. Finally, the optimal number of neurons in the hidden layer of the network was found. Output threshold levels were tested on the output of the "final" network. It was found that a neural network trained with a technical indicator can be useful in predicting the price movement of a financial market.

INTRODUCTION

For many years there has been a great desire to understand the stock market. To most people, the rise and fall of the market is unclear, and the factors affecting market moves are obscure. However, involvement in the stock market has been rising. The growth of the Internet has, in part, facilitated the rise in the interest in stocks as well as the amount of money invested. Different on-line trading sites, such as E-Trade, have made it possible for virtually anyone to invest in the market. Investors are becoming more dependent on advanced computer and communication technologies to benefit from a wider range of investment choices (Elton and Gruber, 1991).

In the past, the financial press has extensively covered the growth of artificial systems in financially based decisions. Much of the initial coverage had been centered on “expert systems” (Trippi and Turban, 1996). In spite of this, expert-systems have posed several problems. First, large computer programs must be written and maintained. This requires an extraordinary amount of time and effort. Also, information from human experts must be gathered and translated into a set of If-Then rules (Trippi and Turban, 1996). Moreover, expert systems are unable to adapt to changing situations. Thus, these systems have to be constantly modified.

To an extent, these problems could be lessened or eliminated with the use of artificial neural networks. Artificial neural networks provide a powerful technique that can theoretically approximate any nonlinear continuous function to any designed degree of accuracy (Cybenko, 1989). In many situations, financial managers have to make decisions based on incomplete, ambiguous, incorrect, and irrelevant information. The decision process must be viewed in an objective manner (Trippi and Turban, 1996). In some cases, humans lack the ability to make such decisions. Neural networks have the ability to learn and generalize. The novelty of neural networks lies in their ability to model nonlinear processes without a priori assumptions about the nature of the generating process (Hagen, Demuth, and Beale, 1996). This proves very useful in the unstructured decision environment of the financial world (Trippi and Turban, 1996), where much is assumed, and little is known about the nature of the processes determining asset prices (Burrell and Folarin, 1997). Numerous researchers have used neural networks within the financial domain (Amornwattana and Enke, 2003; Chenoweth and Obradovic, 1996; Desai and Bharati, 1998; Motiwalla and Wahab, 2000; Thawornwong and Enke, 2003a,b).

For this project, a neural network was created to predict a financial market. In this case, the S&P 500 composite index was used as the measure of the total stock market. The S&P 500 index is made up of the 500 most widely held US common stocks. It is often regarded as an accurate measure of the total US equity market. The Moving Average Convergence/Divergence (MACD) technical indicator, including signal line, was included as inputs to the network, along with closing price and volume of the index.

BACKGROUND

Technical analysis is the study of prices, primarily using charts. The roots of technical analysis reach back to Charles Dow and his creation of the Dow Theory at the beginning of the twentieth century (Achelis, 2001). Technical analysis is made up of technical indicators, which are mathematical formulas used to analyze price, volume, or some combination (Chande and Kroll, 1994).

The MACD is a trend following momentum indicator. It shows the differences between two moving averages of price, often the difference between the 26-day and 12-day exponential moving averages. A signal line, the 9-day exponential moving average, is plotted along with the MACD. In terms of percentages, the 26-day, 12-day, and 9-day exponential moving averages are the 7.5%, 15%, and 20% moving averages, respectively. If the MACD crosses the signal line from below, then a buy signal is produced, and when the MACD crosses from above, a sell signal is produced. In wide-swinging markets, also known as trending markets, the MACD performs very well. In markets in which price stays in a certain range, the MACD performs poorly (Achelis, 2001).

NETWORK DESIGN

For this research, the feed-forward neural network trained with standard backpropagation was designed using the Neural Networks Toolbox in Matlab 6.5. Feed-forward neural networks have been widely used for financial forecasting due to their ability to classify and predict the dependent variable (Vellido, Lisboa, and Vaughan, 1999). A detailed explanation of the backpropagation algorithm that is used to train feed-forward neural networks can be found at (Rumelhart, and McClelland, 1986). Moving windows were also introduced for the inputs, such that the current input, as well as a certain number of delayed inputs, act as the actual inputs of the neural networks. Table 1 gives the initial neural network parameters. The network was trained from 1998 to 2002 to expose it to examples of both a bull and bear market. The market experienced large gains from 1998-2000 and declined in 2001 and 2002.

Parameter	Value
Training Function	gradient decent with momentum
Number of Layers	2 (hidden layer and output layer)
Weight and Bias Initialization	Ngyuen-Widrow
Learning Rate	$\mu = 0.01$
Momentum Rate	$\alpha = 0.1$
Maximum Number of Epochs	5000
Mean Squared Error Goal	0.048
# of Neurons in the Hidden Layer	8
Transfer Functions	hidden layer: tangent sigmoid output layer: tangent sigmoid
Inputs*	closing price, volume, MACD, signal line
Size of the Moving Window**	closing price = 3, volume = 10, MACD = 5, signal line = 5
Target***	closing price_{t+1} – closing price_t

Table 1: Initial Neural Network Parameters

* The data used to train the network was daily data for the S&P 500 composite index from January 2, 1998 to December 31, 2002. The data was normalized between -1 and 1.
** The number of inputs is defined as the size of the moving window for each input. For example, since the size of the moving window for the price is three, the moving window for price is made up of price_t, price_{t-1}, and price_{t-2}, where t is measured in days.
*** The target was set to the price move for the next trading day, normalized between -1 and 1.

NETWORK TESTING METHODS

The network was simulated using the S&P 500 composite index data from January 2, 2003 to March 18, 2004. A positive output was translated as a prediction of a positive market move for the given day. To test the efficiency of the network, the percentage of times the network correctly predicted a positive move in the S&P 500 price was found. For each input, different window sizes were tested and the ability of the network to predict positive price movements were calculated. For each input, different window sizes were tested three separate times and the average efficiency was taken. In Table 2, the range for the moving window sizes tested for each input are defined.

After the optimal window sizes were found for each input, the optimal number of neurons in the hidden layer was obtained. The testing range for the number of neurons in the hidden layer was eight to fourteen. Finally, different output threshold levels were tested on the output of the network. Only simulated outputs with a value above the threshold were considered and the efficiency of the network was observed. The range of output thresholds tested was between 0.05 and 0.25, in increments of 0.05.

Input	Range of the Moving Window Sizes Tested
Closing Price*	3-11
Volume**	5-16
MACD	5-15
Signal Line	5-15

Table 2: Range of the Sizes of the Moving Windows Tested

* The range of the windows sizes for closing price was originally between three and ten. However, since the highest network efficiency occurred when the size of the windows was ten, an additional window was tested at size of eleven.
** The range of the windows sizes for volume was originally five to fifteen. However, since the highest network efficiency occurred when the size of the windows was fifteen, an additional window was tested at size of sixteen.

NETWORK TEST OBSERVATIONS

The optimal window sizes were found as given in Table 3.

Input	Optimal Window Size
Closing Price	10
Volume	15
MACD	12
Signal Line	5

Table 3: Optimal Window Sizes for Each Input

For the most part, as the output threshold increased, the efficiency of the network increased. However, at an output threshold level of 0.20, the efficiency was suddenly reduced. For further investigation, the output thresholds were tested for the network with optimal neurons in the hidden layer.

It was found the optimal number of neurons in the hidden layer was twelve. For the research, this network was considered the "final" network. With twelve neurons in the hidden layer, the correlation between the output threshold level and the efficiency of the network was similar to the network with eight neurons in the hidden layer. When the output threshold layer was 0.10 or smaller, the network produced more accurate results. During financial predictions, correctly predicting market moves at a percentage above 60% is considered acceptable. Though further researched needs to explored, a small output threshold level seemed to increase the efficiency of the network.

For this research there were several factors that may have been responsible for limiting the success of the network. First, only four inputs were used to predict the S&P 500 composite index. In *Neural Networks for Financial Forecasting*, Gately (1996) was able to accurately predict the S&P 500 index using thirteen inputs. Thus, the number of inputs may have limited the performance of the network. Second, the MACD indicator was used as an input. The MACD works well in trending markets, but not in markets in which price moves within a certain range. Thus, the predictive capabilities of the network may have been affected when the market was range bound.

RESEARCH ISSUES

In hindsight, there were several issues that developed during the research. These issues should be evaluated and modified in order to test the validity of future research. The issues are listed below:

- For an input, a window size was only evaluated for three trials.
  - The data collected from a neural network was sometimes inconsistent. In order to remove these inconsistencies, the efficiency of the networks should be tested over more trials.
- The efficiency of the network was the only test for the performance of the network.
  - In future studies, other network performance measures, such as the R^2 statistical measure should be used to give further insight into the network. Furthermore, the efficiency of the network was determined through trial-and-error. A more formal approach should be investigated.
- The network was only simulated over one time period.
  - The network was only simulated from January 2, 2003 to March 18, 2003. All network performance judgments were based on this time period. However, financial markets are always changing. Thus, a network with excellent performance during a certain time period may produce poor results for another time period. During future studies, the network should be simulated over multiple time periods.
- Profitability and transaction cost were not studied.
  - In financial prediction models, the system should be profitable. The transaction costs of investing in the market should not be greater than the profits predicted by the network. A system should take into account the magnitude of the price move in order to be truly valuable to an investor. This will be an area of future research.

CONCLUSIONS

The Financial forecasting using artificial intelligence has become increasingly popular over the past few years. Some of the past research has centered on expert systems. However, expert systems have limitations. These limitations include: a large time requirements for coding and maintenance, an inability to generalize, and the difficulty of translating the knowledge of human experts into conditional statements. Neural network have the ability to eliminate or reduce these problems.

For this research, a neural network was designed with four inputs: closing price, volume, MACD, and signal line. The MACD is used in technical analysis to determine when a security should be bought or sold. The MACD works best in trending markets. Thus, the network may have performed erratically in times when the price stayed within a small range.

The inputs were tested using different window sizes. A window size determined how many delays were associated with a given input. The efficiency of each network was tested. For this research, the network efficiency was defined as the number of correctly predicted positive market moves over the total number of predicted positive market moves. The result was expressed as a percentage. After the optimal number of windows was found for each input, the network was trained and tested. Furthermore, a threshold level was placed on the output of the network, and the results were investigated. Next, the optimized network was tested with different numbers of neurons in the hidden layer. After the optimum number of neurons in the hidden layer was found, output threshold levels were again tested. It was found that small output threshold levels could possibly increase the efficiency of the network. Finally, project limitations and issues were discussed.

In the final network, the model efficiency reached a maximum of approximately 66%. For financial forecasting, this is considered an acceptable value, and one that will often result in profitability. However, with further modifications, this network should be able to realize even higher levels of efficiency.

REFERENCES

Achelis, Steven B. Technical Analysis from A-Z. New York: McGraw Hill, 2001. April 2004 <http://www.equis.com/Education/TAAZ> .

Amornwattana, S., and D. Enke, "A Hybrid Option Pricing Model Using a Neural Network for Forecasting Volatility", *Intelligent Engineering Systems through Artificial Neural Networks*, Vol. 13 (2003): 725-730.

Burrell, P.R. & Folarin, B.O. (1997). "The impact of neural networks in finance", *Neural Computing & Applications*, 6, 193-200.

Chande, Tushar S., and Stanley Kroll. The New Technical Indicator: Boost Your Profit by Plugging into the Latest Indicators. New York: John Wiley and Sons, 1994.

Chenoweth, T. & Obradovic, Z. (1996). "Embedding technical analysis into neural network based trading systems", *Applied Artificial Intelligence*, 10, 523-541.

Cybenko, G. (1989). "Approximation by superpositions of a sigmoidal function", *Mathematics of Control, Signals, and Systems*, 2, 303-314.

Desai, V.S. & Bharati, R. (1998). "The efficiency of neural networks in predicting returns on stock and bond indices", *Decision Sciences*, 29, 405-425.

Elton, E.J. & Gruber, M.J. (1991). Modern Portfolio Theory and Investment Analysis. 4th edition, New York, NY: John Wiley & Sons.

Gately, Edward. Neural Networks for Financial Forecasting. New York: John Wiley and Sons, 1996.

Rumelhart, D.E. & McClelland, J.L. (1986). Parallel Distributed Processing: Explorations in the Microstructure of Cognition, vol. 1, 318-362. Cambridge, MA: The MIT Press.

Hagen, M.T., Demuth, H.B., & Beale, M. (1996). Neural Network Design. Boston, MA: PWS Publishing Company.

Motiwalla, L. & Wahab, M. (2000). "Predictable variation and profitable trading of US equities: a trading simulation using neural networks", *Computer & Operations Research*, 27, 1111-1129.

Thawornwong, S., and D. Enke, "The adaptive selection of financial and economic variables for use with artificial neural networks", *Neurocomputing*, Vol. 56 (2003a): 205-232.

Thawornwong, S., D. Enke, and C. Dagli "Neural Networks as a Decision Maker for Stock Trading: A Technical Analysis Approach," *Journal of Smart Engineering Systems Design*, Vol. 5 (2003b): 1-13.

Trippi, Robert R., and Efraim Turban. Neural Networks in Finance and Investing. Chicago: Probus Publishing Company, 1996.

Vellido, A., Lisboa, P.J.G., & Vaughan, J. (1999). "Neural networks in business: a survey of application (1992-1998)", *Expert Systems with Applications*, 17, 51-70.

BEATING THE HOUSE: A STUDY ON IMPROVING BOLLINGER BANDS USING NEURAL NETWORKS

DUSTIN TRINKLE AND DAVID ENKE
Engineering Management Department
Laboratory for Investment and Financial Engineering
Center for Intelligent Systems
University of Missouri – Rolla
Rolla, MO 65409-0370

ABSTRACT
Much has been written and analyzed when it comes to stock market prediction. Through this discussion, analysts have proven time and time again that linear solutions do not fair well in the prediction of stocks and show little promise that they ever will (Falas et al, 1994). In fact, technical analysts appear to have a leg up when it comes to the debate as they attempt to look for more nonlinear solutions. One of these technical solutions is the use of the Bollinger Band in hopes to better map the volatility of a stock over time (Stridsman, 1997). This band has its flaws, however, and it is the goal of this research to apply a neural network to help aid the band to become more effective in a trending market.

INTRODUCTION AND BACKGROUND

Stock market forecasting is an art that attracts the masses in an effort to find the inefficiencies in the market. People and companies spend countless dollars every year just to find arbitrage opportunities within the trading systems that fuel economies. Most have computer systems and programs such as STS that seek out the most efficient trading strategies and aid paying customers with their portfolios (Brennan, 1988).

All of these "strategies" of course undermine the most traditional argument that many forecasters have to acknowledge - the efficiency of the market (Bollinger, 2002). This efficiency makes the argument that the market seeks out the most efficient level as its participants buy and sell securities. If everyone is seeking to benefit, then theoretically there should be no benefit of doing technical analysis other than examining the random walk model (Cowles, 1994). The random walk model simply states all of this in simpler terms: that the best prediction for the next day's stock price is the current day's price.

There have been numerous studies conducted on the lack of performance of some very well known financial forecasters when compared to a simple random model. Financial forecasters have been cited as being everything from ignorant to thieves. Researchers such as Alfred Cowles go as far as to extensively study the forecasts of specific renowned forecasters and report failures across the board (Cowles, 1994), although it is still a matter of opinion on how the results are tabulated.

These forecasters, of course, were in question prior to widespread computer use for analysis. Nonetheless, pattern following should still prove useful if the market is in fact inefficient. One of the most versatile of these pattern matching technical indicators is the Bollinger band (Bollinger, 2002), which was conceptualized by the widely respected financial analyst, John Bollinger. Since they came to fruition, the bands have been both widely welcomed and criticized at the same time. One such criticism is the observation that the bands are practically useless in a trending market by generating incorrect sell and buy signals (McNicholl, 1998).

It goes without saying that the markets are of a nonlinear fashion and there are numerous believers in Bollinger bands, which obtain respect from reacting so well to volatility of the price (Bollinger, 2002; Renshaw, 1993). The third part of the suggestive equation is the encouragement that the market is not completely efficient and there are indeed flaws to exploit. Thus it is evident that there is a possibility that the application of a neural network applied to a Bollinger band pattern recognition scheme following the price of an index would aid the band to better acknowledge a trending market. There have been other such studies with positive results of looking at applying neural networks to technical indicators, so this provides further encouragement that the networks should not fail in this situation (Safer and Wiliamowski, 1999).

METHODOLOGY AND DATA SET-UP

To examine the methodology, the study must first demonstrate some background on the factors of the equations being considered.

Bollinger Bands

The Bollinger Band is essentially a price envelope that follows a price of a stock or index as it goes through time. The bands contain a middle, upper, and lower band. The middle band is nothing more than a moving average of the price averaged over varying look back periods. For the purpose of this study, all look back periods for Bollinger band calculations are set to 20 days as suggested by Bollinger himself (Bollinger, 2002). The 21 day value would be considered statistically significant in most cases, but the stock market does not follow a normal distribution anyway (Bollinger, 2002).

The upper and lower bands are calculated as being two standard deviations above and below the middle band and the equations are given below. Although there are varying values for the suggested use of the standard deviation calculation, two were chosen for our purposes because of the 20 day look back period (Bollinger, 2002). The calculations of the bands are as follows:

$$\text{Upper Band} = \text{Middle Band}+(2)*\text{sqrt}(\text{sum}(\text{close}-\text{Middle Band})\text{^}2)/20) \quad (1)$$

$$\text{Lower Band}= \text{Middle Band}+(2)*\text{sqrt}(\text{sum}(\text{close}-\text{Middle Band})\text{^}2)/20) \quad (2)$$

$$\text{Middle Band} = \text{sum}(\text{close})/20 \quad (3)$$

Figure 1 shows the bands plotted against the price. The data used for the calculation is based on the closing price of the S&P 500 index from July 1, 2002 thru December 31, 2003. Notice how as the market trends upward that the price is still fluctuating up and down across the general sell signal of 80% b (Bollinger, 2002), with percent "b" being calculated as the price minus the lower band, and dividing that quantity by the quantity of the upper band minus the lower band, as given in Equation 4.

%b=(closing price-lower band value)/(upper band value-lower band value) (4)

Figure 1: Bands plotted against Price

This calculation produces a number that is generally within the 0 and 1 range but can fall out of this range. The typically accepted sell signal is generated when this value drops below the 80% mark. As one can see though, in a trending market, the bands become useless (McNicholl, 1998). Bollinger as well acknowledges this problem but doesn't provide a solution to the problem (Bollinger, 2002). He does however make mention that another type of indicator should be used to confirm a buy or sell signal on the bands, such as the relative strength index.

Relative Strength Index

The relative strength index, RSI, is the second input and was first introduced by J. Welles Wilder and has essentially been around for decades (Elder, 1990). It is deeply imbedded in technical analysis and looks to create values between 0 and 100, based on the following formula:

$$RSI = 100-(100/(1+(U/D))) \quad (5)$$

U represents the average upward price change over the look back period
D represents the average downward price change over the look back period

The look back period used for this study was the generally accepted 14 day period. The RSI has also been suggested by other researchers as a good counterpart to the %b indication in stock market prediction (Stridsman, 1997). Bollinger even cites an alteration to his equations for the normal bands and offers a suggestive band strategy for applying them to the RSI indicator. This essentially creates a normalized value for the use of the bands, which might work well for other studies (Bollinger, 2002).

Backpropagation

There exists several studies on the backpropogation learning rules and stock market prediction, but none could be found involving Bollinger bands. Furthermore, one study goes at great length to suggest parameter values when predicting the stock market using the steepest descent algorithm. The particular study suggested a low number of neurons for the few amount of inputs that we are looking to use for the network (Tan and Wittig, 1993).

Further research on the matter, along with several failed attempts into the process, it was discovered that the Levenberg-Marquardt training algorithm would be more suited to the process. It was thought to be more efficient and train much quicker (Safer and Wiliamowski, 1999). Although some studies suggested minimal neurons in the hidden layer, most suggested that trial-and-error methods were best for determining the right parameters for a network.

ARCHITECTURE

Originally, a basic backpropagation model was attempted in this study, but the results were poor. The magnitude and percent correct direction of the prediction did not provide much help for the model.

The Levenberg-Marquardt training algorithm was widely suggested and seems to predict stock prices well. Nonetheless, after further review and training a network to predict based on previous day price alone, it is found that this algorithm appears to represent the random walk model. The random walk model appears to lag behind the actual data when the prediction of the model is plotted. This is the same pattern produced by Levenberg-Marquardt. For our inputs, it was eventually found that resilient backpropagation learned quickly but not to the extremities of Levenberg-Marquardt. It also did not seem to focus in on price in the input set as much either. Thus, with the resilient algorithm in mind, the study continued.

The study eventually settled on a 50 neuron structure in a single hidden layer. Fewer amounts of neurons were suggested and tried, but the results were poor. Fewer neurons created a network close to the random walk model, which just focuses on price. These networks lag behind the price and only predict the direction of the next day 48% of the time. With RSI and percent b as inputs, the more neurons that were added (up to 50), the better the network became at being predictive, instead of reactive. Other research has also indicated that the addition of more than one layer of hidden neurons is no more effective than a single hidden layer. Thus, this study settles on a single layer of hidden neurons with a tangential sigmoid activation function in the first layer and a pure linear function in the second layer.

The inputs to the network were essentially normalized values of the price, relative strength index, and percent b. Percent b was thought to reflect the input of the Bollinger band in the equation. The target of the network was simply a normalized version of the next day's closing price. It is important to note that the prices in question for training were the daily closing prices for the S&P 500 index from January 1997 thru June 2002. The network was then tested over the period of July 2002 thru December 2003.

The weights were initialized to random values. After numerous trials, the network was allowed to train for only 210 iterations with a average mean square error goal of approximately 0.0096. Further runs with varying iterations were attempted without better results. Further inputs, such as using more than one day's previous price, were examined but produced no more promising results. After each training, the test data was simulated through the network and results analyzed based on actual versus predicted graphs and a percent correct direction calculation. Most of these results were stored and then set aside for comparison with other models.

RESULTS

The results produced a prediction that gave the correct direction 53% of the time and a percent error of magnitude of 0.0169. Nonetheless, the first part of the prediction appeared to be better than the later values. It is for this reason that the study continued in order to exploit this disparity.

Moving Window

To take advantage of this disparity, the network was "moved" over a quarter's worth of time (roughly 61 days at a time) and retrained on the same amount of data points but now 61 days forward into the future. This process was repeated five times until the network had retrained and obtained better results for each quarter of the test data in question. The new results yielded a correct percent direction of 62% and a percent error in magnitude of 0.0157. Thus, the moving window helped improve the direction prediction of the network drastically.

Trading Strategy

After the network was trained and tested, a trading strategy was employed to see if the network could actually aid the Bollinger band in its prediction capabilities. The results of these strategies can be seen in Table 1. While both performed well, the 2nd is the strategy that is essential for our purposes. This strategy examines the problem of the band's prediction ability in the upward trending market. The strategy was first employed with only the bands, trying to compensate for their problem by allowing them to only sell at the 80% b mark if they had seen five days of negative stock movement. These results and the buy and hold strategy (for comparison) are shown in the table.

The strategy was then re-employed with the network's aid to give a prediction for the fifth day and hopefully allow the trader to get out at an earlier time if they need to, but otherwise stay in the position if the market is in fact going to go back up. The results are encouraging with the network help beating both the original band and the buy and hold strategy. It must be noted that the strategies listed in Table 1 do not take into account transactions costs. To increase profits even more, network confirmation was also used in buy decisions at the bottom of the bands.

Table 1. Trading Strategy Results

	Profit for Strategy 1	Strategy 2- Without buy aid	Strategy 2- With Buy aid
Buy and Hold ($)	143.27	143.27	143.27
Bollinger Bands (BB) ($)	139.38	134.81	276.69
Bollinger Bands with Network ($)	281.34	197.74	339.62
% increase over BB (%)	**101.85**	**46.7**	**22.7**

CONCLUSIONS

From this study it is reasonable to suggest that the trending problem of the Bollinger band can be corrected to some extent over the cycle of time that was examined on the S&P 500 index. The study also showed that it was possible to accurately predict the market direction over the same index and test period over 62% of the time, which essentially "takes the house" if you are in a casino, for which the stock market is often compared. Also, it has been shown through trading strategies that the Bollinger Band indicator can be improved upon in a trending market. This study would also suggest that the basic gradient descent training algorithm is not a good training algorithm for the prediction of stock market values. This, however, may not necessarily the case, as it just did not work well for this purpose. Furthermore, this study went beyond what has been demonstrated here and several other methods have been tried in order to obtain the results that were presented, but these go beyond the scope of this study. Some of the other methods involve a drastic overhaul of input and target parameters.

REFERENCES

Brennan, Peter J., Tracking Stocks Like an Expert, Business Publications Inc., 1988.

Bollinger, John. Bollinger on Bollinger Bands, *McGraw-Hill*, 2002.

Cowles, Alfred. "Stock Market Forecasting", *Econometrica*, Vol. 12, No. 3 (Jul.-Oct.,1994), pp. 206-214.

Elder, Alexander "RSI's Variety of Messages", *Futures*, Vol. 19, (April 1990) pp. 38.

Falas, Tasos; Charitou, Andreas; and Charalambous, Chris. "The Application of Artificial Neural Networks in the Prediction of Earnings", *IEEE International Conference*, Vol. 6, (June 1994) pp. 3629-3633.

McNicholl, Dennis "Better Bollinger Bands", *Futures*, Vol. 26, (October 1998).

Renshaw, Edward "Modeling the Stock Market for Forecasting Purposes", *Journal of Portfolio Management*, (Fall 1993) pp. 76-81.

Safer, A.M.; Wiliamowski, B.M. "Using Neural Networks to Predict Abnormal Returns of Quarterly Earnings", *International Joint Conference on Neural Networks*, Vol. 6, (July 1999) pp. 3840-3843.

Stridsman, Thomas. "Bollinger Bands are more than meets the eye", *Futures*, Vol. 26, Issue 13, (Nov 1997) pp. 42-46.

Tan, C.N.W.; Wittig, G.E.. "A Study of the Parameters of a Backpropagation Stock Price Prediction Model", *First New Zealand International Two-Stream Conference on Artificial Neural Networks and Expert Systems*, (Nov. 1993) pp. 288-291.

A NEURAL NETWORK APPROACH TO FORECASTING INVENTORIES FROM INTEREST RATES

ANTHONY JOSEPH, PH.D.
Computer Science Dept.
Pace University
163 William Street, 2nd Floor
New York, New York 10038

NORMAN MOSELEY, M.Sc.
Computer Science Dept.
Pace University
163 William Street, 2nd Floor
New York, New York 10038

ABSTRACT
Inventory investment, which is 0.6% of gross national product (GNP), accounts for about half the size of the changes in GNP and inverted interest rates are predictors of economy activity. Business people see evidence that interest rates affect inventory behavior. Nevertheless, the interest rates inventory relationship remains an important open and difficult research problem. Therefore, we propose to use a time-delayed neural network trained with the Levenberg-Marquardt backpropagation algorithm to determine the relationship between inverted nominal interest rates and aggregate inventory as well as to then predict inventory behavior from interest rates. We did not achieve a unique prediction. We achieved many statistically accurate predictions at the 95% confidence level. Our inconclusive result suggests a complex interest rates aggregate inventory relationship that might be resolved by studying the relationship between interest rates and inventories' components.

INTRODUCTION

Inventories play a dominant role in a nation's economy and their changes are important features in business cycles. Changes in inventory investment have more influence on changes in the gross national product (GNP) than any other economic variable. The 10 recessions in the United States between 1945 and 2001 have been generally attributed to inventory adjustments (Larrain, 2002). This may be attributable to their size and volatility: the stock of real inventories was 155% the gross domestic product (GDP) in year 2000. Blinder and Maccini (1991) showed that typically in these recessions a fall in inventory investments caused a subsequent fall of 87% in GNP. Inventory behavior is basically explained using the production smoothing model and the multiplier accelerator model. These respective models represent the microeconomic and macroeconomic views of inventories (Blinder and Maccini, 1991).

Real sales, real inventories, and nominal interest rates are interrelated and important business cycle variables. Changes in interest rates produce lagging changes in the economy. A basic premise of monetary policy is that interest rates' changes affect and predict many macroeconomic variables. Real nominal interest rates are 'inverted leading indicators' of real economic activity – a high interest rates now is a predictor of low real economic activity 6-12 months hence (King and Watson, 1996). Larrain (2002) used spectral analysis to investigate the macroeconomic interrelationship between nominal interest rates, real sales, and real inventories. He showed that changes in inverted nominal interest rates lead changes in sales by an average of about 17 months while changes in sales lead changes in inventories by an average of about nine months. Joseph and Moseley (2004) confirmed the sales inventory relationship using neural networks and then proceeded to show that changes in aggregate sales now is a predictor of changes in aggregate inventories eight months in the future. Larrain's cross-spectral analysis of changes in nominal interest rates and changes in inventories revealed an ambiguous relationship. Since changes in inverted nominal interest rates lead changes in sales and changes in sales lead in changes inventories, one might suspect that changes in inverted nominal interest rates lead changes in inventories. Therefore, in this study we propose to develop a focused time lagged feedforward neural network (TLFN) model trained with the Levenberg-Marquardt backpropagation algorithm to empirically determine the exact relationship between changes in inverted nominal interest rates and changes in aggregate inventories. We will then use this information to help predict changes in inventories from changes in interest rates. To substantiate the goodness of the prediction, we will test for a structureless prediction error using power spectrum density, autocorrelation, and partial autocorrelation statistical tests.

Artificial neural network models are analogous to a simplistic mathematical description of a biological nervous system operation: an adaptable, nonlinear, highly interconnected parallel system. Their essential features include massively parallel and distributed processing elements, knowledge acquisition from the environment through learning, and memory for acquired knowledge (Haykin, 1999). They can be interpreted as adaptive nonlinear filters that may be static or dynamic. Neural Network models are particularly effective on data sets typified by nonstationary, non-Gaussian, and or nonlinear dynamic characteristics. They have a nonparametric structure, which allows them to learn about relationships in the data directly from the data. Moreover, they are noise and fault tolerant with adjustable network weights and a high degree of redundancy making them relatively more complex, versatile, and flexible than the standard statistical tools.

In economics and finance, neural network models find applications in such areas as financial modeling, stock performance modeling, 30-year U.S. Treasury bond forecasting, end-of-year net asset value of mutual funds, and the stock ranking problem (Refenes et al, 1994; Cheng et al, 1996; Chiang et al, 1996; Refenes et al, 1994).

From the statistical results of the experiment, it was found that the positive lead of inverted nominal interest rates over aggregate inventory is not unique to a specific duration. It was possible to develop neural network models that yielded statistically accurate prediction of inventories from interest rates for leads of 6 months, 17 months, 19 months, 25 months, and 29 months. These predictions were within the 95% confidence limit. We concluded that the relationship between interest rates and inventories is complex and may, in some cases, be indirect. That is, there might be many factors that affect the relationship between interest rates and inventories. Therefore, the result of this experiment is inconclusive.

MATERIALS and METHODS

The raw data used in this study were equivalent to those Larrain (2002) used in his work, except they extended over the period from January 1965 to December 2000. The data sets included aggregate real total business inventories, nominal interest rate (3-month Treasury (T) bills), and aggregate real total business sales obtained from the U.S. Department of Commerce. The inventories and sales data were representative samples from the manufacturing and trades sector of the economy. Manufacturing and trades inventories exceeded 87% of the "nonfarm inventories" in 1989 (Blinder and Maccini, 1991). The data were preprocessed to remove serial correlation as well as some nonstationary characteristics. The preprocessed interest rates, inventory, and sales data sets consisted of 420 12-month backward first difference samples with means removed. Nonetheless, the data sets may still have been nonstationary. The data sets were nonlinear--exponential trend. These types of data sets can be adequately processed using neural networks.

Neural networks can be designed to model any nonlinear data set without having much information and prior knowledge (Haykin, 1999). The feedforward multilayer perceptron, with as few as one hidden layer, is a universal approximator (Haykin, 1999). It is the most widely used neural network structure for time series prediction. The focused TLFN, a dynamic version of the multilayer perception, can process nonstationary nonlinear data with the present output dependent on the present and past input values. We used the focused TLFN implemented in the MATLAB environment. This network consisted of 30 input nodes, a 10-node hidden layer, and an output node. The learning algorithm was the Levenberg-Marquardt backpropagation functioning in the sequential mode and characterized by the minimization of the *mean square error* between the network's output and the target data set. For this experiment, the network was trained with input from interest rate and target from inventory and sales data sets. The activation functions used were the hyperbolic tangent sigmoid function with range from –1 to +1 (Haykin, 1999) for the hidden layer and the linear transfer function for the output layer. In addition, the data sets were arbitrarily partitioned into training set, validation set, and testing set beyond the first 7.1%, which was used for initialization of the focused TLFN input memory unit. These subsets of data were further decomposed according to the rule $\theta = n_i + n\Delta n$, where θ represents the training set if $i = 0$, θ represents the testing set if $i = 1$, and θ represents the validation set if $i = 2$; $\Delta n = 4$, a fixed number; and $n \in \mathbb{Z}^+/360$ for the training, validation, and testing sets. For this experiment, $n_0 = \{n_{00}, n_{01}\} = \{30, 32\}$, $n_1 = 31$, and $n_2 = 33$. The training set consisted of 46.3% of the data, the validation set consisted of 19.5%, the testing set consisted of 19.8%, and the unused consisted of 7.3%.

The results of the experiment's statistical accuracy were validated using power spectral density, autocorrelation, and partial autocorrelation tests (Manolakis et al, 2000). These tests determined whether the prediction error, the difference between the output of the neural network model and the corresponding target, was structureless. The prediction error is structureless if any of the following is true: its standardized cumulative periodogram is approximately linear at the 5% significance level, the distribution of its estimated autocorrelation coefficients is essentially zero at the 5% significance level, or its partial autocorrelation sequence is approximately independent with values falling within the 5% significance level. A presence of structure in the prediction error would indicate that the focused TLFN failed in the prediction process. Of the three tests, the power spectral density test produces the most definitive results (Manolakis et al, 2000). Therefore, we attached more weight to the power spectral density test and substantiated its results with the autocorrelation and the partial autocorrelation tests.

RESULTS

We did not achieve a unique prediction of the changes in aggregate inventory behavior from the knowledge of the changes in inverted nominal interest rate. We achieved many statistically accurate predictions, at the 95% confidence level, corresponding to changes in nominal interest rates leading the changes in aggregate inventory by 6 months, 17 months, 19 months, 25 months, and 29 months. The predictions occurring when interest rates lead inventories by 17 months, 19 months, 25 months, and 29 months were noteworthy, since they were almost statistically equivalent. When interest rates led inventories by an average of 17 months, the focused TLFN was trained in 14 epochs with a mean square error of 0.0022 when the validation phase stopped. The predicted aggregate inventory output was a reasonably good estimate of the actual inventory data. It followed the highs and lows in the behavior of the actual data with many of the slopes overlapping. Its jaggedness was similar to those in the actual data set. These results that are shown in Fig. 1 were validated with power spectral density, autocorrelation, and partial autocorrelation statistical tests. The prediction error was not significantly different from zero within the 95% confidence limits (± 0.22) for the power spectral density test. The autocorrelation and the partial autocorrelation test results were similar and supportive of the power spectral density test. These tests also had confidence limits of ± 0.22 . Since there appeared to be no unique mapping between changes in inverted nominal interest rates and changes in aggregate inventory, we examined the predictive relationship between the changes in inverted nominal interest rates and the changes in aggregate sales. We obtained the best statistically accurate prediction of sales at the 95% confidence level when inverted interest rates led it by an average of 10 months. Affirming a previous study that sales are a predictor of inventory when sales are leading by 8 months, we found that with an assumed additive relationship inverted nominal interest rates lead inventory by an average of 18 months via an indirection through sales. In addition, we established that while the levels of aggregate sales and aggregate inventory were positively correlated with essentially a one-to-one relationship, their changes were not as positively correlated. Also, the correlations of the levels of nominal interest rates and sales as well as of nominal interest rates and inventories were both negative with that between interest rates and inventory being greater than -0.1 , but their changes were positively correlated (> 0.3).

DISCUSSION

King and Watson (1996) stated that current inverted interest rates are leading predictors of the economy's behavior in 6-12 months from now. Furthermore, Larrain (2002) used spectral analysis to establish that the changes in inverted nominal T-bill interest rates lead changes in aggregate real sales by an average of 17 months over 11 dominant frequencies. His result for the relationship between the changes in inverted interest rates and aggregate real inventories is not clear – it showed ambiguity. However, Blinder and Maccini (1991) reported that business people generally state that "higher interest rates induce firms to reduce inventories." Nonetheless, this evidence that changes in interest rates cause changes in inventory remain empirically unsubstantiated and is still an important, open, but difficult research problem. One reason for the disparity between the reported evidence and the empirical research to support it might lie in the complexity of the interest rates inventory relationship and the inadequacy of the tools employed to divulge it. Neural networks have the ability to perform reasonably well on "real world" data, which are usually noisy, partially erroneous, and incomplete; and that may be nonstationary, nonlinear, and non-Gaussian. They infer the correct solution to a problem from the input and their experience with related data.

We found relationships exist between changes in interest rates and changes in inventories. Since we did not find a unique relationship, our results are inconclusive. Nonetheless, we were able to predict changes in inventory from changes in interest rates in each of the five relationships discovered. The existence of so many relationships suggests that the interest rates inventory relationship is complex. This complexity might be at the root of the reported apparent insensitivity of inventory investment to changes in interest rates (Blinder and Maccini 1991). Because these relationships were derived from knowledge of a subset of interest rates and inventory data sets, each might be representative of the relationship between inverted nominal interest rates and a major component of inventories. Manufacturing consists of finished goods, work-in-progress, and raw materials and supplies; trade consists of wholesale and retail. In addition to what business people know to be a direct relationship between interest rates and inventories, economists have long known of an indirect relationship between interest rates and inventories. For example, retailers' stock of durable finished goods responds to changes in real sales. Changes in interest rates have a direct impact on sales of durable goods such as automobiles. Automobiles are a significant percentage of retailers' finished goods. Since most durable goods are bought on credit, higher interest rates would mean fewer purchases unless prices are sufficiently discounted: higher interest rates are a disincentive for retailers to hold inventories. In either case, this would have a delayed downward ripple effect on inventory investments in the related industries, affecting manufacturers' purchases of raw materials and supplies as well as their incurred costs for associated work-in-progress. A resultant effect on real output would then mean reduced deliverables to wholesalers and retailers. It may take a few to many months for a change in interest rates to ripple through the components of inventories.

In looking at the interest rates to sales and sales to inventory relationships, we discovered unique relationships with 10 month and 8 month leads respectively. We were then able to use interest rates as a predictor of sales and sales as a predictor of inventory for the duration of the respective leads. The summing of the leads equaled 18 months, which was sufficiently close to the 17 month lead of interest rates over inventories that led to a statistically accurate prediction.

CONCLUSION

The inconclusiveness of our results has shed more light on the interest rates inventory relationship. Unlike Larrain (2002), our results show complexity and a possible confirmation of business people's observation that changes in interest rates cause changes in inventories. These findings suggest that one or many relationships exist between interest and inventories. One result points to an indirect relationship via sales. Two questions now arise:

- What are the major factors that affect the interest rates inventory relationship?
- How do these factors affect this relationship?

Although we have shed some light on the problem, we believe that this problem requires further empirical research to expand upon our results and to further address business people's claim of the interest rates inventory relation. We suggest for further research a determination of the relationship between interest rates and each component of inventory investments. From this determination, it would be necessary to explore and unravel the apparent complexity in the relationship between interest rates and real aggregate inventory.

FIGURES

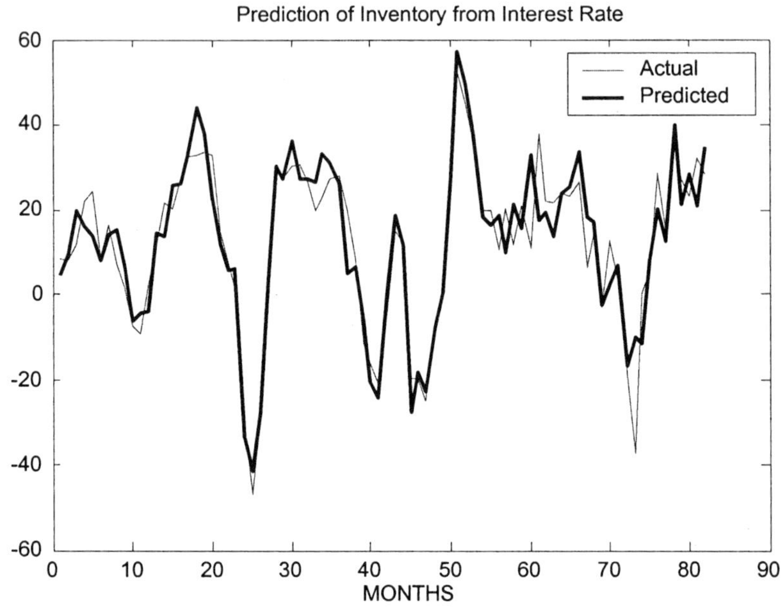

Figure 1. A focused TLFN prediction of changes in aggregate inventory based on knowledge of the changes in inverted nominal 3-month T-bill from 17 months prior. Months are in increments of four starting at the equivalent of month 31 and ending at month 391.

REFERENCES

Blinder, A. and Maccini, L., 1991, "Taking Stock: a Critical Assessment of Recent Research on Inventories," *Journal of Economic Perspective*, Vol. 5, Winter, pp. 73-96.

Cheng, W., Wagner, L., and Lin, C., 1996, "Forecasting the 30-year U.S. Treasury Bond with a System of Neural Networks," *Journal of Computational Intelligence in Finance*, Vol. 4, pp. 10-16.

Chiang, W., Urban, T., and Baldridge, G., 1996, "A Neural Network Approach to Mutual Fund Net Asset Value Forecasting," *Omega – International Journal of Management Science*, Vol. 24, pp. 205-215.

Haykin, S., 1999, *Neural Networks: A Comprehensive Foundation*, 2nd edition, Prentice Hall, Upper Saddle River, pp. 156-247, 635-659.

Joseph, A. and Moseley, N., 2004, "A Neural Network Model for Simulating Inventory Data from sales Data," *Proceedings of 2004 Hawaii International Conference on Computer Sciences*, January 15-18, 2004, ISSN# 545-6722, pp. 20-26

King, R. and Watson, M., 1996, "Money, Prices, Interest Rate and the Business Cycle," *The Review of Economics and Statistics*, February, pp. 35-53.

Larrain, M., 2002, "Do Interest Rates Lead Real Sales and Inventories? A Spectral Analysis Approach," *Business Economics*, pp. 33-43.

Manolakis, D., Ingle, V., and Kogon, S., 2000, *Statistical and Adaptive Signal Processing: Spectral Estimation, Signal Modeling, Adaptive Filtering, and Array Processing,* Mc Graw Hill, New York, pp. 395-498.

Refenes, N., Zapranis, and Francis, G., 1994, "Stock Performance Modeling Using Neural Networks: A comparative Study with Regression Models," *Neural Networks*, Vol. 7, pp. 375-388

IDENTIFYING EFFECTS OF LOW SENSITIVITY INDICATORS IN A STOCK MARKET FORECASTING MODEL.

GARY WECKMAN
Industrial & Manufacturing Systems Engineering
Ohio University
Athens, Ohio 45701, USA

SRIRAM LAKSHMINARAYANAN
Industrial & Manufacturing Systems Engineering
Ohio University
Athens, Ohio 45701, USA

ABSTRACT

Stock markets are active systems that are frequently biased by complex input factors. Some of the input variables may be steady, such as the closing price of stock, high price, low price and volume. A large number of indicators are currently used for stock market forecasting. This paper deals with a technique of pruning indicators and obtaining a simpler model without a trade-off in the accuracy of the forecast. Typically, sensitivity analysis is carried out in forecasting models to identify the effect of input indicators on the forecast. An analysis of the sensitivity of the indicators is completed. The indicators are then classified according to low, medium and high sensitivity. Subsequently different models are created on the same data with a balanced mix of indicators. With the creation of these different models, the authors plan to analyze the effect of indicators on the output and the sensitivity of other input indicators. This could reduce a large forecasting model based on the sensitivity of input indicators while maintaining its accuracy.

INTRODUCTION

An indicator may be defined as a series of data points that are derived from the price data of a security by applying a basic formula. Price data is a combination of open, close, high, or low over a period of time. For example, the average of 3 closing prices is one data point ((41+43+43)/3=42.33). However, one data point does not offer much information and does not make an indicator. A series of data points over a period of time is required to create valid reference points to enable analysis. By creating a time series of data points, a comparison can be made between present and past levels. An indicator offers a different perspective from which to analyze the price action.

The function of indicators may be classified into three broad categories: to alert, to confirm, and to predict.An indicator can act as an alert to study price action a little more closely. If momentum is waning, it may be a signal to watch for a break of support. Or, if there is a large positive divergence building, it may serve as an alert to watch for a resistance break-out.

Indicators can be used to confirm other technical analysis tools. If there is a break-out on the price chart, a corresponding moving average crossover could serve to confirm the break-out. Or, if a stock breaks support, a corresponding low in the On-Balance-Volume (OBV) could serve to confirm the weakness.

Technical Indicators

Relative Strength Index (RSI): This function is used to determine the strength that is inherent in a field using the amount of upward and downward price changes over a given period of time. It has a range of 0 to 100 with values typically remaining between 30 and 70. Higher values indicate overbought conditions while lower values indicate oversold conditions. The Relative Strength Index at the beginning of a data series is not defined until there are enough values to fill the given period. In addition, the value is defined as 100 when no downward changes occur during the given period. The RSI usually leads the price by forming peaks and valleys before the price data, especially around the values of 30 and 70. In addition, when the RSI diverges from the price, the price will eventually correct to the direction of the index.

Money Flow Index (MFI): The Money Flow Index is a measure of the strength of money flowing into or out of a security. It is derived by by comparing the volume of upward and downward price changes over a given period of time. It is based on the Money Ratio, which is the ratio of positive money flow to negative money flow over the given period. Positive money flow is defined as the sum of the prices multiplied by the volume on days when the price increases. Negative money flow is defined similarly, except that it includes only days when the price decreases. It has a range of 0 to 100 with values typically remaining between 20 and 80. Higher values indicate overbought conditions while lower values indicate oversold conditions. This is similar to the Relative Strength Index (RSI), except that it includes the volume as a measure of strength. It also typically uses a more complex price model. The Money Flow Index at the beginning of a data series is not defined until there are enough values to fill the given period.. In addition, the value is defined as 100 when no downward changes occur during the given period, resulting in no negative money flow.

Moving Average (MA): This function returns the moving average of a field over a given period of time. The moving average is calculated by averaging together the previous values over the given period, including the current value. The moving average at the beginning of a data series is not defined until there are enough values to fill the given period. Moving averages are useful for eliminating noise in raw data. Analysis of the moving average of the price yields a more general picture of the underlying trends.

Stochastic Oscillator (SO): The stochastic oscillator is a measure of the difference between the current closing price of a security and its lowest low price, relative to its highest high price for a given period of time. The value is a percent rating for the closing price, relative to the trading range between its recent highest and lowest prices. A value of zero indicates it closed at its lowest recent low. A value of 100 indicates it closed at its highest recent high. The value is often smoothed using a "slowing" period.

Moving Average Convergence/divergence (MACD): The MACD is the difference between the short and the long term moving averages for a field. The MACD is generally a specific instance of a Value Oscillator and is mostly used on the closing price of a security to detect price trends. When the MACD is increasing, prices are trending higher. If the MACD is decreasing, prices are trending lower. The MACD is traditionally traded against a 9-day exponential average of its value, called its signal line. The MACD Signal Line function is provided to generate this value. When the MACD increases above its signal line, a buy signal is generated. When the MACD decreases below its signal line, a sell signal is generated.

Generalized Feed Forward and Multilayer Perceptron Architectures

The multilayer perceptron (MLP) is one of the most commonly used neural network topologies. Generally speaking, for static pattern, the MLP with two hidden layers, is a universal pattern classifier. The discriminant functions are very flexible and can take any shape, as required by the input exemplars. When the weights are properly normalized and the output classes are normalized to 0/1, the MLP is optimal from a classification point of view. The MLP can also approximate arbitrary functions.

MLPs are normally trained with the backpropagation algorithm. In fact the new interest in ANNs was in part triggered by the discovery of backpropagation. The backpropagation rule propagates the errors through the network and allows adaptation of the hidden PEs.

Two important characteristics of the multilayer perceptron are its nonlinear processing elements (PEs), which have a nonlinearity that must be smooth (the logistic function and the hyperbolic tangent are the most widely used); and their massive interconnectivity (i.e. any element of a given layer feeds all the elements of the next layer). The multilayer perceptron is trained with error correction learning, which means that the desired response for the system must be known. An example of this is pattern recognition, since we know which data belongs to which experiment.

Generalized Feedforward Networks are a generalization of the MLP, which contains connections that can jump over one or more layers. In practice, generalized feedforward networks can often solve a problem much more efficiently. The GFN architecture is used in this study for forecasting stock market closing prices and is defined as follows:

Generalized Feed Forward:	
Input Layer Processing elements:	9
Hidden Layer Processing elements:	12
Output Layer Processing elements:	1
Number of Exemplars:	1,569
Hidden Axon:	Tanh Axon
Output Axon:	Tanh Axon

Sensitivity Analysis

Sensitivity analysis is a process by which the relationship between the inputs and outputs of the network can be extracted. After training a neural network, the sensitivity analysis can be used to analyze the effect that each of the network inputs has on the network output. A common method used in sensitivity analysis is when each input channel to the network is varied between its mean +/- 1 standard deviation, while all other inputs are fixed at their respective means. The network output is computed and the corresponding change in the output is reported. The input channels that produce low sensitivity values can be considered insignificant and can usually be removed from the network. This will reduce the size of the network, which in turn reduces the complexity and the training time, and typically improving the network's performance. This process is repeated for each input variable.

METHODOLOGY

For this study, the Hewlett Packard stock market data set was chosen and the data was validated. The data set consisted of 1,569 exemplars.This data set was divided into 80% for training, 10% for cross validation and 10% for testing. The data was split into such a biased ratio because the emphasis of the research is on the sensitivity analysis of the indicators. A large amount of training data eliminates errors due to under-training of the data set. This collection of data is then trained using the specified neural network architecture for 2,000 epochs and 5 runs. The training results were as follows:

Table1: MSE Training statistics

All Runs	Training Min	Training SD	CV Min	CV SD
Min MSE	0.000478	0.000158	0.040766	0.004287
Final MSE	0.000478	0.000158	0.041508	0.004053

Table 1 specifies the average values Mean Square Error (MSE) which was the considered performance measure to assess the network learning. The training and the cross validation minimum and standard deviations are also specified. The best learning was found to occur in the fourth run and the network learning details are in Table 2 as follows:

Table 2: Best Network Training Properties

Best Networks	Training	Cross Validation
Run #	4	4
Epoch #	2000	2000
Minimum MSE	0.000277546	0.036145076
Final MSE	0.000277546	0.036145076

The sensitivity anlalysis was then done on the testing data set retaining the best weights of the network after training. This analysis was carried out by analyzing the mean of the input factor values and varying them on either side of the mean by a factor of one standard deviation. The standard deviation of the computed output value, namely the closing price of the stock yields the sensitivity of that indicator to the output. This was carried out on all of the input factors. The resulting sensitivity values were then multiplied by a factor of 8 so that it was in the same scale as the subsequent analysis. The bar chart in Figure 1 was obtained. MACD decreases below its signal line, a sell signal is generated. Each indicator is now left out of the analysis and the network is tested for sensitivity with the remaining eight indicators. The sensitivities in all these nine experiments are added, grouped by indicator type resulting in eight values that were analyzed cumulatively. The resulting bar chart is shown in Figure 2:

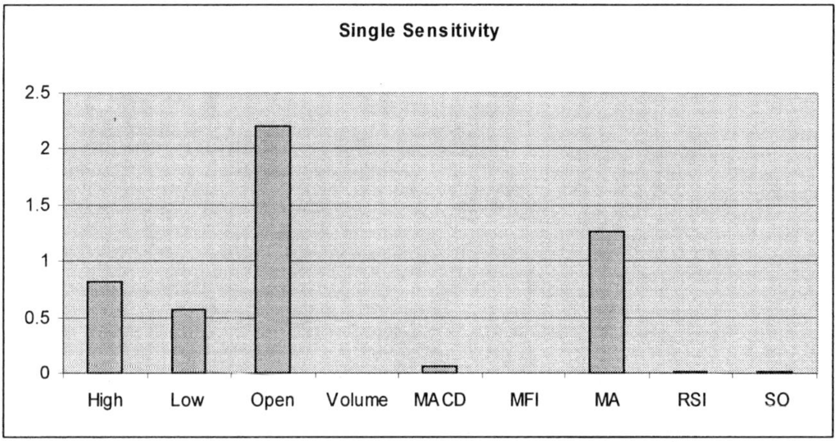

Figure 1. Single Sensitivity of Indicators

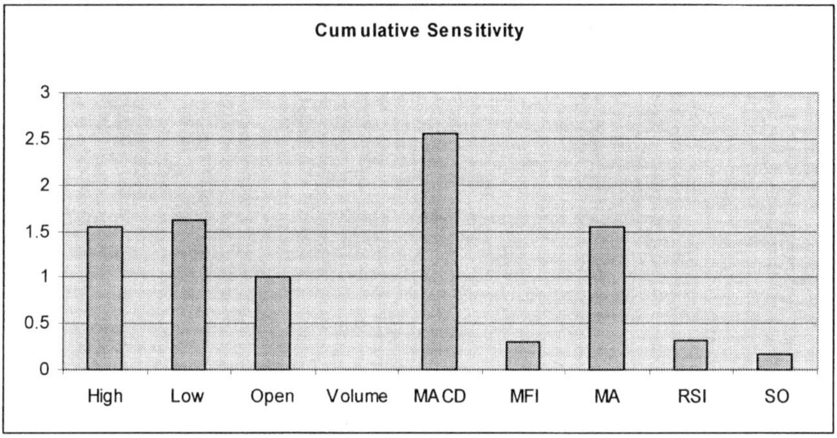

Figure 2. Cumulative Sensitivity of Indicators

RESULTS AND CONCLUSION

The sensitivity analysis demonstrated in Figure 2 suggests that Open and Moving Average indicators are the most valuable indicators for the forecast of the closing price. The process of pruning the number of indicators we are logically consistent in the removal of the indicators with low sensitivity values. This suggests that important and proven indicators such as MACD, MFI, RSI, SO will be omitted from further analysis.

The second stage of the analysis is completed by omitting out one indicator in turn and then analyzing the cumulative sensitivity of the indicators. Essentially, this is an analysis of the effect of the absence of one indicator on the rest of the indicators. The cumulative sensitivity graph as shown in Table 3 suggests that only the volume indicator is redundant or one that can be omitted.

As a rule of thumb, any indicator that has a weight of 10% or less of the indicator with the maximum weight is omitted when pruning a neural network. On analysis of Figure 3, it is clear that the only indicator that can be pruned without affecting the performance is the volume indicator. Thus, by using this method of analysis while pruning, some key indicators may not be omitted.

Table 3: Sensitivity Analysis Results

Indicator Type	Single Sensitivity	Cumulative Sensitivity
High / Low	1.550 / 1.617	0.823 / 0.568
Open	1.005	2.205
Volume	0.000	0.000
MACD	2.555	0.061
MFI	0.296	0.005
MA	1.544	1.258
RSI	0.315	0.014
SO	0.171	0.013

REFERENCES

1. Agarwala, R, Weckman, G. R., and McLauchlan, R., 2002, "Optimization of Data Collection and Training Time for Forecasting Stock Market Trends Using Artificial Neural Network", Proceedings of the ANNIE '02, ASME, St. Louis, Missouri, pp. 707-712.
2. Bogullu, V.K., Enke, D., and Dagli, C., 2002, "Using Neural Networks and Technical Indicators for Generating Stock Trading Signals", Proceedings of the 2002 Artificial Neural Networks in Engineering Conference (ANNIE '02), ASME, St. Louis, Missouri, pp. 721-726.
3. Gately, Edward, 1996, Neural Networks for Financial Forecasting, New York, Wiley.
4. Kohara, Ishikawa, and Fukuhara, Nakamura, 1997, "Stock price prediction using prior knowledge and neural networks", International Journal of Intelligent Systems in Accounting, Finance and Management, 6 (1), pp. 11-22.
5. Kohonen T. "The self-organizing map." Proc. IEEE 78, 1464-1480, 1990.
6. Kyoung-jae, Kim, and Ingoo, Han, 2000, "Genetic algorithms approach to feature discretization in artificial neural networks for the prediction of stock price index", Expert System with Applications, 19 (2), pp. 125-132.
7. Lee, K. H., and Jo, G. S., 1999, "Expert System for predicting stock market timing using candlestick chart", Expert Systems with Applications, 16, pp. 357-364.
8. Saad, E. W., Prokhorov, D. V., and Wunsch, D. C., 1998, "Comparative study of stock trend prediction using time delay, recurrent and probabilistic neural networks", IEEE Transactions on Neural Networks, Vol. 9, No. 6, pp. 1456-1470.
9. Shadbolt, J., and Taylor, J.G., 2002, Neural Networks and the Financial Markets: Predicting, Combining and Portfolio Optimization, Springer, New York.
10. Smith, K. A., and Gupta, J. N. D., 2000, "Neural networks in business: techniques and applications for the operations researcher", Computer& Operations Research, 27, pp. 1023-1044.
11. Strand, Sverre, 1999, "Forecasting the future: pitfalls in controlling for uncertainty", Futures, 31, 333-350.
12. Thawornwong, S., Enke, D., and Dagli, C., 2001, "Using Neural Networks and Technical Analysis Indicators for Predicting Stock Trends", Proceedings of the 2001 Artificial Neural Networks in Engineering Conference (ANNIE '01), ASME, St. Louis, Missouri.
13. Turban, E., and J. E. Aronson, 2001, Decision Support Systems and Intelligent Systems, Sixth Edition, Prentice Hall, New Jersey.
14. Weckman, G. R., and Agarwala, R., 2003, 'Identifying Relative Contribution of Selected Technical Indicators in Stock Market Prediction" Proceedings of the IIE Annual Conference 2002, May 18-21, Portland, Oregon.

A NEURAL NETWORK FOR INFLATION FORECASTING

CHAKKAPHAN TIRASIRICHAI, DAVID ENKE, and RAYMOND CHAFIN
Engineering Management Department
Laboratory for Investment and Financial Engineering
Center for Intelligent Systems
University of Missouri – Rolla
Rolla, MO 65409-0370

ABSTRACT

Currently most of the methods for inflation estimation in the economic area are based on an auto-regressive approach, mainly methods that are Vector Autoregressive (VAR). Concurrently, knowledge in the area of artificial intelligence is growing, especially with neural networks. With its power and flexibility, neural networks can also be applied to the estimation of inflation, which tends to be nonlinearly related with its indicators. This study utilizes the Generalized Regression Neural Network (GRNN) and Time-delay Backpropagation (BP) Network to develop an approach for monthly inflation estimation using the historical inflation rate, interest rates, Commodity Research Bureau (CRB) index, Chicago Fed National Activity Index (CFNAI), oil prices, and the unemployment rate as inputs to the network. The performance of the network for prediction of the inflation value and trends is observed. The performances of both networks are compared. The results illustrate that the BP Network outperforms the GRNN, while the CFNAI appears to be an important inflation indicator.

INTRODUCTION

Inflation is considered an important input in monetary policymaking and has become one of the most closely observed macroeconomic variables. Therefore, economists attempt to explain and predict the behavior of inflation based on economic principles. One of the early theories was introduced by economist A. W. Phillips in 1958 (Abel and Bernanke, 2001). Phillips examined British historical data of the unemployment rate and nominal wage growth from 1861 to 1957. He discovered that there was a negative relationship between the increased rate of wages and the rate of unemployment. This later leads to the conclusion of the existence of a negative relationship between the inflation rate and the unemployment rate. However, this negative relationship was, some years later, proved by Edmund Phelps and Milton Friedman to hold for only short-lived time periods (Lansing, 2002). Lately, Atkeson and Ohanian (2001) demonstrate that the regression coefficient between the unemployment rate and inflation was strongly negative during the 1960 – 1983 periods, and then becomes weak for the post 1983 period. This implies that even the short-run Phillips Curves does not represent a stable empirical relationship between inflation and the unemployment rate.

Since the Phillips Curves is proven to be inconsistent along the time horizon, economists need other models to forecast inflation. Another well-known time series approach that is used by most economists is the autoregressive model (AR), especially the vector-autoregressive (VAR) approach. The VAR model is a group of linear prediction formulas that attempt to predict a desired output based on the previous output(s) and the joint behavior of other input variables (Moshiri and Cameron, 2000). The forecasts results from VAR will depend on the period of estimation, choice of data, and some particular combinations of variables (Fujiwara and Koga, 2002). Moreover, data preparation and the selection of suitable input variable combinations are difficult for this technique.

Recently, artificial neural networks (ANN) have been found to be a useful forecasting method for many fields of study. ANNs have the ability to find the solution for complex problems. They are also free from the linearity assumption. Macroeconomic time series, such as inflation forecasting, are another appropriate field for which ANNs can be applied. Some studies have already been made in the area of neural network applications for inflation forecasting (Moshiri and Cameron, 2000),(Nakamura, 2004),(McNelis et al., 2004). The following study is conducted to investigate the performance of ANN applications for inflation forecasting using economic indicators as inputs. Both the magnitude and trends of forecasted values will be examined to measure the ANN model performance.

BACKGROUND

Artificial Neural Networks are dynamic systems loosely modeled on the human brain. The network consists of multiple layers of simple processing elements called neurons. Each neuron is linked to certain neighbors with varying coefficients of connectivity and synaptic weight. Neural networks have the ability to learn from example and generalize characteristics. The network will learn patterns from the given examples during the training process and store the information in the form of synaptic neuron weights (Ham and Kostanic, 2001). There are many structures of neurons for ANNs. The more complex the problem to be solved, the more complex the neurons and architecture will need to be. In this study, two network architectures are selected for application to inflation forecasting.

Generalized Regression Neural Network (GRNN)

The GRNN is a one-pass learning algorithm with a highly parallel structure. The GRNN is basically a normalized radial basis function network (RBF) in which there are hidden neurons centered at every training case. The hidden-to-output weights are just the target values. Therefore, the output is simply a weighted average of the target values of the training cases close to the given input case. The generalization ability of the network will depend on the spread value. The spread value is a parameter in the GRNN which allows the network the ability for smoothing the output. The GRNN can be applied with any regression problem to estimate the continuous variables, regardless of justification of the linearity assumption (Specht, 1991). It also has the advantage over other ANN architectures in that there is no need to worry about the local minima problem or long training times.

Backpropagation (BP)

Backpropagation is a supervised learning algorithm for a feed-forward multilayer perceptron. The standard BP algorithm for training is based on the steepest descent gradient approach applied to the minimization of an energy function representing the instantaneous error (Ham and Kostanic, 2001). BP is the most popular algorithm used in the neural network field. In this study, a tapped delay line will be added to the input layer of the network. This will give the network the historical information of the inputs which will improve network prediction ability.

DATA PREPARATION

Inflation is an increase in the price of goods and services. In order to measure inflation, information concerning the increase in prices has to be examined. For this study, the monthly increase in the product consumer price index (CPI) by the Bureau of Labor Statistic is used to represent the monthly inflation. Base on economic theories, there are many factors that influence inflation, such as interest rates, the money supply, capacity utilization, etc. Among these many factors, the following five factors are selected to be used as the inflation indicators in this study:

Chicago Fed National Activity Index (CFNAI) is a weighted average of 85 existing monthly indicators of national economic activity designed to better gauge overall economic activity and inflationary pressure. It was recommend by Fisher (2000), and based on study of James Stock and Mark Watson who used the activity index as their inflation indicator. The activity index was also used as an input for an inflation forecasting model by Gosselin and Tkacz (2001).

Commodity Research Bureau (CRB) index is the spot market price index measuring the price movements of 22 basic commodities whose markets are presumed to be among the first to be influenced by changes in economic conditions.

Unemployment rate is one of the earliest inflation indicators used by economists. Even when the Phillip Curve has been proven to be inconsistent along the time line, the unemployment rate is still able to correctly predict the direction of change of future inflation about 60-70% of the time (Lansing, 2002). The unemployment rate still appears to have an influence over inflation.

Oil price has historically had an important influence on inflation. During the last two oil price shocks in 1973–1974 and 1979–1980, the US inflation rate was driven to new levels. Because it is one of the important supplies for production, changes in oil price will have an effect on the U.S. economy. Therefore, oil price should be a good inflation indicator.

Interest rates have a strong relationship with inflation based on money growth and inflation theory. Both the nominal interest rate and inflation rate tend to move together (Abel and Bernanke, 2001). In order to represent the nominal interest rate, three values are selected, i.e., the monthly federal funds rate, the 1-Year Treasury, and the 10-Year Treasury Constant Maturity Rate. These values will be used one at a time in network development to find which value is the best monthly inflation indicator.

All of the above variables, along with the historical value of monthly inflation, are used as inputs to the neural network. These data are colleted from the reliable sources. The CRB indexes are obtained from CRB database itself, whereas the CFNAI information is obtained from Chicago Federal Bank. The other three factors are acquired from Federal Bank of St. Louis Economic Research. The frequency of the data used in network development is monthly data for each variable from the years 1973 thru 2004. The data will be divided into two sets. The first 26 years (1973-1998) will be used as the training set and the last 5 years (1999-2003) as the testing set. There is a wide range in values among these six variables. Therefore, data normalization will be done to remove the network bias. The min-max normalization method (Fisher et al., 2002) was applied to map the data into the range -2 to 2. The normalization equation is as shown below, in Equation 1. The min and max value of the input are the minimum and maximum values of the data from the training set. Two of the inputs, inflation and CFNAI, are not normalized because their values are already in the desired range.

$$v'(i) = \left(\frac{(v(i) - \min)}{(\max - \min)} \times (new\_\max - new\_\min) \right) + new\_\min \qquad (1)$$

where v = current value
v' = normalized value

MODEL SELECTION

The objective of the network is to predict the monthly inflation based on monthly historical data. The GRNN and BP with a time delay line are applied in this study. The GRNN utilizes a one-pass learning model. There is no need to train the network. The inputs to the GRNN include each of the six selected inflation indicators. Each of the input data values will consist of the latest 12 months of data for each indicator, while the output will be the inflation level for the next time period. Three GRNNs were developed with different spread values. The network structure of the GRNN architecture is highlighted in Figure 1.

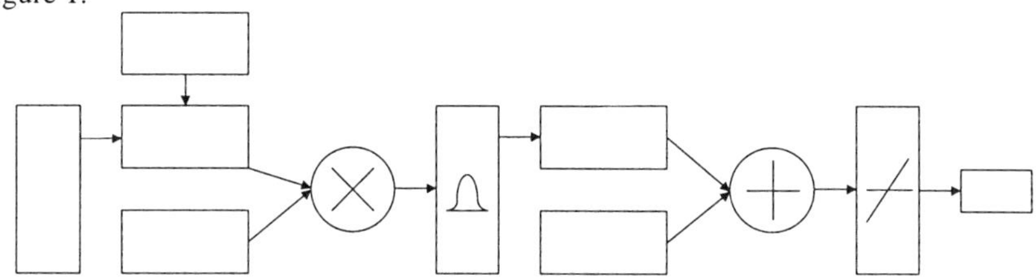

Figure 1. GRNN Architecture

The BP networks are also developed to predict the future monthly inflation. All BP networks developed in this study utilize a two layer network, with a linear transfer function in the second layer. The neurons in first layer are varied from 1 to 6 neurons with two different transfer functions – the hyperbolic tangent sigmoid and logarithmic sigmoid transfer function. The networks have different numbers of inputs, ranging from 1 to all 6 inputs, or with different combinations of inputs. Moreover, some of networks do not utilize a time delayed input. Since there is no validation dataset for the early training process, all networks are trained for 50 epochs and then stopped to avoid the over-fitting problem. The trained weights of the network will be different based on the initialized weight value. Therefore, each configuration is trained for 50 trials with different initial weights and the best performance model is selected to represent that network configuration. The network structure for the BP network with a time delay input is shown in Figure 2.

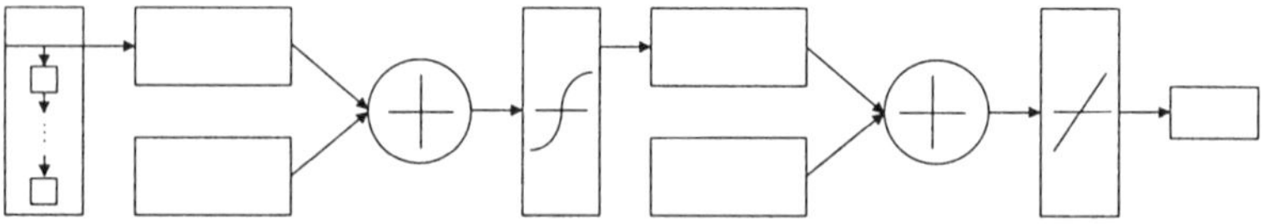

Figure 2. BP Network with the Delay Architecture

The performance of each network is determined from its forecasting ability in terms of both magnitude and direction of the inflation. The mean square error (MSE) will be used to examine the magnitude of the prediction accuracy - the smaller the MSE value, the better the forecasting performance of the network. The definition of MSE for this study is defined by Equation 2.

$$MSE=\frac{1}{n}\sum_{i=1}^{n}(target_i - predict_i)^2 \qquad (2)$$

where n = *total number of data*

The forecasting direction will be investigated by comparing the last actual inflation value with the future value predicted by the model. If the predicted value is larger than the latest actual value, the direction is +1. The direction value will be -1 if the predicted value is less than the latest actual value, and will be equal to 0 when both values are the same.

RESULTS

The random walk model and Phillips Curves are considered as benchmarks for the direction forecasting. Base on an earlier study (Atkeson and Ohanian, 2001), it was demonstrated that the Phillips Curve model can correctly predict the direction of change of future inflation about 60-70% of the time. This ballpark number will be used as the benchmarking number for the Phillips Curve. The random walk model basically assumes that the direction of inflation in the next time period will be in the same direction as the current time period. The random walk model was conducted on the same data to generate the benchmark numbers. The testing dataset direction accuracy for each model is shown in Table 1. The neural network performance is better than both the Phillips Curves and the random walk model.

In terms of the magnitude of network forecasting performance, the random walk model was again introduced as the benchmark model. The random walk model assumes that the future value will be equal to the latest time period value. It was investigated by (Atkeson and Ohanian, 2001) that the random walk model outperformed the Phillips Curve in terms of forecasting magnitude. The MSE of the testing dataset for each network is shown in Table 2. The result shows that most of the networks have a performance that is better than the random walk model.

The best network will be considered using both MSE and direction accuracy, such that the network which is in the top five for both categories will be carefully investigated. There were two BP networks which were in the top five for both performance measures. In addition, the best GRNN is also considered. Based on both performance measures, GRNN7 has the best performance. This network is using Generalize Regression as network architecture with all available inputs, along with a 0.7 as spread value. However, the GRNN7 could not follow the pattern of the inflation value very well. Considering two performance measures and the inflation pattern recognition, the best network for the monthly inflation forecasting is network G1M – the time-delayed feed-forward neural network trained with backpropagation, which included all six data sources provided as input to the network.

CONCLUSIONS

The ANN has better performance than simpler models, such as the random walk model and the Phillips Curve. Research has shown that the ANN could be used as another inflation forecasting tool. However, the neural network models still lacks an explanation of the economic fundamentals. Moreover, not all types of ANN could be used for inflation forecasting. The GRNN does not perform well in forecasting magnitude. This is due to the non-stationary data, which is a limitation of the GRNN algorithm.

For use as a suitable inflation indicator, it was found that the CFNAI contains important information regarding inflation. By adding CFNAI as another input to the same configuration network, the forecasting direction accuracy improved by approximately 10% and network MSE was reduced by half. Finally, the 1-month federal funds rate makes the best representation of interest rate, when compared against long-term vehicles, such as the 10 year bond.

	Direction Accuracy
Network A	58%
Network D	58%
Network B	60%
Network C	61%
Network E	63%
Network H	68%
GRNN1	68%
Network G	69%
Network G1Y(2)	69%
GRNN5	70%
Network I	71%
Network G1M(2)	71%
Network J	71%
GRNN7	72%
Network F	74%
Network G1Y	74%
Network H1M	74%
Network G1M	76%
Phillips Curves	60 - 70%
Random walk	47%

Table 1. Direction Accuracy

	MSE
Network D	0.273
Network E	0.135
Network C	0.116
Network B	0.107
Network H	0.093
Network G1Y	0.089
Network A	0.085
Network G1Y(2)	0.073
Network I	0.063
Network G	0.061
Network F	0.060
GRNN5	0.060
GRNN7	0.057
Network G1M	0.056
Network G1M(2)	0.055
GRNN1	0.054
Network J	0.051
Network H1M	0.045
Random walk	0.089

Table 2. MSE Performance

REFERENCES

Abel, A. and Bernanke, B., 2001, Macroeconomics, 4th Edition, *Addison-Wesley Publishing Company*, New York.

Atkeson, A. and Ohanian, L., 2001, "Are Phillips Curves Useful for Forecasting Inflation?", *Federal Reserve Bank of Minneapolis Quarterly Review* (Winter), pp. 2-11. http://www.mpls.frb.org/research/qr/qr2511.html.

Fisher, J., 2000, "Forecasting inflation with a lot of data", *Chicago Fed Letter*, The Federal Reserve Bank of Chicago, number 151, March 2000.

Fisher, J., Liu, C. and Zhou, R., 2002 "When can we forecast inflation?", *Economic Perspectives*, Federal Reserve Bank of Chicago, first quarter, 2002.

Fujiwara, I. and Koga, M., 2002, "A Statistical Forecasting Method for Inflation Forecasting", *Working Paper, Research and Statistics Department*, Bank of Japan, July 2002.

Gosselin, M. and Tkacz, G., 2001, "Evaluating Factor Models: An Application to Forecasting Inflation in Canada", *Bank of Canada Working Paper 2001-18*, November 2001.

Ham, F. and Kostanic, I., 2001, Principles of Neurocomputing for Science and Engineering, *McGraw-Hill, Inc.*, New York, 2001.

Kamber, M. and Han, J., 2001, Data Mining: Concept and Techniques, *Morgan Kaufmann Publishers*, San Francisco.

Lansing, K., 2002, "Can the Phillips Curve Help Forecast Inflation?", *Federal Reserve Bank of San Francisco Economic Letter*, November 2002-29, October 4, 2002.

McNelis, P., Camba-Mendez, G. and McAdam, P., 2004, "Forecasting Inflation with Thick Models and Neural Networks", *Working Papers no. 352, European Central Bank*, April 2004.

Moshiri, S. and Cameron, N., 2000, "Neural Network Versus Econometric Models in Forecasting Inflation", *Journal of Forecasting*, April 2000, vol. 19, issue 3, pp. 201-217.

Nakamura, E., 2004, "Inflation Forecasting using a Neural Network", *Department of Economics, Harvard University*, February 10, 2004.

Specht, D., 1991, "A General Regression Neural Network", *Brief Papers, IEEE Transaction on Neural Networks*, vol. 2, no. 6, November 1991.

AN APPLICATION OF NEURAL NETWORKS WITH THE BOLLINGER BAND TECHNICAL ANALYSIS INDICATOR FOR STOCK TRADING

THIRA CHAVARNAKUL, DAVID ENKE, AND RAYMOND CHAFIN
Laboratory for Investment and Financial Engineering
Smart Engineering System Lab
Intelligent System Center
University of Missouri - Rolla

ABSTRACT
The Bollinger Band technical indicator can be used for measuring and displaying the volatility of securities and highlighting if security prices are high or low at any point in time. However, in some cases the trading signals produced by Bollinger Bands do not provide a proper confirmation of the price trend and give false signals during trending markets. A continuation of the trend, or a reversal in the opposite direction, is not always evident or predicted, even though the typical trading heuristic is to trade against the direction of the most recent trend. The following research proposes using neural networks in conjunction with the Bollinger Band technical indicator model to predict the future trend of security's prices and create a trading system, given the Bollinger Bands signal, the previous prices, and volume indicators. The predicted trend of security's prices will produce a signal identifying overbought and oversold conditions and will allow for more specific and reliable trading signals. The profitability of the neural network model will be tested on past S&P 500 index data. The results of the neural networks will also be compared against results generated from the Bollinger Bands heuristic trading rules and the buy-and-hold trading strategy.

INTRODUCTION

Stock markets are affected by many highly interrelated economic, political, and even psychological factors, each interacting in a complex manner (Yao et al., 1998). Therefore, predicting stock movement is a very difficult task. Technical analysis is one of the general techniques used to forecast future stock behavior. It is the process of analyzing a security's historical prices in an effort to determine probable future prices (Achelis, 1995). For many investors and institutions, technical analysis has proven to be powerful for evaluating securities prices. In stock market prediction, many methods for technical analysis have been developed and are being used (Pring, 1985). Neural networks (NNs), which are one of many artificial intelligence methods, have performed well for classification, recognition, and forecasting. They have become very important method for stock market prediction because of their ability to deal with uncertain, fuzzy, or insufficient data which may fluctuate rapidly over a very short periods of time (Schoeneburg, 1990). As a result, researhers have used many types of neural networks for technical analysis and stock market prediction. Yao et al. (1998) presented a study of feedforward neural networks using backbropagation learning (BPN) for use in stock index forecasting. Yao et al. (1998) used data from the Kuala Lumpur Stock Exchange as a case study. Mizuno et al. (2001) also presented a neural network model for technical analysis of stock market, and its application within a buying and selling prediction system for a stock index. Bautista (2001) attempted to predict the Philippine stock price index using feedforward neural networks. Networks other than feedforward neural networks have also been used by researchers. Saad et al. (1998) compared time-delay neural networks (TDNN) with recurrent neural networks (RNN), and probabilistic neural networks (PNN) for low false alarm stock trend predictions.

The motivation for this research is to apply neural networks with Bollinger Bands (Bollinger, 2002), a common technical analysis indicator. Eventhough Bollinger Bands can be used for measuring and displaying the volatility of securities and highlighting if securities prices are high or low at a given point in time, false trading signals can be produced by Bollinger Bands, especially in trending markets. Bollinger (2002), who developed the indicator, showed that using only simple trading signals from Bollinger Bands may not always work well, such as when price squeezes and false breakouts occurr, or when prices walk the upper or lower bands.

For this research the TDNN is applied with Bollinger Bands trading model to predict the future trend of security's prices. A trading system based on the Bollinger Band signal and neural network output is then created. The results show that the neural network assisted trading system is better when compared against the results from the isolated Bollinger Bands heuristic traidng rules and the buy-and-hold trading strategy.

BOLLINGER BANDS

Bollinger Bands were created by John Bollinger in the early 1980s (Bollinger, 2002). Bollinger Bands are one of the most popular forms of envelope or channel technical indicators. The difference between Bollinger Bands and envelopes is that envelopes are plotted at a fixed percentage above and below a moving average, whereas Bollinger Bands are plotted at standard deviation levels above and below a moving average, which are usually defaulted at 2 standard deviations and 20 days, respectively. Since standard deviation is a measure of volatility, the bands are self-adjusting – they widening during volatile markets and contract during calmer periods (Achelis, 1995). The purpose of Bollinger Bands is to provide an indication of whether prices are relatively high or low, whether current trends are likely to continue or reverse, and whether the volatility of a market (based on the width of the band) is changing.

Two indicators, %b and BandWidth, can be derived directly from Bollinger Bands. %b depicts where the last price is in relation to the bands and is useful in creating trading systems and signals, whereas BandWidth depicts the width of the bands in a relative manner and is useful for indentifying price squeezes, as well as the beginning and ends of trends.

METHODOLOGY

For this research there are three major processes: preprocessing, the neural network, and post processing. Preprocessing classifies the data inputs, transforms the data by normalizing it into a defined range [-1 1], and provides the input data to the neural networks architecture. The neural network then trains, tests, and evaluates the network to recognize the desired output from the input patterns. Finally, post processing develops a trading system from the resulting outputs of the neural network. More details on each of these three processes are presented in the following sections.

PREPROCESSING AND DATA SET

Past daily S&P 500 index data from March 2nd, 1998 to December 26th, 2003 (1,466 days) was utilized for this research. The data was divided into two periods. The first period served as the training set and included data from March 2nd, 1998 to June 24th, 2002 (1,085 days) and was provided to the model for determining the specifications and parameters of the network models. The second period, which included 381 days of data collected from June 25th, 2002 to December 26th, 2003 served as the testing set in order to perform out-of-sample evaluation among the forecasting models. For this research, the raw data included the daily opens, closes, highs, lows, and volumes of the index price.

Eight variables were selected as inputs to the neural networks and calculated from the daily S&P 500 index data. The first four variables included closing prices and volumes, along with the calculated signals from the Bollinger Band's %b and Bandwidth. The other four variables included popular technical indicators, including the money flow index (MFI), a momentum indicator (M), on balance volume (OBV), and intraday intensity (II). The technical indicators were chosen since according to Bollinger (2002), these indicators can help to empower the Bollinger Bands signals to distinguish between a confirmation and a non-confirmation trading signal. He suggested a choice of volume indicators to combine with the Bollinger Bands. However, in order to avoid the multicollinearity trap (several series containing very similar information used as though they were separate), each of four basic categories of volume indicators based on different computational methods were used. Therefore, OBV was chosen for considering periodic price change, MFI for volume weighting, and II for considering the intraperiod structure of categories of volume indicators that were selected as input of neural networks. Finally, momentum indicator (M) was employed as an input for comparing changes of stock index price movement.

A default of 20 days for the moving average and 2 standard deviations were used to calculate % b and the Bandwidth, a 14 day moving average was used for MFI, a 20 day moving average was used for OBV, a 21 day moving average was used for II, and M was calculated from the closed prices_t – closed prices_{t-1}.

In order to minimize the effect of magnitude among the inputs due to differences in range, a normalization technique was used to scale the input variables between -1 and 1. It was shown by Thawornwong and Enke (2003) that the normalization facilitated the neural network model in learning the relevant relationships. The formula that was used for input normalization for this research is given in Equation 1.

$$x^* = \frac{(2x - (\max.(x) + \min.(x)))}{(\max.(x) - \min.(x))} \tag{1}$$

where x is the input before normalizing and x^* is the input after normalizing.
The max. and min. of x are derived from data in training set.

NEURAL NETWORK ARCHITECTURE

As mentioned before, the time-delay neural networks (TDNN) (Ham and Kostanic, 2001) was applied as the main neural network model. The TDNN architecture is chosen in this research because it is appropriate for trend prediction that requires a recent memory, as is often the case in most time series prediction (Saad et al., 1998). The TDNN uses time delays to perform temporal processing (Ham and Kostanic, 2001). The typical structure of the TDNN is a layered architecture with only delays at the input of the network; however, it is possible to incorporate delays between the layers. The standard backpropagation algorithm with two days of time lag time are used to train the TDNN in this research. It is assumed that the training set consists of neumerous inputs corresponding to the target (output) data, allowing the network to learn the salient features of the input patterns (Thawornwong and Enke, 2003). For example, inputs from date 07/08/2002 are input at time (t-2), 07/09/2002 are input at time (t-1), and 07/10/2002 today (t) are used to predict trend on 07/11/2002 at time (t+1).

As previously mentioned, many researchers have successfully utilized feedforward neural networks driven by backpropagation learning (BPN) to forecast stock returns and their corresponding trends. Therefore, this research will also employ a BPN to compare its results of future trend prediction against the TDNN.

Simulations found that BPN does not perform as well for providing trend predicting accuracy when compared to the TDNN since it gives results that are similar to the random walk model. Thus, only the future trend results from the TDNN are used for the trading systems. For the networks, one hidden layer was selected for use in both the TDNN and the BPN. The Hyperbolic Tangent Sigmoid (tansig) and Log-Sigmoid (logsig) transfer functions were used at hidden layer and the linear (purelin) transfer function was used at output layer. Variations of 4, 5, 6, and 7 neurons within the hidden layer, 1 neuron in the output layer, and various types of transfer function were combined, trained, and simulated over 50 trials to find the three best results for each network architecture. The outputs of the network models were the closing prices at time (t+1). No validation sets were used for this research.

MEASUREMENTS OF NEURAL NETWORKS TRAINING

The Mean Square Error (MSE) was one of the measurement methods used to compare the performance of the neural networks models. The MSE can evaluate and compare the productive power of the models by finding the error between the predict output value and the actual value.

Another method of measuring the performance of neural networks models for stock trend forecasting is to calculate the percentage accuracy of correctly predicting the proper direction of the trend, or sign (SIGN) of the price movement. This measurement can be expressed as

$$\text{SIGN} = \frac{\sum_{i=1}^{n} s_i}{n} \tag{2}$$

where $s = 1$; if $(cp'_{t+1} - cp_t)*(cp_{t+1} - cp_t) > 0$ or $(cp'_{t+1} - cp_t)$ and $(cp_{t+1} - cp_t) = 0$

$s = 0$; otherwise

cp' = predict closed prises, cp = actual closed prices

n = numbers of output value

Although MSE is a very useful and a widely used method to measurement the performance of the neural networks models, lower MSE does not always indicate a higher percentage of SIGN direction accuracy. The results, as expressed in the Table 1, confirm that low MSE may not always be the good measurement for predicting the direction of the trend, as compared to the overall recognition of the trend. As a result, the trading systems will be developed based on the best results of SIGN, along with an acceptable MSE measurement. Model 1-3 within Table 1 represent three of the best models that were found during the network development and simulations.

Table 1. MSE and SIGN of the best three models for each TDNN and BPN

	TDNN				BPN			
	Model #1	Model #2	Model #3	Average	Model #1	Model #2	Model #3	Average
MSE	0.003472	0.005294	0.003118	0.003961	0.002737	0.003022	0.004513	0.003424
SIGN	57.37 %	53.42 %	53.16 %	54.65 %	52.89 %	52.89 %	51.84 %	52.54 %

POSTPROCESSING (THE TRADING SYSTEMS)

The trading system proposed in this research paper is a combined result of the neural network forecast of future stock index trend for the next day, along with a traditional trading Bollinger Bands rule (using % b). The trading system is given in the Table 2.

Table 2. The trading system proposed in this research

Strategy #1	Strategy #2
If $(cp'_{t+1} - cp_t) < 0$ and $\% b_t >= 1.0$, then sell ; If $(cp'_{t+1} - cp_t) > 0$ and $\% b_t <= 0$, then buy ; Else hold position	If $(cp'_{t+1} - cp_t) < 0$ and $\% b_t >= 0.9$, then sell; If $(cp'_{t+1} - cp_t) > 0$ and $\% b_t <= 0.1$, then buy; Else hold position

The benchmarks for this research were the traditional trading rules from the Bollinger Bands, along with the buy-and-hold strategy. These two benchmarks can be expressed in the Table 3 as follow:

Table 3. The Bollinger Band trading rule and Buy-and-Hold strategy

BB. trading rule #1	BB. trading rule#2	Buy-and-Hold Strategy
If $\%b_t >= 1.0$, then sell; If $\%b_t <= 0$, then buy; Else hold position	If $\% b_t >= 0.9$, then sell; If $\% b_t <= 0.1$, then buy; Else hold position	Buy at the first day of the holing period, hold the position until the last day of the holding period, and then sell the entire position.

RESULTS AND ANALYSIS

The three best SIGN results during the testing period from the TDNN which had an acceptable MSE were selected for trading systems development. These systems were compared against the Bollinger Band trading rule and the buy-and-hold strategy as shown in Table 4.

Table 4. Result of expected return from TDNN along with Benchmarks

TDNN	Strategy #1	Strategy #2	BB.trading rule #1	BB.trading rule #2	Buy-and-Hold
Model#1	12.62 %	14.68 %	11.86 %	11.85 %	12.27 %
Model#2	16.68 %	19.49 %	11.86 %	11.85 %	12.27 %
Model#3	15.59 %	15.37 %	11.86 %	11.85 %	12.27 %
Average	14.69%	16.51 %	11.86 %	11.85 %	12.27 %

Based on the results from Table 4, the expected return for each trading strategy was calculated by assuming that $100,000 was invested during the testing period. This money is used to buy (sell) a number of stocks index shares in the right proportion for the entire testing period when the buy (sell) signal was advised. After investors enter a position, they will hold the position until an opposite trading signal (buy or sell) is advised. Another assumption is that investors buy or sell at the market open, therefore, they buy or sell at time (t) with opened prices that are equal to the close prices at time (t-1).

The result from Table 4 shows that the expected returns from the combined trading strategy performed by the TDNN and %b are better than trading strategy developed from the simple Bollinger Bands trading rule using only the %b, as well as the buy-and-hold strategy. The results also illustrate that strategy #2 may provide a better return than strategy#1.

CONCLUSIONS

This research demonstrates the benefits and usefulness of combining neural networks and Bollinger Bands for stock trading. This was expected since neural networks can be used to learn historical data to predict the future trend of the stock market. The Time-Delay Neural Networks (TDNN) with the backpropagation learning algorithm was used in this research. The basic Backpropagation Neural Networks (BPN) was also used to compare the results of future stock trend using the mean squart error (MSE) and percentage diection accuracy (SIGN) for predicting the trend. This research finds that the BPN does not perform well since it gives a similar result as the random walk model. Furthermore, the low MSE does not always give a high SIGN. The trading systems that utilize a combination of the TDNN and Bollinger Bands trading rule give a better rate of return as compared to the simple Bollinger Bands trading rule or the Buy-and-Hold strategy. Further research should examine other technical indicators in different categories as inputs to investigate the sensitivity of the results. Additional neural networks architectures should also be considered.

REFERENCES

Achelis, S.B. (1995). Technical Analysis from A to Z: Covers Every Trading Tool From the Absolute Breadth Index to the Zig Zag. Probus Publisher: Chicago, IL.

Bautista, C.C., (2001) "Predicting the Phillippine Stock Price Index Using Artificial Neural Networks". UPCBA Discussion Paper No. 0107.

Bollinger, J., (2002) Bollinger on Bollinger bands, McGraw-Hill, New York, 2002.

Ham, F. and Kostanic, I.(2001), Principles of Neurocomputing for Science and Engineering, McGraw-Hill, INC., New York, 2001.

Mizuno, H., Kosaka, M., Yajima, H., and Komoda, N. (2001) "Application of Neural Network to Technical Analysis of Stock Market Prediction". (http://nas.cl.uh.edu/boetticher/ML_DataMining/Kimoto.pdf).

Pring, M.J., Technical Analysis Explained, McGraw-Hill, 1985.

Saad, W.E., Prokhorov, V.E., and Wunsch, C. D.,(1998) "Comparative Study of Stock Trend Prediction Using Time Delay, Recurrent and Probabilistic Neural Networks", *IEEE Transactions on Neural Networks*, vol. 9, no.6.

Schoenberg, E., "Stock Price Prediction Using Neural Networks: A project Report," *Neurocomputing*, vol. 2, 1990, pp. 17-27.

Thawornwong, S., and D. Enke, "The adaptive selection of financial and economic variables for use with artificial neural networks", *Neurocomputing*, Vol.56 (2003): 205-232.

Yao, J., Tan, L. C., and Poh, H. (1998) "Neural Networks For Technical Analysis", *International Journal of Theoretical and Applied Finance*, vol. 2, no. 2, pp. 221-241.

USING COALITION FORMATION AND GAME THEORY FOR ALLOCATING CAPITAL TO NEW TRANSMISSION INVESTMENT

J. MEPOKEE, D.ENKE
Laboratory for Investment and Financial Engineering
Smart Engineering System Lab
Intelligent System Center
University of Missouri- Rolla

B. CHOWDHURY
Department of Electrical & Computer Engineering
University of Missouri-Rolla

ABSTRACT

The following presents issues and techniques for new innovation in addressing the problem of allocating cost in the competitive deregulated power markets. Due to deregulation, higher competition in the generation sector of the energy market has occurred. The same has not been true for investment in transmission. The socialization methods of the past have been shown to be unfair to some market and network participants. The decentralization of cost allocation must be considered. In order to help consumers receive cheaper electricity prices while also increasing the reliability of the power grid, a new cost allocation method is needed. To achieve these two goals, new transmission investment (new/upgraded transmission line) must be made to prevent market power and remove congestion cost in order to reduce the locational marginal price of electricity. The following will provide a comparison between traditional cost allocation methods and a new cost allocation method based on agent-based game theory. The performance of the model will be tested on a multi-bus system.

INTRODUCTION

The deregulation of the power industry has resulted in a new level of competition among generators. This new competition raises both technical and economic issues related to the use and the enhancement of the existing transmission system. Problems develop when the expansion rate of transmission cannot keep pace with the expansion rate of generation. This imbalance can result in market power and congestion in some areas, decreasing reliability, causing outages, and inflating market prices for electricity. The imbalances can also result in improper signals being sent to the generation providers, possibly slowing competition.

The primary indicator in making a decision whether to build a new transmission line is congestion. The new or upgraded line will relieve constraints and increase access of lower cost generation (Palmer, 1997). In the past, the cost of new/upgraded transmission is socialized to all users in the network. This practice is not fair to the user who does not get any benefit from a new/upgraded line. Cost allocation from the benefit standpoint can provide a better solution for allocation of investment costs (Gendra, 1999). For the following research, a game theory method is applied to allocate the cost of new investment to the users in the network in a fair manner.

MULTI-AGENT AND GAME THEORY

The planning of transmission has moved from centralization towards decentralization. The main advantage of a centralized planning system is its simplicity. In decentralized systems, the information exchange among the coordinator (ISO, RTO) and agents is required, making the system more complex. Multi-agent systems are one approach that is used to solve this kind of problem (Gil et al, 2002, Hogan, 1999, Mepokee et al 2003).

An agent is an entity that makes decisions according to his/her own interests, as well as the actions of other agents. In transmission planning problems, there are many agents that can make a decision about expanding the network. Several entities can be represented by agents, such as generators, loads, and transmission line owners, each making a decision about the expansion of the network. It is not easy to determine how these agents can obtain the maximum individual benefit from expanding the transmission line, and if it is better to form coalitions to gain more from the line. Therefore, it is difficult to determine which agents are going to pay for the new transmission line investment. Thus, we propose a multi-agent approach to cost allocation of a new investment that takes into account the benefits of each player in the system from the addition of the new line (Zolezzi and Rudnick, 2002, Yan et al, 2003, Coleman, 1995).

COALITION FORMATION AND COST ALLOCATION

The Shapley Value (SV) has been used to solve similar types of allocation problems (Kahan and Rapoport, 1984, Owen, 1995, Contreras et al, 1998). The SV calculates a value based on an individual's contribution among all members in a coalition. It is a concept from the n-person corporate game. SV is a weighted average of marginal contributions of a member to all the possible contribution coalitions that a member participates. It is assumed that a grand coalition is formed. The formula for the Shapley Value is given by:

$$\phi_i = \sum_{S, i \in S \subset N} \frac{(|s|-1)!(n-|S|)!}{n!}\left[v(S) - v(S - \{i\})\right] \tag{1}$$

where i is the ith player, S is a coalition of players, $/S/$ is a number of players in coalition S, n is the total number of players, N is the set of all players, and $v(S)$ is the characteristic function associated with coalition S.

The Banzhaf-Coleman Index has been suggested by Banzhaf and Coleman (Banzhaf, 1968; Coleman, 1971). Assuming v to be simple game normalization, a swing for player i is defined as a set S, N such that S wins and S-$\{i\}$ loses. Letting θ_i be the number of swings for player i, the equation can be written as

$$\beta_i[v] = \frac{\theta_i}{\sum_{j=1}^{n} \theta_j} \tag{2}$$

The process to form a coalition among agents is based on the approach of (Klusch and Shehory, 1996).

A. Self Value Calculation: Each agent uses all available information to calculate its initial self-value. This value is calculated by the maximum value that the agent can get from the new line.

B. Communication and Security Check: All agents send their self-value and the coalitions to independent coordinators (ISO, RTO). The ISO or RTO will check the security of the coalitions and publish to all agents and each coalition.

C. Rank Payoff for Each Agent: After receiving messages from the RTO, each agent proceeds to rank the order to form a coalition with other agents.

D. Negotiation: Every agent begins to negotiate with other agents to get the optimum benefit for each agent.

APPLICATION IN TRANSMISSION PLANNING

A centralize method such as the postage stamp method (Shirmohammadi et al, 1996) does not offer efficient price signals. This is because all customers will be charged an even amount. This method does not provide proper signals to the system operator with regard to either congestion or which area is needed for new generation. A new pricing method is needed to provide such a signal to the system operator. The Locational Marginal Price (LMP) is one such solution.

When the securities system decreases due to congestion, the system operator will act as a last stop. Since the system security has priority, the least-cost generation is passed on when congestion occurs. Thus, the difference of the LMP between two nodes is their transmission costs (Rudnick et al, 1999). The lower biding customers will not get their desired amount because the open access rules are applied on LMP, leading to each bus's competitive prices. The ISO must replace a lower cost generation from an unconstrained area with more expensive generation in the constrained area. This leads to a difference in load serving marginal costs for different areas, resulting in different LMP values. It also represents the incremental costs of re-dispatching the system to accommodate the flows between those two locations within the security constraints (NERC, 2000). If traders face higher congestion charges, they will compare them against the costs of any new investment that would relieve the congestion. The allocation process begins with a Cost-Benefit Analysis (CBA) using game theory as the allocation tool. Again, the overall benefits must increase after adding a new line to the network. The reliability must also increase, and the overall LMP should be cheaper.

ILLUSTRATION

Previous research has shown that loads have seasonal and time of the day effects. For the following, Monte Carlo simulation is used to generate the future load demand (Certo and Saraiva, 2001) for the next 10 years. The test system is a five-bus system, as shown in Figure 1. The demand growth is assumed to include a 2% incremental increase every two years. There is no change in the supply side during this period. The interest is assumed to be constant at 5%. The

Net Present Value (NPV) is applied to judge the project from a benefit standpoint.

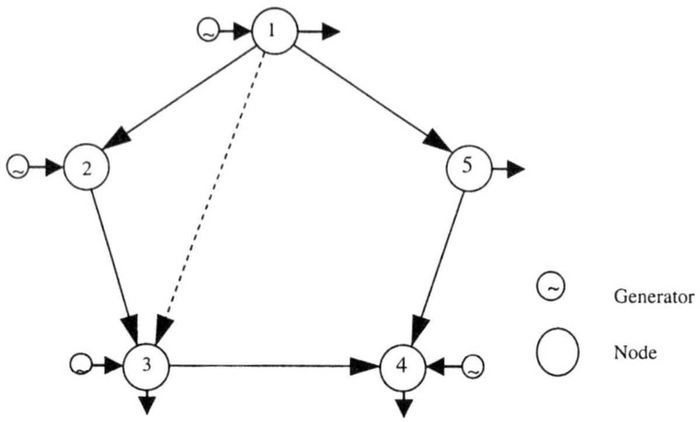

Figure 1: Five-bus test system (--- line is the new transmission investment)

Figure 1 illustrates the system before/after the new investment. The new investment takes place between nodes 1 and 3. After the line is built, the LMP at each node will be changed. The benefit of the new line is determined from the change in LMP at each node. This line will remove some congestion and increase system reliability. The system consists of four loads and four generators. The lines have resistance 0.01, reactance 0.1, and a rating of 800. The generator details are shown in Table 1. The average price of each generator is different to make the system more realistic.

Table 1: Detail of generators

GENERATION OFFERS		
Unit	Generation, MW	Average Price
1	2500	\$15.00
2	500	\$35.00
3	800	\$20.00
4	1000	\$25.00
Total	4800	

Table 2: Load demand detail in MW

	Load 1	Load 3	Load 4	Load 5
Year 0	960.8462	952.8296	564.1727	571.028
Year 1	980.0632	971.8862	575.4561	582.4485
Year 2	980.0632	971.8862	575.4561	582.4485
Year 3	999.6644	991.3239	586.9653	594.0975
Year 4	999.6644	991.3239	586.9653	594.0975
Year 5	1019.658	1011.15	598.7046	605.9795
Year 6	1019.658	1011.15	598.7046	605.9795
Year 7	1040.051	1031.373	610.6787	618.099
Year 8	1040.051	1031.373	610.6787	618.099
Year 9	1060.852	1052.001	622.8922	630.461
Year 10	1060.852	1052.001	622.8922	630.461

The LMP calculator program from PA consultants is used to find the LMP at each node. The benefit of each agent is calculated from cost savings before and after the new investment takes place. This criterion is used to form a coalition, as shown in Table 3.

From the cost-benefit analysis, the overall cost saving of the system will be 490M for the next 10 years if the new line is built. This means if the cost of the new investment is less than $490M, this line should be built. Customers will get benefit from cheaper electricity cost in the future. The next step is to apply game theory methods to allocate the cost of this investment and compare it to the social welfare and load proportional methods.

Table 3: Benefit of each coalition

Coalition	Benefit	Coalition	Benefit
0	0	34	$471,071,712.10
1	-$31,405,479.72	35	$406,383,618.08
3	$356,566,928.37	45	$164,321,473.44
4	$114,504,783.73	134	$439,666,232.38
5	$49,816,689.71	135	$18,411,209.98
13	$325,161,448.65	145	$132,915,993.72
14	$83,099,304.01	345	$520,888,401.81
15	$18,411,209.98	1345	$489,482,922.09

The assumption was made that the new line cost 400M to build. The feasible coalitions are {34}, {35}, {134}, {345}, {1345}. Comparisons between each method, along with the results, are shown in Table 4. Each method gives different results due to the different perspectives being considered. From the game theory methods, none of the players receives a worse payoff from coalition {1,3,4,5} for the Banzhaf-Coleman Index. The Shapley Value also covers the lost of agent {1} from agents {3}, {4}, and {5}. This situation will motivate the new investment to take place faster. From the game theory point of view, the Shapley Value and Banzhaf-Coleman show better results in the allocation of cost to all players in the network in the sense of fairness. The social welfare method and proportional load method are not concerned with the benefits of adding the new line. The costs of the new transmission line should not be socialized since it will harm the players who do not receive any benefits from the new investment. The players who do not receive benefits pay nothing from the game theory method.

Table 4: Cost allocation result of each method

Method	1	3	4	5
Shapley Value	-6.32%	72.86%	23.47%	10.2%
Banzhaf-Coleman	0%	50%	30%	20%
Social Welfare	25%	25%	25%	25%
Proportional Load	31.56%	31.16%	18.54%	18.74%

CONCLUSIONS

Techniques from game theory, including the use of the Shapley Value and the Banzhalf-Coleman Index, are used to allocate costs to participating agents. When combined with agent-based modeling, game theory will allow for a fair and proper allocation of costs to market participants. The coalition facilitates the cost allocation of each agent for upgrade or transmission line expansion in the new environment of power deregulation. Competition in the new environment forces all participants in the network to produce additional profit and/or reduce their costs. The coalition will be formed based on the benefits gained by each agent. From the results, the game theory based method is better in the sense of fairness. The agents that will not get benefit from the new investment have been treated fairly. The agents who have received increased benefit from this investment will pay more. Future work will develop a price forecasting model to deal with long-term investment, along with uncertainty in supply and demand.

REFERENCES

Banzhaf J.F., "A Mathematical Analysis of the Electoral College", Villanova Law Review, Vol. 13, No.2, 1968.

Certo, J., and J Saraiva,. T., "Evaluation of Target Prices for Transmission Congestion Contracts using a Monte Carlo Accelerated Approach," IEEE Porto Power Tech Conference, 10th-13th September, Porto, Portugal, 2001.

Coleman, A.M., Game Theory & its Applications, Butterworth Heinemann, 1995.

Coleman, J.S., "Control of Collectivities and the Power of a Collectivity to Act", In Lieberman (ed.) Social Choice, New York, Gordon & Breach, 1971.

Contreras,J., Klush,M., and Yen, J., "Multi-Agent Coalition in Power Transmission Planning: a Bilateral Value Approach," American Association for Artificial Intelligence, 1998.

Gedra, T. W., "On Transmission Congestion and Pricing," IEEE Transactions on Power Systems, Vol 14, No. 1, February 1999.

Gil, H. A., Silva, E. L. and Galiana, F. D., "Modeling Competition in Transmission Expansion," IEEE Transactions on Power Systems, Vol. 17, No. 4, November 2002.

Hogan, W., "Market-Based Transmission Investment and Competitive Electricity Markets," 1999, available at: http://ksghome.harvard.edu/~.whogan.cbg.ksg/tran0899.pdf.

Kahan, J., Rapoport, A., Theories of Coalition Formation, Lawrence Erlbaum Associates, 1984.

Klusch, M., Shehory, O. "Coalition formation among Rational Agents," Proc., 7th European Workshop on modeling Autonomous Agents in a Multi-Agent World, January, 1996.

Mepokee, J., Enke, D. and Chowdhury, B., "Cost Allocation using Intelligent Agents for New Transmission Investment under Electricity Restructuring," 35th North American Power Symposium, October 20-2, 2003.

North American Electricity Reliability Council: Reliability Assessment 2000-2009: The Reliability of Bulk Electric System in North America, 2000, Page 33.

Owen,G., Game Theory, Academic Press, 1995.

Palmer, R., "Transmission Network Privatization-pricing, Investment, and Access," Power Engineering Journal, April, 1997.

Rudnick,H., Soto M., and Palma, R., "Use of System approaches for transmission Open Access Pricing", International Journal of Electrical Power and Energy Systems, vol.21, no.2, pp. 125-135, 1999.

Shirmohammadi, D., Filho, X. V., Gorenstin, B., and Pereira, M. V., "Some Fundamental Technical Concepts about Cost Based Transmission Pricing," IEEE Transactions on Power Systems, Vol.11, No.2, May 1996.

Yan, Y., Yen, J., and Bui, T. X., "A Multi-Agent Based Negotiation Support System for Distributed Transmission Cost Allocation," Proceedings of the 33rd Hawaii International Conference on System Sciences, 2000.

Zolezzi, J. M., Rudnick, H., "Transmission Cost Allocation by Cooperative Games and Coalition Formation," IEEE Transactions on Power Systems, Vol. 17, Issue: 4, November 2002.

TESTING FOR NONLINEARITIES IN EXCHANGE RATES: AN APPLICATION TO CURRENCY CRISIS

GHASSAN DIBEH
Lebanese American University
Department of Economics
Byblos, Lebanon
gdibeh@lau.edu.lb

GEORGE E. NASR
Lebanese American University
Department of Electrical and Computer Engineering
Byblos, Lebanon
genasr@lau.edu.lb

ABSTRACT
In this paper the correlation dimension is used to detect determinism in an economic time series generated by speculative behavior of market participants during a currency crisis. The time series are from the emerging market of Lebanon, which experienced episodes of severe currency fluctuations in the years 1985-1992. The detection of determinism and nonlinearities in the stationary time series is done through the estimation of the correlation dimension. The time series is shown to have low and finite dimensionality. Furthermore, a significance test for the correlation dimension is applied using Fourier-transformed surrogate data. The results show strong evidence of a nonlinear structure, which lends support to the hypothesis that the currency crisis in Lebanon was driven by deterministic speculative activity.

INTRODUCTION

The detection of nonlinear deterministic generating mechanisms of economic and financial time series has provided the empirical grounds for questioning the adequacy of stochastic linear models of variables such as GNP, exchange rates and stock prices in explaining the stylized facts of market dynamics. Fundamentally, the extraction of deterministic dynamics from such time series reveals prevalent market inefficiencies and the existence of underlying nonlinear generators created by speculators. The speculators forecast the future paths of prices causing herd behavior that drive the market dynamics. Such behavior can be detected empirically by searching for deterministic structures or signatures in the data (Guarda and Salmon, 1996; Serletis and Dormaar, 1996). Such deterministic structures have an impact on the construction of forecasting models and predictability of many financial and economic time series (Sarno et. al (2004); Qi andYu (2003)). In this respect, Hu and Tsoukalas (1999) have shown that during the period of crisis in the European Monetary System (EMS) of August 1993 an Artificial Neural Network (ANN) model outperformed linear models in accounting for the volatility of the European exchange rates during this period. In a theoretical model that attempts to explain the empirically observed chaotic dynamics of monetary data, Auray et al. (2002) show that a simple monetary economy model in which money is used for transaction motives can generate deterministic cycles and chaotic equilibria. Panas and

Ninni (2000), using oil markets data, have shown that oil markets exhibit evidence of chaos with implications for the predictability of future oil prices. Artificial Neural Network (ANN) models have also been used to predict the future behavior of asset prices. Lisi and Schiavo (1999) showed that neural networks compare with chaotic models and both types of models do substantially better than models based on the random walk hypothesis.

In this paper, the correlation dimension is used to detect nonlinearities in daily exchange rate time series. The time series represent a case study of a currency crisis in the emerging market of Lebanon, which experienced episodes of severe currency fluctuations in the years 1985-1992. The detection of determinism and nonlinearities in the stationary time series is done through the estimation of the correlation dimension. The time series is shown to have low and finite dimensionality. Furthermore, a significance test for the correlation dimension is applied using Fourier-transformed surrogate data. The results show strong evidence of a nonlinear structure, which lends support to the hypothesis that the currency crisis in Lebanon was driven by deterministic speculative activity. Although such a result is of historic interest, the detection of deterministic structures in the exchange rate data of Lebanon for the period 1984-1992 may have implications for researchers empirically investigating currency crises that have developed lately in many countries including Russia, East Asia and Argentina. Policy implications follow from such detection for formulating policies that prevent speculative activities that cause bandwagon and herd effects in an otherwise stable foreign exchange markets.

THE CORRELATION DIMENSION

Deterministic dynamical systems such as those that are modeled with differential or difference equations produce a specific type of geometrical signatures (attractors) in phase space formed by the non-transient trajectories of the system. These attractors of deterministic systems (chaotic or limit cycles) are characterized by a *finite dimensionality* of the attractor. In contrast, random systems such as a geometric Brownian motion have no specific signature in phase space and the dynamics fill the whole space generating a dimension of infinity. The estimation of the correlation dimension for a time series data then becomes a crucial test for the detection of nonlinearities. The correlation dimension reconstructs the geometry from a finite sample of data points which are most likely to contain some errors as well (Kantz and Schreiber, 1997). The first step is to define the correlation sum for points x_n in some vector space to be the fraction of all possible pairs of points which are closer than a given distance ε in a particular norm. The basic formula is

$$C(\varepsilon) = \frac{2}{N(N-1)} \sum_{i=1}^{N} \sum_{j=i+1}^{N} \Theta(\varepsilon - \|x_i - x_j\|)$$

where $\Theta(x) = 0$ if $x \leq 0$ and $\Theta(x) = 1$ for $x > 0$

The sum counts the pairs (x_i, x_j) whose distance is smaller than ε. For infinite amount of data and small ε, C is expected to scale like a power law

$$C(e) \sim e^D$$

where D is the correlation dimension defined by

$$d(N,\varepsilon) = \frac{\partial \ln C(\varepsilon, N)}{\partial \ln \varepsilon}$$

$$D = \lim_{\varepsilon \to 0} \lim_{N \to \infty} d(N,\varepsilon)$$

For data exhibiting nonlinear deterministic dynamics, the estimated D will have low-dimensionality. This measure for the detection of chaos and nonlinearities has the advantage over other measures such as the Lyapunov exponent and entropy measures in that the correlation dimension is very suitable for the case in hand of detecting deterministic structures in an economic time series. Deterministic structures whether generated by chaotic underlying dynamics (such as a tent map) or generated by a more limit cycle producing system (such as a nonlinear differential equation) can be detected by the correlation dimension as the phase space trajectories of such systems have finite dimensionality. In such non-chaotic but nonlinear deterministic systems, measures such as entropy and the Lyapunov exponent may not be ideally suited for detecting crucial determinism.

ESTIMATION AND SURROGATE DATA

The estimation of the correlation dimension was done using daily spot Lebanese Pound (LP) to $US exchange rate for the period January 2, 1985 to December 30, 1992 for a total of 2917 points. Due to war interruptions, holidays and weekends missing data exist. These were replaced by the value of the exchange rate in the preceding day.

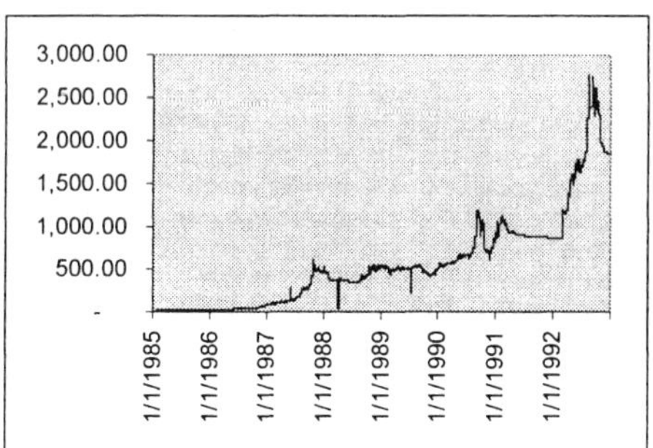

Figure 1. The Exchange Rate Time Series (LP/$US)

The data presented in Fig. 1 shows significant non-stationarity. In order for the data to be analyzed properly, it has to be rendered stationary. The choice of detrending methodology is important in this respect. Since Nelson and Plosser (1982) have shown that economic time series can exhibit unit root phenomena, the preferred method of detrending is first differencing. However, this method can amplify the noise that exists in the data (Sprott and Rowlands, 1995). Diebold and Rudebush (1999) take issue with the stochastic trend (or difference-stationary) approach to modeling macroeconomic time series and argue that a linear deterministic trend would be a good approximation for the trend modeling of the data. Wen (1996) suggests a practical approach to overcoming the problem of noise amplification. In his approach the time series is decomposed into a long-term trend and a fluctuating component around the trend. In this paper a middle ground approach is used to make the data stationary. A first difference is applied to raw data then to eliminate the effect of amplified noise a smoothing process using a third-order moving average process MA (3) is applied to the differenced data.

The program used for numerical calculations on the stationary data is the *Chaos Data Analyzer* (Sprott and Rowlands, 1995). The correlation dimension is calculated when there is saturation in the correlation dimension as T, the embedding dimension, is increased. The correlation time for the data is $\tau = 1.9$. Hence, the correlation dimension was calculated for time delay, T = 8. The calculated D= 2.726 +/- 0.256 lends evidence to a nonlinear deterministic generating process. The correlation dimension is low and finite and it saturates as the embedding dimension increases. Despite the low-dimensionality of the correlation dimension, this result must be further scrutinized for the detection of possible spurious results. Kantz and Schreiber (1997) have argued that in many applications of nonlinear time series analysis, the determinism is weak. This occurs in the domains of economics, finance, medicine and population dynamics where linear structures can be mistaken for determinism. Kantz and Schreiber (1997) suggest the following test. Let D be the correlation dimension estimate. The null hypothesis is that the time series is generated by a linear stochastic process. The procedure calls for the creation of *surrogate* data sets. Suppose that D_0 is the correlation dimension for the original data and D_i, for i=1,….., k surrogate data sets that are generated using a phase-randomizing Fourier transform. Using a rank based test, if $D_0 < D_i$ for all i where $1/\alpha$ is the total number of sets with $1/\alpha - 1$ surrogate date sets, then the null hypothesis is rejected with α significance. This method is applied to our data set using $\alpha = 0.05$ (5 % significance) and surrogate data sets that are phase randomized but that maintain the Gaussian distribution. Table 1 shows the D_i for the surrogate data sets. The results clearly reject the null hypothesis of a Gaussian linear stochastic generating mechanism.

SHUFFLE NUMBER	DIMENSION
1	2.485 +/- 0.184
2	2.422 +/- 0.1098
3	2.594 +/- 0.062
4	2.412 +/- 0.250
5	2.699 +/- 0.180
6	2.581 +/- 0.429
7	2.542 +/- 0.222
8	2.507 +/-0.221
9	2.490 +/- 0.227
10	2.694 +/- 0.176
11	2.349 +/- 0.199
12	2.456 +/- 0.297
13	2.738 +/- 0.229
14	2.802 +/- 0.146
15	2.902 +/- 0.167
16	2.773 +/- 0.265
17	2.599 +/- 0.349
18	2.620 +/- 0.246
19	2.983 +/- 0.355

Table 1. Shuffled Data Estimation of the Correlation Dimension

CONCLUSION

The correlation dimension estimation has shown that the exchange rate time series has a deterministic structure. The result lends support to the widely held view that speculative activities by market participants generated the currency crises of 1985-1992. However, further tests of nonlinearity can be applied to the data in order to confirm the above results. The models that can be used include ANN models. In this respect, ANN models are very suitable for application in predicting currency crises which remains until today a very inexact and uncertain field of study. Since ANN are more adaptable to changes in data sets than linear or chaotic models, they could perform better in predicting changes in foreign exchange rates under currency crisis conditions. Further investigation should also study the effect of dertrending and noise-reduction techniques implemented on the estimated measures of nonlinearity.

REFERENCES

Auray, S., Collard, F., and Fève, P., 2002, "Money and External Habit Persistence: A Tale for Chaos," *Economics Letters*, Vol. 76, Issue 1, pp. 121-127

Diebold, F. X., and Rudebusch, G.D., 1999, *Business Cycle: Durations, Dynamics and Forecasting*, Princeton University Press, Princeton, NJ.

Guarda, P., and Salmon, M., 1996, "Detection of Nonlinearity in Foreign Exchange Data," *Nonlinear Dynamics and Economics: Proceedings of the Tenth International Symposium in Economic Theory and Econometrics,* Cambridge University Press, New York, pp. 77-111.

Hu, M. Y., and Tsoukalas, C., 1999, "Combining Conditional Volatility Forecast Using Neural Networks: an Application to EMS Exchange Rates," *Journal of International Financial markets, Institutions and Money,* Vol. 9, pp. 407-422.

Kantz, H., and Schreiber T., 1997, *Nonlinear Time Series Analysis,* Cambridge University Press, Cambridge.

Lisi, F., and Schiavo, R. A., 1999, "A Comparison between Neural Networks and Chaotic Models for Exchange Rate Prediction," *Computational Statistics and Data Analysis*, Vol. 30, pp. 87-102.

Nelson, C., and Plosser, C.I., 1982, "Trends and Random Walks in Macroeconomic Time Series: Some Evidence and Implications," *Journal of Monetary Economics*, Vol. 10, pp. 139-162.

Panas, E., and Ninni, V., 2000, "Are Oil Markets Chaotic? A Non-linear Dynamic Analysis," *Energy Economics*, Vol. 22, pp. 549-568.

Qi, M., and Wu, Y., 2003, "Nonlinear Prediction of Exchange Rates with Monetary Fundamentals," *Journal of Empirical Finance*, Vol. 10, Issue 5, pp. 623-640.

Sarno, L., Taylor, M.P., and Chowdhury, I., 2004, "Nonlinear Dynamics in Deviations from the Law of One Price: a Broad-based Empirical Study," *Journal of International Money and Finance*, Vol. 23, Issue 1, pp. 1-25

Serletis, A., and Dormaar, P., 1996, "Chaos and Nonlinear Dynamics in Futures Markets," *Nonlinear Dynamics and Economics: Proceedings of the Tenth International Symposium in Economic Theory and Econometric,* Cambridge University Press, New York, pp. 113-132.

Sprott, J. C., and Rowlands, G., 1995, *Chaos Data Analyzer*, American Institute of Physics, New York.

Wen, K., 1996, "Continuous-time Chaos in Stock Market Dynamics," *Nonlinear Dynamics and Economics: Proceedings of the Tenth International Symposium in Economic Theory and Econometrics,* Cambridge University Press, New York, pp. 133-159.

A COMPARISON OF METHODS FOR DERIVATIVE TRADING USING STOCK RETURN FORECASTS

SUNISA AMORNWATTANA AND DAVID ENKE
Engineering Management Department
Laboratory for Investment and Financial Engineering
Center for Intelligent Systems
University of Missouri – Rolla
Rolla, MO 65409-0370

ABSTRACT
Neural networks have been widely used for strategic decision making. The learning capability and flexibility of neural networks can overcome many of the problems with other methodologies. They can deal with the fuzziness and biases of the human decision processes. Many researchers and investors are interested in the area of stock return forecasting. This study involves training neural networks to forecast next trading day stock returns to generate derivative trading signals and compares the results in term of trading loss or profit and accuracy of trading signals between three different models: feed-forward networks with backpropagation, generalized regression neural networks, and Elman recurrent neural networks. These models are trained and tested on historical data of the Standard & Poor's Composite 500 (S&P 500) stock index (symbol: SPX) and stock index options for derivative trading.

INTRODUCTION

Neural networks are statistical methodologies for inductive inference. They need no prior assumptions of models and are able to infer complex non-linear relationships. The use of neural networks as non-linear forecasters in financial engineering seems very promising, however, development of financial applications using neural network is a complex process. Extensive data pre-processing and experimentation with network parameters in the application development is a time comsuming process.

Stock return is an interesting area and has been extensively studied by many researchers. Jansen and Verschoor [1] studied the relationship between expected stock returns and sizes, and market-to-book ratios. Dumas et al. [2] proposed a framework that contains a statistical model for output and an intertemporal financial market model for stock returns. Vuolteenaho [3] decomposed an individual firm's stock return using a vector autoregressive model and provided the result that firm-level stock returns are driven by cash-flow news. Stock return distribution was studied by Linden [4]. A Bayesian model was used to explore the support on return predictability by Avramov [5]. Lanne [6] proposed a general test of whether the return can be predicted by any highly persistent variables. Kanas [7] investigated the performance of parametric and non-parametric models to forecast stock return accuracy. Neural networks have also been studied in other financial areas such as stock trading [8], currency option trading [9], mutual fund performance forecasting [10], foreign exchange rate forecasting [11], and prediction of corporation bankruptcy [12].

The purpose of this papar is to investigate the probability of using neural networks for derivative trading by forecasting the next day trading stock returns. The results of three different neural networks are compared in terms of profitability and prediction accuracy. Networks are trained and tested by the same historical S&P 500 index period. After the neural networks generate the trading signal, the front month options nearest to at-the-money options are studied in this paper.

OPTIONS

The option market has been of great interest for decades due to its monetary benefits and multifunctions. An option is a type of derivative, definded as a financial instrument whose value is derived from the values of underlying asset(s). An option is a right to take action in the future without any obligation. There are two basic types of options. A call option gives the holder the right to buy the underlying asset by a certain date for a certain price. A put option gives the holder the right to sell the underlying asset by a certain date for a certain price.

Options can be applied by three different types of traders for different purposes. First, options can help hedgers to minimize risks by avoiding exposure to adverse movements in the price of an asset. Second, using option can help speculators to take a position in the market - either they are speculating that the prices will go up or they are speculating that the prices will go down. Third, applying options can help arbitrageurs to lock in a riskless profit by concurrently entering into transactions in two or more markets. This paper focuses on speculation. In the current market, there are two major alternatives to speculate on the price of stocks: the stock itself and derivatives. Option markets allow speculators to obtain leverage. Investors are able to take a large speculative position using a small amount of capital. However, investment in options allows for greater potential loss. Fortunately, the loss is limited to the amount paid for the options, called the option price or premium.

REVIEW OF NEURAL NETWORK ARCHITECTURES

Three neural network architectures used in this paper are briefly reviewed. First, a feed-forward network with backpropagation is chosen because of its use as a standard benchmark. Second, the generalized regression neural network (GRNN) [13] is chosen because it provides comparable accuracy to the backpropagation architecture with substantially less training time. Third, the Elman network [14] is chosen because it is widely claimed for accurrate performance in time-series prediction.

BACKPROPAGATION NEURAL NETWORK

Backpropagation learning is derived from the Widrow-Hoff [15] learning rule in multiple-layer feedforward networks using nonlinear differentiable transfer functions. A network is trained until it is able to approximate a function or classify patterns using associated input vectors with specific output vectors. There are many backpropagation training algorithms. The gradient descent algorithm is the standard method, although typically it is too slow. For this research, the Levenberg-Marquardt algorithm is applied due to its faster training time.

GENERALIZED REGRESSION NEURAL NETWORK

The genearlized regression neural network (GRNN) is significantly different from the feed-forward backpropagation model in both algorithm and architecture. It obtains the estimate in a single pass, therefore no iterative training is needed. The network also performs well under noisy environments when given sufficient data. The GRNN is a supervised feed forward network, subsuming the radial basis-function method. It is based on nonlinear regression theory and computes its output using a variation of the "nearest-neighbor" approach. The forecast value for an input vector is a weighted average of the outputs in the training sample. The closer an input vector in the training sample, the larger the weight of its corresponding output. Usually, the GRNN is used for function approximation. It has been shown that the GRNN can approximate a continuous function when given a sufficient amount of training data.

ELMAN NEURAL NETWORK

The Elman recurrent network is a two-layer backpropagation network, with the addition of a feedback connection from the output of the hidden layer to its inputs. This feedback allows the network to detect and generate time-varying temporal patterns. An Elman network normally requires more hidden neurons in its hidden layer than other methods.

DATA SETS

The S&P 500 stock index is a broadly based index of 500 large cap firms. It is a market-value-weighted index. This research applies this index to train networks for the next day trading return. The training dataset covers the period of two calendar years from January 2, 2001 to December 31, 2002, with 501 records. After receiving trading signals from the networks, the front month option nearest to the at-the-money option is applied to observe profit and loss. The testing dataset is in the period of 45 day calendar from January 2, 2003 to February 15, 2003 with 31 records. This study focuses on the daily closing S&P 500 index and S&P 500 option price.

IMPLEMENTATION

Data preparation is one of the most important steps to obtain an effective result in financial modeling, and neural network training can be made more efficient if preprocessing steps are performed. Initially, daily closing stock indexes are transformed into returns. Then a mean and standard deviation approach is applied to normalize the data sets. After preprocessing, inputs and targets have zero mean and unity standard deviation. Next, appropriate thresholds are derived by sorting the results of the testing dataset. Finally, thresholds are used to generate trading signals. This study uses the mean squared error (MSE), mean absolute deviation (MAD), and acccracy percent of stock return direction to benchmark the performance of each model as shown below in equations 1, 2, and 3. The degree of being in or out of the money are also used to compare the performance.

$$\text{MSE} = \frac{\sum (Actual - forecast)^2}{(n-1)} \tag{1}$$

$$\text{MAD} = \frac{\sum | Actual - forecast |}{n} \tag{2}$$

$$\text{Accuracy percent of direction} = \frac{\text{Correct direction trading signals}}{\text{Total number of trading signals}} \tag{3}$$

RESULTS

Table 1 gives the results of the mean absolute deviation, the mean squared error, and accuracy percent of direction for the training dataset for the three tested networks. Table 2 shows the same set of results for the testing dataset.

Network	MSE	MAD	% Direction
Backpropagation	0.0544	0.1775	55.91 %
GRNN	0.0503	0.1711	59.92 %
Elman	0.0551	0.179	54.71 %

Table 1. Training dataset results for each model

Network	MSE	MAD	% Direction
Backpropagation	0.0442	0.1762	64.52 %
GRNN	0.0463	0.1827	67.74 %
Elman	0.0452	0.1779	61.29 %

Table 2. Testing dataset results for each model

From the results in Table 1 and 2, the mean absolute deviation and the mean squared error results from each model for both the training and testing dataset are not much different. On the other hand, the GRNN seems to provide a more accurate direction prediction of around five percent for both datasets. Next, thresholds for each model are derived from sorting results from the training dataset. Then the accuracy percents at each result or threshold are calculated. In other words, determining the correct percentage, if this threshold is applied. In this research, thresholds at different levels of accuracy are observed for their sensitivity of profit and loss.

After sorting the training results of each model, backpropagation provides thresholds at the 100 and 80 percent levels of accuracy. The Elman network provides threshold at only the 100 percent level of accuracy. On the other hand, the GRNN provides a threshold at different levels of accuracy - 100, 90, 85 and 80 percent. Each threshold for each model was also tested to generate trading signals. In general, if the stock market tends to increase, the call option contract is bought and this position will be closed on the next trading day. In the same manner, if the stock market tends to decrease, the put option contract is bought and this position will be closed on the next trading day. The results are investigated in terms of percent of profit, number of trades, and percent accuracy of direction, as shown in Tables 3 and 4. In reality, the number of trades also plays an important role in investment, since each trade incurs a transaction cost.

In this analysis, transaction cost are included using the rate at $8.5 per option contract, referenced from http://www.scottrade.com/frame_reasons.asp?r=5. Therefore, each investment costs $17 to open and close the position.

Network	Threshold	Profit	# of trades	% Direction
Backpropagation	100 %	0 %	0	0 %
	80 %	- 8.25 %	1	0 %
Elman	100 %	- 8.25 %	1	0 %

Table 3. Results at different thresholds for the Backpropagation and Elman networks

Network	Threshold	Profit	# of trades	% Direction
GRNN	100 %	+ 24.9 %	2	100 %
	90 %	+ 24.9 %	2	100 %
	85 %	+ 24.1 %	5	60 %
	80 %	+ 14.1 %	9	67 %

Table 4. Results at different thresholds for the GRNN network

Even though the MSE and MAD results for each model are very close and show no different in term of accuracy, the results in terms of profit and loss are substantially different, as shown in Tables 3 and 4. The backpropagation and Elman networks do not provide useful information in terms of being in or out of the money. The GRNN provides at least 14% in the period of 45 calendar days and up to 25.6% for the same testing dataset. Table 4 also shows that the higher the accuracy percent of threshold, and the more percent of profit, the less the number of trades, and the less amount of investment. The closing S&P 500 stock index on January 2, 2003 is 909.03 and February 14, 2003 is 834.89. If the buy and hold strategy is applied, this portfolio will have lost 8.2%. This shows that the backpropagation and Elman results cannot outperform the market, while the GRNN is able to outperform the market in this research.

CONCLUSIONS AND FUTURE WORK

The research demonstrated the potential benefits of using neural networks in the financial area, since neural networks can learn from the past data to predict and solve the non-linear forecasting problem. However, solving problems with neural networks requires both a theoretical and practical foundation. No one network can be an efficient tool for every problem. Therefore, experimentation and research are needed to explore this possibility. For example, this experiment shows that GRNN network is more suitable than a feedforward network with the backpropagation and Elman networks. In some experiments, MSE and MAD can be used as a preliminary error measurement. However, other techniques might require the researcher to extract useful information. Further research should examine a larger dataset to confirm the capability of the GRNN to solve this problem and also show the robustness of the system. Fundamental factors might also be considered as an additional input parameter to investigate whether they will improve the profitability.

REFERENCES

[1] Jansen, PFG. and Verschoor, WFC., (2004) "A Note on Transitional Stock Return Behavior", *Applied Economics Letters*, vol. 11, no. 1, pp. 11-13.

[2] Dumas, B., Harvey, CR. and Ruiz, P., (2003) "Are Correlations of Stock Returns Justified by Subsequent Changes in National Outputs", *Journal of International Money and Finance*, vol. 22, no. 6, pp. 777-811.

[3] Vuolteenaho, T., (2002) " What Drives Firm-Level Stock Returns?", *Journal of Finance*, vol. 57, no.1, pp. 233-264.

[4] Linden, M., (2001) "A Model for Stock Return Distribution", *International Journal of Finance and Economics*, vol. 6, no. 2, pp. 159-169.

[5] Avramov, D., (2002) "Stock Return Predictability and Model Uncertainty", *Journal of Financial Economics*, vol. 64, no. 3, pp. 423-458.

[6] Lanne, M., (2002) "Testing the Predictability of Stock Returns", *Review of Economics and Statistics*, vol. 84, no. 3, pp. 407-415.

[7] Kanas, A., (2003) "Non-Linear Forecasts of Stock Returns", *Journal of Forecasting*, vol. 22, no. 4, pp. 299-315.

[8] Wilson, C.L., (1994) "Self-Organizing Neural Network System for Trading Common Stocks ", *IEEE World Congress on Computational Intelligence*, vol. 6, no. 27, pp. 3651-3654.

[9] Quah, T.S., The, H.H. and Tan, C.L., (1995) "Neural Logic Hybrid System for Currency Option Trading", *IEEE International Conference*, vol. 2, no. 27, pp.824-828.

[10] Carhart, M. and Karaali, O., (1996) "Neural Network Forecasting of Mutual Fund Returns" , *Sixteenth Annual International Symposium on Forecasting Proceedings.*

[11] Pecen, L., Beran, H. and Pelikan, E., (1994) "Short-Term Foreign Exchange Rate Forecasting from High Frequency Data", *Neural Networks in the Capital Markets NNCM94 Proceedings.*

[12] Atiya, Amir, (2001) "Bankruptcy Prediction for Credit Risk Using Neural Networks: A Survey and New Results", *IEEE Transactions on Neural Networks*, vol. 12, no. 4, pp. 929-935.

[13] Specht, Donald ,(1991) "A General Regression Neural Network", *IEEE Transactions on Neural Networks*, vol. 2, no. 4, pp. 568-576.

[14] Elman, J.L., (1990) "Finding Structure in Time", *Cognitive Science*, vol. 14, pp. 179-211.

[15] Window, B. and Hoff, M.E. (1960) "Adaptive Switching Circuits", *Institute of Radio Engineers, Western Electronic Show and Convention, Convention Record*, part 4, pp. 96-104.

PART X: BIO MEDICAL ENGINEERING

CLASSIFICATION RESULTS FOR SIX ORGANOPHOSPHATE NERVE AGENTS USING SUPPORT VECTOR MACHINES

WALKER H. LAND, JR.,
Research Professor
Dept. of Computer Science
Binghamton University
Binghamton NY

LUT WONG
Graduate Student
Dept. of Computer Science
Binghamton University
Binghamton, NY

MARK J. EMBRECHTS
Associate Professor
Dept. of Decision Sciences and
Engineering Systems
Rensselaer Polytechnic Institute
Troy, NY

ABSTRACT

References 1 and 2 (Land, et. Al., 2003, and Sadik, 2004) describes classification results for a bio-terrorism relevant dataset. These publications established: (1.) SVM classification performance for the detection of organophosphates nerve agents using four separate model stimulant compounds, and (2) evaluated architecture of EP SVMs, which were upgraded to run on multiple machines simultaneously, by using a client-server architecture (Distributed EP). This paper extends these results in the following two ways: (a.) we establish classification accuracies using the following six organophosphate agent pairs: (1.) Parathion vs. Paraoxon, (2.) Dichlorvos vs. Trichlorfon, (3.) and Malathion vs. Diazinon, and (b.) this research also uses a larger data sets of 350 samples/agent with the objective of ascertaining more representative SVM classification performance.

INTRODUCTION

The US is experiencing increasing threats from chemical and biological weapons of mass destruction by international terrorist organizations. Consequently, there is a great deal of interest in developing tools that can be used not only to detect, but also to effectively combat biochemical warfare. Recent events in the country have increased the awareness that biochemical agents (BCA) may become the preferred weapons of mass destruction because these agents can effectively attack large populations cheaply.

Despite the existence of numerous sensing devices and systems, intelligent hybrid sensors that can detect and degrade BCAs are currently nonexistent. To fully realize a hybrid, chemical or biological sensor, as part of a functional system several areas of fundamental and technological research must be addressed. These include controlling the immobilization chemistries used in sensor design in order to minimize false positives and false negatives, designing and constructing a self-powered sensor system, and combining novel sensor mechanisms with artificial intelligence Ritter ,2001 (ref. 3)). Others include identifying specific blocking agents that can counteract the effects of these agents, thus preparing reactive chemical or biological systems that can degrade the agents, as well as effectively destroying the chemical/biological wastes generated from the degradation products.

Most Weapons of Mass Destruction (WMD) technologies emphasize early detection prior to any contact, detecting attacks on the battlefield, either at or near their source. Current BCA detectors (references 4 and 5) fall under four categories: (i) biochemical systems, which can detect a DNA sequence or protein that is unique to the bioagent through its interaction with a test molecule, (ii) immunodetection systems, which uses antibodies that are specific to the BCA agent of interest, (iii) tissue-based systems, in which a bioreagent or biotoxin affects live mammalian cells, causing them to undergo some measurable response, and (iv) purely instrumental mass spectrometry systems, which work by breaking down a sample into its components and then comparing these samples according to their mass-to-charge ratios. Existing detection systems tend to be fairly large and not terribly accurate (5 through 7) . Most often, they require human operation and are not capable of identifying specific agents.

This paper examines the use of multi array sensors coupled with support vector machines for the identification, detection, and classification of chemical warfare agents for a larger data set. A typical EN system consists of an array of chemical sensing elements coupled to headspace sampling, pattern recognition modules and appropriate transducer, references 8 through 10. We have preliminary evidence demonstrating the effective use of the electronic nose coupled with a SVMs for the detection and classification of a smaller data set of organophosphate nerve agent stimulants than reported here (Land, 2003, and Sadik, 2004). These chemicals were paired based on their structural similarity. For example, the difference between Paraoxon and Parathion compounds is only the presence of the sulfur and oxygen atoms, respectively, to the phosphorous atom. These two chemicals should be very difficult to correctly classify and will provide a good test for the SVM classification process.

The theory and background of Support Vector Machines and their operation will not be discussed here. This information, however, may be found in references (1, 2 and 11 through 22).

EXPERIMENTAL RESULTS

Organophosphates (OPs) are among the most toxic substances and are thus commonly used as pesticides and nerve gases. As stated, this research uses six

OP pesticides as nerve agent stimulants. These were Parathion, Paraoxon, Dichlorvos, Trichlorfon, Malathion, and Diazinon (Fig. 1), which were evaluated by pair wise testing.

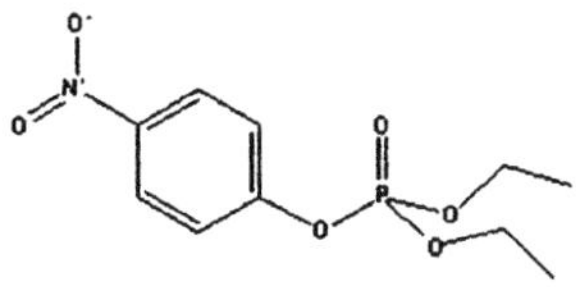

Paraoxon

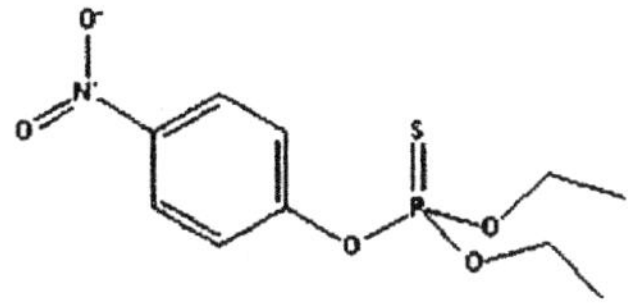

Parathion

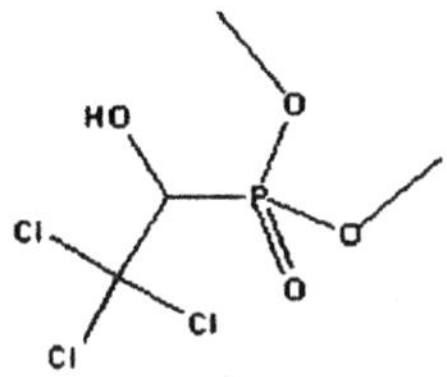

Trichlorfon

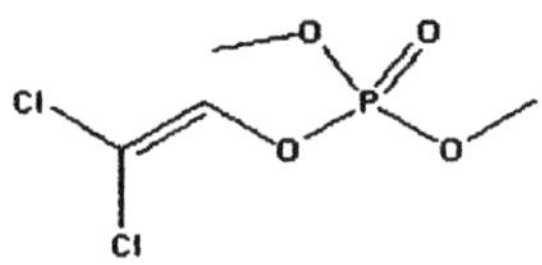

Dichlorvos

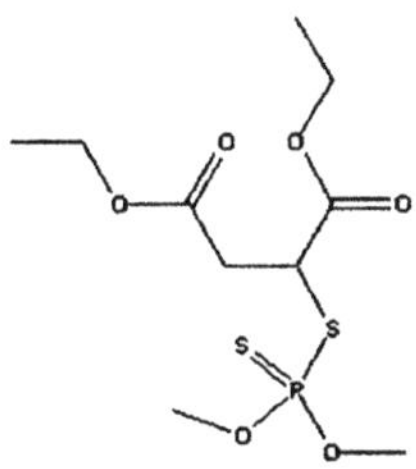

Malathion

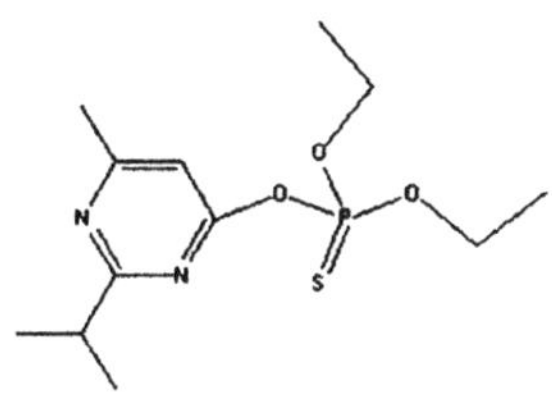

Diazinon

Figure 1. Organophosphate molecules

The last two OPs to undergo pair wise comparison testing, and most difficult to classify, were Paraoxon and Parathion. These OPs were paired because of their structural similarity. As previously stated, the only difference in the structures of the 2 compounds is that the P=O bond in Paraoxon is replaced by P=S bond in Parathion. Trichlorfon and Dichlorvos were also paired because of their structural similarities.

Parathion vs. Paraoxon

The difference between Paraoxon and Parathion compounds is only the presence of the sulfur atom attached to the phosphorous for Parathion, and the oxygen atom attached to the phosphorous for the Paraoxon. Consequently, these two chemicals should be very difficult to correctly classify and will provide a good test for the SVM classification process.

Table 1 depicts the classification accuracy of three kernels when compared to the old data set, which was considered as the baseline performance. When compared to the baseline system there is: (1) a 7.3% improvement in the overall ROC Az index using the radial basis function (rbf) kernel, (2) a significant 22.5 % improvement in specificity with the rbf kernel. This means that the number of false negative errors were reduced by 22.5%, while making no false positive errors, when compared to the base line performance. (3) The Schölkopf (S2000) and polynomial kernels demonstrated 88% specificity and 90% specificity respectively at 100% sensitivity. (4) One would expect slightly better performance at 98% sensitivity, and this generally happens. However, because of the small validation sample size, the results from the old data set were the same. These results improved as larger sample sizes were processed.

	Old S2000	New S2000	% improv	Old rbf	New rbf	% improv	Old poly	New poly	% improv
Az	0.984	0.994	0.98	0.927	0.99	7.38	0.991	0.99	0.24
spec 100%	0.870	0.882	1.44	0.763	0.93	22.53	0.873	0.90	3.55
PPV 100%	0.835	0.865	3.56	0.730	0.92	25.98	0.836	0.91	8.45
spec 98%	0.870	0.947	8.86	0.763	0.95	24.7	0.873	0.95	9.21
PPV 98%	0.835	0.930	11.34	0.730	0.93	28.51	0.836	0.95	14.2

Table 1. Classification Accuracy for the Parathion vs. Paraoxon Pair

Dichlorvos vs. Trichlorfon

Table 2 shows the SVM classification Measures of Performance (MOPs) for the Dichlorvos vs Trichlorfon pair. The results in this table show: (1) almost perfect (> 99%) ROC AZ values form all three kernels, (2) almost perfect partial Az values (Az values over the top 90% of the ROC curve), which are also > 99%, and (3) **comparable (almost perfect) values for the specificity and PPV from 98-100% sensitivity. In summary, *all three SVMs are essentially perfect classifiers for this chemical pair.***

	Az	Az90	100% spec	100% PPV	98% spec	98% PPV
rbf	1.0	1.0	1.0	1.0	1.0	1.0
S2000	0.9989	0.9962	0.9900	0.9902	0.9972	0.9977
poly	0.9999	0.9990	0.9928	0.9925	1.0	1.0

Table 2. Classification Accuracy for Dichlorvos and Trichlorfon

Malathion vs. Diazinon

Table 3 contains the classification results for the Malathin vs Diazinon organophosphate pair. The results using the three SVM kernels show: (1) ROC

Az indices greater than 99%, (2) partial Az values from ≈ 96% to 98%, (3) specificities from 85% to ≈ 95% at 100% and 98% sensitivities, and (4) PPVs from ≈ 95% to 98% at 100% and 98% sensitivities.

	Az	Az90	100% spec	100% PPV	98% spec	98% PPV
rbf	0 .9980	0. .9801	0.8906	0.9596	0.9392	0.9770
S2000	0.9940	0.9635	0.8580	0.9498	0.9529	0.9807
poly	0. 9961	0. 9618	0. 8923	0. 9615	0. 927	0. 973

Table 3. SVM Classification Performance for the Malathion vs. Diazinon Pair

A previously verified software package was used in order to guarantee that the new grid enabled architecture produced accuarate results. The Legion system generates a best result after completing the evolutionary process. This best result is then processed on the linear SVM and the result of the linear SVM is compared to the result from Legion. All reported results have been verified in this way. Information about the SVM software package used for verification can be found in (Land, 2003 and Sadil ,2004) references 1 and 2.

CONCLUSIONS

Preliminary results thus far achieved are: for the **Parathion vs. Paraoxon** pair: First, a 7.3% improvement in the overall ROC Az index using the radial basis function (rbf) kernel, and ,secondly , a significant 22.5% improvement in specificity using the RBF kernel. Consequently, the number of false negative errors were reduced by 22.5%, while making **no** false positive errors, when compared to the previous data set performance. These are excellent results, considering that only one atom differentiates these two nerve agents. Third, the Gaussian and polynomial kernels demonstrated similar specificity at 100% sensitivity. All SVM classifiers provided essentially perfect classification performance for the **Dichlorvos vs. Trichlorfon** pair. Finally, for the classification task of the **Malathin vs Diazinon** pair, the following results were achieved : (1) ROC Az indices greater than 99%, (2) partial Az values from ≈ 96% to 98%, (3) specificities from 85% to ≈ 95% at 100% and 98% sensitivities, and (4) PPVs from ≈ 95% to 98% at 100% and 98% sensitivities.

ACKNOWLEDGMENTS

This work was supported in part under NSF grant no. CHE-0210968.

REFERENCES

1. Land W., Sadik O. A., Embrechts M. J., Wong L., Wanekaya A., Uematsu M., "Distributed evolutionary programming formulation of support vector machines for detecting and classifying organophosphate nerve agents," ANNIE 2003, pg 811.
2. Sadik O. A., Land W., Wang J., "Targeting Chemical and Biological Warfare Agents at the Molecular Level," Electroanalysis 2004 (In Press).
3. Stephen Ritter, Chemical & Engineering News, November 26, 2001, 24, and 44; (b) Walt D. R., Franz D. R., Anal Chem, 2000, 738A; (c) Ligler F., Guest Ed., Biosens. Bioelectronics 2000, Special Issue 14.

4. Institute of Medicine and National Research Council Chemical and Biological Terrorism: Research and Development to Improve Civilian Medical Response. Washington, D.C., National Academy Press, 1999.
5. "Chemical Warfare Agents: An Overview of Chemicals defined as Chemical Weapons." Organization for the Prohibition of Chemical Weapons, April 29, 1997. On-line 11/20/2001, **http://www.opcw.nl/chemhaz/cwagents.thm**.
6. Igbal S., May W., Bruno J., Bronk B., Batt C., Chambers J., Bios. & Bioelectronics, 2000, 15, 549.
7. NSF Workshop on "The New Challenges for Chemical and Biological Sensing" Arlington, VA, January 9-10, 2002; (b) Workshop Report on the "Detection of Chemical and Biological Agents in Water, Opportunities, Requirements and Challenges," Rodman Materials Research Laboratories, Aberdeen proving Ground, MD, August 24-25, 2000; (c) National Research Council Workshop on "Challenges for the Chemical Sciences in the 21st Century Workshop on Homeland Defense & national Security, Arnold & Mabel Beckman center, Irvine, CA January 14-16, 2002.
8. Gardner, J. W.; Bartlett, P. N. Sensors and Actuators B 1994, 18-19, 211-220, (b) Nagle, H. T.; Gutierrez-Osuna, R.; Schiffman, S. S. IEEE Spectrum, pp. 22-34, September 1998; (c) Grate J. W., Abraham M. H., Sensors & Actuators, B 3, 1991, 85; (c) Steter J. R., Jurs P. C., Rose S. L., Anal. Chem., 58, 1986, 860.
9. Pearce T. C., Gardner J.W., Friel S., Bartlett P. N., Blair N., Analyst, 118, 1993, 371; (b) Rose-Pehrsson S. L., Grate J. W., Ballantine D. S. Jr., Jurs P. C., Anal. Chem., 60, 1988, 2801.
10. Zellers E. T., Batterman S. A., Han M., Patrash S. J., Anal. Chem., 67, 1995, 1092; (b) Grate J. W., Rose-Pehrsson S. L., Venezky D. L., Klusty M., Wohltjen H., Anal. Chem., 65, 1993, 1868.
11. V.N. Vapnik. The Nature of Statistical Learning Theory, Wiley, New York, 1995.
12. V.N. Vapnik. Statistical Learning Theory, Wiley, New York, 1998.
13. Cristianini, N., and Shawne-Taylor, Support Vector Machines and other Kernel-Based Learning Methods, Cambridge University Press, 2000.
14. Platt, "Fast training of Support Vector Machines Using Sequential Minimal Optimization", In B. Scholkopf, C. Burges, and A. Smola, Editors, "Advances in Kernel Methods: Support Vector Training", MIT Press, 1998
15. M. J. Embrechts, K. P. Bennet, and C. Breneman, www.drugmining.com, 2000.
16. S. S. Keerthi, and .S. K. Shevade, "SMO Algorithm for Least Squares SVM Formulations," Neural Computation, Vol. 15, pp. 487-507, 2003.
17. T. Evgeniou, M. Pontil, and T. Poggio, "Statistical Learning Theory: A Primer," International Journal of Computer Vision, Vol. 38(1), pp. 9-13, 2000.
18. T. Evgeniou, M. Pontil, and T. Poggio, "Regularization Networks and Support Vector Machines," in Advances in Large Margin Classifiers, MIT Press, 2000.
19. Fung and O. L. Mangasarian, "Proximal Support Vector Machine Classifiers," in Proceedings KDD 2001, San Francisco, CA, 2001.
20. T. Poggio, and S. Smale, "The Mathematics of Learning: Dealing with Data," To appear in Notices of the AMS, May 2003.
21. B. Schölkopf, and A. J. Smola, Learning with Kernels, MIT Press, 2002.
22. J. A. K. Suykens, and J. VandeWalle, "Least-Squares Support Vector Machine Classifiers," Neural Processing letters, Vol. 9(3), pp. 293-300, Vol. 14, pp. 71-84, 1999.

CLASSIFICATION OF PULMONARY DISEASES USING ARTIFICIAL NEURAL NETWORKS

MIROSLAVA BARÚA
Dept. of Electrical and Comp. Engr.
University of Texas at El Paso
El Paso, Texas USA

HOMAYOUN NAZERAN
Dept. of Electrical and Comp. Engr.
University of Texas at El Paso
El Paso, Texas USA

PATRICIA A. NAVA
Dept. of Electrical and Comp. Engr.
University of Texas at El Paso
El Paso, Texas USA

BILL M. DIONG
Dept. of Electrical and Comp. Engr.
University of Texas at El Paso
El Paso, Texas USA

VIRGINIA D. GRANDA
Dept. of Electrical and Comp. Engr.
University of Texas at El Paso
El Paso, Texas USA

ABSTRACT
Pulmonary diseases are divided into central and peripheral conditions, depending on the area affected. Making this distinction is difficult for the untrained eye, but using Artificial Neural Networks (ANN) can help to classify and characterize these diseases by analyzing physical parameters of the lung's mechanics. Impulse Oscillometry (IOS) provides values of resistance and reactance of airways as a function of frequency, from the Pressure/Flow ratio. IOS has brought a sense of fresh air to clinicians because it's a highly reproducible, non-invasive and sensitive test. This study utilizes IOS to create an input set for training a backpropagation ANN seeking to classify pulmonary diseases. Using 131 records for training and testing, the classification accuracy is 98.5%. Using 79 training records and 52 for testing, the accuracy is 61.5%. This ANN tool, although quite accurate in the first case, is envisioned as an aid to the knowledgeable physician, not a stand-alone entity.

Keywords: **Artificial Neural Networks, IOS, Backpropagation, Pulmonary Disease Classification.**

INTRODUCTION

Learning about human physiology has been facilitated by the advances in biomedical instrumentation. Understanding how biological systems, like the respiratory system, behave in health and in disease is crucial in identifying disease, developing treatments and advancing medicine with the noble purpose of helping those who suffer from disorders that make breathing hard or even painful. Having a wide range of possible pulmonary diseases makes it desirable to group them according to which area of the lung they affect. Two possible categories of classification are central and peripheral pulmonary diseases.

Impulse Oscillometry (IOS) is a new method recently introduced as a practical and user-friendly pulmonary test based on the widely-used force oscillation technique (FOT). Careful analysis of respiratory data has found IOS parameters as the most discriminating among the lung function indices (Ortiz and Menendez, 2002).

Distinguishing amongst diseases and making a categorization by looking at these values is a very difficult task, even for the experienced IOS user. For this reason, incorporating a powerful instrument of classification that can use experiential knowledge, such as an Artificial Neural Network (ANN), becomes an attractive proposal.

The purpose of the research study presented in this paper is to show the performance results of an ANN trained to classify pulmonary diseases of 131 adult patients based on their IOS data.

BACKGROUND

The respiratory system is composed of a group of organs that carry oxygen from the air into the bloodstream and expel carbon dioxide produced by the body's cells.

The airways of the lung divide into smaller and smaller cylinders called bronchioles, which in turn have small air sacs called alveoli. Air enters the system through the nose or mouth and follows a long path. (Freudenrich, 2004). While traveling through this path, enough pressure must exist to overcome the resistance presented by the friction associated with air flow, the collision of gas molecules, and other factors, such as airway diameter. As the lung enlarges during inspiration, the airways expand and the diameter increases, while the resistance decreases. Conversely, at low lung volumes during expiration, airways are compressed, therefore resistance increases.

When applying forced oscillations into the respiratory system, fast frequency pressure waves move easily in large airways, while only the slow frequencies reach the small airways. This behavior occurs due to the level of resistance encountered through the system.

Airway resistance is expressed as cm H_2O/L/sec and is defined as the ratio of driving pressure (ΔP) to airflow (V). For total airway resistance (R_{aw}), the driving pressure is the pressure difference between the mouth (P_{mouth}) and the alveoli (P_A). This is expressed as $\mathbf{\Delta P = V{*}R_{aw}}$ (Rhoades and Pflanzer, 2003).

Obviously in disease conditions, airflow can become more restricted, thus making it harder to breathe. This is a common situation in asthma, bronchitis or emphysema where the airways become swollen, presenting more resistance to airflow, as shown in Fig.1.

The most common clinical signs of lung disease are cough, chest pain, chest tightness, shortness of breath, and abnormal breathing patterns. Because most individuals have enormous reserves of lung tissue, the disturbances in lung function may have begun some time before the clinical symptoms appear. Identifying these changes is crucial in early detection of pathological impairments of the small airways (Jaeger, 2000).

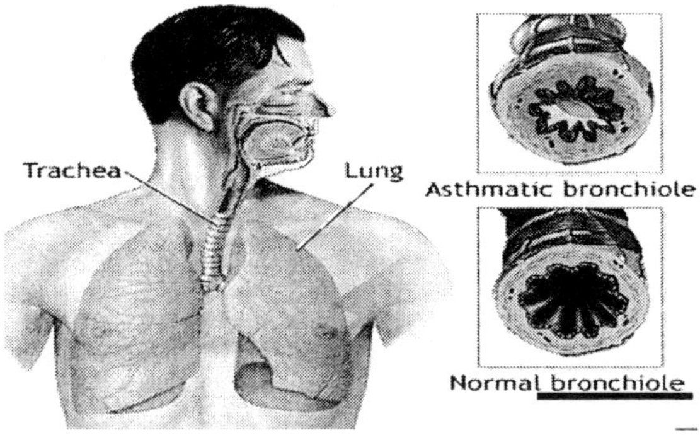

Figure. 1: Airway resistance in health & disease

MATERIALS AND METHODS

Spirometry is a traditional technique for obtaining numerical parameters such as volumes and capacities of the lung as a function of time. Forced Expiration uses spirometric tracings and, although the results are useful for studying the pulmonary ventilation, a successful measurement requires maximal coordination and great effort from the patient in order to obtain two or more flow curves.

Body plethysmography is another popular method that determines resistance by the measurement of pressure and flow, but it adds variables while measuring, such as incrementing the resistance values due to compression inside this large airtight box. In addition, this test can cause people to feel claustrophobic (Vogel and Smith, 1995).

A less disturbing method is the forced oscillation technique (FOT) developed by Dubois in 1956. It uses a superimposed pressure burst at the airway to gain information about airflow obstruction by measuring the respiratory impedance (Z) and its two components, resistance (R) and reactance (X) over a wide range of frequencies (Dubois, et al., 1956). Pulmonologists were limited to these techniques until a short time ago, when Impulse Oscillometry (IOS) was introduced. IOS provides respiratory impedance with very precise results. Even in the early stages of airflow obstruction, IOS is more sensitive to baseline abnormality than spirometry. In more severe diseases, the increase in sensitivity is more pronounced (Jaeger, 2000).

Impulse Oscillometry

The IOS technique consists of applying a rectangular electrical impulse through an external loudspeaker and converting it into a mixture of pressure waves at different frequencies by the mechanical properties of a stimulated loudspeaker (Vogel and Shmidt, 1995). The resulting pressure waveform is applied to the patient's mouth.

IOS provides total respiratory impedance ($Z=R+jX$), which is composed of resistance (R) and reactance (X) and displays these values as a function of frequency. On the plot, resistance is in phase, while reactance is out of phase.

These measurements are recorded at 5 Hz intervals, from 5Hz to 35 Hz: R_5, R_{10}, R_{15}, R_{20}, R_{25}, R_{35}, X_5, X_{10}, X_{15}, X_{20}, X_{25}, and X_{35}.

Each of these values gives information about the lung's mechanics. For instance, in the example shown in Fig. 2, R_5 reflects total respiratory resistance at 5 Hz, while R_{20} is linked to proximal respiratory resistance and X_5 is related to distal capacitive reactance (Jaeger, 2000). Making a reliable reading from these impedance curves requires the knowledgeable opinion of an experienced user. Although IOS has been used in Europe for a long time, in the USA, this technique is not widely available in community practice yet. But the benefits are attracting a lot of attention, making this technique broadly desirable (Smith and Vogel, 2003). These shortcomings yield interesting research areas that can improve familiarity with the system and obtain a standardization of IOS measurements in the USA. Recent reports have described IOS as being more sensitive than conventional spirometry in assessing airway abnormalities in asthmatics and in children at risk for developing persistent asthma. IOS may be feasible for use in children about 3-4 years old, an age when the usefulness of conventional spirometry is questionable. (Marotta, et al.,2003). The sensitivity of the IOS permits the observation of even small changes in bronchoreactivity, as well as the detection of improvements resulting from drug treatment.

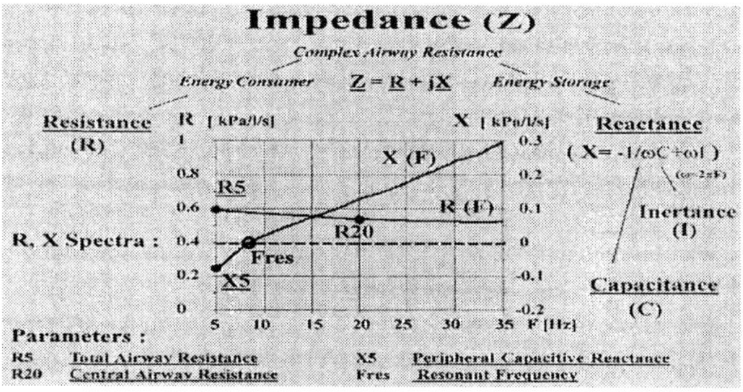

Figure. 2: Impedance gives information about the lung's mechanics

Artificial Neural Networks

Artificial Neural Networks (ANNs) can be characterized as parallel distributed processing systems capable of solving complex problems of classification. The main motivation for creating these models is to try to mimic the biological function and computational power of the human brain as it deciphers difficult pattern recognition dilemmas or other complex problems.

ANNs can be viewed as systems that implement mapping functions, and are characterized by their flexibility and generalization abilities. ANNs can process the given inputs and develop a categorization strategy after learning from examples defined in the appropriate training set. Hence, even new, previously unseen input patterns can be correctly classified, provided the training set is representative of the different diseases to a general extent.

The structure of an ANN consists of many weighted computational nodes (neurons) that are arranged in layers and connected to each other to communicate as they process the information and reach a categorization. The ANN utilizes the provided data as inputs to the nodes and, by using a learning algorithm, adjusts the weights of the nodes accordingly until it matches the known categorization within a specified error range.

AN ANN FOR CLASSIFICATION OF IOS DATA

Although IOS is a good method for obtaining respiratory impedance values, making a categorization of pulmonary diseases by looking at the plotted curves is a very difficult assignment, even for the experienced user. Being excellent classifiers, ANNs can perform this function with efficient and accurate results as a consequence of their massively parallel nature that allows computation to occur at a very high rate (Lau, 1992).

Before the ANN was designed, extensive research was conducted to determine how the IOS works and if the respiratory impedance measurements were meaningful input variables to the network in the effort of deciphering this classification dilemma.

Resistance values reflect the forward pressure or need to push flow, while the more sensitive reactance values indicate the back pressure, or echo. As IOS mouth pressure pulses move towards the lung periphery, damping of the pressure pulse is greater for high frequencies than for low, as shown in studies of high frequency (Frantz and Close, 1985).

By having values of resistance at many frequencies, FDR (Frequency Dependence Resistance) can be detected, hence signaling airway obstruction. Reactance values at many frequencies help detect small airway obstruction.

It has been shown that the pattern of differential transmission of low- and high-frequency oscillations results in a fall in resistance with increase in oscillation frequency in the presence of peripheral airway obstruction. In other words, FDR is observed (Grimby, et al, 1968) in this case. In the opposite case, subjects that are normal would have an almost constant resistance as frequency increases (Goldman, et al., 2002).

In this study, these key respiratory impedance parameters at different frequencies were obtained by IOS. A data set was created, composed of 131 adult (67 females and 64 males) patients' IOS test measurements, along with the patients' demographics: subjects between the ages of 13 and 85, with a varying height from 1.40 m. to 1.85 m. and a weight range from 35 to 176 Kg. Because there is no standard for the diagnosis of pulmonary diseases based on IOS measurements, the expert opinions of pulmonologists were used to provide the appropriate diagnoses, based on the forced expiration test results, in order to define the categorization of the training data.

The ANN used in this study has 3 layers: input, hidden and output, with 17 neurons in each layer. This network was trained using the backpropagation learning rule characterized by using the gradient descent method to minimize total squared error (Faussett, 1994).

CONCLUSIONS

When using the full 131 patients' records for both training and testing phases, the ANN correct classification accuracy was a very impressive 98.5%. After this result, the data set was divided: 79 records used for training and the remaining 52 used for testing. This time, the ANN correct classification accuracy dropped to 61.5%.

These promising results show that an ANN can be trained with IOS measurements and patient demographics as inputs to yield a network capable of classifying pulmonary diseases according to the area being affected.

The performance of this ANN can be improved by providing it with more training data. Currently, a bigger data set is being collected to help in this respect.

The obtained results are encouraging and further research is being performed in this area. The resultant ANN is envisioned to be an aid to the knowledgeable physician, and by no means a stand-alone entity.

ACKNOWLEDGEMENTS

This research was supported in part by the National Science Foundation under grant #EIA-0325024.

REFERENCES

Dubois, A. B., Brody, A. W. and Lewis, D. H., 1956, "Oscillation mechanics of lungs and chest in man," *J. Appl. Physiol.*, vol. 8, pp. 587.

Faussett, L., 1994, "Fundamentals of neural networks: architectures, algorihms, and applications", Prentice Hall, pp. 289-325

Frantz, ID, Close, R., 1985, "Alveolar pressure swings during high frequency ventilation in rabbits." Pediatr. Res., 19:162-6.

Freudenrich, C., "How Your Lungs Work", http://science.howstuffworks.com/lung.htm/.

Grimby G, Takishima T, Graham W, Macklem P, Mead J., 1968 "Frequency dependence of flow resistances in patients with obstructive lung disease" J Clin Invest; 47: 1455-65.

Goldman, MD, Carter, R., Klein, R., Fritz G, Carter B, Pachucki P., 2002, "Within- and between-day variability of respiratory impedance, using impulse oscillometry in adolescent asthmatics", Pediatr Pulmonol. Oct;34(4):312-9.

Jaeger E., 2000, "MasterScreen IOS - Follow the Impulse", Erich JAEGER GmbH, Hoechberg,, http://www.jaeger-toennies.com/english.html.

Lau C., 1992 ,"Neural Networks. Theoretical Foundations and Analysis", IEEE Press, pp. 1-3.

Marotta, A., *Klinnert MD, Price MR, Larsen GL, Liu AH*, 2003 ,"Impulse oscillometry provides an effective measure of lung dysfunction in 4-year-old children at risk for persistent asthma", J Allergy Clin Immunol, 112(2):317-22.

Ortiz, G. and Menendez, R., 2002, "The effects of inhaled albuterol and salmeterol in 2- to 5-year-old asthmatic children as measured by impulse oscillometry," *J. Asthma*, vol. 39, no. 6, pp. 531-536.

Rhoades R., Pflanzer R, 2003, Human Physiology, 4th edition, Thomson, Brooks/Cole, pp. 630-653.

Smith HJ, Vogel J., 2003, "Oscillometry" Australian & New Zealand Society of Respiratory Science Annual Scientific Meetings, VIASYS Healthcare GmbH, Wuerzburg FRD, Berlin, www.anzsrs.org.au/asm2003pp2.pdf.

Vogel J., Shmidt U., 1995, "Impulse Oscillometry. Analysis of lung mechanics in general practice and the clinic, epidemiological and experimental research", pml Verlagsgruppe Gmbh, Frankfurt am Main, pp. 6-16,76-81.

AUTOMATIC SLEEP STAGE CLASSIFICATION UTILIZING FUZZY LOGIC AND NEURAL NETWORKS WITH THE EEG SIGNAL

ELVIA MARTINDELCAMPO
Dept. of Electrical and Comp. Engr.
University of Texas at El Paso
El Paso, TX USA

EDSON ESTRADA
Dept. of Electrical and Comp. Engr.
University of Texas at El Paso
El Paso, TX USA

JAIME BARRAGAN
Dept. of Electrical and Comp. Engr.
University of Texas at El Paso
El Paso, TX USA

PATRICIA A. NAVA
Dept. of Electrical and Comp. Engr.
University of Texas at El Paso
El Paso, TX USA

HOMER NAZERAN
Dept. of Electrical and Comp. Engr.
University of Texas at El Paso
El Paso, TX USA

ABSTRACT

Different features are extracted from the EEG signal through the application of different mathematical models, which are: Relative % Spectral Energy Band, Harmonic Parameters, Itakura Distance and Detrended Fluctuation Analysis. The data sets obtained from extracted features, as well as the features' gaussian distributions, will be employed to develop two systems capable of classifying the Sleep-Stages. Such systems will be developed through different approaches: Fuzzy Inference System (FIS) and Artificial Neural Network (ANN), where both systems have proven to yield an accuracy of 80% for the FIS and 90% for the ANN, respectively.

INTRODUCTION

The objective of sleep-stage classification is to identify the six stages of sleep associated with different characteristics: Wake, NREM1, NREM2, NREM3, NREM4 and REM. Currently, sleep-stage classification is performed by analyzing the Electroecephalogram (EEG), the Electromyogram (EMG), and the Electro-oculogram (EOG), in a process known as Polysomnography. The EOG signal contributes largely in the correct classification of REM and Wake stages, while the EMG contributes only in the classification of the Wake stage (Estévez, 2000). The goal of this investigation is to achieve the 6-stage classification utilizing only the EEG signal. Since only the EEG is used, it was studied extensively to determine what kind of features can be extracted from this signal, and analyze them for their effectiveness in aiding the classification process. The extracted features data, as well as their data distribuiton sets, are used for the sleep-stage classification realized with two separate methods: an Artificial Neural Network (ANN), and a Fuzzy Inference System (FIS).

DATA COLLECTION AND PREPROCESSING

The data used in this study was acquired from one subject who was referred to the Sleep Disorder Clinic. A total of 7 hours and 4 minutes of sleep data were recorded for this subject. One EEG Channel was stored using a sampling frequency of 1000 Hz. An experienced sleep specialist scored the EEG epochs, of 30 seconds in duration, based on depth of sleep. Table 1 shows the percentage and the number of scored segments. This information was saved by the Sleep Laboratory into a binary file.

Table 1. Polysomnography Information

Stage	*30 second scored epochs*	*% of entire recording*
Awake	185	21
Stage 1	52	6
Stage 2	314	36
Stage 3	84	10
Stage 4	128	15
REM	86	10

For simplicity of further processing, this file was restructured into two principal vectors: one containing the sampled EEG information (with $f_s = 1000$ Hz), and the other containing the Sleep Stage information (1 occurrence for each 30-second epoch). The complete EEG vector is then processed using a sixth-order Butterworth bandpass filter with cutoff (corner) frequencies of 0.5 - 50 Hz. A zero-phase digital filter was realized by filtering the EEG signals in both forward and reverse directions resulting in its filtering by a 12th order filter. The filtered EEG had exactly zero-phase distortion. EEG signals were then decimated by a factor of 10 resulting in signals with a new sample frequency of 100 Hz.

Feature Extraction: For implementation of the feature extraction schemes, the following procedure is applied to obtain the statistics for each measure: (1) The EEG signal is partitioned into different epoch lengths, determined by the fact that the EEG is scored in segments of 30-second epochs. In addition to the 30-second epochs, partitioning is performed by taking new epoch lengths of the multiples of 30 (e.g. 1, 3, 5, 6, 10, 15, 30). These multiples provided the flexibility to minimize the probability of having segments with more than one sleep stage present. (2) After running the feature extraction algorithm, it is possible to collect the measures into different groups using the annotations in the sleep stage vector. This allows computation of the mean, standard deviation, maximum and minimum value for each sleep state.

Relative % Spectral Energy Band: For this analysis, the total power content (TPC) of the power density function, $P(f)$, from 0.5 to 45 Hz. is computed. $P(f)$ is divided into seven different energy bands, and the respective power energy bands (PEB) are calculated. The spectral density function is estimated using the AR parametric Method (Hayes, 1996). The relative percent spectral energy band (RPEB) is then expressed as:

$$RPEB = \frac{PEB}{TPC} x100 \tag{1}$$

The partition of *P(f)* and the bandwidth used for each bin or energy band are as follows: Delta-1 (0.5-2.5Hz), Delta-2 (2.5-4Hz), Theta-1 (4-6Hz), Theta-2 (6-8Hz), Alpha (8-12Hz), Beta-1(12-20Hz), Beta-2(20-45Hz) (Principe, 1989).

Harmonic Parameters: The harmonic parameters (Van Hese, 2001; Donohue), which are the frequency versions of the Hjorth parameters, are: the center frequency, the bandwidth, and the value at the central frequency. These parameters are defined as follows:

$$f_c = \int_{f_L}^{f_H} fP(f)df \,/\, \int_{f_L}^{f_H} P(f)df \tag{2}$$

$$f_\sigma = \sqrt{\int_{f_L}^{f_H} (f - f_c)^2 P(f)df \,/\, \int_{f_L}^{f_H} P(f)df} \tag{3}$$

$$Pf_c = P(f_c) \tag{4}$$

Itakura Distance: Itakura distance is used widely in speech processing applications to measure the distance between 2 AR processes (X. Kong, 1995; Muthuswamy, 1998). Here the Itakura distance is used to measure the similarity of a baseline EEG epoch (Awake, Stage1, Stage2, Stage 3, Stage 4, REM) with the rest of the epochs in the EEG vector. Let the baseline epoch, x[n], be an AR process given by $a_x = [1\ \ -a_1\ -a_2\ \ldots\ldots -a_p]$ and the segment y[n], to be compared to it, be given by $a_y = [1\ -a_1\ -a_2\ \ldots\ldots -a_p]$, then the Itakura distance of the baseline to the other epochs is defined as:

$$d_{I_{y,x}} = \log\left(\frac{MSE_{x,y}}{MSE_{x,x}}\right) = \log\left(\frac{a_y^T R_x(p) a_y}{a_x^T R_x(p) a_x}\right), \tag{5}$$

where the $R_x(p)$ is the autocorrelation matrix for the baseline epoch of size p+1. Furthermore, an analysis of how well y[n] is modeled can be done via the AR parameters of x[n]. Thus the new Itakura distance is:

$$d_{I_{y,x}} = \log\left(\frac{MSE_{y,x}}{MSE_{y,y}}\right) = \log\left(\frac{a_x^T R_y(p) a_x}{a_y^T R_y(p) a_y}\right) \tag{6}$$

Combining (5) and (6), we obtain the symmetric Itakura distance as:

$$d'_{I_{x,y}} = \frac{1}{2}\left(d_{I_{x,y}} + d_{I_{y,x}}\right) \tag{7}$$

Detrended Fluctuation Analysis (DFA): This method was conceived to detrend variability in a sequence of events. The DFA computation involves the calculation of the summed series:

$$y(k) = \sum_{t=1}^{k} \{X(t) - E[X]\}, \tag{8}$$

where *y(k)* is the kth value of the summed series, *X(t)* represents the sequence (epoch to be evaluated) at time *t*, and *E[X]* denotes the average of the entire time series {*X(t)*}. The summed series is divided into sub-sequences of length m, and a least squares fit is performed on each of the data segments, providing detrends for the individual segments. Detrending is carried out by subtracting the local trend $y_m(k)$ in each segment. The root-mean-square fluctuation of the resulting series is then

$$F(m) = \left\{ \frac{1}{L} \sum [y(k) - y_m(k)]^2 \right\}^{1/2} \tag{9}$$

The fluctuation dependence of *F(m)* is obtained by evaluations over all segments of size m (Akay, 2001).

FUZZY INFERENCE SYSTEM APPROACH

Fuzzy Logic systems have proven to work effectively in many engineering applications. Lately, they have been widely employed in control systems for the medical field, and as an aid for medical diagnosis. Fuzzy Logic has already been used, with excellent results for sleep-stage classification utilizing the EEG along with the EMG and EOG (Estévez, et al, 2000).

A Fuzzy Inference System is a system based on rules that utilize Fuzzy Logic. Its basic structure, shown in Fig. 1, consists of 4 main components: (1) a fuzzifier, which translates crisp (single, non-fuzzy valued) inputs into fuzzy values; (2) an inference engine that applies a fuzzy reasoning mechanism to obtain a fuzzy output; and (3) a defuzzifier. These three elements utilize a knowledge base which contains an ensemble of fuzzy rules, known as the rule base, and an ensemble of membership functions known as the database (Yen, 1999).

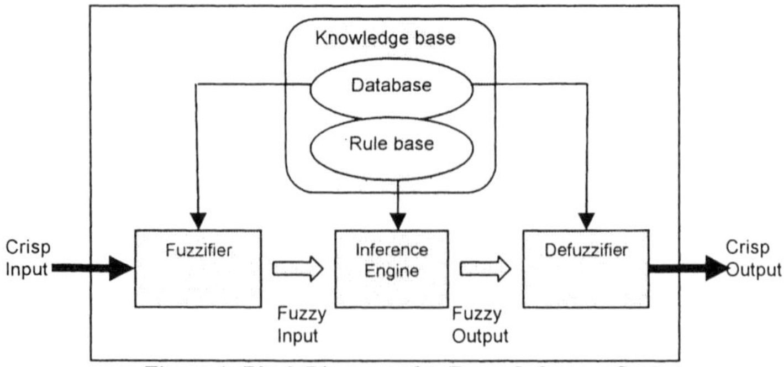

Figure 1: Block Diagram of A Fuzzy Inference System

The Itakura distance as well as the Detrended Fluctuation Analysis (DFA) datasets are used as input to the FIS. Both datasets give meaningful information for sleep-stage classification. The Gaussian distributions of the Itakura distance and DFA, offer a clear scenario to design the Membership Functions, MFs (Cano, 2002), allowing the creation of rules for the system. The Gaussian distribution of the Itakura distance is depicted in Figure 2.

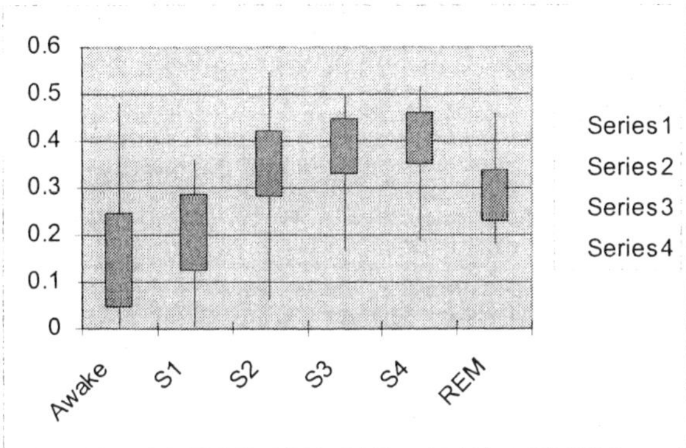

Figure 2: Gaussian distribution of Itakura distance

ARTIFICIAL NEURAL NETWORK APPROACH

An Artificial Neural Network (ANN) with a feed-forward of topology 5-15-3 is designed for this application. That is, 5, 15 and 3 neurons in each of the input, hidden and output layers, respectively. The network is trained using the Back propagation training algorithm, implementing the ANN's ability to map extracted feature values in the EEG to corresponding sleep-stages.

The five inputs for this ANN are EEG signal features: Destructed Fractal Analysis (DFA), Amplitude, Harmonic Hjorth Bandwidth, Itakura distance, and Harmonic Hjorth Central Frequency. Each input is normalized based on the maximum and minimum value from data set, then, values are scaled to a bipolar representation, where -1 is the smallest value, and +1 is the largest value. The three bipolar outputs allow each of the six sleep stages to be encoded, with two unused patterns.

Table 1. Bipolar Encoding of Sleep Stages

Sleep stage	**Bipolar Representation**
Awake	-1 -1 -1
REM	-1 -1 1
Stage 1	-1 1 -1
Stage 2	-1 1 1
Stage 3	1 -1 -1
Stage 4	1 -1 1
Unused	1 1 -1
Unused	1 1 1

CONCLUSIONS

Systems reported in the literature have proven to yield an accuracy of 80% for the FIS (Estévez, 2000) and 90% for the ANN (Estévez, 2000). These systems, however, have had more signals to work with, not just the EEG. When using solely EEG values, extensive feature extraction is necessary to obtain satisfactory results. Similarities between awake, REM, and stage 1 features (Sun, 1993), makes it difficult to detect sleep stages without the help of the EOG and EMG signals. The FIS has yet to provide good results, but the ANN trained with 600 input patterns show an initial efficiency of about 46%, showing misclassification mainly between awake, REM, and stage 1. These preliminary results are less than stellar, but two facts must be kept in mind: (1) this study uses a single EEG signal, as opposed to other studies that used the full suite of polysomnographic signals; and (2) the study has yet to explore other methods for improving performance, such as using a larger data set, and using other methods of feature extraction.

Future work for this study includes exploring other methods of data feature extraction, automatic membership function generation (Cano, 2002) for the extracted features, the use of ANNs to extract the rules for the FIS and quality control for the training data set.

ACKNOWLEDGEMENTS

The data used for this study was provided by Sleep Specialists Inc., Fort Worth, Texas.

REFERENCES

Cano, Janette C., "A Fuzzy Method for Automatic Generation of Membership Functions Using Fuzzy Logic Relations," Master's Thesis, The University of Texas at El Paso, 2002.

Cano, J.C. and P. A. Nava, "A Fuzzy Method for Automatic Generation Of Membership Function Using Fuzzy Relations from Training Examples," *Proc. 21st NAFIPS Int. Conf.*, pp. 158-162, June 2002.

Estévez, P. A., Fernández, et al. "Classification of Sleep-Waking States using Modular Neural Networks," University of Chile, 2000.

Fausett, Laurene, Fundamentals of Neural Networks, Architectures, Algorithms, and Applications, Prentice -Hall, 1994.

Principe, J.C., and A.M.P. Tome, "Performance and Training Strategies in FeedForward Neural Networks: An Application to Sleep Scoring" *Int. Joint Conf. on Neural Networks*, pp. 341 – 346(1), 1989.

Sun, M., N.D. Ryan, R.E. Dahl, H. Hsin, S. Iyergar, and R.J. Sclabassi, "A Neural Network System for Automatic Classification of Sleep Stages," *Biomed. Engr. Conf.*, pp. 137 – 139, 1993.

Yen, John and Langari, Reza. Fuzzy Logic: Intelligence, Control, and Information, Prentice-Hall, Upper Saddle River, NJ, 1999.

A STUDY FOR CONTROL OF A WEARABLE POWER ASSIST SYSTEM

– RECOGNITION OF HUMAN MOTIONS BY SURFACE EMG SIGNALS –

SATOSHI KAWAI
Department of Complex Systems Engineering
Hokkaido University, JAPAN
skawai@complex.eng.hokudai.ac.jp

KEITARO NARUSE
The School of Computer Science and Engineering
The University of Aizu, JAPAN
naruse@u-aizu.ac.jp

HIROSHI YOKOI
Department of Precision Engineering
The University of Tokyo, JAPAN
hyokoi@prince.pe.u-tokyo.ac.jp

YUKINORI KAKAZU
Department of Complex Systems Engineering
Hokkaido University, JAPAN
kakazu@complex.eng.hokudai.ac.jp

ABSTRACT

This paper shows the development of a wearable power assisting system, which helps people lifting a heavy object like a person who cannot move alone in daily life. When we lift something heavy, we use both hands. That is why a control system that can automatically switch on/off without using hands is necessary. In this paper for utilizing the automatic control, we analyze lifting motions and other motions and EMG signals detected from a body surface in order to measure the human intention. For this purpose, utilizing artificial neural networks (ANN) for control of the wearable power assist device, is proposed, and the detail design of ANN is discussed. The experiment results show the adaptability of the proposed ANN controller, which can adapt to the difference of individuals, and it can recognize the five patterns of human motions in the daily life.

INTRODUCTION

Our recent aged and aging society increases the number of people who work for daycare, which is getting heavier and more frequent, particular for the support of moving an aged or disabled person who cannot move around by himself. Not only the supported person, but also the supporting person can be injured himself by the heavy load of the support, particularly in a lower back. According to a report(Troup,1965), most of nurses and workers have had lumbago resulting from a lifting task. However they had few measures against the lumbago. Therefore, we need a mechanical supporting device for the assisting person for protecting his lower back.

There are several projects about a wearable power asssist device. Target portions of assisting in the projects are arms, legs, back and so on. Some projects about power assisting systems are summarized below.

First of all, there is the project of Exoskeletons for Human Performance Augmentation(EHPA), which Jhon A. Main et. al. are carrying out at Defense

Science Office(DSO), Defense Advanced Research Project Agency(DARPA), USA(John, Website). The purpose of this project is to be used by soldiers, who have to move long-distance with heavy loads. Because of the purpose, they are interested in walking or running with the heavy loads. So, they analyze a gait of walking in these conditions.

The full body type assist system has been developing also in Kanagawa Institute of Technology Japan(Yamamoto, 2001), and the University of Electro-communications, Japan(Aoki, 2003). These devices are designed for daycare, so their target load is about 60[kgf] and the device supports many DOFs of a full body. However, these devices are large and heavy. Therefore it is hard to use these devices in a small rooms, as we see in a house.

The device that we propose is to help daycare in a small room as we often see in Japan. Therefore, the device should assist at least 60[kgf] and should have many DOFs. But if the device have many motors to make a large force, and many frames to have many DOFs, the device becomes too large, and it will not be used in daily life. Here, we focus only on bending(flexion and extension) of a lower back, often injured by carrying heavy load. So the size of this device is not so large as the other above devices. Further, for the portability of the device, we introduced a DC motor and a battery without any cables to the outside, which means a person wearing this device can walk easily. Figure 1. illustrates the device, and a photograph of wearing person is shown in Fig.2.

Fig.1 Overview of the power assisting device.

Fig.2 A picture of a person wearing this device.

RECOGNITION OF HUMAN MOTIONS BY SURFACE EMG SIGNALS

In this section, the EMG signals are analyzed. The purpose of this paper is to control this device. So our focus is at the beginning of lifting up and putting down. In Kawai, 2004, we have shown that the EMG signals of the front thigh muscles(vastus lateralis and vastus medialis) are larger than that of biceps femoris while lifting up heavy loads. On the other hand, EMG signals of the biceps femoris are larger than that of front thigh muscles while putting down heavy loads.

From these results, we have developed a controller of the power assist device utilizing the lower back angle and the processed surface EMG signals on the thigh. The objective of the controller is to switch either winding up or down the cable in the device, or stopping the winding. Figure 3. illustrates a schematic diagram of the controller, and the flow of control is shown in Fig.4.

From the above results, we proposed the controller utilizing the lower back angle and EMG signals on the thigh. However, from the viewpoint of safety, it is more important that this device must not make sudden movement in daily life activities other than it moves voluntary. Then, to verify our proposed controller, we have an experiment that shows the EMG signals discrimination possibility, which implies the device moves only when a wearing person needs the assist.

EMG electrodes are placed on vastus lateralis, vastus medialis and biceps femoris. A subject is asked to perform the following actions, which we expect in the case that a person transferred from a bed to a wheelchair as one of representative motion of daycare.

1) Actions when a person needs assistance.
   a) Lifting up heavy loads.
   b) Putting down heavy loads.
2) Actions when the device must not move.
   c) Walking.
   d) Side stepping.
   e) Left turning.

The subject is asked to perform the above five actions with wearing this device. The heavy load is dumbbell of 20[kg].

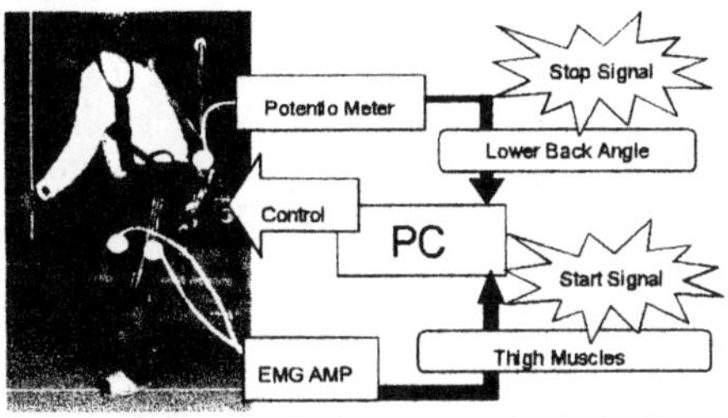

Fig.3 Schematic diagram of controller for the power assist device for switching the motor.

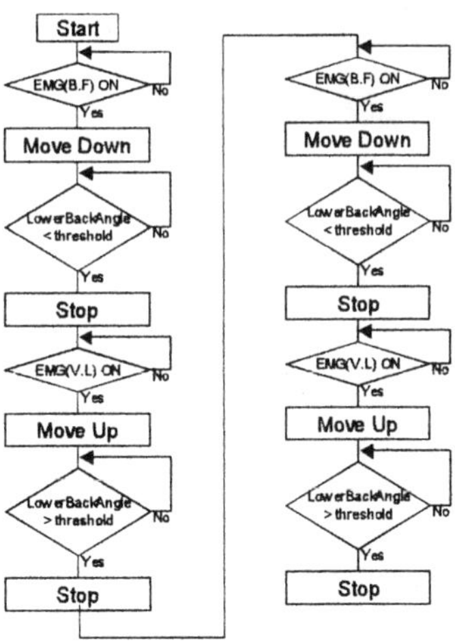

Fig.4 The flowchart of control of this device. V.L means vastus lateralis, and B.F means biceps femoris.

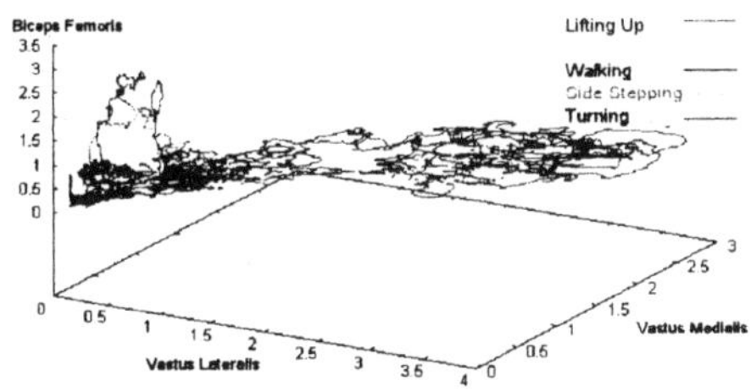

Fig.5 The result for each motion wearing Power assist device with 20[kg] weight.

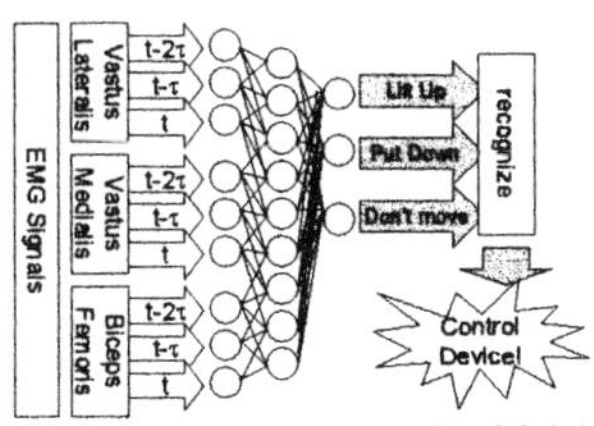

Fig.6 The model of our proposed artificial neural network.

The results are shown in Fig.5. From there we can recognize when a person needs the assist and when the device must not move. It represents that we can design a controller that recognize lifting, putting down, and stopping from EMG signals of three thigh muscles. The motions of lifting up and putting down are spread into horizontally, while the other motions are distributed vertically.

DESIGN OF ARTIFICIAL NEURAL NETWORK

Although automatic recognition of the human motions is important, it is difficult. The same EMG signal can not be measured for the same motion even from the same person, because it is a biologically generated signal. Many factors, such as fatigue, affects the biological signal(Park, 1993). Furthermore, another person generates different level of the EMG signal. Then, it is important that the device has an ability to adapt itself to the wearing person.

In this section, we introduce an artificial neural network(ANN) controller shown in Fig.6, and discuss about improvement of ANN.

The ANNs are designed as follows. The ANNs are constructed in a three layers manner. Nine neurons receive EMG signals from vastus lateralis, vastus medialis and biceps femoris in the input layer. The ANN learns and recognizes the human motions using these signals at the time t, t-τ and t-2τ(τ is the time delay) since we focused not only the value of EMG signals but also the change of it. Figure 6. shows our proposed ANN. There are nine neurons in the hidden layer, and three neurons in the output layer. These three neurons in the output layer sends to the controller the motion command, where the commands are to lift up, to put down, and not to move.

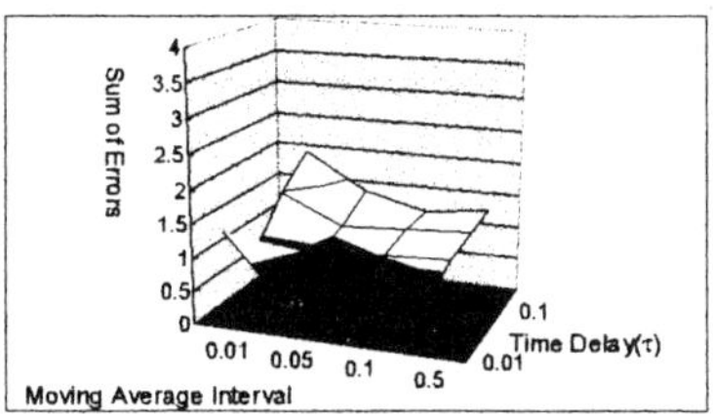

Fig. 7. The relations between moving average interval (horizontal axis), time delay (vertical axis) and sum of errors (height axis) in ANN of type A. Teaching signals are sampled three months ago.

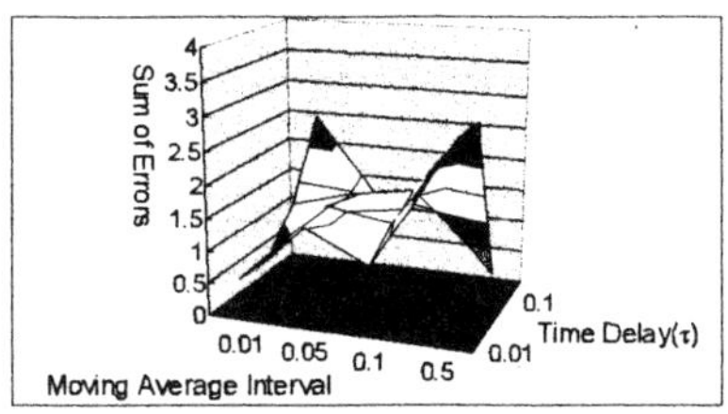

Fig. 8. The relations between moving average interval (horizontal axis), time delay (vertical axis) and sum of errors (height axis) in the ANN of type A. Teaching signals are sampled on the same day.

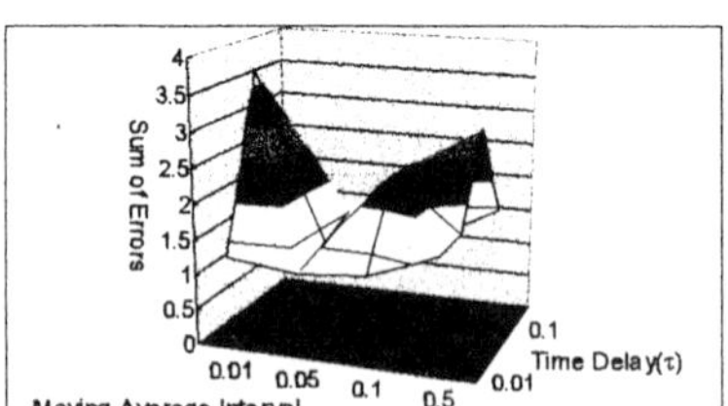

Fig. 9. The relations between moving average interval, time delay and sum of errors in the ANN of type B. Teaching signals are sampled three months ago.

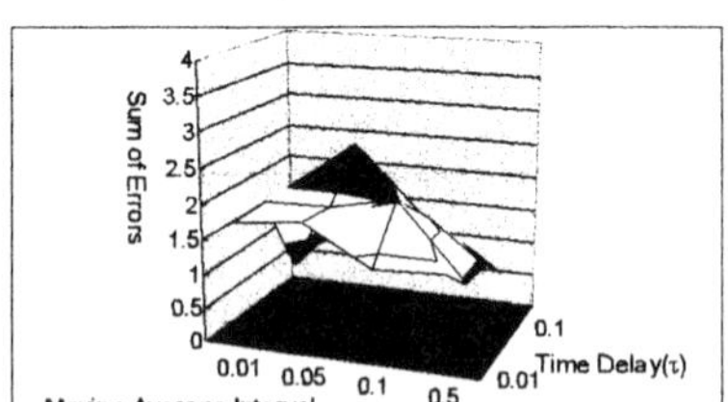

Fig. 10. The relations between moving average interval, time delay and sum of errors in the ANN of type B. Teaching signals are sampled on the same day.

We made a preliminary experiment with τ=0.3[sec]. The result shows that the sum of errors becomes almost zero after this network learn about 500 times. After that, this network received another EMG signals from the same person, and recognized three human motions successfully.

The controller should recognize the motion as soon as possible after received the EMG signals, however, the controller must not make any mistakes. So the relationship between the moving average interval(MAI) and the time delay(τ) received in ANN are important and they are investigated in the following.

We compare two types of ANN, and carry out two experiments on the two ANNs. Table 1 shows the imprementation.

Table 1. Imprimentation of two artificial neural networks.

	INPUT 1	INPUT 2	INPUT 3	
TYPE A	$x(t)$	$x(t-\tau)$	$x(t-2\tau)$	(Absolute value)
TYPE B	$x(t)$	$x(t)-x(t-\tau)$	$x(t)-x(t-2\tau)$	(Relative Value)

The two networks are trained by the same data, changing MAI and τ, for seeing the change of recognition ability. Furthermore, in order to clarify about the effect that are sampled another conditions, we compare the pair of results, those are signals sampled on the same day and three months before. The results are shown in Fig.7-10.

Figure 7. and 8 are the results of type A. In Fig.7, teaching signals are sampled three months ago, and in Fig.8, teaching signals and input signals are sampled in the same day. Both results show we can find areas where the sum of errors are small, we can use it for control of our device.

Figure 9. and 10 are the same results of type B. These results show that the errors became worse than results of type A, and there are few areas which the sum of errors are small.

DISCUSSION

In the previous section, we compared the two types of ANNs. On the whole, the sum of errors of type A are less than the one of type B. (The average of errors in type A is about 1.3 and in type B is about 1.5.) The result shows that the amplitude of the EMG signal is more important than the rate of the amplitude change with respect to time. The thigh muscles always generate the same tension to hold the weight of bust and the load in hands. That is, the amplitude of EMG signals becomes important.

Comparing Fig.7 with 8 means how this controller adapts itself to a wearing person even in the condition change. In general, EMG signals are not always the same because of many factors such as fatigue, positions of sensors and so on. However even in another condition, while MAI is in between 0.05 and 0.1, and while τ is in between 0.05 and 0.1, the sum of errors became small. This result means a controller can be stable in the range, and type A can be used for control of our device. This result of MAI is reasonable since the fundamental frequency is about 30[Hz]-50[Hz].

On the other hand, the robustness of the motion recognition depends on the value of τ. If τ is over 0.1, the change in the input signals for ANN increase when the muscle is elastic in a moment. However, if τ became properly short, the difference does not tend to appear. Furthermore, if τ becomes less than 0.1, the input signals which the neural network receives are affected by a little muscle contraction.

From the above all results, it is reasonable that when MAI is between 0.05 and 0.1, and when τ is between 0.05 and 0.1, this controller recognizes human motions correctly.

As discussed earlier, we proposed the controller including an ANN. Our proposed ANN learns in off-line, which means that once the systems enters into the operation mode, network weights are fixed and do not change any more. The above results showed that our proposed ANN was useful for recognition of human motions by the EMG signals which were sampled in the same time. However, the rate of correct recognitions is not high enough. In order to make this device adaptive for a wearing person, on-line learning is necessary.

CONCLUSIONS

In this paper, we proposed the power assist device which prevents lumbago. And after the analysis of the human motions, we showed that we can control this device utilizing EMG signals of three thigh muscles and the lower back angle.

Also, we analyzed the EMG signals of the three thigh muscles not only signals when lifting up or putting down heavy loads, but also the ones in daily life activities of motions. From these results we discussed about the design of ANN and proposed better values of moving average interval(MAI) and time delay (τ). The results showed that when MAI is between 0.05 and 0.1, and when τ is between 0.05 and 0.1, this controller recognizes human motions correctly.

For the future development, the on-line learning method of ANN to adapt itself to a wearing person at any time should be developed, and an embedded controller should be designed in order to control without notebook PC for walk around easily while wearing.

REFERENCES

TROUP, J.D.G, "The relation of lumber spine disorders to heavy manual work and lifting", Lancet, 1, pp.857-861, 1965.

JOHN. M, "Exoskeletons for Human Performance Augmentation", http://www.darpa.mil/dso/thrust/matdev/ehpa.htm.

YAMAMOTO. K, HYODO. K, ISHII. M, MATSUO. T, "Development of Power Assisting Suit for Assisting Nurse Labor", Transactions of the Japan Society of Mechanical Engineers, Vol.67, No.657, pp.1499-1506, 2001 (in Japanese).

AOKI. T, TAGUCHI. K, "A Study of Human-Assist-Robot -Development of a Prototype Robot for Nursing Use-", Journal of the Robotics Society of Japan, Vol.21, No.2, pp.157-163 (in Japanese).

KAWAI. S, NARUSE. K, YOKOI. H, KAKAZU. Y, "An Analysis of Human Motion for Control of a Wearable Power Assist System", Journal of Robotics and Mechatronics Vol.16, No.3, pp.237-244, 2004.

PARK. E, MARK. S. G, "Fatigue compensation of the electromyographic signal for prosthetic control and force estimation", IEEE Transactions on Biomedical Engineering, Vol.40, Issue.10, Oct. 1993, pp.1019-1023.

FEATURE EXTRACTION USING TIME-FREQUENCY AND WAVELET ANALYSIS FOR CLASSIFICATION OF HEART SOUNDS

MATIAS BRUSCO
Department of Electrical and Computer Engineering
The University of Texas at El Paso
El Paso, TX USA

HOMER NAZERAN
Department of Electrical and Computer Engineering
The University of Texas at El Paso
El Paso, TX USA

SERGIO D. CABRERA
Department of Electrical and Computer Engineering
The University of Texas at El Paso
El Paso, TX USA

ABSTRACT

Many pathological conditions of the cardiovascular system cause murmurs and aberrations in heart sounds much before they present as other symptoms. With the use of modern time- and frequency-domain analysis techniques it is possible to extract valuable information from the heart sounds and perform computer-based pattern classification. In this paper we use a number of advanced signal processing methods for extraction of effective features from heart sounds. We perform Fourier Transform (FT), Short Time Fourier Transform (STFT), Spectrogram (SPEC) and Wavelet Transform (WT) to compare their efficacy in extracting an optimal set of features for neuro-fuzzy classification of heart sounds. We then classify a number of normal and abnormal heart sounds to validate the effectiveness of our feature extraction methods for computer-based recognition of heart sounds.

INTRODUCTION

The timing and pitch of heart sounds reflect the structural condition of the atria, ventricles and valves. As phonocardiography (graphical recording of heart sounds) is noninvasive and provides valuable information on the integrity, function, and hemodynamics performance of the valves, it has a high potential for detecting cardiac valvular diseases (Durand and Pibarot, 1995).

Digital analysis of the phonocardiogram allows extracting features from the heart sounds that could not be detected by the human ear, such as muffled components of heart sound, musical murmurs, rumble, or whiffs. As heart sounds are non-stationary signals, it is important to study both their temporal and frequency contents.

Previous publications (Obaidat and Matalgah, 1992; El-Asir et al, 1996; Lee et al, 1999; and Doyle et al, 2003) have shown that time-frequency/scale methods applied for the characterization of the heart sounds were suitable for heart sounds analysis and feature extraction. Nardiz and Tamer (2002) and Özgür et al (2002) have demonstrated that wavelet decomposition can be used for features extraction and classification.

In this study, time-frequency/scale techniques and wavelet decomposition are applied, special attention is given to wavelet decomposition in the sense that it can be used to: graphically expose more details, segment the heart sound in S_1 & S_2 and form feature vectors for classification. A new feature vector is proposed using decomposition levels 4 and 6 for the decomposition tree using the Daubechies 6 wavelet.

METHODOLOGY

Fourier Transform (FT) is applied to two heart sounds (normal and abnormal) to show their frequency spectra. Time-frequency domain analysis is then performed by using Short Time Fourier Transform (STFT) and Wavelet transform methods. Wavelet decomposition of four heart sounds is finally performed to investigate the sensitivity and specificity of these methods for heart sound segmentation and feature extraction.

Frequency Spectrum - Fourier Transform Method

The Fourier Transform $S(\omega)$ of a signal is defined as:

$$S(\omega) = \int s(t)e^{-j\omega t}dt \tag{1}$$

where t and ω are time and frequency parameters, respectively.

Figure 1 shows an example of a normal and an abnormal (Mitral Regurgitation) heart sounds recordings. The scale of both time and frequency axes is linear. The frequency scan is from 1 Hz to 500 Hz. A sampling rate of 22,050 Hz is used. Figures 1(a) & 1(b) show the time-domain signal and its basic frequency components detected by the Fourier transform for the normal heart sound (frequency components in the range 30 – 150 Hz and 200 – 280 Hz). Figure 1(c) clearly shows the presence of a systolic murmur in the time-domain signal along with its frequency components (Fig. 1d) up to 500 Hz (or more) as a result of turbulent blood flow. Since the time information is lost in this transformation, it is impossible to tell when a particular event took place. Therefore, the conventional Fourier transform spectral analysis method may not be able to provide accurate diagnosis of heart diseases. Therefore, it is essential to investigate deployment of a transform which preserves the temporal component of the signal as well.

Time-Frequency/scale – Spectrogram and Continuous Wavelet Transform

The Fourier transform is adapted to analyze only a small section of the signal at a time (signal windowing) constituting a two dimensional function of time and frequency. The Spectrogram or Short-Time Fourier Transform (STFT) of a signal is defined as:

$$S(t,\omega) = \int s(\tau)W(\tau - t)e^{-j\omega t}d\tau \tag{2}$$

where $W(t)$ is the window applied to the signal, ω is the frequency and t is time.

The wavelet transform of a signal s(t) with respect to an analyzing wavelet g(t) is defined as:

$$S(t,a) = \frac{1}{\sqrt{a}}\int s(t)g^{*\left(\frac{\tau-t}{a}\right)}d\tau \quad = \sqrt{a}\int S(\omega)G^{*}(a\omega)e^{j\omega t}d\omega \tag{3}$$

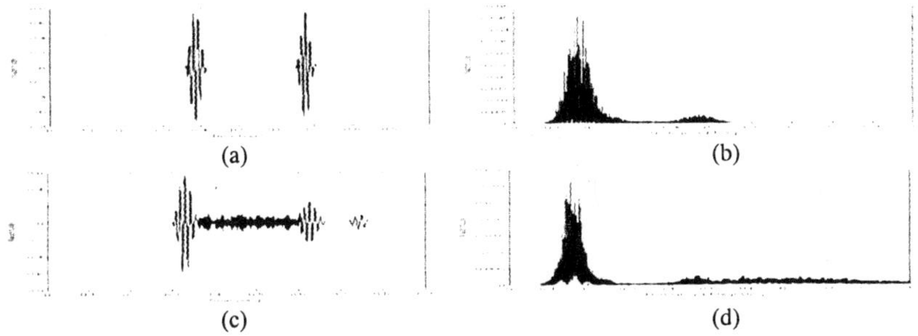

Figure 1: (a) Normal Heart Sound, (b) Spectrum of a, (c) Abnormal Heart Sound (mitral Regurgitation), (d), Spectrum of c.

where * denotes a complex conjugate, and $g(t)$ is the so called analyzing wavelet. $S(\omega)$ and $G(\omega)$ are the Fourier Transform of $s(t)$ and $g(t)$, respectively. The parameter "a" is a scaling parameter which is inversely related to the frequency.

Figure 2 shows an abnormal heart sound (Mitral Stenosis), its frequency spectrum, and contours of both, Spectrogram and Continuous Wavelet Transform (CWT). It has been shown by Ergen and Tatar (2003) that the Morlet wavelet is the most suitable wavelet in the time-frequency analysis of the phonocardiogram to extract the more exact features of the heart sounds, S_1 and S_2, and the heart murmurs, therefore, Morlet wavelet was selected for the CWT.

In spite of the similarity between the contours in Fig. 2, it should be emphasized that in Fig. 2(c) there are frequency components appearing almost at zero frequency, but Fig. 2 (b) clearly shows that there are not significant components below 45 Hz. This discrepancy is due to the time-frequency trade off in the Spectrogram. Figure 2(d) shows how this discrepancy is overcame by the CWT since frequency components appear exactly distributed as the frequency spectrum of Fig. 2(b). It should be also noted that the contour of the CWT provides more detailed information compared to the contour of the Spectrogram.

Wavelet Decomposition – Segmentation of the Heart Sound

As Liang et al (1997) have shown, the important components of the Heart Sound (S_1 and S_2) can be separated calculating the normalized average Shannon Energy for selected approximations and details. Figure 3 shows an example for an abnormal heart sound (Aortic Regurgitation) that was decomposed by using Daubechies 6 wavelet. Its detail 5 level was then reconstructed and the average Shannon energy was calculated over windows of 0.02 sec with a 0.01 sec overlap. It is observed that by setting a correct threshold the main components which are contaminated with noise can be separated.

Wavelet Decomposition – Feature Extraction

In a study Özgür et al (2002) splitted the signal formed by the wavelet detail coefficients at the second and sixth level into 64 windows, each window containing 128 discrete data points. However, since the duration of a single period is not constant (it varies with heart rate), the size of the window should decrease or increase with lower or higher heart rates, respectively. Also the sub-bands should be chosen by considering the concentration of energy for normal and abnormal heart sounds.

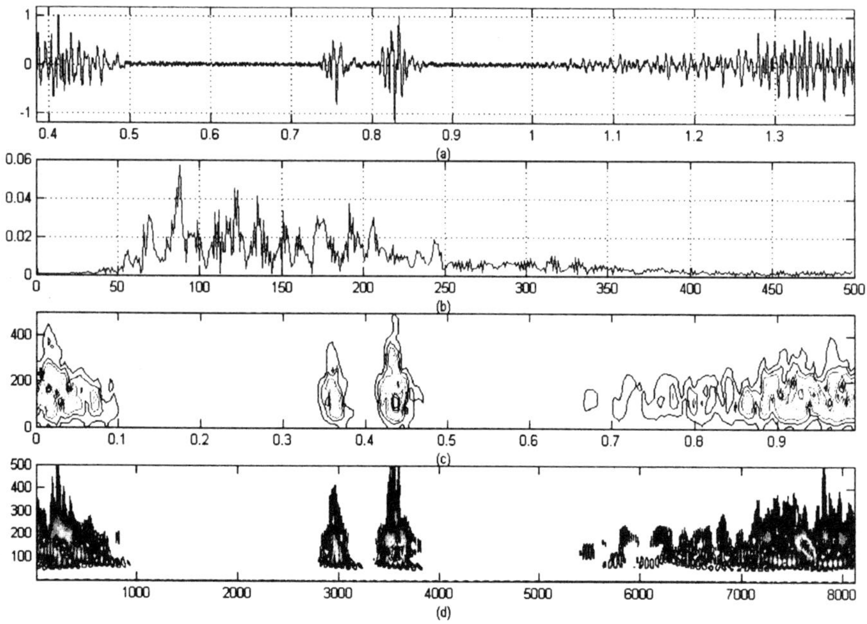

Figure 2: (a) Abnormal Heart Sound (Mitral Stenosis), (b), its Frequency Spectrum, (c) Contour of the Spectrogram of Figure 1-a, (d) Contour of the CWT of a Figure 1-a.

In this study, four heart sounds were analyzed, Normal (from four different sources), Mitral Stenosis, Mitral Regurgitation and Aortic Regurgitation (the last three from 3 different sources). All heart sounds were downsampled to 8,012 Hz in order to use the same decomposition levels for all of them. With this sampling frequency, the sub-bands corresponding to decomposition levels Detail 4 (250 – 500 Hz) and Detail 6 (75 - 125Hz) were selected by using the wavelet Daubechies 6. This was performed to obtain discriminating information Detail 4, which provides more information about the main components of a heart sound and Detail 6 provides extra information about components of abnormal heart sounds.

By selecting S_1 as the starting point, a window which contained a single period of the heart sound was formed. The wavelet detail coefficients at the forth and sixth levels were then subdivided in 32 windows and used to determine the elements of the feature vectors. The feature vector corresponding to a single period is composed by the power of the sub-windows of the decomposition levels giving a vector of size 64 (32+32). The first 32 components correspond to the Detail 4 and the rest to Detail 6.

Figure 4 shows the wavelet detail coefficients at levels 4 and 6 for the heart sounds mentioned above (Normal Heart Sound, Mitral Regurgitation, Mitral Stenosis and Aortic Regurgitation). It is observed that level 6 (left) contains more information about the main components (S_1 and S_2) while level 4 (right) contains discriminating information of the abnormal extra components originated by valvular pathologies.

Figure 5 shows the feature vectors corresponding to the four heart sounds. Each element of the feature vector is characterized by its maximum, minimum and average values. The feature vector for the normal heart sounds were constructed from a space sample of 4 sources, while the vectors for abnormal sounds were constructed from three sources.

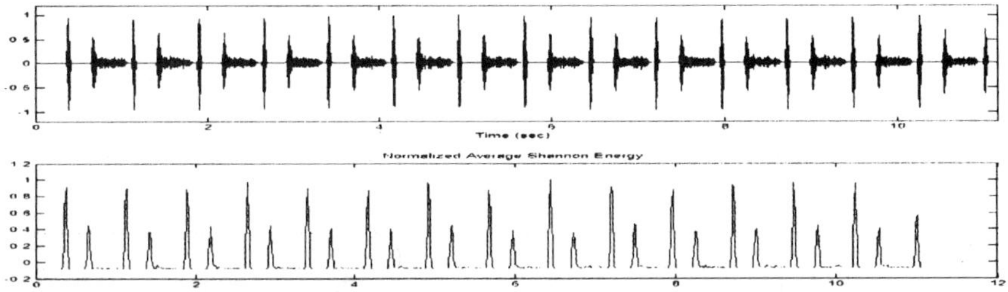

Figure 3: An Abnormal Heart Sound and its Average Shannon Energy of the Wavelets Coefficients of the decomposition level Detail 5.

CONCLUSIONS

We have shown that wavelet decomposition allows the formation of discrete discriminating vectors from analog heart sound signals. These vectors were derived based upon "discriminating information" embedded in time domain heart sound signals. These feature vectors efficiently characterize the heart sounds and serve as a set of reliable parameters in their computer-based classification. It is concluded that there is a clear and robust one-to-one correspondence between each feature vector and its corresponding heart sound signal. This unique correspondence makes the developed approach attractive and motivates the search for improved wavelet-based decomposition to develop an optimal set of feature vectors for neuro-fuzzy classification of heart sounds.

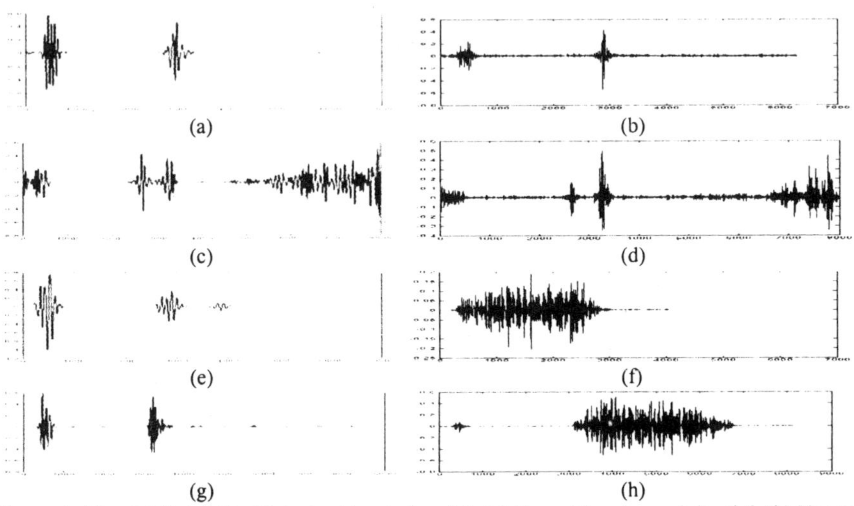

Figure 4: Wavelet Detail Coefficients at levels 4 and 6: (a) Normal heart sound, level 6, (b) Normal heart sound, level 4, (c) Mitral Stenosis, level 6, (d) Mitral Stenosis, level 4, (e) Mitral Regurgitation, level 6, (f) Mitral Regurgitation, level 4, (g) Aortic Regurgitation, level 6, and (h) Aortic Regurgitation, level 4.

ACKNOWLEDGMENTS

The authors would like to acknowledge the support of Texas Instruments Fund.

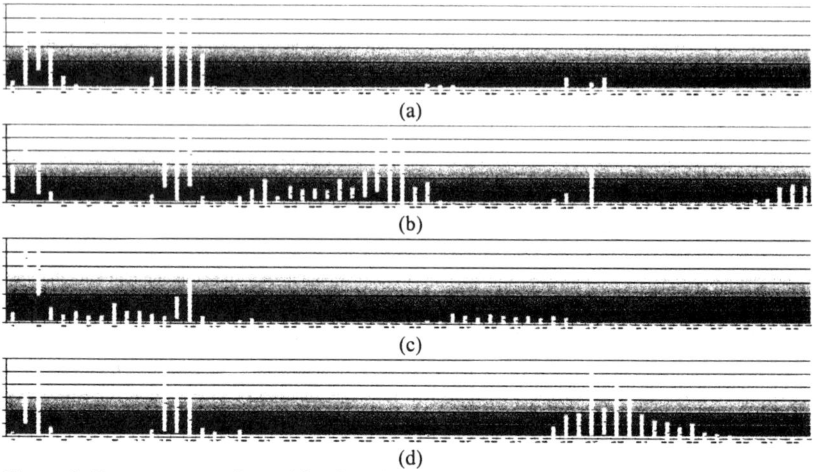

Figure 5. Feature vectors formed by the 64 power components of the wavelet coefficients at Details 4 and 6. (a) Vector of a Normal Heart Sound, (b) Vector of Mitral Stenosis, (c) Vector of Mitral Regurgitation and (d) Vector of Aortic Regurgitation.

REFERENCES

Doyle J. D., Gopakumaran B., and William A. Smith W.A., 2003, "Color Spectrographic Analysis of the Phonocardiogram: A Future Noninvasive Cardiac Monitoring Technology?", *IEEE Engineering in Medicine and Biology Conference (EMBC), Cancun, Mexico,* pp. 2251 - 2554.

Durand L. G., and Pibarot P., 1995, "Digital Signal Processing of the Phonocardiogram: Review of the Most Recent Advancements", *Critical Review^{TM} in Biomedical Engineering* , Vol. 23, pp. 116-219.

El-Asir, B., Kahadra, L., Al-Abbasi, A.H., and Mohamed M. M. J., 1996 , "Time-Frequency Analysis of Heart Sounds", *IEEE TENCON – Digital Signal Processing Applications,* pp. 553 – 558

Ergen, Buthan and Tatar Yetkin, 2003, "Optimal Continuous Wavelet Analysis of Phonocardiogram Signals", *Proceedings of International Conference on Signal Processing,* ISSN 1304-2386, Vol. 1, Number 2, pp. 188-192

Lee J.J., Lee S.M., Young K., Min H K., Hong S. H., 1999, "Comparison between Short Time Fourier and Wavelet Transform for Feature Extraction of Heart Sound", *IEEE TENCON,* pp1547-1550

Liang, H., Lukkarinen S., and Hartimo I., 1997, "Heart Sound Segmentation Algorithm Based on Heart Sound Envelogram", *Computer in Cardiology*, Vol. 24, pp. 105-108.

Liang, Huiying, Lukkarinen Sakari and Hartimo Iiro., 1997, "A Heart Sound Segmentation Algorithm Using Wavelet Decomposition and Reconstruction", *Proceedings – 19th International Conference – IEEE, Chicago*, pp. 1630-1633.

Nardiz Kurnaz M., Tamer Ölmez, 2002, "Determination of Features for Heart Sounds by Using Wavelet Transforms", *Proceedings of the 15th IEEE Symposium on Computer-Based Medical Systems.*

Obaidat M. S., and M. M. Matalgah, 1992, "Performance of the Short Time Fourier Transform and Wavelet Transform to Phonocardiogram Signal Analysis", *Symposium on Applied computing: technological challenges of the 1990's,* pp.856 - 862

Özgür Say, Zümary Dokur and Tamer Ölmez, 2002, "Classification of heart Sounds By Using Wavelet Transforms", *Proceedings of the Second Joint EMBS/BMES Conference, Houstoun, TX, USA,* pp. 128-129.

Rangayyan, R. M., and Lehner, R.J., 1988, "Phonocardiogram Signal Analysis: A review", *Critical Review in Biomedical Engineering,* Vol. 15, Issue 3, pp. 211-236.

Tilkian-Conover, 2001, "Understanding Heart Sounds and Murmurs, With an Introduction to Lung Sounds", W.B. Saunders Company, fourth edition.

NEW RESULTS IN COMPUTER AIDED DIAGNOSIS (CAD) OF BREAST CANCER USING A RECENTLY DEVELOPED SVM/GRNN ORACLE HYBRID

WALKER H. LAND, JR.,
Research Professor
Dept. of Computer Science
Binghamton University
Binghamton NY

TIMOTHY MASTERS
President ,TMAIC
Brackney , Pa.

FRANCES ANDERSON
Lourdes Hospital and the Regional Cancer center
Binghamton, NY

DOUGLAS M. RITZ
Graduate Student
Dept. of Computer Science
Binghamton University
Binghamton, NY

LUT WONG
Graduate Student
Dept. of Computer Science
Binghamton University
Binghamton, NY

DAN MCKEE
Graduate Student
Dept. of Computer Science
Binghamton University
Binghamton,NY

JOSEPH Y. LO
Duke University Medical Center
Duke University
Durham, NC

ABSTRACT

This research consisted of evaluating diagnostic performance results using SVM outputs previously obtained from an integrated Duke/DDSM USF data set and the GRNN oracle. The SVM kernels used in this research included Additive, Multiplicative, S2000, and Spline kernels. GRNN results are presented for the following combinations of gate variables: age, mass margin (MM), age and MM, and all 6 BIRADS™ indicators plus age. For all experiments, Differential Evolution (DE) was used to train the GRNN. A summary of the DE process is described, independent of the software application. The experiments described in this paper show that the GRNN oracle, with all of the gate variable combinations, performed better than any of the individual SVM kernels alone at or below 98% sensitivity.

INTRODUCTION

Carcinoma of the breast is second only to lung cancer as a tumor-related cause of death in women. For 2003, it has been reported that 211,300 new cases and 39,800 deaths will occur just in the US . It has been proposed, however, that mortality from breast cancer could be decreased by up to 25% provided that all women in appropriate age groups were regularly screened . Currently, the method of choice for early detection of breast cancer is mammography, due to **its general widespread availability, low cost,** speed, and non-invasiveness. At the same time, while mammography is sensitive to the detection of breast cancer, it has a low positive predictive value (PPV), resulting in costly and invasive biopsies that are only 15%-34% likely to reveal malignancy at histological examination [15].

Computational intelligence has been applied to the problem of breast cancer screening by several researchers. Earlier work by Floyd et al. [5] and Lo et al. [16] demonstrated the applicability of back propagation-trained Multiple Layer Feed forward Neural Networks (MLFNs) to this task. EP-based feed forward networks were applied by Fogel et al. [7-9] and Land et al. [13]. These applications were able to achieve similar or better results than those trained by back propagation, but with much simpler architectures (i.e., fewer nodes in the hidden layer). Evolutionary-Programming (EP) based linear discriminate analysis [10], and an adaptive boosting/EP hybrid [14] also were investigated as potential classification mechanisms. This paper extends the knowledge gained from previous breast cancer research through a description of the development and preliminary evaluation of a new SVM/GRNN oracle hybrid.

THE GENERALIZED NEURAL NETWORK (GRNN) ORACLE

Designing the GRNN Oracle

We have two or more different models, each of which predicts the same scalar output variable [17]. (Extension to multiple outputs is easy, but in practice we never want to do this.) If there are multiple outputs, use a separate oracle for each.) We do not care about the nature of these models, nor do we care about their inputs. In fact, the model inputs do not enter into this discussion in any way. We also have one or more *gate variables* whose values presumably have an effect on deciding which of the competing models is most valid. For our purposes now, we do not care about the individual prediction models. They are assumed to be black boxes that work reasonably well. Our current goal is to design an oracle that used the gate variables to intelligently combine the outputs of the competing models.

EXPERIMENTAL DESIGN TO EVALUATE INTEGRATED HARDWARE/SOFTWARE SYSTEM AND SENSITIVITIES ANALYSIS

This section describes the experiential design approach that will be used. The measures of performance which will be used are: the overall ROC Az index, the specificity and PPV at 95% (5% false positive errors (FPE)), 98% (2% FRE) and 100% sensitivities (0% FPE). As previously described, these MOPs provide a quantities measure of how well the system decreases false negative errors (FNE), while maintaining the 95%, 98%, and 100% sensitivities. K-fold cross will be employed.

Using the GRNN oracle.

We will accomplish data fusion of several learning machine models using the GRNN oracle. This oracle intelligently combines the outputs of several of these models by using gate variables. The inputs are from several Support Vector Machine models (to be described subsequently). These sevearl SVM learning machines are comprised of the following kernel types: s2000, Gaussian Radial Basis Function (GRBF), polynomial kernels, spline kernels, sum and product kernels whose components are the GRBF and polynomial kernels. Secondly, the gate variables used in this research are (also subsequently described): (1.) age, (2) mass margin (MM) and (3) age and MM. Suppose we have two or more prediction models of any type, each of which predicts the same scalar output variable. Extension to multiple outputs is easy, but in practice we never want to do this. If there are multiple outputs, use a separate oracle for each.)

Our current goal is to design an oracle that uses the gate variables to intelligently combine the outputs of the competing models. Once the expected error of each prediction model is estimated, we use these expected errors to compute the weights for each model. When an unknown case is processed, the gate variables are used by the GRNN to decide which models are likely to be best for this particular case. These models are weighted more heavily than the likely inferior models.

SUPPORT VECTOR MACHINES AND DIFFERENTIAL EVOLUTION

Several references are available that provide extensive information about development of the mathematical foundation of SVMs [3,4,11,12]. The key concepts of SVMs generally are covered in these references and will not be discussed here.

DIFFERENTIAL EVOLUTION

Price and Storn [18] reported on a variation of genetic optimization called *differential evolution*. This variation appears to be much more appropriate than traditional genetic methods when optimizing a multivariate function. It is especially valuable when the scalings in the different dimensions are not commensurate, a situation commonly found in GRNN training using poorly prescaled or highly correlated variables. Unfortunately, differential evolution shares the principal weakness of all stochastic methods in that it can arrive frustratingly close to the global minimum, then fail to converge to the minimum in a reasonable period of time. The problem is that these algorithms generally operate in total ignorance of the local properties of the function being minimized. Sometimes this is out of necessity because the derivatives cannot be computed. More importantly, it is because we must be careful to avoid excessive use of local information if we are to preserve the global quality of the search for the minimum. But when we do have easy access to local information, it often makes sense to make modest use of it. Such is the case when using differential evolution to train a GRNN.

Differential evolution is similar to ordinary genetic optimization in that it starts with a collection of parameter sets that we will call the *source population*. The individuals comprising this population are combined with each other via *crossover* and subjected to *mutation* to produce the members of the *destination population*. The members of the destination population, taken as a group, are generally expected to be superior to the members of the source population. By repeating this process enough times, the best member of the final population is hopefully close to the global optimum.

There are several important differences between traditional genetic optimization and differential evolution. Probably the most important difference is in the nature of the mutation. In traditional genetic optimization, mutation takes the form of a random perturbation of a fixed type, such as flipping bits in a binary representation of a parameter set, or adding random numbers to individual parameters. The problem with this approach is that it fails to account for the fact that what might be a small perturbation for one parameter might be gigantic for another. Also, random bit flipping can be extremely destructive. Differential evolution avoids these problems by using the source population itself to determine the nature and degree of mutation. It does this by randomly selecting a pair of individuals and computing the difference between their parameter vectors. This difference vector is multiplied by a fixed constant (typically around 0.5 or so) and added to the individual being mutated. When the optimization begins, the average difference will be about the same for all variables being optimized. But as generations pass, the difference will tend to adapt to the natural scaling of the problem. Variables having a large natural scale will be distributed over a larger range in the population, so mutations for these variables will also be relatively large. As convergence approaches, those variables having a narrow and well defined range around the minimum will have small variation among the population members, resulting in their mutations being relatively small. This automatic adaptation significantly improves behavior of the algorithm as convergence nears.

Another important difference is that differential evolution does not involve selection of parents based on fitness. Instead, fitness determines which children are kept. In particular, one parent, called the *primary parent* is selected deterministically: each individual in the source population is chosen as a primary parent exactly once. The other parent, called the *secondary parent*, is randomly chosen. Two other individuals which make up the *differential pair* are also selected randomly. These two are subtracted and their difference is multiplied by a small fixed constant. This scaled difference vector is added to the secondary parent to induce mutation. Ordinary crossover is applied to the primary parent and the mutated secondary parent. The resulting child's fitness is compared to that of the primary parent. The winner becomes a new member of the destination population. This entire process is illustrated in Figure 2.

PRELIMINARY RESULTS

This section describes the experiential design approach that will be used. The measures of performance which will be used are: the overall ROC Az index, the specificity and PPV at 95% (5% false positive errors (FPE)), 98% (2% FRE) and 100% sensitivities (0% FPE). These MOPs provide a quantities measure of how well the system decreases false negative errors (FNE), while maintaining the 95%, 98%, and 100% sensitivities. K-fold cross will be employed.

Several research experiments were performed to evaluate the performance of the seperate support vector machine models, and the use of differential evolution to train the GRNN oracle. These familes of SVMs were evolved over 40 genrtations , with a population size of 30, using Evolutionary Programming.

	GRNN	SVM	Difference (GRNN – SVM)	% Improvement
Az	81.62%	81.21%	0.41%	**0.51%**
Az-90	32.01%	29.61%	2.4%	**8.11%**
100% Spec	5.56%	3.27%	2.29%	**70.03%**
100% PPV	48.23%	47.59%	0.64%	**1.35%**
98% Spec	22.15%	17.85%	4.3%	**24.09%**
98% PPV	52.67%	51.33%	1.34%	**2.61%**
97% Spec	24.23%	23.46%	0.77%	**3.28%**
97% PPV	53.16%	52.81%	0.35%	**0.66%**
95% Spec	32.38%	29.44%	2.94%	**9.99%**
95% PPV	56.96%	54.27%	2.69%	**4.96%**

Table 1: Performance Comparsion betweeen SVMs and GRNN oracle

CONCLUSIONS

The experiments just described demonstrated the following: (1.)No measurable performance accuracies difference resulted for variation in the differential evolution crossover constant, (2.)The Az and partial Az are essentially constant for all values of the differential evolution crossover constant, holding at values of 81.6% and 32%, respectively. A patrial Az of 32% means that , on the average, approxiamtely 432 women would avoid biopsy when compared to all cases being biopsied, (3.)Produces a PPV of from 48% to 55% as the sensitivity is decreased from 100 to 95%, respectively, (4.) specificity is increased from about 5% to about 36% as sensitivity is decreased from 100 to 95%, and (5.)Improvements from about 0.5% to 24% were observed in the GRNN oracle performance when compared to the SVM diagnostic accuracy. This is not surprising when one observes that SVMs can be trained to a global minimum, given that the learning machine parameters are properly computed.

ACKNOWLEDGEMENTS. This work was supported in part by the New York state breast cancer research and education fund through department of health contract C017939.

REFERENCES

1. J. A. Baker, P. J. Kornguth, J. Y. Lo, M. E. Williford, and C. E. Floyd, Jr., "Breast Cancer: Prediction with Artificial Neural Network Based on BI-RADS Standardized Lexicon", *Radiology*, Vol. 196, pp. 817-22, 1995.
2. *BIRADS, Breast Imaging - Reporting and Data System (BI-RADS)*, American College of Radiology, 1993.
3. C. J. C. Burges, "A Tutorial on Support Vector Machines for Pattern Recognition," *Data Mining and Knowledge Discovery*, Vol. 2, No. 2, pp. 121-167, 1998.
4. N. Cristanini, and J. Shawe-Taylor, *An Introduction to Support Vector Machines and other Kernel-Based Learning Methods,* Cambridge University, 2000.
5. C. E. Floyd, J. Y. Lo, A. J. Yun, D. C. Sullivan, and P. J. Kornguth, "Prediction of Breast Cancer Malignancy Using an Artificial Neural Network", *Cancer*, Vol. 74, pp. 2944-98, 1994.
6. D. B. Fogel, *Evolutionary Computation: Toward a New Philosophy of Machine Intelligence*, IEEE Press, Piscataway, NJ, 1995.
7. D. B. Fogel, E. C. Wasson, and E. M. Boughton, "Evolving Neural Networks for Detecting Breast Cancer", *Cancer Letters*, Vol. 96, pp. 49-53, 1995.
8. D. B. Fogel, E. C. Wasson, E. M. Boughton, and V. W. Porto, "A Step Toward Computer-Assisted Mammography using Evolutionary Programming and Neural Networks", *Cancer Letters*, Vol. 119, pp. 93-97, 1997.
9. D. B. Fogel, E. C. Wasson, E. M. Boughton, and V. W. Porto, "Evolving Artificial Neural Networks for Screening Features from Mammograms", *Artificial Intelligence in Medicine*, Vol. 14, pp. 317-326, 1998.
10. D. B. Fogel, E. C. Wasson, E. M. Boughton, V. W. Porto, and P. J. Angeline, "Linear and Neural Models for Classifying Breast Masses", *IEEE Trans. Medical Imaging*, Vol. 17, No. 3, pp. 485-488, 1998.
11. S. Gunn, *Support Vector Machines for Classification and Regression,* ISIS Technical Report, Image Speech and Intelligent Systems Group, University of Southampton, May 14, 1998.
12. S. Haykin, *Neural Networks,* Prentice Hall, New Jersey, 1999.
13. W. H. Land, T. Masters, J. Y. Lo, and D. McKee, "Using Evolutionary Computation to Develop Neural Network Breast Cancer Benign/Malignant Classification Models", *4th World Conference on Systemics, Cybernetics and Informatics*, Vol. 10, pp. 343-7, 2000.
14. W. H. Land, Jr., T. Masters, and J. Y. Lo, "Application of a New Evolutionary Programming/ Adaptive Boosting Hybrid to Breast Cancer Diagnosis", IEEE Congress on Evolutionary Computation Proceedings, 2000.
15. J. Y. Lo, J. A. Baker, P. J. Kornguth, J. D. Iglehart, and C. E. Floyd, "Predicting Breast Cancer Invasion with Artificial Neural Networks on the Basis of Mammographic Features", *Radiology*, Vol. 203, pp. 159-163, 1997.
16. J. Y. Lo, J. A. Baker, P. J. Kornguth, and C. E. Floyd, Jr., "Effect of Patient History Data on the Prediction of Breast Cancer from Mammographic Findings with Artificial Neural Networks", *Acad. Radiology*, Vol. 6, pp. 10-15, 1999.
17. T. Masters, and W. H. Land, Jr., "A New Training Method for the General Regression Neural Network", IEEE International SMC Conference Proceedings, pp. 1990-5, 1997.
18. K. Price, and R. Storn, "Differential Evolution", *Dr. Dobb's Journal*, pp. 18-24, April, 1997.

MEDICAL IMAGE RECOGNITION BY USING THE MULTI-LAYERED GMDH-TYPE NEURAL NETWORKS WITH RADIAL BASIS FUNCTIONS

TADASHI KONDO
School of Health Sciences,
The University of Tokushima,
Tokushima 770-8509, Japan

ABHIJIT S. PANDYA
Computer Sciences & Engineering,
Florida Atlantic University,
Boca Raton, FL33431,U.S.A.

ABSTRACT

In this paper, medical image recognition by using the multi-layered GMDH(Group Method of Data Handling)-type neural networks with RBF(Radial Basis Functions) is developed. The multi-layered GMDH-type neural network algorithm can automatically generate the optimal neural network architectures fitting the complexity of the nonlinear system. The structural parameters such as the number of the layers, the number of the neurons in the hidden layers, the useful input variables are automatically determined so as to minimize the error criterion defined as PSS(Prediction Sum of Squares) or AIC (Akaike's information criterion). In this paper, the multi-layered GMDH-type neural network algorithm with RBF is applied to medical image recognition. The RBF neural networks, which are suitable for the medical image recognition, are identified automatically by using the multi-layered GMDH-type neural network algorithm. It is shown that this algorithm is both very easy and useful in medical image recognition because the RBF neural network architecture can be automatically organized so as to minimize the error criterion PSS or AIC.

INTRODUCTION

The GMDH-type neural networks and their applications have been proposed in our early works (Kondo 1998, Kondo, Pandya and Zurada 1999a and Kondo, Pandya and Zurada 1999b). The GMDH-type neural networks can automatically organize the neural network architecture by using the heuristic self-organization method (Ivakhnenko 1970 and Farlow 1984) and they can also determine structural parameters such as the number of layers, the number of neurons in the hidden layers and the useful input variables. These structural parameters are automatically determined so as to minimize the error criterion defined as PSS (Allen 1974 and Tamura and Kondo 1980) or AIC (Akaike 1974). Therefore, it is very easy to apply the GMDH-type neural network algorithm to the practical complex problem whose architectures are unknown.

In the medical image recognition, there are many kinds of medical images such as MRI image, X-ray CT image, X-ray image, mammography and others and these image characteristics are different from each other. Therefore, it is very difficult to find out the optimum neural network architectures fitting the characteristics of medical images when we apply the neural networks to the medical image recognition.

In this paper, the multi-layered GMDH-type neural network algorithm with RBF is applied to medical image recognition. The RBF neural networks, which are suitable for the medical image recognition, are identified automatically by using the multi-layered GMDH-type neural network algorithm. It is shown that this algorithm is both very easy and useful in medical image recognition because the RBF neural network architecture can be automatically organized so as to minimize the error criterion PSS or AIC.

THE MULTI-LAYERED GMDH-TYPE NEURAL NETWORK ALGORITHM WITH RADIAL BASIS FUNCTIONS

The multi-layered GMDH-type neural networks with radial basis functions have a common feedforward multi-layered architecture. Figure 1 shows the architecture of the multi-layered GMDH-type neural networks with radial basis functions. This neural networks are organized by using the heuristic self-organization method. But this algorithm does not need the separation of the original data into the training and test sets because PSS and AIC can be used instead of test errors. So all the data are used as the training data. In this case, the application of PSS and AIC is similar to Tamuka and Kondo's heuristic self-organization approach (Tamura and Kondo 1980) for the conventional GMDH algorithm.

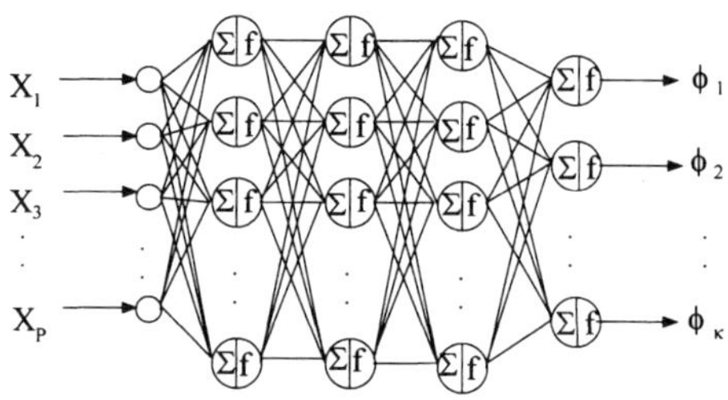

Fig.1 Architecture of the multi-layered GMDH-type neural network.

PSS is described by the following equation:

$$PSS = \sum_{\alpha=1}^{n} (\phi_\alpha - y_\alpha^*)^2 \tag{1}$$

where

$$y_\alpha^* = b_{0\alpha} + b_{1\alpha}x_{i\alpha} + b_{2\alpha}x_{j\alpha} + b_{3\alpha}x_{i\alpha}x_{j\alpha} + b_{4\alpha}x_{i\alpha}^2 + b_{5\alpha}x_{j\alpha}^2, \qquad \alpha=1,2,\dots,n \tag{2}$$

n is the number of training data, ϕ_α is the α-th observed value for the output variable, $x_{i\alpha}$ is the α-th observed value for the input variable x_i and y_α^* is the α-th estimated value obtained by the linear regression analysis of all the data except the α-th datum. In order to compute PSS of Eq. (1), the linear regression analysis must be repeated n times, and the amount of computation increases in the number of data. But PSS of Eq. (1) can be reduced as follows,

$$PSS = \sum_{\alpha=1}^{n} \left((\phi_\alpha - y_\alpha)/(1-\mathbf{x}_\alpha^T (X^T X)^{-1} \mathbf{x}_\alpha) \right)^2 \tag{3}$$

where

$$y_\alpha = b_0 + b_1 x_{i\alpha} + b_2 x_{j\alpha} + b_3 x_{i\alpha} x_{j\alpha} + b_4 x_{i\alpha}^2 + b_5 x_{j\alpha}^2, \tag{4}$$

$$\mathbf{x}_\alpha^T = [1,\ x_{i\alpha},\ x_{j\alpha},\ x_{i\alpha}x_{j\alpha},\ x_{i\alpha}^2,\ x_{j\alpha}^2], \quad \alpha=1,2,\dots,n \tag{5}$$

$$X^T = [\ \mathbf{x}_1, \mathbf{x}_2, \dots, \mathbf{x}_n\ ] \tag{6}$$

y_α is the α-th estimated value obtained by the linear regression analysis of all the data. With this procedure, we need not repeat the regression analysis n times. In the multi-layered GMDH-type neural network algorithm, Eq.(4) is called as the partial description of the nonlinear system.

In the multi-layered GMDH-type neural network algorithm, we can also use the error criterion defined as AIC to organize the optimum network architecture.

AIC is described by the following equations:

$$AIC = n \log_e S_m^2 + 2(m+1) + C \tag{7}$$

$$S_m^2 = \sum_{\alpha=1}^{n} (\phi_\alpha - y_\alpha)^2 / n \tag{8}$$

$$y_\alpha = b_0 + b_1 x_{i\alpha} + b_2 x_{j\alpha} + b_3 x_{i\alpha} x_{j\alpha} + b_4 x_{i\alpha}^2 + b_5 x_{j\alpha}^2, \qquad \alpha = 1,2,\ldots,n \tag{9}$$

Here, m is the number of terms in Eq.(9), n is the number of training data and C is a constant.

The procedures for determining the architecture of the multi-layered GMDH-type neural networks with radial basis functions conform to the following:

(1) The first layer

$$u_j = x_j \quad (j=1,2,\ldots,p) \tag{10}$$

where x_j $(j=1,2,\ldots,p)$ are the input variables of the system, and p is the number of input variables. In the first layer, the output variables are equal to the input variables.

(2) The second layer

Many combination of r input variables are generated. For each combination, the neuron architectures are automatically selected from the following neurons so as to minimize PSS or AIC value.

i) The first type neuron

Σ: (Nonlinear function)

$$z_k = w_1 u_i + w_2 u_j + w_3 u_i u_j + w_4 u_i^2 + w_5 u_j^2 + w_6 u_i^3 + w_7 u_i^2 u_j + w_8 u_i u_j^2 + w_9 u_j^3 - w_0 \theta_1 \tag{11}$$

f : (Nonlinear function)

$$y_k = \exp(-z_k^2) \tag{12}$$

Here, $\theta_1 = 1$ and w_i $(i=0,1,2,\ldots,9)$ are the weights between the first and second layer. The value of r, which is the number of input variables u in each neuron, is set to two for the first type neuron.

ii) The second type neuron

Σ: (Linear function)

$$z_k = w_1 u_1 + w_2 u_2 + w_3 u_3 + \cdots + w_r u_r - w_0 \theta_1 \quad (r<p) \tag{13}$$

f : (Nonlinear function)

$$y_k = \exp(-z_k^2) \tag{14}$$

Here, $\theta_1 = 1$ and w_i $(i=0,1,2,\ldots,r)$ are the weights between the first and second layer. The value of r, which is the number of input variables u in each neuron, is set to be greater than two and smaller than p for the second type neuron. Here p is the number of input variables x_i $(i=1,2,\ldots,p)$.

The optimum neuron architecture for each combination is selected from the first and the second type neuronal architectures. The weights w_i $(i=0,1,2,\ldots)$ are estimated by the stepwise regression analysis (Draper and Smith 1981) using PSS or AIC.

[The estimation procedure of the weight w_i]

First, the values of z_k are calculated by using the following equation:

$$z_k=(-\ log_e\ \phi')^{1/2} \tag{15}$$

where ϕ' is the normalized output variable whose values are between zero and one. Then the weights w_i are estimated by using the stepwise regression analysis (Draper and Smith 1981) which selects useful input variables by using PSS or AIC. Only useful variables in Eq.(11) and Eq.(13) are selected by the stepwise regression analysis using PSS or AIC and the optimum neuronal architectures are organized by the selected useful variables.

From these generated neurons, the L neurons which minimize PSS or AIC value are selected. The output variables y_k of L selected neurons are set to the input variables of the neurons in the third layer.

(3) The third and succeeding layers

In the third and succeeding layers, the same computation of the second layer is iterated until PSS or AIC value of L neurons stop decreasing. When iterative computation is terminated, the neural network architectures are produced by the selected neurons in each layer.

By using these procedures, the multi-layered GMDH-type neural networks with radial basis functions can be organized.

APPLICATION TO THE MEDICAL IMAGE RECOGNITION

In this study, the outline of the lungs is recognized automatically by using the multi-layered GMDH-type neural networks with radial basis functions and the regions of the lungs are extracted. The X-ray CT images of the lungs are used in this study. The identification results of X-ray CT image are shown as follows:

Identification results of the X-ray CT image.

In this study, an original image shown in Fig. 2 is used for organizing the multi-layered GMDH-type neural networks. Then, image features are extracted and used as the input variables of the neural networks. The statistics of the image densities in the neighboring regions, the N×N pixel regions, are used as the image features. The following statistics are used as the input variables. 1) mean, 2) standard deviation, 3) variance, 4) median, 5) minimum, 6) maximum, 7) range. Out of these statistics, only four parameters namely, mean, standard deviation, variance and (mean × standard deviation) are selected as the useful input variables. The output value of the neural networks is zero or one. When N×N pixel region is contained in the regions of the lungs, the neural networks set the pixel value at the center of the N×N pixel region to one and this pixel is shown as the white point. The neural networks were organized when the values of N are 5, 10 and 15. It was determined that when N equals 5, the neural network architecture had the smallest recognition error. The calculation of the multi-layered GMDH-type neural networks was terminated at the fifth layer. Four useful neurons were selected in each hidden layer. The multi-layered GMDH-type neural networks output the lungs image and the post-processing analysis of the lungs image was carried out, based on which the regions of the lungs were extracted. In the post-processing of the output image of the neural networks, the small isolated regions were eliminated and the outlines of the regions of the lungs were expanded outside by N/2 pixels. Then, the outline of the lungs were extracted. Fig.3shows the output image after this processing. In order to check the matching between the original image and the output image of the neural networks, the output image was overlapped on the original image in Fig.2 after the post-processing. The overlapped image is shown in Fig.4 From Fig.4 we can see that the extracted regions were very accurate.

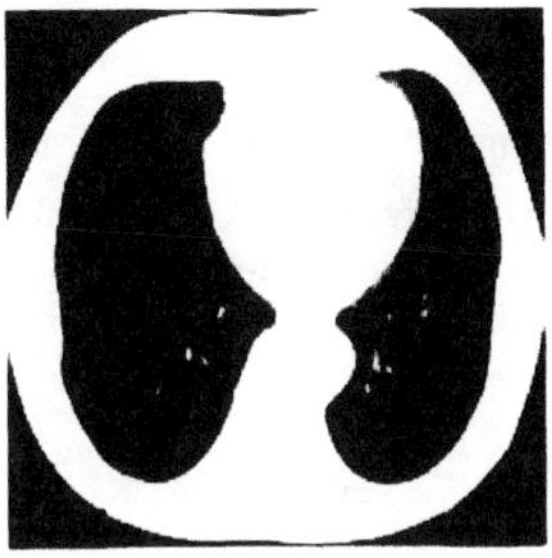

Fig.2 Original image

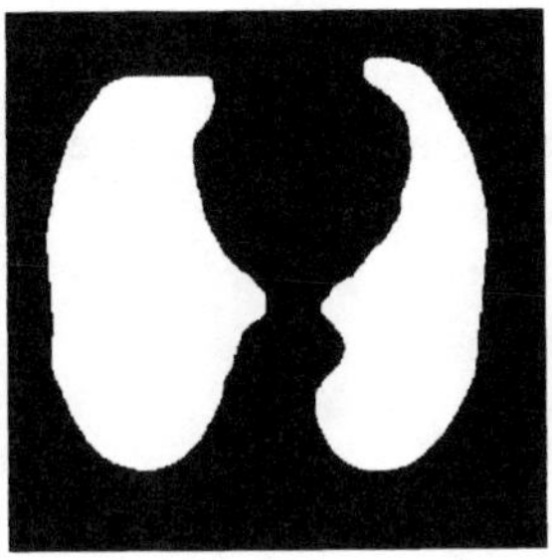

Fig.3 Output image

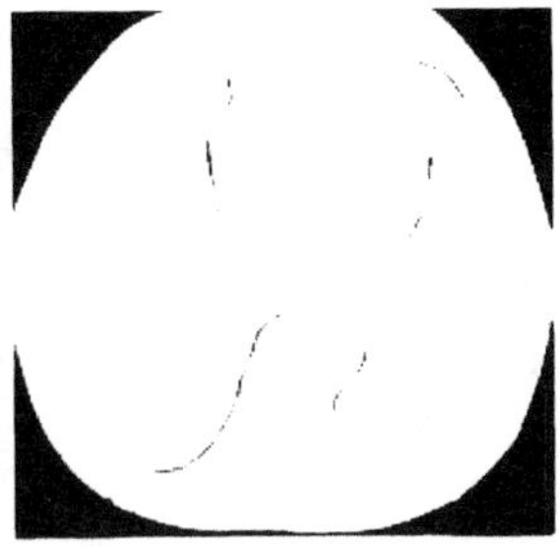

Fig.4 Overlapped image

Check of the generalization ability.

In order to check the generalization ability of the multi-layered GMDH-type neural networks with radial basis functions, the multi-layered GMDH-type neural networks, which were organized by using the original image of the lungs in Fig.2 are applied to another original image of the lungs shown in Fig.5 The multi-layered GMDH-type neural networks output the lungs image and the post-processing analysis of the lungs image was carried out, based on which the regions of the lungs were extracted. Fig.6 shows the output image after the post-processing. In order to check the matching between the original image and the output image of the neural networks, the output image was overlapped on the original image in Fig.5 after the post-processing. The overlapped image is shown in Fig.7. From Fig.7, we can see that the multi-layered GMDH-type neural networks with radial basis functions could extract new regions of the lungs accurately and it was shown that the multi-layered GMDH-type neural networks with radial basis functions had a good generalization ability.

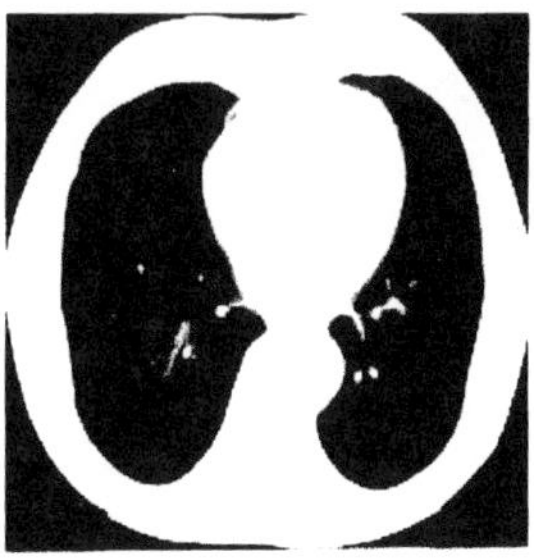

Fig.5 Original image

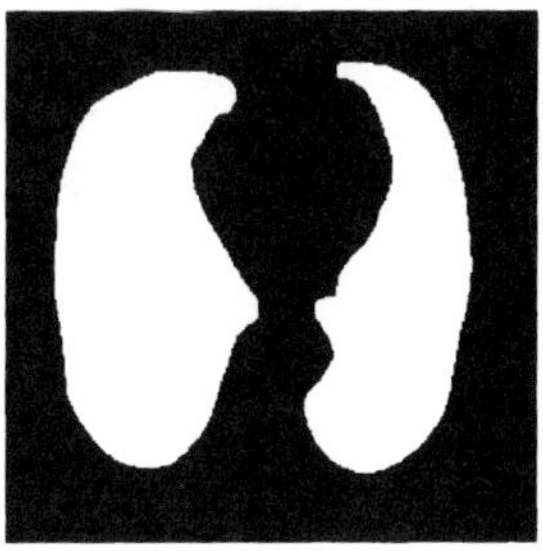

Fig.6 Output image

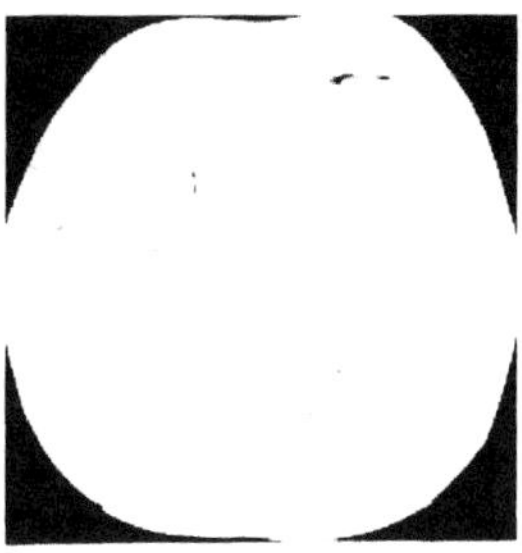

Fig.7 Overlapped image

CONCLUSION

In this paper, the multi-layered GMDH-type neural networks with radial basis functions were proposed and X-ray CT image was identified by using this multi-layered GMDH-type neural networks. In the multi-layered GMDH-type neural networks, the structural parameters such as the number of neurons, the number of layers and the useful input variables are automatically determined so as to minimize PSS or AIC value. Therefore, the multi-layered GMDH-type neural networks can identify the nonlinear system very accurately.

In this paper, this algorithm was applied to the medical image recognition of the lungs and it was shown that the multi-layered GMDH-type neural network algorithm with radial basis functions was a useful method for the medical image recognition of the lungs.

REFERENCES

Akaike H., 1974, " A new look at the statistical model identification", *IEEE Trans. Automatic Control*, Vol.AC-19, No.6, pp.716-723.

Allen D.M., 1974, " The relationship between variable selection and data augmentation and a method for prediction" , *Technometrics,* Vol. 16, No.1, pp.125-127.

Draper N.R. and Smith H., 1981,"Applied Regression Analysis", John Wiley and Sons, New York.

Farlow S.J. ed., 1984, " Self-organizing methods in modeling, GMDH-type algorithm", Marcel Dekker, Inc., New York.

Ivakhnenko A.G., 1970, " Heuristic self-organization in problems of engineering cybernetics", *Automatica*, Vo.6, No.2, pp.207-219.

Kondo T, 1998, "GMDH neural network algorithm using the heuristic self-organization method and its application to the pattern identification problem", *Proc. of the 37th SICE Annual Conference*, pp.1143-1148.

Kondo T, Pandya A.S., Zurada J.M., 1999a, "GMDH-type neural networks with a feedback loop and their application to nonlinear system identification", *Intelligent Engineering Systems through Artificial Neural Networks*, ASME Press, Vol.9, pp.117-124.

Kondo T., Pandya A.S.and Zurada J.M., 1999b, "Logistic GMDH-type neural networks and their application to the identification of the X-ray film characteristic curve", *Proceeding of IEEE international conference on systems, man and cybernetics*, Vol.1, pp.437-442.

Tamura H. and Kondo T., 1980, " Heuristics free group method of data handling algorithm of generating optimum partial polynomials with application to air pollution prediction", *INT.J.SYSTEM SCI.*, Vol.11, No.9, pp.1095-1111.

SIMULATION OF PULSE DISTRIBUTION OBSERVED IN OLFACTORY BULB

HEMACHAND NAREM
University of Louisville
Kentucky
Department of Electrical and Computer Engineering

JACEK M. ZURADA
University of Louisville
Kentucky
Department of Electrical and Computer Engineering

ANDRZEJ G. LOZOWSKI
Southern Illinois University, Edwardsville,Illinois
Department of Electrical and Computer Engineering

Abstract

According to experimental studies, interspike intervals (ISI) are responsible for odor information encoding occurring in the olfactory bulb. In this paper a method is described for generating ISI that hypothetically mimics the temporal encoding of odor information. The ISI is generated by the dynamical system derived from a Markov process synthesized to incorporate the ISI as its invariant distribution. The ISI distribution is the principal eigenvector of the transition matrix of Markov process. An algorithm using Nelder - Mead to synthesize the transition matrix through a cost function minimization is presented.

1 INTRODUCTION

A sense on smell (or Olfaction) allows vertebrates and other organisms with olfactory receptors to identify the odorant molecules. A particular group of receptors is excited by a specific group of odorants (Dickson et al. 1998). The sensory olfactory receptors response to the odorants is then passed to the olfactory bulb for detection. The function of the olfactory bulb is to relay the input obtained from the olfactory receptors into a set of easily interpretable signals to the brain. The characteristics of the signals is assumed to be the following (Lozowski et al. 2004):

1. The spikes mark instances of time when the neurons fire and their shape is not a significant factor.

2. The average value of the signal is affected by spikes since signal is a time sequence of spikes and also they fluctuate between occurring more or less frequently.

3. The code division of information conveyed by a single signal is possible because the interspike intervals may follow a distinct and a repetitive behavior, in simple words spikes may occur in a certain temporal pattern.

4. Synchronization between the signal sources may cause two or more signals to exhibit cross-correlation.If the synchronized signals assume a certain spatial distribution, a set of such signals will manifest a spatio-temporal pattern.

According to a recently proposed principle of pattern processing with ISI distribution which hypothetically mimics the olfactory system encoding (Lozowski et al. 2004), the feature of odor molecules could be encoded with ISI distribution produced by a dynamical system. The dynamic system is derived from a Markov process synthesized to incorporate the ISI distribution which is the principal eigenvector of Markov process.

This paper discusses the means of encoding odor information in the olfactory bulb and suggests an implementation for encoding by using a biological neural circuit of spiking integrate-and-fire neurons. This paper also discusses an algorithm using Nelder - Mead to synthesize the transition matrix through a cost function minimization.

2 SIGNAL ENCODING IN OLFACTORY BULB

Olfactory receptors located in the olfactory epithelium region are hardwired to detect a specific odor component. On one end of the receptor there is a dendrite which receives signals from odorants, on the other end is an axon, which projects to the olfactory bulb. Thus olfactory epithelium the input stage to the olfactory system.

The olfactory receptors also called sensory neurons produce spikes, whose frequency (f) of spiking depends on the concentration of the odorants at olfactory epithelium. The larger the intensity of the odorants at olfactory epithelium the more frequent the sensory neurons spike (White et al. 1991).

The concentration information is temporally modulated at the glomerular inputs of the olfactory bulb, therefore the perception of odor intensity must be related to the interspike intervals ($\tau = 1/f$) (Lozowski et al. 2004). If the odor intensity increases, the intervals of spiking decreases at a different rate for each basic odorant due to the differences in their conversion gains.

A much more compressed way to describe odors is through distributions of interspike interval probabilities, which is more relevant to the signals presented to the mitral inputs. Let the interspike intervals be quantized into N ranges with cutoff τ_{max}. Maximum time difference between evoked and spontaneous activity of the receptors is τ_{max}. A single neural signal can represent an odor with the interspike interval τ probability distribution $\mathbf{a}$=$(a_1, a_2, ...a_N)$,which is formally a vector of probabilities by Lozowski et al.(2004):

$$a_n = \begin{cases} Pr(\frac{n-1}{N} < \tau \leq \frac{n}{N}\tau_{max}) & \text{if } n < N \\ Pr(\tau_{max} < \tau) & \text{if } n = N \end{cases} \tag{1}$$

The transformation of the odor into spikes is a dynamical process. The odor information is embedded in the time realizations of signals and can be retrieved only through observation of these signals for a period of time. Statistical analysis of the neural signals retrieves the probability distribution of the interspike intervals. A simple stochastic process can be modeled to have the statistical properties representing a given odor through the probability distribution.

Let a^* according to Lozowski et al.(2004) represent the probability distribution of odor at a steady state, i.e. after all transient response has vanished. A first order approximation of a dynamical system for the odor leads to Markov process with an invariant probability distribution of a^*. Let A $(N \times N)$ be the transition matrix of the Markov process (Lozowski et al. 2002)

$$a(k+1) = Aa(k) \tag{2}$$

The invariant distribution is the eigenvector of transition matrix A associated with the unit eigenvalue: $a^* = Aa^*$, thus we call the invariant distribution as the principal eigenvector of the Markov process.

The realization of the introduced Markov process is a sequence of interspike intervals τ_k. The interval range is defined to be $T_n = [\frac{n-1}{N}\tau_{max}; \tau_{max})$ if $n < N$, and $T_n = [\tau_{max}, \infty)$ otherwise, where the interval range index n is defined in the same manner as in Rospars et al. (2001). Operator A may be developed by using optimization to have a^* as its invariant distribution of interspike intervals over a period of time. The elements of the operator are denoted by A_{ij}, so that $A = [A_{ij}]$, where i and j are the row column indices. Number A_{ij} is the probability that in the Markov process (Lozowski and Noble 2002) an interval from the range τ_i will follow the interval from the range τ_j (Lozowski et al. 2004):

$$A_{ij} = \frac{Pr(\tau_{k+1} \ \in \ T_i \ and \ \tau_k \ \in \ T_j)}{Pr(\tau_k \ \in \ T_j)} \tag{3}$$

For a given a^* starting with some random A_{ij}'s, Nelder-Mead Simplex method of optimization can be used to find the A_{ij}'s corresponding to a minimum cost function value. As all A_{ij}'s are probabilities, they must be real numbers in the range (0,1). Based on this we define a components of cost function Eq. (4) namely quadratic error Eq. (5) and penalty function Eq. (6).

$$F(A) = F_q(A) + F_c(A) \tag{4}$$

Operator A is a probabilistic matrix whose column vectors are normalized probability distributions. Therefore, the columns of A sum up to 1. The cost function component $F_q(A)$ calculates the error of deviation for this condition (Lozowski et al. 2004):

$$F_q(A) = \sum_{j=1}^{N} \left(1 - \sum_{i=1}^{N} A_{ij}\right)^2 \tag{5}$$

The penalty function component of the cost function $F_p(A)$ calculates the sum of individual element penalties, which defines the error due to a particular element swaying out of range 0 to 1. This can be represented by the Eq. (6).

$$F_p(A) = \sum_{i=1}^{N} \sum_{j=1}^{N} \begin{cases} -A_{ij} & \text{if } A_{ij} < 0 \\ (A_{ij} - 1) & \text{if } A_{ij} > 1 \\ 0 & \text{otherwise} \end{cases} \tag{6}$$

Operator A is a well defined transition matrix of Markov process Eq. (2) if $F(A)$=0. The goal of optimization procedure is to develop operator A with the constraint that a^* is its principal eigenvector associated with eigenvalue 1. To simplify the operator synthesis, matrix A will be assumed to be diagonalizable : $A = B\Lambda B^{-1}$. The diagonal matrix $\Lambda = \text{diag}(\lambda)$ is composed of N eigenvalues λ=$(\lambda_1, \lambda_2, \ldots.., \lambda_N)$ of A. Let $\lambda_1 = 1$. The convergence of the dynamical system Eq. (2) depends on the radius of the remaining λ_i's, for $i > 1$, assuming that $|\lambda_i| < r < 1$ and the radius is kept low to improve the convergence rate. In this paper the value of r was fixed to be equal to 0.2. Operator A is diagonal in the basis constructed with the column vectors of B. Since λ_1=1, the first column vector of B is a^*. All other entries B_{ij}, $j > 1$, are the variables in the optimization process. Their initial values are selected randomly from the uniform distribution in the range (-1;1). The optimization process is explained in the next section.

3 SIMPLEX METHOD FOR FUNCTION MINIMIZATION

The Nelder-Mead Simplex method for function minimization (Nelder and Mead 1965) of multiple variables is a classical, very powerful local descent algorithm, which depends on the comparison of function values at the vertices of a general simplex and not on the objective function derivatives. The comparison of function values at vertices is followed by the replacement of the vertex with the highest value by a new point generated in the process of optimization. The simplex adapts itself to the local landscape, and contracts on to the final minimum.

As described in the previous section the first column of the matrix B is the principal eigenvector a^*, the remaining $N(N-1)$ variables in matrix B have to be adjusted to obtain optimum operator A. So, initially considering minimization of a function of $N(N-1)$ variables, thus a simplex of $N(N-1)$ dimensions needs $N(N-1)+1$ points which are formed by randomly selecting values (in the range (-1;1)) for the variables in matrix B and corresponding transition matrices, cost functions $(Y_{(1\times N(N-1)+1)})$ are formed. The $N(N-1)$ variables in each matrix are treated as vertices of the simplex, thus the vertices of simplex are $P_0, P_1, ..., P_{N(N-1)}$. The cost function at point P_i is denoted as Y_i, the highest value among the cost functions is denoted as Y_h (Y_h=$max_{i=0}^{N(N-1)} Y_i$), and the lowest value among the cost functions is denoted as Y_l(Y_l=$min_{i=0}^{N(N-1)} Y_i$). $\overline{P}$ is defined as the centroid of the points with $Y_i \neq Y_h$ and the distance from point P_i to P_j is represented by $[P_iP_j]$.

The simplex goes through a sequence of geometric transformations (expansion-step 1, reflection-step 2, contraction-step 6 and multi-contraction-step 7) at each stage of comparison by replacing the highest by a new point. The optimization process is as follows (R. Chelouah et al. 2003):

1. Determine the $Y_l, Y_h, \overline{P}$ and calculate $P^* = (1+\alpha)\overline{P} - \alpha P_h$ calculate

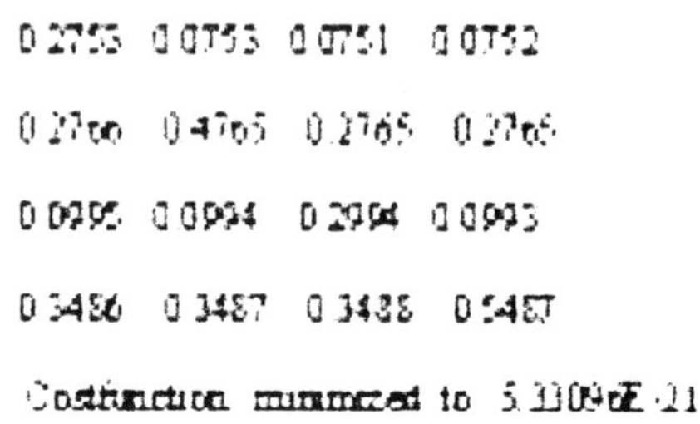

Figure 1: **An example for transition matrix of a four stage Markov process generated by simulator using simplex minimization method**

the cost function at P^* as Y^*.

2. If $Y_l < Y_l$ then form p** and go to step(3) else go to step(4) $P^{**} = (1+\gamma)P^* - \gamma\overline{P}$. calculate the cost function at P^{**} as Y^{**}.

3. If $Y^{**} < Y^*$ then replace P_h by P^{**} and go to step(5).

4. If $Y^* > Y_i$ for all Y_i except Y_h go to step(6).

5. Replace P_h by P^* and go to step(8).

6. If $Y^* < Y_h$ replace P_h by P^*. Form $P^{***} = \beta P_h + (1-\beta)\overline{P}$ and calculate the cost function at P^{**} as Y^{**}.

7. If $Y** > Y_h$ then replace P_i by $\frac{(P_i+P_l)}{2}$, i =0:N, else replace P_h by P^{**}

8. Check if Y_l has reached satisfactory value or zero, if so the optimum value for the matrix B is P_l.

The transition matrix A shown in Fig. 1 is formed with the matrix B obtained from simplex method of minimization. A simple shift-map can be constructed from the probabilistic operator by used in approximation Eq. (7), as described in detail Pingel et al. (2000).

$$f(x) = \frac{1}{A_{ij}}\left(x - j + \sum_{m=1}^{i} A_{mj}\right) + N - i, if j - \sum_{m=1}^{i} A_{ij} \leq x < j + A_{ij} - \sum_{m=1}^{i} A_{mj} \tag{7}$$

A piece-wise linear map as shown in the Fig. 2 $f : [0; N] \rightarrow [0; N], [0, N] \subset R$ is derived from probabilities included in the operator P.

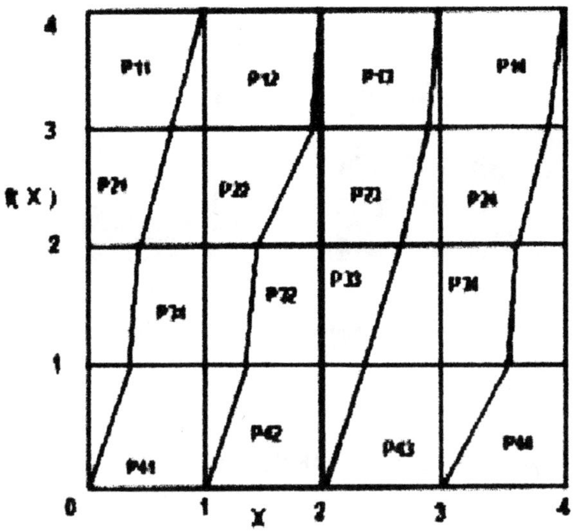

Figure 2: **Example of a piece-wise linear shift map $f(x)$ for the transition matrix shown in Fig. 1**

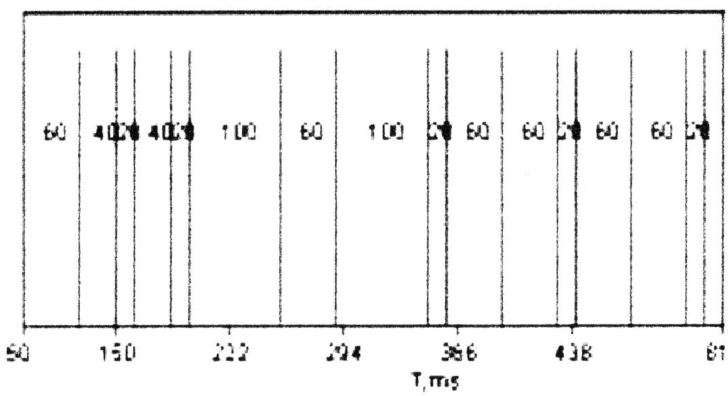

Figure 3: **An example of spike train with specific ISI distribution produced in response to the input pattern *I*={*0.41,0.28,0.41,0.31,0.34*}**

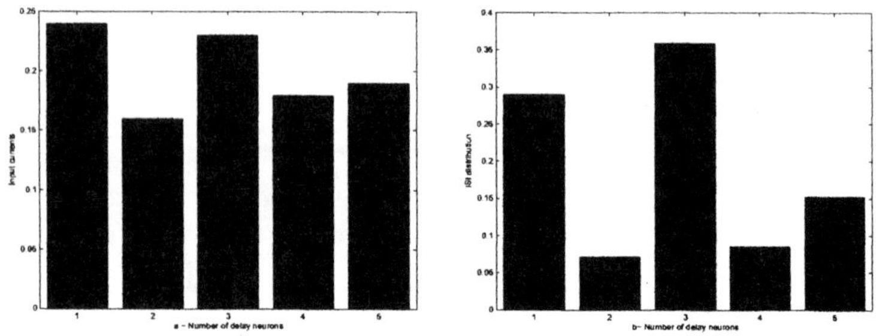

Figure 4: **The pattern of normalized input currents (a) and the resulting ISI distribution (b) of the spike train.**

4 INTERSPIKE INTERVAL GENERATOR

An example of a spike train produced in response to the input pattern $I = \{0.41, 0.28, 0.41, 0.31, 0.34\}$ is shown in Fig. 3. The diagram of the normalized input pattern $I_{norm} = \{0.24; 0.16; 0.23; 0.18; 0.19\}$ and the resulting ISI distribution of 10 seconds spike train are shown in Fig. 4. Here $\rho(ISI_n)$ is the probability of occurrence of the interspike intervals.

Simulator for the interspike interval generator and can be visited at '$http://ci.uofl.edu/currentwork/narem/SIMULATOR/spikegen$'. Fig. 5 shows the example of a spike train produced in response to the input pattern $I = \{0.34, 0.55, 0.27, 0.44, 0.40\}$ and the resulting ISI distribution of 10 second spike train.

Simulator for transition matrix generator can be visited at '$http://ci.uofl.edu/currentwork/narem/SIMULATOR/tranmatrix$'. Transition matrix generated by the simulator and the cost function for the transition matrix with principal eigenvector a^*={0.117,0.3755,0.4047,0.1025} is shown in the Fig. 6. The resulting shift map of the transition matrix is shown in the Fig. 7.

5 CONCLUSIONS

This paper describes a simplest method of encoding information in temporal sequences and show input-output interactions which lead to an odor detection and encoding mechanism. This paper also describes a simulator which generates spike trains with the input controlled distributions of interspike intervals. This paper also describes Simplex method for function

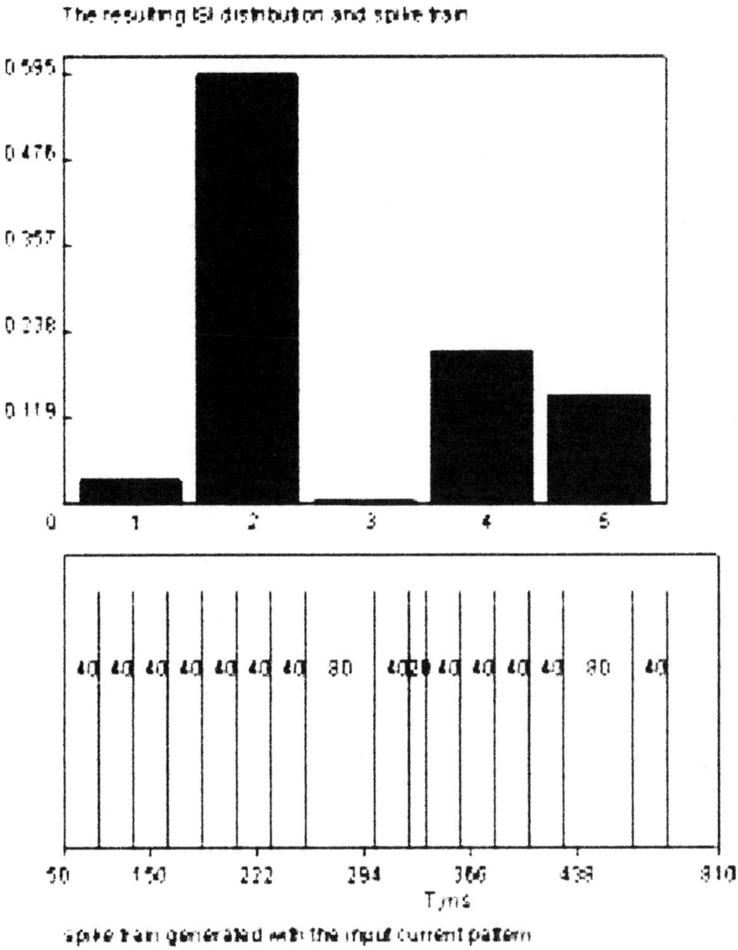

Figure 5: **ISI distribution and spike train produced by the ISI simulator**

```
0.2936 0.0936 0.09367  0.0936

0.3004 0.5004 0.3005   0.3005

0.3236 0.3239 0.5236   0.3239

0.082  0.082  0.0821   0.282

Costfunction minimized  to 1.2413E-20
```

Figure 6: **Transition matrix with principal eigenvector** a^***={0.117,0.3755,0.4047,0.1025} generator generated by the simulator**

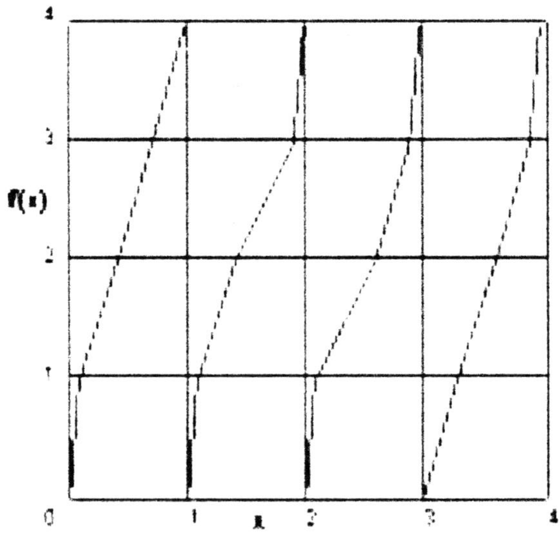

Figure 7: **Shiftmap of the transitoin matrix shown in the Fig. 6**

minimization, a multi-variable function minimization technique.

ACKNOWLEDGMENTS

This work was sponsored by the Department of Navy, Office Of Naval Research, Grant N00014-01-1-0630. The contents of this information does not necessarily reflect the position of the U.S. government.

REFERENCES

Chelouah, R., and Siarry, P., 2003, "Genetic and Nelder-Mead Hybridzed for a more accurate global optimization of continuous multimina functions" *European Journal of Operational Research*, vol. 148, Iss 2, pp.335-348.

Dickson, A.T., White, J., Kauer, J.S., and Walt, R.D., 1998, "Current trends in 'artificial-nose' technology," *Trends in Biotechnology*, Vol. 16,pp.250-258.

Lozowski, G.A., and Noble, L.B., 2002, "Processing Temporal Sequences," in *proc. of the 45th Midwest Symposium on circuits and systems (MSCAS'02)*, vol. 1, (Tulsa, Oklahoma), pp.180-183.

Lozowski, G.A.,Lysetskiy, M., and Zurada, M.J., 2004, "Signal Processing with Temporal Sequences in Olfactory systems," *IEEE Transactions on Neural Networks* (to be published).

Lysetskiy, M., 2003, "Input-Controlled Neural Dynamics And Its Statistics In The Olfactory System Pattern Processing," Ph.D. Dissertation, *University Of Louisville,Louisville,Kentucky.*

Nelder, A.J., and Mead, R., 1965, "A Simplex method for function minimization," *Computer Journal*,vol.7, pp.308-313.

Pingel, D., Schmelcher, P., and Diakonos, F.K., 2000, "Theory and examples of the inverse Frobenius-Perron problem for complete chaotic maps," *Chaos*, vol. 9,no.2,pp.357-366.

Rospars, P.J., Lansky, P., Duchamp-Viret, P., and Duchamp, A., 2001, "Characterizing and modeling concentration response curves of olfactory receptor cells," *Neurocomputing*, vol. 38-40,pp.319-325

White, J., Hamilton, A.K., Neff, R.S., and Kauer, S.R., 1991, "Emergent properties of odor information coding in a representational model of the salamander olfactory bulb," *Journal of Neuroscience*, Vol. 12. pp.

MODELING THE LOCAL BENDING REFLEX OF THE LEECH

CHRIS COULSTON
Electrical and Computer Engineering
Penn State Behrend

THOMAS L. HEMMINGER
Electrical and Computer Engineering
Penn State Behrend

STEFANIE SCHARF
Raytheon Company

THERESA M. VITOLO
Computer and Information Science
Gannon University

ABSTRACT
The first step in a connectionist approach to creating an artificial life form is the reproduction of behaviors using a neurologically accurate simulation. A good model organism is the leech *Hirudo Medicinalis* because it has a simple repertoire of behaviors which are easy to elicit and consistently repeatable. This paper focuses on simulating the local bending reflex, an avoidance behavior used to move away from painful stimulus. Physiological studies have revealed the neurons involved, their interconnections, and their activity during the expression of this behavior. A neurologically accurate simulation of the information processing that occurs during the local bending reflex is created using the GENESIS software package. The parameters of the GENESIS model are derived using an artificial neural network. Experiments show that the simulation mimics observed neurological activity.

INTRODUCTION

The connectionist approach to intelligence argues that the intelligent computing will be actualized by a bottom up approach; intelligence emerges as a byproduct of the neuronal information processing. This thesis implies that models of intelligent information processing must be based on accurate models which capture the salient electronic features of neuronal processing. Nature has a habit of making a virtue out of necessity, consequently introducing too much abstraction may create a model which misses essential details.

Given the complexity of an evolved organism's central nervous system a bottom-up approach to intelligent information processing should start by modeling simple organisms. An ideal starting point is the leech local bending reflex of the leech *Hirudo Medicinalis*. A leech is an aquatic worm with a primitive nervous system and unusually large neurons. Consequently, much is known about the neuronal basis for many of its behaviors [4,5,6].

This paper is organized as follows. The model organism, the leech *Hirudo Medicinalis* is introduced in the second section. The third section introduces the chemical basis for neuron activity. This background is necessary for any detailed simulation. The fourth section introduces the modeling language GENESIS and details of the computational model. The fifth section outlines how the weights are extracted from the artificial neural network, put into the GENESIS model and tested. The fifth section presents our conclusions..

THE LEECH *HIRUDO MEDICINALIS*

The medicinal leech, *Hirudo Medicinalis*, is a segmented aquatic worm [7]. Each segment is a cylindrical portion of the longitudinal axis of the leech's body, see Fig 1. Each cylindrically shaped segment can be further partitioned into four quadrants, dorsal left, dorsal right, ventral left and ventral right, abbreviated Dl, Dr, Vl and Vr respectively. Each of these quadrants has its own sensory input and motor output as discussed below.

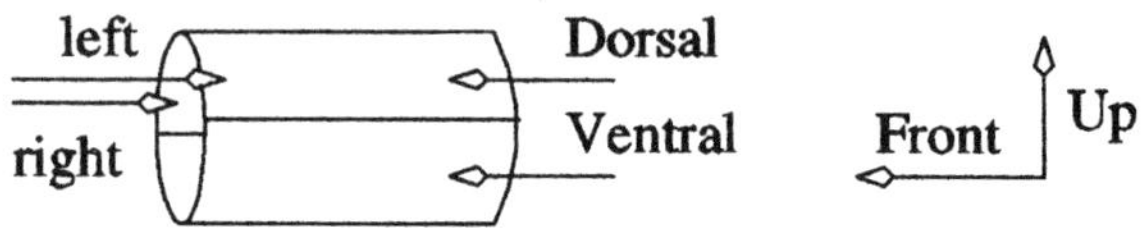

Figure 1: The morphology of the leech body.

Associated with each of its 21 body segments is a nerve packet or ganglia consisting of about 400 neurons [7]. The 21 ganglia are arranged along a spinal cord whose ends are terminated with specialized head and tail ganglia. Each ganglia receives sensory information from its segment and subsequently controls the musculature in its segment. In addition, ganglia receive and transmit information along the spinal cord. Simplifying the study of the leech nervous system is the fact that all 21 ganglia are nearly identical in their structure and functioning.

Each segment has three levels of mechanical perception; touch, pressure and noxious. Each of these three levels is elicited with increasingly vigorous stimulation of the leech's skin. Each of these levels has sensory neurons which become activated with the appropriate stimulation. Because of its role in the local bending reflex, we will focus on the intermediate level perception mode detected by pressure cells, or P-cells for short. There are four P-cells per segment, one for each quadrant. Each is given a label depending on the region from which they receive sensory input; PDl, PDr, PVl and PVr.

Each ganglia has motor neurons which, when stimulated, cause movement in the musculature of the associated segment. Each of the four quadrants of a segment has two types of motor neurons, excitors and inhibitors. When an excitor is stimulated the associated region of the segment contracts. When an inhibitor is stimulated, it inhibits its associated excitor and its associated region of the segment can expand. These eight motor neurons are identified by the abbreviations DEl, DEr, VEl, VEr, DIl, DIr, VIl and VIr.

Interneurons provide the processing interface between sensory input and motor neuron output; interneurons govern the expression of behavior. Structurally, interneurons receive input from sensory neurons and interneurons from their own and neighboring ganglia. Thus, behaviors can be coordinated among segments.

Of the numerous behaviors expressed by the leech, the Local Bending Reflex (LBR) is among the most studied [4,5,6]. The LBR is an avoidance response to mechanical stimulation of the leech body. Initial physiological investigations into the LBR focused on the input/output mapping of this behavior. That is, P-cells were stimulated with current injections and the response elicited at the motor neurons were recorded. The results are reproduced in Table 1 [3]. A "1" entry for a P-cell indicates current was injected (resulting in stimulation) of that neuron. The values for the output neurons represent the mean deviation (in millvolts) from the nominal activity levels.

Left		Right		Left				Right			
PV	PD	PD	PV	DI	VI	DE	VE	DI	VI	DE	VE
0	1	0	0	-3.4	-1.4	5.0	-2.6	-0.1	3.9	3.2	-6.5
1	0	0	0	-0.2	-2.9	-3.7	4.8	5.1	3.7	-7.6	-3.6
0	1	1	0	-4.7	1.8	7.6	-7.1	-4.7	1.8	7.6	-7.1
1	0	0	1	4.3	1.2	-9.0	3.8	4.3	1.2	-9.0	3.8
1	1	0	0	-2.9	-2.4	3.6	2.9	3.5	5.0	-1.9	-6.3
0	0	1	0	-0.1	3.9	3.2	-6.5	-3.4	-1.4	5.0	-2.6
0	0	0	1	5.1	3.7	-7.6	-3.6	-0.2	-2.9	-3.7	4.8
0	0	1	1	3.5	5.0	-1.9	-6.3	-2.9	-2.4	3.6	2.9

Table 1: Input output behavior of the LBR.

After determining the I/O behavior of the neurons involved in the LBR, a painstaking search identified 9 interneurons which are both necessary and sufficient to express the local bending reflex [5]. The topology is a completely connected 3-layer feedforward network shown in Fig 2. As can be seen from this figure the motor neurons of the leech have self inhibiting connections which ensure exclusive activity of the inhibitors and excitors [7].

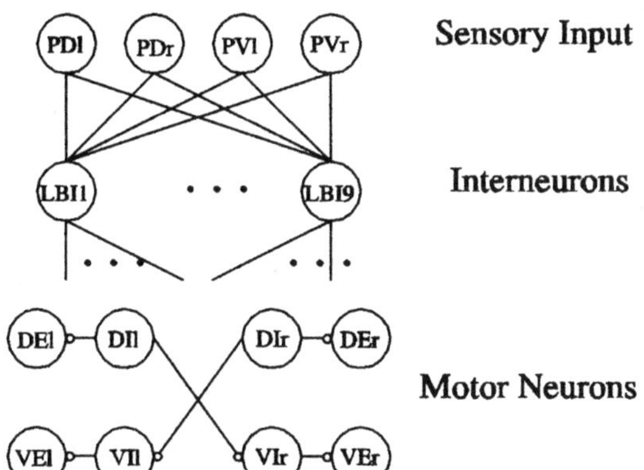

Figure 2: The neurons invoved in the LBR and their interconnections.

Unfortunately, the data gathered from these experiments does not describe the connection efficiency to/from the interneurons. These connection strengths will be determined using a standard back propagation algorithm.

NEURAL INFORMATION PROCESSING

Neurons are living cells which participate in those processes required to sustain themselves. In addition to these processes, neurons have the remarkable ability to integrate and transmit electrical signals over a distance. The electrical properties of the neuron can be categorized into passive and active components. The passive behavior of a neuron is characterized by a internal voltage of -50mV with respect to the extracellular environment. This voltage represents an equilibrium between two ions, sodium (Na^+) and potassium (K^+). The "+" sign indicates that each of these ions carries with it an excess positive charge. In its nominal state, the cell membrane of a neuron actively moves K^+ ions into the neuron and Na+ ions out of the neuron. This imbalance of ions induces a voltage to develop across the cell membrane. The potential induced by an ion type X^+, denoted E_x is given by the Nerst equation [2].

$$E_x = C \ln(X^+_o / X^+_i)$$

C is a constant equal to 25 at room temperature, X^+_o is the concentration of X^+ ions outside the membrane, and X^+_i is the concentration of X^+ ions inside the membrane. In a typical cell the ratio of potassium K^+_o:K^+_i is 1:20 and sodium Na^+_o:Na^+_i is 8:1. Consequently, the nominal potential of a neuron is somewhere between that established by potassium, -75mV, and sodium,+52mV.

Small perturbations of the cell membrane voltage fall off as 1/r, where r is the distance from the site of the disturbance. The relationship is derived from the fact that the cell membrane acts as a resistive element and that the area of membrane at a distance is linear in r. Since the amplitude of the disturbance diminishes rapidly as it travels along the neuron, this phenomenon cannot account for signal transmission over long distances.

The active behavior of a neuron is characterized by the action potential; a pulse of electrical activity which propagates down the axon. An action potential is initiated by a voltage disturbance which exceeds a constant firing threshold. When this happens the neuron reacts by increasing the permeability of the neuron to Na^+. This causes the voltage to increase further increasing the permeability to sodium. As the membrane nears its peak of 52mV, the membrane becomes permeable to K^+. This induces K^+ to move out of the cell dropping the potential back toward the resting potential

The propagation of an action potential relies on two mechanisms. Since the membrane is resistive in nature then a voltage perturbation of 40mV will increase the potential of the neighboring membrane. Second, after it has experienced an action potential, a membrane patch has a refractory period during which it cannot be induced into having another action potential. Hence, an action potential will cause the neighboring patches of membrane to exceed their firing threshold. However, since the membrane to the rear is still recuperating, only the membrane in front of the action potential will be induced into generating an action potential and thus propagating the action potential down the neuron.

THE GENESIS MODELING PARADIGM

GENESIS, the General Neural Simulation System, was developed in 1985 at Caltech in order to provide a means of creating biologically realistic neural simulations [1]. GENESIS allows a user to create an arbitrarily refined model of neural computation and neural networks. In addition, GENESIS provides users the ability to create graphical interfaces to their simulations using an intuitive scripting language. The electrical activity of a neuron is based on the Hodkins Huxley equations [2]. These equations describe the passive and active modes of neuron activity in terms of the equivalent electrical circuit shown in Fig 3.

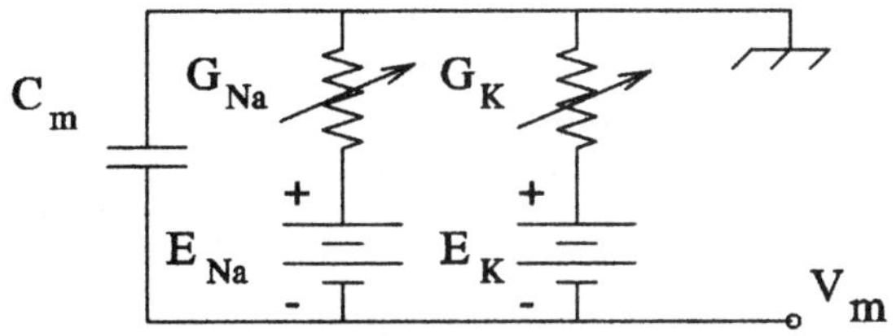

Figure 3: An equivlent circuit of a neuron membrane.

This circuit describes the membrane potential V_m in terms of the passive ion potentials E_{Na} and E_k given by the Nerst equations and the impedance of the membrane to sodium and potassium G_{Na} and G_k respectively. An action potential is generated by this model by the appropriate manipulation through time of $G_k(t)$ and $G_{Na}(t)$.

A generic GENESIS neuron was developed, replicated and connected together to form a network identical to that shown in Fig 3. The only piece of information missing in this model is the strength or efficiency of the connections between the neurons. Since each of the 4 input neurons makes 9 connections to the interneurons, and each interneurons makes 8 connections with the motors neurons, there are a total of 4x9+9x8=108 weights. Artificial Neural Networks (ANNs) were used to provide a systematic method of deriving these weights.

A 3-layer neural network was trained with the data in Table 1. In order to produce an output over the entire range, all the neurons were given linear activation functions. After the weights were determine by the ANN they were plugged into the GENESIS simulation.

A graphical interface was created to enhance the interaction with the GENESIS model. This interface allows users to stimulate any combination of the sensory neurons and observe the activity of any neuron in a voltage vs. time graph.

EXPERIMENTS

A 2-layer feedforward ANN was created and trained, using backpropagation, on the data in Table 1. The ANN trained in a remarkably short period of time. Within 20 epochs the error would consistently come within 4% of the best solutions. The weights derived from the ANN were then exported into the GENESIS model of the LBR. The P-cells of the GENESIS model were then stimulated and the responses of the GENESIS model were then compared against observed values from physiological experiments given in Table 1. This process was repeated 8 times.

On average the sign of the GENESIS response agreed with the observed response 68% of the time with a standard deviation of +/- 4%. For each motor neuron, the average absolute error in the response was 75%. The was significant deviation in these errors.

CONCLUSIONS

It seems obvious that the solution space for the ANN is rich with good solutions; the 108 dimensional solutions space need only accommodate 8 patterns. Consequently, the ANN converged very rapidly (within 20 epochs) and there were many good solutions. Many different ANN solutions were submitted to the GENESIS model for testing.

While these errors may seem high, there is a significant deviation in the motor neuron responses in different leech preparations. From published data [5], there is an average deviation of 5% in the magnitude of the motor neuron responses.

Future work will be aimed at creating better GENESIS models of the leech motor neurons. Future work will also be aimed at investigating what effect the activation function has on the resulting GENESIS model. Its possible that a new activation function may better capture the dynamics of the motor neurons. While there is a lot of work left to be done, this work represents the first steps towards a constructionist, bottom-up, approach towards behavior.

REFERENCES

[1] B.Bower and D. Beeman, *The Book of GENESIS*. Springer-Verlag, NY, 1995.

[2] S.W. Kuffler and J.G. Nicholls, *From Neuron to Brain*. Sinauer Associates, Sunderland MA, 1975.

[3] S.R.Lockery. Personal communication.

[4] S.R.Lockery and W.B. Kristan, Distributed Processing of Sensory Information in the Leech. I. Input-Output Relations of the Local Bending Reflex. *The Journal of Neuroscience* .pp. 1811-1815, 1990.

[5] S.R.Lockery and W.B. Kristan, Distributed Processing of Sensory Information in the Leech. II. Identification of Interneurons Contributing to the Local Bending Reflex. *The Journal of Neuroscience*. pp. 1816-1829, 1990.

[6] S.R.Lockery and T.J. Sejnowski, Distributed Processing of Sensory Information in the Leech. III. A Dynamic Neural Network Model of the Local Bending Reflex. *The Journal of Neuroscience*. pp. 387-404, 1992.

[7] K. Muller, J. Nicholls and G. Stent, G. 1981. *Neurobiology of the Leech*. Cold Spring Harbor Laboratory, Cold Spring Harbor NY, 1981.

MODELING AND SYNTHESIS OF HUMAN GROWTH HORMONE SECRETION MECHANISM USING CAD TOOLS

Nazeih Botros, Jaafar Alghazo, Adil Akaaboune, John Shell
Southern Illinois University at Carbondale
Department of Electrical and Computer Engineering
Carbondale, Illinois.

ABSTRACT
In this paper we present a hardware realization of Human Growth Hormone (HGH) secretion mechanism. The mechanism is developed into a mathematical model and then modeled using Hardware Description Languages (HDL). Computer Aided Design (CAD) tools are implemented to synthesize the mechanism onto Xilinx FPGAs chip. The chip is tested by inputting signals with values corresponding to the concentrations of GHRH and SRIF. A user-selected output pins on the chip show the concentration of HGH. The output of the chip is compared with those generated by the simulation. Both the simulation and the chip generate identical patterns.

INTRODUCTION

To understand the function of biological mechanisms in human body and to develop drugs to treat the malfunction in a particular mechanism, scientists and researchers need to carry out extensive investigations of the mechanisms. Because of ethical issues or other constraints, performing medical experiments on humans and animals are extremely limited and in some instances are prohibited. The goal of this paper is to model the Human Growth Hormone (HGH) secretion mechanism and to realize the model on an integrated electronic chip. After realization, the chip mimics the realized mechanism. Figure 1a shows a general diagram of how the chip may be interfaced with the human body and tested to explore the effect of external stimuli such as drugs on the mechanism. Effect of drugs on the body is detected by appropriate sensors and the output signals of the sensors are transmitted to the input pins of the chip. Figure 1b shows another set up where the realized mechanism on the chip may be tested in lab environment with no human contact.

The Hormones of the anterior pituitary are synthesized and secreted in response to hypothalamic releasing hormones. These releasing hormones either stimulate or inhibit the secretion of a particular pituitary hormone. Growth Hormone Releasing Hormone (GHRH) stimulates the secretion of HGH. On the other hand, Somatostatin or Somatotrophin Releasing Inhibiting Factor (SRIF) inhibits the secretion of HGH/GH. Releasing hormones are secreted in response to neural inputs from the

Central Nervous System (CNS). The neural inputs are produced by external affects to the body or by changes happening within the body. Physiologically the main action of HGH is its stimulatory effects on the growth of the body during childhood

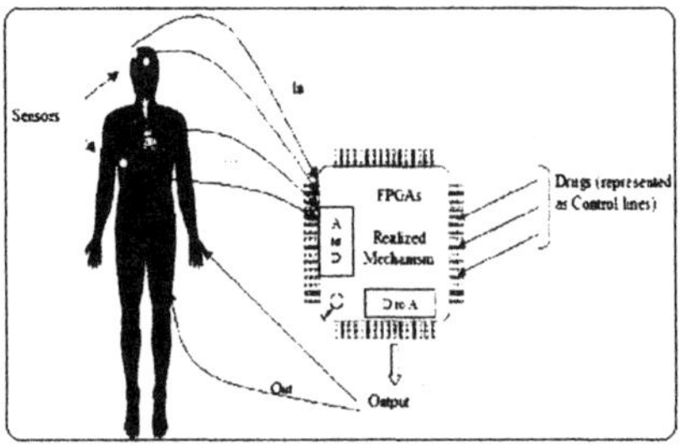

Figure 1a. Real environment

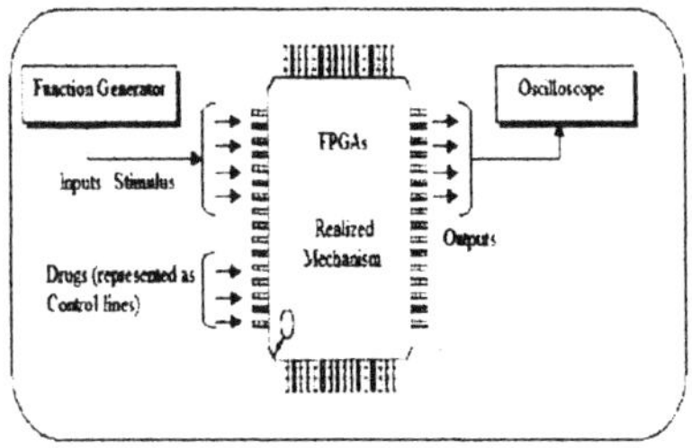

Figure 1b. Lab environment

Verilog Hardware Description Language is implemented to model the behavior of the HGH secretion mechanism, [Botros et al 2000][Botros and Abdul-Aziz 1999]. Xilinx tools are implemented to realize the model onto a Field Programmable Gate Arrays (FPGAs) chip such as the chip used in this paper, Xilinx XSA-50. After realization, the chip mimics the HGH secretion mechanism. To test the realization, input signals representing the value of Growth Hormone Releasing Hormone (GHRH) and Somatotrophin Releasing Inhibiting Factor (SRIF) are applied to user-selected pins on the chip. The output signals representing HGH can be viewed at user selected pins. Both the input and output signals can be in digital (discrete) form or analog (continuous) form. In case of continuous, Analog-to-Digital (A/D) and Digital-to-Analog (D/A) converters must be used.

HUMAN GROWTH HORMONE MECHANISM

Two opposing hypothalamic releasing hormones regulate HGH secretion. Growth Hormone Releasing Hormone (GHRH) as a stimulator of the secretion of HGH, and Somatotrophin Releasing Inhibiting Factor (SRIF) as an inhibitor that inhibits the action of GHRH. The predomination of one of these two hormones determines the level of secretion of HGH. Figure 2 shows the human growth hormone secretion mechanism.

Mathematical Model for GROWTH HORMONE MECHANISM

The rate of concentration of growth hormone (GH), rate of concentration of Somatotrophin Releasing Inhibiting Factor (SRIF), and the rate of concentration of Growth Hormone Releasing Hormone (GHRH) can be written as follows [Farhy et al. 2001 and 2002]:

$$\frac{dGH}{dt} = = -k_1 GH + \alpha\, k_{r,1}\left[\frac{(Pool/t_0)^{n_0}}{(Pool/t_0)^{n_0}+1}\,\frac{(GHRH/t_1)^{n_1}}{(GHRH/t_1)^{n_1}+1}\,\frac{1}{(SRIF/t_2)^{n_2}+1}\right] \quad \ldots\ldots.(1)$$

$$\frac{dSRIF}{dt} = -k_2\, SRIF + S_{min} + k_{r,2,gh}\frac{GH(t-D)/t_3}{1+GH(t-D)/t_3} + k_{r,2,ghrh}\frac{(GHRH(t-T)/t_6)^{n_6}}{(GHRH(t-T)/t_6)^{n_6}+1} \quad \ldots\ldots\{2\}$$

$$\frac{dGHRH}{dt} = -k_3 GHRH + k_{r,3}\left[\frac{1}{(SRIF/t_4)^{n_4}+1}\frac{1}{(GH/t_5)^{n_5}+1}\right] \quad\text{........(3)}$$

$$\frac{dPool}{dt} = k_{r,4}\frac{(GHRH/t_7)^{n_7}}{(GHRH/t_7)^{n_7}+1}[M-Pool] - k_{r,1}\left[\frac{(Pool/t_0)^{n_0}}{(Pool/t_0)^{n_0}+1}\frac{(GHRH/t_1)^{n_1}}{(GHRH/t_1)^{n_1}+1}\frac{1}{(SRIF/t_2)^{n_2}+1}\right] \quad \ldots \{4\}$$

Pool is the amount of releasable GH concentration levels stored in the pituitary gland. *M* defines the maximum amount of GH in the pool. *Smin* is the minimum baseline required for SRIF release. α is a scaling constant that is used to relate the pituitary and circulatory distribution volume. The constants k_1, k_2 and k_3 describe the rates of hormonal elimination. The other constants $k_{r,1}$, $k_{r,2,gh}$, $k_{r,2,ghrh}$, $k_{r,3}$ and $k_{r,4}$ signify the rate of release. Whereas t_1, t_2, t_4, t_5, t_6 and t_7 are the threshold levels eliciting a response in the interfaces in Figure 4.

The constants n0, n1, n2, n4, n5, n6 and n7 are the Hill Coefficients. Hill coefficients are a measure of how hormones might bind to a receptor site. D is the time delay for the GH feedback effect on SRIF and T is the time delay for the GHRH feed-forward effect on SRIF. The four nonlinear delay differential equations depicting the model are solved using MATLAB to produce GH, SRIF and GHRH concentration levels changing over time. Figures 3 shows GH, GHRH and SRIF concentration as a function of time for male and female. The pulsatile behavior of GH is evident in these figures.

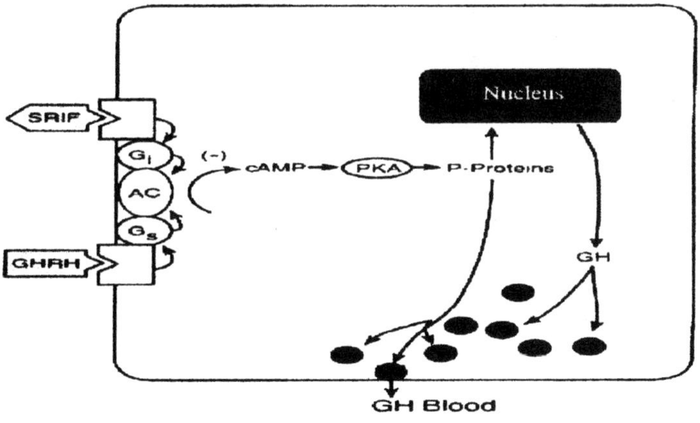

Figure 2. HGH secretion mechanism

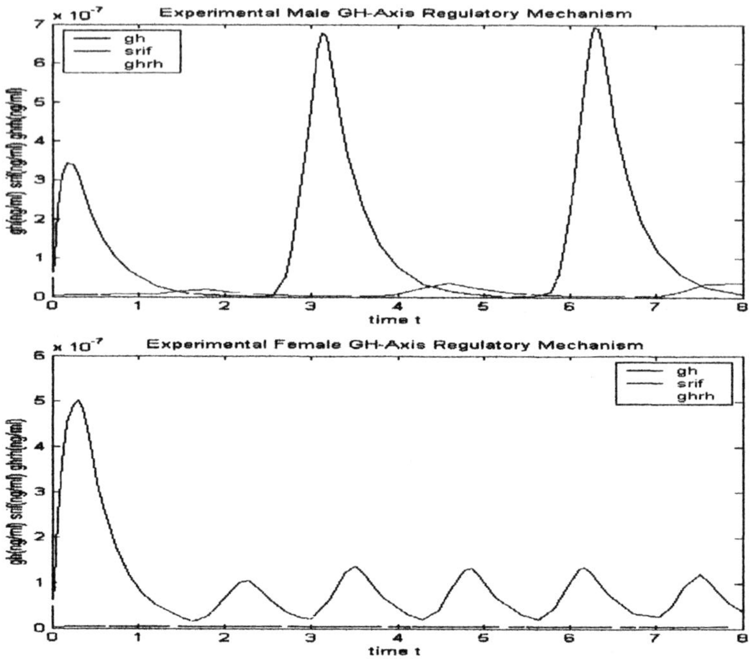

Figure 3: Combined Simulated GH, SRIF, and GHRH Profiles.

RESULTS

Figure 4 shows the steps implemented to realize the mechanism. These steps can be generalized to realize more complex mechanisms. A Verilog HDL code has been written to describe the mechanism. Figure 5 shows the simulation results based on that code. Figure 6 shows the hardware realization of the HGH mechanism on a Xilinx FPGAs chip. Binary representations of the hormonal concentrations are displayed relative to time and driven by the internal chip oscillator. The decimal representations of the binary output are time = 5, GH = 84 ng/ml, GHRH = 1854 pg/ml and SRIF = 32 pg/ml. The programmable oscillator of the chip was reprogrammed to allow a casual observation of the output concentration levels of the hormones relative to time.

CONCLUSION

In this paper we have presented an approach for modeling and realization of Human Growth Hormone (HGH) Mechanism using VHDL and FPGAs. The mathematical model is developed and Verilog HDL modeling is used to simulate the mechanism. After verification of the simulation, the mechanism is realized on FPGAs chip using Xilinx CAD tools. Signals on the input and output pins of the chip are checked to verify that the chip mimics the mechanism. The experimental results show that the desired specifications are achieved.

The same technique presented here can be implemented to realize more complex systems. With the continuous growth of digital technology in terms of new upgraded CAD tools and larger density storage electronic chips, realization of more complex mechanisms can be achieved in the near future.

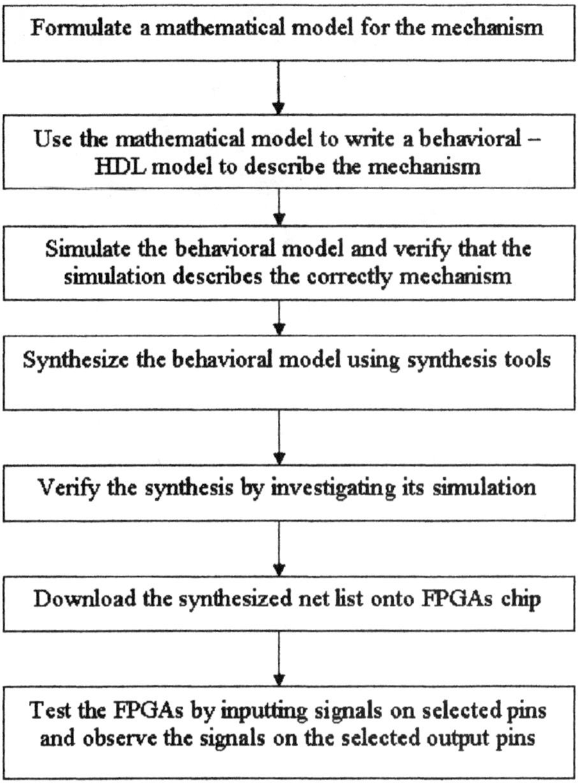

Figure 4: steps for realizing the HG Mechanism.

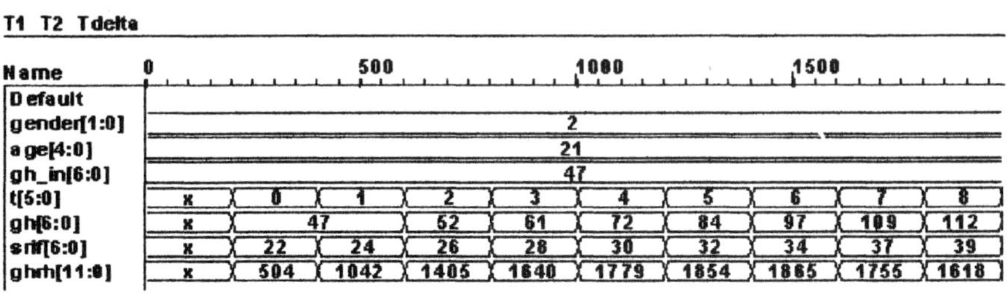

Figure 5: Simulation results at t =5.

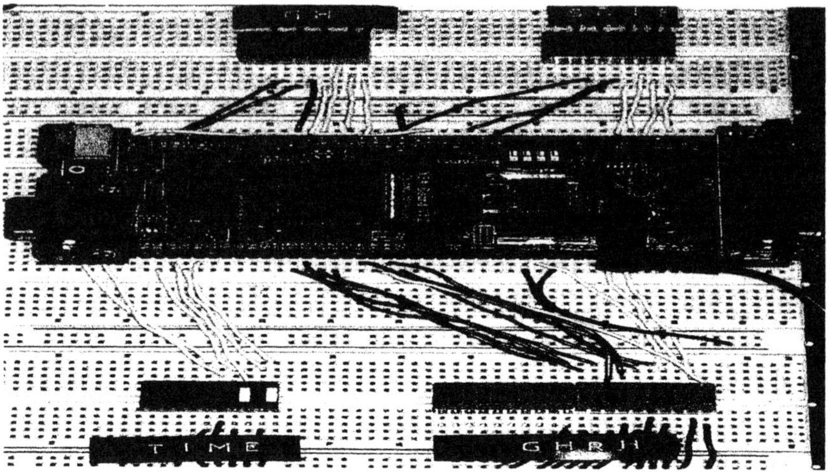

Figure 6: Hardware realization of GH secretion at t=5.

REFERENCES

[1] Botros, N., Akaaboune, M., Alghazo, J. and Alhreish, M., 2000, " Hardware Realization of Biological Mechanisms Using VHDL and FPGAs," *Technical Proceedings of the Third International Conference on Modeling and Simulation of Microsystems, San Diego, CA,* pp. 233-234.

[2] Botros, N. and Abdul-Aziz, M., 1999, " Hardware Implementation of an Artificial Neural Network Using Field Programmable Gate Arrays (FPGAs)," *IEEE Tran. Ind. Electron.*, Vol. 46, no. 1, pp. 3-12.

[3] Farhy, L. S., Straume, M., Johnson, M.L., Kovatchev, B. and Veldhuis, J.D., 2002, "Unequal autonegative feedback by GH models the sexual dimorphism in GH secretory dynamics", *Am J Physiol Regulatory Integr Comp Physiol* 282, pp 753-764.

[4] Farhy, L. S., Straume, M., Johnson, M.L., Kovatchev, B. and Veldhuis, J.D., 2001, "A Construct of interactive feedback control of the GH axis in the female", *Am J Physiol Regulatory Integr Comp Physiol* 281, pp. 38-51.

ANALYSIS OF EQUINE GAITPRINT

ELLEN BAJCAR
University of Guelph
Computing and Information Science
Guelph, Ontario, CANADA

DAVID CALVERT
University of Guelph
Computing and Information Science
Guelph, Ontario, CANADA

JEFF THOMASON
University of Guelph
Biomedical Science
Guelph, Ontario, CANADA

ABSTRACT

Early detection and evaluation of lameness in horses can be achieved by visual assessment by an expert. This evaluation is difficult for non-experts and it would be beneficial if a tool existed to assist with the task. This work evaluates strain measurements taken from the hoof of a moving horse in an attempt to identify characteristics of the horse. A Self-Organizing Map is trained to cluster strain data and the results are analyzed. This method successfully identifies various stride characteristics such as shoeing, gait, speed, and direction of movement and produces a unique cluster for each horse's gait.

INTRODUCTION

Studies [2][4] indicate that there is an unexploited potential of using Artificial Neural Networks to assist in the diagnosis and assessment of lameness, classification of gait characteristics and other kinematic features that may influence the way in which a horse's hooves are maintained. For clinical analysis it seems that a small number of kinematic parameters is sufficient to classify a movement pattern [5]. The objective of this work was to develop a system which demonstrates that the strain measurement data collected from a single hoof of a moving horse can be analyzed with a Self-Organizing Map (SOM) in order to classify various stride characteristics of the horse.

STRAIN DATA

The data is part of a database from the Ontario Veterinary College which includes a collection of strain gauge measurements from the hooves of over 150 thoroughbreds. The subset used for this work includes 35 horses of various breeds. The data set provides a variety of combinations of features, including the type of shoe, direction and how the horse was moving during each run, the gait, the speed, the substrate, the foot to which the sensor is attached, if the horse was ridden, and the angles of the toe and heel. The measurements have been captured by placing a rosette of five sensors on a single hoof of a horse for the duration of each three-minute run. The sensors were placed around the hoof, evenly spaced between the medial heel, anterior and the lateral heel. The data used were sampled at a frequency of 67 hertz. Each sensor measures three values representing the 90-degree vector components of the strain force exerted on the hoof wall by each of the five sensors. Measurements are converted into the two principle forces and the angle between them. The data spans the stance phase of the stride, during which the foot is in full contact with the ground and the horse's weight passes over the limb. Fifty measurements of strain are used and these are evenly distributed over this timeframe.

Individual sensors and force components were used to create an input vector of fifty components. The fifty measurements from the individual sensors are concatenated for each of the five sensors, creating new pattern that had a length of 150 components using the medial, lateral, and anterior sensors, and a length of 250 using all five sensors. Each of these input patterns were used to train the SOM.

DATA ANALYSIS

For each data point in the sample, the maximum, minimum, average, standard deviation, and variance were calculated and graphed. Although each horse appears to have its own unique pattern, it is visually difficult to identify what differentiates one pattern from the others. The patterns indicated the high dimensionality of the data and complexity of the relationships among the features.

Knowing that the data contains samples from a lame horse, an attempt was made to detect significant variation in the hope of identifying the lame horse. Since the diagnosis of lameness is based on specific deviations from normal movement patterns, all data and statistical results were examined for unusual patterns that may represent the changes in the strain pattern of a lame horse. The patterns were examined for indications of reduced weight bearing, delayed impact, and early lift-off during the stride. It was found that each horse is unique, some have longer strides, others are lighter on the hoof. Instead of finding a single cluster which identified lameness, the search lead to the discovery that each horse has a unique gait which is more similar to itself than to the gaits of other horses. The gait can be further analyzed to reveal characteristics of the horse's movement.

GAIT FINGERPRINT EXPERIMENT

This experiment uses a SOM to reduce the high dimensionality of the strain date into a two-dimensional map. The best results were achieved using a hexagonal lattice topology, Gaussian kernel neighborhood, linear initialization, and neighborhood radius of 10 for the initial epoch and radius of 3 for the fine-tuning epochs. The map size was optimized by the network. At least 20 epochs are required to obtain these results.

The most interesting results were produced by the SOM in clustering the strides of the individual horses. The dataset contained 10,387 samples from 21 different horses and an input vector of 33 elements from the anterior, medial, and lateral sensors each, as the input. The SOM organized the samples in a hexagonal lattice of 513 units. Samples from each horse formed 22 distinct labeled clusters, one for each horse in the sample population, as illustrated in Figure 1. Horse 11 was the exception and always formed two clusters.

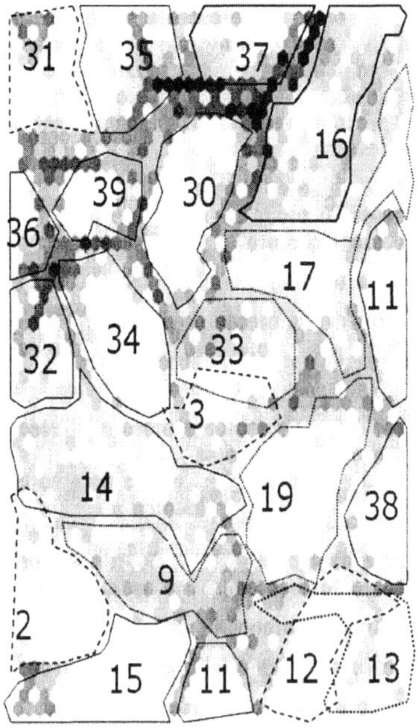

Figure 1: Map showing 22 distinct clusters, one for each of the 21 horses and two for Horse 11.

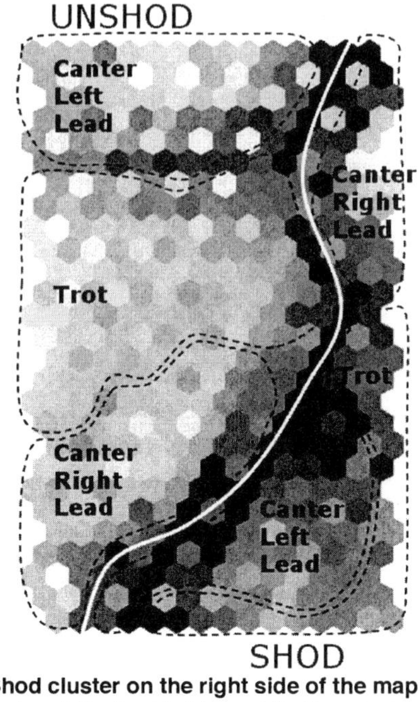

Figure 2: Subclusters for Horse 12. Shod cluster on the right side of the map is grouped by gait--Canter Left Lead, Trot and Canter Right Lead (bottom to top) and unshod cluster on the left side of the map grouped by gait, same clusters, top to bottom.

These results indicate that a natural clustering occurs based on the individual horse's gait characteristics. Each horse appears to develop its own unique "gait fingerprint", and the similarity of the stride characteristics for a single horse is greater than the similarity of strides between different horses.

SUBDIVISION OF CLUSTERS

Initially the samples for an individual horse appear to overlap, making the partitioning based on other features difficult. A closer examination of the clusters reveals a hierarchical relationship among the features. This hierarchical class relationship is observed to hold for the following features: {horseID (shoeing (gait (direction, speed)))}. In other words, the horse's gait fingerprint divides into the shoeing classes, namely {shod, unshod, corrective shoe}, each of which further divides into direction or speed groups. The relationship between direction and speed could not be identified. Similarly, the hierarchy did not identify whether the horse was moving on a treadmill, lunged or was ridden.

Each cluster is divided into two sub-clusters, one corresponding to the shod and the other to the unshod samples. Each shoeing sub-cluster exhibits grouping based upon the different gaits. Each gait sub-cluster in turn is organized by the speed. Although the horse clusters can also be subdivided into how the horse is ridden and how it is moving, there is not sufficient data to determine where in the hierarchy this sub-clustering belongs. Whether or not the horse is wearing a corrective shoe is grouped at the same level as the shod and unshod clusters.

When examining individual horse's clusters, the sub-clusters exist first at the shoeing level. Such as for Horse 12, the cluster is clearly divided into shod and unshod sub-clusters, illustrated in Figure 2. Then each shoeing sub-cluster is further divided into the gait sub-clusters. In the shod sub-cluster, three distinct clusters appear, one for trot, one for canter left lead, and the third for canter right lead. The same gait clusters can be observed in the unshod sub-cluster. When only shod and trot examples are clustered, a different grouping can be detected. It is evident that a sub-clustering occurs in terms of speed, illustrated in Figure 3. As the horse increases speed, the samples are grouped to best match units near the same location on the map, starting at the bottom row and terminating at the top row.

In Figure 4, a similar pattern can be observed in terms of direction. The samples representing the left turn aggregate in the top third of the map, across both the shod and unshod clusters. The samples when the horse was moving straight, aggregate in the middle third of the map, and those representing a right turn fall in the bottom third of the map. The centre for both shod and unshod strides when the horse is moving straight, appears on the left-end of the middle third. All the other combinations fan outwards from this point.

The hierarchy suggests that each horse has its own *gait fingerprint* or *gaitprint*. For each horse the strongest factor that influences the horse's stride is shoeing. The gait characteristics differ if the horse is shod or not shod or wearing corrective shoes. The gait in turn determines how the pattern differs for the direction the horse is moving or how it is ridden. The only clustering that does not appear to follow the same pattern is Horse11 data. In this case, no known characteristic appears to overlap the distribution of the two clusters.

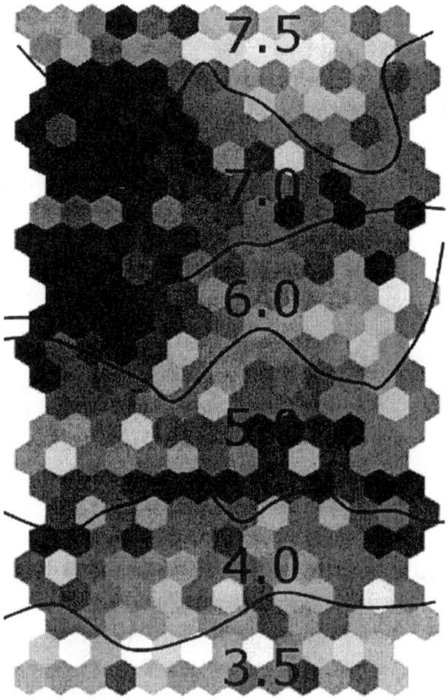

Figure 3: Clustering at the Speed level for Horse 35. The cluster at the bottom of the lattice corresponds to 3.5 m/s, the cluster at the top of the lattice to the fastest speed of 7.5 m/s.

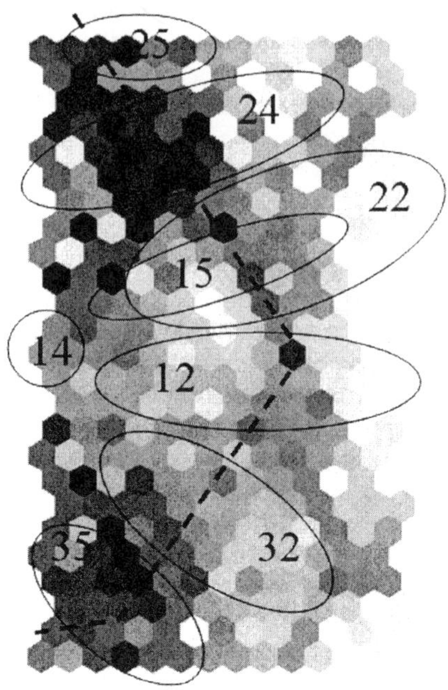

Figure 4: Samples clustered by direction: 25 left turn canterRL, 24 left turn canterLL, 22 left turn trot, 12 straight trot, 14 straight canterLL, 15 strainght canter right lead, 32 right turn trot, 35 right turn canterRL.

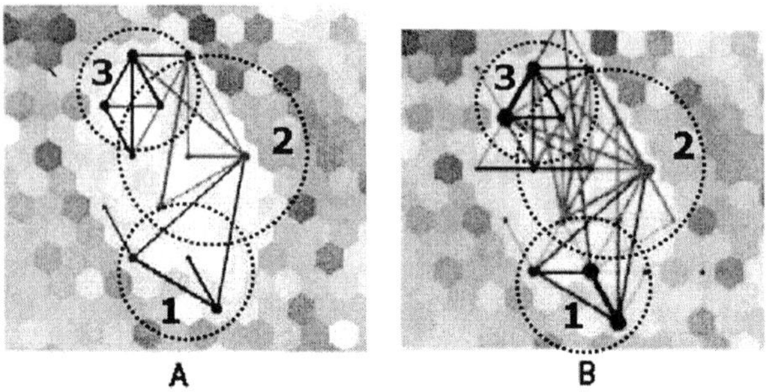

Figure 5: Segment of the distance map for Horse 35, showing the trajectory of the sequence of stride samples. Circle 1: samples from the beginning of a single run. Circle 2: samples from the middle of the run. Circle 3: samples from the end of the run.

PROGRESSION THROUGH THE RUN

Further analysis was performed to examine the local structure of the clusters as the stride changes. The method used was to visualize the trajectory of the successive samples, monitoring the pattern's best matching unit (BMU) on the map. In Figure 5A, the dark dots and lines in Cicle 1 represent the BMU for the first seven strides, the light dots and lines in Cicle 2 represent seven strides in the middle of the run, and dark dots and lines in Cicle 3 represent the last seven strides of the same run. The dots increase in size with each stride and the lines thicken to indicate the more frequented path between the hits. Each part of the run appears to have its own centre, the beginning is distinct from the middle and the end of the run. The latter two groups overlap more than the first two groups. Figure 5B illustrates representation of the same run, tracing 30 strides instead of seven. The transition between early, mid, and late run clusters is still visible.

CONCLUSIONS

Based on the results of this work, it has been shown that the SOM can be used to analyze hoof strain data and that it has the ability to distinguish stride characteristics, to organize the relationships among the features in a hierarchical manner, and to classify the indicators of the hoof's conformity and other kinematic features.

REFERENCES

[1] Simon Haykin, *Neural Networks, A Comprehensive Foundation*, 2nd ed. Prentice Hall, 1999.

[2] Saira Ahmad, D. Calvert, D.A. Stacey, and J.J. Thomason, *Architectures for Equine Gait Analysis*, Intelligent Engineering Systems Through Artificial Neural Networks, 2001.

[3] David Calvert, Neil Harvey, and J.J. Thomason, *Identification of lameness in horses using strain data*, Artificial Neural Networks in Engineering, 2002.

[4] H.H.C.M. Salvelberg, J.P. Loon, and H.C. Schamhardt, *Ground Reaction forces in horses assessed from hoof wall deformation using artificial neural networks*, Equine Veterinary Journal, 1997.

[5] H.M. Clayton, and H.C. Schamhardt, *Measurement Techniques for Gait Analysis*, 1996.

PART XI: SMART SYSTEMS ENGINEERING

A NEURAL NETWORK MODELLING OF LOOK-AHEAD TIME IN BOOK-AHEAD RESERVATION IN QoS-ENABLED NETWORKS

I. AHMAD, J. KAMRUZZAMAN, S. ASWATHANARAYANIAH
Gippsland School of Computing and IT, Monash University, Australia

ABSTRACT- This paper proposes an application of Artificial Neural Network (ANN) in modelling of look-ahead time in Book-Ahead (BA) reservation to control the preemption rate of on-going calls in a QoS-enabled network. Resource sharing between Book-Ahead (BA) and Instantaneous Request (IR) reservation often results in high preemption rate of on-going IR calls. A number of call admission control models have been proposed in literature to reduce IR preemption rate. Most of the models use a tuning parameter which is adjusted manually to achieve desired level of preemption rate. This paper uses an ANN-based model which is trained to map network traffic parameters and preemption rate to appropriate tuning parameter. Once trained, this model can be used to automatically produce correct parameter value necessary to achieve desired preemption rate. Simulation results show that desired level of preemption rate is achievable with high accuracy using the proposed ANN-based model.

INTRODUCTION

For decades, Artificial Neural Network (ANN) has been a useful tool to solve a number of complex problems in Quality of Service (QoS) provisioning in communication research. Neural networks have been successfully exercised in solving QoS related problems like routing, resource allocation, call admission control, traffic pattern estimation, packet loss estimation, network parameter control etc. Chou *et al.* [7] proposed a neural network based model which adaptively adjusts network parameters like threshold, push-out probability and incremental bandwidth size of virtual path to maintain guaranteed QoS in ATM networks. Kumar *et al.* [12] showed that reduction of assigned resources needed to maintain guaranteed QoS under network overload conditions could be successfully done in real time with the assistance of neural network. Rovithakis *et al.* [8] proposed a method which uses neural network as a controller to map QoS at the application level for multimedia applications into appropriate values for the media characteristics in order to achieve the required user satisfaction without violating the available bandwidth constraints.

In this paper a novel application of ANN is shown in modelling of look-ahead time to maintain service continuity in a QoS-enabled network with Book-Ahead reservation. Resource reservation is one of the widely practiced techniques that are used to ensure guaranteed QoS of applications. Two types of reservation techniques have been proposed by researchers: i) Book-Ahead (BA) reservation and ii) Instantaneous Request (IR) reservation. Multimedia and distributed applications which require long duration, high bandwidth demand and have time sensitive significance are good candidates for Book-Ahead reservation [1]-[6]. Resource reservation is made well in advance from the announced starting time in BA reservation to ensure that the application does not experience scarcity of resources at the point of its start. IR reservation makes resource reservation for immediate transfer of traffic. Resource sharing between BA and IR requests imposes a number of challenges. One of them is to keep the preemption rate of on-going IR calls low as preemption is considered as a break to service continuity and is thus perceived as a serious issue from qualitative QoS point of view [13].

A number of researchers proposed different models to maintain low preemption rate in a QoS-enabled network. Greenberg *et al.*[1] proposed an approximate interrupt probability based admission control scheme that showed that resource sharing between IR and BA calls achieves better network performance than strict partitioning of resources proposed in [9]. Schelen *et al.* [2] proposed a constant look-ahead time (CLAT) based call admission control (CAC) model to reduce the number of preemption by introducing the concept of look-ahead time. Look-ahead time is defined as the pre-allocation time, i.e., the time for starting to set aside resources for advance reservations so that there is no resource scarcity at the stating time of a BA call. Ahmad *et al.* [3],[4] proposed a Dynamic Look-Ahead Time (DLAT) based CAC model that considered network dynamicity and attained better performance than CLAT based CAC model. Desired level of preemption rate is not a fixed value at all operating points of a network. Desired preemption rate is governed by interest of both users and network provider and can be best addressed by an optimization approach. If the on-going applications are highly sensitive to service interruption then preemption rate should be very low and vice versa. Desired level of preemption rate is thus subject to change and should be adaptive with changing network scenario. CLAT model uses look-ahead time as the tuning parameter to achieve different levels of preepmtion rate while DLAT model uses a tuning parameter '*c*' to achieve operating preemption rate. No model has been proposed to map the desired preemption rate into tuning parameter which when fitted into the models proposed in [2] and [3] gives the desired preemption rate in real time network. There is no straight forward relationship among the tuning parameter, preemption rate and other traffic parameters. The non-linear regression approach proposed in [3] to find the relationship is highly constrained to a fixed set of traffic parameters and suffers from the problem of higher complexity in terms of effort and time with increasing number of variable traffic parameters. This paper proposes an ANN model to map the desired preemption rate and traffic parameters to the tuning parameter. The mapping of users' and network provider's interest to the desired level of preemption rate is not within the scope of this paper. This paper describes a technique on how to find the tuning parameter value given that desired level of preemption rate is known.

DYNAMIC LOOK-AHEAD TIME (DLAT) BASED MODEL

A BA call request is characterized by two additional parameters, starting time and call holding time along with other QoS parameters. If the request is granted, the application is guaranteed to have required resources at the time of its start. In contrast, starting time for an IR call is immediate and call holding time is open ended. Problem occurs when a BA call becomes active at certain point of lifetime of an on-going IR call and there is no resource available to support the BA call. On-going IR calls are required to be preempted to meet BA request. Preemption probability which indicates the ratio of preempted IR calls to accepted IR calls should be reasonably small in a QoS-Enabled network. It is the responsibility of CAC model to keep the preemption probability low.

Dynamic Look-Ahead Time (DLAT) based CAC model calculates look-ahead time taking the dynamicity of traffic pattern and network state into consideration. Look-ahead time is calculated periodically by the following equation [3]:

$$LAT(t,s) = [\{A(s) + R(t) + (1+l)\sigma(\mu_{IR}) - C\} / \mu_{IR}\lambda_{IR}(1-b)] + \sigma(1/\lambda_{IR})c \quad (1)$$

Here, *LAT(t,s)* is the look-ahead time w.r.t traffic condition at current time *t* and BA activation time *s* (*t<s*). *A(s)* is the aggregate bandwidth reserved for BA calls to be activated at time *s*, *R(t)* is the aggregate bandwidth used by IR calls at time *t*, μ_{IR} is the mean bandwidth demand of IR calls, λ_{IR} is the mean arrival rate of IR calls, *l* is the normalized BA limit which determines maximum allowable aggregate BA load, *b* is the call blocking probability for IR calls, σ(.) is the standard deviation and c(>1) is the tuning parameter which is used to achieve desired preemption probability.

LAT(t) is calculated at regular intervals of operating time. It is calculated only when the numerator of Eq. (1) is found positive, otherwise it is always zero. An IR call with *r* bandwidth requirement is checked against the following rule at call admission time.

$$C > \max_{s \in LAT} (r + R + A(s)) \quad (2)$$

Look-ahead time is computed at each interval for a number of entries in the Book-ahead table. Those entries are taken into calculation for which the following rule satisfies:

$$t > s_i - \{A(s_i) - A(t)\}/(1-b)\mu_{IR}\lambda_{IR} \quad (3)$$

The right hand side is conservatively computed on the worst case assumption that the network is fully utilized. A detail description of this model and algorithm is given in [3].

ANN BASED MODEL OF LOOK-AHEAD TIME

A network is characterized by network parameters like mean bandwidth demand of BA calls μ_{BA}, mean bandwidth demand of IR calls μ_{IR}, mean arrival rate of BA calls λ_{BA}, mean arrival rate of IR calls λ_{IR}, mean call holding time of BA calls T_{BA}, mean call holding time of IR calls T_{IR}, BA limit *l* and preemption probability *PP*. The nature of distribution for bandwidth demand, arrival rate and call holding time is found from proper traffic analysis. Preemption probability is a complex non-linear function of the network parameters. The aim of this work is to find the value of tuning parameter 'c' which when fitted into Eq. (1) provides the desired preemption probability. The variable network parameters, as shown in Fig. 1 are the inputs to the ANN and 'c' is the output. Parameters *l*, μ_{IR}, λ_{IR}, μ_{BA}, λ_{BA}, T_{IR}, T_{BA}, *l* and 'c' are the inputs to the DLAT model which again provides look-ahead time *LAT* as the output. New calls are checked against the *LAT* according to Eq. (2).

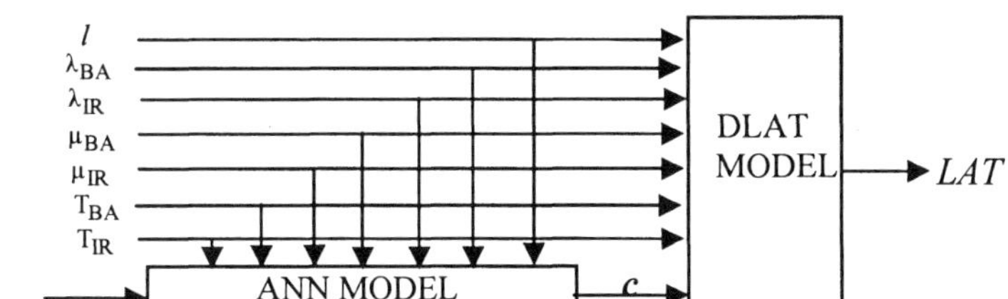

Figure 1: Proposed ANN model.

The ANN is trained with varying values of network parameters. The training dataset is created by simulating the DLAT model as follows: for a particular set of mean bandwidth demand of IR call μ_{IR} , mean bandwidth demand of BA calls μ_{BA}, mean arrival rate of IR calls λ_{IR}, mean arrival rate of BA calls λ_{BA}, mean call duration of IR calls T_{IR} , mean call duration of BA calls T_{BA} , BA limit l and tuning parameter 'c' the simulation is done for $2.5\text{x}10^6$ sec calculating look ahead time at 10s interval At the end of each simulation the number of calls pre-empted is calculated and preemption probability is determined. To cover a wide spectrum of network operating points, the parameters were varied over a wide range. For each combination of parameters the value of 'c' was varied from 1-21 yielding different preemption probability. This procedure generates a data set where each set of traffic parameters and preemption probability is associated with a 'c' value. Once the ANN model is trained with sufficient amount of training data, the network is expected to predict the appropriate value of 'c' in both on-line and off-line for a target preemption probability given the other traffic parameters. The non-linear regression approach proposed in [3] is constrained to a fixed set of network traffic parameters and suffers the problem of complexity with increasing variable parameters. This makes the curve fitting approach practically unusable in real time network solution.

In this study, we used scaled conjugate gradient feed forward learning algorithm to train neural network. In conjugate gradient methods, a search is performed along conjugate directions, which produces generally faster convergence than steepest descent directions [10]. In conjugate gradient method, a new search direction spoils as little as possible the minimization achieved by the previous direction and the step size is adjusted in each iteration. The general procedure to determine a new search direction is to combine the steepest descent direction with the previous search direction so that the current and previous search directions are conjugate. Denoting the fan-in weights to a single neuron by a weight vector **w**, the weight changes in successive steps are given by the following equations.

$$\mathbf{w}_{t+1} = \mathbf{w}_t + \alpha_t \mathbf{d}_t \tag{4}$$

$$\mathbf{d}_t = -\mathbf{g}_t + \beta_t \mathbf{d}_{t-1} \tag{5}$$

$$\mathbf{g}_t \equiv \nabla E(\mathbf{w})\big|_{\mathbf{w}=\mathbf{w}_t} \tag{6}$$

$$\beta_t = \mathbf{g}_t^T \mathbf{g}_t / \mathbf{g}_{t-1}^T \mathbf{g}_{t-1} \quad \text{or} \quad \Delta\mathbf{g}_{t-1}^T \mathbf{g}_t / \mathbf{g}_{t-1}^T \mathbf{d}_{t-1} \quad \text{or} \quad \Delta\mathbf{g}_{t-1}^T \mathbf{g}_t / \mathbf{g}_{t-1}^T \mathbf{g}_{t-1} \tag{7}$$

where $\mathbf{d}_t$ and $\mathbf{d}_{t-1}$ are the conjugate directions in successive iterations. The step size is governed by the coefficient α_t and the search direction is determined by β_t. In scaled conjugate gradient the step size α_t is calculated by the following equations.

$$\alpha_t = -\mathbf{d}_t^T \mathbf{g}_t / \delta_t \tag{8}$$

$$\delta_t = \mathbf{d}_t^T \mathbf{H}_t \mathbf{d}_t + \lambda_t \|\mathbf{d}_t\|^2 \tag{9}$$

where λ_t is the scaling co-efficient and $\mathbf{H}_t$ is the Hessian matrix at iteration t. With sufficiently large λ, the modified Hessian is guaranteed to be positive ($\delta > 0$). However, for large values of λ, step size will be small. If the error function is not quadratic or $\delta < 0$, λ can be increased to make $\delta > 0$. In case of $\delta < 0$, Moller [11] suggested the appropriate scale coefficient $\bar{\lambda}_t$ to be

$$\bar{\lambda}_t = 2\left(\lambda_t - \delta_t / \|\mathbf{d}_t\|^2\right) \tag{10}$$

Rescaled value $\bar{\delta}_t$ of δ_t is then be expressed as

$$\bar{\delta}_t = \delta_t + (\bar{\lambda}_t - \lambda_t)\|\mathbf{d}_t\|^2 \quad (11)$$

A detailed description of the algorithm is given in [11].

SIMULATION RESULTS

Both training and testing data have been collected from the simulation results carried by Ahmad *et al.* [3]. A dataset consisting of 880 data has been used in the proposed ANN model. The dataset covers different combinations of network parameters. 85% of the total data set was used for training purpose and the rest 15% was used to test the ability of the model to produce correct value of 'c' (tuning parameter). The network consists of 8 inputs and 1 output. The experiment was conducted using different combination of hidden layers and hidden units. Three hidden layers consisting of 40, 25, 15 neurons respectively were found to provide the best match on the test data measured in terms of mean squared error. Since the performance of an ANN network depends on the initial weights and other learning parameters, a number of trails were conducted until each trail was continued for 40,000 epochs unless terminated at a predefined mean squared error. For the best trial, mean square error on test data was found as low as 0.0764 and the maximum deviation with respect to correct 'c' was found as 12.7%.

Result found on the test data is reported in Fig. 2. It shows the frequency distribution of achieved 'c' value for different error range. In almost 40% of the test data, the 'c' value predicted by the ANN model lies within 1% error w.r.t the target value. In only 10% of the test data predicted value is found to differ by 5% or more from the target value. These data are mainly for higher target value of 'c' (c>11.0) for which preemption probability approaches very close to zero and successive 'c' values result in very small difference in preemption probability. Only 1.44% of test data suffers 10% or more error. The value predicted by ANN model is then fed to DLAT model. Because of the deviation of the predicted 'c' value from the target value, network performance parameter in form of preemption probability deviates from the desired values. Further investigation was done to assess this impact. Since the test data is quite large (132), representative test samples were chosen for presentation in the paper following the frequency distribution shown in Fig. 2. These samples, target and predicted 'c' values and their deviations are shown in Fig. 3: sample number 1-4 (<1%), 5-6 (1~2.5 %), 7-8(2.5~5%), 9(5~7.5%), 10(7.5~10%) and 11 (>10%), the number within the bracket indicates the error range.

Figure 3 shows that actual value of 'c' provided by the ANN model is very close to the target value of 'c'. Impact of actual and target value of 'c' on preemption probability is reported in Fig. 4. In the worst case for sample no.11 which is the representative of ANN model output with the maximum error, the difference in preemption probability is found to be 5.75%. For most of the data the achieved preemption probability is found to be very closely matching with the preemption probability corresponding to target value of 'c'.

For further investigation of the suitability of the proposed ANN model a complete set of data with network parameters of mean BA bandwidth demand 1.25 Mbps, mean IR bandwidth demand 128 kbps, mean call duration of BA and IR calls 300s, mean IR arrival interval 2.78s, mean BA arrival interval 70s and BA limit l=0.1~1.0 was separated from the training set and tested in the trained ANN model.

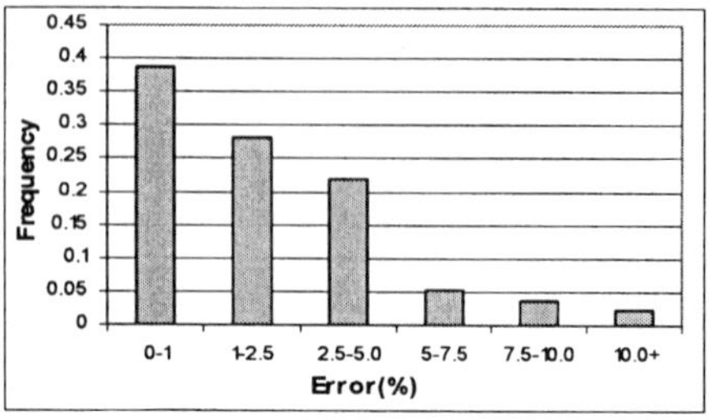

Figure 2: Frequency distribution of error on test data.

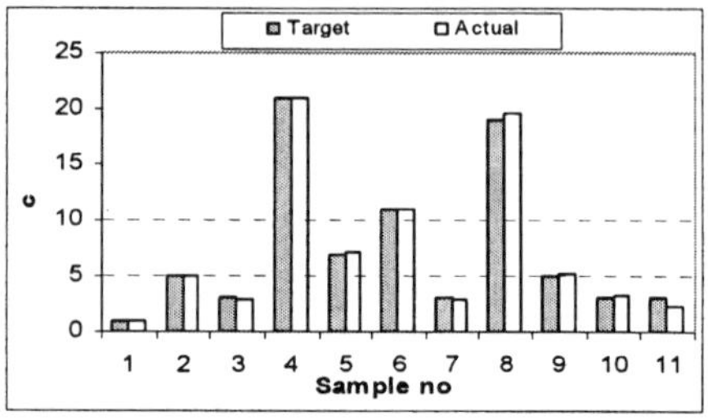

Figure 3: Comparison of 'c' values on test data.

The aim was to investigate the performance of the model for a whole set of BA limit. Observation confirms that for all BA limits, the actual output of ANN model closely matches with the target value of 'c'. Maximum difference in 'c' value was found for BA limit 0.7 which amounts 2.56% on the target value of 13. The impact of target value and actual value of 'c' in terms of preemption probability is reported in Fig. 5. Average amount of deviation $(pp_{target}-pp_{actual})/pp_{target}$ in preemption probability is observed as 1.09% while the maximum deviation is 2.34% for BA limit 0.7.

The motivation of this work is to propose a model which is capable of estimating the value of 'c' so that the target preemption probability is achieved under all possible network operating conditions. To assess whether the proposed ANN model is capable of targeting any range of preemption probability, simulation was done with a random target value of preemption probability. The value of 'c' produced by the model for all BA limits was then fitted into the DLAT model and actual preemption probability was found. Comparison of target and actual

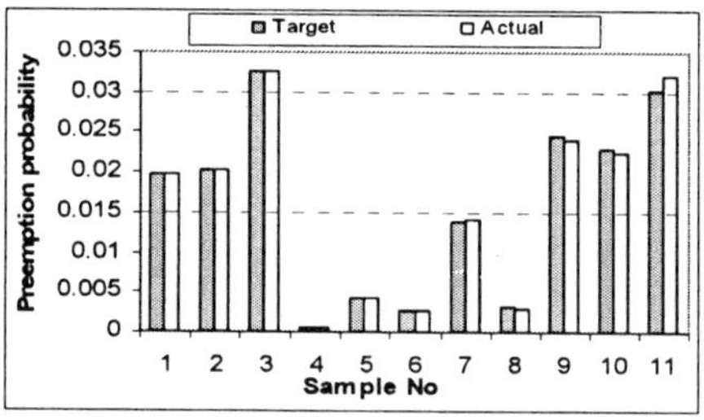

Figure 4: Comparison of preemption probability on test data.

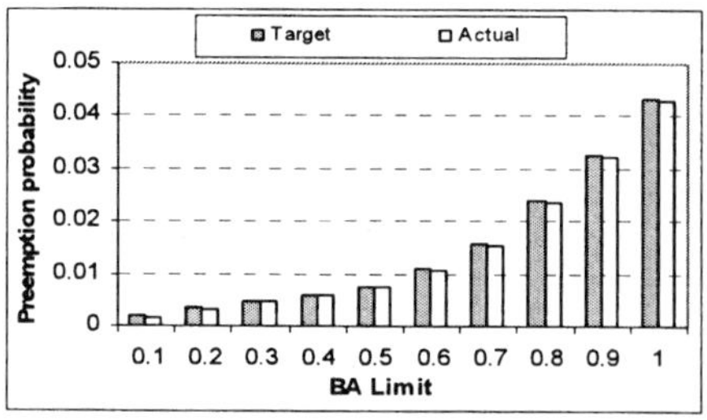

Figure 5: Comparison of preemption probability on fixed data set.

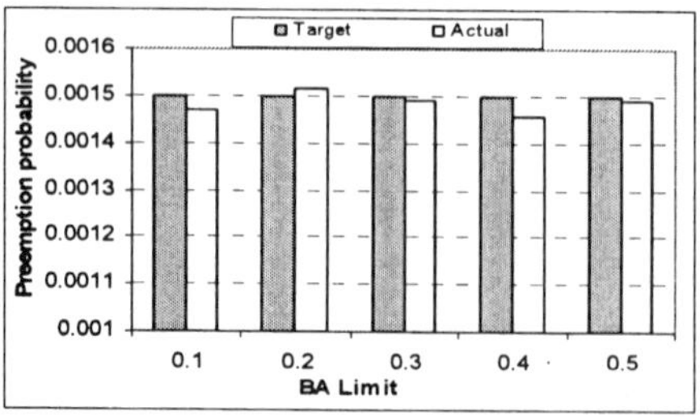

Figure 6: Comparison of preemption probability BA Limit 0.1~0.5.

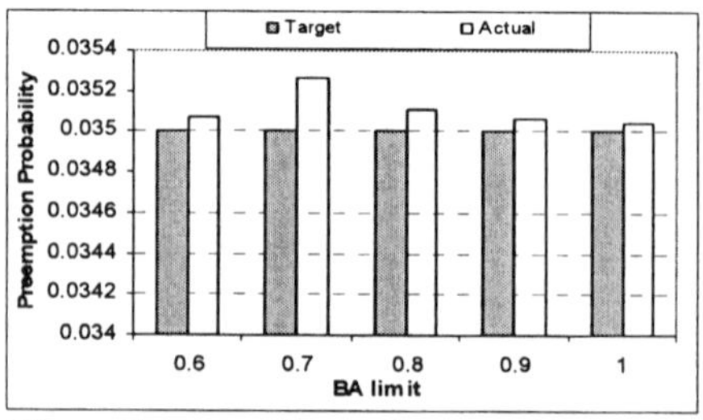

Figure 7: Comparison of preemption probability for BA limit (0.6~1.0).

preemption probability is shown in Fig. 6 and 7. Two different target values were chosen, 0.0015 for BA limit $l = 0.1 \sim 0.5$ and 0.035 for BA limit $l = 0.6 \sim 1.0$. From the figure it is clearly evident that the proposed model is capable enough to achieve the target preemption probability. The maximum mismatch is found for target preemption probability at BA limit l=0.7 and the amount of deviation is recorded as 0.74% which is very small in consideration of network dynamicity. At all other BA limits the error lies well within the range of 0-0.74% error.

CONCLUSION

This paper demonstrates the use of ANN in modelling of look-ahead time used for IR call admission control in a QoS-enabled network. The data set to train the model was created by simulating the previously proposed DLAT based CAC model with different traffic and tuning parameter values that govern the preemption rate. Once the network is trained, it can estimate the value of tuning parameter under all network operating conditions to achieve the desired preemption rate. Simulation results demonstrate close match between the target and actual value of tuning parameter and preemption rate. The proposed model overcomes the problem of higher complexity of effort and time evident in curve fitting approach with large number of variable traffic parameters.

REFERENCES

[1]. A.G. Greenberg, R. Srikant, and W. Whitt, "Resource sharing for book-ahead and instantaneous-request calls," *IEEE/ACM Trans. Networking*, vol.7, pp.10-22, 1999.

[2]. O. Schelen and S. Pink, "Sharing resources through advance reservation agents," *Journal of High Speed Networks*, Special issue on Multimedia Networking, vol. 7, no. 3-4, 1998.

[3]. I. Ahmad, J. Kamruzzaman, and S. Ashwathanarayaniah, "Dynamic look-ahead time in book-ahead reservation," submitted to *IEEE ICON* 2004, USA.

[4] I.Ahmad, J. Kamruzzaman, and S. Aswathanarayaniah, "Dynamic look-ahead time with conditional call admission based on predicted lifetime ", to appear in Proc. *IEEE ICCS*, 2004.

[5] Y.Lin, *et.al.*, "Bandwidth brokers of instantaneous and book-ahead requests for differentiated services networks," *ICICE Trans. Comm.*, vol. E85-B, no.1, 2002.

[6]. F. Breiter *et. al.*, "The usage of advance reservation mechanisms in distributed multimedia applications," *Computer Networks and ISDN Systems*, vol. 30, pp. 1627-1635, 1998.

[7]. L. Chou, and J. Wu, "Parameter adjustment using neural network based genetic algorithms for guranteed QoS in ATM networks," *IEICE Trans. on Comm.*, vol. E78-B, pp. 572-9, Japan, 1995.

[8]. G. Rovithakis *et al.*, "Controlling QoS at the application level of multimedia applications using artificial neural networks: experiment results," *Proc. EUSIPCO 2000*, vol. 2, pp.849-52, 2002.

[9]. D. Ferrari, A. Gupta, and G. Ventre, "Distributed advance reservation of real-time connections," *Proc. NOSSDAV*, pp. 15-26, Durham, New Hamshire, 1995.

[10]. M.T. Hagan, H.B. Demuth and M.H. Beale, *Neural Network Design*, PWS Publishing, Boston, MA, 1996.

[11]. A.F. Moller, "A scaled conjugate gradient algorithm for fast supervised learning," *Neural Networks*, vol. 6, pp.525-533, 1993.

[12]. V. Kumar, and P. Venkataram, "An efficient resource allocation scheme for mobile multimedia networks, " *Proc. Mobile and Wireless Communication Networks 2002*, pp. 88-92, 2002.

[13]. M. Campanella, P. Chivalier, N. Simar, "Quality of Service Definition", http://www.dante.net/sequin/QoS-def-Apr01.pdf.

AUTOMATIC RECOGNITION AND SAFETY ESTIMATION OF VOICE COMMANDS IN NATURAL LANGUAGE GIVEN BY THE OPERATOR OF THE TECHNOLOGICAL DEVICE USING ARTIFICIAL NEURAL NETWORKS

WOJCIECH KACALAK
Department of Mechanical Engineering
Technical University of Koszalin
Koszalin, Poland

MACIEJ MAJEWSKI
Department of Mechanical Engineering
Technical University of Koszalin
Koszalin, Poland

ABSTRACT

In this paper there is a review of the selected issues on recognition and safety estimation of voice commands in natural language given by the operator of the technological device. A view is offered of the complexity of the recognition process of the operator's words and commands using neural networks made of a few layers of neurons. There is also an intelligent layer of two-way voice communication between the technological device and the operator presented, which consists of the intelligent mechanisms of operator identification, word and command recognition, command syntax and result analysis, command safety assessment, technological process supervision as well as operator reaction assessment. The paper presents research results of speech recognition and automatic command recognition with artificial neural networks.

INTRODUCTION

In the future, voice messages in natural language will undoubtedly be the most important way of communication between humans and machines (O'Shaughnessy 2000). Great progress is made in many fields of science, where communication between the technological devices and the operator is an important task, e.g. motorization, road traffic, etc.

The advantages of intelligent two-way voice communication between the technological devices and the operator (fig. 1) include the following (Kacalak and Majewski 2003):

- More resistance from the operator's errors and more efficient supervising of the process with the chosen level of supervision automation.
- Elimination of scarcities of the typical co-operation between the operator and the technological device.
- Reaching a higher level of organizing realization of a technological process equipped with the intelligent two-way voice communication system, which is relevant for its efficiency and production humanization.
- No need of an operator being present at the work stand by the device; i.e., the operator may be any distance from the device.

According to the new conception, the intelligent layer of two-way voice communication between the technological device and the operator (fig. 2), is equipped with the following intelligent mechanisms: operator identification, recognition of words and commands, command syntax analysis, command result analysis, command safety assessment, technological process supervision, and also operator reaction assessment (Kacalak and Majewski 2004).

The condition of the effectiveness of the presented intelligent two-way voice communication system between the technological device and the operator (fig. 3) is to equip it with mechanisms of command verification and correctness. In operations of the automated technological processes, many process states and various commands from the operator to the technological device can be distinguished. A large number of combined technological systems characterize the realization of that process. In complex technological processes, if many parameters are controlled, the operator is not able to analyze a sufficient number of signals and react by manual operations on control buttons.

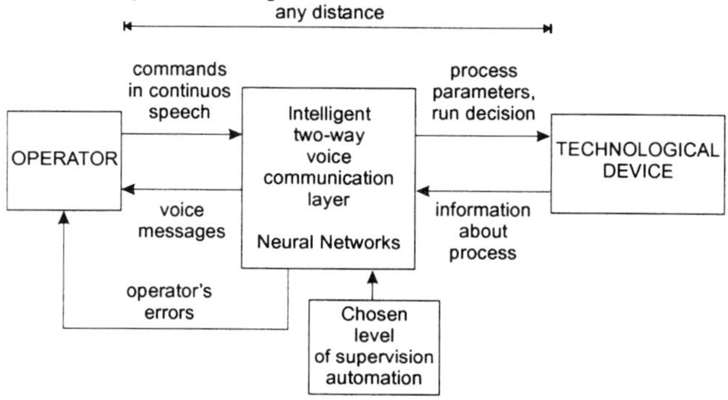

Fig. 1. General Scheme of Intelligent Two-Way Voice Communication between the Technological Device and the Operator

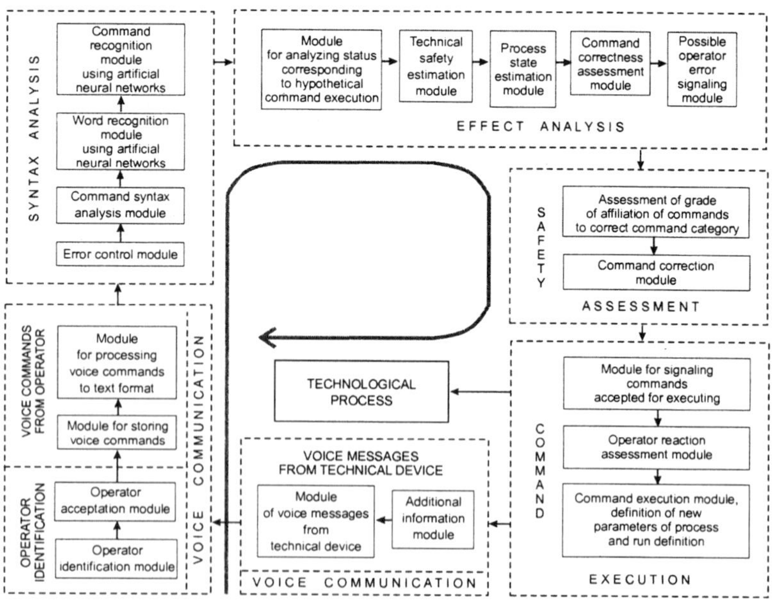

Fig. 2. Scheme of the Intelligent Layer of Two-Way Voice Communication between the Technological Device and the Operator

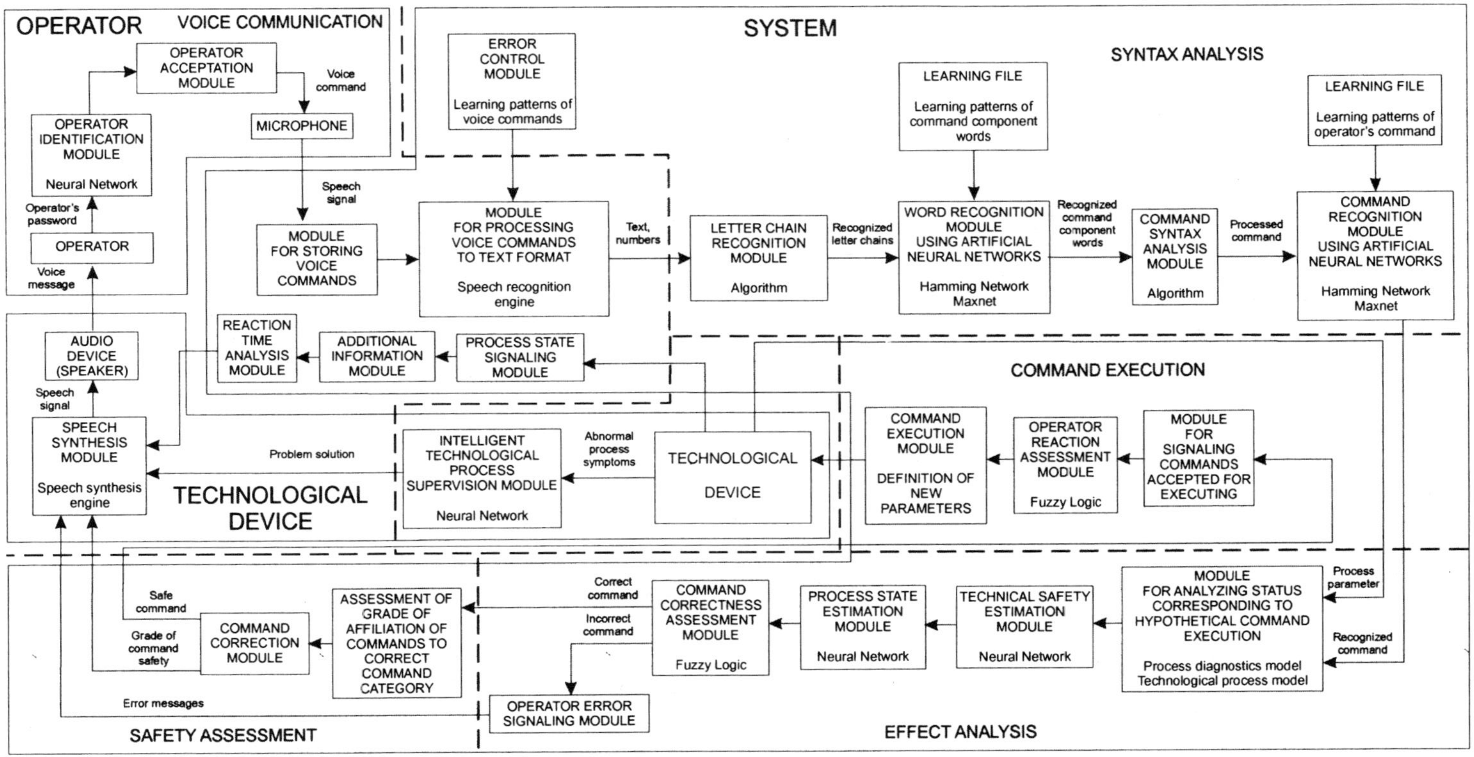

Fig. 3. Detailed architecture of the intelligent two-way voice communication system

AUTOMATIC COMMAND RECOGNITION SYSTEM

In the automatic command recognition system (fig. 4), the speech signal is processed to text and numeric values with the module for processing voice commands to text format using the speech recognition engine. The words of the text are the input signals of the neural network for recognizing words.

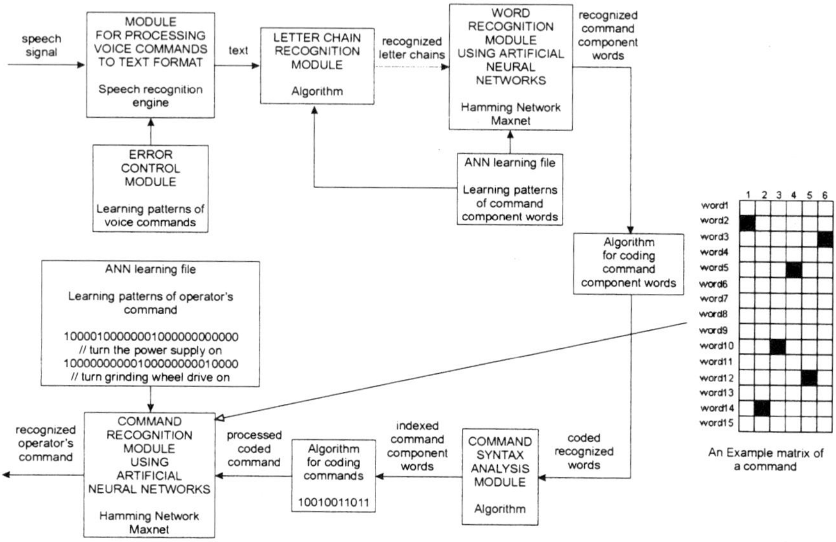

Fig. 4. Scheme of the Automatic Command Recognition System

The network has a training file containing word patterns. As the work result, the network recognizes words as the operator's command components, which are represented by its neurons. The recognized words are sent to the algorithm for coding words. Next the coded words are transferred to the command syntax analysis module. The commands are coded and they are input signals of the command recognition module using 3-layer neural networks, which are equipped with training files containing the learning patterns.

COMMAND SAFETY ESTIMATION SYSTEM

The effect analysis module, shown in (fig. 5a), makes analysis of the recognized command. The technical safety of the technological device is checked by analyzing the state of execution of the commands required to have been done as well as the commands to execute in next decisions. The process parameters to be modified by executing the command are checked and the allowable changes of the parameter values are determined. The analysis of the parameter values is based on the technological process features. The values of the parameter changes are the input signals of the neural network of the process state assessment system (fig. 5b). The neurons of the neural network represent solutions to the diagnostics problem (Principe et al. 2000). The neural network also makes an estimation of the grade of safety of the recognized command. The system for checking the state of the automatic device for grinding of small ceramic elements that is shown in (fig. 5c), before executing next commands is presented in (fig. 5d).

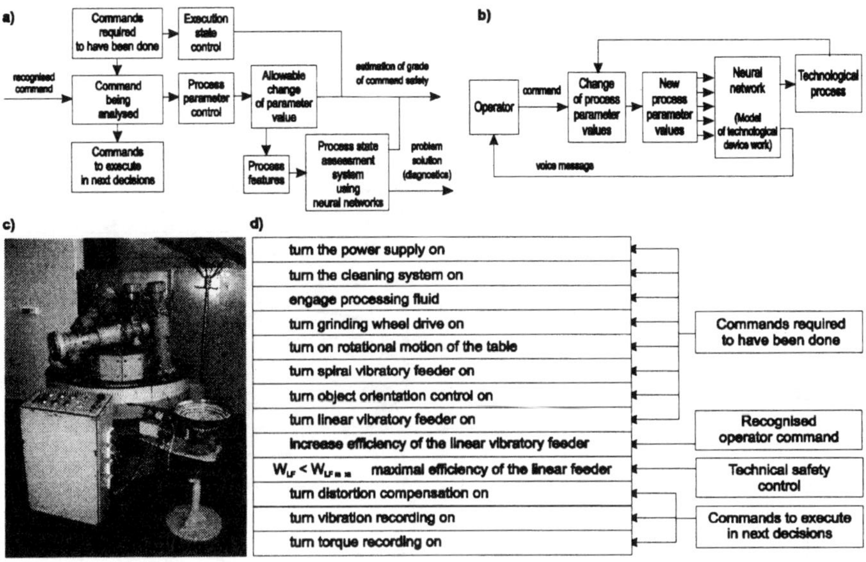

Fig. 5. Scheme of the command effect analysis and safety assessment system

AUTOMATIC SPEECH AND COMMAND RECOGNITION RESULTS

As shown in (fig. 6a), the speech recognition module recognizes 85-90% of the operator's words correctly. As more training of the neural networks is done, accuracy rises to around 95%. For the research on word recognition at different noise power, the microphone used by the operator is the headset. As shown in (fig. 6b), the recognition performance is sensitive to background noise. The recognition rate is about 86% at 70dB and 71% at 80dB. Therefore, background noise must be limited while giving the commands. For the research on word recognition at different microphone distances, the microphone used by the operator is the headset. As shown in (fig. 6c), the recognition rate decreases when the headset distance increases. Also for the research on word recognition at different microphone distances, the microphone used by the operator is the directional microphone. As shown in (fig. 6d), the recognition rate after 50cm decreases reaching rate about 65%. The command recognition module using the Hamming Maxnet neural networks is capable of recognizing different commands of the same meaning in natural language. The ability of the 3-layer neural network to learn to recognize commands depends on the number of learning patterns of possible operator commands. The specified number of the patterns enables the network to learn and work efficiently and quickly (fig. 6e). It could be said that the fewer patterns the neural network is trained with, the faster it works and learns. If the Hamming Maxnet network was trained with the number of patterns bigger than 16, it begun to mix up and overlay the gathered experience information. It is caused by the limited number of neurons storing the training patterns. As a consequence of that fact, there are sometimes considerable errors while recreating the knowledge by the neural network. As shown in (fig. 6f), the ability of the neural network to recognize the command depends on the number of command component words. Depending on the number of component words of the command, the neural network requires the minimal number of words of the given command as its input signals.

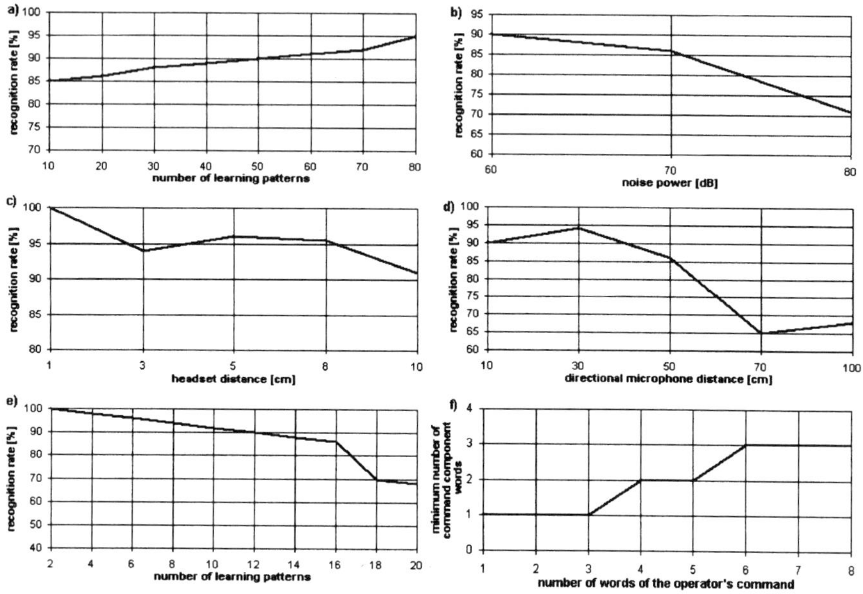

Fig. 6. Speech and command recognition rate

CONCLUSIONS AND PERSPECTIVES

In the automated processes of production, the condition for safe communication between the operator and the technological device is analyzing the state of the technological device and the process before the command is given and using artificial intelligence for assessment of the technological effects and safety of the command. The research aiming at developing an intelligent layer of two-way voice communication is very difficult, but the prognosis of the technology development and its first use shows a great significance in efficiency of supervision and production humanization.

Acknowledgements: The support of the Polish State Committee for Scientific Research (KBN grant 5 T07D 036 24) is highly appreciated.

REFERENCES

Kacalak W., Majewski M., 2003, “Intelligent Two-Sided Voice Communication System Between the Machining System and the Operator”, Proceedings of the ANNIE 2003 Conference, Artificial Neural Networks in Engineering ANNIE 2003, Vol. 13: Smart Engineering System Design, St. Louis 1-4 November 2003, ASME Press, New York 2003, pp. 969-974.

Kacalak W., Majewski M., 2004, “Intelligent Layer of Two-Way Voice Communication of the Technological Device with the Operator”, Lectures Notes in Artificial Intelligence 3070, Subseries of Lecture Notes in Computer Science, Springer-Verlag 2004, pp. 610-615.

O'Shaughnessy D., 2000, "Speech Communications: Human and Machine", IEEE Press, New York 2000.

Principe J. C., Euliano N. R., Lefebvre W. C., 2000, "Neural and Adaptive Systems: Fundamentals through Simulations", John Wiley & Sons, Inc., New York 2000.

SECONDARY STRUCTURE PREDICTION OF HEMOGLOBIN BY NEURAL NETWORKS

İREM ERSÖZ
Department of Technical Education
Mersin University
Tarsus, Turkey

TURGAY İBRİKÇİ
Department of Electrical-Electronics Engineering
Cukurova University
Adana, Turkey

AYÇA ÇAKMAK
Department of Electrical-Electronics Engineering
Cukurova University
Adana, Turkey

OKAN K. ERSOY
School of Electrical and Computer Engineering
Purdue University
West Lafayette, Indiana, USA

ABSTRACT

Proteins are one of the most important parts of an organism because of their vital tasks. Consequently, it is necessary to know both the primary and secondary structure of a protein as closely related to its biological function. Artificial Neural Networks (ANNs) are a useful methodology for secondary structure prediction of proteins. In this study, a generalized regression neural network (GRNN) and a backpropagation algorithm (BP) were investigated with different window sizes of amino acid sequences to predict the hemoglobin secondary structure from the hemoglobin primary structure. All the outputs of the networks were further combined with another GRNN for possible increase in accuracy rates. The data sets were prepared with alpha-141 and beta-146 hemoglobin chains from the Protein Data Bank. The overall success rate of GRNN was around 90.2-91.7% for beta chains and 85.9-87.3% for alpha chains. The BP had an overall accuracy rate of 89.9-92.5% for beta chains and 86.5-90.3% for alpha chains.

INTRODUCTION

The protein molecules represent much of the bulk of an organism and accomplish almost all of its biochemical activities. To understand the life process of an organism, it is necessary to know the structure of a protein since it is closely related to its biological function. Routine and reliable methods to determine the structure of a protein are laborious techniques such as X-ray crystallography and nuclear magnetic resonance spectroscopy (NMR). Since biological techniques are quite expensive and time consuming, scientists have used computer and statistical modeling for protein secondary structure prediction in recent years. In this study, the aim is to investigate the success rate of neural network algorithms as a function of window size and type of neural network in predicting the secondary structure of a protein as a first step towards determination of the overall structure.

All proteins are composed of linear unbranched combinations of twenty different amino acids. The structural and functional properties of the proteins primarily depend on this linear sequence of amino acids. Protein structures are described through four main hierarchical levels; *Primary, Secondary, Tertiary, Quaternary*. There are three common secondary structures in proteins, namely, **alpha helices (H)**, **beta sheets (E)**, and **turns or coils (C)** (Denniston et al., 2001, Solomons, 1995).

Hemoglobin is one of the most important proteins and is frequently investigated because the various types of disorders in its structure cause many diseases in the human body. The oxygen, carried via the hemoglobin protein is a main element of the human and animal physiology (Rinsho, 1998). The hemoglobin molecule is made up of four polypeptide subunits that are known as globins and four heme groups for each globin chain, as its name states (Pauling, 1952). The four globins of normal adult hemoglobin consist of two identical alpha chains, each with 141 amino acids and two beta chains, and each with 146 amino acids. All adult hemoglobin throughout the world has the same structure. However, sometimes some defects can occur in the genetic code for hemoglobin and cause abnormalities. The types of disorders that can result include sickle cell disease and thalassemia (Pauling, 1952).

ANN's are a useful approach for prediction of secondary structures of proteins (İbrikçi, 2000). They have the capability of analyzing the overwhelmingly big data sets and mapping the relationships between the protein sequences.

Studies on the protein secondary structure prediction by computational and statistical methods started with Krigbaum and Kuntton (Cai et al., 2002). They used multiple linear regression algorithms to predict the amino acid composition of a protein. This attempt continued with the Chou-Fasman method that achieved a three-state (Q_3) accuracy of 52% (Chou and Fasman, 1978). This method is a well-known empirical statistical algorithm that is based on the frequencies of the secondary structure types.

In the last decade of the 20th century, the accuracy percentage level rose over 70%. During this period, Rost et al. extensively studied the prediction of secondary structure (1993a, 1993b). The accuracy rate of the network, which trained a set of profiles of multiple alignment sequences, was about 70%. They also used an ensemble of networks, and combined predictions from 10 distinct neural network systems. They observed over 1% improvement in accuracy rate with 72% (1994). In 1998, one of the combination methods, Jpred, was applied by Cuff (1998). This method combined the outputs of several specific methods such as PHD, NSSP, etc. by using a consensus method, and achieved 72.9% accuracy rate. More recently, three and eight classes of protein secondary structures were predicted with the performance of about 78% accuracy rate by using recurrent neural networks and profiles in the study of Pollastri et al. (2002).

DATA SETS AND METHODS

The dataset was taken from the Protein Data Bank, USA and consists of 2820 alpha-141 and 2920 beta-146 hemoglobin chains. The hemoglobin datasets are divided into two parts as training and testing sets. The networks are trained to predict three categories, helix, strand, and coil, on a secondary structure assignment reduced from the eight-category assignment produced by the DSSP program (Kabsch and Sander, 1983). In this dataset, there is no strand (E) structure, and thereby only helix and coil represent the secondary structure. The training files contain a primary structure and its corresponding secondary structure. These structures are manipulated by determining a certain size of sliding windows that consist of contiguous amino acid residues. Prediction is applied by labeling the secondary structure corresponding to the input pattern. The centering technique is based on the assumption that the central amino acid has a large influence in the structural classification of that window (Qian and Sejnowski, 1988).

Since there are 20 known amino acids in nature, each of them is coded as a 20-bit string with all but one bit turned on, and each output is coded as a 1-bit string that can be 0 for helix and 1 for coil. In this study, the eight different sizes of windows in each dataset were chosen as *11-13-15-17-19-21-23-25*. The training dataset and testing dataset are used with these eight different window sizes to obtain comparative accuracy rates of secondary structure prediction for two classes. The accuracy rates for helix and coil are separately denoted by Q_1. Then, all results are calculated for overall accuracy rates in which the accuracy Q_2 is computed with the following formula:

$$Q_2 = \frac{H + C}{N}\% \tag{1}$$

where N shows the total number of predicted residues.

In this study, the two algorithms, GRNN and BP as the subunits are combined by another GRNN that functions as the combiner. The combiner can be another neural network, a statistical method or some other prediction algorithm like the consensus method (Benediktsson et al., 1997).

The GRNN introduced by Donald Specht in 1990 is a memory-based feed forward neural network based on the estimation of the probability density function (pdf) from observed samples using Parzen-window estimation (Specht, 1991). It approximates any arbitrary function between input and output vectors. This approach removes the necessity to specify a functional form of estimation.

The method utilizes a probabilistic model between an independent random vector X (input) and a dependent scalar random variable Y (output). Let x and y be the particular measured values of X and Y, respectively, and $g(X, Y)$ be the joint continuous probability density function of *X and Y*. A good choice for a non-parametric estimate of the probability density function g is the Parzen window estimator as proposed by Parzen and performed for multidimensional cases by Cacoullos (1966). Given a sample of n real D dimensional x_i vectors and corresponding scalar y_i values, the estimate of joint probability density is given by

$$\hat{g}(x,y) = \frac{1}{(2\pi)^{(d+1)/2}\sigma^{(d+1)}}\frac{1}{n}\sum_{i=1}^{n}\left[\exp\left(\frac{(x-x_i)^T(x-x_i)}{2\sigma^2}\right)\exp\left(\frac{(y-y_i)^2}{2\sigma^2}\right)\right] \tag{2}$$

where σ is the window width of a sample probability, called the smoothing factor of the kernel (Cacoullos, 1966).

The expected value of Y given x (the regression of Y on x) is given by using Eq. (2)

$$\hat{y}(x) = E[Y / x] = \frac{\sum_{i=1}^{n}[y_i \exp(d_i)]}{\sum_{i=1}^{n}\exp(d_i)} \tag{3}$$

where d_i is the distance function between the input vector and the ith training vector, and is given by

$$d_i^2 = -\frac{(x-x_i)^T(x-x_i)}{2\sigma^2} \tag{4}$$

The estimate $\hat{y}(x)$ is thus a weighted average of all the observed y_i values where each weight is exponentially proportional to its Euclidean distance from x (Niwa, 2003).

The only adjustable parameter of the network is σ, the smoothing factor for the kernel function. It is critical to decide an optimum value for σ (Specht, 1991).

RESULTS

According to the training and testing results of the 141 alpha set with GRNN, the saturation of accuracy level is observed during training as 99% for helix and around 95.6% for coil. The window size of 17 amino acid residues of the testing dataset provides slightly better prediction of the secondary structure of protein in overall prediction with 87.3% (Figure 1). The GRNN algorithm correctly-classified 93.4% of the helix classes and 69.6% of the coil classes with this window size. If the classes are examined individually, the helix class has the best result with a window size of 11; the best coil results were obtained with a window size of 19 and 21 with 70.7 % accuracy rate. The window size of 13 gave the best overall testing accuracy rate with 91.7% on a 146 beta set (Figure 2). This window also gives the best accuracy for coils with 76.1% and for helix with 95.8%. With respect to these results, it can be said that the small window sizes give better results for the 146 beta test set with the GRNN, in general(Ersoz, 2003).

It is observed in Figures 1 and 2 that the results for different window sizes are close to each other with the BP algorithm. This is believed to be due to larger number of weights in the BP algorithm as well as more complex representation so that very high accuracy is obtained during training. The BP has more accurate results on coil prediction than the GRNN, but the overall results are worse because of the lower success rate in helix prediction. The accuracy rate of our study is better than Rost and Sander's study at the window size of 13 with 87.2% for the 141 alpha set and with 91.7% for the 146 beta set. They predicted the secondary structure of proteins at 70.8% accuracy with a two-layered feed forward neural network at the window size of 13 (Rost and Sander, 1993). The BP training accuracy rates of the 141 alpha set are quite good for helix with 98.4%, for coil with 97.4% and overall with 98.1%. The overall result is worse than the GRNN. The testing dataset with the window size of 13 amino acids provides a slightly better prediction of the secondary structure of protein with 87.2% overall, and 90% in helix, respectively, with the alpha set (Figure 2). The best of the beta set helix prediction and coil prediction are 85.6% with the 17 window size, and 91.7% with the 13 window size, respectively (Figure 2). Like in the 141 alpha results, the small window sizes give better prediction accuracies.

Generally, CNN has not given any improvement in the accuracy of the results in comparison with other individual methods. The CNN method gives the same result on the 141-alpha test set as GRNN that has the best overall test result of the 141-alpha set. In the 146 beta set test, there is a minor improvement that can be neglected, with 0.5% for overall accuracy results. Similarly, Rost et al. reported that the individual methods were more successful than the combined one. They observed an improvement of about 1%-2% on the accuracy rate in their studies (Rost and Sander, 1994).

DISCUSSION AND CONCLUSIONS

The networks successfully handle the problem of predicting the hemoglobin secondary structure. As we can observe from the testing results that were obtained, the algorithms GRNN, BP and CNN are quite successful in terms of accuracy rate if the window size is carefully chosen, and generally give stable results.

Because of its one-pass learning algorithm, GRNN has the advantage of fast training time when it is compared with the BP training time. Another advantage of the GRNN is the fact that adding new samples to the training set does not require re-calibrating the model. Furthermore, GRNN has only one parameter, whereas BP has many parameters to be learned. On the other hand, the main disadvantage of GRNN is that there is no intuitive method for selecting the optimal smoothing parameter. In this study, the chosen value of σ was 0.3 as in references (Niwa, 2003). The use of CNN appears to have no advantage, as it did not give any significant improvement in results. It also increases the computational time.

Since the networks compared gave similar results, it appears very important to choose theoptimal window size given a particular network to be used to achieve best results.

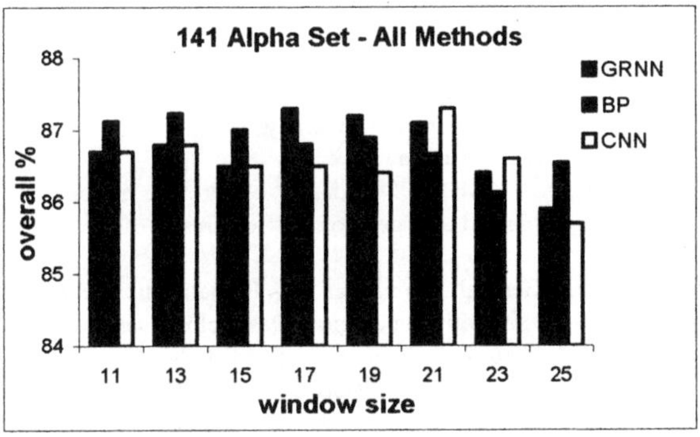

Figure 1. Overall results of the 141 alpha set for each window size with all the methods.

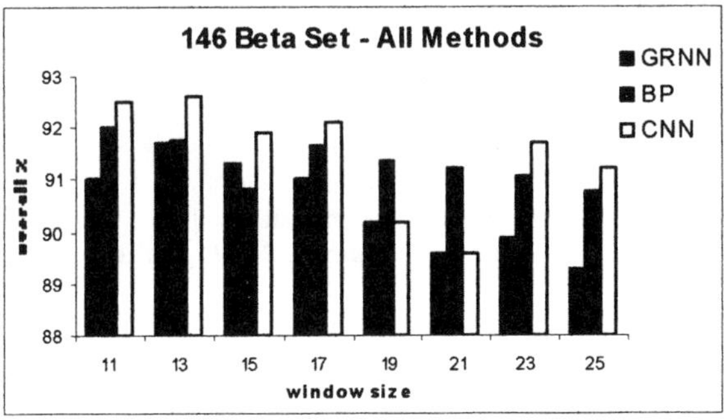

Figure 2. Overall results of the146 beta set for each window size with all the methods.

ACKNOWLEDGEMENTS

This research was supported by Cukurova University Research Foundation FBE2002-YL328 and TUBITAK-EEEAG-100E037. We thank Prof. Dr. Kiymet Aksoy and Erdinç A. Yalin, our colleagues at the Medical School of Cukurova University for their help in understanding the hemoglobin structures.

REFERENCES

Benediktsson, J., Swain, P. H., Ersoy, Okan K., 1997, "Parallel Consensual Neural Networks", IEEE Tran. Neural Networks, Vol. 8, No. 1, pp. 54-64.

Cacoullos, T., 1966, "Estimation of a multivariate density", Annals of Inst. Stat. Math., vol. 18, pp. 178-189.

Cai, Y., Liu, X., Xu, X., Chou, K., 2002, "Artificial Neural Network for Predicting Protein Secondary Structure Content", Computers and Chemistry, 26, 347-350.

Chou, P.Y., Fasman, G.D., 1978, "Empirical Predictions of Protein Conformation", Annual Review Biochemistry, Vol. 47, pp.251-276.

Cuff, J.A., Clamp, M.E., Barton, G.J., 1998, "JPred: A Consensus Secondary Structure Prediction Server", Bioinformatics, 14, 892-893.

Denniston, K.J., Topping, J.J., Caret, R.L., 2001, "General, Organic and Biochemistry", Third International Edition, McGraw-Hill Companies Inc., New York.

Ersoz, I. 2003, " Master Thesis", Cukurova University

Ibrikci, T. 2000, "PhD Thesis", Cukurova University

Kabsch, W., Sander, C., 1983, "Dictionary of Protein Secondary Structure: Pattern recognition of hydrogen-bonded and geometrical features", Biopolymers, 22: 12, pp. 2577-637.

Niwa, T., 2003, "Using General Regression and Probabilistic Neural Networks to Predict Human Intestinal Absorption with Topological Descriptors Derived From Two-Dimensional Chemical Structures", J. Chem. Inf. Computer Sci., 43, 113-119.

Pauling, L., 1952, "The Hemoglobin Molecule in Health and Disease" Proceedings of the American Philosophical Society, Vol. 96, No: 5, October, 555-565.

Pollastri, G., Przybylski, D., Rost, B., Baldi, P., 2002, "Improving the Prediction of Protein Secondary Structure in Three and Eight Classes Using Recurrent Neural Networks and Profiles", Proteins, 47, 228-235.

Qian, N., Sejnowski, T.J., 1988, "Predicting the Secondary Structure of Globular Proteins Using Neural Network Models", J. Mol. Biol., Vol.202, pp. 865-884.

Rinsho, N., 1998, "Human Hemoglobin Structure and Respiratory Transport. Department of Human Genetics", National Institute of Genetics, 9, 54, 2320-2325.

Rost, B., Sander, C., Schneider, R., 1994, "Redefining the Goals of Protein Secondary Structure Prediction", J. Mol. Biol., 235, 13-26.

Rost, B., Sander, C., 1993, "Improved Prediction Of Protein Secondary Structure by Use of Sequence Profiles and Neural Networks", Proc. Natl. Acad. Sci., U S A, 90, 7558-62.

Solomons, T.W.G., 1995, "Organic Chemistry", Fifth Edition, John Wiley & Sons Inc, New York.

Specht, D., 1991, "A General Regression Neural Network", IEEE Trans. Neural Networks, Vol. 2, No 6, pp. 568-576.

Zhang, X., Mesirov, J.P., Waltz, D.L., 1992, "Hybrid System for Protein Secondary Structure Prediction", J. Mol. Biol., 225, 1049–1063.

TIME SERIES ANALYSIS OF ARM MOTIONS CYCLIC MOVEMENT IN A DANCE

SHIHOKO KAMISATO,
Faculty of Engineering,
University of the Ryukyus

KOJI YAMADA
Faculty of Engineering,
University of the Ryukyus

ABSTRACT

The purpose of this study is quantitative description of physical motions characteristics of dance classed by subjective impression. We measured the dancer who was judged "skillful" by previous research at three dimensional motion capture system of a magnetic formula and examined the relationship among motions and impulse response of the multivariate autoregressive model. The results of cumulative power contribution and impulse response showed that "skillful" high scores in subjective evaluation is defined as of wrist-rotation response from shoulder impulse.

1. INTRODUCTION

The concern with elucidation of body intellect has been growing for the last several years. The human motions produce various kinds of impressions. In the field of dance, there are some researches which clarify the relationship between impression and physical exercise so as to investigate the impression structure of the dance. Several studies have been made on sensitivity information and relevance with human motion characteristics by dance [1] - [3].

The purpose of this study is quantitative description of physical motions characteristics of dance classed by subjective impression.

In our previous researches, the relationship between impression and kinetic characteristics of arm motion has been examined in the dance, where the arm motion of the dance seems to be the spatiotemporal features of trajectories of finger, hand, or wrist.

However, analysis of time series seems to be necessary in order to evaluate skillful movement. In addition, on relevance of joint combination and movement of the arms joint making an exercise characteristic, most investigation is not done. Therefore, we measured the dancer who was judged by previous research at three dimensional motion capture system of a magnetic formula for the purpose of quantitative description of characteristic and contingency of motion in free style dance. Next, we examined the relation among motions of shoulder, elbow and wrist through the cumulative power contribution and impulse response of the multivariate autoregressive model. In a study about "Subjective evaluation of dancing motion model with a limited degree-of freedom" by Nakazato, there is a report that it is important as the joint which the arms, legs and body rotation and flexion-extension give an impression [3]. In addition, be reported that more a lot of the degree of freedom is necessary in order to express a "feeling of throbbing pulse" and "beauty" [4].

In this study, pay its attention to only the arm motion. As the reason, there is much the degree of freedom and the arms can invent movement by a combination of joint movement innumerably. In addition, there is the point that can generate complicated movement.

When a person dancing well points at beauty of hand gesture and dancing cleverly points, there can be a thing meaning that beauty and harmony of a dancing figure such as a facial expression, movement, progressing of a leg are produced in Okinawa Japan [5]. From this thing, the arms motion is because I thought that it can give various impressions such as an expert or poor to an observation person only by movement of the body location in complicated movement as a dance.

2. EXPERIMENT METHOD

2.1 EXTRACTION OF MOVEMENT PATTERN BY SENSITIVITY INFORMATION

This study is intended to clarify the relationship between the motion characteristics behind humans and the subjective impressions of the observer and uses dancing as the impressions based on body information to measure sensitivity information received by the observer in a quantitative manner. They used Kachasi, one of the traditional dances in Okinawa Japan, as an object dance. The reason is that this dance is characterized by no fixed pattern and freely moving the hands and legs to express the mood of a dancer to change this dance depending on the personality of dancer.

However, although it is a free-style dance, it gives impressions common to the observer feels from human movements, which is applicable to not only art or entertainment field, but also giving a specific impression to overall human gestures as a communication means.

There are two patterns timewise by a classification of motion to change. When put a pattern of various motions together and there is a case to repeat a motion pattern of one.

For the selection of each of the arm motion dance patterns, the authors tried to collect as many dance patterns as possible regardless of the presence or absence of age, sex and dance experience. They classified the collected patterns of each dance by impressions. For the arm motion, they eventually selected 26 patterns of dance under the condition of the area size, location, direction, speed, and complication of the motion and the length of one cycle and the presence or absence of wrist rotation [6], [7]. One experienced dancer reproduced these 26 patterns, which were used as the videos used for sensitivity evaluation. The questionnaire paper used for sensitivity evaluation was provided with the pairs using a 7-stage evaluation scale. The authors used 30 pairs of adjectives for 26 dance patterns of arm motion to make a sensitivity evaluation experiment was made on 30 college students without dance knowledge and 20 dance instructors with dance knowledge. Pursued an average score of result that evaluated an impression of "skillful - poor" from the inside of 30 pairs of adjectives that did sensitivity evaluation. Selected the movement which 50 subjects evaluated with "skillful – poor".

2.2 MULTIVARIATE AUTOREGRESSIVE MODEL

Multivariate autoregressive model is used for feedback analysis to put in the biochemical systems [8], [9]. So, we searched time series angle change of each joint, "mutual relevance" and "time concomitant" of motion using the multivariate autoregressive model in a frequency domain and a time domain. Multivariate autoregressive model thinks about a system of simple feedback system to mechanism of two variables of x_1, x_2. This shows it in fig.1.

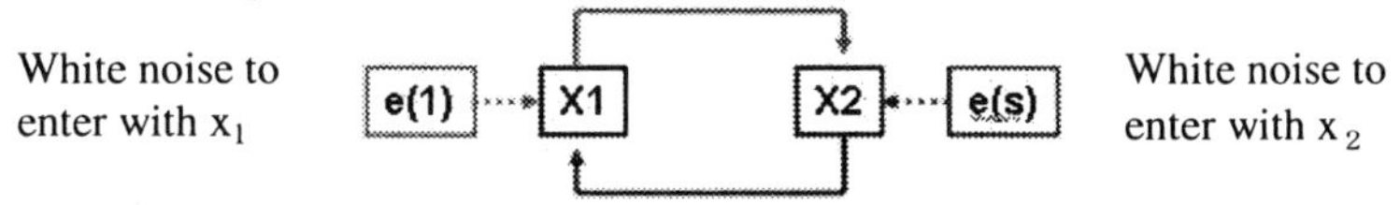

Fig.1. A simple feedback system to mechanism of two variables of x_1 ,x_2.

It is assumed that a change of x_1 is transmitted through in x_2. And a change of x_2 is transmitted through in x_1. However, do not understand it when we examine only a change state of x_1 and x_2 which moves the other. So, in addition to the past linear sum of x_1 and x_2, suppose if there are input e_1 and e_2 to set up a change peculiar to it in a variable of each. Autoregressive model of 2 variable quantities is shown by an equation (1) and an equation (2). Both variables take out input e_1, e_2 producing a change to be peculiar to each from x_1 and x_2. These equations are things the same as Autoregressive model of 1 variable quantitative essentially.

$$x_1(s)=\sum_{j=1}^{2}\sum_{m=1}^{M}a_{1j}(m)\,x_j(s-m)+e_1(s) \quad (1) \qquad x_2(s)=\sum_{j=1}^{2}\sum_{m=1}^{M}a_{2j}(m)\,x_j(s-m)+e_2(s) \quad (2)$$

So expand it in case of K variable quantities. An equation (3) becomes Multivariate autoregressive model.

$$x_i(s)=\sum_{j=1}^{2}\sum_{m=1}^{M}a_{ij}(m)\,x_j(s-m)+e_i(s) \quad (3) \qquad e_i(s)=x_i(s)-\sum_{j=1}^{k}\sum_{m=1}^{M}a_{ij}(m)\,x_j(s-m) \quad (4)$$

And can transform an equation (3).

An equation (5) can show variance and covariance of $e_i(s)$, like the next equation.

$$\mathrm{Re}_{i}e_{j}(n)=\sum_{l=0}^{M}\sum_{m=0}^{M}\sum_{r=1}^{k}\sum_{s=1}^{k}a_{ir}(l)\,a_{js}(m)\,R_{rs}(n-l+m) \quad (5)$$

-A "Yule-Walker" equation of next equation is provided.

$$\sum_{j=1}^{k}\sum_{m=1}^{M}a_{ij}(m)\,R_{jh}(s-m)=R_{ih}(s) \qquad (i,h=1,2,\cdots k) \quad (6)$$

Autoregressive coefficient $a_{ij}(n)$ is demanded by solving this simultaneous equations.

3. KINEMATIC ANALYSIS OF THE ARMS

3.1 MEASUREMENT OF JOINT MOTION

We are here concerned with interrelationship with the arms joint of dance motion and impression of subjectivity. We did three dimension motion measurement of dance movement taken as "skillful" and "poor" using motion capture system by impression of an observation person. A time series transformation of rotation was measured for movement of 6 joints of these 'shoulder: flexion - extension, shoulder: adduction - abduction, elbow: flexion - extension, wrist: pronation - supination, wrist: flexion - extension, wrist: adduction - abduction'. The sampling frequency measured it with 20[Hz] for 15 seconds. The results show time series transformation of joints rotation by fig.2, fig.3. Fig.2 and Fig.3 show a big 3 joint of the influence which motion characteristic in phase difference between 2 joint gives to impression with earlier literature. Fig.2 shows time series changes of three joint rotations in a dance to give "skillful" impression. And Fig.3 shows time series changes of three joint rotations in a dance to give "poor" impression. Compare a time series change of joint rotation of two graphs. The time series of joint rotation of skilful dance motion is bimodal distribution a little and there is phase difference between each joint. The time series of joint rotation of poor dance motion is small angular variation and a peak of angle is prepared. Furthermore, plus and minus direction of a peak is opposite only "pronation - supination" of wrist joint.

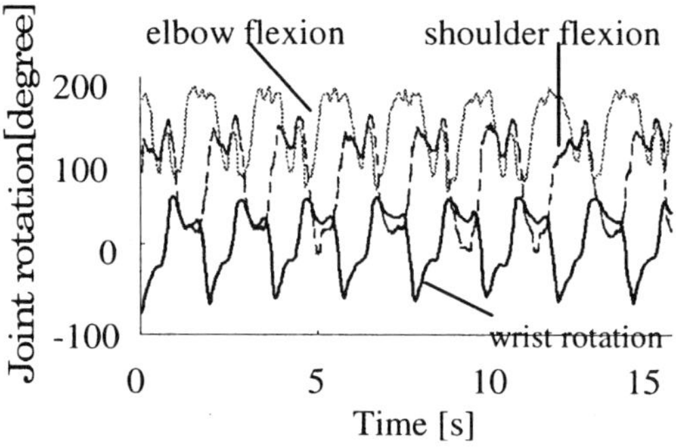

Fig.2 Time series changes of joint rotation in a skillful dance

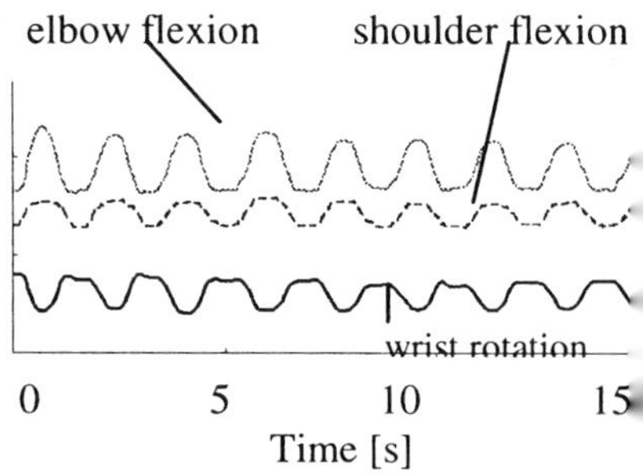

Fig.3 Time series changes of joint rotation in a poor dance

3.2 RESULTS AND DISCUSSION

The time series of joint rotation was analyzed using multivariate autoregressive model. Fig.4 shows result of the power contribution proportion which showed relationship between joint of skillful dance motion with frequency region. Fig.5 shows result for poor dance motion. We compared result of two power contribution proportion. As for the skillful dance motion, there is a little influence of "flexion - extension" of elbow joint compared with poor dance motion. Furthermore, motion of "pronation - supination" of wrist joint gives influence for other joint. As for the poor dance motion, there is big influence of "Flexion - extension" of elbow joint first. And movement of "flexion – extension" of shoulder gives influence. We examine skillful dance motion with frequency region. Skillful movement seems to go along with "flexion - extension" motion of shoulder joint, and move "pronation - supination" of wrist joint. Next, we searched multivariate autoregressive model from time domain, and searched response of other joint for input of impulse to each joint. Fig.6 shows result of impulse response of skillful motion. Fig.7 shows result of impulse response of poor motion. However, vibrated while other joint produced a difference of time by impulse response for "pronation - supination" of wrist joint and "flexion - extension" of elbow joint. And skillful movement goes along with shoulder joint and wrist to begin to move. Furthermore, that it is movement getting skillful evaluation is considered when the phase difference which is time-variant has elbow joint for two other joint. And as a result, as for the poor motion, only motion of elbow characterized it.

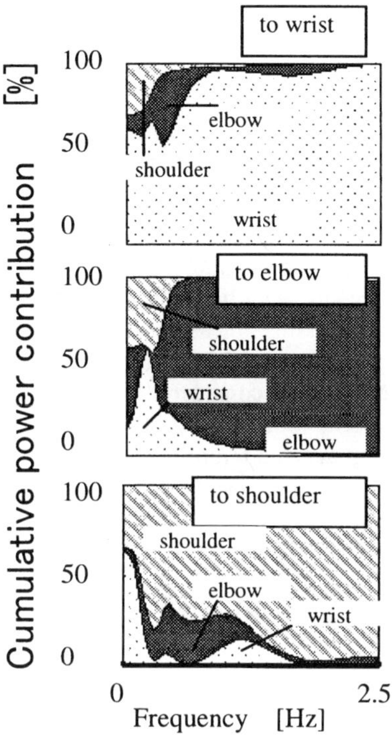

Fig.4 Relative power contribution in joint rotation of a skillful dance.

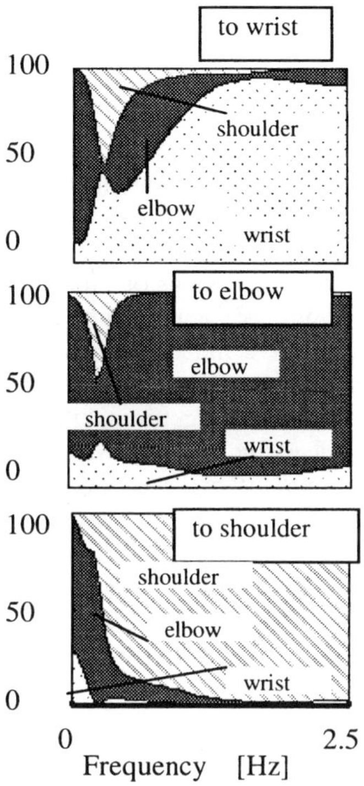

Fig.5 Relative power contribution in joint rotation of a poor dance.

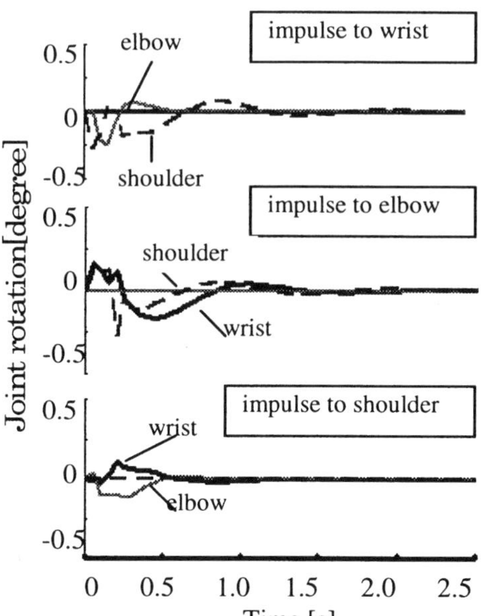

Fig.6 A skillful dance responses of two joints to impulse.

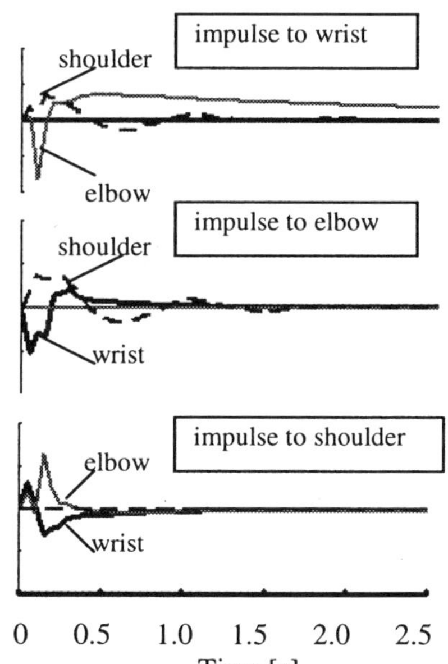

Fig.7 A poor dance responses of two joints to impulse.

CONCLUSIONS

In this research, we measured the dancer who was judged by previous research at three dimensional motion capture system of a magnetic formula for the purpose of quantitative description of characteristic and contingency of motion in free style dance. And we examined the relation among motions of shoulder, elbow and wrist through the cumulative power contribution and impulse response of the multivariate autoregressive model. As a result, skillful movement seemed to go along with "flexion - extension" motion of shoulder joint, and move "pronation - supination" of wrist joint in the result which watched multivariate autoregressive model from frequency domain. Furthermore, on the result which looked at multivariate autoregressive model from time domain that it was movement getting skillful evaluation is considered when the phase difference which is time-variant has elbow joint for two other joint. That it was important to let motion of upper arm and motion of forearm link skillful of dance motion was suggested by these results.

REFERENCES

[1] Shihoko Kamisato, Satoru Odo, Kiyoshi Hoshino, Yoshino Ishikawa: Extraction of motion characteristics corresponding to sensitivity information using dance moveme, Journal of Advanced Computational Intelligence, pp.168--180, 2004.

[2] Shihoko Kamisato , Satoru Odo , Kiyoshi Hoshino , Kouji Yamada : Quantitative Analysis of relation between subjective impressions and characteristics of arm motion in free-style dance, INTELLIGENT ENGINEERING SYSTEMS THROUGH ARTIFICIAL NEURAL NETWORKS, vol.13 (editor C. H. Dagli et al.), ASME PRESS SERIES, pp. 987--992, 2003.

[3] Mariko Shiba, Extraction of kansei information in dance movements: ATR workshop on virtual communication environments, pp.66--88, 1998.

[4] Hisashi Nakazato, Ryojun Ikeura, Hikaru Inooka : Subjective evaluation of dancing motion model with a limited degree-of freedom, Japan Ergonomics society, vol.32, No.4, pp.189--196, 1996.

[5] Shihoko Kamisato, Koji Yamada, Shiro Tamaki,: Sensitivity evaluation and three-dimensional motion analysis of arm motion in dance, The 18th Annual Conference of the Japanese Society for Artificial Intelligence, 2004.

[6] Shihoko Kamisato and Kiyoshi Hoshino : Relationship between subjective impressions and motion characteristics finger and wrist trajectories in dancing, Information technology letters, vol.1, pp.195--196, 2002.

[7] Shihoko Kamisato and Kiyoshi Hoshino : Evaluation of subjective impressions and motion characteristics in a free-style dance, ASOR 2000 Proceedings, pp.309--314, 2000.

[8] Takao Wada, Makoto Jinnouchi and Yasuo Matsumura : Application of autoregressive modeling for the for the analysis of clinical and other biological data, Annals of the Institute of Statistical Mathematics, vol.40, No.2, pp.211-227, 1988.

[9] Hirotsugu Akaike: On the use of a linear model for the identification of feedback system, Annals of the Institute of Statistical Mathematics, vol.20, pp.425-439, 1968.

POSITION DETECTION SENSOR BASED ON CMOS FLOATING-GATE DEVICES

VICTOR H. PONCE-PONCE
CINVESTAV-IPN, Mexico, City.

FELIPE GOMEZ-CASTAÑEDA
CINVESTAV-IPN, Mexico, City.

JOSE A. MORENO-CADENAS
CINVESTAV-IPN, Mexico, City.

LUIS M. FLORES-NAVA
CINVESTAV-IPN, Mexico, City.

ALFREDO REYES-BARRANCA
CINVESTAV-IPN, Mexico, City.

ABSTRACT
This work presents a novel position-detection sensor based on CMOS technology. It uses floating-gate transistors to perform signal aggregation computation, as part of the centroid approximation for 1-D real-time tracking of a regular-shape object. In fact, the object is detected from binary images, which are captured within the field of view of this sensor. The analog-weighting process for the spatial column-components, in the associated algorithm, is realized by using MOS transistors operating in the triode region. Only binary images are considered, even though image information is sacrificed, faster operation speed and increased functionality is obtained. The position-detection sensor was fabricated using a 1.2μm, n-well, CMOS process. The design contains a 17×18 cell-array with a fill-factor of 35.6%. The electrical analysis supported by PSpice of this initial CMOS integrated circuit, demonstrates that its extension to a larger prototype for robotic applications is attractive.

1. INTRODUCTION

The joint integration on a single-chip of image sensor devices and parallel-processing information circuits is known as smart-sensors. This kind of sensors, which are information-oriented systems, obtain the best performance from sensors and also make the sensing and processing information tasks more compact. The design of a smart-sensor is generally targeted for a specific application, where speed, dynamic range, size, power dissipation and system integration are important issues to take into account. Some examples have been introduced in the literature (Shibata and Ohmi, 1998), that attempt to track in real-time the center-of-mass of a regular object using CMOS floating-gate transistors, or ordinary CMOS-based circuits (Meitzler, et al., 1995)(Burns, et al., 2003). We use clock-controlled floating-gate CMOS transistors (FGMOS) in this design (Kotani, et al., 1998), since this technique eliminates the intrinsic charge that is acquired and stored in the floating-gate terminal during the fabrication process of the circuit.

In this work, binary images are captured and their center-of-mass computation (COM) is partially processed on the same chip. The system generates the histograms by projecting the number of pixel in on-state (M_i), for each column of the pixel array, on the coordinate-axis in response to a certain visual scene, as is sketched in Fig. 7. Then the algorithm computes a weighted-voltage summation operation for the numerator and denominator terms and followed by a division according to Eq (1).

$$COM = \frac{\sum_{i=1}^{18} x_i M_i}{\sum_{i=1}^{18} M_i} \qquad (1)$$

Where M_i, is the magnitude of the *i-th* component of the histogram and x_i represents the column position on the coordinate axis and is implemented by a voltage level.

2. SYSTEM ARCHITECTURE

The global architecture for the position detection sensor (PDS) is introduced in Fig. 1(a-b). The system approach consists of a 17×18 cell-array of variable threshold photogate-type active-pixels sensors. Each pixel delivers a binary voltage (0, 5V), that is coupled capacitively via the in-pixel column capacitor C_j, with the floating-gate of a NMOS transistor. This transistor produces a voltage signal V_{SFi}, representing nearly the average sum of the binary voltages, V_{outj}, supplied by the pixels of an entire column. This averaged voltage contributes to evaluate the size of the columns in the histograms on the respective coordinate axis. The histograms are next processed by a weighted-voltage multiplier circuit.

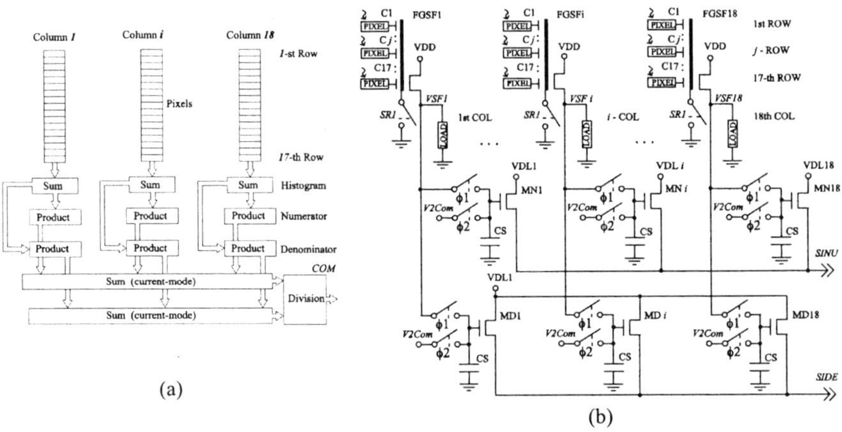

Figure 1. (a) Block level presentation of the PDS and (b) Schematic diagram.

3. PIXEL CIRCUIT

A schematic of the baseline pixel design is introduced in Fig. 2(a), and is partially based on early structures introduced in literature (Mendis, et al.,1997). The photogate is separated from the two-input floating-gate CMOS inverter (FGMI) by a transfer gate (MX). The pixel uses a reset transistor (MRD), for pre-charging the floating-capacitor array (C_{FD}), formed at the source and drain terminals of MRD and MF1, and also at the right-side terminal of MX (FD), where the conversion to voltage takes place.

Also, it has been placed, three transistors (MF1, MF2 and MF3) on the pixel. They are used to discharge the floating-gate of FGMI. An ordinary CMOS inverter (MP y MN) reinforces the binary voltage level provided by FGMI.

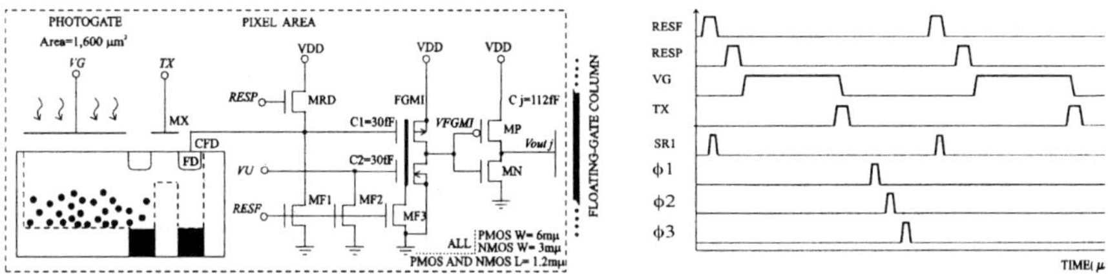

(a) (b)

Figure 2. (a) Schematic circuit of the pixel element, (b) Timing diagram for the PDS operation.

3.1 Operation

Firstly, a brief pulse is applied to MF1, MF2 and MF3, for discharging the floating-gate of FGMI. Next, capacitor C_{FD} is preset to approximately 3.8V by pulsing the gate of MRD. Then VG goes high (5V), starting an integration period. During this integration period (about 40μs), electrons are collected under the surface of the photogate. At the end of this period, MX is pulsed on and electrons are transferred to the FD, changing its surface potential. The potential there is read by C_1. A reference voltage V_U, is used to change the intrinsic inverter switching-point of FGMI.

4. MULTIPLIER CIRCUIT

4.1 Generation of histograms

In Fig. 1(b), we present the proposed circuit for the pixel-column weighted-voltage multiplication process. In each column of pixels, the source terminal of the floating-gate source follower transistor (FGSF) produces a signal-voltage V_{SFi}, (i=1,2,..,18) given by Eq. (2), where, g_{FGSF} is the transconductance parameter of the associated n-channel transistor in the FGSF and g_{LOAD} represents the active-load transconductance, respectively. V_{FGi} is the potential induced in the floating-gate terminal in the respective FGSF, by a column of pixels, and is given by Eq. (3).

$$V_{SFi} = V_{FGi} \cdot \left(\frac{\frac{1}{g_{FGSF}}}{\frac{1}{g_{FGSF}} + \frac{1}{g_{LOAD}}} \right) \tag{2}$$

$$V_{FGi} = \sum_{j=1}^{m} \left(\frac{C_j \cdot V_{outj}}{C_j} \right) \tag{3}$$

Where C_j, is the in-pixel control capacitance. Voltage V_{outj} is the binary voltage delivered by the pixel in the j-row, and m=17. Voltage V_{SFi} represents the magnitude of the i-component of the histogram generated at the i-column of pixels and is proportional to the summation of the pixels in on-state (5V). Voltage V_{SFi}, will start generating a valid voltage level for a potential in the floating-gate, which fulfills $V_{FGi} > 2\Delta V + V_{th}$ setting $2\Delta V + V_{th} \cong 1.86$ as the minimal voltage required by each cascode current source in all the FGSF for operation in the saturation region.

4.2 Multiplication for histograms

The column multiplication circuit requires a three-phase non-overlapping clock scheme. For each column of pixels (i=1,2,...,18), and during the first phase (ϕ_1 active), (see Fig. 1(b)) voltage V_{SFi} is applied to the gates of MN_i and MD_i, contributing to the generation of the currents *SINU* and *SIDE*. As shown in Fig. 3, these currents are converted to voltage and sampled in $C_{1\phi 1}$ and $C_{2\phi 1}$, respectively. Next, during ϕ_2, V_{2Com} is applied to the gate of MN_i and MD_i. Then, *SINU* and *SIDE* are converted to voltage and sampled in $C_{1\phi 2}$ and $C_{2\phi 2}$. During the third phase (ϕ_3 active), the difference of voltages stored in $C_{x\phi 1}$ and $C_{x\phi 2}$ is computed and stored in C_{Sx} (where x, stands for 1,2). This difference is the aggregated multiplication of the corresponding applied drain to source voltage in MN_i and MD_i, times the weighted-difference voltage $k \cdot \beta (V_{SFi} - V_{2Com})$.

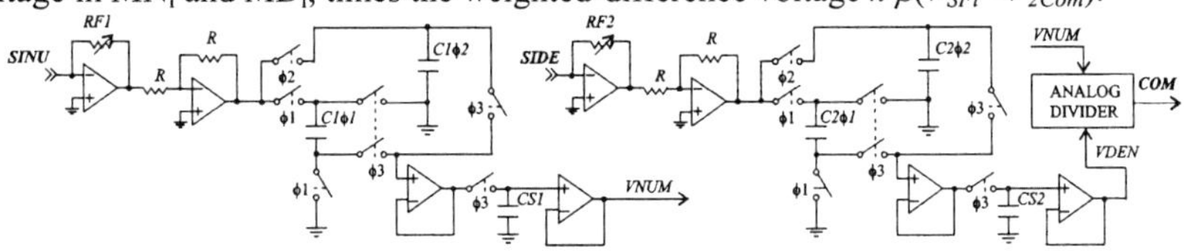

Figure 3 Off-chip multiplication-supporting circuit for the PDS.

Where k is the transresistance factor of the current-to-voltage conversion stage, β is the transconductance of MN_i and MD_i, and n=18. Then, as the source terminal of each FGSF is connected to a common node, see Fig. 1(b), current sum is performed resulting in the following pair of equations.

$$V_{NUM} = k \cdot \beta \sum_{i=1}^{n} V_{DLi} \cdot (V_{SFi} - V_{REF1}) \tag{4}$$

$$V_{DEN} = k \cdot \beta \cdot V_{DL1} \sum_{i=1}^{n} (V_{SFi} - V_{REF1}) \tag{5}$$

Finally, the COM computation can be calculated as follows.

$$COM = \frac{V_{NUM}}{V_{DEN}} \tag{6}$$

5. RESULTS

5.1 Pixel transient response

For this test, we used a photocharge-integration period, t_{int}=40μs, and an illuminance of 0.146mW/cm^2. Then a potential decrease in FD of 2.4V, from reset level (V_{reset}=3.8V) is calculated and measured. Fig. 4(a) shows a PSpice simulation of the transient response for the complemented-buffered output of the pixel structure {NOT($Voutj$)}.

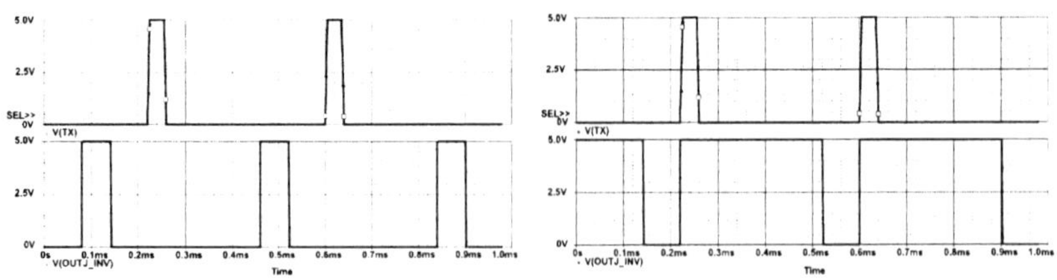

(a) (b)

Figure 4 Complemented-buffered output simulation response of the pixel, using t_{int}=40μs. Case (a) for E=0mW/cm^2, and case (b) for E=0.146 mW/cm^2, and V_u=3.85V.

Without illumination, a low-output level in the pixel, at the onset of TX signal, is found as expected. In Fig. 4(b) an illuminance of 0.146mW/cm^2 from a fluorescent-lamp light source is applied. The lowering in the floating-diffusion potential is now enough to change the output-state of FGMI, therefore a high-level output is achieved at the onset of TX signal. Measured response is shown in Fig. 5(a-b).

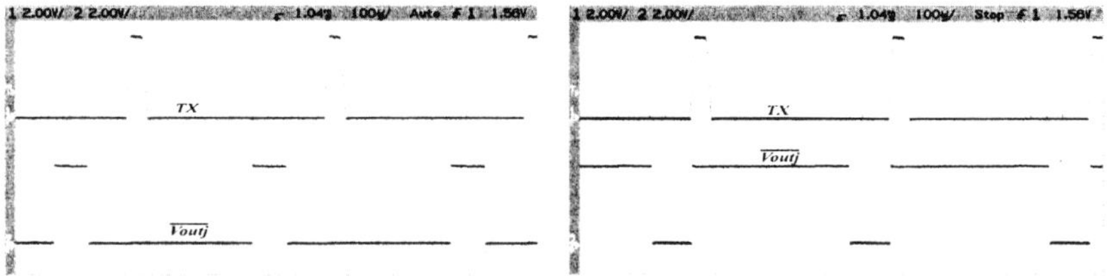

(a) (b)

Figure 5 Complemented-buffered output measured response of the pixel, using t_{int}=40μs. Case (a) for E=0mW/cm^2, and case (b) for E=0.146 mW/cm^2, and V_u=3.85V.

5.2 Column multiplication process

A simulation of the weighted-voltage multiplication response for all the columns appears in Fig. 6 (a). Horizontal axis represents the number of pixels in on-state. The trace labeled as COL1, at the bottom place in the graph, is the response contribution for the first column of pixels for the numerator term, at the node V_{NUM}. The second trace, from the bottom place, corresponds to the second column, and so on for the rest.

5.3 Center-of-mass simulation

For this test, a 1-D COM processing was carried-out by sweeping the PDS in time, with a delta-like histogram scene. The COM simulation response of the system was satisfactory and is introduced in Fig. 6 (b). In this case, COM position is monitored as a voltage level in the vertical axis.

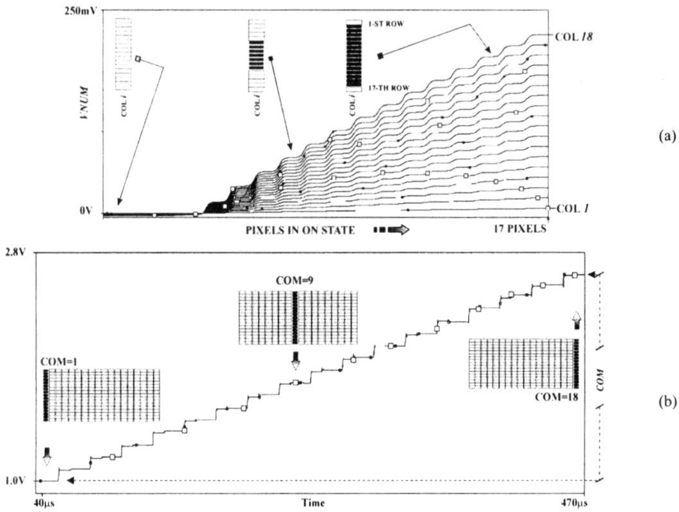

Figure 6. (a) Weighted-voltage column multiplication response for a varying number of pixels in on-state. (b) COM-computation applying a delta-like histogram swept for the 18-input PDS.

6. PROTOTYPE INTEGRATED CIRCUIT

The PDS described in this report was fabricated using double-poly, double metal CMOS process with 1.2μm design rules, using MOSIS services (Run-T39TAM). The microphotography of the silicon chip is shown in Fig. 7.

7. CONCLUSION

We have designed a test chip for detecting binary images and computing in real-time the COM position in 1-D, of regular objects. The chip is expected to perform 10×10^3 COM operations per second. This initial integrated circuit may easily expand to a 2-D COM scheme by incorporating in each row of pixel-circuit a multiplication stage.

Center-of-mass measurements have not been performed by the time of the submission of this paper. However, they will be presented in due course.

Higher resolutions can be achieved by larger silicon real estate with another advanced technology process with extra metal layers to facilitate routing, as we have used metal 2 for shielding active areas from light.

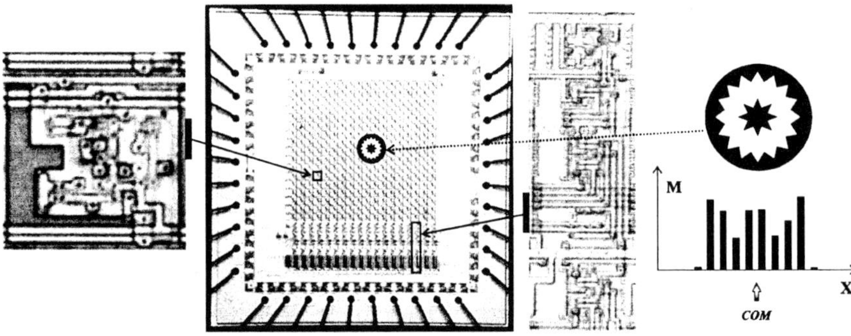

Figure 7. Microphotography the PDS using double-poly, double metal CMOS process with 1.2μm design rules and a histogram sketch from a projected object on the cell-array.

8. ACKNOWLEDGMENTS

This work was supported under project number 41251-A from CONACyT.

9. REFERENCES

Burns, R., Shah, J., Hong, C., Pepic, S., Lee, J., Hornsey, R., and Thomas, P., 2003 ,"Object Location and Centroid Techniques with CMOS Active Pixel Sensors," *IEEE Transaction on Electron Devices*, vol. 50, No. 12, pp. 2359-2377.

Kotani, K., Shibata, T., Imai, M., and Ohmi., T., 1998, "Clock-Controlled Neuron-MOS Logic Gates," *IEEE Tran. on Circuits and Systems-II: Analog and Digital Signal Processing*, vol. 45, No. 4, pp. 518-522.

Meitzler, R., Strohbehn, K., and Andreou, A., 1995, "A Silicon Retina for 2-D Position and Motion Computation," *Proc. IEEE Int. Symposium on Circuits and Systems*, pp. 2096-2099.

Mendis, S., Kemeny, S., Gee, R., Pain, B., Staller, C., Kim, Q., and Fossum, E., 1997, "CMOS Active Pixel Image Sensor for Highly Integrated Imaging Systems," *IEEE Journal of Solid-State Circuits*, vol. 32, No. 2, pp. 187-197.

Yu, N., Shibata, T., and Ohmi, T., 1998, "A Real-Time Center-of-Mass Tracker Circuit Implemented by Neuron MOS Technology ," *IEEE Transactions on Circuits and Systems-II: Analog and Digital Signal Processing*, vol. 45, No. 4, pp. 495-503.

TOP-DOWN VS. BOTTOM-UP NEUROCOMPUTER DESIGN

JOSEPH T. WUNDERLICH
Elizabethtown College Computer Engineering Program
Elizabethtown, Pennsylvania, USA

Abstract - Artificial neural networks are a form of connectionist architecture where many simple computational nodes are connected in a fashion *similar* to that of biological brains for the purpose of solving problems that require rapid adaptation or where underlying governing equations are not known or cannot be easily computed. This paper first discusses the use of various computer platforms for neurocomputer implementation. Two designs are then presented: (1) An artificial dendritic tree "bottom-up" VLSI chip; and (2) A vector-register microprocessor "top-down" design with on-chip learning and a fully-parallel, entirely-digital implementation.

INTRODUCTION

A discussion of machine intelligence *types* is a good place to begin a neurocomputer design process. Machine intelligence includes both "symbolic" AI and artificial neural networks. Symbolic AI programs use heuristics, inference, hypothesis testing, and forms of knowledge representation to solve problems. This includes "Expert Systems" and programming languages such as Prolog or LISP, with knowledge contained in logic, algorithms, and data structures. A neural network (NN) is a form of connectionist computer architecture (hardware or software) where many simple computational nodes are connected in an architecture *similar* to that of a biological brain. Neurocomputers implement NN's [1]-[3], [5]-[9]. A first step in designing a neurocomputer is choosing an architecture that is either structurally similar to, or merely produces results in a *similar fashion* to the human brain (i.e., "bottom-up" vs. "top-down" design).

Most NN's are top-down designs trained to react to external stimuli. They learn via iterative mathematics to change inter-neuron connection strengths (weights) until outputs converge to desired tolerances. The NN learns such that multiple input/desired-output pairs are satisfied simultaneously; the final set of weights represents compromises made to satisfy the constraints. Once trained, the NN can react to new stimuli (i.e., other than the training-set). An implementation problem to consider is that the matrix and vector calculations common to most NN's are often run on von Neumann uniprocessor machines with a "bottle-neck" forcing non-parallel computation. SMP (Symmetric Multi-Processing) architectures improve performance; however the best machines for these calculations are MPP (Massively Parallel Processing) or vector-register supercomputers; or embedded, application-specific, highly parallel systems – especially those providing learning in real-time. An all-digital vector-register NN processor (with on-chip learning) is presented below.

The bottom-up approach is to build a system which functions like a biological brain at the circuit-level. The artificial dendritic tree hybrid-analog/digital chip presented below is an example of this [6], [7].

Predictions of when computer performance will reach that of the human brain often employ Moore's Law to predict computing speed or number of transistors per chip:

$$Q_{NEW} = Q_{OLD}\left(2^{\left(n/1.5\right)}\right) \qquad (1)$$

where Q_{old} is today's computing speed (or chip density), and Q_{new} is computing speed (or chip density) n years in the future (i.e., speed and chip density double every 18 months).

Although this law remains valid to-date, it must eventually break down; in less than 100 years, assuming a present day Q_{old} speed of 6Ghz and a chip density of 50 million transistor per chip, Moore's Law predicts a Q_{new} that would require electricity to travel through a transistor faster than the speed of light and more transistors on a chip than the number of atoms that could fit in the volume of a typical computer "case." This type of prediction can also be misleading if the degree of parallel processing (and pre-processing) that occurs in most biological brains is not considered. Multitasking manmade subsystems as efficiently and elegantly as the human brain is a major undertaking. The degree of parallelism (DOP) of the human brain is simply not found in PC's, workstations, or even mini-computers. Only in some supercomputers does parallelism come close to what might be required [1]. Embedded systems could eventually achieve these goals with many simple devices working independently; however embedded systems often lack the computation power (and precision) of even the simplest PC [5]. A comparison of computing platforms and their use for implementing machine intelligence is shown in Table 1.

Multitasking is a significant part of NN's where learning occurs between the many simple computational nodes. If an MPP machine could be built with billions of nodes (like the human brain), instead of just thousands (to-date), it could possibly implement an NN to rival the functionality of the human brain. Vector-register architectures are also well suited to the many parallel computations involved in the millions of "multiply-accumulates" often required for even the simplest of NN training.

Table 1. Levels of computing and machine intelligence use.

LEVEL	HARDWARE and DEVICES	OPERATING SYSTEM	MACHINE INTELLIGENCE USE
Em-bedded	**Microcontroller:** (Intel, Motorola, PIC) **Microprocessor:** (Intel/AMD, Motorola, PowerPC) **Application Specific IC's**	Typically none or custom	Not typical for symbolic AI. NN ASIC's excellent for high-speed real-time-learning NN applications.
PC	**Microprocessor** (Intel/AMD, PowerPC)	Windows, DOS, MAC OS, B, Linux	Acceptable for NN simulations and symbolic AI.
Work-station	Silicon Graphics , SUN, IBM RS6000 with multiple **Microproc's** (MIPS, SPARC, Intel/AMD, PowerPC)	Windows NT, UNIX, AIX	Good for NN simulations and symbolic AI.
Mini-Comp.	IBM AS400, Amdahl, HP, Hitachi (typically **SMP**)	UNIX, MVS, VMS, OS 390	Good for NN simulations and symbolic AI.
Super-Comp.	**SMP**: (IBM S/390) **MPP**: (IBM SP2, Cray) **Vector-register**: (Cray, IBM S/390 w/vector-register unit)	**SMP**: UNIX, MVS, OS 390 **MPP**: custom **Vector**:custom	Very good for symbolic AI, NN simulations, and real-time NN learning. **MPP** and **Vector-register** especially good for NN's.

DESIGN METHODOLOGY

The following steps can be used for any engineering design [2]:

(a) Define problem
(b) Simplify
(c) Find governing equations
(d) Build
(e) Test and rebuild as needed

Defining a problem includes creating or selecting the concepts to model, observe, and/or derive. An assessment is made of data needed and mathematical tools required. The "simplify" step involves making assumptions and considering different approaches. The selection of hardware platforms and programming languages can significantly effect the complexity, precision, and speed of both simulations and real-time systems. Finding governing equations involves identifying fundamental principles and may require deriving new equations. Different equation-solving techniques are considered; this may include selecting a solution for the fastest real-time response. For simulations, the selection and implementation of a solution may be more dependent on available programming constructs and functions, or on a choice of available numerical techniques. Care should be taken to ensure that the chosen approach does not cause discrepancies between simulations and real-time systems. The "build" step involves fabricating devices after simulating. Engineering of hardware and software may require real-time systems to interactively communicate with a concurrently running simulation [4]. Testing (and rebuilding as needed) involves verifying performance of hardware and software under various operating scenarios. This includes hand-checking computations and assessing resultant data for realistic results (e.g., *order-of-magnitude* checks). It can also involve gathering empirical data from observing real-time system performance, then modifying a simulation to create a more accurate model -- or possibly redesigning and rebuilding the real-time system. Assumptions made during the "simplify" step may need to be reconsidered.

NEUROCOMPUTER PROBLEM DEFINITION

Two methods for designing neurocomputers are presented below. Both can be classified as embedded systems. The first is a bottom-up design; an artificial dendritic tree where biological brain function is modeled as RC analog circuit elements that produce signals *similar* to those propagating through the dendritic tree inter-neuron connections of the human brain. This approach is modeled after the concept shown in Fig. 1. The second design is a top-down design that can process the vector and matrix operations of a typical NN mathematical model; and although it is designed as an embedded device, it has many of the design features of a vector-register supercomputer. The "behavioral" model shown in Fig. 2 inspired this approach.

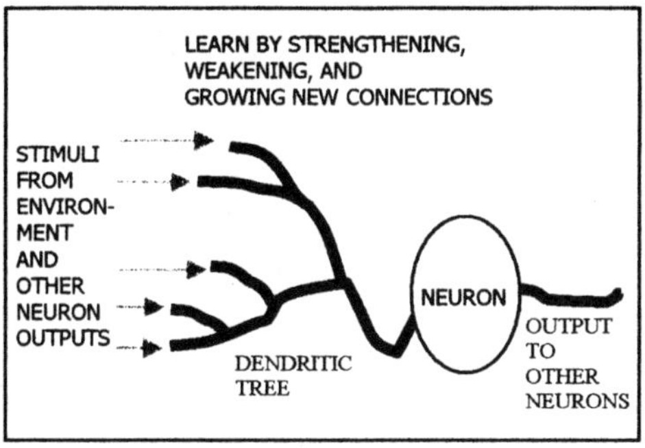

Figure 1. Biological neuron for bottom-up neurocomputer design.

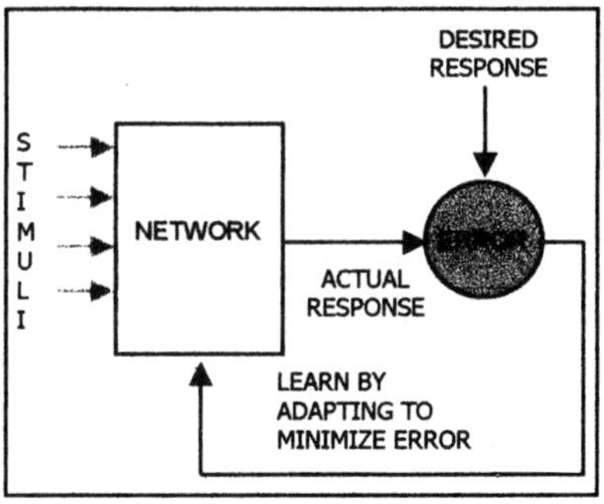

Figure 2. Behavioral model for top-down neurocomputer design.

SIMPLIFICATIONS AND ASSUMPTIONS

The bottom-up neurocomputer design is modeled and simplified by substituting analog circuit transient responses for the electrochemical signals and activations that occur in biological brain function. A design assumption is made that all neurons have fixed connections to all other neurons so that learning can take place by strengthening or weakening connections; the biological growing of new connections is mimicked by electrical connections that are simply inactive until a new connection is desired. The governing equation for the bottom-up neurocomputer presented here is based on the theory in [7] and the biology in Fig. 1. This is modeled as shown in Fig.3.

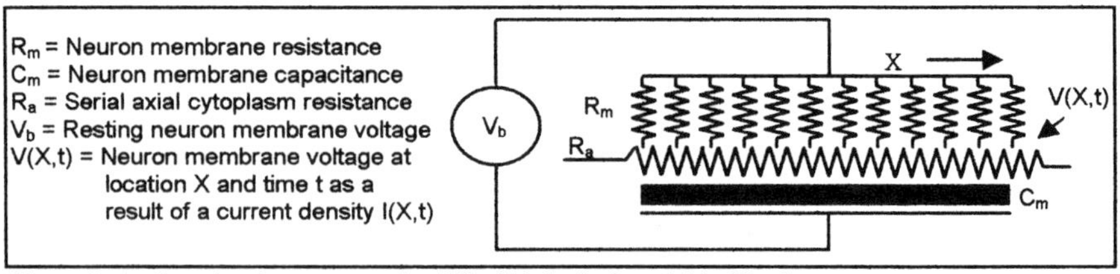

Figure 3. Analog circuit representation [7] of biological model in Fig. 1.

and where neuron membrane voltage V(X,t) is found by solving:

$$R_m * C_m * \frac{\partial V(X,t)}{\partial t} = \frac{R_m}{R_a} * \frac{\partial V^2(X,t)}{\partial X^2} - V + R_m * I(X,t) \qquad (2)$$

The selection of a NN model for a top-down neurocomputer implementation is made here by analyzing historical advances in NN's while keeping in mind the relative success of models to be implemented in hardware or software. The following models were considered [8]-[11]:

(a) Backpropagation, (b) MADALINE III, (c) Hopfield, (d) BOLTZMANN MACHINE, (e) BAM (Bi-directional Associative Memory), and (f) NEOCOGNITRON

The relatively limited applications of the BAM and the NEOCOGNITRON eliminated these two from consideration. The BOLTZMANN MACHINE was eliminated next since the generalized delta rule of backpropagation is a faster learning algorithm for multilayered NN's [9]. Although there have been a number of successful applications of the Hopfield model, the exhaustive connectivity between neurons is less desirable for a single-chip implementation. MADALINE III and Backpropagation function in a similar fashion, however backpropagation exhibits faster learning [10]. Backpropagation is therefore the model chosen for implementation here. A backpropagation neurocomputer chip can be implimented in several ways:

1. Discrete analog components for all computations [9], [13], [14].
2. Digital circuits for all computations except transfer function implemented as serial or parallel analog circuits [9].
3. Digital circuits for all computations including transfer function implemented as serial or parallel look-up tables [15].
4. Parallel vector-register digital circuits for all computations including a polynomial approximation of the transfer function.

The first two approaches rely on analog circuits that can suffer from a number of limitations (e.g., drift, fabrication inconsistencies, conversion delays. etc.) [13], [14]; and although methods have been proposed to somewhat compensate for these problems [14], the approach chosen here is all-digital. The third approach, although entirely digital, would require large on-chip memory to yield the precision required for parallel on-chip learning; look-up table approaches often restrict transfer function computations to serial (one neuron at a time) execution. They may also require learning to be done off-chip with weights down-loaded onto the chip after learning completed. A technique to improve this is proposed in [15] where a "Symmetric Table Addition Method" uses two or more table lookups per transfer function evaluation. However the fourth approach (using a polynomial approximation of the transfer function) is likely to *scale* better when the architecture is expanded to thousands of neurons. This method is therefore chosen here; and on-chip learning is accomplished by defining a new transfer function, the "clipped-sigmoid," which is non-linear over an input domain wide enough to allow the generalized-delta, gradient-decent learning of backpropagation to work. Conversely, this domain is narrow enough to allow the transfer function to be approximated with a relatively high degree of precision; and since the approximation is a simple polynomial, it is easily implemented in digital hardware. For any top-down neurocomputer design, assumptions must be made for the magnitudes and precision needed for weights. Hardware can be simplified by designing the NN to have the minimum required computational precision [2]. It's important to recognize that *greater* precision is needed for evaluation of each neuron transfer function during training [15], [16].

GOVERNING EQUATIONS

The governing equation for the bottom-up neurocomputer design presented here is based on the theory in [7]. This implementation is shown in Fig 4. and is represented by equation (2) above. The field effect transistors (FET's) in Fig. 4 act to inhibit or stimulate by pulling the effected node *down* to the Inhibitory voltage (i.e., V_I=GND=0volts) or *up* to the Excitation voltage (i.e., $V_E > V_b$).

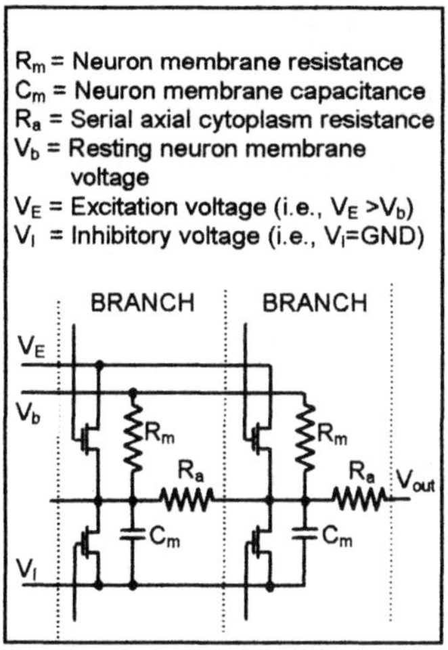

Figure 4. Analog circuit for "bottom-up" design [7].

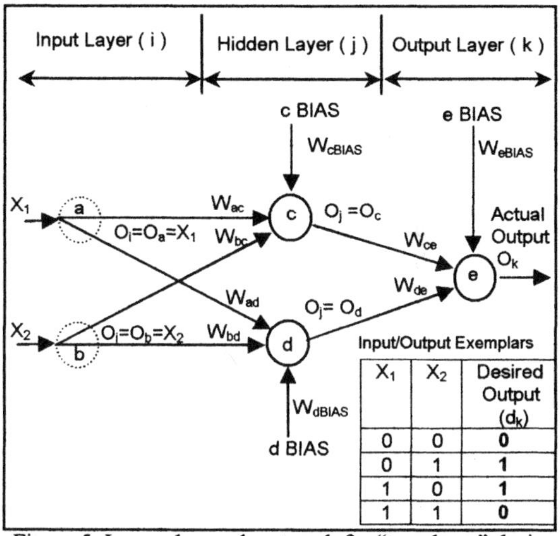

X_1	X_2	Desired Output (d_k)
0	0	0
0	1	1
1	0	1
1	1	0

Figure 5. Layered neural network for "top-down" design.

The architecture for the top-down backpropagation neurocomputer design is shown in Fig. 5 including exemplars (i.e., desired outputs paired with corresponding inputs) for the simple XOR. Here, NN learning involves repeatedly feeding the network exemplars; each time changing weights as a function of a backpropagated error between the desired output and the actual output, until the approximate desired outputs are observed [10], [11]. This is performed as follows:

1. Choose small random initial values for weights (W's), and choose BIAS' (typically set to 1).
2. Feed the input layer an input vector (X_1, X_2) from an exemplar.
3. Propagate the signals forward via non-linear neuron transfer functions (i.e., "sigmoids"):

$$O_j = \frac{1}{1 + e^{-(jBIAS * W_{jBIAS}) + \sum_i (-O_i * W_{ij})}} \quad (3)$$

$$O_k = \frac{1}{1 + e^{-(kBIAS * W_{kBIAS}) + \sum_j (-O_j * W_{jk})}} \quad (4)$$

4. Create an error signal from the difference between actual and desired output for the exemplar, and use it to change the weights between the output layer (k) and the hidden layer (j), and also between the output neuron and bias:

$$\Delta W_{jk} = \eta * [(d_k - O_k) * O_k * (1 - O_k)] * O_j \quad (5)$$

$$\Delta W_{kBIAS} = \eta * [(d_k - O_k) * O_k * (1 - O_k)] * kBIAS \quad (6)$$

where η is the learning rate (typically set between 0.01 and 1).

5. Backpropagate a weighted error signal from the hidden layer (j) to the input layer (i) and use it to change the weights between the hidden layer (j) and the input layer (i), and also between the hidden layer neurons and bias':

$$\Delta W_{ij} = \eta * (O_j * (1 - O_j)) * \sum_k [(d_k - O_k) * O_k * (1 - O_k) * W_{jk}] * O_i \quad (7)$$

$$\Delta W_{jBIAS} = \eta * (O_j * (1 - O_j)) * \sum_k [(d_k - O_k) * O_k * (1 - O_k) * W_{jk}] * jBIAS \quad (8)$$

6. Repeat steps 2 to 5 for each exemplar.
7. Repeat steps 2 to 6 until desired outputs have been *approximately* obtained (i.e., within a specified tolerance).

The neuron transfer function presented here is a polynomial approximation that can be easily implemented using parallel vector-register digital circuits. In preliminary research, the polynomial chosen was a Taylor approximation expanded about a point $f(x_0)=0$ [8]. The Taylor polynomial approximation of any function $f(x)$ is given by:

$$P_{Taylor}(x) = f(x_0) + f'(x - x_0) + f''(x_0)\left[\frac{(x - x_0)^2}{2!}\right] + \dots\dots\dots + f^n(x_0)\left[\frac{(x - x_0)^n}{n!}\right] \quad (9)$$

where $P(x_0) = f(x_0)$, and where the error for all other x points is:

$$Error_{Taylor} = f(x) - P_{Taylor}(x) = (x - x_0)^{(n+1)}\left[\frac{f^{(n+1)}(\xi(x))}{(n+1)!}\right] \quad (10)$$

for some number $\xi(x)$ between x and x_0 [17].

The error for a 15th degree Taylor polynomial approximation of the sigmoid neuron transfer function of equation (3) for (x_0=0) is shown in figures 6 and 7. Large approximation errors are encountered for ($X < -2.5$) and ($X > 2.5$). Through experiment, a better approximation was found to be a 10th degree Taylor polynomial approximation of the e^{-x} part of the sigmoid; this results in a good approximation of the sigmoid for ($-3.5 > X < 3.5$) as shown in Fig. 7. This approximation is termed the "Clipped Sigmoid" and yields sufficient accuracy to allow learning to occur; however certain network initializations need to be specified.

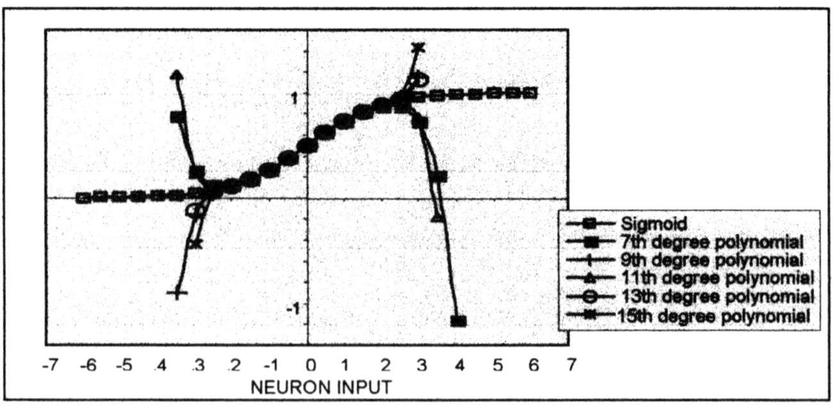

Figure 6. Neuron output for Taylor polynomial approximations of sigmoid: 1/(1+e^-x) expanded about x = 0.

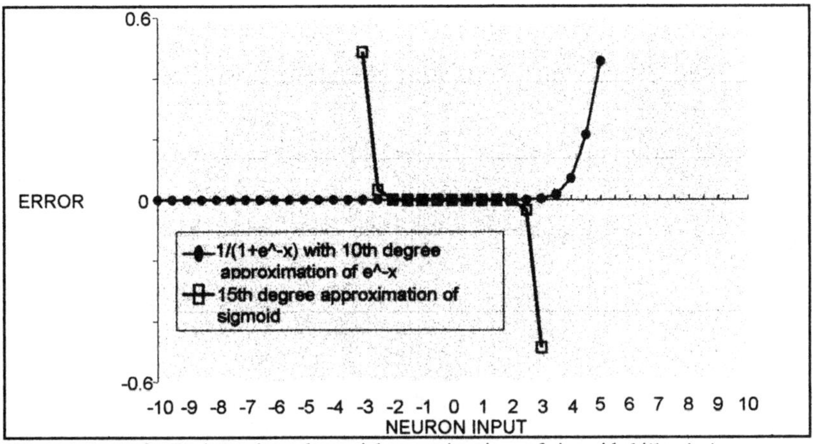

Figure 7. Error for Taylor series polynomial approximations of sigmoid: 1/(1+e^-x).

The initial research of [8] is extended here to include more precise polynomial approximations of the sigmoid (and an initial hardware implementation using FPGA's). The approximation techniques considered are: **(a) Cubic Spline Polynomial, (b) Hermite Polynomial, and (c) Divided-Difference Polynomial**

Cubic Spline is eliminated from further consideration since it is "piecewise" requiring different polynomials for different parts of the input domain. This would require each neuron computation to include a check for input values before applying one of several polynomial approximations. The remaining approaches are better suited for a fully parallel implementation; and will scale better to thousands of neurons.

A $(2n + 1)$ degree Hermite polynomial approximation of a function $f(x)$ with points evaluated at $(x_0, x_1, \ldots, x_n)$ is given in [17] by:

$$P_{Hermite}(x) = \sum_{j=0}^{n} f(x) H_{n,j}(x) + \sum_{j=o}^{n} f'(x) \hat{H}_{n,j}(x) \quad (11)$$

where
$$H_{n,j}(x) = \left[1 - 2\left(x - x_j\right) L'_{n,j}(x_j)\right] L^2_{n,j}(x) \quad (12)$$

$$\hat{H}_{n,j}(x) = \left(x - x_j\right) L^2_{n,j}(x) \quad (13)$$

$$L_{n,j}(x) = \prod_{\substack{i=0 \\ i \neq j}}^{n} \frac{\left(x - x_i\right)}{\left(x_j - x_i\right)} \quad (14)$$

with error:

$$Error_{Hermite} = f(x) - P_{Hermite}(x) = \left[\frac{\prod_{i=0}^{n} \left(x - x_i\right)^2}{(2n+2)!}\right] f^{(2n+2)}(\xi) \quad (15)$$

for some number between adjacent points in $(x_0, x_1, \ldots, x_n)$. This Polynomial is shown approximating $f(x)$=("sigmoid" of equation (3)) in figures 8 and 9. Here, a 12th degree Hermite polynomial yields a relatively good approximation for $(-3.5 > X < 3.5)$.

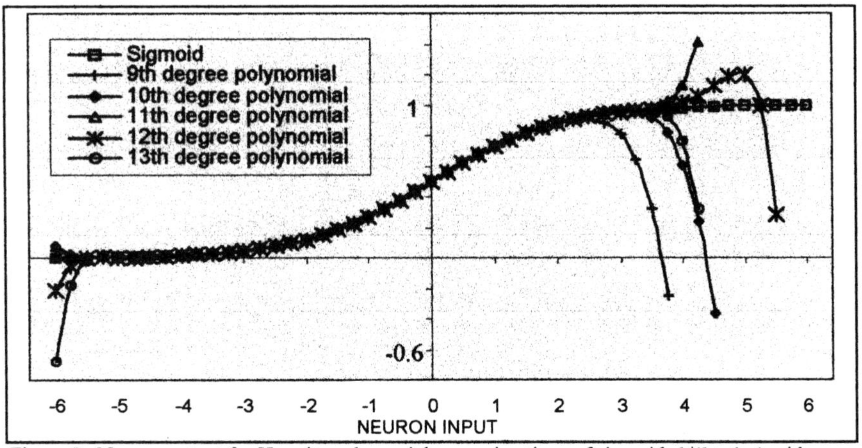

Figure 8. Neuron output for Hermite polynomial approximations of sigmoid: 1/(1+e^-x) with evaluation points at x = [-6 to +6] at 0.25 intervals.

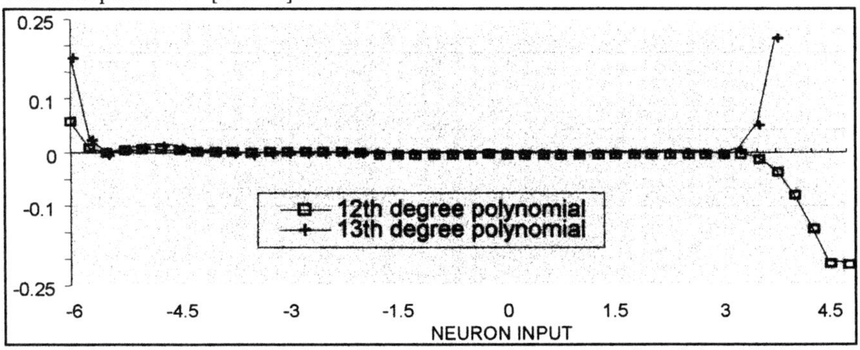

Figure 9. Error for 12th and 13th degree Hermite polynomial approximation of sigmoid: 1/(1+e^-x).

An nth degree Divided Difference polynomial approximation of any function $f(x)$ with points evaluated at $(x_0, x_1, \ldots, x_n)$ is given in [17] by:

$$P_{DivDiff}(x) = a_0 + a_1(x - x_0) + a_2(x - x_0)(x - x_1) + \ldots + a_n(x - x_0)(x - x_1)\cdots(x - x_{n-1}) \quad (16)$$

where

$$a_0 = f[x_0] = f(x_0) \quad (17)$$

$$a_1 = f[x_0, x_1] = \frac{f[x_1] - f[x_0]}{(x_1 - x_0)} \quad (18)$$

$$a_2 = f[x_0, x_1, x_2] = \frac{f[x_1, x_2] - f[x_0, x_1]}{(x_2 - x_0)} = \frac{1}{x_2 - x_0}\left[\frac{f(x_2) - f(x_0)}{x_2 - x_1} - \frac{f(x_2)}{x_1 - x_0}\right] \quad (19)$$

$$= \frac{f(x_0)}{(x_0 - x_1)(x_0 - x_2)} + \frac{f(x_1)}{(x_1 - x_0)(x_1 - x_2)} + \frac{f(x_2)}{(x_2 - x_0)(x_2 - x_1)}$$

$$a_n = f[x_0, x_1, \dots x_n]$$
$$= \frac{f(x_0)}{(x_0 - x_1)\cdots(x_0 - x_n)} + \frac{f(x_1)}{(x_1 - x_0)\cdots(x_1 - x_n)} + \dots + \frac{f(x_n)}{(x_n - x_0)(x_n - x_{n-1})} \quad (20)$$

Divided-Difference polynomial approximations of the sigmoid are shown in figures 10 and 11, and provide the *best* approximations here (i.e., best precision over the widest domain of input values). Two 12th degree Divided Difference polynomial approximations are shown in Fig. 11; one with evaluation points over an X domain from –6 to 6; the other from –10 to 10. The second one yields an approximating error of (0.01) over a relatively wide domain and is the polynomial chosen for implinentation.

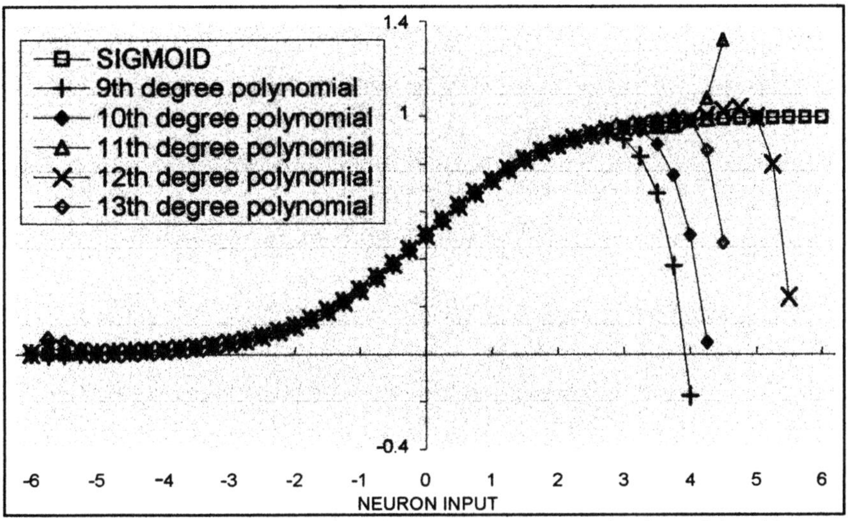

Figure 10. Neuron output with Divided-Difference polynomial approximations of sigmoid: 1/(1+e^-x) with evaluation points at x = [- 6, - 5, - 4, - 3, - 2, - 1, -0. 5, 0.5, 1, 2, 3, 4, 5, 6]

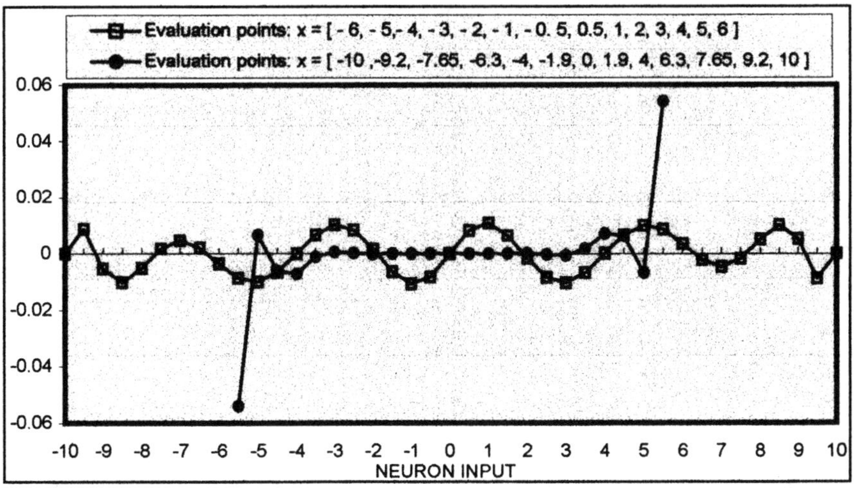

Figure 11. Approximation error for 12th degree Divided-Difference polynomial approximations of sigmoid: 1/(1+e^-x)

To validate this choice, all two-input logic gates were simulated. Tests included evaluating the effect of clipping the standard sigmoid (i.e., no polynomial approximation) which even improved learning for some cases. In Fig. 12, the Divided-Diffence polynomial sigmoid approximation is shown to allow successful learning. This XOR simulation is clipped at -5.25 > X < 5.25 to show the robostness of the method (i.e., it also works with a domain of –10 > X < 10).

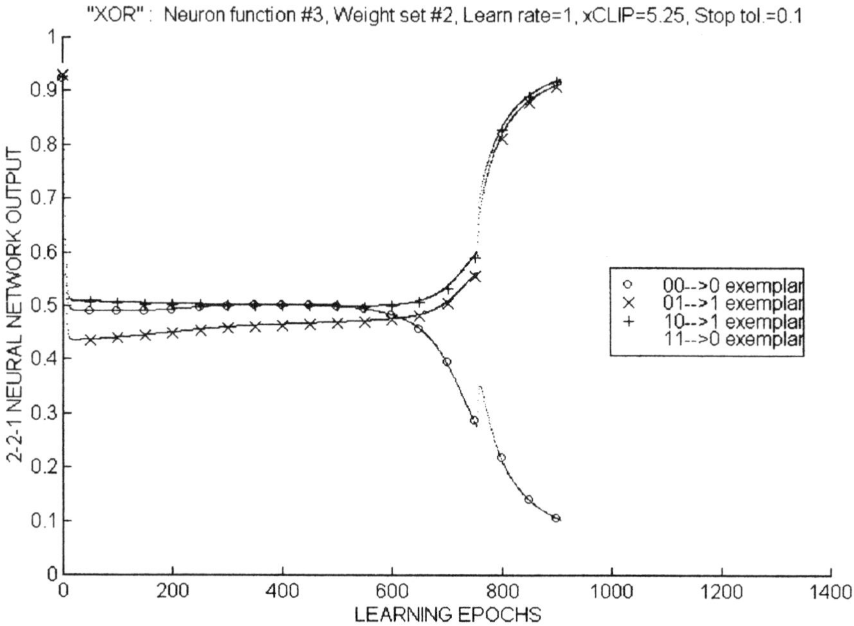

Figure 12. Backpropagation learning using 12th degree Divided-Difference polynomial approximation of sigmoid, and "clipping" outside of domain –5.25 >X <5.25.

BUILDING AND TESTING

The bottom-up design in Fig. 13 is an artificial dendritic tree VLSI chip. It has 64 neurons and combines the analog circuits of Fig. 4 with digital circuits to latch in 4-bit values allowing each node to be excited or inhibited for 16 different "pulse-lengths." The chip has the equivalent of 10,000 transistors on a 2mm x 2mm die [6].

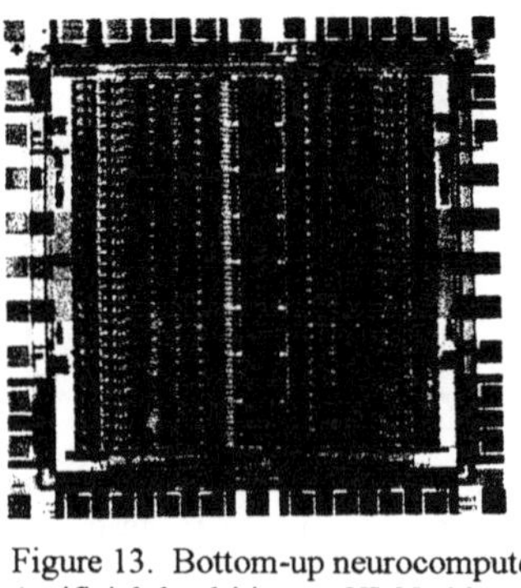

Figure 13. Bottom-up neurocomputer (artificial dendritic tree VLSI chip).

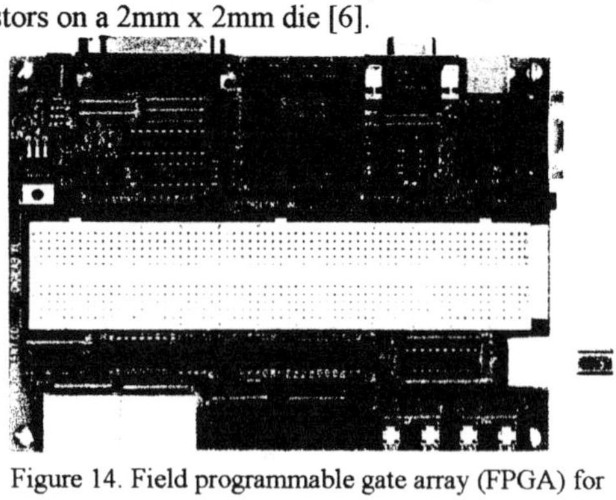

Figure 14. Field programmable gate array (FPGA) for top-down neurocomputer development.

This chip was fabricated and bench-tested by latching in various pulse-length values, then measuring outputs for desired transient output voltage responses.

The top-down neurocomputer design is presently under development using the Field Programmable Gate Array (FPGA) shown in Fig. 14. Testing any digital circuit implementation (FPGA, discrete IC chips, VLSI, etc.), or even an analog circuit implementation of a backpropagation model, involves feeding the network each exemplar after training is completed to verify desired outputs are obtained. This can be followed by testing *never-seen* inputs. Testing complex NN hardware can also involve developing verification programs for both simulated and physical prototype architectures [18].

CONCLUSIONS

The top-down design presented here can process the mathematics of the well-known backpropagation NN model; and although designed as an embedded device, it has an architecture similar to a vector-register supercomputer. This design is entirely digital, fully parallel, and implements a polynomial approximation of the sigmoid transfer function to allow parallel on-chip learning.

Even though the semiconductor industry continues to increase the number of transistors per unit area, the chip-area required to include the neurons needed for a bottom-up neurocomputer to produce useful *higher-reasoning* would need to be much larger than a typical chip. Biological brains have the advantage of being three-dimensional whereas integrated circuits are mostly two-dimensional (despite multiple levels of *layerization*). Another problem is connecting all of these neurons since wire routing would be in mostly two dimensions. Even with several layers of *metallization* (for wires), it would be very difficult to connect all neurons (with each potentially connected to all others). Perhaps the most difficult problem to overcome in mimicking biological learning is that inter-neuron connections are not only strengthened or weakened, but are grown. Wires on chips are fixed, and considering the required extensive connectivity between neurons, useful bottom-up designs can be difficult to realize.

Future research will investigate merging bottom-up techniques for pre-processing sensory data (e.g., visual, auditory, olfactory) with top-down techniques for higher reasoning; including combining neural networks with symbolic AI programming.

References

[1] J. T. Wunderlich, " Defining the limits of machine intelligence," in *Proc. of IEEE SECon 2003 Nat'l Conf.*, Ocho Rios, Jamaica, 2003.

[2] J. T. Wunderlich, "Simulation vs. real-time control; with applications to robotics and neural networks," in *Proc. of ASEE Nat'l Conf.*, Albuquerque, NM, 2001.

[3] Seiffert, U., "Artificial neural networks on massively parallel computer hardware," in *Proc. ESANN 2002 European Symposium on Artificial Neural Networks*, Bruges, Belgium, 2002.

[4] Campos, D. and Wunderlich, J. T., "Development of an interactive simulation with real-time robots for search and rescue," in *Proc. of IEEE/ASME Int'l Conf. on Flexible Manufacturing*, Hiroshima, Japan, 2002.

[5] Wunderlich, J. T., "Focusing on the blurry distinction between microprocessors and microcontrollers," in *Proc. of ASEE Nat'l Conf.*, 1999, Charlotte, NC.

[6] J. T. Wunderlich, et al., "Design of an artificial dendritic tree VLSI microprocessor," University of Delaware research report, 1993.

[7] Elias, J. G., "Artificial dendritic trees," *Neural Computation, vol. 5*, pp. 648-663, 1993.

[8] Wunderlich, J. T., "Design of a Neurocomputer Vector Microprocessor (with on-chip learning)," Masters thesis, Pennsylvania State University, Jan. 1992.

[9] Soucek, B., "*Neural and Concurrent Real-Time Systems, The Sixth Generation*." New York: John Wiley & Sons, 1989.

[10] Widrow, B., "30 years of adaptive neural networks: perceptron, madaline, and backpropagation," in *Proc. 2nd IEEE Intl. Conf. on Neural Networks*, 1990.

[11] Rumelhart, D.E., and McClelland, J. L., "*Parallel Distributed Processing*." Cambridge, MA: M.I.T. Press, 1986.

[12] Mirhassani, M., Ahmadi, M., Miller, M. C., "A mixed-signal VLSI neural network with on-chip learning," in *Proc. of the 2003 IEEE Canadian Conference on Electrical and Computer Engineering*, 2003.

[13] Liu, J., and Brooke, M., "Fully parallel on-chip learning hardware neural network for real-time control," in *Proc. IEEE International Symposium on in Circuits and Systems*, 1999.

[14] Card, H. C., McNeill, D. K., and Schneider, R. S., "How forgiving is on-chip learning of circuit variations?," in *Proc. of the 5th Irish Neural Networks Conference*, Maynooth, Ireland, 1995.

[15] Nihal, K. S., Schlessman, J. A., and Schulte, M. J., "Symmetric table methods for neural network approximations, " in *Proc. SPIE: Advanced Signal Processing Algorithms, Architectures, and Implementations XI*, San Diego, CA., 2001.

[16] Beiu, V., "How to build VLSI-efficient neural chips," *in Proc. ICSC Symp. On Engineering Intelligent Systems, Tenerife*, Spain, 1998.

[17] Burden, R. L., and Faires, J. D., *"Numerical Analysis, "* Brooks Cole publishing, 7 ed., 2000.

[18] Wunderlich, J. T., "Random number generator macros for the system assurance kernel product assurance macro interface," *Systems Programmers User Manual for IBM S/390 Systems Architect ure Verification*, IBM S/390 Hardware Development Lab, Poughkeepsie, NY, 1997.

JOSEPH T. WUNDERLICH

Dr. Wunderlich is the primary Computer Engineering Program Coordinator for Elizabethtown College. Previously, he worked for Purdue University as an Assistant Professor and for IBM as a researcher and hardware development engineer. He received his Ph.D. in Electrical and Computer Engineering from the University of Delaware, his Masters in Engineering Science/Computer Design from the Pennsylvania State University and his BS in Engineering from the University of Texas at Austin.

Optimized Low Power Techniques for Cache Architecture Using WTS Buffer with Tag Skipping and SF-LRU Algorithm

Nazeih Botros, Adil Akaaboune, Jaafar Alghazo
Southern Illinois University at Carbondale
Department of Electrical and Computer Engineering
Carbondale, IL.

Abstract: In this paper we present two novel approaches to reduce the power consumption for a 4-way set-associativity cache. The first approach is a modification of the technique proposed by [Choi et al. 2000], which allows skipping tag look-ups to achieve better power consumption design. In this paper we use a Write tag-skipping (WTS) Buffer (WTSB) that reduces the number of misses by 50-80% therefore reducing accesses to power consuming devices such as memory. The second approach is a robust replacement algorithm, SF-LRU . This algorithm is proposed to improve the performance of the LRU algorithm through the integration of the LFU using the second chance concept. Experimental results show that the SF-LRU significantly reduces the number of cache misses providing a maximum value of approximately 6.3% improvement in the miss ratio over the LRU algorithm in data cache and approximately 9.3% improvement in miss ratio in instruction cache.

INTRODUCTION:

Decreasing power consumption in hand-held devices and high-performance processors is now one of the most critical design concerns. In order to reduce power consumption we are focusing on reducing the miss rate [Chakrabarti, 2001][Memik et al. 2003]. In this paper, we propose a new technique to reduce the number of cache miss on architectures that support Not-load-on-write-miss (NLOWM) and uses tag-skipping technique. Our proposed technique significantly reduces the number of accesses to main memory, thereby reducing the overall energy consumption.

FIRST APPROACH (WTS BUFFER WITH TAG SKIPPING)

To explain the tag skipping for unnecessary tag lookups, we first define the unnecessary tag lookups with the following example. Given two memory-read accesses, if we assume that the first access results in a cache-hit. For the second memory read, the tag is looked up, and if it happens to result in a hit the instruction (data) is read from cache. This is the normal operation of cache. The cache-line in our design consists of four words all sharing the same tag, since the cache line has only one tag. Now if the two consecutive memory-read accesses were from the same cache line, we clearly see that the tag lookup for the second is unnecessary and that if the first resulted in a hit, then definitely the second will result in hit also. By skipping the unnecessary tag lookups the power consumption of tag accessing is reduced significantly.

We propose NLOWM with WTS buffer, a one-cache line buffer, to be placed between the cache and lower level memory. This buffer acts as a temporary storage for the requested block on a write miss. The write buffer miss-handling procedure consists of fetching the requested block from main memory to the WTS buffer. The proposed architecture always results in a hit for sequential accesses to the same cache line stored in the buffer. It is apparent that the new architecture reduces power consumption through the reduction of the number of accesses to lower memory hierarchies. It is found that the tag skipping technique is appropriate for three instances as shown in Figure 1. The three instances are:

1. If the first access read (write) resulted in a cache-hit, then definitely the cache contains the requested data (instruction) cache line. Thus the second access read (write) from the same cache line always results in a cache-hit. Tag comparison is skipped and hit information is sent and treated.
2. If the first read access resulted in a cache-miss, then definitely the cache does not contain the requested data's cache line. The miss-handling procedure is applied where the cache-line is brought from the main memory to the cache. The second read access would automatically result in a hit if it corresponds to the same cache line because the hit information was updated in the miss-handling step. Thus tag comparison is skipped in the second access since it corresponds to the same cache-line.
3. If the first write access resulted in a cache-miss, then definitely the cache does not contain the corresponding cache-line. The WTS buffer write miss-handling procedure is applied and the cache-line is transferred to the buffer from the main memory. The second write access would also automatically result in a buffer hit if it corresponds to the same cache line; therefore the tag look-up is skipped (tag-skipping-hit) since we already know it is a hit from the updated hit information.

THE SECOND APPROACH (SF-LRU ALGORITHM)

In this paper, we introduce a cache replacement algorithm based on LRU and LFU. The algorithm combines both the frequency and recency of blocks in making the decision to replace blocks. The basic philosophy is to modify the LRU so that not only is there a counter to count the number of times a memory block has been referenced but also to give a second chance to those memory reference that have been referenced to the maximum of the counter before being thrown away. This combined number we will call RFCV (Recency-Frequency Control Value). Figure 2 shows hardware architecture of the calculation implementation for the RFCV value.

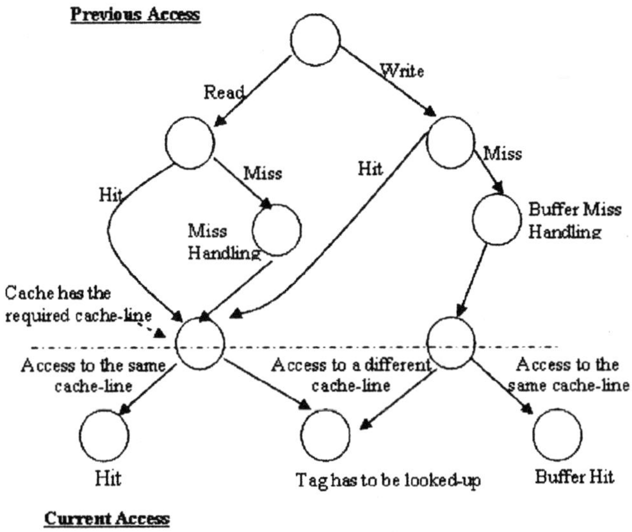

Figure 1: Flow of Tag skipping operations integrating the WTS buffer.

Using this implementation of calculating the RFCV value, the algorithm determines either to delete the last block from the memory or a previous one. The algorithm actually compares the RFCV values for all the blocks in the set and deletes the one with the lowest value:

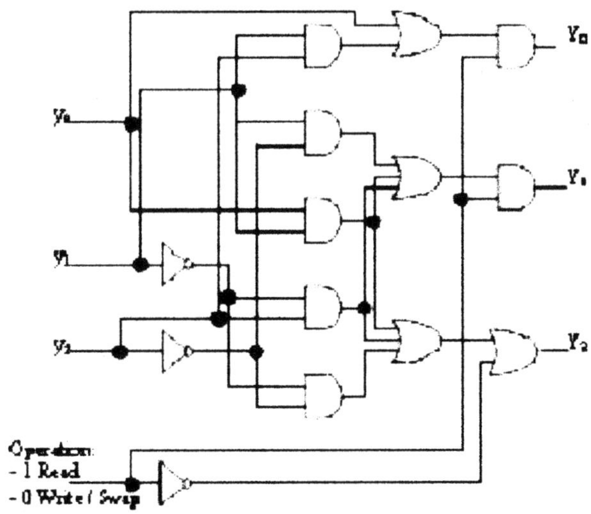

Figure 2: Hardware representation of the RFCV (RFCV=Y=(y+1)) operation.

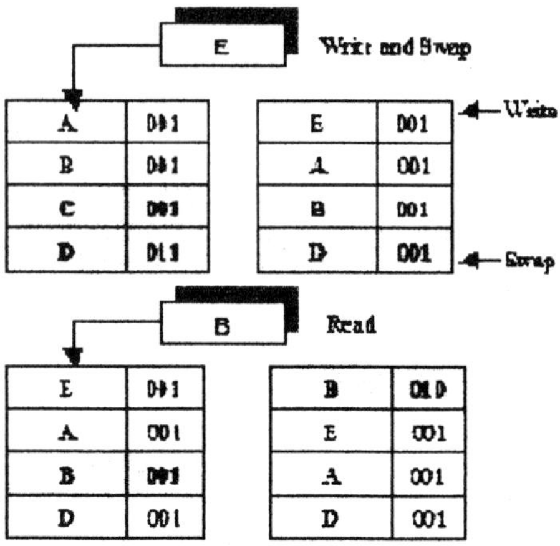

Figure 3: SF-LRU operation

Figure 3 shows the flow of SF-LRU algorithm for two cases. For write, the RFCV values are checked for the last two blocks. Since the last is greater than the previous SF-LRU gives a second chance for the last block and evicts the previous. Swapping the two blocks then executing the LRU algorithm accomplishes this task. As shown in the figure that RFCV values are then updated.

EXPERIMENTAL RESULTS

We implement the proposed techniques using a trace driven simulator. The base configuration for the first approach is 64K bytes, 32 bytes per cache line 4-way set associative data cache. The WTS buffer is one line entry buffer with 32 bytes size. A set of programs is picked up from SPEC92 benchmark suites. We first implement and investigate the Tag-Skipping technique on two cache architectures; one that supports LOWM and another that supports NLOWM using [Choi et al. 2000]'s technique. Then we compare our technique, which we refer to as NLOWM-WTSB with that of Choi et al.'s on NLOWM architecture.

Our experimental results as shown in Figures 4 and 5 reveal the following:

- Enormous decrease in miss rate in the LOWM and NLOWM-WTSB architectures.
- All tag-skipping operation that occurs in LOWM and NLOWM-WTSB architectures are tag-skipping-hit operations.
- The rate of tag-skipping-hit operations increases in LOWM and LOWM-WTSB architectures.
- The miss rate in LOWM and LOWM-WTSB being significantly reduced results in a significant power consumption reduction.

The base configuration for the second approach is 2K to 128K bytes, 8 bytes per cache line for I-cache and 32 bytes per cache line for

D-cache, 4-way set associative cache. A set of programs is picked up from SPEC92 benchmark suites. Figures 6-11 shows the simulation results. Through comprehensive comparison between SF-LRU, LRU and LFU, It is shown that the SF-LRU outperforms the latter two. In particular, the SF-LRU can provide a maximum value of approximately 6.3% improvement in the miss ratio over the LRU algorithm in data cache and approximately 9.3% improvement in miss ratio in instruction cache. This improvement in miss rate implies that the number of accesses to lower level memory is reduced thereby reducing the overall power consumption.

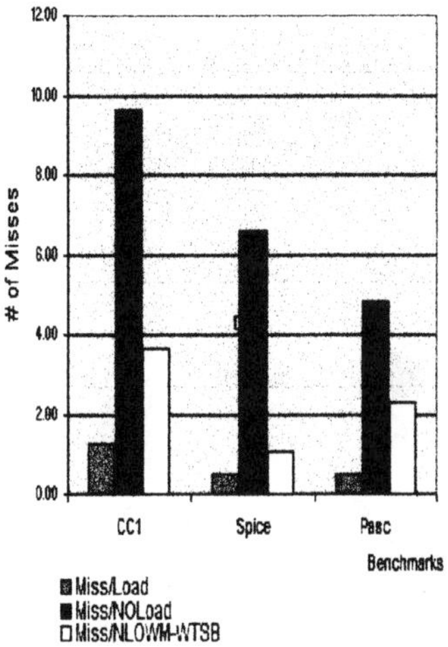

Figure 4: Comparing Misses between Load and not Load on Write Miss

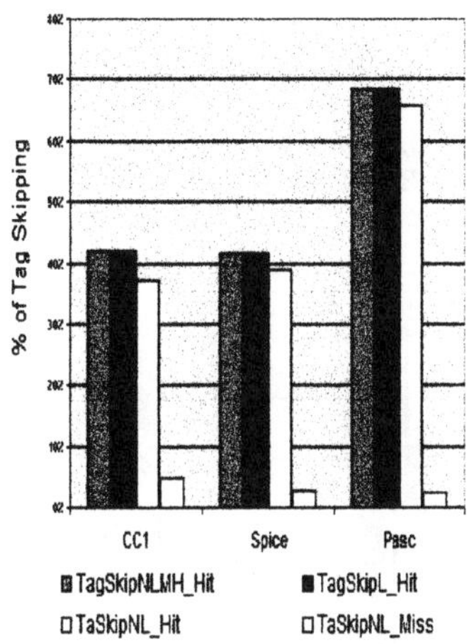

Figure 5: Comparing # of Tag Skipping between Load and not Load on Write Miss

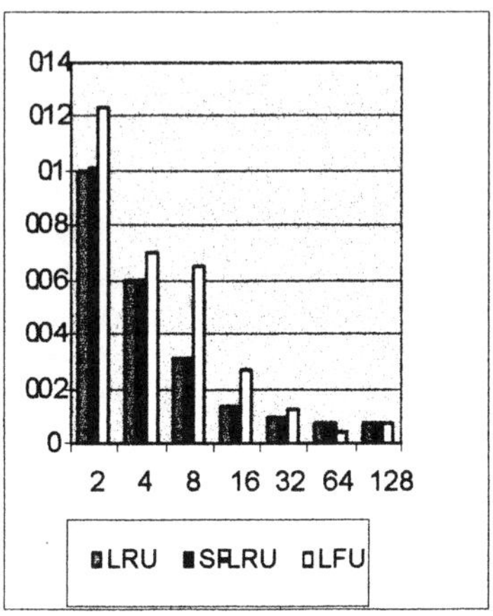

Figure 6: 32 block size D-cache for CC1 Benchmark

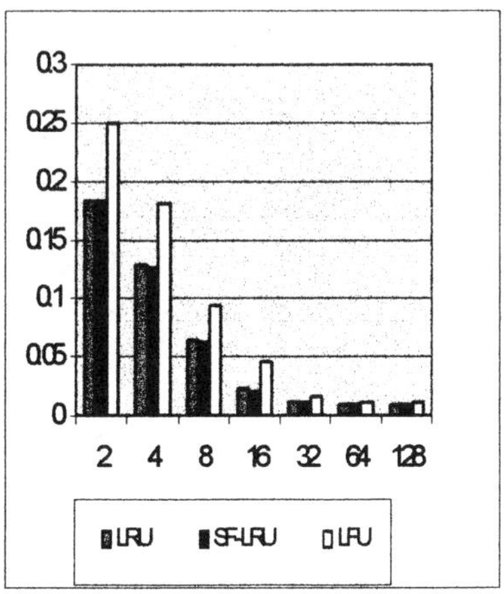

Figure 7: 32 block size D-cache for Pasc Benchmark

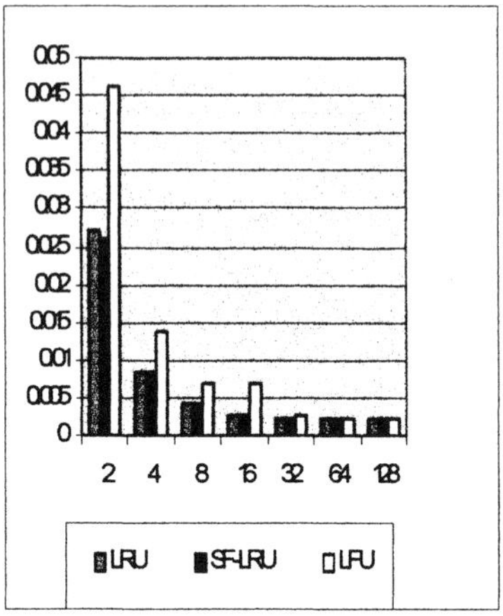

Figure 8: 32 block size D-cache for Spice Benchmark

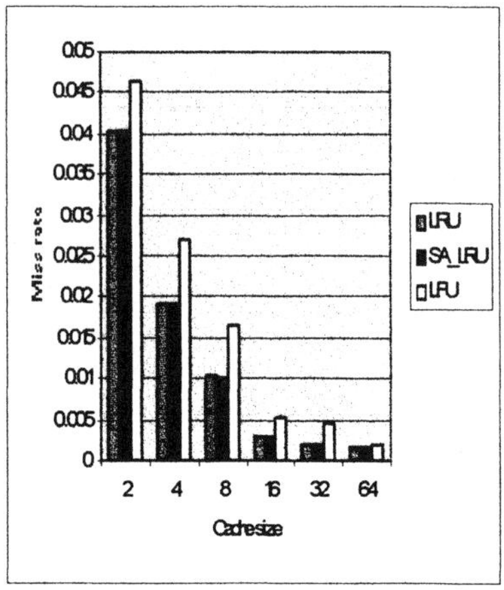

Figure 9: 8 block size I-cache for Spice Benchmark

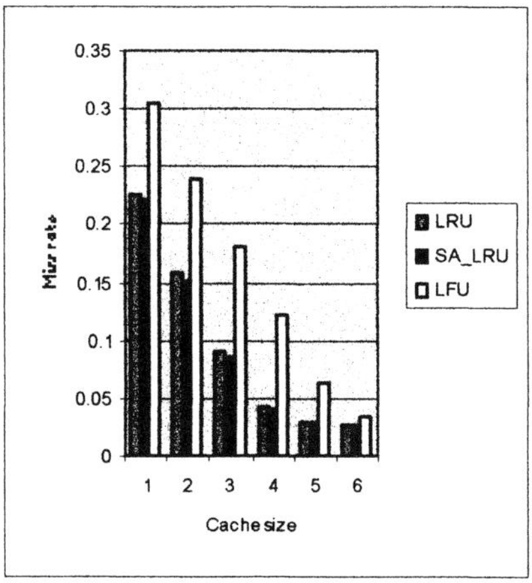

Figure 10: 8 block size I-cache for CC1 Benchmark

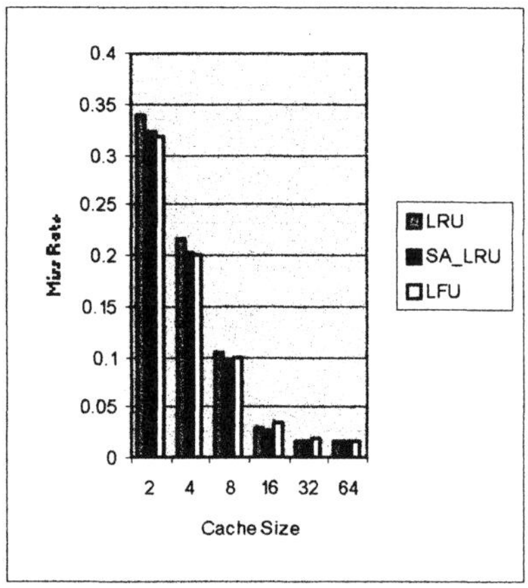

Figure 11: 8 block size I-cache for Pasc Benchmark

REFERENCES

[1] Chakrabarti, C., 2001," Cache Design and Exploration for Low Power Embedded Systems," IEEE International Conference on Performance, Computing, and Communications, pp. 135 – 139.

[2] Memik, G., Reinman, G., and Mangione-Smith, W., 2003," Reducing Energy and Delay Using Efficient Victim Caches," ISLPED '03.

[3] Choi, H., Yim, M.K., Lee,J.Y., and Lee, Y.T., 2000, " Low Power 4-Way Associative Cache For Embedded SOC Design," Proceedings of the 13th Annual IEEE Int'l ASIC/SOC Conference., pp.231-235.

HIGH PERFORMANCE REAL-TIME FUZZY LOGIC SYSTEM USING FIELD PROGRAMMABLE GATE ARRAYS AND VHDL

BRIAN T. HEMMELMAN
South Dakota School of Mines and Technology
Electrical and Computer Engineering Department
Rapid City, South Dakota

ABSTRACT

A hardware implementation of a real-time fuzzy logic system has been developed on a low-cost Xilinx Spartan IIe Field Programmable Gate Array using VHDL. The parallelized architecture developed is suitable for standalone fuzzy controllers or for embedding in larger systems such as fuzzy image processors. Testing so far indicates that system clock speeds of 120 MHz are possible, with the system output being updated approximately every 100 ns. While the Mamdani fuzzy inference engine itself can operate at much greater speeds, its effective throughput in the design is roughly 250 million fuzzy logic inferences per second for a two-input, one-output system with five membership functions per input. The defuzzification method used is a weighted average technique. The architecture can be easily scaled without significant impact on the output update rate due to its parallel operation.

1. INTRODUCTION

Fuzzy logic has been successfully used in a wide variety of applications including language processing (Sun, et. al, 2002), decision support (Richards, 2002), data clustering (Leski, 2003), and control systems (Chandrana, 2002). While some applications of fuzzy logic can be done offline, others require real-time operation. Most often fuzzy logic computations have been done with software, but the need for real-time operation has led to the development of several types of hardware implementations. Early development was based more on analog circuits such as those created by Sasaki and Ueno (1993) and Patyra and Long (1994). Subsequent digital approaches have largely been based on custom ASIC design (Evmorfopoulos and Avaritsiotis, 1999, and Ascia and Catania, 1999). In this paper we present a parallelized fuzzy logic architecture that can be implemented in low-cost Field Programmable Gate Arrays (FPGAs).

2. INTEGER BASED FUZZY LOGIC

Historically, fuzzy logic applications (e.g. control systems) have essentially three stages in the system: fuzzification, rule inference (or rule evaluation), and defuzzification. Our basic design uses symmetric triangular and plateau-like membership functions as seen in Fig. 1 to fuzzify the crisp inputs. Most fuzzy logic systems have a range of 0.0 to 1.0 for the degree of membership. However, since it is really only the relative degree of membership that matters in many applications, there is no reason why the height of membership functions can't be integer (or even fixed-point) values if a sufficient number of values are allowed. In this architecture we assume the crisp inputs are 8-bit integers. The height of the input membership functions are then chosen as suitable integer values such that the slopes of the membership functions are convenient integer or fixed-point values. A typical "convenient" value would be an integer power of two for instance. Figure 1 shows the specific values used for the design described in this paper. Mamdani rule inference has been used to determine integer degrees of membership to the output membership functions which are also symmetric triangles as well as plateaus. We use a weighted-average defuzzification technique to compute a crisp 8-bit integer output.

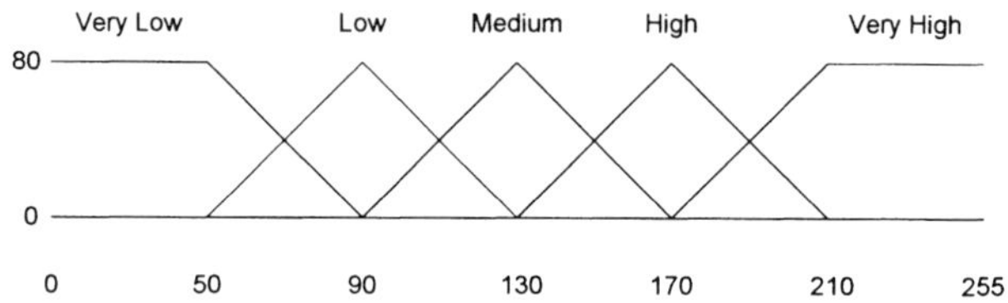

Figure 1. Input membership functions. The horizontal axis spans the input range of 8-bit integers. The vertical axis plots the degree of membership as integer values.

3. FUZZY ARCHITECTURE

Our fundamental architecture for the fuzzy system is shown in Fig. 2. The degrees of membership for any crisp input are computed using a vector of Membership Function Circuits (MFCs). In addition to the degree of membership, each MFC has a single-bit output that indicates whether the crisp input belongs to the that membership function. The outputs of the MFCs are then directed to a matrix of Fuzzy Inference Nodes (FINs).

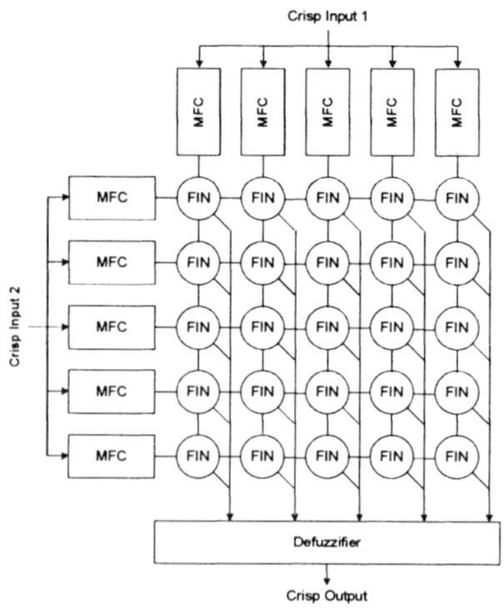

Figure 2. Fuzzy logic chip architecture. Crisp inputs are fuzzified by MFCs. A matrix of FINs then perform rule evaluation, subsequently leading to defuzzification.

Each FIN essentially performs one Mamdani rule evaluation to determine the degree of membership to the corresponding output membership function. All of the FIN outputs are then fed to the weighted-average defuzzifier unit.

3.1 Membership Function Circuit

The MFC architecture for a symmetric triangular membership function can be seen in Fig. 3. Given that the slopes of the membership function are "convenient" numbers (positive or negative two, in this particular design), there is no need for multiplication in order to determine the degree of membership. Any value on the upslope line or downslope line can be computed by simple shifting and addition. One line equation circuit computes the intersection of the crisp input with the upslope line. Another computes the intersection with the downslope line. For the arbitrary triangular membership function illustrated in Fig. 4 we use a set of comparators to determine whether the crisp input is less than c1, between c1 and c2, between c2 and c3, or greater than c3. The comparator outputs are transformed into select bits allowing the MFC multiplexer to output the appropriate degree of membership. The comparator outputs are also used to signal whether the degree of membership is nonzero. This signal is called a trigger bit. A similar approach is used for plateau membership functions.

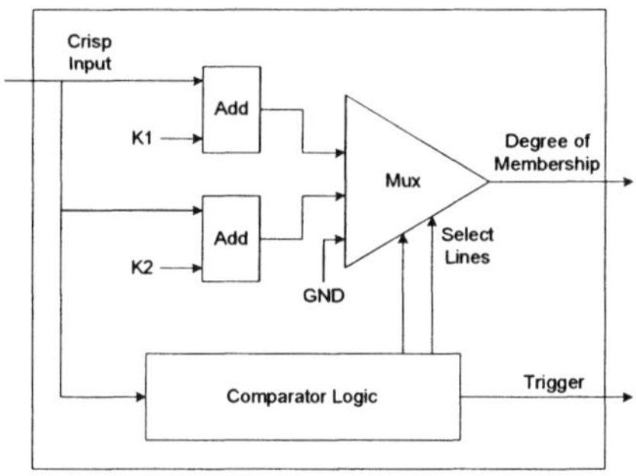

Figure 3. Membership Function Circuit architecture for a triangular membership function. Comparator logic determines where the crisp input lies within the membership function and then selects the appropriate degree of membership.

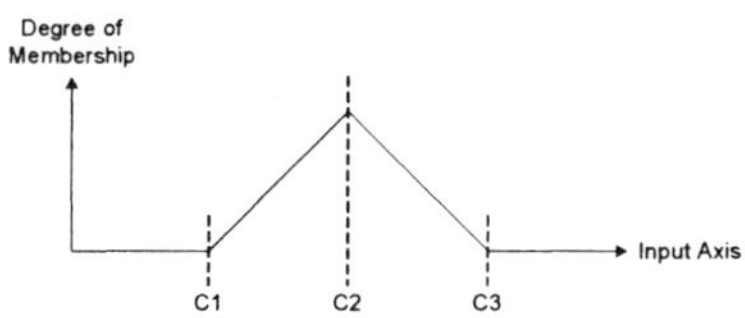

Figure 4. Important sections of a symmetric triangular membership function. C1, C2, and C3 separate the various piecewise linear sections.

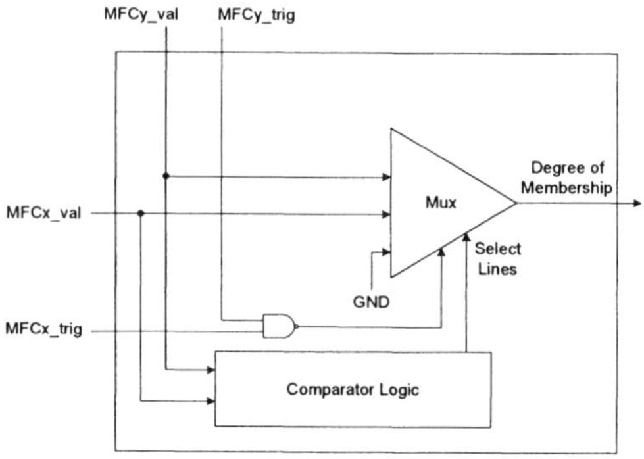

Figure 5. Fuzzy Inference Node architecture. If both trigger bits are asserted the comparator will select the minimum degree of membership, otherwise the output is zero.

3.2 Fuzzy Inference Node

Since the MFCs output trigger bits, the architecture of a FIN is quite simple, as is seen in Fig. 5. The trigger bits that intersect at a particular FIN are ANDed to indicate whether a Mamdani rule inference should take place at that particular node. If no rule needs to be evaluated the FIN outputs a zero degree of membership for the output membership function corresponding to that rule. Otherwise, a single comparator can be used to determine how to multiplex the minimum input degree of membership to the output.

3.3 Defuzzifier

The defuzzification process implemented in this specific design is a weighted average approach. The specific calculation performed is

$$OUTPUT = \frac{\sum_i \mu(z_i) * C_{z_i}}{\sum_i \mu(z_i)} \tag{1}$$

where z_i is the i'th output membership function, $\mu(z_i)$ is the maximum degree of membership in the i'th output membership function and C_{zi} is the "center" of the i'th output membership function. While perhaps not quite as popular as other defuzzification methods (e.g. centroid), this weighted average lends itself well to simple calculations (and therefore simple circuitry). Given that the number of output membership functions is relatively small, combinational multipliers and adders for every mathematical operation have been built, and all operate in parallel to compute both the numerator and denominator in Equation 1. These are fed into a simple sequential divider to yield a crisp 8-bit output as seen in Fig. 6. By far, most of the time delay in the current design is due to the divider.

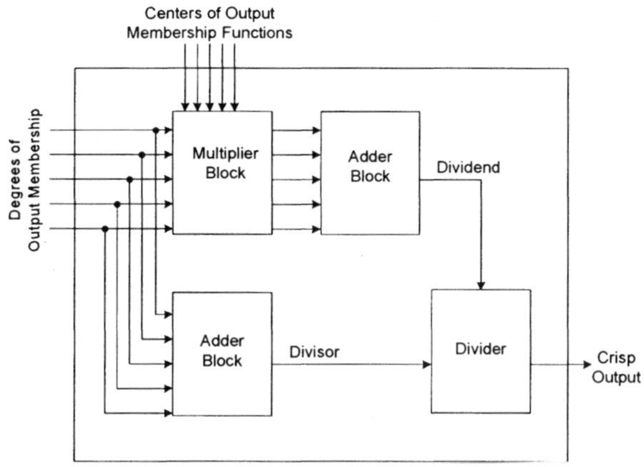

Figure 6. Defuzzifier block architecture. All multiplies and adds for the weighted average are done in parallel and then fed to the divider.

4. SIMULATION RESULTS

The architecture from Section 3 was coded in VHDL and compiled for an XC2S50E-6FT256 Xilinx Spartan IIe target device. After synthesis, a post-place and route timing model was created for detailed timing simulations. These simulations indicate that 120 MHz+ clock speeds are possible, allowing the crisp output to be updated approximately every 100 ns. A typical simulation run can be seen in Fig. 7. Simulation work shows that the MFC and FIN blocks can actually operate within an 8.33 ns window which equates to a rule evaluation rate of approximately 3.0 billion fuzzy logic inferences per second (3.0 GigaFLIPS). However, the multiple clock cycles consumed by the sequential divider reduces the overall throughput to about 250 MegaFLIPS.

5. CONCLUSIONS

This paper presents a high-performance real-time parallelized fuzzy logic architecture designed for low-cost FPGAs. Current simulation results indicate that the maximum effective rule evaluation rate is approximately 250 MFLIPS with the system output being updated every 100 ns. The parallel nature of the MFCs and FINs allows additional input membership functions to be easily added (and thus increase the FLIP rate). However, this would not particularly change the output update rate as that is primarily determined by the speed of the division circuit in the defuzzification unit. A more efficient division circuit should improve the output update rate.

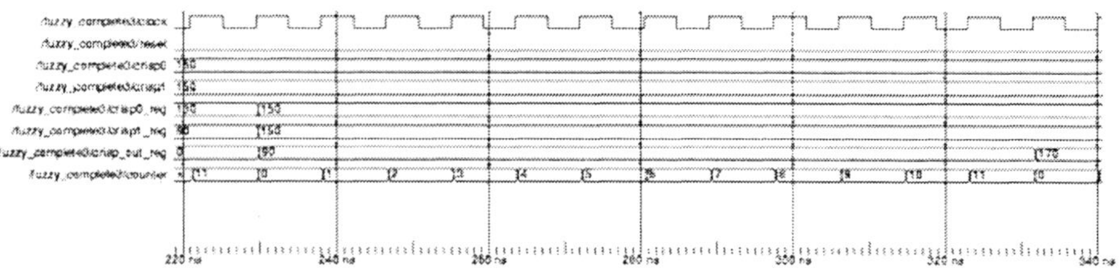

Figure 7. Typical simulation results for the fuzzy logic chip. Approximately 100 ns elapse between the latching of the crisp inputs and the update of the crisp output.

6. REFERENCES

Sun, J., Karray, F., Basir, O., and Kamel, M., 2002, "Natural Language Understanding Through Fuzzy Logic Inference and Its Application to Speech Recognition", Proceedings of the 2002 IEEE Intenational Conference on Fuzzy Systems, Honolulu, HI, pp. 1120-1125.

Richards, Robert, 2002, "Application of Multiple Artificial Intelligence Techniques for an Aircraft Carrier Landing Decision Support Tool", Proceedings of the 2002 IEEE International Conference on Fuzzy Systems, Honolulu, HI, pp. 7-11.

Leski, J.M., 2003, "Generalized Weighted Fuzzy Clustering", *IEEE Transactions on Fuzzy Systems*, vol. 11, pp. 709-715.

Chandrana, C., 2002, "Implementation of Real Time Fuzzy Logic Controller Using Field Programmable Gate Arrays (FPGAs)", Master's Thesis, South Dakota School of Mines and Technology, Rapid City, SD.

Sasaki, M., and Ueno, F., 1993, "A VLSI Implementation of Fuzzy Logic Controller Using Current Mode CMOS Circuits", Proceedings of the 1993 Conference on Industrial Fuzzy Control and Intelligent Systems, pp. 215-220.

Patyra, M., and Long, J., 1994, "Synthesis of Current Mode Building Blocks for Fuzzy Logic Control Circuits", Proceedings of the 1994 Conference of Circuits and Systems, pp. 283-286.

Evmorfopoulos, N.E., and Avaritsiotis, J.N., 1999, "Adaptive Digital Fuzzy Hardware in Application-Specific Integrated Circuits", Proceedings of the 1999 IEEE International Conference on Electronics, Circuits, and Systems, pp. 1635-1638.

Ascia, G., and Catania, V., 1999, "A High Performance Processor for Applications Based on Fuzzy Logic", 1999 IEEE International Fuzzy Systems Conference Proceedings, Seoul, Korea, pp. 1685-1690.

USING ARTIFICIAL NEURAL NE-ITWORKS COMBINED WITH PCA IN AN OPTICAL FIBRE SYSTEM THAT MONITORS FOOD COLOUR IN A FULL SCALE PRODUCTION ENVIRONMENT

C. SHERIDAN
ECE Department,
University of Limerick
Castletroy, Limerick, Ireland
W. B. LYONS
ECE Department,
University of Limerick
Castletroy, Limerick, Ireland
C. FLANAGAN
ECE Department,
University of Limerick
Castletroy, Limerick, Ireland
M. O'FARRELL
ECE Department,
University of Limerick
Castletroy, Limerick, Ireland
E. LEWIS
ECE Department,
University of Limerick
Castletroy, Limerick, Ireland
N. JACKMAN
Food Design Applications Ltd.
Ardcavan, Wexford, Ireland

ABSTRACT
An optical fibre sensor system has been developed for the on-line measurement of food quality in large-scale industrial oven applications. The quality of the food is determined by its internal and external colour as it cooks. By automatically classifying the food at different stages it is possible to determine whether the food is cooked to the desired colour, thus maximising profits. Spectroscopic techniques are employed to determine the colour of the food. Developments have been made, based upon previous works by the authors, by further analysing the spectral patterns using Principal Component Analysis (PCA) before the application of the data to the Artificial Neural Network (ANN). Results are presented that show the use of PCA significantly reduces the dimensions of the spectral information and thus reduces the number of processing units in the neural network.

INTRODUCTION

The food preparation industry is under increasing pressure to reach high standards and as well as maintaining production numbers. The throughput can be very high and the likelihood of occasional lower quality goods' being erroneously produced is correspondingly increased. This is particularly apparent in the cooking of large quantities of different food types in large-scale ovens. The conveyor belts of these ovens are frequently fully laden with food in order to make the most efficient use of the oven as a result. Any error in the cooking process (over-cooking a batch, for example) incurs a large cost. Automation of the cooking stage can be achieved by monitoring the food colour (internally and externally) as it passes through the oven and determining if that colour is optimum for maximising profits.

Grading the quality of a product in terms of its colour [3] or shape and size [4] ensures consistency in the product. Colour, in particular, has a sizeable influence over a customers decision in buying a product as many consumers have pre-conceived ideas of how a product should look when properly cooked e.g., a roast chicken should be golden brown in colour, flame-grilled hamburgers should have black lines and sausages must have a rich golden brown colour.

There are many advantages in developing a system, described here, that can take *on-line* measurements of internal and external food colour. The system utilises an optical fibre probe that can be installed directly into the oven itself as it has the ability to withstand the high temperatures. Traditional colour vision systems do not allow internal readings without cutting the product open and, as a result, having to discard it whereas a 2.5mm probe can be both non-destructive and quick. This system can also be used in microwave ovens, as the optical fibres are immune to electromagnetic interference.

Using a broadband tungsten halogen lamp, the food sample is illuminated through an optical fibre. The reflected light is returned to the spectrometer (Oceanoptics S2000) and the spectrum is sent to the host P.C. for subsequent analysis using Principal Component Analysis (Karhunen-Loeve Decomposition). The resultant data is further analysed using Artificial Neural Networks. The software utilised to implement the neural network is the Stuttgart Neural Networks Simulator (SNNS).

This paper discusses how the use of PCA – a method of feature extraction and dimension reduction – makes it possible, using Karhunen Loeve decomposition, to reduce the dimensions of this solution to a smaller subspace compared to the standard neural network previously used, by only including the most significant data and thus eliminating redundant or highly correlated information.

EXPERIMENTAL SETUP

Food producers often employ a technique to colour the food by using surface air-blowing towards the end of the belt to colour the food. It is clear from the diagram (Fig. 1) that there are five main stages involved in the cooking, represented by the five stages in the oven. The colour sensing is performed between the fourth and fifth stages, after "colouring by roasting" has taken place.

As previously described [3], the colour is measured using a reflective probe and recording the light reflected in the visible spectrum, which is representative of the colour. Illumination of the food is performed with 6 fibres attached to a tungsten halogen white light source. One fibre returns the reflected light to an Ocean Optics s2000 spectrometer, controlled by a host P.C., Fig. 2(a). The data is then saved for subsequent analysis using Principal Component Analysis and, following this, the Stuttgart Neural Networks Simulator (SNNS) the Neural Network Software [4]. Examples of the use of artificial intelligence for decision-making in the food industry are plentiful [5], [6].

The probe for measuring the external readings is required to have a diameter that is as large as possible in order to cover a greater area. The fibres used are 400μm in diameter. For testing a single probe was used, as for initial measurements, it was important for the investigators to have full and free control over where it is placed in order to train the Neural Network with correct data; it is envisaged to have 5 or 6 separate probes placed around the surface of the food sample to read the colour over a greater area. The internal readings need to be unobtrusive so it is important that the diameter is kept to a minimum. The fibres for this probe are 200/220 μm. Fig. 2(b).

Both probes are encased in stainless steel. This material was chosen to allow the probe to be regularly sterilised, something that is essential in the food industry. Its robustness allows the probe to be injected at high speed into the product and puncture without causing damage to the product or itself.

RESULTS

Results are presented for two product types, namely puff pastry and beef. These were chosen as they offer a good selection of spectral grouping for the various cooking stages encountered in the cooking progress. These results were obtained with Food Design Applications, Wexford.

Puff Pastry

Tests were carried out on puff pastry products, i.e. sausage rolls and Cornish pasties. These products colour quite quickly and can become burnt in a matter of seconds. It is important to monitor the edge of the food, as burnt patches will appear there first. The graph of Fig. 3(a) represents the variations in 400 spectra, i.e. 100 per class - raw, too light, correct colour and too dark.

Beef Burgers

Testing was also carried out on beef burgers. The external colour of this product varies from red when raw to a rich brown when correctly cooked to a dark brown colour when over-cooked. Fig. 4(a) shows the variations in 560 spectra, i.e. 140 per class - raw, too light, correct and too dark.

Data Conditioning – PCA

The x-axes of each of the graphs represent the amount of data points that were used to represent the spectra. Each spectral reading from the S2000 spectrometer has 2048 data samples, resulting in high resolution, in the range between 200nm and 900nm. Principal Component Analysis was then used on the data set from the S2000. PCA is a method of grouping non-linearly separable data sets. It provides a much more accurate and reliable method of feature extraction as compared with the previous method used of taking every n^{th} sample. It is also computationally much quicker as it significantly reduces the number of inputs to the neural network. The PCA algorithm was implemented as follows:

Each spectrum in the data set was normalised against itself to account for intensity errors. The mean spectrum was determined using Eq. (1).

$$\bar{v} = \frac{1}{N}\sum_{x=0}^{N-1} \vec{v}_x \qquad (1)$$

The deviation vectors were generated next using Eq. (2).

$$\vec{u}_x = \overline{v} - \vec{v}_x \qquad (2)$$

and are arranged in a dataset matrix, D, as shown in Eq. (3).

$$D = \{ \vec{u}_0 \vec{u}_1 \ldots \vec{u}_{N-2} \vec{u}_{N-1} \} \qquad (3)$$

The covariance matrix C is then calculated from Eq. (4).

$$C = D' \times D \qquad (4)$$

The eigenvalues and eigenvectors are then calculated using the Matlab 'eig' function. A plot of the eigenvalues calculated shows the most significant eigenvalues are at the end of the plot (Fig 5). The eigenvectors that contain the most information about the spectrum correspond to the position of these eigenvalues. The PCA coefficients are computed as shown in Eq. (5), using only the eigenvectors that correspond to the significant eigenvalues:

$$c_{xj} = \vec{u}_x \times \hat{e}_j \qquad (5)$$

Plots of the coefficients for both pastry and beef are given in Fig 6(a) and (b), respectively. They show, for pastry and beef training sets, how the PCA coefficients group together, as expected.

THE NEURAL NETWORKS

Two Feed Forward multilayer neural networks were configured with the number of input nodes corresponding to the number of eigenvectors chosen during the PCA process. For both pastry and beef it was decided that 3 coefficients were sufficient to represent the spectra. This can be seen in Fig. 5 where the largest eigenvalues are the final three. At the output layer of each network one node was chosen for each condition to be sensed. This represents 4 nodes for puff pastry and beef – raw, light, correct and dark.

Neural Network for Puff Pastry

Various network configurations were tested and it was decided that a hidden layer of 4 units was most suitable. Using the standard training algorithm of Backpropagation with Momentum the network was trained using the Neural Network software, SNNS. The following parameters as required by η(learning rate) = 0.8, μ (momentum term) = 0.3 and δ (maximum error) = 0.1. The trained network distinguished between 4 conditions: raw, undercooked, correctly cooked and over cooked. 400 test patterns, 100 for each condition, were used to train the network. When the network was tested using a test set of 280 test patterns, 70 of each condition, it correctly classified the majority of these test patterns. Any patterns it failed to classify had characteristics of two or more of the sets defined, i.e., the pattern had both raw and light colour characteristics as shown in Fig. 7.

Neural Network forBeef

Following a comparison of different configurations, a hidden layer of 4 nodes was chosen for the neural network for external beef readings.The parameters used with SNNS are η = 0.8, μ = 0.3 and δ = 0.1. A total of 560 result patterns were used to train the network, 140 of each condition; raw, too light, optimum colour and dark. The trained network was then tested using an independent set of 360 data patterns (90 of each condition) to that which had been applied previously in the training of the network. The network correctly classified the majority of these test patterns. Any patterns it failed to classify had characteristics of two or more of the sets defined, i.e., the pattern had both raw and light colour characteristics.

Analysis of Results

The results presented here show the combination of using ANNs in association with PCA improves the accuracy of classification – these results agree with the results found by O'Farrell et al [9]. Furthermore, the use of PCA component analysis allows for a significant reduction in the number of nodes used in the netowrk. This accounts for the reduction in computation time of the trained network. This method is faster than other methods, such as knn classifiers or using ANNs without using PCA.

The failure of the network to correctly classify some spectra is due to the cooking process itself. This process is a continuous development that has to be arbitrarily segemented into various classes.

This means that there can exist spectra that are moving from a lighter classification to a darker one and therefore, this is "unseen" data and highlights the need for the generalistion skills of neural networks and the requirment for their use in this project. This point is illustrated in Fig. 7.

CONCLUSION

A fibre optic based spectroscopic technique, coupled with Principal Component Analysis methods and Artificial Neural Network signal processing techniques, has been developed for the purpose of the recognition and classification of the various cooking stages of pastry and marinated chicken. This paper further expands on previous research carried out by the authors [3], [9]. It explores the effects of using Principal Component Analysis on the spectral information, the result being a reduction in neural network nodes and an decrease in the computation time required for the neural network, thus strengthening the viability of the system.

ACKNOWLEDGMENTS

The authors wish to thank the Enterprise Ireland for supporting the research through provision of Innovation Partnerships Grant Award IP-2003-171.

REFERENCES

[1] McConnell RK Jr., Blau HH Jr. "Colour classification of non-uniform baked and roasted foods." *Proc. Food Processing Automation IV, pp.40 –46, 1995*

[2] Aleixo N., Blasco B., Molto E., Navarron F., "Assessment of citrus fruit quality using a real-time machine vision system" *Pattern Recognition, 2000. Proc. 15th International Conference pp. 482 –485 vol.1, 2000*

[3] O'Farrell M., Lewis E., "An Intelligent Optical Fibre based System for Monitoring Food Quality" *IEEE Sensors 2002 Proc. 1st International Conference pp. 308-311 vol.1, 2002*

[4] SNNS, Stuttgart Neural Network Simulator, User Manual version 4.1 or http://www-ra.informatik.uni-tuebingen.de/SNNS/

[5] Shiranita K., Hayashi K., Otsubo A., Miyajima T., Takiyama R., "Determination of Meat Quality by image processing and Neural Network Techniques" *The ninth International Conference on Fuzzy System, pp 989 –992, vol.2, 2000*

[6] Abdesselam A., Abdullah R.C., " Pepper Berries Grading using Artificial Neural Networks" *TENCON 2000. Proceedings pp 153 –159, vol.2, 2000*

[7] Mignani, A., et al, "Spectral nephelometry for making extravirgin olive oil fingerprints", *Sensors and Actuators B Chemical, Volume 90, Issues 1-3, Pages 157-162, 2003*

[8] Jebra, T., "Karehun-Loeve Decomposition for Statistical Recognition and Detection" http://www1.cs.columbia.edu/~jebara/htmlpapers/UTHESIS/node64.html

[9] M. O'Farrell, E. Lewis, C. Flanagan, W.B. Lyons, N. Jackman, "Combining Principal Component Analysis with an Artificial Neural Network to perform Online Quality Assessment of Food as it cooks in a Large-scale Industrial Oven" Sensors & Actuators: B. Chemical, 2004, (In Press)

FIGURES

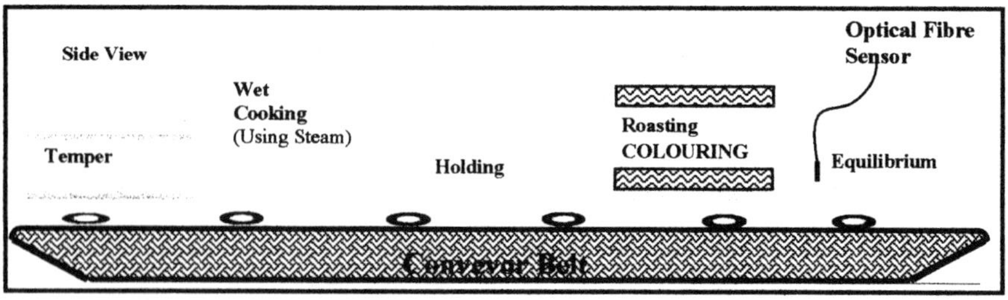

Figure 1: Industrial oven used in on-site testing

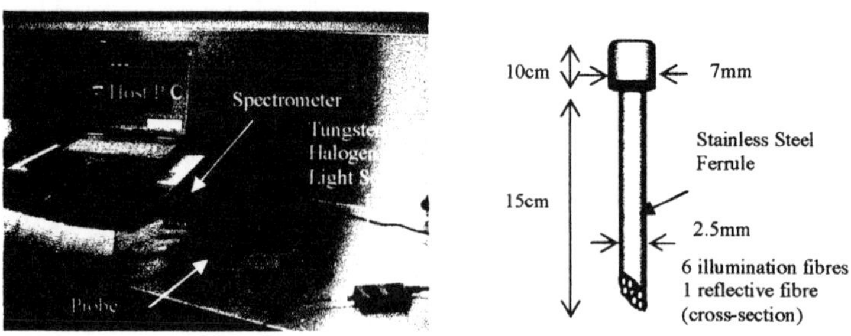

Figure 2: (a) Photo of the System Set-up (b) Probe for internal colour readings.

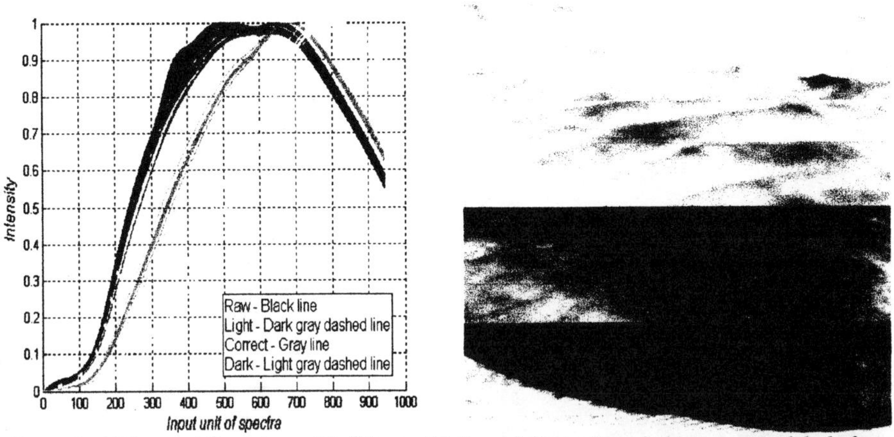

Figure 3: (a) Spectral Variations of Puff Pastry (b) Cornish Pasty; Raw, light, correct and dark, from top to bottom respectively

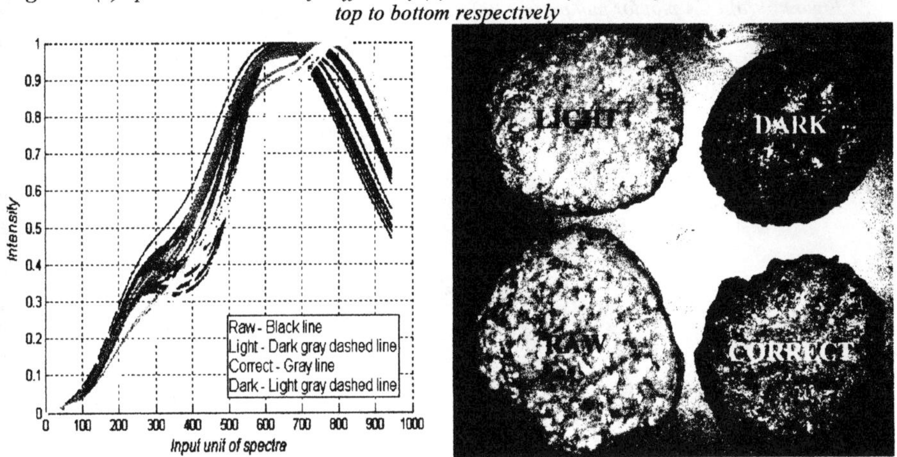

Figure 4: (a) Spectral Variations of Beef (external readings) (b) Photo of External Beef products

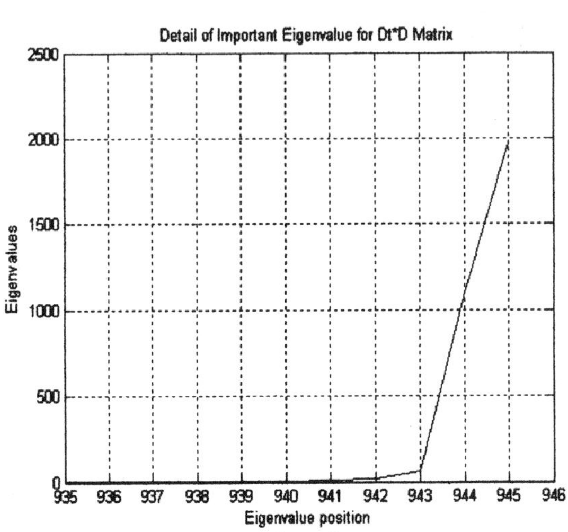

Figure 5: A detailed look at the final eigenvalues, demonstrating an increase in the magnitude of the eigenvalues

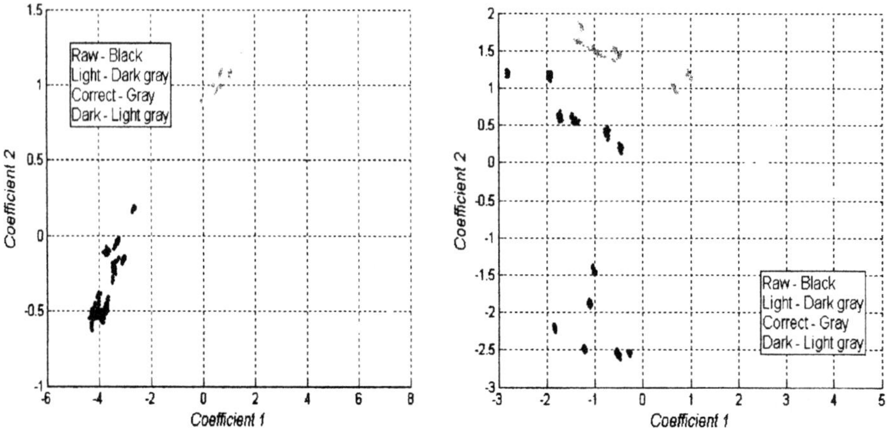

Figure 6: (a) PCA plot for puff pastry, 100 spectra were used to generate these principal components for each stage – raw light correct and dark (b) PCA plot for external beef readings, 140 spectra used to generate these principal components for each stage – raw light correct and dark

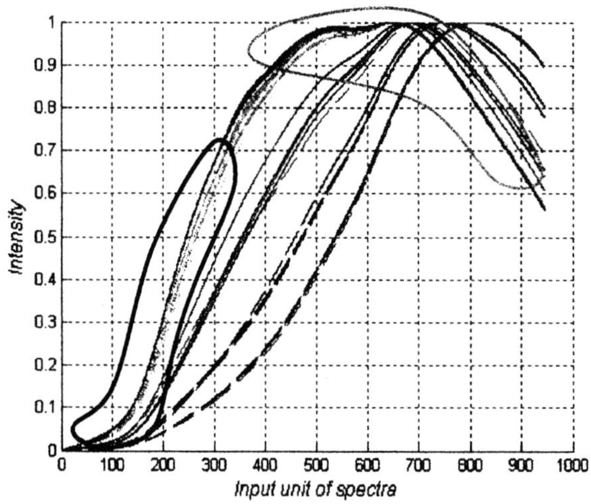

Figure 7: Plot of the spectra of the test data (puff pastry) used to test the neural network. The black line indicates a set of spectra the network was unable to classify. The lower circle (the area between input unit 0 and ~330) highlights that the shape is very similar to the raw spectra while the upper, gray circle (the area between ~400 and 934) highlights how the shape is very similar to undercooked spectra. Thus, as the black spectra have the characteristics of two different stages, it will not classify.

ANALYZING FINITE TIME SERIES WITH DEDICATED NEURAL NETWORK HARDWARE

KARL MATHIA
Newport Corp.
750 National Court, Richmond, California 94804
kmathia@newport.com

ABSTRACT
The Correlation Network (CN), an efficient computational tool for the analysis of finite, real-valued time series, is introduced. When implemented on dedicated, parallel neural network hardware, this feedforward network can process signals in real time. Here the CN computes a moving-average autocorrelation algorithm in order to improve the analysis of finite time series subject to random, uniform noise. It is outlined how the CN is implemented on a commercially available neural network processor. Test results are presented.

INTRODUCTION

Neural networks have been applied and tested for many signal processing applications [1][2]. The Correlation Network (CN) for example, when implemented on dedicated neural network hardware, is an efficient computational tool for the real-time analysis of finite time-series. Here the CN improves the signal-to-noise ratio of a finite time-series by computing a moving-average autocorrelation (MAAC) algorithm. Both autocorrelation and moving average algorithms are well-known numerical tools frequently used for signal processing, statistical analysis, and other scientific and economic purposes [9].

It is further shown that the graphical representation of the average autocorrelation algorithm resembles the structure of feedforward neural network with linear transfer functions. This intuitive notion is formalized mathematically and demonstrated using numerical results. The CN architecture is derived and implemented on a commercially available neural network processor (NNP), an example of dedicated neural network hardware with parallel processing power. The NNP's performance was compared to that of generalpurpose computers in [8], demonstrating the capability for real-time signal processing. Put the introduction text here.

THE ALGORITHM

Autocorrelation sequence and moving average algorithms are common numerical tools. The autocorrelation of a random sequence is a measure for the time variation of a random signal. The moving average may be considered a noise filter [9]. Here these tools are applied to finite, real-valued time series.

Autocorrelation. The autocorrelation of an infinite time series, i.e. a continuous stream of sampled data, can be estimated from a finite time series $x_{fin}[n]$, $-\infty < n < \infty$. The sequence $x[n]$ for computing the autocorrelation is 'extracted' from $x_{fin}[n]$ via multiplication with a time window $w[n]$ of size N:

$$w[n] = \begin{cases} 1, \text{ if } & 0 \le n \le N-1 \\ 0, & \text{otherwise} \end{cases} \quad (1)$$

$$x[n] = x_{fin}[n]w[n] \quad (2)$$

$$= \begin{cases} x_{fin}[n], \text{ for } 0 \le n \le N-1 \\ 0, \text{ otherwise} \end{cases} \quad (3)$$

This is illustrated in Figure 1.

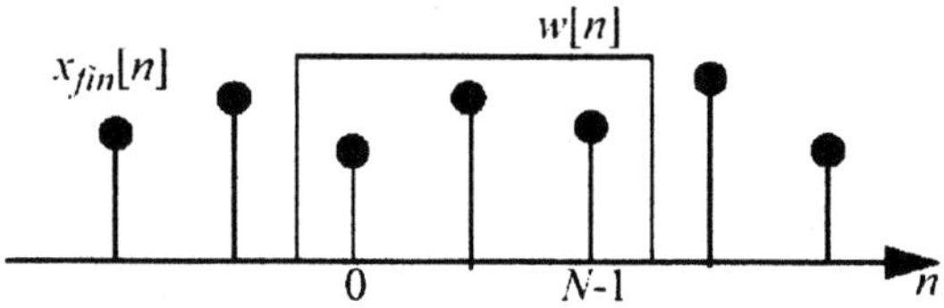

Figure 1. The time window $w[n]$ selects $x[n]$.

The autocorrelation sequence for $x[n]$, given its symmetry $y[m]=y[-m]$, is defined by

$$y[m] = \frac{1}{N}\sum_{n=0}^{N-1} x[n]x[n+m], \quad (4)$$

with $-(N-1) \le m \le N-1$. See also [9], p. 743. The autocorrelation algorithm in Equation 4 is illustrated in Figure 2. The sequence $x[n]$ is 'fixed' in time, while its copy $x[n+m]$ moves along the discrete time axis, beginning with the first sample at time instant $m=N-1$. For each time instant m the overlapping samples at are multiplied and the products accumulated.

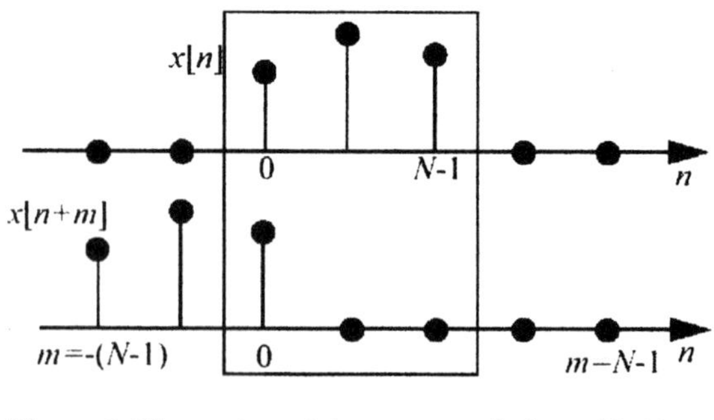

Figure 2. Illustration of the autocorrelation with N=3.

Moving Average. Noise in $x[n]$ also affects the autocorrelation sequence $y[m]$, but can be reduced, for example, by computing the moving average of $y[m]$ ([9], p. 840):

$$\bar{y} = \frac{1}{2N-1} \sum_{m=-(N-1)}^{N-1} y[m] . \qquad (5)$$

The MAAC, the moving average of the k-th sequence $y[m]$, denoted $\bar{y}_k$, is determined by moving $w[n]$ and computing $\bar{y}_k$ for the selected $x_k[n]$. See below.

THE CORRELATION NETWORK

Network Design and *A Priori* Knowledge. It is good practice to maximize the use of *a priori* knowledge for neural network design [6]. The parameters of the above algorithm provide the *a priori* knowledge for fully pre-specifying the CN. No weight training or other parameter adjustments are required. The four pre-specified parameters defining the CN are listed in Table 1. See also [5].

Table 1: Pre-specified network parameters.

Network Parameter	**Pre-Specified By...**
Directed Connectivity Graph	Multiply-accumulate pattern in Figure 3
Number of neurons/layer	Size N of window $w[n]$
Neuron transfer function	Product $x[n]\ x[n+m]$: linear operator
Connection weights w: 1	Product $x[n]\ x[n+m]$: no other factors

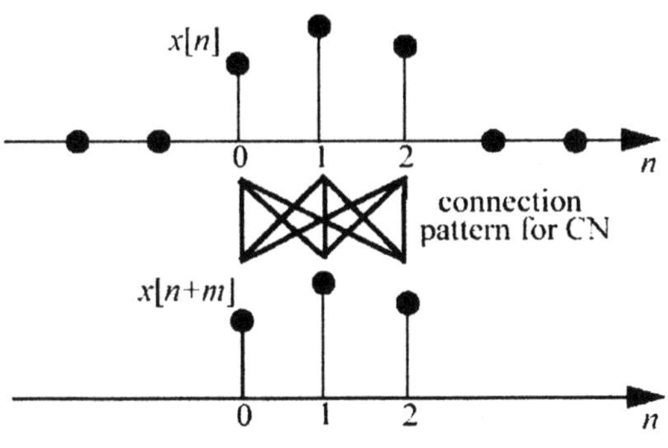

Figure 3. Obtaining the CN connection pattern, N=3.

The 'connection pattern' obtained from multiplying the sequences $x[n]$ and $x[n+m]$, is illustrated in Figure 3. Together with the network parameters in Table 1 it results in the CN architecture illustrated in Figure 4. The CN employs an N-N-1 structure, i.e. one hidden layer, and the number of input nodes equals the number of hidden neurons, determined by the window size N (here: N=3). All neurons perform the usual multiplyaccumulate operations with a subsequent linear transfer function. Note the double connection from i-th input node to i-th hidden neuron. The CN architecture is scalable and suitable for implementation on dedicated neural network hardware, here the NNP.

Proof. It is easy to show that the CN in Figure 4 computes the average $\bar{y}$ in Equation 5, i.e. $y_{CN} = \bar{y}$:

$$y_{CN} = \frac{1}{2N-1}\sum_{n=0}^{N-1} y[n] \tag{6}$$

$$= \frac{1}{2N-1}\sum_{n=0}^{N-1}\left(\frac{1}{N}\sum_{l=0}^{N-1} x[n]x[l]\right),\ l = n+m \tag{7}$$

$$= \frac{1}{2N-1}\sum_{n=0}^{N-1}\left(\frac{1}{N}\sum_{m=-(N-1)}^{N-1} x[n]x[n+m]\right) \tag{8}$$

$$= \frac{1}{2N-1}\sum_{m=-(N-1)}^{N-1}\left(\frac{1}{N}\sum_{n=0}^{N-1} x[n]x[n+m]\right) \tag{9}$$

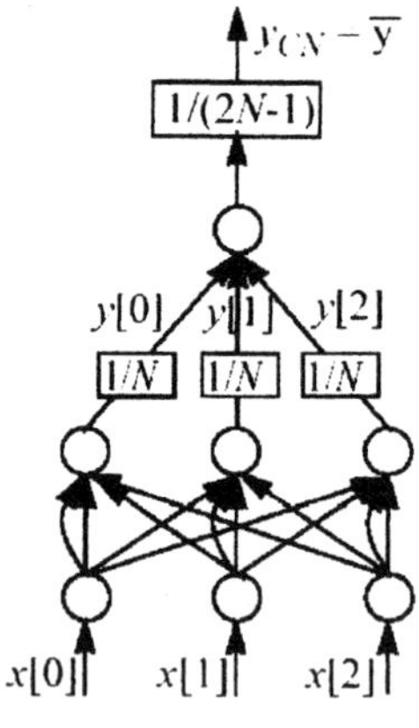

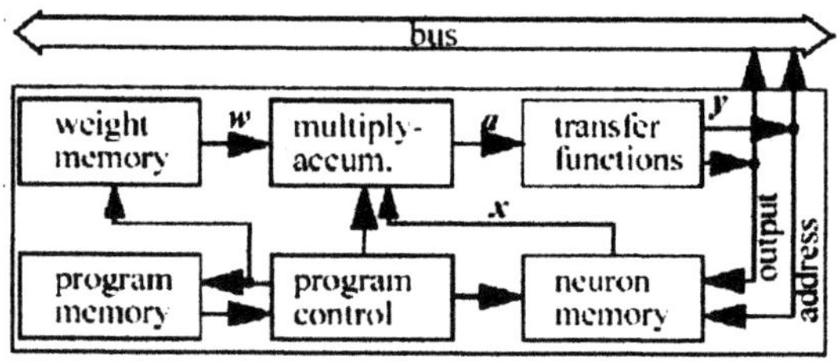

Figure 4 (left). Correlation Network for N=3.

Figure 5 (right). Block diagram of a single NNP.

IMPLEMENTATION ON NEURAL NETWORKS HARDWARE

The Neural Network Processor®. The CN was tested with the commercially available Neural Network Processor NNP® by Accurate Automation Corp. [8][10]. Below its design concept is reviewed.

Architecture. The NNP® architecture provides features for fast processing of neural connections and transfer functions, and it is well suited for feedforward ANN architectures. Up to eight NNPs can be integrated in a parallel multiprocessor environment, resulting in a multiple instruction/multiple data (MIMD) platform. Figure 5 shows the block diagram of a single NNP®.

A multiply-accumulate unit, lookup tables for transfer functions, and 16-bit integer arithmetic emphasize the above feature. Figure 5 illustrates the dataflow of activation values, neuron inputs and weight values. The neuron output, i.e. the transfer function, is read from a preloaded lookup table. Weights are usually learned offline, but on-chip learning is possible [7].

Efficiency is further increased by instruction pipelining, enabling the completion of one instruction, but several data, per clock cycle (single instruction/multiple data, or SIMD). Pipelined events in overlapped time periods are often referred to as temporal parallelism, optimizing the use of a single processor. Parallelism through the replication of physical devices is referred to as spatial parallelism [3]. In this sense a single NNP with instruction pipelining implements temporal parallelism. Spatial parallelism is realized by parallel NNPs, whose performance increases linearly with the number of NNPs.

Programming Paradigm. The NNP programming paradigm emphasizes layered, well-structured, feedforward ANN architectures. Accordingly, its programming language comprises only nine powerful commands, tailored for the efficient computations of appropriate ANN primitives, in particular connections and nonlinear transfer function. For example `mula' (multiply and accumulate) and `lbtf' (compute transfer function). A sigmoidal neuron with three inputs and weights would be implemented using four commands:

Typical neural network	Correlation Network
`mull x1,w1`	`mull x1,1`
`mula x2,w2`	`mula x2,1`
`mula x2,w2`	`mula x2,1`
`lbtf c,sigmoid`	`lbtf c,linear`

The cornerstone of an NNP assembler program is the multiply-accumulate command, which multiplies one weight value with one input value and adds the product to the existing activation value. For larger yet wellstructured neural networks a code generator in the Cprogramming language creates the NNP programs.

CN Implementation. For the Correlation Network with unit weights and linear transfer functions the above command sequence for one neuron changes (listed above). The string 'linear' points to the appropriate transfer function look-up table. NNP code equivalent to the above four lines are programmed per neuron. As such, for the CN in Figure 4 with four neurons a total of 16 lines of code, plus the program overhead, is required.

Implementation Example. Implementing the moving average autocorrelation (MAAC) on the NNP is illustrated with a simple example. Consider an infinite discrete-time sine wave with amplitude 0.5 plus uniform random noise with amplitude in [-0.5,+0.5]. This infinite signal can be represented by a finite time series $x_{fin}[n]$, n=1..,N. Here x_{fin} is sampled with 100

Hz for 10 seconds, resulting in N=1000 samples (Figure 6). Its autocorrelation $y_{fin}[n]$, n=1,..,2N-1 is an estimate for the autocorrelation of the original infinite time series. It was computed with Matlab [4] and all 1999 data points are shown in Figure 7.

How does $x_{fin}[n]$ relate to the MAAC? Assume that $x_{fin}[n]$ is measured and buffered, and five new samples become available every 0.05 seconds. As such, $x[n]$ moves along $x_{fin}[n]$ with a step size of 5, resulting in 196 sequences $x_k[n]$ = $x_{fin}[5k+1,...5k+20]$; k=0,..,196. The NNP was programmed to compute the MAAC for all $x_k[n]$ per Equations (4) and (5). Figure 8 shows $y_1[n]$, the first autocorrelation sequence for k=1, comprising 2N-1=39 samples.

Finally, the MAAC, the average $\bar{y}_k$ for each of the 196 autocorrelation sequences $y_k[n]$, is shown in Figure 9. The MAAC exhibits features similar to y_{fin}, i.e. oscillation frequency and amplitude. It may be concluded that the MAAC provides the information similar to the estimate of an autocorrelation for finite time series, and it can be efficiently computed on neural hardware.

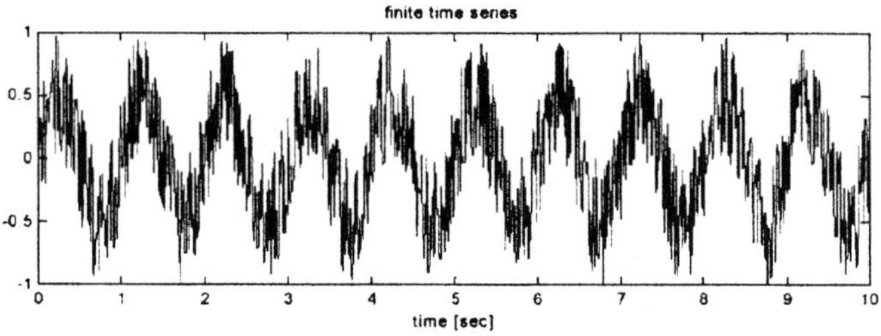

Figure 6. Finite time series $x_{fin}[n]$, N=1000 samples.

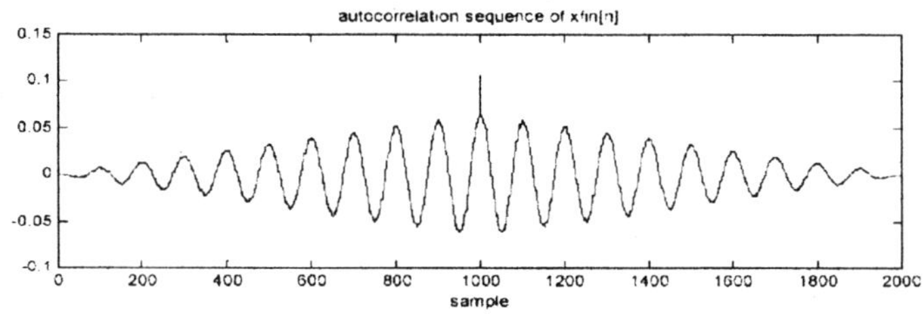

Figure 7. Autocorrelation sequence $y_{fin}[m]$ for $x_{fin}[n]$.

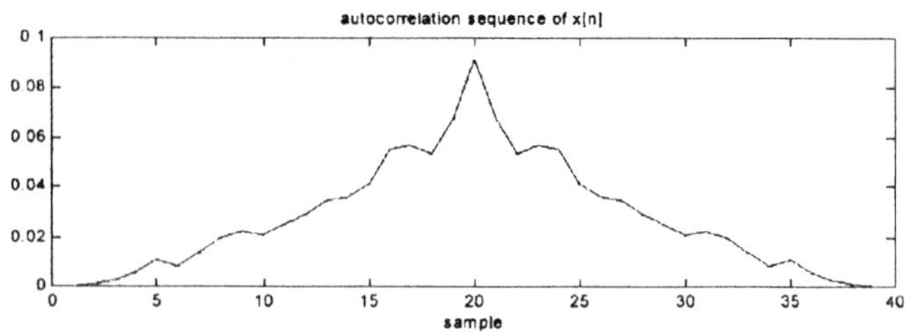

Figure 8. Autocorrelation for sequence $x_1[n]$.

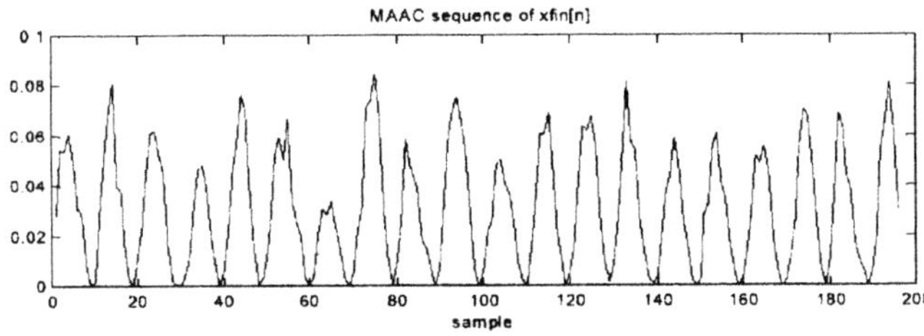

Figure 9. MAAC sequence, 196 samples.

CONCLUSIONS

The Correlation Network (CN), an efficient computational tool for the analysis of finite, real-valued time series, was introduced. When implemented on dedicated, parallel neural network hardware, this feedforward network can process signals in real time. Here the CN computes a moving-average autocorrelation algorithm in order to pre-process and improve the analysis of a finite time series subject to random, uniform noise. It was shown how the CN is implemented on a commercially available neural network processor, whose performance allows the real-time execution of the MAAC for many time-critical applications.

REFERENCES

[1] F.L. Luo, Applied Neural Networks for Signal Processing, Cambridge Univ. Press, Cambridge, Mass., 1999.

[2] S. Haykin, Neural Networks - A Comprehensive Foundation, IEEE Press/Macmillan College, New York, 1994.

[3] Hennesy J.L. and D.A. Patterson, Computer Organization and Design: The Hardware/Software Interface, Morgan Kaufman, San Mateo, California, 1993.

[4] J. Little and L. Shure, Signal Processing Toolbox, User's Guide, The MathWorks, Inc., South Natick, Mass., 1988.

[5] Karl Mathia, "A Variable Structure Learning Algorithm for Multilayer Perceptrons," Proc. ANNIE'04, Rolla, Missouri, 2004.

[6] G.G. Lendaris and K. Mathia, "Using A Priori Knowledge to Prestructure ANNs", Australian Journal of Intelligent Information Processing SYstems, Vol. 1, No. 1, pp. 25-30, May 1994.

[7] K. Mathia, and J. Clark, "On Neural Network Hardware and Programming Paradigms," Proceedings International Joint Conference on Neural Networks'02, May 12-17, Honolulu, Hawaii, 2002.

[8] K. Mathia, J. Clark, B. Colbert, and R. Saeks, "Benchmarking an MIMD Neural Network Processor", Proc. World Cong. Neural Networks '96.

[9] A.V. Oppenheim and R.W. Schafer, Discrete-Time Signal Processing, Prentice-Hall, Englewood-Cliffs, New Jersey, 1989.

[10] R. Saeks, K. Priddy, K. Schnieder, and S. Stowell, "On the Design of an MIMD Neural Network Processor," Proc. World Cong. Neural Networks '95, San Diego/California, pp. 590-595, June 1995.

;ELF ORGANIZING GLOBAL RANKING ALGORITHM AND ITS APPLICATIONS

MEHMET IZZET SAGLAM
Istanbul Technical University,
Faculty of Electrical and
Electronic Engineering, Maslak,
Istanbul 34469 Turkey
misaglam@be.itu.edu.tr

OKAN ERSOY
Purdue University, School of
Electrical and Computer
Engineering, West Lafayette,
Indiana, USA
ersoy@ecn.purdue.edu

ISIN ERER
Istanbul Technical University,
Faculty of Electrical and
Electronic Engineering, Maslak,
Istanbul 34469 Turkey
ierer@ehb.itu.edu.tr

BSTRACT

ı this paper, we discuss a new competitive learning classifier called Self Organizing Global Ranking ;OGR) algorithm and discuss its application in multispectral remote sensing problems. In experiments ıvolving supervised classification of the Colorado data set used, the new method is compared to .ohonen's Self Organizing Map (SOM), Learning Vector Quantization and a hybrid algorithm called SMVDT including Support Vector Machine (SVM) and Decision Tree (DT). The proposed algorithm is ısed on a new concept of global neighborhood generated by ranking. The neighborhood is global, ıeaning that the neighbors are dynamic at each iteration during learning, and they can be anywhere in the ıta space, instead of being adjacent or nearby in a geometric sense. Because the neighborhood concept is əry much simplified, the computational load is considerably reduced, resulting in a very fast algorithm.

INTRODUCTION

Competititive learning algorithms such as Self Organizing Map (Kohonen, 1990) and vector ıantization has many applications such as in remote sensing, data compression, signal processing, and ıta mining. As an example, SOM uses a 2-dimensional (2-D) grid in which every node represents a ɔdebook vector. During training, the node with the codebook vector nearest the input vector and its ighbor nodes are updated. In SOM, the topology of the data can also be preserved. That is, if the ɔdebook vectors are near each other, the corresponding nodes will also be close in the grid geometrically, d vice versa.

Distribution of the codebook vectors on the grid can be considered to be one of the handicaps of the)M algorithm. All codebook vectors are distributed locally. SOM can save the topology of the data, but it ay use unnecessary codebooks vectors whose update is computationally intensive due to neigborhood operations. Therefore, the training and testing time may be substantial. Furthermore, the map size of the SOM must be chosen before starting of the SOM algorithm. Choosing appropriate map size affects the performance of the algorithm.

The proposed algorithm is based on a new concept of global neighborhood generated by ranking with respect to a distance metric. A major advantage of this approach is low computational load. An improved classification performance is also achieved.

The paper is organized in five sections. Section 2 describes the proposed algorithm. Section 3 introduces a difficult multispectral remote sensing classification problem. The comparative experimental results are discussed in Section 4. Conclusions are given in Section 5.

2. SELF ORGANIZING GLOBAL RANKING ALGORITHM

Two important properties of the SOGR are simplicity, and order based on global ranking. The SOGR is an iterative algorithm in the same way as other competitive algorithms. Similar to SOM, there are codebook vectors which are updated iteratively. However, the neighborhood concept is different. The neigborhood is global, meaning that the neighbors are dynamic during iterations, and they can be anywhere in the data space, instead of being adjacent or nearby in a geometric sense. Because the neighborhood concept is very much simplified, the computational load is considerably reduced, resulting in a very fast algorithm.

In order to generate the dynamic neighborhood during iterations, the codebooks are ranked according to their closeness to the current input vector at each iteration. The measure of closeness used is the Euclidean distance even though other measures can also be utilized. We define R to be the membership size of the dynamic neighborhood. During training, at each input vector presentation, the distances between all codebook vectors and the input vector are calculated. The closest R codebook vectors are chosen and updated according to the following update equation:

$$m_i(t+1) = \begin{cases} m_i(t) + \beta_i(t)\left[x(t) - m_i(t)\right] & i \in R \\ m_i(t) & \text{otherwise} \end{cases}$$

where $x(t)$ is the input vector, $m_i(t)$ is the ith codebook vector, and β_i is the learning rate. Learning rate is decreased with time exponentially. It is also important to choose it differently for each value of R. The learning rate is decreased linearly with increasing R.

The initial values of the codebook vector can be chosen randomly among the input data to achieve fast convergence. Furthermore, as the number of iterations increases, R is decreased linearly. Such a strat ıelps achieve the global minimum or a very deep minimum. If R is not decreased linearly with time, a local ninimum may result.

After updating the codebook vectors, a set of counters equal in number to the number of classes are ıttached to each codebook vector. The distance between each training input vector and all codebook ectors are calculated. Then, the codebook vector nearest to the input vector is found, and its counter for he class of the input vector is increased by one. After all the inputs are processed, the counter which has he highest number decides the class label of the codebook vector. Once all the codebook vectors are abeled, the training process is completed.

The testing process is simpler than the training process. At each testing input vector, the distance etween the input vector and all the codebook vectors are calculated. The label of the codebook vector earest the input vector decides the class of the input vector.

. MULTISPECTRAL REMOTE SENSING CLASSIFICATION

As an application domain to test the algorithm, we will describe a particular multispectral remote ensing classification problem. The Colorado data set used for classification consists of 7 data channels btained from the following 4 data sources (Valafar, 1994):

- Landsat MSS data (4 data channels)
- Elevation data (in 10m contour intervals, 1data channel)
- Slope data (0-90 degrees in degree increments, 1 data channel)
- Aspect data (1-180 degrees in 1 degree increments, 1 data channel)

The area which has 10 ground cover classes, is a mountainous area in Colorado. The ground cover lasses are listed in the following table.

Table 1. The Ground Cover Classes of 10 Class Colorado Data.

Class	Field
1	Water
2	Colorado blue spruce
3	Mountain/Subalpine meadow
4	Aspen
5	Ponderosa pine
6	Ponderosa pine/Douglas fir
7	Engelman spruce
8	Douglas fir/White fir
9	Douglas fir/ Ponderosa pine/Aspen
10	Douglas fir/White fir/Aspen

Each channel comprises an image of 135 rows and 131 columns, all of which are co-registered Ground reference data are compiled for the area by comparing a cartographic map to a color composite of the Landsat data and also to a line printer output of each Landsat channel. By this method, 2019 grounc reference points (11.4% of the area) are selected. Ground reference consists of two or more homogeneou fields in the imagery for each class. For each class, the largest field is selected as a training field. The othe fields are used for testing. With the 10-class Colorado data set, 1188 pixels are used for training, and 83 pixels for testing the classifiers. The numbers of samples from each class are shown in Table 2. There ar similar data sets with eight classes and thirteen classes, respectively.

Table 2. Numbers of Samples of each Class with the 10-Class Colorado Data Set.

Class	Training (1188)	Testing (831)
1	408	195
2	88	24
3	45	42
4	75	65
5	105	139
6	126	188
7	224	70
8	32	44
9	25	25
10	60	39

One problem with the data set discussed above is that some of the classes are extremely und represented. For example, class 9 has only 25 samples in the training set. This is 2.1% of the training s The number of samples in classes 1, 5, 6, and 7 constitute more than 72% of the set. This unev representation of classes in training causes the network to ignore the under-represented classes and o learn the well-represented ones unless special precautions are taken. An additional problem is the hig nonlinear separability of the classes. Such problems result in an extremely difficult classification problen

4. EXPERIMENTAL RESULTS

Four algorithms were investigated on a comparative basis with the Colorado data set. These are SC Learning Vector Quantization (LVQ), LSMVDT, and the proposed SOGR algorithms. For SOM and LV the ClassifyIt program of the CIM VisionSolutions Ltd was chosen in order to achieve unbiased resu ClassifyIt can be downloaded from http://cimvisionsolutions.com/cim_uk/tuotteet/ohjel.htm.

All the 8-class, 10-class, and 13-class Colorado data sets were investigated in terms of classification ccuracy on a comparative basis. SOM map sizes of 10*15 and 20*30 yielded good results. 600 codebook ectors were used with the LVQ.

The results of the LSVMDT were obtained with Chi's Matlab toolbox [3]. All the data vectors were ecursively separated into two subsets by a linear decision hyperplane generated by a linear SVM at each ree node. Some data vectors were inevitably classified incorrectly by the first linear decision hyperplane, ecause the data is linearly nonseparable. The LSVMDT then continued to draw linear decision yperplanes to separate the data vectors until all were in the correct decision regions.

The programming of the proposed algorithm was done in Matlab. The number of codebook vectors hosen was 300. This was less than the number of codebook vectors used in SOM. The training vectors vere chosen randomly during iterations, and the total number of iterations was chosen equal to three times e number of input vectors. During iterations, the learning rate was changed between zero and one. In the eginning it is approximately equal to one. After five hundred iterations, it was decreased exponentially. nd the second one is the number of the winning vector. The neighborhood variable R was decreased nearly during iterations. R was chosen as 9 in the beginning. If these two variables were not decreased fter each iteration, a local minimum solution was obtained. The results obtained with SOGR were better an the results with the other classification algorithms, as observed in Table 3. SOGR is also the simplest d fastest of the algorithms investigated.

able 3. The classification results of the Colorada data sets.

%	SOM	LVQ	LSVMDT	SOR
8 Class Colorado	85.97	92.50	92.83	94.10
10 Class Colorado	49.34	51.62	51.38	51.75
13 Class Colorado	66.17	71.41	70.52	71.54

ONCLUSIONS

The proposed algorithm SOGR is considerably simpler and faster to train with and shows competitive rformance as compared to the other competitive learning supervised classifiers investigated. Its ighborhood function is global, based on ranking with respect to a distance metric. It is also dynamic at ch iteration.

There are a number of directions in which SOGR can be further investigated and developed. The oice of distance metric, the size of neighborhood and how it evolves in time, more effective use of nking information generated to achieve higher classification accuracy are some such topics.

CKNOWLEDGEMENT

We would like to thank CIM Vision Solutions Ltd for their kind collaboration.

REFERENCES

H-C. Chi, O. K. Ersoy, "Support Vector Machine Decision Trees with Rare Event Detection," *Int. Journa for Smart Engineering System Design*, Vol. 4, pp 225-242, 2002.

Kangas, J. A., Kohonen, T. K., Laaksonen, 'Variants of Self-Organizing Maps, *IEEE Transaction on Neural Networks*, Volume 1, pp. 93 – 99, 1990.

Valafar, F., Parallel Probabilistic Self Organizing Hierarchical Neural Network, *ECE Technical Report* No 1025-5818, and PhD Thesis, School of Electrical and Computer Engineering, Purdue University, 1994.

HIGH-PRESSURE GAS LEAK DETECTION BY A CHAOTIC APPROACH IN A PETROLEUM REFINING PLANT

TETSUJI TANI
Manufacturing Dep. Idemitsu Kosan Co., Ltd.
Ichihara, Japan

TORU NAGASAKO
Manufacturing Dep. Idemitsu Kosan Co., Ltd.
Ichihara, Japan

TADASHI IOKIBE
Research Institute of Application Technologies for Chaos & Complex Systems Co., Ltd.
Yokohama, Japan

ABSTRACT
It is difficult to detect high-pressure gas leaks using a noise meter or a frequency analyzer, in the case of a low-amplitude or no unique frequency leak sound. To solve these problems, we assumed that the background noise represents the normal condition of a refining plant, and that the structure of an acoustic time series may change when highly pressurized gas is leaked. Using a directional ultrasonic microphone, we measured background noise and an artificially induced leak sound. Subsequently, we generated composite data from the background noise and leak sound using various mixing ratios for transient stage analysis. We applied chaos theory to examine the topological structure and prediction accuracy of the time series mentioned above. We then estimated threshold levels, using nonlinear statistics and the prediction accuracy, for detecting a leak sound.

1. INTRODUCTION

In a petroleum refining plant, detection of high-pressure gas leak depends on an experienced field worker's investigation. Better high-pressure gas leak monitoring systems are required as such workers become fewer (Ohba, et al. 1999). High-pressure gas leaks resulting from equipment failures may lead to disasters. Technology for the early detection of leak sound is indispensable to prevent or minimize these disasters. However, some cases exist in which leak sounds are not detected by a noise meter or a frequency analyzer. This can occur even when the high-pressure gas is actually leaking because of the sound's small amplitude or lack of a unique frequency. Topological analysis is useful in such cases.

As shown in Fig. 1, we assumed that background noise in a petroleum refining plant is a steady sound that is generated by various devices under normal conditions: it has no dominant sound. On the other hand, a high-pressure gas leak has a dominant sound. We have employed chaos theory to identify these dominant sounds.

We have examined the topological structures of twelve different time series, including background noise, leak sounds, and ten composite time series composed of background noise and leak sounds in differing mixing ratios. We then used nonlinear statistics and prediction accuracy to estimate threshold levels for detecting leak sounds.

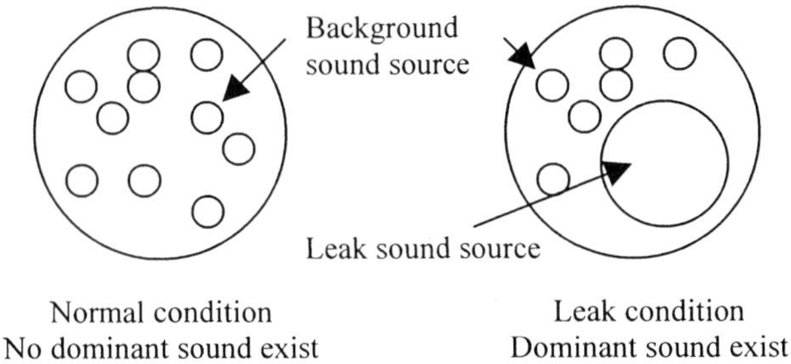

Figure 1 Assumption on background noise and leak sound

2. EXPERIMENTAL METHOD

We observed background noise and leak sounds using a directional ultrasonic microphone near a steam conversion valve attached to an electric power generator in a petroleum refining plant. The leak sound source was 0.35 MPa steam that was artificially leaked from a narrowed nozzle. This steam and nozzle simulated a high-pressure gas leak. The microphone was set 16 m distant from the leak sound source. The background noise amplitude was 34 dB; that of the leak sound was 54 dB.

We observed 10 samples each of background noises and leak sounds. One sample was 1024 points per 5 ms.

3. SIMULATION DATA AND CHAOTIC ANALYSIS

3.1 Simulation data

We selected one time series each from background noise and leak sound samples. We examined not only the background noise and leak sound, but also ten time-series, each of which comprised a composite of background noise and a leak sound. Thereby, we estimated the precise threshold levels for detecting a leak sound in a transient condition. Monitoring sound in a plant continuously, we usually observe background noise. If high-pressure gas leaks, we detect a leak sound after the background noise. For that reason, we generated time series that consisted of a leak sound following background noise. For example, Composite 10 is generated by replacing the last 100 data of background noise with the first 100 data of the leak sound. Table 1 shows a composite time series; Fig. 2 shows a time series of Composite 10.

Table 1 Composite time series

Composite time series	Replaced data	Background noise : Leak sound
Composite 10	100	924:100
Composite 20	200	824:200
Composite 30	300	724:300
Composite 40	400	624:400
Composite 50	500	524:500
Composite 60	600	424:600
Composite 70	700	324:700
Composite 80	800	224:800
Composite 90	900	124:900
Composite 100	1000	24:1000

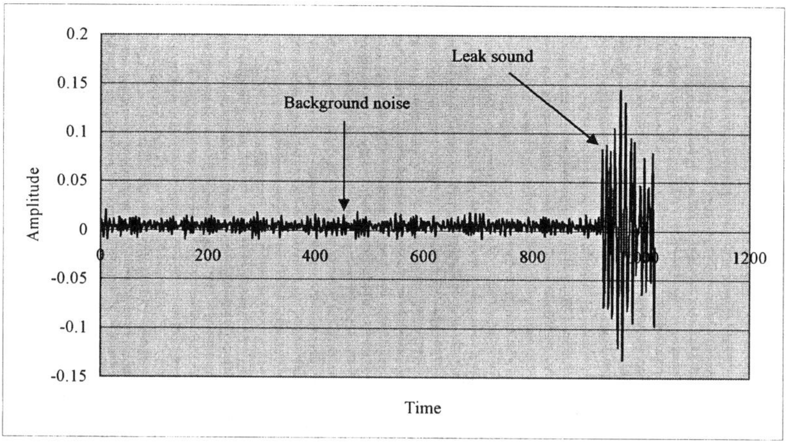

Figure 2 Time series of Composite 10

3.2 Analytical procedure

The analytical procedure for the sound time series is as follows.

Step (1) The latter half of each time series is predicted by the local fuzzy reconstruction method (Iokibe et al. 1994, 1999). The optimum embedding parameter is the following. Embedding dimension "d", delay time "τ" and the number of neighboring trajectories "N" are parameters set for the least root mean square error (RMSE) among original values and predicted values. For this reason, the attractor considered to offer the smoothest manifold can provide the highest prediction accuracy.

Step (2) Reconstruct the attractor with an optimum embedding parameter.

Step (3) Calculate the trajectory parallel measure (TPM) (Fujimoto and Iokibe, 1997) and Kolmogorov-Sinai (KS) entropy (Ott, 1993).

Figures 3 and 4 show attractors of background noise and leak sound at analysis procedure of Step (2). We use the software "ChaosClub" for chaotic analysis.

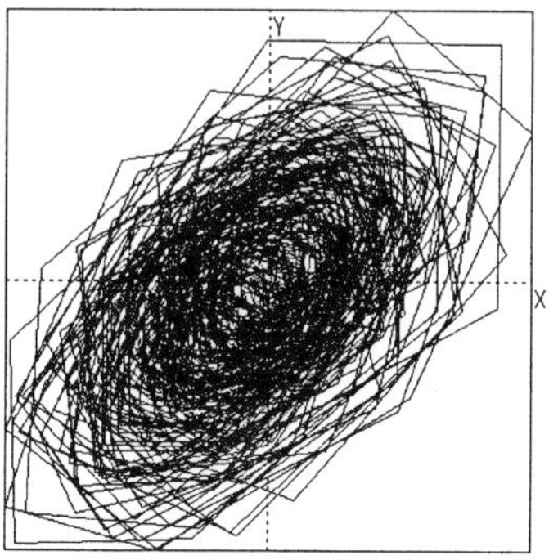

Figure 3 Background noise attractor

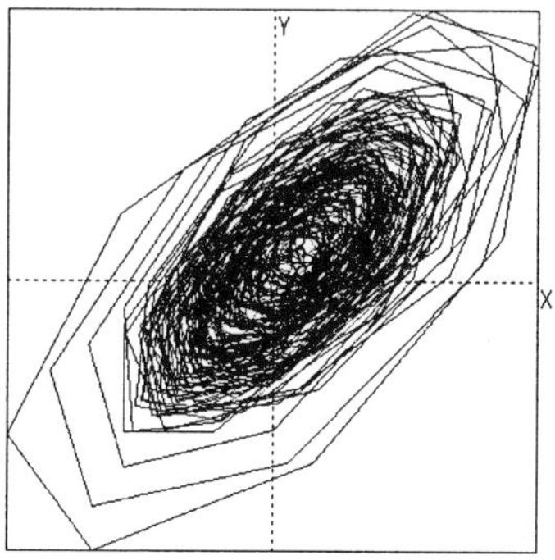

Figure 4 Leak sound attractor

4. EVALUATION AND LEAK-SOUND DETECTABILITY

From the analysis procedure step (1) stated in Section 3.2, optimum embedding dimensions and delay times in all time series are 2 and 1, respectively. This fact demonstrates that all sound time series examined here have almost identical topological structure from the viewpoint of embedding.

Horizontal dotted lines shown in Figs. 5–7 indicate threshold levels.

4.1 Evaluation and detectability by RMSE

Evaluation by RMSE shows the relative degree of determinism on time series. If the time series behavior of is more deterministic, the RMSE is smaller.

In the case of background noise, the RMSE is 0.0028. For Composite 10, the RMSE is 0.0143. The RMSE of Composite 10 is 5.13 times greater than that of background noise. The RMSE of Composite 50 is highest, and leak sound is 0.0196, as shown in Fig. 5.

Comparing a time series comprising a greater proportion of background noise and a leak sound in the latter half of the time series, the RMSE is smaller in the former. For this reason, the leak sound and background noise amplitudes are 54 dB and 34 dB, respectively. That is, the amplitude of 54 dB for the leak sound is 15 times that of 34 dB for background noise. Therefore, the value 0.0196 for the leak sound should be considered to be 0.0013 if both amplitudes are same. This means that leak sound is more deterministic than background noise.

As shown in Fig. 5, if the threshold is 0.0112 – four times of background noise RMSE level – the leak sound will be detectable if it exists with a mixing ratio over 10%.

Assuming that the leak sound amplitude is the same as that for background noise, the RMSE of the leak sound is half that of background noise.

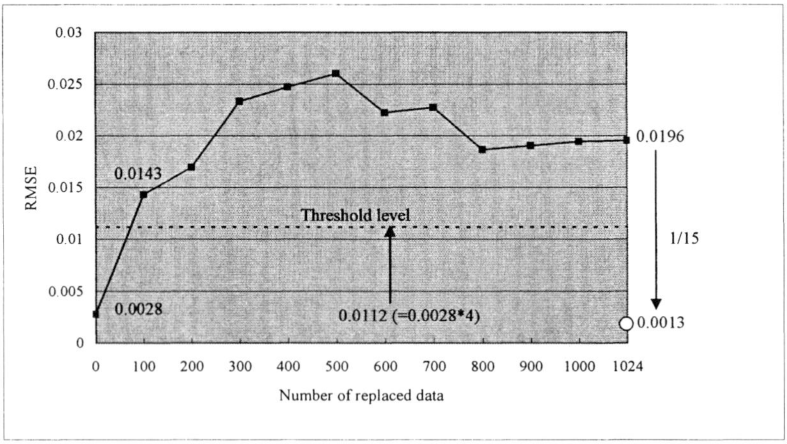

Figure 5 Evaluation by RMSE

4.2 Evaluation and detectability by TPM

Trajectory parallel measure topologically evaluates the trajectory condition in a local subspace containing an attractor. Figure 6 shows that the directions among neighboring trajectories on attractor are almost identical if the attractor is reconstructed from the time series with determinism. In contrast, directions among trajectories are random if the time series is not deterministic. If the TPM value is zero, trajectories are completely parallel, and thereby aligned in the same direction. If the value is 0.5, the trajectories are orthogonal and random.

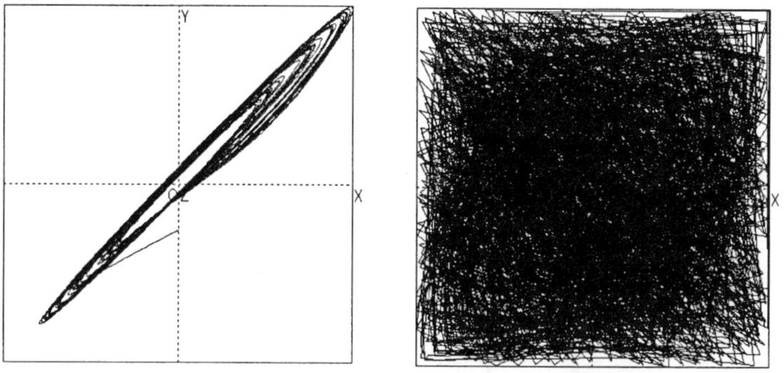

(a) Deterministic (b) Random

Figure 6 Trajectories for determinism and random

Figure 7 shows that the TPM values of background noise and leak sound are 0.103 maximum and 0.062 minimum, respectively. As the number of data replacements is increased, TPM decreases, implying that the leak sound is relatively more deterministic than background noise.

If the threshold level in TPM is less than 90% of background noise, the threshold level is 0.093. The leak sound is detectable when the mixing ratio is over about 40%.

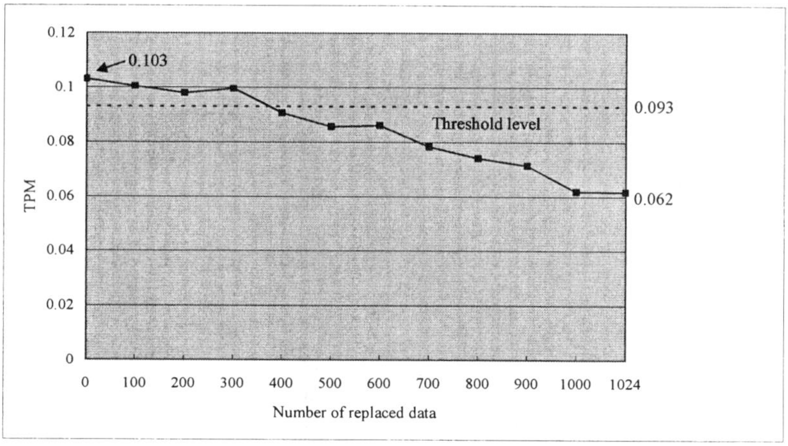

Figure 7 Evaluation by TPM

4.3 Evaluation and detectability by KS entropy

Kolmogorov-Sinai entropy represents a reciprocal for the predictable term; it is also almost equal to the summed values of positive elements for Lyapunov spectra.

As shown in Fig. 8, if the mixing ratio is increasing, KS entropy is decreasing in the former half of the time series. However, if the mixing ratio is above 70%, KS entropy is increasing. The attractor structure will be changed by half at that mixing ratio.

KS entropies of the background noise and leak sound are 2.15 and 1.99, respectively. These values are not significantly different. KS entropy decreases as the mixture ratio increases up to 60–70%; KS entropy increases when the mixture ratio is more than 70%. The reason for this increase is not clear, but it may be related to mixing ratio and amplitude. If the threshold is 1.93, the leak sound will be detected with a range of over 30%.

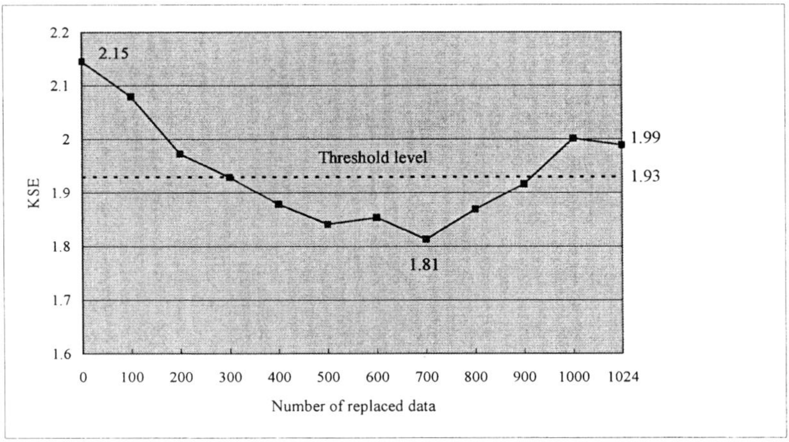

Figure 8 Evaluation by KS entropy

5. CONCLUSIONS

This study examined the topological structure and prediction accuracy of an ultrasonic time series of a background noise, leak sound, and composite sound in a petroleum refining plant. Threshold levels for detecting the leak sound were then estimated. Evaluation by TPM is most practical because amplitude can be ignored as a factor and because its value decreases with the mixing ratio. It is expensive to measure an ultrasonic sound using a directional microphone. Early detection of leak sounds in audible sounds detected by an ordinary microphone remains a subject for future study. This research was subsidized by the Petroleum Energy Center (PEC).

REFERENCES

Ohba, R., Tamanoi, Y., Tokui, I., and Takeshima, M., 1999, "Intelligent robot watchdog for leak monitoring in oil refinery", *Sensors and their Applications X*, (eds. N. M. White and A. T. Augousti) IOP Publishing (Bristol), pp.239-244

Iokibe, T., Kanke, M., Fujimoto, Y., and Suzuki, S., 1994, "Short-term Prediction on Chaotic Timesereis by Local Fuzzy Reconstruction Method," *Proc. of the 3rd International Conference on Fuzzy Logic, Neural Nets and Soft Computing*, 1994/8/1-8/7, Iizuka, Japan, pp.491-492

Iokibe, T., 1999, "Time Series Prediction," *Handbook of Fuzzy Computation*, (eds. E. Ruspini, P. Binissone and W. Pedrycz), Joint Publication of Oxford University Press and Institute of Physics Publishing, pp. G16.4:1-G16.4:11

Fujimoto, Y., and Iokibe, T., 1997, "Measuring Determinism in Time Series by Chaotic Approach," In *Proc. of the 1997 International conference on Neural Information Processing and Intelligent Information Systems*, 1997/11/24-11/28, Dunedin, New Zealand, Springer-Verlag Singapore Pte. Ltd., pp.174-177

Ott, E., 1993, *Chaos in Dynamical Systems.* New York: Cambridge University Press, p.138.

A NEURAL NETWORK-BASED ROUTING ALGORITHM WITH AN IMPROVED ENERGY FUNCTION

DONG C.PARK†, KYO R. KEUM†, and SANG J.HONG‡
†Dept. of Information Eng.
‡Dept. of Electronics Eng.
Myongji University
Yongin, Korea

ABSTRACT

A shortest path routing algorithm using the Hopfield Neural Network (HNN) with a modified Lyapunov function is proposed. Experiments are performed on 30,000 networks with randomly selected link costs. The results show that the proposed algorithm outperforms conventional methods both in route optimality and convergence rate.

INTRODUCTION

In a communications network, efficient routing is a very important factor that has a significant impact on the network's performance. An ideal routing algorithm should find the shortest path within a very short time so as to satisfy the user's demand. Hopfield and Tank's inspirational contribution of the neural network solution to the travelling salesman problem provides us with a new tool to solve many combinatorial search problems [1].

After the pioneering works on the communication traffic routing problem by Rauch and Winarske [2] and Zhang and Thomopoulos [3], Ali and Kamoun proposed an adaptive routing algorithm [4]. However, this algorithm suffers from loops or partitions in the solution path. Park and Choi proposed an algorithm that can remove loops or partitions by adding a new term to the energy function [5]. Most recently, Ahn and Ramakrishna added two new terms to Park and Choi's energy function and proposed a new algorithm for faster convergence [6]. However, the solution quality with the new two terms in the energy function of Ahn and Ramakrishna's algorithm has been left in question for the networks with more than 14 nodes. In this paper, we propose a new energy function for improving both the route quality and convergence rate.

DEFINITION OF THE PROBLEM

With the definition of an undirected graph, the underlying topology of a network can be given with **G = (V,E)**, where **V** is the set of vertices(N nodes), and **E** is the set of its edges (link costs) [4]-[6]. Note that a link cost matrix **L**$= [L_{ij}]$ is defined where L_{ij} is a cost from node i to node j and $L_{ij} = L_{ji}$ since the network is given by an undirected graph.

In HNN modelling, the shortest path routing problem can be represented by the logical algebraic expression of a constrained combinatorial optimization problem as follows :

$$Minimize \sum_{i=1}^{N}\sum_{j=1}^{N} L_{ij}V_{ij} \qquad (1)$$

$$Subject\ to\ \left(\sum_{\substack{j=1\\j\neq i}}^{N} V_{ij} - \sum_{\substack{k=1\\k\neq i}}^{N} V_{ki}\right) = \begin{cases} 1, & \text{if } i = s \\ -1, & \text{if } i = d \\ 0, & \text{otherwise} \end{cases} \tag{2}$$

where s and d represent the source node and the destination node, respectively.

In Eq. (2), the state of a neuron, V_{ij}, is defined as:

$$V_{ij} = \begin{cases} 1, & \text{if the link from node } i \text{ to node } j \text{ exists in solution.} \\ 0, & \text{otherwise} \end{cases} \tag{3}$$

HNNs FOR ROUTING ALGORITHM

The application of the HNN to constrained combinatorial optimization problems was first introduced by Hopfield and Tank [1]. Later, Ali and Kamoun proposed an adaptive algorithm with an energy function that forces the neural network into the lowest energy state. In fact, they first proposed an adaptive algorithm for a network structure using the topological information. The energy function of Ali and Kamoun is defined as follows [4]:

$$\begin{aligned} E \ = \ & \frac{\mu_1}{2}\sum_{i=1}^{N}\sum_{\substack{j=1\\j\neq i}}^{N} L_{ij}\cdot V_{ij} + \frac{\mu_2}{2}\sum_{i=1}^{N}\sum_{\substack{j=1\\j\neq i}}^{N} \gamma_{ij}\cdot V_{ij} \\ & + \frac{\mu_3}{2}\sum_{i=1}^{N}\left(\sum_{\substack{j=1\\j\neq i}}^{N} V_{ij} - \sum_{\substack{j=1\\j\neq i}}^{N} V_{ji}\right)^2 \\ & + \frac{\mu_4}{2}\sum_{i=1}^{N}\sum_{\substack{j=1\\j\neq i}}^{N} V_{ij}\cdot(1 - V_{ij}) + \frac{\mu_5}{2}(1 - V_{ds}) \end{aligned} \tag{4}$$

where the μ_1 term minimizes the total link cost of a routing by taking the cost of existing links into account. The μ_2 term prevents nonexistent links from being included in the chosen routing path. The μ_3 term makes sure that if a node has been entered it will also be exited by a path. The μ_4 term enforces the states of the neural network to converge to a valid route. The μ_5 term makes sure that the source node and the destination node are included in the formed path.

As far as the optimality of the solution is concerned, Ali and Kamoun's algorithm seldom finds a good solution when the number of nodes increases due to loops or partitions in the solution. To remove loops or partitions existing in solutions, Park and Choi proposed an improved routing algorithm with the following energy function [5]:

$$\begin{aligned} E_{PC} \ = \ & \frac{\mu_1}{2}\sum_{i=1}^{N}\sum_{\substack{j=1\\j\neq i}}^{N} L_{ij}\cdot V_{ij} + \frac{\mu_2}{2}\sum_{i=1}^{N}\sum_{\substack{j=1\\j\neq i}}^{N} \gamma_{ij}\cdot V_{ij} \\ & + \frac{\mu_3}{2}\sum_{i=1}^{N}\left(\sum_{\substack{j=1\\j\neq i}}^{N} V_{ij} - \sum_{\substack{j=1\\j\neq i}}^{N} V_{ji} - \phi_i\right)^2 \\ & + \frac{\mu_4}{2}\sum_{i=1}^{N}\sum_{\substack{j=1\\j\neq i}}^{N} V_{ij}\cdot(1 - V_{ij}) + \frac{\mu_5}{2}\sum_{i=1}^{N}\sum_{\substack{j=1\\j\neq i}}^{N} V_{ij}\cdot V_{ji} \end{aligned} \tag{5}$$

where the μ_1 term, the μ_2 term, and the μ_4 term are the same as those in Ali and Kamoun's energy function. There is a slight change in the μ_3 term over Ali and Kamoun's. The μ_5 term was introduced by Park and Choi to ensure that the flow vector $V = [V_{ij}]$ is one directional. This means that $V_{ij} \cdot V_{ji}$ is always zero for all (i, j) and this prohibits a solution route from forming loops or partitions by not allowing $V_{ij} = V_{ji} = 1$.

Ahn and Ramakrishna, later, proposed an energy function for faster convergence with the following [6]:

$$E_{AR} = E_{PC} + \frac{\mu_6}{2}\left[\sum_{i=1}^{N}\sum_{\substack{j=1\\j\neq i}}^{N}\left(\sum_{\substack{k=1\\k\neq i,j}}^{N} V_{ik} - 1\right)\cdot V_{ij}^2\right] + \frac{\mu_7}{2}\left[\sum_{i=1}^{N}\sum_{\substack{j=1\\j\neq i}}^{N}\left(\sum_{\substack{k=1\\k\neq i,j}}^{N} V_{kj} - 1\right)\cdot V_{ij}^2\right] \quad (6)$$

The two new terms, μ_6 and μ_7, in Eq. (6) were introduced to eliminate the possibility of forming loops and partitions in a solution path and to increase the speed of convergence.

THE PROPOSED ALGORITHM

In order to improve the quality of the solution and convergence rate of Park and Choi's algorithm [5], the following energy function is proposed in this paper:

$$\begin{aligned} E \;=\; & \frac{\mu_1}{2}\sum_{i=1}^{N}\sum_{\substack{j=1\\j\neq i}}^{N}\left(V_{ij}\cdot\sum_{\substack{k=1\\k\neq i}}^{N}(1-C_{ik})\cdot C_{ij}\right) + \frac{\mu_2}{2}\sum_{i=1}^{N}\sum_{\substack{j=1\\j\neq i}}^{N}\gamma_{ij}\cdot V_{ij} \\ & + \frac{\mu_3}{2}\sum_{i=1}^{N}\left(\sum_{\substack{j=1\\j\neq i}}^{N} V_{ij} - \sum_{\substack{j=1\\j\neq i}}^{N} V_{ji} - \phi_i\right)^2 \\ & + \frac{\mu_4}{2}\sum_{i=1}^{N}\sum_{\substack{j=1\\j\neq i}}^{N} V_{ij}\cdot(1-V_{ij}) + \frac{\mu_5}{2}\sum_{i=1}^{N}\sum_{\substack{j=1\\j\neq i}}^{N}\left(V_{ij}\cdot\sum_{\substack{k=1\\k\neq i}}^{N} V_{ki}\right) \end{aligned} \quad (7)$$

In Eq. (7), the three terms, (μ_2, μ_3, and μ_4), are the same as those of [4]-[6]. The term μ_1 related with the total link cost is now revisited and modified in this paper. When a node of interest considers which link to take for a path out of all connected links, the newly modified μ_1 term not only takes the costs of the immediate links into account but also the link costs of the nodes connected with the immediate links as well. Furthermore, the μ_5 term related with loop and partition prevention is also revisited in this paper and the μ_5 term doesn't allow any path to the node i when node i selects an outgoing path and can efficiently prevent the solution from forming loops or partitions.

EXPERIMENTS AND RESULTS

In order to have a general performance assessment of various algorithms, a total of 30,000 network topologies (10,000 for each of 3 groups) with sizes up to 50 nodes and randomly assigned link costs are used for our experiments. An example of the network topologies is given in Fig. 1. The proposed algorithm is compared with the routing algorithms of Park and Choi and Ahn et al. in terms of the convergence rate

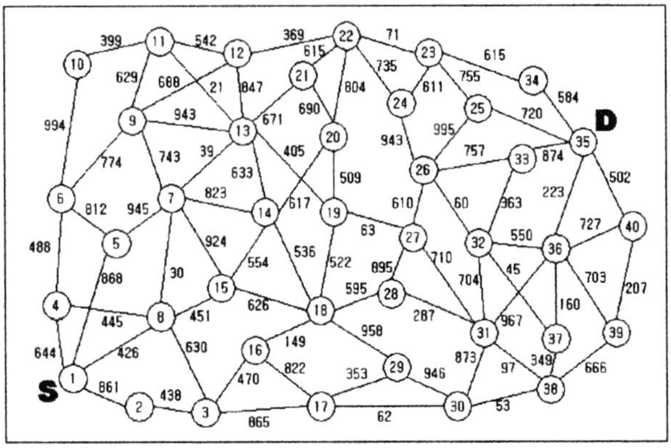

Figure 1: An example of network topologies used in experiments.

and the optimality of solutions. Convergence of a solution is defined as a source-destination pair for which an algorithm find a connected path in finite iterations (in our case, 20,000 iterations). Table 1 shows the parameters used in our experiments.

The convergence rates are shown in Table 2. As can be seen from Table 2, all the algorithms except the proposed one suffer from low convergence rates as the size of the network grows. Note that convergence rates of Ahn et al.'s algorithm are considerably deteriorated when the size of network is over 40. This problem of a low convergence rate on Ahn et al.'s algorithm witnessed in Table 2 was expected because the energy function was intended for faster convergence to any solution while paying less attention to the convergence rate. The μ_5 term proposed in this paper, however, can efficiently prevent solution paths from forming loops and partitions and this greatly aids in higher convergence rates in the proposed algorithm.

Table 3 shows a summary on the optimalities of the routing paths found by various algorithms. Note that the routing paths of Dijkstra's algorithm were used as the reference for optimal results. All the three algorithms give fairly good results on the networks of Group 1. However, when the number of nodes grows to 50 in Group 3 networks, the two conventional algorithms, Park and Choi's and Ahn et al.'s, severely suffer from an unacceptable quality of routing paths. It is quite a contrast because the proposed algorithm shows over 79% of optimality on average for these Group 3 networks. This result of Ahn et al.'s algorithm is far different from the results claimed in [6], where experiments were performed on 14-node networks. For the networks with more nodes, the performance on optimality and convergence rate of solutions become more discriminative depending on the algorithms used. Ahn et al.'s algorithm shows that the inability of obtaining quality solutions regarding route optimality is somewhat obvious because their algorithm

TABLE 1: PARAMETERS USED IN EXPERIMENTS

Parameter	A	B	C	D	F	τ	Δt	λ
Value	950	2500	1900	100	500	1	10^{-4}	1

Table 2 : COMPARISON OF CONVERGENCE RATE (%)

# of nodes / Algorithm	Group 1 (12 ~ 25)	Group 2 (26 ~ 40)	Group 3 (41 ~ 50)
Park & Choi[5]	99.57	99.20	46.13
Ahn & Ramakrishna[6]	98.85	76.20	13.34
Proposed	99.85	99.40	94.23

is intended to have a faster convergence to any solution while paying less attention to the quality of the solution. However, the first term of the energy function of the proposed algorithm tries to find an optimal path by searching not only the immediate links connected to the node of interest but also the links of the nodes connected with the immediate links, as well.

CONCLUSIONS

A routing algorithm for communication networks is proposed in this paper. The proposed algorithm modifies the Lyapunov energy function in order to utilize all the information on the links connected with the node of interest. This results in far better route optimality and higher convergence rates over conventional algorithms such as Ali & Kamoun's, Park & Choi's, and Ahn & Ramakrishna's, especially when the network size increases. The simulation results on 30,000 networks with up to 50 nodes reveal that the proposed algorithm gives on average at least 94.23% of the convergence rate while Ahn & Ramakrishna's algorithm, the most recent one on this subject, is as low as 13.34% of the convergence rate. Regarding the solution quality; the proposed algorithm shows 79.99% of route optimality performance for the networks with 41 to 50 nodes while the other algorithms show 11.21% to 24.20% of route optimality. This confirms that the proposed algorithm is a very effective tool for the routing of communication networks when the convergence rate and route optimality are considered.

ACKNOWLEDGMENT

This work was supported in part by the grant from Korea Science and Engineering Foundation (Grant # R05-2003-000-10992-0).

Table 3 : COMPARISON OF ROUTE OPTIMALITY (%)

# of nodes / Algorithm	Group 1 (12 ~ 25)	Group 2 (26 ~ 40)	Group 3 (41 ~ 50)
Park & Choi[5]	82.65	63.76	24.20
Ahn & Ramakrishna[6]	65.82	52.63	11.21
Proposed	87.97	82.20	79.99

References

[1] Hopfield, j.j., Tank, D.W.,(1980). Neural computations of decisions in optimization problems, *Biol. Cybern.*,42,141-152.

[2] Rauch,H.E., Winarske, T., (1988). Neural Networks for Routing Communication Traffic,*IEEE Cont. Syst. Mag.*, Apr,26-30

[3] Zhang, L., Thomopoulos,S.C.A.,(1989).Neural Network Implementation of the Shortest Path Algorithm for Traffic Routing in Communication Networks, *Proc. of IJCNN*, JUN, II-591

[4] Ali, M.K., Kamoun,F.,(1993). Neural Networks for Shortest Path Computation and Routing in Computer Networks, *IEEE Trans Neural Networks*,TNN-4(6), 941-953

[5] Park, D.C., Choi, S.E.,(1998). A Neural Network based Multi-destination Routing Algorithm for Communication Network, *Proc. of IJCNN*, 1673-1678

[6] Ahn C.W., Ramakrishna,R.S.,(2002). Neural Network Based Near-Optimal Routing Algorithm, *Proc. of ICONIP*, **4**, 1771-1776

[7] Araujo,F., Ribeiro, B.,and Rodrigues,F., (2001). A Neural Network for Shortest Path Computation, *IEEE Trans Neural Networks*,TNN-12(5), 1067-1073

POSSIBILITY DYNAMIC PROGRAMMING

HENRY L. PFISTER, PHD.
Air Force Research Laboratory
Munitions Directorate
Eglin Air Force Base
email: pfister@eglin.af.mil

ABSTRACT

Possibility dynamic programming models extend classic probabilistic dynamic programming models to include a unique measure of uncertainty not currently addressed. The resulting replacement of the probability in the state variables with a possibility evaluation leads to a new method for analyzing stochastic systems. A sample dynamic stochastic policy decision problem is examined in detail to illustrate the unique results of the possibility dynamic programming model. An analysis of the non-intuitive nature of these results is presented that support further research into the value of using possibility reasoning to generalize traditional probability theory in dynamic decision models. This larger set of decision models provided by possibility, as compared with probability, allows for more realistic modeling of complex stochastic systems. These models are employed to analyze the steady state conditions in power grids, in transportation networks, in production planning, and in military operations. A possibility dynamic programming model provides a new capability to extend probabilistic dynamic programming to explicitly include uncertainty in the computation of the optimum stochastic system decisions.

INTRODUCTION

This research is a generalization of probabilistic dynamic programming to create possibility dynamic programming that includes an explicit measure of uncertainty not currently addressed by probability theory. The resulting replacement of the probability in the state variable computation with a possibility value leads to a new method for analyzing stochastic decision systems. A sample dynamic production policy decision problem is examined in detail to illustrate the unique results available from the possibility dynamic programming model. An analysis of the non-intuitive nature of these results is presented that support further research into the value of using possibility reasoning to generalize probability theory in dynamic decision models.

The resulting analysis of the optimum system characteristics provides new decision interpretations using the possibility reasoning. A classic production decision model is analyzed using the possibility dynamic programming model. It is shown that the probabilistic dynamic programming model is a proper subset of the possibility model and it is concluded that the possibility model generalizes the probability model. This generalization provides for the computation of additional information for the analysis of stochastic decisions and the addressing of a larger set of models with explicit uncertainty.

The possibility-reasoning approach used in this research is to explicitly include "uncertain" as a logic state along with the classic logic "true" and "false" states. This leads to logic reasoning decisions using possibility variables that can be computed in terms of the maximum possibility value similar to the use of maximum likelihood for probability. This approach does not depend on the usual randomness concepts in probability theory or any of its underlying distribution assumptions; it is developed from the point of view of uncertainty and numerically computed using fuzzy logic methods.

POSSIBILITY DYNAMIC PROGRAMMING

Probabilistic dynamic programming differs from deterministic dynamic programming in that the state at the next stage is not completely determined by the state and policy decision at the current stage. A probability distribution is used to determine the next state, which is then fully described by the state and policy decision at the current stage; a typical objective is to minimize the expected sum of the cost contributions from the individual stages. The expansion of all states and decisions at each stage results in a decision tree. Possibility dynamic programming explicitly includes uncertainty in the state evaluation and relaxes the requirement for a probability distribution at each stage. In this case the objective is still to minimize the expected sum of the cost contributions. By restricting the uncertainty to zero, possibility dynamic programming is identical to probabilistic dynamic programming. Allowing for uncertainty in the decision model then gives an added dimension to selecting decision strategies.

EXAMPLE PRODUCTION PLANNING PROBLEM

An engineering company has received a competitive government request to create a single prototype item. The item production requirements are so stringent that the company may have to produce more than one item to obtain an acceptable item from a batch of produced items. The company estimates that the probability of producing an acceptable item is 0.5 and for a defective item as 0.5 with no possibility of rework. Then the expected number of acceptable units in a lot size of L can be modeled as a binomial distribution given by the product formula: pr(L) = 0.5 ^ L.

If the marginal production costs are $1,000 per item and excess items are worthless and if each production batch run has a setup cost of $3,000 and the production capacity and delivery schedule allows for no more than three production runs with no more than four units in any production run. Then what is the decision policy for determining production batch sizes that minimizes the total expected cost to the manufacturer?

A probabilistic dynamic programming approach is to treat the three possible production runs as sequential decision stages. The decision variables x(n) are the production lot size at each stage n = 1, 2, and 3. The state of the system at each stage is the number of acceptable items that still need to be produced either 0 or 1. Define $f_n(s, x_n)$ as the total expected cost for stage n onward given the state s and policy x decisions and compute:

$$f_n^*(s) = \min f_n(s, x_n) \quad for\ x_n = 0,...,4 \quad \text{where} \quad f_n^*(0) = 0$$

The dynamic programming recursive decision stage equation is then:

$$f_n^*(1) = \min\{K + x_n * 1000 + pr(x_n) * f_{n+1}^*(1)\}\ for\ x_n = 0...4$$

Where:

$$K = \begin{cases} 0 \ \ if\ x_n = 0 \\ 3000 \ \ if\ x_n > 0 \end{cases}$$

Accounts for the production set up costs and the maximum final cost is set as:

$$f_4^*(1) = 16000$$

A spreadsheet implements this dynamic programming model and the optimum decision policy is to make 2 items in production run 1 and stop if one is good, or else to make 2 items in run 2 and stop if one is good, and finally to make 3 items in run 3 for an expected total cost of $6,750.

It is typical to test the uncertainty in decision models by varying the probability of failure such as from 0.5 to 0.2 to get the following result where the optimum decision policy remains the same with a decrease in the expected total cost to $5,026 indicating a stable decision model.

By increasing the probability of failure to 0.6 we get the following result, where the optimum decision policy is to make 3 items in production run 1 and stop if one is good, then to make 3 items in run 2 and stop if one is good, and finally to make 4 items in run 3 for an expected total cost of $7,719. This result is a bit unsatisfactory since a relatively small increase in the probability of failure results in very different decision policies but not a great deal of difference in the average expected cost. Clearly an explicit way to incorporate uncertainty into this model could provide better policy decision analysis and cost estimates.

USING POSSIBILITY TO REPLACE PROBABILITY

A simple way to replace the probability of a proposition with the pair of possibility values (Sn, Sp) for example where p = 0.5, is to set the necessary support Sn = p and the possible support Sp = 0.0, which yields the following possibility states for the proposition:

Not True:	1 – Sn	= 0.5
True:	Sn + Sp	= 0.5
Uncertain:	1 – Sn – Sp	= 0.5

Note: it is not required that the possibility states sum to 1.0 as it is required that probability states sum to 1.0 in order to from a probability distribution function.

If a product event combination function is used to model the necessity of success for L trials then the function:

$$\prod_{L} Sn = Sn^{L}$$

Is the same formula as the binomial probability distribution and the results for the possibility model and probability model for the sample problem are identical. In addition for the three cases in the previous section the uncertainty can be compared as 0.5, 0.2, and 0.6.

By adjusting the necessary support to be equal to the possibility support so that uncertainty does not change, then the (Sn, Sp) parameter values for the cases becomes: (0.25, 0.25), (0.4, 0.4), and (0.2, 0.2).

Then the dynamic programming stage decisions change to become:

For Sn = 0.25 -> Produce 4 units at each stage
For Sn = 0.4 -> Produce 3 units for stages 1 and 2 and 4 units in stage 3
For Sn = 0.2 -> Produce 4 units at each stage

By considering the highest constant necessary support value so that uncertainty is maintained as before for all cases then the parameter values are: (0.4, 0.1), (0.4, 0.4), and (0.4, 0.0). The resulting dynamic programming solution is the same for all three cases: to produce 2 units in stages 1 and 2, and to produce 3 units in stage 3.

By adjusting necessary and possible support values so that uncertainty is at the maximum value and the possibility is the same for all cases then the parameter values are: (0.5, 0.3), (0.8, 0.0), and (0.4, 0.4). The dynamic programming solution remains the same as the original probabilistic model but now information is available about the imputed possible support values. These are the values required to achieve the maximum constant uncertainty in all cases, which also implies a dual variable relationship for the constant possibility value for each case. For case 1 this implies the need for additional possible support of Sp = 0.3 to achieve an equal uncertainty of 0.2, while for case 3 the required possible support rises to 0.4. As anticipated the high possibility goal of 0.8 requires significantly higher possible support to achieve the low uncertainty.

It should be noted that the explicit inclusion of uncertainty results in a more analytic decision model than by just using probability distributions and performing Monte Carlo sensitivity analysis. This technique of replacing probability with possibility in decision models results in identical results as the probability model. The possibility parameters can then be generalized to determine the possibility support needed to achieve low uncertainty in the decisions. The result is an analytic rather than statistical model of uncertainty that is applicable to more complex decision evaluations. This leads to a generalization of probability using possibility that provides additional modeling capability to explicitly analyze uncertainty.

POSSIBILITY EVALUATION FUNCTIONS

A key component in the probabilistic dynamic programming model is the use of the binomial distribution function to estimate the expected number of acceptable units in a production lot size of L units. It was shown that using the product combination of necessity values for possibility dynamic programming results in the same solution. However, more realistic estimations of acceptable unit production are possible by using the two parameters Sn and Sp in possibility theory. Economics of scale in production can be modeled by assuming constant necessity support Sn with increasing possibility support Sp and by replacing the product combination production function with an increasing function for Sp:

$$\text{Number of successful items: prod(L)} = \left(1 - S_n - S_p(L)\right)^L$$

This assumption is similar to the binomial distribution function but contains state dependent values for the possibilities. As production size increases the possibility of a successful item also increases rather than remaining constant. This situation is often observed as a learning effect but is difficult to model with simple probability distributions. An example of the possibility dynamic programming solution with this production model was solved that has an average failure rate of 0.5 as in the original model.

That leads to selecting an equal production amount decision strategy of 3 units per stage while still using an overall average failure rate per state of 0.5 in the economics of scale production model. The overall expected cost decreases to $6,413 from the original $6,750 or by 5%. This model uses the same dynamic programming sequential decision structure, the same product model for production, and the same average unit failure value to arrive at a very different decision strategy with a lower expected cost by only considering a more realistic non constant production model based on possibility values.

When the same changes are applied to the average failure rate model of 0.6, less change is observed in the decision strategy. The previous production strategy does not change and the expected cost goes from $7,719 to $7,220 or is reduced by 6%. One conclusion is that as failure rate increases the effect of economics of scale is not as influential on the optimum production strategy.

When the changes are applied to the average failure rate model of 0.2, a large change is observed in the decision strategy. The previous production strategy does change to equal amounts per stage and the expected cost only goes from $5,206 to $5,209 for a negligible difference. One conclusion from this example is that a low failure rate that favors the effect of economics of scale is very influential on the optimum production strategy. These examples and conclusions are directly attributable to using possibility models to generalize the simpler probability model assumptions to provide greater modeling power.

CONCLUSION

The classic model of probabilistic dynamic programming for decision optimization of stochastic systems is extended to use possibility theory rather than probability theory in the state evaluation. This results in a unique way to explicitly include uncertainty as a logical state in this new possibility dynamic programming model. The resulting analysis of the decision characteristics provides new information using the possibility modeling interpretations. A classic dynamic programming stochastic production cost model is analyzed using the possibility model. It is shown that the probability model is a proper subset of the possibility model and it is concluded that the possibility model generalizes the possibility model. This provides for a richer decision analysis with many more alternatives by using possibility theory to include uncertainty in the decision model.

A generalization of probability to model the economics of scale in production with possibility was modeled by assuming constant necessity support Sn with increasing possibility support Sp and by replacing the product combination production function with an increasing function for Sp. This assumption is similar to the binomial distribution product combination function but contains state dependent values for the possibilities. As production size increases the possibility of a successful item also increases rather than remaining constant. This situation is often observed as a learning effect but is difficult to model with simple probability distributions.

This is an example of the larger set of decision models provided by employing possibility theory, as compared with classic probability theory, to allow for more realistic modeling of complex stochastic systems. These models can be employed to analyze the dynamic conditions in power grids, the dynamic routing in transportation networks, the dynamic decisions in production planning, and the dynamic planning and engagement in military operations. The concept of a possibility dynamic programming model provides a new capability to extend probabilistic dynamic programming to explicitly include uncertainty in the computation of the optimum stochastic system decisions. The result is a generalization of probability to explicitly include uncertainty. Uncertainty is difficult to capture in any decision model but possibility theory provides a unique approach to incorporate it explicitly as a state variable.

REFERENCES

[1] Zadeh L., "Fuzzy Sets," *Information and Control 8*, 1965.

[2] Baldwin J., "Support Logic Programming", *International Journal of Intelligent Systems 1*, 1986.

[3] Zimmerman H., *Fuzzy Set Theory and It's Applications* – Second Edition, Kluwer, 1991.

[4] Pfister H., "Possibility Reasoning With Uncertainty," Artificial Neural Networks in Engineering Conference, St Louis – ANNIE 2003, November 2003.

[5] Pfister H., "Uncertain Reasoning with Linear Programming," Institute for Operations Research and Management Science, INFORMS 2003, Atlanta, October 2003.

[6] Bellman, R., (1957) *Dynamic Programming*. Princeton University Press.

[7] Hillier, F. & Lieberman, G., *Operations Research,* Holden-Day, Second Edition, 1974.

GENERATION OF PARETO OPTIMUM MAP FOR JOB-SHOP SCHEDULING

MICHIKO WATANABE
Asahikawa National College of Technology
ASAHIKAWA, JAPAN

MASASHI FURUKAWA
Asahikawa National College of Technology
ASAHIKAWA, JAPAN

MASAHIRO KINOSHITA
Hokkaido Institute of Technology
SAPPRO, JAPAN

TAKASHI KAWAKAMI
Hokkaido Institute of Technology
SAPPRO, JAPAN

KATSUMI HAMA
Hakodate National College of Technology
HAKODATE, JAPAN

NORIHIKO TAKATORI
Rakuno Gakuen University
EBETSU, JAPAN

KEITARO NARUSE
Aizu University
AIZU, JAPAN

YUKINORI KAKAZU
Hokkaido University
SAPPORO, JAPAN

ABSTRACT

In this study, we propose the immune algorithm (IA) based on GA using a new chromosome representation to solve the job-shop scheduling problem (JSP). IA realizes to collect various kinds of schedule solution (pareto solutions). Because a weighted scalar function is used to represent the multi-purpose function on JSP, it is important to explore a proper combination of weights for the weighted scalar function responding to manufacturing situation. However, it is hard to find out the proper combination of weights. We propose a knowledge acquiring method based self-organizing maps (SOM) to obtain a relation between the weights and pareto schedule solutions, which are obtained by the proposed IA. This relation is so named the pareto optimum map. Numerical experiments verify that IA can obtain various types of schedules and that the pareto optimum map generated by IA and SOM can indicate the relation between the weights and schedule solutions.

INTRODUCTION

Solving a job-shop scheduling problem (JSP) used to depend on experts who have a skillful experience and intuition in manufacturing industry. However, the more manufacturing systems become complex and deal with various kinds of products with small volume, the more it becomes difficult for scheduling experts to make a good schedule, because it belongs to a class of NP complete problems. Since old days, many methods have been proposed for solving JSP such as heuristic rules (Furukawa M., Arai M., Yoshimura H., and Hama K. (2000)), branch and bound methods (Nabeshima I. (1975)) and GAs (Watanabe M., Furukawa M., Mizoe M. Watanabe T. and Kakazu Y. (2000)).

The purpose of this research is to develop a new method that makes it possible to acquire the relation between the weighted scalar functions and scheduling solutions for the multi-purpose JSP. To obtain such a relation between the weighted scalar functions and their solutions, the proposed method adopts the immune algorithm (IA) and self-organizing maps (SOM) (Kohonen T. (1993), Kohonen T. (1996)). Numerical experiments are performed to obtain the knowledge mentioned above by making the pareto map based on the proposed method and it is confirmed that the obtained pareto map is useful to choose a proper weighted function responding to the changeable manufacturing situations.

JOB SHOP SCHEDULING PROBLEM

A job-shop scheduling problem (JSP) is a combinatorial optimization problem. When a set of jobs and a set of shops (machines) are given, it is to determine a jobs' sequence on the processed machines, in other words to make a jobs' schedule. Several criteria are utilized to make a schedule. Namely, JSP has multi-purpose functions. Typical criteria are a maximum makespan time F_1, a minimum due date F_2, and a minimum machine idle time F_3. Since it is difficult to apply these three functions to JSP at once in general, a scalar function, which is a sum of criterion's values multiplied by some weighted values, is introduced into JSP, such as

$$F = W_1F_1 + W_2F_2 + W_3F_3 \tag{1}$$

where W_1, W_2, and W_3 are the weight coefficients of each criterion. We call the equation (1) the weighted scalar function. JSP has the following constraints.

1) Each job has a machine processing.
2) Processing time of jobs for each machine is given before scheduling.
3) Each machine cannot process two or more jobs at the same time.
4) A due date for each job is specified before scheduling.

JSP is to make a schedule so as to minimize the equation (1) subject to the constraints described above.

RESEARCH OBJECTIVE

The objective of this research is to acquire the knowledge on the relation between the weighted function (a combination of the weight values) and an expected solution. To do so, it is described how to collect a group of schedule solutions by use of IA at first. Then, it is proposed how to show the relation between the weighted function and an expected solution in visual based on SOM. After that, results of numerical experiments are shown to conform the proposed method and finally the conclusion is described.

IMMUNE ALGORITHM APPLIED TO JSP

Immune Algorithm

IA artificially realizes to simply model the creature's immune system. In brief, it is a search method with an ability of exploring a large area of solutions based on the genetic algorithm (GA), a memory mechanism for searched solutions, a solution suppression mechanism using the stored solutions in the memory, and an updating mechanism for exchanging a stored solution with a better one. Therefore, it is expected to obtain various kinds of solutions as a group more than the solutions obtained by the genetic algorithm.

Representing a chromosome by multi-gene representation

In order to apply IA to JSP, we have to design a chromosome at first, because IA is based on GA. The multi-gene representation (MGR), developed by authors for JSP (Watanabe M., Furukawa M., Mizoe M. Watanabe T. and Kakazu Y. (2000)), is adopted to compose this chromosome. MGR basically stands on the order representation (OR), which Grefenssette designs as a chromosome for applying GA to the traveling salesman problem (TSP). OR can be directly applicable to JSP when a single machine is treated as JSP. MGR is modified for use of GA to solve JSP.

Immune algorithm for JSP

After a weighted scalar function is set to a fitness function like GA and some memories are prepared for the sake of keeping the better schedule solutions, IA is applied to JSP as follows.

1) N chromosome lists are generated as initial schedule solutions at random and their weighted scalar functions are calculated based on a job-number list in the chromosome list just as GA. Set $g = 0$, $t = 0$, and $k = 0$.
2) If g=0, t is replaced with t+1, and GA is executed until $t = T$. The best solution searched by GA is registered to memories. Then, g and k are replaced with 1, respectively.
3) Set $t = 0$, and g is replaced with g+1. If $g = G$, terminate the procedure.
4) N chromosome lists are newly generated and their weighted scalar functions are calculated based on a job-number part list in the chromosome list.
5) t is replaced with t+1 and genetic operations are operated to the solutions. A similarity s of each solution with ones stored in the memories is subsequently calculated. If the similarity of solution is less than a threshold value and its weighted scalar function is better than the compared solution, then replace the schedule solution with the compared one in the memory, remove the stored schedule solution, generate the new solution, and add it to the GA solutions.
6) If $t \neq T$, return to the step 4). If $t = T$, the best schedule solution is added to memories and k is replaced with k+1. If $k \geq Mem$ at this time, the worst solution between the added solution and stored solutions in the memories are compared and the worst solution is removed from the memories. Go back to the step 2).

In the above-mentioned procedure, *Mem* is the number of the memory capacity, T is the terminated number of GA operations' iteration, and G is the iteration number of GA. Moreover, The similarity s is calculated by the following equation.

$$s = \sum_{q=1}^{n} \delta_{c_{uq}, c_{vq}} \qquad (2)$$

where c_{uq} and c_{vq} are job-numbers stored in the job-number part list parts in two compared chromosome lists.

SELF-ORGANIZING MAPS

Self-organizing maps and its algorithm

Self-Organizing Maps (SOM) is well known as the neural network without teacher, consisting of hierarchical layer architecture, proposed by Kohnen, T (Kohonen T. (1993), Kohonen T. (1996)).

Let $\{x_i(t)\}$ and $\{\mathbf{m}_j(t)\}$be a set of reference vectors and a set of synopsis vectors at time t, respectively. When the reference vector $\mathbf{x}_i(t)$ is given at random, an activated unit (the unit whose synopsis vector is closest to the reference vector) c is selected by calculating a distance between $\mathbf{x}_i(t)$ and $\mathbf{m}_j(t)$ as follows.

$$c = \arg\min_j \{ |\mathbf{x}_i(t) - \mathbf{m}_j(t)| \} \tag{3}$$

Let N_c be a set of the activated unit and neighborhood units topologically connected to the activated unit. Then, the units belong to N_c learn according to the following equations.

$$\mathbf{m}_j(t+1) = \mathbf{m}_j + \alpha(\mathbf{x}_i(t) - \mathbf{m}_j(t)) \qquad (j \in N_c) \tag{4}$$

$$\mathbf{m}_j(t+1) = \mathbf{m}_j(t) \qquad (j \notin N_c) \tag{5}$$

NUMERICAL EXPERIMENT

Numerical experiments on IA applied to JSP

Numerical experiments are executed to verify that IA collects various kinds of schedule solutions. IA is applied to 10-jobs 5-machines JSP. Table 1 shows parameter values used for IA.

Table 1 Parameters used for experiments

Number of chromosomes generated in GA	10	GA iteration number T	20
Number of chromosomes Stored in the memory *Mem*	5	IA iteration number G	500
Crossover rate in GA	0.3	Similarity threshold value between two chromosomes	20
Mutation rate in GA	0.3	Weight W_1	1.0
Weight W_2	1.0	Weight W_3	0.0

Figures 1-5 show Gantt charts with different schedules remained in the IA memory. As seen in the figures, IA successfully collects a different type of solutions.

Numerical experiments for making pareto maps by SOM

SOM is applied to the solutions maps on the different weighted scalar functions obtained by IA to make the pareto map. Two weights, W_1 and W_3, are used for these experiments. W_2 is set to be zero.

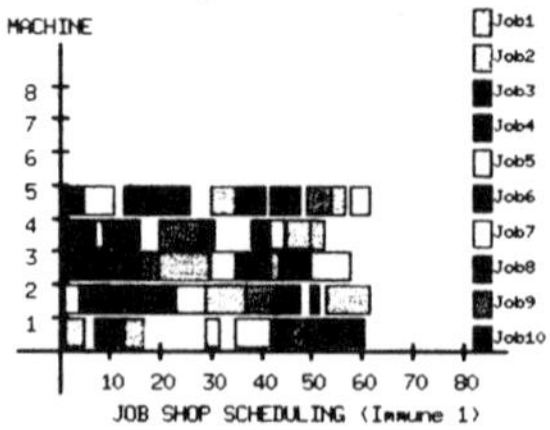

Fig.1 The best schedule obtained by IA

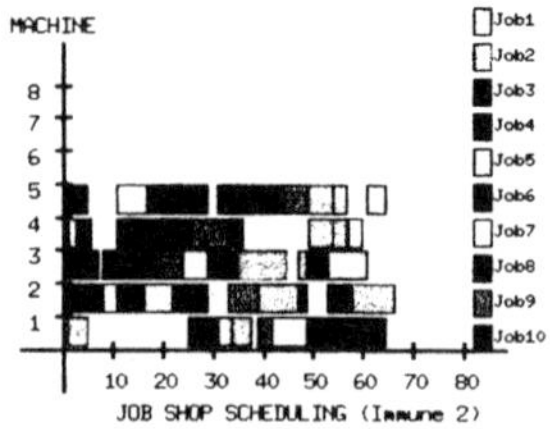

Fig.2 The second schedule obtained by IA

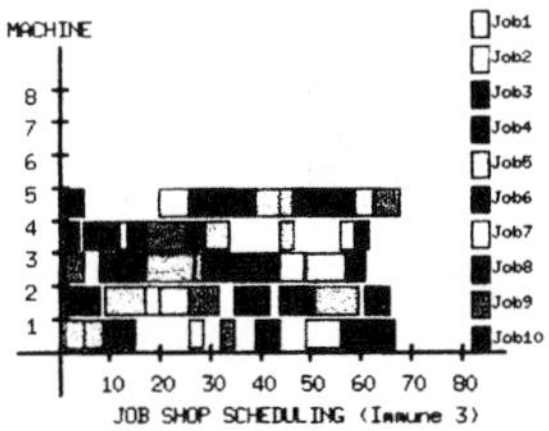

Fig.3 The third schedule obtained by IA

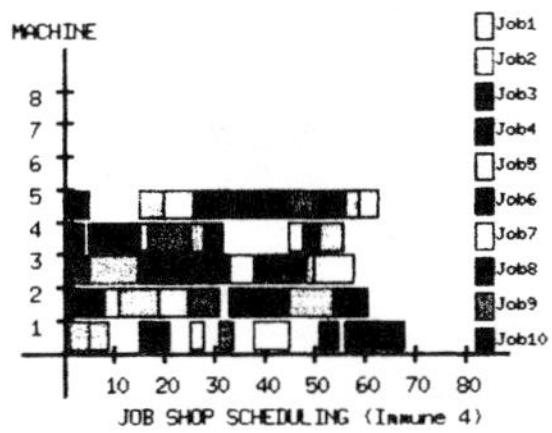

Fig.4 The forth schedule obtained by IA

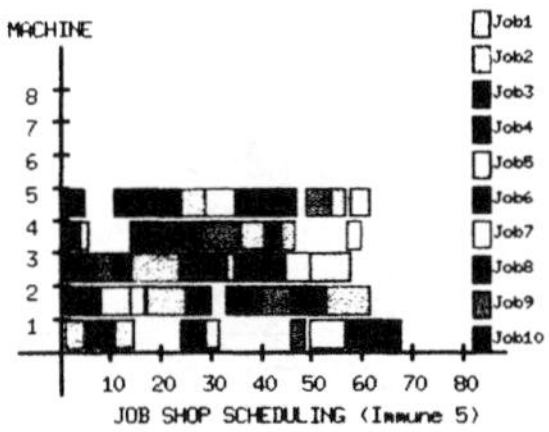

Fig.5 The worst schedule obtained by IA

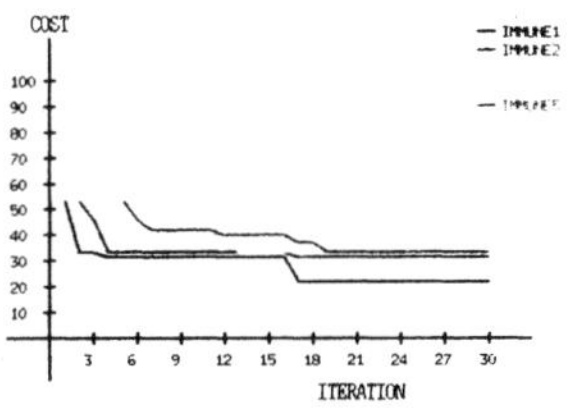

Fig. 6 Aspects in changing five weighed functions stored in memory

Both of weights are digitized by 0.1 from 0 to 1. The reference vector is set by $\mathbf{x}_i = [W_1 \quad W_3 \quad F_1 \quad F_3]$. Experimental conditions are set as referred to Table 2.

Table 2 Parameters for SOM

Number of units	20x20
Learning coefficient α	0.1
Learning iteration number T	20,000
Number of reference vectors	150

Figure7 shows an initial self-organizing map on the weights W_1 and W_3. The horizontal and vertical axis shows the weights W_1 and W_3, respectively. Fig.8 shows a resultant self-organizing map on the weight W_1 and W_3. The self-organizing map is distinguished by four regions, $(0 \le W_1 \le 0.5,\ 0 \le W_3 \le 0.5)$, $(0.5 \le W_1 \le 1.0,\ 0 \le W_3 \le 0.5)$, and $(0 \le W_1 \le 0.5,\ 0.5 \le W_3 \le 1.0)$. Figure 9 and others shows a unit map on the weights W_1 and W_3 drawn by the result shown in Fig. 8. Pareto solutions are divided and clustered into three regions, each of which corresponds to $(0 \le W_1 \le 0.5,\ 0 \le W_3 \le 0.5)$, $(0.5 \le W_1 \le 1.0,\ 0 \le W_3 \le 0.5)$, and $(0 \le W_1 \le 0.5,\ 0.5 \le W_3 \le 1.0)$, respectively. Fig. 10 shows a grey map of SOM, where dark gray cells show boundaries. Figs. 11 and 12 respectively show unit vector maps on the weights W_1 and W_3 and the criteria F_1 and F_3.

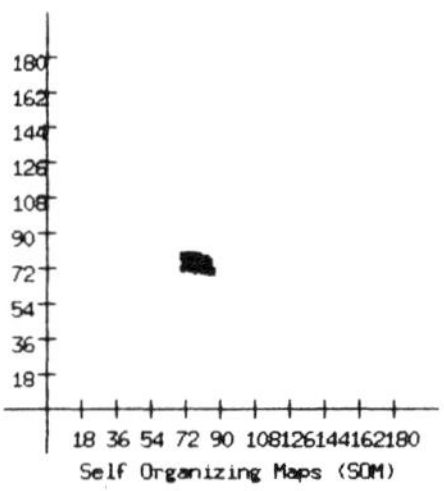

Fig.7 An initial SOM on W_1 and W_3

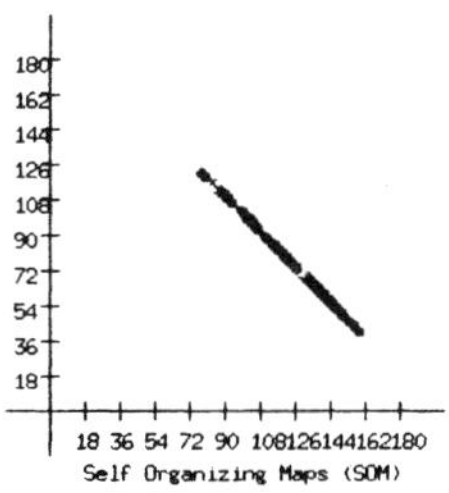

Fig.8 A resultant SOM on W_1 and W_3

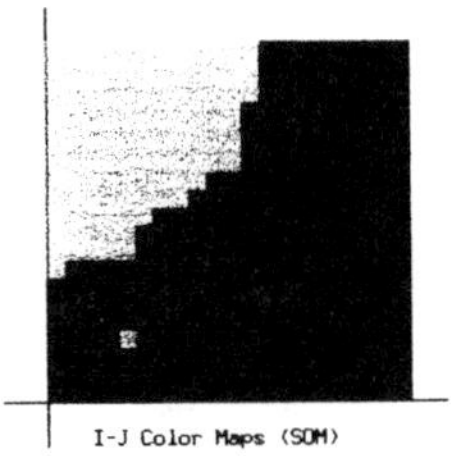

Fig.9 A color pareto map on W_1 and W_3

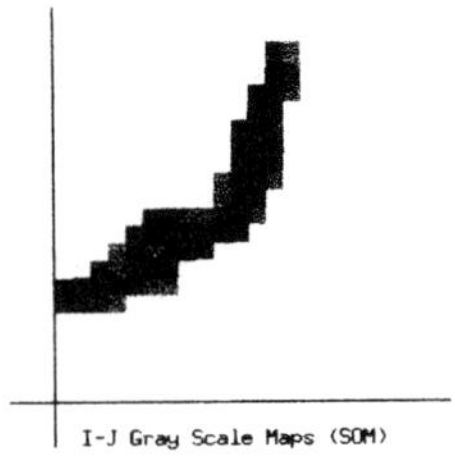

Fig.10 A gray pareto map on W_1 and W_3

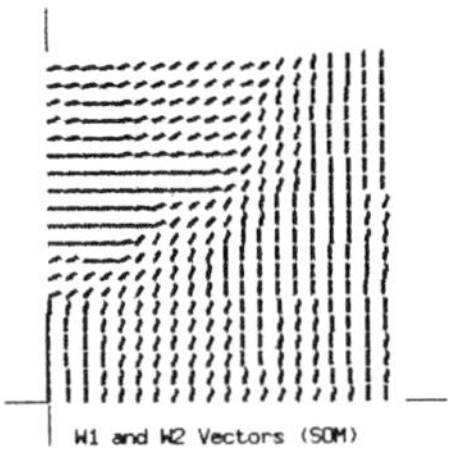

Fig.11 A pareto vector map on W_1 and W_3

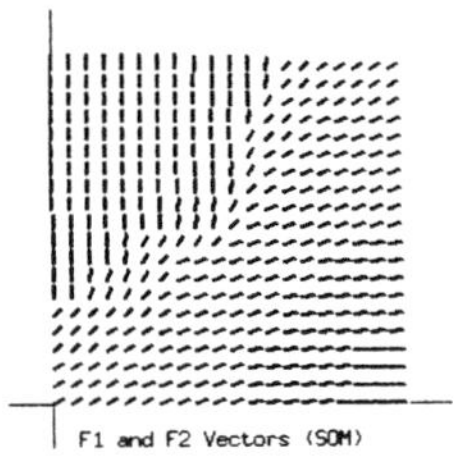

Fg.12 A pareto vector map on F_1 and F_3

Vectors in Fig. 11 represents $[W_1 \quad W_3]$ and the vectors in Fig. 12 represents $[F_1 \quad F_3]$. By comparing Fig. 11 with Fig. 12, it becomes clear to know the relation between the weights and pareto schedule solutions.

CONCLUDINGS REMARKS

The followings are summarized as concluding remarks.

1) It is confirmed that the proposed IA can collect a various type of schedule solution, responding to various manufacturing situations.
2) By use of SOM cooperated with the proposed IA, it becomes possible to acquire the knowledge on the relation between the weighed scalar functions on JSP and their solutions. Output maps by SOM is named the pareto maps and the pareto maps can indicate the relation between the weighed scalar functions on JSP and their solutions.

REFERENCES

Furukawa M., Arai M., Yoshimura, H. and Hama K., 2000, "System Engineering (In Japanese)", Corona Publishing Company

Nabeshima I., 1975, "Scheduling Theory (in Japanese)", Morikita Publishing Company

Watanabe M., Furukawa M, Mizoe, A, Watanabe T. and Kakazu Y., 2000, "Development of a Practical Scheduler Taking into Account in Assignment of Jigs and Machines to Jobs (in Japanese)", Journal of the Japan Society for Precision Engineering, Vol.66, pp1185-1189

Kohonen T., 1993, "Self-Organization and Associative Memory, Springer-Verlag", Tokyo

Kohonen T., 1996, "Self-Organizing Maps", Springer-Verlag, Tokyo

AN APPLICATION OF THE HOPFIELD NN TO REAL-TIME MONOPHONIC NOTE TRANSCRIPTION

GRACE WOO
Department of Electrical and Computer Engineering, University of Illinois Urbana-Champaign

TING FENG TOH
Department of Electrical and Computer Engineering, University of Illinois Urbana-Champaign

PENG YUNG WOO
Department of Electrical Engineering, Northern Illinois University

ABSTRACT
Polyphonic note transcription is a topic of interest to many researchers as the collection of digital music is growing comprehensively and the need for automatic management is taking place slowly. The first step to achieving such a goal is to approach monophonic note transcription. While this is virtually a solved problem for a single known instrument, little has been done to apply this accomplishment to either an all-encompassing management system or a real-time polyphonic transcription service. This paper presents an upgrade to determine the instrument in the Fourier domain by using the Hopfield NN as a part of a complete transcription system.

INTRODUCTION

There are a few different schemes in developing a real-time monophonic note transcription system. The real-time system implemented in this paper utilizes the Fourier domain (by means of a radix-4 FFT) and the cyclical buffer capabilities of the TI-320C549 DSP chip.

A single note on the piano is defined in the frequency domain by both its fundamental frequency as well as its harmonics. The fundamental frequency is assigned with equation (1).

$$f = f_0\left(2^{N/12}\right) \tag{1}$$

where f_0 is generally defined to be 440Hz. N is the index assigned to each note. When $N = 0$ and $f_0 = 440$ Hz, the frequency corresponds to the musical note A in the third octave. Equation 1 contains $N/12$ in the exponential, as it corresponds to the significance of twelve notes in a musical scale [1].

Unfortunately, in the practical musical world, a note is characterized by more than just its fundamental frequency. The additional critical definitions are the harmonics. The complementing harmonics of any note are simply the consecutive integer multiple of the fundamental frequency. Furthermore, in tones from a piano[1], the fundamental frequency is usually greater in magnitude than the harmonics. It is, however, not always the case. A sample frequency domain note is shown in Figure 1.

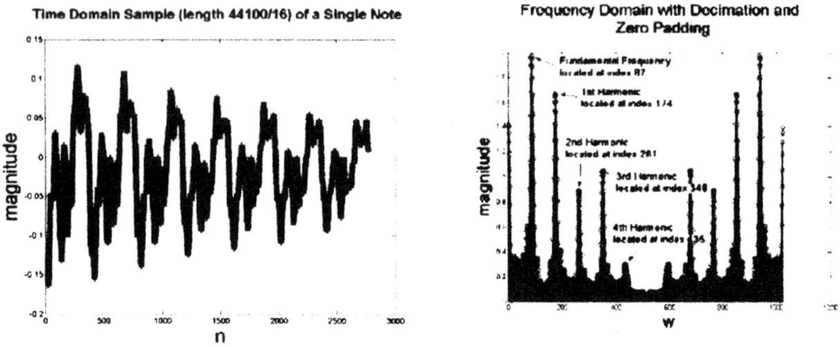

Figure 1
Time Domain Sample and Corresponding Frequency Domain Spectrum Distribution

The design of this real-time monophonic note transcription system is implemented according to the block diagram in Figure 2.

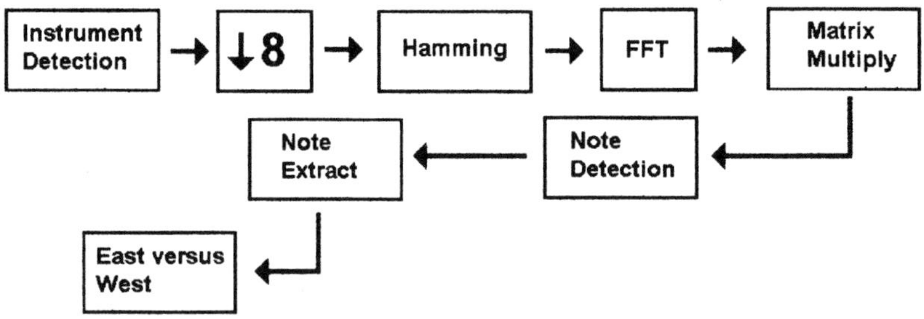

Figure 2
Basic Block Diagram of System Being Implemented

Prior to the application of the Hopfield algorithm, the method used to implement the detection of instruments was a look-up matrix. While this may be legitimate for one or two instruments, it would definitely not work for a larger instrumental database. As a result, the Hopfield algorithm is applied here in this block and is discussed in the remaining sections of this paper.

---

[1] All sample tones in this paper are collected using Visual Music v6.0 and 3D MP3 Sound Recorder

INSTRUMENT DETECTION BLOCK USING THE HOPFIELD NN

The key component that characterizes the nature and sound of each instrument is the energy distribution of the same note in the Fourier domain. Figure 3 depicts the superposition of three instruments: the piano, the violin and the trumpet in the Fourier domain.

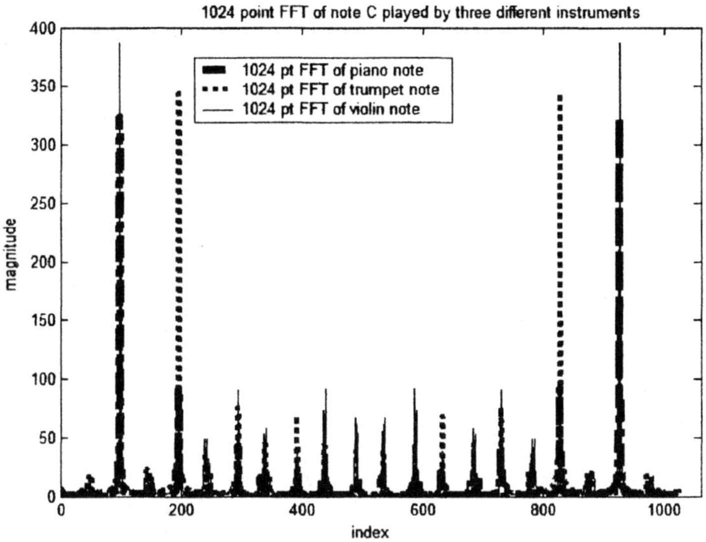

Figure 3
Superimposed Graphs of the Energy Distribution of Each Instrument

As observed from this energy distribution, it is legitimate to characterize each instrument by ratios of the fundamental frequency and the harmonics. Hence, each instrument can be characterized by the "envelope" of its FFT, which depends on the distribution of energy amongst its fundamental frequency and harmonics. Hence, it is desirable to implement a system such that for any given non-discrete input vector A, the "closest" matching vector may be found.

SIMULATING THE HOPFIELD NN WITH THE GRAY CODE

The classical Hopfield NN consists of creating the connection matrix. This is constructed as a closed form in equation (2) [2][3].

$$T_k = x^{(k)}(x^{(k)})^T - I_n \tag{2}$$

I_n is the n x n identity matrix and $x^{(k)}$ indicates each memory vector where each value is either a "*1*" or a "*–1*".

In the case of representing each spectral value at a particular index, there is a problem since the values are not quantized to only two different levels. In fact, there is an infinite range of possible spectral values. As a result, we quantize to a distinguishable number of levels.

Initially, the different quantized levels are attempted to be represented through the use of a 3 bit Gray Code, as shown below in Figure 4.

Decimal value	Gray code representation	Decimal value in this implementation	Modified for Hopfield
0	000	1	{-1,-1,-1}
1	001	2	{-1,-1,1}
2	011	3	{-1,1,1}
3	010	4	{-1,1,-1}
4	110	5	{1,1,-1}
5	111	6	{1,1,1}
6	101	7	{1,-1,1}
7	100	8	{1,-1,-1}

Figure 4
Table of Coding Assignments Used for Each Energy Bin

Since the Hopfield NN requires only the values of -1 and 1, each energy level is distributed into one of the eight bins. As a result, its corresponding values can be represented by using a Gray code sequence. The advantage of using the Gray code in this implementation is that only one bit changes from one decimal value to the next. This is believed to find the "closest" matching vector. When a probe vector is fed into the Hopfield matrix, the 12 number sequence consisting of "1"s and "–1"s are a result of quantizing and assigning an appropriate Hopfield value according to the chart in Figure 4.

However, it is realized that this implementation does not work, due to the modular nature of the Gray Code. Since only one bit changes from one Gray Code to the next, vectors which are similar to the ones "memorized" in the Hopfield matrix can be recalled easily. However, problems arise due to the modular nature of the Gray Code. This implies that bit 1 and 8 are only a single bit apart. Hence, distance wise, bit 1 and 8 are more similar than, say, bit 4 and 8. This results in the Gray Code being unsuitable for our purposes.

SIMULATING THE HOPFIELD NN WITH THE CUSTOM CODE

By using eight bits instead of four bits, this unreliability can be fixed. The eight bit code is simply using {1 1 1 1 1 1 1 1} for the decimal value 8, {1 1 1 1 1 1 1 -1} for the decimal value 7, {1 1 1 1 1 1 -1 -1} for the value 6 and so on. This is at the cost of additional bits and additional multiplies on the digital signal processor. Figure 5 displays the setup of such a Hopfield matrix and Figure 6 displays the simulation results.

Instrument	Ratio[2]	Memory Entrys
Piano	(8 , 2 , 1)	(1 1 1 1 1 1 1 -1 -1 -1 -1 -1 -1 1 -1 -1 -1 -1 –1 -1 -1)^T
Violin	(8 , 2 , 2)	(1 1 1 1 -1 -1 1 1 -1 -1 1 1 -1 -1 -1 1)^T
Trumpet	(4 , 8 , 2)	(-1 1 1 1 1 1 1 1 -1 -1 1 1 -1 -1 1 1)^T

Figure 5
Predetermined Settings for Each Instrument

Probe	Nearest Instrument	No. of iterations taken to reach stable state	Stable state reached	Instrument mapping
(8,4,2)	Violin	2	(8,2,2)	Violin
(4,6,3)	Trumpet	3	(4,8,2)	Trumpet
(6,2,1)	Piano	2	(8,2,1)	Piano
(8,2,1)	Piano	1	(8,2,1)	Piano
(5,8,2)	Trumpet	2	(4,8,2)	Trumpet

Figure 6
Simulation Results

As can be seen from these results, the second eight-bit coding method gives virtually 100 percent accuracy.

Furthermore, for instrument recognition as implemented on a TI DSP, this method is exceptionally useful as the number of instruments (variable m) recognizable by the Hopfield matrix increases. The size of the matrix remains a $n \times n$ matrix where n is the number of bits within each energy vector. As long as m remains significantly smaller than n, the Hopfield matrix is guaranteed to be virtually 100% effective. Furthermore, as m (the number of desired recognizable instruments) increases, n can increase as well by increasing the number of quantized levels and/or the number of harmonics that are taken into account. This results in more detailed storage of the characteristics of each instrument vector. All of this simulation implies that the proposed system is faster with a large number of desired recognizable instruments since external memory need not be accessed. This is because a small increase in the value m with respect to the value n does not affect the size of the $n \times n$ matrix.

---

[2] Ratio of energy between the fundamental frequency and first three harmonics

SUMMARY

In all, the Hopfield method may be modified to be applied to the identification of instruments in monophonic note transcription using the following steps:

1. Quantize the energy distribution between the fundamental frequency and the harmonics of any given note in the Fourier domain.
2. Using the custom 8-bit code, represent the relatives energies of the fundamental frequencies and harmonics of each instrument representative note with a two-value length eight vector with "1"s and "−1"s
3. Construct the Hopfield matrix using equation (2) with each length-eight vector.
4. Iterate with any input probe quantized to the same vector format until the sign of the entries in the result vector is the same as the corresponding entries in the test probe.

CONCLUSION

The application of the Hopfield NN to instrument recognition is useful in practical applications. Its benefits include an ability to handle a large matrix of many different desired recognizable instruments. It is one step closer to a more comprehensive music recognition system.

The simulations presented in this paper are currently being implemented on the TI DSP. If successful, we will pursue other NN techniques and apply them to an ultimate automated musical system.

REFERENCES

1. White, John David (1995), Theories of Musical Texture in Western History, Garland Publishing, New York, NY.

2. Gerasimas, Bernard F. (1988), MS Thesis: Analysis of the Hopfield Neural Networks and Their Application to Pattern Recognition, Department of Electrical and Computer Engineering, University of Illinois Urbana-Champaign. Champaign-Urbana, IL.

3. Mitra, Sundari Samir (1988), MS Thesis: Simulation-Based Comparison of Hopfield and Projection Neural Network Models, Department of Electrical and Computer Engineering, University of Illinois Urbana-Champaign. Champaign-Urbana, IL.

RULE DRIVEN JOB-SHOP SCHEDULING DERIVED FROM NEURAL NETWORKS

GARY WECKMAN
Industrial and Manufacturing
Systems Engineering
Ohio University

CHANDRASEKHAR GANDURI
Industrial and Manufacturing
Systems Engineering
Ohio University

DAVID KOONCE
Industrial and Manufacturing
Systems Engineering
Ohio University

ABSTRACT
This paper focuses on the devolopment of a rule-based scheduler, based on production rules derived from an artificial neural network performing job shop scheduling. This study constructs a hybrid model utilizing genetic algorithms for optimization and neural networks as learning tools. Genetic algorithms are used for obtaining optimal or near optimal schedules and the neural network is trained on these schedules. After successful training and validation of the network's performance, knowlege extraction is performed to yield production rules. The performance of this extracted rule set is then compared to the performance of genetic algorithms and other dispatching rules on a benchmark 6x6 scheduling problem. The capabilitiy of the rule-based scheduler in providing near optimal solutions is discussed.

INTRODUCTION

The deterministic job shop scheduling problem (JSSP) is one of the most widely investigated scheduling problems. The problem's sheer intractability has inspired researchers to develop a broad spectrum of strategies, ranging from simple heuristics to adaptive search strategies based on conceptual frameworks borrowed from biology, genetics and evolution. Adaptive search algorithms like Genetic Algorithms (GAs), Tabu Search and Simulated Annealing have been applied to JSSP with success and are capable of providing optimal or near optimal solutions to many problems. However, a key shortcoming of these approaches for scheduling problems is their lack of insight into the scheduling process. Further, these search-based methods are computationally intensive and often prove unwieldy in a dynamic shop environment.

An interesting line of investigation would be to cast the scheduling problem as a learning task. In such a formulation, the optimal schedules generated by efficient optimizers provide the desired learning material. These schedules contain valuable information such as the relationship between an operation's attributes and its position in the sequence. An exploration of these schedules by machine learning techniques would capture predictive knowledge regarding the assignment of operation's position in a sequence based on its attributes. This extracted knowledge allows for the development of a rule-based scheduler, which is computationally less intensive than search methods, but still provides good solutions. A further benefit of such a system is the provision of knowledge in the form of human comprehensible rules.

Koonce and Tsai [1] use attribute-oriented induction methodology to mine for relationships between an operation's priority and its attributes. The authors report that the developed rule-based scheduler consistently provided superior solutions to the Shortest Processing Time (SPT) heuristic and could duplicate the genetic algorithm's performance on identical problems. The goal of the current research is to utilize neural networks as the choice machine learning tool for understanding the scheduling process.

BACKGROUND

The Job Shop Scheduling Problem

The deterministic job shop scheduling problem (JSSP) consists of a set of m jobs to be machined on a set of n machines and is denoted as an m x n problem. It is a constrained optimization problem, where the precedence constraints on the problem are given by a predetermined order of operations for each job. Capacity constraints require that a machine may process only one operation at any given time. Preemptions of jobs and machine repetitions, absences and breakdowns are not allowed throughout the scheduling process. The objective of the scheduler is to determine the starting time for each operation to achieve the desired performance measures, while satisfying the various constraints. Performance measures used to evaluate the schedules range from minimization of makespan, tardiness and process cost to maximization of throughput and resource utilization.

Approaches to JSSP

The JSSP is considered as a particularly tough combinatorial optimization problem as the solution space increases exponentially with problem size [2]. While exact or optimization methods yield optimal solutions, they cannot solve a problem in polynomial time. Approximation methods include priority dispatch rules, bottleneck based heuristics, connectionist and local search methods.

Priority dispatch rules operate by assigning a priority index to each job. Scheduling of the jobs is then accomplished based on the priority. Some commonly used elementary priority dispatch rules are SPT, Minimum Slack Time (MST), First Come First Served (FCFS), Last Work Remaining (LWKR) and Shortest Remaining Processing Time (SRMPT). The main drawback in using these rules is that different rules perform best in different scenarios and no single rule dominates the rest across all scenarios. The most successful heuristics-based approach is the Shifting Bottleneck procedure by Adams et al. [3]. The local search methods involve a metastrategy that guides an algorithm to optimality by accepting non-improving solutions [4]. Some examples of algorithms in this category include Tabu Search, Simulated Annealing and Genetic Algorithms. These techniques explore a vast search space to find optimal or near optimal solutions. Vaessens *et al.*, [5] provide a detailed review of application of local search methods to JSSP.

Jain and Meeran [6] proposed a modified back-error propagation (BEP) model, where the neural network performs the task of optimization. Although the method has been able to handle large problems compared to other neural network based approaches, the generalization capability of the model was limited. Many hybrid techniques have been developed combining neural networks with local search methods or expert systems. Dagli and Sittasathanchai [7] use a genetic algorithm as a local search technique and the neural network performs multiobjective schedule evaluation. The trained network maps a set of scheduling criteria (flowtime, lateness) to appropriate values provided by experienced schedulers. Rabelo and Alptekin use neural networks have also been used to rank or select priority rules [8].

Machine Learning Applications in JSSP

Koonce and Tsai [1] use attribute-oriented induction methodology to mine for relationships on near optimal schedules generated by a genetic algorithm. Yoshida and Hideyuki [9] apply data mining methodology to extract association rules between the performance measure and the dispatching rules. Kwak and Yih [10] use data-mining based control approach for a testing and rework cell in a computer-integrated manufacturing environment.

Decision Tree Induction

Decision trees are knowledge representation structures, where the classification of an instance is determined by testing its values for specific attributes at each node. The ID3 and C4.5 algorithms developed by Quinlan [11], are capable of inducing decision trees from data. These algorithms use the concept of information entropy to choose a node in building a decision tree. C4.5 is similar to the ID3 algorithm, but can handle continuous attribute value ranges, pruning of decision trees and rule derivation.

METHODOLOGY

The training data for the learning task was provided by the genetic algorithm's solution to the job shop problem. Knowledge was then extracted from the trained neural network as simple propositional rules and decision trees. The following methods and tools were utilized to extract knowledge relevant to the scheduling process.

Genetic Algorithm (GA) Scheduler

For this research, a well-known 6x6 problem JSSP instance, ft06 devised by Fisher and Thomson [12] has been chosen as the benchmark problem. This problem has six jobs, each with six operations to be scheduled on six machines, and has a known optimal makespan of 55 time units. Each gene in the GA is an encoded form of the job shop schedule. The representation of a chromosome is shown in Figure 1.

Job	1	3	2	4	6	2	3	4	3	6	6	2	5	5	3	5	1	1	6	4	4	4	1	2	5	3	2	3	6	1	5	2	1	6	4	5
Operation	1	1	1	1	1	2	2	2	3	2	3	3	1	2	4	3	2	3	4	3	4	5	4	4	4	5	5	6	5	5	5	6	6	6	6	6

Figure 1. GA solution representation

The Operation-based representation of Tsujimura *et al.*, [13] was used to encode the chromosome. Each gene in the sequence is representative of the job number and the operation it is undergoing. The makespan, computed by a FIFO schedule builder incorporated into the GA, was used as the fitness function. Crossover of the chromosomes was done using Syswerda's Position-based Crossover operator [14]. Position-based mutation operator was used to add variation to successive generations. The GA was used to generate 1000 schedules (chromosome sequences with an optimal makespan of 55 units), which formed the training data for the neural network.

Neural Network Model

The learning task for the neural network is to predict the position of an operation in the sequence based on its features or attributes. Based on a study of job attributes commonly used in priority dispatch rules, the following attributes have been identified as features: operation, process time, remaining time and machine load. These features have been clustered into different classes using the hierarchy developed by Koonce and Tsai [1]. Table 1 identifies the possible classes for each input feature.

Table 1. Assignment of class labels to input features.

Feature	Classes	Class Description
Operation	First, Middle, Later and Last	The operation number of a job
ProcessingTime	Short, Middle and Long	The processing time for the operation
RemainingTime	Short, Middle and Long	The sum of processing times for the remaining operations
MachineLoad	Light and Heavy	The utilization of the machine assigned to the operation

The target attribute, priority determines the range of positions in the sequence where the operation can be inserted. The possible range of positions have been split into six classes, and assigned class labels from zero to five.

As each GA sequence has 36 operations, the data set had 36000 (36x1000) exemplars. This data set was split into training, cross validation and testing data sets with 70%, 15% and 15% memberships. For classification, two different network architectures, Multilayer Perceptrons (MLP) and Radial Basis Function networks (RBF) were chosen. After considerable experimentation, a two hidden layered MLP (12-12-10-6) with hyperbolic tangent transfer functions at the hidden layers was chosen, as it had the best classification accuracy for the testing data set.

The number of classes in the *Operation* feature, *ProcessingTime* feature, *RemainingTime* feature and the *MachineLoad* feature are four, three, three and two respectively. Hence, the number of possible feature combinations in the rule space is 4 x 3 x 3 x 2 = 72. These 72 feature combinations form the antecedents of the rules in the production data set. The trained network computes priorities for these 72 antecedents. Each antecedent with the computed priority can be mapped into a simple propositional rule with the structure – If {Antecedent}, then Priority. Though 72 rules are possible in principle, some of these rules can be redundant, as a rule can be subsumed within a more general rule, without losing classification accuracy.

Decision Tree Induction

A more comprehensible representation of the knowledge would be a decision tree structure, which removes redundancy in the rule set and provides an alternate interpretation of the extracted knowledge. An open source software, Weka that provides an implementation of the ID3 algorithm [15] was used for inducing a decision tree from the 72 rules in the production data set. The induced tree has 48 leaf nodes.

RESULTS AND CONCLUSIONS

To schedule the benchmark ft06 instance, two rule sets are used. The first rule set was obtained by mapping the production data set with the computed priorities into simple propositional rules. This rule set, referred to as NN-PR, has 72 rules. The decision tree was also decomposed into a propositional rule set (NN-DT) yielding 49 distinct rules. Sample rules from the latter rule set are shown in Table 2.

Table 2 Sample rules

Operation	ProcessingTime	RemainingTime	MachineLoad	Priority (0-5)
First	Medium	Long	Heavy	One
Middle	Long	Short	*Any*	Three
Later	Long	*Any*	*Any*	Three
Last	Short	Medium	Heavy	One

By matching the attributes of each operation in the 6x6 instance with the induced rules, priorities are assigned to operations. The operations, based on the assigned priorities, are sequenced on each machine and schedules are built. Table 3 gives a comparative summary of the makespans of schedules generated by the GA, the two developed rule sets, and other priority dispatching rules. The performance of the Attribute-oriented induction (AOI) rule set is reported from the work of Koonce and Tsai [1]. Makespans for the schedules built by using dispatching rules are from an empirical study conducted by Kaschel *et al* [16].

Table 3 Makespans of schedules for ft06

Scheduler	Makespan
Genetic Algorithms, GA	55
Neural Network Production rule set , NN-PR	59
Neural Network Decision Tree rule set, NN-DT	59
Attribute-oriented Induction, AOI	67
Shortest Processing Time, SPT	83
Most Work Remaining (MWKR)	67
Shortest Remaining Processing Time (SRMPT)	84

As can be seen from the table, only the GA was able to achieve an optimal makespan of 55 units. The two rule sets, PD-RS and DT-RS, developed in the current work could achieve a makespan of 59 units, a deviation of 4 time units (7.27 %) from the optimum. The deviations of other methods ranged from 6 to 29 units (10.9% - 52.7%). The performance of the developed rule sets is considerably better than the performance of priority rules in scheduling the 6x6 problem. The better performance of the current approach compared to the attribute-oriented induction data mining methodology proves the feasibility of neural network based data mining. Future work will include testing the performance of the rule sets on randomly generated test 6x6 scenarios and exploring the scalability of this method to larger problems.

REFERENCES

[1] Koonce, D. A., & Tsai, S. -C. (2000). Using data mining to find patterns in genetic algorithm solutions to a job shop schedule. *Computers & Industrial Engineering*, 38 (3), 361-374.

[2] Jain, A. S., & Meeran, S. (1998). *A state-of-the-art review of job-shop scheduling techniques*. Technical report, Department of Applied Physics, Electronic and Mechanical Engineering, University of Dundee, Dundee, Scotland.

[3] Adams, J., Balas, E., & Zawack, D. (1987). The shifting bottleneck procedure for job shop scheduling. *International Journal of Flexible Manufacturing Systems*, 34, 391-401.

[4] Jain, A. S., & Meeran, S. (1999). Deterministic job-shop scheduling: Past, present and future. *European Journal of Operations Research*, 113, 390-434.

[5] Vaessens, R.J.M., Aarts, E.H.L, & Lenstra, J.K. (1994). Job-Shop Scheduling by Local Search, COSOR Memorandum 94-05, Eindhoven University of Technology, Eindhoven, The Netherlands.

[6] Jain, A. S., & Meeran, S. (1998). Job-shop scheduling using neural networks, *International Journal of Production Research*, 36(5), 1249-1272.

[7] Dagli, C. H., & Sittasathanchai, S. (1995). Genetic neuro-scheduler: A new approach for job shop scheduling. *International Journal of Production Economics*, 41, 135-145.

[8] Rabelo, L., & Alptekin, S. (1990). Adaptive scheduling and control using ANNs and expert systems for a hierarchical-distributed FMS architecture. *Proceedings of the International Conference on CIM* (pp. 538-545). Troy, NY: IEEE Computer Society Press.

[9] Yoshida, T., & Hideyuki, T. (1999). A study on association among dispatching rules in manufacturing scheduling problems. *Proceedings of Seventh IEEE International Conference on Emerging Technologies and Factory Automation* (pp. 1355-1360). Barcelona, Spain.

[10] Kwak, C., & Yih, Y. (2004). Data-mining approach to production control in the computer-integrated testing cell. IEEE Transactions on Robotics and Automation, 20(1), 107-116.

[11] Quinlan, J. R. (1993). *C4.5: Programs in Machine Learning*. San Mateo, CA: Morgan Kaufmann.

[12] Muth, J., & Thompson, G. (1963). *Industrial Scheduling*. Englewood Cliffs, NJ: Prentice Hall.

[13] Cheng, R., Gen, M., and Tsujimura, Y. (1999). A tutorial survey of job-shop scheduling problems using genetic algorithms, part I: Representation. *Computers and Industrial Engineering*, 30, 983-997.

[14] Syswerda, G. (1991). "Schedule optimization using genetic algorithms". In Davis L. (ed.), *Handbook of Genetic Algorithms*, New York, NY: Van Nostrand Reinhold, 332-349.

[15] Witten, I. H., & Frank, E. (2000). *Data Mining: Practical machine learning tools with Java implementations*. San Francisco, CA: Morgan Kaufmann

[16] Käschel, J., Teich, T., Köbernik, G., & Meier, B. Algorithms for the job shop scheduling problem - a comparison of different methods. *European Symposium on Intelligent Techniques*, Greece, June 3-4, 1999.

MODULAR NEURAL NETWORKS FOR SEMICONDUCTOR MANUFACTURING PROCESS MODELING AND CHARACTERIZATION: APPLICATIONS TO PLASMA PROCESSING

SANG JEEN HONG
Institute of Fluid Science
Tohoku University, Japan
DONG-CHUL PARK
Dept. of Information Engineering
Myongji University, Korea

SONG JAE LEE
Dept. of Information Engineering
Myongji University, Korea
GARY S. MAY
School of ECE
Georgia Institute of Technology

ABSTRACT
Modular neural networks (MNNs) are applied for the purpose of modeling and characterization of semiconductor processes. An MNN consists of a number of local expert networks (LENs) and one gating network. LENs compete using supervised learning to learn different regions of the data space under the supervision of the gating network, while the same inputs are provided to each. The gating network, which is unsupervised, has as many outputs as of LENs. The combination of the supervised and unsupervised learning paradigms takes place in a seamless fashion during training. As examples of process modeling and characterization, surface responses of reactive ion etching and plasma enhanced chemical vapor deposition are presented. As either an alternative or an augmentation to existing methods, this provides a reliable and flexible platform of process modeling and characterization in the area of semiconductor manufacturing.

INTRODUCTION

Semiconductor manufacturing requires high capital investment in equipment, materials, facilities, and technology. It involves sophisticated fabrication equipment and hundreds of sequential fabrication processes. To ensure the successful process integration, a thorough understanding of unit process cannot be overemphasized. Therefore, characterization and modeling of these processes must be performed. In semiconductor manufacturing applications, complex and nonlinear fabrication processes are ubiquitous. Plasma processes, such as reactive ion etching (RIE) and plasma enhanced chemical vapor deposition (PECVD), are typical examples. Both RIE and PECVD are workhorses in semiconductor fabrication, and due the nature of the complexity and nonlinearity of the plasma process, they can also act as yield limiters. Therefore, RIE and PECVD are good candidates for the development of a modeling tool.

Neural networks have become useful tools in process modeling and have demonstrated the capability of learning complex relationships between groups of related parameters (May, 2001). It has been reported that neural networks can provide higher accuracy and robustness over statistical approach with added degree of freedom that is not available in statistical regression technique (Himmel, 1993). For these reasons, neural networks have been extensively used for modeling of etch process (Kim, 1996), characterization of PECVD (Han, 1994), and lithography (Hong, 2004).

In this paper, modular neural networks (MNNs) have been constructed and evaluated for use in process modeling. The processes under consideration are the RIE of benzocyclobutene (BCB) and the PECVD of silicon dioxide. Once an acceptable process

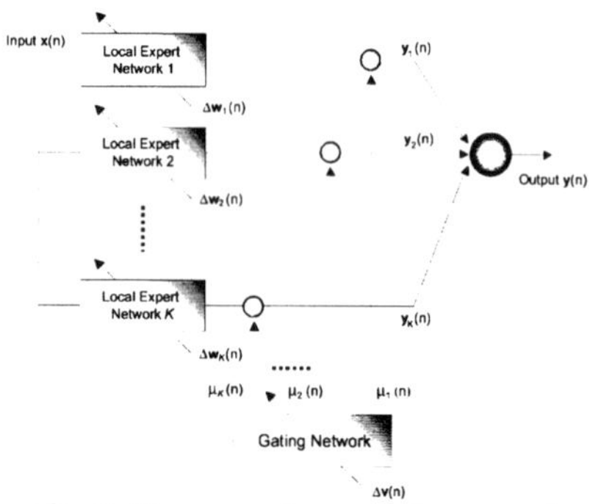

Fig. 1. Diagram of a modular neural network (MNN).

Table I. RIE process parameters

Parameters and the ranges	
RF power	200-400 (watt)
Pressure	100-300 (mTorr)
Gas 1: O_2	20-60 (sccm)
Gas 2: SF_6	2-6 (sccm)

Table II. PECVD process parameters and responses

Parameters and the ranges	
RF power	200-400 (watt)
Pressure	100-300 (mTorr)
Gas 1: O_2	20-60 (sccm)
Gas 2: SiN_4	2-6 (sccm)
Temperature	(°C)

model is established, three-dimensional response surfaces characterizing any selected process parameters can be generated. This approach provides a reliable and flexible platform for semiconductor process modeling and characterization.

MODULAR NEURAL NETWORKS

A neural network is said to be modular if the computation performed by the network can be decomposed into two or more modules (subsystems) that operate on distinct inputs without communicating with each other. The outputs of the modules are mediated by an integrating unit, which is not permitted to feed information back to the modules (Haykin, 1994). A MNN consists of a number of local expert networks (LENs) and a gating network, as shown in Figure 1. LENs with the same inputs compete to learn different regions of the data space under the supervision of the gating network. The gating network, which is unsupervised, has as many outputs as the number of LENs, and its outputs are normalized to sum to unity. The normalized output values are used to weight the output vector from the corresponding LEN. The combination of the supervised and unsupervised learning paradigms takes place in a seamless fashion during training.

Among many competitive learning procedures that have been developed for unsupervised learning in artificial neural networks, the fuzzy *C*-means (FCM) clustering algorithm is the most commonly used competitive clustering algorithm for complicated classification tasks. Suppose that an input vector $\boldsymbol{x}$ is contained in a domain $\mathbf{I}$. The FCM clustering algorithm finds an appropriate partition $\mathbf{I}=[\mathbf{i}_1,\mathbf{i}_2,\cdots,\mathbf{i}_K]$ and a set of reference vectors $\mathbf{c}=[c_1,c_2,\cdots,c_K]^T$ that minimizes an error cost function. The FCM algorithm provides the fuzzy membership grade. The goal of this learning algorithm is to model the probability distribution of the set of training patterns $\{\mathbf{x} \text{ and } \mathbf{d}\}$. Based on the multivariate Gaussian distribution of the desired response vector $\mathbf{d}$ with given input vector $\mathbf{x}$, the conditional probability density function is defined as:

$$f(\mathbf{d}\,|\,\mathbf{x})=\sum_{i=1}^{K} g_i f(\mathbf{d}\,|\,\mathbf{x},i)=\frac{1}{(2\pi)^{q/2}}\sum_{i=1}^{K} g_i\cdot\exp\left(-\frac{1}{2}\|\mathbf{d}-\mathbf{y}_i\|^2\right)\quad i=1,2,\cdots,K \qquad (1)$$

where $\|\bullet\|$ is the Euclidean norm of the enclosed vector, q is the dimension of input vector $\mathbf{x}$, g is activation generated from the gating network, and i denotes the ith local expert network. This conditional probability density function $f(\mathbf{d}|\mathbf{x})$ is called an *associative Gaussian mixture model*, and it can be regarded as a *likelihood function* with the whole synaptic weight vector $\mathbf{w}$ and the activation vector $\mathbf{g}$ playing the roles of unknown parameters. Taking the natural logarithm of $f(\mathbf{d}|\mathbf{x})$ for a monotonically increasing function of its argument and ignoring the constant term, a log-likelihood function can be defined as (Haykin, 1994):

$$l(\mathbf{w},\mathbf{g}) = \ln f(\mathbf{d}|\mathbf{x}) = \ln \sum_{i=1}^{K} g_i \cdot \exp\left(-\frac{1}{2}\|\mathbf{d}-\mathbf{y}_i\|^2\right) \tag{2}$$

By employing the membership grade of the FCM, a prior probability μ_i and posterior probability h_i are defined as:

$$\mu_i = 1\Big/\sum_{j=1}^{K}(\beta_i/\beta_j)^2 \quad \text{and} \quad h_i = \frac{\mu_i \exp\left(-\frac{1}{2}\|\mathbf{d}-\mathbf{y}_i\|^2\right)}{\sum_{j=1}^{K}\mu_j \exp\left(-\frac{1}{2}\|\mathbf{d}-\mathbf{y}_i\|^2\right)} \tag{3}$$

where β_i is the distance from the center of the ith cluster and K is the number of local expert networks.

Adapting the local expert networks is accomplished using the *gradient descent* method that minimizes the log-likelihood function l. Apply the chain rule for $\Delta\mathbf{w}$

$$\frac{\partial l}{\partial \mathbf{w}_i} = \frac{\partial l}{\partial y_i}\cdot\frac{\partial y_i}{\partial \mathbf{w}_i} = h_i(\mathbf{d}-\mathbf{y}_i)\mathbf{x} \tag{4}$$

where

$$\frac{\partial l}{\partial y_i} = \frac{\mu_i \exp\left(-\frac{1}{2}\|\mathbf{d}-\mathbf{y}_i\|^2\right)}{\sum_{j=1}^{K}\mu_i \exp\left(-\frac{1}{2}\|\mathbf{d}-\mathbf{y}_i\|^2\right)}\cdot(\mathbf{d}-\mathbf{y}_i) = h_i(\mathbf{d}-\mathbf{y}_i) \quad \text{and} \quad \frac{\partial y_i}{\partial \mathbf{w}_i} = \mathbf{x} \tag{5}$$

Therefore, the weight adapting equation for the local expert networks is

$$\mathbf{w}_i(n+1) = \mathbf{w}_i(n) + \Delta\mathbf{w}_i(n) = \mathbf{w}_i(n) + \eta_{LEN} h_i(\mathbf{d}-\mathbf{y}_i)\mathbf{x} \tag{6}$$

where η_{LEN} is learning rate of a local expert network.

In the similar manner, the learning algorithm for the gating network can be derived by applying chain rule

$$\frac{\partial l}{\partial \mathbf{v}_i} = \frac{\partial l}{\partial \mu_i}\cdot\frac{\partial \mu_i}{\partial \beta_i}\cdot\frac{\partial \beta_i}{\partial \mathbf{v}_i} \tag{7}$$

where $i = 1,2,\cdots,K$ and $\mathbf{v}_i$ denotes the weight vector of the gating network associated with i^{th} local expert network. Then

$$\begin{aligned}\frac{\partial l}{\partial \mu_i} &= \frac{\partial}{\partial \mu_i}\ln\sum_{i=1}^{K}\mu_i \exp\left(-\frac{1}{2}\|\mathbf{d}-\mathbf{y}_i\|\right)^2 = \frac{\exp\left(-\frac{1}{2}\|\mathbf{d}-\mathbf{y}_i\|^2\right)}{\sum_{i=1}^{K}\mu_i \exp\left(-\frac{1}{2}\|\mathbf{d}-\mathbf{y}_i\|^2\right)} \\ &= \frac{1}{\mu_i}\frac{\mu_i \exp\left(-\frac{1}{2}\|\mathbf{d}-\mathbf{y}_i\|^2\right)}{\sum_{i=1}^{K}\mu_i \exp\left(-\frac{1}{2}\|\mathbf{d}-\mathbf{y}_i\|^2\right)} = \frac{h_i}{\mu_i}\end{aligned} \tag{8}$$

$$\frac{\partial \mu_i}{\partial \beta_i} = -\frac{\frac{\partial}{\partial \beta_i}\left[\sum_{j=1}^{K}(\beta_i/\beta_j)^2\right]}{\left[\sum_{j=1}^{K}(\beta_i/\beta_j)^2\right]^2} \tag{9}$$

The numerator becomes

$$\begin{aligned}\frac{\partial}{\partial \beta_i}\left[\sum_{j=1}^{K}\left(\frac{\beta_i}{\beta_j}\right)^2\right] &= \frac{\partial}{\partial \beta_i}\left[(\beta_i)^2\sum_{j=1}^{K}\left(\frac{1}{\beta_j}\right)^2\right] = 2\beta_i\sum_{j=1}^{K}\left(\frac{1}{\beta_j}\right)^2 - 2(\beta_i)^2\left(\frac{1}{\beta_i}\right)^3 \\ &= \frac{2}{\beta_i}\sum_{j=1}^{K}\left(\frac{\beta_i}{\beta_j}\right)^2 - \frac{2}{\beta_i} = \frac{2}{\beta_i}\left(\sum_{j=1}^{K}\left(\frac{\beta_i}{\beta_j}\right)^2 - 1\right) = \frac{2}{\beta_i}\cdot\left(\mu_i^{-1} - 1\right) \\ &= \frac{2}{\beta_i}\cdot\frac{1-\mu_i}{\mu_i}\end{aligned} \tag{10}$$

Therefore,

$$\frac{\partial u_i}{\partial \beta_i} = -\left(\frac{2}{\beta_i}\cdot\frac{1-u_i}{u_i}\right)\Big/ u_i^{-2} = \frac{2u_i(u_i-1)}{\beta_i} \quad \text{and} \quad \frac{\partial \beta_i}{\partial \mathbf{v}_i} = \mathbf{x} \tag{11}$$

Finally, $\partial l/\partial \mathbf{v}_i$ for $\Delta \mathbf{v}_i$ becomes

$$\frac{\partial l}{\partial \mathbf{v}_i} = \frac{\partial l}{\partial \mu_i}\cdot\frac{\partial \mu_i}{\partial \beta_i}\cdot\frac{\partial \beta_i}{\partial \mathbf{v}} = \frac{h_i}{\mu_i}\cdot\frac{2\mu_i(\mu_i-1)}{\beta_i}\cdot\mathbf{x} = \frac{2h_i(\mu_i-1)}{\beta_i}\mathbf{x} \tag{12}$$

Therefore, updating the gating network can be defined by

$$\mathbf{v}_i(n+1) = \mathbf{v}_i(n) + \Delta\mathbf{v}_i(n) = \mathbf{v}_i(n) + \eta_{GN}\cdot\frac{2h_i\cdot(\mu_i-1)}{\beta_i}\cdot\mathbf{x} \tag{13}$$

where η_{GN} denotes the learning rate of the gating network.

APPLICATIONS AND RESULTS

A. Reactive ion etching

Reactive ion etching (RIE) is a plasma etching process that uses an electrical discharge to ionize gases and induce ion bombardment on a semiconductor wafer surface in order to etch patterns on that surface. Both chemical and physical mechanisms contribute to the etching process. Detailed etch mechanisms of reactions are described in the literature, and it is widely accepted that these physical and chemical reactions represent complex and nonlinear multivariate processes (Hong, 2003).

The statistical experimental design technique requires that a relatively small number of process characterization experiments be performed using orthogonal combinations of values associated with each process variable (factor) (Box, 1978). To reduce the number of experiments, a 2^4 factorial design was initially considered and later further augmented with a central composite circumscribed design. The parameters, their ranges, and responses appear in Table I.

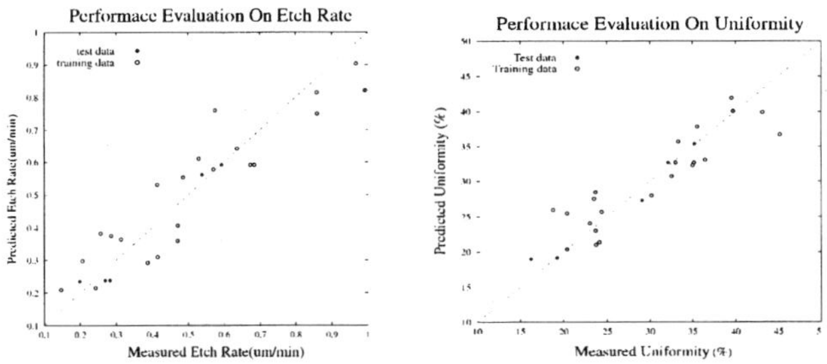

Fig. 2. Performance evaluation of process models. The plot on the left is etch rate, and on the right is uniformity.

Once modular neural networks (MNNs) were trained, they were tested with the data not introduced during training. The established models of etch rate and uniformity are graphically evaluated in Figure 2. Response surfaces were generated to illustrate the relationships between any two parameters and responses of interest (etch rate and uniformity in this study). Any two selected input variables can be simultaneously varied within their ranges while the remaining parameter is set to be its mid-range value. Sample predictions of the neural process models are plotted Figure 3. The figures illustrate the relationship between process parameters and an etch response. It can be seen that maximum gas flow rates (O_2=80 sccm and SF_6=10 sccm) may provide highest etch rate, but to improve uniformity, about 60 sccm of oxygen is desired. We can infer that SF_6 has a strong correlation with both responses in the etching of BCB. This is true because BCB contains silicon, and fluorinated gases can break Si bonds.

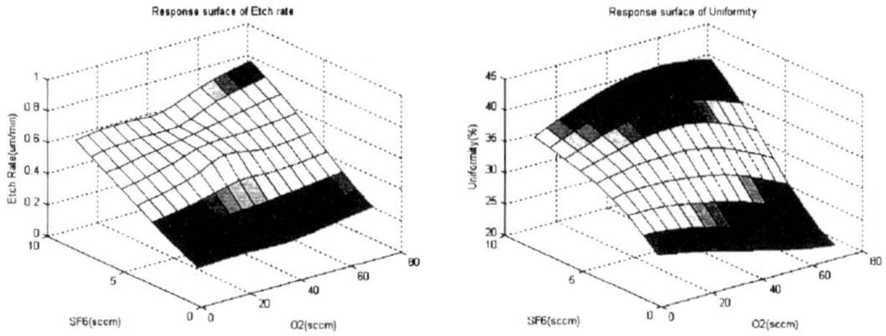

Fig. 3. Response surface plots for etch rate and uniformity associated with two gas flows (RF power is 300 Watts, and pressure is 200 mTorr.)

B. Plasma Enhanced Chemical Vapor Deposition

Chemical vapor deposition (CVD) is a process where one or more gaseous species react on a solid surface, and one of the reaction products is a solid film on the substrate. One of the most frequently used CVD technique is plasma-enhanced CVD (PECVD). PECVD also uses an RF-induced glow discharge to transfer energy into the reactant gases, allowing the substrate to remain at a relatively low temperature (below approximately 300°*C*).

In a similar manner to the RIE example, a 2^{5-1} factorial experiment was performed to characterize a PECVD process (Han, 1997). The parameters and their ranges are listed in Table II. Only the deposition rate of SiO_2 is considered in this example. Modular neural networks were established and evaluated, and response surfaces were generated to illustrate the relationships between two parameters and the response (Figure 4). From the response surface, in order to produce an adequate deposition rate, more than 100 watts of

RF power is desired. It also can be inferred that too low a pressure setting (below 1 Torr) slows down the deposition rate, even with large amount of RF power. This can be interpreted as fewer molecules being deposited may reside in the chamber at lower pressure, thus slowing deposition.

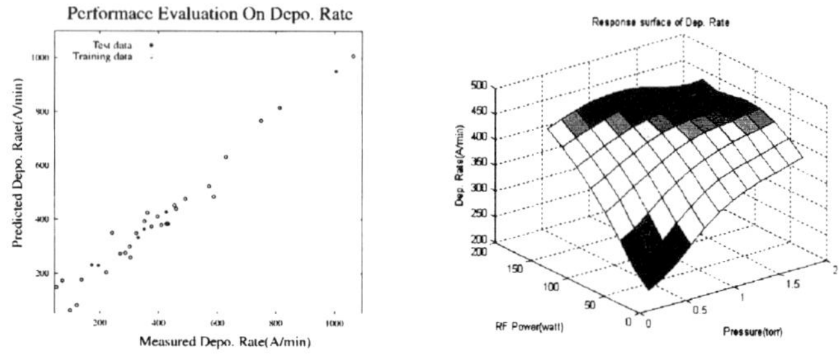

Fig. 4. Performance evaluation and response surface plot for PECVD example.

CONCLUSION

In this paper, the MNN approach is introduced as a means of constructing accurate and robust process models in semiconductor manufacturing. Modular neural networks are capable of generating response surfaces in conjunction with Matlab. The MNNs' added degrees of freedom compared to statistical regression methodd can provide more accuracy, reliability, and flexibility. MNNS therefore represent either an alternative or an complementary approach to statistical modeling and characterization.

REFERENCES

Box, G., Hunter, W., and Hunter, J., 1978, *Statistics for Experimenters*, New York: Wiley.

Han, S., Ceiler, M., Bidstrup, S., Kohl, P., and May, G., 1994, "Modeling the Properties of PECVD Silicon Dioxide Films Using Optimized Back-Propagation Neural Networks," *IEEE Trans. Comp., Pack. & Manufac.*, vol. 17, no. 2, pp. 174-182.

Han, S., and May, G., 1997, "Using Neural Network Process Models to Perform PECVD Silicon Dioxide Recipe Synthesis via Genetic Algorithms," *IEEE Trans. Semi. Manufac.*, vol. 10, no. 2, pp. 279-287.

Himmel, C. and May, G., 1993, "Advantages of plasma etch modeling using neural networks over statistical techniques," *IEEE Trans. Semi. Manufac.*, vol. 6, no. 2, pp. 103-111.

Haykin, S., 1994, *Neural Networks*, New York, NY: Macmillan College Publishing.

Hong, S., May, G., and Park, D., 2003, "Neural Network Modeling of Reactive Ion Etch Using Optical Emission Spectroscopy Data," *IEEE Trans. Semi. Manufac.* vol. 16, no. 4, pp. 598-608.

Hong, S., Choi, S., Choi, Y., Allen, M., and May, G., 2004 "Characterization of Low-Temperature SU-8 Photoresist Processing for MEMS Applications," *Proc. of IEEE Advanced Semiconductor Manufacturing Conference,* Boston, MA, pp. 404-408.

Kim, B., and May, G., 1996, "Reactive ion etch modeling using neural networks and simulated annealing," *IEEE Trans. Semi. Manufac.*, vol. 19, no. 1, pp. 3-8.

May, G., 2001, "Computational Intelligence in Microelectronics Manufacturing," Chapter 13, *The Handbook of Computational Intelligence in Design and Manufacturing* (J. Wang and A. Kusiak, Eds.), Boca Raton, FL: CRC Press.

REAL-TIME SENSORY UPDATING OF RESIDUAL LIFE DISTRIBUTIONS FOR REPLACEMENT MANAGEMENT

NAGI Z. GEBRAEL
School of Mechanical and Industrial Engineering
University of Iowa
Iowa City, AI

MARK A. LAWLEY
School of Industrial Engineering
Purdue University
West Lafayette, IN

ABSTRACT

There is a growing need for designing manufacturing systems able to sustain the implementation of lean concepts, Kanban systems, total productive maintenance, etc. A sophisticated maintenance system able to predict the future performance of equipment is a major requirement for such systems. This work develops a methodology for determining residual life distributions for degrading components by combining reliability information associated with the component's population with condition-based sensory information. This research develops a neural network based approach for predicting a component's failure time at any point during its operating life using vibration-based sensory signals. An empirical Bayes methodology is then used compute posterior residual life distributions using the neural network outputs. We then incorporate these distributions with a simple age-replacement model to estimate the optimal replacement times.

INTRODUCTION

In today's global economy, industries are trying to attain and maintain a competitive edge in productivity and quality. This has resulted in an increased trend to acquire sophisticated technology and increase plant automation, however, few industries recognize the importance of establishing a sophisticated maintenance system that will sustain such advances. For example, applying modern production strategies results in minimal improvement if machinery and equipment are unreliable due to increased breakdowns and high levels of unscheduled downtime. Consequently, many companies have begun to realize that these costs are among the largest controllable expenditure in a plant. Most of the accepted methods of minimizing such costs utilize rigid preventative maintenance schedules and monitoring of warning signs. On the other hand, condition based maintenance (CBM) plays a proactive maintenance role by using sensory information to monitor the condition of various equipment.

This research focuses on condition monitoring of bearings mainly because they are an inherent component of any rotational equipment. Neural networks and fuzzy logic approaches are among the most common techniques used for classification of bearing health and life prediction. Most of these articles attempt to classify the bearing as good or bad, healthy or defective and if defective, identify the defect in the bearing Alguindigue at al. (1993), Choudhury et al. (1999), Haddad et al. (1994), and Huang et al. (1996). Shao and Nezu (2000) model the health of the bearing as a time series for making short term life predictions. Most of this work relies on artificially induced defects, which does not represent the natural modes of bearing failure.

This work is motivated by the need to develop a decision support framework that combines reliability information with real-time condition monitoring sensory signals to estimate residual life distributions of partially degrading components. The importance of these distributions lies in the decision making process regarding maintenance, replacement, and inventory decisions. Lu and Meeker (1993) develop a statistical random coefficients model to estimate remaining life distributions. Considerable work has also been done on modeling preventative maintenance strategies aimed at optimal replacement Wang (2000) Christer and Waller (1984), and Chen and Meher (1994).

This paper presents a neural network model that uses vibration data to predict a bearing's failure time based on sensory data. The paper also develops an empirical Bayes procedure that uses this information to derive posterior residual life distributions based on the latest sensory data. The main contributions of this research include, (1) the capability of updating residual life distributions in real-time using latest vibration-based sensory data, (2) the use of sensory information corresponding to natural failure processes (without any artificially induced defects), (3) the processing of the residual life distributions to estimate optimal replacement times.

BEARING DEGRADATION

Bearing degradation is mostly due to fatigue and wear. The stages of bearing failure are generally the same Alexej (1995). Degradation begins with subsurface cracks occurring within the raceway material. These cracks propagate to the surface of the raceway resulting in a spall. The rotation of the rolling elements excites what is referred to as a bearing defective frequency, which depends on the number of rolling elements, rotational speed, and geometry of the bearing. Consequently, vibration analysis is among the best techniques for bearing condition monitoring.

An experimental setup is used to perform accelerated testing on a set of rolling element thrust bearings Gebraeel et al. (2004). We then develop a vibration-based degradation signal and moel it as a exponential model. Indeed, exponential models have been used often to model fatigue and and bearing wear Shao and Nezu (2000). We develop a degradation database composed of degradation information for 25 bearings (training bearings), which consists of bearing defect times, failure times, vibration spectra, degradation signals, and exponential parameters α and β.

NEURAL NETWORK MODEL

We present a neural network model for estimating bearing failure times. This model is composed of several modular feed forward back propagation neural networks. Each network is trained using the degradation information from an individual bearing. A 7-element vector $A_{in}=[a^n_{i1}, a^n_{i2}, a^n_{i3}, \ldots a^n_{i7}]$ representing the seven amplitudes of the defective frequency and its first six harmonics for bearing i (B_i) at the nth sampling epoch represents the training input to neural network i, (FN_i), where i = 1, . . ., 25. The sampling epoch, n, is the time instant at which a data acquisition is performed. Let N_i be the total number of sampling epochs for bearing B_i from the onset of the defect until failure, thus, n=1, . . ., N_i. The network's output is a single-element vector of B_i's operating time at the nth sampling epoch, $[\,t_i^n\,]$, computed by network FN_i. During training, FN_i sees the following input sequence: $\{[A_{i1}]\ldots[A_{in}]\ldots[A_{iN}]\}$. The output sequence corresponding to this input is: $\{[t_i^1]\ldots[t_i^n]\ldots[t_i^N]\}$ where t_i^N is B_i's failure time. Each FN_i is associated with a two vectors ofexponential parameters $\langle\alpha_1 \ldots \alpha_{25}\rangle$ and $\langle\beta_{1,} \ldots \beta_{25}\rangle$, which is then used to predict failure time. We evaluate the predictability of the neural network model by using another set of 25 partially degraded field bearings (validation bearings).

Consider a bearing B_k with an amplitude vector $[A_{kn}]$ and with a known operating time. The amplitude vector is input to each of the 25 neural networks. Each FN_i outputs an operating time $[\,t_i^n\,]$ resulting in 25 estimated bearing operating times $\{[\,t_1^n\,], [\,t_2^n\,], \ldots [\,t_i^n\,], \ldots [\,t_{25}^n\,]\}$. The estimated operating times are used to compute a squared error, e_{ik}^n, between the estimated operating time output by FN_i and the actual operating time of B_k. The squared error associated with FN_i at sampling epoch n is defined as $e_{ik}^n = \left(t_i^n - p_k^n\right)^2$ where p_k^n is the actual operating time of B_k.

The result is a 25-element vector of squared errors one from each neural network. This vector is then used to calculate a corresponding vector of weights, which is then used to estimate a field bearing's failure time. The weight associated with FN_i (at the nth sampling epoch) is given by equation (1)

$$W_i^n = x_{ik}^n \Big/ \sum_{i=1}^{25} x_{ik}^n \qquad (1)$$

where, x_{ik}^n is given by $x_{ik}^n = \sum_{i=1}^{25} e_{ik}^n \Big/ e_{ik}^n$

Based on equations (1), larger weights are coupled with neural network that have a lower squared error value and the vice versa is true. The weights are used to calculate a weighted average of the exponential parameters. At sampling epoch 'n', the predicted failure time of B_k is computed using (2)

$$t_k^N = \left(1 \Big/ \beta_k^n \right) \times \ln\left(D \Big/ \alpha_k^n \right) \qquad (2)$$

where: D ~ failure threshold; $\alpha_k^n = \sum_{i=1}^{25} W_i^n \alpha_i$; and $\beta_k^n = \sum_{i=1}^{25} W_i^n \beta_i$.

The neural network model is validated using the 25 validation bearings. In the next section, we uses a sequence of predicted failure times coupled with Empirical Bayes methods to derive a bearing's residual life distributions

COMPUTING RESIDUAL LIFE DISTRIBUTIONS

Bayesian analysis is used to compute residual life distributions by combining prior knowledge of a distribution (θ) with observed sample data (x). The posterior distribution is defined to be the conditional distribution of θ given the sample observation x. The posterior distribution is given by (3)

$$\pi(\theta \mid x) = \frac{\pi(\theta) f(x \mid \theta)}{\int f(x \mid \theta)\, \pi(\theta)\, d\theta} \qquad (3)$$

The posterior distribution reflects the updated beliefs after observing a sample observation. In this work, we use empirical Bayes to evaluate the prior and compute posterior distributions. Consider a partially degraded field bearing (one of the validation bearings) that is being monitored continuously. Each vibration data acquisition that is input to the neural network model results in an output representing the predicted bearing failure time. Assume that the failure times are from independent $N(\theta_i, \sigma_f^2)$ distribution (i=1, . . ., p) where σ_f^2 is known, and θ_i's are assumed to be independently distributed and follow $N(\mu_\pi, \sigma_\pi^2)$. We are interested in finding the posterior distribution of θ_i given an observed sample x_i.

We now collect an initial set of 10 consecutive output values (p=10). These values are then used to estimate the hyperparameters μ_π and σ_π^2 using the following expressions; $\mu_\pi = \bar{x}$ and $\sigma_\pi^2 = \max\left\{0, \frac{1}{p}s^2 - \sigma_f^2\right\}$

The parameter σ_f^2 represents the variance of bearing failure times and is calculated using the actual failure times of the training bearings (degradation database). The expression $s^2 = \sum_{i=1}^{10} (x_i - \bar{x})^2$ can be calculated using the observed sample data which is represented by subsequent predictions made by the neural network model. According to Berger (1985), the posterior distribution of θ_i for a given μ_π and σ_π^2 and an observed sample x_i is $N(\mu_i^{EB}(x_i), V_i^{EB})$ where μ_i^{EB} and V_i^{EB} are determined using equations (4) and (5), respectively,

$$\mu_i^{EB}(x_i) = x_i - \hat{B}(x_i - \bar{x}) \qquad (4)$$

$$V_i^{EB}(x_i) = \sigma_f^2\left(1 - \frac{(p-1)}{p}\hat{B}\right) + \frac{2}{(p-3)}\hat{B}^2 (x_i - \bar{x})^2 \qquad (5)$$

The posterior distribution of the failure time coupled with the current operating time allows us to derive the remaining life distribution of the bearing. Initially, we subtract the current operating time of the bearing (t_c) from failure time distribution which results in a. Since the remaining life distribution cannot be less that zero, the distribution is truncated at zero. Thus, the probability of the residual life T_R being less that some time t is given by expression (6),

$$P\{T_R \le t \mid \mu_\pi, \sigma_\pi^2, T_R \ge 0\} = \frac{P\{0 \le T_R \le t \mid \mu_\pi, \sigma_\pi^2, T_R \ge 0\}}{P\{T_R \ge 0 \mid \mu_\pi, \sigma_\pi^2, T_R \ge 0\}} = \frac{\Phi(g(t)) - \Phi(g(0))}{1 - \Phi(g(0))} \qquad (6)$$

where $g(t) = \frac{\mu_i^{EB}(x_i) - t_c - t}{\sqrt{V_i^{EB}}}$ and $\Phi(.)$= cdf of a standard normal distribution.

Figure 1 presents probability density functions (pdf.) of the posterior residual life distributions at four different life percentiles (0%, 20%, 40%, 60%) of one of the validation bearings. These densities are calculated using the empirical Bayes coupled with the latest sensory acquisition. We emphasize that the posterior distributions of a bearing's residual life are evaluated in real-time (during the bearing's operation) and are truncated at zero.

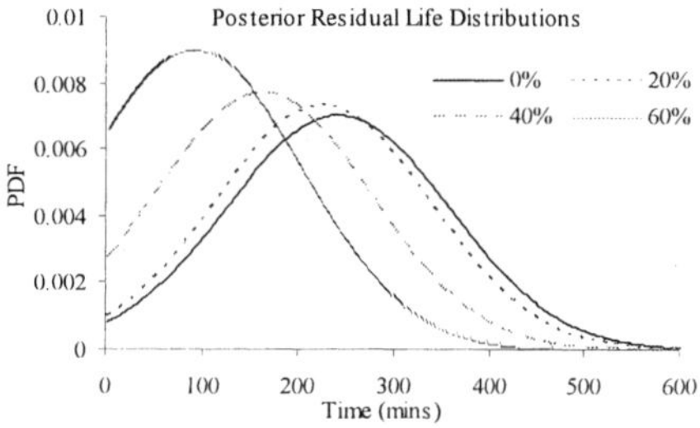

Figure 1 Residual life distributions

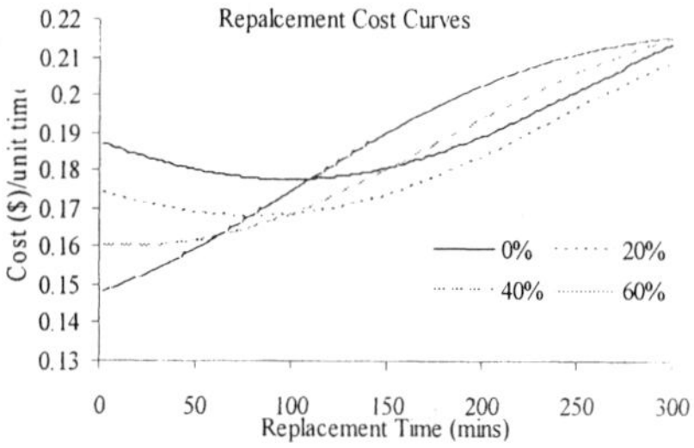

Figure 2 Replacement cost curves

REPLACEMENT STRATEGY

The posterior residual life distributions developed earlier are incorporated into a simple age replacement policy that has been developed based on the theory of renewal processes Karlin and Taylor (1974). The model computes the replacement time, T, that minimizes the long run average cost. The age replacement policy used in this work calls for replacing an item upon failure (failure replacement) or upon reaching age T (planned replacements), whichever occurs first. Thus, we would expect the long-run fraction of failure replacements will be F(T), and the corresponding fraction of planned replacement will be 1-F(T), where F(T) is the cumulative density function of the remaining life distribution. Furthermore, let the cost of planned replacement be c_1 and the cost of failure replacement be c_2.

In order to compute these cost curves, we define $F_k(x)$ as the cdf of the posterior residual life distribution calculated at time t_k. The long-run average replacement cost (LRC) per unit time is then expressed by equation (7). Figure 2 presents a set of replacement cost curves corresponding to the posterior residual life distributions shown in Figure 1 given that c_1 = \$75 and c_2 = \$125. The optimal replacement time T corresponds to the minimum cost value.

$$LRC = \frac{c_1\left[1 - F(T)\right] + c_2\, F(T)}{t_k + \int_{t_k}^{T}\left[1 - F_k(x)\right]dx} \qquad (7)$$

RESULTS AND CONCLUSIONS

A neural network model was developed to estimate failure times of partially degraded bearings using real-time vibration signals. A set of 25 training bearings were used to train the neural network model while another set of 25 validation bearings were used to evaluate the performance of the proposed model. Given the failure times output by the neural network model and the current operating time of the bearing, we estimate the prior distribution of a bearing's residual life. Subsequent vibration acquisitions are then used to update the prior distribution (posterior). Tthe posterior remaining life distributions are then used to compute optimal replacement times corresponding to the minimum long run average replacement cost using single component age replacement models from Renewal theory.

We believe the main contribution of this research is providing a framework for making maintenance and replacement decisions using real-time sensory information. This work can be extended to encompass large scale condition monitoring of multiple components at geographically remote locations and developing multi-criteria decision procedures for maintenance and replacement .

REFERENCES

Alexej Barkov, "Condition assessment and life prediction of rolling element bearings – part 1", *Sound and Vibrations*, vol. 29(6), pp. 10-17, 1995.

Alguindigue I. E., Loskiewicz-Buczak A., and Uhrig R. E., "Monitoring and diagnosis of rolling element bearings using artificial neural networks", *IEEE Transactions on Industrial Electronics*, vol. 40(2), pp. 209-217, 1993

Berger J. O., "Statistical Decision Theory and Bayesian Analysis", New York: Springer-Verlag, c1985.

Chen W., Meher-Homji C. B., and Mistree F., "COMPROMISE: and Effective Approach for Condition-Based Maintenance Management of Gas Turbines", *Engineering Optimization*, vol. 22, pp. 185-201, 1994.

Choudhury S. K., Jain V. K., and Rama Rao Ch V. V., "On-line Monitoring of Tool Wear in Turning Using a Neural Network", *International Journal of Machine Tools & Manufacture*, vol. 39(3), pp. 489-504, 1999.

Christer A. H. and Waller W. M., "Delay Time Models of Industrial Inspection Maintenance Problems", *Journal of the Operational Research Society*, vol. 35(5), pp. 401-406, 1984.

Gebraeel, N., and Lawley, M., "Life Distributions from Component Degradation Signals: A Neural Net Approach" *IEEE Transactions on Industrial Electronics*, vol. 51 (3), June 2004.

Haddad S. D., Chatterji G. B., and Ogunfunmi T., "A ball bearing Fault Detector Using Neural Network Based Vibration Algorithms", *Artificial neural networks in engineering – proceedings*, vol. 4, pp. 967-972, 1994

Huang,Hsin-Hao. and Ben Wang, H. P., "Integrated monitoring and diagnostic system for roller bearings", *International Journal of Advanced manufacturing Technology*, vol. 12(1), pp. 37-46, 1996.

Karlin, S. and Taylor, H. M., "A first course in stochastic Processes", Academia Press, Inc. 1975.

Lu C. and Meeker W., " Using Degradation Measures to Estimate a Time-to-Failure Distribution", *Technometrics*, vol. 35 (2), pp. 161-174, 1993

Shao Y. and Nezu K., "Prognosis of remaining bearing life using neural networks", Proceedings of the Institute of Mechanical Engineer, Part I, Journal of Systems and Control Engineering, vol. 214 (3), pp. 217-230, 2000.

Wang W., "A Model to Determine the Optimal Critical Level and the Monitoring Intervals in Condition-based Maintenance", *International Journal of Production Research*, vol. 38(6), pp. 1425-1436, 2000.

INTELLIGENT PATH PLANNING AND SCHEDULING FOR AUTOMATED GUIDED VEHICLES USING EVOLUTIONARY ALGORITHM

LAKSHMANAN MEYYAPPAN *
University of Missouri-Rolla
Engineering Management Department
Smart Engineering Systems Lab
Rolla, MO 65409
E-mail: laksh@umr.edu
Phone: (573) 341-6558

NEBIL BUYURGAN
University of Arkansas
Department of Industrial Engineering
4207 Bell Engineering Center
Fayetteville, AR 72701
E-mail: nebilb@uark.edu
Phone: (479) 575-7423

CIHAN H. DAGLI
University of Missouri-Rolla
Engineering Management Department
Smart Engineering Systems Lab
Rolla, MO 65409
E-mail: dagli@umr.edu
Phone: (573) 341-4374

CAN SAYGIN
University of Missouri-Rolla
Engineering Management Department
Integrated Systems Facility
Rolla, MO 65409
E-mail: saygin@umr.edu
Phone: (573) 341-6358

ABSTRACT

This paper presents a new intelligent path planning and scheduling method for automated guided vehicles in a flexible manufacturing system. The main objective is to minimize the total distance traveled by a loaded vehicle. The path planning and scheduling algorithm is coded in MATLAB® using evolutionary algorithm. The proposed algorithm has considerable advantages over a number of previous efforts and produces reasonably good results very quickly and hence can be used for real time planning and scheduling of automated guided vehicles. The evolutionary algorithm presented is also flexible, in the sense that it can be used for any number of vehicles and any number of machines in the shop floor with slight modifications.

INTRODUCTION

Flexible manufacturing systems (FMS) consist of number of integrated numerical controlled machine tools with automated material handling systems and are controlled by centralized or decentralized computer systems [Saygin et al. 2001]. Automated guided vehicles (AGVs), which are used to transport loads, large and small, from one location on the shop floor to another have become popular in FMS [Broadbent et al. 1985, Daniels 1988, Kim et al. 1991, Akturk et al. 1996]. Traditionally, AGV's movements are restricted by guide paths such as cables buried underground, some chemical paints or sensors. However recent advances in technology allow AGVs to travel without guide paths and are known as free ranging AGVs [Gaskins et al. 1989].

---

* *To whom all correspondence should be addressed.*

Evolutionary algorithms are known for producing near optimal solution in a very short time and this advantage of evolutionary algorithm is very useful for solving routing problems in FMS in real time. The proposed path planning algorithm using an evolutionary algorithm solves the routing problem very quickly in real time and produces reasonably optimal results. The proposed approach has the considerable merit over most other prevalent evolutionary routing algorithms, that crossover and mutation will always produce legal routes and no separate correction algorithms are required which may take additional running time. A legal route is one which preserves the job's task order, and does not offer multiple jobs to the same machine.

This paper presents a scheduling algorithm using evolutionary algorithm for AGVs in a FMS. Slightly modified versions of greedy crossover and scramble mutation operators are used in the evolutionary algorithm to determine the shortest path. The use of these operators guarantees legal routes. The entire algorithm is coded in MATLAB®. The major motivation for this research was to produce a flexible and scalable scheduling algorithm that can be used for any number of AGVs and any number of machines in a FMS.

LITERATURE REVIEW

Intelligent path planning of AGVs is very essential for FMS to be efficient and economical. Maxwell et al. (1982) developed a method for determining the AGV routes so that the material handling load is satisfied. Blair et al (1985) also addressed the problem of vehicle routing. In both of the above two studies, the main objective was to develop AGV routing schedule resulting in the maximum distance that an AGV travels being minimized. Minimizing AGV travel is also the objective of the approach presented in this paper. However, there are some differences. First, in this approach path planning is done only for loaded vehicles. Unloaded vehicles take the shortest Manhattan distance or rectilinear distance as defined by Francis et al (1974). A second difference in this approach is the assumption that the AGVs are free ranging which allows vehicles to move in any desired direction without physical guide paths and the travel paths from one location to another is pre set to avoid AGV collisions.

Taghaboni et al. (1995) proposed a dynamic routing technique, namely incremental route planning, which can route AGVs relatively quickly. The algorithm selects the next location for an AGV to visit based on the status of neighboring nodes and information about the global network. This algorithms works perfectly as long as the number of AGVs and number of tasks remain small and fairly constant. In the approach presented in this paper, only the global network information is used in determining the AGV route. Hence, the throughput remains fairly constant for varying number of AGVs and machines.

Based on dynamic programming, Langevin et al. (1996) presented an algorithm which could give an optimal integrated solution for scheduling and routing of AGVs. The algorithm defines a partial routing plan for each AGV satisfying a subset of transportation tasks. States are defined based on partial transportation plans. The dynamic programming operations work on the states to find the best final state set which contains the optimal route. However, as stated in their work, the number of states could be astronomical for large systems. This will basically increase the computational time and hence, the throughput of such a system may not scale up with the number of tasks.

Davis (1985) was the first to suggest and demonstrate the feasibility of using evolutionary algorithms for scheduling and routing of AGVs, employing an ad-hoc set of genetic operators and a memory intensive chromosome representation, paving way for future improvements. Meanwhile, the general success of evolutionary algorithms on other similar hard NP complete problems, such as the traveling salesman problem (TSP), accelerated the use of evolutionary algorithms to solve AGV routing and scheduling problem. In general evolutionary algorithms provide a quick near optimal solution to any problem. The approach presented in this paper uses a modified variant of evolutionary crossover and mutation operators discussed by Papadimitriou (1997) for TSP. This representation has the merit of producing only legal routes under crossover and mutation and it is computationally less intensive.

In the approach presented in this paper, global network information is used in determining the AGV route. Hence, change or increase in number of AGV's and number of tasks does not affect the efficiency of the algorithm. Use of modified evolutionary crossover and mutation operators, and clustering greatly reduces the operational time and can effectively route AGVs.

PROPOSED EVOLUTIONARY PLANNING AND SCHEDULING ALGORITHM

Evolutionary algorithms are probabilistic search algorithms which simulate natural evolution. It was proposed about 40 years ago [Bremermann et al. 1965]. Their application to NP-Complete optimization problems, however, only recently gained momentum. In this approach an evolutionary algorithm is developed to determine the jobs to be handled by the available AGVs and to find the optimal routes for each AGV. The path and distance between any two stations are preset and remains constant and is assumed to be collision free.

The input to the evolutionary algorithm is a list of parts with their pick-up and drop-off station numbers, respectively. The output of the evolutionary algorithm is the optimal route to be taken by each AGV in order to accomplish all the jobs optimally. An optimal route is one where the maximum distance traveled by all the AGVs to accomplish the job is minimized.

A clustering approach is used to make the algorithm more time efficient. A pick up point based clustering is used. The stations which are close to each other are clustered together. The number of clusters is based on the number of available AGVs. The AGVs in general pick up the materials from a set of stations and drop them off in their respective drop off points. Clustering the stations based on their location and then applying the evolutionary algorithm separately on each of the clusters greatly reduces the search space and the computation time. The procedure of the evolutionary algorithm is described as follows:

- Initialization – Determination of initial population
- Evaluation of fitness of an individual

- Selection
- Breeding – Mutation and Crossover
- Population update

As mentioned above, the first step is to determine an initial population. It is basically a set of randomly generated candidate solutions. The population size determines the number of candidates created initially. This can be kept constant or can be varied as per the need. The routes will be denoted as 1-2-3 during computation. This basically means that the AGV travels from its home base to station 1, then to station 2 and then to station 3 picking up the parts from these locations and then drop them of in their corresponding drop off locations in the reverse order and go back to its home base. As can be seen above, this consists of only the pick-up points. The drop-off points are not considered to make it computationally less intensive. The route based on first in first out becomes the first candidate. If the first candidate looks like 1-2-3-4-5, some of the randomly generated population will be 4-1-3-2-5, 2-4-1-3-5, and 4-2-1-3-5 and so on.

During the evaluation process, the total distance traveled by each candidate is calculated. Before selection process the entire population is allowed to mutate. This is known as co-evolution. The mutation that takes place initially is called the cycle mutation. For example if the original route is "1-2-3-4-5", after a single mutation it would look like "5-1-2-3-4". This process will be done N times where N denotes the number of stations in the candidate. This process helps in the starting and ending point optimization, i.e. to find as which object is closest to the home base of the AGV and it takes very less time to perform N iterations. After N iteration the best population is pooled and taken to the next age. An elitist principle is followed in selection process and 50% of the best population is kept and allowed to breed.

Crossover operation is then performed. Normal crossover and mutation operators are not very suitable for this particular problem because they can result in a number of illegal tours. Hence the Greedy Crossover [Papadimitiriou, 1997] is used. Greedy crossover selects the first station from parent 1, then compares the stations leaving that station in both the parents, and chooses the one that result in a shorter path to extend the route. If one station has already appeared in the route, the other station is chosen. If both stations have already appeared, a station is chosen in random. This is shown in figure 1.

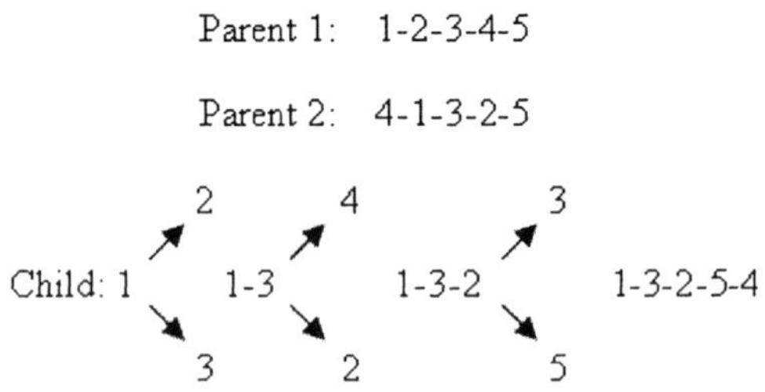

Figure 1. Greedy Crossover Operation

The crossover operation is again followed by mutation. This time instead of cycle mutation described above a scramble mutation is done. The scramble mutation [Syswerda, 1991] selects a random sub portion of the route and scrambles the stations in it. For example, consider the route 1-2-3-4-5, and suppose the sub portion 2-3-4 is chosen, the child might look like 1-4-2-3-5. The mutation process helps in not getting lost in a local minima or maxima. After this, selection process is repeated and the population is updated. This will be the next generation. This process is iterated many times until it doesn't yield any significant difference in distance traveled. The best candidate from the final generation of population is chosen as the optimal route.

Even though most approaches including the one proposed in this approach can be used in various situations with very minimal modifications, it is very difficult to directly compare the algorithms with one another on a one to one basis and suggest that one of them is better in all cases. However, we have compared and stated the major differences of the proposed algorithm as against some popular algorithms in table 1.

Table 1. AGV Routing and Scheduling Algorithms

	Broadbent et al. 1985	Tachaboni et al. 1995	Langevin et al. 1996	Proposed Algorithm
Problem Solved	Finding shortest route for AGV. No scheduling	Finding conflict free shortest route for AGV. No scheduling	Routing and scheduling of two AGVs	Routing and scheduling of multiple AGVs
Basic Algorithm	Dijkstra's shortest part algorithm	Incremental route planning	Dynamic programming	Evolutionary algorithm
Optimality of solution	Near optimal solution	Near optimal solution	Near optimal solution	Near optimal solution
Routing Technique	Static routing	Dynamic routing	Dynamic routing	Static routing
Scalability and Flexibility	Efficient only as long as the number of AGVs and tasks remain fairly small and constant	Works well for any number of AGVs. But the number of tasks needs to be small for it to be efficient	Designed for only two AGVs	Throughput remains fairly constant for any number of AGVs and tasks

RESULTS

Various tests were conducted to test the speed and efficiency of the proposed algorithm. For the first test, the number of AGVs and stations were fixed at four and forty respectively. Thirty data sets consisting of pick-up and drop-off locations were generated randomly. These data sets were solved using the proposed algorithm, a brute-force method and a transportation model variant. The brute-force method arrives at the optimal solution by searching the entire search space and solving all possible routes. The transportation model is basically a linear program operational research approach used in general, to solve scheduling problems efficiently. The computation times were recorded and a paired-t test statistical analysis was performed. The proposed algorithm produced results 4-5 times faster than the other two algorithms for a confidence level of 90%.

For the second test, the number of machines was kept constant at forty and the number of AGVs was varied between two and ten. For the third test, the number of AGVs was kept constant at four and the number of machines was varied between two and forty. The results showed that the change in number of AGVs and machines did not affect the computation time.

The above algorithm produces a near optimal solution in less than a minute on a Pentium IV 2 GHz machine, making it extremely suitable for real time applications. On NP-Complete problems like routing & scheduling of AGVs, researchers routinely need to use problem specific algorithms as the algorithm will vary slightly or drastically based on the plant layout, plant size, type and number of AGVs used and so on. However, the proposed algorithm offers the required flexibility and scalability.

CONCLUSIONS

In this paper, an intelligent path planning algorithm using evolutionary algorithm for AGVs in a flexible manufacturing system is proposed. Table 1 compares the proposed algorithm with a number of other popular algorithms. As can be seen from the above discussion, the proposed algorithm has a number of advantages over various other algorithms. The proposed evolutionary routing algorithm for AGVs produces near optimal routes in real time with minimal computation. The proposed algorithm is both flexible and scalable. Future work includes performing clustering based on drop-off stations instead of pick-up stations or a combination of the two. Fuzzy clustering can be used instead of the simple mathematical clustering proposed here. Research is under way to improve the performance of this algorithm and to obtain optimal solution.

REFERENCES

Akturk,M. S. and Yilmaz, H., 1996, Scheduling of automated guided vehicles in a decision making hierarchy. *International Journal of Production Research,* 32, 577-591.

Blair, E. L., Charnsethikul, P., and Vasques, A., 1985, Optimal routing of driverless vehicles in a flexible material handling system. Texas Tech University and Rensselaer Polytechnic Institute, U.S.A., November.

Bremermann, H. J., Rogson, M. and Salaff, S., 1965, Search by Evolution, Biophysics and Cybernetic Systems, Spartan Books, Washington, 157-167.

Broadbent, A. J., Besant, C. B., Premi, S. K. and Walker, S. P., 1985, Free ranging AGV systems: promises, problems and pathways. In *Proceedings of the 2nd International Conference on Automated Materials handling* (IFS/Springer), 221-237.

Daniels, S. C., 1988, Real-time conflict resolution in automated guided vehicle scheduling. PhD thesis, Department of Industrial Engineering, Pennsylvania StateUniversity, USA.

Davis, L., 1985, Job shop scheduling with genetic algorithms. In *Proceedings of the 1st International Conference on Genetic Algorithms and their Applications*, 136-140.

Francis, R. L., and White, J. A., 1974, Facility Layout and Location – An Analytical Approach (Englewood Cliffs, NJ: Prentice Hall)

Gaskins, R. J., Tanchoco, J. M. A., and Taghaboni, F., 1989, Virtual flow paths for free ranging automated guided vehicle systems. *International Journal of Production Research,* 27, 91-100.

Kim, C. W. and Tanchoco, J. M. A., 1991, Conflict-free shortest-time bi-directional AGV routing. *International Journal of Production Research,* 29, 2377-2391.

Langevin, A., Lauzon, D., and Riopel, D., 1996, Dispatching, routing and scheduling of two automated guided vehicles in a flexible manufacturing system. *International Journal of Flexible Manufacturing System,* 8, 246-262.

Maxwell, W. L., and Muckstadt, J. A., 1982, Design of automatic guided vehicle systems. I.I.E. Transactions, 14, 114-124.

Papadimitiriou, C. H., 1997, The Euclidean traveling salesman problem is NP-Complete. Theoretical Computer Science, 4, 237-244

Saygin, C., Chen, F.F., and Singh, J. 2001, "Real-time Manipulation of Alternate Routings in Flexible Manufacturing Systems: A Simulation Study," International Journal of Advanced Manufacturing Technology, 18(10), 755-763.

Syswerda, G., 1991, Schedule optimization using genetic algorithms, Handbook of Genetic Algorithms, New York, pp332-349

Taghaboni, F., and Tanchoco, J. M. A., 1995, Comparison of dynamic routing techniques for automated guided vehicle systems. *International Journal of Production Research,* 30, 665-681.

FUZZY NEURAL NETWORK MODELS FOR ELECTRICAL LOAD FORECASTING

JAKAPUN MEPOKEE, DAVID ENKE, AND CIHAN DAGLI
Laboratory for Investment and Financial Engineering
Smart Engineering System Lab
Intelligent System Center
University of Missouri- Rolla

ABSTRACT
The following illustrates some initial research activity conducted by the authors in the field of electrical load forecasting based on Artificial Neural Networks (ANN). This paper outlines the use of two neural network architectures: multi-layer feedforward and generalized regression neural networks. The best model had its performance improved by adding fuzzy logic to create a Fuzzy Neural Network (FNN).

INTRODUCTION

Across the country, many established electric power providers are finding themselves being deregulated. The customer base they once controlled is now being inundated with offers of lower prices from new competitors. As such, cost cutting and the bottom-line are becoming more important for power providers. Providing an accurate forecast of electric supply, price, and customer demand is also becoming more critical for capital budgeting, planning, and investment. Estimates show that a 1% reduction in forecasting error for a 10000 MW utility can save up to $1.6 million annually (Hobbs et al., 1999).

When utilizing regression, the load is modeled as a function of a set of independent and deterministic random variables, allowing for extended forecasts (Papalexopoulos et al., 1993). When using expert systems, the load is simply forecasted on a day-to-day basis. However, ANN are preferred over expert systems due to their inherent advantages. For instance, a major advantage of using ANNs over expert systems is that they do not need to depend on an expert (Srinivasan et al., 1999). ANNs also model the non-linear relationships among load and weather patterns, allowing for extended forecasts, similar to regression models. Due to their accuracy and decreased processing time, ANN are also often superior to classical statistical models like regression and time series analysis (Drezga and Rahman 1999; Desouky and Kateb, 2000; Specht, 1996). Furthermore, ANN have the advantage at being able to deal with irregular circumstances (Vaithianathasamy and Enke 2001, Kim 2000), such as noise to the network. Many ANNs are resistant to low levels of noise, and perform better to increase levels of noise, as compared to other more traditional techniques.

The following research modeled the relationship of electrical load with various relevance factors, such as temperature, humidity, wind speed, cloud cover, and previous load. To achieve this, the multi-layer feed-forward and generalized regression neural networks are used to capture and model the nonlinear load profile. The performance of the individual networks, as measured using Mean Absolute Percent Error (MAPE), are also compared to forecasts of electrical load generated by a traditional regression model. Of interest is how the different models perform in both the linear and non-linear regions of the load profile.

INPUT DATA SELECTION AND SYSTEM DATA

Most models for short-term load forecasting rely on weather parameters, such as temperature factors, wind factors, and pressure factors, among others. Some researchers have found that the temperature factors are the most important factors affecting the load. Wind factors typically include humidity and wind speed. Pressure factors are often measured at either stationary level or sea level. Other factors have also been considered, although most models omit these other factors since they are often considered to be too noisy to the network and/or model (Enke and Vaitianathasamy, 2000).

Apart from weather factors, there are also time factors that effect load pattern, such as hour of the day, day of the week, and seasonal cycles. A significant difference in electric power usage can also be seen when comparing between weekdays, weekends, and holidays. Using two models to forecast, one for weekdays and one for weekends, will often give better results (Gao et al., 2000).

The data for this study came from the region serviced by PJM. PJM is one of the most sophisticated, centrally dispatched electric control areas in North America, as well as being the third largest control area in the world. Their service area includes all or part of Pennsylvania, New Jersey, Maryland, Delaware, Virginia, and the District of Columbia. All the electric load data of PJM is reported hourly and available on their website. Load data was downloaded for a period of three years from 1998 to 2000. The load data is aggregated and covers large areas in several states. As such, it is difficult and unreliable to only use one city's weather parameters to forecast the load. Therefore, weather parameters from three cities, Washington DC, Allentown, and Philadelphia were used to represent the overall PJM load region. For the simulations, the chosen weather parameters included temperature, humidity, wind speed, and cloud cover. By examining the historical loads, characteristics of the load data become apparent. First, the load curve is low during the late evening and higher after 9 am every morning. This pattern seems to hold throughout the year.

ANN MODEL AND FUZZY LOGIC

Test results have shown that applying ANN for electrical load forecasting produces results that are limited to the reported data sets. Furthermore, many of the case studies involve different architectures, number of hidden layers, number of hidden nodes, type of transfer function in the hidden and output layers, and learning algorithms. From the literature, multi-layer feed-forward networks (FNN) seem to be the most popular ANN for load forecasting. This architecture has an ability to find a function approximation between inputs and outputs. Another popular architecture, the Generalized Regression Neural Network (GRNN), has also been successful and provides a useful comparison with multi-layer feed-forward neural networks due to its ability to perform of form of non-linear regression. Another advantage of the GRNN is that it does not require an interactive training procedure. The GRNN is used for the estimation of continuous variables, as in standard regression techniques. For this research, three different scenarios were used to forecast electrical load. Results were compared with a regression model to show the difference between linear and nonlinear models. The three different scenarios for comparison include:

a. Forecast the whole data set with one model.
b. Forecast the whole data set with two different models, one weekday and one weekend model.
c. Forecast the whole data with twenty four models, one for each hour.

To improve the training efficiency, the data set was normalized before training the network. In addition, when the networks started to over-fit the data, the error will increase. As a check, when the error began to increase with additional training, the training was stopped and the weights and biases were then returned to their previous values. All models improved generalization by using early stopping to reduce over-fitting the data.

FORECASTING PROCEDURE

Before starting the training process, all input and output parameters have been normalized. For the regression and GRNN models, normalization was not necessary. During training, the parameters of the neural network are based on the availability of the data. The accuracy of the forecast depends on the data sets and the selected time period for the load forecast. Once training is complete, the ANN is ready to forecast hourly load for a given forecast horizon. Four different methods were compared in the analysis:

1. Regression model
2. Back Propagation Neural Network (BP)
3. Generalize Regression Neural Network (GRNN)
4. Fuzzy Neural Network (FNN)

The Mean Absolute Percent Error (MAPE) was used to analyze the results, and is defined by the following equation:

$$MAPE = \frac{1}{N}\sum_{i=1}^{N}\frac{|p_i - a_i|}{a_i} \qquad (1)$$

Where p_i is the predicted and a_i is the actual load for hour i . N is the number of hours.

CASE STUDY RESULTS

All the inputs for Scenarios 1 and 2 were the same. In Scenario 3, the hour is not included because 24 networks are used to define each hour. From the results in Tables 1 and 2, Scenario 2 yields a better forecast when compared to Scenario 1. This shows that separating weekday from weekend can yield a better performance in both the neural network and regression models. Even in Scenario 3, separating the whole data set into 24 hourly data sets can yield better forecasting performance for both the neural network and regression models.

The results of the three scenarios for MAPE have been compared. According to Scenario 1, both artificial neural network models, the backproapagation neural network (BPN) and generalized regression neural network (GRNN), yield better forecast than the regression model. The MAPE of the BPN yields a 2.25% error, the GRNN yields a 3.69% error, while the regression model yields a 3.75% error. When comparing both the weekday and weekend models, ANNs consistently yield better forecasting results compared to the more traditional techniques. In addition, the weekday BPN model yields a 1.96% error, while the GRNN model yields a 3.56% error, which is more accurate than the 3.63% error of the regression model. Furthermore, for the weekend model, the BPN yields a 1.78% error and GRNN yields a 3.37% error when compared to the 3.29% error from regression model. Finally, Scenario 3, where data for the entire day is separated into 24 data sets (for each hour), both the ANN and regression models resulted in higher accuracy when compared to the first and second scenarios. The regression model yields better forecasting results when compared with ANN model. In Scenario 3, the regression model has an average error of 1.17%, while the BPN model has the average MAPE error of 1.29% for the 24 hourly networks. The GRNN model has the average MAPE of 1.66% for the 24 hourly networks.

Table 1: Results from the First and Second Scenarios (MAPE)

	Neural Network			Regression
	BP	GRNN	FNN	
Whole year	2.25	3.69	2.10	3.75
Weekday	1.96	3.56	1.91	3.63
Weekend	1.78	3.37	1.76	3.29

Table 2: Results of Each Hour for the Third Scenario (MAPE)

Hour	Neural Network		Regression
	BP	GRNN	
1	1.44	0.99	0.6641
2	0.98	1.19	0.5036
3	0.65	1.2	0.4997
4	0.71	1.04	0.4079
5	0.75	1.24	0.6085
6	1.23	2.55	1.5719
7	1.71	3.93	2.5495
8	1.46	1.42	1.1671
9	1.75	1.95	1.5413
10	1.01	2.15	1.3401
11	1.32	1.94	0.8952
12	0.86	1.65	0.7322
13	1.33	1.23	0.6404
14	0.79	0.95	1.1311
15	0.85	0.74	1.565
16	0.9	0.66	1.7497
17	1.78	1.92	1.1736
18	1.78	3.95	1.7556
19	1.52	1.8	1.7643
20	1.84	1.72	1.3781
21	1.66	1.44	1.6633
22	1.99	1.49	1.2833
23	1.27	1.44	0.7781
24	1.55	1.21	0.7177
AVG	*1.297083*	*1.658333*	***1.1701***

CONCLUSIONS

The research results above show that in the first scenario the FNN and GRNN give superior results when compared to the regression model. The most probable reason being that the load pattern in the first scenario is non-linear, such that the multiple linear regression model is not capable of producing a good forecast. The width of the load profile in Scenario 1 is more than the width in the other scenarios. The data had been separated into weekday and weekend data for Scenario 2, resulting in some improvement in percent error for both the FNN and GRNN models since the neural network was able to learn the pattern of the load more effectively. Even the linear regression showed some improvement from the separated data. Nevertheless, in Scenario 3, when the data was separated into 24 datasets for each hour, the results were better. By building separate models for each hour (each model is independent), the load pattern can be modeled more efficiently. The mean average percentage error for each method has decreased.

From the results in Scenario 1 and Scenario 2, after adding fuzzy logic to create a new set of inputs to the neural network, some improvement in forecasting results. It was shown that for datasets with more uncertainty or error, fuzzy logic can improve the forecasting results.

Neural networks are able to obtain the relationship between input parameters and output load during the forecasting day. Therefore, the network should be able to forecast a better result during times of rapid changes in inputs, such as temperature changes. From the results, the neural network performed better as compared to the regression model when using the entire yearly data set. On the other hand, when using the weekend and weekday data set for 24 individual hours, the neural network cannot produce a better result than the regression since the 24 sets of data seems to be more linear than the more complete data sets.

Finally, another point that has to be considered is that all the weather parameters, including temperature, humidity, and wind speed are actual data, not forecasted data. Therefore, there is less error in each data set. In a real situation it is not possible to get actual weather parameters to use as inputs - forecasted data must be used. Therefore, the forecasted electrical load will have more error than the results in this paper.

REFERENCES

Desouky, A.A., and M.M.EI Kateb, "Hybrid adaptive techniques for electric-load forecast using ANN and ARIMA," IEE Proceedings: Generation, Transmission, and Distribution., Vol. 147. No. 4, July 2000.

Drezga, I., and S. Rahman, "Short Term Load Forecasting with Local ANN Predictors", IEEE Transactions on Power Systems, Vol.14, No. 3, August 1999.

Enke, D. and S. Vaitianathasamy, "Electric Load Forecasting Using Trend Data and a Feed Forward Neural Network," Intelligent Engineering Systems through Artificial Neural Networks, Vol. 10 (2000): 1019-1024.

Hagan, M.T., and H.B. Demuth, Mark Beale, Neural Network Design, PWS Publishing Co, 1996.

Hobbs, B.F., S. Jitprapaikulsarn, S. Konda, V. Chankong, K.A. Loparo, and D.J. Maratukulam, "Analysis of the value for unit commitment of improved load forecasting," IEEE Transactions, Power Systems, Vol. 14, No.4, pp. 1342-1348, 1999.

Kim, K.H., H.S. Youn, and Y.C. Kang, Member, "Short-Term Load Forecasting for Special Days in Anomalous Load Conditions Using Neural Networks and Fuzzy Inference Method," IEEE Transactions on Power Systems, Vol. 15, No.2, May 2000.

Papalexopoulos, A.D., H. Shangyou, and T.M. Peng, "Application of Neural Network Technology to Short-Term System Load Forecasting Paper", APT 263-16-13 IEEE/NTUA, Athens Power Tech Conference: Planning, Operation and Control of Today's Electric Power Systems, Athens, Greece, 1993.

Specht, D.F., "A general regression neural network," IEEE Transactions on Neural Networks, vol. 2, no.6, pp. 568-576, 1996.

Srinivasan, D.; Swee Sien Tan; Cheng, C.S.; Eng Kiat Chan, "Parallel neural network-fuzzy expert system strategy for short-term load forecasting: system implementation and performance evaluation," IEEE Transaction on Power systems, Volume: 14, Issue: 3, 1999.

Vaithianathasamy, S., and D. Enke, "Comparison of Hourly and Daily Neural Network Models For Forecasting Hourly Electric Load", Intelligent Engineering Systems through Artificial Neural Networks, Vol. 11 (2001): 715-720.

Subject Index

B

C

E

F

I

K

L

O

P

T

Author Index

A

B

C

H

I

J

K

L

M

N

O

P

R

S

T

V

W

Y

Z